W9-AFP-957

Valparaiso Public Library
103 Jefferson Street
Valparaiso, IN 46383

ENCYCLOPEDIA OF
STREET CRIME
in
America

Dedicated to the memory of Irving Louis Horowitz (1929–2012), scholar, publisher, mentor, and friend.

ENCYCLOPEDIA OF

STREET CRIME
in
America

Editor
JEFFREY IAN ROSS

PORTER COUNTY PUBLIC LIBRARY *University of Baltimore*

Valparaiso Public Library
103 Jefferson Street
Valparaiso, IN 46383

Foreword by Francis T. Cullen

REF   364.97303 ENC   VAL

Encyclopedia of street crime i
33410012492593

07/16/13

⑤SAGE reference

Los Angeles | London | New Delhi
Singapore | Washington DC

Los Angeles | London | New Delhi
Singapore | Washington DC

FOR INFORMATION:

SAGE Publications, Inc.
2455 Teller Road
Thousand Oaks, California 91320
E-mail: order@sagepub.com

SAGE Publications India Pvt. Ltd.
B 1/I 1 Mohan Cooperative Industrial Area
Mathura Road, New Delhi 110 044
India

SAGE Publications Ltd.
1 Oliver's Yard
55 City Road
London EC1Y 1SP
United Kingdom

SAGE Publications Asia-Pacific Pte. Ltd.
3 Church Street
#10-04 Samsung Hub
Singapore 049483

Senior Editor: Jim Brace-Thompson
Project Editor: Tracy Buyan
Cover Designer: Anupama Krishnan
Reference Systems Manager: Leticia Gutierrez
Reference Systems Coordinators: Laura Notton,
                                Anna Villasenor
Marketing Manager: Carmel Schrire

Golson Media
President and Editor: J. Geoffrey Golson
Author Manager: Lisbeth Rogers
Production Director: Mary Jo Scibetta
Layout Editors: Kenneth Heller, Lois Rainwater
Copy and Development Editor: James Mammarella
Proofreader: Rebecca Kuzins
Indexer: J S Editorial

Copyright © 2013 by SAGE Publications, Inc.

All rights reserved. No part of this book may be reproduced or utilized in any form or by any means, electronic or mechanical, including photocopying, recording, or by any information storage and retrieval system, without permission in writing from the publisher.

Library of Congress Cataloging-in-Publication Data

Encyclopedia of street crime in America / Jeffrey Ian Ross, editor.

    pages cm
  Includes bibliographical references and index.
  ISBN 978-1-4129-9957-1 (hbk.)
  1.   Crime--United States--Encyclopedias. 2.   Criminal justice, Administration of--United States--Encyclopedias. I. Ross, Jeffrey Ian.
  HV6789.E435 2013
  364.97303--dc23

                                2012032642

SFI® Certified Sourcing
www.sfiprogram.org
SFI-00453

13 14 15 16 17 10 9 8 7 6 5 4 3 2 1

Contents

List of Articles *vii*
Reader's Guide *xi*
About the Editor *xiv*
List of Contributors *xv*
Foreword *xix*
Introduction *xxiii*
Chronology *xxvii*

Articles

A	*1*	M	*247*
B	*15*	N	*281*
C	*57*	O	*297*
D	*129*	P	*303*
E	*155*	R	*345*
F	*161*	S	*363*
G	*165*	T	*409*
H	*193*	U	*427*
I	*207*	V	*437*
J	*215*	W	*447*
K	*227*	Z	*457*
L	*235*		

Glossary *461*
Resource Guide *469*
Appendix: Street Crime Trends in America's 25 Largest Cities Over the Past 24 Years *479*
Index *511*
Photo Credits *538*

List of Articles

A

Alcohol and Drug Testing, On-Scene
Alcohol and Drug Use
Arrest
Arson
Asian Gangs

B

Bail
Baltimore, Maryland
Bank Robbery
Bar Personnel
Bars and Pubs
Bicycle Theft
Black Market
Blackmail
Bloods
Blue Laws
Bootleggers
Boston, Massachusetts
Bounty Hunters
Bratton, William
Brawley, Tawana. *See* Tawana Brawley Incident
Broken Windows Theory
Buffalo, New York
Burglary
Bystander Apathy

C

Central Booking
Central Park Jogger Incident
Chicago, Illinois

Child Molesters
Children, Commercial Sexual Exploitation of
Children as Victims
Cincinnati, Ohio
Cleveland, Ohio
Closed-Circuit Television
Code of Silence/Stop Snitching
Code of the Street
Community Policing
Community Resources Against Street Hoodlums
CompStat
Counterfeit Goods
Courts
Courts, Drug
Courts, Mental Health
Crack House
Credit Card Theft
Crime, Displacement of
Crime Mapping
Crime Patterns
Crime Prevention, Environmental
  Design and
Crime Prevention, Situational
Crime Scene Investigation
Crime–Consumerism Nexus
Crips

D

Day Reporting Center
Defensible Space Theory
Detroit, Michigan
Diallo, Amadou

Domestic Violence
Door-to-Door Scam Artists
Drinking, Underage
Drinking Establishments,
    Unlicensed
Drive-By Shooting
Drug Dealing
Drug Markets, Open-Air
Drugs, Prescription

E
Environmental Criminology
Exposure, Indecent

F
Fear of Crime
Flash Mobs

G
Gambling, Street
Gangs (Street)
Gated Communities
Genovese, Kitty
Gentrification
Giuliani, Rudolph
Goetz, Bernhard
Graffiti
Grand Theft Auto (Video Game)
Guardian Angels
Guns and Weapons
Gunshot Detection System

H
Hate Crime
History of Street Crime in America
Homelessness
Homophobic Assault
Hooliganism
Hot Spots

I
Immigrant Neighborhoods
Indianapolis, Indiana

J
Jails
Jaywalking
"Johns"
Juvenile Curfews
Juvenile Offending

K
Kansas City, Missouri
Kansas City Preventive Patrol Experiment
Kerner Commission on Civil Disorders
Kidnapping

L
La Eme (Mexican Mafia)
Latin Kings
Loitering
Looting
Los Angeles, California

M
Maple, Jack
Mass Transit, Crime on
Massage Parlors
Mental Illness
Metal Theft
Miami, Florida
Milwaukee, Wisconsin
Minneapolis, Minnesota
Miranda Warnings
Mobs and Riots
Motor Vehicle Theft
Motorcycle Clubs
MS-13
Mugging
Murder/Homicide

N
Needle Exchanges
Neighborhood Watch
New Orleans, Louisiana
New York City
Newark, New Jersey
Newark Foot Patrol Experiment

O
Open-Container Laws
Operation Ceasefire
Organized Crime and Violence

P
Panhandling or Begging
Patrol Cars
Peep Shows
Peeping Toms
Philadelphia, Pennsylvania
Pickpocketing

Pimp
Pittsburgh, Pennsylvania
Police (Overview)
Police Brutality/Excessive Force
Police Corruption, Street-Level
Police Detectives
Policing, Problem-Oriented
Pool Halls
Projects, The
Prostitute/Streetwalker
Prostitution, Houses of

R
Racial Assault
Racial Profiling
Rape and Sexual Assault
Risky Lifestyles
Road Rage
Routine Activity Theory

S
San Francisco, California
Seattle Crime Places Study
Security, Private
Serial Killers, Spree Killers, and
    Mass Murderers
Sex Crimes
Shoplifting
Skid Row
Skinheads
Speakeasies (1920s)
St. Louis, Missouri
Stalking
Sting Operations
Stop and Frisk
Street Art

Street Corner Society
Street Crime (Online Game)
Street Crime, Popular Portrayals of
Street Crime Defined
Street/Block Parties
Suite Crimes Versus Street Crimes
Swarming

T
Tawana Brawley Incident
Television Shows
Terrorism
Theft and Larceny
Tompkins Square Riots/Tent City
Truancy

U
Urban Ethnography
Urban Incivility
Urban Planning
Urbanization

V
Vandalism
Victims, Immigrant
Victims, Senior
Victims, Tourist

W
Washington, D.C.
Weed and Seed
Women

Z
Zero-Tolerance/Saturation Policing

Reader's Guide

History and Popular Culture of Street Crime
Bratton, William
Broken Windows Theory
Central Park Jogger Incident
Community Policing
Community Resources Against Street Hoodlums
  (CRASH)
Diallo, Amadou
Genovese, Kitty
Giuliani, Rudolph
Goetz, Bernhard
Grand Theft Auto (Video Game)
History of Street Crime in America
Immigrant Neighborhoods
Kansas City Preventative Patrol Experiment
Kerner Commission on Civil Disorders
Maple, Jack
Neighborhood Watch
Newark Foot Patrol Experiment
Prostitution, Houses of
Seattle Crime Places Study
Skid Row
Speakeasies (1920s)
Street Crime, Popular Portrayals of
Tawana Brawley Incident
Television Shows
Tompkins Square Riots/Tent City

Law Enforcement, Courts, and Corrections
Alcohol and Drug Testing, On-Scene
Arrest
Bail

Bounty Hunters
Closed-Circuit Television
Code of Silence/Stop Snitching
CompStat
Courts
Courts, Drug
Courts, Mental Health
Crime Mapping
Crime Scene Investigation
Crime–Consumerism Nexus
Day Reporting Center
Guardian Angels
Gunshot Detection System
Jails
Miranda Warnings
Operation Ceasefire
Patrol Cars
Police (Overview)
Police Brutality/Excessive Force
Police Corruption, Street-Level
Police Detectives
Policing, Problem-Oriented
Racial Profiling
Security, Private
Sting Operations
Stop and Frisk
Street Crime Defined

Nonviolent Crimes
Alcohol and Drug Use
Bicycle Theft
Black Market

Blackmail
Blue Laws
Bootleggers
Counterfeit Goods
Credit Card Theft
Door-to-Door Scam Artists
Drinking, Underage
Drug Markets, Open-Air
Gambling, Street
Graffiti
Jaywalking
"Johns"
Juvenile Curfews
Loitering
Looting
Metal Theft
Motor Vehicle Theft
Needle Exchanges
Open-Container Laws
Panhandling or Begging
Peep Shows
Peeping Toms
Pickpocketing
Pimp
Prostitute/Streetwalker
Prostitution, Houses of
Shoplifting
Truancy

Organized Crime and Gangs
Asian Gangs
Bloods
Crips
Flash Mobs
Gangs (Street)
La Eme (Mexican Mafia)
Latin Kings
MS-13
Skinheads
Swarming
Theft and Larceny
Vandalism
Weed and Seed
Zero-Tolerance/Saturation Policing

Perpetrators
Child Molesters
Crack House
Crime Patterns
Crime Prevention, Environmental Design and

Drug Dealing
Drugs, Prescription
Exposure, Indecent
Mental Illness

Street Crime in Cities
Baltimore, Maryland
Boston, Massachusetts
Buffalo, New York
Chicago, Illinois
Cincinnati, Ohio
Cleveland, Ohio
Detroit, Michigan
Indianapolis, Indiana
Kansas City, Missouri
Los Angeles, California
Miami, Florida
Milwaukee, Wisconsin
Minneapolis, Minnesota
New Orleans, Louisiana
New York City
Newark, New Jersey
Philadelphia, Pennsylvania
Pittsburgh, Pennsylvania
San Francisco, California
St. Louis, Missouri
Washington, D.C.

Urban Life/Criminology Theory
Bar Personnel
Bars and Pubs
Bystander Apathy
Code of the Street
Crime, Displacement of
Crime Prevention, Situational
Defensible Space Theory
Drinking Establishments, Unlicensed
Environmental Criminology
Fear of Crime
Gated Communities
Gentrification
Homelessness
Hooliganism
Hot Spots
Mass Transit, Crime on
Massage Parlors
Pool Halls
Projects, The
Routine Activity Theory
Stalking

Street Art
Street Corner Society
Street Crime (Online Game)
Street/Block Parties
Suite Crimes Versus Street Crimes
Urban Ethnography
Urban Incivility
Urban Planning
Urbanization

Victims

Children, Commercial Sexual Exploitation of
Children as Victims
Risky Lifestyles
Victims, Immigrant
Victims, Senior
Victims, Tourist
Women

Violent Crimes

Arson
Bank Robbery
Burglary
Domestic Violence
Drive-By Shooting
Guns and Weapons
Hate Crime
Homophobic Assault
Juvenile Offending
Kidnapping
Mobs and Riots
Mugging
Murder/Homicide
Organized Crime and Violence
Racial Assault
Rape and Sexual Assault
Road Rage
Serial Killers, Spree Killers, and Mass Murderers
Sex Crimes
Terrorism

About the Editor

Jeffrey Ian Ross, Ph.D., is a professor in the School of Criminal Justice, College of Public Affairs, and a research fellow of the Center for International and Comparative Law at the University of Baltimore.

He has researched, written, and lectured primarily on corrections, policing, political crime (especially terrorism and state crime), violence (especially criminal, political, and religious), crime and justice in American Indian Communities, and global crime and criminal justice for over two decades. Ross's work has appeared in many academic journals, books, and popular media. He is the author, co-author, editor, or coeditor of 17 books, including his most recent work, *An Introduction to Political Crime*, published in 2012.

Ross is a frequent and respected subject-matter expert for local, regional, national, and international news media. He has made live appearances on CNN, CNBC, and Fox News Network. Additionally, Ross has written op-eds for the (Baltimore) *Sun*, the (Maryland) *Daily Record*, *The Gazette* (weekly Maryland community newspapers), the *Baltimore Examiner*, and the *Tampa Tribune*.

From 1995 to 1998, Ross was a social science analyst with the National Institute of Justice, a division of the U.S. Department of Justice. In 2003, he was awarded the University of Baltimore's Distinguished Chair in Research Award. During the early 1980s, Ross worked almost four years in a correctional institution.

List of Contributors

Beth Adubato
New York Institute of Technology

J. Keith Akins
University of Houston, Victoria

Donald Anthony
Vanderbilt University

Joyce A. Arditti
*Virginia Polytechnic Institute and
State University*

Abby Bandurraga
Portland State University

Maya Pagni Barak
American University

Paolo Barbaro
École Pratique des Hautes Études

Terressa A. Benz
University of Idaho

Michael M. Berlin
Coppin State University

P. Colin Bolger
University of Cincinnati

Amanda Bolton
*University of Missouri,
St. Louis*

Clairissa D. Breen
Cazenovia College

Sarah Britto
Prairie View A & M University

David C. Brotherton
John Jay College of Criminal Justice

Michael P. Brown
Ball State University

Sarah Browning
North Dakota State University

Bradley Buckmeier
University of Cincinnati

Kristen Budd
Miami University of Ohio

Jennifer M. Burke
University of Cincinnati

George W. Burruss
*Southern Illinois University,
Carbondale*

Velmer S. Burton, Jr.
University of Minnesota-Twin Cities

Frank Butler
Saint Joseph's University

Vincent Carducci
The New School for Social Research

Patrick J. Carr
Rutgers University

John R. Cencich
California University of Pennsylvania

Michael Chou
University of Cincinnati

James J. Chriss
Cleveland State University

Susan Clampet-Lundquist
Saint Joseph's University

Colleen Clarke
*Minnesota State University,
Mankato*

Jeffrey E. Clutter
University of Cincinnati

Victoria Ellen Collins
  Old Dominion University
Scott H. Decker
  Arizona State University
Andrew Denney
  University of Louisville
Steven Downing
  University of Ontario Institute of Technology
M. George Eichenberg
  Tarleton State University
Patricia E. Erickson
  Canisius College
Kenneth E. Fernandez
  Elon University
Jeff Ferrell
  Texas Christian University/University of Kent
Benjamin W. Fisher
  Vanderbilt University
Mark S. Fleisher
  Case Western Reserve University
Kelly Frailing
  Texas A&M International University
Teresa Francis
  Central Washington University
Laurence Armand French
  University of New Hampshire, Durham
Kathleen Gallagher
  University of Cincinnati
James Geistman
  Ohio Northern University
Camille Gibson
  Prairie View A&M University
L. Kris Gowen
  Portland State Unversity
Amy Hyman Gregory
  Central Connecticut State University
Jennifer N. Grimes
  Indiana State University
Garrett Grothoff
  University of Cincinnati
Elaine Gunnison
  Seattle University
Colin Hammar
  University of Indianapolis
Dee Wood Harper, Jr.
  Loyola University New Orleans
Aida Y. Hass
  Missouri State University
Frederick Hawley
  Western Carolina University

Keith Hayward
  University of Kent
Jacqueline B. Helfgott
  Seattle University
Melissa L. Jarrell
  Texas A&M University, Corpus Christi
Michael J. Jenkins
  University of Scranton
Eric L. Jensen
  University of Idaho
Rebecca S. Katz
  Morehead State University
David Kauzlarich
  Southern Illinois University,
  Edwardsville
Daniel R. Kavish
  Southern Illinois University, Carbondale
Maria J. Kefalas
  Saint Joseph's University
Sesha Kethineni
  Illinois State University
Theo Kindynis
  University of Kent
Timothy Kinlock
  Friends Research Institute and
  University of Baltimore
Susan V. Koski
  Central Connecticut State University
Jorja M. Leap
  University of California, Los Angeles
Paul Leighton
  Eastern Michigan University
Michael Lenza
  University of Wisconsin Oshkosh
Keith Gregory Logan
  Kutztown University
Brenda J. Lutz
  Indiana University-Purdue University
  Fort Wayne
James M. Lutz
  Indiana University-Purdue University
  Fort Wayne
Michael D. Lyman
  Columbia College
Michael J. Lynch
  University of South Florida
William Mackey
  Indiana State University
Peter K. Manning
  Northeastern University

Eric S. McCord
University of Louisville

Tana McCoy
Roosevelt University

Jill McCracken
University of South Florida, St. Petersburg

John (Jack) McDevitt
Northeastern University

Phyllis P. McDonald
Johns Hopkins University

Zina T. McGee
Hampton University

Jennifer McMahon-Howard
Kennesaw State University

Susan McNeeley
University of Cincinnati

Robert Meier
University of Nebraska at Omaha

J. Mitchell Miller
University of Texas at San Antonio

William J. Miller
Flagler College

David R. Montague
University of Arkansas at Little Rock

Richard K. Moule, Jr.
Arizona State University

Christopher W. Mullins
Southern Illinois University Carbondale

Glenn W. Muschert
Miami University

Stephen L. Muzzatti
Ryerson University

Peter Norton
University of Virginia

Julia Noveske
Case Western Reserve University

Patrick K. O'Brien
University of Colorado Boulder

Allan L. Patenaude
University of Regina

Douglas D. Perkins
Vanderbilt University

Barbara Perry
University of Ontario Institute of Technology

Rebecca Pfeffer
Northeastern University

David Polizzi
Indiana State University

Elizabeth Rholetter Purdy
Independent Scholar

William E. Raffel
Buffalo State College

Prashan Ranasinghe
University of Ottawa

Wendy C. Regoeczi
Cleveland State University

Sadie Reynolds
Cabrillo College

Stephen C. Richards
University of Wisconsin Oshkosh

Christopher Richardson
University of Western Ontario

Scott A. Richmond
Wayne State University

James C. Roberts
University of Scranton

Jennifer J. Roberts
Indiana University of Pennsylvania

Carlos E. Rojas-Gaona
University of Cincinnati

Jeffrey Ian Ross
University of Baltimore

Jeffrey J. Roth
Indiana University of Pennsylvania

Dawn L. Rothe
Old Dominion University

Rick Ruddell
University of Regina

Jeffrey P. Rush
Austin Peay State University

Meghan Sacks
Fairleigh Dickinson University

Patti Ross Salinas
Missouri State University

Jenna Savage
Boston Police Department

Renita L. Seabrook
University of Baltimore

Jeffrey Shantz
Kwantlen Polytechnic University

Zachary Shemtob
Central Connecticut State University

Martha L. Shockey-Eckles
Saint Louis University

Aiden Sidebottom
University College London

Douglas M. Smith
University of Texas at San Antonio

Lionel Smith
University of Delaware

Martha Jane Smith
Wichita State University
Patric R. Spence
University of Kentucky
Philip Stinson
Bowling Green State University
Cody Stoddard
Central Washington University
Amy L. Stutzenberger
University of Cincinnati
John P. Sullivan
Independent Scholar
Richard Tewksbury
University of Louisville
Tracy Faye Tolbert
California State University, Long Beach
Lawrence F. Travis III
University of Cincinnati

Robert F. Vodde
Fairleigh Dickinson University
Norman A. White
Saint Louis University
Kevin Whiteacre
University of Indianapolis
Julie B. Wiest
High Point University
Pamela Wilcox
University of Cincinnati
Aaron Winter
University of Abertay Dundee
Benjamin S. Wright
University of Baltimore
Barbara H. Zaitzow
Appalachian State University
Glenn Zuern
Albany State University

Foreword

It is wrong to equate the nation's "crime problem" with "street crime," especially with those offenses committed by the inner-city poor. Criminologists have done much to deconstruct this limited view of reality. In fact, most forms of lawlessness are spread rather evenly across the social order. More salient, as repeated waves of corporate scandals reveal, white-collar crimes can cost society enormous sums of money and contribute to financial disaster. Less well known is that each year, illegal practices by corporations—maintaining unsafe or unhealthy workplaces, selling harmful products, or polluting the environment—arguably kill, injure, and sicken far more people than are physically harmed by street crime.

It would be equally wrong, however, to ignore that street crime has qualities and consequences that make such illegality central in the public's mind when its members think about criminal conduct and the need to control it. Again, scholars are correct to fight the myopic vision that focuses on crime in city streets while turning a blind eye to crimes in corporate suites. But this effort to illuminate the true breadth of the crime problem should not be taken to imply that street crime is unimportant. Nothing could be further from the truth.

Thus, no matter what kind of measures are used—official, victimization, or self-report statistics—it is clear that millions of street crimes are committed annually in the United States. Most are trivial and only a minor bother, and are soon forgotten. But others shatter the lives of victims and their families. When a youngster dies in a senseless shooting; when a woman is callously raped, whether by a stranger or on a date; when a gun is thrust in a person's face and a wallet taken; or when a home is burglarized and cherished property appropriated, the world is not quite the same thereafter. Grief persists, the feeling of personal safety is undermined, and a sense that one's daily existence can be taken for granted is forfeited.

This reaction occurs because street crime is often personal and predatory, with a perpetrator violating the sanctity of a victim's life space: the individual's car window is shattered and global positioning system (GPS) stolen, a door lock is broken and residence trashed, or a body is touched or bruised. The immediacy and physicality of the offense can trigger feelings of anger and injustice at having been harmed for no reason. Such criminality can incite emotional responses even when not personally experienced. So-called vicarious victimization—witnessing or hearing about the victimization of others—can engender fear and make people, such as the elderly, wary of venturing outside their homes.

The effects of street crime are felt across the social order. Regardless of our class status, most of us either have been or know someone who has been victimized in a troubling way. But the stubborn reality is that the most damaging illegalities—homicide and other kinds of violence in public spaces—are not evenly distributed. Another cost of American inequality is that it is the poor and people of color who bear this burden most heavily.

Since scholars in the Chicago School of criminology started to map the location of crimes and criminals across geographical areas in the first part of the 1900s, it has been known that the risk of victimization is highest for those living in inner-city neighborhoods marked by poverty, structural density, transience, and social disorganization. Although the groups have changed—mainly from European immigrants in past times to people of color today—the pattern has remained largely stable. It now appears that the connection between concentrated disadvantage and high rates of street crime and violence is an enduring criminological fact. It is a fact, moreover, that raises daunting questions about how best to control crime.

Over the past four decades, one option has dominated crime-control policy: Put the criminals behind bars. At first blush, incapacitating the wicked seems sensible. If chronic street offenders are victimizing innocent citizens, then why not send them to prison? In particular, if their predation is visited most often on the urban poor, why is not a stiff sentence a form of social justice? After all, this would be a case of the government allocating its financial resources—paying to incarcerate dangerous criminals—to protect and improve the welfare of its most vulnerable citizens.

There is a kernel of truth to this line of reasoning—but only a kernel. It breaks down for three reasons. First, a prison term is a blunt and often ineffective way to persuade a street offender to desist from a wayward life. To be sure, some crime is saved; during the time a person sits in a prison cell, further offenses are not committed by that person. This incapacitation effect, as it is called, is estimated to lower the crime rate about one-fourth from what it would be if all inmates were turned loose. But the crime savings come at an inordinate price: placing about 2.4 million people—or about 1 in 100 adults in the United States—behind bars on any given day. Many governors today, regardless of their political party, have recognized that this level of incarceration is financially unsustainable and are seeking ways to limit their states' prison populations. Equally relevant, prisons do not have a specific deterrent effect on offenders. Systematic reviews of the evidence have consistently shown that compared to a community-based penalty, a custodial placement does not reduce reoffending and may, in fact, be criminogenic.

Second, prisons are disproportionately repositories for poor, minority offenders—another ghetto, as some commentators have suggested, but one created by the state. Given that these custodial institutions often serve to cage and inflict pain and not to correct and improve, it is hard to argue that such facilities are instruments of social justice. In fact, they tend to function as temporary homes for inner-city offenders who, unreformed and undeterred by their incarceration, are released into the streets where the cycle of crime, imprisonment, and more crime is initiated once again. The effect of this churning process is to disrupt families and communities that are unprepared to absorb the stream of offenders constantly reentering their neighborhood—a phenomenon that commentators argue is criminogenic and undermines public safety. Most disquieting, some areas are known as "million dollar blocks"—streets whose residents' incarceration is costing the state $1 million a year. Might not this money have been spent in more productive ways?

Third, and to answer the question just posed, there are far more constructive options to choose in the attempt to reduce street crime. There is now a powerful, evidence-based treatment approach that has been shown to reduce the recidivism of high-risk offenders. To not try to reform street offenders who enter the correctional system is thus inexcusable. Much can be done as well with at-risk youngsters who are showing signs of early antisocial behavior or who have already begun criminal offending. For example, multisystemic therapy is a widely used program that brings an effective intervention into the home, working with troubled youths as well as with their families and schools to diminish the kids' exposure to criminogenic risk factors and to stave off their nascent criminal careers.

Further, many urban law enforcement departments have fundamentally changed their practices. These organizations now map hot spots for crime, engage in problem-oriented analysis seeking to uncover why crime is concentrated as it is, and work with community groups to try to lower street offending. They employ a combination of strategies such as situational crime-prevention programs that block access to criminal opportunities, shutting down bars or nightclubs that have high call rates for police service and victimization incidents, and sponsoring violence-reduction programs aimed at simultaneously disrupting criminal networks and offering offenders a way out of crime. The larger point is that the efforts to address street crime must not be fixated on prison as the only, or the best, policy alternative. A comprehensive approach to crime control must recognize the limits of imprisonment and embrace diverse, empirically-based intervention strategies.

Importantly, despite the harm caused and challenges posed by street crime, there is much good news to share: Rates of street crime have been on a historic downward arc for two decades. To illustrate this point, Franklin Zimring has calculated the percentage decline in homicide for six major cities between 1990 and 2009: New York (82 percent), Los Angeles (71 percent), Houston (64 percent), San Diego (75 percent), San Jose (36 percent), and Boston (68 percent). To place these statistics in perspective, Zimring further discloses what he calls an "astonishing" fact: The 2009 homicide rate in New York was only 18 percent of the city's 1990 rate. Notably, in the late 1980s, declines of this magnitude were not forecasted, and they defy standard criminological explanation today. Part of the crime drop can be attributed to mass imprisonment and to shifts in population (the aging of the baby boomer generation). But the cause of most of the lower offense rates remains a mystery, and the best accounts offered by scholars amount to no more than plausible speculation.

Still, Zimring leaves us with a telling observation. Many of the inner-city poor and people of color who engaged in serious street crime in past decades were depicted as cold-blooded superpredators beyond reform. Crime and the core features of urban life that arguably produced this cohort of unredeemable thugs were seen as inextricably linked—an ironclad relationship that could never be broken. As it turns out, however, these groups were hardly intractably criminal but rather were quite "malleable"—as the large crime declines show. Zimring thus reminds us of the "inessentiality of urban crime"—that street offenses are perhaps only loosely coupled to, not rigidly determined by, the people, culture, economic structure, or institutions that characterize inner cities. Actions can be taken to encourage conformity and to discourage crime; and when they coalesce in the right mixture at the right point in time, they lead many people who once might have broken the law to make different choices.

In this context, it seems critical that the origins, effects, and means of controlling street crime be intimately understood. In this volume, Jeffrey Ian Ross thus provides a critical service in compiling informative essays on virtually every aspect of this phenomenon—from celebrated cases to crime in cities and places, from theories and types of street crime to diverse prevention strategies. Notably, this encyclopedia is like a criminological Walmart—everything you need to know about street crime contained under one cover.

This organization of knowledge has been an editorial challenge—and one, I might add, that Professor Ross has admirably surmounted. Despite the salience of street crime, much criminological scholarship has paid scant attention to such offending. This seems an odd omission for a discipline named criminology—the study of crime. However, spurred in particular by Travis Hirschi's *Causes of Delinquency* published in 1969, most scholars turned their attention away from detailed studies of street offenders, including from what lures youngsters into a criminal career and how they then go about a life of thievery, burglary, hold-ups, shootings, and so on. Instead, the focus was directed to developing rival theoretical perspectives and then testing them with self-report studies of high school students, selected more for convenience (easily accessible) than for substantive reasons (they were perpetrators of serious illegal acts).

This line of inquiry produced a wealth of publications and much invaluable knowledge, especially on likely criminogenic risk factors (for example, weak social bonds, associating with delinquent peers). But the relative ease of conducting studies on students—and the advent of desktop computers for simply downloading secondary self-report data sets collected by others—had the unfortunate side effect of becoming a method of doing criminology that was too tempting for scholars to pass up (alas, including this author). Thus, rather than venture into real-world environs so as to spend time chronicling the daily lives of street offenders and the nature of their criminal acts, most scholars became—and now remain—armchair researchers who crunch data on computers and turn out publishable articles from the comfort of their offices.

Again, these considerations supply a context for appreciating the unique contribution of Jeffrey Ian Ross's *Encyclopedia of Street Crime in America*. By presenting a compelling roster of essays, this volume allows us, in an unprecedented way, to travel inside the world of street crime—a world rarely visited by most criminologists. Embarking on such an excursion, with Professor Ross as one's able tour guide, is well worth the investment of time and energy. Indeed, truly learning about the complexities of street crime not only is an endlessly fascinating experience but also is essential to achieving a rich understanding of the criminal enterprise.

Francis T. Cullen
Distinguished Research Professor
University of Cincinnati

Introduction

Street crime is a prevalent factor in cities and urban locales in the United States and around the world. The headlines of major daily newspapers and the lead stories on the local nightly news are replete with reported incidents of street robberies, carjackings, sexual assaults, and missing children. The news media and the public appear to have an insatiable appetite for information on this kind of social behavior. Although street crime has existed since humans decided that it would be in their best mutual interests to live close to their neighbors and form communities, street crime in America reached a crescendo in terms of public attention and official rates (as measured by the Uniform Crime Reports) in the 1980s and lasted well into the remaining decade of the 20th century. The fact that violent crime and property crime started declining in the mid-1990s and hit an all time low in 2003 has been ignored by many members of the public, reporters, and politicians alike. Needless to say, street crime remains a fact of life for city dwellers and criminal justice practitioners alike.

Although few definitions exist, in general, street crime refers to crimes connected to the urban lifestyle, against people and property, committed in both public and private places. Indeed many of these types of crimes can occur in suburban and rural areas, but urban locales are unique in many respects. With few exceptions, cities have higher population densities, more attractive targets for victimization, and house a disproportionate number of the country's poor than suburban and rural

parts of the United States. The fact that most introductory textbooks on criminology and criminal justice do not define street crime per se is ironic and contradictory in many respects, but this discussion is best left for a different venue.

This essay is intended to provide a brief overview of the content of the encyclopedia so readers will have a sort of road map of what to expect. It also provides a brief history on scholarship in this area of inquiry. The encyclopedia includes entries concerning the major actors (that is, not only types of criminals, but also the victims), affected by street crime. It also identifies and analyzes the variety of perpetrators (from street gangs to organized crime) and those who get involved after the fact when street crimes are reported, from private citizen groups (such as the Guardian Angels and vigilantes) to publicly-chartered criminal justice agencies (for example, police, courts, and jails). The encyclopedia also reviews important figures who have attempted to control and/or respond to street crime in America (William Bratton, Rudolph Giuliani, etc.). Not content to simply mention the individuals, the *Encyclopedia of Street Crime in America* also looks at some of the major criminal justice initiatives to study and monitor street crime (for example, the Kerner Commission and the Kansas City Preventive Patrol Experiment). Some of the more important street crime cases that garnered public attention are included in this encyclopedia are the 1964 murder of Kitty Genovese, the 1987 Tawana Brawley "assault," and the 1989 Central Park Jogger cases, all occurring in New York City. Theories and debates concerning street crime causation are also examined, such as the Broken Windows Theory, and the debate concerning the disproportionate attention among criminologists and the popular media on street crimes versus suite crimes.

The encyclopedia has entries focusing on street crime in the largest cities in the United States (such as New York City, Los Angeles, and Washington, D.C.). These topics review street crime trends in each of these cities, and the major players, including the civic organizations, political leaders, and criminal justice actors that have been involved in combating and responding to street crime over the past six decades.

Entries review the history and dynamics of street crime and scholarship on this topic. In so doing, they trace both the empirical research, news reporting, and government documentation that has developed, and the moral panic that arose in the United States concerning this topic.

Brief History of Street Crime in Contemporary America

Crime has always been part of the American social fabric. Street crime became an important public policy concern during the 1960s. The federal government sponsored a number of commissions, partially because of the increased number of street demonstrations and riots in connection with public demands for increased civil rights, racial inequality, and America's military participation in Indochina (Vietnam in particular). The first, the Commission on Law Enforcement and Criminal Justice, released its well-cited report, *The Challenge of Crime in a Free Society*, in 1967. The second, the National Advisory Commission on Civil Disorders (often referred to as the Kerner Commission), published its findings in 1968.

In the 1960s, a series of federally funded commissions, including the U.S. National Commission on the Causes of Crime and Disorder (1968), investigated race riots and increasing crime in the country. The reports made several recommendations, one of which was the passage of the Omnibus Crime Control and Safe Streets Act, which established a separate branch of the Department of Justice called the Law Enforcement Assistance Administration.

The administration's mission was to provide funds for postsecondary institutions of higher education to train criminal justice personnel; give out grants and low-cost loans to practitioners pursuing higher education; give money to universities to develop programs in criminology and criminal justice; increase specialized knowledge about criminology/criminal justice; and improve education for practitioners.

Crime was and is a politically charged social problem and methods to reduce its frequency were embraced by the administration of Democratic President Lyndon Johnson in his War on Crime. His administration's failure to make a meaningful dent in the crime rate gave conservative elements (that is, the Republicans) an easily identifiable policy failure to point to. This helped usher Richard Nixon into the White House and laid the seeds of the later failed anticrime policies and practices generally referred to as the War on Drugs, and changes in laws and sentencing, which was a "tough on crime" approach (for example, truth in sentencing, or three strikes you are out).

While the public channeled their discontent to local criminal justice agencies, their mayors, and other elected officials in their cities and states, some individuals were not content to have local law enforcement be responsible for public safety. Although neighborhood self-help groups such as the Black Panthers in the Watts neighborhood of Los Angeles, California, started appearing during the 1960s, it was not until the late 1970s that groups like the New York City–based Guardian Angels started emerging. Distinctive in their red berets and jackets, they would patrol high crime areas on foot such as the subway and housing projects, hoping to act both as a deterrent to criminals and to apprehend individuals (by using a citizen's arrest) if they witnessed them committing a crime. This coproduction of public safety manifested itself in neighborhood watches and crime prevention programs that citizens were encouraged to participate in.

During and since the 1980s, a handful of notable incidents, trends, and seminal pieces of research have affected policing. These include the introduction of community policing, zero-tolerance policing, and CompStat. In 1979, Herman Goldstein published his quintessential article on problem-oriented policing. He suggested that since the development of motorized patrol, police had become increasingly out of touch with the communities they served. This resulted in an increase in both crime and citizens' disrespect for the police. To change this state of affairs, police needed to shift their focus ever so slightly from crimes that have already occurred to the problems that lead to crime. Goldstein advocated that police departments form true partnerships with the communities in which they work to solve mutually identified problems. Problem-oriented policing became one of several strategies embedded in community policing. It took another 15 years for his ideas to result in the formation and passage of the 1994 Violent Crime Control and Law Enforcement Act (also known as the Crime Act), which, among its major components, led to the creation of the Office of Community-Oriented Policing Services in the Department of Justice.

In 1982, James Q. Wilson and George Kelling wrote a seminal article called "Broken Windows: The Police and Neighborhood Safety," which argued that small-scale deviance and neighborhood disorder (for example, houses boarded up, in disrepair, lawns not being cut, or graffiti) can have a big effect on neighborhood deterioration and thus crime. This article provided the intellectual groundwork for the slow and selected introduction of zero-tolerance policing—that is, the aggressive enforcement of one or more criminal laws in a particular jurisdiction and/or during a specific period; no discretion is allowed on the part of officers. It was also seminal for the introduction of CompStat (short form for Computer Analysis of Crime Statistics, or Comprehensive Computer Statistics) in the New York City Police Department. In essence, through the CompStat program, on a regular basis, the police department converts crime statistics into maps of criminal events. This information is then used by senior management to regularly monitor the performance of precinct-level staff in crime reduction efforts.

By the 1990s, street crime was still a prominent part of the urban experience with young economically disenfranchised African American and Hispanic males disproportionately being both perpetrators and victims. By this time, scholars were trying to make sense of the empirical reality of this phenomenon and to understand the wider implications of this trend. Diana Gordon, in her book *The Justice Juggernaut: Fighting Street Crime, Controlling Citizens*, warned readers that because street crime is a dominant social problem, it is easy to assume that rationale responses have been crafted. On the other hand, those that do get passed disproportionally are at the behest of the powerful and loudest segments of society, and this can be dangerous, if not a waste of taxpayers' funds.

As we entered into the 1990s, the street crime rate started leveling out and a Democrat (Bill Clinton) was elected to the White House. One of his first acts of business was the passage of the Crime Bill. Not only did it establish the Office of Community Policing Services, but it also provided funds to eligible law enforcement agencies to hire 10,000 new police officers who would be doing community policing. It also provided funding for research on community policing. Numerous pilot projects were implemented, some were even evaluated. Though street crime appears to be in decline in our major centers, alternative challenges seem to dominate both law enforcement and current headlines. Police departments, particularly large urban ones, are now being drawn into terrorism investigations and into the monitoring of illegal immigration. Both of these tasks are being asked of our criminal justice practitioners while we cut their budgets.

Conclusion

The *Encyclopedia of Street Crime in America* is the most up-to-date work on the subject. The encyclopedia should appeal not only to criminologists, but also to criminal justice practitioners, students of criminology/criminal justice, members of the media, and to politicians seeking an overview on the problem of street crime. The public should also find many of the entries informative, interesting, and engaging.

Jeffrey Ian Ross
Editor

Chronology

1630: The City of Boston passes a law banning all cards, dice, and gambling tables and establishes penalties for violators.

1781: Reverend Samuel Peters coins the phrase *blue laws* in his work published under a pseudonymn, the *General History of Connecticut.*

1783: First reports surface of gang activity along the east coast of the United States after the Revolutionary War. These gangs, known as Smith's Vly gang, the Bowery Boys, the Broadway Boys, the Long Bridge Boys, and the Fly Boys, are made up of local youths defending their turf with their fists.

1820: Following a large wave of immigration, ethnic gangs begin forming in New York City. The new gangs are deemed more structured and considerably more dangerous than gangs of earlier eras.

1823: Congress approves a national lottery with proceeds earmarked for beautifying Washington, D.C. Unfortunately, the private agency that organized the lottery absconds with money garnered from the sale of tickets. The Supreme Court later rules that the winner of the $100,000 prize be paid by the District of Columbia.

1825: The Forty Thieves, which becomes the most notorious youth gang of the period, is founded in Lower Manhattan. Gang members are typically bouncers, laborers, longshoremen, butchers, and carpenters to whom violence and turf wars are a way of life.

1830: The combined earnings of legal and illegal lotteries rises to $60 million. That amount is five times the current federal budget.

1832: Massachusetts and Pennsylvania outlaw all lotteries, and other states soon follow their lead.

1835: Antigambling vigilante groups drive gamblers out of Natchez, Mississippi; Memphis, Tennessee; and a number of other river towns.

1837: Approximately 400 schools in Massachusetts are vandalized.

1840: Pistol- and knife-carrying gangs such as the Bouncers, Rats, and Skinners appear in Philadelphia, Pennsylvania.

1855: A New York City historian estimates that at least 30,000 members of gangs operating in the city are connected to political leaders associated with Tammany Hall, the Know Nothing Party, or the Native American Party.

1860: The first Chinese gangs (tongs) begin appearing in New York City. They are involved in the sale of opium, gambling, and political patronage.

1866: Forming themselves from the defunct Chinchesters, the Wyos begin absorbing other former rivals to become Manhattan's most-feared gang. They offer a menu of crimes for hire that range from punching someone to murder.

1871: In October, a white mob attacks 20 Chinese immigrants in Los Angeles, burning and looting both private homes and stores.

1883: During what becomes known as the Snake River Massacre in Oregon, 31 Chinese miners are murdered by disgruntled cohorts.

1895: Congress passes the Federal Lottery Act, banning lotteries in all types of interstate commerce, as a result of individuals attempting to transport foreign lottery tickets across state lines.

1900: Approximately a quarter of a million Americans are reportedly addicted to opiates.

1910: James R. Mann (R-IL), chair of the Interstate Commerce Committee, steers a "white slavery" bill through the House of Representatives, making it a violation of federal law to aid, abet, or transport females across state lines for "immoral purposes."

1912: The American Purity Alliance and the American Vigilance Committee merge into the American Federation for Social Hygiene to combine efforts to work toward banning all forms of prostitution and halting the spread of venereal disease.

1913: In Atlanta, Jewish American Leo Frank is found guilty of murdering a teenage girl who works in his factory. The conviction is based on circumstantial evidence, and Governor John Slaton commutes the sentence to life in prison. A mob storms Frank's cell and lynches him. Decades later, evidence is produced proving that a janitor in the factory committed the murder.

1914: Congress passes the Harrison Narcotic Act, regulating the production and sale of opium, morphine, heroin, cocaine, and coca products, and requiring licensing of all distributers.

1914: The last major downtown gang battle takes place in New York City.

1918: In response to an outbreak of syphilis during World War I, Congress passes the Chamberlain-Kahn bill, requiring the internment of any female suspected of being a prostitute. The average term of internment is 10 weeks, but minor females are sometimes held for a year or until they reach maturity.

1918: Congress passes the Mann Act, which bans the transportation of any person across state or territorial lines for the purposes of prostitution or other forms of illegal sexual activity. Violators could be fined, serve up to five years in prison, or both.

1919: Fleeing gangland-style murder charges in New York, notorious gangster Al Capone relocates to Chicago.

1919: Following the drowning of an African American youth on a section of beach designated for whites, a race riot rages in Chicago from July 27 to August 2. Before it is over, 38 people are dead, 537 are injured, and 1,000 people have been rendered homeless.

1920: On January 16, the Eighteenth Amendment takes effect, restricting the sale of alcohol and establishing an environment in which speakeasies, organized crime, and the Italian Mafia flourish.

1922: The Narcotic Drugs Import and Export Act tightens existing restrictions on the sale of mind-altering drugs in the United States.

1925: Moving away from the ethnic gangs of the past, 40 percent of all gangs operating in Chicago are composed of mixed ethnicities.

1928: With Chinese immigration banned, racists turn their attention to Filipinos, and rioting breaks out in both California and Washington State.

1930: Anti-Filipino rioting again breaks out in California and Washington State.

1931: In Alabama, nine African American men are arrested for the alleged rape of two white women on a train. Although the charges prove to be unfounded, the defendants spend most of the rest of their lives trying to clear their names and recover damages.

1931: After Thalia Massie is raped in Honolulu, Hawai'i, her husband murders one of her alleged assailants. The case receives national attention when noted attorney Clarence Darrow defends the husband.

1931: In order to combat the Great Depression, the state of Nevada legalizes gambling within its borders, paving the way for its future role as the gambling capital of the United States.

1931: The state of Massachusetts decriminalizes the game of Bingo.

1933: Ratification of the Twenty-First Amendment overturns the Eighteenth Amendment, signaling the end of Prohibition.

1933: Michigan, New Hampshire, and Ohio legalize pari-mutuel betting.

1934: Sexual deviant Albert Fish is apprehended in White Plains, New York, and charged with the murder, mutilation, and cannibalism of 12-year-old Grace Budd.

1934: Bruno Hauptmann is charged with the kidnapping and murder of the infant son of aviator Charles Lindbergh.

1936: New Yorker prosecutor and future Republican presidential candidate Thomas Dewey successfully prosecutes Mafia member Charles "Lucky" Luciano on charges of prostitution and pandering. Doubts continue to surface concerning his guilt.

1937: Passage of the Marijuana Tax Act gives the federal government the authority to control production and distribution of marijuana.

1942: Congress passes the Opium Poppy Control Act, making it a violation of federal law to grow opium poppies without a license, which is issued only to those engaged in growing the seeds for medical or scientific purposes. In California, growers are granted an exception for current crops.

1942: On August 2 in the Sleepy Lagoon area of Los Angeles, the body of Jose Diaz leads to the arrest of 300 Mexican American youths. Twelve are convicted of murder, and five are found guilty of assault in what is subsequently labeled a kangaroo court.

1943: In May, during a high school dance in Venice, California, allegations surface that local Mexican American Zoot Suiters have stabbed a sailor. A crowd of 500 sailors and civilians begins attacking Mexican Americans in retaliation. Over the next few days, the mob grows to 5,000, and the attack spreads to the African American section of Watts.

1944: A U.S. Appeals Court overturns the convictions of those charged with murder or assault in the Sleepy Lagoon Murder.

1946: With the debut of the Flamingo Casino in Nevada, the notorious Benjamin "Bugsy" Siegel becomes the first gangster to build a casino controlled by racketeers.

1948: World War II veteran Otto Friedli founds the Hells Angels Motorcycle Club in Fontana, California. The club eventually goes global, attaining iconic status.

1951: The Special Committee to Investigate Organized Crime of the U.S. Senate holds televised hearings on mob involvement in gambling.

1953: Marlon Brandon stars in *The Wild One*, a movie about two rival motorcycle gangs terrorizing a small town. Brando becomes a cultural icon, but critics contend that the movie glorifies violence.

1955: On August 24, Emmett Till, a 14-year-old Chicago youth visiting his uncle in Money, Mississippi, incurs the wrath of white racist Roy Bryant by "flirting" with his wife while hanging out on a local street. J. W. Milam forcibly removes Till from his uncle's home in the middle of the night, and his mutilated body is later discovered. Both men are exonerated of Till's murder by an all-white jury.

1958: Respected CBS journalist Edward R. Murrow narrates *Who Killed Michael Farmer*, a documentary about the beating death of a handicapped 15-year-old in a New York City park during a gang war.

1961: The Supreme Court upholds Maryland's blue laws in *McGowan v. Maryland*.

1962: The notorious Boston Strangler begins his two-year spree of rape and murder.

1963: On June 12, civil rights activist Medgar Evers is murdered as he arrives at the driveway of his own home. It is not until 1994 that Byron de la Beckwith is successfully prosecuted for the crime and sentenced to life in prison.

1963: On September 15, an African American church in Birmingham, Alabama, is bombed during Sunday school, killing four young girls. The bombing is one of the many incidents that heighten pressure for comprehensive civil rights legislation at the federal level.

1963: On November 22, Lee Harvey Oswald allegedly fires on the presidential motorcade traveling through downtown Dallas, Texas, killing President John F. Kennedy and wounding Governor John Connally.

1964: While returning home from work, in two separate attacks, 28-year-old bar manager Kitty Genovese is repeatedly stabbed and raped in Queens, New York, by Winston Mosley. While as many as 28 neighbors hear her calls for help, no one intervenes. She dies as a result of her wounds.

1964: Arizona Republican Barry Goldwater focuses national attention on street crime by making it a major issue in his presidential campaign.

1964: New Hampshire institutes the first statewide lottery of the postwar period, permitting gambling on two horse races each year.

1965: On August 11, racial rioting begins in Watts, an impoverished Los Angeles neighborhood, after the arrest of an African American motorist by a white police officer. The riot continues for six days, results in the loss of 34 lives, and inflicts $40 million dollars in damages.

1966: On June 12, rioting breaks out during a Puerto Rican Day parade on Chicago's Division Street after the shooting of a Puerto Rican male by police officers. The riot continues for two days as residents express their dissatisfaction with economic and social conditions.

1967: Rioting breaks out in the African American ghettos of Newark, New Jersey, on July 12 after police arrest an African American cab driver. The riot rages for four days, leaving 26 dead, including a 10-year-old child, and results in $10 million in damages.

1967: On July 23, rioting in Detroit is precipitated by a police raid on an unlicensed after-hours drinking club located at Twelfth Street and Clairmont Avenue. Alleging police brutality, African Americans riot for five days, engaging in rampant looting and arson.

1967: President Lyndon B. Johnson appoints Illinois Governor Otto Kerner, Jr., to chair the National Advisory Commission on Civil Disorders following a series of urban racial riots.

1967: In response to President Johnson's War on Poverty, the Spartican Army, a New York Puerto Rican gang, opts to join the Establishment, opening a child-care facility and offering summer classes for inner-city youths.

1967: New York City relaxes its antiprostitution laws, clearing the way for prostitutes to openly seek business in public places such as Times Square. Pimps begin frequenting bus terminals, targeting young Scandinavian girls arriving from the midwest along what becomes known as the "Minnesota Strip."

1968: The National Advisory Commission on Civil Disorders, popularly known as the Kerner Commission, issues a 426-page report detailing the existence of two separate societies in the United States and calling for increased opportunities for African Americans and an expanded police presence to forestall potential rioting.

1969: After being ejected from the Stonewall bar in New York City by police, gay patrons in Greenwich Village initiate a riot. That action sets off a period of increased activism within the gay and lesbian communities.

1970: African American gangs begin resurfacing in Los Angeles, with most members gravitating to either the Crips or the Bloods.

1971: President Richard Nixon creates the Special Action Office of Drug Abuse Prevention to coordinate aspects of his drug policy and programs.

1971: Feminists hold the first public speak-out against rape in St. Clement's Episcopal Church in New York City.

1971: New Jersey launches the first successful modern lottery with 50-cent tickets and weekly drawings, netting $30 million within the first six months of operation.

1972: Officials report that there are 500 gangs operating within Los Angeles.

1972: In Jacksonville, Florida, eight individuals are convicted of "prowling by auto" and loitering under a local ordinance. The ordinance is subsequently found unconstitutional on the grounds of vagueness because its intentions were not made clear, which was perceived as potentially leading to innocent activity being labeled illegal.

1973: The Supreme Court establishes a constitutional right to abortion on the grounds of privacy in *Roe v. Wade*, and antiabortionists embark on a wave of violence against reproductive clinics.

1973: President Richard Nixon establishes the National Institute of Drug Abuse to bring all federal prevention and treatment programs under one umbrella.

1973: Margo St. James and a group of San Francisco prostitutes establish COYOTE, an advocacy group for prostitutes, and begin holding the Hooker's Ball.

1973: The National Organization for Women calls for the decriminalization of prostitution.

1975: The American Civil Liberties Union joins other liberal groups in demanding that prostitution be decriminalized.

1976: Anti-abortionists begin using arson to shut down clinics that provide abortion services.

1977: In *Coker v. Georgia*, the Supreme Court rules that that invoking the death penalty in cases involving the rape of an adult amounts to "cruel and unusual punishment" in violation of the Eighth Amendment to the U.S. Constitution.

1978: A wave of bombings at abortion clinics occurs throughout the year.

1978: In San Francisco on November 27, Harvey Milk, an openly gay member of the Board of Supervisors, and Mayor George Moscone are killed by Dan White, a former supervisor whose reappointment to the board has been blocked by Milk. White is eventually sentenced to only seven years in prison for the murders.

1979: In Atlanta during the summer, two 14-year-old African American youths disappear and are found murdered. The killing spree, which becomes known as the Atlanta Child Murders, continues for two more years, claiming a total of 28 victims ranging in age from 7 to adulthood. Wayne Williams is ultimately convicted of two of the murders. The murder spree ends, but controversy concerning Williams's conviction rages for decades.

1979: In New York City on May 25, 6-year-old Etan Patz disappears while on his way to school and is never seen again. Beginning in 1983, that date is celebrated each year as Missing Children's Day in the United States.

1979: McDonald's night manager Curtis Sliwa founds the Magnificent 13, a voluntary group of unarmed New Yorkers who patrol subways, streets, and neighborhoods to prevent crime. The group, eventually named the Guardian Angels, gains a global following.

1981: Seven-year-old Adam Walsh is kidnapped from a shopping mall in Hollywood, Florida, on July 27. In August, his decapitated body is discovered in a canal in Vero Beach. Serial killer Ottis O'Toole confesses to the crime but is never charged. Adam's father John helps found the National Center for Missing and Exploited Children and becomes the host of the television show *America's Most Wanted*.

1982: Eighty percent of President Ronald Reagan's drug budget targets efforts to reduce the flow of banned substances into the United States.

1982: Chrysler plant superintendent Ronald Ebens and his stepson Michael Nitz beat Chinese American auto worker Vincent Chin to death over their anger at the impact of Japanese manufacturers on the American auto industry. After a plea bargain, they are given probation and a fine. The incident helps inspire the Asian American civil rights movement.

1983: The gang rape of a female occurs at Big Dan's Tavern in New Bedford, Massachusetts, amid cheers of encouragement. Four of the six perpetrators are later convicted.

1983: Some 400 Americans participate in the first annual National Night Out to focus public attention on the need to combat street crime and drug abuse at the local level.

1984: Congress passes the Missing Children's Assistance Act and establishes the National Resource Center and Clearinghouse on Missing and Exploited Children. That role is filled by the National Center for Missing and Exploited Children, which sets up a 24/7 hotline (1-800-THE-LOST).

1984: Self-employed Bernhard Goetz, a former mugging victim, shoots four African American teenagers with an unlicensed revolver during what he characterizes as a mugging on a Manhattan subway. The press dubs him the Subway Vigilante and he is hailed as a hero by many New Yorkers.

1986: President Ronald Reagan formalizes his war on drugs on August 4, initiating a national crusade against drugs.

1986: On December 20, in Howard Beach in Queens, New York, Michael Griffith, an African American construction worker, and his companions seek help after their car breaks down. Griffith is subsequently struck and killed by an automobile while fleeing white teenagers wielding baseball bats and tree limbs and shouting racial epithets.

1986: Florida becomes the first state to mandate human immunodeficiency virus and acquired immune deficiency syndrome (HIV/AIDS) testing of prostitutes.

1987: Bernhard Goetz is cleared of attempted murder charges of the four teenagers who threatened him on the subway, but is found guilty of illegal possession of a firearm

1987: The Reagan administration doubles the amount of federal funding allotted to drug control, focusing chiefly on expanding the reach of law enforcement and shifting efforts to states through block grants.

1987: On November 28, reports surface that Tawana Brawley, a 15-year-old New Yorker, had been abducted and repeatedly raped by six white men, including one wearing a police badge. Her story is later discredited because no evidence substantiates her claim that abduction or rape ever occurred.

1987: Newspapers in southern California report that "road rage" has been responsible for 70 shootings and one stabbing during the summer months.

1987: In New York City, Arthur K. Saloman, a former investment banker, engages in an argument with an unarmed college student over whose vehicle has the right to pass the other. As the student walks back to his car, Saloman shoots him. Convicted of first-degree assault, Saloman receives an 18-month prison sentence.

1988: Congress restores much of the antidrug funding cut by the Reagan administration and passes the Anti-Drug Abuse Act, creating the Office of National Drug Policy Control and increasing penalties for drug traffickers.

1988: Wisconsin passes a new hate crime law that allows judges to add up to five years to the punishment of anyone convicted of attacks in which selected victims are chosen solely because of their race, religion, color, disability, sexual orientation, national origin, or ancestry.

1988: Rioting breaks out in New York's Tompkins Square Park when park habitués protesting a 1 A.M. curfew are assailed by police officers.

1989: Following complaints of heavy late-night activity in a Los Angeles neighborhood warehouse, federal and local police officers discover 47,554

pounds of cocaine protected only by a $6 lock. The street value of the cache is estimated at a value of $6 to $7 billion. The incident nets the largest cocaine recovery in history.

1989: While returning from a convenience store, 11-year-old Jacob Wetterling is kidnapped near his home in St. Joseph, Minnesota, by a gun-wielding masked man. He is never seen again, and no one is ever brought to trial in the case. The incident leads to the 1994 passage of Jacob's Law, requiring registration of those convicted of sexual crimes against children.

1989: The public responds with widespread outrage to reports that a group of popular athletes in Glen Ridge, New Jersey, have raped a mentally handicapped teenager.

1989: Nationwide, school officials report that 15.3 percent of schools are experiencing gang activity. In urban schools, that number rises to 24.8 percent.

1989: On April 19, investment banker Trisha Meili is brutally attacked and raped while jogging through New York's Central Park. Five Hispanic youths are convicted of the crime.

1989: In July in Raleigh, North Carolina, two brothers who believe Jim (Ming Hai) Loo, a Chinese American, is Vietnamese, accuse him of being responsible for American deaths during the Vietnam Conflict. They strike him with a baseball bat, and he falls face down on a broken bottle, which pierces his brain. Robert Piche is sentenced to 37 years in prison, and Lloyd Piche is found guilty of violating Loo's civil rights. This is the first time the federal government has successfully prosecuted a civil rights case involving an Asian American victim.

1989: In Kenosha, Wisconsin, on October 7, a group of black teenagers led by Todd Mitchell attack a white passerby after viewing the civil rights-era movie *Mississippi Burning*. Mitchell is charged with violation of Wisconsin's new hate crime law and has two years added to his two-year sentence for aggravated battery. He appeals the conviction.

1989: Portland, Oregon, passes a local ordinance allowing police officers to impound the vehicles of customers visiting prostitutes. Owners must pay approximately $300 in fines and processing costs to reclaim their vehicles, and the signatures of other owners, including wives or employers, are required.

1990: Contrary to popular belief, an analysis of National Crime Victimization Surveys reveals that 70 percent of assaults on white Americans are committed by white assailants.

1990: In New York, Hispanics replace African Americans as the dominant force in street gangs.

1990: Congress makes it a felony violation to bring guns within 1,000 feet of any school.

1990: Boston turns to community policing after experiencing 152 homicides and 1,000 aggravated assaults in a single year. Homicides rates drop 50 percent overall. The homicide rate among people younger than 24 decreases by two-thirds.

1990: A study released by the Commission on Public Health reveals that 75 percent of 201 prostitutes surveyed claim that they would perform any sex act without using a condom if the price were right.

1991: On May 20, the cargo ship *President Truman* arrives in Oakland, California, from Bangkok, Thailand. Acting on a hunch, customs agents board the vessel, where they discover 1,071 pounds of heroin estimated at a street value of $2.5 billion. It is the largest stash of heroin ever discovered in a single incident in the United States.

1991: A poll released by the National Opinion Research Council indicates that 42 percent of Americans living in suburban areas of large cities are afraid to walk their own neighborhoods at night because of street crime.

1991: On March 3, a home video captures the beating of African American motorist Rodney King by four Los Angeles police officers. Their subsequent acquittal sets off a wave of rioting that leads to 53 death and $1 billion in damages.

1991: Jewish civil rights groups report that the number of anti-Semitic attacks has reached an all-time high.

1991: Antihomosexual attacks rise by almost one-third in the five large American cities that monitor such incidents.

1991: Yankel Rosenbaum, a visiting Jewish scholar, is fatally attacked in an anti-Semitic rampage in the predominantly African American section of Brooklyn's Crown Heights. The person responsible for Rosenbaum's death is later acquitted.

1991: The International Narcotics Control Board of the United Nations reports that there are 12.6 million drug abusers in the United States. The report also states that the number of cocaine abusers in the United States has risen from 1.6 million to 1.9 million over the past year.

1991: According to Federal Bureau of Investigation records, 81,536 arrests are made on charges of engaging in prostitution or providing commercial sex in this year alone.

1991: With the sixth-highest violent crime rate in the nation, New Haven, Connecticut, institutes community policing, setting off a trend of declining crime rates.

1992: The Campus Sexual Assault Victims Bill of Rights is passed, protecting the rights of victims of sexual assaults on college campuses, mandating public reporting of campus sexual assaults, and allowing victims to report assaults to the police rather than to campus security.

1992: In *R.A.V. v. St. Paul*, the Supreme Court overturns the local hate crime ordinance that had been used to prosecute a white teenager who burned a cross in the yard of a black family, setting off a national debate on the constitutionality of similar ordinances and campus speech codes.

1992: The state Supreme Courts of both Ohio and Wisconsin overturn state hate crime penalty-enhancement laws.

1992: The City Council of Chicago passes an anti-gang ordinance prohibiting gang members from congregating on streets or in public places, leading to 89,000 dispersal orders and 42,000 arrests over a three-year period. The ordinance is subsequently overturned in *City of Chicago v. Morales* after being deemed vague.

1992: Suburban Los Angeles schools confiscate a total of 405 guns during the school year, and 28 of these are taken from elementary school students.

1993: In March, abortion provider David Gunn is murdered in Pensacola, Florida.

1993: On October 1, 12-year-old Polly Klaas is taken from her home in Petaluma, California, during a slumber party by a man who enters her home from the street outside. Her strangled body is discovered on December 3, focusing national attention on the issue of the registration of known sexual offenders who prey on children.

1993: The number of participants in the National Night Out event designed to fight crime in local communities grows to 8,500.

1994: In July, abortion provider John Bayard Britton and his escort are murdered in Pensacola, Florida.

1994: In December, Shannon Lowney and Leanne Nichols are shot and killed in separate incidents at abortion clinics in Brookline, Massachusetts.

1994: After luring her into his home in Mercer County, New Jersey, with promises of a puppy, convicted sex offender Jesse Timmendequas rapes and strangles 7-year-old Megan Kanka. Public outcry leads to the passage of Megan's Law, a federal requirement that sex offenders against children register their whereabouts with law enforcement, and that law enforcement make registry information available to the public.

1994: Congress passes the Violence Against Women Act, establishing federal penalties for interstate stalking and assault and setting up the National Domestic Violence Hotline.

1994: Congress passes the Gun-Free School Act, making it mandatory for school officials to expel for one year any student bringing a gun to school.

1994: President Bill Clinton's anticrime legislation the Violent Crime Control and Law Enforcement

Act is signed into law, with the ultimate goal of putting 100,000 new police officers on American streets.

1994: New York City Deputy Police Commissioner Jack Maple introduces CompStat, a computerized analysis of crime statistics that places officers according to recognized patterns of criminal activity, resulting in a reduction in the city's crime rate, leading other cities to adopt the system.

1995: School officials report the presence of gang activity in 28.4 percent of American schools. In urban areas, that figure climbs to 40.7 percent.

1996: On January 13, 9-year-old Amber Hagerman is kidnapped during a bike ride while visiting her grandparents in Arlington, Texas. She is molested and killed, but no one is ever brought to trial for the crime. Her father and a friend initiate the idea that the media and the public can work together to locate missing children immediately after they are abducted by using what becomes known as an Amber Alert system.

1996: Congress passes a federal Megan's Law, mandating registration of known sex offenders.

1996: "Road rage" is reported to be responsible for two-thirds of the 41,000 automobile-related deaths. These incidents involve speeding, cutting off other motorists, and following too closely.

1996: In April, two dueling male drivers traveling at a speed of 80 miles per hour lose control of their vehicles and cross the median, hitting two oncoming vehicles. Only one of the four drivers involved in the crashes survives.

1996: Matthew Shepard meets Aaron McKinney and Russell Henderson at the Fireside Lounge, near Laramie, Wyoming. Offended by his homosexuality, the two take Shepard to a remote location where they tie him to a fence post and torture him until he lapses into a coma. He dies in a hospital days later. The incident focuses national attention on hate crimes motivated by sexual orientation.

1997: In five separate incidents, students open fire at schools, killing 11 classmates and two teachers. Another 47 individuals are wounded.

1997: The video game *Grand Theft Auto* makes its debut, setting off a storm of controversy and complaints that it glorifies street crime. The controversy continues to build as sequels are periodically introduced.

1997: An unnamed physician who provides abortion services is murdered in Rochester, New York.

1997: In San Jose, California, officials use an injunction and public nuisance laws to prevent local gangs from congregating on city streets. The California Supreme Court subsequently rejects gang members' attempts to invalidate the injunction and the laws.

1998: In January, Officer Robert Sanderson is murdered while protecting an abortion clinic in Birmingham, Alabama.

1998: In October, Dr. Barnett Slepian, an abortion provider, is murdered in Amherst, New York.

1998: The four states with the largest number of active gangs are identified as California (363), Illinois (261), Texas (156), and Florida (125).

1998: According to official government reports, 13,000,000 Americans used illicit drugs during the year.

1999: Unarmed West African immigrant Amadou Diallo, while reaching for his wallet, is shot and killed by four New York City police officers who believe he matches the description of a serial rapist. All four are acquitted, inspiring public outcry over racial profiling.

1999: On April 20, in Littleton, Colorado, teenagers Eric Harris and Dylan Klebold initiate a massacre at Columbine High School, killing 12 classmates and one teacher.

1999: The National Youth Gang Survey reports that 90 percent of all gang members are male; 79 percent are Hispanic or African American; 71 percent are between the ages of 15 and 24; and 16 percent are under the age of 14.

2000: After the Supreme Court overturns the Gang Congregation Ordinance on the grounds of vagueness, Chicago's City Council enacts a new law giving police officers the authority to disperse gang members who are congregating solely for the purpose of establishing control over specific areas of the city.

2002: While imprisoned for murder, Matias Reyes confesses to the rape and brutal assault of the Central Park Jogger, Trisha Meili, in 1989. In response to his confession, which is supported by DNA evidence, the previously charged Central Park Five are cleared of all charges.

2002: The 14th state passes an Amber Alert law. A federal law is enacted the following year.

2002: Forty percent of police agencies report that local gang activity has risen 50 percent that year.

2002: The Department of Justice reports that 9,369 homicides have occurred in the United States.

2003: The bipartisan Gang Prevention and Effective Deterrence Act seeks to authorize $100 million in federal funding to assist local law enforcement in areas with intense gang activity. It takes two years to garner sufficient support to become law.

2004: Former drug dealers Ronald Moten and Jauhar Abraham found Peaceoholics to fight violent crime in inner-city neighborhoods in Washington, D.C.

2005: Nine-year-old Jessica Marie Lunsford is abducted from her home in Florida by a convicted sex offender who buries her alive after sexually assaulting her. In the aftermath, states begin passing Jessica's Law to enhance the tracking of released sex offenders through the use of DNA samples, ankle bracelets, and global positioning systems.

2005: The 45th state passes its version of Megan's Law, requiring registration of known sex offenders. Many states also prohibit sex offenders from living near schools or other places where children gather.

2005: Using statistics gathered from the Centers for Disease Control and Prevention, the Violence Policy Center finds that homicide is the leading cause of death for African Americans. Some 90 percent of those crimes are committed using guns.

2005: Danny Ledonne, allegedly a former victim of bullying, releases *Super Columbine Massacre*, a free online role-playing game in which players take on the role of shooters Harris and Klebold.

2006: Texas courts uphold blue laws requiring car dealerships to close on either Saturday or Sunday.

2007: Despite a drop in the national violent crime rate, Atlanta, Baltimore, Dallas, New Orleans, and Miami all report significant increases.

2007: State legislatures in 26 states begin addressing sentencing laws as a means of preventing prisons from being used to train inmates in the perpetration of further crimes.

2008: The Federal Bureau of Investigation reports that there are 640 gangs with 17,250 members operating within the New England states.

2009: Abortion provider Dr. George Tiller is murdered while attending church in Wichita, Kansas.

2009: President George W. Bush releases a proposed budget slashing aid to state and local law enforcement agencies by $400 million.

2009: In February, the Department of Justice issues the National Gang Threat Assessment Report stating that 1 million members of 20,000 street, prison, and biker gangs operating in the United States commit approximately 80 percent of all crimes.

2009: On February 11, Jack Thompson, an Alabama attorney, files suit against the creators and marketers of the *Grand Theft Auto* video game, charging them with inciting a teenager to go on a game-inspired rampage that resulted in the deaths of two police officers and a dispatcher.

2009: In Baltimore, Maryland, on September 2, a gunman carrying a semiautomatic weapon opens fire at a backyard party memorializing two men previously slain by a neighborhood gang. The 12 victims include a pregnant woman and a 2-year-old child.

2010: In June, 52 people are shot by Chicago gang members in a single weekend. The following weekend brings the death of 29 others. The violence leads the Supreme Court to overturn a citywide ban on handguns.

2010: The number participating in the National Night Out program expands to 37 million.

2011: The Central Park Five bring suit against the city of New York, asking for $50 million each in damages for being falsely accused in the 1989 attack of the Central Park Jogger, Trisha Meili.

2012: On February 26, 17-year-old African American Trayvon Martin is shot dead by 28-year-old white George Zimmerman while walking home from the convenience store. Because of Florida's "stand your ground" law, Zimmerman feels his actions are justified as self-defense, as he claims that he felt threatened. The circumstances surrounding the case inspire a nationwide conversation about stand your ground laws and self-defense.

2012: On June 24, the Supreme Court rules in *Miller v. Alabama* that mandatory sentences of life without parole for minors committing certain major crimes are a violation of Eighth Amendment prohibitions on cruel and unusual punishment, requiring 39 states to amend their criminal statutes. The issue of what to do about 2,100 inmates serving life sentences for crimes committed as juveniles remains to be addressed.

2012: On July 20, James Holmes opens fire with a semiautomatic weapon at a midnight showing of The Dark Knight Rises, in Aurora, Colorado. Twelve people are killed, 58 are wounded. Holmes's apartment is discovered to be booby-trapped with explosive devices, necessitating the evacuation of nearby homes for several days.

2012: On August 5, white supremacist and discharged soldier Wade Michael Page enters a Sikh temple in Oak Creek, Wisconsin, and opens fire, killing six before fatally shooting himself in the head after being fired upon by the responding officer, Lieutenant Brian Murphy (who was himself shot 15 times).

2012: Colorado and Washington become the first states to legalize marijuana for recreational use, with age and other restrictions.

2012: Voters in California pass Proposition 36, reforming the state's infamous "Three Strikes law" requiring draconian mandatory minimum sentences; the law had become responsible for California's prison overpopulation and exacerbated state budget problems.

2012: On the Monday after Thanksgiving, November 26, for the first time in recent memory, New York City goes a full day without a single report of violent crime. New York City also makes the news for launching an initiative with investment bank Goldman Sachs to fund "social investments" aimed at reducing youth incarceration rates through programs funded by private investors.

2012: New York State announces a first-in-the-nation change to its state bar requirements, requiring 50 hours of pro bono service from any applicant to the bar. One of the aims of the change is to improve legal access for poor criminal defendants.

2012: On December 14, Adam Lanza shoots and kills his mother Nancy before driving to the school where she sometimes worked, Sandy Hook Elementary in Newtown, Connecticut. There he kills 20 children and six adults, in the second-deadliest school shooting in American history. Lanza, who commits suicide before he could be apprehended, is alternately described as mentally ill and suffering from Aspergers syndrome. The gun he uses for the mass murder belongs to his mother, with whom he lived, raising questions about firearm access and mental health.

2013: Despite initiatives by gun control advocates after the Aurora shooting, it is not until the Sandy Hook shooting that the president and vice president create a special task force to investigate and suggest immediate changes. In January 2013, President Barack Obama issues a series of executive orders related to gun control and school safety on the advice of Vice President Joe Biden's task force.

Elizabeth Rholetter Purdy
Independent Scholar

Alcohol and Drug Testing, On-Scene

On-scene drug and alcohol testing refers to the battery of tests conducted by a police officer after a traffic stop when the officer suspects that the person pulled over is under the influence of either alcohol or illegal drugs. The U.S. Department of Transportation (DOT) has come up with a standardized test that is to be completed by all officers while on a traffic stop suspecting the influence of illegal substances. This standardized test has 94 percent accuracy overall, with most inaccuracies stemming from the presence of false positives (a result when the technology indicates that a given condition is present when it is not). These tests are used to assess the motor skills and involuntary movements that occur when an individual is under the influence of alcohol and drugs. There are also tests available to measure the amount of illegal substances in the bloodstream of an offender.

On-scene drug and alcohol testing has become increasingly important to the American judicial system as the prevalence of science has grown in sophistication, and as precedence has been established in many courts. While decades ago it was largely up to the word of a police officer whether someone was physically able to control a motor vehicle, juries—along with the justice system at large—now expect there to be more proof.

However, as scientific testing became more prevalent, new concerns emerged. For example, while it may only take 30 minutes to transport a suspect to a police station for testing, the individual's blood (or breath) alcohol content will have changed in that time frame, making it more difficult to determine what the level was at the time the suspect was initially stopped. Such nuances presented difficulties for police; it was not necessarily any easier to prove impairment by means of the scientific approach. As a result, we have seen a conscious effort to determine ways to quickly and accurately make an on-scene determination whether a driver is capable of operating a motor vehicle or not.

The advent of better test technologies, as well as social pressure upon law enforcement agencies to combat impaired driving (galvanized by such organizations as Mothers Against Drunk Driving), has led to broader use of drug and alcohol testing. In addition to individual stops by police officers, the use of sobriety checkpoints on a periodic basis is another scenario where drug and alcohol testing can be deployed not only to counter driving under the influence (DUI) or driving while intoxicated (DWI) offenses, but also to interdict or deter the commission of drug- and alcohol-related street crimes.

Motor Skills Test

The U.S. DOT standardized test has three distinct parts to it that are meant to test both the motor skills and involuntary movement of a suspect. The inclusion of involuntary movements assures that officers are not merely fooled by a suspect passing a basic motor skills section.

The first part of the test is horizontal gaze nystagmus testing. When people become impaired by alcohol, their eyes tend to jerk when following an object into the area of peripheral vision instead of following a smooth, continual direction. If an officer notices an eye jerk, the suspect is presumed to be above the legal limit for driving. The second test is the walk and turn test. This test is used to determine whether a person can keep balance while moving and taking directions. The suspect is told to take nine steps in a straight line, heel-to-toe, then turn around on one foot and repeat the steps again. If the person cannot hold his or her balance or has trouble paying attention to directions, then he or she is assumed to be

intoxicated and unable to command a vehicle. The final test is the one-foot test. In this test, the suspect is told to stand on one foot while counting by thousands. The police officer times the suspect for 30 seconds and then allows the person to put his or her foot down. If the person cannot do either of these at the same time, he or she is likely intoxicated and has failed the exam. These tests have become well known by average citizens due to their presence on television shows such as *Cops* and *Campus P. D.* They have come under criticism at times, given the subjective nature by which they can be administered. Despite a scientific backing, the results of the tests are largely dependent on the decision of a single officer. As a result, segments of society have argued that there is a potential bias in the results, along with a lack of actual proof of insobriety. Given these factors, there has been a movement toward objective technical testing at the time of suspicion.

Blood Alcohol Level

One form of on-scene detection is the use of a handheld breathalyzer to obtain a generalized sense of the level of intoxication of a person. The handheld breathalyzer does not directly measure the blood alcohol content of a person—instead, it approximates the blood alcohol content through a chemical reaction that detects ethanol. This method has proven over time to be highly reliable. These breathalyzer results can be used in court as evidence of a person operating under the influence, because as of 2011, it was illegal in most states to be operating a vehicle with a blood alcohol content of over 0.08 percent. Such tests are legally admissible and typically accepted by jurors, judges, and prosecutors as proof of intoxication. There are a number of myths regularly perpetuated that breathalyzer tests can be beat by sucking on pennies, charcoal tablets, or batteries. Yet none have been shown to work. Instead, tight controls are in place to ensure that individuals receive accurate measurements that do not allow false positives measured by improperly calibrated machines or the use of high-alcohol-content mouthwashes.

Other Drugs

At present, commonly accepted or reliable instant technologies to measure the presence in a person's system of many types of drugs do not exist. Yet recent technological advances indicate that such tools will soon be developed. One type of new technology

The Governors Highway Safety Association implemented the 2010 nationwide "Drunk Driving, Over the Limit, Under Arrest" campaign to prevent fatalities using high visibility law enforcement and public education, like this poster.

uses intelligent fingerprinting, which analyzes perspiration contained in a latent fingerprint for metabolites of cannabis, cocaine, and different opiates. In the future, it is expected that it will also be able to detect methamphetamine and ecstasy.

A second developing technology uses work currently employed by the U.S. Navy for identifying biological warfare agents through optical sensors. In the field, officers will have suspects place test swabs in their mouths to collect saliva. The sample will then be put into a cartridge which in turn is inserted into a sensor device. In approximately two minutes, the sensor will indicate whether cocaine, methamphetamine, or cannabis were present in the sample. All of these new technologies, however, will need time to be fine-tuned and tested in the field. Like breathalyzer technology, they will then take a period of time to gain full acceptance by law enforcement and within the judicial complex as accurate indicators of possible impairedness. This is particularly germane considering the longer amount of time after consumption that many drugs can still be identified within our system, compared to the relatively quick bodily elimination of alcohol.

William J. Miller
Southeast Missouri State University

See Also: Alcohol and Drug Use; Arrest; Courts, Drug; Crime Prevention, Situational; Drinking, Underage; Police (Overview); Policing, Problem-Oriented.

Further Readings

Miller, Ted R., et al. "Costs and Benefits of a Community Sobriety Checkpoint Program." *Journal of Studies on Alcohol and Drugs,* v.59/4 (1998).

Ternes, Keith, et al. *Understanding Field Sobriety and Breath Testing Procedures.* New York: Thomson West, 2009.

Wells, Helen. *The Fast and The Furious: Drivers, Speed Cameras and Control in a Risk Society.* Aldershot, UK: Ashgate Publishing, 2012.

Alcohol and Drug Use

Drugs and alcohol are fundamental elements of street crime in multiple respects. A generally recognized drugs-crime nexus has generated multiple theoretical explanations accounting for the central role that drugs and alcohol assume in the occurrence of street crime. Criminologists recognize that substance abuse is associated with crime in either a causal (drug use results in crime) or co-varying (drug use and certain forms of crime naturally coexist) relationship. There has been considerable debate over whether drug use is a precursor to involvement in violent and property crime to maintain addiction and dependency or whether drug use and crime are organic behavioral by-products influenced by a combination of neighborhood characteristics and social dynamics. Accordingly, explanations of drug and alcohol use and their effects on crime range from individual and cultural responsibility to social inequality and constructionist perspectives. Theoretical perspectives regarding drug use facilitate policy position development and philosophical justification of official action, and are thus important in pragmatic terms.

Linking Alcohol and Drugs to Crime

A traditional school of thought defining the drugs-crime relationship is conceptually rooted in the idea of cultural transmission, the belief that various groups internalize subcultural values favorable to drug use and crime. Unprecedented levels of political initiative and media attention on crime in recent decades have thematically reoriented formal social control policy around drug war initiatives. Drug enforcement activity is often conducted in urban underclass settings where drug trafficking and use are heavily intertwined with vice, violence, and property crime.

The U.S. Bureau of Justice Statistics' definitional overview of the drugs-crime relationship, for example, is comprised of three terms with descriptive language suggestive of subcultural reference. The terms *drug-defined offenses* (possessing, dealing, or manufacturing illicit substances); *drug-related* (offenses in which drugs contribute, such as armed robbery and assault, offenses specific to drug distribution, and offenses motivated by user need for money to support use); and, especially *drug-using lifestyle* (high frequency drug use, distance from legitimate economy, and immersion in situations encouraging crime) are illustrated by references to forms of drug crime, violent behavior, theft, and drug-specific violence (such as violence focused against rival drug dealers) that, while generalizable, indicate underclass settings. The

Bureau of Justice Statistics' example of drug-using lifestyle (life orientation emphasizing short term goals, criminal learning, and co-offending) reflects the lingering influence of 1950s perspectives such as Walter B. Miller's focal concerns and Albert Cohen's general subculture theories more so than the social support advocacy positions developed over the last half century. In short, this view maintains that rates of drug use and crime are high because offenders enjoy and choose to offend as a function of normative learned behavior.

Shaping Perceptions

Official portrayals and popular cultural wisdom alike acknowledge that inner city minority neighborhoods are characterized by high levels of alcohol and drug use, drug and alcohol availability, and thus trafficking. The popular reference to subculture in the 1950s and 1960s has been rejargoned as urban underclass and minority-majority, marking inner city neighborhoods as unsafe areas wherein street codes specify conduct norms that facilitate alcohol abuse and drug crime and invite proactive law enforcement intervention.

While such areas are characterized by high rates of street crime, some social scientists contend that the degree to which inner cities areas have been portrayed as drug-crime-ridden is inaccurate, and represent the foremost implication derived from social constructionist accounts of the politicization of the drug war. Within the social constructionist framework, it is more so the definitional activity of the state and the media—rather than the actual reported incidence of drug crime and substance abuse—that influences public awareness and attitudes regarding alcohol and drug abuse as a social problem. In particular, social constructionist theorists argue, how can the reported incidence of drug use during the 1980s and 1990s decline while drug issues increasingly assumed greater attention in the national media?

For social constructionists, the answer lies in the processes by which much of the public came to view drugs as a major national problem in which the behavior of state actors captured media attention that, in turn, shaped popular belief to the point of moral panic regarding an imminent drug crisis. Social constructionism of a drug problem, then, serves the interests of state social control policy and initiatives, a view consistent with critical interpretations of the drugs–crime phenomenon.

Sociological Models and Crime Policy

Critical criminologists recognize that the relationship of drugs with street crime is subjectively tainted by state definitions and innuendo, including the observation that street crime is not a legal category nor is it a major classification in a crime typology, as individual offenses are subsumed under either violent, property, or morality violation categories. In that the street crime category is generally used in reference to stranger victimization, wherein a stereotyped perpetrator reference point is instrumental to social control advocacy, the very discussion of street crime is utilitarian to incumbent political interests consistent with an objectivist model. According to the objectivist model, an increase in the incidence of street crime and drug use has led to a necessary "get tough" approach to crime that has been maintained relatively uninterrupted since the Ronald Reagan administration. Racial profiling, disproportionate minority contact with law enforcement, "Stop Snitching" movements, and disproportionate representation of minorities and the socioeconomically disadvantaged throughout the criminal justice system are unintended consequences and apparently acceptable collateral by-products of conservative drug control policy.

A critical account of the drug-crime situation also recognizes the role of the media in shaping popular opinion. The fundamental assumption is that public level of concern is largely a function of state claimsmaking, not empirical realities. Through drug war activity, the state has a basis for selective intervention that, to some, is racist and classist. To the extent that the fluidity of public opinion is shaped by the media that, in turn, is aligned with and dependent on access to state officials, government is well positioned to define social problems and their solutions. From a critical criminological viewpoint, then, the drug war is less about addressing substance abuse and street crime and more about pronouncing drug use and related criminal activity to maintain the current system of law and order toward continuation of the status quo.

Data From the Front

The state's inability to reconcile increases in undercover activity and drug arrests during periods of drug use decline opens the possibility of latent drug war objectives. While most researchers and informed observers of the drug war are indeed left-leaning and do not accept that decreased substance abuse is a function of drug enforcement effectiveness, official data suggests that illicit drug use and drug trafficking are entrenched social problems in many areas. The Arrestee Drug Abuse Monitoring Program (ADAM II), sponsored by the U.S. Office of Drug Control Policy, gathers information on drug use and related issues from adult male offenders through face-to-face interviews within 48 hours of arrest. The ADAM II reports that over 40 percent of arrestees tested positive for marijuana at time of arrest and that the majority of illicit drug purchases occurred indoors rather than in open-air drug markets, suggesting middle-class involvement as much as an underclass presence typically associated with an outdoors public form of dealing. The second-most commonly used drug among arrestees was crack cocaine, with between 17 and 44 percent of those arrested testing positive for the presence of cocaine in their system at the time of arrest. Respondents from poorer metropolitan areas had the highest percentage of usage.

In addition to monitoring drug use among arrestees, a number of large-scale projects also attempt to measure levels of substance use and abuse in the United States. For example, the National Survey on Drug Use and Health (formerly the National Household Survey on Drug Abuse) is conducted annually by the Substance Abuse and Mental Health Services Administration (SAMHSA) and collects information on the prevalence, patterns, and consequences of alcohol, tobacco, and illegal drug use and abuse in the general U.S. population. Similarly, the Monitoring the Future study (MTF), funded by the National Institute on Drug Abuse (NIDA), also assesses the prevalence and incidence of both licit (alcohol or tobacco) and illicit substances, but focuses exclusively on high school students in eigth, 10th and 12th grades. Other major surveys that collect data on drug use and abuse include the Behavioral Risk Factor Surveillance System (BRFSS) and the Youth Risk Behavior Surveillance System (YRBSS), both of which are funded by the Centers for Disease Control and Prevention.

Efforts to disrupt the drugs–crime nexus include a wide range of diversionary and specialty court programs to re-entry and second-chance act initiatives. Best practices for disrupting drug involved offending include a seamless continuum of services beginning prior to release and maintained throughout transition from incarceration back into the community, family and social support from the community, and avoidance of delinquent and criminal associates. Such observations are problematic for street crime reduction per se. While drug treatment is almost categorically coupled with anger management, cognitive behavioral therapy and awareness of criminal thinking patterns, the underclass settings where the majority of street crime occurs is characterized by realities unfavorable to disrupting drug crime—familial instability, unemployment, homelessness, household overcrowding, and, most significantly, normative substance consumption.

Conclusion

In light of these realities, street crime, along with drug and alcohol use and abuse, has become culturally embedded within underclass contexts. Unfortunately, social policy and programming efforts intended to reduce use and harm run the risk of being counterproductive through glamorizing criminal lifestyles and solidifying antisocial subcultural belief systems through collective reaction formations against state intervention.

J. Mitchell Miller
Douglas M. Smith
University of Texas at San Antonio

See Also: Bootleggers; Code of the Street; Drinking Establishments, Unlicensed; Drug Markets, Open-Air; Drug Dealing; Drugs, Prescription; Gangs (Street).

Further Readings
Anderson, Elijah. *The Code of the Street: Decency, Violence and the Moral Life of the Inner City*. New York: Norton Paperbacks, 1999.
Fagan, Jeffrey. "Intoxication and Aggression." In *Drugs and Crime, Crime and Justice: A Review of Research*, Vol. 13, Michael Tonry and James Q. Wilson, eds. Chicago: University of Chicago Press, 1991.
Hagedorn John M. *People and Folks: Gangs, Crime and the Underclass In a Rustbelt City*. Chicago: Lakeview Press, 1988.
Miller, Walter B. "Lower-Class Culture as a Generating Milieu of Gang Delinquency." *Journal of Social Issues*, v.14/5–11 (1958).
Office of National Drug Control Policy. *Arrestee Drug Abuse Monitoring Program II*. Washington, DC: Executive Office of the President, 2011.

Arrest

Arrest is defined as the taking into custody of a person for purposes of prosecution. The term is of Anglo-Norman origin and related to the French word *arret,* meaning stop. Arrest is one of the primary mechanisms by which individuals are brought before the courts to answer criminal charges against them, particularly for street crimes. Other mechanisms to deter criminal acts, typically involving less serious crimes, include citations or summonses. This entry begins with the definition of arrest and discussion of formal elements of arrest. It then addresses Fourth Amendment requirements for arrest, probable cause, and arrest with and without a warrant, and compares guidelines for felony and misdemeanor arrests. It discusses the critical distinction between stop and arrest, as well as postarrest issues including Miranda rights and search incident to arrest. The entry concludes with a brief overview of the literature and research concerning arrest.

Definitions and Probable Cause

Formal elements of arrest include intent, authority, submission, and understanding. There must be an intent to arrest the offender; a show of authority, real or implied; a seizure of the person to be arrested, involving either physical touching or submission to the authority; and an understanding by the arrestee that he or she is being arrested.

An arrest constitutes a seizure of the person and falls within the ambit of the Fourth Amendment of the U.S. Constitution. Therefore Fourth Amendment reasonableness requirements apply; arrestees are granted all of the protections afforded by the Fourth Amendment, in particular, the requirement that arrests be supported by probable cause. *Bringer v. United States* indicates that probable cause exists where the

. . . facts and circumstances within their [the arresting officers'] knowledge and of which they had reasonably trustworthy information [are] sufficient in themselves to warrant a man of reasonable caution in the belief that an offense has been or is being committed [by the person to be arrested].

Gates v. Illinois further describes the standard for probable cause as:

. . . it is a practical, non-technical conception. In dealing with probable cause . . . we deal with probabilities. These are not technical; they are the factual and practical considerations of everyday life on which reasonable and prudent men, not legal technicians, act.

Stop and Frisk

The traditional test for whether an arrest has occurred is whether a reasonable person would feel free to leave under the circumstances. However, a distinction must be made between an arrest and a *Terry* stop, a brief detention for investigative purposes which may be accompanied by a limited pat down of the outer garments, termed a frisk. The legal standard for stop and frisk is reasonable suspicion based upon articulable facts, as set forth in *Terry v. Ohio.* Arrest is distinguishable from a stop based upon the fact that an arrest involves taking an individual into custody as a prelude to prosecution, and represents a more significant intrusion on an individual's liberty. A stop and frisk is a much lesser intrusion than an arrest and search, and as such it requires less legal justification than an arrest. An individual who has been taken into custody without meeting the formal elements of arrest may fall into a category defined by the U.S. Supreme Court as a "seizure tantamount to arrest," as defined in *Dunaway v. New York.*

Warrants and Misdemeanors

Depending upon the circumstances, type of offense, and relevant state statutes, arrest may be made with or without a warrant. While there is a constitutional preference for arrest with a warrant, the Supreme Court recognizes that the common law permits warrantless felony arrests based upon probable cause and that most states follow this rule; examples are discussed in *Ker v. California* and in *U.S. v. Watson.*

Significant differences exist between the states with regard to misdemeanor arrests. The early English common law, which was built upon previous judicial decisions, permitted police officers to make misdemeanor arrests only for offenses committed within their presence. Many states have modified the common law rule by statute and now permit warrantless misdemeanor arrests for certain offenses which occurred out of the presence of police officers.

These offenses are enumerated by statute and often include domestic violence. Substantial variations exist among the states with regard to warrantless arrests for misdemeanors which occurred out of the presence of law enforcement officers. The U.S. Supreme Court took an expansive view of the permissible scope of misdemeanor arrests in the case of *Atwater v. City of Lago Vista*, which held that custodial arrests for misdemeanors punishable only by a fine did not constitute a constitutional violation. While most of the case law and criminal justice literature addresses arrest from the perspective of law enforcement officers, many states permit citizen's arrests under certain circumstances. State laws concerning citizen's arrest vary widely. However, citizens generally enjoy far less protection from false arrest and false imprisonment suits than police officers.

Postarrest Matters

The U.S. Supreme Court decision in *Gerstein v. Pugh* requires that individuals who have been arrested without a warrant be brought before a judge or magistrate for a prompt determination of probable cause. *County of Riverside v. McLaughlin* requires that this

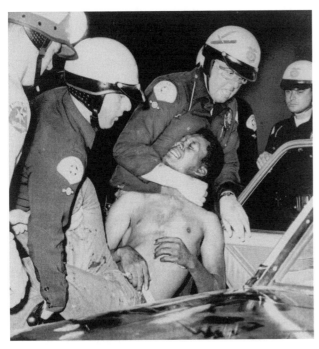

Police arrest a man during the five-day Watts Riots in Los Angeles in 1965. The rioting occurred after police used physical force to subdue a young African American man who had been pulled over. More than 3,400 were arrested by the riot's end.

typically occur within 48 hours. States must meet the minimum 48-hour requirement; they are free to establish more stringent standards requiring lesser periods within which arrestees be brought before the court. Some states have adopted a 24-hour rule.

Individuals placed under arrest are subject to a thorough search of their person, clothing, items in their possession, and the immediate vicinity surrounding where they are arrested. The "search incident to arrest" exception to the general requirement that warrants are required for search and seizure was established by the U.S. Supreme Court in *Chimel v. California*. Searches of vehicles incident to arrest are now governed by the U.S. Supreme Court decision in *Arizona v. Gant*, which dramatically altered the previous rule and requires that police officers demonstrate an actual or continuing threat from the arrestee or have probable cause to believe that evidence is located in the vehicle to justify a search of the vehicle. Individuals arrested and taken into custody are required to be advised of their Miranda rights prior to questioning, based on the decision in *Miranda v. Arizona*. *Miranda* remains in effect but its protections have been eroded—most recently in *Berghuis v. Thompkins*, in which the Supreme Court held that a defendant must unambiguously assert his Miranda rights, and waives his right by answering questions even hours later.

Arrest Literature

There is also a substantial body of criminal justice and law enforcement literature relating to arrest. Much of this literature concerns officer discretion, including research by Richard Groeneveld on the impact of organizational structures on the exercise of arrest discretion, and by Edith Linn on arrest decisions as personal adaptive behavior by the police officer. The benefits and drawbacks of CompStat and the quality of life enforcement obtained by increasing the numbers of misdemeanor arrests has been documented by Eli Silverman, John Eterno, and others. Earlier coverage of arrest discretion arises in the context of broader studies of police personality, such as the work by Jerome Skolnick, and officer typologies by James Q. Wilson and others.

The evolving body of literature concerning arrest-related discretion dates back to at least the 1950s, includes early work by the American Bar Association and Kenneth Culp Davis, and continues through the present. Variables analyzed include: environmental, managerial, adaptive personal, policy, process, situational, organizational, training, values, and others. Methodologies vary substantially, and findings are often contradictory.

Michael M. Berlin
Coppin State University

See Also: Alcohol and Drug Testing, On-Scene; CompStat; Crime Prevention, Situational; Jails; Miranda Warnings; Racial Profiling; Stop and Frisk; Zero-Tolerance/Saturation Policing.

Further Readings

Arizona v. Gant, 556 U.S. 332 (2009).

Atwater v. City of Lago Vista, 532 U.S. 318 (2001).

Berghuis v. Thompkins, 560 U.S. (2010).

Bringer v. United States, 338 U.S. 160 (1949).

Chimel v. California, 395 U.S. 752 (1969).

County of Riverside v. McLaughlin, 500 U.S. 44 (1991).

Davis, Kenneth Culp. *Police Discretion.* St. Paul, MN: West Publishing, 1975.

Dunaway v. New York, 442 U.S. 200 (1979).

Gates v. Illinois, 462 U.S. 213 (1983).

Gerstein v. Pugh, 420 U.S. 103 (1975).

Groeneveld, Richard F. *Arrest Discretion of Police Officers.* New York: LFB Scholarly Publishing, 2005.

Ker v. California, 374 U.S. 23 (1963).

Linn, Edith. *Arrest Decisions: What Works for the Officer?* New York: Peter Lang, 2009.

Miranda v. Arizona, 384 U.S. 436 (1966).

Roberson, Cliff, et al. *Procedures in the Justice System.* 9th ed. Upper Saddle River, NJ: Prentice Hall, 2010.

Silverman, Eli. *NYPD Battles Crime:.* Lebanon, NH: Northeastern University Press, 1999.

Skolnick, Jerome. *Justice Without Trial.* Hoboken, NJ: John Wiley & Sons, 1966.

Terry v. Ohio, 392 U.S. 1 (1968).

U.S. v. Watson, 423 U.S. 411 (1976).

Wilson, J.Q. *Varieties of Police Behavior.* Cambridge, MA: Harvard University Press, 1968.

Arson

Fire setting as a form of criminal behavior is referred to as arson. Arson can be defined as the intentional and malevolent burning or attempted burning of a home, building, motor vehicle, or other personal property. Starting a fire or causing an explosion that recklessly places a person in danger of death or serious physical injury is also considered arson. Targets often include abandoned buildings, schools, retail stores, vegetation, and cars.

Arson involves the introduction of a heat source that can be simple, such as a match, or complex, such as chemicals with very low ignition temperatures. A fire is considered arson when all other accidental causes are ruled out. There are a variety of motives for the crime of arson that can range from the very rationally calculated decision making of profit-motivated offenders to the irrational fantasies of thrill-seeking offenders.

The Incidence of Arson

More than 500,000 arson fires occur each year. According to Uniform Crime Reports data compiled by the Federal Bureau of Investigation, during 2004–10, the percentage of reported arsons decreased each year with the exception of 2006, in which the percentage of arson increased from 2005, but only by 2.1 percent. When comparing the type of property where arson is more likely to occur, residential structures are the most common, followed by community or public structures. Motor vehicles constitute the main type of mobile property where arson is most likely to take place.

Rates of intentional structure fires or arson offenses, relative to population, are highest in large cities but are also higher in rural communities (under 2,500 population) than in small towns (2,500 to 9,999 population). Arson is a very serious crime. It is the second-leading cause of death by fire in the United States, and the main cause of property damage due to fires, making it arguably the most expensive crime in America, costing more than $2 billion a year in property loss. The majority of offenders (55 percent) arrested for arson are under 18 years of age. Only 16 percent of arson offenses ever lead to arrest, however, and a scant 2 percent of those arrested are convicted.

Types of Arsonists

While the motivations for arson are quite diverse, researchers have been able to compile information that yields various categories of arson based on patterns of offending and characteristics of offenders. One pattern of arson offending is perpetrated by

The Skyline Parkway Motel photographed in 2004 in Afton, Virginia, after an arson fire destroyed the structure's roof and center portico. The building in the the unincorporated community of Afton was abandoned for years after the fire and was not torn down until 2007. Rates of arson are higher in rural communities with less than 2,500 residents than in small towns.

younger adolescents who are termed delinquent arsonists. These individuals have a tendency to exhibit poor judgment and a lack of self-control. They often set fires to schools or abandoned buildings and other hidden locations. Their primary motivation is mischief; their methods are fairly unsophisticated and marked by a desire to maliciously harm and rebel against authority.

Some arson offenders have a long history of fire-setting behavior that includes a highly sophisticated method of operation. They have a distinct, often ritualistic approach that leaves a path of destruction the arsonist becomes extremely proud of. These types of fire setters are referred to as pathological arsonists. Unlike most delinquent arsonists, pathological arsonists often suffer psychiatric difficulties and emotional conflicts

that contribute to their fire-setting behavior. These individuals generally do not feel any remorse for their behavior or the destruction it has caused. Their crime is a symptom of a generalized pattern of antisocial behavior and inability to identify with the feelings of others.

Fire setting to get a rush or thrill from its destructive power, to draw attention or gain recognition, or even to find sexual gratification is called excitement-seeking arson. It is rarely intended to harm people or even create large-scale damage but rather serves an expressive purpose. A typical excitement-seeking fire setter may set fire to trash, a dumpster, or recycling bin, then call for help or put it out—appearing as a hero to those around and often basking in the glory of the reaction to his or her accomplishment.

Some arsonists are motivated by a desire for revenge, or to right a wrong. Revenge-seeking arsonists set fires in order to retaliate for either an imagined or real injustice. These types of arson are usually the outcome of conflicts within interpersonal relationships, business partnerships, commercial transactions, or criminal exchanges. This type of crime is usually carefully planned, with a very specific target. It can be a one-time event against a specific individual, or a series of fires over time to avenge a grievance or make a political statement to some type of organization such as a church or clinic, the government or military, or society in general.

Sometimes fire setting can be a secondary pattern of behavior to achieve the primary goals of material profit or personal gain. This pattern is perpetrated by the instrumental arsonist. Personal gain is often the motive when arson is used to cover up a crime that has already taken place, such as burglary, motor vehicle theft, or homicide, in which the fire is an attempt to conceal fingerprints, blood stains, and other forensic evidence that can identify the offender. The desire for material gain can also be a primary motive in the destruction of a property for the purpose of fraud or to collect insurance, conceal loss, or destroy documents. In both cases, instrumental arsons are very carefully planned to create a significant amount of destruction in order to achieve the intended purpose. This category of fire setters is not likely to reoffend—once they have achieved their goal, the motive to set a fire no longer exists.

Arson Investigation

Investigating a suspected act of arson is no easy task, given the physical damage often present at the scene. Moreover, the variety of motives and patterns behind the crime of arson often makes prevention strategies challenging. Arson comprises two aspects: a fire and a criminal act. Consequently, it has not historically fit exclusively into the domain of either the fire department or police department; therefore specific disciplines are essential in providing expertise in order to solve arson cases.

The ideal arson investigator should have qualities and knowledge of fields such as: fire chemistry and behavior; construction methods and materials; reaction of materials to fire exposure, including burn rate and heat release; knowledge involving the investigation procedures and methods for securing and preserving evidence; skills in questioning and interviewing; arrest and judicial procedures; criminal typologies, and psychological profiles. It is often difficult to find one person who possesses all of these components. Thus, successful investigation of arson is best achieved when the fire and police departments work together, and share knowledge and information in order to fully understand and investigate the incidences of arson. Once it has been determined that the cause of a fire was arson by the investigator and/or fire marshal, the investigation commences in a manner similar to any criminal investigation, and is subject to the same sanctions and punishment put in place for other crimes by the criminal statutes of a given state.

Arson investigators are usually called to the scene of the fire after it has been put out by firefighters. Much of the evidence is destroyed by this time, and all that remains are the burn patterns. In some cases, arson investigators will recreate fires in an attempt to find out what the origins of the fire were, doing their best to replicate what the arsonist would have done. One thing investigators might learn from the outcome of the fire they set is the identification of the point of origin of the fire, or where it started. Sometimes, multiple points of origin are indicative of the presence of an arsonist. This is why it is important for arson investigators to work with the firefighters who were first on the scene, because they will have the most information about the appearance of the structure before water and other firefighting materials were used to extinguish the flames. The firefighters may possibly have noticed evidence of arson that does not exist at the time of investigation.

Aida Y. Hass
Missouri State University

See Also: Crime Scene Investigation; Juvenile Offending; Organized Crime and Violence; Vandalism.

Further Readings

Decker, John F. and Bruce L. Ottley. *Arson Law and Prosecution.* Durham, NC: Carolina Academic Press, 2009.

Keyworth, Richard J. *Fires . . . Accidental or Arson? Fire Investigations.* Parker, CO: Outskirts Press, 2010.

Miethe, Terance D., Richard C. McCorkle, and Shelley J. Listwan. *Crime Profiles: The Anatomy of Dangerous*

Persons, Places, and Situations. Los Angeles: Roxbury Publishing, 2006.

Redsicker, David R. and John J. O'Connor, eds. *Practical Fire and Arson Investigation.* 2nd ed. Boca Raton, FL: CRC Press, 1996.

Williams, Dian L. *Understanding the Arsonist: From Assessment to Confession.* Tucson, AZ: Judges and Lawyers Publishing Company, 2005.

Asian Gangs

Asian gang is a generic definition that refers to groups formed, in most cases, by individuals of Filipino, southeast Asian, or Far Eastern backgrounds. The term is also employed for the emerging gangs whose members are of southern-Asian origin, and is occasionally applied to groups made up of Pacific Islander descendants. It therefore indicates a highly diversified set of organizations displaying more than a century of history, a branched-out pattern of ethnic composition, and diversified behaviors, activities, and forms of structure.

Demographic Diversity

Asian gangs represent a relatively small percentage of the total of gangs in the United States. As a whole they share very few—if any—traits of peculiarity, as may be expected from a category based on a racial feature which ties together a complex polyethnic ensemble. There are over 30 ethnic/linguistic Asian groups in the United States, showing an extremely diversified combination of social, economic, and cultural backgrounds, which have mingled in equally diversified environments, in different modes, and in various historical phases over 150 years. It is not surprising, therefore, that key data on Asian gangs differ greatly from one historical period to another and even from one gang to the next, suggesting that the description as a homogeneous group is inadequate and can dangerously lean toward the use of stereotypes, producing biased or even imaginative representations.

Asian gangs include a relatively small percentage of the total amount of gangs identified in the United States. Their quantity varies greatly diachronically and according to the estimates, which usually target the race/ethnicity of members and not of the gang.

Individuals of Asian descent are reckoned to represent 7.5 percent of the total gang members in 1975, around 4 percent in 1982, 5 to 6 percent in 1998 and in the following decade. In order to get some perspective, it should be considered that multiethnic/multiracial gangs are estimated to form about one-third or even as high as 40 percent of all American gangs; that in 2000 Asian Americans represented 3.7 percent of the total U.S. population, and expanded rapidly to about 5 percent of U.S. population in 2010; that in Orange County, California, in 1997, the Asian community made up about 13.3 percent of the total population, and reported crime committed by Asian gang members was 11 percent of the total of gang crimes there.

Asian gangs display a variety of possible ethnic compositions which are rarely stable over time and space. Moreover, ethnicity is seldom the primary bonding factor of any one group, although it can play an important role as an identity referent, while sharing a foreign language can give important logistic advantages. Nevertheless, groups composed by one ethnic group, like the Hmong gangs active in Minnesota since the 1990s, are numerous. Pan-Asian gangs, formed by members belonging to different Asian ethnicities, are also common. Gangs composed mostly by Asians and including non-Asian members are less frequent.

Ethnic composition seems to be related to the gang's size, age, and environment. New cliques and small-sized gangs tend to be more ethnically/racially exclusive, while for bigger (often older) gangs the necessities of recruiting often prevail over ethnic preferences. The Tiny Rascal Gang, for example, one of the largest contemporary Asian macrogangs, was originally formed by a small group of Cambodian youths. It evolved, inviting in Laotian, Vietnamese, and Filipino acquaintances and then, growing exponentially, recruited members of all ethnic/racial backgrounds. Urban environments display a higher number of multiethnic gangs (especially pan-Asian), likely due to the greater variety of interacting communities found in cities, while environments with fewer identities (usually rural) engender more frequently monoethnic groups.

Ethnic Identity and Image

Chinese and Indochinese gangs constitute the majority of contemporary Asian gangs and are the most visible in the media, in academic research, and in law enforcement reports. Incidence of gangs among Asian communities is therefore not proportional to demography, considering that in 2000 the main Asian American ethnic groups in the United States were Chinese (23.7 percent), Filipino (18.1 percent), Indian (16.4 percent), Vietnamese (11 percent), and Korean (10.5 percent).

Indochinese gang is a generic term referring to groups mainly constituted by individuals of Vietnamese, Cambodian, or Laotian descent, but also by ethnic minorities from Indochina like the Viet-Ching (ethnic Chinese from Vietnam) or the Hmong. There are reports of few Thai gangs, sometimes classified as Indochinese. To this day there seem to be no gangs inside the United States from Indonesia, Burma, or Malaysia.

Japanese American street gangs were reported from the 1930s to the 1950s in southern California. These groups were often involved in confrontations with other gangs, in turf-related issues, sometimes in petty and minor crimes. They were often transitional and age-related groups of males that show resemblances with many other similar loosely organized bands of youth that existed during that time.

Korean gangs have formed in the last 30 years and show a wide range of typologies. There are groups of youths mimicking gangsters and involved mainly in weekend fist fights, but also street gangs of embittered criminals engaging in heavy criminal activities such as drug trafficking, robbery, assault, rape, and homicide. Filipino gangs have a fairly long history and are active especially in California, and sometimes emerge from well-educated and wealthy communities. Moreover, the number of Filipinos joining gangs founded by other ethnic groups seems to be relatively high. Gangs whose members' ancestors are from the Indian subcontinent have recently appeared in New Jersey and New York.

Chinese gangs have the longest history and constitute a macrogroup often subdivided according to political geography (e.g., mainland China, Taiwan, Hong Kong) or to ethnic subcategories (e.g., Cantonese, Viet-Ching). Gang-like groups of Chinese youths emerged in many cities throughout the United States at the end of the 19th century, the first ones that attracted attention being those in New York City's Chinatown. However, the development and great diffusion of Asian gangs—in the most commonly employed acceptation of the term—dates to the period between the 1960s and

the 1990s. The process of formation of new Asian gangs and development of old ones is vigorous to this day, as shown by the appearance of numerous new groups in the last 20 years (both in the old locations and in new regions), by the continuation of activities and recruiting of some historical groups, and by the emergence of cliques composed of ethnicities previously not associated with gangs.

Historical Influences

The history of Asian gangs is greatly shaped by the history of migrations from Asian countries, but it is dependent on the modes and patterns of integration and opportunities. Chinese gangs, for example, grew greatly at the turn of the 20th century and during the 1960s and 1970s, both periods following an important migration of Chinese people and the lack of integration or economic opportunities in very challenging social environments. Indochinese gangs started appearing after the great migration waves that, following the end of the Vietnam War in 1975 and other tragic conflicts in Indochina, brought into the United States hundreds of thousands of individuals from southeast Asia, mainly refugees.

Among the most common causes of Asian gang formation are the frictions between earlier settlers and the newly arrived, often including racism and forms of violence (from bullying to racial assaults), which favors the creation of groups of youths (mainly males) who band together for solidarity and self-protection, eventually leading to the formation of a distinctive ethnic gang. The first Hmong gang of Minnesota, for example, began in the 1970s as a self-defense group of Hmong players on a soccer team. The breakdown of traditional social structures and values following the disrupting course of the migration phases and the difficulties of adapting and integrating have also been important propellants for the rise of Asian gangs.

However, not all the Asian gangs originated from underprivileged or problematic environments, as the example of Filipino gangs show. This has led some researchers and many nonspecialists to assert that Asian gangs form in all socioeconomic environments and defy the definition of the gang as a phenomenon related to low socioeconomic standards. Indeed, the existence of these groups raises some interesting theoretical questions. On the other hand, the number of causes likely contributing to the emergence of Asian gangs forms a polythetic ensemble that includes for example the material and immaterial benefits (e.g., money, status, power, a surrogate family, sex, drugs) gained by joining the gang, as well as social factors such as single-parenting, lack of parental supervision, or conversely extreme parental control and high expectations. In all cases, the socioeconomic environment represents a main component.

Structure and Activities

Asian gangs generally reproduce the mainstream features of American gang culture, such as dress code, gang names, slang, hand signs, and graffiti. A number of Asian gangs have aligned with either side of the Crips and Bloods rivalry. The use of tattoos, scars, and burn marks (often cigarette burns) are inspired both by American gang culture and by Far East Asian underworld traditions.

Asian gangs are oriented toward economic activities; inclined to target individuals of their own ethnic group; insular; less turf-oriented; inclined toward crimes like illegal gambling, extortion, home invasions, and prostitution; and having deep connections to (or being manipulated by) organized crime syndicates. Most of these allegedly unique characteristics are specificities of a cluster of gangs and not of the whole ensemble. Some are false claims reproducing ethnic stereotypes.

Asian gangs are clearly involved in all kinds of criminal activities, and are not culturally insular, as shown by their network of relationships. Moreover, although it is true that some street gangs have or had connections with crime syndicates, the great majority of Asian gangs show loose and infrequent ties with larger criminal organizations, and are not more secretive than other gangs. Asian criminal organizations and Triad-like secret societies—which appear to be a stimulating factor for the development of gangs—have existed in the United States since the 19th century; there is sometimes a fine line between gangs and organized crime, the latter often originating from or being a more sophisticated form of the former. Studies describing Japanese and Chinese gangs as less turf-oriented and more secretive, internally organized with a pyramidal structure, and having important international connections, however, tend to focus only on a limited number of groups, often including some which clearly belong to the *yakuza* or Triad world and are more business-like than average street gangs.

Finally, territorialism is not an Asian ethnic/racial specificity. The propensity to victimize people of the same ethnic group is statistically confirmed among Indochinese, Korean, and some Chinese groups, but is not seen as historically continuous. It is related to some cultural factors, such as, for example, the popular custom of storing valuables at home (attracting predators); or a proclivity to conceal crimes committed by members of the community, only partially due to the fear of retaliation; and related to a long-lasting mistrust of law enforcement authorities and to the perception of "communal shame," the negative impact of the misbehavior of a community member on the image of the entire community.

Gender studies focused on Asian gangs are virtually nonexistent. Indirect sources suggest the widespread existence of a sexualized hierarchy where female members have a lower status and often secondary, assistant-kind roles. In some cases they are objectified and become status symbols or, very rarely, "common goods." Male-only gangs are common in the first stages of a gang's history, usually being the consequence of contingencies and not of men-only policies. Many Asian gangs are composed of individuals from both genders, with a higher percentage of males. Very approximately, between 4 to 12 percent of existing Asian gangs can be estimated as female-only, often associated with a predominantly male gang. From an age point of view, Asian gangs do not differ greatly from other gangs.

The west coast, and California in particular, have been among the first regions and one with the highest concentration of Asian gangs. The New York metropolitan area is also a place where Asian gangs have more than a century of history. However, Asian gangs are found in most of the states, especially in major cities. Some major Asian gangs have developed a network of gangs and cliques on an interstate or national scale, although the great majority remain confined in neighborhoods, cities, or counties. Their presence in rural areas is also attested and in the last several decades has arguably grown at a faster pace than in urban areas.

Law Enforcement Response

The anti-gang activities of law enforcement have grown to encompass a range of initiatives specifically targeting Asian gangs. For example, the Los Angeles County Sheriff's Department formed an Asian Organized Crime Unit that is deployed against gang members for which the department has obtained warrants relating to carjackings, homicide, and other violent crimes, as well as illegal gambling, prostitution, and extortion. The unit also acts upon intelligence gathered during times of intergang conflict, often moving to break up such strife prior to all-out "war."

Such efforts often can utilize federal antiterrorism funding and other types of support. Relevant federal agencies providing intelligence-gathering and other resources include the Drug Enforcement Administration, Immigration and Customs Enforcement, and the Internal Revenue Service, as well as the U.S. Justice Department's nearly 200 local Violent Gang Safe Streets Task Force teams, administered through the Federal Bureau of Investigation.

Paolo Barbaro
École Pratique des Hautes Études

See Also: Drive-By Shooting; Graffiti; Immigrant Neighborhoods; Los Angeles, California; New York City; Organized Crime and Violence; Racial Assault; San Francisco, California.

Further Readings

Chin, Ko-Lin. *Chinatown Gangs: Extortion, Enterprise, and Ethnicity*. New York: Oxford University Press, 1996.

Du Phuoc Long, Patrick and Laura Ricard. *The Dream Shattered: Vietnamese Gangs in America*. Lebanon, NH: Northeastern University Press, 1997.

McIllwain, Jeffrey Scott. *Organizing Crime in Chinatown: Race and Racketeering in New York City, 1890–1910*. Jefferson, NC: McFarland, 2004.

Tsunokai, Glenn and Augustine Kposowa. "Asian Gangs in the United States: The Current State of the Research Literature." *Crime, Law and Social Change*, v. 7/1 (2003).

B

Bail

The right to bail has its origins in the Eighth Amendment to the U.S. Constitution, which prohibits the use of excessive bail for defendants charged with a crime. Although the exact origin of bail is not clear, the Eighth Amendment is modeled after English common law.

The practice of releasing the accused prior to trial dates back to 13th-century England, when judges rode circuits deciding criminal cases and it could be months, and sometimes years, before cases were tried. Sheriffs held criminal defendants in local prisons, but the costs and burden of maintaining the prisons was so overwhelming that sheriffs frequently released defendants to family member and friends who pledged their return to future court appearances.

Eventually the authority to set bail was transferred from local sheriffs to judges, who were subject to the influence of the king and often held prisoners without bail at the order of the king. English lawmakers sought to remedy this abuse of power and finally in 1689, the English Bill of Rights prohibited the use of excessive bail. When the American colonies gained independence beginning in 1776, Virginia was first to pass laws emulating English law. The drafters of the U.S. Constitution used the language found in the Virginia Constitution when they drew up the Eighth Amendment.

Many observers have interpreted this amendment as a constitutional right to bail, citing the Federal Rules of Criminal Procedure, which provide that all defendants not charged with a death-penalty crime have the right to bail. The Supreme Court weighed in on the issue with its decision in *Stack v. Boyle*, holding that bail is a traditional right that prevents punishment before adjudication and allows defendants to fully aid in their defense. The court also clarified that the purpose of bail was to ensure the defendant's presence at future court proceedings. Researchers in the field, however, exposed the use of de facto preventive detention, whereby the courts could set monetary bail at amounts that could not be met by poor defendants who would have to remain in detention prior to trial. Opponents criticized a system so reliant on cash bail.

General Bail Options

There are several types of financial bail available to criminal defendants. The strictest is full cash bail, whereby the defendant must pay the bail amount in full to the court to be released prior to trial. A property bond is a second option used by the court and requires the defendant to pledge property deed(s) to obtain pretrial release.

A third option, known as a surety bond, is perhaps one of the most controversial bail options. A surety is when a third party, referred to as a bail bondsman, agrees to pay a defendant's bail to the court in exchange for a fee (typically 10 percent) paid by the defendant. This bail bond industry is profit-driven and is contingent on the court's decision to require financial bail from criminal defendants.

The notion that bail release decisions are decided by profit-seeking bondsmen has led to yet another harsh criticism that defendants with economic resources can purchase their freedom in a system dominated by financial bail. More specifically, if a defendant fails to appear in court, the defendant's bail is forfeited to the court. Similarly, a bail bondsman forfeits the bail amount if a defendant fails to appear. In serious cases, bail bondsmen sometimes enlist the assistance of skip tracers to locate missing defendants. A skip tracer is most commonly known to the public as a bounty hunter, which is a somewhat antiquated but well-known term. Recent reality televisions shows, and most notably *Dog the Bounty Hunter,* have sensationalized the bail bond industry, showing that bounty hunters gallantly track fugitives. Although this is not the norm, it is one potential outcome of a financial bail requirement.

Nonfinancial Bail

Nonfinancial bail options are also available to the court; following the first bail reform movement in the 1960s, they grew in popularity. Most notably, the Vera Foundation formed the Manhattan Bail Project in 1961, which led to a significant increase in the use of release on recognizance (ROR). Although researchers would later question it, initial claims of Vera's success spurred national interest and led to the development of similar programs across the country. Opponents of the cash bail system exposed systematic disparities in bail operations which further fueled reform efforts and led to the passage of the Federal Bail Reform Act of 1966. This act focused on increasing the use of the ROR option. The 1966 act mandated the use of ROR in noncapital cases where this type of release would reasonably ensure the defendant's return to court appearances. The 1966 act, and the increased use of nonfinancial bail, also led to the development of pretrial service agencies.

Pretrial agencies have a variety of responsibilities. While specific duties vary by agency, ultimately they are responsible for assessing pretrial release eligibility of criminal defendants and supervising defendants who have been released prior to trial. Conditional release is a form of nonfinancial release that is similar to ROR but entails some restrictions. Specifically, defendants who are granted a conditional release are free to remain in the community but under the supervision of a pretrial officer and within specific conditions set by the court. Although pretrial agencies have become a common feature of the criminal justice system, the popularity of nonfinancial bail options was short-lived.

Preventive Detention

Rising crime rates, evidence of sentencing disparities, and changing politics all contributed to the move away from rehabilitation and toward a focus on crime control in the 1980s. Consistent with this "tough on crime" movement, a new bail reform effort was undertaken with the goal of protecting the public from potentially dangerous individuals. The Bail Reform Act of 1984, diametrically opposed to the first Bail Reform Act of 1966, authorized the use of preventive detention to protect the safety of the community. This act was upheld in the Supreme Court's decision in *United States v. Salerno*, in which the court opined that protection of the community, in addition to flight risk, was a legitimate goal of bail. Federal law provides that preventive detention can be sought in cases that involve violent and/or serious drug crimes, offenses for which punishment is either life in prison or the death penalty, and for specific repeat offenders.

Since the *Salerno* court upheld the "dangerousness" standard under the Eighth Amendment, 48 states and the District of Columbia amended their bail laws to align with the federal system to allow preventive detention and pretrial release decisions based on potential dangerousness. Although all states and the federal system claim to consider the traditional criteria of flight risk, only two states, New York and New Jersey, have retained flight risk as the sole criteria for pretrial decisions and have banned the use of preventive detention prior to trial. While the criteria for pretrial release decisions varies, offense type and prior criminal history are the two most significant legal factors affecting determinations of potential dangerousness and, ultimately, pretrial release decisions. Judges will often also consider the defendant's history of court appearances and community ties, particularly in those jurisdictions concerned with flight risk.

Size of the Bail "Industry"

Research on bail operations and interest in pretrial detention has gained in popularity, which is understandable given that approximately 62 percent of the 748,000 individuals who occupy U.S. jails are being held in pretrial detention. It is estimated that this pretrial population consumes $9 billion in yearly spending by federal and state authorities. This is the total of administrative, security, and related expenses necessary to hold these criminal defendants who cannot afford bail—many of whom are accused of nonviolent crimes.

Overall, approximately 40 percent of criminal defendants are held prior to trial, a number that has remained fairly stable for several years. Bail researchers have examined factors that affect pretrial decisions and outcomes, concluding that both demographic factors, such as race and gender, and legal factors, such as offense type and criminal history, strongly impact bail decisions. Researchers also continue to focus on the inequities resulting from a system that is generally dominated by financial bail.

Meghan R. Sacks
Fairleigh Dickinson University

See Also: Arrest; Bounty Hunters; Courts, Drug; Courts, Mental Health; Jails; Police (Overview); Street Crime, Popular Portrayals of; Television Shows.

Further Readings

Cohen, Thomas H. and Brian A. Reaves. *State Court Processing Statistics, 1990–2004: Pretrial Release of Felony Defendants in State Courts.* Washington, DC: U.S. Department of Justice, Bureau of Justice Statistics, 2007.

Goldkamp, John. S. *Two Classes of Accused: A Study of Bail and Detention in American Justice.* Cambridge, MA: Ballinger Publishing, 1979.

Harr, J. Scott, et al. *Constitutional Law and the Criminal Justice System.* 5th ed. Belmont, CA: Wadsworth, 2011.

Open Society Justice Initiative. *The Socioeconomic Impact of Pre-Trial Detention.* New York: Open Society Institute, 2011.

Smith, Rich. *Eighth Amendment: The Right to Mercy.* Minneapolis: ABDO and Daughters, 2007.

Stack v. Boyle, 342 U.S. 1, 4 (1951).

United States v. Salerno, 481 U.S. 739 (1987).

Baltimore, Maryland

Baltimore, Maryland, is one of the largest mid-Atlantic cities in America. Its street crime rate consistently ranks in the top 10 of all municipalities in the United States.

Since the early 1960s, Charm City, as Baltimore is affectionately called, has suffered from numerous and persistent urban social problems including: high rates of poverty and sexually transmitted disease; illegal drug use, especially heroin, cocaine, and crack; teenage pregnancy; economic decline; poor public housing; homelessness; an abysmal public-education system; and high rates of violence and crime.

Vividly featured in the 2000 David Simon book *The Corner*, the creatively seminal television series *Homicide: Life on the Street*, and the critically acclaimed HBO television series *The Wire* (each set in Baltimore), these longstanding challenges interact with each other and compound the commission of crime and violence in the city.

Structural Concerns

There are numerous reasons why these social and criminal problems have occurred in Baltimore, including a declining tax base as a result of the shuttering of businesses; and the cycle of poverty that has existed in some underserved communities in the city.

Despite several bold attempts by politicians at the local and state level to redevelop certain areas (e.g., the Inner Harbor and Fell's Point) with the hope of bringing in more tourists and helping the local economy, such efforts do not seem to have been sufficient to radically turn the tide citywide.

There are clear overall reasons that may underlie the current malaise. In 2010 Baltimore had a population of approximately 621,000 individuals. This number has been declining since the 1950s, when the population peaked at about 950,000.

Considerable out-migration to the suburbs of neighboring Baltimore County and elsewhere has caused this decline. The undercurrent of lost jobs has made it difficult to boost the tax base. Further, the neighborhoods that remain heavily populated are often the most crime-ridden. Most homicides are committed against people who know each other, and are connected to the thriving drug trade as well.

A koban in 2009 in Baltimore, Maryland, based on a similar Japanese police practice. The box is staffed by one or more police officers and contains an exterior emergency phone.

Crime

Baltimore has one of the highest homicide rates in the United States. Its violent crime rate is also high. In 1993, homicides peaked at 353 individuals. In 2011, the police reported 196 homicides. Not only was this considerably down from 1993, but it was a tremendous one-year drop compared to the 223 homicides recorded in 2010.

Over the past decade, however, the official crime rates (in reporting years such as 2003, 2005, and 2006) have been disputed. The police department has been accused on several occasions of manipulating the data for political purposes. Regardless, much of the violence is in connection with the illicit drug trade. It is also gang-related with gangs jockeying for control over the lucrative drug markets. In contrast, the city has also been recognized as a leader in drug reform efforts, including "treatment on demand," methadone treatment, and needle exchanges.

Police and Law Enforcement

The problem of street crime has captured the interest not just of victims, their loved ones, clergy, and politicians, but also well-meaning community activists. The latter often form neighborhood self-help organizations to lobby for more police presence and/or engage in patrols themselves. They frequently get temporary news media attention and tend to last for limited periods of time. Over the past two decades, the Baltimore Police Department, the state of Maryland, and the U.S. Department of Justice have implemented numerous programs with the hope of reducing the amount of crime in the state and in Baltimore, its major city.

Between 1994 and 2012 alone, there have been at least eight major crime suppression programs including: the identification and policing of Hot Spots, the Boston Crime Reduction strategy, Break the Cycle, Comprehensive Communities Program, Project Exile, Weed and Seed, Operation Ceasefire, CompStat, and a fledgling gun buyback program.

In many respects Baltimore has led the nation in its willingness to adopt these types of programs. The city has a heritage along these lines, including the time-honored Police Athletic League (PAL) centers (now disbanded), which placed both police officers and Teach for America volunteers to run after-school programs in disadvantaged communities.

Conclusion

Most of these crime-deterrence programs have been ushered in by or required the participation of each new successive commissioner of policing. In fact, between 1998 and 2012, Baltimore had six different police commissioners. The locus of support for these programs has come from a number of different sources. Sometimes these anticrime initiatives have been pushed by the mayor's office, and others have been supported by private foundations like the Baltimore-based Annie E. Casey Foundation, which targets at-risk youth and teen pregnancy. At various times, the federal government has funded these programs and experiments.

Unfortunately, few evaluations of these programs have been conducted; it is difficult to separate out which ones work and those that do not. Some seemed to be in competition with each other. Meanwhile, during the 1990s and 2000s, the Baltimore Police Department has been faced with repeated but short-lived scandals involving corruption, problematic arrests, and police brutality.

Jeffrey Ian Ross
University of Baltimore

See Also: Drug Dealing; Gangs (Street); Hot Spots; Murder/Homicide; Needle Exchanges; Neighborhood Watch; Operation Ceasefire; Street Crime, Popular Portrayals of; Television Shows; Weed and Seed.

Further Readings
Harries, Keith D. "Violence Change and Cohort Trajectories: Baltimore Neighborhoods, 1990–2000." *Urban Geography,* v.25/1 (2004).
Moscos, Peter. *Cop in the Hood: Policing Baltimore's Eastern District.* Princeton, NJ: Princeton University Press, 2008.
Roth, Jeffrey A. and George L. Kelling. *Baltimore's Comprehensive Communities Program: A Case Study.* Cambridge, MA: Botec Analysis Corporation, 2004.
Simon, David with Edward Burns. *The Corner: A Year in the Life of an Inner City.* New York: Broadway Books, 2000.
Taylor, Ralph. *Breaking Away From Broken Windows: Baltimore Neighborhoods and the Nationwide Fight Against Crime, Fear, and Decline.* Boulder, CO: Westview Press, 2000.

Bank Robbery

The banking industry is an essential component of American economic life, giving citizens a sense of enhanced security by providing them with a secure repository for monetary savings and valuable property, as well as loans for purchase of property and other investments, such as business start-ups and expansions. Banks also provide financial services including investment opportunities, electronic transfer of funds, and financial planning advice. As critical components of our economic and social structure, banks are generally well secured with a variety of technical and human controls.

Robbing a bank thus requires a level of audacity perhaps greater than for most other street crimes. While infamous bank robbers such as Frank and Jesse James, Bonnie and Clyde, and Willy Sutton have become icons of popular culture, bank robbery is a serious and dangerous crime. The environment of commercial activity, the level of protection afforded banks, and the daring needed to flaunt those protections create a greater potential for extreme violence than is present in many other types of street crime.

Definition and History
Bank robbery is a federal felony as well as a felony crime in all states, falling under each state's robbery statute or a separate state bank robbery statute. Robbery may generically be defined as the unlawful taking of the property of another through force or the threat of the use of force. The term *bank robbery* is usually used to refer to the taking of property (usually cash held in trust for depositors) from bank employees through force or threatened force. Federal law defines bank robbery as the use of

. . . force and violence or intimidation [to] take or attempt to take, from the person or presence of another . . . any property or money or any other thing of value belonging to or in the care, custody, control, management, or possession of any bank, credit union, or any saving and loan association. (U.S. Code, Title 18-Part I-Chapter 103-Section 2113)

While banks have long been a feature of American life, bank robbery is a comparatively recent development. Popular legend holds that the first bank robbery was committed by the James Gang on February 13, 1866, when they entered the Clay County Savings Association in Liberty, Missouri (near Kansas City), and left with $60,000 after shooting an unarmed bank employee. Allowing for inflation, this would be the equivalent of nearly $900,000, a take all but unheard of today. The Malden Bank in Malden, Massachusetts, also claims the dubious honor of being the first bank robbed. In December 1863 an unidentified person entered the bank, murdered a teller, and departed with $5,000 (approximately $75,000 in today's terms).

Bank robbery was a common crime during the last part of the 19th century, being a Wild West mainstay of such famous criminal gangs as the aforementioned James Gang as well as the Younger Gang, which sometimes operated with the James brothers, and the Dalton Gang. The James and Younger Gangs were decimated during a botched robbery of the bank in Northfield, Minnesota, in September 1876—celebrated there in modern times with re-enactments and an annual festival. The Dalton Gang was similarly hurt while attempting to rob the First National Bank of Longview, Texas, in May 1894.

Bank robbery may have reached its pinnacle during the 1930s. A time of grave financial hardship, some people turned to bank robbery out of economic necessity. Others saw the banks as the cause of their financial hardships and robbery as a means of retaliation, almost a revolutionary act. Regardless, bank robbery came to national prominence during this era in large part due to systematic, serial robberies conducted over multistate areas by well-armed criminals who openly flaunted their guilt with seeming impunity. Up until 1934, bank robbers could elude capture and prosecution by merely crossing a state line. To solve this jurisdictional problem, Congress made bank robbery a federal crime in 1934, and expanded the mission of the U.S. Bureau of Investigation (renamed the Federal Bureau of Investigation [FBI] in 1935) to include bank robbery, a core responsibility of the FBI to this day.

Bank robbery again rose to national prominence during the 1970s when a series of robberies by left-wing radical groups occurred. These gangs perhaps saw themselves following the example of the early-20th-century Russian Communist Party, among whose members future Soviet dictator Joseph Stalin advocated and participated in robbing banks to finance the revolution. Most infamous among these was the 1974 robbery of a branch office of the Hibernia Bank of San Francisco by the Symbionese Liberation Army. The robbery made national headlines in large part because newspaper heiress Patricia Hearst, who had allegedly been kidnapped by the group some weeks earlier, participated in the robbery and reportedly fired several shots.

Popular Culture

When prolific bank robber Willie Sutton was asked why he robbed banks he allegedly replied, "Because that's where the money is." Sutton later denied the quip, but it gave rise to Sutton's Law, which informs medical students that when assessing a patient, always first consider the obvious. As with many other criminal typologies, Americans have long held a fascination with bank robbers, elevating some of them to mythic status. The James and Younger Gangs, for example, as former Confederate guerrilla fighters, were seen by some as continuing the fight of the Lost Cause by striking a blow

against the northern bankers who were profiting at the expense of the defeated South.

During the Great Depression, figures such as Bonnie Parker, Clyde Barrow, and John Dillinger were sensationalized as Robin Hood-like figures that were robbing the rich and giving to the poor. Many of these poor had had their property seized by these very same banks when they fell behind on loan repayments and so may have viewed the robberies as vicarious revenge. Parker and Barrow become the subjects of a controversial 1967 feature film *Bonnie and Clyde*, directed by Arthur Penn, that brought their notoriety to the attention of some of the 1960s generation who, through the film, saw them not as criminals but as antiestablishment types who were striking out at a repressive society.

Even if not seen as cultural heroes, bank robbers may capture the imagination of the public. An example of this occurred February 28, 1997, when two heavily armed and armored robbers entered

An armed Patty Hearst photographed by a closed-circuit security camera during an April 1974 bank robbery in San Francisco, California. Hearst was thought to have been kidnapped prior to her involvement with the Symbionese Liberation Army.

the North Hollywood branch of the Bank of America. A passing Los Angeles Police Department (LAPD) patrol officer spotted the pair entering the bank and radioed for assistance. When the robbers, Larry Phillips, Jr., and Emil Matasareanu, exited the bank they were confronted by several dozen officers. In the ensuing 44-minute shootout, both criminals were killed and 11 LAPD officers and seven bystanders were wounded. The gunfight was covered live by local news helicopters and broadcast nationally.

Scope and Character

According to the FBI there were 5,546 bank robberies nationally during 2010, down some 10 percent from 2009 (there were 5,943 bank robberies that year). Bank robberies have steadily declined from a 1993 peak of 11,876 with a few fluctuations. The total gross loss in cash, checks (including traveler's checks), and other property was $43,016,099 in 2010 or about $7,800 per incident, the FBI reported. In 2010, law enforcement officials recovered $8,193,065, about 19 percent of that gross loss.

Bank robbers are overwhelmingly male (about 95 percent) and variably ethnic; in 2010, 2,936 were white, 2,920 black, 494 Hispanic, 77 classified as other, and 242 for whom race was unknown. About one-third of bank robbers are under 30 years of age. The FBI states that on average about one-third of bank robbers are drug addicts who are looking for quick cash to support their addiction.

About 20 percent of bank robbers have previous convictions for bank robbery and may be considered professionals. Bank robberies tend to occur most frequently on Fridays and Tuesdays; the lowest rates are on weekends. Freestanding branch offices were nearly 40 times more likely to be robbed than main offices, and 52 times more likely to be robbed than offices located in stores or other facilities. Most of the branch offices robbed (3,689) are located in some type of commercial district, or in a shopping center or strip mall (1,339). Bank robberies are most likely to occur in urban areas, followed by small cities or towns and suburban areas. Rural bank robberies are rare, accounting for about just 2 percent of the total.

In about half of the 2010 robberies, the perpetrator gave the teller a note demanding cash; the demand was made verbally in the other half. A firearm, usually a handgun, was used in 25 percent of bank robberies. For a crime with a reputation for being violent, physical injury occurs in only slightly more that 2 percent of incidents; murder, hostage taking, or kidnapping in less than 1 percent. The FBI reports that historically, 75 to 80 percent of bank robberies are solved; only murder has a higher clearance rate. Recently, the clearance rate has dropped; this is mainly due to the fact that several high-rate offenders are still at large. It should be noted that a single arrest often clears numerous robberies.

While most bank robbers are amateurs (about 80 percent), there has been an increase over the past decade in "takeover robberies" perpetrated by professional gangs. While the amateur usually waits in line and presents a note, the visibly armed gang will storm the bank, usually shortly after it opens, making everyone lie on the floor while gang members clean out cash drawers. While relatively uncommon (less than 10 percent), such events have a nightmarish quality producing fear beyond their actual likelihood for bodily harm.

Countermeasures

Banks have long employed security personnel and/or technology to deter robbery. Traditionally, these measures centered around locked tellers' cages, which have evolved into more inclusive bandit barriers fronted with bullet-resistant glass with transactions taking place through shielded drawers. Banks have also employed uniformed, armed guards; quite often these were retired police officers. Silent alarms, triggered by bank personnel and ringing into police stations or monitoring companies, have been employed at least since the 1960s.

Beginning in the early 1980s, banks began using exploding dye packs that indelibly mark stolen cash (and often the robber) with red or purple dye as robbers leave the bank. These packs generally resemble a standard cash packet and are mixed with money given to the robber. As the criminal leaves the bank, a radio transmitter in the doorway sets off a trigger which begins a chemical reaction lasting several seconds; this reaction causes the dye packet to explode, staining the cash.

As closed-circuit television (CCTV) technology has improved and become less expensive, CCTV cameras have proliferated with many banks setting up multiple cameras per teller station. Finally banks, in cooperation with law enforcement agencies, have been providing more sophisticated training to their employees aimed toward preventing robberies and hostage situations, preserving the crime scene and evidence, and identifying perpetrators.

M. George Eichenberg
Tarleton State University

See Also: Closed-Circuit Television; Defensible Space Theory; Guns and Weapons; Security, Private; Street Crime, Popular Portrayals of.

Further Readings

Dillow, Gordon and William J. Rehder. *Where the Money Is: True Tales From the Bank Robbery Capital of the World.* New York: W. W. Norton, 2004.

Federal Bureau of Investigation. "Bank Crime Statistics (BCS) Federal Insured Financial Institutions January 1, 2010–December 31, 2010." March 1, 2011. http://www.fbi.gov/stats-services/publications/bank-crime-statistics-2010/bank-crime-statistics-2010 (Accessed June 2012).

Porrello, Rick. *Superthief—A Master Burglar, the Mafia, and the Biggest Bank Heist in U.S. History.* Novelty, OH: Next Hat Press, 2005.

Weisel, Deborah Lamm. *Bank Robbery: Problem-Oriented Guides for Police.* Guide No. 48. Washington, DC: U.S. Department of Justice Office of Community-Oriented Policing Services, 2007.

Bar Personnel

Bar personnel are at the center of problems occurring in and around licensed drinking establishments, which can range from random disorder to chronic, hardened street crime. While some bar personnel function in a capacity that quells disorder or prevents it from happening in the first place, others exacerbate problems by showing little concern or regard for the patrons they serve.

Instigators of Violence

In their groundbreaking study of bars and pubs in Vancouver, Canada, K. Graham and colleagues identified aggressive and unfriendly bar staff as a significant predictor of alcohol-related aggression. These researchers also noted bar staff's willingness to serve patrons to the point of intoxication and beyond in problem bars and identified excessive drunkenness as another significant predictor of violence and aggression in these establishments. Other researchers also documented extreme patron intoxication and unfriendly and aggressive bar staff as significant predictors of barroom aggression. Observers in a study led by R. Homel reported witnessing bouncers initiating fights with bar patrons, with some going so far as to follow patrons outside to continue altercations that began inside the bar.

Such research placed bar personnel, particularly bouncers and bartenders, under the microscope. Recent strategies aimed at reducing and preventing problems occurring in and around licensed drinking establishments focus on altering and improving the behaviors of bar staff, particularly that of bouncers and servers of alcohol.

S. Wells and colleagues provided one of the first investigations focused specifically on security staff responses to incidents of violence and aggression occurring in bars. Data in this late-1990s study came from unobtrusive observations conducted in licensed drinking establishments, as well as interviews with persons aged 19 to 25 who had previous experience with aggression in bars. Data analysis involved examining summary accounts of aggressive incidents from these observations and interviews and categorizing security staffs involvement as "good," "neutral," "bad," or "ugly."

"Good" responses involved preventing or minimizing the impact of aggressive behavior; "neutral" responses involved permitting the escalation of aggressive behavior; "bad" responses involved unfair or inconsistent treatment of patrons; and "ugly" responses involved bullying and harassing patrons, as well as being physically or verbally abusive. Wells and colleagues reported few examples of "good" bouncer behavior, as security personnel rarely acted in a proactive manner to prevent or minimize aggressive behavior. "Bad" responses by bouncers to aggressive incidents were more common than both "good" and "neutral" responses. These findings led to the conclusion that many security personnel do not behave in a manner that discourages violence or aggression—and suggest that aggressive behaviors by bouncers set the tone for the night and may actually promote aggressive behaviors among bar patrons.

Door Culture and the Bouncer

S. Winlow and colleagues are part of a growing number of researchers who have employed a "covert ethnography" approach to studying the behaviors of bouncers and their contribution to barroom aggression, which entails relying on bouncers themselves to collect data on incidents of aggression occurring in licensed drinking establishments. Dismissing methodologies such as accompanying bouncers while they work as being inappropriate and potentially obtrusive, these researchers recruited an individual who they believed had the necessary academic, social, and cultural skills to serve as an ethnographer in their research. His employment as a bouncer and immersion experience in connection with this study allowed for several valuable insights into the occupational culture of bouncers.

In regard to bouncer recruitment, findings from this study revealed that most bars rely on word of mouth rather than posted advertisements. In addition to an individual's size and physique, one's reputation for using violence is an attractive attribute considered by prospective employers. According to the ethnographer used in this study, employment as a bouncer confers on one a certain degree of respect and deference by both bar patrons and other staff members, as well as more tangible benefits such as free admission to other bars.

D. Hobbs and colleagues, who also employed a bouncer to collect data, suggest that there exists a door culture that is separate and distinct from public police entities, which allows security personnel in bars to wield great discretion in enforcing behavioral codes of their respective places of employment. Like Winlow and colleagues, they suggest that many bar owners and managers seek out bouncers who "look the part." These researchers also found that some bars attempt to minimize security costs by employing large bouncers rather than large staffs of bouncers. While size and physique are usually prerequisites for gaining employment as a bouncer, training in how to handle disorderly behavior and de-escalate altercations between bar patrons is usually not.

Servers and Intoxication

Concerns about the quality and effectiveness of security personnel usually take a back seat to concerns about alcohol beverage service in most bars and pubs. While barroom researchers have identified numerous situational variables in bars that contribute to violence and aggression, many individuals outside this area of research still believe that alcohol is the sole or primary factor responsible for problems occurring in and around licensed drinking establishments. For this reason, much of the programming that takes place in bars and pubs focuses on altering the behaviors of servers of alcohol, rather than altering or improving the behaviors of bouncers.

Ever since K. Graham and colleague's pioneering study, in which they identified continued alcohol service to obviously intoxicated patrons as a significant predictor of violence and aggression, researchers have been studying the behaviors of servers of alcohol and the effectiveness of programs aimed at teaching bar staff how to dispense alcohol responsibly. In addition to observations conducted in natural drinking settings and surveys conducted with bar staff and patrons, researchers have employed the use of "pseudointoxicated" bar patrons in an attempt to better understand the nature of irresponsible alcohol service in barrooms. Phillip Rydon and colleagues were among the first to employ this methodology. Over the course of 120 visits to 23 different licensed drinking establishments, pairs of pseudodrunk actors placed more than 350 drink orders. Bar staff in this study refused alcohol service during only 10 percent of the visits and implemented partial interventions, such as offering food or nonalcoholic drinks, during only 5 percent of visits.

A. James McKnight was another pioneer to use covert actors trained in exhibiting signs of intoxication as a means of evaluating the effectiveness of a responsible beverage service (RBS) training program. While the RBS training program examined in this study led to significant overall changes in knowledge of, attitudes toward, and practices and policies pertaining to responsible alcohol service among bar staff, there was little increase in the refusal of alcohol to trained observers feigning intoxication. Numerous studies have shown similar poor results in terms of RBS training programs altering the behaviors of servers of alcohol and increasing the likelihood that these individuals decline alcohol sales to obviously intoxicated bar patrons. This, however, is not surprising considering that many servers of alcohol see few incentives in refusing alcohol service to bar patrons, as doing so usually leads to loss of gratuities

The visible presence of a person employed as a bouncer can often serve to prevent mischief or violence from taking place. While most bouncers are competent professionals who are more interested in preventing trouble rather than engaging in aggressive behavior, the profession can attract individuals who may abuse their power and position.

or even verbal or physical altercations with those who have been "cut off."

Research shows that many servers, particularly those who have not gone through any sort of RBS training program, are not aware of the legal consequences of their actions or of the laws that exist prohibiting alcohol sales to obviously intoxicated individuals. Regardless of their potential for reducing irresponsible alcohol service and associated problems with alcohol-related harm, RBS training programs will not have the desired effect in establishments whose management does not truly embrace responsible alcohol service. While owners and managers may require that all of their servers go through RBS training, some do this simply to look like they are doing something, possibly for insurance purposes or for protection from potential lawsuits.

Studies indicate that it is rather common to find trained servers in bars in which owners and managers advertise drink specials and allow drinking contests, both of which contribute to increased intoxication and problems with violence and aggression. In his study of barroom aggression in Hoboken, New Jersey, J. Roberts reported observing bar staff who had undergone RBS training drinking on the job, sometimes with or in front of bar managers. Servers of alcohol drinking on the job was a significant predictor of both service of alcohol to intoxicated patrons and of violence and aggression in Hoboken barrooms.

Managers Flirt With Negligence
Through their actions, bar personnel undoubtedly contribute to problems not just in, but also around licensed drinking establishments. In his study of

Hoboken barrooms, Roberts witnessed numerous occasions in which drunken participants in violent altercations were ushered out of bars and onto streets and sidewalks where they would resume verbally and physically assaulting one another if there were no police in the area. Very rarely did bouncers attempt to intervene in patron altercations once they were moved outside the bar. It is well known that many managers and owners instruct bar personnel to remove unruly patrons from the premises and get themselves back inside as quickly as possible.

Furthermore, most bar owners and managers avoid involving the police in such matters when possible and instruct their employees to do the same out of fear of drawing unwanted attention to their bar. Once unruly patrons are ejected from licensed drinking establishments, they become someone else's problem. More often than not, local law enforcement is left to deal with drunken and aggressive individuals once they leave or are ejected from barrooms.

Unfortunately, the training and regulation of bouncers and security personnel is lacking throughout most countries, including the United States, while research suggests that training programs for servers of alcohol are largely ineffective. Too many bartenders are willing to serve bar patrons to the point of intoxication and beyond, and too many bouncers allow patron altercations to escalate before intervening—and rely too little on communication skills and too much on physical force when they do. Even more unfortunate than problems with the training and regulation of bouncers and bartenders is the lack of concern some owners and managers have for the behaviors of their bar staff or the well-being of their patrons, as maximizing profits and avoiding potential lawsuits and unwanted attention by the police takes precedence in most barrooms.

Conclusion

In response to weak internal and, at times, external regulation of barrooms by city officials, a growing number of researchers have proposed implementing community-based interventions that seek to bring together all relevant stakeholders, including bar owners, community members, and government regulators, in coordinated efforts to address problems in and around licensed drinking establishments and put pressure on problem bars. Interventions

that hold bar owners and managers accountable for their behavior, as well as the behavior of their bar staff, have shown promising results both in terms of improving the behaviors of bar personnel and reducing and preventing problems occurring in and around licensed drinking establishments.

James C. Roberts
University of Scranton

See Also: Alcohol and Drug Use; Bars and Pubs; Crime Prevention, Situational; Drinking, Underage; Drinking Establishments, Unlicensed; Environmental Criminology; Hot Spots; Risky Lifestyles; Routine Activity Theory; Security, Private; Street/Block Parties; Victims, Tourists.

Further Readings
Graham, Kathryn, Linda La Rocque, Rhoda Yetman, T. James Ross, and Enrico Guistra. "Aggression and Barroom Environments." *Journal of Studies on Alcohol*, v.41/3 (1980).
Hobbs, Dick, et al. "'Door Lore': The Art and Economics of Intimidation." *British Journal of Criminology*, v.42/2 (2002).
Homel, Ross, et al. "Public Drinking and Violence: Not Just an Alcohol Problem." *Journal of Drug Issues*, v.22/3 (1992).
McKnight, A. James. "Factors Influencing the Effectiveness of Server-Intervention Education." *Journal of Studies on Alcohol*, v.52/5 (1991).
Roberts, James C. "Accessories to the Crime: 'Secondary Servers' and Alcohol Sales to Obviously Intoxicated Barroom Patrons." *Journal of Current Issues in Crime, Law and Law Enforcement*, v.2/2–3 (2010).
Roberts, James C. "Bouncers and Barroom Aggression: A Review of the Research." *Aggression and Violent Behavior*, v.14/1 (2009).
Rydon, Phillip, et al. "Pseudo-Drunk-Patron Evaluation of Bar-Staff Compliance with Western Australian Liquor Law." *Australian and New Zealand Journal of Public Health*, v.20/3 (1996).
Wells, Samantha, et al. "'The Good, The Bad, and the Ugly': Responses by Security Staff to Aggressive Incidents in Public Drinking Settings." *Journal of Drug Issues*, v.28/4 (1998).
Winlow, Simon, et al. "Get Ready to Duck: Bouncers and the Realities of Ethnographic Research on Violent Groups." *British Journal of Criminology*, v.41/3 (2001).

Bars and Pubs

Bars and pubs are locations known for problem behavior, including violence and aggression, which in many cases makes them ignition points for street crime in their immediate vicinity. Those who study barroom aggression contend that social contexts within bars and pubs have a direct effect on the behaviors of individuals who frequent these establishments. Furthermore, it is widely accepted that violence and aggression in bars and pubs is not attributable to any single "situational variable," but rather the subtle interaction in one time and place of several such variables.

Root Cause Studies

Researchers who study aggression in bars do not discount the contribution of various biological, psychological, psychopharmacological, or cultural explanations of alcohol-related aggression. Instead, they take for granted that individuals bring to drinking episodes a variety of unique characteristics, including unique propensities for aggression. However, even individuals who are predisposed to act out aggressively may be unlikely to exhibit such behavior unless exposed to various environmental instigators found in problem drinking establishments. The identification of situational variables that contribute to violence and aggression in bars and pubs is critical to the development of strategies aimed at reducing and preventing such incidents.

Kathryn Graham and colleagues were among the first to study aggression in bars and pubs in their work from the 1970s onward. Methodology used in their studies would become the standard for observing and recording incidents of aggression in licensed drinking establishments. Teams of observers (male-female pairs) spent three months and over 600 hours in the first such study, conducting structured observations in nearly 200 bars and pubs located throughout Vancouver, Canada. Data from this study revealed several characteristics of aggressive drinking environments, including unpleasant and unclean physical surroundings, irresponsible alcohol service, unfriendly bar staff, and poor ventilation.

Relying heavily on these findings, sociologist Ross Homel and colleagues conducted the second major research study of barroom aggression. Relying on structured observation sheets listing a large number of variables to be observed, including several predictors of aggression identified by Graham and colleagues, observers spent 300 hours conducting observations in 23 sites within 17 separate bars and pubs. The major aim of this study was to contrast situational variables in a sample of bars known to be high-risk for violence, with the same variables in a sample of bars known to be low-risk for violence. Data from this study revealed groups of male strangers, high boredom, high drunkenness, and aggressive bouncers as the primary variables present during violent episodes and in bars known to be high-risk for violence.

Bar Environments

The aforementioned studies provided the impetus for subsequent research on barroom aggression, which has spread in recent years to several different countries and entails an increasingly diverse range of research methodologies. While few barroom researchers would contend that any single variable is responsible for aggression in bars and pubs, it is widely agreed that some variables are better predictors of aggressive incidents than are others.

Commonly cited situational variables found to contribute to violence and aggression in licensed drinking establishments include: poor barroom management; poor barroom designs that increase discomfort among, as well as unwanted contact between, bar patrons (e.g., bars with dance floors that intersect with routes to bathrooms); later closing hours; a high proportion of young male strangers; drink specials that encourage rapid drinking; lack of food and nonalcoholic drink options; competitive activities such as drinking contests and wet T-shirt contests; poor quality entertainment that causes boredom, as well as annoyance when combined with high cover charges; low ratio of staff to patrons; failure to check patrons for identification and underage drinking; bar staff drinking on the job; bar staff's tolerance of disorderly behavior among bar patrons (e.g., dancing on bars and tables, spraying beer, and roughhousing); and availability of potential weapons like pool sticks, darts, and glass bottles, mugs, and ashtrays.

Again, researchers studying aggression in barrooms take for granted that bar patrons bring to drinking episodes a variety of unique characteristics, including unique propensities for aggression. Brian Quigley and colleagues are among the few to study the characteristics of bar patrons, finding that those who frequented violent bars were more likely to be young, to have alcohol dependency problems, and to express their anger openly. However, these researchers found that the strongest predictors of bar violence in their study were the characteristics of bars themselves. Most barroom researchers agree that the easiest and most practical approach to reducing aggression in bars is regulating the routine activities of licensed drinking establishments, rather than attempting to modify the routine activities of bar patrons.

Key Factors to Target

Three factors that have received particular attention by barroom researchers are aversive environmental stimuli, aggressive bouncers, and irresponsible alcohol service. Many strategies aimed at reducing and preventing aggression in bars and pubs focus on removing or alleviating aversive environmental stimuli and altering the behavior of bouncers and servers of alcohol. Aversive environmental stimuli include such things as excessive heat, noise, smoke, and crowding.

James Roberts, one of the few American researchers who studies aggression in bars, suggests that factors such as these, each of which has been shown to contribute to problems with violence and aggression in bars and pubs, can be addressed with minimal effort and usually very little cost. For example, the installation of air conditioning units or ceiling fans might reduce problems associated with excessive heat. Similarly, the addition of air filtration units or bans on smoking within licensed drinking establishments might reduce problems associated with excessive smoke.

While there are numerous alcohol beverage service programs that aim to teach bar staff how to identify visible signs of intoxication and dispense alcohol more responsibly, evaluations of these programs have shown mixed results. Unfortunately, most attempts to deal with aggressive and unruly bouncers have been handled "in house," and there are few training programs aimed at teaching security personnel how to do their job more safely and effectively. External regulation of security personnel in bars and pubs by city and county agencies is lacking in many jurisdictions. Few bouncers have to undergo background checks or register with local police departments. Also, in regard to the role of

police agencies in addressing barroom aggression, some departments allow their officers to conduct patrols within bars, while most concentrate on the streets outside, as drunken and unruly patrons inevitably find their way into public spaces after a bar has closed or upon being ejected for bad behavior.

Conclusion

While still in its infancy, barroom research has yielded a good deal of information about the causes of violence and aggression in bars and pubs. Future research should focus on a more diverse population of bars and bar patrons, as most of what is currently available focuses primarily on establishments that cater to young, college-aged individuals. There is also a need for continued studies of barroom aggression in the United States, as most contemporary barroom research emanates from locations throughout Canada, Australia, and the United Kingdom. The identification of a comprehensive group of situational variables that predict violence and aggression in bars and pubs is critical to the development of effective strategies aimed at reducing and preventing problem behaviors both in and around licensed drinking establishments.

James C. Roberts
University of Scranton

See Also: Alcohol and Drug Use; Bar Personnel; Crime Prevention, Situational; Drinking, Underage; Environmental Criminology; Hot Spots; Risky Lifestyles; Routine Activity Theory; Street/Block Parties; Tourists; Drinking Establishments, Unlicensed.

Further Readings

Fox, James G. and James J. Sobol. "Drinking Patterns, Social Interaction, and Barroom Behavior: A Routine Activities Approach." *Deviant Behavior: An Interdisciplinary Journal*, v.21/5 (2000).

Graham, Kathryn, et al. "Aggression and Barroom Environments." *Journal of Studies on Alcohol*, v.41/3 (1980).

Graham, Kathryn and Ross Homel. *Raising the Bar: Preventing Aggression in and Around Bars, Pubs, and Clubs*. Devon, UK: Willan Publishing, 2008.

Green, Joanna and Martin Plant. "Bad Bars: A Review of Risk Factors." *Journal of Substance Use*, v.12/3 (2007).

Homel, Ross and Jeff Clark. "The Prediction and Prevention of Violence in Pubs and Clubs." In *Crime*

Prevention Studies, Ronald Clarke. Vol. 3. Boulder, CO: Lynne Rienner Publishers, 1994.

Quigley, Brian M., Kenneth E. Leonard, and R. Lorraine Collins. "Characteristics of Violent Bars and Bar Patrons." *Journal of Studies on Alcohol,* v.64/6 (2003).

Roberts, James C. "Barroom Aggression in Hoboken, New Jersey: Don't Blame the Bouncers!" *Journal of Drug Education,* v.37/4 (2007).

Bicycle Theft

Bicycle theft is defined as the unlawful taking of a nonmotorized pedal cycle. Typically this refers to the theft of an entire bicycle, but can also include theft of component parts and accessories. Compared to other common types of street crime, bicycle theft has rarely featured in academic research, whether in criminology or related fields such as transport and town planning. The research that has been undertaken shows that the risk of cycle theft, real or perceived, is a significant barrier to cycle usage. In an era where cycling is increasingly promoted as a sustainable alternative to motorized transport in urban and suburban settings, enriching our understanding of cycle theft and its prevention is of social as well as academic importance.

Extent of Bicycle Theft

Data from the International Crime Victims Survey (ICVS) suggest that levels of bicycle theft remained stable in the United States between 1998 and 2004, with a mean rate of 2.8 victims per 100 population. In terms of recorded crime, the Federal Bureau of Investigation (FBI) classifies bicycle theft as an example of larceny-theft, alongside offenses such as shoplifting and pickpocketing. In 2009, bicycle theft accounted for 3.4 percent of all incidents of larceny, equating to over 200,000 reported offences.

This is likely to underestimate the problem, given that many bicycle thefts are not reported to the police; this is illustrated by comparison with figures from the 2008 National Crime Victimization Survey that suggest a fivefold difference between reported bicycle thefts and those that actually occurred. Interviews with bicycle theft victims attribute low reporting levels to a general assumption that the police are unlikely to apprehend offenders or recover stolen bicycles. This notion has some merit. Clearance rates for bicycle theft are consistently low, with typical estimates ranging from 2 percent to 4 percent of stolen bicycles being returned, and an even lower fraction of cases resulting in an arrest. This is in contrast to overall national rates of clearance by arrest for all larceny-theft crimes, which averages between 15 percent and 20 percent. One explanation is that, unlike many comparable crimes, there typically exists little relationship between the cyclist and cycle thief, thus reliable identification of suspects is rare. Another explanation concerns the proof of ownership problem: because many cyclists cannot prove that they own the bicycle recovered by the police, detained offenders will often be released without charge, and may even be given the stolen cycle on release.

Correlates of Victimization

An abundance of opportunities helps explain the prevalence of bicycle theft. National rates for cycle theft year to year strongly correlate with trends in bicycle ownership levels. Similarly, cycle theft is found to concentrate at locations where criminal opportunities are more plentiful, such as on-street parking facilities and transport hubs. Urban areas are ideal for theft, as they present numerous ways to "disappear into the crowd." However, cycle theft is relatively prevalent in suburban areas and in such small town and rural locales as college campuses.

The basic character of the bicycle—lightweight, easy to operate, highly mobile— make it a near-ideal target for theft. Furthermore, many contemporary bicycles are of fairly high monetary value, adding to the criminal lure. The New York City bicycle advocacy organization Transportation Alternatives has conservatively estimated that at least 40,000 bicycles—with a value of $10 million—are stolen annually in the city. The FBI posited an average price value of $276 for bicycles that were stolen in 2000; this extrapolates to a total value of at least $86 million in stolen bikes that year. Beyond theft aimed at obtaining a bike's resale value on the black market, it should be noted that may bicycle thefts are opportunistic, impulse crimes—the cycle is stolen for "joy riding" purposes and later abandoned.

Another factor is simply that stolen bicycles are most likely to be those that were locked insecurely. A study comprising over 8,500 observations of cycle-locking events found "secure" locking practices to be less common than other ways of parking a bicycle. How secure a cycle will be is partly a function of what it is locked to. In urban settings many bicycles are "flyparked," that is, fastened to street furniture not designed for that purpose (e.g., railings, parking meters, signposts) or to trees. Flyparked cycles often suffer higher rates of victimization because such fixtures afford little scope for more secure locking.

For bicycle theft, as with many crime types, a reliable predictor of future victimization is previous victimization. Cycle theft is highly concentrated: a small number of cycle theft victims disproportionately account for a large proportion of cycle theft victimizations. Furthermore, victimization risk displays a contagion-like quality both spatially and temporally; a phenomenon known as near-repeat victimization. Research has demonstrated that for a period of three to five weeks in the wake of a bicycle theft, further incidents were more likely to occur to cycles located nearby and up to a distance of about 450 yards.

The relatively scant data on bicycle theft offenders does indicate that they tend to be repeat offenders. Also, offenders tend to be male and youthful, with late-teens to mid-20s being the most common range in those apprehended. This is in opposition to bicycle theft victims, which research shows to be of diffuse demographics, covering both genders and occurring across all age and occupation ranges.

Prevention

Bicycle theft prevention strategies tend to take one of four forms: (1) interventions designed to detect bicycle thieves in the act; (2) interventions which seek to deter bicycle thieves by focusing on the registration and recovery of bicycles, thereby making stolen bicycles more risky to dispose of; (3) schemes to improve the security of bicycle parking facilities (both bicycle parking fixtures and parking facilities as a whole); and (4) programs to increase the security of locks and the manner in which they are used.

Reliable evaluations of prevention initiatives are limited. However, situational crime prevention measures aimed at altering cyclists' behavior in ways that increase the effort and risk associated with removing bikes appear most promising. In this vein, two design-based interventions have shown advantages in reducing opportunities for bicycle theft. The first is a targeted publicity campaign in which stickers—designed to improve cyclists' locking practice by depicting how to lock a bicycle securely—are attached to a series of bicycle parking stands on public street cycle parks. The second involves the use of on-street parking furniture designed to encourage locking practices known to be more effective, such as locking both the wheels and frame. Both initiatives have been shown to significantly improve locking practices, and thereby deter theft.

Outstanding Questions

Little is known about the market for stolen bicycles. The proof-of-ownership problem implies that few bicycles can easily be identified as stolen, which aids the sale of stolen bikes and reduces the risk of apprehension. Research concerned with disrupting the market for stolen bicycles holds much potential for making significant inroads into the problem. Rental bike and free bike programs are growing exponentially in various cities. As these become increasingly common, research should explore the impact, positive or negative, of such programs on the levels and patterns of cycle theft.

Aiden Sidebottom
University College London

See Also: Black Market; Crime Prevention, Environmental Design and; Crime Prevention, Situational; Pickpocketing; Policing, Problem-Oriented; Shoplifting; Theft and Larceny; Urban Planning.

Further Readings

Armendariz, Agustin and Mihir Zaveri. "Bike Theft on the Rise at BART Stations." California Watch. February 8, 2012. http://californiawatch.org/dailyreport/bike-theft-rise-bart-stations-14522 (Accessed May 2012).

Dragon. "Bicycle Theft vs. Reported Bicycle Thefts in Oregon." May 5, 2012. http://journalism.uoregon.edu/journalist_in_residence/?p=17 (Accessed May 2012).

Green, Stuart P. *Thirteen Ways to Steal a Bicycle: Theft Law in the Information Age.* Cambridge, MA: Harvard University Press, 2012.

Johnson, Shane D., Aiden Sidebottom, and Adam Thorpe. "Bicycle Theft: Problem-Specific Guides Series, No. 52." U.S. Department of Justice, Office of

Community Oriented Policing Services, 2008. http://www.popcenter.org/problems/pdfs/bicycle_theft.pdf (Accessed May 2012).

Sidebottom, Aiden, Shane D. Johnson, and Adam Thorpe. "Using Targeted Publicity to Reduce Opportunities for Bicycle Theft: A Demonstration and Replication." *European Journal of Criminology*, v.6/3 (2009).

Transportation Alternatives. "Bicycle Theft." 2009. http://www.transalt.org/files/resources/blueprint/chapter11 (Accessed May 2012).

Black Market

The underground economy, the "black market," or the shadow economy, consists of economic exchanges that exist outside the state-taxable market. This illicit marketplace consists of both illegal goods and services as well as legal goods, and is occupied by a number of players who also operate in both economies. Goods exchanged in the underground economy include illegal immigrant workers, humans sold for sexual slavery, prostitution (where it is illegal), guns and weapons, and illegal sales of alcohol and drugs, drug manufacturing, smuggling, and fraud. Many street crimes, from robbery to homicide, are generated in the course of black market dealings—either in individual cases, in gang-related crimes, or through the activities of organized crime syndicates. The three most profitable items trafficked by organized crime groups across the United States are guns, drugs, and people.

A Persistent Plague

Historians have presented evidence that the underground economy has existed across time and place. For example, in the south during times of slavery, many slaves bought and sold goods in exchange with poor whites in order to survive under the conditions of debt bondage and slavery that constrained decent living conditions. These exchanges included food, alcohol, clothing, and other perishable goods, as well as a range of mechanical and craft services. Congruent with this historical evidence, other scholars argue that a legitimate and illegitimate economy normatively coexist and have a reciprocal relationship with another that sustains both.

This complementary relationship acts to reduce the disparities produced by the formal economy. In 2002–03 the shadow economy's share of the U.S. gross domestic product (GDP) was 8.5 percent; by 2010 this figure was at 9 percent.

Recent ethnographic research reveals that poor inner-city American communities, with few available legitimate job opportunities, are characterized by a large underground economy that intersects with and interacts with legitimate economic activities and individuals on a daily basis. Researcher S. A. Venkatesh's observation of the inner-city gang networks involved in drug sales reveals that some gang members also act as community leaders giving money to charity, acting as local policing agents, as well as receiving counsel from local religious leaders. The unavailability of public services and jobs creates dynamics that force local gang

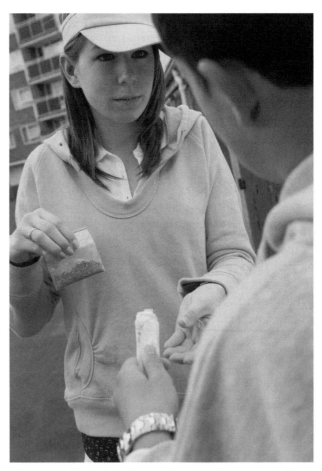

Teenagers buying and selling marijuana. Marijuana or cannabis is the largest black market cash crop in the United States, valued at $35.8 billion, exceeding the value of corn and wheat combined.

members and non-gang members to interact with one another to survive.

Drug sales in urban areas are mirrored to some degree by drug sales in rural areas. Specifically, in rural Kentucky evidence is growing that not only the illicit market for marijuana but also the market for the analgesic oxycodone, other pain killers, and methamphetamine are expanding across rural communities where joblessness and a sense of powerlessness continue to grow. Areas like Appalachia, where a long history of exploitation of the environment and local workers exists, is a prime breeding ground for such activities.

Research illustrates that the underground economy across poor urban landscapes is growing across the United States, even including tent cities characterized by the increasingly growing number of homeless. Many such individuals are not simply homeless as the result of drug addictions, but rather as the result of joblessness, home foreclosures, the absence of shelters, and newly implemented policing strategies referred to as trespass admonishments, parks exclusion orders, and stay-out-of-drug-use-area (SODA) orders or stay-out-of-areas-of-prostitution (SOAP) orders that have forced them from their homes. K. Beckett and S. Herbert refer to these policing strategies as a form of banishment orchestrated by middle-class business motives to rid the urban landscape of the unsightly poor and thereby increase trade and profits.

Calculating Causes and Costs

Some observers argue that the accumulation of private wealth creates conditions under which many people become excluded from the legitimate economy and thus have no other recourse than to become involved in the informal economy. This line of thought holds that some of these activities are criminal and thus harm both the person involved and the sometime unsuspecting others who purchase the goods or services.

Conversely, some economists argue that an underground economy only exists in countries in which excessive regulation and heavy tax burdens drive businesses out of bounds of legitimate trade. However, other scholars insist that there are multiple causal factors that lead to the development of the shadow or illicit economy. Empirical work by sociologist R. Debula has demonstrated minimal support for the tenet that high corporate taxes

increase the size of the shadow economy, but rather that higher personal income tax rates increase the size of the underground economy. Some studies reveal that economic difficulties and feelings of powerlessness can lead to the collective need to mask or suppress feelings through drug demand, drug use, and the need for economic resources. Research perspectives that provide multiple causal explanations seem to have more support than simplistic models, particularly when historiographies are used to examine underground economies.

There seem to be positive elements mixed in with the negative ones. Illegal immigration from Mexico into the United States, for example, provides illegal and sometimes legal work that in the end appears to benefit the legitimate economy. However, this economic boon primarily comes from taxes which are paid by illegal immigrants when they buy legitimate goods through legitimate markets. Some legitimate employers benefit by taking the opportunity to pay illegals under the table without paying employment taxes. However, some illegal immigrants are involved in the drug trade across urban and rural landscapes and bring with them violence and organized criminal networks to compete with homegrown gangs who also sell drugs. Thus the illegal immigration business infiltrates both the legitimate and the illegitimate economies.

Illegal goods are often purchased in poor neighborhoods, characterized by few legitimate job opportunities, smaller grocery stores with higher prices, less banks, and fewer general merchandise stores—in general, fewer legitimate businesses of any kind with the exception of liquor stores. Within these concentrated centers of poverty, the workplaces that do exist pay wages considerably lower than those available in wealthier parts of urban areas. Scholars argue that these are among the factors that push young males into drug sales while similarly often pushing females into prostitution. By extension, an economy that both devalues the work of women while simultaneously sexually objectifying women's bodies provides a mechanism to exploit women's domestic as well as women's sexual services.

Prostitution and Sex Trafficking

Government agencies spend as much as $16 million annually to enforce antiprostitution laws while some of the root causes of individual involvement in prostitution remain very tough to root out: early histories of child abuse, current intimate partner violence, economic exclusion, few job opportunities, and drug abuse.

National estimates suggest that as many as 1 million women are now or have worked as prostitutes, and that 50 to 80 percent of women in this illicit business have never been arrested. The annual arrest rate is about 80,000 sex workers. Similarly, trafficking women and children into the United States from abroad for the purposes of sexual exploitation remains a salient problem. Internationally, the United States remains one of the highest receiving nations; between 14,000 and 17,000 people are trafficked to the country annually, often through organized crime groups.

Criminologist D. Hodge, surveying the two dozen nations where prostitution is legal, as well as those where it is not (such as the United States), argues that legalizing prostitution does not seem to alter illegal levels of prostitution or trafficking. Perhaps the most harmful aspect of the black market is the multibillion-dollar sexual exploitation and forced prostitution of children and adolescents. Estimates are that almost 300,000 children and adolescents are at risk of being sexually exploited in the United States. Earlier familial abuse and neglect are risk factors for youth, while the pornographic industry and the Internet are risk factors for perpetrators and pimps who target disaffected middle-class suburban white girls with the promise of wealth and companionship. Unfortunately, it is the girls of color who are more likely to be arrested while white girls are more likely to get referrals to social service agencies for help.

Conclusion

Clearly, the exclusion of viable legitimate work opportunities resulting from increasing levels of economic inequality may be facilitating the growth in demand for prostitution and drugs across the United States in both urban and rural areas. These economic dynamics in conjunction with the devaluation of women's bodies and the devaluation of legitimate wages may continue to lead toward expanding growth of underground markets in drug sales and prostitution, as well as gun sales to support the previous two markets.

Rebecca S. Katz
Morehead State University

See Also: Children, Commercial Sexual Exploitation of; Drinking Establishments, Unlicensed; Drug Dealing; Gangs (Street); Guns and Weapons; Homelessness; Organized Crime and Violence; Prostitute/Streetwalker; Sex Crimes; Skid Row.

Further Readings
Beckett, Katherine and Steve Herbert. *Banished: The New Social Control in Urban America.* New York: Oxford University Press, 2010.
Dabla-Norris, Era and Andrew Feltenstein. "The Underground Economy and its Macroeconomic Consequences." *Journal of Policy Reform,* v.8/2 (2005).
Debula, Richard J. "An Empirical Analysis of the Impact of Government Tax and Auditing Policies on the Size of the Underground Economy: The Case of the United States, 1973–1994." *American Journal of Economics and Sociology,* v.56/2 (1997).
Ford, M. Julie and Andrew Beveridge. "Bad Neighborhoods, Fast Food, Sleazy Businesses, and Drug Dealers: Relations Between the Location of Licit and Illicit Businesses in the Urban Environment." *Journal of Drug Issues,* v.4/1 (2004).
Forret, Jeff. "Slaves, Poor Whites, and the Underground Economy of the Rural Carolinas." *Journal of Southern History,* v.70/4 (2004).
Goodwin, Michele. *Black Markets: The Supply and Demand of Body Parts.* Cambridge: Cambridge University Press, 2006.
Hodge, David R. "Sexual Trafficking in the United States: A Domestic Problem With Transnational Dimensions." *Social Work,* v.53/2, 2008.
Nadadur, Ramanujan. "Illegal Immigration: A Positive Economic Contribution to the United States." *Journal of Ethnic and Migration Studies,* v.35/6 (2009).
Venkatesh, Sudhir Alladi. *Off the Books: The Underground Economy of the Urban Poor.* Cambridge, MA: Harvard University Press, 2009.
Williams, C. Collin. *The Hidden Enterprise Culture: Entrepreneurship in the Underground Economy.* Northampton, MA: Edward Elgar, 2008.

Blackmail

Blackmail is a criminal offense whereby a person tells another that he or she will disclose specific information not intended for disclosure, or engage in some act or omission that is undesired by the other—unless the other party renders something of value. The item of value, though commonly money, could be anything.

Its Difference From Extortion, Bribery

While blackmail is an uninvited solicitation, if a person initiates the offering of something of value to another to avoid the disclosure of information, then there is no blackmail. If an authority figure is being solicited to alter the proper performance of his or her duty, the offense would be bribery. The key element of the crime of blackmail is the demand for something of value; otherwise the undesired action or disclosure is such that it would not be illegal. This element is what separates blackmail from extortion. During extortion, the person soliciting an item of value threatens to do something illegal if the item is not received, for example, breaking the victim's limbs or assaulting a family member.

The nature of blackmail makes it a frequent addon to personal property crimes and violent street crimes—as well as an element in the functioning of street crime gangs.

Prevalence and History

Statistics on blackmail are difficult to find. In part, this is because most of the victims are so intent on secrecy that the offense goes unreported. It is also less likely than many other crimes to be cited in victimization surveys. In some cases, blackmail victims, instead of turning to law enforcement, will hire a private investigator to assist them. Another reason for sparse research data is that the offense in question might frequently be charged as a different crime, such as mail fraud or wire fraud.

Blackmail is sometimes characterized as a victimless crime. Indeed, many legal scholars and criminologists query whether it should be a crime at all, because blackmail is so close to legal conduct. This refers to the fact that, if the undesired threatened action occurs—such as revealing a secret—without a demand for something of value, there would be no crime. How is blackmail a street crime? The term *blackmail* originated in Scotland in the 16th century; it referred then to an illicit extraction of payment from persons who worked the land in exchange for protection, hence its similarity to extortion. Later, with English urbanization,

the term became associated with the victimization of prostitutes, in that a revelation of the prostitute's activity would be a threat to any level of respectability that she held.

Nowadays, it is the prostitute's customer or "john" who is more likely to be subject to blackmail. Researcher Helen Rappaport notes that in Victorian times, blackmail was associated with women who used their husband's funds secretly for activities such as paying for questionable beauty products. If the respectable woman wanted the relationship with a merchant or other individual to remain discrete, she might be blackmailed to hand over her jewels or other valuables.

Attack on Respectability

Blackmail remains an offense about threatened respectability. One example reported widely in the news media in 2012 was the case of Louise Neathway, who was charged with stalking and attempting to extort $6,000 from the New York Yankees baseball team's general manager, Brian Cashman, a married man. Neathway threatened to reveal their alleged secret love affair. Cashman, as the victim, was said in court documents to have paid the $6,000—but his reputation seemed more damaged by the subsequent action of his wife, who filed for divorce when the situation became public.

Another recent high-profile example was that of talk show host David Letterman. He was blackmailed in 2009 by a television producer, Robert Halderman, who threatened to reveal that Letterman, a married man, had affairs with female staff members unless Letterman gave him $2 million. The outcome: Halderman pleaded guilty to attempted second-degree grand larceny; he served four months in jail.

Gang Fealty

The application of contemporary blackmail, however, is not limited to persons of means. For example, the potential for blackmail is also utilized by street gangs to maintain the loyalty of members. This tends to involve requiring the commission of a serious offense, even murder, as part of a gang initiation. Thereafter, loyalty is expected given the threat that anything less could result in a revelation of the initiation offense to the authorities.

Other cases of street blackmail include cases where young females are enticed by an attractive male to accompany him to a location where, unbeknownst to her, a group of boys or men are waiting to coerce her into sex with them. The incident is photographed or videotaped. The girl is then threatened with revelation of the incident, which would be to her embarrassment, unless she cooperates with them in future sex escapades or in commercial sex trafficking which may include the creation of pornography.

Organized crime syndicates have also been involved in blackmail. The syndicate may threaten some undesirable action (for example, a work slowdown or strike, if it controls a labor union) unless private businesses render to the syndicate something of value, often funds. Unlike many other cities, New York City's trash collection policies in the 1950s rendered businesses vulnerable to such blackmail, in that the city made businesses responsible for disposing of their own garbage. The local government set maximum collection rates—yet crime syndicates, such as the Gambino organization, would blackmail business owners to pay more or suffer city fines when their garbage collection service fell below standards (a legal, but undesired and painful action).

Victimizing Dependency

The proliferation of visual recording devices has made just about any potentially embarrassing conduct on the street potential fodder for electronic capture and blackmail. Thus, persons have been threatened with the release of sex tapes, information about an affair, about the existence of unacknowledged offspring, homosexual encounters, work as a stripper, and illicit drug use. Persons have also been blackmailed regarding the privacy of their children; this includes a large number of celebrities.

Dependent persons are also quite vulnerable to blackmail. Some single mothers have been threatened by new husbands or boyfriends with abandonment and loss of economic support, unless they permit their child to be sexually exploited by these men in their lives—although that would result in a crime, turning the blackmail into extortion and likely bringing up more serious sexual assault charges. Elderly male widowers often with some means, who have come to depend on someone for daily support, are also vulnerable to blackmail lest he loses that support and companionship. The blackmailer in these cases is often a much younger woman. Some

adults with a substantial disability have had similar experiences; they might be threatened to turn over most or all of their disability benefits or lose that human support on which they depend.

Camille Gibson
Prairie View A&M University

See Also: Domestic Violence; Gangs (Street); Pimp; Prostitute/Street Walker; Risky Lifestyles; Sex Crimes; Suite Crimes Versus Street Crimes.

Further Readings
Block, Walter. "The Crime of Backmail: A Libertarian Critique." *Criminal Justice Ethics*, v.18/2 (1999).
Block, Walter, Stephan Kinsella, and Hans Hermann Hoppe. "The Second Paradox of Blackmail." *Business Ethics Quarterly*, v.10/3 (2000).
Katz, Leo. *Ill-Gotten Gains: Evasion, Blackmail, Fraud, and Kindred Puzzles of the Law*. Chicago: University of Chicago Press, 1996.
McLaren, Angus. *Sexual Blackmail—A Modern History*. Cambridge, MA: Harvard University Press, 2002.
Rappaport, Helen. "Beauty and the Whiter-Than-White Blackmail." *Mail on Sunday* (March 6, 2010). http://www.dailymail.co.uk/home/you/article-1255741/Beauty-whiter-white-blackmail.html (Accessed June 2012).

Bloods

The Bloods are a street gang established in south Los Angeles, California, during the early 1970s and engaged in violent, varied street crime including drug trafficking, homicide, robbery, extortion, and prostitution. Their early membership can be traced to the criminal organization that later became their hated rivals, the Crips. In honor of their name and in contrast with the Crips, the color red has long been associated with the Bloods and is worn in many forms—bandanas, T-shirts, even shoelaces.

Similar to the Crips and other African American gangs originating in Los Angeles, the Bloods do not form one uniform, cohesive street organization. Instead they are broken down into constantly shifting subgroups or cliques commonly

A man, who is not a member of the Bloods gang, "flashes" the Bloods sign. Gang signs and other hand signs are a silent method of relaying information or showing allegiance to a gang.

known as *sets*. Each set will adopt unique hand signs, criminal practices, and even strategic morality to distinguish them from other Bloods sets. Just like their Crips rivals, the Bloods have migrated beyond southern California, developing a national and international profile, including a presence in the U.S. military. However, unlike the Crips, the Bloods remain an almost exclusively African American gang, although they too now include women in their membership.

Origin in Strife

The Bloods represented the first serious break in the street monopoly of the Crips in south Los Angeles. In 1972, the Pirus, a Crips set that took its name from Piru Street in the Compton neighborhood, severed all ties with their parent organization amid an internal gang war. Together with other loose, unaffiliated smaller gangs, they bonded to create the gang that would ultimately become the Bloods.

Originally the Bloods focused on petty crime: running numbers and selling marijuana while engaging in fist fights and knife duels. However, with the adoption of firearms, there was an increase in the lethality of gang activity that grew to include homicide, physical assault, and other violent crimes. With the introduction of crack cocaine in the 1980s, the Bloods' business grew to include large-scale drug production and distribution.

In gang culture, legends and acronyms abound. Bloods is often claimed to be an acronym for

Brotherly Love Overcoming Our Depression. Other accounts maintain that the Pirus derived their name from the Swahili word for blood. However, the name is more generally attributed to the traditional, southern African American term used to connote family members—a cousin was considered a blood brother or blood. This term had the added attraction of avoiding the Crips-associated nickname *cuzz*.

Whatever their unique parts of their history, consistent with other street gangs, Bloods gang membership is signified through various behaviors and rituals that constantly change. Although the gang has traditionally identified with the color red, this practice has dwindled. Instead, one of the most commonly recognized Bloods symbols is the number 5, to match the five letters in the word Blood. While tagging is also used to indicate streets that fall into Bloods territory, graffiti frequently includes references to the Crips as well as the word Piru.

A great deal of Bloods graffiti is dedicated to discrediting the Crips: C's are crossed out, the word *cripple* is never spoken, and words beginning with the letter C are avoided unless it is absolutely necessary to use them. This is because any reference to Crips, however oblique, must be undone as part of the Bloods' practice of "affirmation by negation." Bloods members also scrupulously avoid certain words—they will not say "cuzz," or "cousin" because of its association with Crips traditions. Instead, cousins are referred to as "relatives." Additionally, Calvin Klein jeans have long been popular attire for Bloods members who co-opt the CK trademark and use it to symbolize their status as "Crip Killers."

Structure and Crime Impact

The Bloods have always operated as a very loose network of independent groupings referred to as "hoods," never gangs. The hood controls a discrete geographic area, with sets within them claiming even more specific streets and city blocks. These streets or projects give each set its unique name. However, despite the differing Bloods sets, there appears to be less in-fighting between sets when compared with the Crips. This is attributed to their smaller overall membership relative to the Crips, with the Crips outnumbering the Bloods by as much as three to one.

Leadership within each Bloods set is determined by age, criminal history, and the ability of an individual to manage the hood's local criminal endeavors and street crimes: any successful Bloods leader exhibits both lethality and command. In turn, general members are referred to as soldiers; they are compelled to exhibit high levels of violence and lethality, particularly toward individuals who show disrespect toward them personally or toward their Bloods set. Female involvement is extremely limited; they are employed as prostitutes or are called upon to hold drugs or firearms.

It is important to note that while the Bloods remain the smaller of these two major African American gangs in operation, their violence level and criminal activity continue more or less unabated, now into a fifth decade.

According to the *Los Angeles Times*, as of mid-2005, the California Department of Justice, in its CAL/GANG database of known gang members, identified 4,209 Bloods gang members in the city of Los Angeles. This was out of a total of 39,000 gang members citywide in the database. Out of some 463 gangs or gang sets in Los Angeles, the database attributed Bloods identification to 45 of them. In a crude approximation, the database suggests that Bloods members committed 766 of the 7,155 gang-related crimes in 2004. These crimes run the gamut from robbery and shots into a residence, to carjacking, witness intimidation, attacks on police officers, and homicide.

The *Los Angeles Times* reported that the city was spending on the order of $80 million annually on anti-gang programs, which are not limited to law enforcement, but also include organized childhood activities, early intervention, and job support initiatives. Police measures feature federally supported investigative and intelligence-gathering methods. Los Angeles has also used the concept of *gang injunctions,* a means to declare a specified neighborhood as subject to special regulations and enforcement; these include a ban on cellphone use and congregating of named gang members, with any violators likely to spend up to six months in jail. Gang injunctions in practice seem to have some moderating effects on neighborhood safety and crime deterrence.

Jorja M. Leap
University of California, Los Angeles

See Also: Asian Gangs; Community Policing; Crips; Gangs (Street); Graffiti; Latino Gangs; Los Angeles, California.

Further Readings

Hayden, Tom. *Street Wars: Gangs and the Future of Violence.* New York: The New Press, 2004.

Leap, Jorja. *Jumped In: What Gangs Taught Me About Violence, Drugs, Love, and Redemption.* Boston: Beacon Press, 2012.

Maxson, Cheryl. "Gang Members on the Move." In *The Modern Gang Reader,* Arlen Egley, Cheryl Maxson, Jody Miller, and Malcolm Klein, eds. Los Angeles: Roxbury Publishing, 2006.

Morris, DaShaun Jiwe. *War of the Bloods in My Veins: A Street Soldier's March Towards Redemption.* New York: Scribner, 2008.

Shelden, Randall G., Sharon K. Tracy, and William R. Brown. *Youth Gangs in American Society.* Belmont, CA: Wadsworth, 2004.

Winton, Richard. "L.A. Home Turf for Hundreds of Neighborhood Criminal Groups." *Los Angeles Times* (May 13, 2005). http://www.lacp.org/2005-Articles -Main/LAGangsInNeighborhoods.html (Accessed May 2012).

Blue Laws

Blue laws restrict commercial activity from taking place on Sundays. They historically regulated a broad range of behaviors, but currently most only limit Sunday liquor sales. Although they were originally designed to promote religious practices, the Supreme Court has held that they do not violate the Free Establishment Clause of the First Amendment.

Origin and Resistance

Blue laws originated when colonists in 1620s Virginia passed edicts regulating moral conduct, including keeping the Sabbath holy by prohibiting trade, travel, and gambling on Sunday. One historian claims that these prohibitions were printed on blue paper, which is why they became known as blue laws. Other historians claim that the name came about because blue traditionally symbolized fidelity, while still others claim that it was derived from *bluenose,* a derisive term used to ridicule prudish persons, or from the term *blue stocking* used to describe Oliver Cromwell's morally righteous supporters in England's Parliament.

Regardless of the name's origin, blue laws were commonly passed during the colonial period. But by the time of the American Revolution, their enforcement was already controversial. Indeed, President George Washington was stopped in 1793 for violating a Connecticut ban on Sunday travel. Blue laws enacted after the American Revolution typically regulated trade and commerce, such as prohibiting merchants from selling goods and people from working on Sunday

A century later, the temperance movement attempted to curb or to prohibit alcohol consumption. It gained ground in the United States after the end of the Civil War and reached its zenith in 1919 when the Eighteenth Amendment to the U.S. Constitution prohibited the manufacture, sale, or transport of liquor. This sanction was unsuccessful— the Eighteenth Amendment was repealed in 1933. But a number of state and local governments passed blue laws restricting the sale of alcohol on Sundays; these statutes were designed to locally further the goals that the temperance movement and Prohibition failed to achieve nationally.

Yet even as blue laws prohibiting liquor sales on Sundays were passed, exemptions to other types of blue laws were simultaneously enacted. These exemptions created a seemingly arbitrary set of restrictions. For example, under Texas blue laws, a hardware store could be open for business and sell nails on Sundays, but it could not sell hammers. These illogical restrictions and the rapid growth of consumerism in the United States caused state and local governments to begin to repeal or refuse to enforce many blue laws that were not related to the sale of alcohol on Sundays. These repeals gathered force beginning in the 1950s; by the 1990s most remaining and enforced blue laws did pertain only to the sale of alcohol on Sundays.

Supreme Court Findings

In 1961, the U.S. Supreme Court decided several cases challenging the constitutionality of blue laws. The most important of these was *McGowan v. Maryland.* In that case, employees of a Maryland department store sold a binder, a can of floor wax, a stapler and staples, and a toy submarine on a Sunday. They were consequently charged with violating one of the state's blue laws which prohibited the sale of all merchandise on Sunday except tobacco, confectionaries, milk, breads, fruits, gasoline, oils, and greases.

The court found that the Maryland blue law did not violate the Equal Protection clause of the Fourteenth Amendment because the state could justify the list of excepted items— the state may have been promoting recreation or health and believed that these items needed to be available to the public on a rest day. The court also held that because the employees did not offer evidence that the laws inhibited the practice of their own religions, they could not claim that the laws violated the Free Exercise clause of the First Amendment. Most importantly, the court found that the law did not violate the Establishment Clause of the First Amendment, which prohibits the government from passing laws creating a state religion.

The court acknowledged that the blue laws at issue were originally motivated by religious forces. Nonetheless, the court found that they were currently designed to promote a legitimate secular goal—establishing a uniform day of rest for all Maryland citizens. That the rest day took place on Sunday, a day of import to Christian-based faiths, did not mean that the law's current purpose was religious, or that the state was promoting Christianity.

Current Thinking

The Supreme Court has yet to hear a challenge to alcohol-related blue laws. Today, 14 states and the District of Columbia have blue laws related to Sunday alcohol sales, although more blue laws may exist at the local level. Proponents of these laws contend that they provide public health benefits by reducing drunk driving and violent crime. Critics contend that any such benefits are marginal because the restrictions are limited to a single day.

Further, they assert that the alcohol-related blue laws are not truly secular and thus they violate the Establishment Clause by compelling citizens to observe the Christian Sabbath. They also argue that blue laws, especially bans on alcohol sales, represent an attempt by the middle class to use the criminal law to control the behavior of the poor. Given the court's ruling in *McGowan,* where the court found other types of blue laws served secular purposes, it is unclear whether these arguments would be successful. Proponents argue that these laws prevent drunkenness and thereby limit public intoxication, drunk driving, and violence. If they actually prevent consumption of alcohol, blue laws may prevent some street crimes. It is also possible, on the contrary, that these laws contribute to a general disrespect for the law as they are often not enforced or supported by the public. Blue laws may likewise provide incentives or opportunities for corruption of criminal justice personnel. We are unaware of research published to date assessing the impact of blue laws on street crime; for now, any such causal link between blue laws and street crime is theoretical at best.

Jennifer M. Burke
Lawrence F. Travis III
University of Cincinnati

See Also: Alcohol and Drug Use; Bars and Pubs; Bootleggers; Crime–Consumerism Nexus; Speakeasies, (1920s).

Further Readings

Bondonno, Franklin E. "First Amendment Rights and Sunday Closing Laws." *Lincoln Law Review,* v.31/51 (2003).

King, Andrew, J. "Sunday Closing Law In the Nineteenth Century." *Albany Law Review,* v.64/2 (2001).

Lawrence-Hammer, Lesley. "Red, White, But Mostly Blue: The Validity of Modern Sunday Closing Laws Under the Establishment Clause." *Vanderbilt Law Review,* v.60/4 (2007).

McGowan v. Maryland, 366 U.S. 420 (1961).

Raucher, Alan. "Sunday Business and the Decline of Sunday Closing Laws: A Historical Overview." *Journal of Church and State,* v.36/1 (1994).

Bootleggers

The crime of bootlegging, or the manufacture, distribution, or sale of contraband items, has significantly broadened in meaning throughout the last century-and-a-half. Though originally referring exclusively to illicit liquor smuggling, the illegal sale of numerous other materials, cigarettes among these, has also fallen under this umbrella term.

History of Alcohol Bootlegging

The term *bootlegging* originally arose in the midwest in the 1880s when individuals would sell illicit flasks of liquor to Native Americans. Unable to openly carry such items, smugglers would hide them from authorities in their boot tops. The phrase took on general usage in 1920 with the passage of Prohibition. During the Prohibition years, from 1920 through 1933, the legitimate commercial trade in alcoholic beverages was in large part banned within the United States. While the Eighteenth Amendment, along with the Volstead Act, did not explicitly ban the consumption of alcohol, they made its sale, manufacture, or transport illegal throughout the country. Consequently, criminal syndicates were able to reap enormous profits from bootlegging contraband alcohol.

The initial bootleggers mainly used the Canadian and Mexican borders to illegally ship liquor into the United States. These shipments were then distributed to representatives throughout the country, who often delivered or sold them to "speakeasies" (i.e., bars whose profit derived from illicit alcohol sales). Since speakeasies were places where alcohol was illegally sold, customers often needed a codeword to enter them, and were encouraged to "speak easy" or not create noise or fights. Over time, the Bahamas, Cuba, and the French islands of St. Pierre and Miquelon became other popular transshipment centers for illegal imports.

The sale of so-called medicinal and denatured alcohol was also common. Regarding the former, bootleggers would label plain alcohol "medicinal" and then sell it across pharmacy counters using fake prescriptions. Denatured alcohol refers to alcohol intentionally mixed with noxious and poisonous chemicals, in the aim of keeping it from being diverted from its intended applications for industrial use, maintenance, or cleaning. Bootleggers would nevertheless divert shipments of this alcohol, "wash" its dangerous chemicals away, mix it with tap water, add additional liquor for taste, and then resell it to speakeasies or individual customers. Other bootleggers, known as moonshiners, even made their own liquor (generally from corn), a sometimes dangerous operation that could potentially result in contaminated liquor largely known as "rotgut."

It is important to note that not all bootleggers were part of larger criminal syndicates. Makeshift bootleggers, both in the nations' cities and countryside, made and sold their own alcohol on a more local scale. Establishing a foothold in the larger market was difficult and potentially dangerous, however, as larger syndicates sought to monopolize this black market. Gang wars were also common, as different organizations sought to enlarge their business by encroaching on one another's territory.

Famous Bootleggers

Two of the more famous alcohol bootleggers, each of whom reflects differently on this illicit activity, were William S. McCoy and Al Capone. McCoy was a sea captain who pioneered rum smuggling from the Bahamas to Long Island. Over time McCoy's operation expanded to an almost industrial scale, recognized nationally. His frequent and reliably good alcohol shipments engendered the excited phrase "It's the Real McCoy!" Al Capone, perhaps the most famous bootlegger of all, used the profits from this illicit business to take over Chicago's underworld. Capone's infamous "rum-runners" then branched throughout the entire country, distributing alcohol to representatives from Detroit to New Jersey, and corrupting many law enforcement and political officials along the way.

Although Capone's was indicted and imprisonmed in 1931 for tax evasion and not bootlegging, the Eighteenth Amendment was repealed shortly thereafter, and Prohibition was formally ended with the ratification of the Twenty-First Amendment in late 1933. Though numerous counties and municipalities continued to ban alcohol, criminal organizations in most areas began to shift to more profitable venues.

Bootlegging Today

Today, alcohol smuggling is fairly rare compared to that bygone era. That being said, it still occurs in "dry" counties, which still ban the sale of alcoholic beverages. Here bootleggers often sell liquor from neighboring "wet" counties (where such commerce is permitted). The United States has hundreds of dry counties, mostly located in a swath extending from southwest Virginia through Kentucky, Tennessee, and Arkansas to Kansas, Arkansas, and Texas.

Selling various other illicit items is also considered bootlegging. Bootlegged cigarettes, though produced and distributed for decades, have become more prevalent and more of a challenge to law enforcement with increased state sales taxes—often at greatly divergent levels—on cigarettes. Cigarette cartons are often snuck across the Canadian border and then sold under-the-counter in legitimate retail stores. Bootlegging also occurs in the entertainment industry. While it is illegal to record and sell movies or music without copyright permission, doing so via the Internet is relatively easy, and is therefore a fairly common practice. Such items are then distributed and sold on the streets.

The current penalties for bootlegging vary considerably. U.S. copyright law makes illegally distributing and selling certain products punishable by up to five years in prison. State laws can significantly stiffen these statutes. For its part, the entertainment industry has mounted high-profile crackdowns and expensive antipiracy public relations campaigns. The availability of illicit items on the Internet, from cigarettes to live concert recordings, has complicated things even further, as such Web sites can be both difficult to track down and are often operated by offshore businesses.

Zachary Shemtob
Central Connecticut State University

See Also: Alcohol and Drug Use; Black Market; Blue Laws; Drinking, Underage; Drinking Establishments, Unlicensed; Gangs (Street); Organized Crime and Violence; Speakeasies (1920s).

Further Readings
Bartlett, Bruce. "Cigarette Smuggling." National Center for Policy Analysis." October 30, 2002. http://www.ncpa.org/pub/ba423 (Accessed September 2011).

Heylin, Clinton. *Bootleg! The Rise & Fall of the Secret Recording Industry*. New York: Omnibus Press, 2004.

McGrew, Jane Lang. "History of Alcohol Prohibition." 1972. National Commission on Marihuana and Drug Abuse. http://www.druglibrary.org/Schaffer/library/studies/nc/nc2a.htm (Accessed September 2011).

Okrent, Daniel. *Last Call: The Rise and Fall of Prohibition*. New York: Scribner, 2011.

Rap Coalition, Inc. "What Is Sound Recording Piracy?" http://www.rapcoalition.org/bootlegging.htm (Accessed September 2011).

Wheeler, Brian. "The Slow Death of Prohibition." BBC News (March 21, 2012). http://www.bbc.co.uk/news/magazine-17291978. (Accessed April 2012).

Boston, Massachusetts

The city of Boston was founded in 1630. The population of Boston grew at a fairly steady pace until the early 1800s when the pace of growth increased dramatically, primarily because of an influx of European immigrants. The population of the city peaked in 1950 with a reported 801,440 residents: The 2012 population of Boston was 625,087.

Boston is a very small city geographically, made up of only 48 square miles of land. It is the third-most densely populated large city in the United States. There are 21 distinct neighborhoods in the city, most having a long history of being populated by certain ethnic or racial groups. For example, the North End section of Boston is the oldest neighborhood in the city and has been populated primarily by Italian immigrants and Italian Americans since the early 20th century.

Boston Police Department

The Boston Police Department (BPD) was the first paid public safety department in the United States, being established by statute in 1838. The first agency had 260 employees. The initial officers were appointed by the mayor or city aldermen and this practice remained until 1878, when hiring was transferred to a three-member board. The BPD hired its first African American officer in 1878. The city adopted a civil-service model for hiring police officers in 1885. In 1919, the officers of the Boston Police Department were dissatisfied with wages and working conditions.

Police officers formed a union as a means to address these concerns, and on September 9, 1919, officers called a strike against the BPD. More than 1,100 officers, or 73 percent of the force, failed to report for work, and violence and looting broke out in certain sections of the city. The Massachusetts governor, Calvin Coolidge, called in the state's national guard to protect the city. Since it was illegal for police officers to strike, the police commissioner fired all the striking officers and eventually hired replacements for all the fired officers. This action set the American labor movement and particularly police unionization back for decades.

As of 2012, the city of Boston had slightly more than 2,100 sworn officers, and the number of patrol officers has remained somewhat stable during the beginning of the 21st century.

Operation Night Light and Operation Ceasefire

As in most major American cities, crime has risen and declined throughout the city's history. During the 1980s, however, the city experienced a dramatic increase in violence and, in particular, homicide. The levels of homicide rose to the highest levels in the city's history: in 1990, Boston experienced 152 homicides. Youth homicides were an area of particular concern, with a 230 percent increase in youth homicides (homicides involving victims under the age of 25) between 1987 and 1990. Of the 152 homicides, 73 involved victims under 25—a shocking 48 percent of all homicides in the city. In 1992, the BPD began a promising program in partnership with the Massachusetts Department of Probation called Operation Night Light. In this program, probation officers joined police officers to patrol selected neighborhoods of the city to check on high-risk individuals on probation. The program developed out of a realization by police and probation officers working in the Dorchester neighborhood of Boston that they were independently dealing with many of the same local youth. The program involved sharing intelligence and joint patrols to send a message to violent youth that future violence will result in swift enforcement actions.

Following the successful implementation of Operation Night Light, the BPD, under the leadership of Police Commissioner Paul Evans, began Operation Ceasefire. Operation Ceasefire was an innovative program developed to reduce gun violence among the most violent youth in Boston's most violent neighborhoods. The program involved two major components. First, forums were held with the most violent youth in target neighborhoods in which police and prosecutors delivered a message that if violence continues, all potential levers—including probation and the possibility of federal prosecution—would be used against them. However, at the same meetings, youths were offered services ranging from education programs to employment services. The second component of Operation Ceasefire involved youths who continued to commit violent acts: all means would be used to take them off the streets and to incarcerate them for as long as possible.

These programs and other BPD initiatives resulted in a remarkable reduction of youth violence in Boston. Youth homicides declined dramatically, the city of Boston experienced a 63 percent reduction ionF youth homicides, a 25 percent decrease in gun assaults citywide, and a 325 percent reduction in shots-fired calls.

These two programs were quickly recognized as national best practices in dealing with youth violence and were adopted by hundreds of police agencies, both nationally and internationally. In 1996, President Bill Clinton came to Boston to highlight the success of the programs, and Attorney General Janet Reno presented the BPD with an award for its innovative programming. These efforts eventually served as a basis for a series of national violence presentation efforts, including the Strategic Approaches to Community Safety Initiative (SACSI) and Project Safe Neighborhoods (PSN).

Current Crime Problems

In December 2006, Edward F. Davis became commissioner of the BPD. Commissioner Davis previously served as chief of the Lowell, Massachusetts, Police Department and had worked with Boston's Mayor Thomas Menino to expand existing programs and implement new, nationally recognized violence prevention programs. Over the past several years, Boston has implemented a wide variety of programs to combat violent crime through concerted prevention, intervention, suppression, and re-entry efforts. As a result, from 2006 to 2011, the city saw a 30 percent reduction in violent Part I crimes, which are aggravated assault, forcible rape, murder, and robbery.

Boston's success in combating violent crime began in the mid-1990s, when Boston's proactive community policing philosophy began. Community policing was supported and reinforced by a number of innovative approaches; from community prosecution partnerships to improved monitoring and suppression and enforcement of impact players (the highest-risk crime-involved youth), in partnership with probation and a wide range of other programs. Boston, like most major cities, generates a disproportionate share of the state's reported crime. According to the 2010 Federal Bureau of Investigation's Uniform Crime Reports, Boston generates 29 percent of the state's murder and nonnegligent manslaughter, 17 percent of the aggravated assaults, and 21 percent of the state's overall violent crime. The majority of violence in Boston is caused by a small number of players who operate out of key "hot-spot" neighborhoods where

Boston's gun violence tends to be concentrated. In 2011, 74 percent of all firearm-related homicides and 71 percent of nonfatal shootings took place in the neighborhoods of Mattapan, Dorchester, and Roxbury. The BPD's Boston Regional Intelligence Center (BRIC) reports that impact players from area gangs are involved in a disproportionate amount of firearm violence in Boston.

As of June 2012, approximately 121 different gangs of varying size and coherence have been identified and considered active in Boston by police gang officers and the BRIC, and 3,206 individuals have been identified and classified as actively gang-involved. Most Boston gangs are loosely organized and neighborhood or street-based, as opposed to being nationally affiliated. They have access to firearms and routinely participate in violence against one another. Historically, most Boston gangs lived within or congregated around housing developments and neighborhoods, with many feuds extending back over several generations. Today, however, gangs have become more fluid. Traditional gang territories have become blurred and, in some cases, nonexistent.

BPD Current Crime Control Efforts

The BPD's Safe Street Team (SST) initiative began in 2006 and stemmed from the recognition that most of the city's violent crime is concentrated in a few, small, geographic hot spots. Each SST consists of six officers and one sergeant who patrol hot-spot areas, for a total of 13 SSTs throughout the neighborhoods of Boston. On foot or riding a bike, these highly visible officers interact with community members, respond to community concerns, develop partnerships with local business organizations, and conduct outreach with high-risk youth, all while maintaining the safety of the neighborhood. SST officers develop a sense of community ownership, engage in strategic problem solving, and sustain presence and guardianship. A recent impact evaluation conducted by Dr. Anthony Braga found that the SST strategy was associated with a 17.3 percent reduction in the total number of violent index crimes, a 19.2 percent reduction in the number of robberies, and a 15.4 percent reduction in the number of aggravated assault incidents, with no evidence of displacement or diffusion effects, according to A. Braga, D. Hureau, and A. Papachristos.

Under the leadership of Mayor Thomas M. Menino, the city of Boston is involved in many ongoing, multidisciplinary efforts aimed at preventing and reducing youth violence. These efforts received national recognition in the spring of 2010, when Boston was one of six cities selected by the Barack Obama administration to participate in a national forum on youth violence prevention. Agencies from across the city and their partners worked together and with the U.S. Department of Justice to assess Boston's strengths and challenges with respect to youth violence and to develop a comprehensive plan to prevent and reduce youth.

Under the broader Ceasefire 2012 umbrella is the PACT (Partnerships Advancing Communities Together) initiative, a citywide effort to increase community safety through targeted enforcement and intervention. Given that a small, concentrated number of violent, high-risk individuals tend to be responsible for a large portion of the gang and gun violence in Boston, a key component of the BPD's violence prevention efforts is to identify these individuals and implement targeted enforcement and intervention efforts. Once impact players have been identified by the BRIC through a set of criteria, they are approached by partner street workers from the Boston Center for Youth and Families (BCYF) and the Boston Foundation. The street workers inform these individuals that they are being carefully monitored by law enforcement and that if they choose to continue their criminal activity, criminal justice measures will be used to remove them from the

Boston Police Commissioner Edward F. Davis, former chief of the Lowell Massachusetts Police Department, monitors the Occupy Boston protest in October 2011.

community. Criminal justice resources are prioritized and coordinated to ensure that these individuals are held accountable to the strictest degree possible. For example, district and special unit officers focus their attention on PACT individuals, using both short-term means such as enforcing trespassing and misdemeanor infractions, and long-term levers such as ongoing drug trafficking investigations. Probation officers request additional conditions of probation, such as curfews, stay-away orders, drug testing, and global positioning system (GPS) monitoring, and they proactively enforce these terms. District attorneys advocate for no bail, prioritize prosecution, and work with U.S attorneys to target the worst firearm offenders for federal prosecution involving armed career criminal statutes.

At the same time, these individuals are offered a wide range of supports and alternatives that will enable them to steer toward a more productive lifestyle, including job readiness training and placement, educational reintegration, temporary housing, substance abuse treatment, health care services, and individual and family counseling, all through the support of a case manager assigned to the family by the referring street worker.

Often, these case managers are assigned through the YouthConnect organization. Through the city's innovative partnership with YouthConnect, licensed clinical social workers are placed in police stations with the highest rates of youth arrests. These social workers provide on-site, in-home, and community-based counseling services, diverting at-risk youth from the justice system, while working with BPD officials to focus their activities on the most crime-involved families in the neighborhood.

Boston also has a re-entry initiative. The Boston Reentry Initiative (BRI) identifies the highest-risk offenders (males, aged 17–30, with a documented history of gang and gun violence) who, after release from the Suffolk County house of corrections, return to one of Boston's hot-spot neighborhoods. Staff from the BRI offers these individuals critical support and reintegration services for 12–18 months after release, while simultaneously sending them a clear message that further violence will not be tolerated.

Finally, led by Mayor Menino, the city of Boston has a multitude of other prevention and intervention efforts in place to address violence. For instance, the Violence and Intervention Program (VIP) initiative of the Boston Public Health Commission (BPHC) provides vital violence prevention services in four key hot-spot neighborhoods throughout Boston. VIP coalitions in these neighborhoods work to improve the safety of community residents by organizing and forming active partnerships between the residents and city departments.

John (Jack) McDevitt
Northeastern University
Jenna Savage
Boston Police Department

See Also: Community Policing; Immigrant Neighborhoods; Operation Ceasefire; Police (Overview); Urbanization.

Further Readings

Braga, A. A., D. M. Hureau, and A. V. Papachristos. "An Ex Post Facto Evaluation Framework for Place-Based Police Interventions." *Evaluation Review*, v.35/6 (December 2011).

Braga, A. A., D. M. Kennedy, and E. J. Waring. "Problem-Oriented Policing, Deterrence, and Youth Violence: An Evaluation of Boston's Operation Ceasefire." *Journal of Research in Crime and Delinquency*, v.38/3 (August 2001).

City of Boston National Forum on Youth Violence Prevention. "Youth Violence Prevention and Reduction Comprehensive City Plan." April 2011. http://www.bpdnews.com/wordpress/wp-content/uploads/National-Forum-Boston-Plan_3-21-11.pdf (Accessed July 2012).

Bounty Hunters

The author Ernest Hemingway is credited with stating, "There is no hunting like the hunting of a man, and those who have hunted armed men long enough and liked it never cared for anything else." The concept of bounty hunting, or chasing and apprehending a fugitive from the law in the expectation of a reward, has a certain romantic appeal, but is part of a set of long-standing legal and court traditions.

Development of Bail and Surety

Beginning in medieval England, the idea of "bail" was designed to allow the release of individuals from jail, pending an often incredibly long wait time before trial. More often than not this release was to a friend or relative of the accused, known as a "surety." The surety guaranteed the appearance of the accused; failure to do so meant the surety took the place of the accused in court. In essence, custody was transferred—not relinquished—from the county (i.e., the sheriff) to the surety. Clearly if the accused ran, the surety would leave no stone unturned in finding and returning him or her. Thus the concept of bail bondsmen and bounty hunters was born.

That concept became official practice in the United States when the country monetized and commercialized the surety process, creating incentives on both sides. There was an incentive for the bondsmen to provide the surety (in the form of the cash bail) and for the bounty hunter to chase after the accused when they ran. Releasing the accused from jail was generally a cost-savings to the state, by reducing expenses and overcrowding.

This practice gained even more of a foothold in 1832 by the U.S. Supreme Court when it gave bounty hunters the authority to pursue their "jumpers" across state lines, arrest them at any time, and to break and enter a fugitive's house in order to affect such an arrest. Of course, it has to be the right house and bounty hunters must comport with the criminal law as written in a given state. Even with these provisos, bounty hunters still generally have more power than the typical law enforcement agent.

The ROR Option

This changed somewhat in the 1960s with the Manhattan Bail Project and the development of pretrial agencies who would decide whether the accused could be released on their own recognizance (ROR). This essentially replaces the supervision of the bail bondsmen with the supervision of those in the professional bureaucracy. Of course when the accused, on ROR, leaves the vicinity or tries to escape justice, police simply do not have the time to actively pursue all those on warrants, whether on a felony or on a misdemeanor, which is not the case with bounty hunters.

Research suggests that the failure-to-appear rate is much lower for those released on commercial bail than either ROR or other kind of government surety. The incentive for bounty hunters is so great that 50 percent of bail jumpers chased by hunters will be inarcerated within one year. In addition to returning defendants to face justice, bounty hunters work at no cost to taxpayers. When the bounty hunter fails to return a defendant, which is often the case, bail reverts to a general court fund. In austere economic times, many states that eliminated or significantly curtailed commercial bondsmanship are rethinking their earlier decisions.

Questions Over Image

Perhaps the best-known bounty hunter currently is Duane "Dog" Chapman, who has captured some popular acclaim through his TV reality show, *Dog the Bounty Hunter*. Dog, however, is not the representative that professional bounty hunter—who often prefer the term *bail agent*—generally would prefer. Chapman brings too much baggage to the game; though having made more than 6,000 captures in a career spanning 27 years, Dog has in his past some less than photogenic qualifications, including having done prison time, illegal drug use, as well as some accusations of racism. However, Dog has a knack for high-profile heroics, such as his 2003 apprehension in Mexico of American cosmetics heir and serial rapist Andrew Luster. The image of the bounty hunter in the United States is certainly in flux. In the past, the Supreme Court has referred to bounty hunting as a "tawdry business" and bounty hunters as "odorous." Yet many of the rank and file want to be seen as professionals working alongside the other professionals of the justice system. As an icon of the trade, Dog doesn't really fit into that category—though he might think otherwise and certainly sees himself as the poster boy for rehabilitation.

Impetus to Professionalize

Over the past decade there have been calls, by various constituencies, for more stringent regulation of the bail industry and of bounty hunters. It is likely that most in the industry would welcome such regulation. The question of exactly what types of regulations are in store, and who will do the regulating, is of great importance to those in the industry. As with many other professions, the bounty hunters themselves have made some moves to self-police, and to provide guidelines under which they wish to operate.

The Professional Bail Agents of the United States (PBUS) claims 17 state associations as members, and bills itself as "the professional association

representing the 150,500 bail agents nationwide as the National Voice of the Bail Agent." Bail agents, according to PBUS, make between $10,000 annually to "hundreds of thousands of dollars/year" depending largely on where they are located. The average, reported income is between $25,000 and $50,000 per year.

In the United States, 46 states have a provision for bail. Bail agents—bounty hunters—likely exist in all these states and, like many professions and professionals, exist at varying levels of competence, success, and professionalism.

Bounty hunting, like any other criminal justice profession, involves hours of combating complete boredom, punctuated by times of high action and stress. The bail agent is, after all, attempting to return individuals charged with criminal offenses to jail. These are individuals who, for whatever reason, have chosen not to return to court to "face the music" on their own. Their crimes range from public intoxication to multiple counts of murder, and certainly the full scope of street crimes. The bounty hunter is keen on recovering the bondsman's money—and denying the fugitive his freedom. Whenever one is dealing with money and freedom, situations can indeed become intense.

Conclusion

Like other members of the criminal justice system, most bounty hunters are professional and deserve similar respect. They do a great service to the system and perhaps more importantly to defendants—many of whom would not have the privilege of being at home with their family. For without the bail bondsmen, they would be sitting in jail. When they run, it is the bounty hunter that gives chase, returning most back to stand trial, thus providing justice for all involved.

Jeffrey P. Rush
Austin Peay State University

See Also: Arrest; Bail; Courts; Jails; Police (Overview); Street Crime, Popular Portrayals of; Television Shows.

Further Readings

Chamberlin, John A. "Bounty Hunters: Can the Criminal Justice System Live Without Them?" *University of Illinois Law Review*, v.1998/4 (1998).

Fisher, Rebecca. "The History of American Bounty Hunting as a Study in Stunted Legal Growth." *N.Y.U. Review of Law and Social Change*, v.33/2 (2009).

Professional Bail Agents of the United States. "Education, Information, and Representation" 2012. http://www.pbus.com/displaycommon.cfm?an=1 (Accessed May 2012).

Supernor, Christopher. "International Bounty Hunters for War Criminals: Privatizing the Enforcement of Justice." *Air Force Law Review*, v.50/215 (2001).

Tabarrok, Alex. "The Bounty Hunter's Pursuit of Justice." *Wilson Quarterly*, v.35/1 (2011).

Bratton, William

William Bratton, former commissioner of police for New York City and Los Angeles, is best known for his seemingly uncanny ability to reduce crime through police agencies including: the New York City Transit Police, New York City Police Department (NYPD), and the Los Angeles Police Department (LAPD). In order to understand his importance for the history of street crime in America, his early years, career, and impact on crime policy and practice in the United States are reviewed.

Early Years

William Joseph Bratton, born in 1947, enjoyed a working-class, loving, and supportive family. In his book *Turnaround*, Bratton provides an extensive description of family life and boyhood interests. His father remained regularly employed, was an understanding and protective figure, and prioritized times with his family.

During his pre-teen years, Bratton spent hours developing clay figures replicating soldiers of specific eras in great detail. As he aged, his figures grew more detailed and eventually he replicated famous battles, preparing him well for his latter police years when he redesigned policing and knew how to motivate officers to develop crime control strategies. He once commented that he regretted having been born too late to experience World War II.

Bratton attended Boston Tech High School and majored in academics, compared to a traditional business program. Upon graduation, he entered the U.S. Army. He declined the offer to attend Officer's Training School in order to pursue his dream of becoming a police officer and became a military police (MP) soldier instead. After serving his tour of duty, he returned home in 1970 and took the entrance exam for the Boston Police Department (BPD), and was accepted into the department. He took advantage of a program encouraging police officers to earn a college degree at Boston State University.

Career Steps

In 1975, Bratton was promoted to sergeant in the BPD, and became a lieutenant in 1978. Two years later, at the age of 32, Bratton was named the youngest-ever executive superintendent, the number-two rank at the BPD. While in this position, he learned the value of crime data to evaluate police strategies, which served him well in future years.

Bratton seemed to endure a pattern of appointment to high position followed by demotion due to political winds. The outspoken Bratton was dismissed from the executive post as the BPD was undergoing restructuring, and he worked in a community liaison position, followed by a labor liaison post. While in one of these "downturn" periods, in 1983, he was offered the position of chief of police for the Metropolitan Boston Transit Authority (MBTA). When he realized the MBTA police agency needed major improvement and restructuring, he accepted, thinking he was leaving the BPD forever. In 1986, Massachusetts governor Michael Dukakis tapped Bratton to lead the Metropolitan District Commission Police, a state agency in need of a major overhaul as the result of cheating scandals on promotion exams. Again, Bratton accepted the challenge.

By 1990, Bratton had become known as a change agent. When the New York City Transit Authority determined to combat crime in the subway system, which was precipitating a general decline in ridership, Bratton was approached to accept the position of chief of police at that agency—already on its way to becoming one of the nation's largest police forces. A mature Bratton, armed with experience and new approaches to managing police agencies, assumed command in April 1990. By October of that year, serious crime rates began a notable decline in New York's subways. Less than two years later, Bratton was recruited back to Boston where in 1993 he was named police commissioner.

Impact on Crime

While crime decreased markedly in the New York City subways, the process to obtain the results was not explicit. Members of the department invited national professionals to review the agency to explain the rapid decrease in crime. It remained a mystery. When Bratton returned to Boston, with Jack Maple (a former New York City Transit Police lieutenant who had developed creative crime reduction strategies when Bratton was chief there) in tow, he applied some of the same principles, strategies, and tactics—and began to obtain similar results.

By the time New York mayor Rudolph Giuliani appointed Bratton commissioner of the NYPD, his crime reduction strategy had become explicit. With Maple to articulate the management system while bringing the NYPD in line with the plans—no easy task—crime began to plummet in the city. Maple dubbed the management system CompStat, getting across the idea that hard information was the key to policing success on the streets. Police from across the country and from foreign national police agencies came to New York to view and understand the management system that proved nearly miraculous in reducing crime.

By then it was not a mystery. The system required that commanders be held accountable in the focus on crime, while using detailed and up-to-date crime data to scientifically identify problem areas. In addition, police units and patrol units worked cooperatively to develop and implement strategies designed specifically for the identified problems and problem areas. Bratton did not use a "zero-tolerance" policy, but methodically arrested selected perpetrators for minor crimes as a way to obtain information regarding larger criminal enterprises.

Bratton had the added advantage of a charismatic personality and the ability to speak extemporaneously; the media sought him out occasionally and his photo appeared on the cover of *Time* magazine. After Bratton resigned from the NYPD, he applied his knowledge of crime reduction through national and international consulting for a few years. In 2002 he became chief of the LAPD, and instituted his unique system to reduce crime there. True to form, once again crime plummeted. After seven years in Los Angeles, he retired from the department, returning to New York City and a consulting career.

Conclusion

Bratton's unique story and many successes is not a mystery. Here is a man who knew from an early age that he wanted to be a police officer, and shaped his life to achieve his goal. At the same time, he followed where his career took him. Bratton wanted to make a difference; as a result he sought out and listened to experts, and he thought through issues and problems very carefully, as he had done as a young boy studying the strategies of famous battles. He was not swayed or deterred by personnel needs; his focus was always policing. Bratton recognized early that police, by being responsive, could design strategies, systems, and programs to effectively impact the behavior of criminals and ultimately reduce crime. Bratton proved the truth of this axiom repeatedly.

Phyllis P. McDonald
Johns Hopkins University

See Also: Boston, Massachusetts; Broken Windows Theory; CompStat; Giuliani, Rudolph; Los Angeles, California; Maple, Jack; Mass Transit, Crime on; New York City; Police (Overview).

Further Readings

Bratton, William and Peter Knobler. *Turnaround: How America's Top Cop Reversed the Crime Epidemic.* New York: Random House, 1998.

Garner, Gerald W. *Police Chief 101: Practical Advice for the Law Enforcement Leader.* Springfield, IL: Charles C. Thomas, 2010.

McDonald, Phyllis. *Managing Police Operations: Implementing the New York City Crime Control Model—CompStat.* Belmont, CA: Wadsworth-Thomson Learning, 2002.

Shane, J. M. *What Every Chief Executive Should Know: Using Data to Measure Police Performance.* Fresh Meadows, NY: Looseleaf Law Publications, 2007.

Brawley, Tawana

See Tawana Brawley Incident

Broken Windows Theory

Researchers James Q. Wilson and George Kelling proposed a causal link between community order and serious crime in a 1982 *Atlantic Monthly* article. Their perspective emerged from Kelling's experiences with the Newark Foot Patrol Experiment. The experiment found police foot patrols to be ineffective in controlling crime rates—but residents in neighborhoods with a foot patrol felt safer because they perceived that it protected the neighborhood's accustomed level of public order. While foot patrol generally may have no direct effect, the researchers posited that police actions supporting community values can indirectly affect crime. As a theory, Broken Windows states that the reduction of disorderly behavior and minor offenses in neighborhoods will prevent and reduce more serious crime. Thus, by corollary disorder, it may have grave consequences for life in neighborhoods and communities.

Disrupting the Spiral

Broken Windows Theory as a catchphrase comes from the fact that Wilson and Kelling explained their hypothesis using the analogy of the broken window in a given neighborhood: "If a window in a building is broken and is left unrepaired, all the rest of the windows will soon be broken." Regardless of the environment, a single unrepaired broken window becomes a signal that nobody cares about the property. The same applies on a broader scope to communities and disorderliness.

The rise in physical and social disorder within a neighborhood can create the perception that nobody cares, leading to a breakdown of neighborhood social self-control. Moreover, increased fear of the disorderly and the delinquent has a psychological effect on residents. They will adopt the mantra "don't get involved" and let fear shape more of their actions. For these residents, adaptation lessens community cohesion by reducing communal social

Trash and graffiti are all that remain at this abandoned urban housing site. Not all neighborhoods can benefit from Broken Windows Theory enforcement strategies. Areas need to be identified at a time when public order may be deteriorating but is still salvageable; attempts to restore order in neighborhoods that are already disorderly and crime-ridden are not likely to be effective.

ties to just a few trusted friends. People keep more to themselves, reducing guardianship and informal control. This makes the community vulnerable to criminal invasion.

Areas affected in this manner are theoretically more likely to see an influx in criminality, as potential offenders observe that residents are indifferent to what goes on in their neighborhood. Although the police can make the occasional arrest, they are unable to replace the effectiveness of bedrock community informal controls in curtailing crime. This ineffectiveness in turn may well lead citizens to stop calling the police because the police "can't do anything." This creates a spiral of decay in which criminals are more likely to operate in areas where potential victims are already intimidated by prevailing conditions, leading to greater citizen fear and social isolation.

In order to prevent this domino-type effect, police must act to prevent physical and behavioral disorder. Left unattended, minor offenses such as vandalism, panhandling, loitering, and public drunkenness will lead to crimes that are more serious. Waiting to intervene until serious crimes occur is too late. While citizens are important to providing a foundation for order to take root, Broken Windows Theory suggests that the police are the key to neighborhood safety. When neighborhood efforts have failed, police are the ones with legal authority to remove undesirable individuals. However, not all neighborhoods can realize the benefits of Broken Windows enforcement strategies. Some neighborhoods are already stable and orderly, rendering these strategies unnecessary. Others are too disorderly and crime-ridden, where relatively minor attempts to restore order are futile. The key is to identify those at the brink, where public order is deteriorating but salvageable.

Revolution and Reaction

The Broken Windows Theory set off a revolution in law enforcement. While the ability of police to affect crime rates has been widely questioned—with broader socioeconomic variables such as poverty and unemployment cited as primary determinants—Broken Windows proposes that the police can have a substantial impact through proactive policing. In turn, police administrators have embraced this theory, launching enforcement strategies to restore public order. In the 1990s, New York City Mayor Rudolph Giuliani and New York City Police Commissioner

William Bratton adopted a plan to reduce crime and reclaim the streets by sending a message that disorderly behavior would not be tolerated. To achieve this, they implemented Broken Windows–based "quality of life" and "zero-tolerance" policing.

Before its implementation, officers had often ignored or informally dealt with disorderliness. With this new strategy, the New York Police Department (NYPD) deployed officers with a mandate to arrest individuals engaging in visible disorderly conduct. For example, officers aggressively cracked down on the "squeegee pest," public drinking, and illegal peddling. The police arrested and detained such individuals for 24 hours for relatively minor offenses. Soon, such disorderly behaviors were few and far between. These strategies have been touted as central to the city's dramatic decline in both petty crime and serious crime rates.

Critics of Broken Windows have questioned its validity as, to date, these strategies have not often enough been implemented within neighborhoods at the tipping point of irrecoverable deterioration. Additionally, Broken Windows policies have been called antidemocratic, since they are sometimes seen as a common justification for aggressive policing strategies that may discriminate against groups on the fringe of community norms. Neighborhoods can designate these populations as "undesirable" and aggressive policing may infringe upon the targeted groups' constitutional rights. Minorities, the poor, and the homeless especially have been targets of "quality of life" policing, leading to disproportionate arrest rates and giving rise to pseudo-offenses such as "driving while black" or "strolling while poor."

Michael Chou
Lawrence F. Travis III
University of Cincinnati

See Also: Bratton, William; Community Policing; Fear of Crime; Giuliani, Rudolph; Newark Foot Patrol Experiment; Racial Profiling; Stop and Frisk; Zero-Tolerance/Saturation Policing.

Further Readings

Bratton, William and Peter Knobler. *Turnaround: How America's Top Cop Reversed the Crime Epidemic.* New York: Random House, 1998.
Kelling, George and Catherine Coles. *Fixing Broken Windows: Restoring Order and Reducing Crime*

in Our Communities. New York: The Free Press, 1996.

Harcourt, Bernard. *Illusions of Order: The False Promise of Broken Windows Policing.* Cambridge, MA: Harvard University Press, 2002.

Wilson, James and George Kelling. "Broken Windows." *Atlantic Monthly,* v.249/3 (1982).

Buffalo, New York

Despite the fact that rates of violent and property crime are now relatively low across the United States, the effects of street crime are still very problematic for many cities across the nation. Classified as a "Rust Belt" city, Buffalo, New York's, situation regarding street crime is noteworthy because the city continues to suffer from the population losses, economic decline, and high rates of poverty that have plagued similar cities over the last few decades. Rates of violent and property crime in Buffalo remain disproportionately high; in 2010, Buffalo had the sixth-highest violent crime rate of any city in the United States with a population of 250,000 persons or greater, according to the Federal Bureau of Investigation's (FBI) Uniform Crime Reports (UCR) data. However, like many cities across the nation, Buffalo has seen its violent and property crime rates decrease since the peak rates seen in the 1990s. While the exact causes of the crime drop have yet to be identified, initiatives by local law enforcement certainly may play a role.

History and Background

Located in western upstate New York, Buffalo is the state's second-largest city behind New York City. Buffalo is the seat of Erie County and sits directly along the United States' border with Canada, serving as a primary port of entry into the United States. According to the U.S. Census Bureau, the 2010 population in Buffalo was 261,310. This figure represents nearly an 11 percent decline in the city's residents from 2000.

Beginning in the 19th century, Buffalo emerged as a leading manufacturing, transportation, and cultural hub in the region and even the nation. For many decades, Buffalo's economy largely consisted of blue-collar sector industries. However, like many other Rust Belt cities across the northeast and midwest regions of the United States, Buffalo has suffered from a continuously declining economic base since the mid- to late 20th century. Buffalo is now among the most impoverished cities of its size in the nation, with a poverty rate of 30.2 percent, according to the Census Bureau's 2010 *American Community Survey.*

Street Crime Trends

Many street crimes, by their nature, are not reported to official law enforcement agencies, and thus not represented in their statistics. For instance, rates of offending for crimes involving illegal drug activity and the general criminal availability of handguns are not directly available in a year-to-year comparative form. It may be no coincidence, however, that the rise and subsequent decline in street crime in America went hand in hand with the rise and decline of the crack cocaine trade in the 1990s, which has been strongly suggested in the empirical research by scholars such as Jeff Grogger and Michael Willis.

To be sure, surveys of individuals' experiences with victimization (e.g., the National Crime Victimization Survey) do provide insight into criminal activity that may go unreported to police, but these data do not sufficiently capture the essence of street crime either. Despite this limitation, a review of official local law enforcement data is the most informative long-term source available in assessing the rate of criminal activity in a given area. The official crime figures presented here for the United States and the city of Buffalo come from FBI's UCR. The Buffalo UCR data was furnished by the city's primary law enforcement agency, the Buffalo Police Department (BPD), and therefore reflect this agency's records of reported crimes.

Rates of violent crime rose rapidly in the United States during the late 1980s and early 1990s. UCR statistics show that the national violent crime rate peaked in 1992, with 785.2 violent crimes committed per 100,000 persons, but in 2010, this rate stood at 403.6. The national property crime rate, which has historically been markedly higher than the violent crime rate, has gradually decreased in the United States since 1991, when the rate was 5,140.2 offenses reported per 100,000. In 2010, the national property crime rate was 2,941.9.

A review of Buffalo crime statistics from 1985 to 2009 shows the dynamic nature of reported street crime in the city. From 1985 to 2009, Buffalo's violent crime rate increased by 45 percent to 1,459.1, but it has decreased from its peak in 1994 by 31 percent. With regard to murder and non-negligible manslaughter, the rate from 1985 to 2009 increased by 145 percent during that span, but was down by 19 percent to 22.3 since the peak rate seen in 1994. The rate of forcible rape decreased by 39 percent from 1985 and 2009 to 52.5, and was down by over 51 percent since peaking in 1990. Concerning robberies, the rate increased by 49 percent between 1985 and 2009 to 609, but the 2009 rate was 40 percent lower than the peak rate seen in 1994. The rate of reported aggravated assaults increased by 55 percent between 1985 and 2009, but was down by 23 percent since peaking in 1994.

Unlike that of violent crime, however, the property crime rate in Buffalo has not fallen as sharply. The rate of property crime decreased by 11 percent between 1985 and 2009 to 5,390.2, with a more dramatic decline of 33 percent occurring since 1992, which is when the rate peaked. The burglary rate in the city of Buffalo decreased by 25 percent during the period between 1985 and 2009. This rate declined by 43 percent to 1,471.8 since the peak rate in 1991. In terms of the larceny-theft rate, it remained stable between the years 1985 and 2009, but in the latter year was down 16 percent to 3,330.3 from the highest rate seen in 1992. The rate of motor vehicle theft has declined by 23 percent from 1985 to 2009 to 588.1, and was down by 65 percent from the peak rate in 1993. While violent and property crime rates do not represent the totality of street crime activity, the data does serve as an indicator of a locality's overall rates of crime. As these statistics show, street crime trends in Buffalo closely mirror rates seen nationally. The early 1990s represents the zenith of street crime in America—and Buffalo.

Response of Law Enforcement

While the exact causes for the decline in street crime in Buffalo cannot presently be determined, one must consider the efforts of local law enforcement to curb crime as part of the equation. With the support of Mayor Byron W. Brown, in office since 2005, the BPD has implemented many anticrime initiatives. One program that the BPD has instituted is a No Questions Asked gun buyback program. This initiative allows citizens to turn in firearms voluntarily in exchange for an incentive. The goal of this program is to reduce the amount of illegal guns and

gun-related violence on the streets of Buffalo. Since 2005, 3,000 illegal guns have been removed from the streets through this "no questions-asked" buyback.

Often, anticrime efforts are aimed at thwarting crime in specific neighborhoods and areas. Buffalo neighborhoods such as the Chippewa Entertainment District, the University District, and Elmwood Village have all been targets of specific anticrime efforts by the BPD. Buffalo has installed a network of surveillance cameras in many areas in the city. The Wireless Security Camera Network, unveiled in 2008, is designed to provide first responders with access to real-time video in emergency situations as well as evidence in criminal proceedings.

The BPD has collaborated with other law enforcement agencies in its effort to combat crime. For example, the Mobile Response Unit, in partnership with the New York State Troopers, is an initiative started in 2007 that is geared toward tackling areas of high crime, illegal guns, gang activity, and drug trafficking throughout Buffalo. Other anticrime initiatives include the Save Our Streets Task Force, neighborhood Clean Sweeps, Mayor Brown's Working Against Violent Events (WAVE) initiative, and the Zero Tolerance Public Safety policy.

Conclusion

Like most cities in the United States, overall levels of street crime in Buffalo are now lower than during the early 1990s, in spite of the current economic recession that persists across the country. While Buffalo continues to have higher than average rates of violent crime compared to most cities its size, the causes of the continued decline in street crime seen here are complex. Criminologists have a wealth of new data to come, however, as the past decade has seen the launch of an assortment of anticrime programs in the city, some community-based, others technology-based, and still others police procedural-based.

Lionel Smith
University of Delaware

See Also: Closed-Circuit Television; Guns and Weapons; Hot Spots; Police (Overview).

Further Readings

City of Buffalo Mayor's Office. "Archived Press Releases." 2010. http://www.ci.buffalo.ny.us/Home/

Leadership/Mayor/Archive_Press_Releases (Accessed October 2011).

Grogger, Jeff and Michael Willis. "The Emergence of Crack Cocaine and the Rise in Urban Crime Rates." *Review of Economics and Statistics*, v.82/4 (2000).

Krivo, Lauren J. and Ruth D. Peterson. "Extremely Disadvantaged Neighborhoods and Urban Crime." *Social Forces*, v.75/2 (1996).

U.S. Census Bureau. "American Community Survey." 2010. http://www.census.gov/acs/www (Accessed October 2011).

U.S. Department of Justice, Federal Bureau of Investigation. "Uniform Crime Reports (UCR) Data Online." 2011. http://www.ucrdatatool.gov/Search/Crime/Local/JurisbyJurisLarge.cfm (Accessed October 2011).

Burglary

Burglary, a property crime, is typically defined as the unlawful entry of a building to remove property or commit some other felony. Though often confused definitionally with other crimes, burglary is distinct from larceny-theft, which is simply the unlawful taking of another's property, and from robbery, which involves taking property through the use or threat of violence. Legal definitions of burglary often stipulate that the unlawful entry element of the crime can either be forceful (e.g., breaking glass, kicking a door in) or not (e.g., entering through an unlocked door). Additionally, while burglary is commonly thought of occurring against a home residence, other structures (e.g., storage facilities, businesses) can be burglarized as well. In these cases, burglary is distinguished from shoplifting, which is stealing merchandise from a commercial establishment while it is open for business.

Rate of Incidence

Both the Federal Bureau of Investigation's Uniform Crime Reporting (UCR) system and the National Crime Victimization Survey (NCVS) collect data on burglary each year allowing for a national picture of the offense. Although the burglary victimization rate in the United States declined by 59 percent from 1990 to 2008, it remains the second-most common serious crime (behind larceny-theft) in the United States according to both the UCR and NCVS. Additionally, UCR figures reveal that suburban areas and small towns (with fewer than 50,000 residents) have burglary rates about 30 percent lower than cities with populations over 100,000.

UCR data also indicate that only 12.5 percent of burglary cases are cleared by law enforcement, a rate which is lower than that of any other serious offense except auto theft. The frequency of this offense and the improbability of recovering stolen property increase the necessity of prevention efforts. These measures seek to deter burglars by boosting signs of occupancy, enhancing supervision of the location, and strengthening resistance of the building to illegal entrance. In general, the success of these efforts depends on the situational elements involved, but in many cases burglary is amenable to prevention.

Motivation and Target Selection

While burglars as a group are diverse both in terms of their demographics and motivation, prior research shows some patterns. For example, arrest data from the UCR indicates that the vast majority of burglars are male, outnumbering their female counterparts more than five to one. White offenders account for nearly seven out of every 10 burglary arrests; African Americans represent nearly three out of 10. Additionally, the majority of persons arrested for burglary are under the age of 25.

While burglars can sometimes be motivated by thrill-seeking, or by a desire for revenge against, for example, an ex-lover or former employer, this crime is far more often the product of an immediate financial need which is frequently the result of substance addiction. Many burglars use the crime as a means of financing partying that includes heavy usage of alcohol or illegal drugs. A smaller number of offenders may use burglary as their profession, although substance abuse remains common in this group. A given offender's motivation and the urgency of his or her financial need are likely to impact the targets they choose.

The likelihood of burglary victimization to a home or business is a function of the presence of desirable goods and features that affect the chances of the offender's apprehension. Burglars view a home or business as potentially rewarding if it appears to contain desirable goods. For example, a large house and the presence of expensive cars in the driveway are indicators that a home contains valuable goods. Homes that are well maintained, expensively adorned, or have ornate landscaping may also be seen as more rewarding targets, although some burglars may avoid well-kept homes out of fear that they are more likely to contain burglary prevention measures like alarms. Burglars may also impute the neighborhood's wealth to a particular home, assuming that any home in a wealthy neighborhood contains valuable property sufficient to justify a burglary. Because the wares of a business are often public knowledge, and because burglars can enter during regular hours to examine the merchandise, commercial establishments are more likely to be rated as rewarding based on their actual contents rather than their external appearance.

Similar characteristics make items desirable to both residential and commercial burglars. Because burglars rarely keep stolen articles for themselves, goods that are valuable, easily transported, and easily resold are especially attractive. For example, items commonly taken during residential burglaries include: laptop computers, jewelry, cash, televisions, and other electronics. Burglars can dispose of stolen property in several ways, usually with the goal of converting the property into cash or drugs. They can attempt to sell the property to a pawnshop, or perhaps on the street. Burglars may attempt to trade the stolen items directly for illegal drugs, and some may utilize a "fence," a broker specializing in disposing of stolen goods.

Preferences of the Burglar

There are essentially four factors that impact the difficulty associated with a burglary: (1) the presence of occupants, (2) the visibility of the structure, (3) the ease of entering, and (4) the offender's familiarity with the location. Burglars generally prefer to enter unoccupied buildings rather than risk an altercation with residents or employees, and will sometimes test the occupancy of a house (e.g., by knocking on the door) before proceeding to victimize it. Occupancy "proxies" that increase the chances of a burglar being discovered can also serve to protect homes and businesses. For example, noisy dogs that draw attention to intruders may deter residential burglaries.

Security alarm systems may serve a similar function for both homes and businesses, although some burglars view them as indicators of the presence of valuables. This preference for unoccupied

buildings impacts the temporal distribution of burglaries. The majority of residential burglary occurs during daylight hours on weekdays when residents are likely to be at work; burglaries are particularly prevalent around mid-morning and mid-afternoon when even frequently occupied houses are likely to be empty.

Burglars also prefer less visible targets. Visibility refers to the way the natural and built environment shapes the capacity of residents and business owners to observe and defend the space around their buildings. Factors that make a location less visible, like shielded doorways, tall hedges, privacy fences, and distance from the road, increase its attractiveness as a burglary target. Because some burglars give an appearance of legitimacy (for example, by carrying clipboards), they do not fear being seen on a property as much as they fear being seen entering the building. Thus the visibility of entry points (i.e., windows and doors) is an important influence on the likelihood of burglary.

A location's accessibility can also impact the likelihood of victimization. At one level, access can refer to the ease of entering and leaving the area. Locations near thoroughfares and at the edge of neighborhoods are at more risk for burglary because the offender can quickly leave the area after the offense, and because residents are accustomed to larger numbers of strangers in the neighborhood. At

Previous burglaries at certain locations are strong predictors of future victimization, as evidenced by this notice posted by a victim trying to recover his or her belongings and warning neighbors.

another level, the burglar must determine whether the building can be easily entered. The term *target hardening* is sometimes used to describe physical security measures that attempt to prevent burglary by making it more difficult for intruders to enter a building. Putting bars and locks on windows, installing deadbolt locks, and using glass block windows are examples of measures intended to decrease a building's accessibility to burglars.

A burglar's familiarity with a location is likely to impact his or her view of its suitability as a target. Knowledge of the routines or security measures at a location can reduce risks associated with burglarizing it. Thus a previous burglary at a location is among the stronger predictors of future victimization, partly because of the knowledge the offender gains of the building's accessibility, layout, and desirable contents. Neighbors of a victimized building also have an elevated probability of victimization because the offender is likely to return to a successful location to commit future crimes.

Burglars can gain familiarity with a location in a variety of legitimate ways. The offender may legitimately scout a site as a relative, acquaintance, or while performing a service in the home or business. Sometimes illegitimate means are used to assess a location. For example, criminologists Richard Wright and Scott Decker interviewed female burglars who frequented bars, feigned romantic interest in men, and went home with them as a means of scouting residences for burglary.

Prevention and Deterrence

Prevention efforts can attempt to impact the factors that influence burglars' target choices (occupancy, visibility, access, and potential rewards). Because most burglars are unwilling to risk confronting residents, preventative measures aimed at increasing occupancy elements are often successful. Efforts at simulating occupancy can include placing interior lights on timers when a home is empty and ensuring that snow is shoveled from walks and driveways during the residents' absence. Similarly, canceling mail and newspaper delivery during vacations prevents a visible backlog that would clearly indicate the prolonged absence of the residents. Dogs and alarm systems create a form of occupancy by drawing attention to intruders.

Others measures attempt to increase visibility by installing closed-circuit television cameras or

removing fences and landscaping that obscure the location from view. Motion sensor lights on a building and improved street lighting can also increase visibility, although these efforts can only impact nighttime burglaries. Another approach is using community watches and other programs to encourage neighboring residents and businesses to watch over each other's buildings. Access reduction efforts usually seek to increase the difficulty of entering a particular building by installing locks, strengthening doors, and in some cases barring windows.

It is often impossible to reduce access to an entire neighborhood, although some gated communities are able to utilize this approach. The effectiveness of these visibility and access measures depends on the particular situational elements that are present. Finally, other measures seek to make it more difficult for offenders to dispose of stolen goods. For example, lawmakers may compel pawnshops to copy the photo identification of those pawning items, and police can attempt to disrupt the sale of stolen property on the streets. However, increasing the difficulty of reselling property may not deter burglars with an established market for their goods. Additionally, news organizations frequently report that burglars have been found selling stolen goods on Internet resale outlets like Craigslist and eBay, which may further reduce the effectiveness of back-end prevention measures.

Jennifer J. Roberts
Jeffrey J. Roth
Indiana University of Pennsylvania

See Also: Alcohol and Drug Use; Closed-Circuit Television; Crime Prevention, Environmental Design and; Crime Prevention, Situational; Defensible Space Theory; Neighborhood Watch; Theft and Larceny.

Further Readings

Cromwell, Paul and James N. Olson. *Breaking and Entering: Burglars on Burglary.* Belmont, CA: Wadsworth/Thomson Learning, 2004.
Weisel, Deborah Lamm. *Burglary of Single-Family Houses.* Rockville, MD: U.S. Department of Justice Office of Community-Oriented Policing Services, 2004.
Wright, Richard T. and Scott H. Decker. *Burglars on the Job.* Lebanon, NH: Northeastern University Press, 1994.

Bystander Apathy

Bystander apathy is a social-psychological phenomenon that occurs during extraordinary events during which the surrounding community or the observers fail or refuse to act to alleviate the suffering or imminent danger of an individual in need of aid.

Historical Example

One of the most infamous incidents of bystander apathy occurred in the Queens borough of New York City. In March 1964, Kitty Genovese was attacked outside her apartment building. Her screams awakened neighbors. The assailant, Winston Moseley, an African American, raped and stabbed Genovese multiple times. Several of her neighbors thought they heard screams but later told police they weren't sure what they heard. One neighbor, Robert Mozer, who heard the attacks, yelled from his window and scared Moseley away. Genovese staggered to the rear entrance of her apartment building but was unable to gain entrance. Moseley returned, searched the area, found Genovese and attacked her again.

Although her neighbors admitted they heard her pleas, none of them called police. Police reports show that many of them thought it was a domestic argument. The media called it a lack of concern. Her neighbors were vilified and described as apathetic and callous. Such a determination, however, failed to include the numerous psychological and sociological implications and motivations of their behavior. Since the Kitty Genovese incident, there have been several studies to determine the cause, roots, and solutions to the phenomenon that has earned the nomenclature bystander apathy.

Social-Psychological Studies

In response to the Genovese tragedy, social psychologists John M. Darley and Bibb Latané published the results of a series of studies in the late 1960s and early 1970s. The psychologists identified three social-psychological processes that may interfere with individuals intervening in emergencies. First, "diffusion of responsibility": the more people there are observing a critical event, the less likely an individual will feel responsible to act. The second process, "evaluation apprehension," occurs when individuals fear being judged by others if they act inadequately and/or fail. The third, "pluralistic ignorance," occurs when individuals rely on the response of others; thus, if no one acts first, there is no perception by others of an emergency.

The outcome of Darley and Latané's studies indicated that the more people present at an event, the lower the likelihood an individual will respond to an emergency or urgent need for aid. The failure to act occurs generally because individuals are unable to communicate with other bystanders; critical discussion is needed before action can be undertaken. Another finding illustrated that when several people are present at a critical event, everyone expects another person will act and will make the appropriate communications. It seems to be a natural assumption to believe someone else will act first. Genovese's neighbors expected someone would respond to the victim's pleas for help. According to police reports, many of the neighbors assumed someone had or would call the police. So, no one physically responded or came to her rescue, demonstrating Darley and Latané's theory of pluralistic ignorance. This theory has been the school of thought for several years and is still used to explain bystander apathy in some textbooks.

Examples in Other Settings

There have been innumerable cases since the Genovese incident that have either tended to strengthen or to bring into question the conclusions and assumptions of earlier studies. For example, the 1983 Big Dan's Tavern case made national news when Cheryl Ann Araujo was assaulted and repeatedly raped in front of about a dozen male tavern customers in New Bedford, Massachusetts. In June 2008, 49-year-old Esmin Green collapsed and died in Kings County Hospital in Brooklyn while awaiting service in the waiting room. She was ignored by others in the room and by two security guards. In April 2010, homeless man Hugo Alfredo Tale-Yax was stabbed to death in New York City after coming to the aid of a woman who was being robbed. Tale-Yax lay dying on a Queens sidewalk for more than an hour during which as many as 20 people walked by.

Instances of bystander apathy occur often in urban centers. Scholars of urban life suggest that the intense stimulation associated with city life results in psychological withdrawal from others. This produces attenuated social relationships and situations where a sharp distinction is drawn between one's friends and others. Suburban populaces, by contrast, may tend to show more willingness to aid others. A meta-analytic review examined 65 tests of the hypothesis that "country people are more helpful than city people." Results demonstrated a significantly greater helping response by nonurban people. This effect was found to be robust across variations in helping requests and experimenter and subject variables.

Divergent Findings

Decades after the Darley and Latané work, a meta-analytic review was completed by a group of authors and published in the 2011 *Psychological Bulletin*, it tended to refute earlier studies. The review covered research from 1960 to 2010 and resulted in different conclusions when compared to past theories. A sizable number of past studies showed that the presence of other people in a critical situation reduced the likelihood that an individual would help. Using evidence from incidents after 1981, the review showed that the more bystanders present, the more likely an individual would be to take action resulting in the perception that the intervening individual is encouraged and empowered by the presence of additional bystanders.

Further, the analysis also proposed that traditional gender roles played a significant factor in the expectation that an individual would act. Another meta-analytic finding indicated bystander apathy often followed an arousal-cost-reward model; that is, the level of perceived danger and physical consequences of intervention influenced the impulse to intervene. In a life-threatening emergency, therefore, helping behavior was less likely in situations where the helper was likely to sustain injury, such as situations that were perceived as mortally crucial or when dangerous perpetrators were present.

Conclusion

Although these more recent hypotheses and surveys aid in understanding how bystander apathy occurs, actual incidents show that a myriad of factors influence behavior. More research in more settings will need to be conducted and analyzed for a fuller comprehension of this phenomenon. Of additional value would be research that investigates ties between bystander apathy syndrome and the chronic under-reporting to police—by both victims and witnesses—of such street crimes as robbery, assault, rape, extortion, prostitution, and child abuse.

Teresa Francis
Central Washington University

See Also: Broken Windows Theory; Community Policing; Fear of Crime; Genovese, Kitty; Neighborhood Watch; Routine Activity Theory; Urban Incivility.

Further Readings

Bergman, Jerry. "The Sociology of Bystander Apathy." *JASA*, v.37/3 (1985).

Fischer, Peter, et al. "The Bystander-Effect: A Meta-Analytic Review on Bystander Intervention in Dangerous and Non-Dangerous Emergencies." *Psychological Bulletin*, v.137/4 (2011).

Helmer, John and Neil Eddington, eds. *Urbanman: The Psychology of Urban Survival*. New York: The Free Press, 1973.

Latané, Bibb and John Darley "Bystander 'Apathy.'" *American Scientist*, v.57/4 (1969).

Latané, Bibb and John Darley. "Group Inhibition of Bystander Intervention in Emergencies." *Journal of Personality and Social Psychology*, v.10/3 (1968).

Manning, Rachel, Mark Levine, and Alan Collins. "The Kitty Genovese Murder and the Social Psychology of Helping: The Parable of 38 Witnesses." *American Psychologist*, v.62/6 (2007).

Steblay, Nancy M. "Helping Behavior in Rural and Urban Environments: A Meta-Analysis." *Psychological Bulletin*, v.102/3 (1987).

Central Booking

Central booking is relevant to the subject of street crimes in America because it is the primary place that all persons are sent after having been arrested for various misdemeanor or felony offenses. The Federal Bureau of Investigation, Uniform Crime Report for 2010 estimated that approximately 13 million arrests were made by various law enforcement agents, mainly for property or drug-related crimes, that year. With each arrest, all offenders are transported to the local police station or county jail where they are formally booked and processed.

There are many functions and procedures that make up the intricate fabric of central booking; these include processing, admission, classification, housing, and release of individuals under arrest. This multifaceted approach to central booking serves an array of purposes: to establish an accurate identification of the arrestee; record the details of the arrest; determine if the defendant is wanted by other local, state, or federal police agencies; and to assess whether the person can be released on recognizance or cash, property, or bail bond.

Sequence and Process of Jail Admissions

Understanding the process of central booking is important for identifying who is being admitted into the system and the eventual release of that person from the system. There are terms that are commonly used that refer to the process and procedures of central booking that include "admissions and processing," "booking," and "intake." In order to gain a full understanding of the phenomenon of central booking, an article written by criminologists Christopher Miller and Richard Southby, "From Arrest to Inmate to Release," brought into perspective the daily routine of the central booking process in the Arlington County (Virginia) Detention Facility. This article described in detail the sequence of events that occur during central booking. Another such source is Tom McLaughlin's "The Art of Jail Admissions and Processing."

On a broader scope, during the intake process, researchers Ira Silverman and Manuel Vega's chapter on "Jails and Detention: The American Jail" discussed certain types of information that must be ascertained from arrested individuals to ensure the overall health and safety of the other inmates and the security of the correctional institution. In addition, all incoming persons are interviewed and screened for medical and mental health conditions.

After the initial assessment, an arrestee is fingerprinted and photographed; these materials are electronically sent to an automated federal database. Once these steps have been completed, inmates that are not released on recognizance or bail are bodily searched; their personal property and clothing are inventoried and stored in exchange for jail issued clothing, and they are classified as to their security level and cell assignment in the housing area within the jail. On average, a person may spend between 18 to 24 hours in central booking, but his or her stay could be as short as four to five hours, depending on the case. By law, all individuals must be booked, that is, charged with a crime, within a 24-hour period.

Problems and Resolutions

The ebb and flow of central booking has presented challenges and problems to the jail correctional staff. Gary Cornelius's article "Problems in the Jail Booking Area" described the problems and dangers that jail officials encounter while performing their duties during the booking process. With the high influx of inmates being admitted and released, jails have been inundated with problems such as releasing the wrong person, or mistakes in offender identification, inmate suicides, persons under the influence of alcohol or drugs, mental or medical health issues, and contraband (i.e., illegal drugs, weapons, or tobacco).

In order to address these problems, jails have recently made improvements to their booking and release procedures. Various local and state jurisdictions have implemented new technological advances that have been designed to save hours of manpower and record keeping. These improvements include using a live scan electronic fingerprint device, the use of a photo mug shot and identification card, and the use of video-link courtroom arraignments to eliminate the transporting of inmates. In essence, central booking is a viable component to jails.

Renita L. Seabrook
University of Baltimore

See Also: Arrest; Bail; Closed-Circuit Television; Courts; Jails; Police (Overview).

Further Readings

Cornelius, Gary. "Problems in the Jail Booking Area." *American Jails*, v.24/1 (2010).

Federal Bureau of Investigation. "Uniform Crime Report—Crime in the United States, 2010." http://www.fbi.gov/about-us/cjis/ucr/crime-in-the-u.s/2010/crime-in-the-u.s.-2010/persons-arrested (Accessed September 2011).

Justice Policy Institute. "Baltimore Behind Bars: How to Reduce the Jail Population, Save Money, and Improve Public Safety." Washington, DC: Justice Policy Institute, 2010.

McLaughlin, Tom. "The Art of Jail Admissions and Processing." *American Jails*, v.23/6 (2009).

Miller, Christopher and Richard Southby. "From Arrest to Inmate to Release: An Account of the Booking Processes and Participation in the Inmate Work Program at the Arlington County Detention Facility." *American Jails*, v.21/1 (2007).

Silverman, Ira and Manuel Vega. *Corrections: A Comprehensive View*. St. Paul, MN: West Publishing, 1996.

Central Park Jogger Incident

On the night of April 19, 1989, Trisha Meili, a 28-year-old white female investment banker at Salomon Brothers, was jogging in New York City's Central Park when she was assaulted and raped in what became known as the Central Park Jogger case. Meili suffered a fractured skull, internal bleeding, and was left in a coma. She also lost a large amount of blood and had hypothermia after being outdoors for approximately four hours before being found. There were no witnesses to the attack, but there had been sightings of approximately 30 African American and Latino youths allegedly assaulting and robbing people in random attacks, including throwing rocks at a taxi, chasing a couple on a bicycle, and hitting a jogger with a pipe, in what became labeled "wilding."

The attack on Meili was thought linked to these events, and five of the wilding group, Antron McCray, Kevin Richardson, Yusef Salaam, Raymond Santana, Jr., and Kharey Wise, were arrested. This Central Park Five group were all identified publicly by the New York City Police Department (NYPD) prior to their arraignment and indictment—in violation of procedure, as all but Wise were under 16. Salaam falsely claimed to be 16 and his name was released on that basis. Meili was not identified, preferring to remain anonymous and known as the Central Park Jogger until 2003, when she confirmed her identity. However, several local television stations did release her name immediately following the attack and arrests, and two African American newspapers in New York City continued to publish her identity as the case progressed.

Yusef Salaam, one of Trisha Meili's alleged attackers, known as the Central Park Five, speaking at a rally for Troy Davis in New York City's Union Square Park in May 2009. The increasingly polarizing racial tensions after the attack on Meili were not contained to New York City and became widespread throughout the country.

Confessions and Convictions

During police interviews, McCray, Richardson, Santana, and Wise confessed to the assault and rape of Meili. The confessions were recorded on videotape. Each of the suspects implicated the others as well as Salaam, who admitted to his presence at the attack but refused to confess on video or in writing. McCray, Richardson, Santana, and Wise soon retracted their confessions, claiming that they were the product of police coercion and deception. It was such deception, the police telling Salaam that his fingerprints were found on the victim, that led to his false admission. Not only were their fingerprints not found, but the only DNA present, semen on the victim, belonged to an unknown male.

Because of the lack of physical evidence, the prosecution relied on the now-retracted confessions. In spite of this, on September 11, 1990, the first of the trials ended with the jury convicting McCray, Salaam, and Santana for rape, assault, riot, and robbery; Judge Thomas Galligan sentenced them to

5 to 10 years in prison. The second trial ended on January 9, 1991, with Richardson being convicted for attempted murder, rape, sodomy, assault, robbery, and riot, and sentenced by Galligan to 5 to 10 years. Wise was convicted for assault, sexual abuse, and riot. As he was over 16, Wise was sentenced to 5 to 15 years. Four of the five launched appeals, but all were rejected.

Response

The attack and response to it took place in and reflected a city that was increasingly fearful of crime and somewhat racially polarized, experiencing an economic downturn, gang and crack cocaine "epidemics," a serial rapist, and general urban decay. This informed "tough on crime" rhetoric from politicians, sensationalist reporting of the case that exploited the public fear of crime and racism, widespread assumption of the five's guilt, and a push to convict them. Mayor Ed Koch told the police commissioner that the case was the highest priority. Leaders of the African American community argued that the assumption of guilt, quick arrests, and fast convictions were examples of racial profiling and wider institutional racism.

Nothing encapsulated the racist response to this case more than the term *wilding*, which the police and media used to describe the youths and their activities that night. Although the police attributed the term to the suspects, they are widely believed to have said "doing the wild thing." The term *wilding* could be linked to racist colonial discourses about black people being primitive, uncivilized, and aggressive, and historical fears of black male crime, violence, and sexuality as a threat to white society and particularly to white women. In the context of New York City in 1990, there was also a fear and a political theme that the city was being overtaken by a black underclass extending out and threatening that beyond the confines of the ghetto.

The fear of crime and racial tensions, which were further exacerbated later that summer with the murder of African American teenager Yusef Hawkins by a group of white males in Bensonhurst, Brooklyn, also played a role in the mayoral contest in which Republican Rudolph Giuliani ran a tough on crime campaign against Democratic African American candidate David Dinkins. Although Dinkins won in the fall 1989 race, he was unseated by Giuliani, running on a law-and-order platform, in 1994.

Convictions Vacated

The Central Park Five contested their convictions, represented by lawyer Michael Warren and supported by the Innocence Project. In 2002, the convictions were vacated when Matias Reyes, a convicted murderer and rapist serving a 33-1/3 year-to-life sentence, confessed to the crime. Reyes' confession was supported by the DNA found on the victim, which matched his. In response to this and questions about the original confessions, District Attorney Robert Morgenthau reinvestigated. The reinvestigation, headed by Nancy Ryan and Peter Casolaro, concluded that the confessions differed from one another in almost all aspects of the crime, as well as not being corroborated by or consistent with the evidence. These new developments led the district attorney to recommend that the convictions for the Meili attack and other crimes to which the five confessed be vacated. On December 19, 2002, the sentences were vacated by Justice Charles

J. Tejada of the State Supreme Court. Although by this time the five had served parts of their sentences, their names were cleared. There was opposition to Morgenthau's recommendation from original prosecutor Linda Fairstein, and to Tejada's decision from the NYPD detectives. NYPD commissioner Raymond W. Kelly commissioned a report, prepared by former prosecutor Michael Armstrong and New York University official Jules Martin, which challenged the charges of police coercion and Reyes' credibility, as well as his claim of acting alone. The NYPD argued that the five had likely been involved along with Reyes.

Aftermath

Following their exoneration, in 2003, Richardson, Santana, and McCray took legal action against New York City, seeking monetary compensation for malicious prosecution, emotional distress, and racial discrimination. As of 2011, the case was not resolved. Meili survived the attack, but was left with brain damage, loss of vision, and loss of all memory of the attack. In 2003, she confirmed her identity and spoke out about the case. She also wrote *I Am the Central Park Jogger: A Story of Hope and Possibility*. Meili lectures on healing and recovery at hospitals, universities, sexual assault centers, and to victims groups.

Writing and Analysis

In addition to Meili's book, the case has been the focus of Timothy Sullivan's *Unequal Verdicts: The Central Park Jogger Trials*, and Sarah Burns's *The Central Park Five: A Chronicle of a City Wilding*. It has also become part of criminology research on crime and race in 1980s America, and a prime example of the emergence of "random violence" as examined by Joel Best in *Random Violence: How We Talk About New Crimes and New Victims*.

Aaron Winter
University of Abertay Dundee

See Also: Fear of Crime; Giuliani, Rudolph; New York City; Racial Profiling; Rape and Sexual Assault.

Further Readings

Best, Joel. *Random Violence: How We Talk About New Crimes and New Victims*. Berkeley: University of California Press, 1999.

Burns, Sarah. *The Central Park Five: A Chronicle of a City Wilding*. New York: Knopf, 2011.

Meili, Trisha. "A Story of Hope and Possibility: Trisha Meili." http://www.centralparkjogger.com (Accessed June 2012).

Meili, Trisha. *I Am the Central Park Jogger: A Story of Hope and Possibility*. New York: Scribner, 2004.

Schanberg, Sydney. "A Journey Through the Tangled Case of the Central Park Jogger." *Village Voice* (November 26, 2002). http://www.villagevoice.com/ne.ws/0247,schanberg,39999,1.html (Accessed June 2012).

Smith, Chris. "Central Park Revisited." *New York Magazine* (2002). http://nymag.com/nymetro/news/crimelaw/features/n_7836 (Accessed June 2012).

Sullivan, Timothy. *Unequal Verdicts: The Central Park Jogger Trials*. New York: Simon & Schuster, 1992.

Chicago, Illinois

One of the most important geographic locations for the study of street crime is the city of Chicago. Chicago is associated with the development of the Chicago School of Sociology and Criminology that originated in the 1920s and 1930s at the University of Chicago.

Members of the Chicago School emphasized the scientific study of society. They were noted for analyzing the relationship of social phenomena to their environment (human ecology). When studying criminal behavior, they examined the social conditions that stimulate and perpetuate street crime. In addition to the Chicago School, Chicago is also noteworthy as the location for some of the most famous examples of street crimes ever recorded in American history and for its reputation as a setting for violent and organized crime.

The Chicago School

By the time of the emergence of the Chicago School, Chicago had become an urbanized, industrial city with a population of more than two million. Urbanization, industrialization, and the rapid growth of a diverse population transformed the city, producing a variety of social problems. The Chicago School utilized the city as a natural laboratory to study these urban challenges. Among the problems studied was street crime. Criminologists at the Chicago School developed social disorganization theory to explain the relationship between Chicago's ongoing transformation and street crime.

The concept of social disorganization refers to a confusion of norms, values, and relationships at a community level. In this kind of community setting, there are weak personal ties between residents and, consequently, weak social control over the individual. Edwin Sutherland, a faculty member at the University of Chicago, developed the concept of social disorganization to explain the increase in crime rates. In *Principles of Criminology,* Sutherland observed that in preliterate and peasant societies, the social control mechanisms influencing a person were steady, harmonious, uniform, and consistent. Modern industrial societies, he claimed, were very different. An individualistic ideology, economic competition, and mobility characterized capitalistic industrial societies. These characteristics of modern industrial societies resulted in the disintegration of the social control that the family and homogenous neighborhoods had over the individual. Instead, in cities like Chicago, people are anonymous, relationships are transitory, and family bonds are weak.

Clifford Shaw and Henry D. McKay, also members of the Chicago School, applied a model of human ecology developed by their colleagues Robert Park and Ernest Burgess. This model begins with the assumption that certain neighborhoods in all cities have more crime than other parts of the city. Moreover, these areas are located near the center of the city, where businesses and industry are also found. Park and Burgess referred to this area as the Zone of Transition. Shaw and McKay emphasized that Zone of Transition neighborhoods have at least three factors in common: physical deterioration, poverty, and racial and ethnic diversity. Zone of Transition neighborhoods also usually have a highly transient population and high unemployment among residents. These social ills create a state of social disorganization.

In *Juvenile Delinquency and Urban Areas,* Shaw and McKay examined delinquency rates in Chicago. They used data from the U.S. Census and city records to demonstrate that neighborhoods with the three common factors of physical deterioration, poverty, and racial and ethnic diversity also had the highest rates of delinquency and crime. The results of their research confirmed that delinquency as well as adult street crime were caused more by social conditions—and less by explanations that placed the cause at the individual level. In further support of social disorganization as the cause of street crime, Shaw and McKay found that relatively high crime rates continued in areas characterized with the common factors of physical deterioration, poverty, and racial and ethnic diversity even when specific racial and ethnic groups moved out of the center of the city. In sum, high crime rates persist in these areas because traditional institutions no longer function locally as agencies of social control over the individual.

In addition to the focus on socially disorganized neighborhoods, the Chicago School of Criminology also developed a subcultural theory of crime to explain how social conditions create deviant values and behaviors among peers, and how these values and behaviors are passed from one generation to the next. In *The Gang: A Study of 1,313 Gangs in Chicago*, Fredric M. Thrasher, a member of the Chicago School, described gangs as "interstitial," meaning that they filled the gaps created by deteriorating neighborhoods, shifting population, and the disorganization of the slum. Thrasher maintained that since socially disorganized neighborhoods were characterized by weak families and schools, they were not effective in socializing youth. Their weakness left an opening for the development of gangs.

The subculture of gangs served as a mechanism for transferring deviant normative values and behaviors from older to younger members. The gist of subculture theory is that values and activities that violate conventional law become viewed by youth in socially disorganized neighborhoods as the positive way to believe and behave.

The contributions of the Chicago School continued to influence the work of criminologists and remain today as a lasting and significant contribution to the study of criminology. Unlike previous explanations that placed the cause of criminal behavior in biological or psychological factors, the Chicago School confirmed that factors external to the individual could go some distance in explaining street crime.

Infamous Chicago Street Crimes

Chicago is the location of some of the most well-known street crimes. Among the most infamous ones are the Chicago Race Riot of 1919, the Leopold and Loeb kidnapping and murder of Bobby Franks

in 1924, the Saint Valentine's Day Massacre of 1929, and the Police Riot at the Democratic National Convention of 1968.

The Chicago Race Riot of 1919. In the summer of 1919, approximately 25 race riots occurred in cities throughout the United States, a consequence of racial tensions following the migration of large numbers of African Americans into cities seeking employment. Labor competition and overcrowding in urban areas created resentment among racial and ethnic groups. Chicago experienced the most intense of the race riots that became known as the Red (i.e., Bloody) Summer of 1919.

The death of an African American teenager triggered the Chicago riot. Swimming in Lake Michigan, the teenager had drifted into an area customarily reserved for white swimmers. A white male threw rocks at the teenager and he drowned shortly afterward. Police refused to arrest the white man believed

A house vandalized during the Chicago race riots of 1919, previously inhabited by an African American family. The windows were broken and the front steps were torn off.

responsible for the death. Shortly after, fighting erupted between African Americans and white gangs. Violence escalated and continued for 13 days. Shootings, arson, looting, and beatings occurred resulting in the deaths of 23 blacks and 15 whites, with injuries to over 500 individuals. Afterwards, city leaders formed the Chicago Commission on Race Relations to study the reasons for the riots and determine how the city could improve race relations.

The Leopold and Loeb Murder of Bobby Franks in 1924. This murder became widely infamous for several reasons. The perpetrators were unusual in terms of their family and educational backgrounds. Nathan Leopold, 19 at the time of the crime, was the son of a millionaire and a law student at the University of Chicago. Richard Loeb, 18, was the son of a retired Sears Roebuck vice president and the youngest graduate ever of the University of Michigan. Leopold and Loeb met at the University of Chicago as teenagers and developed a close, intimate relationship. Loeb decided he wanted to commit the "perfect crime." On May 21, 1924, as 14-year-old Bobby Franks was walking home from school, Leopold and Loeb, driving a rented car, lured him into the car and killed him. They drove out of town, poured hydrochloric acid over his body, and stuffed his body into a drainage culvert. A laborer discovered the body and called police. Next to the body was a pair of horn-rimmed tortoise shell glasses belonging to Leopold. The glasses had an unusual hinge traced to a single optometrist who had only written three such prescriptions. Additional evidence tied Leopold and Loeb to the crime; during police questioning, they confessed.

The perpetrators' families hired celebrated attorney Clarence Darrow to represent the boys. Darrow decided to change their initial pleas from "not guilty" to "guilty" so that the sentencing decision could be made by a judge instead of a jury who would, in all likelihood, vote for the death penalty. Darrow's summation to the judge emphasized the young men's youth, genetic inheritances, and external influences. The judge sentenced Leopold and Loeb each to life imprisonment for the murder and 99 years each for the kidnapping.

The Saint Valentine's Day Massacre of 1929. This event refers to the murder of gangsters on February 14, 1929, on the streets of Chicago during Prohibition, an era in which gangsters controlled illegal activities such as speakeasies, breweries, and brothels. The Saint Valentine's Day Massacre involved Al Capone and George "Bugs" Moran, leaders of two rival Chicago gangs.

Capone placed his associate Jack "Machine Gun" McGurn in charge of organizing the assassination of Moran and his gang. He hired gunmen and lookouts, and he obtained a stolen police car and two police uniforms. McGurn contacted a local booze hijacker to contact Moran to tell him that he had obtained a shipment of whiskey that he was willing to sell at a reasonable price. Moran agreed to meet him the next morning—February 14—at his garage. The next morning, gunmen climbed into the stolen police car, two dressed in police uniforms. The seven Moran men inside the garage thought the men who entered were police and dropped their weapons and faced the wall. The gunmen then opened fire, killing them. However, Capone did not succeed in killing Moran. When Moran arrived at the garage, he noticed the police car and stayed away from the building. While police believed Capone was involved in the murders, he was living in Miami at the time and had an airtight alibi. Police charged McGurn but later dropped the charges because of a lack of evidence. No one was ever tried or convicted for the murders.

The Police Riot at the Democratic National Convention of 1968. This convention was held during a year in which American society had experienced wide violence and civil unrest. President Lyndon Johnson had decided not to seek a second term because of the turmoil in society created by American involvement in the Vietnam War. In addition, in April, race riots had erupted in more than 100 cities, including Chicago, following the assassination of Dr. Martin Luther King, Jr. In June, Senator Robert F. Kennedy, a Democratic presidential contender, was shot and killed in California after winning that state's primary election. Against this background, the Democratic National Convention convened in Chicago August 26–29 to select the Democratic nominee for president of the United States.

Several months prior to the convention, antiwar leaders met to plan a protest march at the convention. Among the groups that would attend were the Students for a Democratic Society, the National Mobilization Committee to End the War in Vietnam, and the Yippie! movement. In the end, more than

10,000 demonstrators gathered in Chicago. The violence began on Sunday, August 25. City officials had denied the request by protesters for permits to sleep in Lincoln Park and demonstrate outside the convention site. Police used tear gas and billy clubs to remove the protesters from Lincoln Park. On Wednesday, August 28, the worst confrontation between protesters and police occurred. In the end, reports indicated that police made close to 600 arrests while over 1,000 protesters were injured.

Eight protest leaders, dubbed the Chicago Eight, stood trial under provisions of the 1968 Civil Rights Act, which made it a federal crime to cross state lines to incite a riot. The defendants disrupted the trial; the judge ordered one of the defendants—Bobby Seale—to be gagged and chained to his chair because of his outbursts. Ultimately the judge severed Seale's trial from the others and sentenced him to four years in prison for contempt of court. The jury acquitted two of the defendants and found the remaining five guilty of crossing state lines with intent to incite a riot. However, an appeal overturned all charges. A federal commission, moreover, later characterized the disorder in the streets around the convention as "a police riot."

Homicide in Chicago

Chicago is often associated with high levels of violent crime, especially homicide. In 1930, the Federal Bureau of Investigation (FBI) began managing the Uniform Crime Reports (UCR) program, collecting data from 400 cities including Chicago. The UCR includes data on murder and manslaughter among its crime statistics. Prior to 1930, available data on homicide in Chicago comes from an analysis of police records conducted at Northwestern University School of Law. The Chicago Historical Homicide Project examined police records of more than 11,000 homicides during 1870-1930. The UCR program and the Chicago Historical Homicide Project make it possible to examine homicide rates in Chicago from 1870 to date.

The homicide rate is expressed as the rate per 100,000 residents. In 1870, the homicide rate in Chicago was 2.6 per 100,000 residents. Like other urban areas, the rate climbed steadily until by 1920 it was 10.5 per 100,000 residents; by 1930 the homicide rate was 14.6 per 100,000 residents. The large upswing in homicides may be due to several factors: the tremendous growth in population, the effects of Prohibition,

and the prevalence of organized crime. Nevertheless, even when Prohibition ended in 1933, homicide rates remained high, perhaps as a consequence of the Great Depression. By 1940, however, the homicide rate had dropped to 7.1 per 100,000 residents and in 1950 the rate was 7.9 per 100,000 residents.

Beginning in the 1960s, again similar to other large cities, Chicago experienced a new, major rise in violent crime, reflected in part by the homicide rate. In 1960, the homicide rate was 10.3 per 100,000 residents; by 1970 it was 24.0. This increase is attributed to a time of much political and social conflict in the United States about race relations and the war in Vietnam. In the 1980s, violent crime was linked with illegal drugs. By 1980, the homicide rate in Chicago had climbed to 28.7 and by 1990 the rate was 32.9.

In 2000, Chicago again mirrored the violent crime rate trends of other large cities with a significant decline in the homicide rate. It fell to 22.1 per 100,000 residents in 2000 and this decline continued to 2010 with a decline to 15.2 per 100,000 residents. Researchers point to community policing, tougher sentencing laws—and most controversially, the role of legalized abortion—as the factors accounting for the decline in violent crime.

Law enforcement in Chicago has fielded a range of responses to deter and contain the street crime rise since 2000. For instance, the Special Operations Section was created to break up gang and organized crime activities. However, it was disbanded in 2007 after a storm of allegations of corruption and brutality. A similar fate befell two subsequent programs—the Targeted Response Unit and the Mobile Strike Force—in 2011. In the most recent anti-gang and antiviolent crime campaign, Chicago police superintendent Garry McCarthy and Mayor Rahm Emanuel in 2012 unveiled a type of hot spot enforcement plan, with concentrated efforts in two districts—Englewood on the South Side, and Harrison on the West Side—where police say nearly one-quarter of all Chicago's 2011 murders and shootings took place.

Patricia E. Erickson
Canisius College

See Also: Gangs (Street); Guns and Weapons; History of Street Crime in America; Immigrant Neighborhoods; Juvenile Offending; Mobs and Riots; Organized Crime and Violence; Racial Assault; Urbanization.

Further Readings

Bienen, Leigh B. and Brandon Rottinghaus. "Learning From the Past, Living in the Present: Understanding Homicide in Chicago, 1870–1930." *Journal of Criminal Law & Criminology*, v.92/3–4 (2002).

Farber, David. *Chicago '68.* Chicago: University of Chicago Press, 1994.

Fentress, James. *Eminent Gangsters: Immigrants and the Birth of Organized Crime in America.* Lanham, MD: University Press of America, 2010.

Higdon, Hal. *Leopold & Loeb: The Crime of the Century.* Champaign, IL: University of Illinois Press, 1999.

McWhirter, Cameron. *Red Summer: The Summer of 1919 and the Awakening of Black America.* New York: Henry Holt, 2011.

Shaw, Clifford R. and Henry D. McKay. *Juvenile Delinquency and Urban Areas.* Chicago: University of Chicago Press, 1942.

Thrasher, Frederic M. *The Gang: A Study of 1,313 Gangs in Chicago.* Chicago: University of Chicago Press, 1927.

Child Molesters

A child molester is a type of sex offender who victimizes children. While often used interchangeably, the terms *child molester* and *pedophile* are two distinct types of sex offenders. Child molesters are classified as pedophiles only when they are diagnosed using the American Psychological Association's *Diagnostic and Statistical Manual of Mental Disorders.* Though characteristics of child molesters vary, general patterns exist: most are white, most are male, and their ages range from teens to middle-age. There are female child molesters, although based on official statistics they are vastly fewer in number that male child molesters. Juveniles are also perpetrators of child sexual abuse.

Evolution of the Criminal

Community members did not always perceive child molesters as the greatest social or criminal threat. Philip Jenkins, the author of *Moral Panic: Changing Concepts of the Child Molester in Modern America*, highlights the role of the media in constructing an image of the child molester as an imminent danger to society, especially a threat to children.

Public reaction to highly publicized sex crimes and resulting government legislation played key roles in reshaping comprehension of the child molester in modern America. Today, the media still play a prominent role in constructing child molesters and their crimes. This perceived threat revolves around community members' concerns and fear about child molesters' access to children. This fear stems from "stranger danger," or the perception that child molesters are more likely to commit sex crimes against unknown victims, even though family members and acquaintances are more likely to be the perpetrators of child sexual abuse than strangers.

Sex Crimes Against Youth

According to statistics from the National Incident Based Reporting System, of all the sexual assaults reported to the police between 1991 and 1996, approximately 67 percent of the victims were 17 years of age or younger. Approximately 46 percent were victims of rape, 79 percent victims of forced sodomy, 75 percent victims of sexual assault with an object, and 84 percent victims of forced fondling.

Of these sex crimes, about 87 percent were committed by someone the victim knew: family members (27 percent) or acquaintances (60 percent). Fourteen percent were committed by strangers. Approximately 24 percent of offenders were arrested for these sex crimes and overall 42 percent were cleared by arrest or by exceptional means. Patterns show that the younger the victim is, the less likely the chance of an arrest.

In general, recording an accurate number of sex crimes committed against children is difficult. This crime type is not included in all national data collection instruments. Also, due to the nature of the crime itself, children may not report; for example, children may be too young to talk, may not realize they are being victimized, or do not know how to report their victimization.

Additionally, some street crimes—assault, rape, trafficking—are linked to child molestation cases, although no hard statistics are kept on such association.

Convicted Molesters and the Community

Federal and state lawmakers implemented sex offender laws in an attempt to better inform and protect community members and children and to aid law enforcement in their mission of public safety. Through registration and notification laws, the public can access an online database to locate sex offenders in their community. Residency restriction laws limiting how close sex offenders can live in proximity to where children congregate, such as schools and parks, were designed to address child molesters' access to potential victims and prevent sex crime recidivism, or the commission of another sex crime against a child.

Approximately 30 states have residency restrictions. Restricted distances vary by state and range from 500 to 2,500 feet. All individuals convicted of child molestation are required by law to comply with residency restrictions. To date there is a lack of scientific support that registration or residency restriction laws are meeting their public safety mission.

Research shows that registration and notification laws do increase the speed at which sex offenders are arrested, but the laws also have unintended consequences. Individuals released from prison with sex crime convictions have extreme difficulty finding employment and housing due to the stigma of the criminal label and the stigma attached to their status of sex offender. Data supports that due to these reintegration problems, sex offenders are more likely to commit non-sex crimes, like property crimes, after release from prison in order to survive on the "outside." There has also been an increase in the number of homeless sex offenders. This creates obstacles for law enforcement officials that monitor sex offenders in the community, and may tend to increase the incidence of certain types of street crimes.

Conclusion

Today there is an ongoing struggle to manage child molesters in the community in order to divert additional sex crimes against youth. The damage inflicted by child molestation has lifelong consequences for victims. One avenue of promise is the continued development of sex offender treatment, such as cognitive-behavioral therapy, that develops coping mechanisms and changes deviant patterns of thinking, with the goal of decreasing recidivism and increasing prosocial and life skills. Community management strategies, such as the containment model where law enforcement officials, probation or parole officers, and treatment providers work together to manage sex offenders in the community, shows promise to reduce recidivism and meet the needs of sex offenders struggling to reintegrate.

Kristen Budd
Miami University of Ohio

See Also: Children as Victims; Exposure, Indecent; Homelessness; Kidnapping; Rape and Sexual Assault; Sex Crimes; Sting Operations.

Further Readings

Federal Bureau of Investigation. "Crimes Against Children" 2012. http://www.fbi.gov/about-us/investigate/vc_majorthefts/cac (Accessed June 2012).

Jenkins, Philip. *Moral Panic: Changing Concepts of the Child Molester in Modern America*. New Haven, CT: Yale University Press, 1998.

O'Connor, Tom and William Carson. "Understanding the Psychology of Child Molesters: A Key to Getting Confessions." *Police Chief*, v.72/12 (2005).

Snyder, Howard, N. "Sexual Assault of Young Children as Reported to Law Enforcement: Victim, Incident, and Offender Characteristics." Washington, DC: Bureau of Justice Statistics, 2000.

Wooden, Kenneth, Rosemary Webb, and Jennifer Mitchell. 2012. "A Profile of a Child Molester." http://www.childluresprevention.com/pdf/Profile-of-Molester.pdf (Accessed June 2012).

Children, Commercial Sexual Exploitation of

The commercial sexual exploitation of children (CSEC) is the sexual exploitation of children for financial gain, that is, pornography, prostitution, child sex trafficking, and child sex tourism. It occurs when a person buys, sells, or trades sexual activity or a sexually explicit performance involving a person under the age of 18. Therefore, CSEC includes employing or utilizing minors as prostitutes and/or exotic dancers/models, as well as using children under the age of 18 in sexually explicit images and shows. Street-level CSEC primarily involves prostitution. In the majority of these cases, adults purchase sex from a child in exchange for money or other valued goods.

Some believe that the term child prostitute *carries problematic connotations, failing to differentiate that children cannot be expected to make informed choices. The act of prostituting a child is sometimes carried out by another party.*

CSEC as a Social Problem

While the involvement of children in commercial sexual activities is not a new social problem, the conceptualization of prostituted children as victims of CSEC is new. Historically, juveniles involved in prostitution have been viewed, processed, and treated as criminals. Over the past dozen years, however, there has been an effort to create a paradigm shift in the way that society and the criminal justice system view prostituted youth. Instead of treating youth prostitutes as criminal offenders, child and victim activists argue that prostituted youth should be viewed and treated as victims of sexual exploitation. These activists have pushed for legislative changes that define prostituted youth as victims, instead of offenders. These efforts have resulted in the social construction of a new social problem—the commercial sexual exploitation of children.

The roots of this paradigm shift in the United States have been traced back to the enactment of the Victims of Trafficking and Violence Protection Act (TVPA) in 2000. In response to growing awareness of the nature and scope of human trafficking, the TVPA was the first antitrafficking legislation that was designed "to ensure just and effective punishment of traffickers and to protect their victims" (22 U.S.C. §§ 7101–7110). Following guidelines set out in the 2000 United Nations Protocol to Prevent, Suppress, and Punish Trafficking in Persons, the TVPA specifies that one "severe form of trafficking in persons" involves "the recruitment, harboring, transportation, provision, or obtaining of a person for the purpose of a commercial sex act [sex trafficking]... in which the commercial sex act is induced by force, fraud, or coercion, or in which the person induced to perform such act has not attained 18 years of age" (114 STAT 1470). Although the primary purpose of the TVPA was to combat international human trafficking, including the forced prostitution of children, it played a major role in starting a discussion about commercial sexual exploitation of children.

Some have argued that since all juveniles involved in prostitution are induced to engage in commercial sex by "pimps" or "johns," all minors involved in commercial sex can be considered victims of sex trafficking under the TVPA. Regardless of whether or not force, fraud, or coercion was used, it is their age that classifies prostituted youth as sex trafficking victims. Thus, according to this view, the commercial sexual exploitation of children is considered to be a "severe form of trafficking in persons," as defined by the TVPA. There are, however, opponents of this view who argue that not all juveniles involved in prostitution are induced to engage in sex in exchange for money. These opponents suggest that for some juveniles, prostitution is a choice; if no one, such as a pimp, directly influenced a juvenile's decision to trade sex for money or anything of value, then the juvenile should not be considered a trafficking victim. As such, these opponents caution against conflating juvenile prostitution, CSEC, and sex trafficking; they argue that while child sex trafficking is a form of CSEC, not all CSEC cases involve sex trafficking.

Nature and Extent of CSEC

In response to the emergence of CSEC as a social problem, researchers and social service organizations have been drawing more attention to concerns about juveniles involved in prostitution. Due to the underground nature of CSEC, however, researchers have been unable to come up with any scientifically valid national estimates of the number of children involved in prostitution in the United States, with estimates ranging from 1,400 to 2.4 million. Some scholars suggest that CSEC youth are more likely to be found in convention cities and tourist destinations with thriving adult entertainment venues and adult prostitution markets. In fact, data from Federal Bureau of Investigation (FBI) investigations indicates that the following 14 cities have the highest incidence of CSEC in the United States: Atlanta, Chicago, Dallas, Detroit, Las Vegas, Los Angeles, Miami, Minneapolis, New York, San Diego, San Francisco, St. Louis, Tampa, and Washington, D.C.

While the full extent of the problem is unknown, Richard Estes and Neil Weiner's national CSEC study and Ric Curtis and colleagues' study of CSEC in New York provide preliminary data on the risk factors and pathways into CSEC. While some findings indicate that the average age of entry into CSEC is 15 for both boys and girls, other estimates suggest that the average age of entry is 11–13 for boys and 12–14 for girls. Researchers agree, however, that the children who are most at risk of CSEC in the United States are homeless and runaway youth. Other risk factors for CSEC include poverty, family dysfunction, physical and/or sexual abuse, parental substance abuse, youth substance abuse, truancy, and school failure.

While some children are kidnapped and forced to work in the commercial sex industry, researchers believe these cases account for only a small proportion of all CSEC cases in the United States. Another small percentage of commercially sexually exploited children are adolescents from less developed countries and/or impoverished areas who are sold to pimps or traffickers by their parents. In some cases, the parents knowingly sell their children to traffickers; however, in other cases, the parents send their child to the United States with a relative or family friend, under the false promise that the relative or friend will provide a better life for their child in the United States.

In the United States, however, the majority of commercially sexually exploited children are children who were sexually abused at home by a family member or friend. For some, this sexual abuse is videotaped and/or photographed and distributed over the Internet for profit. There are also cases where parent(s) or family member(s) arrange or allow another person to have sex with the child in exchange for money, rent, food, drugs, etc. Other CSEC youth are those who have run away from an abusive and/or dysfunctional home environment; these youth often engage in "survival sex" while living on the streets and/or end up being exploited by pimps.

Pimps and CSEC

Some CSEC youth first engage in prostitution in response to being approached by a stranger who saw them on the street and offered to help them out (e.g., give them some money and/or a place to stay) in exchange for sex. Other CSEC youth are recruited by "boyfriends" or pimps. The majority of the CSEC youth, however, are recruited by "friends," or same-age peers, who are already involved in prostitution; some of these "friends" recruit other youth into prostitution for pimps, while others introduce the youth to prostitution and tell them where and how to engage in prostitution in order to help them survive on the streets. Also, while over half of CSEC youth work on the streets, there is a current trend toward using the Internet to set up "dates" or appointments to meet customers.

While research clearly indicates that girls are more likely than boys to become involved with a pimp, it is unclear what percentage of CSEC girls end up under the control of a pimp, with recent estimates varying from 16 percent, to 40 percent, to 75 percent. Often targeting homeless and runaway youth, many pimps use seduction and deception to recruit vulnerable young girls into the sex trade. In addition to recruiting girls themselves, pimps also send peer recruiters, who are young girls already working for them, to bus stops, train stations, shopping and tourist locations, and areas near youth service centers to look for vulnerable young girls to recruit. Pimps befriend the young girls, buy them clothes and jewelry, take them out to eat, buy them drugs, and offer to provide them with protection and a place to stay. While the girls may be impressed and flattered by this attention, thinking that this older man is their boyfriend, the pimp soon asks them to trade sex for money in order to pay him back or to do him a favor. By promising to love and protect them, pimps are able to convince many girls that working for them is a better alternative to trying to survive on the streets alone.

Although a small proportion of CSEC youth believe there are benefits to being with a pimp (i.e., protector and father figure), most have negative experiences with their pimp. For instance, while the majority of CSEC youth currently earn between $100 and $400 per night, the pimp-involved CSEC youth rarely get to keep any of that money as their pimps take most, if not all, of the money that they earn. Most pimp-involved CSEC youth also experience severe and horrific violence at the hands of their pimp.

Violence is a common occurrence for most CSEC youth, especially for those who work the streets. In addition to violence from pimps, CSEC youth also experience violence from customers. Their experiences with violent customers include being raped, beaten, kidnapped and held hostage. For the CSEC youth who work the streets, there are also violent encounters with other CSEC youth as well as older sex workers. The violence between CSEC youth, including physical attacks and robberies, may occur as a result of turf disputes and arguments over stealing customers. Similarly, the older sex workers who work well-known prostitution tracks may use violence to force out new CSEC youth who try to work the same tracks.

Prevention and Intervention

As researchers have been uncovering the nature and extent of the commercial sexual exploitation of children, advocacy groups have been working to develop prevention and intervention programs to help CSEC youth and those at risk for CSEC. A number of nonprofit organizations have been established to help provide outreach services to youth who may be at risk for CSEC and to help CSEC youth exit "the life." Working with a number of community partners, these nonprofit agencies also have helped raise awareness about CSEC and lobby for social and legal changes.

In order to improve the criminal justice system's response to CSEC, state and local CSEC task forces have been created. For example, the Federal Bureau of Investigation has established multiagency task forces to coordinate the response to CSEC among local police departments as well as state and federal agencies. Also, as a part of the effort to improve the criminal justice system's ability to detect, prosecute,

and punish sex trafficking offenders, activists have lobbied for changes in state laws that would increase penalties for the customers, pimps, and traffickers, while also recognizing CSEC youth as victims instead of offenders. These efforts have been met with some success. For example, in 2011, Georgia passed a law that defines commercially sexually exploited children as victims of crime, provides an affirmative defense for sex crimes for trafficking victims when coercion or deception was used to induce them to perform the act, and mandates training to improve law enforcement's response and treatment of trafficking victims.

Statistical compilation of the first several years since the passage of TVPA show some movement toward the detection and interdiction of higher-level forms of CSEC. In a study by the Justice Policy Center of the Urban League, using data on federal prosecution of CSEC defendants, this trend is reflected in the drop of the proportion of CSEC crime cases that were strictly pornography-related. Child pornography defendants dropped from 82 percent of CSEC defendants in 1998 to 72 percent in 2005. Child prostitution/sex trafficking defendants expanded from less than 10 percent of defendants in 1998 to 18 percent in 2005. Defendants charged with sexual exploitation of children made up about 8 percent of CSEC defendants in 1998, expanding to 10 percent in 2005. During the period of this study (1998–2005) the total number of federal CSEC prosecutions overall increased threefold nationally.

While these prevention and intervention efforts have improved the legal and societal response to CSEC cases, there is no evidence to suggest that these efforts have actually reduced the incidence of CSEC in the United States. There also is little reason to expect these efforts to reduce the incidence of CSEC in the United States. That is, in order to reduce CSEC, efforts must also address the demand that drives CSEC. Unfortunately, very little is known about the customers, or "johns," who drive the demand for CSEC youth. Thus, future research and prevention efforts must focus on those who buy sex from children. Also, since our current knowledge about CSEC youth is based upon the first generation of research studies on this topic, additional research is needed on CSEC youth in the United States

Jennifer McMahon-Howard
Kennesaw State University

See Also: Children as Victims; Homelessness; "Johns"; Juvenile Offending; Peep Shows; Pimp; Prostitute/Streetwalker; Prostitution, Houses of; Sex Crimes; Truancy.

Further Readings
Adelson, Wendy J. "Child Prostitute or Victim of Trafficking?" *University of St. Thomas Law Journal,* v.6/1 (2008).
Curtis, Ric, Karen Terry, Meredith Dank, Kirk Dombrowski, and Bilal Khan. *The CSEC Population in New York City: Size, Characteristics, and Needs. Vol 1 in Commercial Sexual Exploitation of Children in New York City.* New York: John Jay College, 2008.
Estes, Richard J. and Neil Alan Weiner. *The Commercial Sexual Exploitation of Children in the U.S., Canada, and Mexico.* Philadelphia: University of Pennsylvania, 2001.
Mitchell, Kimberly J., David Finkelhor, and Janis Wolak. "Conceptualizing Juvenile Prostitution as Child Maltreatment: Findings From the National Juvenile Prostitution Study." *Child Maltreatment,* v.15/1 (2010).
Urban Institute. *An Analysis of Federally Prosecuted CSEC Cases Since the Passage of the Victims of Trafficking and Violence Protection Act of 2000.* Washington, DC: Urban Institute Justice Policy Center, 2008.
U.S. Congress. "Victims of Trafficking and Violence Protection Act of 2000, Public Law No. 106-386, 114 Stat. 1464 (22 U.S.C. §§ 7101-7110)." U.S. Department of State. http://www.state.gov/j/tip/laws/61124.htm (Accessed May 2012).

Children as Victims

Children are vulnerable to various forms of violence, including violent offenses such as murder, physical assault, rape, and robbery; property offenses, such as larceny-theft, burglary, and auto theft; abuse and neglect; commercial sexual exploitation; and online victimization. These crimes have devastating impact on children in both the short and long term. In the long term, violent and sexual victimization at a young age often contribute to an intergenerational cycle of violence: these child victims are likely to become either victims or perpetrators of adult violence and abuse.

Categorizing the Offenses

Sociologists David Finkelhor and Jennifer Dzuiba-Leatherman grouped child victims into three categories: the pandemic, which include sibling assaults that affect a large number of children; the acute, which include physical assaults that are less frequent yet significant in terms of the percentage affected; and the extraordinary, such as homicide, which affects a small number of children.

The Crimes Against Children Research Center identifies violence against children into criminal acts defined by law (sexual assault, abduction, theft, robbery, and aggravated assault against children); child abuse (physical, sexual, and emotional abuse; and child neglect); child-on-child violence (peer and sibling assaults); and indirect victimization (children witnessing violence at home or against family members, classmates, or friends). The Federal Bureau of Investigation's (FBI) Supplementary Homicide Reports for 1980 and 1997 listed homicide as the third-leading cause of death for children between the ages of 5 and 14.

According to the FBI Uniform Crime Reports (UCR), in 2010 there were 1,277 juvenile (under the age of 18) murder victims, of whom 24.5 percent were between 1 and 4 years of age. Most of these victims were male; females represented about 23 percent of the victims. The National Crime Victimization Survey (NCVS) for 2010, which generates victimization rates for various demographic groups, reported that children between the ages of 12 and 14 experienced simple assaults, rapes, and sexual assaults at rates higher than older age groups. A 2008 National Survey of Children's Exposure to Violence documented the incidence and prevalence of children exposed to violence, including school violence and threats, Internet victimization, and street crimes. The report found that one-half of the children surveyed were victims of assault in the past year, and one in four (24.6 percent) were victims of robbery, vandalism, or theft.

As there is no single source that provides comprehensive data, it is difficult to gauge the complete picture. For example, the UCR includes data on homicide, arson, commercial crimes, and crimes against children under age 12, while the NCVS excludes such data. Furthermore, the UCR compiles data on crimes reported to law enforcement, while NCVS collects data on many unreported crimes. In addition, children exposed to violence, regardless of the type of crime, experience long-term consequences that may have multiplier effects. As a result, researchers have focused on various forms of child victimization using multiple sources of data.

Property Crimes

Juveniles are much more likely to be victims of property crimes than other crimes, yet research in this area is scant. Finkelhor and Richard Ormrod studied juvenile property victimization and its specific features. Between 1996 and 1997, they found, one in six juveniles were victims of property crimes; the rates were highest among African American juveniles living in urban areas. The majority of property crimes occur at schools, followed by the victims' residence or neighborhood. The most common items stolen were backpacks, electronics, and clothes.

Victimizations involving burglaries and auto theft make up less than 5 percent of crimes against juveniles. In addition to the FBI data, the NCVS and the National Incident-Based Reporting System (NIBRS) document property victimization. Although specific studies on the impact of property crime on young children have not been conducted, studies on adult victims indicate that they experience fear, anxiety, hostility, and sleep deprivation. As the incidence of property victimization is much higher among young people, one expects that children face similar symptoms but at much higher levels and likely with more profound impact.

Physical Abuse and Neglect

In 2007, approximately 62 percent of referrals of child abuse and/or neglect were investigated by child protective services. About 25 percent (794,000) of the investigations resulted in the determination that at least one child had been a victim of abuse or neglect. Researchers have tried to find the connection between childhood maltreatment and later crime victimization.

Sociologists J. K. McIntyre and C. S. Widom reported that the relationship between childhood maltreatment and later victimization is not direct but rather mediated through behaviors that are common among children of abuse and neglect. These behaviors include running away,

homelessness, prostitution, substance abuse, and delinquency. Abused and neglected children are not only at high risk for physical and sexual assault, but also face death. The Children's Bureau's National Child Abuse and Neglect Data System (NCANDS) report, *Child Maltreatment 2009*, documents 1,770 child fatalities. Of these deaths, children less than 1 year old accounted for 46.2 percent of all child fatalities; children younger than 4 years represented 80.8 percent of all child fatalities.

Young children are most vulnerable because of their size, their dependence on adults, and their inability to defend themselves. NCANDS differentiates fatalities resulting from repeated abuse (e.g., battered child) and those resulting from a single impulsive act (e.g., drowning, suffocation, shaking the baby). Fatal neglect is identified as either chronic neglect or acute neglect. When a child is extremely malnourished, it is considered chronic neglect, whereas drowning in the bathtub due to neglect is acute neglect. In addition, there are a small number of child fatalities that occur due to medical neglect (e.g., failure to provide appropriate health care).

The 2009 NCANDS data on child fatalities reported neglect in 35.5 percent of cases, followed by physical abuse in 23.2 percent of cases, and medical neglect in 1.8 percent of fatalities. Although there is no single profile of perpetrators of these crimes, studies have indicated that young adults in their mid-20s, who lack a high school education, have lower socioeconomic status, and have mental disorders (e.g., depression) are more likely to abuse children. Fathers and boyfriends of mothers are the likely perpetrators in abuse fatalities, whereas mothers are more often the perpetrators in neglect fatalities. To improve the reporting, investigation, and prevention of child fatalities, states have developed multidisciplinary and multiagency child fatality review teams. Federal legislation, specifically the Child Abuse Prevention and Treatment Act (CAPTA), requires states to include child death reports (CDR) in their program plan.

Commercial Sexual Exploitation

Children are at high risk for commercial sexual exploitation. Researchers have reported that approximately 200,000 to 300,000 individuals in the United States are at risk for commercial sexual exploitation of children (CSEC). Children are often lured into the trade in exchange for promises of a better life in the form of food, shelter, clothing, money, employment, or a better education, either for the child or other family members. According to the National Center for Missing and Exploited Children (NCMEC), children are forced into participating in child pornography, prostitution, sex tourism, and extrafamilial molestation of children.

Children can also receive obscene unsolicited materials via the mail, or can be subject to online enticement. The organization to End Child Prostitution in Asian Tourism (ECPAT) includes pedophilia, child marriages, and forced marriages under the definition of CSEC.

These crimes can occur in the streets or indoors at bars, brothels, restaurants, clubs, or hotels. The recruiters target poor families, homeless, runaways, refugees, addicts, and other vulnerable children. The U.S. Department of Justice classifies the players into seven types: investors/arrangers, recruiters, transporters, purveyors of documents, informers, debt collectors, and money movers. Investors provide money for the operations. Recruiters work with families offering false promises of hope. Transporters are in charge of moving the children from one destination to the other. Purveyors of documents create false identity documents. Informers gather information about law enforcement, border security, and so forth, for the transporters. Debt collectors charge trafficking fees for children arriving at their final destination. Money movers serve as money launderers.

An AMBER Alert highway sign alerts motorists to a suspected child abduction in Northern California. AMBER is an acronym for America's Missing: Broadcasting Emergency Response, but was originally named for Amber Hagerman, a 9-year-old child who was abducted and murdered in Arlington, Texas, in 1996.

Nonfamily Child Abductions

Child abductions are classified into abductions by family members and abductions by nonfamily members. Research has shown that almost half of abducted children are sexually assaulted. Although younger children are at greater risk of family abductions, older children are more likely to be abducted by nonfamily members and face secondary victimization.

Criminologists have categorized secondary victimization as physical assault or attempted physical assault, sexual assault or attempted sexual assault, and robbery or attempted robbery. Children of 7 to 12 years are at a higher risk of all types of secondary victimization than those 6 years old and younger. With regard to gender, girls are more likely to face sexual assault as a secondary victimization than boys, whereas boys encounter more physical assaults than girls. This theory applies routine activity and lifestyle theories to explain the re-victimization of children who were abducted. The routine activity theory posits that the likelihood of victimization depends on the exposure to a motivated offender, the availability of suitable victims, and the lack of guardians.

Online Victimization

Researchers Finkelhor et al. surveyed three specific types of online victimization: sexual solicitation, unwanted exposure to sexual materials, and harassment. One in five study subjects reported unwanted sexual solicitation; two-thirds of victims were female; and three-quarters of the victims were between the ages of 14 and 17. Children between the ages of 10 and 13 represented one-quarter of the victims.

Regarding unwanted exposure, almost 25 percent of children surveyed reported that they received such messages or materials. Boys are victims of unwanted exposure to sexual materials at a slightly higher rate than girls. About 6 percent of children surveyed received harassing messages in the form of threats, rumors, or other offensive behaviors. In recent years, sexual predators have used the Internet to target and make contact with young children. The FBI and local law enforcement agencies have special Internet crime units to investigate such crimes. In addition, the NCMEC Cyber-TipLine also conducts investigations of online victimization of children.

Conclusion

Research on child victimization has primarily focused on a specific type or a relatively few types of victimization. In the opinion of several scholars, these studies underestimate children's exposure to different types of victimization. For example, property crimes against children and nonforcible sex crimes are often not included.

In addition to underestimating the nature and extent of child victimization, the fragmented approach fails to show the interrelations among various forms of victimization. For example, bullying may involve physical assault, destruction of property, and sexual harassment. The Developmental Victimization Survey by Finkelhor et al. incorporated a comprehensive juvenile victimization questionnaire covering a wide range of victimizations, including different assaults with or without weapons, assaults with injuries and without, genital assaults, kidnappings, dating violence with or without injury, child maltreatment (e.g., physical abuse, sexual abuse, emotional abuse, neglect, family abduction, or custodial interference), sexual victimization (e.g., sexual assault, rape, sexual exposure, sexual harassment), property victimization (e.g., robbery, vandalism, theft), and bullying or teasing. Studies such as these will help us achieve a more comprehensive understanding of the nature, extent, and the relationships among various forms of victimization.

Sesha Kethineni
Illinois State University

See Also: Child Molesters; Children, Commercial Sexual Exploitation of; Kidnapping; Rape and Sexual Assault; Routine Activity Theory; Sex Crimes; Theft and Larceny; Truancy.

Further Readings

Albanese, Jay. *Commercial Exploitation of Children: What Do We Know and What Do We Do About it?* Washington, DC: National Institute of Justice, 2007.

Best, Joel. *Threatened Children: Rhetoric and Concern About Child-Victims.* Chicago: University of Chicago Press, 1993.

Finkelhor, David, Heather Turner, Richard Ormrod, Sherry Hamby, and Kristen Kracke. *Children's Exposure to Violence: A Comprehensive National*

Survey. Washington, DC: U.S. Department of Justice, Juvenile Justice Bulletin, 2009.

National Center for Victims of Crime. "Child Victimization." 2011. http://www.ncvc.org/ncvc/main.aspx?dbName=DocumentViewer&DocumentID=38709 (Accessed May 2011).

Schwartz, Lita Linzer and Natalie K. Isser. *Endangered Children: Homicide and Other Crimes.* 2nd ed. Boca Raton, FL: CRC Press, 2011.

Cincinnati, Ohio

While the United States has experienced an overall reduction in crime, some municipalities continue to address unsettling conditions and street crime problems. In recent years, Cincinnati has suffered from job and population losses, as well as increasing poverty.

Challenges and History

In 2010, the U.S. Census Bureau reported that Cincinnati's population was 296,943, a 10.4 percent decrease from 2000. More notably, Cincinnati has experienced four riots since 1967, three of them race-related; the city has struggled with racial and cultural tensions across the city. Shortly after the riots, Cincinnati had an increase in reported violent and property crimes. For example, during 2001–2006, Cincinnati averaged 73.3 homicides a year, which was a dramatic increase from the 41.3 homicides that the city averaged yearly before 2001.

More recently, in comparison to other cities with populations between 250,000 and 499,999, Cincinnati had the third-highest property crime rate and the eighth-highest violent crime rate in the United States. Despite spikes in crime, the Uniform Crime Reports (UCR) of the U.S. Department of Justice highlights a fairly steady decline overall in violent and property crimes in Cincinnati, similar to national trends.

Situated on the Ohio River, Cincinnati is the third largest city in the state of Ohio and is the seat of Hamilton County. During the early 19th century, Cincinnati quickly established itself as a hub of industry and trade, being labeled the Queen City of the West. Spurred by steamboat trade on the Ohio River, entrepreneurs built the Miami and Erie Canal, connecting to the booming Erie Canal (out of New York City) at its Toledo, Ohio, juncture with Lake Erie, leading to faster population growth and development of Cincinnati. By the mid-19th century, population growth slowed and there was less reliance on river and canal trade—but the railroad system largely took up the slack. Today, the central location of Cincinnati to a major portion of America's population makes it a prime location for shipping and manufacturing businesses, as well as a key hub for commuters from Kentucky and southeast Indiana.

Trends in Street Crime

A reasonably accurate comprehension of street crime in Cincinnati is derived from those crimes that are reported to local police agency officials. These data are voluntarily provided to the Federal Bureau of Investigation (FBI), which is compiled into the national Uniform Crime Reports (UCR). The UCR provides annual crime rates and total counts for violent crimes—counting murder, nonnegligent manslaughter, robbery, forcible rape, and aggravated assault—and property crimes, including burglary, larceny-theft, motor vehicle theft, and arson.

The UCR only captures data on reported crimes. Most reported figures of street crime come from the UCR and/or law enforcement agencies as they tend to focus on major and some minor forms of street crime. The following figures were extracted from the UCR data for Cincinnati, Ohio, as provided to the FBI by the Cincinnati Police Department.

Crime across the United States has been in decline since the early 1990s. Prior to the decline, violent crime showed a rise throughout the 1980s, with the peak generally seen in the early 1990s. As of 2010, the violent crime rate was 403.6 reported offenses per 100,000 population, which is significantly lower than the rate of 747.1 in 1993. Similarly, the rate of property crime has steadily dropped since 1992. According to UCR national figures, the property crime rate in 2010 was 2,941.9 reported offenses per 100,000 population, far lower than the rate of 4,903.7 in 1992.

In a parallel trend with the U.S. rates, the reported crime rates for Cincinnati reflect the increase in violent crime through the late 1980s and the decrease in the mid-1990s. In 1985, Cincinnati's violent crime rate was 884.7 reported offenses per 100,000 population. By 1991, the violent crime rate peaked at 1,578.2 and dropped to 840.1 reported offenses per 100,000 population by 2000. Similarly, in 1985, Cincinnati's property crime rate was 6,822.8 and by 1991 it reached a high of 8,144.1 reported offenses per 100,000. By 2000, Cincinnati's property crime rate dropped to 5,864.7 per 100,000.

Spike From 2001 to 2002

However, in 2001 and 2002, Cincinnati experienced a dramatic increase in reported violent and property crime. More specifically in 2001, Cincinnati's violent crime rate increased from 840.1 to 1,207.1 reported offenses per 100,000. From 2001 to 2002, the violent crime rate experienced an additional, small increase to 1,275.2. Similarly, in 2001, Cincinnati's property crime rate increased from 5,864.7 to 7,035.5 reported offenses per 100,000. In 2003, the property crime rate peaked at 7,475.2. The spike in reported violent and property street crimes experienced in Cincinnati from 2001 to 2003 coincide with riots that occurred in 2001. The relationship between these riots and street crime in Cincinnati will be discussed in the following section.

From 2003 to 2007, Cincinnati's violent crime rate fell from 1,127.4 to 1,081.6 reported offenses per 100,000. However, by 2010, the violent crime rate rose to 1,217.4 Similarly, Cincinnati's robbery rate increased from 673.5 reported robberies per 100,000 in 2003 to 757.6 in 2006. In 2007, the robbery rate decreased to 590.3, but by 2010, the rate was 712.9. Like the violent crime rate from 2003 to 2007, the property crime rate in Cincinnati slowly fell from 7,475.2 to 6,196.4. By 2010, the property crime rate increased to 6,937.4. During 2003 to 2007, the reported larceny-theft rate in Cincinnati decreased from 4,581.0 to 3,723.7 and increased to 4,198.1 in 2010. The motor vehicle theft rate also experienced a decline during 2003-09. In 2003, the reported motor vehicle theft rate was 1,065.4 and by 2009, it dropped to 466.8. In 2010, the motor vehicle theft rate increased to 545.2 reported offenses per 100,000.

Cincinnati's recent violent and property crime rates are persistently higher than the reported national averages. In 2010, Cincinnati's violent crime rate was 1,217.4 while the national violent crime rate was 403.6. Cincinnati's property rate for 2010 was 6,937.4 while the national property crime rate was 2,941.9. Though these differences

appear to be extreme, it is important to consider that the UCR averages reported crime across all cities. Therefore, the recent crime rates for Cincinnati may appear to be higher than the national average, but not much different from rates in other large cities. Despite this difference from the national average, the reported violent and property crime rates for Cincinnati generally appear to follow national crime rate trends—for increase or decrease—for the United States.

Law Enforcement Response

In 2001, while national crime rates were in decline, the city of Cincinnati experienced a rise in reported violent and property crime. This rise coincides with race riots that occurred after a fatal shooting by police. On April 7, 2001, a Cincinnati Police Department (CPD) officer shot and killed an unarmed 19-year-old Timothy Thomas, an African American male, who was attempting to avoid arrest for unpaid traffic citations. This shooting spawned allegations of racial profiling and misuse of force by the CPD in part because Thomas was the 15th African American male to be killed by CPD since 1995. The incident led to a public outcry over violence and enflamed distrust in law enforcement and other public officials.

The summer after the April 2001 riots, the CPD formed a 70-officer unit, Violent Crimes Task Force (VCTF), in order to address the rise in violent street crime. The VCTF's role was to respond to and investigate all violent crime under CPD's jurisdiction, while also serving outstanding warrants and arresting the violent perpetrators of these crimes. The proactive controversial efforts of the VCTF led to it being restructured; the VCTF later became the Violent Crimes Squad (VCS), with one squad assigned to each of the five Cincinnati police districts.

In 2006, in addition to increasing patrols on the streets, CPD created a specialized permanent unit, Safe Streets (formally known as the Vortex Unit), to tackle violent crime across the city. More specifically, Safe Streets was designed to take a zero-tolerance approach to street crime and drug trafficking. Composed of 50 officers, Safe Streets specializes in targeting high crime areas. To assist officers with responding to street crime and calls for service, CPD strategically installed cameras throughout the city of Cincinnati. This public safety camera network is comprised of real-time cameras that have the capability to be monitored any time by police officers and emergency dispatchers. Some of the cameras have specialized functions, such as reading license plates in order to retrieve motor vehicle registration information, and changing position to focus on activity based on direction of gunfire.

Conclusion

To address the increase in gun violence, in 2007 political leaders in Cincinnati partnered with law enforcement officials, academics, social service agencies, community agencies, street advocates, and medical and business professionals. This partnership, known as the Cincinnati Initiative to Reduce Violence (CIRV), is modeled after Boston's Operation Cease Fire, a focused deterrence strategy that communicates the consequences of violence to active group or gang members and known associates. With the efforts of law enforcement, services, community, and systems strategy teams, CIRV is intended to make involvement in criminal violence risky and costly, while also providing prosocial pathways away from violence and encouraging communities to spread the no-tolerance message for violence.

Years after the riots, the property crime rate in Cincinnati is still only slightly lower than it was during the early 2000s. While on average national crime rates have been in decline since the early 1990s, CPD continues to address highly resistant pockets of street crime in Cincinnati, especially those areas that harbor violent crime and illegal drug activity.

Amy L. Stutzenberger
University of Cincinnati

See Also: Closed-Circuit Television; Crime Prevention, Situational; Fear of Crime; Guns and Weapons; Kansas City Preventive Patrol Experiment; Operation Ceasefire; Street Crime Defined; Urban Ethnography.

Further Readings

City of Cincinnati. "Cincinnati Police Department— Serving & Protecting the People of Cincinnati." 2012. http://www.cincinnati-oh.gov/police/pages/-3039 (Accessed April 2012).

Engel, Robin S., Marie Skubak Tillyer, and Nicholas Corsaro. *Reducing Gang Violence Using Focused Deterrence.* Cincinnati, OH: University of Cincinnati Policing Institute, 2011.

Hurley, Daniel. *Cincinnati: The Queen City.* Cincinnati, OH: Cincinnati Historical Society, 1982.

Mrozowski, Jennifer. "Racial Strife Not New to City." *Cincinnati Enquirer* (April 11, 2001).

Prendergast, Jane. "Cincinnati Police to Install 120 Crime Cameras." *Cincinnati Enquirer* (June 25, 2008).

Cleveland, Ohio

Like most major American cities, Cleveland has had an historic problem with street crime. During Prohibition, organized crime flourished and was involved in bootlegging and gambling through the 1920s. Illegal gambling remained a problem after Prohibition ended, as both wealthy and not-so-wealthy citizens took advantage of it. Wealthier people frequented illegal casinos in the cities, while the less wealthy played various numbers games and slot machines. Pressure from the city police pushed most of these games into the suburbs and surrounding countryside. However, the combination of the economic hardships of the Depression and the higher levels of crime in gambling "Hot Spots" laid the foundation for street crime that would plague Cleveland throughout the 20th and into the 21st century.

The issue of race and its bearing on crime became an issue after World War II. Experts identified various sources of a rise in juvenile delinquency: availability of liquor, availability of guns, and broken homes. Debates on who was to blame for the rise in crime rates exacerbated racial tensions through the 1970s.

Street crimes such as murder, rape, and robbery that happened to people who came from the suburbs either to visit or to work in Cleveland increased fear of crime, its causes, and the role played by race. As in many cities, arguments arose as to whether an increase in police patrols or more sophisticated police techniques would lessen street crime, or if it was more important to provide greater economic opportunities to those who were low on the socioeconomic ladder.

Police Department Strife

A key issue affecting street crime in Cleveland was the contentious nature of the relationship

Table 1 Violent[1] and property crime[2] rate comparison for Cleveland, Ohio, and the United States, 1985–2009

Year	U.S. violent crime rate	Cleveland violent crime rate	U.S. property crime rate	Cleveland property crime rate
1985	558.1	1,204.9	4,666.4	6,681.8
1986	620.1	1,301.8	4,881.8	6,791.8
1987	612.5	1,270.4	4,963.0	7,013.1
1988	640.6	1,346.7	5,054.0	6,886.5
1989	666.9	1,520.3	5,107.1	6,829.7
1990	729.6	1,817.6	5,073.1	7,297.0
1991	758.2	1,831.9	5,140.2	7,113.0
1992	757.7	1,661.6	4,903.7	6,622.2
1993	747.1	1,643.2	4,740.0	6,267.2
1994	713.6	1,529.7	4,660.2	5,926.4
1995	684.5	1,646.2	4,590.5	6,163.7
1996	636.6	1,538.4	4,451.0	6,003.0
1997	611.0	1,458.6	4,316.3	5,996.9
1998	567.6	1,307.9	4,052.5	5,673.3
1999	523.0	1,215.3	3,743.6	5,528.0
2000	506.5	1,262.7	3,618.3	5,548.3
2001	504.5	1,340.4	3,658.1	5,558.7
2002	494.4	1,322.3	3,630.6	5,577.9
2003	475.8	1,323.5	3,591.2	5,566.9
2004	463.2	1,299.5	3,514.1	5,868.6
2005	469.0	1,400.6	3,431.5	6,248.0
2006	473.6	1,552.7	3,334.5	6,279.5
2007	466.9	1,468.6	3,263.5	6,169.5
2008	457.5	1,419.8	3,211.5	5,804.3
2009	429.4	1,395.5	3,036.1	5,621.1
2010	404.5	1296.8	2945.9	5500.9
2011	386.3	1366.8	2908.7	6736.9

Source: Federal Bureau of Investigation's Uniform Crime Reports.
[1]Violent crimes: murder and non-negligent manslaughter, forcible rape, robbery, and aggravated assault.
[2]Property crimes: burglary, larceny theft, motor vehicle theft.

between the Cleveland Police Department (CPD) and black residents. Race relations between the CPD and the city's black community soured throughout the 1960s. Cleveland, like many other cities, experienced race-related riots during what became known as "the long, hot summers" of the mid-1960s. The nadir in racial relations occurred when the CPD was involved in a gun battle, known as the Glenville Shootout, with black militants in the summer of 1968, a battle that resulted in the deaths of four citizens and three police officers. Residents, especially African Americans, as well as the African American mayor, Carl Stokes, were highly critical of the police department, which continued to struggle against street crime.

Concerns continued into the next decade, especially budgetary in nature, which led to a loss of over 600 officers between 1970 and 1980. Organizational continuity and guidance was also an issue; 12 different chiefs served from 1966 to 1979. Combined with rises in crime and citizen demand, these factors led to a belief that the police were incapable of doing their jobs.

Although 40 percent of Cleveland's population consisted of minorities in the 1970 census, minorities composed just 6.2 percent of the CPD in 1966 and only 8.1 percent by 1972. This disparity led to a lawsuit by a group of minority police officers, citing discriminatory hiring and promotion policies. The CPD was found guilty and placed under a consent decree which mandated that, by the end of 1992, 33 percent of the CPD would consist of minority-group members.

Consistent fears about street crime led one U.S. congressman to invite the Guardian Angels to open a chapter in Cleveland. Organized by Curtis Sliwa in 1979 in New York City, the Angels consisted of volunteers who would patrol public areas, such as streets, buses, and trains, in an effort to deter and intervene in street crimes. Wearing distinctive red berets, they patrolled in groups of eight. In 1982, they made two arrests and helped police apprehend 13 people. Citizens welcomed them, and the general consensus was that they did in fact deter crime. The first chapter disbanded in 1983, but a new chapter formed in 1993. According to the Guardian Angels Web site (www.guardianangels.org), the Cleveland chapter is still active.

In 2004, concerns over a projected $61 million deficit led to the layoff of 252 police officers and the shutdown of numerous specialized, proactive units, among them the Strike Force, Fugitive, and Street Crimes units. These units were forced to put team members on patrol in an effort to calm public fears about the limited number of officers. In 2011, a loss in state aid led to the layoff of 81 officers in Cleveland, which at the time was considered the eighth-most dangerous city in the United States. Layoffs continued into 2012, and morale in the CPD was running low. Officers were being pulled from policing in dangerous schools in order to patrol the streets. Union leaders claimed that the job was getting too dangerous for the thin contingent of officers remaining. Relationship with Cleveland residents remained strained, especially in May 2011 when police union president, Steve Loomis, complained that taxpayers and businesses were rapidly abandoning Cleveland, leaving behind them the "dregs of society."

Persistent Crime

Given this history, it is not surprising that Cleveland often has one of the higher rates of street crimes,. Table 1 presents a comparison between violent and property crime rates for the United States and those of Cleveland.

While it is clear that violent crime and property crime rates peaked in 1991 and 1990, respectively, and have drifted downward since, Cleveland's violent crime rate in 2009 was 3.3 times the national violent crime rate, while the property crime rate in the city in 2009 was 1.85 times the national property crime rate. Street crime undeniably remains a problem in Cleveland.

In 2010, Cleveland was ranked as the nation's seventh-most crime-ridden urban area in the CQ Press's City Crime Rankings 2010–2011, despite a 21 percent drop in violent crime and a 15 percent drop in property crime during 2006-10. Police argue that during this period, street crimes such as homicide fell 40 percent, rape fell by 16 percent, robbery fell 26 percent, felonious (aggravated) assault fell 14 percent, theft fell 10 percent, and vehicle theft fell 46 percent. Burglary was the only crime which rose, by 2 percent.

Conclusion

While some of the decrease in crime is believed to be a result of a general drop in the population and thus a decrease in criminal opportunities, police argue that their use of technology, especially to aid in crime analysis, and reaching out and forming alliances with community and social groups have led to more effective policing techniques. Police have begun the use of two-officer patrols during evening shifts to concentrate on "hot spots" as well as forming a Community Services Unit to focus on quality-of-life issues. They argue that this shift toward a community-policing philosophy has also helped lead to a decline in street crime, especially burglary.

James Geistman
Ohio Northern University

See Also: Burglary; Community Policing; Fear of Crime; Guardian Angels; Hot Spots; Juvenile Offending; Murder/Homicide; Police Brutality/Excessive Force; Street Crime Defined; Theft and Larceny; Urban Ethnography.

Further Readings

Baird, Gabriel. "Cleveland Police Officers Charged with Assault Had Criminal and Financial Troubles Before Receiving Their Badges, Records Show." *Cleveland Plain Dealer* (April 17, 2011). http://blog.cleveland .com/metro/2011/04/cleveland_police_officers _char_1.html (Accessed October 2011).

Case Western Reserve University and the Western Reserve Historical Society. "The Encyclopedia of Cleveland History." http://ech.cwru.edu (Accessed October 2011)

Federal Bureau of Investigation. "Crime in the United States 2009." http://www.fbi.gov/stats-services/ crimestats (Accessed October 2011).

Gillispie, Mark. "Cleveland Crime Statistics Show Little Change in Six Months, But Big Drop From 2006." *Cleveland Plain Dealer* (July 3, 2011). http://blog.cleveland.com/metro/2011/07/cleveland _crime_statistics_sho.html (Accessed October 2011).

Closed-Circuit Television

Closed-circuit television (CCTV) is a method of surveillance using video cameras connected to a centralized control room. The cameras can be mounted on light posts, the sides of buildings, inside public transportation vehicles, or on the dashboards of police cars. Cameras have been placed near traffic lights to ticket drivers who speed through red lights, or snap photos of toll evaders' license plates. Some can pan, tilt, or zoom in using remote controls, or connect with face recognition software to automatically identify alleged criminals. Other programs can automatically detect suspicious behaviors such as abandoning a package in a public place.

Video from some or all of the cameras can be recorded for later playback in courts or on local television in an effort to request witnesses to contact authorities. While advocates point to the efficiency of monitoring activities at many locations simultaneously, and in helping deter street crime victims and identify crime suspects, critics dislike the lack of privacy and question the cameras' effectiveness in reducing crime.

Development and Spread

Cameras may be placed overtly so the general public is aware of their presence, or hidden behind frosted domes to not reveal in which direction they are aimed. Some anti-rape installations are identified by their distinctive blue lights to draw public attention and potentially deter crime before it occurs. The images from CCTV cameras are either relayed to a centralized, stationary monitoring station or to officers with a control unit in police cars. In most cases, CCTV cameras are semicovert, so that while people know a camera is there, they may be unsure about the direction it is pointed. These cameras proliferated in installations in many cities across the United States following the 9/11 terrorist disaster, largely funded by grants from the federal government.

Surveillance is designed to prevent crimes before they occur, but for this to happen criminals must believe their behavior will be noticed and that the authorities are capable of apprehending them. Cameras may also encourage local citizens to be more willing to report crimes—though the prevalence of cameras can also scare them into having a greater fear of it. For example, in places with higher rates of violent crime, many such criminal acts go unreported. A CCTV is capable of bringing more of these cases into the legal system, but this may in turn cause a statistical rise in crime in that locality.

The United Kingdom has been a recent pioneer in using CCTV technology. As of the early 2000s, 4.2 million or one out of every five security cameras in the world was placed there, for a rate of one per 14 residents. As much as $400 million was spent on these systems that seem to be accepted enthusiastically by the public. In the United States an experiment with surveillance cameras began in 1973 in New York City's Times Square—but was quietly abandoned two years later when it was found to be ineffective. The post–9/11 expansion of camera installation saw state-of-the-art systems cropping up in Boston, Washington, D.C., New York City, and Chicago, among other major U.S. cities.

A public opinion poll in 2007 found that 71 percent of Americans favored video technology to improve public safety, with about 25 percent opposed.

While the American Civil Liberties Union (ACLU) does not oppose placing cameras at high-profile places to deter terrorist attacks, it considers their more widespread implementation a violation of citizens' Fourth Amendment rights. The ACLU further questions the ability of police officers to focus on television monitors for long periods of time and challenges their ability to use information gathered via CCTV without harassing and intimidating bystanders, even to the extent of focusing cameras on the private parts of attractive people. Another fear is that basic cameras will be replaced by more advanced technology, giving greater detection powers at night, and there will be a chilling effect on people's public lives, out of fear of attracting unwarranted attention from the official person monitoring the cameras. Other critics charge that cameras are most often placed in areas where wealth is concentrated, to the neglect of communities with less affluence but potentially higher crime rates.

Probing Effectiveness

The cameras have been shown to have a modest effect in reducing property crimes. In a meta-analysis of 44 studies concerning their effectiveness, Researchers Brandon Welsh and David P. Farrington found an 8 percent reduction in crime overall could be attributed to CCTV. However, they were far more effective in such specific uses as preventing damage to cars in parking lots—where crime rates fell by an average 41 percent. The effect on the rate of violent crime was found to be statistically insignificant. Critics also argue that security cameras can displace criminal activities to places outside the cameras' range, as street criminals learn to distinguish places being monitored and those that are not. Drug dealers can also use tactical displacement of crime by changing their methods, such as taking orders by phone and delivering them later, rather than standing on a street to meet with customers.

A study in Philadelphia used two different methods to analyze data after CCTV cameras were installed; the report found them responsible for a 13 percent reduction in "serious and disorder offenses." However, the crime rate did not fall at all in half of the sites that were monitored. Some criminologists recommend placing cameras near clusters of intersections with high crime rates, as opposed to isolated problematic corners. This could make CCTV systems more cost-effective.

Local conditions account greatly for the effectiveness of CCTV systems. Long, straight streets are easier to monitor than curvy ones, for instance. Police staffing must be sufficient to respond to the additional "eyes and ears" provided by security imaging systems. Some publicity should accompany their installation, to increase the deterrent effect. Cameras should be located in areas with specific problems, while taking blockage by foliage or other barriers into account.

Academic studies note a lack of sufficient literature about CCTV cameras in the United States, and also note that cities continue to install these systems despite this shortcoming. Researchers almost unanimously encourage other scholars to conduct more studies so that future security systems can be installed more effectively.

William E. Raffel
Buffalo State College

See Also: Crime, Displacement of; Crime Mapping; Gunshot Detection System; Policing, Problem-Oriented; Security, Private.

Further Readings

American Civil Liberties Union. "What's Wrong With Public Video Surveillance?" February 25, 2002. http://www.aclu.org/technology-and-liberty/whats-wrong-public-video-surveillance (Accessed June 2011).

Fennelly, Lawrence. *Effective Physical Security.* 3rd ed. Oxford, UK: Butterworth-Heinemann, 2003.

Nemeth, Charles. *Private Security and the Law.* 4th ed. Oxford, UK: Butterworth-Heinemann, 2011.

Ratcliffe, Jerry. *Video Surveillance of Public Places.* Washington, DC: U.S. Justice Department. http://www.cops.usdoj.gov/files/ric/Publications/e02061006.pdf (Accessed June 2011).

Ratcliffe, Jerry, Travis Taniguchi, and Ralph B. Taylor. "The Crime Reduction Effects of Public CCTV Cameras: A Multi-Method Spatial Approach." *Justice Quarterly,* v.26/4 (2009).

Robb, Gary C. "Police Use of CCTV (Closed Circuit Television) Surveillance: Constitutional Implications and Proposed Regulations." *University of Michigan Journal of Law Reform*, v.13/3 (1980).

Welsh, Brandon and David P. Farrington, *Making Public Places Safer.* New York: Oxford University Press, 2009.

Yesil, Bilge. *Video Surveillance: Power and Privacy in Everyday Life.* El Paso, TX: LFB Scholarly Publishing, 2009.

Code of Silence/ Stop Snitching

Though codes of silence have long been staple criminal norms, the recent evolution of the practice into the so-called Stop Snitching phenomenon has proven divisive in many cities and has been blamed for low clearance rates for serious violent crime, and for an increase in witness intimidation. Stop Snitching, like variants of codes of silence that have gone before, exhorts people involved in criminal and deviant activity to stay silent and not cooperate with law enforcement, much like La Cosa Nostra's code of *omerta*.

Riding a Style Wave

The recent iteration of Stop Snitching can be traced to several sources. Boston rapper Tangg The Juice recorded tracks in the late 1990s and early 2000s such as "N***az Told on Us," in which he used the phrase. In 2004 an underground digital video disc (DVD) titled *Stop Snitchin',* produced by Rodney Thomas (also known as Skinny Suge) in Baltimore, became a cause célèbre because it included National Basketball Association star Carmelo Anthony.

The furor over Anthony's brief appearance masked a more important development, namely that it was no longer the case that only those who were engaged in crime were duty bound to stay silent. Rather, the message in the DVD was that everyone in the community had to toe the line or suffer the consequences. At the same time the DVD became popular, T-shirts emblazoned with a red octagonal stop sign with the word *Snitching* tagged underneath started to appear in many urban areas; these were followed by shirts with smiley face emoticons with zippered mouths.

Though this underground movement is part fashion statement, some of the real consequences of the Stop Snitching movement are a perceived lack of cooperation between citizens living in disadvantaged high-crime communities and law enforcement. Moreover, a crisis of faith in the legal system is part and parcel of this perception. Several police chiefs and district attorneys in large cities have gone on record to exhort witnesses of recent serious crimes to come forward. In Philadelphia, the catchphrase was "Stand Up, Speak Out" and elsewhere there have been attempts to engage a "Start Snitching" campaign in response.

Social Pressure and Response

Research at the Community College of Philadelphia by Rick Frei has shown that the more a situation requires the person to take the initiative, the more likely it is to be viewed as snitching. For instance, it takes more initiative to actually call police than it does to answer questions if one is already at the scene of a crime. In other research also in Philadelphia, Maria Kefalas, Patrick Carr, and Susan Clampet-Lundquist found that young people in high-crime areas have a complex understanding about when it is and is not permissible to cooperate with authorities. This "sliding scale of snitching" distinguishes between the person who informs to escape prosecution or to receive leniency—a bona fide snitch—and the person whose family member has been violently victimized, who is permitted to opt for legal recourse. Exceptions to the Stop Snitching rule can also be made in the case of a person who shares information about a child molester, rapist, or someone who beats up women.

There are several explanations for the Stop Snitching phenomenon. Some argue that Stop Snitching is an extension of the code of the street, a subcultural response to the disadvantage and social isolation of ghetto life. Others say that it is a contextual response to the decades-old War on Drugs that has fundamentally reshaped the urban justice system in America. For instance, legal scholar Alexandra Natapoff has written about how the use of snitches to secure convictions has operated without oversight and has contributed to an erosion of trust in the justice system. So in these terms, Stop Snitching is a response to decades of overincarceration in high-crime neighborhoods, and to a system that makes ample use of informants.

More worrying for authorities than the cynicism and distrust that a reliance on informants has brought, is the use of Stop Snitching to intimidate witnesses scheduled to testify in high-profile criminal cases. Many witnesses are not there as part of a deal, but are trying to do what is right. Some of these witnesses recant previously given statements or refuse to show up in court because they have been threatened or intimidated.

There has been a push-back from law enforcement, politicians, and community leaders. In some cases, ordinances have been passed outlawing the wearing of Stop Snitching T-shirts in courtrooms, or, in the case of Boston, their sale in the city. Smaller-scale grassroots protests against the proliferation of the Stop Snitching message have occurred in Philadelphia and Baltimore, and in the latter city the Police Department even crafted its own video in response to the Stop Snitching DVD, titled *Keep Talking*, which they focused on individuals featured in the original video whom police had subsequently arrested.

Conclusion

Despite the efforts from law enforcement to blunt the impact of Stop Snitching, lack of cooperation with police remains a pressing issue for many big cities. With the War on Drugs showing no signs of abating and incarceration rates at or near all-time highs, the Stop Snitching phenomenon may well be a feature of our most dangerous cities for many years to come.

Patrick J. Carr
Rutgers University
Susan Clampet-Lundquist
Maria J. Kefalas
Saint Joseph's University

See Also: Baltimore, Maryland; Boston, Massachusetts; Bystander Apathy; Code of the Street; Courts; Fear of Crime; Neighborhood Watch; Philadelphia, Pennsylvania; Police Detectives; Street Crime, Popular Portrayals of.

Further Readings

Brown, Ethan. *Snitch: Informers, Cooperators, and the Corruption of Justice.* New York: Public Affairs, 2007.

Grimes, Michael E. *Informants—A Guide for Developing and Controlling Informants.* San Clemente, CA: LawTech Publishing, 2009.

Hill, Marc Lamont. "Damned If You Do. Damned If You Don't." Buzzmedia. http://www.popmatters.com/pm/column/hill060224-1 (Accessed May 2012).

Kefalas, Maria, Patrick J. Carr, and Susan Clampet-Lundquist. "Rules for Snitching." *The Root* (May 17, 2011). http://www.theroot.com/views/my-turn-rules-snitching (Accessed May 2012).

Natapoff, Alexandra. *Snitching: Criminal Informants and the Erosion of American Justice.* New York: New York University Press, 2009.

Code of the Street

The sociologist Elijah Anderson developed the concept of the Code of the Street in 1994, and fully articulated the notion in his book by that title published in 1999. At its most fundamental level, the code involves the use or threat to use violence as the main way for people to achieve respect on the streets of the inner city. The code involves sets of rules and norms that govern how one behaves on the street, and by extension how one is treated by others in public places. If one gains respect on the street, he or she can decrease their chances of being bothered or victimized, but if a person has low credibility on the street, he or she is at higher risk for being violently victimized. The code, according to Anderson, is like a "street justice" system that has replaced what he sees as a negligent and indifferent official criminal justice system known to many in the middle class.

Alienation and Approaches

Without other forms of social capital (i.e., wealth, education, or living-wage employment), the code serves as both a technique of survival and a way to engender status in the inner city, according to Anderson's analysis. Anderson is very careful to point out that the code is not a trait of individuals or a matter of free will/rational choice, but that it is in direct response to the lack of jobs, institutional racism, and the unavailability of basic social services, as well as drug use and a sense of hopelessness in the inner-city African American communities he studied. He consistently points out that the code develops and sustains itself because of larger sociological and economic forces, which all lead to

The most powerful force counteracting the code of the street in the inner city is the presence of strong, loving, "decent" families. The culture of the street thrives, unfortunately, and often defeats decency because it controls public places so that individuals with higher aspirations are often entangled in the code and its self-destructive behaviors. An individual's safety and sense of worth are determined by the respect he or she commands in public—a deference frequently based on an implied threat of violence.

inner-city residents' high levels of alienation from "mainstream" society.

Anderson bases the concept of the code on his intense ethnographic and interview research in some of the most economically disadvantaged communities in Philadelphia, Pennsylvania. Among the more impressive examples of field research to date, Anderson interviewed a range of people and studied numerous social settings from public schools, playgrounds, and retail stores to jails and taverns. Importantly, Anderson interviewed many people who do not subscribe to the code, but who occasionally practice the ritual to survive. These "decent" families (a term not applied to this group by Anderson himself, but rather by the people he interviewed) are in the statistical majority in the inner city and seem to hold middle-class values

such as politeness, saving money, emphasizing the importance of education, and more even-handed child supervision and discipline.

On the other end of the spectrum are the "street" or "ghetto" families, who Anderson found to be most heavily invested in the code and whose anger and lack of ability to deal with such difficult economic situations leads them to engage in more violence than other groups in the inner city. Importantly, however, Anderson notes that many people may not actually believe in the value system of street justice—but simply use it on occasion, or when otherwise necessary, to survive a threat. Further, some people are known to "code switch," which involves adopting street or decent behavior depending on the circumstance. As such, the code should not be confused with the notion of subcultures, because the code is fluidly used and only truly embraced by a small amount of people.

Academic and Policy Responses

Several empirical studies have tested or used Anderson's concept to help understand a variety of issues, such as the lyrical content in "gangsta rap," how the code concept fits into other explanations of crime, and youth violence in areas outside Philadelphia. Most of these studies have found at least limited support for the value of Anderson's concept. Moreover, Anderson's study is valued outside of criminology, as it contributes to the understanding of urban sociology, the family, stratification, and race and ethnic relations. Although not a primary interest, Anderson's work can also speak to how gender is performed in inner-city communities.

In terms of the policy implications of the concept, Anderson argues that the main way to reduce the code is by opening up economic opportunities that provide good paying and rewarding jobs to inner-city residents. Given that the code is fueled by larger institutional structures beyond the control of its adherents, Anderson's concept calls for structural change, although not necessarily radical change to capitalism, as Marxist scholars would advocate.

David Kauzlarich
Southern Illinois University, Edwardsville

See Also: Juvenile Offending; Philadelphia, Pennsylvania; Projects, The; Urban Ethnography.

Further Readings

Anderson, Elijah. *Code of the Street: Decency, Violence, and the Moral Life of the Inner City*. New York: Norton, 1999.

Anderson, Elijah. "The Code of the Streets." *Atlantic Monthly*, v.273/5 (1994).

Anderson, Elijah. "The Ideologically Driven Critique." *American Journal of Sociology*, v.107/6 (2002).

Brezina, Timothy, Robert Agnew, Francis T. Cullen, and John Paul Wright. "The Code of the Street: A Quantitative Assessment of Elijah Anderson's Subculture of Violence Thesis and Its Contribution to Youth Violence Research." *Youth Violence and Juvenile Justice*, v.2/4 (2004).

Kubrin, Charis. "Gangstas, Thugs, and Hustlas: Identity and the Code of the Street in Rap Music." *Social Problems*, v.52/3 (2005).

Community Policing

Community policing refers to a departure from traditional policing strategies to one in which the police work closely with the community to define problems and arrive at solutions. A central idea is that the police can best reduce crime by attacking its causes through crime prevention strategies that involve community residents. Community policing recognizes that crime prevention and control must involve a partnership between the police and the community.

Background

Community policing emerged in the 1980s and 1990s as a virtual revolution in American police practice. President Bill Clinton's initiative to put 100,000 more police officers on the street required those officers to engage in community policing. The federal government invested billions of dollars in this new strategy; and by the end of the 20th century, almost all police departments in the country reported they had adopted community policing.

Policing research established that much of the crime problem was beyond the control of traditional policing. Police are dependent on citizens for information about crime, yet citizens were not reporting most crimes. Poor relations between the police and citizens hampered crime prevention and control.

Research into new police tactics, especially foot patrol, revealed that when citizens got to know officers, cooperation increased. More importantly, foot patrol experiments revealed that most citizens wanted closer relationships with police. Researcher Robert Trojanowicz, sometimes called the "father" of community policing, observed that increased contact between officers and citizens led to improved cooperation, better public support of the police, and reductions in citizen fear of crime.

Investigations into the state of police relations with the community also revealed that the police were not focusing on those factors that the public found most important—including order maintenance, tangible service, and fear of crime. Order maintenance and service issues involve minor disturbances that professional police sometimes see as less important than combating violent street crimes and other highly visible disorders. By ignoring these types of incidents, however, the police were missing important opportunities to address community concerns and improve community relations. Similarly, traditional policing did not emphasize or directly address fear of crime. Fear of crime differs from crime rates and is not necessarily addressed when police emphasize law enforcement. The realization of the shortcomings of professional policing and a desire to address other important issues led to the development of community policing.

Theory and Practice

In community policing, the police focus shifts from reacting to criminal incidents to adopting crime prevention strategies. It also shifts tactics from a reliance on law enforcement to addressing community concerns through attending to order maintenance and service activities. Community policing incorporates citizens and nonpolice services to achieve reductions in crime and improvements in community order. Academics universally agree that community policing involves incorporating the community in crime prevention; however, further agreement is difficult to find. This confusion may have stemmed from the simultaneous development of a separate, but similar, strategy: problem-oriented policing. Some authors have attempted to clarify this problem by providing specific definitions of the two strategies. Gary Cordner provides an example of such an attempt with his classification of three dimensions: philosophical, strategic, and programmatic. Herman Goldstein for his part delivers the most renowned description of problem-oriented policing.

Cordner's description of the philosophical dimension involves the central tenets of community policing. As is the case with all definitions of community policing, he begins with the reorientation of policing to include citizens in the ultimate direction and execution of police strategies. This results in an increased focus on less severe offenses, because they are more likely to occur in view of the public. The strategic dimension contains police operations used to achieve the new objectives of community policing. In particular, officers are permanently assigned to specific geographic areas for longer periods of time so that they can become sufficiently familiar with residents. This increased familiarity allows officers to organize citizens in efforts to curb community problems and be held accountable for the success in eliminating these problems.

The final dimension of Cordner's overview, the programmatic, describes specific tactics used to implement community policing. Officers engaged in community policing are directed to use problem solving to address community problems. This involves responding in an analytic manner to patterns of problems, rather than specific incidents. Possible responses include options beyond traditional law enforcement, but this does not mean the strategy abandons the importance of law enforcement. Rather, patrol officers should implement whatever tactic (or combination of tactics) will best reduce the problems identified by residents.

Problem-oriented policing, as described by Goldstein, proposes the same methods of police interventions, but differs in focusing police efforts on different sorts of incidents. As is the case with community policing, problem-oriented policing advises that the police should target the underlying causes of a crime problem rather than only reacting to criminal events. The focus of what institutes a problem deserving of police attention, however, differs for this strategy. Rather than incorporating community residents into deciding the primary problems faced by the community, it is the police who must identify these problems and attend to them. Avoiding the prejudicial focus of many resident perceptions, patterns of more serious criminal offenses are thus put at the forefront.

Conclusion

Like problem-oriented policing, community policing requires police to take a broader view of their responsibilities. Trojanowicz described community policing as a "philosophy" of policing in which police bear responsibility for community health and welfare. The police, in other words, should work with the community to overcome what the community sees as its most pressing problems. In this synthesis, the police play a central role as the link between the citizens and all types of local, state, and federal government services, whether primarily engaged in crime fighting on the one hand, or in community-building on the other.

P. Colin Bolger
Lawrence F. Travis III
University of Cincinnati

See Also: Broken Windows Theory; Crime Prevention, Situational; Fear of Crime; Kansas City Preventive Patrol Experiment; Neighborhood Watch; Newark

Foot Patrol Experiment; Police (Overview); Policing, Problem-Oriented.

Further Readings

Cordner, Gary. "Community Policing: Elements and Effects." *Police Forum*, v.5/3 (1995).

Goldstein, Herman. *Problem-Oriented Policing.* New York: McGraw-Hill, 1990.

Kelling, George and Mark Moore. "The Evolving Strategy of Policing." Washington, DC: U.S. Department of Justice, 1988.

Skolnick, Jerry and David Bayley. *The New Blue Line: Police Innovation in Six American Cities.* New York: The Free Press, 1986.

Trojanowicz, Robert and Bonnie Bucqueroux. *Community Policing: A Contemporary Perspective.* Cincinnati, OH: Anderson Publishing, 1990.

Community Resources Against Street Hoodlums

The crime unit Community Resources Against Street Hoodlums (CRASH) was established by the Los Angeles Police Department (LAPD) in 1977 to deal with gang-related crimes and gang members.

Mission of CRASH

The unit was started during the tenure of Chief Daryl Gates to address the increasing problem of gangs and gangsters in Los Angeles. CRASH was composed of some of the best LAPD officers at the time. These were officers who would not be intimidated by the gangsters, who would be able to engage them and gather intelligence to develop a better understanding of gangs and their activities.

Chief Gates believed the unit to be effective, successful in reducing gang crime through the 1970s and 1980s. Assigned to specific gangs and their inner workings, CRASH duty was different than regular patrol duty. CRASH officers did not answer regular, routine calls. Their only job was to work on drug, extortion, firearm, and other deals; intervene; and suppress the gang crime activities. CRASH was deployed in a variety of places and public and private events, all to gather intelligence and to identify and keep the gangs in check during many specific times and events. To many a Los Angeles gangster, CRASH was simply a rival, if legal, gang: a group of police officers whose job it was to arrest as many gang members as possible.

Rampart Scandal

While CRASH existed in all 18 LAPD divisions throughout the city, what brought the unit the most notoriety (apart from the movie *Colors*) was the scandal that developed in the Rampart division. The area known as Rampart—comprising the near-to-downtown districts of Echo Park, Pico-Union, and Westlake—was a mixture of different ethnicities and recent immigrants. Physically located away from the LAPD Rampart station, CRASH officers assigned to Rampart were essentially unsupervised, or at best loosely supervised. They developed what came to be known as the Rampart Way, a unique yet not formally defined set of methods for dealing with the gangsters and the people of the Rampart area.

Without question, prior to the Rampart scandal, CRASH was an effective gang unit, engaging gangsters in a variety of ways and carrying out gang sweeps, hot spot targeting, and intensified patrols to apply pressure on gangs. One of their most effective operations, known as Operation Hammer, took place over a Friday and Saturday netting 1,400 arrests. One author referred to this and similar operations as remarkably inefficient generally for so few felony arrests and subsequent charges. Members of CRASH, however, would no doubt see it differently—as would many of the residents of the various communities in which Operation Hammer was carried out.

In the late 1990s, after working close to 20 years, CRASH was hit with the Rampart scandal. Beginning slowly, with officers assigned to CRASH becoming involved in non-CRASH and in some cases non-gangster related criminal activity, it all came to a head with the arrest of Officer Rafael Perez.

Arrested for the theft of cocaine from the LAPD evidence room, Perez in turn agreed to "rat" on other officers. Of the hundreds of officers assigned to CRASH, Perez implicated 70 CRASH officers. Of these, 58 were brought up on charges of one sort or another. Of these, only 24 were found to have committed wrongdoing. Of these 24, 12 were administratively dealt with, seven resigned, and five were fired. Only three or four officers, all CRASH officers assigned to Rampart, were ultimately prosecuted for one or more charges.

The Rampart investigation implicated the same four officers who were subsequently found guilty as having worked for Suge Knight of Death Row Records. Knight was known to be a Bloods gang member (or have ties thereto). The resulting investigation found evidence suggesting that all four of the Rampart officers were tied themselves to the Bloods gang, with one openly joining the Bloods in prison. A lawsuit implicated three of these Rampart officers in the murder of rapper Notorious B.I.G.

The scandal also led to just over 100 criminal cases being overturned, almost $140 million in lawsuits, and of course accusations of cover-up throughout the entire process.

Legacy

Various enterprises of the entertainment media as well made their mark with CRASH. The motion picture *Colors* was based on the unit (pre-Rampart), as were the television show *The Shield*, the video game *Grand Theft Auto: San Andreas*, and the movies *Cellular* and *Faster*. The latter came more than 10 years after the Rampart scandal.

The LAPD replaced CRASH with new Special Enforcement Units to deal with gang activity, this one reportedly staffed with better, more educated, and more experienced officers under tighter supervision and control. So tight, in fact, that the unit lost many of its members and had difficulty filling many of the positions on the unit. To date, however, there have been few if any reported problems.

Jeffrey P. Rush
Austin Peay State University

See Also: Bloods; Bratton, William; Crips; Gangs (Street); *Grand Theft Auto* (Video Game); Los Angeles, California; Police Corruption, Street-Level.

Further Readings

Drooyan, Richard. "Report of the Rampart Independent Review Panel." Los Angeles: Rampart Independent Review Panel, 2000.

Frontline. "L.A.P.D. Blues: CRASH Culture." PBS, 2001. http://www.pbs.org/wgbh/pages/frontline/shows/lapd/scandal/crashculture.html (Accessed September 2011).

Kaplan, Paul J. "Looking Through the Gaps: A Critical Approach to the LAPD's Rampart Scandal." *Social Justice*, v.36/1 (2009).

Sullivan, Randall. *LAbyrinth: A Detective Investigates the Murders of Tupac Shakur and Notorious B.I.G., the Implication of Death Row Records' Suge Knight, and the Origins of the Los Angeles Police Scandal*. New York: Grove Press, 2003.

CompStat

The managerial approach to policing called "CompStat" was developed in the early 1990s by the then commissioner of the New York City Police Department (NYPD), William Bratton, and his associates. Epidemiologists and geographers as well as students of urban poverty have used mapping—representations in space and also in time—systematically since the early 19th century. They combined these techniques with interventions to prevent and/or reduce negative risks. The mapping idea was first used systematically in the United States by members of the Department of Sociology at the University of Chicago. Maps were hung and colored dots used to mark crimes, juvenile offenses, and other social matters to characterize areas of the city. Mapping was central to the Chicago School's approach, combining ecology, and demography, and using intense fieldwork. It was used to plot crime by Clifford Shaw and Henry McKay, Frederic Thrasher, Thorsten Sellin and others in the 1930s. CompStat thus stands in a long tradition of using mapping to guide interventions and improve the quality of life in cities.

All such maps and their symbols (representations standing for something else), icons (miniature versions of something), and indicies (conventionally understood pointers) are meaningful only as constituted social objects: they are made sensible by collective discussion, indication, and mutually shared understandings. Maps are meaningful because of the knowledge that is brought to bear in their interpretation. They do not and cannot "speak for themselves." People have to learn about maps and to communicate to each other what they mean.

This idea of mapping diffused to police departments began in the 1950s, and was adopted using pins placed at addresses and locations where reported, and validated crime or calls for service clustered in given periods of time, whether days, weeks, or months. The idea was to chart crime and alert patrol officers to clusters and trends. There was more concern with incidence (recent events) than prevalence (total number of events over a longer period of time). As is true now, if the mapped trends in reported crime did not continue over the following few weeks or months it was viewed as having been "prevented." However, it was not prevented—because that connotes actions had changed it; variations up or down do not in themselves indicate prevention has occurred.

Mapping Crime

Crime mapping and map-based analysis is used by police and criminologists to augment and refine policing ideas. Crime mapping has a number of constitutive elements. It is a technique based on software (usually ERSI, ArcView, or MapInfo) that converts geo-coded addresses or locations (one set

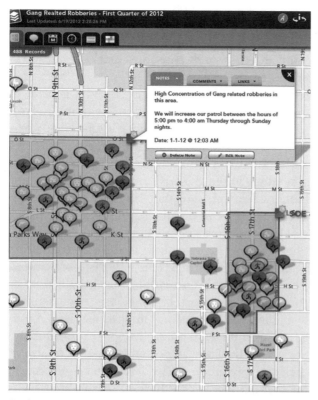

During a CompStat meeting, computer screens are shown at the front of the room showing maps and data for the area under examination.

of files) so that maps, tables, and figures (another set of files) can be merged with them. The map's content of symbols is selectively chosen by those who create the maps. The content can vary as to form, size, color, and scale, and the perspective, size, and point of view of what the map reveals can be altered. These maps can display an array of representations (tables, bar graphs, pictures, icons, cartoons, videos, embedded text, or figures) characterizing a city or political area. A wide range of facts can be included, sometimes in drop down menus, such as fire risks, demographic characteristics, indices of disorder and quality of life offenses, addresses of those on parole, registered sex-offenders, and more conventional police-generated data concerning juvenile gangs, patterns of adult crime, and traffic. Other data have been added by some fire and police departments such as addresses where restraining orders are to be enforced, gang territories, the location of chemical storage or past fires, as well as the demographics of areas of the city. Variations in density by location, types of crimes, or days of the week can be mapped, as can offenders' residences and patterns of co-offending. Anything that can be plotted spatially can be represented. The map can be printed out, projected on large or small screens, used as a basis for zooming in or out, and transmitted widely electronically. In effect, these displays, including hot spots or clusters of crime, have created a context for problem solving and reflection, what is called loosely "crime analysis."

Crime mapping using indices, marks, and other representations of crime as the focal displayed matter has at least four components.

- *Infrastructure:* Developing the software and knowledge needed to make tables, graphs, figures and models. This is the job of technicians, repair people, and civilian analysts. It requires budgeting, serving, repairing, and maintaining this infrastructure.
- *Implementation:* Fitting crime mapping materials into organizational planning, strategic plans, unit objectives, evaluations, and operating procedures.
- *Integration:* Utilizing the techniques in day-to-day police operations.
- *Sense-making activity:* Making sense of the maps and imagining what actions they suggest.

Crime mapping became a more feasible and practical tool for police between 1980 and 1990 as computers were adopted by many large police departments for dispatching, record keeping, and other managerial functions. It was also nurtured and made viable as a research technique by a generation of social scientists. Early research on calls for service stimulated descriptive studies of the spatial distribution of repeat calls for service, clusters of crime, or other indices. Studies attempting to combine problem solving, spatial analysis, and crime reduction were published. In time, the technique evolved from a descriptive, geographically-based way to present data spatially, to a means by which data can be aggregated, displayed, and applied in practice.

CompStat and the NYPD

The most visible, known, and evaluated studies of crime mapping are associated with a management strategy called CompStat, which itself is shorthand for "compare statistics." As noted above, this innovation was introduced into the NYPD and was designed to apply computer technology and regular meetings to increase the accountability of divisional level police (captains) in order to reduce crime. Commissioner Bratton organized his top command and staff, set out specific objectives within the context of crime-reduction strategy, and reorganized and demoted some command staff. Four principles governed the CompStat process according to Bratton:

- Accurate and timely information
- Rapid, focused deployment of personnel and resources
- Effective tactics
- Relentless follow-up and assessment

These procedures were implemented along with the politically tinged element of many meetings attended by the media, other top command, and visiting police. Precinct heads were called upon randomly, and on short notice (a few days), to appear at the meetings and defend their performance in regard to crime in their jurisdiction. As it developed, between 1994 and 1996, a trickle-down effect emerged, with local commanders developing tactics to reduce crime stimulated by the meetings and the possibility of being called upon to defend variations in crime (increases being most feared). Top command identified clusters of crime for attention and this idea was refined to focus attention on "hot spots," typically guided by selections by sergeants or higher ranks. The celebration of successes in 1994-96 was followed by a media backlash, increased complaints of police incivility and brutality, and later evidence. Researchers Eli Silverman and John Eterno argue that social pressure to conform and appear successful led to systematic, persistent, conscious, and possibly illegal manipulation of crime statistics during the 1994–98 period (not all of this occurred under Bratton; the meetings continued under Commissioner Howard Safir).

In spite of the inflated claims and initial media frenzy, after 1996 little or no research sought to evaluate or validate independently many of the claims made about reorganization, smart management, or the effect of any of Bratton's four principles on practices in the NYPD. The general public and the police remained convinced of the value of the approach, and focused almost exclusively on the decline in reported crime.

Developments Since CompStat

Three strands have coiled out from the ideas expressed in CompStat. First, the combination of publicity, reduction in crime in New York attributed to management moves, and the media amplification of this gave birth to a flurry of CompStat adoption by police departments elsewhere, such as CitiStat in Baltimore. Like community policing, the idea of CompStat meetings swept the country. They were reported to be present in all major and even smaller police departments within a year or two. Studies of CompStat-like meetings were positive, although they showed little or no direct impact on reported crime. The continuing decline in reported crime makes it difficult to sort out the effects of such meetings. Second, research concluded that it is implausible that these meetings and changes in management style alone had such an effect on crime. Research published recently by Eterno and Silverman make abundantly clear that pressures to manipulate figures were present at the level of patrol officers and sergeants, and that they are still present under NYPD commissioner Raymond Kelly. A third strand concerns research; the use of mapping and crime analysis has stimulated more sophisticated experimental studies of police effects on crime, although not based on CompStat meetings or studies of the internal management of crime analysis.

Street Crime and CompStat

The foundational idea, that by rational planning and administration top command could sanction efforts to reduce reported crime, is mainly a rhetorical shift from "crime fighting" without content or strategy, or periodic crackdowns targeting the usual suspects in the usual disadvantaged areas of large cities. Crime mapping, when combined with management strategies to induce patrol officers to attend to time-sensitive empirical patterns, also permits the public demonstration of police achievement and competencies. Success or failure becomes less anecdotal: these achievements can be archived, memorialized, and repeatedly shown in the mass media and in annual reports. They make police craftwork visible for others. On the other hand, the pressure to make traffic stops, stop and frisk stops, and misdemeanor arrests, while refusing to take reports of some more serious crime categories—such as robbery, aggravated assault, extortion, and related violent street crimes—and downgrading other reports, directly shapes the life chances of young men in disadvantaged areas.

Turning to the management claims, according to Peter K. Manning's research, these exercises do not lead to an elaboration or refinement of police strategies or tactics. They amplify the usual and well-understood tactics of an attack on crime. It is possible to use hot spot tactics and mapping to make arrests without articulating an underlying causal link between the maps, the incident, the motivation, or the offenders and/or the dynamics of offending. These attack tactics prevent nothing, and can cause chaos in the selected areas. It is clear that the implementation of hot spots policing, augmented by mapping, increases stops and arrests in already high-crime areas, and creates marginal reductions in reported crime. This could be called a more efficient means of increasing inequalities in the life chances for the young, poor, and black. The role of CompStat in street crime is or was to amplify attention to such crimes, mobilize rapid deployment, and make such activities "relentless."

Peter K. Manning
Northeastern University

See Also: Arrest; Bratton, William; Crime Mapping; Crime Patterns; Crime Prevention, Situational; Giuliani, Rudolph; Hot Spots; New York City; Seattle Crime Places Study; Stop and Frisk; Urbanization.

Further Readings

Bratton, William and Peter Knobler. *Turnaround: How America's Top Cop Reversed the Crime Epidemic.* New York: Random House, 1998.

Erez, Edna, ed. "Experimental Studies of Crime Control." *Justice Quarterly*, v.12/4 (1995).

Eterno, John and Eli Silverman "The New York City Police Department's CompStat: Dream or Nightmare?" *International Journal of Police Science & Management*, v.8/3 (2006).

Manning, Peter K. *Technology of Policing.* New York: New York University Press, 2008.

Sherman, Lawrence W., Patrick R. Gartin, and Michael Buerger. "Hot Spots of Predatory Crime: Routine Activities and the Criminology of Place." *Criminology*, v.27/1 (1989).

Silverman, Eli. *The NYPD Battles Crime.* Lebanon, NH: Northeastern University Press, 1999.

Walsh, William. "CompStat: An Analysis of an Emerging Managerial Paradigm." *Policing: an International Journal of Police Strategies and Management*, v.24/3(2001).

Counterfeit Goods

Counterfeit goods, commonly known as "knock-offs," are products that infringe upon the intellectual property rights of others through unauthorized use of trademarks, copyrights, patents, and related claims of ownership. Counterfeit goods are perceived to be a significant economic, political, and social problem. They accounted for an estimated $200 billion in illegal commerce worldwide in 2005, according to the Organisation for Economic Cooperation and Development (OECD), eroding sales income, profits, tax revenues, and jobs in the legitimate economy. They also pose problems for public safety and health. This illicit activity has additionally been linked to other types of street crimes, as well as to international terrorism and organized crime.

Types of Goods

A wide range of products are subject to counterfeiting and piracy, including luxury goods, pharmaceuticals, computer software, and other consumer and industrial products. As a category of street crime in America, markets for counterfeit goods may be most noticeably found in urban enclaves such as the shopping district along Canal Street near Chinatown in New York City.

The traffic in counterfeit and pirated products in these districts can be best categorized under what the OECD terms *secondary market* activity, that is, transactions in which both seller and buyer acknowledge the bogus nature of the items being proffered. This contrasts with "primary markets," where consumers are led to believe that the products are genuine. In the latter case, products are often materially deficient and may pose health and safety risks, as in the sales of counterfeit prescription and over-the-counter drugs or substandard automotive parts. The former impinges on the revenue streams from lost sales of legitimate intellectual property owners, and also has the potential effect of brand degradation by reducing the market value of trademarks and copyrights through the distribution of products in unauthorized channels. The most commonly found items available in the urban American black market are counterfeit luxury items, such as designer handbags, fashion accessories, watches, fragrances, and clothing, all of which are copies of lesser value than the original goods; and pirated entertainment products, such as digital video discs (DVDs), compact discs (CDs), and digital video games, which are direct copies of intellectual creative property.

Imports and Attitudes

Policing the illegal activity in counterfeit and pirated products has proven difficult. Many counterfeit and pirated items enter the country by passing under the scrutiny of the U.S. Customs surveillance system. The paperwork accompanying shipping containers being imported may misrepresent its cargo with knowledge that only a very small percentage are ever actually physically inspected and verified. Components may also be imported that individually do not violate intellectual property rights, only to be assembled into products that do, once they are safely inside the border.

Another impediment to policing illegal products of this type is the attitude among many consumers that purchasing such goods is not really harmful and in fact constitutes a rational decision when weighing cost versus perceived value. And as opposed to copyright violation with the illegal downloading of music and films, the sanctions for possessing counterfeit and pirated products outside of the intent to distribute are relatively modest. Vendors have also become more sophisticated, using mobile communications and multistep fulfillment techniques to avoid detection and arrest.

Immigration and Globalization

The trade in counterfeit and pirated products in New York City's Chinatown is abetted by patterns of immigration from lesser-developed areas, especially Asia, and the changing nature of "gateway" entry-level work. Prior to the decline of the city's garment industry, it was common for women emigrating from China to work in the needle trades. With those jobs now mostly gone, many immigrants, especially undocumented Asian women, find work as black market street vendors a viable, if risky, employment option. Another factor in the creation of a ready workforce is the enormous debt illegal immigrants typically incur in order to be smuggled into the United States, an obligation which must be serviced often under threat of bodily harm. The trade in both goods and people has an elective affinity, in that China is generally recognized as the primary producer of counterfeit and pirated products with the Asian criminal gangs, known as "tongs," that in many cases oversee both types of operations.

Certain perspectives on the trade in counterfeit and pirated goods point to the ways in which it is linked to globalization. The disaggregation of the value chain under late-modern mass manufacturing, in the form of outsourced production to remote offshore locations and the longer lines of supply that have resulted, provide myriad opportunities for unauthorized goods to proliferate and for the diversion of even legitimate products into gray and black markets around the globe.

Culture is another factor. Sensitivity to intellectual property concerns that have long been commonplace in the West have only recently been embraced in China, prompted largely by its entry into the World Trade Organization in 2001. From this perspective it is argued that China is still emerging from a "premodern" phase of production whereby imitation was an accepted aspect of traditional craft manufacture. As China continues to develop, the argument continues, its focus will shift to more innovative production in order to better compete in the global economy over the long term.

Conclusion

Intellectual property owners have adopted a number of strategies in their efforts to combat product counterfeiting and piracy, beyond relying on legal enforcement. These include modifying products to make them more difficult to copy; incorporating various methods of authentication, such as holograms, digital watermarks, and trace codes; and mounting awareness campaigns geared to different constituents on the harmful effects of counterfeiting and product piracy. These efforts have been to varyingly degrees successful, although they tend to add costs to brand ownership and product manufacture.

Vince Carducci
New School for Social Research

See Also: Asian Gangs; Black Market; Crime–Consumerism Nexus; Immigrant Neighborhoods; New York City; Sting Operations; Victims, Tourist.

Further Readings:

Carducci, Vince. "Confidence Games on Canal Street: The Market for Knockoffs in New York City." *Consumers, Consumption, and Commodities,* v.6/2 (2005). http://csrn.camden.rutgers.edu/newsletters/6-2/Carducci.html (Accessed June 2011).

Organisation for Economic Co-operation and Development (OECD). "The Economic Impact of Counterfeiting and Piracy: Executive Summary." Paris: OECD, 2007.

Pang, Laikwan. "'China Who Makes and Fakes': A Semiotics of the Counterfeit." *Theory, Culture, and Society,* v.25/6 (2008).

Paradise, Paul R. *Trademark Counterfeiting, Product Piracy, and the Billion Dollar Threat to the U.S. Economy.* Westport, CT: Quorum, 1999.

Philips, Tim. *Knockoff: The Deadly Trade in Counterfeit Goods.* London: Kogan-Page, 2005.

Courts

The United States has a dual federal and state court system. The vast majority of criminal cases, particularly those arising from street crimes, involve violation of state laws and are tried in state courts.

James Earle Fraser's statue, The Contemplation of Justice, *sits outside the Supreme Court Building. The building was designed as a temple of justice, keeping with the importance and dignity of the U.S. court system.*

Crimes involving violation of federal statutes are tried in federal court, but federal courts also play a critical constitutional role with regard to state cases. This entry discusses the functions and purposes of the courts. It describes state and federal court structures and processes and explains the relationship between the two systems. It also addresses critical judicial issues confronting courts today, including increasing caseloads, plea bargaining, selection of judges, wrongful convictions, and the recent trend toward problem-solving courts.

Broad Court Functions

Criminal trial courts have two essential functions: adjudication of facts, that is, the determination of guilt or innocence; and sentencing. Within these two areas, criminal justice literature discusses 10 broad purposes or goals of the courts. First, courts are intended "do justice." How this purpose is interpreted depends not only on the interests of the parties before the court but also on the values and views of the public. Second, courts are expected to "appear to do justice." This function is accomplished primarily through adherence to principles of procedural due process, including the right to notice of charges and hearing dates, the right to counsel, and the right to call and cross-examine witnesses. The appearance of justice is also achieved through appropriate judicial temperament and demeanor and the respectful treatment of litigants.

Third, courts provide a forum for peaceful dispute resolution and adjudication of facts, which, in criminal cases, leads to a determination of guilt or innocence. In the absence of such a forum, individuals might easily resort to vengeance or violence. The fourth purpose of the courts is to censure wrongdoing and publicly condemn illegal acts. Additionally, courts determine legal status, for example, marital status and child custody, and protect against arbitrary government actions. The remaining purposes—punishment, deterrence, incapacitation, and rehabilitation—relate to sentencing criminal offenders.

The U.S. Constitution created the federal court system. Article III, Section 1 provides for "one Supreme Court" and "such inferior courts as the Congress may from time to time ordain and establish." State court systems originated independently in the 13 colonies.

Tiers and Jurisdictions

State court systems typically have a four-tier structure that includes two trial courts (a court of general jurisdiction and a court of limited jurisdiction) and two appellate courts. Trial courts adjudicate cases, hear testimony from witnesses, review evidence, rule upon applicable law and procedure, and make decisions of fact. Trial courts hear both criminal and civil cases. Criminal cases involve charges brought by the state against one individual or multiple defendants, provide for sentences which carry the possibility of incarceration, and require proof beyond a reasonable doubt for conviction. Civil cases typically involve disputes between individual parties, provide for an award of money damages or decrees of specific performance, and require proof by a preponderance of the evidence.

The court of general jurisdiction is usually located in the county seat. It hears serious criminal cases, primarily felonies, as well as substantial civil cases. Courts of general jurisdiction are known by a variety of names in different states, including

circuit courts, courts of common pleas, district courts, superior courts and, sometimes, supreme courts. There are approximately 3,000 trial courts of general jurisdiction in the United States. In 2004, courts of general jurisdiction heard just over 19 million cases, of which approximately one-quarter were criminal cases. On average, a judge sitting in a court of general jurisdiction hears approximately 1,800 cases per year.

State courts of limited jurisdiction hear less serious criminal cases, often misdemeanors, as well as smaller civil cases. Like courts of general jurisdiction, courts of limited jurisdiction are known by different names in different states, including county courts, magistrate courts, municipal courts, and district courts, among others. One estimate puts the number of courts of limited jurisdiction in the United States at approximately 13,500. In 2004, courts of limited jurisdiction heard nearly 26 million cases of which approximately 14 million were criminal cases. Just over 26,500 trial judges were assigned to state courts of general jurisdiction and limited jurisdiction.

Case Volume

The number of new case filings skyrocketed during the 2000s, with approximately 106 million new cases being filed in state courts in 2009. Of these, 66 percent were filed in courts of limited jurisdiction and 17 percent were filed in courts of general jurisdiction. The remainder were filed in single-tier or unified courts. Traffic cases composed the largest caseload in courts of limited jurisdiction (61 percent) followed by criminal cases (21 percent).

Trial judges in courts of limited jurisdiction have been known to try as many as 10,000 to 20,000 cases per year. Dockets can be so overcrowded that some cases may receive no more than a minute each. Assembly-line justice is well documented statistically. In criminal cases, the most common methods of dealing with crushing caseloads are plea bargaining and preliminary dispositions such as dismissals.

A recent trend in state court systems has been the development of problem-solving or specialty courts. Drug courts, which originated in Florida in 1989, were in operation in 49 states by 2004. Domestic violence courts, mental health courts, and community and teen courts have all experienced growth in recent years. In general, these problem-solving courts are based on five principles: a tailored approach to justice, creative partnerships, informed decision making, accountability, and a focus on results.

Procedures and Processes

Court processes follow a similar pattern across the United States. Federal constitutional law requires that a criminal defendant be presented for an initial appearance before a judge or lesser judicial official, such as a court commissioner or magistrate, within 48 hours of arrest. States are free to mandate a shorter (but not longer) period between arrest and presentment, and some require presentment within 24 hours of arrest.

At the initial appearance, defendants are advised of the charges against them and of their right to counsel. Typically, the initial appearance also includes a review of the adequacy of probable cause and a determination of the conditions of release, if any. The court may detain a defendant prior to trial or release a defendant on recognizance, based on a promise to appear for trial at a later date. The court may also set bail, which requires the posting of money, property, or a bond with the court to guarantee the defendant's appearance.

Misdemeanors are generally scheduled for trial in the court of limited jurisdiction. Procedures vary dramatically for misdemeanor defendants who request a jury trial. Certain courts of limited jurisdiction are authorized to conduct jury trials. Other jurisdictions require that jury trial requests be transferred to the court of general jurisdiction. Felonies are scheduled for preliminary hearing, grand jury indictment, or information. Felony defendants will be arraigned in the court of general jurisdiction, where they will be advised of the charges against them and of their right to counsel and asked to enter a plea. Trial will be scheduled for a future date following opportunities for pretrial discovery and pretrial motions, which include motions to suppress evidence and statements obtained in violation of the Constitution and motions to dismiss.

A defendant generally has the option to select either a bench (judge) or jury trial. Certain minor or petty misdemeanors, however, do not carry the right to a jury trial. In a bench trial the judge is the final arbiter of both law and fact. In other words, the judge decides both the legal issues and the guilt or innocence of the defendant. In a jury trial, the judge decides issues of law, and the jury makes factual determinations. Juries are traditionally composed of 12 citizens from a pool selected randomly by the clerk of the court or jury commissioner. Some states have opted for smaller juries, subject to minimums established by the U.S. Supreme Court. Smaller juries are more common in civil than in criminal cases.

Jury trials begin with the process of jury selection. During voir dire, prospective jurors are examined to determine whether they can be fair and impartial. The state and defense may move to strike an unlimited number of prospective jurors for cause, if those individuals demonstrate bias. Additionally, both the state and defense are allotted a specified number of peremptory challenges to be used at their discretion, subject to constitutional limitations; for example, preemptory challenges may not be exercised to reject jurors based on their race.

Trial Ways and Means

Once the jury is sworn, the judge typically gives preliminary instructions to the jury, and lawyers for the parties deliver opening statements. The state presents its case first; witnesses are called to testify and are subject to cross-examination by the defense. "Jeopardy" typically attaches when the first witness is called in a bench trial or the jury is sworn in a jury trial. Documents or exhibits are typically entered into evidence through witnesses or by means of stipulations or agreements.

At the conclusion of the state's case, the defense typically makes a motion to dismiss or for judgment of acquittal, arguing that the state has not proven sufficient facts to let the trial proceed. Such motions are rarely granted. Next, the defense has the opportunity, but is not obligated, to present evidence and call its own witnesses. Following the defense's case, the state may present rebuttal evidence to contradict or refute evidence presented by the defense. At the conclusion of all evidence, the defense typically renews its motion to dismiss or for judgment of acquittal. Again, such motions are rarely granted.

After attorneys have the opportunity to make closing arguments, the judge gives final instructions to the jury, typically concerning the law applicable to the case. In some states, jury instructions may precede closing argument. The standard of proof required to convict a defendant in a criminal case is proof beyond a reasonable doubt and to a moral certainty. This is the highest standard of proof required in any court proceeding.

If the jury finds the defendant not guilty, the defendant is acquitted, the proceedings end, and the defendant is free to go. If the jury is unable to reach a verdict, it is said to be a hung jury. The judge declares a mistrial, and the prosecutor has the option to retry the case. Retrials under these circumstances do not violate the principle of double jeopardy.

If the defendant is convicted, the judge generally sentences the defendant immediately after trial in minor cases, or at a later date in more serious cases. While several states provide a sentencing role for the jury in noncapital cases, the vast majority limit the jury's sentencing role to death penalty cases.

Sentencing

Sentencing serves four distinct and sometimes competing purposes: punishment, deterrence, rehabilitation, and incapacitation. Punishment fulfills society's need for vengeance and prevents victims and their friends and families from taking the law into their own hands and retaliating against the perpetrator. Punishment and deterrence are closely related. Under classical and neoclassic theories, the purpose of punishment is to deter the offender from repeating counterproductive behaviors, or specific deterrence. Punishment also sends a broader message to society about the consequences of committing a crime, which serves the goal of general deterrence.

Rehabilitation suggests a treatment model based upon changing the behavior of convicted offenders. Finally, incapacitation refers to the "lock 'em up and throw away the key" philosophy of warehousing inmates. One problem associated with incapacitation is the cost of incarcerating inmates, whose number now exceeds 2 million in the United States.

Depending on the seriousness of the crime, the facts of the case, applicable law, and the defendant's background, possible sentences include fines, incarceration, restitution to the victim, community service, or suspended sentences and probation, subject to a variety of conditions, including drug and alcohol testing and counseling, mental health evaluation, employment, and other conditions deemed appropriate by the court. Many states

and the federal courts have sentencing guidelines based upon the seriousness of the offense and the offender's prior history. As a result of recent U.S. Supreme Court decisions in *U.S. v. Booker* and *Blakely v. Washington*, federal and state sentencing guidelines are largely advisory rather than mandatory. However, certain crimes may carry mandatory minimum sentences.

The vast majority of criminal cases are disposed of through plea bargaining and preliminary dispositions. Only about five percent of all criminal cases are actually tried. The benefits and detriments of plea bargaining have been extensively debated. Given enormous caseloads and limited judicial resources, this practice is likely to continue at both the state and federal level.

Appeals System

Appellate courts review decisions of the lower courts, generally based on the record, which includes trial transcripts, docket entries, and exhibits. Their caseloads are dramatically lower than those of trial courts. Most states have a two-tier appellate system, consisting of an intermediate appellate court and the highest court (or court of last resort). Intermediate appellate courts are often called courts of appeal. Defendants convicted in courts of general jurisdiction usually have an appeal as of right to the intermediate appellate court.

To prevail on appeal, the defendant must typically demonstrate that the trial court made an error of law or otherwise abused its discretion. Errors of law most frequently involve trial court rulings on the admissibility of evidence, jury instructions, and other technical issues. If the defendant prevails on appeal, the case is typically reversed and remanded back to the trial court for a new trial consistent with the findings of the appellate court. In some instances, however, the appellate court may simply reverse the decision of the trial court.

The states' highest appellate courts are often known as supreme courts. Relatively few cases are appealed to the state supreme courts, especially in the vast majority of states which have intermediate appellate courts. Some state statutes provide for automatic appeals to the state's highest appellate court in death penalty and certain other cases. More often, states require the petitioner, or appealing party, to file a writ of certiorari requesting permission to appeal. For permission to be granted, the petitioners must usually demonstrate that the appeal involves either an unsettled area of law requiring the court's guidance, or an important public policy issue.

Cases tried at the state level may enter the federal court system only after all state appeals have been exhausted. One mechanism by which state criminal decisions come to be reviewed by the federal courts is the writ of habeas corpus. Once his state court remedies are exhausted, a defendant may file a writ of habeas corpus with the U.S. District Court, which is the federal trial court, alleging that he is being detained illegally.

There are 94 U.S. District Courts, with at least one in each state and U.S. territory. U.S. District Courts adjudicate both civil and criminal cases, and have original jurisdiction over violations of federal criminal statutes. In recent years, state and federal prosecutors have worked together to bring targeted handgun and other prosecutions traditionally tried in state courts into the federal court system. Generally, prosecutors in the federal courts have more resources than their state counterparts, sentences tend to be harsher, and federal parole has been abolished.

The intermediate federal appellate court is the U.S. Circuit Court of Appeals. There are 12 Circuit Courts of Appeal, divided by geographical region. These courts hear appeals of federal civil and criminal cases. Criminal defendants convicted in the U.S. District Court are typically entitled to an appeal as of right to the U.S. Circuit Courts of Appeals. The U.S. Supreme Court is the highest court in the land and the court of last resort. While the U.S. Supreme Court has original jurisdiction in a few special types of cases, the vast majority of its cases involve judicial review of lower court decisions that raise important federal questions or constitutional law issues.

Critical constitutional issues often arrive at the U.S. Supreme Court from the state's highest court by way of a writ of certiorari. Landmark criminal procedure cases such as *Miranda v. Arizona*, involving the right to counsel prior to a custodial interrogation; *Mapp v. Ohio*, establishing the exclusionary rule, which prevents prosecutors from using evidence obtained in violation of the Constitution; and *Terry v. Ohio*, setting forth the standard for stop and frisk, were brought to the U.S. Supreme Court as a result of this process. Each of these cases involved what we would consider "street crime."

Conclusion

State and federal courts currently face a number of important issues. One issue involves the selection of judges. While federal court judges are appointed by the president, confirmed by the Senate, and have lifetime tenure, state court judges are selected in a variety of ways and serve limited terms. The most common methods are public elections and merit selection by the governor from a list of qualified attorneys nominated by a nonpartisan commission. Advocates for both methods make compelling arguments that their way most effectively reduces inappropriate political influence in the judicial selection process and potential judicial bias. Increasing caseloads and shrinking resources present an ongoing problem. Threats to impeach judges for unpopular decisions and legislative efforts to limit judicial jurisdiction or overturn judicial decisions through legislation are problems at both the state and federal level. There are also concerns with regard to campaign finance issues associated with state judicial selection processes and partisan politicization of the Senate confirmation process at the federal level.

Public perception of the courts is another issue that warrants serious consideration. In recent years, the problem of wrongful conviction has garnered a great deal of publicity and threatens to undermine public confidence in the courts' ability to determine guilt or innocence. On the other end of the spectrum, the courts may be perceived as too lenient and unable to reduce persistent criminal activity.

Michael M. Berlin
Coppin State University

See Also: Arrest; Bail; Central Booking; Courts, Drug; Courts, Mental Health; Day Reporting Center; Miranda Warnings; Police Detectives; Television Shows.

Further Readings

Berman, Greg, John Feinblatt, and Sarah Glazer. *Good Courts: The Case for Problem-Solving Justice*. New York: The New Press, 2005.

Blakely v. Washington, 542 U.S. 296 (2004).

Bogira, Steve. *Courtroom 302: A Year Behind the Scenes in an American Criminal Courthouse*. New York: Knopf, 2005.

Cronkhite, Clyde L. *Criminal Justice Administration: Strategies for the 21st Century*. Sudbury, MA: Jones and Bartlett, 2008.

LaFountain, Robert C., Richard Y. Schauffler, Shauna M. Strickland, Sarah A. Gibson, and Ashley N. Mason. *Examining the Work of State Courts: An Analysis of 2009 State Court Caseloads.* Williamsburg, VA: National Center for State Courts, 2011.

Langton, Lynn and Thomas H. Cohen. "Bureau of Justice Statistics Special Report, State Court Organization, 1987–2004." Washington, DC: U.S. Department of Justice Office of Justice Programs, 2007.

Mapp v. Ohio, 367 U.S. 643 (1961).

Mays, G. Larry and Peter R. Gregware. *Courts and Justice: A Reader.* 3rd ed. Long Grove, IL: Waveland Press, 2004.

Meyer, Jon'a and Paul Jesilow. *'Doing Justice' in the People's Court: Sentencing by Municipal Court Judges.* Albany: State University of New York Press, 1997.

Miranda v. Arizona, 384 U.S. 436 (1966).

Robertson, Cliff, Harvey Wallace, and Gilbert B. Stuckey. *Procedures in the Justice System.* 9th ed. Upper Saddle River, NJ: Prentice Hall, 2010.

Rottman, David B. and Shauna M. Strickland. *State Court Organization, 2004.* Washington, DC: U.S. Department of Justice, Bureau of Justice Statistics, 2006.

Terry v. Ohio, 392 U.S. 1 (1968).

U.S. v. Booker, 543 U.S. 220 (2005).

Courts, Drug

Perhaps the most influential changes in the scope of the contemporary U.S. criminal justice system have come from the War on Drugs initially declared by President Ronald Reagan in 1986 and expanded by Congress and President George H. W. Bush in 1988. In 1979, 40,237 adults were incarcerated in the U.S. for drug offenses. By 1989 this number had increased to 224,974 individuals or 459 percent. This increase in adults incarcerated for drug offenses took place at the same time that the overall estimates of illegal drug use had declined.

Concerned about drug policy failures, and dealing with a growing felony caseload of drug offenders, former Florida State Attorney Janet Reno joined with local stakeholders to design and implement a diversionary treatment drug court in 1989. Offenders were to be provided an opportunity to change by participating in a demanding regime of drug treatment and monitoring. Later that year, the first drug treatment court (DTC) was established in Miami. Thus began the drug court movement.

In 1995, the U.S. Department of Justice opened the Drug Courts Program Office to plan, implement, and provide funding for drug courts across the country. The rapid growth in drug courts began with the availability of federal funding under the Clinton Administration. By late 2009, 1,317 adult drug courts and 476 juvenile drug courts were in operation.

In 1997 the U.S. Department of Justice published a document that identified the 10 key components of a drug court. Since the operation and structure of drug courts differ considerably from traditional criminal courts, the framework provided by these components is critical to the success of drug courts. A well-known study of a Las Vegas drug court that resulted in an increase in arrests of its clients found that it did not implement many of the key components recommended.

Drug courts combine drug treatment with supervision using a team approach that involves the cooperation and collaboration of judges, prosecutors, defense counsel, probation authorities, treatment providers, and ideally evaluation researchers. This cooperation can be difficult for some members of the team since not all are accustomed to working with other professionals in the context of the criminal justice system.

For example, the prosecutor and defense counsel must extricate themselves from their adversarial courtroom relationship and work together on the team. This change is often difficult for attorneys who have been trained to work within the adversarial criminal justice system. Team members also need continuing interdisciplinary education to effectively implement drug court operations. The federal government has sponsored a number of drug court trainings for team members and prospective DTC team members.

Drug courts should employ a treatment process that is divided into three phases: a stabilization phase, an intensive treatment phase, and a transition phase. During the stabilization phase the client is expected to desist from drug use and begin establishing a conventional lifestyle. The treatment phase is the longest and most important stage of the process. The transitional phase follows success in the treatment stage and should contain supports for continuing a drug- and crime-free life. The treatment process typically lasts from nine months to two years. Eligible individuals should be promptly placed in the drug court program as previous research suggests that the period immediately following an arrest or apprehension for a probation violation provides a critical window of opportunity for intervening and explaining the value of treatment.

Drug courts should provide access to a continuum of services. While primarily concerned with substance abuse and criminal activity, the drug court team should also address co-occurring problems such as medical and dental problems, lack of adequate housing, educational deficits, unemployment and poor job skills, and spouse and family relations. These services are often difficult to obtain for drug court clients. Many social service systems do not have the resources to provide adequate services for their existing caseloads. This component is often the weakest link in the drug court system. The massive cuts in social and health services to disadvantaged persons as a result of the Great Recession will exacerbate this problem.

Participants' drug use is monitored by frequent drug testing. Random drug testing is the most effective method since clients cannot predict when the testing will take place. A combination of

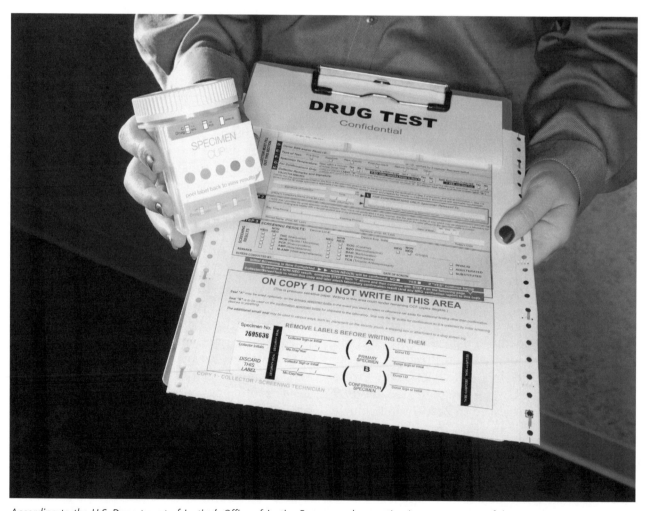

According to the U.S. Department of Justice's Office of Justice Programs, drug testing is a cornerstone of drug court operations. Courts can only operate effectively if drug tests are conducted randomly and on a frequent basis (as often as two or three times a week), if test results can be obtained immediately, and if test results are accurate and reliable.

rewards and sanctions is used by the drug court team to respond to clients' compliance with program requirements. Small rewards such as congratulations by other drug court clients or candy for incremental successes reinforce a participant's progress. Sanctions include chastisement by the judge, increased drug testing, and brief stays in jail. Relapse is expected and must be dealt with appropriately. This approach is more pragmatic than the traditional punitive handling of relapse by the criminal justice system.

Ongoing judicial interaction with each drug court participant is essential. Clients are required to appear before the judge frequently. Drug courts require judges to step beyond their traditional roles and develop new expertise in substance abuse and its treatment. Many drug court judges enjoy the sense of accomplishment they receive from helping clients to change their lives.

Creating partnerships among drug courts and stakeholder organizations generates local support and enhances drug court program effectiveness. The ability of drug court teams to achieve this goal varies widely according to the stigma placed on both drug court participants and DTCs in the local community, however.

Numerous studies have been conducted on adult drug courts. Recent reviews of the research on DTCs conclude that they are successful in reducing recidivism and subsequent drug use, improving family relationships, and providing a substantial cost savings to the criminal justice system. The most recent benefit/cost analysis concluded that DTCs produce an average savings of $2.21 for every $1.00 expended when the outcomes are limited to criminal incidents. Since this is an average, some courts produce much higher savings while others result in virtually no savings. The research found that the most substantial savings were gleaned from DTCs that targeted higher risk offenders. When benefit/cost analyses included indirect benefits, such as healthcare usage and child protective services, the amount of savings increased substantially.

Although the underlying premise is the same, juvenile drug treatment courts (JDTCs) differ from adult DTCs in some important ways. First, juveniles are often referred to JDTC for offenses that are not directly related to substance use. Moreover, due to their age juveniles often have much shorter

substance use and criminal histories than their counterparts in DTCs. Together these factors have made the identification of an appropriate target population for JDTCs more difficult. Finally, many communities lack treatment providers that are equipped to provide treatment for the special needs of adolescents. The reviews of JDTCs suggest that the treatment components are often a hodgepodge of techniques taken from adult treatment models, rather than evidence-based practices for adolescent substance users.

Evaluations of JDTCs are not as common as evaluations of adult drug courts. A meta-analysis of JDTCs suggested that they produced very small effects on reducing delinquency (3–5 percent reductions on average). Later evaluations are showing somewhat more favorable results as the model is adjusted to better serve the juvenile population. While few benefit/cost analyses of JDTCs have been completed, the benefits appeared to be substantially smaller than those found for DTCs. Some researchers have argued that much of the cost savings of JDTCs are eliminated by the overuse of detention (i.e., short-term incarceration) as a sanction.

Numerous discussions about developing best practices for JDTCs have taken place. The suggestions focus on the need to implement treatments that are evidence-based, include family members/caregivers, and the need to modify the drug court model for the appropriate developmental level of participants. Juveniles are at an earlier developmental stage than are adults yet the adult drug court model is the basis of JDTCs.

JDTCs face two other important issues: problems in the family of origin and peer relations. Inadequate parental supervision, erratic parenting practices, substance abusing parents, abuse/neglect of their children, and associations with deviant peers are well-established correlates of antisocial behaviors by youth. JDTCs face the unique challenge of convincing the parents and/or guardians of the youth to make changes to their own behavior without having the authority to compel them to do so. A recent study suggests that requiring a parent or guardian to attend status hearings with the juvenile increases positive outcomes. Theoretically the parent or guardian learns about appropriate parental monitoring by watching the judge interact with the juvenile. Some programs have attempted to deal with the problem of deviant peers by establishing alumni programs that keep graduates connected with other youth that are attempting to maintain a sober and crime-free life.

While the evaluations of adult DTCs are generally positive, drug courts are not without critics. Due to the expanded role of the judge in DTCs, some argue that DTCs provide too much power and discretion to judges without a specific set of guidelines, or checks and balances, to regulate this power. Supporters of "get tough" policies claim that DTCs are too "soft" on drug offenders. Others argue that DTCs deprive offenders of their due process rights.

Typically defendants give up some or all of their due process rights (i.e., the presumption of innocence) as a condition of participating in drug court. Proponents of the DTC model argue that the benefits of participation in the DTC outweigh these costs. Net-widening could also be a problem with drug courts. Net-widening refers to the possibility that individuals who would not have been charged with a felony in the absence of a DTC are now being charged at this higher level so they can be coerced into participating in the DTC.

Eric L. Jensen
University of Idaho
Sarah Browning
North Dakota State University

See Also: Alcohol and Drug Testing, On-Scene; Alcohol and Drug Use; Courts; Courts, Mental Health; Drug Markets, Open-Air; Jails; Juvenile Offending; Needle Exchanges; Risky Lifestyles.

Further Readings

Bouffard, Jeff and Faye Taxman. "Looking Inside the 'Black Box' of Drug Court Treatment Services Using Direct Observations." *Journal of Drug Issues,* v.34/1 (2004).

Butts, Jeffrey A. and John Roman, eds. *Juvenile Drug Courts and Teen Substance Abuse.* Washington, DC: Urban Institute Press, 2004.

Jensen, Eric L., Jurg Gerber, and Clayton Mosher. "Social Consequences of the War on Drugs." *Criminal Justice Policy Review,* v.15/1 (2004).

Jensen, Eric L., Nicholas Parsons, and Clayton Mosher. "Adult Drug Treatment Courts: A Review." *Sociology Compass,* v.1/1 (2007).

National Association of Drug Court Professionals. "National Drug Court Institute." http://www.ndci.org/ndci-home (Accessed May 2012).

Courts, Mental Health

Dedicated lawyers and judges determined that there had to be a better solution for offenders with mental illness who continued to cycle through the criminal justice system. As a result, the first mental health courts were developed in the late 1990s. Today, there are about 250 mental health courts in the United States. This entry introduces the concept of mental health courts and examines the research on mental health courts to date.

The Concept

Mental health courts are one type of specialty court. Specialty or problem-solving courts provide treatment in lieu of incarceration with the hope that participants, as a result of the treatment, will not have future contact with the criminal justice system. This is a revolutionary idea, the criminal justice system providing treatment instead of punishment for lawbreaking.

The first specialty courts were drug courts. They were developed because so many nonviolent drug offenders continued to cycle in and out of the criminal justice system. Research on outcomes for drug court participants has shown that they have less contact with the criminal justice system after participating in the drug court. Mental health courts are one type of specialty court designed to steer willing and eligible offenders with mental illness toward treatment in lieu of incarceration or other punishment with the goals of reducing recidivism, reducing jail overcrowding, improving offenders' quality of life, and preserving public safety.

Upon arrest for a crime, offenders with mental illness are referred to the mental health court, usually by their public defender or another court. The mental health court staff then makes a decision on whether the person referred is eligible to participate. This decision is based primarily on the presence of a qualifying mental illness and the seriousness of the current crime and criminal history. If the offender is deemed eligible to participate by court staff, he or she is given an offer to participate in the mental health court. If the offender accepts, he or she becomes a participant in the mental health court and develops a treatment plan with court staff.

The treatment plan is highly individualized. Participants follow the treatment plan by receiving the services listed. These services include but are not limited to: check-ins with court staff, drug and alcohol tests, psychiatric medication, psychological counseling, drug and alcohol treatment, and housing and job acquisition. Participants are also required to appear before the mental health court judge during the mental health court sessions that are held once a week.

The length of enrollment varies from one jurisdiction to another, from eight months at one extreme to five years on the other. The typical enrollment is about a year. Participants who fail to follow their treatment plan—for example if they fail to check in with court staff, if they miss a medication appointment, or if they test positive for drugs—may receive a sanction for noncompliance.

The use of sanctions varies from court to court as well; many courts use sanctions such as closer supervision, observing specialty court sessions, community service, jail, and removal from mental health court and return to traditional court for the most serious breaches. Participants who successfully complete all court requirements for the length of enrollment successfully graduate and may be eligible to have the charge that brought them into mental health court expunged from the criminal record and/or to receive early and honorable release from probation.

Regional Differences

Each mental health court in the United States operates a little differently in terms of four things. First, they operate differently in terms of the participants they accept. The courts that were developed first, in the late 1990s, accept primarily those offenders who have committed misdemeanors. Those courts developed later, the second-generation mental health courts, accept both misdemeanants and felons; some even accept violent felons on a case-by-case basis. Second, they differ in terms of the services they can offer. Those mental health courts that are situated in communities rich in mental health and drug and alcohol services are able to offer more and a greater variety of services to participants than those mental health courts situated in communities with fewer services. Third, mental health courts differ in the sanctions they use for noncompliance.

The older, first-generation courts tend not to use jail as a sanction, while many of the second-generation courts use jail as a sanction with some frequency. At least one study has found a positive correlation between the number of felons enrolled in mental health court and the use of jail as a sanction for noncompliance.

Finally, mental health courts differ in the requirements for participants to graduate. Some courts include a sustained period of sobriety or securing housing as requirements for graduation, while others do not. As implied here, each mental health court is different. This is positive in terms of specificity, as each mental health court is tailored to the community in which it is located, but it makes comparison of mental health courts to one another quite challenging.

Research on Effectiveness

Research on mental health courts has focused on a number of areas, including referrals to the court, outcomes for participants, and participants' perceptions of the mental health court. Most recently, research has probed the mental health court process, in particular examining what occurs during enrollment, that is most associated with a successful outcome.

A handful of studies have expressly focused on who is referred and accepted to the mental health court. One found that a history of felony convictions, a current charge of a crime against a person, and being male were all associated with rejection from the mental health court. Another study found that those referred to the court were more likely to be older, white, and female than the local jail and prison populations, and that those diagnosed with schizophrenia or bipolar disorder were more likely to be accepted than those without these characteristics. Both studies raise the concern that mental health courts may be accepting those they believe are going to be successful in the court. As there are only two studies in this area to date, it is unsurprising that those characteristics associated with acceptance or rejection are not yet fully elucidated.

A variety of studies have found that the mental health court is associated with reduced recidivism for participants. Mental health court participants had fewer arrests than before mental health court, and fewer arrests than a comparable traditional court group. Mental health court participants had fewer jail days than before mental health court and fewer jail days than a comparable traditional court group. Mental health court participants were less likely to be charged with crimes of any kind and also with violent crimes than a comparable traditional court group.

No matter how it is measured, then, the mental health court is associated with reduced recidivism for participants. Other studies have examined the relationship between length of enrollment and recidivism, and the duration of the effects of mental health court. Researchers have found that it is not just participation in the mental health court, but successful graduation that is associated with the positive outcomes detailed above. For those who successfully graduate, the mental health court's positive effects on recidivism have been observed one and two years after graduation.

In two studies on participants' perceptions of the mental health court, researchers found that participants were generally positive about the court and perceived little coercion during the enrollment process. However, many participants in both studies claimed not to know that the court was voluntary and that they could choose not to participate.

Conclusion

The latest wave of mental health court research is focusing on the mental health court process, probing that which occurs during enrollment that is associated with the positive outcomes. Studies in this area have focused on the use of court appearances to more closely supervise mental health court participants, and on the role of the judge in reducing recidivism.

Interactions with the judge during mental health court sessions are overwhelmingly positive, with participants often receiving praise or encouragement. These affirming interactions with the judge may be the first such interactions mental health court participants have had with a judge. Researchers maintain this rapport and this demonstration of investment in the participant is instrumental in keeping the participant engaged in the treatment offered by the mental health court.

Kelly Frailing
Texas A&M International University

See Also: Courts; Courts, Drug; Day Reporting Center; Homelessness; Mental Illness; Women.

Further Readings

Almquist, Laura and Elizabeth Dodd. *Mental Health Courts: A Guide to Research-Informed Policy and Practice.* New York: Council of State Governments, 2009.

Frailing, Kelly. "How Mental Health Courts Function: Outcomes and Observations." *International Journal of Law and Psychiatry,* v.33/4 (2010).

Herinckx, Heidi A., Sandra C. Swart, Shane M. Ama, Cheri D. Dolezal, and Steve King. "Re-Arrest and Linkage to Mental Health Services Among Clients of the Clark County Mental Health Court Program." *Psychiatric Services,* v.56/7 (2005).

Hiday, Virginia A. and Bradley Ray. "Arrests Two Years After Exiting a Well-Established Mental Health Court." *Psychiatric Services,* v.61/5 (2010).

Luskin, Mary L. "Who is Diverted? Case Selection for Court-Monitored Mental Health Treatment." *Law and Policy,* v.23/2 (2001).

McNiel, Dale E. and Renee L. Binder. "Effectiveness of a Mental Health Court in Reducing Criminal Recidivism and Violence." *American Journal of Psychiatry,* v.164/9 (2007).

Moore, Marlee E. and Virginia A. Hiday. "Mental Health Court Outcomes: A Comparison of Re-Arrest and Re-Arrest Severity Between Mental Health Court and Traditional Court Participants." *Law and Human Behavior,* v.30/6 (2006).

Poythress, Norman G., John Petrila, Ann McGaha, and Roger A. Boothroyd. "Perceived Coercion and Procedural Justice in the Broward Mental Health Court." *International Journal of Law and Psychiatry,* v.25/1 (2002).

Redlich, Allison D., Henry J. Steadman, John Monahan, Pamela C. Robbins, and John Petrila. "Patterns of Practice in Mental Health Courts: A National Survey." *Law and Human Behavior,* v.30/3 (2006).

Steadman, Henry J., Allison D. Redlich, Pamela Griffin, John Petrila, and John Monahan. "From Referral to Disposition: Case Processing in Seven Mental Health

Courts." *Behavioral Sciences and the Law,* v.23/2 (2005).

Crack House

A crack house is a house, apartment, or other type of building; either privately or public owned, sometimes abandoned, where crack cocaine is cooked and sold to users who congregate to buy, use, and sometimes exchange sex for the drug. In addition to drug sales and drug use, research on crack houses indicate they are associated with violence, property crime and violent personal crime, risky sexual behavior, prostitution, community fear, and disorder.

Scales of Crime and Disorder

Crack houses present a major challenge to the community and law enforcement agencies in the jurisdictions where they are found. A number of initiatives have successfully been employed to dismantle crack houses. However, some of these efforts have been criticized as displacing crime related to crack houses to other communities or of violating civil rights. While a reliable estimate of the number of crack houses operating at any one time is unavailable, they are known to operate in every major American city: nevertheless, scholars have criticized media reports dating from the early-1980s crack "epidemic," as well as some law enforcement agencies, as exaggerating many aspects of the crack cocaine trade including the prevalence of crack houses.

Research on crack houses has focused on issues including risky sexual behavior, crime, and prevention strategies. Ethnographic research conducted in the field has attempted to define different types of crack houses. One typology focuses on the amount of social interaction occurring in different crack houses. Some crack houses will only sell drugs, significantly limiting the interaction between dealers and customers since users must smoke elsewhere. Others allow users to smoke crack on premises. This arrangement keeps the customer nearby to assure repeat business once the originally purchased crack is gone. Still others also allow sexual activities.

Research examining Philadelphia in the late 1980s described four types of crack houses primarily differentiated by the social status of the owner and customers. Relatively stable female crack users operated "party houses" visited by employed men with whom the proprietor traded sex for crack. Women were selective in those men allowed to visit; activities were restricted and closely monitored to avoid attention from neighbors or law enforcement. This type represented the most tightly controlled environment for the group consumption of crack.

In contrast, the most disorganized and dangerous was the "bandominium" (abandoned house, apartment, or other building). Characterized by squalor, such crack houses rarely had electricity or running water; they attracted the most dangerous and unpredictable patrons, many homeless due to their drug addiction. Monitoring of activities was minimal, with no particular person in charge.

Violence and Women

A variety of social and economic roles are unique to crack houses. At the top of the hierarchy are those directly dealing the drug in exchange for cash. Crack subcultures have historically been dominated by males who manufacture and sell the drug at the higher or middleman levels. They determine who can enter, purchase drugs, and also direct all other activities in houses that allow smoking and sex. Lookouts are responsible for detecting the arrival of the police; "catchers" responsible for removing the drugs if a police raid does occur.

Some such men do not smoke crack, but frequent crack houses to provide drugs to addicted women in exchange for sex. More common is the male user who may or may not engage in sexual activities. While critical to the financial success of the house, users are often viewed with contempt and ridiculed for crack-specific behaviors such as obsessively looking for crack on the floor. The lowest social role is occupied by the woman willing to trade sex for crack, commonly known as a "crack whore." Many of these women are subject to emotional, sexual, and physical abuse on a regular basis.

Economic exchanges are central to all activities in the crack house. Large amounts of money change hands on a nightly basis. Male users quickly become unwelcome when their money runs out. Females with no cash may be allowed to stay if able to induce males to purchase additional crack to trade for sex. Some crack houses charge for a wide variety of services such as a room for sex, paraphernalia, even a mattress for a sexual act. Some crack houses charge an entrance fee or require the person to provide a rock of crack in exchange for entry. Users who have exhausted their cash will often exchange personal items such as electronics or jewelry.

The exchange of sex for crack is common and has a number of public health repercussions. Desperately addicted women often perceive themselves as powerless in sex-for-drugs exchanges. This imbalance of power often results in acts of severe degradation and leads women to engage in unprotected

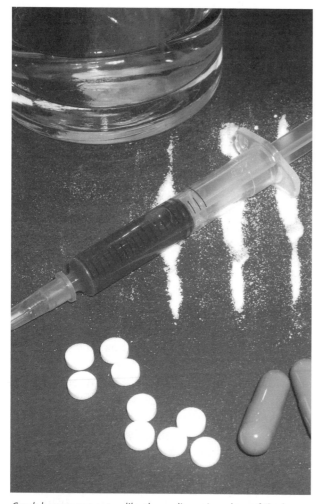

Crack houses are not unlike the earlier opium dens of the late 19th and early 20th centuries. Increased law enforcement activity is causing some drug operations to relocate to the suburbs with an effort to blend in to the neighborhood.

sex. Interviews of crack-addicted women indicate that some women have as many as 100 sexual partners within a 30-day period. While males also trade sex for drugs, research indicates this behavior is less common among crack-addicted men. However, both male and female crack users have higher rates of all sexually transmitted diseases, including human immunodeficiency virus (HIV) infection.

Some women live at the crack house, essentially employed as a sex worker for the proprietor. Women are expected to provide a variety of services with multiple men on demand. In return, these women are provided shelter, food, and crack. Often young, homeless runaways known as "house girls," they are subjected to constant degradation given that the crack house has a continuous flow of customers throughout the day and night. Many prostitutes or street walkers are also addicted to crack but able to exercise far more control than the house girl. Street workers are mobile and can negotiate price, services performed, and customers serviced. In contrast, females who live at crack houses are completely controlled by the men selling the crack. In essence, they are sexual slaves.

Violence is a common feature of crack houses. Prolonged cocaine use is associated with cocaine psychosis characterized by hallucinations, paranoia, and violence. Violence can also be associated with withdrawal symptoms that appear relatively quickly after the last hit of crack. Extreme moodiness, irritability, and mood swings are common. Violence may also occur from those dealing to establish the security of the crack itself. Given the large amount of cash and drugs on premises, robberies sometimes are attempted against which dealers arm themselves. Research has further shown women to be at substantially greater risk of violent victimization than men who are also involved in crack subcultures.

Levels of Enforcement

Drug trafficking associated with crack houses has presented tough challenges for communities and law enforcement. Public disorder, violence, open drug use, and fear cause law abiding citizens to withdraw from the community. Community engagement is necessary to establish informal social control that discourages criminal behavior. In public housing, the negative impact of crack houses is intensified because of the large number of families nearby. A number of community policing strategies have been utilized to disrupt and eradicate crack houses, including the development of meaningful relationships and trust with community residents to encourage the reporting of drug hot spots. Cameras, publicizing drug arrests, and focusing on probationers and parolees who are involved in drug trafficking have also been successful in dismantling crack houses.

In some cities such as New York, Detroit, Philadelphia, and Miami, residents have committed arson against crack houses. In public housing, federal laws have been enacted to evict tenants who are accused of using, possessing, or selling drugs from their residence. The law also extends to family members and visitors. These laws have been challenged by civil rights advocates as violating basic civil rights. At the same time, communities consistently call for tougher enforcement.

Tana McCoy
Roosevelt University

See Also: Alcohol and Drug Use; Crime, Displacement of; Crime Mapping; Fear of Crime; Projects, The; Prostitute/Streetwalker; Risky Lifestyles; Sex Crimes; Skid Row; Urban Ethnography; Women.

Further Readings

Carlson, Robert G., Merrill Singer, Richard C. Stephens, and Claire E. Sterk. "Reflections on 40 Years of Ethnographic Drug Abuse Research: Implications for the Future." *Journal of Drug Issues*, v.39/1 (2009).

Curtis, Richard. "The Improbable Transformation of Inner-City Neighborhoods: Crime, Violence, Drugs, and Youth in the 1990s." *Journal of Criminal Law & Criminology*, v.88/4 (1998).

Erickson, Patricia G., Jennifer Butters, Patti McGillicuddy, and Ase Hallgren. "Crack and Prostitution: Gender, Myths, and Experiences." *Journal of Drug Issues*, v.30/4 (2000).

Geter, Robert S. "Crack User Settings: A Crack House Typology." *International Journal of the Addictions*, v.29/8 (1994).

Inciardi, James A., Hilary Surratt, and Steven P. Kurtz. "HIV, HBV, and HCV Infections Among Drug-Involved, Inner-City, Street Sex Workers in Miami, Florida." *AIDS and Behavior*, v.10/2 (2006).

Maranda, Michael J., Han H. Chenglong, and Gregory A. Rainone. "Crack Cocaine and Sex." *Journal of Psychoactive Drugs*, v.36/3 (2004).

Saxe, Leonard, Charles Kadushin, Elizabeth Tighe, Andrew A. Beveridge, David Livert, Archie Brodsky, and David Rindskopf. "Community-Based Programs in the War on Drugs." *Journal of Drug Issues*, v.36/2 (2006).

Sharpe, Tanya Telfair. *Behind the Eight Ball: Sex for Crack Cocaine Exchange and Poor Black Women*. London: Haworth Press, 2005.

Walsh, William F., Richard Tewksbury, and George P. Wilson. "Fighting Back in Bright Leaf: Community Policing and Drug Trafficking in Public Housing." *American Journal of Criminal Justice*, v.25/1 (2000).

Credit Card Theft

Credit cards were first used in the early 1900s. These cards were issued by oil companies and department stores. These were known as charge cards, and differed from modern credit and debit cards in that they could only be used at the establishment that issued them. Charge cards were created to develop loyalty to the merchant; consumer convenience was a secondary matter. Bank cards joined this system starting in 1940. Well into the 1950s, charge card crime was minimal as the restrictions on card use made crime difficult, with relatively low return. Early card were part of a closed loop system (transactions only occurring between one bank, one merchant, and one person) made up of the consumer, the merchant, and the issuer of the card. Card balances were generally paid each month.

Increasingly street criminals began to steal credit cards. This occurred in 1959 as the the ability to maintain balances and make payments was introduced to credit card holders. With the increased use—and the revolving credit—credit card crime began to rise. Cards, after being stolen could be used for longer periods of time. It could take days and even months to stop the use of the card. Still, the criminal was limited by the nature of the closed loop system, in which the issuer of the credit card authorizes and processes transactions and settles debts directly with merchants and consumers.

The advent of Visa and MasterCard, based on an association of banks with third-party transaction houses, (bank customers that provide payment processing services to merchants), formed an open-loop system. In this system, diverse banks cooperated and made transfers between each other in support of the Visa or MasterCard credit card, while an exploding number and variety of merchants also joined the pool. This boom time for credit cards in the 1960s and 1970s created new theft and robbery opportunities for street criminals, dovetailing with credit card crime that would often follow a purse snatching, pickpocketing, or other form of street theft.

Processing of cards began to change, partly to address the new security challenges. Street criminals, who previously could steal a card and use it for long periods, now faced a system that shut down cards rapidly. When a credit card is stolen it remains usable until the issuer is notified by the user. Most issuers have 24-hour hotlines where card owners can report the theft of a card. Other security measures include a signature panel on the back of cards, and the requirement of a picture ID for a transaction to be completed. In most cases the ID is not requested by merchants; many merchants routinely process cards without signatures.

With the advent of self-serve and online merchandising, many more transactions are handled completely by the card owner; this allows for security measures to be remotely circumvented by criminals. A common security measure against this form of card theft is the requirement of the member's zip code being keyed in at the self-service terminal. The efficacy of this measure is limited; in the case of stolen wallets or purses, for instance, that type of personal information is readily available to the thief. The use of personal identification numbers (PIN) is yet another security measure that is often foiled by a lack of proper use by consumers.

Identity Theft

Street crime has changed from the direct theft of cards to downloading card information. Even as the rate of direct theft has declined, as reflected in the Uniformed Crime Reports (UCR) compiled by the Federal Bureau of Investigation (FBI), the incidence of remote, online theft using credit card and other personal identity information has skyrocketed. UCR statistics document the continued decline of robbery, the violent street crime associated with credit card theft in the past. In 2010 there were 367,832 robberies reported by police departments nationally. This was a 10 percent decline from 2009 and an 18 percent decline since 2008.

While violent street crime credit card theft declined, nonviolent forms continued to increase. Data from the Federal Trade Commission (FTC) released in 2008 stated that there were 8.3 million victims of identity theft in 2005. These victims spent over 200 million hours to recover their money and identities. Currently the FBI is involved with over 21 task forces throughout the country working on identity theft. Mail order and Internet purchases completed by credit card, already an significant source of crime during the 1990s, expanded rapidly after 2000. Countermeasures have increased and much has been learned by law enforcement, banks, and merchants. Two types of credit card crime are directly related to street crime: account takeover and skimming.

In an account takeover, the criminal stealthily gathers crucial information on an individual. This can be done by stealing and then returning wallets, purses, or even burglarizing a house for information. The next step is to contact the card issuer and pretend to be the legitimate cardholder; then the criminal asks that the address of the card be changed. A new card is then requested and sent to the new address.

Skimming is the theft of credit card information during the course of a legitimate transaction. A dishonest merchant or a dishonest employee of a legitimate merchant obtains a person's credit card number by looking at receipts, or using an electronic scanner. Any additional identity data—such as PIN numbers, zip codes, security codes—is also stolen as available. Scanners can be placed over legitimate automated teller machines (ATMs), allowing criminals to steal from unsuspecting ATM customers. Skimming commonly occurs in restaurants and bars where the person's credit card is carried out of sight by the server to complete the transaction.

Industrial-Scale Crime

Organized crime has moved into identity theft, and deployed more robust operations. For

The purpose of credit card theft is generally to obtain goods without paying or to obtain unauthorized funds from an account. The cost of card fraud, due to the high volume of transactions, translates into billions of dollars.

old-style stolen card street crime—although that version of credit card theft is sure to remain a concern as long as consumers avail themselves of the convenience of credit cards for routine transactions.

Glenn Zuern
Albany State University

See Also: Bar Personnel; Bars and Pubs; Counterfeit Goods; Crime–Consumerism Nexus; Pickpocketing; Theft and Larceny; Victims, Tourist.

Further Readings
Brickey, Kathleen F. *Corporate and White Collar Crime.* Waltham, MA: Aspen Publishers, 2006.
Federal Bureau of Investigation. "Leader of Large-Scale Identity Theft Ring and Co-Conspirator Plead Guilty, Admit Roles in Fraud Enterprise." January 9, 2012. http://www.fbi.gov/newark/press-releases/2012/leader-of-large-scale-identity-theft-ring-and-co-conspirator-plead-guilty-admit-roles-in-fraud-enterprise (Accessed June 2012).
Hastings, Glenn and Richard Marcus. *Identity Theft, Inc.: A Wild Ride With the World's #1 Identity Thief.* New York: The Disinformation Company, 2006.
Woolsey, Ben and Emily Starbuck Gerson. "The History of Credit Cards." May 2009. http://www.creditcards.com/credit-card-news/credit-cards-history-1264.php (Accessed June 2012).

example, in 2011 the FBI cracked an operation in Bergen County, New Jersey, headed by Sang-Hyun Park that allegedly involved some 43 codefendants engaged in large-scale credit card fraud, bank fraud, and tax fraud. Park's criminal staff, working as "identity brokers," obtained Social Security numbers and used them to create and sell false identities complete with elevated credit scores. The high credit scores were used to open bank accounts, generate new credit cards, and fraudulently obtain and spend millions of dollars worth of cash by coercing dishonest merchants to charge the cards for goods and services that were never delivered. The people whose Social Security numbers were illegally used in this manner were victimized, as were many honest merchants, banks, and other consumers.

Authorities are increasingly focused on this type of sophisticated operation as supplanting the

Crime, Displacement of

The concept of displacement of crime is based on the belief that the motivation levels of offenders and the opportunities for offending are constant. This belief leads to the assumption that offenders who are blocked from committing an offense in one geographic or temporal area will simply turn to an alternative opportunity to complete their offending. As a result of displacement, crime levels in areas where offenders are blocked from offending may decrease, but levels of crime in other areas, times, or types of offenses may increase due to the altered patterns of offenders.

The potential for displacement has served as a criticism of crime prevention programs out of the concern that the programs will not reduce overall crime but will displace the targeted crime out of the target area. Thus, designers of programs to reduce or deter street crime should consider how their project might displace crime and how to control that displacement. Recent research on the effects of displacement have identified new techniques and technologies that the police may use to better measure and anticipate displacement as the result of street crime reduction efforts.

Types and Levels of Displacement

Thomas Repetto conducted one of the first examinations of the impact of displacement on crime reduction programs. In his analysis, Repetto identified five different ways in which displacement could occur, including changes to offending which are temporal, tactical (method), target-related, territorial (location), or functional (offense type). Subsequent researchers noted that a sixth form, perpetrator displacement (previous offenders replaced by new ones), was also possible.

Although a variety of types of displacement are possible, Repetto argued that the likelihood of displacement was largely dependent on the ability of the offender to adapt to new circumstances. In particular, he found that some offenses were so opportunistic as to not be displaceable because they required that offenders and victims come in contact at a specific location and time. Among offenders and offenses that are displaceable, Repetto suggested that it might be possible for practitioners to predict how and where displacement would occur and potentially further intervene to block offending.

Repetto's work provided an example of the potential for variation in levels of displacement, specifically identifying that full displacement is an unlikely result of crime prevention efforts. This general finding has led to displacement levels being categorized as malign or benign. Malign displacement is the result of an increase in crime in the community or a change in offending that leads to an overall negative effect for the community when compared to the preprogram levels. Benign displacement is the result of some, but not all, crime being displaced in a manner that results in a general improvement for the greater community. The likelihood of displacement will increase when the intended offense can easily be moved or altered to a different place, time, or offense type. The potential for displacement will decrease when the offenses are situational in nature and require specific elements to be present simultaneously in order for the offense to occur.

The exact opposite of displacement, the diffusion of crime control benefits has also been found to occur as the result of crime prevention efforts. A diffusion of benefits occurs when the effect of a specific crime prevention project spreads beyond the borders of the target area and into the surrounding community. The diffusion of the prevention efforts results in a reduction in crime for the greater community, beyond what is found in the project area. This reduction in crime may be from increases in the perceived risks of crime (deterrence) or decreases in the perceived rewards (discouragement) as a result of crime reduction efforts.

Empirical Evidence

In a meta-analysis of situational crime prevention programs that evaluated the impact of displacement and diffusion, Rob Guerette and Kate Bowers found that crime displacement or diffusion of benefits were equally likely to occur. However, when displacement did occur following the introduction of a crime prevention program, the displacement effect was often benign and less powerful than the crime reduction program's effect—resulting in an overall improvement for the community. A limitation of this review and many other assessments of displacement is that the included programs focused on reducing crime through situational crime prevention efforts primarily, and only examined the impact of displacement or diffusion of benefits on the community secondarily, and occasionally after the fact.

In contrast, in a unique experiment conducted in Jersey City, New Jersey, David Weisburd and colleagues developed a test that primarily focused on measuring the effect of spatial displacement and diffusion. In Jersey City, the researchers were focused on measuring the levels of displacement or diffusion of benefits that occurred following the introduction of prostitution and drug dealing reduction efforts in two neighborhoods. In particular, the research team wanted to test whether crime was spatially displaced and "moved around the corner" when the crime prevention program was implemented, or if there were other patterns of crime displacement or diffusion that occurred.

Following several months of observations, interviews, and other data collection efforts, the researchers found that the drug and prostitution reduction programs were successful in reducing crime in the target area and resulted in a small, but general, diffusion of benefits to the community immediately surrounding the project areas, rather than a displacement of the targeted crimes.

Conclusion

Concerns related to the displacement of crime as the result of crime reduction efforts have served as criticisms of crime prevention programs for several decades. However, recent research suggests that a diffusion of benefits is just as likely to be the result of crime prevention efforts as is displacement. Future crime prevention efforts to reduce street crimes should be undertaken with the understanding that the potential for both displacement and diffusion of crime control benefits may occur.

Kathleen Gallagher
Pamela K. Wilcox
University of Cincinnati

See Also: Crime Mapping; Crime Patterns; Environmental Criminology; Hot Spots; Policing, Problem-Oriented; Routine Activity Theory; Seattle Crime Places Study; Urbanization.

Further Readings

Clarke, Ronald and David Weisburd. "Diffusion of Crime Control Benefits: Observations on the Reverse of Displacement." In *Crime Prevention Studies,* Ronald V. Clarke, ed., Vol. 2. Monsey, NY: Criminal Justice Press, 1994.

Cornish, Derek and Ronald Clarke. "Understanding Crime Displacement: An Application of Rational Choice Theory." *Criminology,* v.25/4 (1987).

Guerette, Rob and Kate Bowers. "Assessing the Extent of Crime Displacement and Diffusion of Benefits: A Review of Situational Crime Prevention Evaluations." *Criminology,* v.47/4 (2009).

Repetto, Thomas. "Crime Prevention and the Displacement Phenomenon." *Crime and Delinquency,* v.22/2 (1976).

Weisburd, David, et al. "Does Crime Just Move Around the Corner? A Controlled Study of Spatial Displacement and Diffusion of Crime Control Benefits." *Criminology,* v.44/3 (2006).

Crime Mapping

Crime mapping is a technique used by law enforcement agencies and academics to visualize and analyze crime data using geographic information systems (GIS). It can be used to map police activity and crime reduction efforts, identify recently committed crimes, "hot spots," predict where crime is most likely to occur in the future, understand the patterning and distribution of crime within a geographical area, and assess and evaluate the impact of crime-combating policies. It has disproportionately been used in urban settings.

GIS is a computer software system developed to capture, manage, integrate, manipulate, analyze, and display spatial data. GIS allows users to layer different maps on top of base maps. Base maps contain geographical data, which depict the spatial landscape of an area. Base maps could be street maps, maps containing housing and building locations, geographic census data, and a variety of other forms of basic demographic data. Top layer maps may include more specific types of data related to crime, such as where crime incidents have occurred or where law enforcement has implemented policies or crime-fighting initiatives. Individual maps can be analyzed, manipulated, or displayed separately, or maps can be combined and layered with others to examine particular relationships between variables of interest. Some popular GIS software packages include: ArchView, ArcGIS, GeoMedia, and MapInfo. For crime-specific data, the following extensions are available for the software packages: CompStat, CrimeStat, CrimeView, Spatial Analyst, and SpaceStat.

History and Development

GIS technology arose through its application in various U.S. federal government sectors. Its earliest use was in planning for the U.S. Census. It provided information as to where the most populous areas in the country were. At this time, the U.S. military was also using GIS technology for intelligence gathering. It provided the armed forces with precise geographical locations, which are useful for accurately targeting military attacks.

In the 1980s more widespread use of GIS occured. This was a result of many technological changes: the price of technology had decreased, operating systems had improved significantly, electronic storage media was becoming more popular, and computer software was becoming far more advanced than in previous generations. GIS software, in particular, had not only become more advanced, but also had become more cost-effective and accessible. All of these technological advancements allowed GIS to be used in fields previously untapped.

GIS found its way into law enforcement and criminal justice agencies following the digitalization of police records. No longer was police data stored solely in file cabinets at local police departments. Rather, data on offenders, victims, and criminal events were stored on computers connected through interdepartmental networks, which allowed for greater ease of accessibility. Having access to a multitude of informational resources encouraged practitioners to identify patterns based on the information provided in police reports.

The National Institute of Justice's Mapping and Analysis for Public Safety (MAPS) Program (formerly the Crime Mapping Research Program) was one of the driving forces in crime mapping advancement. Since its inception, the group has brought attention to crime mapping as an effective method for examining crime. It has organized conferences and seminars, published articles and books, and funded research on the topic. The MAPS program has also created new crime mapping tools and software particularly for criminological use. Today, it continues to further awareness and support the continued development of crime mapping innovation worldwide.

Applicability to Criminology

The GIS method is ideal for the study of crime data because every criminal event has a particular geographic location in which it occurs. The notion that GIS could be used to investigate crime problems arose from the school of environmental criminology, a subset of criminology that focuses on the spatial ontology of crime. Environmental theorists argue that crime is not a random phenomenon that is equally distributed across time and place. Rather, there are temporal and spatial patterns in the organization and orientation of criminal activity.

Routine activity theory, in particular, asserts that crime trends change over time as a result of the movement of legitimate routine activities. The movements of activities in public spaces allow more opportunities for the convergence in time and space of three necessary elements of a criminal act: a motivated offender, a suitable target, and the lack of capable guardianship. Crime pattern theory, an extension of routine activity theory, adopts and expands upon these propositions. According to the crime pattern theory, potential offenders search for criminal opportunities in locations that are familiar to them—in locations where they participate in their own daily activities and routines. The aforementioned theories prescribe situational crime prevention as a practical response to crime problems. Situational crime prevention implements initiatives aimed at reducing opportunities for crimes to occur.

Following the recommendations put forth by situational crime prevention, there are various ways that crime mapping can be used in the fields of criminology and criminal justice to police and prevent crime. Particularly, crime mapping can be used for crime auditing. Auditing is the measurement and analysis of crime problems through the use of descriptive statistics and detailed criminal event information. Auditing relates to describing and displaying current crime levels and examining how these levels have changed over time in particular geographical locations. During the auditing process, crime mappers can identify patterns over time which consequently can determine where "hot spots" are located.

Crime mapping can also be applied to problem-solving crime analysis. This is an action-research approach that focuses on targeting specific and recurrent crime problems. Its goal is to reduce crime by identifying the underlying causes. Using crime mapping techniques, the practitioner is able to first identify a crime problem, and consequently, conduct an in-depth investigation of it. Using this information, policy makers can create and implement practical responses to the issue. Finally, crime mapping provides tools to assess the impact of actions designed to address the crime problems. The use of crime mapping is often an integral component of problem-oriented policing strategies.

Geographic profiling can also be completed using crime mapping methods. Geographic profiling allows law enforcement agencies to track the location of an offender using known information as to his or her whereabouts. This technique is used when criminal justice agencies are aware that an unidentified suspect has carried out a series of criminal activities at several geographic points. Geographic profiling can determine the next probable location of attack.

Conclusion

Crime mapping data can assist in the implementation, monitoring, assessment, and evaluation of programs aimed at reducing crime. Visualizations can determine if initiatives have been successful by creating comparative reports of before and after crime levels since the implementation of the program. Maps can demonstrate whether displacement of crime has occurred as a result of preventative efforts. Crime mapping also assists police departments with assessing whether the work of their officers is sufficient. It can provide knowledge regarding what areas need more patrolling and what areas are doing well in terms of crime levels.

Like any other technique or methodology applied within the law enforcement realm, the value of adopting crime mapping in any given jurisdiction will depend on the expectations and challenges of the department, and commitment to testing its efficacy over time. As has been seen in the case of CompStat, adopted by the New York Police Department in the 1990s and a focus of much approval—as well as disdain—care must be taken in the evaluation of crime mapping not to overvalue its effectiveness, nor to undervalue its use in combination with altered management approaches.

Certain types of violent street crimes, as well as gang-related activities, are among the priorty targets for crime mapping use by numerous police departments. As such crimes are often addressed by multijurisdictional teams, crime mapping has become part of the police toolkit at the local, state, and federal levels. Due to its diverse applicability and its ability to answer a plethora of criminological questions, crime mapping is an indispensible new technology for law enforcement agencies and academics alike.

Amanda Bolton
University of Missouri, St. Louis

See Also: CompStat; Crime, Displacement of; Crime Patterns; Crime Prevention, Situational; Environmental Criminology; Hot Spots; Policing, Problem-Oriented; Routine Activity Theory.

Further Readings

Brantingham, Paul and Patricia Brantingham. *Patterns in Crime.* New York: Macmillan, 1984.

Chainey, Spencer and Jerry Ratcliffe. *GIS and Crime Mapping.* Chichester, UK: John Wiley & Sons, 2005.

Clarke, Ronald and Marcus Felson. *Routine Activity and Rational Choice.* New Piscataway, NJ: Transaction Publishers, 2004.

Cohen, Lawrence and Marcus Felson. "Social Change and Crime Rate Trends: A Routine Activity Approach." *American Sociological Review*, v.44/4 (1979).

Longley, Paul, Mike Goodchild, David Maguire, and David Rhind. *Geographic Information Systems and Science.* Chichester, UK: John Wiley & Sons, 2001.

Ratcliffe, Jerry. "Crime Mapping and the Training Needs of Law Enforcement." *European Journal on Criminal Policy and Research*, v.10/1 (2004).

Crime Patterns

Variation in the social, spatial, and temporal patterns of street crime has long drawn attention from scholars, practitioners, and the media. Measures of crime rates are considered important social indicators reflecting the health of our society and are often used to judge the effectiveness of our criminal justice system. Because of the importance of these measures, scholars are greatly interested in the reliability of sources of information on criminal behavior. The relatively recent availability of systematic and nationwide estimates of crime has greatly enhanced our understanding of how and why crime varies across social groups, geographic areas, and time periods. The rapid rise in crime from the 1960s to the mid-1980s inspired a wide range of theories of crime patterns. However, the historic declines in crime in more recent decades have challenged many of the explanations derived from earlier trends.

Observing Crime Patterns

Historical analysis of patterns in crime suffered from the lack of systemic national data until the development of the Uniform Crime Reports (UCR) in the 1930s. Prior to the UCR, historical studies were based on the few cities or counties that collected crime statistics in a systematic manner. The availability of national crime statistics was a major turning point in the study of the distribution of crime, but concerns over reliability remained. The UCR estimates are based upon figures provided to the Federal Bureau of Investigation (FBI) by local law enforcement agencies. Unfortunately, the quality of this information may differ across agencies. Furthermore there is concern that many crimes go unreported to authorities. This is especially true for crimes such as forcible rape or for victims who experience victimization repeatedly (e.g., victims of domestic violence).

To address the problems with crime estimates based on official police reports, the National Crime Victimization Survey (NCVS) was implemented in 1973. The NCVS collects information from approximately 49,000 households (over 100,000 individuals) twice a year, every year. The survey asks respondents about the variety and frequency of criminal victimization; it was designed to produce reliable measures of victimization that could be compared across time. Although the NCVS was designed to overcome some of the problems with the UCR, the NCVS is not without its limitations. Although the sample is large, the number

The Charleston, South Carolina, Police Department is working with IBM to assist the city's more than 400 police officers to more accurately evaluate and forecast crime patterns. The officers' ability to input data from their patrol cars regarding arrests and disturbances assists in collecting accurate crime patterns.

of individuals surveyed in a particular area is relatively small and does not allow accurate comparisons across jurisdictions. In addition, the NCVS, for obvious reasons, does not collect information on homicides, nor does it include crimes affecting businesses. Even with their noted limitations, the UCR and NCVS are the two most authoritative sources of crime and victimization in the United States. With this systematic collection of crime statistics came the ability to measure crime patterns across time and space, and the ability to test competing explanations of the distribution of crime and victimization.

Individual, Spatial, and Temporal

Researchers have been interested in how crime varies among individuals, regions, and time. Scholars interested in understanding who commits crimes or who are likely victims focused their attention on individual-level characteristics in explaining patterns. These studies found that criminal behavior and victimization varied in predictable ways by age, gender, race, income, and a host of other microlevel variables. Young minority males living in inner-city areas, for example, tend to have higher rates of both criminal behavior and victimization.

Other scholars are concerned with why different areas suffer higher crime rates. Cross-sectional studies of different communities observed predictable differences between areas and found that poverty, population density, and ethnic heterogeneity, among other macrolevel variables, were closely associated with higher crime rates. Still others have focused on how crime varies across time. These studies have frequently looked to demographic variables, economic conditions, and other temporal factors in understanding patterns in crime.

Recent trends in the study of crime patterns have seen the development of multilevel models that incorporate both micro- and macrolevel variables. The availability of quality crime estimates and the development of crime mapping and geographic information system (GIS) software have made the multilevel analysis of crime patterns possible. These studies have illustrated how crime is linked to a complex interrelationship between personal lifestyles, community contexts, and temporal changes in society. These multilevel studies have found evidence that earlier studies may have overestimated the importance of individual-level characteristics (such as race) by not accounting for spatial factors. Furthermore, studies examining spatial patterns of crime using longitudinal data have found that previously estimated declines in crime in a location were in part due to the displacement of crime (pushing crime to another jurisdiction) rather than an overall reduction in criminal activity.

Explaining Crime Trends

Temporal changes in crime rates have been the most difficult to explain by scholars and practitioners. Some of the most common explanations use demographic variables, such as age and ethnicity, to predict fluctuations in crime. James Allen Fox, in his work *Forecasting Crime Data: An Econometric Analysis*, found that demographic shifts can have a large effect on crime rates. Fox correctly forecasted the peak in violence in the 1980s and the following decline by tracking the movement of the baby-boomer generation in and out of the age associated with increased criminal activity.

Yet demographic models failed to anticipate the increase in crime beginning in the mid-1980s which was associated with access to guns and the appearance of crack cocaine, rather than demographic shifts. Moreover, the more recent decline in crime is not readily explained by demographic factors since the 18–24-year-old segment of the population, both black and white, began to increase during this time period.

Models focusing on economic conditions have also had difficulty in explaining fluctuations in crime patterns. Given that many crimes are motivated by economic need or desire, economic models predict that changes in economic conditions and opportunity would be associated with changes in crime rates. However, many longitudinal studies have shown the correlation between economic variables and crime trends often run in the opposite direction than predicted. In his book *Thinking About Crime*, James Q. Wilson referred to the observed increase in crime rates in the presence of strong economic indicators as the "paradox . . . of crime amidst plenty." Wilson noted that during some of the most rapid crime increases in the United States (e.g., between 1960 and 1970) unemployment and poverty were in decline. The continued decline in violent and property crimes from the early 1990s to the present has also caused numerous scholars to conclude that the direct connection between crime rates and economic conditions is limited.

The recent and historic declines in crime rates have also challenged the social disorganization perspective. This viewpoint is widely used to account for the variation of crime across geographic units, but has been less successful in explaining variation across time. From this perspective, communities with certain socioeconomic conditions (e.g., poverty, higher ethnic heterogeneity, more single-parent families) are also likely to be the communities with higher rates of criminal activity. Although some of these indicators have improved in recent years, the improvement has been slow and modest and not clearly connected to the decline in crime since the early 1990s.

One theory that has been used to explain the stable crime rates from the early 1930s to 1960, the rapid rise in crime from the 1960s to the mid-1980s, and the more recent declines is the routine activity theory. This approach argues that crime requires the presence of three elements: a motivated offender, a suitable target, and the absence of a capable guardian. Studies using this approach have suggested the increase in crime observed in the post–World War II period was a product of the increase in supply of attractive goods; a reduced capacity of traditional guardians, fueled in part by the breakdown of the traditional family; and targets (potential victims) whose routine activities (work, school, leisure) are associated with increased exposure to criminal activity.

The routine activity approach has also been used to explain the decline in crime in the last two decades. Although the supply of goods has increased over time, the value, because of lower costs of production, has declined. In addition, potential targets have adapted to crime risk and modified behavior (e.g., avoiding areas, installing car alarms). Furthermore, the increase in the number of police on the streets, mass incarceration, and new policing strategies (community and problem-solving policing) may have increased the capability of authorities.

Kenneth E. Fernandez
Elon University

See Also: Crime, Displacement of; Crime Mapping; Environmental Criminology; Kerner Commission on Civil Disorders; Policing, Problem-Oriented; Routine Activity Theory; Seattle Crime Places Study; Urban Ethnography.

Further Readings
Fox, James A. *Forecasting Crime Data: An Econometric Analysis.* Lexington, MA: Lexington Books, 1978.
Lynch, James P. and Lynn A. Addington, eds. *Understanding Crime Statistics: Revisiting the Divergence of the NCVS and UCR.* New York: Cambridge University Press, 2007.
Miethe, Terance D. and David McDowall. 1993. "Contextual Effects in Models of Criminal Victimization." *Social Forces*, v.71/3 (1993).
Wilcox, Pamela, Kenneth C. Land, and Scott A. Hunt. *Criminal Circumstance: A Dynamic Multi-Contextual Criminal Opportunity Theory.* New York: Walter de Gruyter, 2003.
Wilson, James Q. *Thinking About Crime.* Rev. ed. New York: Basic Books, 1983.

Crime Prevention, Environmental Design and

In an effort to reduce street crime and improve quality of life in certain geographic locations, place-based crime prevention efforts have emphasized environmental modification as a way to control human behavior. Formally known as crime prevention through environmental design (CPTED), these efforts focus on changing the environment to influence the behavior of criminal offenders and those able to intervene in criminal offenses (e.g., bystanders). CPTED methods can be introduced into the initial environmental design of a property as well as incorporated as modifications of buildings, roads, and other aspects of the physical environment with the aim of reducing crime.

Theoretical Development

The term *crime prevention through environmental design* was first coined by C. Ray Jeffrey in his 1971 book by the same title. But the concept as it is understood today is more often linked to the theoretical ideas developed earlier by Jane Jacobs and

Oscar Newman. In her 1961 book titled *The Death and Life of Great American Cities*, Jacobs posited that neighborhoods could benefit from enhanced passerby surveillance (what she termed *eyes on the street*) with the addition of bringing increased activity to an area through commercial development. More specifically, she was a vocal advocate of high-density, mixed-use areas, which combined residential and commercial development, as opposed to urban development strategies that separated residential and commercial areas. Her work thus highlighted the importance of understanding the relationship between the physical construction of cities and their neighborhoods, and opportunities for crime.

In particular, Jacobs's work highlighted how physical design could reduce criminal opportunities indirectly, by enhancing resident-based surveillance. Decades later, as urban police departments strove to counter growing levels of street crime and to employ better antigang crime measures, some of the core principles in these earlier researchers' work became tied into related ideas, such as the Broken Windows Theory and Routine Activity Theory. Applications that combined elements of these studies became championed as results seemed to imply at least partial success in some cities' efforts to combat street crime.

Newman provided an extension to Jacobs's earlier theoretical work through his 1972 book, *Defensible Space: Crime Prevention Through Environmental Design*. In his discussion of the idea of "defensible space," Newman suggests that the physical design of residential communities—including things like street design, building height, placement of buildings in relation to one another, and building relation to sidewalks and streets—was important in affecting crime rates. He suggested that these sorts of physical design features affect to what degree an area is perceived by outsiders as communal space that is "socially defended" or controlled by its inhabitants.

Newman advocated physical design modifications that created clearly defined spaces, so as to delineate territory and enhance surveillance. He also emphasized the need for spaces to be attractive and to feel safe. Newman argued that housing communities that had territorial markings, strong surveillance potential, a pleasing appearance, and were located near safe areas would foster resident-based, informal social control. Through this process, according to Newman, the opportunity for crime to be committed in residential communities would be reduced. In other words, he suggested that appropriate physical design reduced opportunities for crime indirectly, through enhancing resident-based territorial behavior and informal social control.

Six Key Aspects

Contemporary notions of CPTED have expanded the ideas of Newman and Jacobs in noting that physical design modifications can directly impact criminal opportunity. The modern-day conceptualizations of CPTED focus on the following important aspects of the design of physical space: territoriality, surveillance, access control, image or maintenance, activity program support, and target hardening.

Territoriality represents the ownership that residents have over private, public, and communal spaces. Certain "territorial markers," such as fences, walkways, gardens, and signs serve as a way to communicate to outsiders that space is "private," "owned," or meant for specific users and uses. Territorial markers provide indications that residents of the physical space are assuming control over that space.

The second key component of CPTED is surveillance. Surveillance represents the various methods of observation over an area. This observation could be informal or formal in nature. Informal surveillance is conducted by residents, while formal surveillance is conducted by police patrol or professional security officers. Surveillance can also be mechanical or natural. Mechanical surveillance is conducted through use of street lighting, cameras, and the like, while natural surveillance refers to surveillance that emerges from the environmental design. Natural surveillance is manifested for instance through use of shrubbery that is kept neatly trimmed or houses that are placed relatively close to public sidewalks and streets.

The third key concept comprising modern-day CPTED is access control. Access control is defined as the actions taken to prevent outsiders from entering a targeted area. Common examples of access control are gated communities/spaces, dead-end and cul-de-sac street patterns, call buttons or buzzer systems at the entrance to buildings, and alarm systems.

The fourth key component of CPTED is image or maintenance. This component refers to the visible condition of an area. Common examples of poor image or maintenance include: dilapidated buildings, graffiti, and street-crime-related activities like panhandling and prostitution. The appearance of an area that is plagued by such disorder suggests to law-abiding outsiders that it is unsafe and lacks ownership. Additionally, areas with a poor image appeal to criminals in search of areas where they can operate freely.

The fifth key component of CPTED is activity support. This concept refers to the extent to which the environment encourages legitimate informal and formal activities. Informal activity support is found in spaces that foster daily interactions among residents, such as places for conversation (e.g., common areas, public benches along sidewalks). Formal activity support is represented by aspects of the environment that foster neighborhood or community meetings and celebrations (e.g., community centers, community parks).

The sixth key component associated with CPTED is target hardening. Target hardening refers to the steps taken to secure a residence and make it less vulnerable to offenders. Common examples of target hardening include locks, window bars, and self-defense training.

In conclusion, over time, the implementation of place-based crime prevention has shifted from informal social-control-focused defensible space theory, to more design-specific crime prevention through environmental design. In early defensible space theory, physical design modifications were expected to increase informal social control, which, in turn, reduced criminal opportunity. The contemporary use of CPTED focuses on how physical design modifications can directly block criminal opportunity, whether or not residents engage in informal social control.

Empirical Evidence

Most evaluations of the effectiveness of CPTED have centered around programs or practices that focus on only one of the mentioned concepts: territoriality, surveillance, access control, image or maintenance, activity/program support, or target hardening. Overall, these evaluations have found support for each component's ability to reduce crime and/or fear of crime. There are fewer examples of

more comprehensive prevention programs—those that address multiple CPTED concepts. Nonetheless, some do exist, and research evaluations have also found support for these more comprehensive CPTED interventions.

One of the first comprehensive evaluations of CPTED was conducted by Richard Gardiner, who evaluated a neighborhood-level CPTED intervention that was applied in the Asylum Hill neighborhood in Hartford, Connecticut. The CPTED intervention's primary goal was to change the design of the neighborhood so as to lower criminal opportunity. Modifications such as the creation of cul-de-sacs and construction of fencing were implemented to prevent through traffic and make the space more private. These alterations addressed the concepts of access control and territoriality, while also enhancing surveillance in the process. Gardiner's three-year collection of data found that the neighborhood design changes lowered the rate of crime in the community. This project and the reported evaluation findings were used to develop federal guidelines for evaluating CPTED interventions across the United States.

Patrick Donnelly and Charles Kimble conducted an evaluation of a CPTED plan for the Five Oaks neighborhood in Dayton, Ohio. The Five Oaks neighborhood was undergoing serious deterioration during the 1980s and early 1990s due to drug and prostitution markets infiltrating the area. Concerned citizens and city agencies worked with Oscar Newman to develop a strategy to alter the environmental design of the neighborhood to prevent crime. Newman developed a plan for Five Oaks that consisted of closing a number of the streets that allowed easy access to and through the neighborhood from major arteries. In addition to restricting access and traffic flow, the street and alley closures created a system of mini-neighborhoods within the larger Five Oaks community, limiting the number of entrances and exits for vehicles, allowing for more surveillance and territoriality among neighbors.

Donnelly and Kimble examined the effects of the physical design modifications (i.e., street closures) by examining survey responses of the Five Oaks residents' perceptions of crime and safety and their participation in informal social control, in conjunction with city crime and traffic data. More specifically, Donnelly and Kimble assessed whether there was a drop in crime, and if so, whether these changes were due to the environmental changes in Five Oaks.

The evaluation determined that there were significant reductions in arrests, reported property and violent crime, as well as residents' concerns and perceptions of crime in the neighborhood. The investigator's analysis of residents' survey responses found that there were no significant changes in neighborhood organization involvement, territoriality, or commitment to the neighborhood, or other indicators of informal social control. However, residents did note improved ability to identify strangers and neighbors after the changes. Furthermore, traffic within Five Oaks dropped dramatically. Thus, Donnelly and Kimble concluded that the street closures reduced crime because they made access to the area by criminals more difficult. However, the street closures did not lead to increased informal social control.

Limitations and Conclusions

Though evaluations and reviews of CPTED interventions indicate promising results, there are also important limitations associated with CPTED. Paul Cozens, Greg Saville, and David Hillier have identified a variety of limitations, some of which are discussed briefly here. First, CPTED may have a difficult time deterring irrational criminals, those under the influence of drugs or alcohol, or who have a psychological or neurological deficiency, such as schizophrenia or damage to the frontal lobe of the brain. These types of offenders would be difficult to deter because their view of the environment might be distorted. Second, it is also possible that certain CPTED measures could create the opportunity for crime to occur or could conflict with the cultural, socioeconomic, or demographic characteristics of the target location. For example, some design modifications might benefit offenders by creating opportunities for them to offend, or might discourage residents from assuming control or ownership over communal space. For example, social conditions in a neighborhood may block a resident's ability to intervene or encourage them to seek protection in their reinforced homes.

In addition, certain CPTED modifications may enable drug dealers' ability to sell drugs in areas that have received design changes. Third, it is also important to consider that if CPTED techniques are not implemented correctly, crime could be displaced to other areas. For example, a crime prevention intervention that is effective in reducing drug dealing in a target area might displace drug dealing to an area that is in close proximity. However, it is also possible that positive effects of the intervention could be diffused to neighboring areas. Last, if a CPTED intervention is implemented without community interaction, then the intervention could reinforce a community that is closed-off and does not ascribe to communal values or behaviors. Such a result would contradict one of the original goals of pioneers within the CPTED tradition (such as Jacobs and Newman), which is to engage social interaction.

Empirical evidence to date supports evaluations of place-based interventions that implement one or many components of CPTED. Research should continue to explore CPTED and agencies should also be encouraged to evaluate CPTED interventions through robust research and statistical techniques. More robust research evaluations can help determine which components of CPTED strategies and interventions are most effective and which may be limited in application.

Amy L. Stutzenberger
Pamela K. Wilcox
University of Cincinnati

See Also: Broken Windows Theory; Crime, Displacement of; Defensible Space Theory; Environmental Criminology; Fear of Crime; Gated Communities; Routine Activity Theory; Urban Planning.

Further Readings

Cozens, Paul M., Greg Saville, and David Hillier. "Crime Prevention Through Environmental Design (CPTED): A Review and Modern Bibliography." *Property Management*, v.23/5 (2005).

Crowe, Timothy. *Crime Prevention Through Environmental Design*. 2nd ed. Oxford: Butterworth-Heinemann, 2000.

Donnelly, Patrick G. and Charles E. Kimble. "Community Organizing, Environmental Change, and Neighborhood Crime." *Crime & Delinquency*, v.43/4 (1997).

Jacobs, Jane. *The Death and Life of Great American Cities*. New York: Random House, 1961.

Jeffrey, C. Ray. *Crime Prevention Through Environmental Design*. Beverly Hills, CA: Sage, 1971.

Moffat, R. E. "Crime Prevention Through Environmental Design: A Management Perspective." *Canadian Journal of Criminology*, v.25/4 (1983).

Newman, Oscar. *Defensible Space: Crime Prevention Through Environmental Design.* New York: Macmillan, 1972.

Crime Prevention, Situational

While crime prevention is broadly defined to include activities aimed at reducing or minimizing crime and its harm, situational crime prevention (SCP) is more narrowly defined as "those prevention efforts that seek to reduce crime by increasing the effort and risk involved to commit a criminal act, while reducing the possible rewards that may accrue from that criminal act."

Modern crime prevention activities may be categorized within one of three general approaches to eliminate or minimize crime. In addition to SCP, they also include crime prevention through environmental design (CPTED, pronounced *sep-ted*), a hypothesis that posits that changes in the physical environment will reduce opportunities for crime; and crime prevention through social development (CPSD), whose hypothesis holds that crime is a product of reduced social opportunities/social environment.

Most American jurisdictions have opted for SCP and/or CPTED with short- to medium-term strategies targeting either offense categories, such as drug trafficking or auto theft; offense locations, like open-air drug markets; or offenders, such as gang members. These police departments have adopted a reactive, localized approach to immediate and short-term crime. (Most European jurisdictions have generally adopted CPSD and thus focused on strategies that seek to ameliorate general social conditions correlated with crime through a long-term approach to preventing crime.)

SCP traces its genesis to criminologist Oscar Newman's concept of defensible space, whereby the design and structure of the built-up area can reduce crime; and also to the *opportunity reduction* beliefs of sociologist Ronald Clarke, holding that specific

approaches can lower the risk of crime by removing/reducing the opportunity. Clarke himself held that SCP is based on three beliefs: (1) most criminal acts require the convergence of motivated offenders, potential victims, and a lack of suitable guardians (i.e., routine activity theory); (2) many types of crime are opportunistic; and (3) most offenders make rational choices that calculate the risk of detection, effort involved, and the advantages and/or disadvantages associated with their chosen action. These beliefs are translated into practice as situational crime prevention when efforts are made to:

- increase the effort required to commit a crime;
- increase the risks of committing a crime;
- reduce the reward derived from crime;
- reduce provocation; and
- remove excuses for doing crime.

Thus, SCP may be classified as opportunity reduction aimed at specific types of crime, specific geographic areas, or specific offenders. It draws its theoretical support from routine activity theory, whose individual-level of analysis is based on the convergence at the same space and time of an offender, target or victim, and the absence of a capable guardian. It also draws upon crime pattern theory, which offers a community or neighborhood analysis based on the study of patterns of movement whereby offenders become more aware of their peripheral areas and the targets within them; the more comfortable they become the more opportunities to commit crime are taken. SCP further draws on rational choice theory, which analyzes individual behavior based on the notion that offenders make rational decisions, weighing the associated rewards and sanctions, to commit or not to commit crime prior to its commission.

SCP programs can provide attractive and low-cost opportunities for governments seeking to reduce criminal activity and the fear of crime. For example, changing traffic patterns through a mixed small business-residential area frequented by prostitutes can reduce both the sex trade in that neighborhood and trace evidence (used hypodermic needles and condoms) found by children in the area; unfortunately we must accept that crime may merely be displaced to a neighboring area. As noted by Marcus Felson and Ronald Clarke, the redeployment of guardians (citizen patrols as well as public and private police) has also contributed to the moving of drug markets out of parks in a number of American cities; guardianship can also take the form of increased/improved street lighting and result in a reduction in crime in and around transit stops or back alleys.

SCP and Specific Offense Categories

Discussions of SCP activities targeting specific offense categories typically have routine activity and rational choice theories as their respective theoretical foundations. This is not surprising since such locations often present opportunities that require little effort, while offering low risk and high rewards for the offender. Auto theft and theft from autos offers a case in point.

Richard Hollinger and Dean Dabney's study of auto theft at shopping centers noted that the presence of motivated offenders and the absence of capable guardians predicted auto theft, while target availability was not a factor in such thefts. They found that increased numbers of security personnel, high-visibility patrol vehicles, and police patrols of parking lots reduced thefts of autos considerably. Rana Sampson's examination of theft of and from autos in Chula Vista, California, identified the absence of guardians in the form of physical security measures as factors that contributed to higher rates of auto theft. Adding physical security measures (cameras, triggered gate alarms), staffed gates, and security patrols increased the effort and risks for the offender while the rewards from the auto theft remained level. The effects were dramatic, as those parking locations implementing SCP measures experienced a reduction of nearly all theft. Auto theft has also been reduced in numerous American and European cities where SCP principles have been introduced.

SCP and Specific Offense Locations

The advancement of technology, notably geographical information systems or GIS, during the past two decades has facilitated the improved mapping of the distribution of crime, including the identification of clusters or "hot spots" of repeat crime and/or victimization. Similar to the previous discussion on specific offense categories, these locations typically present a convergence of motivated offenders, suitable targets, and a lack of guardians. Nearly two decades later, Felson and Clarke employed these

concepts and noted that specific categories of crime are often concentrated in time and space and that such concentrations, in turn, provide an opportunity to translate SCP principles into action. Two examples are targeting crime in or near public transit and residential buildings.

Washington, D.C.'s, Metro subway system offers an example of the application of SCP principles in its design and operation. Nancy La Vigne's study of that system noted the effectiveness of multi-use fare cards and the absence of bench seating, public washrooms, shops, and kiosks in reducing the potential rewards of robbery, while continuously staffed entrances, closed-circuit television, and roving police patrols increased the risks of committing crime.

Alex Hirschfield, Andrew Newman, and Michelle Rogerson's examination of burglary and the effects of target hardening, that is, increasing the physical security to reduce situational opportunities, offered an excellent example of SCP applied to specific offense locations. They found that 1,270 of the 1,739 residences (73 percent) in a high-crime area that added new door and window locks, door security chains, alarm systems, and motion-sensitive detection lighting were not victimized in the first instance, while only 15 percent (261 residences) of previously victimized residences experienced a repeat victimization. This example offers an integration of defensible space with the five techniques of situational crime prevention.

SCP and Specific Offenders

In addition to specific offenses and locations, SCP has also proven effective in targeting specific offenders to reduce their criminal activities. Campaigns aimed at reducing impaired driving/driving under the influence have increased the risks of detection, reduced the rewards by increasing the sanctions, and, most notably, removed excuses for driving while intoxicated. The effectiveness of check stops and other programs during the Christmas season has seen "Christmas in July" programs suggested to reduce intoxicated driving and boating during the summer.

Another group of offenders that may be targeted using SCP approaches are cyberstalkers. Cyberstalking is stalking conducted in an online environment using instant messenger, e-mail, blogs, text messages, photos, and viruses to bully, harass, and threaten individuals. Recently, cyberstalking/cyberbullying has been identified as one of the major causes for teens that have committed suicide. Bradford Reyns noted that SCP principles may be applied to the online environment in a similar manner to the way they are applied in the physical environment. The social networking site replaces the geographical site. The network provider can increase the efforts of the cyberstalker by restricting the age of participants, limiting access to personal information, and using filters such as sex offender registries to deny access. So, too, can the risks of detection be increased by requiring verification of identity and including a button to allow reporting inappropriate users. Although Reyns noted that it is possible to reduce the rewards and provocation by limiting access (for example, only friends can access photos or contact information), "sexting," or e-mailing photos of naked body parts, to so-called friends as a form of harassment shows how such prevention efforts can be bypassed.

Conclusion

If we accept Clarke's claim that most criminal activity is opportunistic and involves a convergence of a motivated offender, a suitable target, and a lack of a capable guardian, then crime prevention efforts should target those opportunities by increasing the effort and risk involved in committing a criminal act while reducing the possible rewards that may accrue. This may offer the best potential for preventing and/or reducing crime. Yet, it must be remembered that just as there is no single cause of crime, there is also no magic bullet that will prevent or solve all crime. The most effective approach may lay in a combination of SCP, CPTED, and CSD activities.

Allan L. Patenaude
University of Regina

See Also: Closed-Circuit Television; Crime, Displacement of; Crime Patterns; Crime Prevention, Environmental Design and Defensible Space Theory; Hot Spots; Routine Activity Theory; Stalking.

Further Readings

Clarke, Ronald V., ed. *Situational Crime Prevention: Successful Case Studies.* 2nd ed. Guilderland, NY: Harrow and Heston, 1997.
Cornish, Derek B. and Ronald V. Clarke. "Opportunities, Precipitators, and Criminal Decisions: A Reply to Wortley's Critique of Situational Crime Prevention." *Crime Prevention Studies*, v.16/1 (2003).
Hirschfield, Alex, Andrew Newton, and Michelle Rogerson. "Linking Burglary and Target Hardening at the Property Level: New Insights Into Victimization and Burglary Protection." *Criminal Justice Policy Review*, v.21/3 (2010).
Hollinger, Richard C. and Dean A. Dabney. "Motor Vehicle Theft at the Shopping Centre: An Application of the Routine Activities Approach." *Security Journal*, v.12/1 (1999).
La Vigne, Nancy G. "Visibility and Vigilance: Metro's Situational Approach to Preventing Subway Crime." Washington, DC: Office of Justice Programs, National Institute of Justice, 1997.
Reyns, Bradford W. "A Situational Crime Prevention Approach to Cyberstalking Victimization: Preventative Tactics for Internet Users and Online Place Managers." *Crime Prevention and Community Safety*, v.12/2 (2010).
Sampson, Rana. "Theft of and From Autos in Parking Facilities in Chula Vista, California. A Final Report to the U.S. Department of Justice, Office of Community Oriented Policing Services." Washington, DC: Department of Justice, 2004.
Sherman, Lawrence W., Patrick R. Gartin, and Michael E. Buerger. "Hot Spots of Predatory Crime: Routine Activities and the Criminology of Place." *Criminology*, v.27/1 (1989).

Crime Scene Investigation

On October 6, 2000, CBS aired the first episode of a new crime drama series that it hoped would bring new life to the network and the genre. The show was *CSI: Crime Scene Investigation*, and over the past dozen years it has revolutionized the criminal justice world in more ways than CBS ever imagined. Most importantly, through multiple seasons and two spin-off series, *CSI* introduced a glorified, and thus not always realistic, portrayal of crime scene investigation and forensic analysis to millions of Americans on a weekly basis. Prior to the creation of *CSI*, U.S. citizens knew little about forensic analysis techniques. In a primitive form, this meant dusting for fingerprints, measuring footprints, and running simple DNA analysis. Yet crime scene investigation is far more than this—although also somewhat less than popular media and television would lead us to believe. In this entry, we will examine the facts and fiction about crime scene investigation.

History and Development

Crime scene investigation is a branch of applied science located within forensic science, which is the study of evidence presentation and deliberation within the legal system. It focuses on the science required to examine a crime scene for evidence, including ballistics, fingerprinting, lie detection, blood splatter, time of death estimation, and establishment of cause of death. The word *forensic* comes from the Latin phrase for "before the forum." Roman trials involved a group of citizens serving as jurors in the forum. Both the accused and accuser would present their case orally and the side with the best argument and delivery was deemed the winner.

While the etymology of forensic science dates to the Romans, citizen fascination with crime scene investigation also has a long historical tradition. We can begin a historical awareness of forensic science by remembering that in ancient China and ancient Greece, citizens took clay impressions of fingerprints for recording purposes. Further

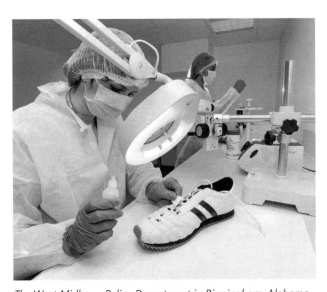

The West Midlancs Police Department in Birmingham, Alabama, has a forensic lab that provides services on all major crime scenes. The investigators search for evidence such as footwear markings, blood, and other materials.

ancient advancements are worth noting. As early as 250 B.C.E., physicians in Greece realized that pulse rate typically rose when suspects were lying. Consequently, Erasistratus used pulse rate to conduct a lie detector exam much like the ones still used today. And if we think about the assassination of Julius Caesar, we can remember that an autopsy revealed that despite being stabbed 23 times, there was just one fatal blow.

What the developments above show is that despite a lack of standardized practices, there were concentrated efforts to use the best available scientific methods to help determine the who, what, where, when, and how of crime. Criminal investigations did not have to rely merely on confessions and written testimony as they had for centuries before.

Throughout the Middle Ages, we witnessed the continued development of forensic science tools to aid in crime scene investigation. Using medical advances in China, doctors became able to distinguish between causes of death—between strangulation and downing, for instance. Likewise, Song Ci would publish *Washing Away of Wrongs* in 1248, which is the first book devoted to crime scene investigation through the study of medicine and related disciplines. Generally, the book attempted to help investigators rule whether a death was caused by murder, suicide, or accident.

Europe in the Middle Ages and into the Enlightenment also saw advances in the examination of body organs and body chemistry to determine pathologies and toxologies, and to isolate the causes and manners of death. Ambroise Pare, Fortunato Fidelis, Paolo Zacchia, Carl Wilhelm Scheele, and James Marsh were among those active in this area. By the 1800s, bullet comparisons began to be used to help identify murder weapons.

These earlier tools have been amplified by today's technologies to help measure body temperature and time of death; examine minute amounts of physical evidence ranging from hair, blood, gunpowder, and other substances; make polygraphs portable; and identify individuals by voice recordings and other techniques.

Double-Edged Technology

The current state of crime scene investigation can be seen as both a blessing and a curse. While new technologies allow investigators to solve and build cases, they also present a series of problems.

First, many of these technologies are still in relative infancy and take a significant amount of time to successfully do what they claim. DNA analysis is a prime example. Second, some techniques are less readily accepted—both socially and by the courts—than others. Lie detectors, for example, are not admissible in criminal court as actual evidence, given the lack of reliability and validity in their answers. Third, some forensic techniques have proven to not be as scientifically reliable as originally hoped or intended. For example, the Federal Bureau of Investigation (FBI) for several decades aimed to utilize comparative bullet-lead analysis, indexing a particular projectile's chemical makeup to that of manufactured batches of ammunition. This method was finally discontinued by the FBI in 2005, after independent testing concluded it was largely unreliable. Lastly, the advance of new technologies and their ability to give jurors peace of mind has led to many myths. With the myths come juror calls for evidence that can potentially not exist at all or may not be retrievable for any number of factors.

Aspects of Procedure

Forensic science professionals are trained to exercise extreme caution in the handling and development of physical evidence. Knowing they are among the very first law enforcement officials to examine a crime scene, these investigators also operate on the assumption that, while the testimony of and descriptions by eyewitnesses, suspects, victims, and even police officers may change between the moment of the crime and subsequent court appearances, the physical evidence must stand a series of tests and scrutiny without changing—thereby serving as perhaps the most solid link to the actual events at the time and place of the crime.

Crime scene investigation embodies aspects of both science and art. While there are key fundamentals to be learned in terms of evidence gathering and handling, there are also tremendous variances in the conditions and situations an investigator can encounter—making every crime scene unique. In addition, investigators must sift through samples characterized as being from both known sources and unknown/questionable sources. Thus, there is no single "right way" to learn how to conduct these investigations; a great deal of on-the-job training is a necessity.

That said, there are standard outlines for how to proceed. A crime scene investigation can be seen as having four regular phases:

1. Initial response to the scene and prioritization of efforts
2. Preliminary documentation and evaluation of the scene
3. Processing the scene
4. Completing and recording the crime scene investigation

These steps can interact with or be followed by coordination with crime lab personnel, the medical examiner's office, various other forensic specialists (e.g., experts in arson and explosives, human remains identifying), photographers, mass disaster specialists, and still other professionals. The steps of investigation are also informed by an understanding of how prosecutors and defense counsel approach the introduction of forensic evidence in both pretrial and courtroom settings.

Standards for procedural approaches vary in different jurisdictions; a range of educational and training resources as well as professional standards guidance is available from such institutions as the American Academy of Forensic Sciences, the American Board of Forensic Odontology, the Federal Law Enforcement Training Center, the Institute of Police Technology and Management, the International Homicide Investigators Association, the National Forensic Science Technology Center, and the U.S. Department of Justice.

Many such organizations provide detailed and field-tested methods and techniques that apply specifically to street crimes. There are separate priorities, for example, in the investigation of traffic incidencts, theft from motor vehicles and auto theft, and carjacking; home invasion or burglary; rape and other sexual crimes; simple assault or larceny-theft; aggravated assault, homicide, and suicide. Methods and priorities also must be tailored to the type of location of a crime scene: rural, suburban, commercial, industrial, institutional, and various classes of urban environments need to be approached in a different manners.

Conclusion

Popular fictional shows like *CSI* have been heavily criticized by some in the legal system who assert that citizen jurors have come to expect evidence provided clearly through investigatory techniques that may be less tangible or reliable than those they have seen portrayed in the media. This so-called *CSI* syndrome in some instances has led to a juror pool that is unwilling to convict someone for a crime regardless of testimony, if the case lacks much in the way of "hard" evidence such as DNA, fingerprints, or other forensic materials. For better or worse, we find ourselves in a society that takes forensic analysis very seriously, and struggles to be able to see beyond a lack of physical evidence. Now that citizens are becoming more aware of what technology can and cannot do, however, it may become easier to convince jurors that not every piece of evidence needs to be present in order to take someone to trial or to prove guilt beyond a reasonable doubt.

At the same time, we want forensic science to continue developing. Continued polishing of DNA identification has led to states being able to go back and test samples and ultimately either release citizens from prison or have their death sentences commuted (even if some exonerations came after the state had already delivered its punishment fully). In short, we want the knowledge and the certainty that science brings with it. What we do not want, however, is for juries to refuse to even consider convicting someone unless strong forensic evidence provides direct links.

William J. Miller
Southeast Missouri State University

See Also: Alcohol and Drug Testing, On-Scene; Arrest; Courts, Drug; Police Detectives; Street Crime, Popular Portrayals of; Television Shows.

Further Readings

Dale, W. Mark and Wendy S. Becker. *The Crime Scene: How Forensic Science Works.* New York: Kaplan, 2007.

Federal Bureau of Investigation. *FBI Handbook of Crime Scene Forensics.* New York: Skyhorse Publishing, 2008.

Horswell, John. *The Practice of Crime Scene Investigation.* London: Taylor & Francis, 2004.

National Institute of Justice. *Crime Scene Investigation: A Guide for Law Enforcement.* Rockville, MD: National Criminal Justice Reference Service, 2000.

Saferstein, Richard. *Criminalistics: An Introduction to Forensic Science.* 6th ed. Upper Saddle River, NJ: Prentice Hall, 1998.

Zonderman, Jon. *Beyond the Crime Lab: The New Science of Investigation.* Rev. ed. Hoboken, NJ: John Wiley & Sons, 1999.

Crime–Consumerism Nexus

The crime–consumerism nexus is a theoretical concept used by (cultural) criminologists to understand the relationships that exist within consumer-driven capitalist societies between the values and emotions associated with consumerism on the one hand, and various forms of expressive and acquisitive criminality on the other.

Conception and Context

Originally conceived by the English criminologist Keith Hayward, the crime–consumerism nexus asserts that consumer culture creates and cultivates—especially among young people—new forms of concomitant subjectivity based around desire, individualism, hedonism, and impulsivity. These, in many instances, can find expression in transgressive behaviour—including various forms of street crime, from street gang activity to arson, mugging, and vandalism. Importantly, this is not to suggest that consumer culture is criminogenic in any simplistic sense of direct correlation/causation; nor is it an attempt to integrate consumerism into a general theory of crime. Rather, the crime–consumerism nexus should be understood simply as an attempt to outline the striking convergence between novel forms of subjectivity propagated by consumerism (as both an economic and a cultural activity), and many of the characteristics identified within the criminological literature as being constitutive of criminality.

To understand the crime–consumerism nexus, you must first know something about what it means to live in a consumer society. This refers to a society in which the creation and expression of identity via the display and celebration of consumer goods has triumphed over more traditional modes of self-expression. Lifestyles become more important than families; individual consumer desires more important than community relations. In countries like the United States and the United Kingdom, the ethos of consumerism is now so encompassing that, for many individuals, self-identity can only be accomplished through consumer products. In the school playground, the bar, or on the street corner, material possessions now serve as the primary indices of self-realization for virtually all strata of society, establishing status and imbuing individuals with a narcissistic sense of who they are.

It is against this backdrop that the crime–consumerism nexus was developed. Interdisciplinary and constitutive in nature, drawing as it does on criminology, behavioral economics, social psychology, consumer research, and the sociology of risk and identity, it is not an easy concept to define. However, for the purposes of this entry, four main themes have been identified: (1) insatiable desire, and its concomitant, perpetual dissatisfaction; (2) new forms of "hyperstrain"; (3) engagement with risk; (4) and instant gratification, or impulsivity. Importantly, these themes are in no way postulated as an exhaustive set of factors; rather they are offered here simply as an introduction to the subject.

Insatiability of Desire

A unique feature of contemporary consumer culture is that insatiable desire—the constant demand for more—is now not only normalized but essential to the very survival of the current socioeconomic order. Far from an unintended or unwanted side effect, insatiable desire is actively cultivated in a consumer culture, most obviously through advertising. Of particular relevance to any criminological analysis of consumerism is the logical flip side of such a situation: namely, a constant sense of unfulfillment, dissatisfaction, and disillusionment. Importantly, this is not disillusionment with consumerism or capitalism per se, but rather with a particular purchase, a specific product.

The criminogenic consequences of this strange combination of perpetual dissatisfaction and a longing for the new hardly need spelling out. At the most obvious level, a lot of crime—from shoplifting to street robbery—can be understood not as a desperate act of poverty or a defiant gesture against the system, but as an attempt to bridge a perceived consumer deficit, and as a form of identity construction

(if it is true of shopping then it is also true of shoplifting). Consequently, street muggers who "tax" you for your mobile phone can be understood as consuming machines, flawed urban entrepreneurs whose primary goal is to get hold of the latest designer accessories: items that in today's consumer society are no longer simply desirable but for many young people are essential to individual identity, shifting as that may be from moment to moment.

New Forms of "Hyperstrain"

Such thinking is reminiscent of Robert Merton's classic Strain Theory. However, today, hyperconsumerism is contributing to the crime problem in ways that are qualitatively different from those expressed by strain theorists. Today, what people are feeling deprived of is no longer simply the material product itself, but rather the sense of identity that products have come to bestow on the individual. Such a situation demands a move away from the instrumentality inherent in Merton's strain theory toward a concept predicated more on the expressivity associated with new forms of desire.

Such a situation has massive implications for our understanding of crime, for this is strain on an unprecedented scale. In his original 1938 formulation, Merton differentiated between the anomie that is a property of the social system, and anomia, a term used to describe the personal, anomic state of the individual. A similar conceptual distinction is useful between hyperanomie and hyperanomia. The former refers to the characteristic state of our current socioeconomic-cultural conjuncture of consumer capitalism, in which there exists an inherent contradiction between the exalted cultural goal of self-realization through consumption and the limits imposed. The latter refers to the lived experience of hyperanomie, that is, the constellation of negative emotional states—the often latent feelings of frustration, injustice, resentment, insecurity, humiliation, and dread—that arise from the perpetual failure to fulfill essentially unattainable consumption-oriented expressive aspirations and which, given the right set of circumstances, can manifest themselves in crimes of passion, retaliation, and illicit acquisition.

Engagement With Risk

A further source of tension exists between the desire for excitement that is so prominent a feature of consumer culture, and the mundane and overcontrolled nature of much modern life—from the encroachment of surveillance to the drudgery of low-wage employment. One way in which individuals attempt to escape this paradox is by exerting a sense of personal control, or more accurately, a controlled loss of control, through engaging with risk. Certainly, within various cultural activities associated with contemporary youth culture there is much evidence to suggest that risk-taking is becoming more common. From the rise of extreme sports to the youthful excesses associated with drug use, car cruising, and binge drinking, it seems that for many young people, the greater the risk, the greater the attraction.

But what happens if a person does not have the money or the opportunity to pursue excitement through legal or socially acceptable avenues? In many instances, the likelihood is that individuals will get his or her kicks in spaces they know well. For example, run-down neighborhoods or lightly patrolled street corners become paradoxical spaces: while they symbolize the systematic powerlessness so often felt by individuals living in these environments, they also become sites of risk consumption that provide numerous opportunities for elicit excitement and thrill seeking. Such spaces serve as performance zones, places in which public displays of risk, gender, and identity abound. In other words, many forms of street crime frequently perpetrated within urban areas, such as peer group fighting or graffiti writing, should be seen for exactly what they are—attempts to construct an enhanced sense of self or a semblance of control by engaging in risk-laden practices on the metaphorical edge.

Instant Gratification or Impulsivity

For some time, instant gratification and impulsivity have featured prominently in psychological models of deviancy and criminality. Most famously within criminology, James Q. Wilson asserted that personality traits including impulsivity may be strongly related to criminal behavior, his central argument being the concept of present orientation: the idea that a rapid cognitive tempo and shortened time horizons are responsible for impulsive and disinhibited behavior. However, outside of a few brief allusions to the rise in individualism and the subsequent breakdown of social cohesion, Wilson and his fellow conservative criminologists offer little in the way of explanation for the rise of these characteristics.

In contrast, the crime–consumerism nexus asserts that such traits are simply the obvious end-products of an unmediated system of consumer capitalism. In addition to being insatiable, consumer culture cultivates a desire for immediate, rather than delayed, gratification. We are, at a societal level, increasingly encouraged to eschew long-term conservatism in favor of instant gratification as evidenced, for instance, by the massive expansion of credit facilities and the constant emphasis on immediacy in the "buy now" language of advertising. The bombardment of stimuli associated with consumer culture fundamentally distorts our experience of temporality, now reduced to a series of pure and unrelated presents.

With its particular emphasis on the new and the now, consumer culture separates people from the consequences of their actions and makes them more likely to pursue excitement without regard for conventional normative constraints. Inevitably, this emphasis on impulsivity, along with the other manifold entanglements of criminality and consumer culture identified above, does much to both problematize and challenge conventional situational crime prevention techniques and other instrumental approaches to the crime problem predicated on rational choice theories of human action.

Conclusion

It is important to reiterate the tentative and heuristic nature of the above themes. Nevertheless, even a cursory theoretical analysis of consumer culture and its associated values and emotions renders the potential criminological implications of our current socioeconomic system impossible to ignore. Furthermore, late capitalism's attendant culture of consumption shows no signs of abating in the foreseeable future, and as such the crime–consumerism nexus seems likely to be of enduring theoretical relevance and utility for contemporary criminology.

Keith Hayward
Theo Kindynis
University of Kent

See Also: Code of the Street; Crime Prevention, Situational; Gangs (Street); Graffiti; Mugging; Risky Lifestyles; Shoplifting; Vandalism.

Further Readings

De Haan, Willem and Jaco Vos. "A Crying Shame: The Over-Rationalized Conception of Man in the Rational Choice Perspective." *Theoretical Criminology*, v.7/1 (2003).

Hayward, Keith. *City Limits: Crime, Consumer Culture and the Urban Experience*. London: GlassHouse, 2004.

Hayward, Keith. "Situational Crime Prevention and its Discontents: Rational Choice Theory Versus the 'Culture of Now.'" *Social Policy and Administration*, v.41/3 (2007).

Gang tagging or graffiti is one of the common practices of the Crips. The Crips are one of the largest and most violent associations of street gangs in the United States.

Crips

The Crips are one of the oldest and most violently active gangs in the United States. While initially involved in petty crimes and random fighting, they have grown into a criminal association engaged in extensive street crimes including drug trafficking, extortion, robbery, and homicide. First established in South Los Angeles, Crips members traditionally identified one another through their use of the color blue, wearing bandanas, hats, and personal accessories in that hue. However, over the past decade, pressure from law enforcement along with community-based gang intervention has caused the Crips to seek other symbols and identifying characteristics.

Although the gang is well known for its historic rivalry with the Bloods, different Crips sets often engage in brutal gang wars with one another that have proven to be of even greater lethality than their outside conflicts. In certain instances, Crips sets will team up with Bloods sets to war with other Crips sets. Much of this conflict is attributed to the lack of centralized authority needed to impose street discipline on warring Crips sets. Nevertheless, despite their internal conflicts, the Crips have maintained control over extensive geographic territory or "hoods." Additionally, their current membership is both large and cross-generational: Many children of Crips members ultimately have joined their parents' sets.

Origins and Symbols

There are numerous accounts of the gang's origins but there is general consensus that the Crips were founded as an African American gang sometime during 1970–71 in Los Angeles by two enterprising teenagers: Raymond Lee Washington, leader of the East Side Crips, and Stanley "Tookie" Williams, leader of the West Side Crips. After several bloody confrontations, the two agreed to a street merger to consolidate their power and territory. Their agreement created what would eventually grow into a loosely connected network of individual sets that engaged in "warfare" with rival gangs, and which included murders, robberies, drug dealing, and other criminal pursuits.

Stories about the origins of the Crips name are as varied as the tales surrounding their establishment. There are claims that the name represents a combination of the word *crib* and R.I.P. ("Rest in Peace"), signifying that membership spans life from the cradle to the grave. There are other reports that Crips stands for Community Revolution in Process or alternately, Continuous Revolution in Process.

Despite the multiple legends, there are certain practices that have evolved through time: All Crips members uniformly follow specific street rituals. These institutionalized Crips gang behaviors require that all speech and tagging omit certain letters of the alphabet—primarily the letter "B" for Bloods. In its most extreme practice, any word that starts out with the letter B will be uniformly disrespected or crossed out with Crips tagging or graffiti. However, not all rituals are negative. Certain behaviors and ritual expressions serve as affirmations. The word *cuzz* is a synonym for Crips, for example, and is used by gang members to refer to one another in an indication of loyalty and belonging.

National and Global Influence

The Crips continue to maintain their greatest concentration in Los Angeles, but their membership has spread throughout California, the United States, and beyond—reportedly operating as far away as the Australian outback, Edinburgh, Scotland, and the foreign and domestic bases of the U.S. military. Still identified as an African American gang, the Crips are no longer exclusively black or restricted to males. They have admitted limited numbers of women who generally become prostitutes or hold drugs and firearms.

As part of their migration and changing demographics, it is critical to note that the Crips are no longer a monolithic gang, but instead a basic identity used by many gangs and neighborhoods. There are even street organizations considered "copy cats" that cannot trace any connection whatsoever to the Los Angeles Crips neighborhoods but simply use the name, applying their own regional identity, and developing new gang behaviors.

Still, while their practices change—identity theft is currently in vogue with some sets—and their membership moves to new locales, the Crips remain one of the largest and most dangerous perpetrators of street crime in the United States today, with no signs of dwindling in volume of operations or lethality.

The *Los Angeles Times* reported in a 2005 article that California law enforcement authorities estimated that the city was home to some 39,000 gang members operating in approximately 463 gangs. Of this number, the Crips membership was projected at slightly over 10,000. Authorities pointed out that the 39,000-member estimate was dramatically down from 1997, when anticrime databases showed about 64,000 gang members active in Los Angeles. Aiming more broadly, the data for Los Angeles County (which includes the city figures) put the 2005 number of Crips at 17,542 distributed across 210 sets.

Additional data from the Los Angeles Police Department (LAPD) identified 7,155 gang-related violent crimes in 2004. Thus a rough extrapolation would have the Crips responsible for about one-fourth of these, or 1,800 violent crimes in Angeles in 2004. The LAPD response, similar to that of many urban police departments, features the assignment of officers to antigang teams that gather information, develop criminal cases against specific gang members, and generally hew to the 10 Percent Factor mode, which posits that about 10 percent of criminals commit about half of all serious crimes, and these are the ideal targets of arrest and prosecution.

Jorja M. Leap
University of California, Los Angeles

See Also: Asian Gangs; Bloods; Community Policing; Drug Dealing; Gangs (Street); Graffiti; Latino Gangs; Los Angeles, California.

Further Readings

Hayden, Tom. *Street Wars: Gangs and the Future of Violence*. New York: The New Press, 2004.

Leap, Jorja. *Jumped In: What Gangs Taught Me About Violence, Drugs, Love and Redemption*. Boston: Beacon Press, 2012.

Maxson, Cheryl. "Gang Members on the Move." In *The Modern Gang Reader,* Arlen Egley, Cheryl Maxson, Jody Miller, and Malcolm Klein, eds. Los Angeles: Roxbury Publishing, 2006.

Shelden, Randall G., Sharon K. Tracy, and William R. Brown. *Youth Gangs in American Society*. Belmont, CA: Wadsworth, 2004.

Simpson, Colton with Ann Pearlman. *Inside the Crips: Life Inside L.A.'s Most Notorious Gang*. New York: St. Martin's Press, 2005.

Williams, Stanley Tookie. *Blue Rage, Black Redemption: A Memoir*. New York: Touchstone Books, 2004.

Winton, Richard. "L.A. Home Turf for Hundreds of Neighborhood Criminal Groups." *Los Angeles Times* (May 13, 2005). http://www.lacp.org/2005-Articles -Main/LAGangsInNeighborhoods.html (Accessed May 2012).

Day Reporting Center

The first day reporting centers opened in Great Britain and Europe in the late 1960s. The first day reporting center in the United States opened in 1986 (in Hampden County, Massachusetts). By 1995 there were at least 114 such programs active in 22 U.S. states. Today, in many U.S. cities, they serve as the innovative option of choice for the structured supervision of prisoners released from jail on bail or serving time on probation or parole. In general, all day reporting centers require clients under court supervision to report at a specific location on a regularly scheduled basis. In contrast to community corrections centers or halfway houses, clients are not confined in day reporting centers. Instead, they live with their families in the community. Unlike probation or parole offices that may send supervised persons to outside treatment programs, day reporting centers tend to have support services for clients on-site. Prisoners report for a few hours, submit to supervision protocols, are provided with services and training, may be directed to participate in scheduled programs or group activities, and then return to their employment or homes.

Range of Service Types

Day reporting centers may be opened in either commercial or residential buildings, in large cities, or small towns. The organization and operation of day reporting centers varies in terms of types of prisoners; the number of people served at each location; hours and days per week required; days, weeks, or months spent at the center; and services rendered. Some centers may require clients to report every day, while others might only report once a week.

Day reporting centers may offer a combination of social work and correction services. For example, studies indicate that centers that provide employment aid, family and life skills, and drug counseling services, as well as formal meetings with probation or parole officers, were more successful than those that did not offer services targeted to their client groups. Researchers have found that day reporting centers offering appropriate rehabilitative risk-focused treatment are consistently more successful in reducing recidivism for violent and nonviolent offenders as well as moderately high-risk offenders than centers without a strong program orientation; however, both types of center still outperformed normal probation or parole supervision.

These correctional centers may serve as one-stop locations for delivery of many services for at-risk populations. They have become successful alternatives to incarceration and may be operated by federal, state, county, or city correctional authorities as well as by profit or nonprofit agencies. The increase in the numbers of such facilities stems from operational cost savings compared to incarceration or reincarceration costs, and does not cause a greater safety risk to the public. Significant savings in tax dollars are realized for each client, as these centers are less expensive to build and operate than jails or prisons.

Jurisdictional Differences

In many jurisdictions, day reporting centers are used to divert people from jail, reduce jail populations, and generally provide a lower-cost alternative to incarceration. The client population in such cases mirrors the local correctional population: Typically, 90 percent or more are male. In large urban centers in the United States, the typical client is a working-class, minority, young, male adult, often referred on drug-related offenses, property crimes, or simple assault. Studies have shown that these centers are especially effective for helping prisoners with previous drug-related offenses. The clients in these studies had more time to interact with staff at the centers, compared to typically short meetings with parole officers.

Many centers, particularly with clients from drug courts, require mandatory attendance in treatment programs and drug testing. Prisoners that fail drug or alcohol tests or who do not otherwise adhere to program rules or guidelines can be subject to immediate incarceration in local jails or prisons. Programs that impose sanctions but not revocation tend to have higher overall success rates and improved long-term outcomes. Infractions may include not reporting as required, being late, failing to appear in court, suspicion of criminal behavior, new arrests, or supervision rules violations. However, the best programs recognize that during alcohol and drug treatment, a client's momentary failure may still be overcome with a supportive staff.

Conclusion

While the wide range in how centers are structured, managed, and integrated with other institutions in a given jurisdiction make it difficult to draw sharp conclusions, day reporting center programs do appear to offer great advantages over the traditional, one-size-fits-all use of jails and prisons, where comparatively few program resources are available. At the very least, they allow prisoners to live and work in the community and maintain their families while receiving supervision and treatment. Implemented correctly, they work; these centers generate significant savings while reducing recidivism.

Implemented poorly, the centers still tend to have lower costs than incarceration, but are not as successful and do not reduce costs as effectively as well-managed facilities.

Stephen C. Richards
Michael Lenza
University of Wisconsin Oshkosh

See Also: Arrest; Courts; Courts, Drug; Homelessness.

Further Readings

Boyle, Douglas J., Laura Ragusa, Jennifer Lanterman, and Andrea Marcus. "Outcomes of a Randomized Trial of an Intensive Community Corrections Program—Day Reporting Centers—For Parolees." 2011. National Institute of Corrections. http://www.nicic.gov/Library/025368 (Accessed May 2012).

Champion, David R., Patrick J. Harvey, and Youngyol Yim Schanz. "Day Reporting Center and Recidivism: Comparing Offender Groups in a Western Pennsylvania County Study." *Journal of Offender Rehabilitation*, v.50/7 (2011).

Marciniak, Liz Marie. "The Addition of Day Reporting to Intensive Supervision Probation: A Comparison of Recidivism Rates." *Federal Probation*, v.64/1 (2000).

Ross, Jeffrey Ian and Stephen C. Richards. *Beyond Bars: Rejoining Society After Prison*. New York: Alpha/Penguin Group, 2009.

Ross, Jeffrey Ian and Stephen C. Richards. *Convict Criminology*. Belmont, CA: Wadsworth, 2003.

Defensible Space Theory

Defensible space theory asserts that the design of physical space influences the way that both residents of an area and outsiders interact with that space, especially in urban areas. A space within or outside a building is considered defensible space when the residents or occupants of the building are able to extend their personal control into that space. Such control may include both resident appropriation and surveillance of the space. According to defensible space theory, urban areas that are designed with defensible spaces promote positive social dynamics while also deterring negative ones such as personal and property crime.

Background

An early forerunner to defensible space theory was urban theorist Jane Jacobs's conceptualization of *eyes on the street*, a phrase she used in her 1961 treatise, *The Death and Life of Great American Cities*, to describe a built environment in which public spaces were always visible. Jacobs criticized modernist urban planning principles that left residents disconnected socially from one another and physically from their surroundings. Among the changes she advocated were increases in density and reorientation of structures toward the street.

Jacobs argued that isolated, dark, closed-off spaces fostered street crime, while visibility acted as a deterrent. Her ideas proved influential on both practitioners and theorists who further elaborated on environmental design as a means of preventing common street crimes such as panhandling, theft, illegal drug use, robbery, extortion, and assault.

Sociologist Oscar Newman expanded on the work of Jacobs and other theorists by introducing defensible space theory in 1972, following years of involvement with various housing projects and related initiatives. A notable catalyst for Newman's theory of defensible space was his observation of the highly publicized rapid decline and ultimate demolition of Pruitt-Igoe, a high-rise housing complex in St. Louis, Missouri, designed by a prominent architect using state-of-the-art design principles. The decision to demolish the entire 33-building project after less than 20 years was a result of pervasive decay, litter, vandalism, gang crime, and the looming threat of physical danger, even though parts of the complex were better maintained and less troubled.

While Pruitt-Igoe had failed, Carr Square Village, a row-house community across the street, continued to thrive, with very low incidence of crime, despite having a very similar demographic

Defensible space is used to describe a residential environment whose characteristics function to allow the inhabitants to become key players in ensuring their own safety. The idea is that crime can be controlled and mitigated through environmental design. If an intruder senses a watchful community, he or she feels less secure committing the crime.

composition to Pruitt-Igoe. Newman analyzed the physical differences between these two housing projects as well as several others across the country; he found that successful housing communities shared several characteristics. His understanding of these commonalities led to the formation of defensible space theory.

Public Space as Private Trust

In the context of housing, defensible space refers to the physical space outside a house that the residents of that house understand as their own private space, which they may occupy and interact with accordingly. Newman argued that a housing community's physical design is a primary determinant in whether outdoor private spaces are defensible spaces. Among Newman's critiques of Pruitt-Igoe was that residents understood the spaces outside the individual housing units as public spaces, not privately controlled spaces. Thus, residents did not exert personal influence over these spaces, which quickly became hotbeds for delinquent and criminal activity. On the other hand, the successful housing project at Carr Square Village consisted of row-house buildings that were conducive to residents claiming and occupying the spaces outside their homes. Newman argued that these privately controlled spaces fostered better social environments than anonymous public spaces, which were often unoccupied and lacked clearly defined social norms.

In addition to this large-scale understanding of defensible space, small-scale physical features in a community are important parts of defensible space theory as well. Features such as lighting, benches, and green spaces promote the occupation of exterior spaces by residents and the reduction of crime. On the other hand, the presence of barriers or other objects may create potential hiding spaces and deter residents from expanding their influence into the spaces outside their homes. Moreover, the presence of these potential hiding spaces makes surveillance more difficult, creating an environment more conducive to criminal activity.

Focus on these smaller-scale elements build on Broken Windows Theory by emphasizing the importance of occupying spaces with a sense of ownership—not just the presence of certain built environmental features. Furthermore, Broken Windows emphasizes physical "incivilities" and other negative symbols signifying social disorder (e.g., graffiti, litter, or unmaintained street furniture) which by extension merely point to the need for reactive property maintenance. Defensible space and territorial markers emphasize positive and proactive design and personalizing improvements to prevent even the initial signs of disorder from occurring.

Social Control Dynamics

Like other physical design safety features, defensible spaces are thought to deter street crime and reduce fear mainly through their impact on various social dynamics in urban residential or business settings. Defensible space encourages greater territorial behavior, such as personalizing and beautifying property, on the part of occupants. In residential areas, it increases informal social control (people's willingness to monitor suspicious behavior and intervene or to simply ask strangers if they need help) and the use of outdoor space. It encourages users to get to know their neighbors, which can lead to greater social capital (or neighboring, sense of community, citizen participation, empowerment, and networking).

In more public spaces, it improves visibility and a sense of security throughout the space, so that workers, shoppers, and pedestrians feel a greater sense of control and so act accordingly. Regardless of these social dynamics, the public space design elements of defensible space theory may deter street crime, as potential offenders may respond consciously or unconsciously to these elements and seek targets in spaces that are less defensible.

Conclusion

Defensible space is just one set among many kinds of built environment elements related to street crime prevention. While there is debate about the nature of the relationship between the built environment and social factors, there is little doubt that defensible space theory at the very least provides a useful lens for analyzing and understanding physical spaces.

Benjamin W. Fisher
Donald L. Anthony
Douglas D. Perkins
Vanderbilt University

See Also: Broken Windows Theory; Community Policing; Crime Prevention, Environmental Design and; Urban Incivility; Urban Planning.

Further Readings

Jacobs, Jane. *The Death and Life of Great American Cities*. New York: Random House, 1961.

Lersch, Kim Michelle. *Space, Time, and Crime*. 2nd ed. Durham, NC: Carolina Academic Press, 2007.

MacDonald, Julia E. and Robert Gifford. "Territorial Cues and Defensible Space Theory: The Burglar's Point of View." *Journal of Environmental Psychology*, v.9/3 (1989).

Newman, Oscar. *Defensible Space: Crime Prevention Through Urban Design*. New York: Macmillan, 1972.

Perkins, Douglas, et al. "The Physical Environment of Street Crime." *Journal of Environmental Psychology*, v.13/1 (1993).

Reynard, Danielle M. and Henk Elffers. "The Future of Newman's Defensible Space Theory: Linking Defensible Space and the Routine Activities of Place." *European Journal of Criminology*, v.6/1 (2009).

Whyte, William H. *The Social Life of Small Urban Spaces*. New York: Project for Public Spaces, 2001.

Detroit, Michigan

The largest city in the state of Michigan and the seat of Wayne County, Detroit serves as a major port on the Detroit River, connecting the Great Lakes with the St. Lawrence Seaway. Data from the 2010 U.S. Census Bureau reveals that Detroit, a Rust Belt city, is still feeling the effects of years of recession. Between 2000 and 2010, Detroit lost a quarter of its population. The housing market collapsed, the automobile industry survived, largely because of government bailouts, and downtown Detroit has been reliant on its role as an entertainment hub in recent years. If not for three casino resorts, two new stadiums, and a redeveloped riverfront, many wonder what would be left of the once great city. Despite rates of violent and property crime falling across most of the United States, street crime still creates extremely problematic effects for large urban areas throughout the country. Detroit is no exception.

Initially discovered in 1679 by Father Louis Hennepin (who believed the north bank of the Detroit River would be a model area to create a new settlement), the city was established in 1701 as Fort Pontchartrain du Detroit by French officer Antoine de La Mothe Cadillac and 51 French Canadians. Detroit grew quickly and eventually became a booming population. In 2011, *Forbes* magazine ranked Detroit as the most dangerous city in the United States because of prevailing trends within the city limits due to street crime. Rates of violent and property crime remain disproportionately high in Detroit compared to similarly sized cities. While most of America has witnessed a dramatic fall in both violent and property crimes since the early 1990s, Detroit's crime rates today remain near their peak levels. In 2010, Detroit had the highest violent crime rate of any U.S. city with a population of 250,000 or greater, according to the Federal Bureau of Investigation's (FBI) Uniform Crime Reports (UCR) data. They also had the 17th-highest rate of property crime. The property crime numbers, however, have significantly fallen over the course of the past 20 years.

Violent crime in Detroit has existed for nearly as long as the city. Problems became more noticeable in the early 1920s with the emergence of the bootlegging Purple Gang. This group—also referred to as the Sugar House Gang—was a mob of predominantly Jewish members of hijackers who utilized Detroit's proximity to Canada to run alcohol during Prohibition. The group was known for being openly violent, and due to convictions and intragang killings was relatively short-lived. In the 1970s, the Errol Flynns were the most prominent street crime figures. This street gang introduced the world to "jitting" (better known as hand signs to identify themselves). They came together out of the racial and economic unrest that existed within inner-city Detroit during the late 1960s. With white flight eliminating much of the economic means for the city, the infrastructure collapsed, leaving the remaining citizens impoverished and angry. Eventually, murder rates soared and gangs took on territories of their own.

One such group, the Errol Flynns, were known for mass robberies and hijackings and controlled the entire heroin industry within the city. With this prominence came attention, and as a result the gang collapsed in the 1980s as crack cocaine became more prominent than heroin, and the group watched as more members found themselves charged and convicted with crimes related to their activities. They would be replaced by Young Boys, Inc. (YBI)—an African American drug cartel that operated on street corners in the Dexter/Webb neighborhood of Detroit's west side. At its height, YBI was selling roughly $750,000 worth of illegal drugs per day.

Statistical Trends of Street Crime in Detroit

By their very nature, many street crimes are never brought to the attention of law enforcement agencies (at any level) and subsequently are missing from official reports. Reliable statistics are not available on handgun ownership and the direct relationship between illegal drug usage and criminal behavior. The National Crime Victimization Survey helps fill some gaps by providing estimates of unreported activity, yet they cannot simply be added to official reports to create a confident measure of street crime. Simply put, crime-related data is somewhat limited on street crime in large urban areas such as Detroit; however, the FBI's UCR does report data from the Detroit Metro Police Department.

UCR reports classify crime into two categories: violent and property. Violent crimes include murder, assault, and manslaughter. Property crimes, on the other hand, involve offenses such as motor vehicle theft, burglary, and larceny. These crimes are typically characterized by a lack of physical harm to the victim. Throughout the 1980s and early 1990s, violent crime rose throughout the country. Peaking at 785 violent crimes committed per 100,000 persons in the population in 1992, UCR statistics in 2010 showed a dramatic fall to only 403 crimes per 100,000. The U.S. property crime rate has been historically higher than the violent crime rate by a wide margin. In 1991, the national property crime rate peaked at 5,140 offenses per 100,000 in the population. By 2010, the rate had gradually fallen to 2,942 property crimes per 100,000.

UCR data from Detroit paints a fairly clear picture of street crime in the city. Looking at statistics related to violent crime between 1985 and 2010, the rate has increased 0.11 percent. This number, however, is deceiving since over the 35-year-period, the rates have fluctuated greatly between years (from a high of 2,669 violent crimes per 100,000 persons in 1990 to a low of 1,740 in 2004). The decrease since the peak in 1990, consequently, is a modest 11.9 percent. Looking at murder and non-negligible manslaughters—the most dangerous and serious crimes reflected in the UCR data, particularly for a city once referred to as Murdertown, U.S.A.—the rate of change from 1985 to 2010 demonstrates a decrease of 25.4 percent. Previously, rates have fluctuated even more than this. In the 1970s, the rate was significantly higher than in 1985 when the current UCR dataset begins. At its highest in the past 25

years, the rate was 62.8 murders per 100,000 in the population (1987); at the lowest, the rate was 35.7 (2008). The rate of forcible rapes has also decreased by a substantial margin of 69.2 percent. This is even more impressive given that there was an increase of 53.1 percent between 2009 and 2010. Looking at robberies, there was a substantial decrease of over 49 percent in the rate in Detroit between 1985 and 2010. This number has consistently fallen over the past two decades, except for a jump up in 2005. Finally, while most violent crimes have decreased in Detroit between 1985 and 2010, reported aggravated assaults increased by almost 137 percent.

Property crime rates in Detroit have also decreased between 1985 and 2010, falling almost 42 percent to 6,698 per 100,000 people. The burglary rate has decreased by 35.3 percent. Likewise, the larceny-theft rate has fallen 39.8 percent between 1985 and 2010. This number could be slightly misleading, as there was a 24 percent increase between 2009 and 2010 taking the number back up to 2,539.6 per 100,000 in population. Motor vehicle theft rates were relatively stable between 1986 and 2006 before beginning to fall between 2006 and 2010. Ultimately, since 1985, the motor vehicle theft rate has dropped by 48.9 percent.

These rates do not represent the entire view of street crime activity in Detroit, yet they do tell a fairly accurate story of a city that witnessed a severe rash of property and violent crime in the 1970s before seeing almost all of its crime numbers fall over the subsequent three decades. What differentiates Detroit from many other large urban areas is the lack of a dramatic increase in crime rates during the early 1990s. The fact that the city has successfully brought rates down since 1985 does not, however, mean that its problems have been eliminated. In 2011, it was found to have the fifth-highest crime risk index in America. With the national average represented by 100, Detroit measured in at 369.

Response of Local Law Enforcement

While the specific causes for the ebb and flow of street crime in Detroit over time cannot be precisely determined, one can examine what local police agencies have done to attempt to limit its occurrence and what outside events and factors have contributed to it. First, one can look at the relationship between gambling and crime. In 1996, the Michigan Gaming Control and Revenue Act was passed via statewide ballot initiative providing for state licensing and oversight of three casinos in Detroit. While casinos have been accused of causing increases in crime in cities where they are opened, the Detroit Police Department's Crime Analysis Unit has actually shown that crime has dropped 24 percent since casino gaming first opened in the city in late 1997. While there is no means to justify this as a causal argument, it does show that the crime rate has clearly not increased, as many feared it would, in response to the opening.

Another established explanation for increased criminal activity is the presence of illegal drugs. In 2007, Detroit officials set out to examine how much of their serious violent crime could be related back to illegal drugs in some way. What they found was that almost 70 percent of all homicides within city limits could be traced back to a narcotics catalyst. As a result, they have stepped up efforts to eliminate illegal narcotics and have achieved some success in lowering homicide rates. Many of these issues have been blamed on white flight in the 1970s, which led to urban decay, high levels of unemployment, and poverty. Since that time, the city has been in a constant push for redevelopment, which has been referred to as a renaissance. Through increased funding from state and federal sources, the city has, in the past 10 years, successfully demolished condemned buildings quickly to limit their potential usage for illegal activities.

The city of Detroit has recently undertaken a series of initiatives to improve the city's image and has worked to eradicate remaining crime problems. The most overarching initiative is called Transforming Detroit, which aims to restructure city government, rethink urban policy, and reclaim the city's future. From a police perspective, a cornerstone of this movement is to create a new, modernized police headquarters that is better able to meet the needs of citizens. Mayor Dave Bing has also signed on to the national Youth Violence Prevention Initiative, which includes a multidisciplinary approach embracing prevention, intervention, enforcement, and re-entry. Finally, the Project 14 initiative aims to encourage police officers, firefighters, homeland security, emergency medical service workers, and city employees to purchase homes and live in the city of Detroit. By having these individuals living in the city, the hope is to deter crime and increase public safety in neighborhoods, strengthen community relations, increase the city's tax base, and leverage federal resources to attract new residents at no cost to the city of Detroit. This program is modeled after similar successful programs throughout the country.

Like most cities in the United States, overall levels of street crime in Detroit are now lower than during the early and mid-1990s, despite current economic conditions that have been historically correlated with high amounts of street crime. What is even more impressive has been the significant decrease since the 1970s, when Detroit's crime rates (both violent and property) per 100,000 citizens were some of the highest ever recorded in our nation. Detroit still suffers from both violent and property crimes (first in the nation in violent crime index and 17th in property crime index out of cities with a population of 250,000 or greater in 2010). Ultimately, the causes of the overall decline in street crime in Detroit cannot at this time be precisely assessed and remain perplexing to many criminologists. Detroit, however, appears to be aware of its current problems and willing to take innovative measures in order to see the numbers continue to shrink.

William J. Miller
Flagler College

See Also: Gangs (Street); Murder/Homicide; Police (Overview); Street Crime Defined.

Further Readings
Bragg, Amy Elliott. *Hidden History of Detroit.* Charleston, SC: History Press, 2011.
Martelle, Scott. *Detroit: A Biography.* Chicago: Chicago Review Press, 2012.
U.S. Census Bureau. "2010 American Community Survey." http://www.census.gov/acs/www (Accessed July 2012).

Diallo, Amadou

On February 4, 1999, Amadou Bialo Diallo was shot and killed at the doorstep of his apartment building in the Bronx by four New York Police Department (NYPD) officers. The shooting of the innocent, unarmed, 23-year-old African street vendor with no criminal record, and the acquittal of the four white police officers involved, became the focus of

A participant in the antipolice brutality protest march in front of the White House in February 1999, holds up a newspaper featuring the story about the shooting of Amadou Diallo, recalling "Cops Fired 41 Shots."

controversy and protests, as well as becoming part of the history of and debate about racism in the New York criminal justice system.

Background and Incident

Diallo was born on September 2, 1975, in Sinoe County, Liberia, where his parents, Kadiatou and Amadou Saikou Diallo, had moved from Guinea for work. Diallo immigrated to the United States in 1996 in order to study. He moved to New York City, where he had family, ran a vending stall on 14th Street, and lived at 1157 Wheeler Avenue in the Bronx, where he was killed. The shooting incident took place at 12:40 A.M. when Diallo was spotted on the stoop of his apartment building by NYPD plainclothed officers from the Street Crimes Unit. The officers— Kenneth Boss, Sean Carroll, Edward McMellon, and Richard Murphy—thought that Diallo matched the description of a suspected rapist. According to the officers, they approached Diallo and identified themselves, at which point he moved toward his building door, ignoring their orders to stop. When Diallo reached into his jacket to show his wallet in the badly lit entrance, Carroll thought he saw a gun and called out, leading the others to begin shooting their 9-millimeter semiautomatic weapons. They fired 41 shots, hitting Diallo 19 times.

Investigation and Trial

Following the shooting, the NYPD's investigation found no weapons on or near Diallo's body, and identified a wallet as the object that he was pulling out of his pocket. Yet, they ruled that the officers had acted in accordance with department guidelines on shooting based on what they reasonably believed to be a threat. In spite of the outcome of that investigation, on March 25 all four officers were indicted on charges of second-degree murder and reckless endangerment by a grand jury in the Bronx. Before coming to trial, the appellate court changed the venue from the Bronx to Albany, the state capital 140 miles north of New York City. This decision was based on the court's belief that a fair trial was impossible in the Bronx due to pretrial publicity that tainted the jury pool.

As much of the controversy surrounding the case was based on suspected racism in the NYPD and racial profiling of Diallo, the makeup of the Albany jury was not immune to questions of bias. The defense tried to use its peremptory challenges to remove three African American women from the jury, which the judge rejected. In the end, the jury consisted of four African American women, one white woman, and seven white men. The defense attempted to lay blame for the shooting on Diallo's "suspicious" behavior, but the prosecution argued that the officers caused the confrontation by prejudging Diallo as a criminal and did not consider that he had a legitimate reason for being at the building. On February 25, 2000, following two days of deliberations, the jury acquitted the defendants of all charges. The following year, the U.S. Justice Department decided against charging the officers with violating Diallo's civil rights.

Protests and Legacy

The Diallo incident occurred while tensions were high between the African American community and the NYPD and Mayor Rudolph Giuliani, whose tough law-and-order rhetoric and policies were seen to legitimize and increase racial profiling and police brutality (e.g., the in-custody assault on Abner Louima by NYPD officers in 1997). The shooting, change of venue, and acquittal led to widespread criticism and daily protests outside NYPD headquarters at One Police Plaza in Manhattan, as well as protests at Diallo's apartment. Critics and those arrested in the protests included high-profile politicians such as former Mayor David Dinkins and civil rights activists such as Rev. Jesse Jackson and Rev. Al Sharpton, as well as community activists and members of the public.

The Diallo case represented a stain on Giuliani's approach to law and order, and led to calls for reform. Thus, in spite of the NYPD clearing the officers and the court acquitting them, reform did occur, including a full review of police training policy and the disbanding of the NYPD's Street Crimes Unit in 2002, 31 years after its formation.

Following the acquittal of the four officers, in April 2000 Diallo's mother and his stepfather, Sankarella Diallo, filed a $61 million lawsuit against the city of New York and the officers for wrongful death, negligence, and the violation of his civil rights; they accepted a $3 million settlement in March 2004. The Diallos also established the Bronx-based Amadou Diallo Foundation, which works on combating racial prejudice and conflict, as well as enhancing police-community relations. Diallo's mother also wrote, with Craig Wolff, *My Heart Will Cross This Ocean: My Story, My Son*.

Other tributes included the event To Amadou With Love: A Night of Healing, which was held on June 19, 2000, at New York's Hammerstein Ballroom and included among the performers Wyclef Jean, who wrote the song "Diallo." Also in response, Bruce Springsteen wrote "American Skin (41 Shots)," which he played during his 2000 Madison Square Garden concerts, leading the Patrolmen's Benevolent Association to call on its members to boycott Springsteen's concerts in terms of both attendance and accepting overtime work as security.

The Diallo case would be examined in academic studies, mostly in the fields of criminology and social psychology, including Beth Roy's *41 Shots . . . and Counting: What Amadou Diallo's Story Teaches Us About Policing, Race, and Justice*, and Saul Kassin, Sharon S. Brehm, and Steven Fein's *Social Psychology*, which contains the section "41 Shots Revisited: Did Racial Stereotypes Make the Police More Likely to Shoot Amadou Diallo?" The relationship between stereotypes and the shooting was also discussed in Malcolm Gladwell's *Blink: The Power of Thinking Without Thinking*.

Aaron Winter
University of Abertay Dundee

See Also: Central Park Jogger Incident; Giuliani, Rudolph; New York City; Police Brutality/Excessive Force; Racial Profiling; Tawana Brawley Incident.

Further Readings

Cooper, Michael. "Officers in Bronx Fire 41 Shots, and an Unarmed Man Is Killed." *New York Times* (February 4, 1999). http://www.nytimes.com/1999/02/05/nyregion/officers-in-bronx-fire-41-shots-and-an-unarmed-man-is-killed.html (Accessed June 2012).

Diallo, Kadiatou and Craig Wolff. *My Heart Will Cross This Ocean: My Story, My Son*. New York: Ballantine Books, 2004.

Fritsch, Jane. "The Diallo Verdict: The Overview; 4 Officers In Diallo Shooting Are Acquitted of All Charges." *New York Times* (February 26, 2000). http://www.nytimes.com/2000/02/26/nyregion/diallo-verdict-overview-4-officers-diallo-shooting-are-acquitted-all-charges.html. (Accessed June 2012).

Gladwell, Malcolm. *Blink: The Power of Thinking Without Thinking*. Boston: Back Bay Press, 2005.

Roy, Beth. *41 Shots . . . and Counting: What Amadou Diallo's Story Teaches Us About Policing, Race, and Justice*. Syracuse, NY: Syracuse University Press, 2009.

Domestic Violence

Definitions of domestic violence vary depending on their utilization. For example, definitions for the purpose of academic research differ considerably from legalistic, or social-historical definitions. Most broad definitions assert that domestic violence is violence perpetrated by intimates who are cohabiting or have previously cohabitated, including physical, sexual, psychological/emotional, and financial abuse. In relation to street crime, domestic violence shares significant characteristics of many such offenses, in that victims are more likely to be attacked by someone they know; the most frequently committed crime categories are basic assault and simple battery, which can escalate to the most violent crimes of aggravated assault, rape, or murder; and in that developing control over one's immediate environment, whether in the home or on the street, is a key element in reducing the risk of the crime being committed as well as reducing the severity of an attack.

Nature of Abuse

Domestic violence is prevalent in the United States, with the Bureau of Justice Statistics reporting

652,660 incidents of domestic violence in 2008. Despite this prevalence, it is estimated that approximately half of all domestic violence incidents are not reported to law enforcement; these incidents are part of what is referred to as the "dark figure of crime." This segment of under-reporting is attributed to the sociohistorical treatment of domestic violence as one that is of lesser importance than other forms of street crime, in addition to the unique dynamics found in a domestic violence relationship.

Psychological abuse is any behavior that causes emotional trauma to the victim, such as name calling, belittling, coercion, isolation, threats, and intimidation. Although in isolation psychological abuse does not constitute a violation of the law, it acts as a predictor of future harm that manifests as physical and sexual violence which are typical of street crime offences. Physical abuse includes acts of physical force with the intention of causing physical harm, injury, disability, or death. Sexual abuse involves forced sexual acts, as well as attempted or completed acts when consent is not given because of illness, disability, intimidation, or the influence of drugs and/or alcohol. Financial abuse includes economic abuses such as one partner preventing another from seeking or holding employment, having access to the household finances, and/or providing an allowance. Not all forms of abuse are present in every domestic violence relationship, and not all forms of abuse are considered criminal. Financial abuse includes economic abuses such as one partner preventing another from seeking or holding employment, having access to the household finances, and/or providing an allowance. As indicated, not all forms of abuse are present in every domestic violence relationship, and not all forms of abuse are considered criminal, but many of the behaviors that are indicative of domestic violence are street crime offenses.

Some research has indicated that domestic abuse, at least that part committed by males, may be more difficult to address in rural communities than in urban areas. Factors include the rural males' average lower employment and education levels, higher arrest rates, and greater incidence of combining pharmaceuticals with alcohol than their urban counterparts. The net effect can be exacerbated by some of the structural components of rural society, such as relative isolation, entrenched patriarchy, fewer institutional resources, and less experience among officials and interveners. Separate studies show that law enforcement, legal, and judicial forces in rural areas tend to be less well equipped than those in urban areas to provide a comprehensive preventive and reactive response to domestic violence.

Cycle and Causes

Lenore Walker, in her 1979 book *The Battered Woman,* asserts that violence in the context of an intimate relationship has a cyclical patterning, termed the "cycle theory of violence." Walker contends that this pattern of domestic violence has three stages: (1) tension-building stage, (2) battering stage, and (3) honeymoon or contrition stage. During the tension-building stage the perpetrator will experience higher levels of tension which may manifest as poor communication, increased control, or increased threats made toward the victim. In response the victim may become more withdrawn and minimize the problem, while also experiencing and reacting to the increased tension in the household, with many victims likening the experience to walking on eggshells. The second stage of the cycle is the battering stage, where the perpetrator becomes very unpredictable and abusive. This often culminates when an acute incident of violence occurs, for which the perpetrator blames the victim. During this time the victim feels isolated, trapped, and helpless, experiencing high levels of trauma.

The honeymoon or contrition stage follows the acute violence incident, and the perpetrator manipulates the victim into forgiveness by apologizing, buying her gifts, acting remorseful, and promising change. The victim often experiences mixed or confused feelings about the incident and may experience feelings of self-blame and guilt. Consequently, the victim often reconciles with the perpetrator and the cycle then repeats itself. There is tremendous variation in duration of the cycle, with some victims experiencing cycles that last weeks, others months, and sometimes years. Irrespective of time frame, as the cycle repeats, the honeymoon or contrition stage shortens with the perpetrator becoming less apologetic or remorseful for the violence.

There are many theoretical explanations offered to explain the gendered patterning of intimate partner violence. One of, if not the most dominant explanations of domestic violence is the feminist perspective; this developed viewpoint links the motivations for intimate partner violence primarily with patriarchal values, and the societal institutionalization of patriarchy. At the individual level, the motivations for the violence center around one partner gaining and maintaining power and control over the other partner. At the societal level, subordination of women is also apparent in many of the institutions in the United States, such as the economy, church, education, politics, and family. This is apparent when examining the history of domestic violence in the United States as women have been disadvantaged, discriminated against, and victimized as a direct result of social stratification, and are largely afforded lesser resources than men. Additionally, unlike other forms of street crime, female victims of domestic violence were historically not afforded any protection through the criminal justice system, as laws preventing domestic violence did not exist in the United States until the 1800s. Even when some states made legislative changes criminalizing domestic violence, the social reality remained the same; domestic violence was not considered a crime. Therefore the traditional criminal justice response to domestic violence was really more of a nonresponse until the 1980s.

Many police departments prior to the 1980s ignored or screened out domestic violence calls, and when police officers did respond to calls for help they often did not arrest the perpetrator. Some police departments had policies that, contrary to the classification of domestic assault as a crime deserving of a legal response equal to that of similar street crimes such as assault and battery between nonintimates, explicitly stated that officers should not make arrests for domestic violence. The civil rights movement of the 1960s, coupled with antiwar sentiment and black liberation, gave rise in turn to the feminist movement. Violence against women was framed successfully by feminist groups as a political and social issue and one deserving of criminal justice response equal to that of other street crimes. This led to the opening of hundreds of local domestic violence programs across the country, in addition to the formation of state and national coalitions.

There was an increase in civil litigation against local police departments for failure to provide adequate protection for victims of domestic violence. Such cases resulted in large monetary settlements being awarded to victims who were not afforded adequate protections from their assailants by their local police department, such as the case of *Thurman v. City of Torrington*. Academic research was also instrumental in providing a catalyst for change. The Minneapolis Domestic Violence Experiment, conducted by L. Sherman and R. Berk in 1984, was an influential study that indicated that arrest, when compared to nonarrest, was more effective in reducing perpetrator recidivism. This study, combined with the increase in litigation against police departments, and further fueled by the political pressures deployed through the feminist movement, led to the enactment of federal legislation: the Violence Against Women Act of 1994. This landmark legislation mandated police departmental policies that required criminal justice intervention to protect domestic violence victims and implemented response mechanisms that afford domestic violence victims the same, if not greater, criminal justice protections as other victims of comparable street crimes. As of 2000, all states permitted an arrest for domestic violence without a warrant, provided there was sufficient probable cause. In addition, most states implemented proarrest policies, and mandatory prosecution policies became more widespread. Such policies require prosecutors to bring criminal charges against batterers.

These legislative changes have led to domestic violence offenses being considered much more seriously than they have been historically, especially considering that many of the crimes perpetrated in the context of these relationships include street crimes such as assault, battery, sexual assault and rape. However, despite the change in approach domestic violence rates in the United States still remain high. Recent statistics from the U.S. Department of Justice has indicated that although the overall violent crime rate in the United States has decreased 30 percent from 2002 to 2011, the rates for domestic violence have remained relatively stable over time, and between 2010 and 2011 there was no measurable change in the rates for intimate partner violence, and serious domestic violence incidents.

Victoria Ellen Collins
Old Dominion University

See Also: Children as Victims; Mental Illness; Rape and Sexual Assault; Sex Crimes; Stalking; Women.

Further Readings
Catalano, S., E. Smith, H. Snyder, and M. Rand. "Female Victims of Violence." In *National Crime*

Victimization Survey, 2009. Washington, DC: U.S. Department of Justice, Office of Justice Programs.

Logan, T. K., Robert Walker, and Carl G. Leukefeld. "Rural, Urban Influenced, and Urban Differences Among Domestic Violence Arrestees." *Journal of Interpersonal Violence,* v.16/3 (2001).

Sherman, Lawrence W. and Richard A. Berk. "The Specific Deterrent Effects of Arrest for Domestic Assault." *American Sociological Review,* v.49/2 (1984).

Thurman v. City of Torrington, DC, 595 F.Supp. 1521.

Truman, J. L. and M. Planty. "Criminal Victimization, 2011." Washington, DC: U.S. Department of Justice Office of Justice Programs, Bureau of Justice Statistics, NCJ 239437, October 2012.

Door-to-Door Scam Artists

A door-to-door sales scam is a mode of fraud that includes a variety of techniques. The practice is widespread throughout the United States, occurring in rural, suburban, and urban communities. Poor urban neighborhoods can be particularly vulnerable because the throng of people passing through makes it easier for itinerate door-to-door scammers to blend in; conversely, door-to-door scams are less likely in gated communities, where strangers are easily spotted, treated with suspicion, and often tracked with some form of identity database. The most common kinds of goods and services used as enticements in such scams include magazine sales, home repairs, asphalt installation, charitable donations, and food.

Structure and Countermeasures

A typical door-to-door scam operates this way: A stranger approaches a residence and offers to sell some good or service at a discounted price or for some beneficial cause. The seller will often use high-pressure sales tactics so that the resident will feel that the offer is too good to pass up or that the charitable cause needs immediate support. In some instances, the seller will appear desperate. For example, young people selling magazine subscriptions will tell residents they are paying their way through college by selling the subscriptions; they

have been sent to the area for the summer with little support. The sellers' desperate situation pressures the buyer to over-pay for goods or services that could be purchased much more economically from legitimate vendors. While selling goods and services door-to-door can be legitimate, the practice becomes a scam or fraud because the seller misrepresents what they are selling or the circumstances in which they are offering the sale. In most states, misrepresentation in the selling of goods and services is a felony, though authorities often invoke civil law over criminal law. Such violations most often fall under the purview of a state's attorney general or a state consumer protection bureau. The sales of some kinds of goods sold door-to-door, such as magazine subscriptions, are regulated by the Federal Trade Commission, which has established a three-day cooling off period in which customers can nullify a subscription or contract.

The illegality of such practices generally falls under states' fraud statutes. In order to be considered a fraudulent act, the misrepresentation must include a clear lie or omission of a material fact (this will differ by state jurisdiction). Such a misrepresentation must be more than advertising puffery. Because the statements made by door-to-door salespersons typically are not put into a contract, proving fraud is difficult. Often, the sales visit is merely a prelude to a more serious crime; in such instances, the door-to-door sales session is a cover for surveillance of a property. That is, the door-to-door scam provides the opportunity for later criminal acts such as a burglary.

Door-to-door scammers are often individuals, but some companies engage in the practice by transporting groups of people to specific locations. The use of students in the above example is a common practice by companies that sell magazine subscriptions or encyclopedias. Other groups caravan across the country selling home repair or asphalt installation. In reported cases, such groups will contract to do home repairs, but then fail to complete the work or do substandard repairs. In an asphalt installation scam, a door-to-door salesman say he has leftover asphalt from a nearby job and will pour a new driveway for a very low price. After the resident pays the salesman full or partial payment in advance, he or she discovers that either the work is incomplete or the driveway is spray-painted black to look like asphalt. By the time the resident realizes what has happened, the crew has fled. Because

In the United States, some communities attempted to criminalize door-to-door sales by passing what is known as a Green River Ordinance. However, the Supreme Court ruled that to totally ban door-to-door sales was unconstitutional.

these scammers are itinerate, the local police are often unable to make an arrest.

Systematic Obstacles to Study

The precise prevalence of door-to-door sales scams is unknown for four reasons. First, like other kinds of fraud, many victims do not report incidents to the police, as noted by researchers H. Copes, K. Kerley, K. Mason, and J. Van Wyk. Often the amount taken is considered too small to bother reporting, or the victim feels foolish or complicit in his or her own victimization. Therefore it is induced that official reports tend to undercount the crime. Second, police are often unable or unwilling to go after the perpetrators because the nature of the fraud makes it a case of the victim's word against the perpetrator; thus, arrests for door-to-door scams are unlikely.

Third, door-to-door scams that are reported are often counted under the general category of fraud in official police reporting, victimization surveys, and other official data. For example, the Uniform Crime Reports has only a general category of fraud

in its Part 2 offenses. Fourth, law enforcement and consumer protection agencies, such as state attorneys general and the Better Business Bureau, that do have jurisdiction over door-to-door scams, typically break down the complaints they receive by kind of goods or services and not by mode of sale. For instance, door-to-door sales are often categorized under the old classification of magazine subscriptions, which include door-to-door sales, telemarketing, and electronic sales.

Other door-to-door scams might be categorized as home repair or charitable contributions. Thus, how these kinds of goods and services were pitched to customers is not noted in the available statistics or tip sheets routinely published by consumer protection agencies.

Victims of door-to-door scams are often stereotyped as being poor and elderly, since these two groups are considered most vulnerable to the scammers' tactics. The available research on low-level frauds, however, suggests that door-to-door scam victims tend to be younger and middle-class. Without better reporting of the practice, its prevalence and victimology remain speculative.

To protect against door-to-door scams, law enforcement and consumer protection agencies may use the media or consumer education campaigns, promoting a caveat emptor or "buyer beware" attitude. Without any kind of reliable data, however, the effectiveness of such policy is unknown. Given that the practice continues to thrive suggests that it remains a profitable enterprise.

George W. Burruss
Southern Illinois University, Carbondale

See Also: Burglary; Credit Card Theft; Crime–Consumerism Nexus; Gated Communities; Suite Crimes Versus Street Crimes.

Further Readings

Copes, H., et al. "Reporting Behavior of Fraud Victims and Black's Theory of Law: An Empirical Assessment." *Justice Quarterly*, v.18/2 (2001).

Huff, R., C. Desilets, and J. Kane. *The 2010 National Public Survey on White-Collar Crime.* Fairmont, WV: National White-Collar Crime Center, 2010.

Kerley, K. and H. Copes. "Personal Fraud Victims and Their Official Responses to Victimization." *Journal of Police and Criminal Psychology*, v.17/1 (2002).

Drinking, Underage

On January 17, 1920, the Eighteenth Amendment to the U.S. Constitution went into effect and prohibited manufacturing, selling, and distributing alcoholic beverages. The 18th Amendment was repealed 13 years later, on December 5, 1933, when the Twenty-First Amendment to the U.S. Constitution was ratified. At that point, each state was expected to write its own drinking laws. But there was a movement across the United States in the early 1980s for the federal government to intervene in what was considered to be a national crisis: teenage drinking and driving. President Ronald Reagan, responding to strong political pressure from Mothers Against Drunk Driving, signed into law the National Minimum Drinking Age Act of 1984, which stipulated that alcoholic beverages could no longer be sold to or possessed by persons under the age of 21.

Compliance with the law was virtually assured by the legislation, because it stipulated that states that failed to comply with this law would face a reduction in federal highway funds. All states conformed to the minimum drinking age act. Unfortunately, we are only now beginning to realize substantial reductions in underage drinking and still more needs to be done.

Age and Ethnic Patterns

Alcohol is the drug of choice among teenagers. More teens use alcohol than use tobacco or other illegal drugs. The age at which teens are having their first drink has become younger in the last four decades. While in 1965 the average age at which teens tried alcohol for the first time was 17.5, the average age today is estimated to be about 11 for boys and 13 for girls. The National Survey of Drug Use and Health, in its 2010 study conducted for the U.S. Department of Health and Human Services, reported that alcohol use increases as adolescents mature. For instance, while 3.1 percent of 12-to-13-year-olds reported using alcohol, by age 14–15 the number had jumped to 12.4 percent. By age 16–17, about one in four (24.6 percent) reported that they had used alcohol, and by age 18–20 that number swelled to 48.9 percent.

The Monitoring the Future survey, conducted by the University of Michigan and published in 2011, revealed that about 40 percent of eighth-graders, 60 percent of 10th-graders, and 70 percent of 12th-graders reported that they had consumed alcohol at least once in their lifetime. Eighty-two percent of college students had used alcohol in the past.

While these numbers seem large, research indicates that there is a general trend toward a decline in alcohol use among teenagers. For example, while 25 percent of eighth-graders in 1991 reported consuming alcohol in the past 30 days, the number dropped to 14 percent in 2010. The percentage of 10th-graders who reported alcohol use in the last 30 days dropped from 43 percent in 1991 to 29 percent in 2010. And for 12th-graders, alcohol consumption dropped from 54 percent in 1991 to 41 percent in 2010. Underage college student drinking over the past month fell the least of all the groups, from 75 percent in 1991 to 65 percent in 2010.

Likewise, binge drinking has been declining. For instance, there was a decrease in binge drinking for eighth-graders from 11 percent in 1991 to 7 percent in 2010. Among 10th-graders, there was a decline from 21 percent in 1991 to 16 percent in 2010. And, among 12th-graders, binge drinking dropped from 30 percent in 1991 to 23 percent in 2010. Binge drinking among college students declined from 43 percent in 1991 to 37 percent in 2010.

According to the most recent survey performed by Monitoring the Future, except for the eighth grade, males were more likely than females to have reported that they had consumed alcohol in the last 30 days. For example, 13 percent of males and 14 percent of females in the eighth grade reported that over the last month they had consumed alcohol. By the tenth grade, 30 percent of males and 28 percent of females reported that they had consumed alcohol. By the 12th grade, 44 percent of males and 38 percent of females reported alcohol use in the last 30 days. By college, 47 percent of underage males and 41 percent of underage females reported that they had consumed alcohol in the last 30 days.

A similar pattern exists for binge drinking. Females reported a slightly higher percentage than males (8 percent versus 7 percent) in the eighth grade, but in the 10th grade, 12th grade, and in college, males were more likely to report binge drinking than females. For example, in the 10th grade, 18 percent of males and 15 percent of females reported binge drinking. In the 12th grade, 28 percent of males and 18 percent of females reported binge drinking. In college, 44 percent of males and 32 percent of females reported binge drinking.

White and Hispanic youth reported more underage drinking than African American youth. For instance, while 14 percent of white youth and 18 percent of Hispanic adolescents in the eighth grade reported that they consumed alcohol in the past 30 days, only 12 percent of African American youth reported that they consumed alcohol in the past month. In the 10th grade, 31 percent of white, 35 percent of Hispanic, and 21 percent of African American youth reported alcohol consumption over the last 30 days. In the 12th grade, 45 percent of whites, 40 percent of Hispanics, and 31 percent of African Americans reported that they had consumed alcohol in the past month. The same is true for binge drinking. With only one exception, white teens reported higher rates of binge drinking among eighth grade (7 percent), 10th grade (17 percent), and 12th grade (28 percent) students than Hispanic youth (11 percent, 22 percent, and 22 percent, respectively) and African American youth (5 percent, 11 percent, and 13 percent, respectively).

Immediate and Later Consequences

The younger the person is when he or she starts drinking alcohol, the greater the likelihood that they will engage in high-risk behaviors, including trying other drugs (especially cocaine and marijuana) and having multiple sex partners. In fact, adolescents who drink before their 15th birthday are five times more likely to become alcohol dependent as an adult than those who wait until they were at least 21. Underage drinkers have higher rates of school absences and poor school performance.

Underage drinking is also associated with fighting and other aggressive acts, suffering unintentional injuries (e.g., from falls), engaging in unprotected sex, being a victim of sexual assault, accidentally drowning, and committing suicide. Delays in brain development may also occur, and these changes may have long-term or even lifelong deleterious effects. Binge drinking may result in alcohol poisoning and sometimes even death, and it generally exacerbates the above-mentioned consequences of underage drinking. There may also be increased risk of cardiovascular disease and cancer.

Preventing Underage Drinking

Through federal and state legislation and the concerted efforts of dedicated professionals and lay people, teenage alcohol use has declined in recent years. But more needs to be done to bring about further reductions in the use of alcohol by teens. The first step needs to be the formulation of an effective response to the influence that marketing has on teen decision making. Research shows strong, positive correlations between alcohol ads—on television and radio, in print, and displayed on outdoor billboards—and increased use of alcohol by adolescents. Alcohol ads raise awareness and reinforce cultural acceptance of alcohol use. Additionally, new products are often packaged and geared specifically toward younger consumers, and marketing portrays drinking as attractive, glamorous, and exciting.

Underage drinking prevention programs have usually taken two approaches to reduce the appeal of alcohol to teens: (1) programs that target adolescents and (2) programs that target the adolescents' environments. Programs that target teens try to change their expectations and attitudes; they seek to educate youths about the dangers of using alcohol; and they attempt to provide the motivations and skills needed to successfully resist the temptation to drink before their 21st birthday. Environmental programs take steps to reduce opportunities for underage drinking through effective law enforcement practices; through consistent enforcement of punitive laws that target those who sell alcohol to or purchase it for minors; and by changing the culture of the community from one that tolerates underage consumption to one that promotes wellness and strongly condemns the use of alcohol before the age of 21.

Underage drinking is also associated with the commission of street crimes (e.g., fighting and other aggressive acts), suffering from unintentional injuries (e.g., from falls), engaging in unprotected sex, being a victim of sexual assault, accidentally drowning, and committing suicide.

Michael P. Brown
Ball State University

See Also: Alcohol and Drug Use; Bar Personnel; Juvenile Offending; Risky Lifestyles; Routine Activity Theory.

Further Readings

Bonnie, Richard J., et al., eds. *Reducing Underage Drinking: A Collective Responsibility*. Washington, DC: National Academies Press, 2004.
Johnston, Lloyd D., et al. *Secondary School Students.* Vol. I in *Monitoring the Future National Survey*

Results on Drug Use, 1975–2010. Bethesda, MD: National Institute on Drug Abuse, 2011.

Miller, Jacqueline W., et al. "Binge Drinking and Associated Health Risk Behaviors Among High School Students." *Pediatrics,* v.119/1 (2007).

U.S. Department of Health and Human Services. *The Surgeon General's Call to Action to Prevent and Reduce Underage Drinking.* Washington, DC: U.S. Department of Health and Human Services, Office of the Surgeon General, 2007.

Drinking Establishments, Unlicensed

One of the sources of street crime—even in rural areas—is the unlicensed drinking establishment where illegal liquor (moonshine), hard liquor, beer, and wine are sold. These establishments go back in recent history to Prohibition, the so-called Noble Experiment that outlawed most alcoholic beverages in the United States pursuant to the Eighteenth Amendment to the U.S. Constitution. During this era, speakeasies, blind pigs, and other unlicensed establishments proffering alcoholic drinks flourished, and the illegal sale of liquor went hand-in-hand with organized crime. The term *speakeasy* is said to have originated during Prohibition, when customers had to speak quietly so as not to draw the attention of the police and federal agents. The etymology of the term *blind pig* is as murky as the establishments themselves. Some attribute the phrase to live animal shows where customers were charged for the performance and alcohol was dispensed at no charge; thus, attempting to circumvent criminal charges of selling alcoholic beverages without a license. Another version came about during Prohibition when police officers were bribed to turn a blind eye to the illegal activities.

The Twenty-First Amendment repealed Prohibition, but the illegal liquor trade produced organized crime as we know it today. Similarly, the modern-day speakeasies often with tinted windows and peepholes that continue to exist throughout the country contribute significantly to criminal activity including street crime. These unlicensed drinking establishments go by different names, which are often colloquial in nature. In Michigan, for example, it was a raid on a blind pig by Detroit Police vice officers that sparked the 1967 summer race riots in the Motor City. In Virginia, they are frequently called nip joints and shot houses, presumably from taking a nip or shot of whiskey.

By whatever name they are called, there are different reasons these illegal clubs exist. Most of the reasons surround the lack of the regulated environment that is typically associated with premises that are licensed to sell alcoholic beverages. For example, at an illegal establishment, liquor can be purchased on credit, sold to underage persons, and sold in dry counties or cities. Other factors that are sometimes associated with the existence of illegal clubs and bars include the limitations in some states and jurisdictions on the number of licenses available in the area; the prohibition of Sunday sales of liquor or blue laws; and the ability to engage in other forms of illegal activities such as gambling, prostitution, and drug dealing. From a sociocultural perspective, one possible reason for the continued existence of unlicensed drinking establishments, particularly in the south, might be the historical discrimination against minority groups relative to the acquisition of liquor licenses, which has emerged into a subculture that has survived the passage of time. There are no known statistics as to the number of illegal bars and clubs in the United States. It is known, however, that unlicensed clubs exist mostly in urban and rural areas. For example, these types of establishments are operated throughout New York City. One recent raid in midtown Manhattan revealed that the unlicensed bar also served as an afterhour's sex club. Shipments of Virginia moonshine, which costs only a fraction of state liquor, make their way to Washington, D.C., Philadelphia, and New York City on a weekly basis where it is sold in mason jars and by the drink. In Richmond, Virginia, alone there are an estimated 200 illegal clubs operating into the early morning hours of any given weekend.

Criminal Investigations and Enforcement

With the repeal of Prohibition, the enforcement of liquor laws was primarily given over to the states. There are different approaches taken toward liquor law enforcement. Some states such as Michigan leave criminal enforcement of the liquor laws to local law enforcement officers, and investigators with the Liquor Control Commission handle administrative matters. Turning in another direction, Pennsylvania employs civilian liquor enforcement officers with the Department of State Police, who are empowered to enforce state liquor laws and related crimes. Virginia takes it even further. There, the Bureau of Law Enforcement of the Department of Alcoholic Beverage Control employs special agents who are police officers vested with the authority to enforce any criminal law throughout the commonwealth.

Other criminal laws that are typically investigated and enforced in and around unlicensed drinking establishments include gambling, prostitution, money laundering, drug dealing, firearms violations, and public disorders. Priorities in law enforcement efforts often include violent crime originating from these illegal establishments. The concept of community policing, which can augment the efforts of uniformed police officers, encompasses quality of life issues and public nuisances created as inebriated patrons spill out into the streets. Fights, public urination, and prostitution are by no means uncommon, and homicides, drive-by shootings, and stabbings are often associated with illegal drinking establishments. Nontraditional organized crime groups such as outlaw motorcycle gangs often run bars out of their clubhouses and sell liquor by the drink. Search warrants at these premises frequently turn up narcotics, illegal firearms, and stolen goods.

A number of law enforcement approaches are taken to contain and eradicate unlicensed drinking establishments. Traditional undercover operations are time consuming, involve the difficulties of infiltration, and indeed are inherently dangerous. However, this approach does produce direct evidence of illegal liquor sales and related crimes such as gambling and narcotics distribution.

Other approaches can involve criminal or civil common nuisance charges that can be developed through evidence demonstrating the premises are frequented by drug users, habitual drunkards, prostitutes, and other persons of ill-repute. Crime statistics demonstrating calls to the premises for police service, as well as documented violent crimes occurring inside the premises or directly linked to the illegal establishments, can contribute to padlocking the unlicensed drinking establishments and preserving the quality of life in communities and neighborhood streets.

John R. Cencich
California University of Pennsylvania

See Also: Alcohol and Drug Use; Bars and Pubs; Blue Laws; Bootleggers; Speakeasies (1920s).

Further Readings
Albanese, Jay S. *Organized Crime in Our Times.* Cincinnati, OH: Anderson Publishing, 2007.
Hirschfeld, Al and Gordon Kahn. *The Speakeasies of 1932.* Milwaukee, WI: Glenn Young Books, 2003.
Tatum, Shirley. "Moonshine Yesteryear." National Geographic (February 2, 2007). http://www.incubator .nationalgeographic.com/inside_ngc/2007/02/moon shine-yesteryear.html (Accessed April 2012).

Unlicensed drinking establishments can be located in dry counties where the government forbids the sale of alcoholic beverages. Hundreds of U.S. dry counties exist, many of them in the south.

Drive-By Shooting

Drive by shootings, colloquially known simply as "drive-bys," are a tactic used by urban guerrillas, political assassins, terrorists, and criminal gangs. Drive-bys are armed attacks made from moving or momentarily stopped vehicles against individuals in the open, in other vehicles, or in structures. Attacks may be made against vehicles or structures with no clear intent to injure or kill personnel but simply to terrorize. Since stealth and speed are key elements of such attacks, they are usually made with automatic or semiautomatic firearms from automobiles capable of fast acceleration—with the intent to surprise the targets, then overwhelm them with rapid firepower. As such, shot placement is secondary to volume of fire, frequently causing collateral damage to bystanders and property. It is, perhaps, this potential to wound and kill innocent persons that has drawn national attention to these criminal acts.

History and Modern Era

Drive-by shootings probably originated as a military tactic long before the invention of motor vehicles. Civil War guerrilla bands such as Quantrill's Raiders employed a "ride-by shooting" stratagem against enemy civilians and soldiers alike with great effect across parts of Kansas, Missouri, and Kentucky. The hit-and-run tactics of the Civil War guerrilla were later adapted as an ideal by the Prohibition-era gangster. The invention of the automobile and relatively compact fully automatic firearms such as the Thompson submachine gun increased the level of stealth and firepower exponentially from the days of the Civil War.

Drive-by shootings today are perhaps best known as a common criminal act perpetrated by modern American street gangs. Certain inner-city areas such as South Central Los Angeles are actually famous for the number of such attacks occurring each year. It has been reported that drive-by shootings are so common in this area that schools, retail stores, and residences have had additional architectural features such as masonry walls built and bullet-resistant windows installed to stop stray bullets. It is, however, difficult to separate fact from myth as there is no real incident reporting system specifically geared to drive-by shootings.

Gangland Use

Drive-by shootings are a common gang tactic used to terrorize if not actually kill and wound members of rival gangs. They may be used to establish territorial boundaries, serve as a warning to rivals, and as a relatively safe means of retaliation and vengeance. These shootings also serve as a rite of passage, initiating new members and testing the loyalty of questionably reliable members. They may serve as a bonding experience between members and may also be a source of prestige to intended targets who survive such attacks.

According to criminologists such as F. Parra, the typical shooter feels no remorse or guilt, celebrating the experience and the accompanying feelings of acceptance and a sense of accomplishment. Drive-bys are stereotypically associated with urban, minority street gangs and there seems to be little research effectively disputing this. Actors in drive by shootings are almost exclusively young males, often juveniles, the idea being that if caught they will receive little in the way of punishment. Victims are predominantly young males as well, but may be any age or sex. Much of the statistical information on drive-by shootings dates to the 1990s. A 1996 study of drive-by shootings in Los Angeles (by researchers H. Hutson, D. Anglin, and M. Eckstein) is fairly typical. The study documented 6,327 incidents occurring between 1989 and 1993. In these incidents, there were over 9,000 persons shot at, 590 of whom were killed. Of those killed, 23 percent were classified as innocent bystanders.

Incidence

One of the more recent studies was published in 2007 by the Violence Policy Center (VPC); it should be noted the VPC is a gun control advocacy group. The researchers used a popular search engine to compile their data. They report that in 2006, California led the nation with 115 drive-by shootings that killed 51 and injured 123. No other state came close; Florida had 57 such shootings in which 18 were killed and 47 wounded; Texas had 56 drive-by shootings killing seven and wounding 41; Illinois had 24 drive-by shootings, killing 11 and injuring 29. There were at least a few such incidents in every state except Maine, North Dakota, South Dakota, Vermont, and West Virginia. All told in 2006, there were 621 persons killed and wounded in such attacks, according to VPC research. For all the publicity surrounding drive-by shootings, they account for less than 0.5 percent of murders in the United States.

According to the VPC study, about 75 percent of drive-by shooting casualties were over the age of 18. Over half the attacks occurred at a residence; in about 21 percent of cases, the attack was made on persons in another vehicle; another 22 percent were against persons in a restaurant, shop, church, basketball court, or other public place. Most drive-by shootings occur during the evening or nighttime hours; 47 percent between 7:00 P.M. and midnight, and 27 percent between midnight and 7:00 A.M. Drive-by shootings peak in July and are lowest in December and January. Researchers were not able to determine from their source material a precise number of such shootings that were confirmable as gang-related.

Conclusion

Although drive-by shootings have been depicted or even celebrated in rap music, movies, and television as elements of pop culture, they are not nearly as prevalent as presented in popular and news media. While any act that claims even a few hundred lives per year cannot be discounted, it should be remembered that these are uncommon events and should be regarded as such by the general populace.

M. George Eichenberg
Tarleton State University

See Also: Bloods; Crips; Fear of Crime; Gangs (Street); Guns and Weapons; Gunshot Detection System; Murder/Homicide; Operation Ceasefire.

Further Readings

Dedel, Kelly. *Drive-By Shootings: Problem-Oriented Guides for Police Problem-Specific Guides Series.* No. 47. 2007. http://www.cops.usdoj.gov/files/ric/Publications/e02072864.pdf (Accessed June 2012).

Hipp, John R., George E. Tita, and Robert T. Greenbaum. "Drive-Bys and Trade-Ups: Examining the Directionality of the Crime and Residential Instability Relationship." *Social Forces*, v.87/4 (2009).

Hutson, H. Range, Deirdre Anglin, and Marc Eckstein. "Drive-By Shootings by Violent Street Gangs in Los Angeles: A Five-Year Review From 1989–1993." *Academic Emergency Medicine*, v.3/4 (1996).

Parra, Fernando. "Good, the Bad, and the Ugly: Veterano (Older) Chicano Gang Members and the (Dys)Functional Aspects of the Role." *Journal of Gang Research*, v.8/4 (2001).

Sanders, William B. *Gangbangs and Drive-Bys: Grounded Culture and Juvenile Gang Violence.* Hawthorne, NY: Aldine de Gruyter, 1994.

Drug Dealing

Concentrated research has shown that the scope of what is typical and atypical in the street dealing of illicit and prescription drugs is undergoing a variety of changes that will impact prevention, deterrence, incarceration, treatment, and other aspects of this societal challenge. Many long-accepted images about the types of drug dealing in the United States no longer reflect the reality on the street; nor do some of the accepted cliches about the individuals and demographic groups most heavily involved still ring true. This entry surveys some of the most recent findings and relevant trends.

Historical and Current Profiles

Street drug dealing remains the province of men who are able to demonstrate aggression and fearlessness in their roles as masters of the trade. However, while they may be masters of the illicit sale of drugs, they are also subjugated by their own drug use and in some instances drug addictions. Males who are more likely to report involvement in drug sales are more likely to be using marijuana, cocaine, hallucinogens, or prescription drugs.

Contrary to the stereotype of the black male drug dealer, analysis of the 2006 National Survey on Drug Use and Health of over 13,000 youth reveals that 6.4 percent of black male youth were dealing drugs, while 4.5 percent of white male youth were dealing. Moreover, 2 percent of white females were dealing, compared to 1.6 percent of black females. Findings also reveal that black youths who use marijuana were 13 times more likely to sell drugs than black youths who did not use marijuana. Among white youth, those who misused prescription drugs and cocaine were three times more likely to sell drugs than white youths who did not misuse prescription drugs. Other work supports this basic tenet that many users later become sellers to subsidize their own use of drugs. The national study also revealed a negative relationship between receipt of public assistance and drug dealing among whites and blacks.

Recent sociohistorical research presents substantive findings revealing that initial drug abuse and drug sales in the United States were neither illegal nor criminalized, but were indeed facilitated by pharmaceutical companies. One such drug in the early 18th century was an opiate called Dover's powder, sold by pharmacies, groceries, and traveling medicine shows. As racial and immigrant fears became more pronounced and stereotypically associated with specific ethnic groups, such drugs were initially regulated and controlled for tax purposes—then later criminalized in accordance with the racial threat hypothesis. That is, as specific types of drugs or forms of drug abuse became associated with minority groups, the drug itself was perceived as more of a threat to the white power structure.

Researchers James Inciardi and Theodore Cicero reviewed the history of drug abuse and sales patterns in the United States, illustrating that while specific substances wax and wane in popularity, sometimes coinciding with legal sanctions, the most recent patterns of drug use and sales since the late 1990s again involve pharmaceuticals. Specifically, oxycodone and other narcotic painkillers sold by physicians and marketed by pharmaceutical firms later end up being sold on the streets. This is also evidenced by recent Drug Abuse Warning System data from emergency rooms around the country that show narcotic analgesics abuse admissions increased by 153 percent from 1995 to 2002. From 2005 to 2009, emergency room admissions of pharmaceutical abuse cases increased again by 82 percent. The most commonly abused or misused substances leading to hospital admissions were pharmaceuticals.

Inicardi and Cicero argue that from Maine through the Ohio Valley across rural communities, physically arduous blue-collar occupations such as mining, logging, and fishing result in chronic pain and often necessitate pain management medications. In 2004, prescription opioids had the highest number of new users, according to the National Survey of Drug Use and Health. By 2009, this survey reflected that rates of abuse of pharmaceutical drugs were second only to abuse of marijuana. Similar findings have been illustrated by the Monitoring the Future study, a leading national survey of adolescents in high schools.

Illicit Channels for Prescription Drugs

Some researchers argue that these legal drugs are unlawfully diverted from regulated pharmaceutical channels to the street market in several ways. There are those among the federal enforcement agencies, however, who insist that most such substances enter the illegal market through "doctor shoppers" (drug-abusing patients making simultaneous requests for prescriptions from multiple physicians), inappropriate prescribing practices of physicians, and inappropriate dispensing practices

of pharmacists. But many respondents in the National Survey on Drug Use and Health continue to report that they get their drugs from friends or relatives; these drug dealers are likely the major source of illicit prescription drugs.

Drug Enforcement Agency evidence reflects indications that these dealers are stealing the drugs from pharmacies, legitimate distributors, hospitals, clinics, and other businesses where controlled substances are stolen. Other work indicates that residential burglaries also result in theft of drugs as self-reported by drug-involved offenders and active street drug users, who report stealing four typical items: money, jewelry, guns, and prescription drugs. Finally, there are doctors who prescribe these drugs illegitimately; sex workers buy or barter from clients; and disability patients sell drugs, as do some Medicaid recipients.

Similarly, while earlier research studies seemed to reflect that drug dealing was the occupation of large criminal organizations with a hierarchical structure and international connections to producers and growers, more recent work reveals that these kinds of structures are somewhat obsolete; many have been replaced by more loosely organized networks of adults who maintain egalitarian relationships with one another. These adults appear to be involved in loosely connected networks of about 40 individuals with roles as brokers, who are described as middlemen between the sellers (mostly men) of quantities of about a pound or more, and retailers who buy smaller quantities from a quarter of an ounce to four ounces from sellers. Sometimes these retailers also included women.

These networks generally also included secretaries who were more likely to be women, and the wives or girlfriends of other active members who acted as messengers between brokers, sellers, and retailers. While researcher Mangal Natarajan's work did not attempt to explore the likelihood that these individuals were also addicted, he did identify small cliques of three to four members within these networks with some overlap between cliques and sellers.

Similarly, other work identifies ecstasy sellers as involved in legitimate paying work as well as being involved in selling drugs, primarily to networks of their friends. Natarajan reveals that there appeared to be one pivotal individual who bridged relationships between street sellers and a number of mid-level drug dealers who scored relatively high on a measure of power; other research reflects that most dealers sell primarily to friends and do not see themselves as drug dealers, nor do they have much power in drug dealing networks.

In work analyzing larger drug dealing networks, players in the network did not specialize in any one area of a given city, but rather patterns of sales were diffuse; for example throughout all five boroughs of New York City, the most active calls by drug dealers were made from Manhattan rather than the poorer boroughs.

Finally, the research suggests that while these weak network ties demonstrated to exist between sellers, retailers, and brokers may not reflect prosecutors' descriptions of criminal conspiracies, their existence would reflect that they may be more likely to survive after arrests are made of some of the players who could easily be replaced by new members. This work resonates with other evidence that drug dealers have multiple social identities; many of them deal in private rather than in public settings, are predominately white, and a significant proportion have college degrees.

Shifts in Cause and Effect

A variety of studies indicate that street drug sales are likely to result in violence, as the result of drug market conflicts or from police crackdowns. Some scholars argue that police crackdowns are not the best response to drug dealing, since so many dealers are drug users and that this policy response may drive intravenous (IV) users away from the community public health and treatment community—increasing rather than decreasing health consequences of IV drug use.

Such community programs, when well planned, implemented, and evaluated, have been shown to be successful in reducing drug use and related crimes. Other work indicates that some prosecutorial descriptions that identify urban drug trafficking networks as structured criminal syndicates may be inaccurate. Rather, research reveals that urban heroin street drug dealing networks are more likely to be characterized by small groups of loosely linked sellers.

Nevertheless, drug trafficking across inner cities contributes to the decline of neighborhoods, absence of jobs, immigrant exploitation, and bank redlining processes. Many of those involved in drug sales are trying to earn a living or are supporting their own drug addiction.

Some of the myths promulgated in the past included the involvement of young black gang members in drug sales, while even in the early 1990s, for example, just 8 percent of youth living in housing projects in one inner city reported being involved in drug sales.

Even more recent research finds that drug dealing also occurs outside the context of the urban poor and housing projects or the "traditional street," but rather occurs in spaces not as prone to the gaze of law enforcement, such as a college dorm. These dynamics reflect the privileges or race and class in that most college campuses are attended by predominately white and middle-class and working-class individuals who are less likely to be subjected to public surveillance.

Conclusion

The change in major drug demand from cocaine to pharmaceuticals may have had a suppression effect on the homicides previously associated with inner-city street drug dealing and the former territorial disputes between gangs selling drugs that lead to the increased violence of the 1990s. These older systemic rates of homicide associated with drug dealing also may be decreasing, as reflected in findings that the new paradigm of drug selling networks necessitate the maintenance of supportive groupings across the drug buying and selling chain.

Nevertheless, there are more proximal effects of drug dealing that are connected to drug use. Specifically, some research reveals that in both homicide and suicide cases with associated drug abuse aspects, the commonly abused substances are alcohol and pharmaceuticals, with the latter likely to be used by two-thirds of the victims of homicides as illustrated in postmortality toxicology reports. Moreover, alcohol was present in almost 40 percent of the victims, illicit drugs in about a quarter of the cases, and pharmaceuticals in another quarter of the victims.

Rebecca Katz
Morehead State University

See Also: Alcohol and Drug Use; Drugs, Prescription; Immigrant Neighborhoods; Needle Exchanges; Policing, Problem-Oriented.

Further Readings

Campbell, Howard. "Female Drug Smugglers on the U.S.–Mexico Border: Gender, Crime, and Empowerment." *Anthropological Quarterly,* v.81/1 (2008).

Floyd, Leah J., Pierre K. Alexandre, Sarra L. Hedden, April L. Lawson, William W. Latimaer, and Nathaniel Giles III. "Adolescent Drug Dealing and Race/Ethnicity: A Population-Based Study of the Differential Impact of Substance Abuse on Involvement in Drug Trade." *American Journal of Drug and Alcohol Abuse,* v.36/2 (2010).

Iavchunovskaia, Tatiana M. and Irinia B. Stepanova. "A Social Description of Female Narcotics Crime." *Sociological Research,* v.48/2 (2009).

Inciardi, James A. and Theodore J. Cicero. "Black Beauties, Gorilla Pills, Footballs, and Hillbilly Heroin: Some Reflections on Prescription Drug Abuse and Diversion Research Over the Past 40 Years." *Journal of Drug Issues,* v.38/4 (2009).

Kerr, Thomas, William Small, Caitlin Johnston, Kathy Li, Julio S. G. Montaner, and Evan Wood. "Characteristics of Injection Drug Users Who Participate in Drug Dealing: Implications for Drug Policy." *Journal of Psychoactive Drugs,* v.40/2 (2008).

U.S. Department of Health and Human Services. "Summary of National Findings." Vol. I in "National Survey on Drug Use and Health." Rockville, MD: Substance Abuse Services and Mental Health Services Administration, 2010.

Drug Markets, Open-Air

There are two types of markets for illicit drugs. Unlike person-specific markets, where people learn from their social networks to locate sellers and potential buyers, what drugs are sold, and at what prices, open-air drug markets operate in specific places at specific times. Researchers Alex Haracopos and Mike Hough emphasized that open-air markets have advantages and disadvantages to buyers and sellers. Regarding advantages, potential buyers have fewer obstacles to access, while sellers can increase access to customers. The disadvantages to market participants are that sellers are more likely to be arrested and buying from strangers is more likely to lead to violent victimization. Because these markets are typically found in such locales as public housing areas, they tend to generate street crime. Because of the attraction of likely victims (drug buyers) and victimizers (sellers), open-air drug markets are, by Routine Activity theory definition, environments that can spawn additional crimes beyond the immediate violations of the drug trade. These additional street crimes include larceny-theft, aggravated assault, homicide, and vandalism.

Adverse Consequences

As noted by Paul Goldstein and Henry Brownstein, who have conducted considerable ethnographic research on illicit drug trafficking, whenever situations arise such as disputes between dealers over territory or potential customers, failure to pay one's debts, or disagreements regarding the price, amount, and quality of drugs, homicide or assault often occurs. Furthermore, local citizens who inform police of drug activity face violent retaliation by dealers. Innocent bystanders can be killed or injured by stray bullets intended for drug market participants. Police officers can be killed or wounded in confrontations with dealers. Additionally, criminologists Haracopos and Hough observed that open-air drug markets contribute to disorder and crime which can damage residents' quality of life. Residents can be robbed and their homes and businesses burglarized. Prostitution, disorderly conduct, loitering, and noise also result from drug market activity. Drug markets can lure local youth away from school and legitimate work, facilitating their involvement in addiction and crime. All of these conditions can increase residents' fear of crime.

Origins and Interventions

According to scholar James Inciardi, open-air drug markets are disproportionately prevalent in poor urban areas with many serious social problems. Within such neighborhoods, such markets tend to emerge where there is poor street lighting, many vacant buildings, and few owner-occupied residences. Furthermore, places where there are many broken windows, malfunctioning locks and security systems, and poorly maintained residences often attract drug markets.

Interventions designed to reduce open-air drug markets and their adverse consequences include criminal justice sanctions such as arresting drug market participants, police crackdowns on "hot spots" (areas in which drug trafficking is disproportionately prevalent), regulatory enforcement, and drug abuse treatment.

Among the more comprehensive summaries of research findings on the effects of various law enforcement procedures have been performed by Haracopos and Hough; David Boyum, Jonathan Caulkins, and Mark Kleiman; as well as by Lawrence Sherman. Arresting large numbers of drug buyers and sellers has been ineffective in reducing the size of a given market and its concomitant drug use and violence. Boyum and his colleagues noted that with massive arrests, there are increased costs of arresting and incarcerating many nonviolent drug offenders, which leads to prison crowding. Also, other dealers typically take the place of those arrested. However, as Boyum, Caulkins, and Kleiman emphasized, longer prison sentences for the most violent dealers can lead to a subsequent reduction in violence emanating from open-air drug markets.

The 1980s crackdown by the New York Police Department on the open-air drug market in Washington Square Park resulted in a 300 percent increase in arrests during the 1984–86 period, as noted by researchers Roger Conner and Patrick Burns. For the reporting year of 1985, this effort resulted in a conviction rate of 70 percent for the 1,490 drug-related cases that went to trial. Unfortunately, in part due to jail overcrowding, only about 100 of the convictions resulted in incarceration of more than 15 days. Sherman found that conducting police crackdowns on drug trafficking hot spots can reduce citizen calls to police about crime and disorder without moving crime elsewhere. Moreover, as Boyum and his colleagues noted, longer police crackdowns on drug trafficking hot spots tend to be more effective than short-term ones in disrupting a drug market—provided sufficient resources can sustain the crackdown.

Other Strategies

Sherman also reported that regulatory enforcement, including meetings between police and property owners to discuss eviction of drug-involved tenants and civil code enforcement, tended to be more effective in reducing reported crime than either police raids or criminal prosecution for most dealers. Haracopos and Hough contended that such a strategy works to the extent that effective sanctions exist for noncompliance.

Haracopos and Hough, along with and Boyum and colleagues, stressed that by disrupting drug markets, enforcement can drive some users into drug treatment. Boyum and his co-authors and Inciardi both noted that many rigorous research studies have shown that methadone maintenance and therapeutic community treatment can reduce drug use and crime. However, many of these studies, while showing that treatment works better than no treatment, found that many users relapse after a treatment episode.

Timothy Kinlock
*Friends Research Institute
and the University of Baltimore*

See Also: Alcohol and Drug Use; Arrest; Broken Windows Theory; Burglary; Drug Dealing; Fear of Crime; Hot Spots; Loitering; Murder/Homicide; Police (Overview); Vandalism.

Further Readings

Boyum, David, Jonathan Caulkins, and Mark Kleiman. "Drugs, Crime, and Public Policy". In *Crime and Public Policy,* James Q. Wilson and Joan Petersilia, eds. New York: Oxford University Press, 2010.

Conner, Roger and Patrick Burns. "The Winnable War: A Community Guide to Eradicating Street Drug Markets." Washington, DC: American Alliance for Rights and Responsibilities, 1991.

Goldstein, Paul and Henry Brownstein. "Drug Related Crime Analysis: Homicide." Rockville, MD: National Institute of Justice, 1987.

Inciardi, James. *War on Drugs IV: The Continuing Saga of the Mysteries and Miseries of Intoxication, Addiction, Crime and Public Policy.* 4th ed. Boston: Allyn & Bacon, 2007.

Sherman, Lawrence. "Democratic Policing on the Evidence." In *Crime and Public Policy,* James Q. Wilson and Joan Petersilia, eds. New York: Oxford University Press, 2010.

Drugs, Prescription

Street-level prescription drug crime (SLPDC) is one aspect of what is commonly known as "prescription drug diversion" (PDD), which involves all efforts to move legitimate drugs into a setting that is not legal. SLPDC deals with this movement at the retail level of the regulated chain of prescription drugs, and most often involves those stakeholders with direct access to the legal drugs, but who choose to sell them on the illegal market.

Changing Enforcement Trends

The scope and history of SLPDC are intertwined in that during a relatively recent period of time, society and even many in law enforcement have denied the extent or even danger of legal drugs entering society illegally via street-level transactions. From the 1970s until the late 1990s or even early 2000s, the most significant response to address SLPDC and PDD generally was at the state and local levels. The primary reason for this was that it was these agencies that encountered the immediate negative impact of pharmaceutical drugs such as Ritalin, Dilauded, Xanax, Librium, and many others flooding communities in the illicit market.

During this same time at the federal level, the more immediate focus was placed on what the public and unfortunately many in decision-making positions considered "street-level" drugs and drug crimes. This meant the focus went toward marijuana, cocaine, heroine, PCP, and so forth. For many in American society, what was commonly thought of as the drug problem in America constrained the law enforcement response generally to those drugs which were already considered street-level, even though SLPDC was occurring at an alarming rate to include not only illegal diversion of legal drugs so that they might be sold at the street level, but also a growing market for counterfeit legal drugs to also be sold at the street level. What is clear today, is that all levels of law enforcement currently understand the reality of SLPDC, its damage to communities, and its international and economic nature, which relies on street-level sales.

By the Numbers

The magnitude of SLPDC is staggering. The U.S. National Institutes of Health's National Institute on Drug Abuse estimates that in 2010, almost 20 percent of people within the United States abused prescription drugs; that is, used them outside of their approved medical purpose. That percentage equates to roughly 60 million people. Between 2000 and 2003, thefts and losses of prescription drugs from pharmacies counted for 89.3 percent of all thefts and losses reported to the U.S. Drug Enforcement Administration.

There was an increase in prescription drug abuse by 212 percent between 1992 and 2003 in teens aged 12 to 17; these drugs were mostly obtained at the street level. Adding to the temptation to commit such crimes at the street level, the potential profitability of OxyContin for instance, can bring approximately 10 times the legitimate value in a nonstreet setting. There has even been an increase on attacks against elderly citizens to gain access to their prescription drugs. Testimony to a congressional committee asserted that the prescription drug abuse issue directly impacts the lives of many nationally, and increases financial costs to our health care system—as well as the increased problem of gaining access to medications by those legitimately needing them.

Clinical Street Setting

Substance abuse treatment clinics or narcotic treatment programs started as a societal response to the heroin addiction issue. The drug used to address treatment and maintenance for these addicts was methadone. As more SLPDC occurred, many substance abuse treatment clinics saw a rise in patients who were polydrug abusers, meaning that they were using multiple drugs simultaneously; prescription drugs were often found to be part of this mixture.

The reasoning was direct; to the addict, the status of prescription drugs indicated they were made in a controlled environment and that they were safer than drugs mixed on the street. Also, these drugs were easy to obtain while avoiding detection, since law enforcement agencies were looking toward drugs like cocaine and heroin, and did not generally consider pharmaceuticals as something to be concerned about at the street level.

What did become a serious phenomenon for law enforcement at all levels was patients associated with treatment programs selling their methadone in clinic neighborhoods to other addicts. Sometimes this even meant vomiting the methadone into a strainer and then handing it to an addict for a price. Many treatment programs have switched to using Methadose (liquid form) in order to reduce this behavior, and ask nurses to monitor administration of the drug to help ensure it is ingested.

Finally, there are some with medical access to legal prescription drugs who misuse their access in order to gain financially: physicians, pharmacists, nurses, and others in the clinical setting. The number of these professionals doing so is small; however, the impact on our legitimate system of legal drugs and the negative impact on society is tremendous, given that these professionals are in a position of trust and essentially have used their access to become street-level drug dealers.

Nonclinical Street Setting

The nonclinical setting of SLPDC involves patients who receive their legitimate prescription drugs and those with access to such drugs due to their connection to the medical industry (including some pharmaceutical company representatives). Some consider this dimension of drug crime at the street level to be more of a problem, although it is difficult to measure the scope of the issue. Whole new populations of addicts have come about, including the average everyday "soccer mom" who develops an addiction to either pain medication or to tranquilizers known as benzodiazepines. Obtaining these drugs in quantity via "doctor shopping" (getting prescriptions from multiple physicians simultaneously) or other connections at the street level has been an exploding issue for law enforcement. Many students have gained access to prescription drugs simply by purchasing pills from dealers near schools or at popular recreational facilities (e.g., arcades and shopping malls).

Drugs such as a formulated fentanyl product called Actiq have become popular; this is a flavored product for oral administration (known as a "narco-pop") to help people primarily suffering from cancer that now sells on the street. Many young users, like longtime drug addicts, associate prescription drugs with a sense of safety. Some youth steal legitimate prescription drugs from their own homes and then sell them to their friends.

Criminal Justice Response

The societal response to this increasing phenomenon varies. Many cities are providing more attention via law enforcement training on investigation and awareness of SLPDC; the National Association of Drug Diversion Investigators is one organization providing a link between law enforcement, health professionals, and pharmaceutical companies. The Rx PATROL (Pattern Analysis Tracking Robberies and Other Losses) is an example of a response by the pharmaceutical industry to assist law enforcement in solving robberies and thefts of prescription drugs at the retail level. The robberies normally involve targeting pharmacies, but an increasing issue for law enforcement is the rise in theft from private homes by family members as well as those temporarily gaining access to homes (e.g., some repair workers).

In today's society, to not consider SLPDC as a serious issue (especially considering polydrug abuse) is finally almost unheard of in many jurisdictions. This type of crime impacts every level of society and connects numerous realities (e.g., gender, race, ethnicity, religious preference, nationality, or age).

Therefore, SLPDC is a complex form of criminality, one which it has taken decades for society to grasp the scope of. The scholarship to reflect this transition of public opinion and views of decision makers toward policies to better address this criminal issue have not yet caught up with the efforts of law enforcement and intelligence officials. However, the scholarship is increasing and is helping shed light on this phenomenon.

David R. Montague
University of Arkansas at Little Rock

See Also: Alcohol and Drug Use; Counterfeit Goods; Courts, Drug; Drug Dealing; Drug Markets, Open-Air; Juvenile Offending; Needle Exchanges; Theft and Larceny.

Further Readings

Burke, John. "Drug Diversion: The Scope of the Problem." Lutherville, MD: National Association of Drug Diversion Investigators, 2011.

Hanson, Glen R., Peter J. Venturelli, and Annette E. Fleckenstein. *Drugs and Society.* 11th ed. Sudbury, MA: Jones and Bartlett, 2011.

Joranson David E. and Aaron M. Gilson. "Drug Crime is a Source of Abused Pain Medications in the United States." *Journal of Pain and Symptom Management,* v.30/4 (2005).

National Institute on Drug Abuse. *Commonly Abused Prescription Drugs.* October 2011. http://www.drugabuse.gov/drugs-abuse/commonly-abused-drugs/commonly-abused-prescription-drugs-chart (Accessed June 2012).

Pharmaceutical Security Institute. http://www.psi
-inc.org/counterfeitSituation.cfm (Accessed June
2012).

Purdue Pharma, L.P. "Rx PATROL—Crime Stoppers
Tip Reward Program." 2012. http://www.rxpatrol.org
(Accessed June 2012).

Environmental Criminology

Exposure to environmental toxins has widespread effects on health and behavior. This issue has been a significant scientific concern for at least 50 years, and for the past two decades it has informed a growing knowledge base in a segment of law enforcement and criminal justice known variously as green criminology, environmental criminology, or environmental justice. This entry examines green/environmental crime issues relevant to urban environments; the unequal distribution of environmental pollution in urban areas relative to neighborhood racial, ethnic, and class characteristics; and the effects of some specific toxins (e.g., heavy metals and endocrine disruptors) on human behavior in urban space.

Unequal Distribution of Toxins

Environmental justice (EJ) is the study of the functioning of the criminal justice system as it applies to unequal exposure to toxic harm by the race, ethnicity, and class of affected neighborhoods, as noted by sociologist Robert Bullard. Minorities and the poor face a disproportionate share of exposure to environmental burdens including hazardous waste, toxic facilities, and chemical pollution, according to the work of many researchers. The recognition of EJ

emerged in the late 1970s, pioneered by Bullard, and soon became nationally recognized as the environmental justice movement, particularly following protests against the placement of a PCB-contaminated landfill in a predominantly African American community in Warren County, North Carolina.

Bullard's original research examined the siting of garbage dumps in Houston, which were disproportionately located in African American communities. In 1987, the United Church of Christ published a groundbreaking study which concluded that commercial hazardous waste facilities and uncontrolled toxic sites were disproportionately located in communities of color and that three out of every five African Americans and Latino residents across the United States lived in communities with uncontrolled toxic waste sites. In eight- and 20-year follow-up studies, researchers including T. J. Roberts and M. Toffolon-Weiss found even greater evidence of such racial disparities.

The body of work by these researchers and others to come has begun to focus EJ on a set of goals, namely to address injustice and the unequal application of criminal justice through study, data presentation, and application in the legal and regulatory dominions. These goals can be accomplished by examining the nature and distribution of pollution, the disposal of toxic waste; habitat destruction, disproportionate exposure to environmental harms, deficiencies in environmental regulation, pressure

Protestors in 1982 marched against dumping toxic polychlorinated biphenyl (PCB) into a landfill located in a predominantly African American community in Warren County, North Carolina. The protests brought attention to the issue of environmental racism. The landfill was constructed to contain 60,000 tons of highly PCB-contaminated soil scraped from 210 miles of roadside shoulders in North Carolina.

exerted on legislatures by corporations engaged in the chemical waste industry, and unequal enforcement of environmental laws.

Scope of Green Damage

The environmental crimes in question include a myriad of unreported events: the siting of waste transfer stations in politically disadvantaged urban neighborhoods; laxity in zoning for incinerators, chemical storage, and waste dumps; illegal reuse of untreated soils, industrial tailings, and toxic building materials in such functions as school and playground construction; and water table pollution in written-off areas of cities, towns, and rural zones. The crimes also include well-known events, such as the Bhopal disaster in India, the Love Canal incident in New York, the *Exxon Valdez* oil spill in Alaska, and the BP oil disaster in the Gulf of Mexico.

The harm from such incidents, however, are rarely depicted as "crimes" despite the fact that researchers suggest that environmental crime may rival street crime itself in the cost of personal injury

and death and property damage it causes. Environmental crimes include acts or omissions that violate federal, state, or local environmental laws, as well as civil laws. Their repeated and unstanched spread also encourages the spread of organized crime enterprises, which often are found to be involved in the waste disposal businesses that operate, often with official corruption at every level of government from the most local to the federal tier.

Hard data on this damage and corruption are difficult to compile and assess—there are few if any uniform, national reporting protocols for EJ crimes similar to those for street crime (e.g., Uniform Crime Reports, National Crime Victimization Survey). This does not mean, however, that this type of research should be ignored; rather it can serve to alert academics and law enforcement policy makers that there is much work to be done.

Toxic Effects on Youth

Environmental justice research within the criminological literature has been limited. However, much of what there is forms a devastating indictment of the chemical waste industry. Researchers Paul Stretesky and Michael Lynch, for instance, found unequal toxic waste exposure patterns for minority populations, including chidlren, that may "affect learning ability, [and] alter behavior in ways that delay school progress and maturation, perhaps leading to poor school performance, an increased likelihood of dropping out, and a diminished ability to obtain a well-paying, satisfying job, or enter a legitimate career path." This conclusion was supported by a Public Citizen study in 2005 on declines in attendance rates at schools in several Texas counties following air emissions events at nearby petroleum refineries.

Medical researchers assert that toxic emissions affect childhood development, that the neurological toxins in industrial pollution are partially responsible for the increased incidence of outcomes such as learning disabilities, and that more than half of all toxic chemical emissions reported to the federal Toxic Release Inventory are known or suspected developmental and neurological toxins.

All in all, an estimated 40 million people—one-sixth of the U.S. population—live in close proximity to one or more hazardous waste sites. An equal number are served by drinking water systems with lead levels exceeding regulatory limits.

Environmental toxins can interact with brain chemistry and development in ways that can stimulate aggression and criminal offending. Exposure to chemicals, pesticides, and heavy metals such as lead, cadmium, and mercury, affect brain and cognitive development, which in turn affects behavior. Lead exposure has been linked to conduct disorders and/or aggressive behavior, delinquency, and criminal behavior, especially homicides and violent crime.

Unequal Environmental Enforcement

Only a small percentage of criminal enforcement efforts are aimed at environmental crime. These efforts, however, are also marked by environmental injustice. Fines imposed on polluters are significantly higher when the pollution affects predominantly white communities than in affected minority communities. As noted in a 1992 study, "There is a racial divide in the way the U.S. government cleans up toxic waste sites and punishes polluters. White communities see faster action, better results, and stiffer penalties than communities where blacks,

Hispanics, and other minorities live." This conclusion has also been extended to the enforcement of state environmental laws, as shown in research by Konisky. Similarly, a study in 2004 demonstrated that while federal sentences for nonenvironmental crime offenders increased, sentences for environmental crime offenders decreased substantially (from 52 percent in 1996 to 23 percent in 2001), and that length of sentences for environmental crime offenders were significantly shorter than for nonenvironmental crime offenders. Similar patterns have been found for financial penalties.

Conclusion

When companies dump chemicals into the environment, legally or illegally, Stretesky and Lynch point out in the results of their 1999 work, "they do so purposefully and with knowledge that the likely results of their actions will include injury and death for those exposed to their waste products. These are not accidents—they are planned actions no less serious than assaults or killings." Environmental crime and injustice are a result of industry and corporate decisions to maximize profits and externalize costs. Environmental injustice and environmental racism are a result of the political and economic processes that exist at all levels of government. Often, economic and political decisions at the state and federal level benefit industry or a segment of the community at the expense of others in the community. "It is time for criminologists to take environmental problems more seriously," Stretesky and Lynch emphasized in a 2007 work, "and engage with the various ways in which environmental and criminological issues intersect."

Melissa L. Jarrell
Texas A&M University, Corpus Christi
Michael J. Lynch
University of South Florida

See Also: Children as Victims; Gentrification; Immigrant Neighborhoods; Suite Crimes Versus Street Crimes.

Further Readings

Bierne, Piers and Nigel South, eds. *Issues in Green Criminology: Confronting Harms Against Environments, Humanity, and Other Animals.* Portland, OR: Willan Publishing, 2007.

Binns, Helen J., Carla Campbell, and Mary Jean Brown. "Interpreting and Managing Blood Lead Levels of Less Than 10 g/dl in Children and Reducing Childhood Exposure to Lead: Recommendations of the Centers for Disease Control and Prevention Advisory Committee on Childhood Lead Poisoning Prevention." *Pediatrics,* v.120/5 (2007).

Bullard, Robert D. *Unequal Protection: Environmental Justice and Communities of Color.* San Francisco: Sierra Club Books, 1994.

Burns, Ronald G. and Michael J. Lynch. *The Sourcebook on Environmental Crime.* New York: LFB Publishers, 2004.

Konisky, David M. "Inequities in Enforcement? Environmental Justice and Government Performance." *Journal of Policy Analysis and Management,* v.28/1 (2009).

Lynch, Michael J. and Paul B. Stretesky. "Green Criminology in the United States." In *Issues in Green Criminology,* Piers Bierne and Nigel South, eds. Portland, OR: Willan, 2007.

Lynch, Michael J. and Paul B. Stretesky. "Toxic Crimes: Examining Corporate Victimization of the General Public Employing Medical and Epidemiological Evidence." *Critical Criminology,* v.10/3 (2001).

Roberts, T. J. and M. Toffolon-Weiss. *Chronicles From the Environmental Justice Frontline.* New York: Cambridge University Press, 2001.

Stretesky, Paul B. and Michael J. Lynch. "The Relationship Between Lead and Crime." *Journal of Health and Social Behavior,* v.45/2 (2004).

Zilney, Lisa Anne, Danielle McGurrin, and Sammy Zahran. "Environmental Justice and the Role of Criminology: An Analytical Review of 33 Years of Environmental Justice Research." *Criminal Justice Research,* v.31/1 (2006).

Exposure, Indecent

As a form of street crime, indecent exposure in public can occur in a variety of ways. The most prominent type includes actions commonly referred to as exhibitionism. Exhibitionism as originally conceptualized referred to a male who exposes his genitals to an unsuspecting victim in a public setting. However, today this term is used to refer to female offenders as well. As a legal issue or crime, such events are typically referred to as "indecent exposure."

Other ways that indecent exposure occurs, other than the stereotypical flasher, includes both men and women exposing their genitals or breasts during party-like atmospheres at activities like Mardi Gras or sporting events, individuals taking and sending nude or partially nude pictures of themselves to others (*sexting*), or individuals making—usually for personal consumption or distribution to only select others—"sexy," "erotic," or "soft-core" types of pictures and videos.

Variables and Profiles

Data on how often and where this offense occurs are widely lacking, due to both an extremely low estimated reporting rate of victims and the lack of clarity in police records, which tend to include all forms of public nudity under indecent exposure, as well as including lewd acts such as public urination.

Definitions of indecent exposure for males means revealing and showing their penis. For females, this means uncovering and displaying their breasts and/or vagina. Due to this narrow definition, this does not leave much room for variation. The most common variables in how this offense occurs hinge on whether the offender speaks to the victim during the act, and whether the offender actively masturbates while exposing himself or herself to the victim. Victims are almost always females, often in groups. However, children may be victims as well.

When examining where indecent exposure incidents are likely to occur, the only pattern revealed in research is a lack of a pattern: this offense can occur at any time of day and in any public setting. However, among the most common places for such incidents are streets, sidewalks, and parking lots.

Numerous stereotypes are common about flashers or exposers in the mainstream news and entertainment media. The typical offender is often portrayed as an extremely reserved individual with few or no social relationships and skills. In addition, the classic image of this offender is generally male, middle-aged, and Caucasian.

Criminological research tends to indicate that common characteristics of indecent exposure offenders include: likely to be shy, struggle with expressing their own personality, experience sexual identity problems, have problems adapting to romantic relationships including marriage, have poor emotional communication skills, and hold negative attitudes toward females.

The main reason individuals expose their genitals to unsuspecting others is for purposes of sexual arousal. This behavior can occur at any given time, largely depending on whether the offender has the urge to commit the act (as opposed to a planned act). The very fact that offenders experience a compulsive urge, and that this urge can increase the frequency of offenses, has led psychologists to believe that the offense is a result of obsessive compulsive disorder (OCD). This suggests that there can be effective medical treatment provided to offenders.

It is also important to recognize that alcohol and drugs may play a factor through the effect of lowering people's inhibitions and making them more likely to expose themselves. Considering the environmental ingredients of an event like Mardi Gras, it is likely that offenders are more apt to flash their genitals or breasts in such a situation because of the general licentiousness of the gathering—and even more likely if they are consuming alcohol.

Victims and Consequences

There are a number of different psychological effects that victims of indecent exposure report. The most commonly noted include shock at the act; fear of not knowing what the offender may do next, such as physical or sexual assault; and some victims have even reported being amused at the act itself. This crime is also severely underreported. As a legal matter, many victims report that they believe that the police did not take this crime seriously and are often dismissive in regard to the crime and the nature of the crime itself. This behavior also has the possibility of increasing the perceived fear of the victims to where they develop an unreasonable fear that this type of attack will impact them again.

Statutes vary widely by state. When the nature of the offense veers into lewd conduct, some state laws even require the convicted person to register as a sex offender. In such states as California and Vermont, however, simple nudity is acceptable in a broad variety of public spaces—still, some localities even within these states enforce their own stricter codes. It is not uncommon for the term *obscene* to be part of a local indecent exposure statute, calling attention to the idea that it is the impact on the victim, and the extent and manner of the nudity, that are key in defining the offense, its severity, and the punishment due.

Richard Tewksbury
Andrew Denney
University of Louisville

See Also: Alcohol and Drug Use; Children as Victims; Fear of Crime; Peeping Toms; Sex Crimes; Urban Incivility; Women.

Further Readings

Bader, Shannon M., Katherine A. Schoeneman-Morris, Mario J. Scalora, and Thomas K. Casady. "Exhibitionism: Findings From a Midwestern Police Contact Sample." *International Journal of Offender Therapy and Comparative Criminology*, v.52/3 (2007).

Johnson, Kelly D. "Illicit Sexual Activity in Public Places." In *Problem-Oriented Guides for Police: Problem-Specific Guide Series.* No. 33. Madison, WI: Center for Problem-Oriented Policing, 2005.

McCreary, Charles P. "Personality Profiles of Persons Convicted of Indecent Exposure." *Journal of Clinical Psychology*, v.31/2 (1975).

Ptacek, James. *Restorative Justice and Violence Against Women.* New York: Oxford University Press, 2009.

Riordan, Sharon. "Indecent Exposure: The Impact Upon the Victim's Fear of Sexual Crime." *Journal of Forensic Psychiatry*, v.10/2 (1999).

Fear of Crime

In addition to the tangible costs of street crime, fear of crime has become a social problem in and of itself, affecting citizens' behavior and quality of life. This problem has inspired a growing body of research, in part because many more people fear crime than are actually victims of crime. The scholarship in this field has struggled with how to define and measure fear and to understand the complex factors associated with fear of victimization.

Effects

Fear of crime, besides having a negative psychological effect on individuals, can influence a person's behavior. Survey research has shown that the insecurity and tension caused by fear frequently causes citizens to limit their activities, thus reducing quality of life and even affecting the local economy. Fear of crime may cause individuals to become isolated by avoiding certain areas or even moving away from neighborhoods, and into gated communities. This isolation can cause a breakdown in social cohesion and can, in turn, cause an escalation in fear and anxiety.

One challenge in studying fear is that it is a difficult concept to measure. Researchers have cautioned that many of the survey measures used to study fear of crime do not directly measure fear—but rather measure a person's perception of the probability of being victimized. In addition, the term *crime* is very broad, and the emotion of fear may only be connected to violent crime, whereas the term *worry* would be a better description of an individual's response to the threat of property crimes. There are also concerns that certain individuals may not be honest about how fearful they really are. Young males are the most likely to be victims of violent crime, but are the least likely to report they are fearful. This may be partly because of the fact that this group is less willing overall to admit they are fearful.

Vulnerability

Despite these challenges in measuring fear, scholars have produced some remarkable and significant studies on this social problem. Perhaps one of the most interesting findings is that fear of crime is generally not correlated with actual risk of victimization. Frequently the least victimized (e.g., the more affluent, older, white, female) are more fearful than their counterparts (less affluent, young, minority, male). This paradox has caused many scholars to look to other factors, besides actual crime, in understanding the dynamics of fear of crime. Some researchers believe fear of crime is more widespread than actual levels of crime would predict because people are exposed to numerous stories of victimization (both real and fictitious).

In addition, populations that are more physically vulnerable to violent crime, such as women and the elderly, are more sensitive to these crime stories which frequently permeate the media. The media is generally believed to have the broadest influence on fear of crime. Studies have found that the number and type of crime reports and images in the media greatly influences the baseline of and fluctuations in our concern and fear of crime. Media reports on crime generally focus on random and sensational violent crime. This helps foster our fear of crime by distorting our perception of the actual risk of being a victim of these types of acts.

There is also a set of studies that link fear of crime to perceived disorder and incivilities within a community. Communities with excessive amounts of graffiti, public drinking and drug use, litter, broken windows, and vacant lots give residents a sense that the neighborhood is in decline. These environmental conditions heighten residents' anxieties and make them feel more vulnerable to crime and other social ills.

Related to this approach are studies theorizing that fear of crime is connected to changes in our society. The latter half of the 20th century saw the United States go through enormous disruptions in social and economic life; the public's fear of crime was in part a function of the uneasiness that these changes caused. Changes in the family, the economic system, and the ecology of cities created feelings of helplessness and vulnerability, such research suggests. Similarly, some scholars posit that the public's fear of crime has not necessarily been a reaction to increasing crime rates, but rather a response to the dramatic changes in ethnic diversity in many cities and suburbs.

Trends and Countermeasures

Despite the complexity in measuring and understanding fear of crime, there are a number of surveys that attempt to gauge the public's level of fear. Two prominent surveys in the United States, the General Social Survey (GSS) and the Gallup Poll, have used similarly worded questions to track the level of fear for several decades. Both show a peak in the early 1980s with almost half of respondents (48 percent in the Gallup survey, and 45 percent in the GSS) stating there was an area near them through which they were afraid to walk alone at night. By 2010 both surveys confirmed a substantial decline in fear, with 37 percent of those surveyed by Gallup and 33 percent in the GSS admitting to being fearful.

Although this decline in level of fear seems to coincide with declining crime rates, scholars and government officials are concerned that fear of crime remains high relative to actual crime risk. This has stimulated research by academics and practitioners that has examined ways of reducing fear of crime. This research has generally suggested that traditional policing strategies (e.g., solving crime, quick response time, high visibility) are not enough. Some recommend government programs that would reduce both crime and fear, such as environmental design (e.g., improved street lighting) and community policing (i.e., foot and bicycle patrols, police storefronts, ministations, and community policing officers). Evaluations of such programs have largely shown that such tactics not only assist in deterring crime and helping police solve crimes, but also help reassure residents and reduce fear.

Kenneth E. Fernandez
Elon University

See Also: Broken Windows Theory; Community Policing; Gated Communities; Graffiti; Crime, Popular Portrayals of; Urban Incivility; Victims, Seniors; Women.

Further Readings

Ferraro, Kenneth F. and Randy L. LaGrange. 1987. "The Measurement of Fear of Crime." *Sociological Inquiry,* v.57/1 (1987).

Lee, Murray J. *Inventing Fear of Crime: Criminology and the Politics of Anxiety.* Abingdon, UK: Willan, 2007.

Stafford, Mark C. and Omer R. Galle. "Victimization Rates, Exposure to Risk, and Fear of Crime." *Criminology,* v.22/5 (1984).

Taylor, Ralph B. and Margaret Hale. 1986. "Testing Alternative Models of Fear of Crime." *Journal of Criminal Law and Criminology,* v.77/1 (1986).

Warr, Mark. "Dangerous Situations: Social Context and Fear of Victimization." *Social Forces,* v.68/3 (1990).

Flash Mobs

Flash mobs are a relatively recent, largely urban phenomenon. They are characterized as a large group of persons congregating together in a particular public place, having been brought together through use of social networking technologies such as Facebook and MySpace, or through cell phones via network contact lists.

Benign or Destructive

Flash mobs can take two broad forms in terms of the aims or goals of the group. One type of flash mob has relatively benign intentions, more along the lines of an expressive or artistic statement. These have been around in one form or another since at least 2003, originally going by the name of "smart mobs." For example, a group of persons may be brought together at a train or bus station with the goal of breaking out in song or dance in unison at a specific time. Such smart mobs first captured public notoriety when the New York City-based writer and critic Bill Wasik used networked e-mail messaging to organize 10-minute-long mass performances in public spaces. A recent television advertisement for the AT&T cell phone network depicted such a benign or artistic flash mob scene. This type of flash mob seems to be concerned with revitalizing the community sense of spectacle: The spontaneous, artistic expression of the flash mob stands in stark contrast to a modern society which has become

A flash mob in July 2011 in Austin, Texas, breaks out into a water fight. A phenomenon that started out as innocent has recently been turned into a "flash rob," where groups of 50 to 100 people descend on a store or area and loot it.

too predictable, too bureaucratic, perhaps even too boring.

It is the second type of flash mob which will be more of a concern here. This is the type of flash mob that has criminal or disruptive intentions, insofar as its participants show up simultaneously in large numbers, thereby overwhelming the locally available police or security forces. There are many recent examples of these types of destructive flash mobs in the United States and Europe. Unfortunately, a number of these incidents have been racially-tinged. In August 2011, an angry mob of black youth descended on the Wisconsin State Fair attacking predominately white fairgoers. As large numbers of persons were leaving the fairgrounds for the evening, causing traffic to come to a standstill in the areas of the disturbance, some persons were being pulled from their cars and beaten. Police in Wisconsin considered filing federal hate crimes charges against those who were identified and arrested.

Also in August 2011, several dozen people "invaded" a 7-11 convenience store in Germantown, Maryland, apparently coordinating their action through social media networking. This flash mob stole a considerable quantity of merchandise and rapidly left the store. The unusual nature of this act and its rapidity—less than a minute from start to finish—caused the store clerk to delay hitting the silent alarm; once activated, it was too late as police did not arrive until well after the looters had dispersed. The National Retail Federation refers to such events not as flash mobs, but as "multiple offender crimes," while acknowledging that the perpetrators do utilize "flash mob tactics."

A Web site has recently been created that lists instances of violent flash mobs in America. As of 2012, the Web site (www.violentflashmobs.com) lists more than 60 flash mob incidents ranging from Philadelphia to Milwaukee, Detroit to St. Louis, and in western locations including Texas, California, and Oregon. Many of these involve bands of youth looting retail establishments or robbing innocent victims of their cell phones or other valuables.

Legislative and Police Response

In addition to the 2012 incidents, on June 26, 2011, in the eastern Cleveland suburb of Cleveland Heights, a flash mob of some 1,500 youth descended upon the Coventry Street Fair. Violence broke out in the streets, and a number of youths participating in the flash mob were arrested. Concerned citizens pressed the Cleveland Heights City Council to hold a series of forums on the problem of youth flash mobs. There seemed to be a consensus arising from the citizens gathered there that the kids involved in these flash mobs have absolutely nothing productive to do and are not being properly supervised by parents or legal guardians. Fearful of a repeat of the June 26 flash mob, the Cleveland Heights City Council instituted a 6:00 P.M. to 6:00 A.M. curfew for youth under the age of 18 in the Coventry Village area.

Attempting to be proactive, Cleveland city councilman Zack Reed proposed a new city ordinance which would prohibit the use of cell phones and Internet sites to plan flash mobs for purposes of inciting disturbances. Even so, Reed acknowledged that the proposed ordinance would be hard to enforce. Flash mobbing would be treated as a misdemeanor with a first offense bringing a $100 fine, $250 for a second offense, and $500 for a third. The proposed flash mob legislation did not get far, however, as Mayor Frank Jackson vetoed it in August 2011.

Another flash mob incident occurred in the Cleveland suburb of Strongsville in late August 2011. A white Cleveland rapper by the stage name of Machine Gun Kelly (real name Colson Baker) tweeted his fans encouraging them to dress up in costumes and meet up at the local Strongsville mall at 5:00 P.M. on a Saturday. By 6:00 P.M., a large group had assembled in the mall to greet Kelly, but local law enforcement had received a tip as well that a flash mob was forming. The rapper was arrested and dragged through the crowd as the officers instructed those assembled there to move away and disperse.

Here was a case of a more or less benign public gathering facilitated by the use of social networking technologies such as Facebook and Twitter. Yet the group still ran into legal barriers, primarily because of restrictions placed on the massing of people in an enclosed space. It was perhaps a flash mob in the making—and Kelly did not help matters by publicly defining it as such—illustrating the tensions and anxieties that city officials face whenever there is a possibility that safety forces may become overwhelmed by the sheer volume and rapid arrival of people at such events. Whether warranted or not, there was a desire on the part of these city officials to avoid a repetition of some of the more destructive flash mobs that had occurred previously around Cleveland and in more distant locations.

Conclusion

It is unclear what the future holds for flash mobs. It is very likely that with each new high-profile case of crimes or disturbances arising from such gatherings, local governments will seek to fashion appropriate responses, both on the legislative side as well as the law enforcement side.

James J. Chriss
Cleveland State University

See Also: Cleveland, Ohio; Loitering; Looting; Mobs and Riots; New York City; Shoplifting; Swarming; Theft and Larceny; Vandalism.

Further Readings

National Retail Federation. "Multiple Offender Crimes" August 2011. http://www.nrf.com/modules .php?name=News&op=viewlive&sp_id=1167 (Accessed May 2012).

Solecki, Susan and Karen Goldschmidt. "Adolescents Texting and Twittering: The Flash Mob Phenomenon." *Journal of Pediatric Nursing,* v.26/2 (2011).

Walker, Rebecca. *Eight Is Not Enough: A Historical, Cultural, and Philosophical Analysis of the Flash Mob.* Baton Rouge: Louisiana State University, Department of Communication Studies, 2011.

Gambling, Street

When most Americans think of gambling, they have visions of Las Vegas, Nevada, Atlantic City, New Jersey: high-end casinos with table games and slot machines. They think of entertainment and opportunity. However, across the country a very different type of gambling occurs daily—illegal street gambling. Street gambling happens in every major urban area and often opens the doors for other related street crimes. While much of the American media focuses on the potential perils of casino gambling (including gambling addiction, prostitution, and the decline of host cities), less attention is paid to the problems associated with rampant street gambling. To a large degree, small games have been all but decriminalized in most areas, given the more pressing issues facing urban police forces. Large-scale games connected with second-order criminal acts (such as robbery, assault, or other acts of violence), often operated by organized crime groups, will typically be shut down by police. This selection will focus on three common variants of street gambling: craps, Three-Card Monte, and the shell game, to name a few—are similar to legalized games that are well-known in modern society.

Street Craps

Street craps is an illegal form of the casino craps game based on Hazard. It originated from the Crusades, based on the dice game known as Hazard. The fundamental differences between the two versions of the game are the lack of a "banker" and craps table in street craps. The main bets that occur in street craps—also referred to as ghetto craps or shooting dice—are between the shooter (the individual who is throwing the dice) and the bettors (those wagering money on the outcome of the throw).

There are two main types of betting that occur within a game of street craps: pass and don't pass. After the shooter and the bettors have made their appropriate bets, the shooter throws the two die. If the shooter throws either a seven or an 11, the pass bet wins. If, however, the shooter throws a two, three, or 12, then the don't pass bets win. If any other number is thrown, it is referred to as the point. From that throw on, the shooter attempts to throw a seven to end the game. If the shooter succeeds in throwing a seven before throwing the point again, then the pass bet wins. If, however, the shooter throws the point before being able to throw a seven, then the don't pass bets win.

Street craps has become popular as a form of illegal gambling because of its simplicity and the lack of need of an elaborate setup. All that is required to successfully host a game are two die and a wall to throw the dice against. The use of a barrier (such as a wall) to bounce the dice off is carried over from the casino game. In casino craps, shooters are expected to roll the dice off of the opposite table wall to assure they are not attempting to manipulate how the dice fall. If rolls do not touch the opposite table wall, dealers are permitted to declare a no roll and force the shooter to throw again.

Likewise, within the context of a casino, other actions by shooters are policed by security. For example, shooters are typically not permitted to hold the dice in both hands as it makes it easier for them to utilize sleight of hand techniques to switch the dice. In fact, in most casinos, to switch the hand you use to shoot, you must place the dice on the table and then pick them back up with the other hand. Clearly, in a street craps game this level of policing only occurs as players monitor each other. Without an authoritative policing mechanism in place, accusations of cheating can lead to violence. Given the lack of formality in street craps games, it is easy for players to avoid the actual police as well. With dice and a wall serving as the only supplies, all players need to do in order to avoid arrest is pick up the dice when they see a police presence.

Three-Card Monte

In contrast to craps, Three-Card Monte is a confidence trick that attempts to fool the marks (intended victims) into thinking that they are gambling, when in fact they are being played for their money. Confidence tricks rely on a dealer who can help exploit the characteristics of the human psyche—particularly greed, vanity, irresponsibility, and naiveté. The setup for Three-Card Monte is simple. The dealer chooses three cards (typically two jacks and one queen) and then makes it known which one of the cards is the money card (almost always the queen). All three cards are then flipped over so they lie face down. The dealer rearranges the cards and through sleight of hand attempts to hide the location of the money card from the mark. At this point, the mark is asked to place a bet on which one of the cards he or she believes is the money card.

While this form of game is illegal already, at this point the game becomes even more questionable. Once a bet has been made, conspirators join with the dealer to assure there are no winners. These conspirators (referred to as shills) pose as passersby but work to either confuse the mark or to outbet the mark in order to assure that money is not lost by the dealer and his cronies. In this way, it takes at least two people to successfully pull off a Three-Card Monte scam.

In its full form, Three-Card Monte is an example of a classic "short con" in which a shill pretends to conspire with the mark, or victim, to cheat the dealer, when in fact he or she is conspiring with the dealer to cheat the mark.

Three-Card Monte has a long history as a form of illegal gambling. It has been played internationally since before the 15th century. If we consider just the alternative names, we can see the reach this confidence game has. Besides Three-Card Monte, it is known as Three-card Marney, the Three-card Trick, Three-way, Three-card Shuffle, Manage-a-card, Triplets, Follow the Lady, *les Trois Perdants, le Bonnetau,* Find the Lady, and Follow the Bee. While the game has quite a history, it is—like street craps—difficult for police to monitor as it relies on only three cards to be played. Perhaps most surprisingly, despite its long history in numerous cultures, dealers and shrills are still able to successfully find marks willing to lose their money in the scam.

Beyond the shrill, dealers have developed other ways to guarantee they always end up on top. They are able to use manipulated cards (arched and folded corners) and expansive sleight of hand tricks (including switching cards when needed or pretending to drop the cards when aware of a likely loss). While the scam itself is illegal in the United States, Canada has taken extra steps to assure citizen protection from Three-Card Monte by criminalizing aspects of how it is played. According to the Criminal Code of Canada, it is illegal to receive bets, to induce a person to hazard any money or property, to carry on play in a public place, to employ someone to carry on play in a public place, or to allow a game to take place in a private place in relation to Three-Card Monte. Anyone found doing so can be indicted and faces a possible two-year prison term.

The Shell Game

The shell game is a variant of Three-Card Monte still popular in the United States, and with roots in ancient Greece. In 1670, we saw reference to Thimblerig—a version of the game played with three thimbles. Eventually walnut shells were used; today we see even bottle caps being utilized as tools. The game grew in popularity in the United States in the 19th century, when it was regularly found being played in or around traveling fairs. At that time, operators were concerned enough about facing criminal prosecution that they refused to stay in one place for too long and instead jumped from city to city seeking individuals they could scam for money. Jefferson Randolph Smith—better known as Soapy—was an infamous shell game organizer throughout the United States during the era. Today we still see the game being played illegally for money in major cities around the world. Typically, it centers on areas with high tourist populations, in hope of finding unguarded and unsuspecting victims to play for marks.

The shell game requires three objects (typically shells, thimbles, bottle caps, or plastic cups) and any object that can be hidden beneath one. The optimal selection for this object has been a small, soft ball sized similarly to a pea. While the shell game can theoretically be played on any flat surface, street games normally happen on the top of a cardboard box or on a makeshift mat. The operator places the ball under a shell and then quickly shuffles them all around. At the end of shuffling, he asks for a bet on where the ball is. Everything else operates the same as in Three-Card Monte.

Conclusion

While seemingly as dangerous to society as casino gambling, street gambling is less understood and noticed by the American public. The games are not large enough to merit concentrated police efforts and would be extremely difficult to track even if police wanted to. Ironically, the types of games we see on the streets—craps, Three-Card Monte,

and the shell game, to name a few—have accepted places in modern society. There are legal (casino) forms of both craps and Three-Card Monte poker. For its part, the shell game is a childhood favorite for many children, and even finds its way onto the scoreboards as participatory activities at major sports stadiums. Yet such activities only go further to show how, in part through such through mass desensitization, street gambling is not typically regarded as a serious concern of the average American citizen—failing to register as a main concern in Gallup public opinion polling.

William J. Miller
Southeast Missouri State University

See Also: Door-to-Door Scam Artists; Pickpocketing; Pool Halls; Victims, Tourist.

Further Readings

Favero, Don. *Craps Across America—A Boomers Guide to the Gaming Life.* Montgomery, AL: E-Book Time, 2006.

Haller, Mark. "The Changing Structure of American Gambling in the Twentieth Century." *Journal of Social Issues,* v.35/3 (1979).

Newman, Paul B. *Daily Life In the Middle Ages.* Jefferson, NC: McFarland & Company, 2001.

Reith, Gerda. *The Age of Chance: Gambling In Western Culture.* London: Routledge, 2002.

Sauerwine, Stan. *Soapy Smith—Skagway's Scourge of the Klondike.* Victoria, BC: Heritage House Publishing, 2005.

Gangs (Street)

Ancient historians as far back as the Late Roman Empire reported unruly, street-based social groups harassing shop owners and disrupting social life in Rome's wealthier suburbs. Today, these groups are called street gangs. Over the past 30 to 40 years, American sociological and criminological research amassed a vast scholarly literature about gangs. This entry draws attention to a cross section of noteworthy topics like gang definitions, gang crime and violence, and gang prevention and intervention. Attention is also paid to how gang membership adversely affects gang members' mental health. Gang members are more frequently exposed to violent incidents like killings and beatings than nongang members. Recent research finds exposure to violence has serious effects on mental health.

Defining Street Gangs

In April 2008 the U.S. attorney general's *Report to Congress on the Growth of Violent Street Gangs in Suburban Areas* reported nationwide findings of a law enforcement agency survey on gangs. The survey finds more than 20,000 gangs and one million gang members in the United States. Those statistics are indeed terrifying; however, the national law enforcement survey did not provide police personnel with a common definition for a gang but rather permitted agencies leeway to define gangs and gang crime.

In the absence of a common definition, law enforcement agencies did not differentiate violent criminal groups (e.g., Latin American drug cartels) from local, neighborhood youth groups that adopted a gang name and insignia for gangs well known in the media (e.g., Latin Kings, Vice Lords), or from outlaw motorcycle gangs (e.g., Hells Angels), or from notorious prison gangs (e.g. Mexican Mafia).

In its effort to be inclusive, the 2008 *Report to Congress* embraces a wide range of social groups as diverse as neighborhood youth gangs who sell illegal drugs and violate curfew regulations to enduring criminal organizations under the same rubric of gangs. Inclusion enables a comprehensive tally of crime-oriented groups valuable to national political leadership. However, gang researchers and community leaders require detailed criteria in order to distinguish clearly youth groups who are a nuisance to a neighborhood from extremely dangerous criminal organizations that pose a serious threat to public order.

The difficulty that various stakeholders in gang research, law enforcement, and gang interventions have in reaching a consensus about gangs reflects their varied motives and interests. Community (e.g., law enforcement, researchers, schools, and the criminal justice system) stakeholders' perspectives depend upon their organizational mission. Schools' educational mission, law enforcement's public-order mission, a criminal justice system's mission to adjudicate criminal offenses, and academic researchers' mission of social scientific inquiry shape their varying perspectives on gangs. Police activities thwart and react to criminal behavior; educators worry about obstacles to learning; jails and prisons impede security threats; and researchers probe cultural, social, economic, and political forces underlying antisocial groups, and across these perspectives we find common traits. An integration of these creates an effective denotative gang definition.

A street gang (versus an outlaw motorcycle gang or prison gang) in its simplest form refers to a social group composed of males or females or both (age 12 to 24), whose members pursue criminal activity as diverse as small sales of illegal drugs and burglary to robbery and armed assault, and share symbols of association (e.g., a name and insignia) over a significant time period. "Significant time period" distinguishes small groups of youth who might call themselves by a gang name for a weekend or a few weeks, and while doing so occasionally shoplift, from youth groups who have been disruptive in a particular neighborhood over years; exhibit some degree of organization; intend to commit criminal offenses; recognize their illegality of behavior; and deliberately disregard formal and informal rules of social regulation.

Crime Activities and Violence

Gangs are controversial, but not illegal. An assessment of the threat that gangs, gang members, and gang crime pose to community safety should not immediately assume that all gang members commit or intend to commit serious, violent or nonviolent criminal offenses. Gangs do not cause members to become violent, although adolescents exhibiting a propensity toward violent behavior gather together in gangs. Causes and conditions of criminal conduct reach well beyond the context of gangs and gang membership. Research shows that adult men and women who say they were adolescent gang members but eventually stop hanging out with crime-oriented gang members often retain their gang member self-identity.

Law enforcement personnel and gang researchers have struggled to identify specific criteria that distinguish gang and nongang crime. A criminal offense committed by a gang member has been commonly labeled as a gang crime, which then poses the conundrum of a gang definition. In the absence of a specific definition of a gang crime, one finds instead examples of crime committed by gang members, for example: lethal and nonlethal fights over gambling debts; fights or shootings that result from an argument over girlfriends; disputes over territory where marijuana and other drugs are sold; street robbery; assault with and without deadly weapons; rape; arson; and domestic violence. To that list can be added statutory offenses applicable only to minors, such as curfew violations.

Some clarity has emerged on types of gang crime. Gang crime falls into two categories known as gang-related and gang-motivated crime. Gang-related crime has a personal motivate (e.g., domestic violence). Gang-motivated offenses support the criminal intent of a gang (e.g., planned and implemented distribution of illegal drugs to deliberately further gang activity). This distinction (personal versus gang group) also distinguishes active, former, and inactive gang members. If aging gang members do not commit gang-motived crime but do commit gang-related crime, one might reasonably consider those gang members as inactive or former gang members.

Violent gangs and gang members have long been fodder of media depictions. Despite stereotypic media characterizations, all gang members are not violent. However, gang groups include individuals with varying propensities toward the perpetration of violent acts. If a street gang has 20 members among them, there may be five who are willing to perpetrate violence. Generally speaking, adolescent street gangs pose less of a collective threat than violent youth who join gangs.

Controversy surrounds gang membership initiation. Research finds that a majority of street gangs do not force prospects, or potential members, to commit heinous acts. Recent research found that adolescent gang girls who reported a sexual initiation (i.e., one female engaging in sexual acts with more than one male) did so under a threat of violence. In other words, the sexual initiation was not consensual; these women in fact were raped. Male initiates reported "beat-downs" when a group of gang members punched and kicked a potential member over a specific time period. Research shows that beat-downs are committed by violent bullies preying on weaker youth; gang members report that initiates who are known as good street

fighters, threatening the physical safety of gang members, are not beaten down.

Once accepted by a gang, new members stay only a short time. Research shows that on average, gang membership occurs at 14 years of age, and that the average amount of time spent as a gang member amounts to less than 24 months. The popularized idea that gang membership lasts a lifetime, that gangs are "blood in, blood out," are fanciful, image-bolstered exaggerations reported to gang researchers decades ago by imprisoned gang members.

Mental Health

There are relatively few studies on chronic, or persistent, gang members' mental health. Recent research shows that adolescent gang members more so than nongang adolescent peers suffer from high levels of anxiety and depression; affective (emotional) disorders; personality disorders; and addiction. These mental health issues are clustered in neighborhoods where children and adolescents are exposed at home, school, and neighborhoods to violent acts. Within those areas children and adolescents are victims of the consequences of witnessing violence; unsurprisingly in these same neighborhoods street gangs have emerged and persisted over generations.

Witnessing violence repeatedly can over time create debilitating consequents on the sociopsychological development of children and adolescents similar to those of direct physical victimization. Gangs expose members to violence, and that exposure has traumatic effects. As children and adolescents mature and expand their participation in community social life, opportunities to witness violence increase and so do the behavioral and psychological consequences of violence exposure (e.g., disruptive behavior at school; chronic discord between children and parents; abuse of alcohol and illegal drugs; and mental illness).

Gang membership and hanging around street gangs do not necessarily increase victimization; however, the likelihood of witnessing degrees of violence from slaps to kicks to punches to stabbing to shooting by gang youth increases. Street gang research reports that witnessing sexual victimization increases as well, and that adolescent male gang members participate in the sexual victimization of children and adolescent females.

Witnessing violence, the emergence and perpetuation of street gangs, and adolescent mental health trauma are bound inextricably in an injurious, difficult-to-break cycle of mutual reinforcement. In a multicity study, psychologists and social workers compared 485 dangerously violent youth—those who reported attacking someone with a knife or gun within the past year—to a group of adolescents of similar size and composition who did not report dangerously violent behavior. Dangerously violent youth reported witnessing significantly more incidents of victimization.

The damage trauma causes can be emotionally severe enough that it contributes to sexually deviant behavior and substance abuse. The behaviors may have a momentary palliative effect on anxiety, stress and depression, engender a fleeting sense of emotional relief, or provide a temporary sense of mutual support and physical protection. However, these transient benefits of drugs and sex often backfire, exposing adolescents to added violence and sexual victimization.

Violence exposure also predicts envelopment within the criminal justice system. Research shows that a high rate of youth enmeshed in the juvenile justice system suffer effects of post-traumatic stress disorder and similar trauma-related symptoms. The precise pathways between violence exposure and perpetration of violence are unclear; however, children and adolescents who are gang members and who hang around gangs witness more violence than nongang youngsters. As a result of repeatedly witnessing violent acts, gang members are poised to incur trauma and suffer its lifelong consequences.

Seeking Solutions

Urban centers and suburban and rural communities have been challenged to solve problems that some gang members cause. Communities' responses to gang crime depend on stakeholders' perceptions of gangs and gang members. In a community-wide response to problematic gang groups, a gang definition becomes more than an academic exercise; a definition lays the groundwork by identifying specific target groups for critical first steps toward curbing gang violence and preventing youth from entanglement in an intractable social situation. Law enforcement agencies use agency-specific criteria to identify gangs. Those agency definitions are guidelines for the assessment of the prevalence of gangs and gang members. However, as definition criteria change over time the prevalence of gangs, gang

members, and gang crime increases or decreases. Gang definitions do more than act as an analytic framework for prevalence assessments; definitions also identify strategies and tactics to guide gang prevention and intervention initiatives.

Citizens in gang neighborhoods are frightened. Challenged with gang violence, worried communities' first response often prescribes increasing the number of gang member arrests. Little doubt shrouds community citizens' desire to rely on police arrests and prosecutions. In the absence of an effective, long-term gang prevention and intervention initiative, community citizens feel physically and emotionally vulnerable to street-corner drug sellers, gunfire, and gang fights in public parks and schools.

When citizens fear for lives in their own homes and are afraid to stroll on neighborhood streets, and when school children hurry home before dark, fearful of corner drug dealers, citizens expect quick action by local, state, and federal law enforcement. However, tens of thousands of gang member arrests over decades has not rid urban areas of gangs. Today a growing consensus among elected public officials and policy makers recognizes that arrest and prosecution, while necessary, cannot address the fundamental causes and conditions leading to the emergence and perpetuation of neighborhood gangs nor stem the flow of youth attracted to street-corner gangs.

Reaching a community-wide consensus on appropriate tactics to effectively alleviate gang crime and slow gang membership is difficult. A community must first endorse policing strategies most suitable and acceptable among constituent subgroups. Then, as a second step, a community must balance police suppression (i.e., arrests) with an integrated package of educational, vocational, and mental health programs. Next, community agencies require a shared methodology to assess gang members' willingness to help themselves, as well as their specific educational deficits and mental health disorders. Finally, a community must ensure funds are readily available at adequate levels to sustain over many years police suppression programs and healing programs.

Policy makers—sensitive to political climate; community citizens—sensitive to public safety; community social service agencies—sensitive to adolescent victimization and its behavior and psychological effects; law enforcement—sensitive to demands to keep the public safe; and neighborhood parents and relatives of gang members—sensitive to the fate of their children: Each of these groups have their own perspectives on response to gangs and gang members. Over years of trial and error, community leaders, police personnel, and gang interventionists have seen firsthand that generic, single-purpose, antigang tactics are inadequate, and that strategies and tactics must offer complementary responses (e.g., suppression and education and mental health treatment).

Conclusion

Intangible causes and conditions embedded in an amalgamation of community, neighborhood, school, and family problems underlie contemporary gang problems. Media coverage of street gangs and autobiographies of imprisoned gang members offer stereotypic and exaggerated depictions, casting gang members as drug-addicted, violent youth whose lives spiraled out of control and who live day to day beyond the reach of community resources. A majority of children and adolescents who are gang members or hang around street gangs are

relatively harmless, engaging in a short-term flight of risk-taking behavior typical of youngsters. There are, however, a small percentage of adolescents and young adults whose early lives were a nightmarish blend of physical, sexual, and emotional victimization. Neighborhood social interaction leads many of them to street corners where they adopt the outward appearance of ruthless rogues. To be sure, some are not only dangerous to others but also to themselves; however, those less traumatized would benefit from the resources available to children and adolescents in American communities.

Mark S. Fleisher
Julia Noveske
Case Western Reserve University

See Also: Alcohol and Drug Use; Arrest; Asian Gangs; Bloods; Code of the Street; Crips; Juvenile Curfews; La Eme (Mexican Mafia); Latino Gangs; Motorcycle Clubs; Organized Crime and Violence.

Further Readings
Buka, Stephen L., Theresa L. Stichick, Isolde Birdthistle, and Felton J. Earls. "Youth Exposure to Violence: Prevalence, Risks, and Consequences." *American Journal of Orthopsychiatry,* v.71/3 (2001).
Decker, Scott H. and Barrick Van Winkle. *Life in the Gang: Family, Friends and Violence.* New York: Cambridge University Press, 1996.
Flannery, Daniel J., Mark I. Singer, and Kelly Wester. "Violence Exposure, Psychological Trauma, and Suicide Risk in a Community Sample of Dangerously Violent Adolescents." *Journal of the American Academy of Child and Adolescent Psychiatry,* v.40/4 (2001).
Fleisher, Mark S. "Coping With Macro-Structural Adversity: Chronic Poverty, Female Youth Gangs, and Cultural Resilience in a U.S. African American Urban Community." *Journal of Contingencies & Crisis Management,* v.17/4 (2009).
Hagedorn, John M. *People and Folks: Gangs, Crime and the Underclass in a Rustbelt City.* Chicago: Lakeview Press, 1988.
Howell, James C. "Menacing or Mimicking? Realities of Youth Gangs." *Juvenile and Family Court Journal,* v.58/2 (2007).
Lynch, Michael. "Consequences of Children's Exposure to Community Violence." *Clinical Child and Family Psychology Review,* v.6/4 (2003).

Dealing drugs in San Francisco's Mission District. Gang members are involved in all areas of street-crime activities like extortion, drug trafficking, and theft.

Stein, Bradley D., et al. "Prevalence of Child and Adolescent Exposure to Community Violence." *Clinical Child and Family Psychology Review*, v.6/4 (2003).

U.S. Department of Justice. "Attorney General's Report to Congress on the Growth of Violent Street Gangs in Suburban Areas." Washington, DC: U.S. Department of Justice, 2008.

Gated Communities

A gated community is a neighborhood surrounded by high walls or natural barriers. Such enclaves usually have a gate, secured either by guards or electronic security systems that may require the entry of access codes or radio frequency identification (RFID) passes. The idea is to give homeowners easy access to their properties while impeding the flow of outsiders into the development.

Concepts and Rationales

Common security strategies include the use of burglar alarms, closed-circuit surveillance cameras, and/or advanced computer controlled security systems with lasers. At many developments, visitors may only enter after a guard checks with a homeowner. Homes are usually moderate- to high-priced to exclude lower-class people (seen as more associated with street crime), and often contain upscale recreational facilities. Homeowners or residential associations place restrictive covenants on properties to specify what owners can and cannot do with them. While residents of these communities feel safer, critics fear their popularity leads to greater social isolation and exclusion.

Sociologists Edward J. Blakely and Mary Gail Snyder identified three broad categories of gated communities. Lifestyle Communities appeal to targeted groups of people, such as senior citizens, through the emphasis on leisure activities and other amenities. Many contain golf courses, tennis clubs, parks, and swimming pools. Prestige Communities are built for upper-class residents, and the gates are a strategy for emphasizing the elite quality of the development. Security Zone Communities use fences as a deliberate strategy to promote security. Instead of new housing, some of this latter type originated

as regular city streets that became barricaded later. Nearly 70 percent of residents of all gated communities indicated that security was a major consideration when deciding to move into one.

The fear of crime extends beyond home invasions or burglaries. Residents often report being concerned about migrations of immigrants or people of a lower socioeconomic status, such that the presence of gates and guards gives added security about their safety. While guards often report they are relatively powerless to intervene in disputes within the walls, and residents acknowledge criminals might still walk into the community or jump a fence, the security features provide a sense of added safety. Still, several residents reported setting their burglar alarms before leaving their homes. Some gated communities are secretive about their locations, with streets not appearing on maps and the gates situated on quiet side streets.

Who Lives Where

The 2000 Census found 5.9 percent of American households lived in an area surrounded by walls, and 3.4 percent had access to their household secured by some means. Renters were 2.5 times more likely than homeowners to live in such communities, as public housing developments are often more highly secured. Caucasian residents were more likely to be homeowners and more wealthy than African Americans.

Within the United States, these structures are more likely to be found in southern cities such as Los Angeles, California; Phoenix, Arizona; Houston and Dallas, Texas; and Miami, Florida—or in the suburbs outside of major northern cities such as New York City and Chicago. They are also located in other countries aside from the United States, especially in those with unequal distributions of wealth. Some scholars note they represent a reversal of a trend toward greater inclusiveness, diversity, and racial integration in housing.

Historical Developments

Gated communities have been called the contemporary versions of walled European cities in medieval times. For example, the Romans erected walls around their settlements in Britain as early as 300 B.C.E. to protect rulers from uprisings from their citizens. Later British kings built castles for similar purposes. America's elite built gated residences, such as

Tuxedo Park in New York City, to protect themselves from working-class people. However, the earliest of the modern gated communities is Leisure Wood in Florida. It was marketed toward retirees.

The increase during the late 20th and early 21st centuries of gated communities in the United States can be attributed to three complementary forces: developers seeking to increase property densities; local governments looking to attract wealthier residents; and homeowners looking for exclusive residences separated from urban blight. Residential associations often assume financial responsibility for services often provided by local governments, such as security. As governments cut some services in response to increasing budgetary problems, gated communities give affluent people a choice to opt out of communities without physically departing from them. Consequently, some scholars view them as being economically rational, as opposed to socially exclusionary.

William E. Raffel
Buffalo State College

See Also: Closed-Circuit Television; Fear of Crime; Gentrification; Immigrant Neighborhoods; Neighborhood Watch; Street Crime, Popular Portrayals of.

Further Readings

Blakely, Edward J. and Mary Gail Snyder. *Fortress America: Gated Communities in the United States.* Washington, DC: Brookings Institution, 1997.

Low, Setha. *Behind the Gates: Life, Security, and the Pursuit of Happiness in Fortress America.* New York: Routeledge, 2003.

Sanchez, Thomas W. and Robert E. Lang. *Security versus Status: The Two Worlds of Gated Communities.* Metropolitan Institute at Virginia Tech. 2002. http://www.scribd.com/doc/8414774/Security-Versus-Status-The-Two-Worlds-of-Gated-Communities (Accessed June 2011).

Genovese, Kitty

On March 13, 1964, Catherine "Kitty" Genovese, a young single woman, was murdered just outside her apartment in the Kew Gardens district of Queens, New York, by a stranger named Winston Moseley, a machine operator who suffered from mental illness. At approximately 3:00 A.M., Kitty had driven home in her red Fiat from her work as manager at a tavern (Eve's Eleventh Hour) and parked her car in a lot next door to her two-story apartment building on Austin Street. The apartment entrance was in the rear.

A few doors away from the apartment, under a streetlight in front of a bookstore, Moseley grabbed her, attacking her with a knife. Genovese screamed for help. Frightened by some shouts from an apartment building across the street, Moseley ran to his car and moved it to a position where its license plate was not so visible.

Meanwhile, Genovese managed to stagger around the corner to the back of a building, evidently seeking the entrance to her apartment, and into its vestibule. Moseley found her and continued to stab her inside the vestibule hallway. He also sexually assaulted her. Approximately 35 minutes after the first attack began, Moseley took $49 from Genovese's pocketbook and drove away as she bled to death. (Moseley was later convicted of Genovese's murder and sentenced to life in prison.)

Front Page Tragedy

The tragedy became a sensation as a result of a front page article in the *New York Times* on March 27, 1964. The headline read: "37 Who Saw Murder Didn't Call the Police. Apathy at Stabbing of Queens Woman Shocks Inspector." The article stated that 37 (originally reported as 38) people had witnessed the attack but none took action to impede it, to offer assistance to the victim, or to contact the police.

There was a nine-story apartment building opposite the bookstore where Genovese was first attacked. During the attack, lights went on in the building. One occupant yelled out his window, "Let that girl alone." Another, a teenager, raised his window and shouted out, "Shut the f— up!" During the attack, Genovese exclaimed, "Oh my God, he stabbed me! Please help me! Please help me!"

Psychology of the Bystander

Though the story was initially presented for its shocking exceptionality, it soon came to be viewed as symbolic of urban apathy, anonymity, and paralysis in the face of danger. In the urban context in which people live insular lives, sound-proofed and sequestered from the concerns of others, helping behaviors can be attenuated or—as in Kitty Genovese's case—nonexistent. From this perspective, the city is a dangerous place that should be feared. In addition to the strangers who lurk there, one should also feel anxiety, fear, and even panic over the insouciant groups who live there.

In their noncommunication and moral indifference, the neighbors are un-neighborly in the extreme. As "unresponsive bystanders" who, as a group, are indifferent to human suffering, even in emergencies, the culture of urban dwellers may be considered pathological. Concomitantly this view is nostalgic for an idyllic, rural existence where helping behaviors are presumed to be natural and endemic.

In social psychology the notoriety of the Kitty Genovese murder contributed to development of the construct known as "bystander effect" (people are more apt to help when alone than when with other bystanders), including the "diffusion of responsibility" (reduction in sense of personal responsibility) that people experience when others are present. The predominance of research in these areas may have contributed to relative neglect in studying potentially more favorable aspects of group behavior, for example, whether cohesive groups actually facilitate helping in emergency situations.

Confusion Over Witnesses

A number of inaccuracies or omissions in early accounts of the Kitty Genovese story have come to light. The early stories implied that she was heterosexual, though she was a lesbian and lived with her girlfriend, Mary Ann Zielonko. The original reports were of three attacks, though there were actually two. There was no list of who the 37 or 38 witnesses were, and it is likely that there were far fewer.

Some witnesses later asserted that they called the police after the first attack; some others who did not said they mistook the event for a quarrel spilling out of the bar at the corner of Austin Street. There was no "911" system at the time, and the police did not necessarily welcome calls in the early-morning hours. There was only one known witness to the second attack (the one in the vestibule). Initially he closed his door, not wishing to be involved, but soon thereafter he phoned Genovese's next-door neighbor (Sophie Farrar), who immediately called the police and went to Genovese, cradling her until

police arrived. Genovese was still alive when the police and medics came on the scene.

Frank Butler
Saint Joseph's University

See Also: Bystander Apathy; Mental Illness; Street Crime, Popular Portrayals of; Urban Incivility.

Further Readings

Darley, John M. and Bibb Latané. "Bystander Intervention in Emergencies: Diffusion of Responsibility." *Journal of Personality and Social Psychology*, v.8/4 (1968).

Fischer, Peter, et al. "The Bystander-Effect: A Meta-Analytic Review on Bystander Intervention in Dangerous and Non-Dangerous Emergencies." *Psychological Bulletin*, v.137/4 (2011).

Manning, Rachel, et al. "The Kitty Genovese Murder and the Social Psychology of Helping: The Parable of the 38 Witnesses." *American Psychologist*, v.62/6 (2007).

Gentrification

Gentrification, or the funneling of middle- and upper-class money, power, prestige, and persons into a working-class or poverty-stricken area of a city is a process thought to lead to the displacement of some or all of the original inhabitants of the area. Gentrification can take place within several years or over a more extended period of time, even decades. As such, its relationship with urban street crime is variable. It is generally agreed that an area undergoing gentrification will in its early stages experience a short-term increase in crime followed by long-term declines for both violent and property crimes.

Three Viewpoints

Crime rates are thought to rise during the beginning stages of gentrification and decline later on in the process for several reasons. It is important to note that this relationship is much stronger for property crime than it is for violent crime. First, crime rates may rise as a result of increased opportunity; this is especially relevant to property crime. Second, drawing from social disorganization theory, the initial increase in crime is thought to be due to the series

Gentrification refers to the changes that result when wealthier people acquire or rent property in low-income and working-class communities. In a community undergoing gentrification, the average income increases and average family size decreases. The last few years have seen dramatic gentrification of downtown Los Angeles, as shown in this construction site.

of rapid changes that the neighborhood is experiencing, which lead to temporary social instability and population heterogeneity (populations made up of many types of subpopulations). A third explanation suggests that the changes in crime rates reflect the process of displacing crime-prone individuals from the area over time. The relationship between gentrification or neighborhood change and street crime is more complex than the above explanations suggest. To begin, methodological issues abound. Scholars have had difficulty agreeing on what constitutes a neighborhood, making cross-study comparisons difficult. Once scholars have decided on a unit of measurement they traditionally focus on the intervening role played by population turnover, the velocity of change, and to a lesser extent the role of the economy and criminal justice interventions, including situational crime prevention and efforts at defensible space.

Displacement and Informal Control

There are two relevant ways to consider the effects of population change: displacement and informal social control. With displacement, the central question becomes if decreases in neighborhood crime rates result from neighborhood-level variables, or if they occur because crime-prone individuals are displaced through the process of the arrival of a more gentrified population. Despite how relevant the role of gentrified displacement on crime rates may be, there is little scholarly work on the subject. One criminologist, Richard Curtis, does examine this relationship in several neighborhoods in Brooklyn. His findings suggest that crime-prone individuals involved in the drug trade have merely moved to adjacent neighborhoods as a result of gentrification. He also found that policing interventions tend to rise in conjunction with an area's gentrification.

When considering the impact of population change on informal social control, we must ask a different question: Does the rapid inflow of new residents into an area undermine the social cohesion of the neighborhood, eroding informal social control? Social disorganization theory suggests that it will. Neighborhood change, even when—as in the case of gentrification—it leads to socioeconomic improvements in the area, tends to have destabilizing effects on the community, which often result in increases in crime, at least during the initial stages. This is a result in large part of original area residents being displaced by upper- and middle-class residents with few ties to the area or one another, which leads to a breakdown of community. That being said, the relationship between gentrification and crime is further complicated by a number of additional factors.

Gentrification as a process can vary greatly in terms of the velocity of change. It is thought that neighborhoods going through more rapid transformation, most often measured in terms of the rise in property value over time, have more difficulty adjusting or metabolizing change and will therefore experience higher levels of social disorganization and higher crime rates. On the other hand, the neighborhood going through a slower process of gentrification, perhaps as a result of a downturn in the economy, will experience lower rates of crime and higher levels of social cohesion resulting from lower levels of social disorganization. and less displacement of original area residents. The velocity of neighborhood change, whether it happens rather quickly like New York City's Lower East Side or more slowly like Los Angeles' Historic Core, is an important variable, yet it is a grossly under-examined aspect of gentrification and crime.

Law Enforcement Effects

Another rarely examined aspect of neighborhood change is the role played by criminal justice interventions on crime. The very process of gentrification requires the transformation of a previously low-income or working-class high-density area with presumably middle to high crime rates. As a result, most gentrification efforts, once established, are accompanied by some kind of supportive change in criminal justice strategy, such as the implementation and enforcement of injunctions and/or a variation in policing technique. These shifts in strategy tend to exhibit a lag time with gentrification and will usually start toward the middle to end of the process. An injunction is a court order banning certain individuals or activities from being present or taking place within a specified geographic area. Injunctions are becoming increasingly popular as a tool to control particular undesirable populations such as gangs and drug dealers. Injunctions are a controversial topic for many reasons that cannot be covered here, yet they are one of the many tools law enforcement may find especially useful in policing a gentrified area. Policing strategies within gentrification zones tend to reflect the growing trend toward a community policing model, in which the construction of a healthy police-citizen relationship is of utmost importance.

In addition, the process of gentrification brings in residents that have more social, political, and economic capital than previous residents. As a result or in response, policing strategy is likely to change in the area in order to better meet the needs of the new population and the capacities of the police department. This change in policing strategy may in fact contribute to the eventual decline of street crime in gentrified areas over the long term.

Another aspect of policing that has not been fully examined is the role that policing interventions in neighborhoods adjacent to gentrifying areas have on increasing crime through displacement. A clear example comes from Los Angeles and the zero-tolerance policing strategy called the Safer Cities Initiative that is being employed in that city's Skid Row (Central City East). The city has assigned 50 additional officers to the relatively compact area; the result is a nearly constant police presence in Skid Row. This must be kept in mind when questioning why crime rates in the area adjacent to Skid Row, the Historic Core (which is undergoing gentrification) are higher than in Skid Row, an area once notorious for its violence and crime. In the end, the role played by changes in criminal justice strategy on crime rates is a vital piece of the puzzle that few researchers of gentrification have yet to consider.

Conclusion

In general, gentrification leads to a short-term increase in crime and long-term declines in crime for both property and violent offenses. Why this is the case is a question that has not yet been fully answered. We do know that population change matters in terms of initial reduced community stability, and perhaps even in terms of the displacement of crime-prone individuals. Also the rate or velocity of neighborhood change informs our understanding of the variability in how communities adjust to change. Less attention has been paid to changes in criminal justice strategy—which can contribute markedly to potentially inflate or deflate crime rates.

Terressa A. Benz
University of Idaho

See Also: Community Policing; Crime, Displacement of; Crime Prevention, Situational; Defensible Space Theory; Gated Communities; Urban Planning; Zero-Tolerance/Saturation Policing.

Further Readings

Covington, Jeanette and Ralph B. Taylor. "Gentrification and Crime: Robbery and Larceny Changes in Appreciating Baltimore Neighborhoods During the 1970s." *Urban Affairs Quarterly*, v.25/1 (1989).

Curtis, Richard. "The Improbable Transformation of Inner-City Neighborhoods." *Journal of Criminal Law and Criminology*, v.88/4 (1998).

McDonald, Scott C. "Does Gentrification Affect Crime Rates?" *Crime & Justice*, v.8/1 (1986).

Van Wilsem, Johan, Karin Wittebrood, and Nan Dirk De Graaf. "Socioeconomic Dynamics of Neighborhoods and the Risk of Crime Victimization: A Multilevel Study of Improving, Declining, and Stable Areas in the Netherlands." *Social Problems*, v.53/2 (2006).

Giuliani, Rudolph

Rudolph Giuliani, former mayor of the city of New York (1994–2001) and presidential contender, appears to always have been controversial, craving approval and notoriety, yet highly successful in almost all endeavors in his public service career.

Rudolph Giuliani, destined to become the 107th mayor of the city of New York, was born in a lower-class Brooklyn neighborhood on May 28, 1944. Many relatives lived nearby and spoiled young Rudy as he progressed through Catholic elementary school. His mother, Helen, represented a typical housewife of the times, but his father, Harold, vacillated between crime, mob activities, and full-time jobs. At the age of seven, Giuliani's family moved to Garden City, Long Island—migrating to an upper-class neighborhood. Interestingly enough, his parents switched their political allegiance from Democratic to Republican, having been advised that they would do better in Nassau County as Republicans.

Giuliani's friends remember him as "charismatic, chubby, and jolly." In 1959, the Giulianis moved to Lynbrook, Long Island, an upper-middle-class town, and this time joined the Democratic Party in order to fit into the neighborhood more comfortably. The family enrolled their son in Bishop Loughlin High School, at the time a gateway to college.

Giuliani graduated from Manhattan College in the Bronx in 1965. His political aspirations began to surface during his years in college. He and other students assembled a new political organization for the college, the Eagle Party, and he won the election to become president of his sophomore class. In 1968, Giuliani graduated from the New York University School of Law.

Legal Career

Following law school, Giuliani had the good fortune to be selected by a most influential judge to serve as law clerk: Judge Lloyd F. MacMahon, chief judge of the Southern District of New York. This effectively launched Giuliani's career in prosecutorial service. During the Vietnam War, Judge MacMahon's intervention kept the future mayor from being drafted. During this same period, Giuliani married his cousin Regina Peruggi. She grew to understand that Giuliani was a workaholic and would not be a devoted husband appearing home for dinner at a regular time every evening. The couple divorced 10 years later, and in 1982 he married Donna Hanover, an attractive TV anchorwoman. Years later, as the media followed the emerging politician, his affair with Judith Nathan was exposed when in 2000 he announced on television that the couple would be married. His wife Donna learned of his pending marriage to Nathan at the same time as did the public.

In 1970, Giuliani achieved his coveted dream when he was sworn in as assistant U.S. attorney for the Southern District of New York. In 1975 he advanced to associate deputy attorney general of the United States. In 1981, he was appointed associate attorney general, the number-three man in the Ronald Reagan Justice Department. In 1983, he began his transition to politics with appointment as U.S. District Attorney, Southern District of New York.

Political Career

Early in his college career, Giuliani knew he would later aspire to the presidency of the United States; he practiced lofty political speeches for his girlfriend and described to her the kind of wife he would need to be president. In 1965, he entered New York University Law School. During these years, he touted himself as a Kennedy Democrat and deeply mourned the assassination of Robert Kennedy, one of his heroes. Over the years, Giuliani slowly migrated toward the right politically, registering as an Independent in the 1970s and finally a Republican early in 1981, as Ronald Reagan ascended to the presidency.

In 1989, Giuliani attempted his first run at public office, campaigning for mayor of New York on the Republican ticket. He lost the election, and David Dinkins achieved the coveted post. In 1993, Giuliani made a second run, campaigning on a platform of crime reduction, noting that the crime rate in New York City had achieved an all-time high. This time he succeeded. One of the most important posts to be filled was the appointment of a commissioner of the New York City Police Department (NYPD). Considering how to fulfill his campaign promises, he selected William Bratton, the outspoken but forward-thinking former chief of the New York City Transit Police and, at the time, chief of the Boston Police Department.

As Giuliani deepened his participation in politics, he indulged a habit of exaggerating current events perhaps in an attempt to heighten his self-importance; this seemed to cost him constant criticism from the media. In his first term as mayor, he claimed credit for Disney's determination to rebuild an old 42nd Street theater by announcing it at a press conference with Governor Mario Cuomo. In fact, Mayor Dinkins had secured the contract that began the gentrification of Times Square on the last day of his administration, December 31, 1993. Regardless of his flubs, Giuliani worked hard with Bratton to keep the NYPD in the forefront of the popular focus on law and order. This tack paid off when Giuliani ran and won reelection in 1997.

Impact on Policing

Giuliani had an impact on crime throughout his career, starting in the practice of criminal law. As Southern District U.S. District Attorney, his goal was to reestablish the Southern District as "the most prestigious and feared federal prosecutor's office in the country." He was once quoted as saying, "It's about time law enforcement got as organized as organized crime." He prosecuted members of five of the most notorious Mafia families in the New York area, including the Colombo and Genovese organizations. He also targeted corrupt Wall Street traders, and two extremely high-profile women: Philippines first lady Imelda Marcos and New York socialite Leona Helmsley.

Perhaps Giuliani's biggest contribution to crime reduction, however, was his appointment of Bratton to helm the NYPD. Bratton had been experimenting with systems to manage operations and various policing methods; he and Jack Maple, deputy commissioner for crime control strategies (a civilian position), together completely transformed the NYPD into one of the most effective crime reduction agencies in the world. The NYPD gained international recognition for its success and many agencies attempted to emulate the processes.

Unfortunately, two years into his mayoralty, Giuliani saw the notoriety gained by Bratton as a threat, especially when Bratton appeared on the cover of *Time* magazine. At about that point, Bratton's time

As mayor of New York City, Giuliani was credited with initiating improvements and with a reduction in crime, pressing through the city's quality of life initiatives.

with the NYPD came to an end. Giuliani claimed credit for the outstanding crime reduction success; after leaving office he occasionally consulted with other nations on the CompStat system developed by Bratton and Maple, often claiming it as his inspiration.

Giuliani surfaced politically again in 2007 to run for president but faded early in his campaign. He continues to do consulting nationally and internationally.

Phyllis P. McDonald
Johns Hopkins University

See Also: Bratton, William; CompStat; Maple, Jack; New York City; Organized Crime and Violence.

Further Readings

Barrett, Wayne. *Rudy! An Investigative Biography of Rudolph Giuliani.* New York: Basic Books, 2000.

Barrett, Wayne and Dan Collins. *Grand Illusion: The Untold Story of Rudy Giuliani and 9/11.* New York: HarperCollins, 2006.

Bratton, William and Peter Knobler. *The Turnaround: How America's Top Cop Reversed the Crime Epidemic.* New York: Random House, 1998.

Newfield, Jack. *The Full Rudy: The Man, the Myth, the Mania.* New York: Nation Books, 2007.

Siegel, Fred. *The Prince of the City: Giuliani, New York, and the Genius of American Life.* New York: Encounter Books, 2005.

Goetz, Bernhard

On December 22, 1984, in the mid-afternoon, a blonde, clean-cut, bespectacled 37-year-old white man boarded a New York City subway train. He was carrying an unlicensed, concealed .38-caliber pistol loaded with five rounds. The man was Bernhard Hugo Goetz, who was about to become a folk hero, a celebrity avenger against street criminals, and a "subway vigilante."

Also in the subway car were four noisy, African American youths, and Goetz chose to sit near them. One youth asked Goetz, "How are ya?" Then another youth joined him, asking Goetz for $5. When Goetz asked what the youth wanted, the youth said, "Give me $5." Goetz rapidly fired four shots, wounding three of the youths. He then approached the fourth youth, and seeing no blood, opined, "You seem to be all right, here's another," whereupon he fired the fifth round, severing the youth's spinal cord.

Most of the 15 to 20 passengers fled the car, in terror of the gunfire. However, two women passengers (one of whom was African American) were immobilized by fear. Goetz said some comforting words to them, then calmly walked to the front of the car and exited via the platform between cars, jumping down onto the tracks.

Details

The four youths were all 18 or 19 years old; all were residents of a housing project in the south Bronx. All were shorter than Goetz. Goetz was sure that none of the four had a gun, but said he feared being "maimed" by them because of a prior mugging.

He said that he established "a pattern of fire" with an intention to murder the youths. Two of the bullets were standard load; the other three were hollow-point bullets ("dum-dums") that were illegal. The youths were Troy Canty, Barry Allen, James Ramseur, and Darrell Cabey, two of whom were shot in the back. One dum-dum bullet, fired at close range, paralyzed Cabey for life.

Media Portrayals

In the aftermath of the shootings, the mass media romanticized Goetz, even as they painted the youths as generic, African American "punks." There were persistent reports that the youths were carrying "sharpened screwdrivers," though the police found only three ordinary screwdrivers (used for breaking into video-game machines).

The media painted the "subway vigilante's" actions as admirable: legitimate vengeance exacted against young, urban, African American villains. In this view, the youths merely got what they deserved, and Goetz became a powerful symbol of avenging the urban street crime that was so widely feared.

Making of a Subway Vigilante

Goetz came from a financially prosperous New York family. His mother was German Jewish, and his father, known for being remarkably cold and dictatorial toward his children, was a German Lutheran immigrant. Bernhard was a studious boy. When he was 12 years old, his father was charged with sexually assaulting two 15-year-old boys. At that point his family suddenly forced him to attend a boarding school in Switzerland, where he remained until high school graduation.

Goetz then majored in nuclear engineering at the Bronx campus of New York University. Fascinated with electronics, he eventually started his own business, run out of his apartment, for repairing electronic equipment. The subway shooting occurred three months after the death of Goetz's father, with whom he had had a tumultuous relationship.

Goetz came to despise New York and to distrust the ability of criminal justice to protect citizens from street crime. In 1981 he was mugged in a subway station, with injuries resulting in lasting damage to his chest, as well as the loss of electronic equipment he was carrying. Of the three assailants, only one was caught. Goetz was disgruntled because he spent the whole day at the police station, filing charges, while the suspect was allowed to leave after a short time (though later pleading guilty to misdemeanor assault). Goetz also faulted the police after he purportedly spent $2,000 to prepare a gun-permit application, only to have it cursorily rejected by the police.

Self-Defense Assertion

Eventually Goetz was charged with assault and attempted murder of the four youths. He asserted self-defense, claiming that as a New Yorker he could read the youth's body language, that they intended to harm him grievously, and that in the subway car he felt "cornered like a rat" with no possibility to retreat.

New York law allowed self-defense if it was necessary to defend oneself from the imminent use of unlawful physical force and if one reasonably believed he or she was either about to be seriously hurt or killed or about to become a victim of robbery. A major difficulty with the defense is the degree to which the jury should consider only what a generic, law-abiding person would do under the circumstances (an objective approach), in contrast to a more flexible standard that also considers the subjective fears of this particular defendant (a subjective approach). In Goetz's case, the latter prevailed.

The jury evidently concluded that based on his prior victimization, Goetz believed—even if

mistakenly—that he was about to suffer grievous bodily harm at the hands of the four youths. This threat was imminent in Goetz's mind, even if that belief was tainted by racism. In this view, Goetz's shooting the four youths was proportionate to the harm he was facing, and his intent was merely to repel the youths' aggression against him. Though it is especially difficult to comprehend the imminence of the harm Goetz faced from the fourth (already wounded) youth at the time of the firing of the fifth shot at close range, the jury found that even that qualified as self-defense.

Conclusion

Ultimately the jury acquitted Goetz of all charges (including attempted murder and assault) except illegal possession of a handgun. Goetz was sentenced to six months in jail, a $5,000 fine, five years of probation, 280 hours of community service, and a requirement that he find psychiatric counseling.

Frank Butler
Saint Joseph's University

See Also: Fear of Crime; Guardian Angels; Mass Transit, Crime on; Mugging; New York City; Panhandling or Begging; Street Crime, Popular Portrayals of; Racial Assault.

Further Readings

Fletcher, G. P. *A Crime of Self-Defense: Bernhard Goetz and the Law on Trial.* New York: The Free Press, 1988.

Lesly, Mark and Charles Shuttleworth. *Subway Gunman: A Juror's Account of the Bernhard Goetz Trial.* Latham, NY: British American Publishing, 1998.

Rubin, Lillian B. *Quiet Rage: Bernie Goetz in a Time of Madness.* Berkeley: University of California Press, 1986.

Graffiti

Graffiti is among the most pervasive and visible of contemporary street crimes. Generally, graffiti denotes the variety of words and figures illicitly inscribed on the alley walls, buildings, trains, and freeway overpasses that collectively make up the spatial environment of "the street." Specifically, graffiti references the particular forms of street marking that have proliferated over the past few decades within various urban subcultures. With this widespread growth and visibility of graffiti have come impassioned public debates over graffiti's role in the urban environment, and ongoing media and criminal justice campaigns against graffiti, many of these founded in new models of urban policing. This public and legal response to graffiti has served to alter the dynamics of graffiti writing over time, as has the increasing merging of graffiti with public art, advertising, and commerce.

Identity and Status

Certainly the most popular and pervasive form of contemporary graffiti throughout the United States, Europe, and beyond is the style of urban graffiti that emerged in the 1970s around hip hop culture and other urban youth subcultures. This form of graffiti is practiced by "writers" and their "crews," who utilize graffiti to negotiate status and subcultural fame. Such fame is based on the visibility of a writer's graffiti, the "spots" where it is written, and the style with which it is designed and executed. Whether writing their subcultural nicknames, or "tags," or painting elaborate murals, practitioners employ graffiti as a form of ongoing symbolic communication by which to issue aesthetic challenges, invitations, and comments to other writers. Using spray paint and ink markers along with etching tools and stickers, they also gain status through the sheer spatial scope of their work.

"Tagging the heavens" involves illicitly writing graffiti atop a building or freeway overpass, and imparts status due to the difficulty and visibility of the spot selected. "Going citywide" denotes writers' success at spreading and maintaining their graffiti throughout an urban area. Increasingly, writers in addition "go nationwide" by painting graffiti on the sides of outbound freight trains; so popular is this practice that distinct aesthetic codes have now evolved in the subculture regarding freight train graffiti.

With the proliferation of graffiti Web sites and magazines, and the emphasis on photographs of graffiti, writers can now go worldwide with their work as well. Nonetheless, they also remain local folk artists within many inner city and ethnic minority communities, painting signs for small businesses

and designing "rest in peace" street memorials for those lost to violence.

Gang Aspects

The graffiti of street youth gangs invokes a different dynamic of status and communication. Such gangs often utilize graffiti to demarcate contested space and to define gang presence and identity; this graffiti writing is at times reinforced by the symbolic degradation of rival gangs through coded threats or the crossing out of rival gang graffiti. This type of graffiti resonates more closely with street crime as conventionally defined, and is often intertwined with other forms of street criminality like drug dealing or assault.

For Latino/Latina gangs especially, such graffiti can also reference historical traditions of public life and public mural painting, and in this way can symbolize community pride and solidarity. Likewise, while such graffiti can invite physical violence, it can also displace the need for physical confrontation by demarcating spatial and cultural boundaries. In contrast, the graffiti of skinheads and neo-Nazi youth gangs is more overtly designed to communicate ethnic domination, terror, and threat in conjunction with campaigns of physical violence against immigrants, gays and lesbians, and others.

Antigraffiti Campaigns

The proliferation of urban graffiti over the past few decades has led to numerous legal and media antigraffiti campaigns and "wars on graffiti," most all of them predicated on a Broken Windows Theory policing model that associates low-order street crime with more serious forms of criminality. In both public pronouncements and day-to-day street policing, such campaigns have regularly conflated the various forms of graffiti under the general heading of gang activity and dangerous youth crime, in part as justification for more aggressive legal penalties for graffiti writing. As a result, public perceptions of graffiti have in many cases hardened, and arrests and convictions for graffiti writing have multiplied.

Graffiti writers themselves have in some cases embraced this public notoriety, becoming more political in their work and moving from subcultural to countercultural orientations. Others have parlayed increased visibility into noncriminal careers, providing graffiti-style images for corporate advertising campaigns and products, and launching their own art and media endeavors.

Jeff Ferrell
Texas Christian University, University of Kent

See Also: Broken Windows Theory; Gangs; Hate Crime; Juvenile Offending; Skinheads; Street Crime, Popular Portrayals of; Vandalism.

Further Readings

Ferrell, Jeff. *Crimes of Style*. Lebanon, NH: Northeastern University Press, 1996.

Iveson, Kurt, ed. "Special Feature on Graffiti, Street Art, and the City." *City*, v.14/1,2 (2010).

Phillips, Susan A. *Wallbangin'*. Chicago: University of Chicago Press, 1999.

Snyder, Gregory. *Graffiti Lives*. New York: New York University Press, 2009.

Grand Theft Auto (Video Game)

The *Grand Theft Auto* (*GTA*) video game series became highly controversial in the late 1990s for allowing players to adopt the personas of violent street criminals. Designed for a variety of computers and gaming platforms, *GTA*'s missions range from stealing cars and rounding up prostitutes to killing competing gangsters and shooting police officers to earn money and rewards.

Evolution and Revenues

The first installment of *GTA* was launched in 1997 and features a two-dimensional, bird's-eye view of three crime-ridden cities modeled on New York (Liberty City), Miami (Vice City), and Los Angeles (San Andreas). Throughout the game, the protagonist responds to phone calls from mob bosses and gang members who instruct the player on which cars to steal and what crimes to commit. The details and nuances of players and missions have increased tremendously since the first edition, offering players entire cities to explore by walking, climbing, swimming, or using a car, motorcycle, boat, or aircraft.

In 2008, *GTA* entered the *Guinness Book of World Records* for generating $310 million in its first 24 hours of sales, and $500 million in its first week, outgrossing virtually all other forms of popular entertainment.

In 2001, *GTA* introduced players to a three-dimensional Liberty City with shipping yards, urban parks, various ethnic neighborhoods and gang turfs, and an elevated train that encircles the city. The character wanders the neighborhoods looking for weapons and drugs with the aid of a global positioning system (GPS) map, and can kill or rob anyone he likes along the way. The city features a range of characters from street thugs and pimps to triad members and mobsters.

In addition to performing theft, arson, and homicide for his bosses, the character can increase his "wanted level" by shooting police officers and running over pedestrians, which eventually leads to a pursuit by helicopters, SWAT teams, and the army. When the player is shot to death or killed in an explosion, his weapons are confiscated and he wakes up in the hospital with money taken from his account to pay for his health care bill. If the character is "busted," he is forced to turn over his weapons and bribe the police to avoid jail. One of the major criticisms from opponents of the game is that despite these penalties, the character can infinitely die or be arrested, giving young players unrealistic ideas about the consequences of street crime and violent actions.

Youth Influence and Reaction

Concerns about the game's influence on youth were heightened in 2003 when police apprehended 17-year-old Devin Moore for stealing a car in Fayette, Alabama. Moore claimed to have played hundreds of hours of *GTA* prior to this event. Inside the police station, the teen seized an officer's gun and shot him in the head. Moore killed two others and fled the station in a police cruiser before being caught. Moore reportedly told an interviewer, "Life is like a video game. Everybody got to die sometime." Attorney Jack Thompson argued that *GTA* was a "murder simulator" that trained Moore to perform such acts and led a lawsuit on behalf of the victims' families against Moore, as well as Walmart and GameShop for selling him versions of the game, Take-Two Interactive for producing the game, and Sony for making the console. While these legal actions garnered international headlines, Moore's video game defense proved unsuccessful, as did Thompson's bid to find the companies criminally responsible.

The most controversial installment in the *GTA* series is arguably San Andreas, released in 2004, in which the African American protagonist Carl Johnson (C J) returns to the city after serving time in prison and is immediately harassed by police officers, who frame him for killing another officer and steal his money. Based on the early 1990s crack epidemic in Los Angeles, the game involves negotiating neighborhoods filled with gun-packing prostitutes and hostile gang members, leading many critics to deplore the racial and gendered stereotypes throughout the fictional city. San Andreas also features a "hot coffee" modification in which the protagonist's girlfriend invites C J inside for coffee. She then takes off her clothes and the player can control C J's movements to increase excitement levels during intercourse.

Revelations of this scene, which requires a special hack to access, led states such as California, Illinois, and Michigan to legislate age restrictions on the purchase of such games. It also moved political leaders Hillary Clinton and Joe Lieberman to introduce the Family Entertainment Protection Act in 2006. In a related legal decision, in June 2011, the Supreme Court ruled 7–2 against a California law barring children from purchasing video games, finding that such practices violate the First Amendment rights of young people. This decision indicates that violent video games such as *GTA* are protected under freedom of speech legislation.

Conclusion

Despite harsh criticism from concerned politicians and citizens' groups, *GTA* remains one of the highest grossing franchises in the entertainment industry, spurring numerous imitations and homages such as *The Simpsons Hit and Run* (2003). For better or worse, the game continues to allow millions of consumers to commit virtual street crimes at their leisure. Its developer, RockStar Games, shows no signs of ending this profitable series in the future.

Chris Richardson
University of Western Ontario

See Also: Drive-By Shooting; Gangs (Street); Mugging; Patrol Cars; Prostitute/Streetwalker; Street Crime, Popular Portrayals of; Urban Incivility.

Further Readings

DeVane, Ben and Kurt D. Squire. *The Meaning of Race and Violence in* Grand Theft Auto*: San Andreas.* Madison: University of Wisconsin, Madison, 2007.

Garrelts, Nate, ed. *The Meaning and Culture of* Grand Theft Auto: *Critical Essays.* Jefferson, NC: McFarland & Co., 2006.

Murray, Soraya. "High Art/Low Life: The Art of Playing Grand Theft Auto." *PAJ: A Journal of Performance and Art,* v.27/2 (2005).

Guardian Angels

The Guardian Angels is a citizens' crime-fighting group started by Brooklyn native Curtis Sliwa in 1977 in response to the growing level of street crime in New York City. While others have been identified as cofounders, only Sliwa remains as the recognized founder and director of the Guardian Angels. What began as a small citizen patrol group in New York City has expanded to 139 chapters in 15 countries. Sliwa reports that, as of 2011, the Guardian Angels had chapters in 82 cities worldwide, comprising approximately 5,000 members.

Origin and Principles

Prior to becoming the leader and organizer of the group, Sliwa had worked as a night manager at a McDonald's restaurant in the Bronx, New York. The Bronx had become notorious in the 1970s as a high-crime area of the city. Sliwa and several coworkers developed the concept of a voluntary citizen patrol group to prevent or reduce crime; the subway system was their first area of patrol concentration.

The original Guardian Angels group consisted of 13 members, originally calling themselves the Magnificent 13. As new members were attracted and signed on, they changed the name in 1979 to Guardian Angels.

The self-defined purpose of the Guardian Angels is to prevent crime through the presence of an unarmed, voluntary citizen patrol group specially trained to handle various situations in high-crime areas. In the original group, particular emphasis was placed on training members to make citizens' arrests for violent crimes. Today, however, this emphasis has shifted toward detaining violent offenders until law enforcement arrives. The group walks the streets in high-crime areas or rides on public transportation to create a visible presence that can dissuade motivated offenders from committing crime. Typical street crimes that the group seeks to deter include the violent crimes of assault, robbery, and rape; and various types of property crime such as burglary, theft from autos, auto theft, and vandalism.

Recognizable by their uniforms consisting of red jackets, white T-shirts with red lettering, and red berets, the group became more active both in direct crime-stopping and in publicizing their efforts. The berets have over time become a worldwide symbol of community crime prevention through voluntary citizen patrol. As the Guardian Angels received nationwide recognition for their crime control and prevention efforts in New York City, chapters in other large U.S. cities began to develop. More than 35 years later, public support and appreciation of the Guardian Angels has grown to the extent that chapters are no longer limited to large cities with serious crime problems; several chapters have also been developed in smaller U.S. cities.

Members of the Guardian Angels are instantly recognizable due to their paramilitary-style uniforms. In order to be acting on behalf of the Guardian Angels, a member is required to be in uniform while on patrol and at the time he or she attempts to intervene during a crime or a situation that is escalating toward a crime. Guardian Angels patrol groups receive training from a designated liaison appointed by Sliwa. They do not consider themselves vigilantes, pointing to their cooperation with law enforcement agencies as evidence that the Guardian Angels do not act outside the parameters of the law. New chapters are developed based upon citizen request or upon Sliwa's determination that a community is in need of the group's assistance.

Troubled History

The Guardian Angels were not initially supported by politicians in New York City, then-Mayor Ed Koch opposed the actions of the group, as did some other prominent figures. As new chapters were in the process of being developed in other cities, these, too, were often met with political opposition, mainly focused on the issue of supposed vigilantism as a hindrance rather than help to local law enforcement. Such resistance escalated in 1992, when

Sliwa admitted to fabricating at least six incidents of the group's claimed crime-fighting exploits in the late 1970s and early 1980s in his effort to raise the profile of the group. Confrontations were staged by Sliwa that typically involved other members of the group in disguise, acting as would-be criminals and engaging in altercations with members wearing the Guardian Angels' uniform. These stunts were staged to draw media attention and increase public support for the group's efforts.

Two actual incidents, both tragic, added to the high-profile controversy. Guardian Angel Frank Melvin, age 26, was shot and killed by Newark, New Jersey, police during a response to a call for a burglary. The district attorney declared the 1981 shooting an "accident," while Sliwa led protests with the cry of racism. Nearly two decades later, a former Guardian Angels member—James Richards, a cofounder of the Los Angeles chapter in the 1980s—was shot and killed in 2000 at age 55, after years of patrolling both as a Guardian Angel and with Neighborhood Watch, and informing the Los Angeles Police Department about drug-related and gang-related crime activity. A federal jury in 2002 convicted a gang member of crimes connected with the homicide.

In another brush with lethal force, an attempt was made on Curtis Sliwa's life in 1992; he was kidnapped and shot after he entered a stolen taxi. Sliwa expected the taxi to take him to midtown Manhattan where he produced his radio program, but instead the taxi turned in a different direction and a masked gunman emerged who had been hiding, crouched down in the taxi's front seat. The gunman began shooting at Sliwa, who wrestled with the gunman. Upon being shot in the leg and lower back, Sliwa jumped out of the taxi's window. This was the second attempt on Sliwa's life: earlier the same year, at the same intersection near Sliwa's home, three men with baseball bats beat him, resulting in head injuries and a broken wrist.

John A. Gotti, son of the leader of the Gambino crime family at that time, was eventually charged by federal prosecutors with plotting to kidnap Sliwa, but three attempts (the last in 2005) to prosecute Gotti for conspiracy to kidnap Sliwa as part of racketeering charges were unsuccessful and the charges were dropped. It was believed Gotti targeted Sliwa due to comments that Sliwa had made about Gotti and his father on Sliwa's radio program. Sliwa's testimony convinced some of the jurors that Gotti had ordered the shooting, but none of the juries could agree to convict on all charges brought in the trials.

Sliwa continues to host a radio program, appears on television, maintains a public blog, and is president of the Guardian Angels. There are some former members who contend that Sliwa has never confessed to all of the fabrications perpetuated by the group, but due to a renewed focus on community crime prevention through activism and education, the Guardian Angels has regained a positive image in much of the United States, as well as abroad. Despite its rocky start and troubled history, the current Guardian Angels enjoy public support from such figures as former New York City Mayor Rudolph Giuliani and Mayor Michael Bloomberg.

Guardian Angels Today

The Guardian Angels is comprised of three separate programs: Safety Patrols, CyberAngels, and the Guardian Angels Education Society. Safety Patrols welcome new members without a criminal record who are not a member of a gang or hate group. While still advocating community crime prevention through voluntary citizen patrol, the Safety Patrols component has refocused its training of new members to emphasize detaining crime suspects until police arrive rather than more aggressive tactics such as conducting citizen's arrests. Members are trained in first aid and cardiopulmonary resuscitation (CPR), conflict resolution, the legal rights of citizens and suspects, and basic self-defense. The volunteer Safety Patrol groups patrol streets, subways, neighborhoods, and community events. They also engage in community service activities such as graffiti removal and safety seminars.

Launched in 1995, the CyberAngels is an Internet safety education program that provides parents and others with the information needed to help keep children safe online. The Web site serves as a resource center on how to secure a computer, prevent predators from interacting with children, and how to handle cyberbullying. The CyberAngels site works to ensure that online activities do not result in crimes on the streets.

The Guardian Angels Education Society is an education program for students and teachers covering topics such as gang resistance, violence prevention, character development, antibullying, and safety education. The goal of the education program is to create safe schools and a positive classroom environment. The Guardian Angels Education Society was developed with the idea that education and intervention can prevent school and personal conflicts from resulting in violence and bullying outside of the school environment.

The most recognized symbol of the Guardian Angels, however, remains the red beret, white T-shirt, and red jacket worn by members of the Safety Patrols who walk city streets and other public spaces for the purpose of deterring crime. The small and controversial crime-fighting group that developed in the late 1970s as a direct response to the increase in violent crime in New York City has now been replicated in cities all over the United States and around the world. International chapters can be found in Canada, Mexico, Brazil, Peru, Italy, the United Kingdom, Israel, South Africa, New Zealand, Australia, Philippines, Japan, and Korea, among other nations. In mid-2011, a business owner contacted the Guardian Angels in response to an increase in crime in West Haven, Connecticut, to explore the possibility of starting a new chapter of the Guardian Angels in that

Curtis Sliwa, photographed at the 2007 West Indian Day parade in Brooklyn, New York, is an American anticrime activist, the founder and chief executive officer of the Guardian Angels, radio talk show host, and popular media personality.

city; this is typical of how the group has expanded. There are also cities where local Guardian Angels chapters, once thriving, have over time shrunk or disbanded. The once-controversial Guardian Angels is now, more often than not, met with public and political support and is welcomed into classrooms and other community forums to work in cooperation with law enforcement agencies in their crime-prevention efforts.

Jennifer N. Grimes
Indiana State University

See Also: Bystander Apathy; Community Policing; Crime Patterns; Gangs; Neighborhood Watch; New York City; Routine Activity Theory.

Further Readings

Kenney, Dennis J. *Crime, Fear, and the New York City Subways—The Role of Citizen Action.* Westport, CT: Praeger, 1987.

Kenney, Dennis J. "Crime on the Subways: Measuring the Effectiveness of the Guardian Angels." *Justice Quarterly,* v.3/4 (1986).

Pennell, Susan, Christine Curtis, and Joel Henderson. *Guardian Angels: An Assessment of Citizen Response to Crime.* Washington, D.C.: United States Dept. of Justice, National Institute of Justice, 1986.

Pennell, Susan, Christine Curtis, Joel Henderson, and Jeff Tayman. "Guardian Angels: A Unique Approach to Crime Prevention." *Crime & Delinquency,* v.35/3 (1989).

Perry, Joseph B. and M. D. Pugh. "Public Support of the Guardian Angels: Vigilante Protection Against Crime, Toledo, Ohio, 1984." *Sociology & Social Research,* v.73/3 (1989).

Sever, Brion, Al Gorman, and Greg Coram. "Curtis Sliwa: Vigilantism, Victims' Rights, and the Guardian Angels." In *Icons of Crime Fighting: Relentless Pursuers of Justice,* Jeffrey Bumgarner, ed. Westport, CT: Greenwood Press, 2008.

Guns and Weapons

Weapons of some sort have been employed in violent crime as long as there has been violent crime; the rocks and clubs employed by our ancient ancestors are no less lethal today than they were in ancient times. While many types of street crime rely on stealth or deception, the average person most fears crimes of direct intimidation and violence. While many street crimes—such as robberies, carjackings, and aggravated assault—are perpetrated through the use of intimidation or physical force alone, weapons are commonly displayed or used to obtain the victim's maximum cooperation with the least effort and the least vulnerability to the offender. Typically, the level of technology in guns and other weapons used by criminals are for all intents and purposes matched by the level deployed by law enforcement agencies.

Clubs and Knives

Early references to violent street crime refer to the use of simple impact weapons such as clubs or cudgels made of wood. Technically, a club is relatively short and wielded with one hand. A cudgel is longer than a club and may double as a walking stick; it is generally swung two-handed, like a baseball bat. The club is a very basic yet extremely functional design that has not changed in thousands of years except in terms of materials.

More modern examples of these impact weapons may be made from aluminum (e.g., aluminum softball bats), steel (e.g., crowbars), or hard plastic, as well as wood. They are easily made and can be concealable or may be carried under the guise of a cane. Injuries caused by the use of such weapons are referred to as blunt force trauma. Blunt force trauma can fracture bones as well as cause bruising and, above all, extreme pain.

As in the case of clubs, knives have been utilized for relieving people of their life or property since ancient times. Perhaps the earliest examples are the single-edged blades made of flint often seen in museums. Double-edged flint blades are not uncommon. The double- and single-edge design was easily transferred to other materials, especially metals.

While these early basic designs continue to the present day, one of the more famous designs originated with slave trader, land speculator, and frontiersman James (Jim) Bowie whose notoriety arose in large part through his design of the large fighting knife that bears his name. The Bowie knife is long (most examples are over a foot in length) and heavy, with a sharp clip point and a single edge. It was invented as a fighting weapon and meant to be used edge up to eviscerate opponents. Considered brutal even by mid-19th-century standards, many states made the public carrying of Bowie knives illegal.

In early modern Europe, swords were popular among highway robbers and other criminals and were used into the 19th century to supplement the unreliable, single-shot firearms of the era. Swords do not seem to have been common among American criminals. Automatic knives, usually referred to as "switchblades," were invented during the mid-18th century as gentlemen's knives. A type of folding knife, switchblades employ a spring-loaded mechanism to open and lock the blade with the push of a button. These were developed as a one-handed convenience type. Automatic knives became quite popular in Europe after World War I due to the large number of men who survived the war as amputees.

Switchblades were issued to U.S. troops during World War II, and thousands of others were purchased and brought back by returning veterans. Most of the privately purchased knives were cheap, poorly made, and probably bought on impulse as novelties with the purchaser harboring no intent that the knives be used as weapons, much less as criminal weapons. While not entirely based in fact, during the late 1940s switchblades became identified with criminals and delinquents. Specifically, they were portrayed in the mass media as a weapon of choice among motorcycle gangs and juvenile street gangs. National media associated these knives with evil, claiming there was no legitimate (noncriminal) use for such items. This led to their actual criminalization during the early 1950s.

While ancient in conception, knives and clubs (clubs are now frequently referred to as impact or kinetic weapons) are still widely used in street crime. Easily purchased, they are also easily improvised. For example, in modern barroom assaults, broken beer bottles often substitute for knives, and heavy beer mugs for clubs.

Guns From Flintlocks to Revolvers

Just as warfare was revolutionized by the invention of firearms, so too was crime. The earliest firearms were too large and unwieldy to be employed in any setting other than battlefield or fortress. By about 1600, firearms had been sufficiently reduced in size to be carried for personal use. They were, however, still relatively cumbersome, and being made one at a time by highly skilled craftsmen, they were also

very expensive, putting their use outside the realm of any criminals other than professional assassins.

By 1750, technology had greatly improved firearms, making them more reliable and more easily carried by the standards of the day. Although still relatively expensive, the proliferation of gunsmiths reduced the price of a pistol sufficiently for many highwaymen, or highway robbers, to acquire. The pistols of the 18th century were most often single-shot flintlocks, over a foot in length, and several pounds in weight. Loaded from the muzzle with loose powder and a lead ball or shot, they could be devastating when employed at close range. Since reloading was not an option during commission of a crime or while defending oneself from a criminal, both criminals and their potential victims usually carried a knife or sword as well.

The invention of interchangeable parts and mass production during the early 19th century made firearms far cheaper than in the past. The introduction of the percussion cap (a copper disk coated with mercury fulminate, a substance highly explosive when struck a hard blow) made for a much handier and more efficient means of firearm ignition than the earlier flintlock. This made pistols more easily carried and concealable, as well as more reliable; percussion caps could be waterproofed, solving a problem that had dogged those using flintlock firearms.

The percussion cap made Samuel Colt's 1836 invention of the revolver, a compact, multishot handgun, possible. The multishot capability, concealability, and reliability of Colt's revolver was a boon to the military that was quickly adopted by criminals as well as early law enforcement officers. Indeed, the small, concealable revolver has remained one of the most common weapons used by criminals and law enforcement officers to the present day, although since the 1980s their numbers have tailed off in favor of contemporary semiautomatic models.

Early Colt revolvers were still difficult to load, as the cap was separate from the powder and projectile. Smith and Wesson developed a self-contained metallic cartridge during the late 1850s. While such cartridges, containing primer, powder, and projectile in a brass case, saw limited use during the Civil War, it was clear that future firearms development would hinge on the self-contained cartridge. By the end of the 1870s metallic cartridges had mostly eliminated the earlier cap and ball revolvers invented by Colt. Indeed, after 1870 few pistols, rifles, or shotguns were produced using flint or percussion ignition and loose powder and bullet.

Semiautomatic Weapons

Development of firearms and ammunition moved quickly between about 1850 and 1950—but firearms development has been relatively slow over the past 50 years. Aluminum alloys were developed to make firearms lighter and cheaper; ammunition has become more reliable. A major development occurred in the mid-1980s, when Gaston Glock, an Austrian clock maker, developed frames for semiautomatic pistols from modern polymer plastics. This reduced weight and production time, and resulted in a high quality, relatively less expensive pistol.

Quickly adopted by the military of several countries, the Glock caught on rapidly as a law enforcement weapon worldwide. The compact, lightweight design of the pistol also made it possible to carry 15 or more cartridges in the magazine. Designs similar to and perhaps better than the original Glock proliferated during the 1990s, making revolvers quasi-obsolescent for police use. Many police agencies still issue or allow their officers to carry revolvers; approximately 10 percent of the New York City Police Department (NYPD), for example, still choose to carry revolvers.

It has been argued that the police adopted high-capacity semiautomatic pistols such as the Glock to keep from being "outgunned" by the criminal element. The same argument has been used in the past when police departments adopted increasingly powerful revolvers and, in some cases, submachine guns. However, the evidence of a police-criminal arms race is tenuous. It seems more likely both police and criminals adopt new firearms because they can, not because either group feels a particular need to better arm itself from the other. This is definitely an area needing further research.

Main Firearm Types

Firearms fall into three broad categories: rifles, shotguns, and handguns (pistols). Handguns are much more commonly associated with crime than rifles or shotguns. Handguns used in crime are generally semiautomatic pistols or revolvers. A revolver is a firearm designed to by fired by one or both hands, having a rifled barrel and a revolving cylinder. The revolving cylinder has five to eight chambers; each chamber holds one cartridge.

A semiautomatic pistol (often erroneously called an "automatic") is a firearm designed to by fired by one or both hands, having a rifled barrel and a removable magazine (usually held within the pistol's grip) with a self-loading mechanism. This self-loading mechanism may be semiautomatic or fully automatic. In a semiautomatic firearm, the mechanism works with each squeeze of the trigger, ejecting a fired round and loading another. In a fully automatic firearm, the process of firing, ejecting, and loading continues so long as the trigger is squeezed, the magazine is emptied, or the gun malfunctions. While some fully automatic pistols have been produced over the past 100 years, they are impractical for most uses, including crime. Finally, derringers and similar pistols firing one or two shots are encountered in the hands of criminals, though rarely.

A rifle is a firearm with a rifled barrel designed to be fired from the shoulder. Rifles may be single-shot, lever-action, bolt-action, pump-action, or auto-loading. Auto-loading rifles may be semi or fully automatic. Rifles generally fire more powerful cartridges than do pistols. A subcategory of the rifle is the submachine gun. A submachine gun is a firearm with a rifled barrel meant to be fired from the shoulder. These have a fully automatic mechanism and fire a pistol cartridge. The Thompson or "Tommy gun" and the Uzi are well-known examples of submachine guns.

Another subcategory of rifle, the assault rifle, has been mentioned frequently by the news media as a weapon of choice among criminals. Most of what are commonly referred to as "assault rifles" actually are not assault rifles. A true assault rifle is a fully automatic weapon firing an intermediate cartridge; that is, a cartridge more powerful than a pistol cartridge but less powerful than a standard military rifle cartridge.

All fully automatic weapons, whether configured as a pistol, rifle, submachine gun, or assault rifle, are closely regulated by federal law and must be registered with the Bureau of Alcohol, Tobacco, Firearms and Explosives. A criminal could not meet the stringent federal standards to own a fully automatic weapon; possession of an unregistered machine gun is a federal felony carrying stiff penalties. Most of the firearms identified by news writers as assault rifles are not; they are look-alike weapons cosmetically resembling military assault rifles but functionally are the same as most semiautomatic rifles used for sporting purposes, and cannot be made to shoot in fully automatic mode.

A shotgun has a nonrifled or smooth bore barrel, is designed to be fired from the shoulder, and fires a cartridge or shell containing multiple projectiles or pellets. Shotguns used in street crimes often have had their barrels shortened to make them easier to carry and deploy. Contrary to popular belief, a short-barreled or "sawed-off" shotgun is no deadlier than one with a longer barrel, just handier and more easily concealed. Shotguns are produced with a variety or action types, pump and semiautomatic

being the most commonly encountered in use by criminals as well as law enforcement personnel. Any shotgun with a barrel shorter than 18 inches is regulated by the federal government in a manner similar to machine guns.

The caliber of a firearm is based on the diameter of the inside of its barrel or bore and the volume or powder capacity of the cartridge case. Firearms most commonly used in street crime are pistols in .22 and .380 caliber, and the 9mm. The .22 was the original self-contained metallic cartridge patented by Smith and Wesson in 1857. The .380, a relatively low-powered cartridge, has become popular over the past few years because of the numerous very lightweight and easily concealed semiautomatic pistols that are being made for the cartridge. Arms

Gun violence in the United States is an intensely debated political issue. Gun-related violence is most common in poor urban areas and often connected with gang violence. Policies at the federal, state, and local levels have attempted to address gun violence through a variety of methods, some of which include waiting periods before purchase, targeted law enforcement and policing strategies, education programs, community-outreach programs, and stiff sentencing of gun law violators.

in this caliber are popular among legally armed citizens as well as criminals, and are frequently carried by police officers as emergency or backup guns.

Firearms in Crime

According to a 1997 survey of state prison inmates, of those who used firearms in commission of a crime less than 2 percent obtained them from a gun show or flea market; 12 percent stated they purchased them at a pawnshop or retail store; while 80 percent stated they obtained them through family, friends, theft, a street buy, or other illegal source. Less than 2 percent stated they had used a true assault rifle or assault rifle look-alike.

According to the National Crime Victimization Survey (NCVS), produced by the Bureau of Justice Statistics, from 1993 through 2001 violent crime declined 54 percent, weapon violence fell 59 percent, and firearm violence was down 63 percent. Overall, the NCVS found that 26 percent of the average annual 8.9 million violent victimizations in the United States were committed by offenders armed with a weapon. "About 10 percent of the violent victimizations involved a firearm," the report stated.

Additionally, the NCVS reported that gun crimes reported to the police peaked in 1993 and have dropped steadily since. In 2010, firearms were used in less than 10 percent of nonfatal violent crimes. By contrast, about 90 percent of homicide victims were killed with a weapon, with firearms making up about two-thirds of those cases.

Guns, knives, or other objects were used in approximately 22 percent of all incidents of violent crime in 2009. Of robberies, 47 percent of occurrences involved a weapon of some type, with about 28 percent involving use of a firearm, most commonly a handgun. In cases of sexual assault, in only 15 percent of cases was the offender armed; in other types of assaults offenders were armed about 25 percent of the time.

Overall, weapons are used in about 22 percent of violent crimes; perpetrators are about as likely to be armed with a firearm (8 percent), as a knife (6 percent), or an impact weapon (7 percent). However, most murders, in the range of 66 percent to 68 percent, are committed with firearms, usually handguns. With a few periodic modulations, this has been the case since 1970. Thus, while the national murder rate has dropped since 1970—the murder rate fell 36 percent in the period from 1993

through 2001—the proportion of murders committed with firearms has remained fairly steady. With the exception of murder, then, the vast majority of violent crimes do not involve the use of a weapon of any kind, and firearms are not disproportionately used in any crime other than murder.

M. George Eichenberg
Tarleton State University

See Also: Fear of Crime; Gunshot Detection System; Mugging; Murder/Homicide; Operation Cease Fire.

Further Readings

Bureau of Justice Statistics. "National Crime Victimization Survey (NCVS): Weapon Use by Offense Type." December 7, 2010. http://bjs.ojp .usdoj.gov/index.cfm?ty=tp&tid=43 (Accessed April 2012).

Hogg, Ian. *Small Arms: Pistols and Rifles.* Barnsley, UK: Greenhill Books/Lionel Leventhal, 2001.

Hogg, Ian and John Weeks. *Pistols of the World: The Definitive Illustrated Guide to the World's Pistols and Revolvers.* Iola, WI: Krause Publications, 2004.

Perkins, Craig. *Bureau of Justice Statistics Special Report—Weapon Use and Violent Crime.* Washington, DC: U.S. Department of Justice, 2003.

Pogrebin, Mark, N. Prabha Unnithan, and Paul B. Stretesky. *Guns, Violence, and Criminal Behavior: The Offender's Perspective.* Boulder, CO: Lynne Rienner Publishers, 2009.

Gunshot Detection System

A gunshot dectection system uses electronic sensor technology to locate the source of gunfire and then send an alert to local law enforcement dispatchers. Usually installed in high-crime areas, such a system can employ a variety of acoustic, optical, seismic, and thermal sensors in distributed arrays that aid triangulation of gunfire sources. Such sensor information can, in some systems, automatically direct nearby surveillance cameras in order to gain additional data, such as the structural nature of the location and potentially even a picture of the shooter or shooters.

In the ideal case, a gunshot detection system captures such information reliably, helps accurately dispatch officers to the scene more quickly, aids in offender identification, and leads to an overall increase in both the opportunity to make arrests and to make charges stick. This type of surveillance enhancement thus can act as a "force multiplier" as it frees officers to respond to other calls, yet alerts them should dangerous situations arise. However on the other hand, the effectiveness of installed gunshot detection systems has been questioned as it relates to an increase in dispatching officers to locations where there is little evidence of a crime and no one to arrest, thus increasing workloads while decreasing efficiency. Still, the technology has shown promise when incorporated in a problem-oriented policing approach.

Capabilities and Utility

Gunshot detection system technology is sufficiently advanced to automatically screen out loud, sudden sounds that are similar to gunshots, such as engine backfires or fireworks. In a field test in Redwood City, California, underwritten by the National Institute of Justice, investigator Cory Watkins and his team found that a gunshot detection system had an 81 percent accuracy level in detecting shots, and an 84 percent accuracy level in triangulating the shots. There are several companies that manufacture gunshot detection systems, either for military or law enforcement applications; their specific technology solutions vary. Brands include Gun-Loc, Sentri, and ShotSpotter. The systems generally work by placing up to 20 sensors per square mile, each equipped with mulitple microphones and other types of detection; these are typically tied in to a global positioning system (GPS) receiver. In the case of ShotSpotter, for instance, when a gun is fired and its audio wave is detected by at least three stations, the direction of the sound and its strength are detected—along with thermometer readings to determine how quickly the sound traveled. All this information is used to triangulate the location of the shooting to within approximately 40 feet; it can also indicate if there were multiple shooters. If shots are fired from a vehicle in motion, the system will also determine its direction on the street.

All the stations of an installed system are linked through a network connection to a central server that reports the location to either dispatchers or directly to officers in patrol cars through the Internet. The sounds are recorded for later reference; some prosecutors have credited the audio playback with encouraging some suspects to plea bargain instead of standing trial. Data from the system can also be used to map the location of gunshots for crime analysis purposes, to reconstruct crime scenes, in addition to corroborating or refuting eyewitness testimony. In the first half of 2009, according to industry data, at least 57 known shooting victims were saved from life-threatening wounds because of the rapid response of emergency medical services personnel alerted by gunshot detection systems. A quicker response time also helps officers to gather crucial evidence, such as shell casings.

The ShotSpotter technology—originally developed from the work of U.S. Geological Survey seismologist John Lahr and Stanford Research Institute accoustics specialist Robert Showen—can be applied in stationary arrays, moveable arrays, a special operations version, and a military version suited for open terrain rather than urban environments.

Conclusion

Installing a gunshot detection system is not a quick and easy solution to crime in a given area. An installed system can cost $500,000 or more; training, maintaining, upgrading, and coordinating with other police techniques brings additional costs. These costs of course must be balanced against the potential yield of benefits, which can be a combination of crime deterrence, public safety and security enhancement, more effective use of patrol and response resources, better arrest rates and higher prosecution success rates. As pointed out by researcher Lorraine Green Mazerolle, the positive results of utilizing a gunshot detection system can be enhanced to the degree that local police departments use publicity to inform the public that illegal discharge of weapons will lead to higher arrest rates in certain neighborhoods. She cautions that police departments thinking about adopting gunshot detection systems must consider the relative efficacy of rapid response measures, as opposed to preventive measures.

William E. Raffel
Buffalo State College

See Also: Closed-Circuit Television; CompStat; Crime Mapping; Drive-By Shooting; Guns and Weapons; Policing, Problem-Oriented.

Further Readings

Mazerolle, Lorraine Green. *Using Gunshot Detection Technology in High-Crime Areas.* Washington, DC: National Institute of Justice, 1998.

Shafer, Rachel. "To Catch a Speeding Bullet." University of California Berkeley College of Engineering. August 2011. http://innovations.coe.berkeley.edu/vol5-issue6-aug11/showen (Accessed May 2012).

Watkins, Corey, et al. "Technological Approaches to Controlling Random Gunfire: Results of a Gunshot Detection System Field Test." *Policing: An International Journal of Police Strategies & Management*, v. 25/2 (2002).

Watters, Ethan. "Shotpotter." *Wired*, v.15/4 (2007). http://www.wired.com/wired/archive/15.04/shotspotter.html (Accessed June 2011).

Hate Crime

Scholars use many terms to describe the specific form of hate crime. Jack Levin and Jack McDevitt would call it "defensive hate crime"; Donald Green et al. would invoke the notion of "defended neighborhoods"; Jeannine Bell would simply call it "move-in violence." These hate crime scholars are all referring to a similar phenomenon: hate crimes motivated by a desire to preserve territory through the violent expulsion of perceived "outsiders."

Such violence might be directed against immigrants "taking over" a nation, migrants taking over a city, or others taking over the neighborhood. The latter, locally situated violence is the focus here. Just as national demographics shift, so too do those at the local level, often resulting in violent efforts to protect one's street from being taken over by the "dangerous other." Such violence is reflective of the geopolitics of race—that is, conflicts over territorial control—in particular, at the most immediate level of "the street."

Definitions and Implications

It is important to define the key phenomenon under investigation here, that is, hate crime. Framing the present understanding of hate crime is sociologist Barbara Perry's definition from 2001, which has come to be widely cited in the relevant literature:

It involves acts of violence and intimidation, usually directed toward already stigmatized and marginalized groups. As such, it is a mechanism of power, intended to reaffirm the precarious hierarchies that characterize a given social order. It attempts to recreate simultaneously the threatened (real or imagined) hegemony of the perpetrator's group and the 'appropriate' subordinate identity of the victim's group.

In the present context, what is especially useful about this definition is that it recognizes that bias-motivated violence is directed toward the preservation of some imagined social order. The emphasis here is on the preservation of a carefully contrived racial order that characterizes local communities.

It is no accident that scholarship on hate crime and related forms of violence uses such terminology as "borders," "boundaries," "transgressions," or "territory." Hate crimes are situationally located; they have a spatial element that is often overlooked, although just as often implied by the language noted above. Hate crime can be seen as one mechanism by which the appropriate "spaces for races" can be created and reinforced. It is a weapon often invoked when victims are perceived to threaten the racialized boundaries which are meant to separate "us" from "them." Racial violence becomes justifiable as a punishment for transgressions of institutionalized codes of conduct, for crossing the boundaries of race. Reactionary violence to such border crossings ensures that white people and people of color will inhabit their appropriate places in physical and cultural terms.

As important as they are for separating "us" from "them," these borders are nonetheless not fixed. In both symbolic and material terms, they are permeable and subject to ongoing tendencies to transgression. So, for example, black Americans or south Asian Americans move into predominantly white neighborhoods to gain access to better schools and other social and economic supports. Yet such movements represent threats; these newcomers have violated the carefully crafted barriers intended to keep them in their respective boxes. It is in these contexts—at the symbolic boundaries—that racialized violence is likely to occur. It thus becomes a territorial defense of cultural, as well as geographical space. It is a means to remind outsiders that they are not welcome. This is especially evident in racialized violence directed toward those moving into what had been traditionally comfortably homogeneous communities, usually white.

Forms of Violence

Several recent studies have uncovered patterns of elevated rates of racial violence in the context of shifting demographics. That is, the movement of nonwhites into largely white strongholds coincides with rising incidents of hate crime. The violence can

President Barack Obama greets the sisters of James Byrd, Jr., and Matthew Shepard's mother to commemorate the enactment of the Matthew Shepard and James Byrd Jr. Hate Crimes Prevention Act in October 2009.

be seen as forms of resistance on the part of white people whose relatively uniform neighborhoods appear to be subject to what they perceive as troubling demographic change. Their intent is to shore up ways of life that have been carefully crafted by a white majority. The fear is that racial difference will also insert moral difference. Long-held stereotypes of racialized others create fears of cultural decay, loss of shared values, and rising crime rates.

Gone are the days of collective violence and race riots intended to chase blacks out of white communities. Far more typical are individual acts of violence directed at those nonwhites who dare to cross the geographical—and often economic—boundaries to "invade" white neighborhoods. In many areas of the country, this has taken the form of move-in violence, wherein nonwhite encroachment on white territory is met with an array of discouraging behavior, ranging from verbal harassment and vandalism to cross-burning, arson, and even murder. Commonly, they take the form of sustained campaigns of intimidation directed toward the newly resident "threat." Daily and ongoing barrages of verbal abuse and graffiti explicitly tell the victims they are not welcome. Malicious acts of vandalism are typical of move-in violence, and often leave the newcomer with few viable options other than withdrawal and escape.

Motivations

Understood in these terms, it is probably obvious that what we now understand to be hate crime is not a new phenomenon. While this term came into vogue only in the 1980s, the violence it describes has a lengthy history in the United States. Racial violence has, in fact, been a persistent feature of American history, from first contact to the present: massacres of Indian villages, attacks on Chinese railway laborers, lynching of African Americans, post–9/11 assaults on Middle Eastern communities are some examples.

Often, what we think of today as hate crime was intended to remove the non-white threat into distinct and isolated communities. Segregated communities do not necessarily occur naturally and of their own accord. Nothing could be further from the truth, given that the geography of race has often been the product of violent repression by the white community. For example, black ghettos were created, in part, as zones of safety, as defenses against collective assaults on blacks migrating to northern cities for work. Retreating into these emerging communities rendered black people relatively safe from the angry attacks perpetrated by threatened white laborers. Thus, they represented a segregated community grounded in violence.

For the most part, however, these actions were normative and rarely seen as a cause for action on the part of law enforcement. Indeed, police were often complicit if not directly involved themselves in the violence. However, the mobilization of a number of key interest groups in the 1980s and 1990s finally spurred the justice system to concerted action. An unexpected coalition of women's rights, gays rights, and victims' rights organizations pressed federal and state legislators to recognize the emerging notion of hate crime. In the closing decades of the 20th century, policy and lawmakers began to take hate crime seriously enough to develop legislation, policy, and procedure in the area.

Legislation

The most momentous piece of federal legislation early on was the Hate Crime Statistics Act of 1990, which mandated the collection of hate crime data by all law enforcement agencies. The HCSA defined hate crimes as: "crimes that manifest evidence of prejudice based on race, religion, sexual orientation, or ethnicity." For the most part, states that subsequently (or previously) introduced hate crime legislation have followed suit, adopting a similar definitional style. What differs across the nation is the breadth of protected classes. Minnesota, for example, records hate crimes motivated by the victim's race, religion, national origin, sex, age, disability, and sexual orientation. In New Jersey, criminal violations of persons or property are designated as hate crimes in which the victim's race, color, creed, ethnicity, or religion was a motivating factor. Oregon hate crime protections are extended to victims violated because of perceived race, color, religion, national origin, sexual orientation, marital status, political affiliation or beliefs, membership or activity in or on behalf of a labor organization or against a labor organization, physical or mental handicap, age, economic or social status, or citizenship of the victim.

There is considerable variation in the victim populations addressed by state hate crime statutes. The common categories are reduced to race, religion, and ethnicity. Sexual orientation and gender, for example, appear in only a handful of statutes, as does country of origin.

Since 1990, there have been some noteworthy revisions and additions to federal hate crime legislation. The 1994 Violent Crime Control and Law Enforcement Act mandated increased penalties for federal crimes committed on the basis of actual or perceived race, color, religion, national origin, ethnicity, or gender. The most recent legislative reform is codified in the Matthew Shepard and James Byrd, Jr., Hate Crime Prevention Act of 2009. This law added protections, at the federal level, for sexual orientation, gender, gender identity, and disability.

Enforcement

What has emerged in the two decades since the passage of the Hate Crime Statistics Act are some very consistent patterns in the social distribution of hate crimes. Race (African American), religion (Jewish), and sexual orientation (lesbian/gay) are the most frequent motivators of hate crime by perpetrators who are typically young, white males. Generally, such crimes occur in or near residences (around 30 percent), or on the street (around 20 percent), according to Federal Bureau of Investigation statistics from 2008 onward. Moreover, hate crimes tend to be urban phenomena, with the vast majority committed in cities.

The latter trend has led police departments in most major cities in the United States to develop what are known as hate or bias crime units. The most effective bias crime units share a number of key characteristics. Among the most important factors is that officers must have full investigative and intelligence gathering capacity. There are agencies that largely restrict their units to providing guidance to frontline officers, or engaging in community outreach to enhance public reporting of hate crime. This is insufficient. Those with the expertise in the nature and dynamics of the problem must themselves be leading the investigative team.

Effective units also tend to be proactive, meaning that the officers must have the capacity to engage in research and fact finding. They must be willing and able to monitor the contexts in which hate crime might emerge—religious holidays, for example, or civil rights initiatives—and be aware of the link between these events and reactionary violence. Their research skills should extend to using the Internet to also monitor the activities of organized hate groups so that they are aware of planned activities, or a rise in the frequency or intensity of online hate.

Another crucial component of their fact-finding role is their ability to connect with the communities most likely to be affected by hate crime. This latter point is especially crucial to any initiatives intended to confront hate crime. Victims and potential victims are in the best possible position to understand the dynamics of their victimization. Thus, their input will be vital to confronting and preventing hate crime intended to exclude them from the rights and mobility that should extend to all citizens and residents of a community.

Barbara Perry
University of Ontario Institute of Technology

See Also: Fear of Crime; Immigrant Neighborhoods; Racial Assault; Terrorism; Urban Incivility; Vandalism.

Further Readings

Bell, Jeannine. "Hate Thy Neighbor: Violent Racial Exclusions and the Persistence of Segregation." *Ohio State Journal of Criminal Law*, v.5/3 (2008).

Jenness, Valerie and Kendal Broad. *Hate Crimes: New Social Movements and the Politics of Violence.* New York: Aldine de Gruyter, 1998.

Levin, Jack and Jack McDevitt. *Hate Crimes Revisited: America's War on Those Who Are Different.* Boulder CO: Westview Press, 2002.

Perry, Barbara. *In the Name of Hate.* New York: Routledge, 2001.

History of Street Crime in America

Few other public policy problems have generated so much discussion and fear than has street crime in the United States. Although present in smaller towns and rural locations, illegal activity is typically associated with America's cities with the largest populations like Baltimore, Boston, Chicago, Cleveland, Detroit, Los Angeles, Miami, New York, Philadelphia, and Washington, D.C. Street crime is part of the steady daily diet of subjects that many of our news media and cultural industries (e.g.,

movies, fiction, etc.) use to attract audiences. Street crime and criminals in the United States; public, media, and political reactions to it, and scholarship surrounding this phenomenon has been a longstanding and contentious issue in American society. The problem of street crime and criminals has been a recurrent issue in the United States almost since the founding period when organized mobs and highwaymen preyed on defenseless citizens. More recently, incidents of drive-by shootings, multiple murderers, and swarming only serve to reinforce public and political concern over this kind of activity. In order to understand the most recent trajectory of street crime, the recent history (1960–2012) of this phenomenon is reviewed. In so doing, it traces both the empirical research that has been conducted and the moral panic that arose in the United States concerning this urban challenge. Street crime generally includes acts such as homicide, forcible rape, robbery, aggravated assault, burglary, larceny-theft, motor vehicle theft, and arson. In general, the legal system considers street crimes to be Type I offenses that are catalogued by the Federal Bureau of Investigation's (FBI) Uniform Crime Reports (UCR). Traditionally, Type I offenses are regarded as the most serious types of crimes.

Running throughout this history is an appreciation that not only is street crime an empirical reality, but that the response to it has been highly political. Consistently, reactions to street crime have invoked a considerable amount of fear and panic that the news media has participated in and contributed to. This reaction has not necessarily been reflective of the empirical reality. Nevertheless, it has created moral panic and/or amplified the deviance that has occurred. According to Ruth and Reitz:

Across much of the 19th and 20th centuries, the reality of crime in America was generally far different from alarmist statements and perceptions. . . . There is now a consensus that crime, including serious violent crime, was dropping from the early 1800s throughout the remainder of the 19th century and for roughly the first half of the 20th century.

The growth of street crime is coterminous with numerous urban social problems like poverty, unemployment, poor housing, a declining manufacturing base, and out-migration to the suburbs.

Urbanization, industrialization, poverty, unemployment, changing demographics, and population dislocation contribute but do not necessarily cause street crime. With respect to the later process, this can include out-migration of middle-class and upper-class individuals, and immigrants and new arrivals to the United States who chose to live in one or more urban enclaves.

During the early part of the 20th century, the federal government, through the FBI, started collecting statistics on crime. Known as the UCR, the FBI depends upon the participation of state and local law enforcement entities to submit their statistics in a timely fashion. The UCR is an inexact measure of the actual crime rate. Alternative measures, such as the Census Bureau's National Criminal Victimization Study (NCVS), have been implemented. The latter measures victimization based on interviews with members of the household. Both have been criticized for underestimating the actual amount of crime.

In terms of arrests, African Americans have been disproportionately represented in this category. Ruth and Reitz report:

> With alarming suddenness in the 1950s and 1960s, U.S. crime rates, especially . . . the number of crimes committed by African Americas per capita is considerably higher than among whites, and this has been true as far back into the 20th century as crime statistics have been gathered. . . . The white arrest rate for each crime category is standardized at a value of 100. . . . For the most feared offenses—murder, rape, and robbery—black arrest rates were more than five times the white rates. For murder, the black arrest rate was greater by more than a factor of eight. . . .

Awareness regarding street crime in America did not really begin until the 1960s.

The 1960s
During the 1960s, student demonstrations and protests against the draft and U.S. participation in Indochina, and race riots in African American communities, led to widespread property destruction and looting on U.S. college campuses and in cities. Some of these actions increased the amount of street crime in the streets of the United States.

After studies by well-known national commissions (e.g., Kerner, Rockefeller, etc.), the federal government started pumping more resources into state and local law enforcement and experiments with street crime took place, involving patrol in particular. The 1968 riots left many big city blocks in flames and ashes. Many merchants and residents decided that enough was enough and they would not rebuild. Some of the properties were insured and the owners simply pocketed the money and invested it in more secure places elsewhere. Many owners were uninsured and lost their assets.

Between 1960 and 1969, according to Dina Gordon,

> . . . official crime statistics show huge increases in both violent (104 percent) and property (123 percent). . . . Some of that increase can be attributed to technological and cultural changes that made the reporting of crimes more likely and professionalization of police that increased the likelihood that citizen reports of crime would be recorded. . . . Even acknowledging these limitations on the reliability of the data, thoughtful criminologists conclude that it is difficult to argue that no real increase in crime has taken place in the United States in the last few decades.

The 1970s
Despite the activities of the 1960s, cities continued to lose their populations and their economic base to the suburbs and the Sunbelt (southern) region of the United States. Those who could move (i.e., the middle and upper class), did. What remained were the poor, marginalized, and socially disadvantaged, who were typically African American and Hispanic. Many big cities lost their sales and property tax revenues and either declared bankruptcy and/or increasingly depended on state and federal governments for assistance (e.g., bailouts). The 1970s was also a time of great experimentation by law enforcement agencies in an attempt to eradicate street crime. Some of these practices were financially supported by the U.S. Department of Justice's National Institute of Justice and/or the Bureau of Justice Assistance. Police departments implemented different kinds of street patrols if not to minimize crime, but to lessen public fear. Additionally, there was a greater effort to monitor

ex-offenders who had been released from prison. By the end of the 1970s, there were numerous parts of well-established cities, such as Harlem, Brooklyn, and the Bronx in New York City, the combat zone in Boston, west Philadelphia, and west Baltimore, that were so plagued by street crime that they resembled war zones.

The 1980s

Between 1984 and 1993, crack, a derivative of cocaine, was made widely available in large quantities and sold cheaply throughout economically depressed areas, especially in U.S. inner cities. This led to increased drug addiction and gang violence in order to control drug markets in major centers in the United States. In order to support themselves, addicts would engage in all sorts of petty and street crimes. This period was called the crack epidemic. More recently, according to Madison Gray, "some experts are beginning to see them as the product of street culture of feuds, vendettas, retribution and violent one-upmanship that pervade what are commonly called gangs but which may not be gangs at all." In the early 1980s, official statistics seemed to indicate a decrease.

The 1990s

Although high rates of street crime were present during the early part of the 1990s, it was not until 1993 that homicide rates began dropping to levels that existed during the 1960s. According to Ruth and Reitz, "Other categories of gravely violent offences declined in the same time period, and the United States enjoyed drop-offs even among less serious offences." Needless to say, Gordon reports, "there is no denying that street crime is a very pervasive and destructive fact of life in the United States at the cusp of the 1990s. . . . Young people, males, and blacks were more likely to be victims of violent crimes than older people, women and whites."

Response to street crimes was not evenly distributed. According to Gordon:

It is easy to assume that because this terrible social problem generates so much concern in all quarters, the policies instituted in its name constitute a rationale response to the focused demands of a representative electorate. But "popular demand," in fact, issues from a highly selective sample of attentive citizens, skewed

The surge of crack cocaine use in the United States in the 1980s was called the crack epidemic. These users were smoking crack cocaine in an alley in 2008 and agreed to pose for a photo.

toward the powerful and the noisy. And that demand is both instrumental and expressive.

The 2000s

By all measures, 2000 was the safest year in the past 50 years in the United States. Homicide rates had reduced to the 1968 level. Both property and violent crimes declined as well. From 2002 to 2008, the homicide rate (5.5 individuals per 100,000 persons) remained relatively stable. A small cottage industry of scholars has devoted a considerable amount of attention trying to explain the decline in crime either in the country as a whole or in New York City in particular.

Criminal Justice Responses

The criminal justice system has responded to street crime not just with lip service, but with a slew of programs and practices, some built on criminological theory, others derived from trial and error experiences, and some based on speculation. Over the past five decades, municipalities have implemented juvenile curfews, gang injunctions, CompStat, zero-tolerance policing, increased stop and frisk actions, Project Safe streets, the Weed and Seed program, and community policing. Some of these programs have suffered from having been implemented in a haphazard fashion, and thus have had predictable results, while others have been undertaken in a logical progression.

Regardless, criminal justice reactions have had a minimal response on lowering the crime rate. At most, law enforcement and correctional activity temporarily removes offenders from the streets, displaces criminal activity from one neighborhood to another, or from the streets (e.g., open-air drug markets, prostitution) to inside buildings, where it is less visible to the public and law enforcement agencies. More important factors such as demographics (i.e., births and deaths) and the age at which individuals are most likely to commit street crimes (i.e., ages 18–35) have much to do with street crime dynamics.

Street Crime Versus Suite and State Crime

This being said, street crime, while important to city residents, seems to pale in comparison with suite crimes (i.e., white-collar and corporate crimes, theft, corruption, injury, and death), and state crime (i.e., human rights violations, extralegal violence, genocide, etc.), in terms of the number of people who are victimized and the extent of their injuries. Conceptually, these later categories of crimes are difficult for many members of the public to understand and accept because of businesses, corporations, and states operating with minimal control. Moreover, statistics on these sorts of crimes are rarely published; if they are, they are often poor or maligned, and thus the public remains ignorant on how widespread these activities are.

Conclusion

Regardless of the country, most incidents of street crime are very visceral and emotional phenomena. As long as people choose to live part of their lives in urban locations and conduct their activities in public, and as long as other people, for one reason or another, decide to rob, rape, and kill them, street crime will remain part of the social and urban fabric of America for years to come. Street crime will also exist as a staple of the news media and politicians' platforms as they clamor for issues to respectively report and/or campaign on. Street crime will remain a controversial issue for years to come.

Jeffrey Ian Ross
University of Baltimore

See Also: Crime Patterns; Drug Dealing; Gangs (Street); Police (Overview); Street Crime Defined; Suite Crimes Versus Street Crimes.

Further Readings

Flamm, Michael W. *Law and Order: Street Crime, Civil Unrest, and the Crisis of Liberalism in the 1960s.* New York: Columbia University Press, 2005.

Friedrichs, David. O. *Trusted Criminals: White Collar Crime in Contemporary Society.* 4th ed. Belmont, CA: Wadsworth Publishers, 2010.

Gordon, Dina R. *The Justice Juggernaut: Fighting Street Crime, Controlling Citizens.* New Brunswick, NJ: Rutgers University Press, 1991.

Gray, Madison. "Experts: Street Crime Too Often Blamed on Gangs." *Time* (September 2, 2009). http://www.time.com/time.printout/0,8816,1919250.html (Accessed June 2012).

Gurr, Ted Robert, et al. *Rogues, Rebels and Reformers.* Beverly Hills, CA: Sage, 1977.

Jencks, Christopher. "Is Violent Crime Increasing?" *American Prospect* (December 4, 2000). http://www.prospect.org/article/violent-crime-increasing (Accessed July 2012).

La Free, Gary. *Losing Legitimacy: Street Crime and the Decline of Social Institutions in America.* Boulder, CO: Westview Press, 1998.

Ross, Jeffrey Ian, ed. *Controlling State Crime.* 2nd ed. New Brunswick, NJ: Transaction Publishers, 2000.

Ross, Jeffrey Ian. *Policing Issues: Challenges and Controversies.* Sudbury, MA: Jones and Bartlett Learning, 2012.

Ross, Jeffrey Ian, ed. *Varieties of State Crime and Its Control.* Monsey, NJ: Criminal Justice Press, 2000.

Rothe, Dawn L. *State Criminality: The Crime of All Crimes.* Lanham, MD: Lexington Books, 2009.

Ruth, Henry and Kevin Reitz. *The Challenge of Crime: Rethinking our Response.* Cambridge, MA: Harvard University Press, 2003.

Sheingold, Stuart. *The Politics of Street Crime.* Philadelphia: Temple University Press, 1992.

Homelessness

Homelessness refers broadly to the experience of people who lack their own regular residence or dwelling. This can include conditions in which people are without a home altogether and are compelled to live or sleep in the open in public spaces such as parks, or private spaces such as parking lots, that are not designed or intended primarily for human accommodation. Such experiences are referred to as street homelessness or visible homelessness, as people living in such conditions are forced to spend much of their time living openly on sidewalks or other visible spaces. At the same time, the street homeless often avoid sleeping on open streets, preferring unoccupied buildings, areas under bridges, and abandoned lots within urban or suburban areas.

Homelessness also refers to conditions of precarious or temporary residence, such as in shelters or drop-ins. These examples provide the most commonly discussed cases of homelessness and the forms of homelessness that are at the center of most public and popular discourse. In addition, however, homelessness also includes situations in which people are compelled to rely on ad hoc housing from friends, neighbors, or relatives. Experiences such as "couch surfing," in which a person is dependent for temporary housing on the generosity of other individuals, are less recognized and less discussed examples of homelessness.

Housing as a Human Right

Decent housing is viewed as a basic human right and recognized as such in the United Nations Declaration of Human Rights. For most of human history, housing has been part of community membership; even nonelites have had claim to some form of basic housing. This has changed with the development of economies based on market exchange and profit. Homelessness has been a regular characteristic of life within capitalist social systems as housing is made into a commodity like any other and people are required to pay rent on their dwelling or purchase their residence.

Homelessness has become a growing problem within wealthier industrialized countries during the last three decades, the so-called period of neoliberalism or neoliberal capitalism. Neoliberalism represents a conservative or New Right ideological approach to social policy in which programs such as welfare, social housing, rent controls, and shelters, which primarily benefit the poor and working classes, are cancelled or defunded in favor of programs such as tax cuts and corporate grants, which

exclusively benefit the wealthy and socially privileged. During the neoliberal period, governments in countries like Britain, Canada, and the United States have systematically cancelled key provisions of the welfare state. One result has been a growth in homelessness as people are left with fewer means to afford housing, and fewer options for lower-cost or subsidized housing. For example, a 1991 study of 182 U.S. cities with populations over 100,000 found that homelessness rates tripled between 1981 and 1989 for the 182 cities taken together.

Unemployment, relating to workplace closures and the shift to a service sector economy during the neoliberal period, has also left large numbers of the working classes in more precarious economic conditions. At the same time, governments have responded to the problems created by social service cuts through an increased emphasis on punitive measures to contain and control growing ranks of the poor. This has meant not only increases in police and prison spending, but also a range of legislation directed at criminalizing the poor and homeless.

Criminializing the Homeless

Homeless people, particularly the street homeless, have been targets of violence, both interpersonal as well as legislative. In cities from Miami to Los Angeles, there have been numerous cases of physical attacks on homeless people by vigilantes, including the killing of a homeless man by armed forces reservists. Each year several homeless people die as a result of the lack of shelter. Governments, particularly at the municipal and state level, have contributed to moral panics around homelessness by publicly associating homelessness with criminal activity.

The history of criminal punishment targeting homeless people shows the class character of governments, policing, and legislation, even within liberal democracies such as Britain, Canada, and the United States. In the mid-1300s, following the Peasants' Revolt, constables in England were given authority to jail so-called vagabonds. During the 1500s, homeless people could be imprisoned and were often branded with a "V" (for vagabond or vagrant) to designate their "crime." A second offense was subject to the punishment of death. The experience of homelessness expanded in the early period of capitalist development following the Enclosure Acts, which closed off the commons and left peasant communities without means of subsistence.

From the 17th to the 19th centuries, successive "poor laws" provided governments in England the legal means to arrest and detain homeless people and vagabonds. Under the poor laws, homeless people could be transferred to workhouses where they were required to labor. Many homeless people were also transported to various colonies as convicts.

More recently legislation has focused on the survival strategies by which homeless people sustain themselves on the streets. This includes prohibitions against public display of possessions to punitive legislation that bans panhandling and squeegeeing car windshields for money. In New York City, the administration of Mayor Rudolph Giuliani initiated policies informed by the Broken Windows Theory—the idea that, left unchecked, visible activities that might be considered a nuisance will result in more serious criminal activity—to remove homeless people from the streets of the city. Homeless people were removed to shelters in suburban areas away from their social networks and the resources they relied on for survival, such as drop-in centers and cheap food sources. Many ended up in hospitals and in prisons, but few were permanently housed.

Survey data from the National Coalition for the Homeless and the National Law Center on Homelessness and Poverty done between 2002 and 2006 indicated a 14 percent increase in laws prohibiting sitting or lying down in public spaces in U.S. cities. In addition, there was an 18 percent increase in laws prohibiting so-called aggressive panhandling, a practice often associated with the homeless.

Clinging to the Commons
The claim that parks are exclusively, or even primarily, for the use of children and families (of the housed), is in fact an ideological, and erroneous, political representation. Never mind that most of humanity has ranged over the land for most of human history. Never mind either that in many places the memory of the commons, prior to enclosure, still holds a powerful place in civic narratives, revived as environmental concerns have caused many to question the broad dangers of private ownership of the planet.

More than that, there have been important moments in history when the poor and homeless have taken to camping in relatively large numbers in parks and other public spaces. Certainly this was the case during the mass economic depressions of the 1910s and 1930s, when economic troubles left many homeless. It was also a common occurrence in certain areas during the 1960s and 1970s, partly an expression of that desire for the commons. That the crisis of homelessness since the 1980s has led more to seek out this option as a means of sustenance or survival is not surprising.

Jeff Shantz
Kwantlen Polytechnic University

See Also: Broken Windows Theory; Juvenile Curfews; Loitering; Mental Illness; Panhandling or Begging; Pickpocketing; Skid Row; Theft and Larceny; Urban Ethnography; Victims, Tourist.

Further Readings
Burt, Martha R. *Over the Edge: The Growth of Homelessness in the 1980s.* Thousand Oaks, CA: Sage, 1992.
Jasinski, Jana L., et al. *Hard Lives, Mean Streets: Violence in the Lives of Homeless Women.* Northeastern Series on Gender, Crime, and Law. Lebanon, NH: Northeastern University Press, 2010.
Schutt, Russell K., et al. *Homelessness, Housing, and Mental Illness.* Cambridge, MA: Harvard University Press, 2011.

Homophobic Assault

The crime of homophobic assault includes verbal, physical, and sexual abuse of individuals who are perceived to be gay, lesbian, bisexual, or transgender. As a crime, homophobic assault generally did not receive much attention until the mid- to late 1980s and early 1990s. However, in the two decades since then, homophobic violence has become more commonly reported, and today is the third-most reported hate crime in the United States (behind racially-biased and religion-biased offenses). The frequency and nature of this type of crime underlines the need for its continued understanding.

Homophobia is a severe negative reaction to those who are perceived to violate the established social norm of heterosexualism. Homophobic assault, then, is a form of response by offenders to victims' perceived deviance; offenders perceive themselves to be appointed gatekeepers of heterosexual identity. Offenders most often target men perceived to be gay, because such men are seen as subverting the traditional male gender role, more than lesbians are perceived deviant from a traditional female gender role.

Offenders may perceive that their actions earn them increased social standing among their own social groups. Although the numbers of reported homophobic assaults have increased dramatically in recent years, this is still widely believed to be a very under-reported offense. The most common reason for victims to not report to the police is fear of their homosexual identity being known, and fear of antihomosexual actions by police officers.

The 2010 Federal Bureau of Investigation (FBI) Hate Crime Statistics showed criminal incidents where offender bias was motivated by sexual orientation of the victim to be the third-most commonly reported form of hate crime; first was race, second was religion, fourth was ethnicity, and fifth was disability. The report showed that of 1,277 sexual-orientation biased incidents, 739 were antimale homosexual, 144 were antifemale homosexual, another 347 were unspecified antihomosexual, and the remainder included 26 antibisexual and 21 antiheterosexual incidents. These incidents impacted 1,528 victims, defined by the FBI report as "a person, business, institution, or society as a whole." There were a reported total of 1,516 known offenders.

The 1,277 incidents reported represented a 4.4 percent increase over the 1,223 such incidents in the FBI's 2009 report. The proportions of the breakout categories were roughly equivalent year to year. Sexual-orientation bias crimes made up 19.3 percent of the total of 6,628 incidents in 2010; they accounted for 18.5 percent of the 6,598 incidents in 2009. The FBI compiles the data based on reports from nearly 2,000 law enforcement agencies. Offense categories tracked in the hate crimes report include murder and non-negligent manslaughter, forcible rape, aggravated assault, simple assault, intimidation, robbery, burglary, larceny-theft, motor vehicle theft, arson, destruction/damage/vandalism, and other crimes against persons, property, or society.

Characteristics of Offenses and Offenders

The majority of homophobic assaults occur in locations frequented by large numbers of gay and lesbian individuals. Such locations include near bars and nightclubs specifically aimed at a gay clientele, reputedly gay-friendly neighborhoods, parks, workplaces, business parking lots, and even private residences. Although there are some patterns of regularity regarding where such offenses occur, these types of locations are not the only places such offenses happen. As a result, one common consequence of such assaults is fear among gay men and lesbians who are living openly.

There have emerged identifiable patterns with the known characteristics of offenders of homophobic assault. The first most identifiable characteristic is that almost all offenders are male. There are very few cases that involve female offenders.

In addition to this, the crime tends to be carried out by groups of individuals, and usually not a lone assailant. This could possibly be because it assures the potential status rewards of this behavior as previously mentioned. Another common characteristic is that almost all offenders are Caucasian and are younger, usually in their 20s or early 30s. It has also been suggested that some offenders are suppressing their own homosexual identity, and therefore assault perceived homosexuals as a result of their inner conflict. However, the most extreme offenders usually have medically diagnosed phobias of homosexuals.

The majority of homophobic assaults fall into three broad categories, which include verbal, physical, and sexual assault. Verbal assault can include incidents where sexually derogatory language and homophobic language is directed toward the victims. Physical assault can include spitting, punching, kicking, and using a weapon. This also includes both simple and aggravated assault, with most incidents of physical assault using a mix of verbal assault as well.

Sexual assault, although rare, does occur. Some of the most common forms of this involve a male offender who will force a perceived male homosexual to perform oral sex on him, or even rape a perceived lesbian. However, the most extreme types of homosexual violence include rape and murder.

Victims of homophobic assault have been reported to face a number of serious mental health aftereffects from these assaults. Many of the common side effects include headaches, trouble sleeping, general fear, depression, problems with substance abuse resulting from coping mechanisms, and perhaps even suppressing their homosexual identity. Although the severity of the aftereffects depends on the severity of their attack and other factors, most keep experiencing these effects years after their attack occurs.

Laws and Enforcement Measures

Legal response to homophobic assault is largely built upon the landmark 1964 federal Civil Rights Act, which permits (encourages) federal prosecution of an offender who "willingly injures, intimidates or interferes with another person, or attempts to do so, by force because of the other person's race, color, religion or national origin." Thirty years later, federal sentencing laws were bolstered with increased penalties for such crimes. Then, in October 2009, President Obama signed into law the Matthew Shepard and James Byrd, Jr., Hate Crimes Prevention Act, which extended the existing statutes to apply to sexual-orientation-bias crimes. At the state level, matters are more complex. While nearly every state has its own criminal statutes covering violence or intimidation motivated by bias, only in 31 states is sexual orientation an enumerated type of bias. Just 14 states specify transgender and/or gender identity as recognized categories of bias-motivated crime.

Homophobic assault, as the most common form of sexual-orientation-biased hate crime, is a critical point of opportunity for education and advocacy—as well as prevention and prosecution—as justice institutions and enforcement agencies attempt to keep pace with cultural trends and expanding civil rights in American society.

Richard Tewksbury
Andrew Denney
University of Louisville

See Also: Fear of Crime; Hate Crime; Rape and Sexual Assault; Routine Activity Theory.

Further Readings

Comstock, G. D. "Victims of Anti-Gay/Lesbian Violence." *Journal of Interpersonal Violence*, v.4/1 (1989).

Garnets, Linda, et al. "Violence and Victimization of Lesbians and Gay Men." *Journal of Interpersonal Violence*, v.5/3 (1990).

Stotzer, Rebecca. *Comparison of Hate Crime Rates Across Protected and Unprotected Groups.* Los Angeles: UCLA School of Law, 2007.

Tomsen, Stephen. "Homophobic Violence, Cultural Essentialism, and Shifting Sexual Identities." *Social Legal Studies*, v.15/3 (2006).

U.S. Department of Justice. "Hate Crime Statistics, 2010." November 2011. http://www.fbi.gov/about-us/cjis/ucr/hate-crime/2010 (Accessed April 2012).

Willis, Danny. "Meanings in Adult Male Victims' Experiences of Hate Crime and Its Aftermath." *Issues in Mental Health Nursing, v.*29/6 (2008).

Hooliganism

Hooliganism is a catch-all term used to describe a range of angry, aggressive, unruly, or destructive behaviors typically carried out in public spaces such as streets, public squares, or parks. Often the term is associated with the rowdy behaviors and conflicts involving sports fan clubs, especially football (soccer) clubs. Sometimes sports hooliganism escalates into large-scale riots.

Hooliganism also refers to politically motivated street fights and intimidating tactics deployed publicly by members of political groups or parties. An example of this type of political hooliganism is provided in the street marches and attacks on political opponents carried out by the Sturmabteilung (SA), or paramilitary "brownshirts" wing of the National Socialist (or Nazi) Party, in Germany during the 1920s and 1930s.

Origins in Europe

Most accounts trace the origin of the term *hooligan* to the 1890s in London, England. Early references to the term appeared in stage musicals and novels, with the first recorded use on court or police records appearing in 1894 in reference to activities of a London gang. Authors Arthur Conan Doyle and H. G. Wells both made reference to hooliganism in novels published in the first years of the 1900s.

By the mid- to late 20th century, the term *hooliganism* developed a very strong association with public acts of violence and property damage carried out by soccer club supporters, particularly supporters associated with English teams. Indeed the contemporary popularization of the term is largely because of its connection with high-profile acts of aggression involving these sport supporters. Hooliganism in soccer can refer to pregame or postgame fights between supporters of rival clubs, sometimes prearranged. It can also include fights during matches and can become stadium-wide clashes involving hundreds of people. In its most extreme outcome, soccer hooliganism has developed into full-scale riots, inside and outside stadiums, and has resulted in the deaths of participants or bystanders.

In some cases soccer supporter clubs bring together sporting and political issues as supporter clubs advocate political positions of the left or right. In such cases political opposition can mesh with fan rivalries to encourage acts of hooliganism against opponents. While soccer hooliganism was little remarked upon before the end of World War II, it drew greater attention, and the term became more widespread, during the 1950s and 1960s. Some scholars suggest that this relates to growing frustration and politicization among working-class, particularly blue-collar youth, expressing their general dissatisfaction with economic and social changes that rendered their status more precarious.

Hooliganism is associated with soccer supporters in every country in Europe, with supporters in Russia, Serbia, Croatia, France, Germany, and Italy gaining particular notoriety. In countries such as Germany, Italy, and Denmark, there have been connections between soccer hooliganism and far-right, neofascist, and racist organizing. North American team supporters, with soccer less prominent than other sports, have fewer associations with hooliganism.

U.S. Sports Troubles

Hooliganism has been associated with numerous sports riots in the United States. Sports riots in the United States, as opposed to Canada and Europe, tend to follow a team victory rather than a loss. The riots are part celebration and part performance. Losses tend to produce feelings of demoralization and retreat. Observer Jerry Lewis concludes from studies of hundreds of sports riots in the United States that there are two common denominators in the riots. First is the availability of a "natural" or familiar urban gathering space. Second is the presence of a large proportion of young (under 30 years old) white males. Indeed sports riots are more gender-exclusive than are political riots. Alcohol also often plays a part in sports riots. The riot in Los Angeles following the Lakers' National Basketball Association victory in 2010 occurred despite a massive riot police presence which had been mobilized as part of preparedness protocol developed after

the 2000 riots that broke out following a previous Lakers championship.

Some sports riots emerge in contexts of social upheaval and rebellion. The riots in Detroit, Michigan, following the Tigers' Major League Baseball World Series victory in 1968 came only a year after that city's devastating so-called race riots of 1967, which had been the largest-scale riot in the United States during the 1960s. The Detroit riots of 1984—following another Tigers championship victory—came in a period of economic decline and working-class dissent in the city. Sports riots have not been without casualties. During the Boston riots following the Red Sox World Series victory in 2004, one young woman was killed by police.

Moral Panics

Hooliganism, or popular constructions of hooliganism within mainstream media and government discourses, has been a common feature within "moral panics" in the late 20th and early 21st centuries. Typically within moral panics, charges of hooliganism are mobilized by local commercial interests intent on controlling youthful activities that they believe will threaten their profits or economic gains. The claims of commercial actors are taken up and magnified by media and local politicians seeking to maintain or extend their relationships with commercial donors or patrons. Within such crises, youthful activities that are not necessarily harmful, such as horseplay or loud arguments, are presented as examples of hooliganism needing to be controlled by police or government. The work of sociologist Stanley Cohen is groundbreaking in examining the formation of moral panics and the attribution of hooliganism, particularly by power holders against members of youth subcultures, in the mobilization of public fear and appeals for law and order policies to clamp down on the supposed hooligans.

Charges of hooliganism have often been leveled by governments against the activities of political opponents or social activists as a way to discredit them and dismiss their political grievances. Politicians often refer to protesters as hooligans, and their actions, which may include property destruction, as hooliganism. Opponents of capitalist globalization have been accused of hooliganism for their part in organizing and carrying out high-profile demonstrations during meetings of representatives of global capital such as the World Trade

Organization (WTO), International Monetary Fund (IMF), or World Bank (WB).

The use of the term *hooligan* provides an easy tool for dismissing acts of social upheaval without actually trying to understand underlying social structural forces, such as class, poverty, racism, unemployment, dispossession, or social stratification. The class or status background of those engaged in acts identified as hooliganism can be telling. In addition, sentences given to people involved in acts labeled as hooliganism are typically disproportionately harsh for those from lower-income backgrounds. In contexts in which people lack legitimized means for expressing social, economic, or political frustration or dissatisfaction, hooliganism will likely become a means of expression. It may even be a necessary social "safety valve" for releasing pent-up pressures. Yet, the term *hooliganism* is largely ideological in character, serving as a way to individualize what are social issues as a method to dismiss them.

Jeff Shantz
Kwantlen Polytechnic University

See Also: Alcohol and Drug Use; Crime–Consumerism Nexus; Flash Mobs; Gangs (Street); Homelessness; Mobs and Riots; Vandalism.

Further Readings

Frosdick, Steve and Peter Marsh. *Football Hooliganism*. London: Willan, 2005.

Humphries, Stephen. *Hooligans or Rebels? Oral History of Working Class Childhood and Youth, 1889–1939*. Oxford: Wiley Blackwell, 1995.

Lewis, Jerry. *Sports Fan Violence in North America*. Lanham, MD: Rowman & Littlefield, 2007.

Millie, Andrew. *Securing Respect: Behavioural Expectations and Anti-Social Behaviour in the UK*. London: Polity, 2009.

Pearson, Geoffrey. *Hooligan: A History of Respectable Fears*. New York: Palgrave Macmillan, 1983.

Hot Spots

Crime is not randomly distributed; it tends to be concentrated in certain areas. Researchers who have found these patterns have taken to calling high-crime areas "hot spots." Identified crime hot spots can be broken down into specific areas, including neighborhoods, streets, housing complexes, public plazas and parking areas, and various other types of spaces. The identification and public knowledge of hot spots not only allows citizens to avoid high-crime areas, but also allows police administrators to concentrate resources in order to maximize their impact against street crime.

Research and Major Theories

Researchers first discovered hot spots while researching domestic assaults and homicides. Studying Kansas City, Missouri, they discovered that in about 85 percent of cases, police had been called to the crime location at least one time before. In about 50 percent of cases, police had been called to that location five or more times. Other research specifically looking to identify hot spots found similar patterns regarding the concentration of crime.

L. Sherman, P. Gartin, and M. Buerger, in their seminal work in the 1980s, reported that relatively few hot spot places generated a majority of calls to police. Around half of all calls came from only 3 percent of places within the city of Minneapolis, one study showed. More importantly, they found that all the calls for robberies, rapes, and auto thefts came from less than 3 percent of all possible places.

There are many criminological theories to explain the existence of crime hot spots, including routine activity theory, offender search theory, the theory of crime generators and attractors, and social disorganization. Each theory explains why more crimes (or criminals) are located in some areas relative to others. Routine activity theory relates instances of hot spots to increased amounts of suitable targets (as in densely populated urban settings) and lack of guardianship or place management at specific places. According to offender search theory, hot spots appear along nodes and paths of potential offenders. Hot spots can also appear in the forms of crime generators, places where noncriminal enterprises generate many crime targets (e.g., bars, automated teller machine [ATM] locations, pool halls), or crime attractors, places where criminals are attracted to other criminal opportunities (e.g., parking lots). Social disorganization theory suggests that hot spots occur in areas where social control is low.

Mapping Down

Hot spots can exist according to many different levels of measurement and analysis. However, researchers primarily use three: neighborhood level, street level, and place level. Neighborhood-level hot spots refer to entire blocks, communities, or census tracts with increased crime. Street-level hot spots refer to individual corridors or blocks of streets with increased levels of crime. Place-level hot spots can refer to many things, such as specific buildings, addresses, or even isolated units such as ATMs.

No matter what level researchers use to define a hot spot, they are mapped in similar ways using spatial analysis tools and geographic information systems. Similar to placing pins on a map, these tools allow crime mappers to quickly visualize hot spots on a map, whether they be crime-specific occurrences or general crime activity rates.

Awareness of hot spots and the ability to map them has affected how both civilian official and police administrators to respond. This is seen every day as public officials, aware that civilians tend to avoid areas where they perceive crime levels to be elevated, can utilize hard data to lobby for increased security measures in sharply identified zones. In the same vein, knowledge of hot spots gives police an avenue to direct their always finite resources to specific areas where they know crime will most likely occur. This policy is often called "intelligence-based policing" or "problem-oriented policing".

Police Response

One police strategy that has stemmed from knowledge of hot spots is the use of crackdowns. Crackdowns, also called sweeps, are police initiatives that focus major resources on specific crimes in specific areas for brief periods. Use of crackdowns has been shown to reduce crime in hot spots, albeit for a limited time.

Another use of hot spots by police has been the CompStat process started in New York City in the early 1990s. Through this process, identified crime hot spots are relayed to precinct commanders, who in turn develop strategies to eliminate them. Weekly and monthly meetings between precinct commanders and police administrators occur in order to update hot spots and develop new strategies to reduce them.

The identification of hot spots of crime also helps police, citizens, and other social and government agencies to prevent crime. The identification of a hot spot directs attention to the characteristics of that place that might explain high levels of crime. In theory at least, changing the nature of a place can change the rate of crime there. Better lighting, changing traffic patterns, installing fences, and similar efforts can help prevent crime. Hot spot comprehension contributes to better understanding of crime and can, in turn, lead to more effective prevention.

Jeffrey E. Clutter
Lawrence F. Travis III
University of Cincinnati

See Also: CompStat; Crime Mapping; Crime Patterns; Policing, Problem-Oriented; Routine Activity Theory.

Further Readings

Braga, Anthony A. "The Effects of Hot Spots Policing on Crime." *Annals of the American Academy of Political and Social Science*, v.578/1 (2001).

Eck, John E, Spencer Chainey, James G. Cameron, Michael Leitner, and Ronald E. Wilson. "Mapping Crime: Understanding Hot Spots" NCJ 209393. Washington, DC: National Institute of Justice, 2005.

Eck, John E. and David L. Weisburd, eds. *Crime and Place: Crime Prevention Studies*. Monsey, NY: Criminal Justice Press, 1995.

Sherman, Lawrence W., Patrick R. Gartin, and Michael E. Buerger. "Hot Spots of Predatory Crime: Routine Activities and the Criminology of Place." *Criminology*, v.27/1 (1989).

I

Immigrant Neighborhoods

There is a popular perception that immigrant neighborhoods are criminogenic. The perception that immigration leads to crime is based partially on early criminological research, such as the seminal work *Juvenile Delinquency and Urban Areas*, written in the early 20th century by Clifford Shaw and Henry McKay. This work found that communities in which immigrants tended to reside had higher rates of street crime than other neighborhoods. In addition to this academic work, widely held stereotypes regarding immigrants and the areas in which they live have contributed to public opinion that immigrant neighborhoods experience high levels of property crime and violence. However, this idea is debated by modern scholars, who argue that immigrant neighborhoods in fact have lower crime rates than communities with fewer immigrants.

This entry reviews the work on crime in immigrant neighborhoods. The first section will discuss important changes to immigration that are believed to be responsible for the change in the effect of immigration on crime. The second section will outline the theoretical explanations for higher and lower rates of crime within immigrant neighborhoods. Third and finally, the state of the empirical research on immigration and crime will be discussed.

Changing Nature of Immigration

Patterns of immigration since the 1980s are vastly different from those seen in earlier eras of American history. Immigration from Europe, which was the major source of immigration in the late 19th and early 20th centuries, has slowed significantly; many recent immigrants come from various parts of Central and South America, Asia, and Africa. Therefore, native-born citizens are typically unfamiliar with the variety of today's (early 21st century) immigrants in terms of ethnicity, languages spoken, religious practices, and cultural backgrounds. These differences are important for understanding native attitudes toward immigration; earlier immigrants had cultural beliefs and practices that were similar to or at least recognizable to the majority of Americans.

The spatial concentration of immigrants within the United States has also changed considerably. Traditionally, immigrants settled in major cities, mainly in the northeast, although other large cities (such as Chicago) experienced high rates of immigration as well. Recently, there have been significant increases in the immigrant populations residing in smaller cities and even rural areas in the south and midwest. Communities within these areas are less accustomed to high levels of immigrants than are neighborhoods within traditional migrant poles. Therefore, immigrant communities within these new immigrant destinations are likely to experience

Shulman's Market in the Southwest Waterfront neighborhood of Washington, D.C., was established by a Jewish Lithuanian immigrant named Harry Shulman. The community remained, along with other immigrant neighborhoods, until urban revitalization and eminent domain forced residents to move. The majority of the buildings in these neighborhoods were razed, including the one pictured above.

more negative consequences than are those in areas with established histories of immigration.

It is important to note that these changes in immigration have occurred during periods marked by major changes to the economy. The economic shift from an industrial to service industry has made it more difficult for both immigrants and native-born residents to obtain employment. This difficulty would be expected to affect communities' abilities to control crime, as well as individual motivations for criminal activity.

Furthermore, changes in immigration laws during the 20th century have made it more difficult for many foreigners to immigrate legally. This difficulty increases the number of undocumented immigrants entering the country and residing in certain neighborhoods. An increase in undocumented immigration makes formal social control within these immigrant neighborhoods difficult, thereby increasing the importance of informal control within the community.

Traditional Theory

Criminologist Charis Kubrin's review of the immigration and crime literature outlines the proposed conceptual links between immigration and crime. The theoretical work in this field has posited several explanations for both increased and decreased crime in immigrant communities. The overview below summarizes Kubrin's discussion of the conceptual advances in immigration and crime research.

There are several theoretical explanations for a positive relationship between immigration and crime. First, the most basic reason to expect immigration to result in an increase in crime is that immigration results in a demographic shift toward crime-prone populations. Immigrants are disproportionately young males, the group most likely to engage in criminal activity. Immigrant women exhibit higher rates of fertility, thus further contributing to the disproportionate youthfulness of immigrant populations in the United States. Finally, current immigrants tend to have low educational attainment and few professional skills, making them less likely to find high-paying jobs. Therefore, increases in immigration are expected to correspond with increases in the proportion of the population that is at high risk for criminal activity, which is expected to increase crime rates.

Second, immigrants are likely to settle in poor areas, which are already inhabited by individuals likely to be financially pressured to commit crime. An influx of immigrants places additional strain on the job market and provides additional competition for other resources, increasing the motivation for crime in native-born residents of immigrant communities. For this reason, immigrant communities are expected to have higher rates of crime committed by native-born residents of the community as well as crime committed by immigrants.

A third explanation of a positive relationship between immigration and street crime comes from the theory of social disorganization. Traditionally, newly arrived immigrants settled into poor areas until they were financially stable enough to move to better neighborhoods. Therefore, immigration caused population instability in these areas, as neighborhoods with high proportions of immigrant residents were likely to experience a great deal of population turnover. This residential instability is believed to decrease the familiarity among residents of a community, decreasing their ability and willingness to exert informal social control by performing surveillance and intervening in criminal situations. Because of this diminished informal social control among neighbors, the neighborhood is expected to experience a higher rate of crime.

Finally, scholars argue that immigrant communities are more likely to experience crime because immigrants are more likely to be recruited into illegal drug markets. Immigrant youth are likely to be recruited into gangs, partly because of their demographic profile (they are generally young males from nonwhite groups) and the social disorganization of the areas in which they reside. In addition to these characteristics, young immigrants or first-generation Americans often experience cultural conflict with the native population, making membership in a gang composed of their ethnic group particularly attractive. Also, immigrants are often coerced to work in illegal markets in order to pay off debts to the gangs that smuggled them into the country.

Current Controversy

While there are several posited explanations for a positive relationship between immigration and crime, scholars have recently suggested that immigration decreases crime, rather than increasing it. There are several arguments that support this viewpoint. First, most individuals who choose to immigrate are not criminally motivated; immigrants generally relocate to the United States in order to find employment and obtain greater financial success than is available in their home countries. Immigrants are highly motivated to live conventional, law-abiding lives. As such, immigrant communities may actually experience below-average levels of crime.

A second reason to expect lower rates of crime in immigrant communities is the potentially strong formal social control exerted in such areas. The police may focus on these areas to a greater extent than other communities due to the general public's belief that immigrant communities are criminogenic. Because an increased police presence is assumed to deter criminals, immigrant communities that receive attention from the police should have less crime than other communities, on which the police concentrate less.

Third, immigrant neighborhoods should experience less street crime because they are now more socially organized than they were previously. As noted above, immigrant communities in the late 19th and early 20th centuries were characterized by residential instability, which decreased the ability of residents to exert informal social control. Changes in the nature of immigration have resulted in less social disorganization in immigrant communities. Rather than settling in disorganized areas for short periods of time, immigrants now tend to settle more permanently in areas inhabited by members of their ethnic group.

Scholars thus argue that modern immigrant communities benefit from social organization due to residential stability and a lack of family disruption. This social organization increases the informal social control practiced by members of the community.

Furthermore, immigrant communities contain ethnic enclaves that provide support in obtaining resources and dealing with cultural differences between the immigrant and native groups. These support systems help alleviate the strain experienced by immigrants within the community, making them less likely to participate in criminal activities.

Empirical Evidence

To date, extensive empirical research has been conducted to determine whether the expected links between immigration and street crime exist. Although there are several reasons to expect immigrant neighborhoods to have high rates of crime, this expectation is not well supported by research. Rather, many studies find that either there is no difference in crime rates between immigrant and native communities, or that immigrant communities experience lower rates of crime.

Early criminological research, such as that originating from the Chicago School, demonstrated the tendency of immigrants to temporarily settle in poor areas that were characterized by high crime rates. The most notable of these early studies is Clifford Shaw and Henry McKay's *Juvenile Delinquency and Urban Areas*, which found that crime clustered in areas within cities, and that these patterns remained constant over time even though the demographic makeup of the areas changed. This discovery that certain areas maintained high crime rates regardless of the group living within them led to the emergence of the social disorganization tradition. Early studies of social disorganization typically included a variable representing immigration, such as proportion of foreign-born, as a structural indicator of social disorganization. These studies generally found that immigrant communities suffered from crime to a greater extent than other communities.

However, due to the changes in immigration patterns discussed above, more recent research does not find the relationship that Shaw and McKay found between immigration and crime. A large body of empirical research demonstrates that communities with high proportions of immigrants experience less crime than communities with fewer immigrants. Furthermore, many individual-level studies find that the foreign-born engage in less crime than their native-born counterparts; such findings suggest that communities with higher percentages of foreign-born residents should experience less crime than similar communities with few immigrants.

There are some major limitations of the current research on immigrant communities that make it difficult to fully understand the relationship between immigration and crime. First, most of the existing studies have simply established correlations between immigration and crime. Few studies test the intervening mechanisms through which immigration is expected to increase or decrease crime. Because of this limitation, it is unknown at this time why immigrant communities experience lower rates of crime than other communities.

Second, most studies test for correlations that exist at one point in time. Therefore, while it is possible to find evidence that immigrant communities experience different crime rates than other communities, these differences are not necessarily attributable to the presence of immigrants within those communities. Finally, most research does not examine possible nuanced effects of immigration on crime. The few studies that do examine such nuances suggest, for instance, that immigration's effects are race specific (i.e., there is some indication that immigration has differential effects on white, black, and Latino crime rates). As another example, there is evidence that immigration influences crime differently in traditional areas of settlement than in newer immigrant locations.

Conclusion

It is popularly believed that immigrant communities experience higher rates of street crime than communities in which few immigrants reside. While traditional theoretical and empirical work demonstrated a higher degree of criminal activity in immigrant communities, more recent work suggests that modern immigration no longer affects crime in the same way. Scholars suggest that changes in immigration patterns have changed immigrant communities, making them less suitable for criminal activity. In fact, modern immigrant communities may be less criminogenic than similar communities made up of nonimmigrants.

There is still debate over the idea that immigrant communities experience less street crime than similar nonimmigrant neighborhoods. Future research should attempt to improve upon the existing work, primarily by conducting more longitudinal research and testing the intervening mechanisms suggested by theory. Longitudinal research will aid in establishing a link between immigration and crime rates. Measurement and inclusion of intervening variables between immigration and crime rates will assist criminologists in understanding the mechanism through which immigrant communities become more or less criminal.

Susan McNeeley
Pamela K. Wilcox
University of Cincinnati

See also: Asian Gangs; Chicago, Illinois; Crime Mapping; Immigrant Neighborhoods; Latino Gangs; Street Crime, Popular Portrayals of; Urbanization.

Further Readings

Desmond, Scott A. and Charis E. Kubrin. "The Power of Place: Immigrant Communities and Adolescent Violence." *Sociological Quarterly*, v.50/4 (2009).

Kubrin, Charis E. "Immigration and Crime." In *The Handbook of Criminological Theory*, Francis T. Cullen and Pamela Wilcox, eds. New York: Oxford University Press, 2012.

Martinez, Ramiro. "Coming to America: The Impact of the New Immigration on Crime." In *Immigration and Crime: Race, Ethnicity, and Violence*, Ramiro Martinez and Abel Valenzuela, eds. New York: New York University Press, 2006.

Sampson, Robert J. "Rethinking Crime and Immigration." *Contexts*, v.7/1 (2008).

Shaw, Clifford R. and Henry D. McKay. *Juvenile Delinquency and Urban Areas: A Study of Rates of Delinquency in Relation to Differential Characteristics of Local Communities in American Cities.* Chicago: University of Chicago Press, 1942.

Singer, Audrey. *The Rise of New Immigrant Gateways.* Washington, DC: Brookings Institution, 2004.

Indianapolis, Indiana

Indianapolis is a large metropolitan area with a significant street crime problem, violent crime in particular. The city's consolidation with Marion County has provided unique opportunities for law enforcement and also posed problems for comparing crime rates over time and with other cities. Numerous public safety initiatives have been implemented in the city to reduce street crime, with some success.

The City

Indianapolis is the capital and largest city in the state of Indiana. With a population of 820,445 as of the 2010 census, the city is the 12th-largest in the United States. Founded in the 19th century to serve as a central locale for state government, the city grew to become a national center of industry, including production of early American automobiles. The latter half of the 20th century saw Indianapolis decline as a base for manufacturing; the city suffered from economic stagnation and a lack of modern development until the recent revitalization of the downtown in the 1990s and a turn to service and other new industries.

Indianapolis serves as the county seat of Marion County, and the city and county share a unique history. In 1970, following action by the Indiana State Assembly, the governments of the city of Indianapolis and Marion County were consolidated through legislation known as Unigov. The city grew from the 26th-largest, with a 1960 population of 476,258, to the 11th-largest in 1970, with a population of 744,624. Under the law's provision, the city of Indianapolis incorporated all the territory within Marion County with the exception of four excluded cities or towns. The excluded cities and towns maintain municipal autonomy, including the ability to maintain police and fire services, but elect members to the government of the consolidated city-county council and vote in Indianapolis mayoral elections. Eleven smaller towns were consolidated into the city while maintaining limited autonomy, such as the right to levy certain taxes and maintain a police force.

Law enforcement in the consolidated city was undertaken jointly by the Indianapolis Police Department (IPD) and the Marion County Sheriff's Department until 2005, when action by the City-county council merged the two entities and formed the Indianapolis Metropolitan Police Department (IMPD). From 2005 until 2007, IMPD was headed by the elected sheriff of Marion County. However, in 2007, the city-county council voted to transfer power over IMPD to the mayor's office.

Several federal enforcement agencies maintain offices in Indianapolis, including the Federal Bureau of Investigation (FBI), the Bureau of Alcohol, Tobacco, Firearms and Explosives (ATF), and the U.S. Marshals Service. Marion County Jail, the largest jail in Indiana, includes four separate locations: the Main Jail (average daily population [ADP]: 936 males), Jail 2 (ADP: 1024), Liberty Hall Women's Jail (ADP: 179), and the Intake Center (ADP: 163).

Crime Trends

For the last half century, the city of Indianapolis has experienced higher than average rates of crime. In 1960, the Indianapolis Police Department reported 836 violent crimes, with an average of 176 violent crimes per 100,000 persons, compared to the national reported average of 161. These numbers included 32 reported homicides (6.7 per 100,000 persons compared to 5.1 for the United States). Property crime rates also exceeded national averages, with a reported 1,928 per 100,000 (including larceny-theft less than $50) compared to the national average of 1,726.

Crime trends continued to outpace the national average and were significantly affected by the Unigov consolidation. The lack of law enforcement agency consolidation for several decades following the Unigov action created inconsistent reporting patterns and the potential to skew reported crime rates. Because the IPD, until its consolidation with the Marion County Sheriff's Department in 2007, continued to patrol only the jurisdiction of the old city limits (with a few exceptions), the data reported in the Uniform Crime Reports only captured a portion of crime in the city and so reflected lower crime rates than were truly present. The concentration of crime in the urbanized city center was diluted by the comparison with population numbers that included the outlying areas of the consolidated city. The numbers reported by the Marion County Sheriff's Department, meanwhile, reflected crimes occurring within the jurisdiction of Indianapolis and crimes occurring in the excluded cities and towns, which cannot be distinguished. Furthermore, the presence of police departments maintained within the new city limits by the smaller included towns is not acknowledged in the data reporting of the IPD.

Through the 1990s, as national trends in crime began to decrease, crime rates in Indianapolis continued to increase, in some cases dramatically. The rate of violent crimes peaked in the mid- to late 1990s when the IPD reported 2,077 violent crimes

per 100,000 persons, compared to the national rate of 611, for 1997. The murder rate in 1997 exceeded four times the national figures, with IPD reporting a murder rate of 31 per 100,000 persons versus 6.8 nationally. Crime rates began to decrease through the 2000s but continue to exceed the national averages, with the consolidated police force still reporting significantly higher rates of murder, forcible rape, aggravated assault, and robbery as well as property crimes.

Public Safety Initiatives

As a large city with its share of street crime, Indianapolis has been the site of many public safety initiatives and experiments addressing the problem. One of the initial efforts to address firearms violence in Indianapolis occurred in the mid-1990s and involved a directed police patrol initiative focused on gun hot spots in two police districts. A research team led by Edmund McGarrell, Steve Chermak, and Alex Weiss found that homicide was reduced in both target areas. The study also found high levels of citizen support in the targeted areas and attributed this to police management efforts to emphasize respectful policing during these directed patrols.

In 1995 Indianapolis began receiving federal grant money for Weed and Seed initiatives, which grew to encompass six sites within the city with high rates of street crimes, such as prostitution and drug violence. The Safe Streets Task Force (SSTF) was one outgrowth of the Weed and Seed initiative, formed by the FBI to address gangs and violence in different U.S. cities. It involved collaboration between state and local law enforcement and the FBI. The SSTF came together for a successful investigation of a new drug-dealing gang, which resulted in multiple charges of gang members for federal drug trafficking offenses.

In 1996 and 1997 a team of researchers conducted the Project on Policing Neighborhoods (POPN) in Indianapolis and St. Petersburg, Florida. Funded by the Office of Community Oriented Policing, it sought, among other things, to better understand community policing and how it affects neighborhood quality of life. This project led to numerous publications on police interactions with the public, perceptions of law enforcement, the effects of institutions on crime rates, police perceptions of intimate partner violence, police coercion, and more.

In response to significant increases in homicides during the 1990s, city officials implemented the Indianapolis Violence Reduction Partnership (IVRP), a coalition-based approach to addressing homicide and serious firearms-related violence based on Boston's Operation Ceasefire. The IVRP was part of a U.S. Department of Justice effort known as Strategic Approaches to Community Safety Initiative that sought to create police-researcher partnerships to support strategic problem solving. Preliminary analysis by Steven Chermak and Edmund McGarrell found a decline in the types of homicide that the intervention focused on, as well as other promising findings. Later research has continued to identify associated reductions in certain types of violent crimes.

One development of the IVRP involved using "call-in" sessions to address issues of inmate reentry. The call-in meetings welcomed the returning former inmate to the community, communicated a deterrence message related to felons carrying firearms, and attempted to link individuals to social support and services. A pilot study found that although program participants reoffended at a slightly reduced rate, the difference was not statistically significant. Another development was the implementation of CompStat crime tracking and mapping through what was called the Indianapolis Management Accountability Program.

The Indianapolis Family Group Conferencing Experiment (FGC) was implemented in 1997 through a partnership among researchers, the Marion County juvenile court, and the prosecutor's office. First-time youthful offenders charged with crimes such as battery, theft, or disorderly conduct were randomly assigned to either the FGC or other diversion programs. After a 24-month follow-up, researchers Edmund McGarrell and Natalie Hipple found that assignment to the FGC reduced youths' probability of reoffending.

Other initiatives related to street crime include Gang Reduction Education and Training (GREAT), a school-based curriculum to prevent youth crime and gang activity, which is taught by law enforcement; the ATF's Project Achilles, an initiative targeting offenders who use a gun while committing a drug or violent crime; and the Indianapolis Ten-Point Coalition, an alliance of urban churches to reduce violence, based on Boston's Ten-Point Coalition.

Kevin Whiteacre
Colin Hammar
University of Indianapolis

See Also: Community Policing; CompStat; Drug Dealing; Gangs (Street); Guns and Weapons; Hot Spots; Operation Ceasefire; Policing, Problem-Oriented; Weed and Seed.

Further Readings

Allender, David M. "Safe Streets Task Force: Cooperation Gets Results." *FBI Law Enforcement Bulletin*, v.70/3 (2001).

Chermak, Steven and Edmund McGarrell. "Problem-Solving Approaches to Homicide: An Evaluation of the Indianapolis Violence Reduction Partnership." *Criminal Justice Policy Review*, v.15/2 (2004).

Mastrofski, Stephen D., Roger B. Parks, Albert J. Reiss, Jr., Robert E. Worden, Christina DeJong, Jeffrey B. Snipes, and William Terrill. "Systematic Observation of Public Police: Applying Field Research Methods to Policy Issues." Washington, DC: National Institute of Justice, 1998.

Although the city of Indianapolis rated very high in violent crime, the downtown area around most main attractions, venues, and museums remains relatively safe.

Jails

The jail plays an important role in the American criminal justice system—and by extension, the larger society.

Jails in Contemporary America

In the 21st century, the United States incarcerates more people per capita than any country in the world, at a rate of 731 per 100,000. When one considers the fact that approximately 11.8 million individuals are admitted to U.S. jails in one year alone, one begins to grasp the impact of the jail in contemporary American society. On any given day in the United States, more than 2.2 million adult prisoners are incarcerated. Almost one-third are held in the nation's jails, or 236 per 100,000. But an average daily count masks the magnitude of the reach of jails. When one considers the fact that approximately 11.8 million individuals were admitted to U.S. jails in 2011 alone, one begins to grasp the impact of the jail in contemporary American society.

The number of jail facilities and the number of people it takes to run them are also notable. There are 3,283 jail facilities in 2,860 jurisdictions in the United States. U.S. jails employ an estimated 234,000 workers as correctional officers, administrators, professional staff, and in maintenance, education, and health services, amounting to a ratio of employees to prisoners of 3.3 to 1. Federal jails constitute one of these jurisdictions, with 12 facilities; the remaining facilities are state, county, and local jails across the nation. They range in size from very small lock-ups in jurisdictions with low populations to what have been called "mega-jails" like the Los Angeles County Jail and New York City's Rikers Island—the two largest jails in the country.

Forty percent of the nation's jails house fewer than 50 prisoners; about 11 percent hold more than 500 prisoners on a given day. In 2006, U.S. jails employed an estimated 234,000 workers as correctional officers, administrators, professional staff, and in maintenance, education, and health services, amounting to a ratio of employees to prisoners of 3.3 to 1.

The Administrative Function of Jail

The jail receives so many people partly because of its role within the larger criminal justice system and the concomitant transient nature of its population. Most jails are local detention facilities that serve the municipalities in which they are sited—arrestees' first point of contact with detention in the criminal justice process. Depending on the disposition of cases, individuals might be released without charge, on bail, or on their own recognizance; held while cases are processed, or to serve time as punishment; or ultimately sent to federal or state prison to serve lengthier sentences. A few jails are used as overflow for prison populations or detention by the Immigration and Customs Enforcement (ICE) agency.

A key distinction among jail prisoners is between individuals who have been convicted of a crime and those who have not. Nationally, more than 60 percent of jail prisoners on a given day have not been convicted of a crime. This group includes persons who have not yet been arraigned and/or charged, and those who have been charged but are awaiting bail or trial. Jails also hold individuals undergoing trial—a sometimes years-long process.

The second major group of prisoners consists of persons who have been convicted and are either awaiting sentencing or transfer to prison, or serving sentences of less than one year, frequently misdemeanors. By contrast, state and federal prisons typically house persons convicted of felonies and sentenced to a year or more.

Jail prisoners are admitted in association with four major types of crime, with about one-quarter of the jail population admitted for each: violent crimes including assault, robbery, mugging, rape, and murder/homicide; drug offenses such as possession and distribution; property offenses like theft, shoplifting, burglary, and fraud; and the public-order offenses of vandalism, driving under the influence, drunk and disorderly, vagrancy/loitering, lewd and lascivious conduct, and prostitution.

The Social Function of Jail

The widely accepted institutional function of the jail is to process criminal cases, and thereby control crime and promote public safety. While the jail serves these ends, some criminologists suggest that a key purpose of the institution is to control the poor. John Irwin argues that the primary social function of the jail is to manage what he calls "undesirables"—social "rabble" whose conduct defies dominant societal norms; incarceration in jail is more a response to behavior that offends members of the dominant class than a response to criminal harm, in his view.

That most jail prisoners serve time for low-level crimes of poverty—that is, the minor types of street crime—lends credence to this claim, as does the reality that jail prisoners are over-represented among the poor. The unemployment rate is 30 percent among jail prisoners; their average wages earned fall far below those in the general population—corresponding to low educational attainment and high rates of homelessness and reliance on public assistance.

Defendants with economic resources are better able to avoid or extricate themselves from jail. In the first place they are more likely to be in a position to shape law and have connections and less likely to be targeted and apprehended by law enforcement. But in cases in which they are charged, the bail, plea bargain, and public defender systems favor them. Posting bail—in the form of money or property—is only an option for those with resources. Furthermore, roughly 95 percent of felony convictions are resolved through plea bargains—in which defendants plead guilty in exchange for sentencing leniency, thereby saving the state the cost of going to trial.

A good defense lawyer dramatically improves one's chances of winning a criminal case, whereas public defenders are notoriously overburdened and unmotivated to take cases to trial. One problem with this system is that it incentivizes false pleas out of fear of longer sentences.

The mammoth growth in the U.S. criminal incarceration and suspect holding system over the last 40 years—prisons and jails alike—has been accompanied by a decline of welfarism, pointing to the idea that the criminal justice system has become a surrogate for a withering welfare state in the United States. Loïc Wacquant suggests that it is more accurate to refer to the United States historically as a "charitable" state—in which public resources are provided only to those deemed "deserving"—and that in recent years this charitable state has transformed into a penal state, wherein poverty is managed through criminal punishment and the poor are punished for their economic position.

Racial Inequality

The U.S. criminal justice system's focus on "crime in the streets" over "crime in the suites" suggests that reproducing class inequality is one of the outcomes of the institution. But an understanding of the ways in which economic inequality operates through the jail requires examining it at its intersections with race, ethnicity, gender, and nation. Young African Americans and Latinos are dramatically over-represented among jail prisoners, and racial discrimination has been documented at every step of the criminal justice process—lawmaking, police stops, arrest, conviction, and sentencing.

Men compose the vast majority of jail prisoners and the crimes for which they and their female counterparts are jailed reflect dominant gender norms. Undocumented immigrants are currently the fastest growing segment of the jail population, who experience poor conditions of confinement in ICE detention facilities and routine denial of constitutional protections and due process.

Historical Development

Examining the history of the jail sheds light on its current institutional form and social functions. The forerunner to the U.S. jail was the early English jail, which also served the social function of controlling

A modern jail cell in Brecksville Police Department, Brecksville, Ohio. Jails have many different security levels, ranging from dormitory-style open housing to ultra-secure lock-downs.

undesirables and managing poverty. Indeed, some of the first jails were poorhouses for English debtors and vagrants. In British jails in the early modern period, quarters were relatively luxurious for those who could pay jailers—and prisoners of means could buy sex, food, and alcohol, as well as free reign of jail grounds. For those without, conditions were notoriously dreadful, though rampant disease in these jails was no respecter of wealthier persons.

With the advent of the Enlightenment a new punishment ethic emerged, one advocating swift and fair punishments with the goal of crime deterrence and reform of the individual. Conditions of confinement became hotly contested and new practices were based on the concept of human perfectibility emerged. The penitentiary was born and the work of trying to correct prisoners began, though prisoners of the lowest social castes were generally viewed as permanently irredeemable, for example, persons of indigenous, African, or Mexican descent, and the poorest whites. Meanwhile the jail continued to administer local justice. While it was affected by the punishment ideology of the day, it retained a primary focus on administrative convenience and expediency and focused less than its offshoot on penitence and rehabilitation.

The goal of administrative expedience continues to drive jail operations, though rehabilitation programs in jails are routine, if experiencing a notable historical lull in the current tough-on-crime zeitgeist. It is common knowledge among prisoners and criminologists alike that jail conditions are generally poorer than conditions in prison—particularly in big city jails and jails in the south—albeit with wide variations depending on a range of factors. Common issues are overcrowding, squalor, violence, and lack of adequate medical and mental health care.

An important development is that jails—and prisons to a lesser extent—have filled the void created by the wide-scale closure of publicly funded mental institutions, which began in the 1960s. As horrendous as many of these institutions were, deinstitutionalization has created homelessness among large numbers of untreated mentally ill individuals who then commit street crimes—overwhelmingly of a petty variety—that lead them to jail.

Poor treatment of prisoners at the hands of jail staff has also been noted. In the 1980s at the height of the War on Drugs and the concomitant escalating criminal justice expenditures, private corrections emerged and has since grown into a multibillion-dollar industry. Proponents of privatization contend that private industry can do a better job than the state because it is unburdened by bureaucratic inefficiencies and operates in the free market. Its detractors claim the drive for profits translates into fewer resources allocated to maintain conditions, along with high turnover among poorly trained and undercompensated staff.

Another reason the jail receives so many people is obscured by a dominant logic of our time—the assumed inevitability of incarceration as the primary response to social problems resulting from violence, poverty, and racism. The economic downturn of 2008 and ensuing budgetary crises faced by municipalities nationwide have led policy-makers to consider alternatives to incarceration that would have been unpopular just a few years ago. Indeed, in 2009 the jail population decreased for the first time since 1982, with consecutive decreases again in 2010 and 2011.

Whether this fiscal impetus is strong enough to translate into substantial reductions in incarceration remains to be seen. Recent developments in California—a bellwether for criminal justice practices nationally, and globally—suggest not. In 2011, Governor Jerry Brown ushered in a policy of managing prison overcrowding by sending state prisoners with fewer than three years to serve into local jails—thus vastly expanding the use of the jail in the correctional archipelago.

Sadie Reynolds
Cabrillo College

See Also: Arrest; Bail; Central Booking; Courts; Courts, Drug; Courts, Mental Health; Day Reporting Center; Immigrant Neighborhoods; Police (Overview); Truancy.

Further Readings
Barak, Gregg. *Class, Race, Gender, Crime: The Social Realities of Justice in America.* Lanham, MD: Rowman & Littlefield, 2007.
Glaze, Lauren. "Correctional Populations in the United States, 2010." Washington, DC: U.S. Department of Justice, Bureau of Justice Statistics, 2011.
Irwin, John. *The Jail: Managing the Underclass in American Society.* Berkeley: University of California Press, 1985.
Minton, Todd. "Jail Inmates at Midyear 2011—Statistical Tables." Washington, DC: U.S. Department of Justice, Bureau of Justice Statistics, 2012.
Stephan, James and Georgette Walsh. "Census of Jail Facilities, 2006." Washington, DC: U.S. Department of Justice, Bureau of Justice Statistics, 2011.
Wacquant, Loïc. *Punishing the Poor: The Neoliberal Government of Social Insecurity.* Durham, NC: Duke University Press, 2009.

Jaywalking

Defined variously by states, local jurisdictions, and common usage, *jaywalking* is a distinctly American term applied to certain disapproved street uses. Typically a jaywalker is a pedestrian who crosses streets without regard to pedestrian regulations—particularly in ways that obstruct traffic or endanger the pedestrian. In most U.S. jurisdictions jaywalking can be a violation of local traffic ordinances; it is therefore a minor crime. The term has found only limited use in Anglophone countries outside of North America.

Onrush of the Automobile
Before automobiles were common—that is before about 1900 or 1910—street use in the United States was generally regulated only by the unwritten common law. Citing precedents, most judges treated all ordinary street uses as legitimate, provided they did not obstruct or endanger other users of the street. Pedestrians' right to use the street surface from curb to curb was thus sanctioned by law and custom. As automobiles flooded city streets after 1910, however, this environment was an obstacle to motorists wherever pedestrian traffic was heavy. Motorists could expect pedestrians to enter the street anywhere, and motorists who struck pedestrians could not expect sympathy from judges, even if the pedestrian was careless.

Early advocates for the automobile, especially auto clubs, promoted changes in the law to better accommodate automobiles and to limit pedestrians' free access to streets—but until the 1920s such efforts generally failed. Reformers were more successful when they tried a more direct approach: aiming terms of ridicule at free-roaming pedestrians. For this purpose, advocates of the automobile requisitioned a relatively obscure midwestern term of derision: *jay walker*. A "jay" was a foolish rural person—a rube. Jay walker (by the mid-1920s more often jaywalker) was an epithet occasionally directed at rural visitors to the big city who obstructed other pedestrians because they were dazzled by the city sights.

Beginning about 1912, and with increasing frequency thereafter, advocates of automobiles began to appropriate jaywalker as a term of derision for pedestrians who obstructed motor vehicles. In public safety campaigns they publicized the term, using inventive techniques.

For example, during "safety weeks," Boy Scouts distributed cards defining jaywalking to pedestrians, clownish jaywalkers dressed as rubes were used to attract ridicule to the practice, and in at least one case such a character was repeatedly struck by a slow-moving Model T Ford to amuse onlookers. In its early years, however, the term was widely regarded as abusive and even offensive, and its use against pedestrians who were not actually violating any city ordinance was controversial. Nevertheless, publicity campaigns were extraordinarily successful in promoting the term; still very rare in 1915, by 1924 it was in general use and, for the first time, had entered a standard dictionary of American English.

From Words to Warrants

Success in this war of words served as a foundation for regulatory change. Los Angeles led the way. Like some other cities, Los Angeles had attempted to regulate pedestrians before the term *jaywalker* was publicized—without success. In 1925, Los Angeles automobile groups secured passage of strict pedestrian regulation, but persuaded police to delay enforcement pending a thorough public relations campaign, including extensive condemnation of jaywalking. The results were impressive; the Los Angeles method served as an example for cities nationwide.

Later that year, when Congress (which in those days had the responsibility of directly appointing the District of Columbia's city government) named an executive of the American Automobile Association to serve as Washington, D.C.'s, traffic director, the new administrator elevated the term *jaywalking* to the name of an official infraction in his jurisdiction. Intensive school safety education programs,

many of them funded by the American Automobile Association, helped instill in later generations a lasting disapproval of jaywalking.

Despite this impressive achievement, advocates of pedestrian control never came close to suppressing jaywalking. Enforcement of pedestrian regulations is practically difficult, and pedestrians who relinquish street space often do so more out of respect for motor vehicles' deadly momentum than for any written regulations.

Most pedestrians retain greater agility than cars and are prepared to use it to their advantage (or peril) against vehicles' superior horsepower wherever long signal timings, infrequent crossings, or other disadvantages make compliance with regulations difficult. Such disadvantages for pedestrians are especially common in cities designed to accommodate automobiles, where pedestrianism can be especially dangerous.

Recent trends in urban planning, such as new urbanism, have challenged such design models in favor of greater freedom of street access for pedestrians. These trends, while limited to date, reflect new values for diverse street uses—and a new favor for practices once condemned as jaywalking. They are indicated by the proliferation of terms such as *walkability, shared space*, and *complete streets*.

Peter Norton
University of Virginia

See Also: Los Angeles, California; Road Rage; Urban Planning; Washington, D.C.

Further Readings

Das, Sanghamitra, Charles F. Manski, and Mark D. Manuszak. "Walk or Wait? An Empirical Analysis of Street Crossing Decisions." *Journal of Applied Econometrics*, v.20/4 (2005).

Ernst, Michelle, Marisa Lang, and Stephen Davis. *Dangerous by Design 2011: Solving the Epidemic of Preventable Pedestrian Deaths.* Washington, DC: Transportation for America, 2011.

Jason, Leonard A. and Richard Liotta. "Pedestrian Jaywalking Under Facilitating and Nonfacilitating Conditions." *Journal of Applied Behavior Analysis*, v.15/3 (1982).

Norton, Peter D. *Fighting Traffic: The Dawn of the Motor Age In the American City.* Cambridge, MA: MIT Press, 2008.

Norton, Peter D. "Street Rivals: Jaywalking and the Invention of the Motor Age Street." *Technology and Culture*, v.48/2 (2007).

"Johns"

The term *john* usually refers to a customer who purchases sex from a sex worker on the street or a higher-end escort or call girl, rather than those persons who purchase sex in other sexual commerce environments such as erotic dance establishments. This exchange can be purchased through currency, drugs, or other material goods. Historically, johns have not been the focus of laws against prostitution and therefore represent only a fraction of the arrests for prostitution. This focus has changed in recent years; johns are increasingly targeted for the act of solicitation of a sex worker. Johns, or clients, often victimize street sex workers and are infrequently held accountable because street sex workers are not willing or able to inform authorities and prosecute these crimes.

Slang for a prostitute or sex worker's male customer or client, the term *john* was first used in 1911 according to the *Online Etymological Dictionary,* and has been attributed to sex customers using the common and therefore anonymous name "John." Other common synonyms for this term include "trick," which reveals the hustling involved in selling sex or as one who is tricked into giving the worker money; or a "date," as in the person with whom the sex worker chooses to spend time in exchange for an agreed upon amount of money.

Within the street context, the john usually decides what sexual act he wishes to purchase, as well as where that act will occur—although these acts and locations can also be negotiated between the client and street sex worker based on the availability of an automobile, motel, or other location, as well as what the prostitute or sex worker is willing to do for an agreed upon amount of money.

Estimates of the number of street-based sex workers in the United States vary. A 1990 analysis by a Colorado health official projected 23 "full-time equivalent prostitutes" per 100,000 population, or approximately 84,000 women nationally on an annual basis. The number of johns would obviously be a fairly high multiple of this figure. A 2004 poll sponsored by *ABC News Primetime Live* found that 15 percent of American men—equating to approximately 15 million adult males—said they had paid for sex; of single men age 30 and up, about 30 percent said they had paid for sex.

Shifting Enforcement, Targeting Demand

Because prostitution is illegal in the United States except for certain counties in Nevada, historically people selling sex have been the focus of most criminal codes as well as resources spent to enforce them. Because sex workers, and those participating in street-based sex work in particular, are often considered to be victims of personal and economic circumstances as well as criminalization, there have been movements to shift the focus of this criminalization to the johns, or clients. Over the past two decades, johns have increasingly become the object of enforcement policies. In certain cases, the act of offering to sell sex has been decriminalized while the penalties have increased for those who offer to pay money for sex. John schools have also been created as a way of educating or "re-educating" customers about prostitution, while simultaneously allowing men convicted of this crime to avoid an arrest record. Developed by police departments, social service agencies, public health departments, community leaders, and former sex workers, such courses are meant to deter men from patronizing sex workers in the future.

Resident or community groups also create tactics that try to intimidate those who purchase sex, in order to remove both sex workers and johns from their neighborhoods. These groups photograph and videotape customers, hold up signs about the risk of acquired immune deficiency syndrome (AIDS) and venereal diseases, and write down license plate numbers in hopes of contacting "the woman of the house." Campaigns have also been developed across the United States to post names and pictures of johns on television, billboards, and posters as a way of shaming both those who have been observed, arrested, and/or convicted of prostitution, as well as those who may be deterred from participating in these activities because of the risk of this public attention.

End Demand campaigns, often based on what is referred to as the "Swedish model," are another result of the increase in criminalization of those who purchase sex. These campaigns specifically target those people, typically men, who are creating the demand side of the exchange of sex for money, as a result of some activists and scholars who argue the exchange of sex for monetary gain constitutes an act of violence against the worker, who is typically considered to be a woman and a victim of prostitution.

Although designed to improve the lives of street sex workers in particular, these campaigns are contested by other scholars, activists, sex workers, and sex worker rights' proponents who argue they are ineffective against curbing street-based sex work and can actually increase violence and harm committed against street sex workers, because it becomes more difficult for sex workers to negotiate the exchange as well as assess the potential risk of the client.

Jill McCracken
University of South Florida, St. Petersburg

See Also: Prostitute/Streetwalker; Prostitution, Houses of; Sex Crimes; Women.

Further Readings

Bernstein, Elizabeth. "Desire, Demand, and the Commerce of Sex." In *Regulating Sex: The Politics of Intimacy and Identity*, Elizabeth Bernstein and Laurie Schaffner, eds. New York: Routledge, 2005.

Harper, Douglas. "John." *Online Etymology Dictionary.* July 6, 2011. http://www.etymonline.com/index .php?term=john (Accessed April 2012).

Kulick, Don. "Sex in the New Europe: The Criminalization of Clients and Swedish Fear of Penetration." *Anthropological Theory,* v.3/2 (2003).

Weitzer, Ronald, ed. *Sex for Sale: Prostitution, Pornography, and the Sex Industry.* 2nd ed. New York: Routledge, 2010.

Juvenile Curfews

Curfews are regulations or laws which require selected classes of people, historically usually poor, lower-class, slaves, minorities, or juveniles, to be off the street during certain hours, usually at night. It is noteworthy that those subject to these controls are almost always politically powerless,

but feared. These rules are aimed at controlling the behavior of subject groups by constraining their mobility. While today's curfews aimed at juveniles generally contain verbiage that implies uniformity of application, discriminatory enforcement is generally or potentially present. Although not restricted to juveniles, temporary curfews are occasionally invoked uniformly in times of disaster, riot, or emergency in order to keep areas clear for rescue efforts and to prevent looting.

Development and Aims

The concept of a curfew originated during the Middle Ages when peasants, villagers, and townspeople were expected to be in their homes, and external fires extinguished, between sunset and sundown. This was announced by the tolling of church bells. At that time, city gates were locked and people were barred from entry or exit. The movement of Jews, and later, Gypsies, was especially tightly regulated.

In the United States before emancipation, the movement of all African Americans, free or slave, was similarly controlled; they were expected to have written permission from their owners or manumission papers when in the community at large, particularly at night. Curfews were enforced during slavery times by patrols made up of plantation owners, sheriffs, or other whites from the community. The restrictions on free movement and association imposed by curfews were much resented by African Americans and by abolitionists at that time.

Curfews today are often applied to juveniles but as such are often clearly aimed at reducing street crime and gang activity among minority groups in the inner city. As such an intent is discriminatory and the laws are seldom aimed at or enforced in largely white suburbs, today's curfews in this sense hark back to slavery times and are accordingly resented by many in minority communities.

The general argument that underlies the logic of curfews is that youth have no business being outside their homes during nighttime hours. Furthermore, it is assumed that the streets are safer and youth also are safer if the mobility of high-risk youth is limited. This seemingly common sense notion presses parents to take more responsibility for the actions of minors under their aegis. It ignores the fact that many young people are subject to minimal parental supervision; indeed, in many cases no parents are present to enforce controls.

Before the 1890s, youth curfew laws were not widely promulgated or, if extant, were not often enforced. This was because children commonly worked long hours and night shifts in various industries. The child welfare movement forced changes that did away with child labor and the already dying apprentice system. Labor unions were anxious to reduce competition in the workplace as well. This left large numbers of idle youth on the streets. Many joined gangs and got involved in criminal activity.

A particular concern of reformers was to prevent young girls from being influenced by unwholesome associations and being lured into precocious sexual activity, prostitution, or pregnancy. Neither boys nor girls had any legitimate or wholesome reason to be abroad in the evening, in the view of reformers. Thus, curfews were seen by progressives and conservatives as a way to keep economically redundant youth and potential victims off the street. It was hoped that the existence of such laws would help stressed parents, many of whom were immigrants, to get control of their children and their communities. Concern with under-regulated youth mounted during the 1900s and the popularity of curfews grew apace. Today the majority of American cities have some kind of youth curfew laws.

Contending Perspectives

Though law enforcement agencies tend to strongly approve of curfews, academic criminologists are not at all uniform in support of their efficacy. The discretionary power that curfews give police agencies, such as the power to stop and question any young person without any real probable cause beyond violation of the curfew itself, is extremely popular with those charged with enforcement. The fact that such discretion invites discriminatory enforcement is simply dismissed as irrelevant by those who pass such laws, as well as enforcement entities.

That notwithstanding, almost all criminologists who have studied curfews find general juvenile curfew laws to be ineffective. Study after study reveals little or no practical impact of the implementation of new general laws or enforcement of existing juvenile curfew laws. Moreover, such studies, at least a dozen, point out that criminal activity by young people is often simply displaced to daylight hours, particularly property offenses such as burglary. Still, specifically targeted "enhanced enforcement" characterized by saturation police patrol and aggressive enforcement of juvenile curfew laws can have statistically significant impact in terms of suppressing gang-related violence. In addition, victimization of juveniles is not impacted in the long term by such laws. Other studies have not demonstrated that juvenile crime is geographically displaced by curfews. That is, juvenile crime does not shift from a jurisdiction with curfews to one where curfews have not been enacted.

Enforcement of curfew laws has not proven effective in uncovering other crimes, contrary to police opinion. One major fact ignored by advocates is that curfew laws simply cannot have much impact, since only one juvenile crime in five actually occurs during the proscribed time period. It must be noted, however, that curfews have been marginally successful in reducing simple assault, larceny, and nocturnal burglary. Parents or youth, or both, may be subject to sanction if juveniles are caught breaking curfew. Punishment may be largely symbolic appearances in juvenile court, or could amount to significant fines, sometimes up to $1,000 depending on ordinances in the local jurisdiction The notion that parents can or will be able to alter children's behavior is questionable, however, and such fines may be seriously punitive on already financially stressed urban citizens but have little practical effect in deterring street crimes.

Conclusion

Criminological research and concerns of minority advocates may dissent, but curfew laws are highly popular with elected civil leaders, politicians, parents, and even with a majority of the juvenile population. While the very existence of such laws upsets civil libertarians and some in minority communities, some who live in the inner city strongly support any efforts, even potentially discriminatory ones such as curfews, to help reestablish order and civility in gang-ridden neighborhoods. And as noted earlier, some evidence exists to support the notion that enhanced police patrol and continued focus on enforcement of juvenile curfew laws can impact gang-related violence.

Francis Frederick Hawley
Western Carolina University

See Also: Drinking, Underage; Gangs (Street); Juvenile Offending; Loitering; Looting; Pool Halls; Racial Profiling; Stop and Frisk.

Further Readings

Adams, Kenneth. "The Effectiveness of Juvenile Curfews at Crime Prevention." *Annals of the American Academy of Political and Social Science,* v.587/1 (2003).

Bernard, Thomas J. and Megan C. Kurlychek. *The Cycle of Juvenile Justice.* New York: Oxford University Press, 2010.

Howell, James C. *Preventing and Reducing Juvenile Delinquency: A Comprehensive Framework.* 2nd ed. Thousand Oaks, CA: Sage, 2009.

U.S. Department of Justice, Office of Juvenile Justice and Delinquency Prevention. "Curfew: An Answer to Juvenile Delinquency and Victimization." Washington, DC: Government Printing Office, 1996.

Juvenile Offending

Juveniles in the United States are involved in various forms of violent offenses, property offenses, drug and alcohol-related crimes, sex offenses, and gang-related offenses. Violent offenses they commit range from murder to robbery to assaults. Property offenses range from burglary to larceny-theft to vandalism. Drug-related offenses include manufacturing, selling, or possession of illegal substances. Sex offenses range from rape to prostitution. In addition, juveniles are also charged with status offenses, such as curfew violations and underage drinking.

Often, public perceptions of juvenile crimes are based on media portrayals of high profile cases such as the Columbine High School shootings of April 1999, where 12 students and a teacher were killed. Thus, it is important for the public, criminal justice professionals, and policy makers to have an accurate picture of juvenile offending in terms of crimes committed, the proportion and characteristics of juvenile offenders, the trends and patterns of offending, theoretical explanations, and prevention through evidence-based programming.

It is, however, impossible to provide comprehensive information from a single source of data or from official records because many juveniles, including those who commit serious crimes, never enter the formal justice system. As a result, researchers must compare multiple sources of official and unofficial data. In addition, understanding the nature and causes of delinquency will enable policy makers to develop prevention/intervention programs.

Sources of Data

Juvenile crime is measured using official and unofficial sources. Official sources include the Federal Bureau of Investigation's (FBI) Uniform Crime Reports (UCR), Bureau of Justice Statistics (BJS) reports, the Bureau of Labor Statistics, the Centers for Disease Control and Prevention's Youth Risk Behavior Surveillance, the National Incident-Based Reporting System (NIBRS), and the National Institute on Drug Abuse Monitoring the Future Survey, from the Office of Juvenile Justice and Delinquency Prevention (OJJDP). In addition to official data, self-report studies, such as the National Crime Victimization Surveys (NCVS) and the National Longitudinal Survey of Youth, are also useful.

Of all the official sources, the UCR is the most often utilized. The UCR provides juvenile arrest rates and demographics. It groups offenses into index and nonindex offenses. Index offenses are further classified into personal: murder and non-negligent manslaughter, forcible rape, and aggravated assaults; and property offenses: burglary, larceny-theft, motor vehicle theft, and arson. The nonindex offenses include simple assaults, forgery, fraud, prostitution, vandalism, stolen property, less serious sex offenses, drug-abuse-related offenses, and curfew violations.

It should be pointed out, however, that the UCR reports on a highly select group of offenders. For example, arrests do not include the actual number of offenders because less than half of violent crimes are reported to the police. Furthermore, most of the arrest data comes from urban police departments; small and rural police departments often fail to report the data. James Lynch argues that using such arrest data to estimate overall offending produces inaccurate rates. He recommends that the use of NCVS data, although it has its own limitations, in conjunction with UCR and other self-report studies produce more meaningful estimates of juvenile offenders and offending rates.

The NCVS gathers data from a national probability sample of households in which individuals are interviewed. This produces data on unreported, as well as reported, serious crimes. The interviews are limited to household members aged 12 and above. The NCVS estimates offending rates for juveniles by gender, race, and index offenses (excluding homicides). Data on specific offenses such as homicide and gang violence are compiled from the FBI's Supplemental Homicide Reports and the National Youth Gang Survey, respectively.

Crimes and Patterns

The Office of Juvenile Justice and Delinquency Prevention (OJJDP) reported 2.11 million arrests of juveniles in 2008. Violent personal offenses accounted for 0.5 percent of juvenile arrests; of these, aggravated assaults accounted for approximately 56 percent, followed by robbery, 37 percent. Murders and non-negligent homicides represented less than 2 percent of juvenile arrests. Most of these murders involved the use of firearms. Seventy percent of males and 35 percent of females admitted to using a firearm during the commission of the crime.

Property offenses accounted for 20.8 percent of total arrests. Of the property offenses, larceny-theft accounted for 75 percent, followed by burglary, 19 percent. Of nonindex offenses—which made up 84.5 percent of all juvenile arrests in 2008—the top five were nonaggravated assaults, disorderly conduct, drug-abuse and liquor offenses, and curfew or loitering violations.

Of all the variables criminologists have studied as contributors to delinquency, the two that consistently stand out are age and gender. The delinquency rate for 16- and 17-year-olds is higher than younger age groups. In addition, high-school age juveniles (14 years and older) represented approximately 80 percent of the delinquency cases in 2002.

The arrests showed a declining trend. There were 3 percent fewer juvenile arrests in 2008 compared to 2007. Overall, the last decade of data indicate that street crime for females increased at alarming rates compared to males, even for serious offenses. For example, between 1985 and 2002, assaults by females rose by 80 percent, whereas assaults by males showed a 20 percent increase. Similar to arrest data, juvenile court caseloads reveal that a higher percentage of females are involved in offenses such as simple assaults or larceny-theft, but in a smaller proportion in cases of robbery, burglary, drug offense, and vandalism. When females commit most the serious offenses (e.g., murder), they tend to commit them alone, unlike their male counterparts.

Regarding race, African Americans are disproportionately represented in the juvenile justice system. Although African Americans represent approximately 13 percent of the population, the delinquency rate is more than twice the rate for whites, and over three times the rate for other racial groups. In addition, African Americans are represented in a greater proportion in personal offenses, and admitted using firearms more often than whites.

Gang Offenses and Make-up

In addition to individual street crimes, the presence of gangs in major cities and midsized towns creates special concerns for law enforcement agencies. To assess the prevalence of gang activity and to develop antigang training for law enforcement agencies, the National Gang Center, in collaboration with the Bureau of Justice Statistics and OJJDP, conducts surveys of law enforcement agencies. The 2009 study showed that gang activity significantly increased between 2001 and 2005, and has remained fairly constant since then. The annual estimate of the number of gangs for the 12-year survey period is about 26,000, accounting for 775,000 members nationally.

The largest cities and suburban areas in the United States account for 80 percent of all gangs, followed by smaller cities (approximately 17 percent), and rural counties (about 3 percent). Some large cities have reported more than 30 different gangs operating, whereas a typical small town or rural area with a gang problem might report the presence of three gangs with a membership of approximately 50 members.

In addition, the presence of a large number of gangs indicates that the gangs have been operating for a long time. Of all the cities and towns, Los Angeles and Chicago are considered to have the most gangs, accounting for half of all gang-related homicides in the United States. The presence of a large number of gangs correlates to an increase in various types of crimes, including murder, drug-related offenses, and gun violence.

The National Gang Intelligence Center identified three basic types of gangs: street gangs, prison gangs, and outlaw motorcycle gangs. There are about 11 national-level street gangs with ties to criminal organizations in other countries. These include Los Angeles-based 18th Street; Latin Kings (operating in major cities such as Chicago and New York); Asian Boyz (based in southern California); Bloods (operating primarily in California); Crips (based in California); Mara Salvatrucha, also known as MS-13 (largest Hispanic gang from California) Sureños and Norteños (Hispanic gangs operating in California); Tiny Rascal Gangsters (the most violent Asian gang, operating in the southwestern, Pacific, and New England regions); and Vice Lord (based in Chicago). Regional-level street gangs include Florencia 13, Fresno Bulldogs, Latin Disciples, Tango Blast, and United Blood Nation.

Many of these criminal gangs recruit young people. Youth gangs are involved in a disproportionate number of homicides; once youth join a gang, they are more likely to participate in delinquency, drug use, and violence.

According to researcher James Howell, gang involvement negatively affects youth, their families, and their communities in several ways. First, youth commit more serious crimes during their stay in a gang, compared to their criminal activity prior to joining a gang or after leaving a gang. Second, gangs commit more serious crimes, such as murder and drug-related violence, than other groups. Third, youth who continue their gang involvement for over a year will continue to commit crimes for a longer period of time. Fourth, youths who join a gang are more likely to go through arrest, conviction, and incarceration—often repeating the cycle after release—and the costs to society are enormous. Howell estimates that it costs taxpayers between $1.7 million and $2.3 million for a single adolescent who maintains a criminal career for 10 years. In recent years, female gang membership has been increasing. For example, OJJDP reports that in high-crime neighborhoods, 29.4 percent of girls claimed gang membership, compared to 32.4 percent of boys.

Laws and Institutionalization

The United States does not have a uniform system of juvenile justice. Rather, it has 50 separate systems created by individual states. Although Supreme Court decisions have brought some uniformity and clarity in terms of juvenile rights and due process rules, each state has its unique body of law, judicial processes, and correctional approach. While founded on a legal-social-welfare approach to deal with needy and troubled juveniles at the turn of the century, the justice system—disillusioned by lagging rehabilitation and an apparent growth in youth crime in 1980s and 1990s—has in many states taken a more punitive approach.

Currently two major approaches, the justice versus welfare philosophies, seem to guide the operations of juvenile justice in individual states. Juvenile courts primarily handle juvenile offenders, although alternative mechanisms in the form of family courts and diversion programs have been developed for status offenders and needy children. Liberalization of waiver or transfer laws has created a system in which youth accused of serious crimes are treated as adults and subject to adult proceedings and sanctions.

Juvenile courts use a range of dispositions such as diversion, fines, brief detention, probation, and prison sentences in juvenile correctional institutions. For more than a century, institutional confinement has been the programmatic choice for juvenile offenders. In 2003, approximately 300 juvenile offenders were in custody for every 100,000 juveniles, which is much higher than many other countries.

Of the juvenile correctional population, the overwhelming majority are held in secure correctional facilities, compared to fewer than 20 percent in private facilities in secure settings. The OJJDP Census of Juveniles in Residential Facilities shows that public facilities house seven out of 10 delinquents, of whom three-quarters are held for technical violations of probation/parole or alternately for committing serious offenses such as homicide, robbery, sexual offenses, aggravated assault, or weapon charges. A slightly lower numbers of juveniles are held in public facilities for committing drug-related offenses.

A typical offender in a juvenile facility is a white male between the ages of 15 and 17 with less than a ninth-grade education, previously convicted of crimes, a regular user of alcohol and drugs, and from a single-parent household with its own criminal history. Regarding gender representation in correctional institutions, males represent the overwhelming majority (85 percent) of juvenile offenders. In addition, female offenders in correctional institutions tend to be at least a year younger than their male counterparts.

Currently, states facing budgetary crises are experimenting with diverse placement options in lieu of incarceration. For example, states such as Illinois, Ohio, and Wisconsin have developed various community-based programs to reduce incarcerations. Redeploy Illinois is a new program designed to provide comprehensive services to youth who are at high risk of being committed to the Department of Corrections. The program offers a range of services based on the individual needs of the youth and has proven to be successful in reducing prison commitments. In addition, the program has reportedly saved millions of taxpayer dollars.

Sesha Kethineni
Illinois State University

See Also: Asian Gangs; Bloods; Gangs (Street); Juvenile Curfews; Vandalism.

Further Readings
Hawkins, Darnell F., John H. Laub, Janet F. Lauritsen, and Lynn Cothern. "Race, Ethnicity, and Serious and Violent Juvenile Offending." *Juvenile Justice Bulletin*, v.2000/6 (2000).
Howell, James C. "The Impact of Gangs on Communities." *NYGC Bulletin*, v.2006/8 (2006).
Loeber, Rolf and David P. Farrington. *Serious and Violent Juvenile Offenders: Risk Factors and Successful Interventions.* Thousand Oaks, CA: Sage, 1999.
Lynch, James P. "Trends in Juvenile Violent Offending: An Analysis of Victim Survey Data." *OJJDP Juvenile Justice Bulletin*, v.2002/10 (2002).
Shoemaker, Donald J. *Theories of Delinquency: An Examination of Delinquent Behavior.* New York: Oxford University Press, 1990.
Snyder, Howard N. and Melissa Sickmund. "Juvenile Offenders and Victims: 2006 National Report." Washington, DC: U.S. Department of Justice, 2006.

Kansas City, Missouri

Located on the border of Kansas and Missouri in northwest Missouri, Kansas City is the largest city in the state, with approximately 150,000 more citizens than St. Louis. It is one of two county seats of Jackson County (along with Independence). According to U.S. Census Bureau data, the population of Kansas City was 459,787 in 2010, reflecting a 4.1 percent increase from 2000.

Violent crime in Kansas City has been prevalent since the Civil War. However, crime in the city became most prevalent during the era of Democratic political boss Tom Pendergast. Under Pendergast, from 1890 to 1940, Kansas City became a "wide-open" town, with absolutely no alcohol-related arrests being made in city limits during the entirety of Prohibition.

In the 1970s, the Kansas City mob was involved in a series of violent acts aimed at assuring continued dominance over the large entertainment district. The activities involved bombings and the deaths of several prominent gangsters. Shortly after these disturbances, the mob lost control of a prominent Kansas City casino and began to fade out of the public eye. Since that time, much of street crime has been attached to gang activity occurring in the urban core, where poverty rates are higher and crime is more likely to remain largely unabated.

A 2007 analysis by the *Kansas City Star* and the University of Missouri, Kansas City, suggested that downtown Kansas City had experienced the largest drop in crime of any neighborhood in the city during the decade. In 2010, however, *Forbes* magazine still ranked Kansas City as the third-most dangerous city in the country, largely because of prevailing trends within the city limits related to street crime.

Rates of violent and property crime remain disproportionately high. In 2010, Kansas City had the ninth-highest violent crime rate of any U.S. city with a population of 250,000 or greater, according to the FBI Uniform Crime Reports (UCR) data. These numbers, however, are still significantly lower than those tracked in the city in the early 1990s.

The official crime figures discussed in this entry are from the Federal Bureau of Investigation's Uniform Crime Reports, which collect data from the Kansas City Police Department.

UCR data from Kansas City reveals the extent of street crime in the city. According to crime statistics from 1985 to 2010, the violent crime rate decreased 31.8 percent. This statistic can be deceiving, however, since the violent crime rate peaked in 1992 at 2,854.7 violent crimes committed per 100,000 persons. The decrease since 1992, consequently, is an impressive 57 percent. The rate of murder and non-negligible manslaughter—the most dangerous and serious crimes committed in the United States—increased by 8.3 percent from 1985 to 2010. This number, however, is not necessarily representative of a complete trend, as rates have fluctuated in the past decade between 20.1 and 35.1 murders per 100,000 in the city's population. The rate of forcible rape has actually decreased in the city, from 95.3 per 100,000 to 52.4—a decrease of 45 percent. The rate peaked in 1992 at 127.8 forcible rapes per 100,000. Regarding robberies, there was a decrease of over 38 percent from 1985 and 2010 in Kansas City. The decrease is even more impressive considering that robberies peaked at 1,130.8 per 100,000 in 1991. The decrease from 1991 to 2010 was over 68 percent. Reported aggravated assaults increased by 27.6 percent between 1985 and 2010, but fell almost 53 percent since hitting a peak in 1992.

Unlike many large cities in the United States, the property crime rate in Kansas City has decreased by over 30 percent between 1985 and 2010 to 5,915.3. A dramatic decline has occurred since 1989, when there were 10,678.5 property crimes per 100,000 citizens in the city. The burglary rate has decreased by 37.7 percent between 1985 and 2010. Since it peaked in 1987, the rate has fallen over 45 percent. Considering the larceny-theft rate, there is a relative stability and only a slight decrease since 2004. Motor vehicle theft decreased rapidly between 1985 and 1990 (almost 91 percent) before falling a further 69 percent since.

These rates do not represent the entire picture of street crime activity in Kansas City, yet they do paint a fairly accurate portrayal of a city that witnessed a severe rash of property and violent crime in the early 1990s before seeing numbers fall over the subsequent two decades. The city has mirrored a pattern witnessed throughout the nation. The positive recent trends, however, do not necessarily mean Kansas City has eliminated its street crime concerns. In 2011, it was found to have the ninth-highest crime risk index in America. With the national average represented by 100, Kansas City measured in at 337.

Response of Local Law Enforcement to Street Crime

While the specific causes for the ebb and flow of street crime in Kansas City over time cannot be precisely determined, police departments in Kansas City have historically been known for a

willingness to experiment with tactics in an effort to limit criminal activity. Between 1972 and 1973, the Police Foundation evaluated a preventive patrol test within the city limits. The study aimed to determine if the presence of police officers in marked cars reduced the possibility of a crime being committed, and if citizens noticed changes in patrol levels or changed their attitudes regarding fear of crime or satisfaction with the police. To execute the study, they used three patrol beats and varied the patrol routine within each group. One group had police only responding to calls, another had regular patrol levels, and the final group received a minimum of double patrols. Ultimately, the results demonstrated that routine patrols in marked cars had little value in preventing crime or helping citizens feel more safe. Richard Wright—a criminologist—spent time researching street crime in Kansas City, including carjackers, armed robbers, drug dealers and residential burglars.

Between 1986 and 1989, Kansas City experienced a significant rise in drug-related crimes; drug-related arrests more than tripled from 1,110 in 1988 to 3,806 in 1989. From 1988 to 1989, there was also an increased perception among citizens that crack houses were spreading in Kansas City. As a result, pressure was put on the Kansas City Police to address the problem. The department introduced a Street Narcotics Unit in 1989 to raid crack houses

In June 2010, Kansas City police outfitted seven patrol cars with a Mobile Plate Hunter license plate reader system, which takes infrared pictures of plates, compares them to a hot list database of warrants and stolen vehicles, and archives the data.

on blocks with high crime rates. Unlike other similar programs, the goal in Kansas City was to restore public order through reducing crack-related crime rather than locking up offenders. Over time, the plan largely succeeded.

More recently, two new programs were developed in Kansas City to decrease property and violent crime rates. First, since 2011, officers are assigned to foot-patrol beats, similar to those common decades earlier. The goal was not to become less reliant on police cruisers, but to learn more about neighborhoods and citizens and develop higher levels of trust. New officers currently begin their careers by spending three months walking a beat in a certain area, generally areas with more rampant crime. Officials have high hopes for the program, which is modeled after a successful program in Philadelphia.

The second program is the Kansas City No Violence Alliance, which uses a focused deterrence approach that has proven to be successful in other cities (such as Boston; Stockton, California; and Cincinnati, Ohio). The alliance consists of Kansas City Mayor Sly James and representatives from the Jackson County Prosecutor's Office, the U.S. Attorney's Office, the Kansas City Metropolitan Crime Commission, and the University of Missouri, Kansas City's, criminal justice and criminology program. To help lower crime rates, the program targets certain offenders and people who are associated with them. These associates are offered opportunities to transition to more productive lifestyles. Ultimately, the hope is to punish the criminals and prevent those around them from following in their footsteps.

Like most cities in the United States, overall levels of street crime in Kansas City are lower than during the early and mid-1990s, despite existing economic conditions that have historically been correlated with high levels of street crime. Kansas City still suffers from both violent and property crimes—11th in the nation in the violent crime index and ninth in the property crime index out of cities with a population of 250,000 or greater in 2010. Ultimately, officials in Kansas City appear willing to utilize new programs in an effort to continue making its streets safer.

William J. Miller
Flagler College

See Also: Kansas City Preventive Patrol Experiment; Patrol Cars; Police (Overview).

Further Readings

Bennett, T. and R. Wright. *Burglars on Burglary: Prevention and the Offender*. Aldershot, UK: Gower, 1984.

U.S. Census Bureau. "American Community Survey." http://www.census.gov/acs/www (Accessed July 2012).

U.S. Census Bureau. "American Fact Finder." http://factfinder2.census.gov/faces/nav/jsf/pages/index.xhtml (Accessed June 2012).

U.S. Department of Justice, Federal Bureau of Investigation. "Uniform Crime Reports (UCR) Data Online." http://www.ucrdatatool.gov/Search/Crime/Local/JurisbyJurisLarge.cfm (Accessed July 2012).

Wright, R. and S. Decker. *Burglars on the Job: Streetlife and Residential Break-Ins*. Lebanon, NH: Northeastern University Press, 1994.

Kansas City Preventive Patrol Experiment

It has been virtually an article of faith that the backbone of modern policing is preventive patrol. This tenet has been around since Sir Robert Peel's founding of the Metropolitan (London) Police Force in 1829. Peel wanted his officers to move from place to place and to be visible to citizens, and presumably to criminals. The use of distinctive uniforms, including high helmets to make the constable even more visible, was a formal part of the patrol function. In spite of its popularity and assumed effectiveness, the idea was seldom if ever tested empirically, with one exception coming nearly 150 years after its inception: the Kansas City Preventive Patrol Experiment.

Structure of the Experiment

Kansas City, Missouri, was seen as a progressive city at the time; its chief of police, Clarence Kelley, would later head the Federal Bureau of Investigation. The city had a population of 500,000 in the city limits in 1970, and about 1.2 million in the Kansas City metro area. The police department numbered some 1,300 officers. The experiment began October 1, 1972, and ended September 30, 1973.

The experiment involved an area that contained 15 beats, which were divided into three groups:

1. *Reactive Beats*: These would have no preventive patrol cars. Police from other beats would respond to calls for service but otherwise the police would not be present in the area on routine patrol.
2. *Control Beats*: These would have a single car on patrol. This is the level of staffing all the beats had before the experiment began. These beats were simply maintaining the status quo.
3. *Proactive Beats*: These would have two or three cars on routine patrol, at least twice as many as existed before the experiment began. If there were to be some preventive effects of patrol, it was thought the evidence of that would occur on these beats.

The zones were arranged so that reactive beats would not be located side by side, to avoid increasing response time to those unpatrolled areas.

Evaluation

Administered in the field by the Kansas City Police Department, the experiment was evaluated by the Police Foundation. The Police Foundation was launched in 1970 with seed money by the nonprofit Ford Foundation, and the very first study it generated in its effort to impact police operational practices was the Kansas City Preventive Patrol Experiment. Researchers from the Police Foundation used a variety of metrics for each experimental condition across the 15 beats to generate data for evaluation, including (1) a victimization survey, (2) an analysis of reported crime rates, (3) attitude surveys of citizens on their perceptions of the experiment, (4) interviews with department personnel, and (5) an examination of other departmental records.

The main findings of the experiment can be summarized as follows: (1) there was no difference by area in level of crime, (2) there was no difference by area in citizen feelings of security, (3) there was no difference by area in citizen perception of speed of delivery of services, (4) there was no difference in fear of crime by experimental condition, (5) there was no difference by area in terms of public satisfaction in

police services, and (6) there was no difference by area in response time by experimental condition.

These results seem to suggest that preventive patrol is not that effective in cutting down on or responding to crime, or even in influencing citizen attitudes toward crime or toward the police—but such a conclusion would be facile. It could be the case, for example, that the three experimental conditions were not optimized to detect whatever differences existed among the conditions. For example, perhaps the results would have been different had the proactive beats used as many as five cars rather than a maximum of three.

This is speculation, but it is possible that the lack of positive measurable results were a function of the closeness of the three conditions, or the wording of survey materials, or the atmosphere under which surveys were conducted, or faulty demographic skewing of data due to the specific nature of the 15 beats selected for the study. While the findings clearly do not emphasize the benefits of preventive patrol, neither do they necessarily condemn the practice. Nevertheless, Chief Kelley's successor, Chief Joseph McNamara, who was in office upon completion of the experiment and publication of the results, stated that the experiment had repudiated "a tradition prevailing in police work for almost 150 years."

Impact on Later Approaches

Empirical evidence accumulated in the experiment tended to validate the survey results; for example, either increasing or decreasing the patrol levels "had no significant effect on resident and commercial burglaries, auto thefts, larcenies involving auto accessories, robberies, or vandalism—crimes traditionally considered to be prevented by random, highly visible police patrol," according to the Police Foundation findings. Among the recommendations by the Police Foundation were that targeted crime prevention activity and resources devoted to service goals might yield more tangible positive results than routine preventive patrol. The Foundation also noted that other police departments could learn about and test new anti-crime approaches and methods, by tapping the technical expertise of outside research bodies.

However, in 1988 researchers Sherman and Weisburd conducted a similar study—but one targeted to known crime "hot spots"—in Minneapolis, Minnesota with the police authorities of that city. This study found what the researchers called "a clear, if modest, general deterrent effect of substantial increases in police presence in crime hot spots." Their work buttressed the idea that stepping up police presence in targeted areas, rather than across a general selection of beats, could provide what they called a "place-specific 'microdeterrence' in the hot spots." Additional studies by other researchers throughout the 1990s, summarized in detail by researcher Braga, has given further credence to this targeted approach.

Robert F. Meier
University of Nebraska at Omaha

See Also: Community Policing; Crime, Displacement of; Crime Prevention, Situational Fear of Crime; Hot Spots; Kansas City, Missouri; Newark Foot Patrol Experiment; Police (Overview).

Further Readings

Braga, Anthony A. "The Effects of Hot Spots Policing on Crime." *Annals of the American Academy of Political and Social Science*, v.578/1 (2001).

Bilodeau, Sara. "Random Preventive Police Patrol." November 12, 2009. http://voices.yahoo.com/random-preventive-police-patrol-4862452.html (Accessed April 2012).

Kelling, George L., Tony Pate, Duane Dieckman, and Charles E. Brown. *The Kansas City Preventive Patrol Experiment: A Summary Report*. Washington, DC: Police Foundation, 1974.

Larson, Richard C. "What Happened to Patrol Operations in Kansas City? A Review of the Kansas City Preventive Patrol Experiment." *Journal of Criminal Justice*, v.3/4 (1975).

Sherman, Lawrence W. and David Weisburd. "General Deterrent Effects of Police Patrol in Crime 'Hot Spots': A Randomized, Controlled Trial." *Justice Quarterly*, v.12/4 (1995).

Kerner Commission on Civil Disorders

The National Advisory Commission on Civil Disorders was established by President Lyndon B. Johnson in 1967 as a response to the numerous so-called race riots that had occurred in the United States in the mid-1960s, including Watts (1965), Chicago (1966), and Newark (1967). The 11-member commission was known popularly as the Kerner Commission after its chair, Governor Otto Kerner, Jr., of Illinois. Other members of the commission included: I. W. Abel, president of the United Steelworkers of America; Senator Edward Brooke (Republican, Massachusetts); Congressman James Corman (Democrat, California); Catherine Graham Peden, Kentucky commissioner of commerce; Senator Fred R. Harris (Democrat, Oklahoma); Herbert Jenkins, chief of police of Atlanta, Georgia; Mayor John Lindsay of New York City; Congressman William McCulloch (Republican, Ohio); Charles Thornton, founder of military manufacturer Litton Industries; and Roy Wilkins, executive director of the NAACP.

"Separate and Unequal"

The commission was formally struck on July 28, 1967, even as rioting and open struggle with police and armed forces was occurring in Detroit, Michigan. In launching the commission, President Johnson entreated its members to provide answers to three primary questions: What happened? Why did it happen? What can be done to prevent it from happening again?

The commission released its final 426-page report on February 29, 1968, following seven months of investigation. Perhaps the most striking passage in the final document, and one which captured public attention, signaled a dire warning: "Our nation is moving toward two societies, one black, one white—separate and unequal."

Perhaps surprisingly, the report became a best seller. Published in paperback by Bantam Books, it quickly sold more than 2 million copies. On the whole it offers a significant work of social-ecological research and cultural criminology. In the end Johnson, frustrated that his administration's efforts to address poverty and civil rights had not been highlighted, chose largely to overlook the report. In any event, only a year later, and a mere month after the release of the report in April 1968, more than 100 cities in the United States were in flames as riots broke out in response to the assassination of Martin Luther King, Jr.

The main conclusions of the commission were that the riots and civil unrest in U.S. cities during the mid- and late 1960s resulted from the ongoing confluence of racist practices and policies within urban centers, both interpersonal and structural, and the economic inequality and worsening material conditions for sections of the working class, particularly among African Americans. Even more, the report highlighted the failures of government-initiated programs and policies, particularly around employment, housing, welfare, and education, to address effectively the needs of poor and working-class residents of the cities.

Frustration with social conditions, and the recognition that governments were unwilling or unable to improve conditions, encouraged outbursts of violence and removed restraints on engaging in riotous activities. The commission concluded that white racism against African Americans played significant parts, perhaps the significant part, in heightening frustrations and contributing to civil disturbances. Of significance remained racist attitudes among police forces in urban centers. That the commission identified white racism as a contributing factor in the riots, and suggested that white citizens bore some responsibility for urban riots, while seeming apparent, would prove to be among the most controversial assertions of the final report.

Recommendations and Responses

Based on its findings, the commission provided a range of recommendations. Among these was for the diversification and sensitization of urban police forces. The commission also advocated increased police surveillance of urban populations and even suggested police infiltration of social and political movement groups and the increased use of informants. The commission also recommended wide-ranging transformations in the structure of urban centers. Part of this transformation should include thoroughgoing desegregation and diversification to end ghettoization. Governments should invest billions of dollars to end residential segregation and move away from public housing based in high-density high rise housing units, and toward smaller-scale and spatially diffuse settlements.

The commission also encouraged government investment in job creation strategies and programs, as well as funding for educational and training projects to address economic inequalities. The commission suggested that government encourage the opening of closed suburban areas to African American residents while also supporting the movement of African American workers to emerging industrial centers outside the traditional cities.

Responses to the report and the issues highlighted by commentators were upon its release, and continue to be decades later, deeply divided along lines of political and theoretical perspective. Indeed, whether the report is viewed positively, as making an important contribution to social understanding, or negatively, as a work of social determinism, corresponds very closely with one's position on the political spectrum (from left to right, respectively).

Conservative commentators have criticized the commission's report for its emphasis on structural inequalities and institutional racism as key conditions contributing to riots in northern urban centers. For conservatives, such structural emphases shift responsibility away from individual actors, the primary focus of conservative critics. In the view of conservatives, the commission report has provided excuses for aggressive behavior rather than highlighting personal factors that might have contributed to the riots. Conservatives even reject the notion that ongoing racism contributed to conflictual social relations that precipitated the emergence of riots.

Other critics, on the left, contend that the commission did not address fundamental structural inequalities and only served as a substitute for real social change. In such a view, the commission served to reinforce law and order policies, which only hindered more progressive, community-based alternatives.

Conclusion

Decades later, in the 21st century, the Kerner Commission is still hotly debated, its findings still relevant both within public discourse and within academic circles. Incredibly, the commission predicted urban and suburban developments that have left many cities in the United States with majority African American (and other ethnic minority) populations ringed by suburbs that are predominantly white. The racialized urban development patterns are matched by class distinctions as the commission suggested.

Jeff Shantz
Kwantlen Polytechnic University

See Also: Closed-Circuit Television; Crime Patterns; Immigrant Neighborhoods; Mobs and Riots; Police (Overview); Racial Profiling; Urban Ethnography.

Further Readings

Boger, John Charles. *Race, Poverty, and American Cities*. Chapel Hill, NC: University of North Carolina Press, 1996.

Graham, Hugh Davis and Ted Robert Gurr. *The History of Violence in America: A Report to the National Commission on the Causes and Prevention of Violence*. New York: Bantam, 1969.

Kerner Commission. *Report of the National Advisory Commission on Civil Disorders*. New York: Bantam, 1968.

Lupo, Lindsey. *Flak-Catchers: One Hundred Years of Riot Commission Politics in America*. Lanham, MD: Lexington, 2010.

Kidnapping

Few crimes elicit the fear that kidnapping does. This is particularly true for the kidnapping of children. High-profile cases both historical (e.g., Charles Lindbergh, Jr., Adam Walsh) and contemporary (e.g., Elizabeth Smart, Jaycee Lee Dugard, and Jessica Lundsford) illustrate this. Subsequent media coverage flames this fear. Indeed, there is concern that the number of kidnappings in America continues to grow from year to year. This fear has resulted in new laws and policies at the state and federal level.

The reality is that kidnapping is understudied. A growing body of research has begun systematically examining kidnapping from both the perspective of the offender and the victim. The resulting literature reflects technological advances related to the collection and dissemination of kidnapping information, and highlights the need for future research.

Dearth of Data

Understanding kidnapping requires an understanding of who is offending, why those individuals are offending, and who is being victimized. There are two limitations to such research. First, inconsistencies between jurisdictions in defining kidnapping have previously hindered efforts to quantify

the phenomenon. In the late 1980s, the federal government funded the National Incidence Studies of Missing, Abducted, Run-Away, and Throwaway Children (NISMART-I). Though limited to only 12 states, the study was the first to explore kidnapping at a national level. A follow-up, NISMART-II, was conducted in the late 1990s, and included a greater number of law enforcement agencies, as well as surveys of homes and interviews with children themselves.

The second limitation is one of reporting. The Uniform Crime Reports (UCR) and the National Crime Victimization Survey do not include kidnapping specifically. To address this, the National Incident-Based Report System (NIBRS) was put in place by the Department of Justice. Drawing from law enforcement records in 31 states, NIBRS includes kidnapping as well as other offenses not broken out in the UCR data.

Estimates from the early 2000s, derived from NIS-MART II, place the total number of caretaker-reported child abductions at approximately 150,000 per year. Estimates of child abductions reported to law enforcement and missing children's agencies from the same time period number slightly more than 68,000.

Types of Kidnapping

Recent scholarship demonstrates that kidnapping is not one-dimensional. There are distinct differences in victimization and offending characteristics between family, acquaintance, and stranger kidnappings. Family abduction is the most common form of kidnapping, with some estimates numbering in the hundreds of thousands. These estimates vary due to different data collection methods, differing definitions between jurisdictions, and combined counts of missing and exploited children.

Infants and small children are the most likely to be victimized by family members, typically parents. Boys and girls are equally likely to be kidnapped by their parents, with the majority being taken from the home. Concerns over child custody and intentions to spite the other parent have been suggested as the main motivations for family kidnapping.

Acquaintance and stranger kidnappings have previously been categorized together, though recent work has separated the two. Acquaintance kidnapping is committed by adults, but also by a large number of adolescents. It is characterized by a higher likelihood of victim injury than other forms of kidnapping, an association with other crimes (e.g., sexual assault, robbery), predominantly male offenders, and a disproportionate number of older, female victims. Like familial kidnapping, most acquaintance abductions are committed in the home.

Abduction of children by strangers has received the greatest amount of scrutiny in the media and among researchers, though it is the rarest form of kidnapping. Most such offenders are males, with school-age and teenage females frequently targeted. As with acquaintances, stranger abduction is associated with the crimes of robbery and sexual assault. Often committed outside, stranger abductions are also the most likely to include firearms, something rare in the context of kidnapping. Further, over half of nonfamilial abductions have reportedly involved sexual assault.

Conclusion

These findings reflect 20 years of research into the phenomenon of kidnapping and child abduction. Contrary to reports in the media, stranger abductions are rare events, while familial kidnappings are the most common. Similarly, the motivations for kidnapping have been found to vary, with some occurring for profit, others for sex, and others to avoid losing custody of a child. Only limited attention has been paid to the contextual nature of kidnapping outside of place (i.e., home or school). However, in spite of limited data and knowledge, the fear of kidnapping has spurred policy changes. The development of NISMART-III is in the early stages, but will continue to enhance knowledge of kidnappings in the United States.

Richard K. Moule, Jr.
Scott H. Decker
Arizona State University

See Also: Children as Victims; Domestic Violence; Fear of Crime; Rape and Sexual Assault; Sex Crimes; Stalking.

Further Readings

Boudreaux, M., W. Lord, and S. Etter. "Child Abduction: An Overview of Current and Historical Perspectives." *Child Maltreatment*, v.5/1 (2000).

Finkelhor, D. and R. Ormrod. *Kidnaping of Juveniles: Patterns from NIBRS.* Washington, DC: U.S. Department of Justice, Office of Justice Programs, 2000.

Miller, M., M. Kurlycheck, J. A. Hansen, and K. Wilson. "Examining Child Abduction by Offender Type Patterns." *Justice Quarterly*, v.25/3 (2008).

Sedlak, A., D. Finkelhor, H. Hammer, and D. Schultz. "National Estimates of Missing Children: An Overview." Washington, DC: U.S. Department of Justice, Office of Justice Programs, 2002.

Tzanelli, R.. "Capitalizing on Value: Towards a Sociological Understanding of Kidnapping." *Sociology*, v.40/5 (2006).

La Eme (Mexican Mafia)

The "Mexican Mafia," also known as La Eme, is a prison gang that originated in California in 1957. La Eme is notable for its domination of criminal enterprises and inmate life in federal and state prison and county jails, and for its projection of power outside the walls in the initiation of and influence on a range of street crimes. The group is considered a correctional security threat group (STG) and a networked criminal gang.

Origins and Characteristics
La Eme is a networked gang with origins in California's prison system. A group of inmates from East Los Angeles formed the group for self protection while incarcerated at the Deuel Vocational Center in Tracy, California. These original *carnales* (i.e., "blood brothers") included Luis "Huero Buff" Flores, Mundo Mendoza, Joe "Peg Leg" Morgan, and Eddie Gonzales. From this initial cadre, the gang has grown to between 200 and 400 actual members with an estimated 40,000 affiliates.

The Mexican Mafia is primarily focused on solidarity and control of drug trafficking, as well as a range of criminal enterprises within prisons and jails and on the streets. Gang activities have included heroin trafficking, drug theft, prostitution, robbery, murder by contract, gambling and loansharking, and extortion, according to the Federal Bureau of Investigation (FBI). La Eme is active in state prisons and county jails throughout southern California, and federal prisons throughout the southwest United States.

A horizontal organization, it lacks a formalized, hierarchical central leadership. Each correctional facility with a La Eme presence has its own separate leaders. The leaders interact in a networked fashion exerting influence rather than direct command and control. Because of the centrality of the Los Angeles gang culture in the group's informal channels of influence, it calls the Los Angeles County Jail "headquarters." La Eme derives its name from the Spanish pronunciation of the letter "M," as in "Mexican Mafia." (It is a separate distinct organization from the Texas Mexican Mafia.) La Eme distinguishes itself with distinctive tattoos. These tattoos generally have Mexican themes, such as the Mexican eagle, the number 13, the letter "M" or "MM," and a black hand. The color blue is also linked symbolically to the gang.

Structure, Links, and Rivals
La Eme emerged as a classic prison gang operating a self-perpetuating criminally oriented entity formed from a select group of inmates with a chain of command and a code of conduct. It retains a high level of racial/ethnic (in this case Mexican) homogeneity, although one of its original members was white. It employs instrumental violence, is entrepreneurial, utilizes covert behavior and actions, engages in

collective drug dealing, and demands unqualified loyalty. All of these are typical prison gang characteristics. La Eme, however, departs from the classic prison gang typology to project power and influence into the street.

In addition to allies behind bars, the gang has a cadre of loyal vassals within the Sureño (Sur 13) street gangs that number 50,000 to 75,000 members in southern California. Affiliates include the Aryan Brotherhood, the "Old" Arizona Mexican Mafia, and Mexikanemi (Texas Mexican Mafia). It is also believed to have ties to the La Cosa Nostra (LCN), providing protection for LCN prisoners. Rivals of La Eme include La Nuestra Familia (and its Norteño gang affiliates), as well as the Arizona "New" Mexican Mafia, the Black Guerrilla Family (BGF), black street gangs, the Texas Syndicate, and Barrio Azteca (Los Aztecas).

Women—wives, girlfriends, and relatives—play a key role in facilitating the gang's external reach by supporting drug transactions, financial activities through mail forwarding, and relaying information garnered during visits. La Eme operates on a "one man, one vote" principle, where its *carnales*, all bonded through a "blood in, blood out" commitment, have input into decisions.

Enterprises and Activities

La Eme emphasizes drug trafficking and collecting "cell" and "street" taxes. It maintains links with several Mexican drug-trafficking organizations and maintains substantial influence over street gangs in its area of operational influence. This influence is derived from the knowledge that members of all gangs will ultimately serve time in jail or prison. The reality of this threat is demonstrated when gangs and their members that fail to pay tribute are targeted for murder in jail and through proxies on the street through the "green light," or *luz verde* for murder.

The gang has also exerted influence over community groups (including drug/alcohol treatment programs) to finance its criminal activities. It is believed to have threatened the Mexican American actor Edward James Olmos, and to have arranged the targeted murder of Ana Lizarraga, a technician from the movie *American Me* that chronicled the gang's activities.

LA Eme members have been the subjects of federal Racketeer Influenced and Corrupt Organizations Act (RICO) indictments. For example, the FBI reports that a single RICO investigation of La Eme resulted in the April 1995 arrest of 22 members or associates, and the seizure of "quantities of marijuana, cocaine, 14 vehicles, 10 weapons, numerous documents, and photographs relating to the Eme's criminal transactions, and in excess of $8,000.00 in U.S. currency." That raid netted seven guilty pleas to RICO charges, one defendant severed for court purposes, one defendant killed before trial, one acquittal after trial, and 12 trial convictions with sentences from 32 years in prison to life imprisonment without the possibility of parole.

John P. Sullivan
Independent Scholar

See Also: Bloods; Crips; Drug Dealing; Gangs (Street); Los Angeles, California.

Further Readings:

Pyrooz, David, Scott Decker, and Mark Fleisher. "From the Street to the Prison, From the Prison to the Street: Understanding and Responding to Prison Gangs." *Journal of Aggression, Conflict and Peace Research*, v.3/1 (2010).

Rafael, Tony. *The Mexican Mafia*, New York: Encounter Books, 2007.

U.S. Department of Justice. "National Gang Threat Assessment, 2009." Johnstown, PA: National Drug Intelligence Center, 2009.

U.S. Department of Justice. "Safe Streets Violent Crime Initiative Report—Fiscal Report 2000." Rockville, MD: National Criminal Justice Reference Service, 2001.

Latin Kings

Among the Latino gangs in the United States that are involved in street crimes, the Latin Kings has long been recognized as both one of the original such organizations and as one of the most violent. The Federal Bureau of Investigation noted in its 2000 "Safe Streets Violent Crime Initiative Report," for example, that some 1,600 self-identified Latin Kings members were imprisoned in Illinois, and that they accounted for more than half of all the violent attacks on other prison inmates and prison guards in the state. The types of crimes for which the Latin Kings have been incarcerated include murder, aggravated assault, racketeering, and carrying firearms while drug trafficking. In terms of its crime record, its network of local chapters across the country, and its internal dynamics, the Latin Kings is a prototypical Latino gang; examining its history and particulars can be useful for understanding the phenomenon of Latino gangs in America.

Origins of the Latin Kings

It is difficult to say exactly when the Latin Kings started. According to its manifesto, it was in the Illinois prison system during the late 1940s, originating as a prisoner self-help group for Latino inmates; whereas community leaders in Chicago recall that it began as a street group called the Latin Angels during the 1950s, and later, according to researchers David Brotherton and Luis Barrios, became the Latin Kings during the 1960s. Another explanation for the group's origin is given by George Knox, director of Chicago's National Gang Research Center, who stated that prior to 1965 there was little evidence of the Latin Kings, but by 1966 the group was "up and going strong throughout the city of Chicago." According to Knox, as well as his colleague Malcolm Klein, it was the focus of Chicago's youth gang workers that gave the Kings its identity. Thus, Knox argues that a detached gang worker program affiliated to the YMCA had the unintentional consequence of facilitating the organization. This occurred after the youth workers organized a "shout out" to gang members in a certain area of Chicago with the result that local gangs like the Spanish Kings, Junior Sinners, and the Jokers came together and somehow formed the Latin Kings.

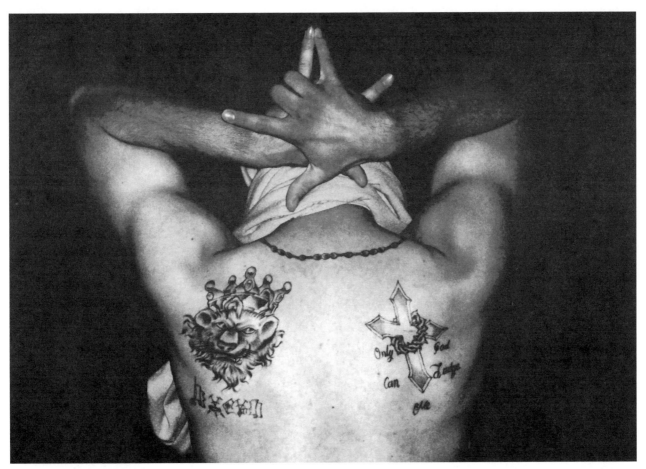

The Latin Kings has long been known as one of the most violent of Latino gangs in the United States. This is an image of a Latin King showing his Latin King tattoo—a lion with a crown, and signifying the five-point star with his hand gesture, which stands for the Almighty in the Almighty Latin King and Queen Nation.

Whatever the precise origins of the group, according to an oft-cited prison study by criminologist Jack Jacobs, the group known as the Chicago Latin Kings moved from the streets to the prisons during the 1960s and 1970s, becoming a "super-gang," a group that was "larger and more violent than their predecessors [whose] . . . location at the intersection of the civil rights movement, the youth movement, and a reconstructed relationship between the federal government and grassroots society suggests a divergence from the traditional street gang."

Geographic Growth
In time, the Chicago Latin Kings developed an auxiliary wing called the Latin Queens, with its own very similar manifesto; both owed allegiance to the Supreme Crown of the entire organization, Gustavo Colón (Lord Gino), also known as the "Sun King," who is currently serving a life sentence in federal prison. During the early to mid-1980s, the Latin Kings spread beyond Chicago to other cities of the midwest, for example Milwaukee, Wisconsin, where a combination of the deteriorating blue-collar job base and the anti-working-class and antiminority political policies of the Reagan administration left a whole strata of youth in conditions described by social scientists as typical of the so-called "underclass."

It is also during this period that the group extended beyond its midwest origins, aided by policies of mass incarceration of lower-class blacks and Latinos, to the East Coast. There it spawned chapters in Connecticut, founded by Felix Millet and Nelson (Pedro) Millan in the mid-1980s; and in New York State, founded by Luis Felipe (also known as King Blood) in 1986 at the Collins Correctional Facility. At this critical juncture, the group on the East Coast became known as the Almighty Latin King and Queen Nation, with separate manifestos (or "bibles," as group members usually refer to them) written by the leaders of each succeeding chapter, all of them pledging their allegiance to the Motherland, that is, Chicago. However, members of the New York faction declared that they were now part of an alternate hierarchy, the "Bloodline," which gave them greater autonomy. Still, there was enough cohesion that members in many locations referred to their allegiance to the overarching Almighty Latin King and Queen Nation (ALKQN).

By the mid-1990s, the Latin Kings could boast substantial prison and civil society memberships in chapters throughout the northeast (e.g., New York City, New York State, Connecticut, Massachusetts, New Jersey, and Pennsylvania) with some areas declaring their allegiance to the Bloodline and others to the Motherland, along with still other groups up and running in Florida, North Carolina, and California.

According to law enforcement officials, the group is said to be in 34 states. Additionally, members of the group can be found in Puerto Rico, the Dominican Republic, Mexico, Peru, Bolivia, and Ecuador in the Americas, and currently much further afield in parts of Europe, where there are now chapters in such countries as Spain, Italy, and Belgium—all nations where a growing segment of the working-class is increasingly globalized and of Latin American origin. It is important to note that the reaction to the group in other countries often contrasts to the repressive approach to gangs that dominates the United States. For example, in Barcelona, Spain, and Genova, Italy, the city councils decided to view the group as a "cultural association" of immigrants rather than as a gang. In Ecuador the country's president met with the group's leaders, welcoming them as a positive force against youth disempowerment.

Secret Society
Originally, membership of the group was open only to those who had traces of "Latin" blood—although researcher Dwight Conquergood observed that Chicago's membership is more reflective of the ethnic make-up of the immediate surroundings. However, to join the group, members must pass through various stages of initiation and show that they are trustworthy and committed to the group under all circumstances, including physical threats coming from rival groups. Once in the group, according to the Chicago manifesto, a member passes through three stages of consciousness: (1) the Primitive Stage, wherein the neophyte member is expected to be "immature" and to be involved in such activities as "gang-banging" and being a street "warrior" without the full consciousness of Kingism; (2) the Conservative or Mummy Stage, which is where a member tires of the street gang life but is still accepting of "life as it has been taught to him by the existing system that exploits all people of color—dehumanizes them and maintains them under the

conditions and social yoke of slavery"; and (3) the New King Stage, where the member "recognizes the time for revolution is at hand. Revolution of the mind! The revolution of knowledge! A revolution that will bring freedom to the enslaved, to all Third World people as we together sing and praise with joy what time it is—it is Nation time!"

The aims of the group originally were to create a semi-secret society which would heighten the notion of Latino/a identity for its members and to increase the possibility of Latino solidarity in a society they saw as endemically racist. Over time, however, the group in Chicago developed like many other gangs into a local, territorially oriented organization that, in turn, became a major player in the umbrella organization of Chicago gangs said to have formed in prison during the 1980s, the People Nation. The People Nation includes other large gangs such as the Black P. Stone Nation, The Vice Lords, and the El Rukns—and stands in opposition to the Folk Nation, which includes gangs such as the Black Gangster Disciples, the Spanish Cobras, and the Simon City Royals.

Organizational Structure

The overall organizational structure of the Latin Kings affiliate group in a particular region is hierarchical, with the leadership typically comprised of the Inca (president), Cacique (vice president), treasurer, enforcer or peacemaker, and spiritual advisor. Within this structure are the local tribes whose leadership posts are known as "crowns" (usually five), with the leader known as the Supreme Crown or Suprema. These structures vary slightly according to different regions. The rank and file of the membership is known as "the body."

There are also other suborganizations of the group such as the females and under-18 youth, with the former known as Latin Queens and the latter known as the Pee Wees. Alongside these organizations are different regional councils that provide overall leadership to the city or to the state, and the local tribes, which are essentially branches that represent specific neighborhoods. Such local branches often adopt names that relate to the indigenous and colonized history of the group's members or to the group's primary signifiers or symbols. For example, in New York City there are branches called the Caribe, the Taino, and the Arawak tribes, which each take their name from once large native

populations inhabiting the Caribbean, particularly Puerto Rico and the Dominican Republic, that were mostly exterminated by the Spanish colonizers during the sixteenth century.

Another important organizational characteristic of the group is its meetings. These take place weekly at the branch level where members come to pay their dues, usually about five dollars, deal with the group's local business, hear about infractions by members, and enforce the discipline of the group. Before each of the group's meetings the ALKQN's prayer is recited and it is important to acknowledge the role that an eclectic religiosity/spirituality plays in the group's rites, rituals, and ideology. In some groups, disciplinary action can include physical punishment, the stripping of a member's rank, community service, or a fine. Once a month, when possible, the group organizes a "universal," which is a mass meeting of the membership that in its most political form can take on the appearance of a grassroots community forum.

Ideology

The ideology of the groups vary to some extent according to region. In New York State, for example, during the late 1990s under the leadership of Antonio Fernández (also known as King Tone), the group took a particularly radical turn with an ideology that drew on the group's original interpretation of nationalism, Third World radicalism, and a melding of social justice and self-affirmation themes from Catholicism, Pentecostalism, and different New World syncretic religions such as Santeria and Yorùbá mythology. During this period of the group's transformation it came to be defined as a street organization, that is, a hybrid street collective that had characteristics of both a social movement and a gang. Other branches of the group, however, were less overtly political and engaged in much more traditional street criminal activity such as drug and weapon sales as well as intergang violence.

Symbolically, the ALKQN is represented by the colors black and gold that adorns a member's clothing and beads, and by its five-point crown, which is also often on a member's attire and tattoos, as well as present in the group's graffiti. There is often an upside-down pitchfork somewhere on the design, which represents the group's historic rivalry with Chicago's Gangster Disciples. These crown points represent the five principal lessons embodied in the group's moral code, which can also vary. For example, in Chicago the core principles of the group are: respect, loyalty, love, wisdom, and obedience; whereas in New York they are: respect, honesty, unity, knowledge, and love. When members greet each other symbolically it is usually in the form of a three-point crown that is first banged hard against the heart area of the upper body, accompanied by the exclamation "ADR" or "Amor de Rey" (King Love) for males and "Amor de Reina" (Queen Love) for females.

Conclusion

U.S. law enforcement almost without exception considers the group one of the most dangerous in the nation and labels it a criminal organization. The hostility of the criminal justice system toward this group is reflected in the life sentence given to Luis Felipe, New York's founder, for ordering the killings of his own gang members while in prison. The judge stipulated that the first 45 years were to be spent in solitary confinement at the nation's most secure prison, the U.S. Penitentiary, Administrative Maximum Facility, ADX Florence in Colorado, amounting to one of the most punishing conditions of any federal inmate since World War II.

In contrast, from a social scientific standpoint, the group may be understood as a subcultural formation developed among lower-class youth and adults under quite specific social, economic, and cultural conditions of marginality. The group is capable of great variability in both its practices and ideology, and while some members are engaged in criminal deviance, others are pursuing quite traditional working-class and lower-middle-class lives with goals such as attending school and college, raising families, and working in legitimate employment.

David C. Brotherton
John Jay College of Criminal Justice

See Also: Bloods; Chicago, Illinois; Crips; Gangs (Street).

Further Readings
Brotherton, David C. "The Latin Kings and the Global Process: An Extended Case Study Analysis." *Journal of Studi Sulla Questione Criminale*, v.4/1 (2011).
Brotherton, David C. and Luis Barrios. *The Almighty Latin King and Queen Nation: Street Politics and the Transformation of a New York Gang.* New York: Columbia University Press, 2004.
Conquergood, Dwight. "Homeboys and Hoods: Gang Communication and Cultural Space." In *Group Communication in Context: Studies of Natural Groups,* L. Frey, ed. Hillsdale, NJ: Lawrence Erlbaum, 1993.
Hagedorn, John. *People and Folks.* Chicago: Lake View Press, 1988.
Jacobs, Jack. B. *Statesville: The Penitentiary in Mass Society.* Chicago: University of Chicago Press, 1977.
Klein, Malcolm. *Street Gangs and Street Workers.* Upper Saddle River, NJ: Prentice Hall, 1971.
Knox, George W. "Gang Profile: The Latin Kings." 2000. http://www.ngcrc.com/ngcrc/page15.htm (Accessed April 2012).
U.S. Department of Justice. "Safe Streets Violent Crime Initiative Report—Fiscal Report 2000." Rockville, MD: National Criminal Justice Reference Service, 2001.

Loitering

Loitering refers to a person or persons remaining in a public place or area for a protracted amount of time without an obvious purpose or reason. Loitering prohibitions are particularly common in the United States, with laws and punishments varying according to local governments. For instance, in some parts of the United States, loitering in public areas is a crime in and of itself, whereas in accordance with local laws elsewhere, loitering is only punishable if it is connected with some other form of illegal conduct. In cases such as this, loitering can be considered illegal if it is done for the purposes of begging, drug trafficking, prostitution, public drunkenness, or in conjunction with other street crimes. According to sociologist William Chambliss, whose work has long been held up as seminal concerning vagrancy ordinances and related statutes, such laws originally emerged as tools to benefit the elite and control the lower class.

Chicago and the Supreme Court

Loitering cases have appeared in the news on multiple occasions in connection with the stalking of or harassment of children, including cases of adults facing police charges for loitering on school grounds during hours when children were present. Loitering has also on numerous occasions been tied into the selling or trafficking of drugs, adding another area of justification for local governments to consider loitering a crime—as opposed to a harmless behavior—and react to such offenses accordingly. According to the Federal Bureau of Investigation, combined cases of vagrancy and loitering accounted for approximately 4.8 percent of total arrests in the United States in 2009.

Due to loitering's connection to gang-related activity, in 1992 the city of Chicago, Illinois, adopted a now-famous antiloitering law. This law gave Chicago police officers the ability to demand individuals move on, provided they were perceived as having no purpose for remaining in a public area. Those accused of loitering in these cases would then face imprisonment, fines, or community service. While the gang-related homicide rate fell 26 percent after the law was passed, in 1999 (although some debate the direction relationship between the reduction in homicide and the passage of the law), Chicago's loitering ordinance was deemed unlawful by the Supreme Court of the United States.

The Supreme Court ruled that the law as it stood was too vague (defining loitering as "to remain in any one place with no apparent purpose"), thus failing to give citizens a clear enough concept of what local officials such as police officers considered loitering. In response to the Supreme Court's decision, the Chicago government redefined loitering in the Chicago area as "remaining in any one place under circumstances that would warrant a reasonable person to believe that the purpose or effect of that behavior is to enable a criminal street gang to establish control over identifiable areas, to intimidate others from entering those areas, or to conceal illegal activities." This definition of loitering was not only one with a great deal more detail; it also more directly enforced the Chicago government's original intentions of loitering laws as a way to control or prohibit gang-related activity.

Conclusion

Loitering as a form of street crime is notable for a distinct lack of detail in what constitutes the activity from area to area. Thus police officials enforce the varying laws with different degrees of severity both due to the specific laws in the area and the specifics of the loitering incident. Depending on the area and any suspected activity connected with the loitering incident (stalking, drug-related crime, gang activity), police may simply request an individual or individuals move on, or take more severe action.

Some constitutional scholars have pointed out that antiloitering laws, much like curfews and antivagrancy ordinances, have been used from time to time to quash citizens' First Amendment rights such as freedom of association and assembly.

Loitering is also notable in that cases in the past have raised concerns of racial profiling by police officials. This has formed part of the Chambliss viewpoint, linked as it is to his class-based analysis. Other researchers take various differing views. Jeffrey Adler, for example, downplays control of the lower-class masses (as cited by Chambliss) as a goal of vagrancy laws—but even he points to the desire of governments to manage "social stability" as a direct influence on writing and enforcing the statutes.

Scott A. Richmond
Wayne State University
Patric R. Spence
University of Kentucky

See Also: Chicago, Illinois; Children as Victims; Drug Dealing; Gangs (Street); Juvenile Curfews; Neighborhood Watch; Panhandling or Begging; Racial Profiling; Stop and Frisk.

Further Readings
Adler, Jeffrey S. "A Historical Analysis of the Law of Vagrancy." *Criminology*, v.27/2 (1989).
Chambliss, William J. "A Sociological Analysis of the Law of Vagrancy." *Social Problems*, v.12/1 (1964).
Livingston, Debra. "Gang Loitering, the Court, and Some Realism About Police Patrol." *Supreme Court Review*, v.1999/1 (1999).
Owens, Patsy Eubanks. "No Teens Allowed: The Exclusion of Adolescents From Public Spaces." *Landscape Journal*, v.21/1–2 (2002).
Rai, Candice. "Positive Loitering and Public Goods: The Ambivalence of Civic Participation and Community Policing in the Neoliberal City." *Ethnography*, v.12/1 (2011).
Rosenthal, Lawrence. "Gang Loitering and Race." *Journal of Criminal Law and Criminology*, v.91/1 (2000).

Looting

Colloquially speaking, looting is easily defined. It is the unlawful taking of goods during a period of civil unrest, social upheaval, or disaster. However, it was not until recently that scholars began to consider when and why looting occurs and what factors are associated with it. This entry describes the concept of looting, examines the debate in the literature as to when looting occurs, identifies verified instances of looting, and explains the implications for prevention.

Criminologist Stuart Green notes that three characteristics are common to all types of looting: unauthorized entry, the taking or damaging of goods, and lack of normal security. However, the moral component of looting is on a continuum. At one end of the continuum is predatory looting in which the goods taken have little to do with surviving the chaos at hand. At the other end is survival looting, the appropriation of goods such as food and water that are necessary to sustain life and health. All other looting falls in between these two extremes. Green argues that the punishment for looting should be mitigated or aggravated by both the circumstances of the offender and the effects of the crime.

Disaster researchers Enrico Quarantelli and Russell Dynes maintain that looting is common after civil disturbances such as riots—but very uncommon after natural disasters such as earthquakes and hurricanes. They believe looting is a response to the new norms that are created during a civil disturbance. The line between public and private property is blurred and the taking of formerly private property is viewed as normative and imbued with function, for example, a way to send a message to society about property rights. The reason looting is less common after a natural disaster is because all formerly private goods are needed by the community to survive and rebuild. To loot after a natural disaster would violate the new norm of sharing all goods.

Verified Instances

Extensive property damage and looting have characterized many of the most familiar contemporary historical civil disturbances, including but not limited to the Watts riot of 1965, the Detroit riot of 1967, and the Los Angeles riot of 1992. While the

Background checks on those arrested for looting during the aftermath of Hurricane Katrina in New Orleans, Louisiana, revealed that 45 percent had some sort of criminal record.

precipitating conditions of riots in the 1960s and 1970s are thought to include minority poverty, unemployment, and residential segregation, the precipitating conditions of the 1992 Los Angeles riot can be traced in part to the criminal justice system. The 1991 beating of Rodney King by police during a traffic stop and subsequent acquittal of the police officers involved set off six days of rioting that effectively shut down the city of Los Angeles. Looting during this riot was ubiquitous in several areas of the city.

However, some type of looting has also followed a number of natural disasters. In the aftermath of the San Francisco earthquake of 1906, looters attempted to steal jewelry from corpses and ransacked the devastated Chinatown, looking for relics. The mayor ordered soldiers in the city to shoot anyone they observed engaged in looting. The Wilkes-Barre, Pennsylvania, flood of 1972 resulted in a significant increase in property crime (where property crime was used as a proxy for looting) in the six months after the flood as compared to the six months before. Media reports of looting strengthened the conclusions drawn based on the proxy measure.

The looting that followed Hurricane Hugo, which hit St. Croix in 1989, was massive. Nearly all consumer goods on the island were stolen, and looters ripped wires, fixtures, and carpeting out of homes. Opportunistic thieves stole cash and jewelry from corpses, and both hotels and relief convoys were looted in the wake of the Indian Ocean tsunami of 2004. Again, using the property crime of burglary as a proxy for looting, the burglary rate in New Orleans increased from 82.3 per 100,000 in the month before Hurricane Katrina in 2005 to 245.9 in the month after, reflecting a jump of nearly 200 percent. This percent increase in burglary from the month before to the month after the hurricane was more than double that for any other storm that directly impacted New Orleans.

It is this long list of verified instances of looting in the wake of natural disasters that caused Quarantelli to eventually revise his and Dynes' initial argument. Quarantelli noted that poor socioeconomic conditions in the area affected by a natural disaster and/or a botched relief response may be associated with looting—even when no civil disturbance occurs. Both poor socioeconomic conditions and a botched relief response characterized the Hurricane Katrina disaster, for example, it is actually unsurprising that so much looting occurred in its aftermath.

Implications for Prevention

Looting should be recognized as a real possibility in both civil disturbances and natural disasters. Both emergency planners and law enforcement authorities should be aware of this possibility and ready to combat this crime in the midst of trying circumstances. Moreover, efforts to improve socioeconomic conditions for minorities in times of normalcy will likely prove useful in preventing or mitigating the extent of looting when hard times befall an area.

Kelly Frailing
Texas A&M International University

See Also: Burglary; Mobs and Riots; New Orleans, Louisiana.

Further Readings

Dynes, Russell and Enrico L. Quarantelli. "What Looting in Civil Disturbances Really Means." *Trans-Action*, v.5/6 (1968).

Frailing, Kelly and Dee Wood Harper. "Fear, Prosocial Behavior and Looting: The Katrina Experience." In *Crime and Criminal Justice in Disaster*, D W. Harper and K. Frailing, eds. 2nd ed. Durham, NC: Carolina Academic Press, 2012.

Green, Stuart P. "Looting, Law, and Lawlessness." *Tulane Law Review*, v.81/1 (2007).

Murty, Komanduri and Julian Roebuck. "The Actions of the Criminal Justice System as a Disaster Precipitant: The 1992 Los Angeles Riot." In *Crime and Criminal Justice in Disaster*, D W. Harper and K. Frailing, eds. 2nd ed. Durham, NC: Carolina Academic Press, 2012.

Quarantelli, Enrico L. and Russell Dynes. "Property Norms in Looting: Their Pattern in Community Crises." *Phylon*, v.31/2 (1970).

Samenow, Stanton E. "Making Sense of 'Senseless Looting.'" *Forensic Examiner*, v.14/4 (2005).

Los Angeles, California

This article focuses primarily on street crime within the city limits of Los Angeles, California, and Watts, a district within southern Los Angeles. The data indicate that crime rate trends in Los Angeles remain roughly constant, and that current law enforcement policies and practices are having a significant effect on controlling and containing the criminal element. Along with the imposition of juvenile curfews, gang injunctions, and increased arrest of the most violent gang members, with the exception of attacks against police officers and gunshots in private dwellings, gang crime has decreased as well.

The City of Angels

Los Angeles is a city of contradictions. Known for its motion picture industry, Los Angeles is often depicted as the city of the rich and famous. Los Angeles hosts a population of approximately 3.5 million people and stands on a land mass of 468 square miles. As the most populous city in California, Los Angeles is located in the southern region of the state, near Long Beach and Santa Ana, and adjacent to several cities constituting the whole of Los Angeles County. Also known as the City of Angels, Los Angeles is highly sought out for its business, international trade, entertainment, culture, media, fashion, science, technology, and educational institutions. As the birthplace of cinema empires in the United States, Los Angeles has attracted many celebrities over the years, many of whom reside in the plush suburbs surrounding the city proper.

Despite this picture of wealth, and local achievement, Los Angeles also has the reputation of being the city of "surplus populations." Unlike the rich and famous, the general perception of this group is that they have little or no attachment to the labor market, and therefore little stake in conformity. Because of the stigma of the label, surplus populations in Los Angeles are also seen as a "marginal" or "dangerous" classes, on whom an anticrime war has been waged almost since the city's inception. Questions have been raised relating to the possibility that the war on crime is actually a war against people who are down and out, or people effected by racial and class inequality.

In Los Angeles, as in most large metropolitan cities, much of this population is located in relatively poor, dense areas of the city, which also tend to correlate with high percentages of street crime. However many community leaders would argue that at least 92 percent of the individuals who make up this theoretically marginalized group are hard working people who attend church, send their children to school, and participate in community activities. They are not criminals, and thus do not constitute the dangerous class. Yet this is one general perception of crime in Los Angeles that persists.

While it is true that a criminal element exists in the urban communities of Los Angeles, street crime is not confined to these areas. Crime in Los Angeles is widespread and reflects a variation in the types of crimes committed and in criminal behavior relative to age, race, social class, gender, sexual orientation, and religion. From the affluent districts of Brentwood and West Hollywood to Korea Town, Little Saigon, South Central, and East Los Angeles, crime is part of the social landscape in Los Angeles.

According to the 2010 Los Angeles Police Department's (LAPD) "Crime and Arrest Weekly Statistics Report," crime declined in Los Angeles by 6.9 percent compared to 2009. From a historical perspective, this downward trend has generally continued for almost two decades, while there appears to be some increase in the surrounding cities of Long Beach, Palmdale, and Lancaster since 2008.

Violent Crimes

In contrast to the 314 homicides reported in Los Angeles in 2009, 297 were reported in 2010, representing a 5.4 percent decrease. The incidence of sexual violence in Los Angeles also seems to have fallen. Against the 823 rapes reported in Los Angeles in 2009, 789 were reported in 2010, representing a 4.1 percent decrease during the more recent period.

Los Angeles also has its fair share of robberies; one of the more spectacular robberies occurred in February 1997. The crime was reported by the media as the North Hollywood Shootout, which was more of a miniwar between two heavily armed and armored bank robbers against the LAPD patrol and special weapons and tactics (SWAT) officers. Although both criminals were killed while attempting to escape, 17 officers and civilians were wounded in what appeared to be a daylong exchange of gunfire. However, for the most part, robberies committed in Los Angeles vary little from this type of violent street crime as characterized in other major cities. Again, the recent statistics are encouraging, showing a notable 10.5 percent decrease from the 12,164 robberies reported in Los Angeles in 2009 to 10,890 robberies reported in 2010.

An even more pronounced decrease was recorded in the category of aggravated assaults, with the 2009 reported total of 10,581 such crimes dropping to 9,265 in 2010, representing a 12.4 percent decrease. Thus, total violent crimes registered a year to year decrease of 11.1 percent citywide between 2009 and 2010. Of the four categories of violent crime, the two-year trend of decreasing frequency was most pronounced in homicide—down 23.5 percent from 2008 to 2010—and aggravated assault, which fell by 23 percent in the same period.

Property Crimes

Reported property crimes were also down in Los Angeles during this period, albeit to a less dramatic degree, with a citywide decrease of 5.8 percent. The crime of burglary is somewhat of a mixed bag of perceptions; pertaining to the notion of the professional criminal, burglars are too often thought of as highly skilled thieves who carefully plan and execute their crimes and reap the glamorous rewards of luxury jewelry and large sums of cash. Ironically, Hollywood is more than somewhat to blame for this misconception. Reflecting the general trend, from the 18,325 burglaries reported in Los Angeles during 2009, reported incidences of this crime category fell to 17,191 in 2010, a 6.2 percent decrease in burglaries. A similar rate of decrease was registered in larceny crimes, with the 28,006 personal thefts reported in Los Angeles during 2009 falling by 5 percent to 26,611 personal thefts in 2010. The number of burglary theft from vehicles (BTFV) reported in 2009 was 29,143; this volume fell to

27,540 BTFV in 2010, a decrease of 5.5 percent. The reported auto theft volume in 2009 was 17,940 incidents; this fell to 16,667 reported auto thefts in 2010, representing a 7.1 percent decrease. Of all property crime categories in 2010, auto theft registered the greatest two-year decline, down 25.1 percent from its level in 2008.

Sifting through this official police department data, it reveals that overall, the city of Los Angeles experienced a 5.8 percent decrease year to year in property crimes in 2010 (93,414 in 2009 versus 88,009 in 2010), as well as an 11.1 percent decrease in violent crimes during the same period (23,882 in 2009 versus 21,241 in 2010). Taken together, the sum total of such direct-contact predatory crimes decreased by 6.9 percent (117,296 in 2009 versus 109,250 in 2010). These figures tend to suggest that current law enforcement policies and practices are having a significant effect on controlling and containing the criminal element. Not included in these figures, however, are direct-contact predatory crimes related to child and spousal abuse, which are calculated from the Part I & II Index of the nationally coordinated Uniform Crime Reports (UCR). From the 12,750 reports of child and spousal abuse taken in 2009, there followed a 6.9 percent decrease to 11,873 reported incidents in 2010. While LAPD officers made 9.9 percent fewer arrests in 2010 than in 2009, it can be argued whether this reflected greater crime prevention or a lower rate of successful interdiction of criminal activity.

Gang Crimes

Gang crime represents the most significant medium through which criminal activity emerges in Los Angeles County. The misconception about this type of street crime is that it is thought to be endemic to urban communities only. In reality, gang activity spans a range of suburban and rural areas of Los Angeles, Watts, Long Beach, Palmdale, Lancaster, and Orange County. To further exacerbate the situation, many gangs have ties to organized crime entities such as the Mexican Mafia (also known as La Eme) or the Yakuza, which originated in Japan and throughout the Far East. Statistics for gang crime are compiled by the Los Angeles Police Department Gang and Narcotics Division. The data in this ongoing compilation indicate that just as violent/property crime decreased in Los Angeles, it appears that—with a few exceptions—gang crime

is decreasing as well. For example, as of June 2009, 74 homicides were committed by gang members, in contrast to the 95 homicides that were committed the previous year, thus constituting a 22.1 percent decrease in gang-related homicides in Los Angeles County. The number of gang-related aggravated assaults also decreased in comparison to the same period. According to the crime database, 1,268 cases of aggravated assault were reported in 2009, in contrast to 1,423 cases reported in 2008, constituting a 10 percent decrease.

In a similar trend, the prevalence of rapes reported in gang-related incidents declined at a faster pace than the decrease in this crime overall. In 2009, the LAPD registered 14 rapes by gang members, in contrast to 25 recorded in 2008. As of June 2009, the 1,054 robberies committed by gang members in Los Angeles contrasted to the 1,252 robberies by gang members committed in the previous year, constituting a 15.8 percent decrease in gang-related robberies. The number of carjackings decreased also in the same period, with 40 such cases reported at the same point in 2009, in contrast to 56 reported in 2008: a 28.6 percent decrease. There were 19 reported cases of kidnapping by gang members in the mid-year 2009 report, as opposed to 22 reported at the same point in the previous year. Thus gang-related kidnappings decreased by 13.6 percent, according to the 2009 report. The number of criminal threats also decreased in comparison to the previous period, with 371 cases in the 2009 data, a decrease of 14.1 percent from the 432 cases reported in the 2008 compilation.

Yet in contrast to the overall decline in gang crime, attacks on Los Angeles police officers increased significantly in the same time frame. In 2008, police were the targets of 22 attacks; the frequency of these gang-member attacks on police climbed to 33 in the following year, reflecting a daunting 50 percent increase in attacks on police officers. In addition to the increase in gang violence against police, the LAPD also reported a definitive increase in gunfire occurring in private dwellings. In 2009, 84 cases were reported, in contrast to the 72 incidents reported in 2009. This figure represents a 16.7 percent increase in gunfire in homes and private dwellings.

Overall the data indicates that gang crimes are on the decline except for increased attacks on police and gunfire in private dwellings. With gang activity in Los Angeles on the rise since the 1970s, the question of the cause of such a slowdown in gang crime is critical. One answer is that the LAPD, like police departments nationwide, created specialized task forces and gang units trained to recognize and understand gang culture. Knowledge of gang signs, tattoos, and codes helped police to identify gang members in specific neighborhoods, which gave rise to efficient enforcement of proactive policing against the most predatory and somewhat organized gangs throughout Los Angeles County. In addition, the city of Los Angeles has developed a program that offers $50,000 rewards to citizens who provide information leading to the arrest and conviction of the city's Ten Most Wanted gang members. This has allowed LAPD gang task force officers to concentrate on the 11 gangs it considers the most dangerous. These most dangerous gangs are as follows:

- 18th Street Westside (Southwest)
- 204th Street (Harbor)
- Avenues (Northeast)
- Black P-Stones (Southwest, Wilshire)
- Canoga Park Alabama (West Valley)
- Grape Street Crips (Southeast)
- La Mirada Locos (Rampart, Northeast)
- Mara Salvatrucha aka MS-13 (Rampart, Hollywood, and Wilshire)
- Rollin 30s Harlem Crips (Southwest)
- Rollin 40s (Southwest)
- Rollin 60s (77th)

These 11 gangs, which operate across a wide range of communities spanning Los Angeles County, constitute the LAPD's "most watched" gangs. They are considered to be the most predatory perpetrators of street crime throughout the region, and have therefore demanded special attention. Along with the imposition of juvenile curfews, gang injunctions, and increased arrest of the most violent gang members, gang crime has decreased significantly in recent years.

Conclusion

The success of the LAPD in stemming the rising tide of street crime in the city of Los Angeles must be commended. It appears that the fear and concerns that many Los Angeles residents have expressed pertaining to their own freedom and safety, and the safety of their children, within many urban communities have been allayed for the present. The decrease in violent/property crime in general and gang crime specifically speaks to the effectiveness of the policies enacted over the past several years. The decrease in street crimes as direct-contact predatory crimes helps restore and maintain the image of Los Angeles as the City of Angels. This bodes well for the business and entertainment community, which depends on tourism and the production of goods and services on a grand scale.

Although many misconceptions about the citizens who inhabit the relatively poorest and most dense areas of the city persists, the fact remains that the criminal class constitutes a rather specific group of violent and predatory offenders. The task of the LAPD is to recognize the difference between these groups and continue to target all resources toward the arrest and incarceration of those who constitute a truly dangerous class.

Tracy Faye Tolbert
California State University, Long Beach

See Also: Asian Gangs; Latino Gangs; Racial Profiling; Routine Activity Theory; Urbanization.

Further Readings

Barak, Gregg, Paul Leighton, and Jeanne Flavin. *Class, Race, Gender, Crime: Social Realities of Justice In America*. Lanham, MD: Rowman & Littlefield, 2010.

Cohen, Lawrence E. and Marcus Felson. "Social Change and Crime Rate Trends: A Routine Activity Approach." *American Sociological Review*, v.44/4 (1979).

Los Angeles Police Department. "Citywide Gang Crime Summary." LAPD Gang and Narcotics Division. June 2009. http://www.lapdonline.org/get_informed/content_basic_view/24435 (Accessed May 2012).

Masters, Ruth E., Lori Beth Way, Phyllis B. Gerstenfeld, Bernadette T. Muscat, Michael Hooper, John P. J. Dussich, and Candice A. Skrapec. *Realities and Challenges*. New York: McGraw-Hill, 2011.

Maple, Jack

Jack Maple, former deputy commissioner for crime strategies (1994–96) in the New York City Police Department (NYPD), is best known for implementing CompStat in the NYPD, to reduce street crime in New York City. In order to understand his work and his contributions to law enforcement, it is important to review his early years, career, and impact on crime policy and practice in the United States.

Early Years

Little biographical information exists on Jack Maple's early years. Born in 1952, his childhood was spent in Richmond Hills, a working-class neighborhood of Queens, New York. His father worked for the U.S. Post Office and his mother became a nurse's aide after raising seven children. Maple himself intimates that he had few advantages: "Growing up, I had never been one of the kids with the big box of crayons. I never played Joseph; I was the beast in the manger." He admits struggling with school work and earned a General Equivalency Degree having been forced to seek employment while in his last years of high school. At age 18, he became a police trainee with the New York City Transit Police Department. By the age of 21, he was married, had one son, a mortgage on a house in Queens, and was sworn in as a New York City Transit police officer.

Maple never attended college. The Transit Police Department policy required a bachelor's degree for the rank of captain. As a result, when Chief William Bratton, for whom Maple worked, returned to Boston policing in 1992, Maple accompanied him to serve as a crime consultant—understanding that otherwise he would forever remain a lieutenant.

By 1992, Maple had already established himself as a flamboyant character. He sported a black Homburg hat, two-tone shoes, and always a bowtie. Maple felt that using police personnel as crime analysts wasted police officers; from time to time he hassled the Transit Crime Analysis Unit. One day all the men in the unit appeared wearing bowties as payback for Maple's ongoing criticisms. Some speculated that Maple attempted to emulate Edward G. Robinson, a famous Hollywood actor of the 1930s and 1940s, whom Maple faintly resembled. The myth states that at one point in his life he borrowed a large sum of money so that he could live on a yacht in New York harbor and indulge in a swinging life style.

Career

In 1972, Maple became a New York City Transit police officer, a position he loved. He advanced to achieve the position of commander of the Central Robbery Bureau while a lieutenant. Maple devised the well-known decoy tactic in which police officers exhibiting gold jewelry posed on the subway as seriously inebriated passengers. As perpetrators approached to steal the valuables, Transit police would apprehend the thieves on the spot.

Maple created a highly successful warrant unit whose members appeared at the doors of "wanteds" at three in the morning within 24 hours of the warrant having been issued, in order to make successful apprehensions. In many police agencies, warrants are simply not acted upon that quickly. While the 24-7 Crime Analysis Unit of the Transit Police produced crime statistics, using electronic mapping, that appeared on commanders' desks at 7:00 A.M. every morning like clockwork, analyzed with hot spots and patterns, Maple continued to rely on hand-plotted maps to analyze robberies on the subways. Maple could be considered a brilliant strategist. It was these innovative and creative tactics and strategies that bought him to the attention of the new police chief, William Bratton, in 1990.

Impact on Crime

In the 1990s, the triumvirate of Mayor Rudolph Giuliani, Bratton, and Maple created the greatest impact on crime reduction policies and practices in a century, according to numerous observers. Serious crime on the New York City Subway system peaked in 1989; Bratton was hired in April 1990 by the NYC Transit Authority to reverse the trend since ridership—and revenue—declined in response to the mounting crime rate. While Maple pursued robberies and warrants, Bratton led the remainder of the police department to reduce crimes significantly through a modified CompStat process. At the time, the agency recognized that crime reduction occurred at a significant rate, but did not recognize the new, unique, and effective crime reduction strategy as a "system" that could be duplicated by other agencies. When Bratton returned to the Boston Police Department in 1992, with Maple as his crime consultant, Bratton emulated the Transit system, labeling the regularly scheduled review meetings as simply Crime Analysis meetings.

In 1994, Bratton returned to New York City, having been appointed to the position of Police Commissioner by Mayor Giuliani, whose campaign included a promise to reduce crime and clean up the city. Bratton immediately appointed Maple as his deputy commissioner for crime control strategies. Maple used this position to provide an operational structure to the system similar to the one that Bratton had applied in the Transit and Boston agencies. Maple not only articulated the process to others, but through great effort forced the process on a highly reluctant NYPD. He ultimately labeled the process CompStat. The legend was born and crime reduced significantly. (In the literature, CompStat is sometimes referred to as evidence-based policing, and/or intelligence-led policing.)

Once institutionalized in the NYPD by Maple's efforts, the success of CompStat quickly spread. By 1997, one-third of large city law enforcement agencies across the United States had implemented a similar process, and another third planned on doing so in the future.

Maple left the NYPD when Giuliani fired Bratton, and continued his career as a consultant, retailoring and revitalizing the New Orleans Police Department, the Baltimore Police Department, and several other agencies. While in Baltimore, he assisted Mayor Martin O'Malley to create Citi-Stat for the City of Baltimore, a more extensive crime database and the first of its kind in the nation. When O'Malley became governor of Maryland, one of his first actions was to implement an expanded version dubbed State-Stat.

Maple died August 4, 2001, a premature end to a brilliant career. His crime-fighting system converted law enforcement from a disorganized intuitive system to a scientific approach to managing police operations: a lasting legacy.

Phyllis P. McDonald
Johns Hopkins University

See Also: Baltimore, Maryland; Bratton, William; Boston, Massachusetts; CompStat; Crime Mapping; Giuliani, Rudolph; Mass Transit, Crime on; New York City; Police (Overview).

Further Readings

Bratton, William and Peter Knobler. *Turnaround: How America's Top Cop Reversed the Crime Epidemic.* New York: Random House, 1998.

Maple, Jack. *The Crime Fighter: How You Can Make Your Community Crime-Free.* New York: Broadway Books, 1999.

Silverman, Eli. *The NYPD Battles Crime.* Lebanon, NH: Northeastern University Press, 1999.

Weisburd, David. "Reforming to Preserve: CompStat and Strategic Problem Solving in American Policing." *Criminology & Public Policy*, v.2/3 (2003).

Mass Transit, Crime on

Mass transit generally refers to urban transportation that is open to the public and carries passengers along fixed routes for a set fare with frequent, scheduled stops. It includes subways, buses, streetcars, trolley-buses, ferries, and commuter- and light–rail systems. Passengers ride in vehicles and are not, strictly speaking, on the street; many systems are completely separated from street and pedestrian traffic. However, for many riders, their transit journey requires them to travel on the street to get to public transit and wait in areas accessible to the nontraveling public. In addition, many riders, having disembarked from the vehicle or left the system, travel along the street until they reach their destinations.

Whether on or off the system, passengers sometimes face and often fear the types of crimes that are most often associated with the term *street crime.* These include predatory person-to-person crimes and those crimes associated with disorder or disorderly people. Some of these crimes (e.g., robbery and sexual assault) rarely occur on most systems, yet that is in part due to robust security and policing measures. The prospect of being victimized can and does affect potential travelers and increases the costs of maintaining safe and secure mass transit service.

Whole Journey Approach

Examining crime on mass transit from the perspective of a hypothetical traveler encountering a series of physical and social environments along the route is known as the "whole journey approach." The term was developed by Peter Maxson and his colleagues at Crime Concern; it was first used to examine passenger safety along a commuter rail corridor in England. However, the general idea of looking at transit crime in terms of a series of interlinked situational contexts can be found in earlier research on bus crime in Los Angeles by Ned Levine and colleagues.

Situational analyses of the physical and social aspects of crime problems and the crime opportunities they provide are now routinely used to look at crime and disorder on public transport. These analyses often distinguish between two main types of crime-facilitating conditions:, overcrowded situations, and those that lack supervision. Different types of crimes tend to be associated with different types of conditions. This supports the practice in situational crime prevention and problem-oriented policing of being crime-specific when doing situational analyses.

Situational Analyses

Walking to a mass transit node is frequently the first stage of the whole journey, and operators should therefore be aware of the need to treat the local neighborhood as part of the mass transit environment. Recent research by Christopher Ferrell and his team examined the effects of neighborhood crime rates in the San Francisco area on travelers' reported decisions to about how to get to a public transit station. Generally, in neighborhoods with a higher level of crime, travelers chose to travel by car rather than walk or take a bicycle. This was seen as supporting the neighborhood exposure hypothesis.

Driving a car to a transit stop offers its own specific risks. Using a parking lot as part of an inbound or outbound journey may present the potential for thefts of and from cars, as well as personal robbery, especially when there is little supervision of the setting. Improving sight lines by removing vegetation and installing better lighting, establishing strong parking lot boundaries, and providing surveillance at times when the lots might be otherwise deserted—and publicizing these surveillance

Despite the occasional highly publicized incident, many U.S. mass transit systems have low crime rates. Criminal incidents at bus stops are not included in data involving crimes on buses.

measures—are considered good practices and ones supported by research.

Waiting at bus or other transit stop accessible to nontravelers is generally safer where there is potential oversight by someone who might be able or likely to intervene, such as a local resident or business owner, or another waiting passenger.

Stations with passenger-only entry points can have crime rates that are lower than those in their surrounding neighborhoods. Research by Nancy LaVigne on crime on the Washington, D.C., Metro subway system suggests that a system's design and the procedures and practices of its staff can help eliminate potential crime opportunities. Operators of transportation systems with older infrastructures have adopted similar designs and strategies by closing off infrequently used entries and exits late at night, improving lighting, and providing better surveillance opportunities (such as increasing staff presence in passenger areas or installing closed-circuit television, or CCTV).

Riding on a bus or other vehicle, particularly during rush hour, can present overcrowded conditions for passengers in which theft, in the form of pickpocketing, is one potential hazard. Crowded conditions make surveillance and detection very difficult, with victims often not discovering their losses until they have exited the vehicle or the transit system. Sexual touching is another problem sometimes associated with overcrowded conditions. Vehicles tend to be much less crowded at off-peak times, removing the conditions conducive to pickpocketing and sexual touching, but increasing those related to robbery, assault, and vandalism of the system itself. To provide more natural passenger and employee surveillance, systems can operate fewer vehicles (and shorter trains), provide concessionary fares to encourage more travelers, install CCTV, and employ staff to check tickets or monitor conditions.

Destinations, such as transportation hubs, can exhibit conditions that foster crime or fear of crime. A study of New York City's Port Authority Bus Terminal by Marcus Felson and his students at Rutgers University documented the crime and disorder problems in and around this massive facility and the steps taken by police and other officials to help tackle them. For example, some areas of the terminal were made inaccessible to nonemployees, preventing both vulnerable homeless people and lost passengers from being victimized there.

Return journeys, which include all of the earlier stages in reverse, can present special challenges at the final stage in some neighborhoods. Richard Block and Sean Davis studied robberies that occurred in Chicago, finding patterns in some areas of the city that could be related to victimization of passengers leaving rapid transit stations and returning home late at night. This research demonstrates the utility of using crime mapping techniques for transit crime analyses involving crime location.

Keeping It Local

Crime prevention challenges vary widely from system to system—and reporting methods also vary, leading to sometimes tricky comparisons. For example, a 2012 comparison of urban transit agency crime reports conducted by the *Washington Examiner* uncovered some widely divergent findings. The study noted that Philadelphia's Southeastern Pennsylvania Transportation Authority (SEPTA) report was limited only to the part of its network in which the agency deploys its own police force. And the New York City Metropolitan Transportation Authority (MTA) report does not include a range of crimes including arson, auto theft, or petty larceny.

Commenting to the newspaper, Washington, D.C., Metro officials pointed out that their system has a greater volume of commuter parking lots than systems like New York's, which tends to swell automobile-related offenses within Metro statistics. They emphasized that crime rates for Metro parking lots have fallen by more than a third since 2008. They also said that 2011 was the first full year that the Metro employed a crime-statistic tracking database similar to the widely applauded one used by the New York Police Department. The problem of comparability was addressed in 1996 by LaVigne in Clarke's volume. She compared Part I crime rates per million riders on transit systems in four cities—Washington, D.C., Chicago, Boston, and Atlanta—and found that D.C.'s Metro had significantly lower rates than the other systems. For her analysis, only crimes on the systems themselves (and not in commuter parking lots) and at times when all systems were open (6:00 A.M. to 1:00 A.M.) were used.

Conclusion

In conclusion, mass transit operators in the United States need to work cooperatively with police and the local community organizations to address the conditions associated with both crime and fear of crime along these "whole journeys." These risks and fears vary not only by setting but also by type of traveler. Recent research led by Anastasia Loukaitou-Sideris found that few U.S. operators have developed programs directed toward women's security concerns, even though women's higher levels of fear of crime on mass transit—in comparison with men's—have been widely documented.

Without these types of programs, many potential passengers may be reluctant to use mass transit, since perceptions of unacceptable risk at any point in a journey may become a reason for not traveling at all.

Martha Jane Smith
Wichita State University

See Also: Crime Prevention, Situational; Environmental Criminology; Fear of Crime; Goetz, Bernhard; Routine Activity Theory.

Further Readings
Clarke, Ronald V., ed. "Preventing Mass Transit Crime." *Crime Prevention Studies*, v.6/1. Boulder, CO: Lynne Rienner Publishers, 1996.

Crime Concern. Secure Transport Route – Manchester (Victoria) to Clitheroe Pilot. London: Department of the Environment, Transport and the Regions, 2001.

Ferrell, Christopher, Shishir Mathur, Justin Meek, and Matthew Piven. *Neighborhood Crime and Travel Behavior: An Investigation of the Influence of Neighborhood Crime Rates on Mode Choice—Phase II.* San Jose, CA: San Jose State University, 2012.

Levine, Ned, Martin Wachs, and Elham Shirazi. "Crime at Bus Stops: A Study of Environmental Factors." *Journal of Architectural Planning and Research*, v.3/4 (1986).

Loukaitou-Sideris, Anastasia, et al. *How to Ease Women's Fear of Transportation Environments: Case Studies and Best Practices.* San Jose, CA: San Jose State University, 2009.

Smith, Martha J. and Ronald V. Clarke. "Crime and Public Transport." *Crime and Justice: A Review of Research*, v.27/1 (2000).

Smith, Martha J. and Derek Cornish, eds. *Secure and Tranquil Travel: Preventing Crime and Disorder on Public Transport.* London: Jill Dando Institute for Crime Science, 2006.

Weir, Kytja. "Metro Crime Rate Tops Other Transit Systems." *Washington Examiner* (February 29, 2012). http://www.m.washingtonexaminer.com/metro-crime-rate-tops-other-transit-systems (Accessed April 2012).

Massage Parlors

Massage parlors are commercial establishments where customers can purchase a massage. Some massage parlors are legitimate businesses offering a wide range of massage and spa services; however, other massage parlors offer erotic or sensual massages and operate illegally by having masseuses (far more prevalent than masseurs) provide sexual services in exchange for money, mainly to male clientele. Although it may be difficult to differentiate between some of the legitimate and illegitimate massage parlors from the outside, there are some illegitimate massage parlors that explicitly advertise "happy endings," which refers to massages designed to bring the client to a point of sexual climax (i.e., ejaculation).

Houses of Prostitution

Those who seek out erotic massages may use online review sites for erotic massage parlors (e.g., www.rubmaps.com) to select a parlor and/or a specific masseuse. On Internet review sites, customers provide information about each masseuse (i.e., age, height, build, hair color, eye color, race/ethnicity, breast size/implants, etc.), report the amount they paid for admission (ranging from $40 to $80 per hour), list the sexual services received, and indicate the amount of the tip or additional fee paid for the "extras" (ranging from $60 to $200). The customers sometimes use a five-star system to rate the quality of the provider, the service, and the massage as well as provide comments detailing their experiences.

When erotic massage parlors first emerged in the United States, during the 1970s, the majority of these massage parlors were "massage and masturbation only" parlors. Today, many massage parlors offer a wider range of services, including oral and/or vaginal sex, by request. In other words, some massage parlors are simply fronts for illegal brothels. As such, massage parlors are believed to be one of the main venues for "indoor prostitution."

Most of the so-called erotic massage parlors operate similarly. When a client arrives at an erotic massage parlor, he first requests a massage at the reception desk. When there are multiple masseuses available, they line up and the client chooses a masseuse. If the client asks about sexual services, the masseuse responds by telling the client that she gives "complete" massages. Clients usually pay an up-front fee that covers the cost of admission and the cost of the massage, then pay an additional fee or tip for "extra" sexual services offered or requested during the massage.

Once the client is taken to a room, he is instructed to undress and is offered a shower before the massage begins; it is common for the masseuse to bathe the client either in a shower room or on the massage table (the latter is referred to as a table shower). Once the client is clean, the masseuse begins the massage and/or negotiates sexual services. During the massage, if the client does not explicitly request sexual services, the masseuse may ask if there is "anywhere else" the client would like to be massaged and, if so, to place her hand on the area to be massaged. Most masseuses will specify a fee for sexual acts, while others expect an unspecified tip for the sexual services.

There is no given or standard length of time that masseuses spend engaging in sexual acts with the client. Regardless of the length of massage the client purchased up front, the massage session ends when the masseuse brings the client to the point of climax. Thus, it is in the interest of the masseuse to bring the client to climax as soon as possible. In these parlors, masseuses work an average of 10 hours a day, five days a week, and service an average of 27 customers per week.

Raids and Crackdowns

Historically, erotic massage parlors, as well as other forms of "indoor prostitution," have been tolerated, for the most part, by the larger society. Despite opposition to street-level prostitution, there was little public concern or opposition raised about illegal massage parlors, as long as they remained discrete. Thus, police raids on massage parlors were rare, being initiated only in response to the occasional complaint. Over the past decade, however, we have witnessed a wave of crackdowns against illegal massage parlors in the United States due to the growing awareness of human trafficking and concerns about the suspected relationship between massage parlors and human trafficking.

When police set up sting operations and raid these massage parlors, they often find illegal immigrant women working as unlicensed masseuses and engaging in prostitution. Some of the women may be working there voluntarily; however, police raids of massage parlors have found a number of Asian women who were smuggled into the United States and forced to work as prostitutes in massage parlors in order to pay off their debt for being brought into the country. For example in 2009, two massage parlor operators in Missouri pled guilty to human trafficking charges and were sentenced to five years in prison after a law enforcement investigation discovered that at least 22 Chinese women were being held inside several of their massage parlors and being forced to work 14 hours a day without pay. Similarly in 2008, a 29-year-old man from South Korea was sentenced to two years for smuggling illegal immigrants into the United States and forcing them to work in massage parlors.

These raids, however, do not always lead to convictions for sex trafficking. For example in 2005, as part of an investigation of a suspected South Korean sex trafficking ring in California, federal and local law enforcement officers conducted a high-profile raid, Operation Gilded Cage, of 10 massage parlors in San Francisco and found over 100 Korean women working as prostitutes. Although 29 people were indicted for allegedly bringing these women from Korea and forcing them to work as prostitutes in these establishments, this case did not result in any convictions for sex trafficking. In fact, the sex trafficking charges were dropped against the suspected ringleader when he pled guilty instead to alien harboring and money laundering. Most of the defendants either had their cases dropped or were sentenced to probation and fined.

As these law enforcement sting operations often involve years of surveillance and undercover work, they can be quite costly. Given that most of the sentences that the massage parlor operations receive are relatively minimal (imprisonment for five years or less), some question whether such expenditures are worth it. Others, however, point to the slave-like conditions that many of the masseuses work under and argue that combating such human rights violations should be made a top priority. Based upon recent police activity across the country, there is evidence to suggest that various jurisdictions are continuing to conduct these stings.

Jennifer McMahon-Howard
Kennesaw State University

See Also: Prostitution, Houses of; Sex Crimes; Sting Operations; Women.

Further Readings

Bryant, Clifton D. and C. Eddie Palmer. "Massage Parlors and 'Hand Whores.' Some Sociological Observations." *Journal of Sex Research*, v.11/3 (1975).

Draper, Bill. "Kansas Massage Parlor Operators Sentenced to 5 Years." *Associated Press State & Local Wire* (October 13, 2009).

May, Meredith. "San Francisco: 17 Massage Parlors Closed by Task Force—Undercover Drive by the City Against Human Trafficking." *San Francisco Chronicle* (May 18, 2007). http://www.articles.sfgate.com/2007-05-18/bay-area/17244817_1_massage-parlors-asian-massage-human-trafficking (Accessed September 2011).

Nemoto, Tooru, Don Operario, Mie Takenaka, Mariko Iwamoto, and Mai Nhung Le. "HIV Risk Among Asian Women Working at Massage Parlors in San Francisco." *AIDS Education and Prevention*, v.15/3 (2003).

Weitzer, Ronald. "Prostitution Control in America: Rethinking Public Policy." *Crime, Law and Social Change*, v.32/1 (1999).

Mental Illness

While it is well documented that mental illness is disproportionate among prison and jail inmates, a consideration of mental illness is particularly relevant with respect to understanding the causes and implications of street crime. Street crime encompasses the most common offenses that contribute to prison and jail population growth (e.g, property theft, illegal drug trade, aggravated assault). Street crime generally excludes organized and commercial crime as well as domestic assault, and is often concentrated in urban neighborhoods with high rates of unemployment and a strong underground economy based in street level drug sales. The emphasis in the United States on zero-tolerance policies and intensive policing as a means to reduce crime and ensure quality of life has fueled increases in arrests for street crimes.

Street crimes such as disorderly behavior, disturbing the peace, loitering, and other behaviors considered to be antisocial and criminal are those for which the mentally ill are more prone. By its very definition street crime is likely to be seen or heard; those individuals who are exposed to the police and other facets of the system may find themselves arrested, and possibly convicted and sentenced to serve jail or prison time. Mentally ill transients are particularly vulnerable in terms of getting caught in the street crime net.

Criminalization and Victimization

It is estimated that approximately 10 percent of individuals with severe psychiatric disorders are incarcerated at any given time. According to the Bureau of Justice, at the end of 2008, federal and state corrections facilities held 1,610,446 prisoners, reaching all time year-end highs. Additionally, at mid-year 2009, another 767,992 offenders were confined to local jails. These figures suggest that there are in the range of 238,000 seriously mentally ill individuals incarcerated in our nation's prisons and jails. Federal reports utilizing broader definitions of mental health difficulties suggest the number of mentally ill is even higher, with more than half of all prison and jail inmates having some kind of mental health problem.

Some critics of the system argue that the mentally ill are being criminalized for demonstrating symptoms of their illness. The mentally ill have more frequent contact with the police than the general population; they are arrested and convicted at rates that surpass their criminal behavior. For example, researcher Linda Teplin found that those exhibiting symptoms of mental illness were arrested at a rate that was 67 percent higher than those who were not displaying those symptoms. Data from the U.S. Bureau of Justice reveal that offenders with mental health problems in state prisons are more likely to receive and serve lengthier sentences than offenders without such problems (although this relationship does not hold for federal prisoners or jail inmates).

Those with mental illness, particularly those with severe mental illnesses, not only are more prone to be criminalized for their mental health symptoms, but also are much more likely to be victims of

The Community Mental Health Act of 1963 was passed to provide funding for mental health centers. It led to considerable deinstitutionalization and patients were released into the community, and many became homeless in larger cities.

crime. Factors associated with crime victimization such as poverty, homelessness, and substance abuse are common among the mentally ill. The vulnerability of the mentally ill makes them easy targets for street crimes such as larceny-theft and robbery. In this manner, the presence of persons with severe and untreated mental illness in the community contributes to street crime rates not only via their criminalization but by their victimization.

The deinstitutionalization movement during the 1970s is seen as a key reason as to why mentally ill persons would end up in the criminal justice system rather than the mental health system. The lack of psychiatric beds and budget shortfalls in community mental health has made it increasingly difficult for the mentally ill to access psychiatric and psychological treatment. Enhancements regarding patients' rights which involve more stringent commitment criteria, as well as confirming the rights of mentally ill persons to live in the community without treatment, may have also inadvertently contributed to the possibility they might be swept up in the criminal justice system via street crime.

Mental Illness and Homelessness

Concurrent with trends impacting the mentally ill is the rising number of homeless individuals, many of whom are mentally ill with nowhere to go but the streets. While there is no definitive answer to the exact number of mentally ill persons who are homeless (due to variation in how mental illness is defined and how and where homeless persons are counted), recent estimates from the National Coalition for Homelessness specify 26 percent of the homeless suffer from severe and persistent mental illness. Using 1996 federal survey data, previous research conservatively estimates that on any given day, as many as 112,000 adults with serious mental illness are homeless in the United States.

Homelessness in and of itself is disproportionately represented in jails and prisons across the country. A study analyzing data from the 2002 Survey of Jail Inmates found that the rate of homelessness among jail inmates was approximately 7.5 to 11.3 times the annual rate of homelessness among the general population. Homeless individuals in jail were also more likely to be incarcerated for street crimes such as a property theft. Past studies have found even higher rates (up to 33 percent) of homeless individuals in jails. Further, time spent in institutions (i.e., jails and prisons) can further perpetuate homelessness after offenders have completed their sentences.

The overrepresentation of homeless and mentally ill persons within the criminal justice system has led many scholars to agree with Teplin's conclusion that jails and prisons have become "the poor person's mental health facility." A 2006 Bureau of Justice Statistics (BJS) report on the status of mental health among prison and jail inmates revealed that 13.2 percent of mentally ill state prison inmates, 17.2 percent of jail inmates, and 6.6 percent of federal prisoners experienced homelessness the year prior to their arrest. Rates of homelessness for mentally ill prisoners were two to three times higher than for prisoners without mental health problems.

From a purely fiscal perspective, the presence of the homeless mentally ill within jails and prisons is a costly means to provide for their care. For example, in 2002, Dennis Culhane and colleagues calculated the cost of one night of supportive housing in New York City at just $41 as compared to a night in state prison or city jail ($74 and $164.5, respectively, excluding mental health treatment). Moreover, these researchers found that the provision of supportive housing for the homeless mentally ill cut prison rates by 74 percent and jail rates by 40 percent. For those homeless and mentally ill persons who received supportive housing but ultimately became incarcerated, placement in supportive housing also reduced the total time spent behind bars.

Mental Illness and Substance Use

In addition to homelessness, comorbid mental illness and substance dependence/abuse is pervasive among prison and jail inmates. According to the 2006 BJS report, not only do a disproportionate number of prisoners report either a history or symptoms (or both) of a mental health problem (56.2 percent of state prisoners, 64.2 percent of jail inmates, 44.8 percent of federal prisoners), there are high rates of mental health problems and substance dependence in jails and prisons across the country (41.7 percent state, 48.7 percent jails, 28.5 percent federal). Earlier studies have found even higher rates of co-occurring substance use and severe mental disorders, with a 72 percent rate among jail detainees. Rates of comorbidity are particularly elevated among female inmates, with women reporting higher rates of mental health problems (approximately three-fourths in both state and federal prisons) and more intense histories of drug use.

The consideration of both mental problems and substance use is relevant for several reasons. Offenders with mental health problems in state prisons are more likely to receive and serve lengthier sentences than persons without such problems (although this relationship does not hold for federal prisoners or jail inmates). Second, inmates with mental health problems are more likely to report having parents or guardians with histories of abusing drugs and alcohol, as well as family members who had been incarcerated, pointing to intergenerational patterns of dysfunction. Finally, many offenders (approximately two-thirds in the BOJ data) who report either mental health problems or substance dependence do not receive treatment during imprisonment, with some studies suggesting even higher rates of nontreatment for women.

The Perfect Storm

The growing numbers of individuals who are mentally ill, possibly homeless, and or dependent on substances is the "perfect storm" with respect to overwhelming an already burdened criminal justice system. A recent report by the Street Crime Working Group (SCWG) in Canada addresses this confluence of factors noting the extent to which both mental illness and addiction contribute to street crime, and how homelessness corresponds to visible disorder. Without comprehensive services addressing mental health, substance dependence, and housing needs, "street criminals" are destined to reoffend, often chronically. The overrepresentation of the mentally ill, their treatment needs, and increasingly their housing needs, within the criminal justice system is a cause for concern among policy makers, criminal justice, and mental health stakeholders alike.

Jails and prisons are typically not adequately equipped to provide psychiatric treatment. Overcrowded facilities further compromise mental health care during a person's confinement. Incarceration may also worsen psychiatric symptoms as a result of the "pains of imprisonment," isolation, or victimization occurring during confinement. Ultimately the mentally ill return to the streets, at great risk of homelessness or hospitalization after release, only to cycle back into the criminal justice system. A study by the Justice Department found that federal inmates with mental illness reported three or more prior convictions. Other studies have pointed to recidivism rates among the mentally ill that are even higher than the general population of offenders for relatively minor offenses.

Responding to the Mentally Ill

In order to reduce street crime and the burden of the mentally ill on the criminal justice system, we must respond to the needs of the mentally ill swiftly and humanely. Recent reports by both the Street Crime Working Group (SCWG) and the World Health Organization identify two key levers for reducing the number of mentally ill individuals who commit low-level offenses in prison. First and foremost is the need to divert people with mental disorders into the mental health system before they reach prison. Early mechanisms for diversion, such as mental health courts, are particularly applicable as they are most likely to be utilized for nonviolent misdemeanors and ordinance violations—common violations of the mentally ill. Mental health courts are useful in lessening criminal justice/confinement costs by (1) reducing the time spent in jail, (2) preventing the unnecessary placement of offenders of minor infractions of the law (much of which can be classified as street crime) into more restrictive settings which can further marginalize individuals and intensify their psychiatric symptoms, and (3) lessening future involvement in the criminal justice system. For example, recent evaluations suggest that mental health court participants have lower subsequent rates of criminal charges than those mentally ill persons going through traditional court procedures.

Second, as noted by the SCWG, public safety, public health, and street crime are closely linked. Hence there is a great need for comprehensive and integrated services within the community as well as adequate health care within the criminal justice system. These services encompass supportive housing, given high rates of homelessness; community mental health treatment; and access to psychotropic medication. The lack of access to appropriate and consistent psychiatric treatment in the community is a particular problem with respect to prisoner reentry. For those offenders who were receiving psychotropic medication during confinement, it is not uncommon for them to experience a disruption in their treatment, effectively undermining the possibility of a successful return to the community.

Joyce A. Arditti
Virginia Polytechnic Institute and State University

See Also: Alcohol and Drug Use; Courts, Mental Health; Homelessness; Jails; Urban Ethnography.

Further Readings
Culhane, Dennis, Stephen Metraux, and Trevor Hadley. "Public Service Reductions Associated With Placement of Homeless Persons With Severe Mental Illness in Supportive Housing." *Housing Policy Debate*, v.13/1 (2002).
Greenberg, Gregg and Robert Rosenheck. "Jail Incarceration, Homelessness, and Mental Health: A National Study." *Psychiatric Services*, v.59/2 (2008).
James, Doris and Loren Glaze. "Mental Health Problems of Prison and Jail Inmates." Washington, DC: U.S. Department of Justice, Office of Justice Programs, 2006.
Lovell, David, Gregg Gagliardi, and Paul Peterson. "Recidivism and Use of Services Among Persons With Mental Illness After Release From Prison." *Psychiatric Services*, v.53/10 (2002).
Steadman, Henry and Michelle Naples. "Assessing the Effectiveness of Jail Diversion Programs for Persons With Serious Mental Illness and Co-Occurring Substance Use Disorders." *Behavioral Sciences and the Law*, v.23/2 (2005).

Metal Theft

Metal theft is the theft of items for the value of their constituent metals. Common targets include copper wires, cable, and plumbing; air conditioners and parts for the copper content; catalytic converters from cars for their platinum, rhodium, and palladium; aluminum siding and gutters; electrical transformers, beer kegs, manhole covers, highway guardrails, and more. Jurisdictions across the country have reported steep increases in metal thefts in the last five years, and numerous local and state legislatures in the United States have enacted, or are considering, new metal theft legislation, regulating sales to scrap yards, and increasing penalties for convicted thieves. Rigorous empirical study of the problem, however, remains sparse.

History
Metal theft is not new. In 1756, Great Britain's George II refined existing laws against receiving stolen goods to explicitly include lead, iron, copper, brass, bell-metal or solder stolen from buildings, ships, vessels, wharfs, or quays. Patrick Colquhoun's classic *Treatise on the Police of the Metropolis* (1795) devoted much discussion to the problems of metal thefts in England and metal dealers as the primary fence for the stolen goods. At the turn of the 19th century, American newspapers published hundreds of articles reporting metal thefts. Both Jane Addams and Jacob Riis decried the problem of metal theft as an entry to crime for youth, and the Juvenile Protective Association of Chicago sponsored a comprehensive study of the problem, *Junk Dealing and Juvenile Delinquency*, in 1919.

Metal theft's growth has followed industrialization and demand. It seems to have decreased substantially during the Great Depression and remained relatively rare until contemporary industrialization in developing countries like China sparked new demand and higher prices for metals.

Prevalence and Cost
Reliable data on the prevalence of metal theft are hard to come by, since few police departments collect information on metal theft separately. The Federal Bureau of Investigation's National Incident-Based Report System, which is associated with the Uniform Crime Reports, does include a field for collecting information on precious metal theft (e.g.,

gold jewelry), but it does not collect information for base metals, which comprise metal theft. Consequently, there are no national data on metal theft and, to date, little incentive for police departments to collect that information separately.

Organizations associated with utilities, one of the larger victim industries, however, have collected baseline data on the theft of copper wires. The U.S. Department of Energy's Office of Electricity Delivery and Energy Reliability conservatively estimated the loss to industries from copper wire theft alone to be $900 million in 2006. From a survey of utilities, the Electrical Safety Foundation International estimated there were more than 50,000 copper thefts from utilities alone in 2008, costing more than $60 million.

Though early accounts of metal theft suggested it was occurring mostly in the west, rural midwest, and south, recent data indicate larger urban areas are likely hardest hit. Data on metal theft insurance claims from the National Insurance Crime Bureau (NICB) identified urban areas in the "Rust Belt" (e.g., Cleveland, Ohio, and Flint, Michigan) and other large cities as having the highest rates of metal theft.

One of the most comprehensive attempts to measure metal theft occurred in Indianapolis. The project counted an average of eight metal thefts every day in the first half of 2008 before a drop in metal prices. The study estimated losses from metal theft to average over $1 million per month. It is worth noting the NICB data did not rank Indianapolis in the top 10 cities for metal theft rates, suggesting that many other cities might have (or at least had in 2008) even more costly problems.

Agricultural areas are affected by the crime, too, as irrigation and other equipment are common targets, but the best evidence suggests metal theft is most common in urban areas, particularly residential neighborhoods with high rates of home vacancies and industrial areas with similarly vacant factories and a lot of metal.

Causes and Prevention

To date, the primary criminological explanations for metal theft have stemmed from the Rational Choice and Routine Activity Theories. Foremost, explanations have focused on the importance of metal goods' value and disposability. It is generally agreed that the rise in metal thefts has resulted from steep increases in the prices of metals, spurred by growing demand for metals and speculative investment in base metals. Studies in America and Britain have confirmed a relationship between copper prices and copper theft, with the effect showing a slight lag between price and theft.

Unlike other commonly stolen items, such as electronics, the resale of stolen metal items, such as catalytic converters and copper wire, requires a very specialized secondhand market, which scrap yards provide. The product, often coming to the yards in pieces, also makes it difficult to distinguish between stolen and legitimate items. By knowingly or unknowingly purchasing stolen items, scrap yards might increase metal thefts by facilitating the disposal of stolen goods. Indeed, research has found evidence of a strong relationship between the number of scrap yards in a city (per 100,000 residents) and the rate of metal thefts. Most prevention discussions focus on Rational Choice and Routine Activity Theories. Suggestions include target hardening through surveillance, marking/identification, and physical protections like cages for air conditioners. Resale of stolen goods must be discouraged through regulations requiring identification from metal sellers, prohibiting cash payments, and other similar measures. Finally, public awareness must be raised through education and collaboration between residents, industries, and law enforcement.

Kevin Whiteacre
University of Indianapolis

See Also: Black Market; Burglary; Crime Prevention, Situational; Indianapolis, Indiana; Routine Activity Theory; Theft and Larceny.

Further Readings

Kooi, Brandon. "Theft of Scrap Metal." Washington, DC: U.S. Department of Justice, 2010.

Posick, Chad, Micahel Rocque, Kevin Whiteacre, and David Mazeika. "Examining Metal Theft in Context: An Opportunity Approach." *Justice Research and Policy*, v.14/2 (2012).

Sidebottom, Aiden, et al. "Theft in Price-Volatile Markets." *Journal of Research in Crime and Delinquency*, v.48/3 (2011).

Whiteacre, Kevin and Raeann Howes. *Scrap Yards and Metal Theft Insurance Claims in 51 U.S. Cities*. Indianapolis, IN: University of Indianapolis Community Research Center, 2009.

Miami, Florida

Few other cities in America have been more saturated with street crime than Miami, Florida. Many books, journal and newspaper articles, films, and even the 1980s television show *Miami Vice* have analyzed, examined, or dramatized the street life, street crime, and newfound ethnic culture of the city. Between 1980 and 1985, Miami experienced several polarizing events, such as the Mariel Boatlift, the Miami River Cops scandal, a major race riot, and the crack-cocaine epidemic that put into perspective the prevalence and types of street crimes committed by various offender populations. In the aftermath, a broad range of scholars and journalists examined the historical framework of Miami and its relevance in explaining the contextual criminological elements of police corruption, the transportation of illegal aliens and drugs, and the city's overall increase in crime.

Critical Components

The types of street crimes that have evolved in Miami have been perpetuated and intensified by the use and distribution of drugs, especially when crack cocaine took center stage from the late 1970s throughout the 1990s. During the latter half of the 20th century, crime rates in Miami soared to new levels. According to the Federal Bureau of Investigation's (FBI) Uniform Crime Reports (UCR) data, between 1985 and 1990 Miami experienced a steady increase in violent and property crimes rates, with highest peaks in and around 1990. For instance, the rate of violent crime in 1985 was 2,898.7 as compared to 4,352.8 in 1990, and the rate of property crime in 1985 was 12,223.4 compared to 14,670.8 in 1990, an increase of 83 percent violent and 66 percent property crimes, respectively.

Miami's plethora of historical events in that period altered the social fabric of the city and no doubt contributed to the elevated levels of crime. In 1980, approximately 125,000 Cubans were given permission by Fidel Castro's regime to migrate to America. With this declaration, Cubans crossed 90 miles of ocean to American shores, making Miami their primary area for resettlement—and subsequent criminal activity. Referred to as the Mariel Boatlift refugees, this heightened flow of immigrants into the Miami-Dade County area fueled criminal activity in part because many of the Cubans who came were political exiles, ex-convicts, mentally ill offenders,

and prison escapees. Some of those immigrants committed various felony and misdemeanor offenses such as homicides, robberies, aggravated assaults, illicit drug activities, and property crimes. According to researchers Dale Sechrest and Pamela Burns, Miami's crime rates began to climb dramatically; they note, for example, that the number of homicides went from 142 in 1979 to 239 in 1980, a 68 percent increase. The increase in homicide rates was largely attributed to the Mariel refugees and the rise in illicit drug-related crimes. Miami's homicide rate led the country at various points throughout the 1980s.

During the same year as the Mariel Boatlift, the city experienced one of the country's major race riots. Stemming from several incidents prior to this May 1980 riot, racial tension between the black community and the Miami Police Department revealed heightened levels of injustice and discrimination. After the acquittal of four Miami-Dade police officers, who had been charged with the death of Arthur McDuffie, a riot ensued that lasted approximately five days; some 3,500 National Guard soldiers were called in to help restore order. The U.S. Department of Justice, in its *Prevention and Control of Urban Disorders: Issues for the 1980s* publication, reported that estimates of the costs related to the race riot included overwhelming losses to human life (at least 15 killed and hundreds injured), fires and burglaries racking the black community, approximately $125 million in property damage, and massive loss of employment. The riot caused many business owners to suffer devastating losses; the destruction in urban black neighborhoods was severe.

The importation and distribution of drugs, especially crack cocaine, was another major contributor to Miami's crime problems. With the increase in the drug industry, Miami's police officers and justice system were constantly inundated with arrests of offenders who committed a variety of drug-related crime offenses. Not only did the police face challenges maintaining law and order in relation to the upswing in illicit drug activities, but there was also corruption within the department.

The 1985 Miami River Cops case is considered one of the chief examples of systemic police corruption in the United States. In brief, three incidents of police drug raids on the Miami River led to the arrest of 19 Hispanic police officers, known as the River Cops." As researcher Kim Lersch denoted, these officers were charged, indicted, and sentenced to prison for an average of 23 years for a variety of state and federal crimes, which included drug racketeering, civil rights violations, robbery, and murder. The scandal, according to criminologist John Dombrink, inevitably changed the nature and scope of the Miami Police Department and the community at large.

Between the late 1970s and early 1980s, Miami-Dade County experienced the introduction of crack cocaine into its community and, along with it, increases in crimes such as illegal substance use and drug trafficking, higher homicide rates, prostitution, and juvenile delinquency. As the number of adult crack cocaine users began to increase, juvenile delinquent crack users emerged, too. A study by James Inciardi, Ruth Horowitz, and Anne Pottieger provided a detailed account of the substance abuse and related criminality of a large sample of juvenile delinquents in Miami. This work revealed that not only were these adolescent offenders using crack cocaine, but also a multitude of other drugs such as alcohol, marijuana, and powder cocaine. Prostitution by the female delinquents was a frequent side effect to the drug enterprises of these youths.

Inciardi pointed out that prostitution and sex-for-drugs exchanges had become a growing concern. Other research showed that many female prostitutes in Miami not only had a criminal history comprising

The distribution of drugs is one of Miami's largest crime issues. The coastline surrounding the city makes it extremely difficult for officials to control the import of illegal substances.

burglary, theft, or drug-related offenses but they also encountered and were often victims of violent criminal acts such as aggravated assault, rape, and other street violence. They were victims of these forms of crimes primarily because of the people they encountered and by being on the streets where the violent crimes occurred. The negative effects this lifestyle had on the women also included exposure to human immunodeficiency virus and acquired immune deficiency syndrome (HIV/AIDS), hepatitis, and other sexually transmitted diseases.

Impact of Street Crime

As a result of this chain of major events, and the street crimes that festered along with them, Miami's challenges of the time included high unemployment rates, increased poverty, and rapid decay in various urban neighborhoods and communities. In addition, the court system was inundated with drug-related criminal cases. In order to gain control over the backlog of court cases for drug possession and drug trafficking, Florida's Eleventh Judicial Circuit developed and implemented a court-based substance abuse treatment program for felony drug abusers.

In 1989, the first drug court model began in Miami, the first ever established in the United States. The drug court model was designed to help and supervise offenders in the hope that this treatment approach could reduce the demand for illegal drugs and drive down recidivism. Based on this model, other cities and jurisdictions in the United States began their own drug courts to provide an alternative strategy for judges and the criminal justice system. As the crack cocaine drug market and the level of violent crime began to diminish in the late 1980s into the early 1990s, the overall level of illicit substance use and drug trading still continued to flourish. Since the year 2000, violent crimes such as murder, forcible sex offenses, robberies, and aggravated assaults—many of them drug-related—have continued to increase in Miami. The *Sourcebook of Criminal Justice Statistics* reported that among cities with population over 100,000, Miami in 2004 ranked 9th out of 241 cities, and in 2005 ranked 12th out of 245 cities in overall violent crime rates.

More recently, however, Miami has seen the start of a decline in the rate of violent crimes committed. Based on a five-year comparison study by the office of Mayor Carlos Alvarez and the Miami-Dade Police Department, the total number of violent crimes between 2006 and 2010 decreased by 22 percent. This is of course good news for the city's economy and residents. Although Miami has been characterized as the illicit drug capital of the United States, millions of people continue to visit this city annually to enjoy the life, culture, and diversity that come with Miami's heritage.

Renita L. Seabrook
University of Baltimore

See Also: Drug Dealing; Immigrant Neighborhoods; Mobs and Riots; Police Corruption, Street-Level; Racial Assault.

Further Readings
Dombrink, John. "The Touchables: Vice and Police Corruption in the 1980s." *Law and Contemporary Problems*, v.51/1 (1988).
Inciardi, James A. *The War on Drugs IV.* Upper Saddle River, NJ: Pearson, 2008.
Lersch, K. M. "Drug Related Police Corruption: Miami Experience." In *Police Misconduct*, M. J. Palmiotto, ed., Upper Saddle River, NJ: Prentice Hall, 2000.
Martinez, Ramiro, Jr., Richard Rosenfeld, and Dennis Mares. "Social Disorganization, Drug Market Activity, and Neighborhood Violent Crime." *Urban Affairs Review*, v.43/6 (2008).
Miami-Dade Police Department. "Five Year Crime Comparison Press Conference" March 3. http://www.miamidade.gov/mdpd/Press_Releases/Crime_Stats/2011_MAYORS_PRESS_CONFERENCE.pdf 2011. (Accessed February 2012).
Surratt, Hilary, et al. "Sex Work and Drug Use in a Subculture of Violence." *Crime and Delinquency*, v.50/1 (2004).

Milwaukee, Wisconsin

In 2010, Milwaukee, Wisconsin, had a population of 594,833. Milwaukee's citizens are less white, more black, less educated, more impoverished, and more likely to be victims of street crime than the average American citizen. Though recent downward trends in Milwaukee's street crime rates outpace crime declines in the rest of the United States (Milwaukee's street crimes were down 7.6 percent from

2009 to 2010 and 19 percent from 2007 to 2010), street crime still exists. Community groups and law enforcement groups continue their work in preventing criminal activity and alleviating its affects on the victims and neighborhoods that experience a disproportionate amount of street crime victimization. A brief history of street crime in Milwaukee situates the more detailed explication of Milwaukee's recent response to combatting street crime. Milwaukee's history reflects the promise that America's manufacturing roots offered to a diverse group of immigrants from Europe and the southern United States. In the decade following 1840, Milwaukee's population increased over 1,000 percent, and in 1855, Milwaukee established its first official police force, to assist the community in apprehending the thieving, robbing, and burglarizing criminals who viewed the burgeoning cities as a playground for their illegal activities.

Police History
As in other industrialized U.S. cities in the late 19th century, and in addition to the multitude of street crimes common in such settings, Milwaukee's citizens were presented with riotous and violent mobs as immigrant groups jockeyed for political and economic power and fought for any number of causes. In 1917, Milwaukee lost nine of its police officers and one civilian when a bomb constructed by an anarchist group exploded. This would be the most deadly single event in American law enforcement history, second only to September 11, 2001.

By the early 1900s, Milwaukee had increased its police department to a relative size much larger than other similarly situated cities at the time. Under the 33-year tenure of Chief John Janssen, the police department implemented a system of photographing and fingerprinting suspects to aid in investigations; began a motorcycle patrol unit and a traffic unit; and opened an additional station house in the city's South Side. Despite these innovations in policing, Milwaukee still depended on informal social control systems for preventing street crime and vice, which was at the forefront of many people's minds at that time.

During the Prohibition era, the Milwaukee Police Department (MPD) turned its attention to organized crime, even purchasing high-powered weapons and armored cars, but also maintained its focus on preventing and detecting the prevalent street crimes. For instance, the MPD instituted a police training course, created auto theft squads, began mounted patrols, increased the numbers of police officers (including their first female and African American hires), and opened more station houses to serve a growing population. By 1950, realizing the importance of youth, drugs, and minority relations in Milwaukee's crime problem, the police department created units to deal with each.

Modern Era

By the 1960s, Milwaukee was a city of 800,000 residents, and was dealing with riotous demonstrations as seen in America's other big cities during the civil rights era. The comparatively low crime rates of the prior decades began to rise. Throughout the 1970s, businesses and socioeconomically-advantaged Milwaukeeans left the city, and crime continued its rise. Both violent and property crime rates continued to increase throughout the 1980s. While violent crime rates remained high into the 1990s, property crime rates began a slow decline, and in 2010 were nearing a 25-year low. Even though violent crime rates declined from 2007 to 2010, the 2010 violent crime rate is still higher than most of the previous 25 years (keeping in mind the limits to comparing Federal Bureau of Investigation Uniform Crime Reports data over time). Today, the historic City of Nations is considered by some to be a "big small town"—a large city made up of smaller, distinct, ethnic neighborhoods. Milwaukee's most recent experiences dealing with various street crimes are understood within the city's move toward community problem-solving, in which law enforcement and community groups define relevant problems and work together to devise and implement the solutions.

Community Problem Solving

In late 2007, the *Milwaukee Journal-Sentinel* held a violent crime roundtable, which included the mayor, the district attorney, the Milwaukee county sheriff, and a number of representatives of community groups and social service organizations. This group met to discuss their views of the priorities facing the incoming chief of police, Edward Flynn, and implicated poverty, unemployment, undereducation, family, culture, and police-community working relationships in contributing to the level of street crime (i.e., they discussed criminal violence in the streets, burglaries, and theft of and from vehicles). The roundtable participants noted the

need for the criminal justice community to work with citizens at the neighborhood level to reduce such crimes. Examples of criminal justice agencies working with citizens to respond to street crimes include: the district attorney restructuring its office to respond to crimes by neighborhood; a community justice model of working with prostitutes to help reduce arrests for prostitution; the Milwaukee Safe Streets Collaborative; and the Milwaukee Police Department's Neighborhood Policing Plans.

Comparing the first six months of 2007 to 2010 reveals that homicides in Milwaukee dropped by 14 percent, sexual assaults by 18 percent, robberies by 21 percent, aggravated assaults by almost 38 percent, burglary by under 1 percent, theft by 22 percent, auto theft by 41 percent, and arson by 20 percent. While no means exhaustively nor exclusively street crimes, these statistics give some insight into Milwaukee's street crime situation. Since Chief Flynn took over the MPD in 2007, all of these crimes have declined.

Nonetheless, a comparison of numbers of crimes over a longer time period supports a continued need to combat street crime. For example, though the 2010 overall violent crime rate in Milwaukee is at a five-year low, it is still the city's seventh-highest annual overall violent crime rate since 1985. The 2010 rate of aggravated assault is also the seventh-highest annual aggravated assault rate for the 26-year period. Though such street crimes may be on the decline in Milwaukee, criminal justice officials and residents alike agree that progress remains to be made in ending street crime and its effects in their city.

Gangs and Drug Trade

The amount of drug use and distribution, the number of juvenile and young adult gangs, and the level of easy access to firearms (notably, from dealers within Milwaukee) contribute to some of the most serious streets crimes that occur in Milwaukee. According to the National Drug Threat Survey, crack cocaine is the drug most associated with both the violent and property street crime problems in Milwaukee. As part of their criminal drug distribution activities, such gangs may also be involved in such street crimes as robbery, theft, burglary, assaults, homicides, auto theft, and prostitution rings.

Research on the interactions of illicit drugs and crime explores the tertiary ways in which drug use and the drug trade can lead to other forms of criminal offending against the community. For instance, drug users may commit burglaries, thefts, or robberies to get fast money for drugs, or the underground nature of the drug and prostitution world may make those involved in it vulnerable targets for other crimes (e.g., robbery or assault).

In 2000, Milwaukee was deemed a high intensity drug trafficking area (HIDTA), which focuses local, state, and national law enforcement agencies on the Hispanic, black, and Asian gangs operating in the Milwaukee area. Under the auspices of HIDTA, law enforcement officials noticed a difference in offense type by geographic location and criminal gang. Specifically, the gangs working Milwaukee's South Side are more likely to engage in violence (between gangs or among group members) over turf, whereas the North Side gangs are more likely to use violence to steal guns, drugs, or money from drug dealers. Additionally, in Milwaukee County in 2005, 196 deaths resulted from ingesting illicit substances. In 2006, after receiving a $2.5 million grant from the U.S. Department of Justice Project Safe Neighborhoods, Milwaukee instituted the Milwaukee Safe Streets Collaborative to attack its gang and gun problem by working with Milwaukee's faith community, targeting neighborhoods, increasing penalties at the state level for gun offenses, and including various law enforcement and community agencies.

In 2007, under the leadership of newly appointed Chief Flynn, the MPD began a new era of community problem solving for his organization. The police department incorporated new technologies to increase the number of interactions it had with citizens both for positive purposes (i.e., problem solving) and on grounds of order maintenance and law enforcement activities. The police and citizens together defined neighborhood-level problems (most of which involve street crimes or public nuisances) and created and implemented solutions to those problems.

Operating with an understanding that even low-level street crimes affect citizen's perceptions of their safety, and acknowledging the contribution that responding to these lower-level street crimes can have on the levels of more serious street crimes, the MPD increased their subject and motor vehicle stops (i.e., police stopping citizens when they have reasonable suspicion to believe a violation has occurred or is about to occur). Data comparing the amount of these stops from 2007 to 2009 show a 150 percent increase. These stops are used not only to respond to the observed violations of any number of street crimes, but also to detect evidence of past or potential street crime activity. The intelligence gathered in such interactions (and added to intelligence gathered in problem-solving meetings with citizens) is also used at daily and weekly crime briefings to reveal patterns of known criminal behaviors. This allows a more precise implementation of crime strategies at the neighborhood level.

Violent and property crimes in Milwaukee steadily decreased from 2007 to 2010, from 1,406 to 1,065 and from 6,698 to 5,340 violent and property crimes (respectively) per 100,000 residents. Even as the amount of street crime diminishes, street crime incidents remain the forefront of concern for citizens and criminal justice officials.

Even as the amount of street crime diminishes, street crime incidents remain at the forefront of concern for citizens and criminal justice officials in the city. Though recent approaches to responding to Milwaukee's street crime problem are associated with street crime reductions, most people would argue that any level of street crime is intolerable.

Michael J. Jenkins
University of Scranton

See Also: Broken Windows Theory; Chicago, Illinois; Community Policing; Crime Patterns; Drug Dealing; Gangs (Street); Guns and Weapons; Police (Overview); Policing, Problem-Oriented.

Further Readings
Brandl, Steven and Meghan Stroshine. "The Relationship Between Gun and Gun Buyer Characteristics and Firearm Time-to-Crime." *Criminal Justice Policy Review*, v.22/3 (2011).
City of Milwaukee. "History of the Milwaukee Police Department." 2008. http://www.city.milwaukee.gov/Police/History779.htm (Accessed June 2012).
Jenkins, Michael J. *Bringing Police into the 21st Century: Police Leaders in the New Community Problem-Solving Era.* Boulder, CO: Lynne Rienner (Forthcoming).
National Drug Intelligence Center. "Milwaukee High Intensity Drug Trafficking Area Analysis" 2007. http://www.justice.gov/ndic/pubs22/22850/index.htm#Contents (Accessed June 2012).
Weisburd, David, et al. "Is Problem-Oriented Policing Effective in Reducing Crime and Disorder?" *Criminology and Public Policy*, v.9/1 (2010).

Minneapolis, Minnesota

Minneapolis is the largest city in Minnesota, covering approximately 58.4 square miles with a population of 382,578, according to the 2010 U.S. Census. English is the predominant language spoken in Minneapolis followed by Spanish, Somali, Hmong, Oromo, Laotian, and Vietnamese. In 2007 Minneapolis ranked 47th out of 100 American cities in foreign-born citizens. As the largest city, Minneapolis also has the highest crime rate in the state.

Crime Trends and Hot Spots

Violent crime in Minneapolis rose dramatically in the mid 1990s—murders/non-negligent homicides rose substantially from just six in 1990 to 96 in 1995—earning the city the reputation of "Murderapolis." By 2000, according to the Uniform Crime Reports (UCR) compiled by the Federal Bureau of Investigation (FBI), the murder/non-negligent manslaughter rate dropped to 50 and declined further, to 32 in 2011. Other violent crime categories mainly followed suit. Robberies decreased from 1,794 in 2002 to 1,589 in 2011; assaults declined from 1,920 to 1,715. However, rapes increased in the 10-year period of 2002-11, from 362 to 386; some researchers suggest this may be due to greater awareness by victims and their increasing readiness to report this crime.

The 10-year trends in property-related crimes presented a mixed picture in the UCR. Motor vehicle thefts were cut roughly in half from 3,433 in 2002 to 1,775 in 2011. Larceny-theft cases fell 15.9 percent, from 14,641 in 2002 to 12,311 in 2011. Burglary, however, increased in number of offenses from 4,433 in 2002 to 5,104 in 2011.

To test the theory that police presence decreases criminal behavior, the Minneapolis police participated in an experiment in areas of the city known for persistent street crimes. In 1995, criminologists Lawrence Sherman and David Weisburd designed and implemented the Hot Spots Experiment, utilizing concentrated police resources in select areas of one city block or more, yet smaller than a neighborhood. The outcome of the study generally was fewer calls to the police of sightings of criminal behavior or complaining of disturbances. The activity by police in the two hot spots in the study appeared to have contributed to a prevention of crime in those areas.

Minneapolis continues to use the hot spot theory regularly, and publicizes the effort by publishing crime maps online. Crime mapping is a means of identifying hot spots using a global positioning system (GPS) for tracking. Although a useful tool, the hard numbers of violent crime as reported via the UCR cannot be disputed. Their fluctuating nature from one year to the next sometimes makes it difficult to evaluate a policing strategy, or even to determine the "big picture" trend as it develops. For one example, Minneapolis was listed as 48th in the nation in the city crime rate rankings at 127.47 in 2009—then jumped to a ranking of 331 for 2010, placing the city in a tie with Cleveland for 10th-most violent city in the nation.

UCR figures are also sometimes hard to decipher. Nationally for 2010, for instance, FBI statistics showed an overall decrease in violent crime by 5.5 percent from the previous year. Regionally, violent crime in the Midwest was down 5.9 percent, but the UCR tracked cities with 250,000 to 499,999 populations—including Minneapolis—at an increase of 3 percent in murder. Thus for 2009–10, Minneapolis registered a change in reported violent crimes that was nearly 9 percentage points at odds with the remainder of its region.

Police Response

Although there is a tendency to slot cities in various crime categories, Minneapolis, as with any city, has its share of merits, including safe places to live, relative wealth, and somewhat better than average employment and cost of living, all against a backdrop of cultural diversity and a higher than average degree of environmental sustainability.

The Minneapolis Police Department (MPD) divides the city into five precincts: the first precinct is the downtown core; the second is in the northeast; the third is south of the core; the fourth is to the north; and the fifth precinct is situated in the southwest.

A housing crisis is evident in the north precinct, where the city's share of the national housing bubble collapse is obviously evident with a number of abandoned homes. The north sector of Minneapolis also has the highest violent crime rate in the city. The majority of murders committed in 2010 were committed with handguns and knives; the police report that many were gang-related crimes. Fear of crime in these north-of-downtown neighborhoods is an aggravated form of the atmosphere in all of the neighborhoods bordering the center of the city.

A passerby witnessed more than a dozen police cars on the scene of a crime in the Cedar-Riverside neighborhood of Minneapolis in April 2008. After the peaceful environment experienced in Minneapolis, Minnesota, in the mid-1900s, the city began to experience an increase in various crimes. Politicians debated the causes and created solutions, including increasing the number of police officers, providing youths with alternatives to gangs and drugs, and providing assistance to families living in poverty.

The most affluent precinct—the southwest—experiences the least amount of violent crime.

Due to the economy, the MPD has lately sustained a hiring freeze in terms of new recruits. Indeed, some observers believe that actual crime has not decreased as much as reported as a result of the fact that with less police officers patrolling, lower numbers of criminal offenses will be recorded, whether property crimes or incidents of cleared violent crimes. Violent incident calls are given precedence, with officers sometimes pressured to complete investigations quickly in order to answer other calls.

The decrease in police personnel also affects the follow-up duties on all crime calls. The property complaints are answered when time allows; victims of property crimes may cancel calls or simply not bother to report when they grow accustomed to believing that police do not respond in a timely manner—thus decreasing the overall crime rate as recorded. In their effort to address the pressing need for an expanded and more productive human resources situation, the MPD has deepened its collaboration with the city's Department of Public Safety, the Minnesota Bureau of Criminal Apprehension, the State Patrol, the Hennepin County Sheriff's Office, and the Metro Transit agency.

Blueprint for Action

Prevention programs investing in youth living in Minneapolis neighborhoods are costly and often the first to be cut in times of economic difficulties. In addition, community policing efforts require the input of the neighborhood to be successful. Unfortunately, neighborhoods requiring the most attention suffer from economic hardship with fewer stable families to invest the time in their youth. These neighborhoods struggle with the issue of youth joining gangs and their subsequent arrests. Equally damaging is the overall fear associated with the violence in these neighborhoods. A recent political intervention titled Blueprint for Action, was initiated to curb violence among youth. The MPD, social service agencies, community groups and the city highlight four main goals: (1) connect every youth with a trusted adult, (2) intervene at the first sign that youth are at risk for violence, (3) restore youth who have gone down the wrong path, and (4) unlearn the culture of violence in our community. The plan includes a hospital-based component where young victims of violent crime are evaluated by social workers and aided through 35 community organizations assisting in breaking from a gang, job training, or education. As of 2012, the Blueprint project is ongoing and gathering some momentum statewide. The long-term effects, however, are impossible to predict.

Another novel approach, called the Downtown 100 Program, targets the 100 most chronic offenders in the downtown core. MPD declared that the program, launched in Aril 2010, led to a 74 percent reduction in crimes committed by the first 50 offenders targeted in the city's Downtown Improvement District (DID). Offenders received the services of dedicated prosecutors and probation officers, leading to a lowering of recidivism rates. Drug offenses, theft, trespassing, and disorderly conduct are among the crimes at the core of this program; it is noted that many such offenses can and do lead to more severe street crimes when left unpunished and the offenders unmonitored.

Colleen Clarke
Minnesota State University, Mankato

See Also: Arson; Broken Windows Theory; Community Policing; Fear of Crime; Gangs (Street); Hot Spots; Neighborhood Watch; Urban Planning.

Further Readings

Berg, S. "Minneapolis Progress: Downtown Has Never Been Cleaner, Safer, or Greener." *MinnPost* (March 7, 2011). http://www.minnpost.com/cityscape/2011/03/minneapolis-progress-downtown-has-never-been-cleaner-safer-or-greener (Accessed June 2012).

Bradshaw, Ted K. "Theories of Poverty and Anti-Poverty Programs in Community Development." *Journal of the Community Development Society*, v.38/1 (2007).

Brandt, Steve. "Minneapolis Claims Success Dealing With Lower-Level Chronic Offenders." *Minneapolis StarTribune* (March 2, 2011). http://www.startribune.com/local/117288673.html (Accessed June 2012).

Frost, Natasha A. and Nickie D. Phillips. "Talking Heads: Crime Reporting on Cable News." *Justice Quarterly*, v.28/1 (2010).

Johnson, Dirk. "Nice City's Nasty Distinction: Murders Soar in Minneapolis." *New York Times* (June 30, 1996). http://www.nytimes.com/1996/06/30/us/nice-city-s-nasty-distinction-murders-soar-in-minneapolis.html (Accessed June 2012).

Minneapolis Department of Health and Family Support (DHFS). "Blueprint for Action: Preventing Youth Violence in Minneapolis." Minneapolis, MN: Minneapolis DHFS, 2008.

Small, Mario Luis, et al. "Reconsidering Culture and Poverty." *Annals of the American Academy of Political and Social Science*, v.629/6 (2010).

Weisburd, D. "Hot Spots Policing Experiments and Criminal Justice Research." *Annals of the American Academy of Political & Social Science*, v.599/1. (2005).

Miranda Warnings

Miranda warnings are a procedural safeguard against self-incrimination. The U.S. Supreme Court created the warnings in 1966 requiring that police inform individuals when taken in police custody of their constitutional rights during interrogation. Police give Miranda rights warnings to suspects in the following form:

You have the right to remain silent. Anything you say can and will be used against you in a court of law. You have the right to an attorney during questioning. If you cannot afford an attorney, one will be appointed to you by the court. Do you understand these rights?

Each legal jurisdiction has its own wording variations, but the Miranda warning must be given and must be substantially similar to the above. The warnings are a result of the landmark case

Miranda v. Arizona. Ernesto Miranda was a mentally challenged young man arrested by police and questioned in police custody for two hours. He confessed to the crimes of kidnapping and rape and was convicted at trial. His attorney appealed, arguing that Miranda was unable to exercise his Fifth Amendment protection against self-incrimination (testifying against himself). Without being told of his constitutional rights prior to questioning, and being in police custody, the attorney argued that Miranda did not realize he could refuse to answer the questions of the police.

Constitutional Grounds

The Supreme Court weighed the issues of whether police must inform those in custody of their constitutional rights and whether statements made without notice of rights are admissible in court. In its 1966 decision, the Supreme Court held that the statements obtained from the suspect while in police custody during questioning could not be used at trial. The circumstances of the interrogation did not provide enough protection of the right against self-incrimination. The court found that the prosecution may not use statements obtained from a suspect in police custody unless police show they provided safeguards to protect the suspect's Fifth Amendment right against self-incrimination; the court argued that the Fifth Amendment protects persons from providing testimony against themselves in any setting in which their freedom is constrained.

In addition, the court held that the questioning must stop if at any time the suspect asks for an attorney or wishes to remain silent during questioning, even if the suspect initially waived the right. The government bears the burden of proof to demonstrate that the defendant voluntarily waived the rights. Since the original decision, the Supreme Court has continued to uphold the *Miranda* ruling. The Supreme Court held that protections in *Miranda* are required by the Constitution and cannot be overruled by Congress through federal law.

Exceptions and Controversy

The court has recognized a few notable exceptions where *Miranda* does not always apply. The court's decision in *New York v. Quarles* allows for a public safety exception. The police may question an individual without giving Miranda warnings in cases in which a concern for the safety of the public exists.

The *Illinois v. Perkins* ruling held that Miranda warnings are not required when a suspect has a conversation with an undercover agent. The privilege against self-incrimination does not apply when suspect are unaware they are conversing with police.

In the case of *Rhode Island v. Innis* the court held that spontaneous statements made in custody are admissible whether or not police gave the Miranda warnings. In *Maryland v. Shatzer* the court held that the protection afforded by *Miranda* does not last indefinitely. The court allowed statements by a defendant who had originally refused to answer police questions when the police returned more than 14 days later.

The original *Miranda* decision was very controversial. The Miranda warnings created new rules for how substantive law would be applied. Critics feared that excluding confessions obtained without a waiver of rights and requiring police to inform suspects of their rights would increase the number of factually guilty suspects found legally innocent. The debate centered on crime control versus due process.

Politicians and the police thought the decision would "handcuff" the police and undermine the ability of the police to obtain confessions as suspects would no longer talk to the police. A fear existed that crime would flourish because of an inability to effectively interrogate and convict suspects. Also, as one of the key goals of a street crime arrest is to get the presumed perpetrator off the street, there was concern that Miranda warnings would hamstring the ability of the police to move smoothly from detaining a suspect, and get through the arrest and booking process and into the hearing and court process. In particular, with a street crime suspect who is apprehended "red-handed," some law enforcement agents wondered how the verbal encouragement to remain silent might upset what could have been a natural flow toward confession by the suspect.

The Miranda decision has not had the dramatic impact that many feared. The confession rate has not markedly changed after the decision. In addition, clearance rates and conviction rates have not had substantial changes. The decision does not appear to have heavily impeded the ability of police to do their job.

Bradley Buckmeier
Lawrence F. Travis III
University of Cincinnati

See Also: Arrest; Courts; Police (Overview); Police Detectives.

Further Readings

Bazelon, Adam S. "Adding (or Reaffirming) a Temporal Element to the Miranda Warning 'You Have the Right to an Attorney'" *Marquette University Law Review,* v.90/4 2007.

Justia.com. *Dickerson v. United States*, 530 U.S. 428 (2000). http://www.supreme.justia.com/cases/federal/us/530/428/case.html (Accessed April 2012).

Justia.com. *Illinois v. Perkins*, 496 U.S. 292 (1990). http://www.supreme.justia.com/cases/federal/us/496/292/case.html (Accessed April 2012).

Justia.com. *Maryland v. Shatzer*, 08-680 (2010). http://www.supreme.justia.com/cases/federal/us/559/08-680 (Accessed April 2012).

Justia.com. *Miranda v. Arizona*, 384 U.S. 436 (1966). http://www.supreme.justia.com/cases/federal/us/384/436/case.html (Accessed April 2012).

Justia.com. *New York v. Quarles*, 467 U.S. 649 (1984). http://www.supreme.justia.com/cases/federal/us/467/649/case.html (Accessed April 2012).

Justia.com. *Rhode Island v. Innis*, 446 U.S. 291 (1980). http://www.supreme.justia.com/cases/federal/us/446/291/case.html (Accessed April 2012).

Leo, Richard A. *Police Interrogation and American Justice.* Cambridge, MA: Harvard University Press, 2009.

Leo, Richard A. and George C. Thomas III, eds. *The Miranda Debate: Law, Justice, and Policing.* Lebanon, NH: University Press of New England, 1998.

Thomas, George C. and Richard A. Leo. *Confessions of Guilt: From Torture to Miranda and Beyond.* New York: Oxford University Press, 2012.

Mobs and Riots

The term *riot* is popularly used to describe collective acts of rebellion, unrest, or disorder, usually resulting in instances of property damage or destruction and/or personal violence. Riots typically occur in public spaces such as urban streets or town squares, but they can also occur in closed spaces such as prisons. Riots are generally portrayed as uncoordinated, spontaneous, and disorganized, though much recent research suggests that riots can involve planning and often develop their own logic and forms of coordinated solidarity within the course of the riot.

Nature of the Beast

Riots erupt for various reasons and there are different types of riots depending on the primary focus of anger or reason for emergence. These include: economic riots (such as those over food or housing), political riots (e.g., over government repression, conscription, or taxation), race riots (based on ethnic or cultural differences), and sports riots (those following team victories or losses or involving clashes between team supporters). Riots usually involve property damage directed at targets perceived to represent the cause of a grievance, such as multinational companies, stores, or government buildings. Targets vary depending on the cause or motivation of the riot.

Regardless of the primary cause of the riot, it is generally acknowledged by analysts of these disorders that there is most usually an economic or class aspect to riots, with economic privation or dissatisfaction playing into the eruptions. Some commentators, such as urbanist M. Barnholden, suggest that in the socioeconomic contexts of class-divided societies marked by economic and political inequalities, riots will be regular, and unavoidable, occurrences.

Sociologists arguing from a social structural perspective, such as Émile Durkheim, suggest that activities like riots can serve as a social safety valve, allowing nonelites to release pent-up anger over social, economic, or political dissatisfaction in a limited way that does not threaten society more fundamentally. For such theorists, riots are understandable occurrences within class-divided and unequal societies where the eruption of riots can serve as a useful warning signal that changes need to occur in society before it faces a larger upheaval or disruption. Without occasional outbursts, social anger could lead to more thoroughgoing or radical dislocations.

Scholars also note that riots are not typically the unorganized and incoherent events that they appear to be from the outside. Sociologists drawing upon Durkheim suggest that participants within crowds develop their own value and belief systems, which serve to order and legitimize their activities. Thus there emerges a "conscience collective," or shared value system, of the crowd which can influence the emergence and/or direction of a riot. Notably, the penetration of the crowd by police or perceived

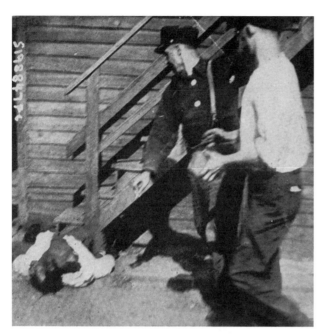

The Chicago Race Riot of 1919 was a major racial conflict, during which dozens died and hundreds were injured. The combination of prolonged arson, looting, and murder led to the worst race rioting in the history of Illinois.

outsiders can spark a defensive reaction contributing to riotous activities.

Politics, Race, Economics

Liberal democracies like the United States have been marked by regular outbreaks of riot and insurrection. Over the first decades of the 21st century there were at least 30 major riots in the United States, including those around Occupy Oakland in 2011, the Santa Cruz (California) May Day riot in 2010, and the riots against the 2008 Republican National Convention in New York City. Some commentators suggest that this reflects the growing disparity of income and wealth in the United States, its larger gap between the very wealthy and very poor, and the sharper class and status divisions, including intersections of race and class and the perceived racialization of poverty.

In liberal democratic polities, riots become more regular occurrences during periods of broader social struggle when organized dissent is more common and social movements are more active. In 1967 alone there were more than 150 riots in the United States occurring in 128 cities (the Long Hot Summer inner-city uprisings) During the 1960s, riots and public uprisings were rather frequent occurrences.

These included explicitly political actions, often spurred by reactions to police violence, such as the riots during the Democratic National Convention in Chicago in 1968 and the Days of Rage actions the following year in the same city. These riots, and the radical movements that developed partly as a result, impacted U.S. politics and have been credited with playing a part in the U.S. withdrawal from Vietnam. There were more spontaneous eruptions, which were also rooted in political frustrations, such as the riots following the assassination of Dr. Martin Luther King, Jr., in 1968. .

In the United States, many of the most notable and infamous riots have been so-called race riots. Indeed the term *race riot* itself emerged in the context of the United States during the late 1800s. Among the most damaging and notorious race riots in U.S. history include: Memphis, Tennessee, 1866; Springfield, Illinois, 1901; East St. Louis, Illinois, 1917; Chicago, Illinois, 1919; Omaha, Nebraska, 1919; Tulsa, Oklahoma, 1921; Detroit, Michigan, 1943; Los Angeles Zoot Suit Riots, 1943; Detroit, Michigan, 1967; Newark, New Jersey, 1967; Akron, Ohio, 1968; and Washington, D.C., 1968.

Originally the term *race riot* was used to refer to acts of mob violence initiated and carried out by numbers of the majority racial, ethnic, or cultural group against members (individually or collectively) of one or more minority groups. By the 1960s the term had come to be applied in situations involving public eruptions of collective violence involving members of racial, ethnic, or cultural minority groups. While the popular term for such events, and the term used by governments, emphasizes racialized aspects of the riots, critics note that modern race riots almost always have economic causes. These include unemployment, job discrimination, inadequate housing, economic depression, or economic transition (as in times of war production).

In response to the riots of the mid-1960s, the U.S. government launched various commissions to study causes of riots and urban violence. The Kerner Commission of 1968 concluded, controversially, that the primary precipitating factor in race riots of the 1960s was ongoing racism by members of the white majority. This included systemic racism within institutions of economic and political authority. Economic conditions caused deeply felt grievances within minority communities but anger was stoked into active aggression following an incident of racism, often including violence committed by a majority member against a minority member, which became amplified through rumor and public representation.

Riots have become more regular occurrences within liberal democracies with the rise of alternative globalization movements and protests. During the late 20th and early 21st centuries, popular mobilizations against capitalist globalization have often been marked by direct actions and the targeting for damage of corporate property, particularly the property of instantly recognizable multinational corporations like Nike, Starbucks, and McDonald's. Of much focus within such protests have been the activities of so-called black bloc anarchists, activists dressed alike in black garb to avoid detection or identification by police. Police aggression, violent arrests, and the indiscriminate use of tear gas, pepper spray, and water cannons against political demonstrators have sparked riots within urban centers in which meetings of global capital are taking place. Riots have erupted during protests against capitalist globalization and following aggressive policing practices, most notably in Seattle during the meetings of the World Trade Organization (WTO) in 1999 and in Miami during negotiation meetings for the proposed Free Trade Area of the Americas (FTAA).

In dealing with protesters during the Miami demonstrations, police and security agencies developed the so-called Miami model of policing demonstrations. The Miami model, which has been applied against citizens in subsequent street demonstrations, involves: establishment of joint, multiagency command networks; mass purchase and deployment of often new or experimental surveillance equipment; use of psychological operations to discredit protesters; association of anarchists with terrorists or criminals; mass arrests and detentions in temporary facilities; disruption of activist media centers and housing spaces; preemptive arrests; use of nonlethal weaponry against protesters; establishment of militarized zones behind fences and barricades; and containment of masses of people on side streets or public squares for lengthy periods of time, followed by mass arrests. Critics suggest that these very practices contribute to the radicalization of demonstrations, thereby increasing the likelihood of riotous activities.

Conclusion

For some commentators, particularly those influenced by Marxism, riots represent forms of "primitive" rebellion, important for mobilizing public dissatisfaction but incapable of effecting real, lasting social transformations. While expressions of class anger, riots lack the organizational forms, such as a political party, that would focus and direct that anger over greater periods of duration. For anarchist commentators, who conceptually reject the necessity of political parties, riots are more properly understood as insurrectionary moments, potentially capable of sparking broader social unrest and raising critical consciousness against economic inequality or state repression. In any event, for anarchists, riots are necessary precursors to larger revolutionary actions and cannot be readily dismissed as "primitive."

Jeff Shantz
Kwantlen Polytechnic University

See Also: Defensible Space; Flash Mobs; Hooliganism; Kerner Commission on Civil Disorders; Looting; Vandalism; Zero-Tolerance/Saturation Policing.

Further Readings

Ellsworth, Scott. *Death in a Promised Land: The Tulsa Race Riot of 1921*. Baton Rouge: Louisiana State University Press, 1992.

Mackay, Charles. *Extraordinary Popular Delusions and the Madness of Crowds*. New York: Farrar, Straus, & Giroux, 1960.

Sugrue, Thomas J. *The Origins of the Urban Crisis: Race and Inequality in Postwar Detroit*. Princeton, NJ: Princeton University Press, 2005.

Motor Vehicle Theft

In the Uniform Crime Reports (UCR) the Federal Bureau of Investigation (FBI) uses a generic definition of motor vehicle theft. This approach is taken so that its national summation of the criminal offense is not burdened with specific state statutory requirements. According to the FBI, motor vehicle theft occurs when someone either steals or attempts to steal a motorized vehicle that runs on land and not on water or rails. Motor vehicle theft is classified in the UCR as a property crime. Some selected examples of motor vehicles include automobiles, trucks, motorcycles, buses, motor scooters, and all-terrain vehicles. Motorized conveyances that would not be considered motor vehicles in the UCR include such vehicles as farm tractors, bulldozers and other construction vehicles, motorboats, sailboats, and airplanes.

Anatomy of a Street Crime

For the average person, a street crime is any type of crime in which he or she feels that they are personally threatened (e.g., robbery) or where their property may be stolen (e.g., burglary) while they are in a public place. Motor vehicle theft generally falls into the category associated with a property street crime. It is a street crime because your motor vehicle could be stolen either from your home, from your job, or from the parking lot at your local grocery store. Under most circumstances it will not matter whether the vehicle is parked on private or public property; it is still exposed to anyone passing by with the criminal intent to steal it. What the vehicle owner has to realize is that in most situations he or she will not be able to directly prevent their property from being stolen. However, what is most interesting about motor vehicle theft is that it usually has the lowest reported property crime rate each year. For example, comparison of the reported property crime rate for larceny-theft, burglary, and motor vehicle theft over a recent five-year period shows that the motor vehicle theft rate is the lowest.

A close inspection of the UCR for 2009 demonstrates that people were more likely to be victims of a larceny-theft (67.9 percent of property crimes in 2009); followed by burglary (23.6 percent of property crimes for 2009); with motor vehicle thefts comprising just 8.5 percent of property crimes that year. There are several possible explanations for these differences. First, it is easier to steal small personal property items, such as a watch or camera. If a thief is looking for an item to steal that can be easily concealed, then he or she will not focus their attention on a motor vehicle. Second, as it relates to crimes of opportunity, a thief is much more likely to steal an unsecured laptop computer than a motor vehicle. The average person may leave a laptop computer unprotected for a few minutes—all the time needed for it to be stolen—but at a minimum, they will usually lock their car when they park. In most instances the average street criminal will steal property that is easily concealed and requires the least amount of time and resistance to steal the

item. Finally, a motor vehicle theft presents a higher level of security for the average street criminal to overcome. At a minimum, people tend to seek high-visibility places to park, and most tend to lock their car doors. Many people, often encouraged by insurance-rate reductions, add simple to very complex security systems to their vehicles in an attempt to prevent a theft.

Security measures as simple as steering wheel lock bars increase the odds in favor of the vehicle owners that their property will not be stolen; if nothing else, the visibility of such devices serves as a deterrent for the opportunistic motor vehicle thief who will more likely select a more vulnerable vehicle. More sophisticated electronic systems—such as those that cut off electronic ignition without proper identity verification—are a further deterrent. Among the most sophisticated technology is the vehicle tracking system (such as the LoJack branded version) that utilizes an installed miniaturized radio transmitter with a tie-in to a vehicle identification number (VIN) database and the National Crime Information Center. Once a victim reports the theft of a LoJack-enabled vehicle, local police departments can tap into the tracking system.

Carjacking

In the UCR, the FBI defines carjacking as a type of robbery where a motor vehicle is taken by force or threat of force. Carjacking is reported as a robbery and not as a motor vehicle theft. In most instances when a person's motor vehicle is stolen, he or she is not directly threatened with physical harm. However, a carjacking places the victim in direct contact with the person who steals the vehicle. The criminal who commits a carjacking uses force or the threat of force to take the vehicle from the victim. The driver of the vehicle is more likely to be harmed during the commission of the carjacking. The use of force reclassifies a motor vehicle theft as a violent crime against the person, as opposed to a property crime.

As a street crime, carjacking places the victim in more danger than a routine motor vehicle theft. Based on data collected from the National Crime Victimization Survey (NCVS), a victim of a carjacking stood a very good chance of facing a car thief with a weapon (74 percent of the time during the period 1993–2002) and a 24 percent chance of being injured if they fought with the thief. The possibility of the victim being physically injured, the data showed, increases the longer that they are in the thief's presence.

The NCVS also found that you have a much higher chance of being the victim of a carjacking if you live in a big city as opposed to a small town. During the period 1993–2002, the NCVS found that 93 percent of carjackings occurred in urban areas. In a big city it would be easier for the thief to commit a carjacking and get lost in heavy traffic, or get out of one jurisdiction quickly and into another. Also, it would not take much effort on the part of the thief to hide the stolen vehicle on a side street or in a garage The propensity for someone to be a victim of carjacking is highest if you live in a city that is in an urban area. The National Crime Victimization Survey reported in 2002 that 93 percent of carjackings for that year occurred in cities located in urban and suburban areas. As a street crime, carjacking resembles a robbery in several aspects. The various "survival tips" on yielding to a robber also apply to a carjacker. The victims decrease their chances of being injured if they do not resist the carjacker. A carjacker is a desperate or risk-taking person; the victims decrease their chances of being seriously injured if they give the thief their car and get away from the theif as quickly as possible.

Organized Motor Vehicle Theft

Due to the relatively high cash value of many vehicles, especially those of recent vintage and wide popularity, theft of motor vehicles is often an enterprise of teams of criminals. In some cases, the stolen vehicles are shipped to neighboring states and resold, using falsified titles and records. In other cases, the vehicles are sent to chop shops, where they are quickly stripped of parts and components that are then sold illegally to less than scrupulous repair stations. In such cases, the stripped shell of the vehicle is typically abandoned.

More ambitious theft rings ship stolen cars—typically luxury models—to foreign countries, making them even harder to trace and where they can command even higher prices than domestic buyers will pay. A typical crime of this sort can involve dozens of perpetrators, scores of vehicles, and be worth several million dollars. Middlemen along the way—container shipping companies, document forgers, import/export firms—all benefit to some degree from the crime.

Conclusion

Law enforcement has access to insurance industry and other databases that can be useful in preventing motor vehicle thefts. Police can also help local residents, business owners, parking facility managers, and motor vehicle dealers understand and utilize both simple and more sophisticated preventive measures to deter such crimes.

Motor vehicle thieves may be operating under the impression that their crime is less likely than other types of larceny to result in arrest—and some statistics bear this out. "Only about 14 percent of motor vehicle thefts known to police were cleared by arrest in 1998, whereas the average for index offenses was about 21 percent," according to research by the Center for Problem-Oriented Policing. The center also pointed to a study, however, that showed a crackdown on persistent offenders within a given jurisdiction can make an oversized impact on the reduction of motor vehicle theft in that area.

In general, property crime rates, both in overall volume and by per capita proportion, are decreasing, and motor vehicle theft rates have been plunging. According to the FBI's Uniform Crime Reports (UCR), over the five-year period 2005–09 the property crime rate per 100,000 citizens dropped from 3,431.5 to 3,036.1—a decline of 11.5 percent. During that same period, the motor vehicle theft rate decreased from 416.8 to 259.2—a dramatic cut of 37.8 percent. While motor vehicle theft remains problematic, its impact on street crime rates has been steadily diminishing. As manufacturers continue to improve vehicle security systems, there will probably be a continued decline in the theft rate to parallel those enhanced security systems.

Benjamin S. Wright
University of Baltimore

See Also: Black Market; Crime Patterns; Organized Crime and Violence; Theft and Larceny; Urbanization.

Further Readings

Bromley, Max L. and John K. Cochran. "Auto Burglaries in an Entertainment District Hotspot: Applying the SARA Model in a Security Context." *Security Journal*, v.15/4 (2002).

Rand, Michael and Jennifer Truman. "Criminal Victimization, 2009." Washington, DC: Government Printing Office, 2010.

Segall, Brad. "International Luxury Car Theft Ring Smashed in Southeastern Pa." April 17, 2012. http://www.philadelphia.cbslocal.com/2012/04/17/international-luxury-car-theft-ring-smashed-in-southeastern-pennsylvania (Accessed April 2012).

U.S. Department of Justice. "Crime in the United States 2009." Washington, DC: Government Printing Office, 2010.

Motorcycle Clubs

Motorcycle clubs consist of bikers from diverse social backgrounds who form associations for the purposes of riding together, sharing mechanical knowledge, and/or partaking in specific motorcycle subcultures such as long-distance cruising, racing, or stunt biking. While the exaggerated image of the outlaw biker persists within popular culture, the reality is that most motorcyclists are law-abiding citizens. Criminal biker clubs, however, remain a significant concern among law enforcement due to their involvement in drug trafficking, prostitution, and racketeering.

History and Image
Although motorcycles have existed in various forms since the late 19th century, a recognizable motorcycle subculture only began to develop in the United States during the 1940s and 1950s. At this time, returning veterans seeking the camaraderie and excitement that they had experienced during the war found it through motorcycle clubs. A number of these ex-soldiers were working-class men who exhibited many of the traits found in popular depictions of outlaw bikers—aggressive behavior, a penchant for drinking and/or recreational drug use, and a desire for power and respect. Most of these men rode large V-Twin Harley-Davidson motorcycles and congregated in bars and pool halls where they formed club rules and regulations.

In 1947, motorcyclists from the Booze Fighters and the Pissed Off Bastards of Bloomington, California, disrupted an event in Hollister, California, sponsored by the American Motorcycle Association (AMA). Known as the Hollister Riots, the violent incident led the AMA to publicly state that the deviant bikers who took over Hollister's main drag were not representative of 99 percent of motorcyclists. This declaration led the outlaws to adopt the title of "one percenter," a moniker that many continue to use with pride.

As news spread of this event, which left 50 people injured and landed nearly 100 bikers in jail, popular depictions of motorcyclists began to focus on the criminal element, as reflected in films like *The Wild One* (1953) and *Easy Rider* (1969); books like Hunter S. Thompson's *Hell's Angels: A Strange and Terrible Saga* (1966) and Danny Lyon's *The Bikeriders* (1968); as well as the 1970s *Ghost Rider* comic book series.

By the 1960s, competition from Japanese manufacturers like Honda, Yamaha, Kawasaki, and Suzuki made pricing more affordable and increased the options available to American consumers. Consequently, many different motorcycle clubs formed during this period and street racing became a greater concern for authorities with the introduction of these new high-speed models. Despite more tattoos, piercings, and other traditional marks of deviance, these motorcyclists are generally not involved in street crimes and may be more accurately classified as "pseudo-deviants," argues social psychologist William Thompson.

Criminal Minority
Many contemporary bikers are termed *weekend warriors* because they follow law-abiding professional schedules five days per week and gather to ride and display their motorcycles on weekends. News reports, however, continue to focus on the criminal minority of bikers. About 300 criminal motorcycle clubs are estimated to exist within the United States—with ties to street gangs, drug cartels, and other organized crime groups.

While some scholars use the term *Big Four* to include Hells Angels, Bandidos, Outlaws, and Pagans, others employ the term *Big Five* and add the term *Sons of Silence*. The customized Harley-Davidson, with its distinct engine reverberation that can be heard from far away, remains a staple of these groups. The Hells Angels and other clubs continue to make these motorcycles mandatory for their members, while generally abhorring foreign-made machines.

Most outlaw motorcycle clubs are composed of heterosexual Caucasian males of different levels of involvement. Clubs usually consist of full-patched members and prospects who take orders from the former. Though uncommon, certain clubs are known to include more diverse ethnicities, such as the Chicano Mongols (Los Angeles), the African American East Bay Dragons (Oakland), and the mixed-ethnicity Wheels of Soul (Philadelphia). For the most part, however, biker clubs of all kinds remain dominated by white men. The women involved in one-percent organizations are generally subservient. Their roles consist of "mamas," who are treated as club property and available for all the men's sexual desires, and "old ladies," who are considered the property of one member (though he may sell or trade her at his discretion).

Hells Angels

Of all the criminal gangs, the Hells Angels is thought to be the most prominent and well-organized. Also known as Local 81 (8=H, 1=A), the Hells Angels are estimated to have more than 700 members nationally and 2,000 worldwide. The first Hells Angels chapter was composed of World War II veterans based in San Bernardino, California, in the late 1940s, some of whom were members of the Pissed Off Bastards of Bloomington.

The contemporary club was formed in 1957 and incorporated in 1966 with leader Ralph "Sonny" Barger at the helm. Despite a film produced in 1927 by Howard Hughes about aviators and titled *Hell's Angels,* and at least two military groups that used the label, Barger claims that the name stemmed from the suggestion of Arvid Olsen, former commander of a Flying Tigers fighter group. Although numerous members are incarcerated for violent and drug-related charges, Barger maintains that the club is for motorcycling purposes and that any criminal acts by members have taken place outside the club.

The Hells Angels' main rivals are the Bandidos, who formed in Houston, Texas, in the late 1960s. Like their adversaries, the Bandidos have chapters throughout the world. In 1978, the Bandidos reportedly struck an alliance with the Outlaws, who are the oldest criminal biker group, having been formed in 1935 outside Chicago. Together, the two groups significantly outnumber their rivals with international membership totaling between 2,000 and 7,900 members. Police continue to cite these groups as among the most violent and dangerous criminal organizations in the country. Their bloody competition with the Hells Angels for turf and control of criminal markets has left hundreds dead and thousands injured.

Conclusion

While few academic studies have been conducted on outlaw motorcycle clubs, much has been written in journalism and popular literature. Most accounts, however, derive from observations made between the 1960s and 1980s. This lack of contemporary information makes it difficult to gauge how these groups and their criminal practices have changed over time. Today, inner-city gangs and organized crime syndicates largely overshadow public concerns about outlaw biker clubs. Nevertheless, a small percentage of motorcycle clubs continue to contribute significantly to American street crime and create problems for law enforcement internationally.

Chris Richardson
University of Western Ontario

See Also: Bars and Pubs; Drug Dealing; Gangs (Street); Organized Crime and Violence; Pool Halls; Risky Lifestyles; Street Crime, Popular Portrayals of.

Further Readings

Barker, Tom. "One Percent Biker Clubs: A Description." *Trends in Organized Crime,* v.9/1 (2005).

Davis, Charles Donald. *Out Bad.* Charleston, SC: CreateSpace, 2011.

Lavigne, Yves. *Hells Angels: Into the Abyss.* Toronto: HarperCollins, 1996.

Lyon, Danny. *The Bikeriders.* San Francisco: Chronicle Books, 1968.

Thompson, Hunter. S. *Hell's Angels: A Strange and Terrible Saga.* New York: Random House, 1966.

Thompson, William. E. "Pseudo-Deviance and The 'New Biker' Subculture: Hogs, Blogs, Leathers, and Lattes." *Deviant Behavior,* v.30/1 (2009).

MS-13

Mara Salvatrucha-13 (MS-13) is a street gang that originated in the barrios of Los Angeles during the 1980s. From its initial ethnic street gang orientation, it has evolved into a transnational criminal network operating throughout the United States and Central America, with a presence in Canada and Europe.

MS-13 formed on the streets of Los Angeles in the Pico-Union and Rampart barrios in the 1980s. Its first members were Salvadoran youths from immigrant families who fled the civil war in El Salvador. To protect themselves from the 18th Street gang (a transnational street gang originating in the Rampart area of Los Angeles also known as Calle 18, Mara 18 or M18, and the chief rival of MS-13), they formed the Mara Salvatrucha Stoners. This gang was a way to deal with social isolation, economic hardship, and attacks from other gangs. Violence and crime became their social bond.

The Mara Salvatrucha Stoners morphed into Mara Salvatrucha-13 when its members encountered members of the Mexican Mafia (La Eme) in the Los Angeles county jail and state prisons. By becoming part of Eme's Sureño constellation of gangs, they became linked with other criminal gangs and were afforded protection by La Eme when incarcerated. By joining this relationship, MS-13 owes fealty to the Mexican Mafia. The 13 in MS-13 refers to the 13th letter of the alphabet—M (Eme)—representing this bond, not the 13th Street frequently mentioned in erroneous accounts.

MS-13 has morphed from a single, turf-oriented street gang to a criminal gang seeking profit, and then into a complex, networked criminal enterprise with transnational reach. Within the United States it is recognized as a national-level street gang with a presence in 42 states and key cities including Los Angeles, Atlanta, Dallas, Washington, D.C., and Northern Virginia. It is also active throughout Central America (where it is also known as Mara 13) with an evolving criminal presence in El Salvador, Guatemala and Nicaragua, as well as Mexico. It has an estimated 30,000-50,000 members or affiliates worldwide, with between 8,000 and 10,000 members in the United States.

Characteristics, Allies, and Rivals

Mata, Controla, Viola (Kill, Control, Rape)—the gang's informal motto—summarizes its ethos. From its starting point as a single-turf gang it has evolved into a criminal network consisting of individual local "cliques" (geographic subsets or factions of a larger gang) linked through social networks, influence, and opportunity. Influence among cliques is allocated through a "hierarchy of respect." This

An MS-13 suspect bearing gang tattoos is handcuffed. In 2004, the Federal Bureau of Investigation (FBI) created the MS-13 National Gang Task Force. A year later, the FBI helped create the National Gang Intelligence Center.

network of influence is reinforced through social bonds and ties and enforced through brutal instrumental violence. While originally a Salvadoran gang, it now has multiethnic membership. MS-13 members are known for distinctive (often full-face and full-torso) tattoos.

The MS-13 cliques employ a distributed form of leadership. Each clique has two primary leaders, the "first word" (*primera palabra*) and the "second word" (*segunda palabra*). The segunda palabra from a large powerful clique frequently exerts influence or suasion over smaller, subordinate cliques. The leaders operate in a neofeudal manner, collecting taxes (a cut of the criminal proceeds) in exchange for protection. Each clique also has a treasurer who collects taxes, and an Eme representative. This representative ensures Eme gets its cut, disciplines MS-13 members, organizes meetings among cliques, resolves disputes, and brokers business transactions and ensures that "respect" is paid to key nodes in Los Angeles and El Salvador.

Relations within and among cells are coordinated through meetings (known as *misas* within cliques and *generales* among cliques) and through targeted violence as a means of enforcing discipline. The "green light" or *luz verde* (i.e., permission to kill transgressors) is the powerful means of ensuring adherence to the gang's "management vision." Within the United States, the gang is primarily allied with La Eme and its constellation of Sureño affiliates in southern California. Outside the Eme sphere of influence, MS-13 cliques affiliate with a range of other gangs (including Eme rivals, such as Barrio Azteca and the Texas Syndicate). MS-13 is also believed to partner with a range of Mexican drug trafficking organizations, including Los Zetas.

Enterprises and Activities

MS-13 activities include drug trafficking and smuggling, human trafficking (of illegal aliens), weapons trafficking, drive-by shootings, robbery, identity theft, extortions, prostitution, assaults, robbery, and murder for hire. As a transnational organization, MS-13 is often characterized as a "third-generation" gang. This connotes: international reach, high degree of sophistication, and mercenary attributes.

John P. Sullivan
Independent Scholar

See Also: Drive-By Shooting; Drug Dealing; Gangs (Street); La Eme (Mexican Mafia); Latin Kings; Murder/Homicide; Organized Crime and Violence; Terrorism.

Further Readings

Logan, Samuel. *This is for the Mara Salvatrucha: Inside the MS-13, America's Most Violent Gang.* New York: Hyperion, 2009.

National Gang Intelligence Center/National Drug Intelligence Center. "National Gang Threat Assessment, 2009." Washington, DC: U.S. Department of Justice, 2009.

Sullivan, J. P. and S. Logan. "MS-13 Leadership: Networks of Influence." *Counter Terrorist*, v.3/4 (2010).

Mugging

Mugging is a term referring to robbery, which is a crime legally differentiated from larceny or larceny-theft by two factors: robbery explicitly requires the removal of property from a person (rather than a burglary or simple theft from a home, office, etc.), and robbery explicitly requires the use of physical intimidation or actual violence. Mugging specifically refers to a robbery that occurs in the street, and as a slang term seems tied to urban areas, rather than small towns or rural areas. The term seems to have orginated in the mid-1800s, stemming from the word *mug*, meaning face, implying a punch in the nose as step one in committing a robbery.

Victims and Degrees

The busy streets in urban areas provide a wealth of potential targets for muggers. Anyone can be chosen as a target for a mugging, although muggers typically choose individuals who display wealth, are distracted or do not appear to know or pay attention to their surroundings, and are of a lesser physical stature than themselves. The targets of muggers can be any age, any ethnicity, male or female. While the majority of individuals who engage in mugging are male, it is not unheard of for women to engage in mugging, especially when targeting other women. Muggings take place on both main streets and side streets or alleyways, but usually in situations where few individuals are available to come to the aid of the target.

Mugging, as a form of robbery, involves physical confrontation between the mugger and his or her target. This means that the experience of a mugging is very personal. A mugging typically involves the direct threat of, or an actual physical attack on, a target, and while the target is either unconscious or disoriented the mugger steals their belongings: jewelry, wallet or purse, personal electronics, anything of value on the target's person, including jackets, shoes, or other items of clothing. A contemporary trend in mugging is to use the items pilfered in the commission of the crime to engage in further crime, such as identity theft.

When compared to other forms of street theft, such as the commission of pickpocketing or purse snatching without a struggle, muggings are more violent. A mugging does not require a weapon. If a weapon is involved and used, the theft may be classified as an aggravated assault or worse.

Variations of the Crime

The physical attack of a mugging can occur from behind, where the target is struck on the head or back by a blunt object, or in more technologically advanced situations by a taser or stun gun. The attack can also be as simple as the target being shoved to the ground. In either situation, the mugger may continue to use physical violence against the target to keep them from protecting their valuables.

In some cases a mugging may involve more than one perpetrator. In these situations the target is not always attacked by all the members of the group. One member of the group may approach the intended target and distract him or her from the activities of the others. This person may even make it appear as though he or she is attempting to help the target keep track of their belongings, only to pocket the items and leave when the others have finished the attack. In other scenarios, a group of individuals perpetrating a mugging may all attack the target, especially if the target appears to be more physically capable of a robust personal defense.

Violence, as a tool in mugging, is used to disorient, intimidate, and terrorize the target. The strike-first element of a mugging ensures the mugger that they will not have to deal with a vocal target, or one that will be fighting to protect his or her belongings. The victim is not given the chance or opportunity to talk to the mugger, to plead with him or her, or to willingly hand over belongings.

The level of violence present in a mugging is in part intended to dissuade victims from reporting the event to law enforcement, or if they do report the event, discourage them from identifying their attacker. However, some data suggest that the use of violence can have the opposite effect. Crime victim survey responses compiled nationally in the National Crime Victimization Survey, 1973–92 include the finding that, based on the 1992 data, "Crimes involving injury are more often reported than those without injury." For example, the study revealed that 70 percent of completed robberies that involved injury were reported to the police that year, versus just 54 percent of completed robberies with no injury to the victim. Similarly, 43 percent of attempted robberies that involved injury were reported, versus 29 percent of attempted robberies with no injury.

In cases where mugging victims are attacked from behind, they may not be able to identify their attacker as they may have not seen the mugger. Because of this inability to identify an attacker, or gaps in memory, muggings are likely under-reported to the police. Depending on the extent of injury, the victim may not be able to remember the attack or may not recover, either due to permanent injury or death. While death is not a common occurrence in mugging, nor the prime purpose of the attack, the level of violence used in some muggings has been known to result in death.

Current Trends

While in the past muggings were rather anonymous crimes, the increased use of closed-circuit television (CCTV) to monitor activity in the streets of larger cities has provided a new way for law enforcement to keep on top of this type of crime and to assist victims in reconstructing the event. However, CCTV is not universal and does not cover every potential location where a mugging may occur. Due to expense, CCTV cameras may be placed on main thoroughfares but not on side streets or alleyways that provide more opportunities for the muggers to shield themselves from a potential target.

Muggings, along with various related types of street crimes, have decreased in volume nationally, according to the local jurisdiction police reports tracked by the U.S. Department of Justice Uniform Crime Reports (UCR). Full-year UCR data for 2010, for example, showed a continuing trend of fewer robberies and violent crimes, both in terms of outright totals and of per capita occurrence. The 2010 count of 367,832 reported robberies in the United States was the lowest volume since 1970. The robbery rate per 100,000 population was 119.1, the nation's lowest rate since 1967.

In the more general classification of violent crimes—reports of which are in some cases generated by muggings attempted or carried out—the 2010 count by the UCR was 1.25 million, lowest since 1979; the rate per 100,000 inhabitants was 403.6, lowest since 1972.

Unfortunately, not all muggings reported to the police are real events. In cities that have developed a reputation for muggings as an everyday occurrence, a mugging can be reported for purposes of insurance fraud or to cover up another crime, such as theft of a package by a courier. In these cases, the victim, either on their own or with the assistance of coconspirators, injures him or herself or reports the event to law enforcement as a legitimate crime. The items reported stolen from their person in these situations are either still in their possession, were never owned, or have been sold or pawned.

Clairissa D. Breen
Cazenovia College

See Also: Closed-Circuit Television; Pickpocketing; Theft and Larceny; Urbanization.

Further Readings

Jefferson, Tony and John Clarke. "Down These Mean Streets: The Meaning of Mugging." *The Howard Journal of Criminal Justice*, v.14/1 (1974).

Lejeune, Robert. "The Management of a Mugging." *Urban Life: Journal of Ethnography*, v.6/2 (1977).

Lejeune, Robert and Nicholas Alex. "On Being Mugged: The Event and Its Aftermath." *Journal of Contemporary Ethnography*, v.2/3 (1973).

U.S. Department of Justice. *Crime in the United States 2010.* http://www.fbi.gov/about-us/cjis/ucr/crime -in-the-u.s/2010/crime-in-the-u.s.-2010 (Accessed April 2012).

Murder/Homicide

Among the most feared crimes of urban dwellers is homicide. Citizens are bombarded with information about these violent lethal acts on a daily basis through the media. One result of the intense coverage of murder in the news is the unrealistically high estimations individuals have regarding the prevalence of homicide. According to the statistics from the Federal Bureau of Investigation's (FBI) Uniform Crime Reports (UCR), murder rates in the 21st century have been considerably lower than the levels reported in the late 1980s and early 1990s. Yet the decrease in homicide rates does not appear to have been accompanied by a comparable decrease in fear of murder.

As it relates to street crime, types of homicide that continue to remain common include felony-related murders (i.e., those committed during the course of other crimes such as robberies or rapes), drug-related killings, gang-related homicides, and arguments arising from confrontations in public places (both indoor and outdoor). A range of prevention strategies has been implemented to reduce the occurrence of these various types of homicides on urban streets.

Felony-Related Homicides

Felony-related murders are likely the most fear-inspiring of all street crime-related killings. The knowledge that victims of robberies, rapes, burglaries, and other crimes are sometimes killed in the course of their commission has had a significant impact on the way in which many individuals navigate their way through the urban landscape. They also attract significant news media coverage when they occur.

Felony-related homicides most closely fit the concept of instrumental crimes that are committed to achieve specific goals such as obtaining money or desired items. In this way, they are distinguished from expressive types of killings that are viewed as more emotionally driven. FBI statistics on the circumstances of murders and non-negligent manslaughters show that the proportion of homicides resulting from felonies is relatively consistent from year to year, hovering around 15 percent. The most common of these are robbery-related homicides, representing about 10 percent of all homicides in the United States in which the motive is known.

Unlike patterns for most other types of homicides, murders resulting from robberies disproportionately involve strangers, guns as the lethal method, multiple offenders, multiple victims, and black offenders killing white victims. These killings are most commonly found in large urban areas and most typically involve deaths during street muggings and robberies of convenience stores. Lethal carjackings receive much media attention, but these types of robbery homicides are extremely rare events. Felony-related homicides as a group have lower clearance rates than other types of homicides, in part due to the disproportionate involvement of strangers in these killings.

Women have a particularly high fear of rape-related homicides. Although they are far more likely than men to be the victims of these types of killings, homicides resulting from rapes account for less than two percent of all felony-related homicides annually. In contrast to the common image of these homicides being committed by total strangers hiding in dark alleys and behind bushes ready to pounce on unsuspecting victims, these killings are more likely to be perpetrated by an individual known to the victim, including friends, family members, neighbors, and acquaintances.

Drugs and Killing

Killings stemming from the use and selling of drugs have long plagued urban areas. Paul Goldstein's well-known tripartite framework for understanding the relationship between drugs and violence describes three models of how drugs can produce lethal violence. The psychopharmacological model explains how the physiological effects on the body from the ingestion of drugs can lead to excitability, irrationality, and violence. The widespread use of alcohol in urban public settings, as well as the emergence of PCP as a significant drug problem in recent decades, contributes to lethal street violence in this manner.

The economic compulsive model explains how violent crime, including homicide, can be driven by the economic need to feed a drug habit. Drugs with higher street values, such as heroin, are often linked to this type of violence. Victims of these kinds of economically motivated attacks often live in the same neighborhoods as the perpetrators.

The final of the three models—systemic— explains how the nature of drug distribution and selling results in disputes over territory and drugs, robberies of drug dealers and subsequent retaliation, and violent enforcement of normative codes within drug distribution networks, all of which can lead to homicides. The diffusion of crack cocaine throughout urban areas in the United States during the 1980s is believed to have been largely responsible for a substantial increase in gun-related homicides among juveniles in the late 1980s and early 1990s. These murders were overwhelmingly systemic in nature. The connection of gangs to drug distribution networks may also contribute to lethal violence generated by drug markets.

Gang-Related Homicides

The extent to which gang-related homicides contribute to the numbers of street crime murders in urban areas has been difficult to establish. The UCR Supplementary Homicide Reports are believed to underestimate the number of gang homicides occurring annually. Furthermore, considerable variation exists across law enforcement agencies in the classification of homicides as gang-related. In Chicago, for example, the homicide must be motivated by gang membership or gang activity for the homicide to be categorized as gang-related. In Los Angeles, on the other hand, it is sufficient that the victim or offender be a known gang member. This broader definition increases the counts of gang homicides in Los Angeles.

A streetside homicide memorial in Buffalo, New York, is a frequent sight. In the United States, murder is the leading cause of death for African American males aged 15 to 34.

In spite of the fear they generate of images of innocent bystanders killed in drive-by shootings resulting from gang warfare, homicides involving individuals who are members of gangs constitute a relatively small proportion of homicides in most cities. Chicago and Los Angeles are the obvious exceptions. As noted previously, gangs contribute to levels of lethal violence through their involvement in drug markets; a number of cities witnessed increases in gang-related homicides in the late 1980s when crack market violence was also escalating.

Gang-related killings also occur from gang rivalries and disputes over turf; however, gang membership may also raise the risk for homicide by increasing gun possession and exposure to high-crime areas. Gang-motivated homicides disproportionately involve males, multiple offenders, and outdoor public locations such as streets. The prevalence of lethal gang-related street violence is higher in disadvantaged, racially isolated neighborhoods.

Criminological Theories

Various types of criminological theories have been used to identify the causes of homicides and their social and spatial distribution within urban environments. For example, some theories emphasize the importance of particular biological traits (e.g., testosterone levels, genetic defects in dopamine and serotonin levels) and psychological risk factors (e.g., high impulsivity, low self control, high sensation seeking) for the onset of lethal violence. Sociological theories, in contrast, explain how aspects of the social structure and culture both enable and constrain the prevalence of homicide in various geographical areas.

Cultural and subcultural perspectives on homicide seek to explain high rates of violence among particular groups, and in particular physical locations, by the existence of a value system that encourages, tolerates, and may even demand a violent response to anger-provoking situations. These pro-violent values and beliefs are learned at home by how parents discipline their children; such values are reinforced in childhood play activities, on schoolyards, and in the routine daily activities on the street.

In his theory of violence in inner city areas in the Code of the Street, sociologist Elijah Anderson bridges structural and cultural explanations of violence in arguing that homicide and violence in urban public locations often center on issues of respect. In his view, being "street" and standing up for oneself is a necessity for many inner-city youth. These kids learn immediately that the quick resort to violence and the defense of one's reputation are important survival skills in these particularly high-crime areas. When they are in public places in disadvantaged neighborhoods, violence is both enabled and constrained by the normative rules of action that underlie this code of the street. The code is reflected in street verbalizations like "watch your back," "protect yourself," "don't punk out," "respect yourself," and "if someone disses you, you gotta straighten them out." In this way, Anderson's work helps explain the pervasiveness of lethal violence in inner-city public areas to the extent that they serve as staging areas for demonstrating, maintaining, and/or enhancing one's reputation as someone with whom one should not mess. Consistent with many structural theories, cities and neighborhoods with higher levels of structural disadvantage are the most likely to develop such codes and consequently experience the highest levels of lethal violence.

Previous research on homicide has also identified the types of interpersonal dynamics that facilitate the occurrence of lethal events in public places such as on the street and in bars. For example, research by David Luckenbill suggests that violent confrontations in public places involve a sequence of actions and reactions that may ultimately have deadly consequences. Six stages represent the sequence of events that often underlie deadly confrontations. These situated transactions begin with a victim making an opening move that the offender interprets as an offense to "face." The victim's actions can take a variety of forms, including a direct verbal expression, the refusal to cooperate or comply with the offender's request, or a nonverbal, physical gesture. Regardless of the specific form, the action is seen as offensive by the offender. This can set into motion a series of stages during which a working agreement is forged between the offender and victim to define the situation as one in which violence is appropriate.

Both participants have a stake in the battle that is often driven by the need to save face or maintain or improve status. Audiences can play an important role in this regard. The transaction culminates in lethal violence. Analyses of case narratives of homicides reveal that these kinds of face-saving, confrontational homicides are relatively common. They disproportionately involve assaults between males in public locations. The notion that lethal street violence in urban public locations is the result of escalating character contests and face-saving efforts that move through a series of stages implies that reducing homicides on the streets and in bars can be achieved through bystander intervention in the early phases of these confrontations.

Countermeasures

A wide range of strategies has been implemented that seek to reduce lethal violence occurring on urban streets. Situational crime prevention initiatives have focused on hardening targets and increasing guardianship in dangerous public places. These strategies emphasize opportunity reduction, and include increasing the visibility of employees in gas stations and convenience stores, adding security cameras to both indoor and outdoor public locations, better lighting, installing metal detectors, and saturated police patrols in dangerous neighborhoods.

Many homicide reduction strategies focus on changes made within the criminal justice system.

These include the increased adoption of three-strikes legislation, mandatory minimum prison sentences, and sentence enhancements for violent crimes committed with firearms, all of which seek to deter potential offenders from committing violence by increasing the penalties for those crimes. Other strategies put forward are based on the logic of the Broken Windows Theory, which argues that a proliferation of less serious crime and disorder leads to more serious crime by creating the impression that such areas lack both formal and informal social control. New York City's CompStat program, implemented by then-Police Commissioner William Bratton, fits this model. Among the various components of this initiative was a crackdown on minor offenses using aggressive, order-maintenance policing that was argued in turn to reduce serious offenses.

Other strategies have more specifically targeted either guns, gangs, or both. For example, using problem-oriented policing tactics, Operation Ceasefire specifically targeted reductions in firearm violence and homicide among youth in Boston. The deterrence-based program directly notified youth gang members of a zero-tolerance policy on gun possession that, through "pulling levers," guaranteed swift and severe punishment of offenders. Project Exile, implemented in Richmond Virginia, invokes federal prosecution with sentence enhancements for offenders committing violent or drug offenses with firearms. This model incorporates both deterrence and incapacitation methods for reducing gun-related violent crime. More contentious has been the movement to ease restrictions on citizens carrying concealed weapons as a means of deterring would-be attackers who will fear potential victims may be armed.

Federal crime control initiatives for reducing gun- and gang-related violent crime on the streets include Project Safe Neighborhoods. Using models like Boston's Operation Ceasefire and Project Exile as a basis, the program seeks to increase federal prosecution for illegal gun use and gun possession by forbidden individuals. Recognizing the need to go beyond these deterrence- and incapacitation-based strategies, the program also emphasizes the need for collaboration and partnerships in designing strategic, research-based initiatives to prevent gun violence tailored to individual localities. Evaluations of the project have shown reductions in violent and gun-related crime.

Wendy C. Regoeczi
Cleveland State University

See Also: Alcohol and Drug Use; Bars and Pubs; Broken Windows Theory; Closed-Circuit Television; Code of the Street; Fear of Crime; Gangs (Street); Guns and Weapons; Mugging; Operation Ceasefire; Zero-Tolerance/Saturation Policing.

Further Readings
Anderson, Elijah. *Code of the Street: Decency, Violence, and the Moral Life of the Inner City*. New York: W. W. Norton & Company, 1999.

Blumstein, Alfred. "Youth Violence, Guns, and the Illicit-Drug Industry." *Journal of Criminal Law and Criminology*, v.86/1 (1995).

Goldstein, Paul J. "The Drugs/Violence Nexus: A Tripartite Conceptual Framework." *Journal of Drug Issues*, v.15/4 (1985).

Luckenbill, David. "Criminal Homicide as a Situated Transaction." *Social Problems*, v.25/2 (1977).

Rosenfeld, Richard, Timothy M. Bray, and Alren Egley. "Facilitating Violence: A Comparison of Gang-Motivated, Gang Affiliated, and Non-Gang Youth Homicides." *Journal of Quantitative Criminology*, v.15/4 (1999).

Wolfgang, Marvin E. and F. Ferracuti. *The Subculture of Violence*. London: Tavistock, 1967.

Needle Exchanges

Syringe exchange and distribution programs for injecting users of illicit drugs were developed to reduce the spread of blood-borne diseases (e.g., human immunodeficiency virus [HIV], hepatitis B virus, and hepatitis C virus). When people who inject illicit drugs cannot obtain sterile syringes due to legal restrictions on purchasing or possessing them, they frequently share needles. Sharing syringes is an extremely efficient method of spreading blood-borne diseases.

Syringe exchange programs give the drug user a sterile syringe when he or she turns in a used needle. Syringe distribution programs give out sterile syringes upon request. Some programs have mobile units that move around the sections of cities in which users, including prostitutes, are known to congregate to improve access to these services.

Although syringe exchange and distribution programs have been in existence in the United States since at least the 1970s, the first organized syringe exchange programs were established in the late 1980s.These programs were started in cities with large populations of illicit drug injectors whose drug of choice was most often heroin. These cities were Tacoma, Washington; Portland, Oregon; San Francisco; and New York City. The acceptance of syringe exchange and distribution programs and therefore the implementation of them vary widely by community within the United States, however.

Syringe programs began to emerge around the country more widely in the 1990s and early 2000s. This spread of syringe exchange programs followed the advent of the HIV/acquired immune deficiency syndrome (AIDS) disease. Once gay males began taking precautions to prevent the spread of HIV/AIDS through sexual contacts, it was discovered that a major factor responsible for the spread of the disease was needle sharing among illicit drug users.

The potential for growth in the number of syringe exchange programs was restricted when the federal government stopped funding these programs in 1988, however. One of the arguments put forth by opponents of syringe exchange programs is that they encourage people to use illegal drugs. There is no research that supports this claim. The federal ban on funding syringe exchange programs was revised for fiscal year 2010. Syringe exchange programs are now eligible for federal funding subject to provisions regarding the location of the program site.

Harm Reduction
Syringe exchange and distribution programs fall within the harm reduction framework. Harm reduction policies can be defined as pragmatic approaches to illicit drug use with the intended outcome of reducing or minimizing harms associated

with this behavior. The most obvious example in this context is the reduction of the spread of blood-borne diseases. But syringe exchange can also reduce other harms such as expenditures of public funding to treat injecting illicit drug users who contract blood-borne diseases from needle sharing, as well as the disposal of used needles in public places which poses a risk to persons who may handle them.

As of 2009, there were 184 syringe exchange programs operating in 36 states, the District of Columbia, and Puerto Rico. In 2008 more than 29 million syringes were exchanged through these programs. Eighty percent of their budgets came from state and local governments. Most syringe exchange programs also offer other services in addition to sterile syringes. These services include HIV counseling and testing, referrals to substance abuse treatment, hepatitis C counseling and testing, sexually transmitted disease screening, distribution of condoms to prevent sexual transmission of HIV and other sexually transmitted diseases, and tuberculosis screening.

Conclusion

A number of reviews of the research conducted in several countries have concluded that syringe exchange programs lead to substantial reductions in HIV incidence among injecting drug users. Between 1988 and 1990 and 2003 and 2006, when numerous syringe exchange programs were initiated, the incidence of HIV among injecting illicit drug users in the United States declined by approximately 80 percent. In addition, syringe exchange programs have been found to be cost-effective in preventing the spread of HIV infection. Some studies show that syringe exchange programs are also effective in reducing the spread of the hepatitis C virus, but more research is needed on this topic. Some studies have found that syringe distribution is more effective than is a strict one-for-one exchange program. In addition, the research has concluded that syringe exchange programs have no negative effects.

Eric L. Jensen
University of Idaho

See Also: Alcohol and Drug Use; Crack House; Courts, Drug; Drug Dealing; Drug Markets, Open-Air; Homelessness; Prostitute/Streetwalker; Risky Lifestyles; Skid Row; Urban Ethnology.

Further Readings

Bluthenthal, Ricky N., Keith G. Heinzerling, Rachel Anderson, Neil M. Flynn, and Alex H. Kral. "Approval of Syringe Exchange Programs in California: Results From a Local Approach to HIV Prevention." *American Journal of Public Health,* v.98/2 (2008).

Centers for Disease Control and Prevention. "Syringe Exchange Programs" 2005. http://www.cdc.gov/idu/facts/AED_IDU_SYR.pdf (Accessed April 2011).

Wodak, Alex and Annie Cooney. "Do Needle Exchange Programs Reduce HIV Infection Among Injecting Drug Users: A Comprehensive Review of the International Studies." *Substance Use and Misuse,* v.41/6–7 (2006).

Neighborhood Watch

Neighborhood Watch (NW) is a community policing and crime prevention program designed to reduce crime through more communication between police and individual citizens. Residents are encouraged to report suspicious activities or persons to law enforcement agencies for a quicker response. It also gives police a communication channel to alert communities to significant crime trends or arrests.

Development and Variations

Founded in 1972 by the National Sheriffs' Association to combat burglaries, the program was renamed USA on Watch following the 9/11 terrorist attacks. Individual neighborhoods form associations, and their scope of activities depends upon the specific problems affecting their areas. Some have citizen patrols to actively look for potential problems, while others encourage residents to take preventative steps to reduce the likelihood of victimization. Either way, citizens are told not to confront people directly but to notify police. Evaluations of NW have produced mixed results, largely because of different evaluation techniques and the problems sustaining these groups over the long term.

There are different rationales behind NW. One is to make criminals believe they are more apt to be noticed and apprehended if they attempt to commit a crime in a location with NW. Citizens are

A neighborhood watch may be organized as its own group or may be a function of a neighborhood or community association. When suspecting criminal activities, members are encouraged to contact authorities and to not intervene.

encouraged to be diligent about locking and closing their windows, doors, and garages in order to reduce opportunities for victimization. They are encouraged to look out for each others' homes, especially when people are away. Creating signs of occupancy such as removing newspapers or taking out garbage can make criminals believe someone is home, with higher odds of their being caught. The greater awareness of crime can exert informal social control by reminding potential offenders of the illegality of certain actions and the likelihood of being prosecuted. It is also hoped that fear of crime will be reduced with increased awareness of how to prevent it, and that citizens will have a higher opinion of law enforcement through the partnership and quicker responses.

Local law enforcement agencies encourage the formation of NW groups by assigning a liaison officer to work with interested volunteers. At least one citizen serves as an area coordinator to facilitate the group's activities. The coordinator may publish a newsletter to mention recent crimes or crime attempts in the area, especially ones that might have been prevented by NW, suggest crime prevention tips, or introduce newly formed NW groups. The coordinator may be formally elected or, in some cases, may have been the initial organizer. Every 10 to 15 homes have a block captain who passes along information to and from the coordinator. This person may also be part of a telephone tree to help disseminate important news about criminal activities. Many organizations also maintain community maps with names of residents and contact information. Some law enforcement agencies have citizens advisory boards to coordinate activities among different NW groups.

NW neighborhoods will typically post signs at key points to alert outsiders about the organization's existence, usually at main entrances. This lets potential criminals know that citizens may be observing them and could potentially alert authorities. Approximately 41 percent of Americans lived in a community with a NW group.

Police and Community Activities

In order to effectively communicate with police, citizens need to be trained in what constitutes suspicious activities. Anything from someone peeking into windows, to a high volume of traffic around a home, can be warning signals. Citizens should write down relevant information including license plate numbers and descriptions of people to tell police. Residents also need to understand when to call "911" or when to use a nonemergency telephone number for more routine matters. Residents are encouraged to protect their own possessions by making inventories with serial numbers, in case they are stolen.

Aside from discussing crime, NW groups are encouraged to schedule social activities to make membership more fun and give members a continuing incentive to participate. First aid training and beautification projects are examples. Several communities had NW groups become inactive because once people believed their neighborhood was safe, the organization's primary purpose disappeared. Crime waves tend to capture people's interest on a short-term basis, and once the problem is solved, they move on to other activities. Researchers James Garafalo and Maureen McLeod estimated that half of all NW programs are dormant because many of their activities, such as engraving household items with security information, need only be performed once.

Because police encourage participants to call them and not confront suspicious people themselves, this gives citizens a more passive role that also makes sustaining long-term interest difficult. Multipurpose organizations, such as block clubs, may stimulate longer-term involvement, as preventing crime would be just part of the reason for joining. The challenge is continuing to hold citizens' interest after a NW group is formed.

The apparent failure of NW to achieve greater results could be attributed to low levels of citizen participation. While 80 percent of survey respondents said they wished to participate in a NW program, only about 5 percent of residents do. Nonparticipants are not likely to be influenced by the informal social control that comes from NW meetings. Participants are usually middle- or upper-class, well-educated, have children, live in racially homogenous residential neighborhoods, and have owned their own homes for five years or more.

Some NW groups have citizen patrols, in which volunteers drive or walk around a community looking for potential problems, including lost children, stray dogs, or vandalized property. These volunteers should not carry weapons and must alert police to any situations they encounter. Patrols are most likely found in working-class areas where surrounding neighborhoods are experiencing influxes of lower-income people or are plagued by high levels of crime.

Research on Effectiveness

Several studies have reached mixed results when evaluating the effectiveness of NW. Many are simple comparisons of crime statistics before a program began with data from a year after. In several cases, the number of reported crimes actually increased. However, this could be in keeping with the community policing philosophy that often results in an increased number of crime reports as a community learns to visibly work with law enforcement, followed by later decreases. An evaluation of NW in two London neighborhoods found no statistically significant influence on crime rates, but fear of crime decreased and the evaluation of police performance increased. The British program was more limited than American ones in that police only had one meeting with citizens and no formal organizations were formed. A narrative and meta-analysis of several studies found 53 percent of NW groups studied did have a decrease of crime in their communities, with the remaining 47 percent either providing uncertain evidence or actual increases.

An effort in Dayton, Ohio, organized by a neighborhood association proved more successful in combating drug and crime problems when measured five years after the organization started addressing them. This effort went beyond a simple NW organization to include barricading streets and improving dilapidated properties, with the city more involved than most communities are. This study illustrates the need for longer-term research to effectively evaluate the impact of NW programs along with improved results from a more multifaceted organization.

Limitations

Lower-class neighborhoods rarely have active NW programs, in spite of the fact that their crime rates are higher, and are more apt to have worse relations with police. The approach may not be suitable for more heterogeneous areas, as "strangers" may be more challenging to detect. The NW concept does not work well in commercial districts as they attract outsiders on a routine basis, making it more difficult to determine who is suspicious as opposed to legitimately conducting business. People may also distrust their neighbors whom they suspect or know are involved with criminal activity.

It is also assumed that citizen interaction will lead to a reduced fear of crime—but discussions of neighborhood activities may actually increase some participants' apprehension. Hearing about other crimes could make them feel more likely to be victimized. One can also question if criminals will respond to the presence of a NW by displacing their activities to communities without one, or change their tactics to diminish the likelihood of being noticed. While NW can be a deterrent to crime, the final results are likely to depend on the dedication of a single group's members.

William E. Raffel
Buffalo State College

See Also: Broken Windows Theory; Burglary; Bystander Apathy; Community Policing; Crime,

Displacement of; Fear of Crime; Immigrant Neighborhoods; Policing, Problem-Oriented.

Further Readings

Bennett, Trevor. *Evaluating Neighbourhood Watch.* Aldershot, UK: Gower, 1990.

Bennett, Trevor, Katy Holloway, and David P. Farrington. "Does Neighborhood Watch Reduce Crime? A Systematic Review and Meta Analysis." *Journal of Experimental Criminology,* v.2/4 (2006).

Donnely, Patrick G. and Charles E. Kimble. "An Evaluation of the Effects of Neighborhood Mobilization on Community Problems." *Journal of Prevention and Intervention in the Community,* v.32/1–2 (2006).

Garafolo, James and Maureen McLeod. "The Structure and Operations of Neighborhood Watch Programs in the United States." *Crime & Delinquency,* v.35/3 (1987).

National Sheriffs' Association. "Neighborhood Watch Manual." Alexandria, VA: National Sheriff's Association, 2010.

Rosenbaum, Dennis T. "The Theory and Research Behind Neighborhood Watch: Is it a Sound Fear and Crime Reduction Strategy?" *Crime & Delinquency,* v.33/1 (1987).

New Orleans, Louisiana

There are a number of issues that account for the most intractable types of street crime in the city of New Orleans, Louisiana: drug-related and retaliatory murder and tourist robbery. The persistence of these types of street crime is largely a function of complex and interrelated factors including the physical location of the events. Changes in the city since Hurricane Katrina in 2005 may one day lead to a lower murder rate, but as discussed below, the storm brought with it new crime problems for New Orleans.

Drug-Related and Retaliatory Murder

In his book on policing New Orleans during the 19th century, Dennis Rousey mentions the English journalist William Howard Russell, who visited New Orleans in 1861. Russell commented on the high incidence of violence and the proclivity of its citizenry to carry weapons. In the four years from 1857 to 1860, at least 225 criminal homicides were committed in New Orleans, for a rate of 35 per 100,000, making it at that time the most violent city in the United States.

According to Rousey, the attorney general at the time complained that the police were ineffective, witnesses were afraid to testify, too many people were exempted from jury duty, the criminal court was dysfunctional for many reasons, and the prosecutor's office was grossly understaffed and overworked. As a result, the criminal justice system was not particularly efficient at apprehending or prosecuting murder suspects. In fact, of the murders committed during this period, only 21.5 percent were closed with convictions for either murder or manslaughter.

The murder rate in New Orleans was considerably lower in the latter part of the 19th century than in the antebellum period, but still 76 percent of murders in New Orleans in the late 1800s were committed with firearms. The overall murder rate for New Orleans at this time was six times higher than that for Philadelphia, a comparably sized city, and the rate of homicides committed with firearms was 23 times higher.

In the 1960s, New Orleans experienced its lowest murder rates, at around 13 per 100,000. However, this was still more than twice the national rate. The city of New Orleans continues to struggle with these same issues of violence. It had far and away the highest murder rate in the country in 1994, at nearly 86 per 100,000 persons. Violent crime rates dropped in the aftermath of Hurricane Katrina with the exodus of the city's population, but have been on the rise again. An estimated 800 murders occurred in New Orleans in the first six years since the storm made landfall.

A majority of murders in the city qualify as drug-related or retaliatory. Drug-related and retaliatory murders tend to occur in neighborhoods that are highly isolated, racially segregated, and have high levels of poverty. William Julius Wilson has noted in his research that the lack of exposure to the constraints and expectations of middle-class society that comes with high rates of poverty, racial segregation, and social isolation are associated with high rates of violent crime. Because there is little in the way of jobs for the unskilled and uneducated, street crime, particularly the drug trade, becomes attractive.

These circumstances tend to push and pull young, usually African American males into the drug trade, the hallmark of which is the use of lethal violence.

Violent crime rarely reaches outside of these isolated neighborhoods even when they are contiguous with some of the most affluent neighborhoods of the city. Central City, historically one of the most violent neighborhoods in New Orleans, is only a few blocks away from St. Charles Avenue, which courses through some of the most elegant Garden District neighborhoods. Yet there is little crime on St. Charles. In fact, most of the neighborhoods of New Orleans are free of violent crime and experience only minor petty theft. Crime is mostly confined to those racially segregated, socially isolated, and high-poverty neighborhoods.

Moreover, the criminogenic neighborhoods in New Orleans are losing population, so that everyone left in these neighborhoods knows everyone else. Residents of these neighborhoods do not in general trust the police; they are unlikely to provide information to the police or to serve as witnesses if a perpetrator is brought to trial. One of the primary reasons for not getting guilty verdicts in murder trials and in the release of those arrested for committing murder is witness reluctance to testify. In a study of 352 homicide cases in New Orleans between 1996 and 2003, the district attorney chose not to prosecute 145 of these cases because a key witness refused to testify. Of these 145 cases, 139 were drug-related or retaliatory murders. Releasing people who have committed murder back on the street sends the message to these perpetrators that murders committed in New Orleans go unpunished. This phenomenon has to fuel the continuing high rate of murder in the city.

Tourist Robbery

Tourist robbery tends to occur in perimeter areas around the French Quarter, the main tourist attraction in the city. This probably occurs for a variety of reasons. First, guardianship in these areas is typically low. Police in the French Quarter tend to patrol on foot on Bourbon and Royal Streets and around the Jackson Square area. The remainder of the quarter, which is largely residential, is dimly lit and is in close proximity to some criminogenic neighborhoods similar to the ones described above. This proximity allows easy ingress to and egress from the French Quarter by would-be perpetrators.

Second, a feature of the quarter that makes tourists easy targets is the architecture. The structures are Victorian with Spanish influence and look quite similar to one another, which makes it easy for visitors to get turned around and wander out and away from the main tourist venues. Third, people come to New Orleans to have a good time. The nickname the Big Easy and the motto "the City that Care Forgot" are not unearned. Tourists often overindulge in food and drink and may also be searching for illicit drugs or sex. Drunkenness and/or their efforts to procure drugs or sex tend to make tourists more vulnerable to street robbery than they might otherwise be.

Another issue that makes tourist victimization an intractable problem is the difficulty of prosecuting the perpetrators. Even when an arrest is made, which is rare, the victim is not likely to return to New Orleans the numerous times it would take to effect a conviction. Only in high-profile cases in which the victim is seriously injured does the prosecutor's office have funds to return the victim to New Orleans to testify.

Changes Since Hurricane Katrina

There is some hope that the ongoing lethal violence in New Orleans might decline in the future. First, in the post-Katrina era (since 2005), improvements in public education have been nothing short of dramatic. The public education system before 2005 was in shambles with many students withdrawing from high school when they reached 16, the legal age to do so. Since Katrina, many public schools have been chartered and school performance scores have improved, as have students' scores on the Louisiana Educational Assessment Program (LEAP) test and graduation rates.

Better education available to more of the city's youth may start a chain reaction in which these children experience less poverty as young adults, are less likely to get involved in the drug trade, and are less likely to become victims or perpetrators of lethal violence.

Second, the exodus out of New Orleans after Hurricane Katrina also led to a significant decline in the city's population of young children. The birth cohorts that would contain future violent criminals are much smaller now because many parents who left the city with infants and small children have not returned. The population of New Orleans is still about 100,000 less than it was in July 2005 before Katrina made landfall.

However, new kinds of crime have surfaced since Katrina. Readers may remember the devastation the storm caused the city of New Orleans. Eighty percent of the city flooded and remained underwater for two weeks. During that time, relief was virtually absent and residents who had not evacuated were left to fend for themselves. During the immediate aftermath of the storm, looting reached epic proportions. Using burglary as a proxy for looting, in part because it limits items stolen to those unnecessary for survival in post-Katrina conditions, the burglary rate in the month after Katrina was nearly 200 per 100,000 persons, much higher than that after any storm before or since.

Rape also characterized the phases of Katrina. Some women who needed assistance to evacuate in advance of the storm were raped, as were those who could not evacuate and were trapped in the city. Some forced into shelters surrounded by strangers were raped, as were some who moved into temporary trailer housing among new and unknown neighbors. Women who moved to the city to procure recovery jobs and those who came as cleanup volunteers were also raped. A principal reason for these rapes was the lack of both formal and informal guardianship in the lead-up to and aftermath of Katrina.

Finally, a new and highly specific form of street crime has emerged since the storm. The devastation caused by the storm necessitated a large number of cleanup workers. Laborers from Central and South America came en masse to New Orleans beginning in 2005. A large majority of the estimated 120,000 workers were undocumented illegal aliens and unable or unwilling to use banks to deposit their wages, which were often paid in cash. These workers quickly became associated with carrying large amounts of cash on their persons and were targeted by robbers. In fact, in the local vernacular, these workers were referred to as "walking ATMs" by perpetrators. A lack of police concern for crimes committed against migrant workers made these laborers all the more susceptible to robberies, including home invasion robberies and robbery/murders.

Dee Wood Harper, Jr.
Loyola University New Orleans
Kelly Frailing
Texas A&M International University

See Also: Burglary; Drug Dealing; Looting; Mugging; Murder/Homicide, Rape and Sexual Assault; Risky Lifestyles; Victims, Tourist.

Further Readings

Harper, Dee Wood, Jr. "The Tourist and His Criminal: Pattern in Street Robbery." In *Tourism, Security, and Safety: A Case Approach,* Yoel Mansfield and Abraham Piazam, eds. Burlington, MA: Butterworth-Heinemann, 2005.
Rousey, Dennis C. *Policing the Southern City: New Orleans, 1805-1889.* Baton Rouge: Louisiana State University Press, 1996.
Thornton, William E. and Lydia Voigt. "Disaster Phase Analysis and Crime Facilitation Patterns." In *Crime and Criminal Justice in Disaster*, Dee Wood Harper and Kelly Frailing, eds. Durham, NC: Carolina Academic Press, 2010.
Wilson, William J. *When Work Disappears—The World of the New Urban Poor.* New York: Alfred A. Knopf, 1996.

New York City

Over the past two decades, New York City, with a population of 8.2 million, has experienced a decrease in both personal and property crimes. The debate over how and why this has occurred has been long and complex and remains hotly contested. Fundamental rationales regarding crime based on urban demographics, economic trends, community policing, and a better-informed and strategically-managed police force have been among the key focal points of contention. It may be wise to consider each of these factors as a contributor to the overall trends in diminished crime rates in New York. This entry will probe the drug-related and gang-related crimes in particular to gain insights into causes, effects, and mitigating factors of these trends as they apply specifically to the street crime profile of this urban area.

Encouraging Trends

First, a look at those trends in the aggregate. Records compiled by the Federal Bureau of Investigation (FBI) in its Uniform Crime Reporting (UCR) Program show declines in New York City in all four categories of crimes committed against persons, with the largest drop being in forcible rape, where reported cases saw a drop of 82 percent, from 54 per 100,000 population in 1985 to 10 per 100,000 in 2009. The drop in reported cases of robbery was nearly as steep, with an 80 percent decline from a rate of 1,107 per 100,000 in 1985 to 221 per 100,000 in 2009—even though the rate peaked at 1,370 in 1990.

Murder and nonnegligent manslaughter peaked in 1990 as well, reaching 31 per 100,000—but the rate showed a drop of 71 percent from 19 per 100,000 in 1985 to 6 per 100,000 in 2009. Cases of aggravated assault, which were recorded at the rate of 701 per 100,000 in 1985, fell 55 percent by 2009, when the rate was 315 per 100,000.

On the property-related crime side of the ledger, motor vehicle theft showed the biggest drop-off, down 88 percent from the rate of 1,106 per 100,000 in 1985 to 127 per 100,000 in 2009. Burglaries were as dramatically stymied; the rate fell 87 percent,

from 1,738 per 100,000 in 1985 to 224 per 100,000 in 2009. The larceny-theft rate was cut by two-thirds; it had peaked at 4,199 per 100,000 in 1988, but dropped to 1,340 per 100,000 in 2009.

While one might gain confidence from these trends, it is prudent to note that they in large part mirror trends across the United States during the same period. However, the trends in all seven UCR crime categories were more dramatic in New York City than those rates compiled nationally—in several cases the decline in reported crimes in New York was double the average decline across the country. On the one hand, this shows great strides. On the other hand, the city was insolvent in the 1970s, with many services and much infrastructure having experienced several decades of neglect and lack of investment prior to this 1985-2009 period. Therefore, compared to numerous other major cities, New York City had more room for dramatic changes to be made in its crime rates. To the credit

The New York City Police Department is the largest municipal police force in the United States, with responsibilities covering the five boroughs of the city. Mounted police who patrol on horseback serve in metropolitan areas such as Manhattan, where their day-to-day function may be ceremonial, but they are often employed in crowd control because of their mobile mass and height advantage and are increasingly used for crime prevention and high visibility policing roles.

of its public officials, the city did make decisive moves to address these challenges.

Anticrime Initiatives

Among the most celebrated—and contested—measures to slash crime rates in New York, still debated even as they have been adapted and implemented in many jurisdictions nationally, was a suite of initiatives that combined: improvements made to the New York Police Department (NYPD) crime reporting and management system including CompStat; the augmenting of the NYPD by 5,000 new officers; stronger penalties for crimes committed with a firearm; and a neighborhood-level commitment to policing minor crimes based on the Broken Windows Theory. These policies and practices were implemented beginning in the 1990s under Mayor Rudolph Giuliani and Police Commissioner William Bratton.

To combat crime in New York City, a quality-of-life initiative was created in 1994. Order-maintenance policing (OMP) is a strategy in which police officers target minor offenses in an effort to curtail major offenses. The minor crimes include vagrancy, loitering, prostitution, littering, graffiti, panhandling, public drunkenness, vandalism, minor drug use, excessive noise, public urination, and related breaches of public order. This OMP plan was a response to the Broken Windows Theory, perhaps the most aggressive and ambitious application attempted in the United States. The theory posits that increased policing of minor offenses proves to the community that the police will enforce quality-of-life issues at every level, and encourages the self-policing of neighborhoods and better community relations that are thought essential to support modern standards of problem-oriented policing. Two key areas of crime where such efforts and their results can be monitored are drug-related crimes and gang-related crimes.

Drug Crime

Drug activity is pervasive, generally private, and attended by social damage that is highly problematic. Substance abuse affects individuals and communities directly, even as it creates incentives for individuals and groups to commit property-related and personal criminal offenses. Results of some studies suggest that virtually all types of crimes are in one way or another related to arrests for the manufacture and sale of "hard drugs." Increases in total per capita drug arrests and arrests for hard drug possession, the study found, are accompanied by higher rates for all crimes except assault. Increased arrests for the manufacture or sale of marijuana, as a further example, are associated with increases in larcenies overall.

New York City has long harbored the largest number of heroin abusers in the United States. The purity of retail-level heroin is very high there, averaging between 60 and 70 percent. Heroin is usually sold in small bags that are stamped with a particular brand name, a practice that began in the 1970s as a way for dealers to establish brand loyalty. According to the Drug Enforcement Administration, New York City remains the main heroin distribution center in the northeast. Latino gangs, whether Mexican, Dominican, Puerto Rican, or others, generally control the street-level distribution, according to several sources. The heroin imported into the city comes primarily from South America and southeast and southwest Asia, with an increasing profile of importation and distribution via Chinese, Pakistani, and Turkish criminal gangs.

Another aspect of drug activity that generates a growing volume of street crime are substances known as "club drugs." Since the 1980s, club drugs have been a concern; among the more common are: ecstasy (3, 4-methylenedioxymethamphetamine or MDMA), GHB (gamma-hydroxybutyrate), ketamine, LSD, methamphetamines, PCP (phencyclidine), and Rohypnol R (flunitrazepam). The National Institute on Drug Abuse's Community Epidemiology Working Group reported that ecstasy, or MDMA, has been moving from clubs into general street use in several cities, including New York, where adoption by minority substance abusers was increasing. Although the sample studied was not representative of all minorities, it provided evidence for growing ecstasy use among African American and Hispanic heroin, crack, and cocaine users, especially in such sections of the city as Harlem and the South Bronx.

Gang Activity

Gangs in New York City have historically been involved in street crime. Traditionally, the Italian Mafia has been seen as a very dominant organized crime group, but—sensational mob trial headlines aside—this is no longer true. "The exclusiveness of gang existence is no longer the case," according to the FBI Organized Crime Unit. Criminal enterprises listed and confronted by the FBI include African, Asian, Balkan, Eurasian, Haitian, Jamaican, Italian, Middle Eastern, and Latin American networks. The National Gang Threat Assessment of 2011 (compiled by the National Drug Intelligence Center or NDIC) reported there are more than 1.4 million active gang members nationally, with the majority residing in major urban areas, and with membership increasing most rapidly in the southeast and northeast regions (which includes New York City).

These individuals include members of street, prison, and outlaw motorcycle gangs. Four of the five most rapidly expanding outlaw motorcycle gangs— the Mongols, Outlaws, Vagos, and Wheels of Soul— are active in New York, the assessment noted. New York is also one of the jurisdictions where gang members are known to have compromised or corrupted either judicial, law enforcement, or correctional staff within the past three years, the assessment reported.

In New York City, gang-related incidents (defined by the NYPD as as any incident of unlawful conduct by a gang member or suspected gang member). increased 47.3 percent and gang-related motivated incident (defined as any gang-related incident done primarily to benefit gang interests) increased nearly 45 percent since 2006 with a steady increase each year, as estimated by the NDIC. Research shows that gangs in New York City such as the Latin Kings have increased their presence in the city through recruiting the city's youth to existing units, forming new chapters, and actively interacting in the city's drug trade. Prospective gang members have the option of seeking recruitment or engaging in illegal activities online, a growing avenue of criminal activity that augments some characteristics of gang crime including distributing drugs to minors, theft in the private and public sectors, and enforcing fear among citizens.

According to the FBI, gangs are multiplying and subdividing now more than ever before, and one aspect of this phenomenon is a spread from urban centers into the suburbs and in some cases to rural areas. This makes New York City a true breeding ground for gang-driven crime, in some cases hundreds of miles beyond the city limits. Factors in this crime advance, according to the NDIC, include expansion of drug distribution territories, increasing streams of revenue, new membership recruiting areas, running from law enforcement, and escaping other gangs.

Gangs growing more active in schools is another front of activity as reported by the National Crime and Victimization Survey (NCVS). Students between the ages of 12 and 18 who reported the presence of gangs in their schools increased 17 percent from 2003 to 2005, the NCVS reported. Gangs are using middle and high schools for recruitment and drug distribution; some gangs in New York and neighboring areas are reportedly instructing teenage members who dropped out of school to re-enroll and recruit new members and sell illicit drugs there. African Americans and Hispanics are more likely to report gangs at their schools than Caucasian students. In public schools 25 percent of students reported gang exposure, compared to 4 percent of private school students.

Conclusion

New York City is a constantly growing city where, according to the UCR, street crime rates have been reduced. Through bold and innovative use of fresh approaches, the NYPD and city government has made great strides in affecting the everyday quality of life for most New Yorkers. However, persistent pockets of street crime, typically fueled by the illicit drug trade and various gang and organized crime activities, remain. Further, the macroeconomic stress of recent years puts into jeopardy some of the gains made over the past several decades. Obviously there is a need for New York City to remain vigilant on the law enforcement front—and for the city to welcome further in-depth probes from the academic researchers who seek answers to our society's crime generation and deterrence measures.

Zina T. McGee
Hampton University

See Also: Bratton, William; CompStat; Counterfeit Goods; Drug Dealing; Gangs (Street); Giuliani, Rudolph; Goetz, Bernhard; Guardian Angels; Homelessness; Immigrant Neighborhoods; Organized Crime and Violence; Policing, Problem-Oriented; Stop and Frisk; Street/Block Parties.

Further Readings

Cerda, Magdalena, Steven F. Messner, Melissa Tracy, David Vlahov, Emily Goldmann, Kenneth J. Tardiff, and Sandro Galea. "Investigating the Effect of Social

Changes on Age-Specific Gun-Related Homicide Rates in New York City During the 1990s." *American Journal of Public Health*, v.100/6 (2010).

Harrell, Erika. "Violence by Gang Members, 1993–2003." Bureau of Justice Statistics. June 2005. http://www.bjs.ojp.usdoj.gov/content/pub/pdf/vgm03.pdf (Accessed June 2012).

Ompad, Danielle M., Sandro Galea, Crystal M. Fuller, Vincent Edwards, and David Vlahov. "Ecstasy Use Among Hispanic and Black Substance Users in New York City." *Substance Use & Misuse*, v.40/9–10 (2005).

Rosenfeld, Richard, Robert Fornango, and Andres F. Rengifo. "The Impact of Order-Maintenance Policing on New York City Homicide and Robbery Rates: 1988–2001." *Criminology*, v.45/2 (2007).

Spunt, Barry. "The Current New York City Heroin Scene." *Substance Use & Misuse*, v.38/10 (2003).

White, Michael D. "The New York City Police Department, Its Crime-Control Strategies and Organizational Changes, 1970–2009." Phoenix: Center for Violence Prevention and Community Safety, Arizona State University, 2011.

Newark, New Jersey

Unlike other cities' more ethereal nicknames—the City of Lights (Paris, France), the City of Angels (Los Angeles)—Newark, New Jersey's, nickname is Brick City. As opposed to something cheerful or inspiring, the name evokes a hardness—something impermeable or something you cannot fight against. In reality, the nickname came about because of all the stunning brick buildings throughout the city, but few residents make that connection anymore. Brick City is now almost synonymous with "concrete jungle."

Keeping up With Crime

Newark has always had criminal gangs. The majority of gang members in Newark today are Bloods. Most of the crime being committed by these gang members is intragang crime; the crimes are block sensitive (meaning gang factions control certain blocks) and drug-related. Newark police have had relative success against gang crime; this is mostly because federal money is available to combat gang violence. While the drug trade is still active, it has been sharply curtailed.

Technological advances have aided these gains against gang crime. The Newark Police Department employs CompStat, holding weekly command meetings to analyze crime trends and identify hot spots of criminal activity. Newark also has positioned 40 closed-circuit televisions around the city in an effort to provide better surveillance. But while other cities are riding technology into the future of crime fighting, for Newark it is not the predominant philosophy of policing. Newark's policing strategy and that of the county where Newark sits—Essex County—focus more on manpower and trying to alleviate the causes of crime. It is a philosophy that takes longer, but if effective could reroute the paths of crime that have been so firmly embedded.

Riotous Fun to Riots in the Streets

In its heyday, Newark was a "swing town," with jazz shows, theater, nightclubs, and after-hour bars. Department stores, such as Bamberger's and Hahne's, enticed the suburban folks to hop on a bus and come spend their money. The area where Springfield Avenue and Bergen Street intersect was considered a shoppers' paradise.

Organized crime was also a presence in Newark. Notorious gang leader Dutch Schultz set up operations in the city, prospered there—and was gunned down at the Palace Chop House on October 23, 1935. When Prohibition ended, Newark continued to swing. The composition of the revelers, however, was markedly divided: African Americans partied in the Third Ward only. The separate but unequal nature of the neighborhoods and the lack of political representation for blacks became increasingly troublesome.

Between 1953 and 1962, Mayor Leo Carlin made an effort to stop businesses and white people from leaving Newark—as sociologists call it, "white flight." Regardless, investment in Newark's infrastructure dissipated as the white population departed, but the city's leaders remained white. Tensions over this disparity in power began to build.

Although fewer white people were living in Newark, yet another white mayor, Hugh Addonizio, was elected to succeed Carlin. The Addonizio years were fraught with racial tensions. He was criticized for not including African Americans in positions of responsibility and for not providing enough opportunity in the black community. Even though Newark was one of the first cities to hire a black police officer, representation of blacks within the force was lacking.

Adding to the problems, the city had reached its peak of small business production by 1958. Between 1950 and 1967, Newark lost nearly 20,000 manufacturing jobs. Finally, blacks felt disenfranchised by the shoddy public housing developments that were being built specifically to house the black population. Just as Jane Jacobs had warned, high-rise industrial-looking housing dampened the spirits of the residents and produced a criminogenic atmosphere, with no sense of community. All of these factors increased the pressure on the already precarious balance of race relations in the city.

At the time of the Newark Riots in July 1967, the city had the highest violent crime rate in the country. The events of July 12–17 left 26 people dead, 725 injured, close to 1,500 arrested, and incurred property damage exceeding $10 million, which the cash-strapped city could ill afford.

Fixing Broken Brick

After the riots, Newark was a city left to die. The only new businesses opening up were bars. Prostitutes freely strolled through the streets. With a dearth of jobs, many unemployed men would gather around the city's two train stations, asking for money and appearing threatening. Whether they all were criminals or not, the fear felt by ordinary citizens was palpable. The city's population fell at the rate of 50,000 per decade during that time, with more than a quarter of the population leaving by 1990.

A couple of corporate entities and some determined leaders did not give up on Newark. Prudential and PSE&G are two companies that maintained their commitment to the city. The city's second African American mayor, Sharpe James, took office in 1986, promising a renaissance. Utilizing government subsidies and with the help of community/private partnerships and philanthropists, this rebirth slowly began. The city selectively demolished public housing high-rises that symbolized poverty and were reminders of the riots.

Rutgers University also greatly expanded its reach in the city of Newark. Its School of Criminal Justice hired George Kelling to its faculty. Kelling and James Q. Wilson were the authors of an *Atlantic Monthly* magazine article in 1982 called "Broken Windows." Their theory posited that disorder

and crime are usually inextricably linked, and they used the metaphor of broken windows in neighborhood buildings leading to further criminal activity. In 2001, Kelling and the Rutgers School of Criminal Justice (RSCJ) founded the Police Institute. Through its implementation of the Greater Newark Safe Cities Initiative (GNSCI), with the partnering of RSCJ, its Police Institute, and the Newark Police Department the effort contributed to a major shift in policing policies.

The GNSCI, focusing on community-based crime prevention strategies, targeted "at risk" probationers and parolees, mostly those with prior or present gang membership. Working with groups comprised of law enforcement, parole officers, social workers, clergy, and family members, these men and women were shown that there is hope in quitting the criminal life and there are grave consequences in not. Bringing together all of these stakeholders in their lives was designed to show that the community would help, if they chose the noncriminal path.

RSCJ worked with the city on other projects, such as advisement on how to make playgrounds safer and adding police kiosks along the streets of Newark. The Broken Windows Theory was utilized throughout the city, and many blighted areas of Newark began to flourish again. An increase in police officers on the streets brought people back to the city.

Perception and Statistics

The perception that Newark is a dangerous city where street crime runs rampant is only reinforced by news media coverage. Because Newark sits between two major media markets (New York and Philadelphia), local coverage is already limited. When Newark is covered, it is mostly for violent crime. When the crime is particularly heinous, such as the 2007 playground killings of three college students by gang members, Newark makes national headlines.

From 1995 to 2005, Newark experienced a murder rate that was 10 times the national average. When Cory Booker became mayor in 2006, he declared that one of his first priorities was to reduce the crime rate. In June of that year, state investigators foiled a plot led by Bloods gang leaders, inside four New Jersey prisons, to assassinate Booker. Booker's promise was kept and crime dropped drastically between 2006 and 2007. Since 2007, however, these numbers have vacillated—with overall crime mostly dropping, but murder rates rising. With cuts to police staff and anticrime projects like Operation Ceasefire, the city will have to find innovations to reduce those homicide rates again.

Newark in 2010 ranked 23rd on the list of the nation's most dangerous cities. Although in its history Newark has held the number one position, 23 is no consolation to those victims of crime. Crime in Newark in 2010 was up 10 percent from the previous year—not an overly alarming increase, but a definite move in the wrong direction for a city battling to change its reputation.

Renaissance

Reducing street crime is one way to entice people back to a city, but other attractions are also needed. The Newark Bears, a minor league baseball team, now play at the newly-constructed Riverfront Stadium, which cost $30 million to build. Opening in 1997, the New Jersey Performing Arts Center has been called one of the nation's greatest concert venues. It has improved the area surrounding the center, as local restaurants accommodate the theatergoers. The Prudential Center opened in 2007 to host sports events and trade shows and is considered the core of the downtown revitalization.

Because of Newark's long-held reputation as a dangerous city, careful planning goes into the policing of any events at these three venues. Incidents of street crime could upset the delicate structure of the rebuilding of Newark's reputation. In March 2011, the Prudential Center hosted the Eastern Regional round of the men's National Collegiate Athletic Association (NCAA) basketball tournament. Then Police Director Garry McCarthy was extremely cognizant of the chance for Newark to prove it is not just a crime city. No criminal incidents occurred anywhere near the arena or near the hotels where the teams stayed. Afterward, the city breathed a collective sigh of relief.

Newark Now

Newark's renaissance has not progressed as quickly as any of its leaders or citizens would have desired, but there are clear differences today. Parts of the city are vibrant, while "socially disorganized" neighborhoods stand in between.

Several nonprofit organizations with the intent to better the overall lifestyle and reduce the crime

Dutch Schultz was a New York City–area mobster who started an operation in nearby Newark, New Jersey, in the 1930s. He made his fortune in organized crime-related activities, such as bootlegging alcohol and the numbers racket.

problems have sprung up since the late 1990s. GlassRoots is an organization that teaches youth the art of glass blowing during those unsupervised after-school hours that are so conducive to delinquent behavior. The Newark Chess Club has a similar mission and includes adult/child mentorship to strengthen positive community bonds. This club will initially be housed in the Boys and Girls Club of Newark, which also provides alternatives to delinquent behavior for youth.

Before Cory Booker became mayor, he founded a nonprofit organization called Newark Now, with the mission to empower residents to transform their neighborhoods. Conducting a survey of 20,000 residents, Newark Now determined that financial problems and fear of crime were the two biggest concerns of Newark residents. Newark Now has developed programs from tax preparation assistance to workforce development to helping exoffenders re-enter their communities. This alone is quite an undertaking, as Newark sees approximately 1,300 former inmates return to the community annually.

While many generations of New Jersey residents moved as far away from Newark as possible, some realize the importance of Newark's success. Even those who live outside of the state have been drawn to helping Newark by donating large sums of money or starting social programs—most notably, celebrities and entrepreneurs such as Oprah Winfrey, Facebook-founder Mark Zuckerberg, and Newark-native, Shaquille O'Neal.

A few of the early stakeholders of this renewal have pulled some of their financial backing from Newark, as evidenced by the owners of the New Jersey Nets selling the team and watching it move to Brooklyn. There is, however, truly promising news—Newark's population has increased for the first time in 60 years (2010 U.S. Census). The grounds where one of the housing projects once stood—the notorious Baxter Terrace—now boasts of an $130 million dollar housing complex, called "Baxter Park."

Its proximity to transportation and the New Jersey Institute of Technology may coax middle-income families back to the area. Newark's comeback, however, remains slow-footed and somewhat teetering. Every news story of murder or gang activity casts a pall on the enthusiasm for the rebirth of a once-great city. It is a slow and arduous process and one that can only be accomplished by laying a strong foundation—brick by brick.

Beth Adubato
New York Institute of Technology

See Also: Broken Windows Theory; Community Policing; Fear of Crime; Gangs (Street); Mobs and Riots; Newark Foot Patrol Experiment; Operation Ceasefire; Street Crime, Popular Portrayals of.

Further Readings

Grogan, Paul S. and Tony Proscio. *Comeback Cities: A Blueprint for Urban Neighborhood Revival.* Boulder, CO: Westview Press, 2000.

Ingle, Bob and Sandy McClure. *The Soprano State: New Jersey's Culture of Corruption.* New York: St. Martin's Press, 2008.

Kelling, George and Catherine Coles. *Fixing Broken Windows: Restoring Order and Reducing Crime in Our Communities.* New York: Touchtone, 1996.

Parks, Brad. "Crossroads Pt. 1: Before 1967, A Gathering Storm." New Jersey On-Line, LLC, July 15, 2007. http://www.blog.nj.com/ledgernewark/2007/07/crossroads_part_1.html (Accessed June 2012).

Newark Foot Patrol Experiment

In the late 1970s, the Police Foundation experimentally assessed the impact of increased police foot patrols on crime, fear of crime, citizen perceptions of police, and police opinions of the public in Newark, New Jersey. Although the foot patrols had little effect on crime, residents' perceptions of crime and the police improved. This research appeared during a time when a number of seminal experimental policing studies were completed. While the study is heavily cited and served as the foundation for James Q. Wilson and George Kelling's well-known "Broken Windows" article on social disorganization, it has also been criticized on a number of methodological grounds.

Study Design and Findings

New Jersey's Safe and Clean Neighborhoods Program began in the early 1970s; it included funding for foot patrol officers in 28 cities. In 1976, the Police Foundation began an evaluation of the foot patrol portion of the program. Although the study included data from the other 27 cities, the experiment focused primarily on Newark, and was one of the fullest tests of foot patrol in the United States up to that point. To test the effectiveness of foot patrols, researchers selected 12 foot patrol beats to study. Eight police beats in Newark already using foot patrol were matched into four pairs based on commercial and residential land usage. In each pair, one beat was randomly assigned one beat to discontinue foot patrol while the other remained the same. Police foot patrols were also initiated in four additional beats where they were previously nonexistent.

The results of the study indicated that crime (measured with both victimization surveys and police records of reported crimes) was unaffected by the foot patrols. However, foot patrol was related to improved perceptions among residents, particularly for those in the four beats where foot patrol was added. For example, in these "added" beats, residents reported improvements in their perceptions of the crime problem in their area, their overall fear of crime, and their personal safety, along with more positive impressions of police services. Similarly, foot patrol officers reported higher job satisfaction and better views of citizens than those on motor patrol.

The findings for commercial establishments were less positive. Establishments in beats where foot patrol was added reported that crime was more severe than establishments in beats where foot patrol was discontinued or sustained. Among businesses, foot patrol did not significantly impact feelings of safety, use of protective measures, or most measures of satisfaction with police. One explanation for these results is that the experimental foot patrol beats were manned during times when most businesses were closed, thus those establishments did not notice changes in police activity. Additionally, during the later stages of the experiment, the city of Newark laid off 200 police officers. Although the experimental foot patrols continued, it is possible that the police union's strong public opposition to the cuts impacted the study's results.

Criticisms

While these researchers attempted to systematically assess the impact of foot patrols on a variety of outcomes, the study is not without flaws. First, the study design is not a true experiment as the beats were not randomly assigned to each condition. Second, the study utilized a small sample limited to one city—begging questions about the generalizability of the results. Third, the intervention period was very short (about 11 months), thus the long term sustainability of the results is questionable. Fourth, the flaws of official statistics and victimization surveys as measures of crime are well-known.

Finally, police scholars note that in experiments like Newark's, it is often difficult to distinguish between a program with no impact and one where police do not patrol as intended. Foot patrol is particularly prone to this problem, given the difficulty of keeping officers patrolling outdoors during bad weather. The Newark researchers acknowledged that foot patrol was not deployed during the experiment in ways that revealed its maximum potential.

Broken Windows

In 1982, Wilson and Kelling expanded on the Newark experiment and social disorganization theory in an article titled "Broken Windows: The Police and Neighborhood Safety." The article contends that although foot patrols did not reduce crime, they did improve public order. These ideas contributed to the development of both "community policing," in which officers work closely with citizens to improve community controls, and "zero-tolerance" policing, which strictly enforces even minor offenses like panhandling and public drunkenness.

Jennifer J. Roberts
Jeffrey J. Roth
Indiana University of Pennsylvania

See Also: Broken Windows Theory; Community Policing; Fear of Crime; Newark, New Jersey; Police (Overview); Zero-Tolerance/Saturation Policing.

Further Readings

Kelling, George L., Antony Pate, Amy Ferrara, Mary Utne, and Charles E. Brown. *The Newark Foot Patrol Experiment.* Washington, DC: Police Foundation, 1981.

Kelling, George L. and James Q. Wilson. "Broken Windows: The Police and Neighborhood Safety." *Atlantic Monthly,* v.249/3 (1982).

Sherman, Lawrence W., David P. Farrington, Brandon C. Welsh, and Doris Layton MacKenzie, eds. *Evidence-Based Crime Prevention.* Rev. ed. New York: Routledge, 2002.

Open-Container Laws

Open-container laws are those that pertain to an open container of alcohol being carried by a citizen outside of an enclosed area, an establishment with legal permission to sell alcohol, or a person's private property. The concern over open containers relates directly to the possible effects of public intoxication. Public drinking—in the eyes of those who support open-container laws—leads to overconsumption and binge drinking. Beyond moral objections to public consumption, proponents of open-container laws argue that the mixing of alcohol and public places increases potential safety issues and encourages irresponsible behavior. Without a bartender or bouncer measuring overconsumption, proponents fear that drinkers can too easily become intoxicated and disruptive. Those who oppose open-container laws, on the other hand, argue that there is a basic right associated with drinking in public and that social problems—not the ability to drink in public—cause overconsumption and violence. If citizens can drink in public, proponents believe, it can work to normalize attitudes toward drinking and ultimately create a healthier drinking culture within our country.

Local Preferences

Most open container laws emerged in the immediate aftermath of Congress passing the Transportation Equity Act for the 21st Century in 1998.

Open-container laws attempt to monitor the behavior of Americans in public places. The most interesting aspect of these laws may be how they work in a federal society. States may not have laws on the books, but local ordinances can work to prevent public drinking. Likewise, cities—or event parts of cities—can move to eliminate open-container laws within their boundaries. There are even particular streets where open containers are legal despite a city's general ban on them.

Most U.S. states and localities do not allow the possession or consumption of open containers of alcohol in public. Only seven states do not have a general ban on the public possession or consumption of alcohol. These seven are Georgia, Louisiana, Missouri, Montana, Nevada, Pennsylvania, and Virginia. In all other states there is a state law that bans the possession or consumption of alcohol in public. Municipal laws may be more restrictive than state laws but cannot be more lax. In situations where and state and municipal law conflict, state law will prevail because of the federal structure of our government. Even in the seven states drivers fail to have a statewide law on the issue, most local jurisdictions take such a stance.

Of the 50 states, at present only 39 have laws that prohibit open containers or consumption of alcohol within a moving vehicle. It should be noted, however, that only the state of Mississippi permits drivers to consume alcoholic beverages while driving the vehicle. Even in this case, they must maintain a blood alcohol content of less than .08 percent and there are counties within the state that prevent the practice altogether. There are also several instances in various states where open containers are permitted in public places by statute. These include Butte, Montana (where an effort to pass a citywide open-container law was recently overwhelmingly voted down); the Las Vegas Strip; Beale Street in Memphis, Tennessee; the city of New Orleans; and the historic district of Savannah, Georgia. These exceptions seem to focus on certain toursit friendly types of areas. Each of the cities mentioned has a vibrant downtown entertainment district with large numbers of bars; these zones also tend to be pedestrian-centered.

Open-container laws are often left to the discretion of police officers to be enforced. For example, even in cities where there are no laws banning public

drinking, public intoxication can still be illegal. Police officers on the ground will largely be left to decide whether someone needs to be arrested for violating these laws or not. In downtown districts and during major athletic events, for example, we have witnessed police officers using their discretion in choosing not to arrest individuals who are potentially violating city or state laws as long as they are exercising caution and not acting in a reckless manner. College towns often take a similar approach in their dealings with students. As long as students are behaving well and not acting irresponsibly, local police officials are more willing to permit them to bend rules.

The United States is unique when it comes to calling these codes open-container laws. Most other nations simply term the possible infraction "public drinking." But in America, the term *open-container law* is used since police are asked to make judgments based on the mere presence of an alcoholic

In the United States, open-container laws regulate the existence of open bottles or cans of alcohol in public places, such as parks and vehicles. The purpose is to restrict public intoxication, especially drinking while operating a motor vehicle. Open-container laws are state laws rather than federal and therfore vary from state to state.

beverage, rather than actually trying to prove that someone was drinking.

William J. Miller
Southeast Missouri State University

See Also: Alcohol and Drug Use; Bar Personnel; Bars and Pubs; Drinking, Underage; Drinking Establishments, Unlicensed; Street/Block Parties.

Further Readings

Fagan, Jeffrey. "Intoxication and Aggression." In *Drugs and Crime, Crime and Justice: A Review of Research,* Michael Tonry and James Q. Wilson, eds.Vol. 13. Chicago: University of Chicago Press, 1991.

Graham, Kathryn and Ross Homel. *Raising the Bar: Preventing Aggression in and Around Bars, Pubs, and Clubs.* Devon, UK: Willan Publishing, 2008.

Homel, Ross, et al. "Public Drinking and Violence: Not Just an Alcohol Problem." *Journal of Drug Issues,* v.22/3 (1992).

National Highway Traffic Safety Administration. "Do Open Container Laws Work?" *State Legislatures,* v.28/10 (2002).

Wells, Samantha, et al. "'The Good, The Bad, and the Ugly': Responses by Security Staff to Aggressive Incidents in Public Drinking Settings." *Journal of Drug Issues,* v.28/4 (1998).

Operation Ceasefire

The Boston Gun Project Working Group was formed in 1995 to address high levels of youth violence in the Boston area. This working group was a collaborative effort incorporating practitioners, including federal, state, and local law enforcement, as well as researchers, including David Kennedy, Anthony Braga, and Anne Piehl from Harvard University, and community groups such as church groups, social workers, and community organizers. The focus was to apply problem-oriented policing to reduce the high levels of youth violence. In spring 1996, the Boston Gun Project Working Group created Operation Ceasefire as a specific program to address the youth homicide problem in Boston. Operation Ceasefire represents an innovative approach toward combating youth violence, using a pulling-levers philosophy of policing that has seen a variety of replications across the United States.

Structure and Implementation

Research by the Boston Gun Project Work Group found patterns in the violence in Boston. In particular, much of the violence was concentrated within the youth demographic (originally defined as under 21 and later expanded to under 24). Additionally, data on violence in Boston indicate that there were other trends related to the violence in that city, including a strong preference for particular types of firearms. Based on this information, Operation Ceasefire utilized a two-prong approach to address youth violence. The first prong focused on the trafficking of firearms. Law enforcement authorities focused on traffickers selling the specific types of firearms most commonly used by youth in Boston as well as traffickers who were supplying firearms to the city's more violent street gangs. The second prong of Operation Ceasefire focused on an innovative application of deterrence referred to as Pulling Levers. Local, state, and federal law enforcement cooperated with a variety of agencies (state, local, and federal prosecutors; probation and parole services; and a variety of community and religious groups) in order to send out a strong, uniform message that violence would no longer be tolerated in the community.

The message that these agencies and community groups hoped to convey was that any form of violence would cause a rapid and significant response. Since gangs are often engaged in a variety of criminal activities, this makes them vulnerable to a variety of criminal justice responses. In essence, any acts of violence perpetrated by these groups would incur a strong response—any and all tools or "levers" that the criminal justice community could use to punish the group responsible for the violence (e.g., enforcing old warrants, increasing probation and parole restrictions on current gang members, cracking down on drug activity, or refusing to engage in plea negotiations) were used by the agencies who agreed to take part in the strategy. In order to spread the word about this newly focused attention on street violence, social workers, community organizers, church groups, and others disseminated the message that violence would no longer be tolerated. Additionally, known gang members on probation or parole were forced to attend meetings or call-ins as part of their release conditions. During these meetings, gang members were told of the new antiviolence stance of the community and informed that if they, or their fellow gang members, were involved in violence, they would be the focus of this coordinated enforcement effort.

Evaluation

The focus on reducing the accessibility of firearms, combined with the focused deterrence efforts and the announcement of these deterrence efforts, were theorized to result in a reduction in violent crime in Boston. If a significant reduction in youth violence could be created, it was hoped that it would lead to a new norm and to a long-term reduction in youth violence. Evaluations of the effectiveness in reducing youth violence have generally indicated that Operation Ceasefire was successful in reducing youth violence. After implementation of Operation Ceasefire, criminologists A. Braga, D. Kennedy, E. J. Waring, and A. M. Piehl found Boston saw about a 60 percent decrease in youth homicide, a 25 percent decrease in gun assaults, and a 30 percent decrease in calls for service resulting from reports of shots being fired. In addition, their work indicates that these reductions in homicide and violent crime were not due to regional effects or nationwide reductions in crime. In other words, all data indicate that these reductions were due, at least in part, to Operation Ceasefire.

Despite the studies showing significant reductions in violent crime, Operation Ceasefire has not been without criticism. One challenge levied against Operation Ceasefire is that the intervention cannot be sustained for long durations of time, and that agency coordination will dissolve over time due to practical, political, and resource pressures. Because of this, pulling-levers deterrence programs cannot have long-lasting effects, it is theorized. This criticism has been seen in the failure of some replications of Operation Ceasefire in other jurisdictions, such as Baltimore, Maryland, and Minneapolis, Minnesota.

Cody Stoddard
Central Washington University

See Also: Boston, Massachusetts; Gangs (Street); Guns and Weapons; Juvenile Offending; Policing, Problem-Oriented; Zero-Tolerance/Saturation Policing.

Further Readings

Braga, Anthony A., et al. "Problem-Oriented Policing, Deterrence, and Youth Violence: An Evaluation of Boston's Operation Ceasefire." *Journal of Research in Crime and Delinquency*, v.38/2 (2001).

Braga, Anthony A. and Christopher Winship. "Partnership, Accountability, and Innovation: Clarifying Boston's Experience With Pulling Levers." In *Police Innovation: Contrasting Perspectives*, David Weisburd and Anthony Braga, eds. Cambridge, MA: Cambridge University Press, 2006.

Kennedy, David M., et al. "Reducing Gun Violence: The Boston Gun Project's Operation Ceasefire." Washington, DC: National Institute of Justice, 2001.

Siegel, Larry J. and Brandon C. Welsh. *Juvenile Delinquency: Theory, Practice, and Law.* Belmont, CA: Wadsworth, 2008.

Tita, George, et al. *Reducing Gun Violence: Results From an Intervention in East Los Angeles.* Santa Monica, CA: RAND Corporation, 2003.

Organized Crime and Violence

Organized crime in the United States is a multifaceted phenomenon. Composed of numerous ethnic groups, organized crime has emerged throughout the nation's history to exploit specific criminal enterprises. The modus operandi of criminal organizations is generally characterized as premeditated criminal acts (i.e., conspiracy), involving numerous offenders who consistently engage and persist in these illicit activities. While organized crime is essentially an ongoing criminal enterprise with the ultimate purpose of economic gain through unlawful means, controversies continue regarding its definition, structure, functions, and how best to deter it. Organized criminals and their perpetration of street crimes are difficult to penetrate and research because of their secrecy, violent nature, and sophisticated organization.

Definitions and Derivations

The U.S. Omnibus Crime Control and Safe Streets Act of 1968 defined organized crime as the unlawful activities of the members of a highly organized, disciplined association engaged in supplying illegal goods and services, including but not limited to gambling, prostitution, loan-sharking, narcotics, labor racketeering, and other unlawful activities of members of such organizations. The Federal Bureau of Investigation (FBI) currently defines organized crime as any group having some manner of formalized structure, and whose primary objective is to obtain money through illegal activities. Such groups maintain their position through the use of actual or threatened violence (including street crimes), corrupt officials, graft, or extortion, and generally have a significant impact on the people in their locales, region, or the country as a whole.

Definitions of organized crime vary from country to country but the fundamental challenge is not defining the word *crime*, but understanding the application of the word *organized*. These broad and far-reaching definitions of organized crime have encompassed political criminal factions and militant social movements (e.g., Ku Klux Klan and Palestinian Liberation Organization); criminal street gangs (e.g., Crips, Bloods, and Hells Angels); and drug trafficking organizations. According to the FBI, American citizens typically picture the Italian and Sicilian mafioso as the face of organized crime. However, organized crime has changed significantly in recent years. Russian crime gangs first entered the United States in the 1970s when the Soviet Union permitted around 300,000 people to emigrate to America. However, the collapse of the Soviet Union in 1991 led to the formation of thousands of criminal gangs, collectively known as the Russian Mafia. These organizations operate predominately in South Brooklyn. Other organized criminal groups include African crime groups involved in drug trafficking and Internet scams, Chinese Tongs, Japanese Boryokudan, and other Asian crime groups, and other organizations based in eastern European nations such as Romania and Hungary.

There are several characteristics indicative of these particular types of organizations that include: lack of political goals, exclusive membership, a stratified and hierarchal power structure, perpetuation without external agency or intervention, use of violence or threats of violence, distribution of illicit services or goods of public demand, assurances of members' immunity through corruption and enforcement, and governance by subculturally explicit rules and laws that are enforced through informal sanctions. In the United States, organized crime groups most visibly involved in street crime include La Cosa Nostra (i.e., Italian/Sicilian Mafia),

outlaw motorcycle gangs, Asian gangs, Russian mafia, and Colombian and Mexican drug cartels.

Historically, the majority of street crime perpetrated has arguably stemmed from the Italian Mafia in New York, New Jersey, and Philadelphia; from the Irish mob in Boston; the Colombian cartels in Miami, Florida; and the Mexican cartels in El Paso, Texas. These organized criminal networks have a strong presence in the United States, but are also transnational, crossing borders in their criminal enterprises. These organized crime groups operate in occasional alliance and apart, as well as in conjunction with legitimate business and political entities. Without the support and assistance of corrupt officials, legitimate entrepreneurs, and political figures, organized crime would not exist as it does today. For these prominent criminal organizations, street crime in the form of ruthless personal violence, such as beatings and killings, and property crimes such as bombings and arson are forms of systematically applied violence for doing business.

According to the FBI, the impact of organized crime on society and its level of involvement in street crime are not easily measured. Given that organized crime often operates under explicit rules and regulations of silence and exclusive membership, it is difficult to disentangle the type and number of street crimes associated with organized crime. The Uniform Crime Reporting Program of the FBI includes data on a vast number of both personal and property crimes that are perpetrated by more tightly or "professionally" organized groups above the average street-level gang. Although organized criminals sometimes eschew common street crimes, as they attract the attention of law enforcement and can be considered "bad for business," such crimes are still required tactically to support their ongoing criminal rackets.

Crime Types and Patterns

Racketeering activities are those criminal acts chargeable under the federal Racketeer Influenced and Corrupt Organizations (RICO) statute and enforced by the FBI. These include: bribery, sports bribery, counterfeiting, embezzlement, mail fraud, wire fraud, money laundering, obstruction of justice, murder for hire, drug trafficking, prostitution, sexual exploitation of children, alien smuggling, trafficking of counterfeit goods, theft from interstate shipment, and interstate transportation of stolen property.

Associated racketeering activities also include: murder, kidnapping, gambling, arson, robbery, bribery, extortion, and drug distribution. The RICO Act was passed into United States law on October 15, 1970, with the explicit purpose of eliminating organized crime and racketeering from legitimate organizations operating in interstate commerce.

Researchers and law enforcement have described a pattern of organized criminality in which there sometimes is a steady movement from typical street crimes, to illegal business activities, and finally to legitimate business enterprises. Alternately, such tactical crimes, which include assault, robbery, coercion, and murder, are considered the essential, bottom-line tools used by organized criminal groups once established. They are employed by these organizations as weapons of last resort to guarantee profits and compliance. These crimes—and the threat of them being applied—provide the money, muscle, and respect (i.e, terror) required for organized crime to operate illegitimate businesses.

The illicit services provided by organized crime—gambling operations, loan-sharking, prostitution, and drug sales—are both in demand by a large segment of American society and are a source of street crime. Extortion, a form of aggravated theft, is categorized as the use or threat of violence to attain criminal compliance. Loan-sharking is the illegal lending of money at exorbitant rates; violence and intimidation are typically used to foster repayment. Similarly, both prostitution and illegal gambling require organized criminals employing force and intimidation either for repayment or compliance by those involved in such illegitimate enterprises. Additionally, protection rackets are a major source of power and cash; this form of extortion threatens legitimate businesses with damage through fire or vandalism, for example, and provides "protection" from such damage through regular off-the-books payments. Organized criminal organizations also hijack cargo trucks, rob goods, steal cars, and rob banks.

Researchers note that alcohol Prohibition in the 1920s was a central catalyst in the rise to power of organized crime in America. Today's current drug prohibitions are not so different; the public demand for illicit drugs creates an enormous black market controlled by organized criminals, especially Mexican and Colombian drug cartels. The intrinsic systemic violence of the illicit drug market is responsible for a great deal of street crime in the United

States. Due to the fact that individuals involved in the illicit drug market cannot defer to formal control agents to solve disputes or handle wrongdoings, organized criminals resort to pay-offs as well as violence and murder to even debts and maintain order.

Street crime related to the drug market and organized crime arises from disputes over drug territory, as a means of enforcing normative codes, retaliation for drug robberies, elimination of informers, punishment for adulterated drugs, and the generally degraded social ecology of drug using areas. The Mexican drug cartels, such as the Juarez cartel and the Cardenas-Guillen, Valencia-Cornelio, and Caro-Quintero organizations, have been responsible for fueling a large portion of street crime in the last decade, especially in states along or near the southern border of the United States. These criminal organizations implement extensive violence to instill discipline, intimidate law enforcement and public officials, and quell power struggles.

Numerous organized crime bosses seem to have learned that it is often safer to be based in a foreign nation than to establish headquarters and run businesses from headquarters in highly industrialized nations such as the United States. Organized crime has taken a global form and has expanded its portfolio of infamy beyond violent street crimes to such modern crimes as identity theft, wire fraud, stock fraud, computer hacking, and economic espionage. Regardless of the numerous high-level crimes committed by organized criminals, however, these organizations at their base continue to rely on street crimes of extortion, violence, and intimidation to assure compliance and continuation of their criminal enterprises on the street level.

Patrick K. O'Brien
University of Colorado Boulder

See Also: Bloods; Bootleggers; Crips; Drug Dealing; Gangs (Street); Guns and Weapons; Immigrant Neighborhoods; Police Corruption, Street-Level.

Further Readings
Abadinsky, Howard. *Organized Crime*. Belmont, CA: Wadsworth, 2009.
Lyman, Michael D. and Gary W. Potter. *Organized Crime*. Upper Saddle River, NJ: Prentice Hall, 2010.
Shanty, Frank G. *Organized Crime: From Trafficking to Terrorism*. Santa Barbara, CA: ABC-CLIO, 2008.

Panhandling or Begging

Panhandling, sometimes referred to as begging, refers to the act of requesting a donation in a public space. The term *panhandling* derives from the shape of the outstretched arm and hand or from the fact that a cup or plate is sometimes used to hold the donations. Without employment, social assistance, or housing supports, people may be left with few options except for panhandling, squeegee-cleaning car windshields, or criminal activities in order to acquire necessities such as food, clothing, or shelter.

While there is no national survey of involvement in panhandling and rates of panhandling among homeless people, comprehensive studies of local surveys suggest most commonly that around 30 to 40 percent of homeless people panhandle. Enforcement and punishments for the crime vary around the world. In the United Kingdom, for example, all forms of begging have been illegal since the Vagrancy Act of 1824—however, there is no jail term associated with violations of the act. In more recent antipanhandling legislation in other jurisdictions, jail time can be given for failure to pay fines or for repeat citations.

Homelessness

Panhandling is directly tied to homelessness, and numerous studies suggest increases in the numbers of homeless people in the United States over the last few decades. A 1991 study of 182 U.S. cities with populations over 100,000 found that homelessness rates tripled between 1981 and 1989 for the 182 cities taken together. The U.S. Conference of Mayors report from 2008 noted that 19 of the 25 cities examined reported an increase in homelessness from 2007. The *State of Homelessness Report* for 2011 reported that the homeless population in the United States increased by approximately 20,000 people from 2008 to 2009 (a 3 percent increase). In a 2011 report, the Homeless Research Institute estimated that over the next three years homelessness in the United States could increase by 5 percent, or by approximately 74,000 people.

With the increases in homelessness in urban and suburban areas, it can be inferred from this that survival strategies on which homeless people depend, including panhandling, have also increased. While there are no systematic statistics on the practice of panhandling, or on incidences of panhandling in U.S. cities, there has been a notable increase in the criminalization of panhandling in numerous jurisdictions.

Over the last decade in cities across North America those who have need to panhandle in public spaces have increasingly experienced a proliferation of laws against begging and panhandling. Numerous local governments have cut or canceled social services such as welfare, subsidized housing, and health care services that benefit homeless people while simultaneously emphasizing criminal justice system approaches that police, regulate, and punish homeless people for engaging in survival activities such as panhandling. The result has been an increase in jail time for panhandlers.

Recent Prohibitions

Researcher James D. Wright showed that a comparison of reported data from 2002 and 2006 by the National Coalition for the Homeless and the National Law Center on Homelessness and Poverty saw a 3 percent increase in laws prohibiting loafing, loitering, or vagrancy. There is also a 14 percent increase in laws prohibiting sitting or lying down in public spaces in U.S. cities. In addition, there was an 18 percent increase in laws prohibiting so-called aggressive panhandling. Wright observed that of all the behaviors associated with homelessness in public discourses, beggary is viewed as the

most offensive, and laws against panhandling are consistently at the center of efforts to "clean up the streets." The implementation of legislation typically follows periods of moral panic over panhandling and squeegeeing in which high-level politicians play important parts in stoking public fear and condemnation of people engaged in such activities.

Various antipanhandling laws prohibit panhandling in a broad range of contexts and practices. While laws differ, certain prohibitions can be found across cases. These include prohibitions against: panhandling near automated teller machines (ATMs) or bank entrances; approaching people in motor vehicles; following people or making repeated requests; panhandling outside stores or restaurants; panhandling in groups; using a loud voice; and panhandling while camping out. Clearly the prohibitions greatly restrict panhandling practices, making it difficult for any panhandling to be carried out at all.

Most panhandlers state that they would prefer a minimum-wage job to begging, typically citing a desire for a steady income. However, many could not handle a conventional job because of mental illness, a physical disability, or a lack of skills. Beggars tend to congregate in public places such as transportation routes, parks, or near busy shopping areas.

Cities such as Santa Cruz (1998) and San Francisco, California, (2004 and 2010) have passed bylaws restricting where panhandling can take place. In Orlando, Florida, the municipal government established a city ordinance in 2006 requiring that panhandlers acquire a permit much like a street vending business would. The Orlando ordinance also prohibits panhandling anywhere in the downtown commercial districts. It also makes it illegal to provide false information while panhandling or to use funds secured from panhandling for purposes other than those stated during the course of panhandling. Atlanta, Georgia, has a law prohibiting any panhandling; arrest and incarceration are used to remove homeless people from view by higher income consumers, tourists, and business owners.

The recent antipanhandling legislation, in various jurisdictions, shows the way in which governments advocate for and implement legislation that does not necessarily reflect the concerns of the population more broadly. Critics note that there was no public outcry for such legislation prior to the moral crisis instigated by local politicians. Furthermore, there is little evidence to suggest that panhandling was a threat to public safety, or that the antipanhandling laws have reduced street crimes or improved the safety of city streets. Critics suggest that, in fact, antipanhandling acts make life less safe for homeless people—and by extension of their desperation, could make them more likely to commit more serious street crimes.

Other Views

Numerous research projects, both prior to and since passage of antipanhandling acts, have shown that homeless youth who were involved in squeegeeing or panhandling had less involvement in criminal activity and drug use than homeless youth who did not squeegee. Even more, there is little legitimate or systematic evidence showing that squeegeeing and panhandling make cities any less safe. In some jurisdictions, security guards have been hired, using public funds, to harass and intimidate panhandlers. In particular, security forces patrol streets in commercial areas to push panhandlers away from those areas. In these cases, governments are acting not to secure the needs of citizens but to fulfill the interests of private businesses by displacing the crime activity. In response, activists have formed panhandlers unions in cities to defend panhandlers against

harassment and criminalization. Interestingly, panhandling and homelessness do not entirely correspond. Many homeless people do not panhandle, often as a result of fear of negative responses from more privileged members of society who may call police or resort to harassment or vigilante violence. Some studies suggest that an estimated 40 percent of homeless people engage in panhandling, although exact numbers are difficult to come by given that many homeless people cannot be reached for surveys and many do not want to disclose involvement in activities that might well be targets of criminalization. This noncorrespondence plays into urban myths about panhandling as a lucrative scam. The myth of the rich panhandler who lives in a gated community and drives a Cadillac at the end of the day is prevalent in different urban contexts.

In the United States, advocates such as the American Civil Liberties Union have achieved greater success having antipanhandling legislation struck down as violations of First Amendment (free speech) rights. They have argued that the First Amendment protects public requests for donations which might include panhandling. In the early 1990s federal courts struck down state laws prohibiting panhandling in New York and California. In the view of those courts, solicitation in public is supported for various causes and interests and therefore panhandling cannot be singled out for differential treatment.

Jeff Shantz
Kwantlen Polytechnic University

See Also: Broken Windows Theory; Homelessness; Juvenile Curfews; Loitering; Pickpocketing; Skid Row; Theft and Larceny; Victims, Tourist.

Further Readings

Feldman, Leonard C. *Citizens Without Shelter: Homelessness, Democracy, and Social Exclusion.* Ithaca, NY: Cornell University Press, 2006.

Gowan, Teresa. *Hobos, Hustlers, and Backsliders: Homeless in San Francisco.* Minneapolis: University of Minnesota Press, 2010.

Lee, Barrett A. and Chad R. Farrell. "Buddy Can You Spare A Dime?: Homelessness, Panhandling and the Public." *Urban Affairs Review,* v.38 (2003).

Mitchell, Don. *The Right to the City: Social Justice and the Fight for Public Space.* New York: Guildford, 2003.

Sermons, M. William and Peter Witte. "State of Homelessness in America." Washington, DC: National Alliance to End Homelessness and Homelessness Research Institute, 2011.

U.S. Conference of Mayors. "2008 Status Report on Hunger & Homelessness." Washington, DC: U.S. Conference of Mayors, 2008.

Wright, James D. *Address Unknown: The Homeless in America*. New Brunswick, NJ: Transaction, 2009.

Patrol Cars

The influence of the police patrol car on street crime began in the late 19th and early 20th centuries in Akron, Ohio. Frank Loomis, a member of the Akron Fire Department, built an electric wagon that was first used to pick up intoxicated residents in 1899. From this modest beginning, the proliferation of gasoline-driven patrol cars began in the 1930s and by 2007, 99 percent of police departments were using automobiles.

Driving Versus Walking the Beat

Rather than walking a beat, most officers use the patrol car as a means of transportation. The patrol car allows police to respond to more calls for service, more rapidly, and across larger geographic areas. The patrol car has influenced street crime response time, calls for service, deterrence, and surveillance. However, patrol cars have also reduced the personal interaction of the beat officer on foot, undermining the officer's knowledge and understanding of residents' problems on specific beats. This isolation has affected the relationship between the police and the public.

Policing street crime was not the first goal of the patrol car. The car was a multipurpose vehicle that could move officers and transport arrestees. The Industrial Revolution and immigration rapidly increased the population and size of cities; these changes created an increased demand for police service and increased the size of metropolitan police jurisdictions. As personal ownership and use of automobiles increased and urban populations began to move away from city centers, police departments adapted with the use of patrol cars to augment or replace foot patrols. Criminologist

Samuel Walker notes that patrol car use still varies, from completely motorized departments to cities that still emphasize foot patrols. Following studies of the effect of foot patrols on crime and public support for police, many heavily motorized departments have returned some officers to foot patrol, typically in densely populated areas.

Observers reported one effect of patrol cars as isolating the officer from the ordinary citizen and damaging police-community relations. Automobiles shifted police contacts from ordinary citizen encounters to "problem persons." They removed the casual contact the officer had with both law-abiding citizens and street criminals. This was a factor supporting the development and spread of community policing throughout the end of the 20th century.

Communications and Hot Spots

Other advances in technology complemented use of the patrol car in policing street crime, specifically the increase in private telephones and in car two-way radios linked to the department. Telephones allowed the average citizen to summon the police at the first sign of trouble. The patrol car, coupled with a two-way radio, allowed for a faster response. It was possible for citizens to call for police to deal with a broad range of problems. The advent of the 911 system increased the need for patrol cars to respond to more calls for service. The patrol car now allowed police the ability to patrol beats more frequently and at varied times. This in turn increased public expectations of police to handle nuisance crimes.

Recent research into the impact of patrol cars on street crime indicates that patrolling specific areas of high crime can deter street crime. The key is the focus of patrols in the specific locations where street crime is habitually worst, or a "hot spot." These studies contradict previous work like the Kansas City Preventative Patrol study that found no significant deterrent effect of street crime by marked patrol cars. The breadth of this research shows automobile patrol can reduce street crime—but results, as with foot patrols, are contingent upon focusing patrol on those areas where it can have the greatest impact.

Advances in technology continue to improve the patrol car as a means to combat street crime. Computer systems within the cars that have geographic positioning systems allow officers to better track their location in conjunction with calls for service and known hot spots.

Conclusion

The patrol car changed the manner in which the police react to street crime. The patrol car is a tool that represents continued application of advanced technology. The advantages of patrol cars allow police to answer more calls for service, across larger beats, while still maintaining a deterrent effect.

Garrett Grothoff
Lawrence F. Travis III
University of Cincinnati

See Also: Community Policing; Hot Spots; Police (Overview); Zero-Tolerance/Saturation Policing.

Further Readings

Braga, Anthony A. "The Effects of Hot Spots Policing on Crime." *The Annals of the American Academy of Political and Social Science*, v.578/1 (2001).

Kelling, George L., Tony Pate, Duane Dieckman, and Charles E. Brown. "Kansas City Preventative Patrol Experiment: Summary Report." Washington, DC: Police Foundation, 1974.

Sherman, Lawrence W. and David Weisburd. "General Deterrent Effects of Police Patrol in Crime 'Hot Spots': A Randomized, Controlled Trial." *Justice Quarterly*, v.12/4 (1995).

Walker, Samuel. "Broken Windows and Fractured History: The Use and Misuse of History in Recent Police Patrol Analysis." *Justice Quarterly*, v.1/1 (1984).

Peep Shows

Peep shows began innocuously enough as innocent amusements to be shown on the streets or at carnivals in the 16th century. Usually called "raree shows," denoting something rare or unusual, in England, they were closed boxes containing peepholes that featured and emphasized drawings of buildings, battles, or current events. The illusion of perspective was maintained by mirrors and lenses which magnified certain vignettes within the box. The box, if small enough, was typically carried on the back of a peddler or solitary showman. Sometimes the boxes were carried like litters, which required two men to carry the attraction.

This sort of peep show was portrayed by William Hogarth, the celebrated English artist and satirist, in 1733. The main operator, often dressed like a soldier, always gave a stentorian running account of the events to be seen within the box. This would attract a crowd and keep it in place. Children, typically, would stand on boxes to peer into the peephole to see the extraordinary contents. Older people could sit in folding chairs and gaze at the rare attraction within. Numerous depictions of this scene show peasant children crowding around a box peering into a porthole-type lens or waiting for their chance to see the show. Occasionally in period art a pickpocket is shown picking the purse of an unwary peeper. This suggests that the showman and the pickpocket may have been in cahoots, an early association of crime and popular entertainment.

Early American Versions

Oddly, few of the early artistic depictions or written accounts suggest that the peep shows viewed at carnivals or on the streets of London had obscene content, though this must surely have followed in the wake of this technology. Peep shows were popular all through Europe and made their way to the North American colonies in the 1700s. They were popular attractions in circuses, fairs, and carnivals throughout the 1800s, and became features of penny arcades in the latter part of that century.

Often found in back rooms of arcades or pools halls, the stationary, coin-fed, film-driven peep shows of the early 1900s, propelled by hand cranks, featured racy content such as belly dancing and "Salome dancing," a rudimentary, relatively tame form of stripping. This additional attraction of pool halls attracted young men to these "dens of inequity" and further excited the ire of antipool reformers. Hand-crank-driven loops featuring mildly racier content could be seen in arcades on New Orleans' Bourbon Street through the 1960s.

Modern Peep Shows

The modern peep show evolved out of the emergence of the adult entertainment industry in the 1970s. One type of attraction is merely a technologically advanced form of the hand-cranked classic arcade type static peep show. It is a stationary booth, closed off from view on all sides, with a screen, a projector (to which the customer has no access), a list of films with illustrations, and a coin box. The customer enters the booth, sits down, selects a film, feeds tokens or coins into the coin box, and watches the film. He can watch the film as long as he has quarters or tokens to feed into the box and is free to change titles and watch a different film should he choose to do so.

TThese sorts of peep shows are often found adjoining adult theaters or as booths attached to an adult bookstore or novelty shop. There are frequently masturbatory aids such as lubricants for sale and towel dispensers for discreet cleanup. The peep show site is dark and frequently is redolent with the smell of disinfectant, body fluids, and bleach.

The other kind of peep show features a more confrontational format in that an actual female performer, not a cinematic "actor," is the main attraction. As in the cinematic peep show, the customer enters a booth and feeds coins or tokens into a box. However, at this point a screen rises and a nude or nearly nude live female begins to gyrate and pose in ways that prominently feature breasts and genital areas. Other men in booths may be situated around the performer in an arena-type seating arrangement, all kept separate from each other by study carrel-type partitions and from said performer by a screen. As the action becomes more explicit, the customer is exhorted to feed more coins into the box to continue the show. If he fails to do so, or runs out of money, the curtain descends and he cannot see the continuing action. The live peep show is more costly than the filmic variety, and tips are encouraged.

Today cinematic peep shows can be found in many cities worldwide. Although notably moved from Times Square, live peep shows are still going strong on New York City's lower East Side. Live peep shows are still found in San Francisco, in the Tenderloin and just north of Chinatown near the old Condor Club and City Lights Bookstore. Southern California has many adult bookstores, many of which contain the cinematic variety, but others have live peep shows. Los Angeles, San Diego, and the surrounding communities have cinematic peep shows of the former variety.

Crime Connections

The question arises: "Do peep shows cause crime?" Certain unsettling and counterintuitive things can happen in that context. Homosexuals, bisexual males, or men on the "down-low" (nominally heterosexual men who meet other men for homosexual

interludes) often use peep shows as places of assignation and furtive sexual performance. Frequently, unambiguously heterosexual men are accosted in this context and react with some surprise, panic, dismay, and occasionally violence. Police may be called in some situations. Pimps frequent some peep shows to line up customers for prostitutes; sexually oriented con games may have their genesis in that environment. Prostitutes may aggressively solicit customers or make an issue over perceived inadequate compensation after performing a peep show sex act. Sometime thefts and muggings occur in the immediate vicinity of a peep show arcade.

That being said, social scientists are not in agreement about peep shows being a stimulus to crime. In fact, an authoritative review conducted in San Diego concluded that in terms of late night police calls for service, that is, incidents that called for a police response and record of same, there was no evidence of heightened law enforcement activity in the immediate environs of peep shows. It should be noted that police officials in general disagree on this issue, and other scholars point to the inadequacy of calls for service as a measure of criminal activity in a given geographic milieu. As adult-oriented businesses are normally located in already depressed, high-crime areas, whether they actually exacerbate crime remains an open question.

Frederick Hawley
Western Carolina University

See Also: Crime–Consumerism Nexus; Exposure, Indecent; Mugging; Pool Halls; Prostitution, Houses of; Risky Lifestyles; Sex Crimes; Skid Row; Women.

Further Readings

Herzog, Amy. "In the Flesh: Space and Embodiment in the Pornographic Peep Show Arcade." *Velvet Light Trap*, v.62/3 (2008).

Linz, Daniel, Bryant Paul, and Mike Yao. "Peep Show Establishments, Police Activity, Public Place, and Time: A Study of Secondary Effects in San Diego, California." *Journal of Sex Research*, v.43/2 (2006).

McCleary, Richard and James W. Meeker. "Do Peep Shows 'Cause' Crime? A Response to Linz, Paul, and Yao." *Journal of Sex Research*, v.43/2 (2006).

Tewksbury, Richard. "Peep Shows and 'Perverts': Men and Masculinity in an Adult Bookstore." *Journal of Men's Studies*, v.2/1 (1993).

Peeping Toms

Peeping Tom is the nickname given to a person who engages in voyeurism. The origin of the phrase comes from the legend of Lady Godiva, in which a man named Tom watched Lady Godiva ride her horse nude through the village. Voyeurism (also called scopophilia) is both a criminal act and a mental health disorder. As a mental health diagnosis, voyeurism involves recurring and intense sexual urges that compel a person to secretly observe an unsuspecting person who is either in some state of undress and/or engaging in sexual activity. Voyeurism as a crime is usually defined as the act of observing a person in a private act without the consent of the observed person, for sexual purposes. This type of crime often happens out in public; that is, the perpetrator commits the crime in a public area, such as a street or outside a property, while the victim is often inside a private location that has been made accessible through an uncovered window or similar means. According to scholars, most perpetrators are male, and are typically unmarried.

Voyeurism is considered illegal primarily because a victim's right to privacy is being violated; in some instances, voyeurism can be considered a sex crime. Usually, voyeurs do not seek any contact with the victim, so most assault and harassment laws do not apply. However, a significant minority of voyeurs have committed sexual assault or rape. Some criminologists believe that voyeurs are likely to possess characteristics that are also found among serious sexual offenders. These include taking considerable time and effort; careful, methodical, and detailed planning; deliberate selection of victim; and purposeful preparation of equipment before executing the crime. Laws within the United States regarding voyeurism vary widely from state to state, but are usually classified as misdemeanors and punishable by fines. However, in extreme cases or instances of repeat offenses, some perpetrators can be accused of committing a felony, and it is possible that someone could be considered a sex offender if found guilty of voyeurism. The seriousness of the crime may also be determined by the extent to which any images made by the offender are published and disseminated.

Video Voyeurism

With the proliferation of small cameras, including those in cell phones and some that can be discreetly mounted on such surfaces as the top of a shoe, video voyeurism has become a concern. In 2004, the Video Voyeurism Prevention Act was signed into U.S. federal law. Under this act, it is illegal for a person to, "capture an image of a private area of an individual without their consent, and knowingly does so under circumstances in which the individual has a reasonable expectation of privacy." Currently, the law primarily has been interpreted to prohibit taking photos of a person without his or her consent in a private place, such as one's home, a dressing room, or public bathroom.

Under the domain of video voyeurism is the phenomenon of upskirting, which is the act of taking unauthorized pictures underneath a person's skirt, and capturing an image of the crotch area. Similarly, downblousing is the act of taking a picture of a woman's cleavage without her knowledge. The legal issue associated with upskirting and downblousing is whether a person can have a reasonable expectation of privacy, despite being in a public place. The debate continues as to whether the Video Voyeurism Prevention Act includes the taking of pictures in public, open areas. Arguments in support of banning upskirting and downblousing include clearly defining the place where one should expect privacy to a very narrow, exact location such as underneath a skirt or shirt, as opposed to the broader location of the person (e.g., shopping mall, park, subway). Some states have specifically outlawed these precise practices in order to avoid the vagueness of the federal legislation.

L. Kris Gowen
Portland State Unversity

See Also: Courts, Mental Health; Exposure, Indecent; Rape and Sexual Assault; Sex Crimes; Stalking; Women.

Further Readings

Hanson, R. K. and A. Harris. "Voyeurism: Assessment and Treatment." In *Sexual Deviance: Theory, Assessment, and Treatment*, D. R. Laws & W. T. O'Donahue, eds. New York: Guilford Press, 1997.

Hazelwood, Robert R. and Janet Warren. "The Serial Rapist: His Characteristics and Victims." *FBI Law Enforcement Bulletin*, v.58/1–2 (1989).

Langstrom, N. "The DSM Diagnostic Criteria for Exhibitionism, Voyeurism, and Frotteurism." *Archives of Sexual Behavior*, v.39 (2010).

Laws, D. Richard and William T. O'Donohue. *Sexual Deviance—Theory, Assessment, and Treatment.* 2nd ed. New York: Guilford Press, 2008.

U.S. Senate. "S. 1301: Video Voyeurism Prevention Act of 2004." http://www.govtrack.us/congress/bill .xpd?bill=s108-1301 (Accessed September 2011).

Winder, Belinda and Philip Banyard, eds. *A Psychologist's Casebook of Crime: From Arson to Voyeurism.* London: Palgrave Macmillan, 2012.

Philadelphia, Pennsylvania

Philadelphia, like many of its big city counterparts, has had a long history with street crime. From the street riots in the 18th century to the drug-related drive-by shootings of today, the city has been host to an array of crime waves and has also been home to innovative crime control responses. Today, the city of 1.5 million has averaged just under 340 homicides and over 1,000 nonfatal shootings a year for the past decade, and while the number of murders is down from a peak of 406 in 2007, Philadelphia ranks as one of the most dangerous big cities in America.

According to the Federal Bureau of Investigation's (FBI) Uniform Crime Reports (UCR) data, between 1980 and 2005 Philadelphia experienced an increase in the violent crime index, increasing from 1,029 total violent crimes per 100,000 people in 1980 to 1,467 per 100,000 people in 2005. The property crime index decreased slightly in the same time period. The 1980 rate was 4,987 people per 100,000 compared to 4,102 in 2005.

Disrupted Economic Base

The bare numbers only tell part of the tale. In Philadelphia, as in many other big cities, street crime is concentrated in a small number of areas. In Philly, most homicides, shootings, robberies, and rapes occur in areas of concentrated disadvantage. In the poorest neighborhoods a multigenerational drug trade is the one of the primary employers, and a vortex around which much street crime plays out.

In many of these communities the factories and businesses that employed thousands of people through the first six decades of the 20th century have long since shuttered, and the decline in economic fortunes has not been reversed in these places. As the formal economy has diminished, an informal drug economy has taken root in many of these areas, and has, over time, flourished. The Kensington neighborhood, for instance, used to be a thriving manufacturing center—once the millinery capital of the United States—but is now more famous for the quantity and quality of the heroin that is trafficked through there than for anything that is actually made in the community.

It is more than simply a tale of the decline of manufacturing and the loss of jobs. The most dangerous parts of Philadelphia are also where rates of infant mortality are among the highest in the nation, where life expectancy is much lower than the national average, and where school dropout rates are extremely high. Philadelphia public schools have been in the news recently mainly because of the high levels of violence there. For the 2009–10 school year, there was an average of 25 violent incidents a day in Philadelphia public schools involving students, teachers, and staff, and ranging from assault to rape and robbery.

A recently published dissertation by University of Delaware researcher Heather Zaykowski, based on in-depth interviews with over 150 Philadelphia youth growing up in high-crime neighborhoods, has illustrated high levels of violent victimization especially among those youth most involved in illicit activity. Much of this victimization is never reported and indeed is accepted almost as an occupational hazard by young people. Most youth spoke of times that they were jumped by others or of fights that broke out in school or in their neighborhoods. Moreover, several said that they had witnessed someone being shot, and a small number had themselves been injured in gun violence. More surprising than the low levels of reporting victimization is the finding that youth don't really see themselves as victims in such situations, preferring to internalize the experience as bad luck, or to retaliate.

Police Tactics and Programs

The ubiquity of guns and violence in certain communities has instigated a response from formal authorities anxious to curb street crime in Philadelphia. The stubborn persistence of violent crime of combating violent crime has been the wider deployment of so-called stop and frisk tactics (brief preventive detainment and cursory search of suspicious persons) by police.

Stop and Frisk

Politics plays a key role in the story of crime and its control in Philadelphia. As with many other big cities, the police commissioner in Philadelphia is a mayoral appointee, and thus must serve the interests of the administration. Mayor Michael Nutter won the election in 2007 in part because of his hard-line stance on the street crime problem, which was the number-one issue with voters in the city at the time. Nutter promised that if he was elected he would declare a crime emergency in several hard-hit neighborhoods and crack down hard on violent crime.

While he did not in the end declare a state of emergency, Nutter, along with his newly appointed police commissioner Charles Ramsey, instituted an aggressive stop and frisk policy in the nine districts (out of the city total of 22) with the highest rates of violent crime. As a result, in 2008 there were over 570,000 officer-initiated stops in Philadelphia. Vehicle stops increased 13 percent to 357,844, and pedestrian stops increased 56 percent to 215,779, with the vast majority of the stops occurring in the areas of concentrated crime.

These Terry stops are named for the 1968 Supreme Court decision in the *Terry v. Ohio* case in which the court held that the Fourth Amendment prohibition on unreasonable search and seizure is not violated when a police officer initiates a pedestrian stop without probable cause to arrest if there is "reasonable suspicion" that the person may have committed, is committing, or is about to commit a criminal offence, or if there is a reasonable belief that the person may be armed and dangerous. In addition to being able to stop someone, police can also perform a frisk of outer clothing if they believe a person to have firearms. The remit of Terry stops was later expanded to include temporary detention of a vehicle, in essence, a traffic stop.

While these stop and frisk tactics are touted as being effective in tamping down violent crime, their deployment is unpopular as they are most often targeted in areas of high crime and concentrated disadvantage, which, in the case of Philadelphia as in other cities, means predominantly African American and

Three Philadelphia police officers and a Highway Patrol lieutenant monitoring the streets: Philadelphia was ranked as the sixth-most dangerous among 32 American cities with populations over 500,000.

and its concentration in the most disadvantaged parts of the city masks the many and varied law enforcement responses to violence. In the past two decades, various forms of saturation policing have been tried out in high-crime areas, ranging from the street sweeps (typically a geographically concentrated campaign of undercover drug purchases and targeted arrests of violent gang members and others with outstanding warrants) and enhanced patrolling of Operation Sunrise (a "quality of life" or Broken Windows theory campaign) in 1999–2000 to the drug corner targeted sweeps of Operation Safe Streets (utilizing a round-the-clock flood of uniformed police patrol presence) and in May 2002. In recent years, the predominant mode

Hispanic neighborhoods. Thus charges of racial profiling frequently arise when stop and frisk is implemented in a given jurisdiction. Recently the opposition to the over-use of stop and frisk in Philadelphia resulted in the establishment of a panel to oversee its deployment. Mayor Nutter declared that it was never his intention to trample the rights of any Philadelphia citizen.

Stop and frisk illustrates the difficulty in crafting a response to high levels of street crime in American cities. It is sometimes possible to reduce crime by deploying draconian measures, but the danger is that this alienates the law-abiding citizens who are caught in the fine mesh of saturated policing and Terry stops. Stop and Frisk policing strategies inevitably deepen the chasm of mistrust between police and community members. Ultimately, this lack of trust can be harmful to crime reduction if a significant portion of the public views many of their local officers as an occupying army.

Philly Rising

In 2010, however, a pilot program in a high-crime neighborhood in North Philadelphia successfully implemented a new approach. Called Philly Rising, this strategy brought police officers and community residents together to discuss problems and create solutions. Through Philly Rising, vacant buildings were demolished, a Police Athletic League was opened, and a computer lab, staffed by volunteers from the nearby university, was established. Moreover, a community center with a pool, which had been abandoned and neglected, was reopened, making it possible for seniors to do water aerobics and children and teens to have a safe place to play.

These actions may sound like they have little to do with reducing crime, but in fact they play an important role in decreasing neighborhood disorder and increasing the ability of community residents to work alongside police officers to cut down on street crime. In fact, after the first year of Philly Rising, violent crime fell by 16 percent in the district. Mayor Nutter is now working to implement Philly Rising in other high-crime neighborhoods; additional aspects are under consideration to augment the program, such as broader use of cash rewards to citizens who help police. For instance, Nutter has proposed a $500 reward for information leading police to an illegal gun, and up to a $20,000 reward for information leading to homicide arrests.

Conclusion

Street crime in Philadelphia has proven to be a persistent and hard to solve problem. Even as violent crime rates have dropped in many large American cities, the rates in Philadelphia have remained stubbornly high. Homicides in 2012 were projected to be the highest since 2007, confirming that the inroads into violent crime made in the early days of the Nutter administration could be diminishing. Though the nickname "Killadelphia," earned at the height of the violent crime spike in the mid-2000s, is probably misleading, street crime in Philadelphia has causes far deeper than the remedies that have been deployed to combat it, and consequences far greater than the mere statistics suggest.

Patrick J. Carr
Rutgers University
Susan Clampet-Lundquist
Maria J. Kefalas
Saint Joseph's University

See Also: Community Policing; Racial Profiling; Stop and Frisk; Zero-Tolerance/Saturation Policing.

Further Readings

CityRating.com. "Philadelphia Crime Rate Report (Pennsylvania)." 2012. http://www.cityrating.com/crime–statistics/pennsylvania/philadelphia.html (Accessed September 2012).

Cornell University Law School. *Terry Versus Ohio* (No. 67). http://www.law.cornell.edu/supct/html/historics/USSC_CR_0392_0001_ZS.html (Accessed September 2012).

Lawton, Brian A., Ralph B. Taylor, and Anthony J. Luongo. "Police Officers on Drug Corners in Philadelphia, Drug Crime, and Violent Crime: Intended, Diffusion, and Displacement Impacts." *Justice Quarterly*, v.22/4 (2005).

Newall, Mike. "Who Will Pray for Camden?" *Philadelphia City Paper* (July 16, 2008). http://www.archives.citypaper.net/articles/2008/07/17/who-will-pray-for-camden (Accessed September 2012).

Philly.com "History of Philly Crime." January 30, 2009. http://www.philly.com/philly/hp/art/history_philadelphia_crime.html (Accessed September 2012).

U.S. Department of Justice. "Philadelphia Division: A Brief History." http://www.fbi.gov/philadelphia/about–us/history/history (Accessed April 2012).

Pickpocketing

In legal codes, pickpocketing is sometimes referred to as larceny from a person. Pickpocketing has historically been an urban crime, occurring in environments and situations characterized by population density and the movement of pedestrians in public. Pickpocketing is also historically related to youth delinquency. Unsupervised youth and rapid growth of urban populations characterized many American cities during the 19th century.

Prototypical Youth Street Crime

Perhaps predictably then, present-day rates of pickpocketing are lower than they have been in the past. The changing nature of personal routine activities and shifts in definitions and supervision of youth have in part led to a decline in rates of pickpocketing. Despite being collapsed into larger larceny categories, pickpocketing remains a codified offense in both the Uniform Crime Reports (UCR) and the National Crime Victimization Survey (NCVS).

Popular culture depictions of pickpocketing draw on both its urban or street nature as well as its relationship to juvenile offending. Charles Dickens's 1838 novel *Oliver Twist*, for example, portrays a wayward youth drawn into the clutches of the dark London underworld by an older, experienced criminal (referred to as a "hook") named Fagin. Organizers of youthful pickpocketing have since been referred to as "fagins." That pickpocketing is a crime associated with youthful offending is important to its overall understanding. Pickpocketing has often been seen as a crime lying at the bottom of a criminal hierarchy, and as such, a gateway crime. The youthful composition of pickpocketers was further facilitated by the nature of urban youth during 19th- and early-20th-century America. Frederic Thrasher, a prominent sociologist at the University of Chicago in the 1920s, would later describe Chicago youth who were bored and in need of financial wherewithal; pickpocketing afforded a solution to both of these dilemmas. That Thrasher describes such delinquency in the context of gangs is also relevant to the technical nature of pickpocketing.

Techniques

There are various pickpocketing techniques, but all of them invariably involve a "mark," or the intended victim, as well as a form of distraction. Distractions range from one offender intentionally stopping in front of or bumping into a mark, to a staged incident such as the dropping of an item in hope that this will prompt the mark to offer assistance, thus allowing a second offender to pickpocket them in the midst of the victim's distraction. This example involves the use of compassion on the part of the mark, which is a compelling type of distraction. By eliciting compassion, the pickpocket in effect temporarily disarms the vigilance of the mark.

The pickpocket is sometimes—especially when working in a team—referred to as a "tool" or "dip." The member of the team whose role is to distract the mark is called the "stall." Pickpocketing teams often use a third type, the "runner," whose task is to disappear rapidly into the crowd with the valuables that have been removed by the tool or dip. Ultimately, the pickpockets most often avail themselves of the services of a "fence," or a trafficker in stolen goods.

Another key component of classic pickpocketing technique is camouflage. The pickpocket, whether working alone or in a team, is most

New Style of Picking Pockets.   Old Style of Picking Pockets.

Pickpockets have a very long history in our society. This 1897 illustration from the book The American Metropolis From Knickerbocker Days to the Present Time *depicts "new" and "old" styles of picking pockets.*

successful when blending in with the average looks and postures of a local population. In an urban rush hour, the pickpocket will dress in office attire; in an area of high tourist traffic, the preferred camouflage will be that of the typical tourist, complete with camera, map, and day bag.

The techniques used to commit pickpocketing relate directly to its nature as a street crime. The London streets described by Dickens share similar characteristics to American cities such as New York. They were densely crowded, with persons travelling from one district to another, and they were often loud, chaotic, and filled with people of varying ages, ethnic groups, and occupations. These characteristics help facilitate a crime that relies on deception and confusion.

Dramatic Decline

Though American cities are still characterized by large amounts of pedestrian traffic, rates of pickpocketing have declined. Currently, the UCR incorporates pickpocketing (or "pocket picking") under the label of personal theft, which also includes purse snatching and attempted purse snatching. Pocket picking in the 2009 UCR accounted for only 0.4 percent of all larceny-thefts. The UCR defines larceny-theft as acts of theft attempted or completed in the absence of violent force or fraud. NCVS data supports that pickpocketing is a relatively uncommon crime, reporting that in 2009, less than 1 percent of all reported crimes were personal thefts (133,210 incidents out of 20,057,180 total victimizations). Furthermore, the NCVS reports that between 2000 and 2009 the number of instances of personal theft dropped by more than 50 percent.

A 2001 report by the *New York Times* showed that New York City had more than 23,000 reported cases of pickpocketing in 1990 (valued at over $10 million in losses), but the rate had dwindled by 50 percent in 1995, and was down to under 5,000 cases in the year 2000. There are many explanations for why pickpocketing has declined so drastically in the past decade, and even more markedly since the 19th century. Shifts from paper money to credit card carrying offer one explanation. More impactful may be the evolution of youth definitions and supervision. Statutory education now requires that youth remain effectively off the streets during what are typically heavy pedestrian traffic hours.

Gentrification of many American cities also may play a role in the decline of pickpocketing. Though youthful offenses still occur, much research has shown that they are committed in close proximity to the homes of these youths. As such, youth living in areas characterized by unemployment and urban decay, and lacking low cost access to mobility, may have reduced access to public places where pedestrian traffic remains high.

Steven Downing
University of Ontario Institute of Technology

See Also: Juvenile Offending; Routine Activity Theory; Theft and Larceny.

Further Readings
Gilfoyle, Timothy J. "Street-Rats and Gutter-Snipes: Child Pickpockets and Street Culture in New York City, 1850–1900." *Journal of Social History*, v.37/4 (2004).

Keohane, Joe. "The Lost Art of Pickpocketing." February 23, 2011. http://www.slate.com/articles/arts/culturebox/2011/02/the_lost_art_of_pickpocketing.html (Accessed April 2012).

Rand, Michael and Jennifer Truman. "Criminal Victimization, 2009." October 13, 2010. http://www.bjs.ojp.usdoj.gov/index.cfm?ty=pbdetail&iid=2217 (Accessed April 2012).

Thrasher, Frederic M. *The Gang: A Study of 1,313 Gangs in Chicago*. Chicago: New Chicago School Press, 2000.

Yeager, Wayne B. *Techniques of the Professional Pickpocket*. Port Townsend, WA: Loompanics, 1990.

Pimp

The term *pimp* is often associated with street prostitution or street-based sex work where those who participate in the exchange of sex for money or drugs are more vulnerable to arrest and assault. Often oversimplified in its use, this term masks the complexity of relationships surrounding sex work. The term *pimp* is often also applied to any person, usually male, that helps manage or profits from the sex industry. For example, strip club owners and motel managers where sex work takes place can also be considered pimps. This term is also used outside its stereotypical and historical meanings by certain subcultures to reflect wealth, status, and sexual appeal.

Roots of the Term

According to linguistic study, from its roots (in 1607), the term *pimp* or *pimper* meant "to dress elegantly" or "alluring in dress," and later, "a knave, rascall, varlet, scoundrell" (1611). Yet this term has moved beyond its stereotypical and historical meanings to reflect wealth and status that is achieved outside middle- and upper-class America. The combination of exploitive behavior with wealthy dress or status is retained in the first recorded use of "pimpmobile" in 1973, which was used to refer to an automobile that was flashy and yet perhaps belonged to someone who did not achieve their wealth in a mainstream or legitimate manner. This term has been embraced by various groups in popular culture and used as a compliment that reflects status, sexual appeal, and respect. As such, the term still retains its outlaw origins and rebellious or even menacing overtone.

Popular culture has presented a mix in its depiction of pimps, as on the one hand their flashy style is inherently good content for entertainment purposes, while on the other hand they are often shown as degenerate, weak, or untrustworthy characters. The 1973 motion picture *The Mack,* which features actor Richard Pryor, portrays both sides of the coin: its hero John "Goldie" Mickens, an ex-con turned pimp, comes into conflict with a rival pimp, Pretty Tony.

In 1972, the seminal blaxploitation movie *Super Fly,* directed by Gordon Parks, Jr., featured a real-life pimp from Harlem named K. C. in a minor role, and more to the point the film spotlighted K. C.'s customized 1971 Cadillac Eldorado. The car featured the largest-ever V-8 engine used in a production vehicle, and it was visually jazzed up for the film with such details as oversize headlights and exhaust pipes, an abundance of chrome, and porthole windows. In a case of life imitating art, this car became the model for countless real-life pimpmobiles.

In the 1974 film *Willie Dynamite,* the title character is a successful pimp complete with pimped-out purple Cadillac. He comes into contact with Cora, an ex-prostitute turned social worker, who tries to convince some of Willie's hookers—and ultimately

Willie himself—to leave behind their illicit life. The final scene indeed shows Willie happily walking away from his Cadillac for good.

Power Over Work and Relationships

The power relationships between pimps and street sex workers vary dramatically. Because prostitution is illegal everywhere in the United States except for certain counties in Nevada, those who exchange sex for money or drugs are vulnerable to arrest. In addition to legal harassment by the police, the illegal status of the work undermines workers' abilities to protect themselves from dangerous clients and then dissuades them from filing charges if such violence does occur. The illegality of the work also requires that negotiations and transactions are speedy and occur in vulnerable locations such as cars, parks, or alleys. As a result of these conditions, many people who participate in these exchanges have someone who works as a lookout against police and/or violence. Many individuals work independently of a pimp. But when they are involved, the relationships between workers and pimps vary considerably.

Although many sex workers do not identify as members of a profession and view their involvement in the sex trade as a temporary activity, the business is often more organized and structured than outsiders realize. This organization is further complicated by the existence of pimps in myriad capacities that can, in some cases, serve to protect while simultaneously further isolate workers. The pimp is usually identified as a man who forces, to various degrees, a worker who is male, female, or transgender to exchange sex for money and then requires that person to bring all or a portion of the money back to him. In exchange for this money, the pimp typically offers some protection for the worker from police and potential assaults and may provide housing, food, and drugs.

In addition to direct needs, a pimp can also provide or withhold affection and social status. The pimp may forcibly control another person in the making of sexual transactions through physical and emotional intimidation by access and control to a woman's children as well as her own personal safety. The pimp can also be a husband, boyfriend, or friend who assists as a lookout or protector. These relationships exist on a continuum that runs from violence to protection and often somewhere in between. Those people associated with the sex trade, specifically prostitution, are subject to laws against pimping and pandering, or profiting from prostitution.

Jill McCracken
University of South Florida, St. Petersburg

See Also: Prostitute/Streetwalker; Prostitution, Houses of; Sex Crimes; Women.

Further Readings

Dalla, Rochelle L. *Exposing the "Pretty Woman" Myth—A Qualitative Investigation of Street-Level Prostituted Women.* New York: Lexington Books, 2006.

Harper, Douglas. "Pimp." *Online Etymology Dictionary.* http://www.dictionary.reference.com/browse/pimp (Accessed April 2012).

Weinkauf, Kathleen. "'Yeah, He's My Daddy': Linguistic Constructions of Fictive Kinships in a Street-Level Sex Work Community." 2010. http://www.appweb .cortland.edu/ojs/index.php/Wagadu/article/view/ 553/788 (Accessed April 2012).

Williamson, Celia and Terry Cluse-Tolar. "Pimp Controlled Prostitution: Still an Integral Part of Street Life." *Violence Against Women,* v.8/9 (2002).

Pittsburgh, Pennsylvania

The city of Pittsburgh, also known as the City of Bridges and the Steel City, has a population of just over 300,000. It is situated in Allegheny County, with a population of approximately 1.2 million. The county includes four cities, four political subdivisions that are referred to as municipalities, 82 boroughs, and 40 townships. The Pittsburgh metropolitan area has a total of almost 2.5 million residents. Like most urban areas, the closer to the inner city, the higher the rate of street crimes. Many of the boroughs that are adjacent to the city also have their share of street crime.

In the late 1800s and early 1900s, the area's coal and steel industries brought immigrants from different European countries, who like many in New York City and other major cities, often became victims of crime. Sneak thieves, con artists, and muggers working the gritty streets were not uncommon. Protection rackets were run by "social organizations" that were believed by the victims to exist for their benefit. Prohibition brought more crime, with

organized crime as we know it today coming into its own. In and around the city, the Pittsburgh Crime Family of La Cosa Nostra (LCN) ran illegal numbers rackets and fenced stolen property. As time went on, LCN mobsters bribed politicians and police officers, which allowed them to progress to prostitution, narcotics, loan-sharking, and extortion.

Through the years, mob activities in the Pittsburgh metropolitan area slowed down, primarily due to the efforts of local, state, and federal law enforcement agencies and prosecutors. Although some organized crime still exists in Pittsburgh, the attention of the police and the public today is directed more toward drug dealing, drive-by shootings, armed robberies, and other street crimes perpetrated by an entirely different breed of criminal. Crimes of this nature were depicted by Steven Bocho, the writer of the 1980s television series *Hill Street Blues,* who is said to have been inspired by the urban crime of Pittsburgh's Hill District.

Pittsburgh, which was listed in 2011 as the "Most Livable City in the United States" by the research unit of the *Economist,* has a police department (Pittsburgh Bureau of Police or PBP) of approximately 900 sworn officers who patrol the streets and investigate crime. The rate of solving or otherwise clearing criminal cases, including street crimes such as robberies and assaults, is considered better in Pittsburgh than in many other cities of similar size.

Compared with national case clearance rates, however, Pittsburgh presents a mixed picture. According to the Pittsburgh Department of Public Safety in its 2010 annual report, the crimes against persons clearance rates for Pittsburgh versus the national clearance rates were 53.7 percent (Pittsburgh) versus 66.6 percent (national) for homicide, 62.1 percent versus 46.2 percent for rape, 39.9 percent versus 28.2 percent for robbery, and 58.0 percent versus 56.8 percent for aggravated assault. For crimes against property the clearance rates were 20.2 percent (Pittsburgh) versus 12.5 percent (national) for burglary, 16.4 percent versus 21.5 percent for theft, and 26.6 percent versus 12.4 percent for motor vehicle theft. Overall then, the Pittsburgh authorities had better rates of clearance for five of the crime categories, and lesser rates for two categories.

Police Cooperation and Key Targets

The PBP is known for specialized detective squads, first-class criminal intelligence units, and a community policing philosophy that has resulted in the reduction of crime. There are other police agencies operating in and around the city of Pittsburgh. The Allegheny County Police Department has a detective division that provides specialized investigative services to most of the boroughs in the county. The Port Authority Police works to reduce street crime within its jurisdiction. In fact, more than 10 years ago the Port Authority Police and the PBP began a joint plainclothes unit to combat street crimes in and around downtown Pittsburgh. The officers ride buses and patrol bus stops and subway stations. Undercover surveillance and technology assist in the anti-crime operations. Purse snatchers, pickpockets, and drug dealers are some of the priorities of the unit.

Pittsburgh continues to experience street crime in many forms. Thefts, armed robberies, and strong-arm robberies are more prevalent in downtown areas. Residential burglaries, as elsewhere in the country, have evolved into violent home invasions, which sometimes lead to shootings and homicides. Sex crimes appear to be more frequent on the city's South Side, which is a mixed residential-commercial nightlife area that is often described as bohemian. Pittsburgh's Strip District, which got its name from a strip of land, is used during the day by merchants to sell wholesale produce, fresh fish, and other products from around the world. By late night, customers of bars and restaurants often become intoxicated, which leads to fights, aggravated assaults, and other public disorders. In other areas of the Strip District, male and female prostitutes walk the dark streets looking for johns. Sometimes the true gender of male prostitutes is not readily apparent, and "trick" sex can lead to violence once discovered. In other areas of the city, brothels operating as so-called legitimate massage parlors have recently been raided by Pittsburgh vice officers.

PBP narcotics and vice officers work aggressively to arrest prostitutes and customers. Traditional undercover operations as well as reverse stings, in which police officers pose as the prostitutes, are regularly employed. Narcotics and vice officers also work other forms of street crime including narcotics, nuisance bars, gang activities, and gambling.

Gambling and Gangs

In spite of the fact that most unlicensed video poker and other types of video gambling devices are illegal under federal law whether gambling occurs or not, the machines are prevalent throughout the area. Often connected to organized crime, some devices generate thousands of dollars in profit each week. Illegal numbers operations based upon the Pennsylvania Lottery's daily number are as frequent as different forms of sports betting such as professional and college football, followed by basketball, baseball, and hockey.

Illegal gambling on the street can sound somewhat benign, but it can be just as malignant as violent street crime. Indeed, whether video poker, craps, or sports betting, arguments over gambling and debts owed to loan sharks can lead to extortion, assaults, and even homicide. Gambling also has more nefarious connections to organized crime, and continues to be one of its primary sources of revenue. In fact, members of organized crime often take the proceeds from illegal gambling and reinvest into other rackets such as narcotics distribution and pornography. The PBP, the Allegheny County Police, the district attorneys offices in Allegheny and Washington Counties, the Pennsylvania State Police, and the Bureau of Liquor Control Enforcement work to eradicate illegal gambling operations and related crimes.

Street crime in and around Pittsburgh is often violent. Contributing to this is the presence and activity of outlaw motorcycle gangs (OMG) such as the Pagans. The Pagans OMG, which started in Maryland in the 1950s, came to Pennsylvania in the following decade and has engaged in a number of illegal activities throughout the Pittsburgh metropolitan area. Pagans are known to have LCN ties and to have run extortion and protection rackets. In 2009, the Pennsylvania State Police led an investigation into Pagan activities in the region, which resulted in charges involving firearms, drug dealing, auto theft, and violent street crime.

Other types of street gangs, including many youth gangs, operate throughout the city. On Pittsburgh's North Side, once a residential area for immigrants who dealt with ordinary street crime and loan sharks, the scene has changed. Now carjacking, assaults, and drug dealing are everyday activities of local Crips. Street gangs of this type are heavily armed, many with illegal firearms, and engage in unprecedented violent criminal activity. There are several different gangs that call themselves Crips, but this is no different that elsewhere in the United States. Some of different Crips gangs work together; others are rivals.

Gangs operate in Pittsburgh communities such as Brighton Place and Northview Heights. Other gangs include the North Charles Street Crips and the Trey-8, which operates out of the North Side's Perry Hilltop. In 2010, the federal Bureau of Alcohol, Tobacco, Firearms and Explosives (ATF), working with the PBP, led an extensive investigation that resulted in numerous arrests for firearms and narcotics violations as well as violent crimes. In early 2011, a member of the leadership of the Brighton Place Crips, which controlled several areas of Pittsburgh's North Side including Brighton Place and Morrison Street, who was known as Mad Cave, pled guilty to conspiracy and racketeering charges and was sentenced in federal court to 20 years in prison.

Additional Allies

The PBP works in close partnership with several other law enforcement agencies toward common goals. The Federal Bureau of Investigation's Greater Pittsburgh Safe Streets Task Force, the Drug Enforcement Administration, and the ATF collaborate to help control what has been traditionally viewed as a local police function. Working with the U.S. Attorney's Office, local, state, and federal law enforcement agencies in Pittsburgh are making an impact on all forms of street crime. The Weed and Seed program, sponsored by the U.S. Department of Justice, is another example. This program is designed to weed out and eradicate guns, drugs, and violence in a targeted area, and to seed the area through social and economic revitalization.

Moreover, in addition to traditional crime prevention programs such as Neighborhood Watch, Pittsburgh worked with professor David Kennedy from John Jay College of Criminal Justice in New York to develop the Pittsburgh Initiative to Reduce Crime, a homicide deterrence strategy. Slow in getting started, this initiative is modeled after a similar program in Boston, which had excellent results relative to the reduction of guns, homicides, and other violent crimes. These efforts are likely to have positive results on the reduction of all forms of street crime. For example, according to data from the 2011 Uniform Crime Report (UCR) from the Pennsylvania State Police, robberies in Pittsburgh occurred at the rate of almost 365 per 100,000 population. Similarly alcohol crimes were recorded as having a rate of approximately 560 per 100,000. Arrests for certain crimes also provide a reflection on the amount of street crime. For example, during 2011 PBP made 290 arrests for prostitution and commercialized vice, 345 arrests for weapons offenses, and almost 1,000 arrests for public drunkenness.

John R. Cencich
California University of Pennsylvania

See Also: Community Policing; Crips; Drive-By Shooting; Drug Dealing; Gambling, Street; Gangs (Street); Motorcycle Clubs; Organized Crime and Violence; Prostitute/Streetwalker; Weed and Seed.

Further Readings

City of Pittsburgh Department of Public Safety. "Bureau of Police 2010 Annual Report." http://www.pittsburghpa.gov/police/crimestatistics.htm (Accessed April 2012).

International Association of Chiefs of Police. "Pittsburgh Bureau of Police: Investigations Staffing and Deployment Requirements." http://www.pghica.org/final_report.pdf May 2005. (Accessed April 2012).

"Pittsburgh Neighborhood Crime Statistics." *Pittsburgh Post-Gazette* (July 30, 2003). http://www.post-gazette.com/neigh_city/20030730crimedatapart1 p9.asp (Accessed September 2011).

Wilson, Jeremy M., et al. *Community-Based Violence Prevention: An Assessment of Pittsburgh's One Vision One Life Program.* Washington, DC: National Institute of Justice, 2012.

Police (Overview)

Policing methods and practices have evolved along with the development of modern civilization, although the fundamental precepts—maintenance of order, protection of property, keeping the peace, enforcement of statutes, and investigation of crimes—have remained essentially the same. This entry reviews the major historical developments of police departments, their executives, and their rank and file, with both an individual and citywide perspective.

Police in America: A Brief History

The history of law enforcement in the United States has its foundation in colonial America. The more

Heavily outfitted riot police formed a line near the September 2009 G-20 summit when about 300 protestors marched without a city permit in Pittsburgh, Pennsylvania. Most larger law enforcement organizations employ specially selected and trained quasi-military units to deal with situations beyond the capability of a patrol officer response.

heavily populated eastern seaboard cities used a night watch to provide security patrols at night to protect the people and businesses. The night watchmen were paid a fee and saw themselves more as private businessmen than public servants. As these cities continued to grow in population and become more industrialized, the night watchman style of policing became more ineffective.

Eventually, these cities found it necessary to merge their day police watch with the night watchman system. The founding of the modern integrated police organization was also precipitated by a wave of riots and public disorder beginning in the 1830s. There were major riots in Boston, New York City, and Philadelphia during this period, fueled by friction between various groups of immigrants and the established propertied class. By 1838, Boston had consolidated its separate day

and night watchman system into a citywide police force. New York soon followed its with own citywide police force in 1845.

These early police departments were established based on the model of the London Metropolitan Police department, which was founded in England in 1829. That first police department in London used a crime prevention strategy. The London police officers, called Bobbies after their founder Sir Robert Peel, were assigned to fixed patrol areas so that they would be highly visible. Peel felt that a very visible police force could deter crime, hence the crime prevention model. Peel also organized the Bobbies around a military model that included uniforms, a rank structure, and a command structure. This quasi-military organizational structure and style of policing was adopted by those first police departments in the United States.

The major difference between the London police and the police in 1840s America was that the American police departments were heavily impacted by local politics. Police officers had no job security, and in many cities their ability to get a job as an officer was based on political patronage. If your candidate won the election, then you stood a good chance of getting a job in law enforcement. And, while politics are not quite so prominent in modern police departments, politics still impact the way that policies and procedures are developed and implemented in the 21st-century police department.

Another interesting development in the history of policing in the United States is the different style of policing that evolved in the large urban centers. In the cities along the east coast, policing could more easily adopt the London style of policing; its crime prevention strategy was more suited to cities that were heavily populated. In an area with a highly concentrated population, the very visible police patrol approach was appropriately designed to deter street crimes.

The basic approach to a regular but random foot patrol strategy was to prevent the occurrence of street crimes. A uniformed police officer walking a fixed geographical area could, in all probability, walk up on a street crime in progress and be able to apprehend the criminal. An officer walking a beat would be highly visible and readily available to private citizens who wanted to report that they were victims of a crime. That officer on foot patrol might influence whether the criminal was willing to risk getting caught in the act. If the potential criminal was uncertain where the police officer was and unable to predict when he might walk by, then that uncertainty would often be enough to deter the individual from committing a crime. However, for the foot patrol style of policing to be effective, a city's population must be heavily concentrated in its core so that walking police officers can respond quickly to calls for service.

Policing Contemporary Society

Law enforcement in the United States today is a large, complex industry that varies in its responsibilities. Various laws and historical traditions combine to present us with the type of police functions that exist in the 21st century. The most dominant tradition in law enforcement is police departments at the city and county level of government. The majority of police agencies come under the authority of local governing bodies, either at the city, town, or county level. There are also state police agencies that have statewide policing responsibilities.

The final tier of policing is found at the federal level. At the federal level, the agencies do not have general police powers nationwide. The colonial leaders, who ultimately codified the democratic principles for the United States, did not want to impose a national police force on the citizens so soon after the Revolutionary War. Therefore, federal police agencies were authorized by U.S. Congress to have a relatively narrow scope of law enforcement duties nationwide. The Federal Bureau of Investigation (FBI) comes closest to being a national police agency. But the FBI is limited to investigating violations of federal statutes and those instances in which individuals commit a crime that involves activity in more than one state jurisdiction (e.g., kidnapping across state lines).

What is common among these different types of law enforcement agencies is that their primary mission is to prevent crimes. Second, at each level of government the police organization is authorized by statutory criminal law to investigate criminal violations and to apprehend criminal suspects. Third, these police agencies strive to maintain order. Finally, police agencies at all levels of government have a general responsibility to protect the domestic peace within the borders of the United States. However, because the United States has a standing military, law enforcement agencies do not have a specific legal responsibility to protect the borders of the United States against foreign invading armies.

As noted earlier, the majority of police agencies are either under the regulatory control of a city or county governing body; there are also 50 state police agencies. And there are about 10 major federal agencies with specific law enforcement duties (e.g., FBI; Drug Enforcement Administration; Secret Service; U.S. Marshall Service; Alcohol, Tobacco, Firearms and Explosives; Border Patrol; Immigration and Customs Enforcement; and several agencies within the Department of Homeland Security). In day to day practice, most of the public's image of law enforcement is shaped by city and county agencies.

Recruiting and Training Officers

All police agencies have some mechanism in place for the recruitment, selection, and training of potential police candidates. At the local level, individuals are usually recruited in very similar ways. When job openings are available, police agencies actively recruit police candidates through various advertising media. Urban police departments spend more of their recruiting budget to attract college students. The big city police departments usually have more funds budgeted for selecting from a more diverse pool of police candidates. These larger police departments strive to recruit and select individuals who can be trained to police in a social setting that is going to be racially, economically, linguistically, and socially diverse.

Once an individual is selected for an urban police department, he or she is assigned to a training academy class that will train them for as little as 10 weeks to as much as six months (training academy time will vary based on the minimum training curriculum mandated by state law). While the training of police candidates can and does vary by local statute, some of the general subject areas include criminal and traffic law enforcement, criminal investigation, patrol tactics, radio communication, vehicle pursuit driving, and firearms training and qualification. The police candidate is tested periodically to ensure that he or she is proficient in the required subject areas. The candidate must achieve a minimum overall score in order to complete academy training successfully.

In urban police departments, once the police candidate completes academy training he or she is usually paired with a veteran police officer and will continue to be trained, on the street, in the specific duties of a patrol officer.

In small, more rural police departments the police candidate may spend time in on-the-job training before being assigned to a formal police training academy class. These small town police agencies most often have to rely on a regional training academy for the formal training of their police candidates. While the agency waits for the next available class it will usually begin some in-house training of its potential police candidate. The police candidate is paired with a veteran police officer and will be taught, in an informal way, how to enforce the law in that town. Candidates will be taught basic patrol strategies and tactics; the enforcement of local ordinances, as well as state criminal statutes; traffic enforcement; radio communication; writing a police criminal complaint; and other duties that may or may not be reinforced once the police candidate begins formal instruction at the police training academy.

Street crime is not a major problem in rural police departments, so neither the police candidate nor the public is placed at uncertain risk when the candidate is trained informally by more experienced police officers. In these rural towns there is typically less social and economic diversity than in an urban setting. Thus on-the-job training can be a functional and effective way to introduce a newly hired police candidate to the law enforcement needs of small town America. In many ways, rural police departments attempt to police to meet the needs of the community. In these small towns there is a bit more agreement on the type and style of policing; the goal is to help the citizens feel protected without intervening too much into their daily lives. The police candidate is taught how to manage people and situations that are usually not life-threatening, and to avoid creating undue fear about the possibility of becoming a victim of a violent street crime.

Highway Patrol Officers

State police agencies are often called "highway patrol" officers; that title accurately reflects their primary role. Within the United States, these state police agencies have somewhat limited law enforcement responsibilities. Their major role is to patrol the state and interstate highways and enforce the traffic laws. They do have statewide police powers and conduct some very specific criminal investigations. However, the types of criminal investigation that is conducted by state police officers usually are offshoots of a traffic stop.

In some states these state troopers can be assigned to statewide drug enforcement task forces and similar projects. But rarely are they involved, on a regular basis, with the investigation of major street crimes like murder, rape, robbery, burglary, or larceny-theft. Motor vehicle theft is one of the street crimes that they do encounter on a regular basis.

The recruitment and selection of potential state police officers parallels that for urban police candidates. They receive formal police academy training before they are allowed to police the public. State police candidates are instructed in the same subject areas as urban police candidates, even though their major role will be to enforce the traffic laws. Once the state police candidates successfully complete the classroom phase of their training, they are assigned to work with an experienced officer who is called a Field Training Officer (FTO). The FTO provides the rookie police officer with the practical, field application of techniques and strategies taught in the training academy. The field training usually moves through various phases of hands-on experience under the supervision of the FTO.

While federal law enforcement agencies are smaller in size and scope in comparison with urban agencies, they are probably the most complex police agencies. Many of these federal agencies have dual enforcement and regulatory responsibilities. The focus here will be primarily on the federal law enforcement function. The federal agency that more closely resembles an urban police department is the FBI. But, as noted, the signers of the Declaration of Independence did not want a centralized national police force. Therefore, the U.S. Congress assigns federal police agencies like the FBI and the Drug Enforcement Administration very specific law enforcement duties that usually require some type of interstate coordination to investigate the most violent street crimes. The responsibilities and powers of these federal police agencies were limited intentionally because the primary protection of citizens was and still is considered to be an issue that can be handled more efficiently by city and county police organizations.

Police Role: The Crime Fighter

Law enforcement organizations tend to perpetuate the image of their role as a crime-fighting force. The crime fighter role is one in which police stand between citizens and criminals, protecting the citizens and their property from harm. Police administrators take the position that by having police officers patrol the streets in their highly visible police cars and uniforms, this strategy will help prevent crime. And if a crime is committed, then that police officer on patrol should be able to respond to the crime scene in a timely manner.

The goal is for the officer to respond quickly enough to catch the criminal in the act and make an arrest. After all, many in the law enforcement community are of the opinion that they are engaged in a war on crime. The image of the police officer as a crime fighter places him on the front lines in that war. The law enforcement establishment strongly desires to be on the front lines preventing citizens from becoming victims of crime. Unfortunately, the crime fighter image is not an accurate depiction of what police do on a daily basis. The crime fighter image is perhaps more accurately a myth.

While law enforcement does strive to prevent crime and apprehend criminals in the act of committing crimes, there are many obstacles to achieving this goal. The commission of criminal acts, and in many cases street crimes, occur in places away from the eyes of the general public and police officers on vehicular patrol. It would require a police officer on every street corner in order to have general success in preventing street crimes. Even if it was possible to get a more visible street presence among police officers, it would still be difficult to prevent those crimes that occur behind closed doors. The prostitution, illegal gambling, and drug activities are extremely difficult for police to prevent. Then there are the rapes and robberies that are committed in the middle of the night that law enforcement will not know about until the victim calls the police for help.

In general, the major obstacle that prevents police officers from being crime fighters is that most crimes are crimes of opportunity. It is the motor vehicle that was left unlocked, with the key in the ignition; it is the person in the bar consuming too much alcohol and flashing large sums of money; and it might also be the man walking down an unfamiliar street in a physically decaying neighborhood after midnight. With each one of these types of situations, the victim has more control over preventing the crime than does a police officer. However, there is a more realistic role that police officers play in a democratic society. The law enforcement community is well versed in maintaining the peace. Indeed in some states, police officers are referred to as peace officers.

Police Role: Order Maintenance

A more accurate image of the police officer is as a peacekeeper. The majority of police work is order maintenance. Order maintenance is nothing more, for instance, than a police officer being in the right place and able to intervene in a public disturbance before it escalates and becomes a riot. Order maintenance is what police officers mostly do while they are on routine patrol. While on patrol the officer is trained to observe people and situations; when they notice that a public disturbance is about to become too heated they can intervene and disperse the crowd, or if needed they can make an arrest to diffuse the disturbance. This is a more accurate portrayal of what police officers do while on patrol.

This is also a role that supports the police patrol function. A police officer, while on patrol, is more likely to observe two people engaged in a physically violent encounter than an individual committing a robbery in some dark alley. The officer can intervene in the physical encounter and prevent it from becoming an aggravated assault or a more serious street crime.

Police patrol is the most proactive aspect of the law enforcement function. The image of the crime fighter was created to give the public the illusion that police officers stood ready to prevent them from becoming victims of crime. But the reality is that for a public agency that is available 24 hours a day and seven days a week, the police officer is most likely to observe some type of public disorder rather than someone committing a violent street crime.

However, the order maintenance part of the police function does not always involve observing and responding to a criminal act. While on patrol, the officer may observe someone who needs medical assistance or someone just asking for directions. These types of activities are also a part of the police function and a police officer on patrol will be sought out to assist citizens with everyday life problems. As noted earlier, the officer drives a highly visible vehicle and wears a highly visible uniform. For various order maintenance activities (e.g., a sick relative or a lost child) citizens are drawn to a recognizable public servant to assist them in resolving their problem. And while this may not be the most glamorous part of the police officer's job, it is probably the most realistic view.

Benjamin S. Wright
University of Baltimore

See Also: Arrest; Community Policing; Kansas City Preventive Patrol Experiment; Newark Foot Patrol Experiment; Police Detectives; Policing, Problem-Oriented.

Further Readings

Bratton, William and Peter Knobler. *The Turnaround: How America's Top Cop Reversed the Crime Epidemic.* New York: Random House, 1998.

Chamlin, Mitchell B. and John K. Cochran. "Social Altruism and Crime." *Criminology,* v.35/2 (1997).

Edwards, Charles. *Changing Policing Theories: For 21st-Century Societies.* Annandale, Australia: Federation Press, 2005.

Greenwood, Peter W., Jan M. Chaiken, and Joan Petersilia. *The Criminal Investigation Process.* Lexington, MA: D. C. Heath, 1977.

Iannone, Nathan, Marvin Iannone, and Jeff Bernstein. *Supervision of Police Personnel.* 7th ed. Upper Saddle River, NJ: Prentice Hall, 2008.

Newburn, Tim, ed. *Policing: Key Readings.* London: Willan Publishing, 2005.

Walker, Samuel and Charles Katz. *The Police in America: An Introduction.* New York: McGraw-Hill, 2004.

Wilson, Orlando W. *Police Administration.* New York: McGraw-Hill, 1950.

Police Brutality/ Excessive Force

The criminal justice system represents one of the most controversial governmental systems known. Perennial concerns abound in the fields of corrections, courts, and police. Of the many concerns prevalent today, few are more concerning than the use of force by our nation's police. Reasonable persons know that police work is a difficult and demanding responsibility and that controlling volatile encounters with the public can be dangerous. The police bear the burden of public scrutiny on many fronts, but none so closely watched as the use of force by police. This is especially so when acts of alleged brutality surface.

Force Versus Brutality

Police brutality, per se, is a broad and general term that means different things to different people. Police brutality can be defined as the intentional use of excessive force, typically physical, but possibly in the form of verbal abuse and intimidation by a police officer. Police brutality exists around the world and is one of several forms of police misconduct, which also include false arrest and excessive use of force.

In 2004, Robert K. Olsen, former Minneapolis police chief and past president of the Police Executive Research Forum (PERF), called the use of force "the single most volatile issue facing police departments." He noted that "just one use of force incident can dramatically alter the stability of a police department and its relationship with a community."

The statistics regarding police use of force are instructive. For example, according to the United States Department of Justice (2001) in 7,512 adult custody arrests, fewer than one out of five arrests involved police use of physical force (defined as use of any weapon, use of any weaponless tactic, or use of severe restraints). Also known with substantial confidence is that police use of force typically occurs at the lower end of the force spectrum, involving grabbing, pushing, or shoving. In the study focusing on 7,512 adult custody arrests, for instance, about 80 percent of arrests in which police used force involved use of weaponless tactics. Grabbing was the tactic used about half the time. About 2.1 percent of all arrests involved use of weapons by police. Chemical agents, such as pepper spray, were the weapons most frequently used (1.2 percent of all arrests), with firearms least often used (0.2 percent).

The origin of modern policing is typically traced back to 17th- and 18th-century France and England, with modern police departments being established in most countries by the 19th and early 20th centuries. According to research, incidents involving police brutality were frequent during these periods of time. Widespread beatings of civilians by officers armed with nightsticks, blackjacks, brass knuckles, or other devices were typical.

Better training and a reliance on enhanced communications and coordination has made routine police work less reliant on such violence. Still, the challenge persists. More recent examples of police brutality include the 1991 Rodney King beating incident when King was stopped by Los Angeles Police Department (LAPD) officers and was excessively beaten. Bystander George Holliday videotaped much of the incident from a distance with a personal video recorder. The footage showed LAPD officers repeatedly striking King with their batons while other officers stood by watching, without taking any action to stop the beating.

Another case is the Danziger Bridge shooting incident occurring in New Orleans in the aftermath of Hurricane Katrina in 2005. On Sunday, September 4, six days after the hurricane, 19-year-old James Brissette and 40-year-old Ronald Madison, both African American, were killed in the gunfire,

and four other civilians were wounded. All victims were unarmed. Madison, a mentally disabled man, was shot in the back. New Orleans police fabricated a cover-up story for their crime, falsely reporting that seven police officers responded to a police dispatch reporting an officer down, and that at least four people were firing weapons at the officers upon their arrival. On August 5, 2011, five officers were found guilty of all charges.

These examples demonstrate that the use of excessive force by police is not without consequences. In addition to being subjected to potential lethal force by those who are the subjects of their abuse, violent officers also risk civil liability and even extended prison sentences.

Necessity of Control

Today, police work continues to be a dangerous profession, and officers, from the moment they enter the basic police academy throughout their careers, are made aware of the many dangers. The Federal Bureau of Investigation annual report of police officers killed and assaulted reflects part of the vast scope of this problem. For example, in the year 2009

On New Year's Day, 2009, Oscar Grant, an unarmed African American young man, was shot and killed by a Bay Area Rapid Transit officer in Oakland, California. Many peaceful and violent protests were held in the following days.

official statistics indicated that 48 law enforcement officers were feloniously killed, an increase of seven from the prior year. Between 2000 and 2009, 536 law enforcement officers were feloniously killed in the line of duty.

As serious as these statistics are, they do not reflect the immense number of unreported and more typical cases in which police officers confront uncooperative suspects who are physically threatening or resistant. Unless handled properly, such situations can and often do escalate into life-threatening confrontations. An officer's use of force in these circumstances must not exceed that which is reasonably necessary to gain control and compliance of suspects. This is taught in police training venues across the nation. While the alarmingly high number of police officer deaths each year explains in part why some officers are overly vigilant about circumstances in which they find themselves, this is not the only explanation. The fact is that some people with a predisposition for violence sometimes become police officers themselves. Detection of such individuals during the screening process and before they become officers is a crucial responsibility of police administrators. Moreover, careful monitoring and tracking of police conduct through supervision is equally as vital in detecting and correcting abusive behavior by officers.

According to the U.S. Department of Justice COPPS Program, for the most part, the general public associates police use of force with the discharge of a firearm. But police use of force includes a much wider range of nonconsensual compliance techniques and devices. These less coercive but more common uses of force may range from command presence to soft hand control procedures such as a firm grip, escort or pain/pressure compliance holds, or the use of other more aggressive measures involving electronic control devices such as the Taser, the use of pepper spray, batons, or other non-deadly force equipment or tactics.

Based on a 1989 United States Supreme Court decision (*Graham v. Connor*, 490 U.S. 386), the use of these or other types of force must be "objectively reasonable." Force that is likely to cause death is properly judged through the eyes of a reasonably prudent and well-trained police officer under the same or similar circumstances.

The variety of coercive options available to police officers in a confrontational setting is generally referred to as the force continuum. From options on this continuum, ranging from so-called verbal judo and command presence to the use of a deadly weapon, officers are expected to employ only the level of force that is objectively reasonable to gain control and compliance of suspects. The decision to employ any force, including the use of firearms, may be considered excessive by statutory law and/or departmental policy if it exceeds a degree of force that reasonably appears necessary in a specific situation.

Lethal and Less-Lethal Force

Police use of force is divided into two categories: deadly and nondeadly force. Simply put, deadly force is defined as force that is reasonably likely to result in a subject's death. The most common example of deadly force is that which employs the use of a handgun or other firearm in an encounter with a violently resistant individual. The vast majority of officers killed in the line of duty during 2009, for example, were shot to death—28 with handguns, 15 with rifles, and 2 with shotguns, according to 2010 Federal Bureau of Investigation data.

In contrast to deadly force, nondeadly force is defined as any force other than that which is considered deadly force. In recent years, these force options are termed less-lethal force. The operational rule of thumb for use of force is any physical effort used to control or restrain another, or to overcome the threat or resistance of another. The difference between deadly and nondeadly force is not determined simply by the nature of the force technique or instrument that is employed by an officer. Numerous force options can result in the death of a suspect depending on the circumstances. For example, a small but significant number of people die suddenly and without apparent reason while being restrained in a prone position by police. The term *positional asphyxia* is commonly associated with this phenomenon that occurs when a person's physical position prevents him or her from breathing properly. The subject essentially suffocates during the restraint process.

Conclusion

Responsible police work challenges the officer on the beat as well as supervisory personnel to identify and properly address abusive behavior. Officers, supervisors, and administrators alike share responsibility for dealing with abusive officers who by virtue of their actions threaten the very citizens they are sworn to protect.

Michael D. Lyman
Columbia College

See Also: Arrest; Courts; Mobs and Riots; Racial Profiling; Street Crime, Popular Portrayals of; Tompkins Square Riots/Tent City.

Further Readings

Community Oriented Policing Services. "Use of Force." U.S. Department of Justice, 2001, http://www.cops.usdoj.gov/default.asp?item=1374 (Accessed April 2012).

Holmes, Malcolm D. and Brad W. Smith. *Race and Police Brutality: Roots of an Urban Dilemma.* Albany: State University of New York Press, 2008.

Ross, Darrell L. *Civil Liability in Criminal Justice.* 4th ed. Cincinnati, OH: Anderson Publishing, 2008.

Ross, Jeffrey Ian. *Making News of Police Violence: A Comparative Study of Toronto and New York City.* Westport, CT: Praeger, 2000.

Police Corruption, Street-Level

Street-level police corruption is the illegal use of police authority for personal gain. It occurs in face-to-face encounters with the public, primarily in urban settings. Police corruption is distinguished from other forms of police deviance (e.g., police brutality, police misconduct, police crime) by the personal gain sought through the misuse of one's official position as a sworn law enforcement officer. It often involves an exchange relationship—money or gifts—and an agreement by a corrupt officer to do or not to do something with an external corrupter. Conversely, police brutality involves the use of excessive or inappropriate force; police misconduct involves violations of administrative policies and rules that are typically handled internally within an agency; and police crime includes those crimes by police officers that do not necessarily involve the misuse of police authority. Street-level police corruption is found in various forms in law enforcement agencies throughout the United States, and much of what is known comes from media reports of police scandals as well as from investigation reports of independent commissions established in the wake of corruption scandals.

Types of Street-Level Police Corruption

As a part of their typology of police corruption as organizational deviance, sociologists Thomas Barker and Julian Roebuck identified types of corruption found in many police departments. The street-level forms of police corruption in the typology are corruption of authority, kickbacks, opportunistic theft, shakedowns, protection of illegal activities, fixing cases, and direct criminal activities.

The most common form of street-level police corruption involves corruption of authority where police officers receive discounted restaurant meals or services from local businesses, often in the nature of a gratuity. In many instances the gratuity is unsolicited by the officer, and all that is needed to induce the discounted or free goods and services is the act of an officer showing up in uniform to a retail establishment, commercial business, or restaurant. Corrupt acts of this type are usually prohibited by police department policies but are seldom violations of criminal statutes. Nevertheless, corruption of authority is common everywhere and often informally viewed as a harmless benefit. Problems develop though, when a benefactor who has provided such a gratuity to an officer wants the favor returned.

Another minor form of street-level police corruption involves officers who receive kickbacks from businesses and professionals for referring business. Often these kickbacks are paid by persons who are interested in securing new business opportunities from persons with whom police officers come into contact with during their normal policing activities. Major scandals have been documented where officers received cash payments from tow truck operators who respond to traffic accidents, funeral directors who are called to the scene of an untimely death, bondsmen who are called to police stations to post bail for arrestees, as well as lawyers, chiropractors, and physicians who seek new business from injured persons. Both kickbacks involving collusion and corruption of authority are often viewed as minor forms of street-level corruption, where officers receive a personal benefit during the normal course of their police work without altering their response nor failing to do some official police function.

More serious forms of street-level police corruption involve situations where an officer fails to perform some official police duty or changes the outcome of a street-level citizen encounter. These are typically police crimes. Opportunistic theft by police officers occurs in street-level encounters with unsuspecting or helpless individuals as well as when an officer finds an unlocked door or unprotected premises at commercial establishments. Some instances involve the theft of building supplies from unguarded lumber yards and construction sites, or merchandise taken from a retail store where a door was inadvertently left often when the store closed for the night.

Other street-level police theft targets persons arrested for drug and alcohol-related offenses, either by stealing cash, drugs, or belongings from a helpless person or by an officer stealing confiscated items meant to be logged in as evidence. Shakedowns occur when an officer accepts a bribe in a street-level encounter with a citizen to alter the official outcome of the encounter by not making an arrest when a crime has occurred, or when an officer extorts money, or even sexual favors, in a street-level encounter with a citizen under the threat of arrest for noncompliance with the officer's extortive demands. Officers engaging in shakedowns who are exposed in the media are often prosecuted criminally and terminated from their positions as sworn law enforcement officers, in part because of the public embarrassment to their employing law enforcement agency.

Protection of illegal activities involves payoffs to police officers so that organized criminals can engage in their ongoing criminal activities without interference or harassment from law enforcement. The protected illegal activities often involve drug distribution, gambling operations, and prostitution rings. In other instances there are legitimate businesses engaging in illegal activities that pay corrupt officers for protection (e.g., trucking firms with overweight trucks, construction companies in routine violation of traffic and parking regulations). Fixing cases involves the dismissal of a traffic or criminal case following an arrest without prosecution. The most common form of the fix is fixing traffic tickets. Sometimes an officer who issued

a traffic ticket accepts cash payment to dispose of the ticket soon after the ticket was issued. Other times there are officers who work in offices controlling the ticket paperwork process who accept cash to destroy or otherwise dispose of the ticket. Direct criminal activities of police officers occur when they engage in street-level drug crimes, burglaries, or robberies. These crimes involve some aspect of information acquired during an officer's street-level policing work and can occur while an officer is on or off duty.

NYPD Street-Level Corruption

The New York Police Department (NYPD) has repeatedly undergone periods of scandal followed by attempts at reform since its inception in 1854. These corruption scandals have occurred cyclically every 20 years since the 1890s, resulting in the appointment of special commissions to investigate allegations of corruption within the NYPD. Much of the knowledge of street-level police corruption in the United States comes from the reports of the two commissions investigating allegations of corruption in the NYPD over the past 40 years.

The Commission to Investigate Allegations of Police Corruption and the City's Anti-Corruption Procedures was established by an executive order of New York City Mayor John Lindsay in May 1970. Two years later, the commission—widely referred to as the Knapp Commission in deference to its chairman, U.S. District Judge Whitman Knapp—issued a report outlining widespread corruption within the NYPD. The Knapp Commission relied on a variety of methods to assess and determine the nature, extent, and patterns of corruption within the NYPD. These included field investigations, issuance of hundreds of subpoenas for document production, countless interviews of police personnel and citizens, as well as public and private hearings. In assessing patterns of corruption within the police department, the commission identified two types of corruption-involved police officers they labeled as grass-eaters and meat-eaters. They defined grass-eaters as those officers who engaged in petty acts of police corruption such as accepting gratuities and soliciting payments in the range of $5 to $20 on a regular basis from businesses. Meat-eaters were a small percentage of officers who were involved in more serious forms of corruption and spent most of their workdays aggressively pursuing gambling, narcotics, and other criminal opportunities they could exploit for personal financial gain.

The Knapp Commission concluded that corruption in the form of petty offenses by grass-eaters was pervasive throughout the NYPD at least at the local precinct level of the organization. Petty corruption was deeply engrained in the police subculture, in which small payoffs were routine occurrences and those officers who refused them were ostracized and viewed with suspicion. The commission noted that it was impractical to arrest all of the officers involved in widespread systemic petty corruption, and suggested that the only viable remedy would be if the NYPD police commissioner could somehow change the existing police culture within the department. The commission took a more critical view of the serious forms of corruption by meat-eaters, suggesting that the best way to handle them would be by ferreting them out one at a time for criminal prosecution. In addition to distinguishing between corrupt police officers who were grass-eaters and those who were meat-eaters, the commission also identified factors that influenced the type and extent of an officer's involvement in corrupt activities—including the character of each officer, the branch within the agency where an officer is assigned, the geographic area within the city where an officer works, the type of assignment (such as foot patrol in midtown Manhattan versus vehicle patrol in Harlem), and officer rank within the organization.

Two decades after the report of the Knapp Commission, in July 1992 New York City Mayor David Dinkins issued an executive order establishing the Commission to Investigate Allegations of Police Corruption and the Anti-Corruption Procedures of the Police Department. It was commonly referred to as the Mollen Commission, in recognition of its chairman Milton Mollen. The mandate of the Mollen Commission was to investigate the nature and extent of police corruption within the NYPD, to evaluate the department's existing procedures for preventing and detecting corruption, and to make recommendations to change and improve procedures to prevent and detect police corruption.

Following a two-year investigation, the Mollen Commission found systemic changes to the nature and extent of police corruption in the NYPD to those observed by the Knapp Commission 20 years earlier. No longer was there a prevalence of grass-eater corruption typified by petty acts of corruption

that were common among many NYPD officers in the early 1970s. The situation was now reversed, with the more serious forms of corruption—what the Knapp Commission previously referred to as meat-eater corruption—prevalent. Police corruption within the NYPD during the 1990s was now characterized by serious criminal activity, and most of it stemmed from the drug trade related to a dramatic rise in cocaine trafficking that created new opportunities for corruption fueled by the drug money on the streets of many neighborhoods in New York City.

Drug-Related Police Corruption

Much drug-related police corruption involves officers using their police authority to allow open-air drug markets to flourish. The Mollen Commission concluded that most drug-related police corruption in the NYPD involves police officers using their police powers to actively assist and strengthen the illegal drug trade in the city. The commissioners learned from numerous sources that street-level drug dealers often paid corrupt police officers to work hand in hand with them to facilitate their drug-related criminal activities and enterprises. The Mollen Commission determined that drug dealers were no longer the victims of shakedowns by corrupt police officers; now the drug dealers were often the direct beneficiaries of police corruption. In recent years, the actual victims of street-level police corruption are often the law-abiding people who reside in the urban neighborhoods where drug-related police corruption now thrives.

The Mollen Commission developed an erosion theory of police corruption; many police officers who engage in street-level police corruption that is drug-related seemed be the result of regular and constant exposure to corruption opportunities in crime-infested police precincts that worked to change the attitudes and behaviors of some police officers. This also worked as erosion on many honest police officers who developed a tolerance for widespread drug-related corruption among their colleagues within the NYPD. The commission found that some corrupt police officers were drug dealers motivated by profit; others were drug users themselves. Some police officers acted as drug dealers in the course of their daily police duties. These drug-dealing officers cultivated connections with drug dealers who lived in the precincts where they worked as police officers, and soon the officers were selling cocaine while wearing their full police uniform.

Other corrupt officers used fellow police officers as fences to sell their stolen drugs. Some acquired illegal drugs while working as police officers and then distributed the drugs while off-duty in their own neighborhoods and towns, often outside New York City. Still other corrupt officers committed off-duty robberies of street-level drug dealers. The Mollen Commission also determined that drug abuse among police officers—especially cocaine and steroids—has grown considerably in the past few decades as a direct result of street-level police corruption.

Philip Stinson
Bowling Green State University

See Also: Drug Dealing; Drug Markets, New York City; Open-Air; Police Brutality/Excessive Force; Sting Operations.

Further Readings

Knapp Commission. "Commission to Investigate Allegations of Police Corruption and the City's Anti-Corruption Procedures: The Knapp Commission Report on Police Corruption." New York: George Braziller, 1972.

Kutnjak Ivkovic, S. *Fallen Blue Knights: Controlling Police Corruption*. New York: Oxford University Press, 2005.

Mollen Commission. "Commission to Investigate Allegations of Police Corruption and the Anti-Corruption Procedures of the Police Department: Commission Report—Anatomy of Failure: A Path for Success." New York: The City of New York, 1994.

Punch, Maurice. *Police Corruption: Deviance, Accountability and Reform in Policing*. Portland, OR: Willan Publishing, 2009.

Sherman, Lawrence W. *Scandal and Reform: Controlling Police Corruption*. Los Angeles: University of California Press, 1978.

Police Detectives

In most police departments police detectives begin their career as uniformed police officers. They are recruited, hired, and trained as generalists at the

A detective (right) at the scene of a crime. Before becoming a detective, an officer must attend a law enforcement academy, studying criminal justice. After graduation, the officer undergoes job training with a field training officer.

start of their law enforcement career. In the police training academy, future police detectives learn the fundamentals of how to police the streets. They are taught policies, procedures, and a sufficient amount of statutory law so that they will be able to recognize and respond to violations of the criminal code. All of the basic skills learned in the training academy will be useful to the rookie police officer and even more useful for those who eventually become police detectives.

Who They Are

The road to becoming a police detective varies, depending on the requirements of a specific city or state police department. However, for most police departments, detectives are either promoted or selected from the ranks of the uniformed police officers. Uniformed police officers who are interested in being promoted to detective will usually have several years of general experience policing street crime on a regular basis.

In some departments the chief or assistant chief will select a uniformed officer to act as the department's detective or lead criminal investigator. The selection of police detectives occurs most often in small, rural police departments. In these smaller police departments (i.e., usually less than 50 police officers) the officers selected to work as detectives are usually those individuals who have exhibited the ability to stay engaged with a criminal case beyond the initial investigation.

A police detective in a small town will usually learn on the job and will act as the primary investigator for the entire police department. He or she will investigate a wide range of criminal offenses, such as murder, forcible rape, robbery, aggravated assault, burglary, larceny-theft, and motor vehicle theft. However, in the larger cities once uniformed officers are promoted to detective they will receive advanced training so that they are especially proficient in investigating one or two types of street crime.

Large, urban police departments provide their newly promoted detectives with advanced training in understanding the nature of the criminal violation, how to manage the victim of the crime, and how to use the facts of the case to identify a possible criminal suspect. These detectives become specialists. They learn in a classroom setting how to investigate a specific type of street crime (e.g., murder or burglary). Their education continues on the street when they are matched with a veteran detective.

What Detectives Do

The major responsibility of a police detective is to investigate crimes that may either cause harm to the victim (e.g., murder, forcible rape, robbery, and aggravated assault) or when the victim's property has been damaged or stolen (e.g., burglary, larceny-theft, and motor vehicle theft). Once again, there are some differences in the duties of a police detective, depending on the size of the police department. In large, urban departments a detective is most likely a specialist.

A uniformed police officer will usually be the first official sent to the crime scene. That officer has the responsibility of conducting the initial investigation. The police detective gets involved in a criminal case once the initial investigation has been completed by the uniformed officer. It is the detective's responsibility to gather the facts and to collect evidence that might be used to identify the criminal

suspect. However, the role of the detective is not quite as straightforward as this. The general public has a distorted view of the police detective based on what they see on TV and in the movies.

The reality of investigating a crime is not as exciting, nor are the results as typcially successful as what the average person will see on TV. Police detectives do not have the luxury of solving the criminal case by the end of an hourly TV show. They will spend days and even months talking to the victim and other witnesses. It is evident that the work of the police detective can be very tedious. Sometimes they will receive critical information on an unsolved case from a person or a source that they were not expecting it from. There are other times when many hours are devoted to solving a case and they are not able to make any progress. The accepted measure of how effective police detectives are in solving crimes is the annual clearance rate which is compiled by the Federal Bureau of Investigation (FBI) in its Uniform Crime Reports (UCR).

During the period 2006–10 the UCR's clearance rate for the most serious street crimes that cause harm to either the victim and/or to their property varied in the following ways. In 2006 the clearance rate for all violent crime was 44.3 percent, but the murder clearance rate was a bit higher, at 60.7 percent. In 2010, the clearance rate for all violent crime was 47.2 percent, but the murder clearance rate was again marginally higher, at 64.8 percent. An examination of the property crime clearance rate for those years was in stark contrast, indicating that for 2006 for all property crimes the clearance rate was 15.8 percent, with larceny-theft having the highest clearance rate, at 17.4 percent. In 2010 the clearance rate for all property crimes was 18.3 percent and larceny-theft was again higher, at 21.1 percent.

The clearance rate is the police detective's traditional measure of success. But based on the UCR reported clearance rate data, police detectives have limited success in solving property crimes (clearance rate up to 21 percent) and violent personal crimes (clearance rate up to 65 percent). This is the reality that police detectives face when they arrive at a crime scene. The police detective goes to work trying to solve the crime long after the criminal has committed the crime and left the scene, and after the victim has reported the crime. These are the obstacles facing a police detective when a criminal incident is submitted to him or her for further investigation.

Conducting the Criminal Investigation

Police detectives do not investigate all street crimes with the same level of time and resources. Traditionally, a violent crime like murder would receive a higher response priority than a property crime like burglary. The determination of which crimes are going to receive the highest investigatory priority are usually based on four factors. First, the seriousness of the crime committed. A murder, or any other violent crime that causes death or personal harm to the victim, would receive the highest priority. Second, property crimes would receive a higher priority than public disorder crimes, like disturbing the peace. Felony property crimes are major street crimes that are usually submitted to the investigation unit for a more thorough follow-up. Many types of public disorder offenses are resolved during the initial investigation by a uniformed police officer.

Third, a criminal complaint that receives a lot of media attention will usually receive more attention from the investigation unit. Many times cases that receive a great deal of publicity are violent crimes such as murder and forcible rape. A police department's top administrators will be under close scrutiny by the media and they are going to ensure that their detectives have the resources that they need in order to attempt to solve the case. Finally, a criminal complaint might be investigated because of pressure from elected political leaders. While the criminal investigation may not be a high priority for the detective unit, it may be for the mayor or other top elected official.

Another factor that can affect the way that a criminal case is investigated is the size of the police department. Smaller, more rural police departments may have only one police detective. If that is the case, then violent crimes will usually receive top investigatory priority.

The limited resources available in a small town police department place some constraints on its police detectives. In small town departments the detective is usually a generalist. He or she is able to investigate a variety of street crimes at a superficial level. While violent crimes may occur infrequently in such locales, the detective must still learn the basics of how to investigate and collect evidence to solve those types of crimes. Property crimes will consume a good bit of the rural detective's investigation time. It is not uncommon for rural police detectives to work a criminal investigation in conjunction with uniformed police officers, because manpower and equipment resources are scarce.

If the small town police detective is known as the generalist, then the urban police detective is the specialist. They are often given the opportunity to spend their law enforcement career investigating one specific type of street crime. The urban police detective assigned to the homicide unit is going to learn various techniques and procedures associated with investigating a murder. As long as that detective works in the homicide unit, then murder investigations will be his or her primary area of responsibility.

The actual process for investigating a street crime will not vary considerably from small town to big city police departments. The primary way that a detective will conduct an investigation is by using observation skills and talking to crime scene witnesses and the criminal suspect, if one has been identified. The detective usually goes to work investigating the criminal incident after the initial investigation by the uniformed police officer; information and evidence collected by the uniformed officer is the starting point of the investigation. The police detective will enter the investigation and will interview the victim and any witnesses who can provide information that will be useful in developing a list of potential suspects. Once the detective begins to focus on one specific suspect, he or she moves away from the interview process and more toward the interrogation process.

The interrogation process involves asking the suspect specific questions that are designed to place them at the crime scene. Even after the interrogation process begins, the police detective continues collecting information, but it is information designed to elicit a confession from the suspect. If the suspect does not confess to the crime, then the second goal of the interrogation is to develop independent information that will either incriminate or exonerate them.

Constitutional Realities

To ensure that the criminal investigation is conducted in a fair way, the police detective's investigation is subject to internal and external measures of accountability. First, within the police department there are certain rules and regulations that must be followed. One such regulation is that the detectives cannot interrogate a suspect until they have collected enough evidence to make the suspect the focus of a criminal investigation. Second, the investigative work of the police detective is also subject to external oversight. Key among these is the power of the U.S. Supreme Court to review a police investigation that may have violated a suspect's constitutional rights.

The investigative work of the detective may come under scrutiny if the criminal suspect accuses them of collecting evidence in a manner that violated their constitutional rights. The first 10 amendments to the Constitution are known as the Bill of Rights; within the Bill of Rights are many of the constitutional rights afforded to criminal suspects. There are two amendments that are especially applicable to the investigative work of a police detective.

The Fourth Amendment, which gives the suspect protection against unreasonable searches and seizures, means that the detective has to collect a sufficient amount of evidence that implicates the suspect. Once there is enough evidence to focus on a suspect, then the detective can arrest them. But, the consequences for an unreasonable search and seizure is that the courts will not allow the evidence to be used at trial. Second is the protection against self-incrimination; this particular protection is contained within the Fifth Amendment. Protection against self-incrimination puts the detective on notice that if he or she was deception or forces the suspect to confess, then there will be constitutional consequences. Similar to the Fourth Amendment, a confession acquired in an unconstitutional manner is at risk of being excluded before the trial.

The internal and external oversight of the detective's investigation is to ensure fairness. The purpose of the investigation is to identify the right suspect, not just any suspect. These oversight measures strive to ensure that the detective is not just trying to close the criminal case, but to solve it.

Benjamin S. Wright
University of Baltimore

See Also: Bank Robbery; Motor Vehicle Theft; Murder/Homicide; Police (Overview); Policing, Problem-Oriented; Rape and Sexual Assault; Theft and Larceny.

Further Readings

Chamlin, Mitchell B. and John K. Cochran. "Social Altruism and Crime." *Criminology,* v.35/2 (1997).

Greenwood, Peter W., Jan M. Chaiken, and Joan Petersilia. *The Criminal Investigation Process.* Lexington, MA: D. C. Heath, 1977.

Inbau, Fred, John Reid, and Joseph Buckley. *Criminal Interrogation and Confessions.* Baltimore, MD: Williams and Wilkins, 1986.

Jackall, Robert. *Street Stories: The World of Police Detectives.* Cambridge, MA: Harvard University Press, 2005.

U.S. Department of Justice. "Crime in the United States, 2010." Washington, DC: U.S. Government Printing Office, 2011.

Walker, Samuel. *The Police in America: An Introduction.* New York: McGraw-Hill, 1992.

Policing, Problem-Oriented

Problem-oriented policing (POP) in America dates back to the 1980s, as a response to the need of an alternative approach to police work. Until then, the field was dominated by the so-called traditional model, in which police departments focus on law enforcement as a primary means to control street crime, using tactics such as preventive random patrol, rapid response, and criminal investigations. However, a decade earlier, scholarly work regarding the police role and empirical studies on the effectiveness of these tactics largely showed that the traditional model of policing was not effective in reducing crime and disorder.

Setting the Stage

In 1979, professor Herman Goldstein published an article in which he coined the term *problem-oriented policing*. Relying on research conducted decades earlier about the nature and functions of police, Goldstein argued that the movement toward professionalism in police departments reflected a managerial perspective. From this perspective, the desired levels of order and accountability within the organization are achieved through features such as higher standards of education among officers, opportunities for training, centralization of decision making, and reduced discretion among police officers.

Yet this trend toward professionalism placed police departments in a vacuum. Operational efficiency was regarded as an indicator of success, despite an apparent disjuncture between the police job and its effects on mainstream society. For example, rapid response to calls for service, random patrol, or the number of arrests per year were the "means" rather than "ends" by which police departments established their efficiency.

By placing more attention on these reactive strategies, police departments were neglecting the quality of the "end product" of their work: the handling of a myriad of problems on a day-to-day basis and finding intelligent solutions to these problems. Goldstein argued that police should be more analytical in dealing with citizen calls for assistance. Rather than responding to each call, he urged police to identify problems—categories, or types of calls—and to identify the conditions that caused those problems as targets for police intervention.

Premises and Principles

Problem-oriented policing is an approach in which police departments seek to understand the causes of crime and disorder and to attack those causes. Police may form partnerships with the community, as well as other agencies/institutions and their managers, in order to assess specific problems of crime, fear of crime, and disorder. As such, POP is a problem-solving approach with emphasis on proactive strategies of crime prevention. One of the interesting features of problem-oriented policing is that police departments adapt their responses to the very specific nature of neighborhood problems. Therefore, it would be misleading to consider POP as a standard program, since each police department can tailor different strategies to assess and analyze problems, based on specific characteristics and needs of the community it serves.

A major premise of POP is that problems must be correctly identified before engaging in responses to them. Correctly identifying a problem entails understanding its underlying causes, which enables police to target its working parts. For example, a neighborhood might be experiencing burglaries, but a further analysis of the environmental characteristics where these incidents occur (e.g., lack of natural surveillance, lack of lighting) and how they occur (e.g., time of occurrence, persons involved, modus operandi) would be necessary to implement

a successful crime prevention strategy. Therefore, there are three key elements of POP. First, POP is used to define problems, rather than just incidents, as specifically as possible. Second, in order to correctly define and analyze specific problems, POP requires police to collect information. In this case, data used to support the implementation of POP relies not only on the information that police departments possess, but also on information provided by other agencies, business managers, or other persons that might be directly affected by the problem. Finally, POP is geared toward implementing alternative responses to arrest, recognizing that a problem might persist if its underlying cause is not directly targeted. For example, the police might advocate for improved lighting to deter burglaries rather than simply try to arrest the burglars.

Building on the Model

As implied earlier, POP offers an innovative approach to policing and a redefined role of police officers as being problem-solvers, instead of crime fighters. After more than 30 years of history and data, there are many examples of the successful implementation of POP in the United States. One of the earliest experiences is worth mentioning. Driven by Goldstein's propositions, a group of scholars and police chiefs from the Police Executive Research Forum (PERF) assessed the extent to which they could successfully apply and evaluate POP. One of the POP efforts conducted in the city of Newport News, Virginia, targeted theft from vehicles, domestic violence, and public housing problems. They found that POP was a successful approach to solving these problems, and the research set the stage for further structuring of POP.

In 1987, John Eck and William Spellman proposed the SARA model, outlining the four basic steps of the problem-solving process: Scanning, Analysis, Response, and Assessment. In general, SARA is a cyclical process designed to identify a problem, collect the necessary information to analyze it, apply the strategies designed to solve the problem, and evaluate their effectiveness during and after the implementation.

Although the SARA model is a primary guide for the design and implementation of crime prevention strategies, other theoretical perspectives complement POP. These include situational crime prevention and routine activity theory. Altogether, these

One of the 10 largest local police agencies in the United States, the Metropolitan Police Department of the District of Columbia (MPDC) uses highly developed modern techniques and a contemporary community policing philosophy, referred to as Customized Community Policing. Community policing joins police and residents in a partnership designed to organize and mobilize residents, merchants, and professionals to improve the quality of life for all who live, work, and visit the nation's capital.

theoretical frameworks aid police departments and scholars in developing structured responses to problems of crime, fear of crime, and disorder. The available research highlights the effectiveness of POP. The National Academy of Sciences reviewed the empirical studies on various policing practices and concluded that POP is more effective than other approaches such as traditional policing or community-oriented policing.

By 2012, the Center for Problem-Oriented Policing had forged an international presence and generated a wealth of support materials, professional reviews, conference programs, and other resources. The center has drawn upon the expertise of its members to expand the application of POP methods and know-how to areas as diverse as scrap metal theft, aggressive driving, sexual assault of women by strangers, crime in urban parks, asset forfeiture, prescription fraud and abuse—to name but a few.

Each year the POP Conference brings together police officers and executives, criminologists, safety and security consultants, and others to share information, news, and analysis of POP successes and challenges. As an example of the scope of POP application to types of crimes, the POP Conference program from 2011 included these workshops and presentations:

- A CPTED (Crime Prevention Through Environmental Design) Approach to Reducing Crime in Privately-Owned Apartment Complexes
- A Situational Approach to Residential Security
- A Strategic Response to Moped Theft
- Addressing the Problem of Prescription Fraud
- CCTV's (closed-circuit television) Impact on Crime and Disorder
- Chronic Mental Health Consumer Stabilization Initiative
- Comprehensive Responses to Crime and Disorder Associated With Large Produce Markets

- Crime and Disorder in Apartment Complexes
- Integration of Problem Analysis in Response to Crime Issues
- Last Call for Unsafe Bars: Dayton (OH) Police Deptartment
- Noise in Neighborhoods: Achieving Community Together (ACT)
- Peek-a-Boo: Responses to Hidden Crime Places
- Policing Problems Associated with Abandoned Buildings
- Reducing Gang-Related Crimes in Maravailla Public Housing
- Repeat Offending
- Safe as Houses: Reducing Residential Burglary
- Taking Action Against Gang Violence
- Taking the Wheels off Bicycle Theft—A Situational Approach
- Urban High School Disorder Reduction Project

Conclusion

The popularity of POP stems not only from its empirical support, but from the collaborative partnerships between scholars and practitioners that it facilitates. The approach has spread not only in America, but also in the Nordic countries, in Australia, and the United Kingdom. As a result, the Herman Goldstein Award was created in 1993 to recognize the best practices in the field of POP conducted by individual officers and police departments around the world, based on their effectiveness in preventing crime.

Problem solving is the underlying rationale for a variety of contemporary and emerging policing strategies. The CompStat program which started in New York City uses police crime data to identify problems that area commanders must solve. A range of geographic or spatial analyses of crime problems emerged in support of efforts to better understand and target crime problems. More recently, police leaders have considered "intelligence-led policing," where data analysis seeks to predict the emergence of crime or disorder problems so police can anticipate them and take preemptive action. The central premise of POP is that most crime and disorder represent symptoms of larger problems. If police understand the larger problems and work

to solve them, the crime and disorder issues can be attacked in a systematic way. While there are no general statistics on the number of jurisdictions that apply POP in a fundamental way, it is clear the key principles of POP have taken root at various levels of the civic and law enforcement infrastructure in the United States and other nations.

Carlos E. Rojas-Gaona
Lawrence F. Travis III
University of Cincinnati

See Also: Broken Windows Theory; Community Policing; CompStat; Crime Prevention, Situational; Fear of Crime; Routine Activity Theory.

Further Readings
Center for Problem-Oriented Policing. "What's POP?" http://www.popcenter.org/about/?p=whatiscpop (Accessed April 2012).
Eck, John E. and William Spelman. "Problem-Solving: Problem Oriented Policing in Newport News." Washington, DC: National Institute of Justice, 1987.
Goldstein, H. "Improving Policing: A Problem-Oriented Approach." *Crime and Delinquency*, v.25/2 (1979).
National Research Council. *Fairness and Effectiveness in U.S. Law Enforcement: The Evidence on Policing.* Washington, DC: National Academies Press, 2004.

Pool Halls

Pool halls were mainly male haunts during the 1800s and into the early 1900s. Since pool halls in most cities were physically linked to bars or saloons and sold alcohol, they were a singular symbolic target of anti-alcohol crusaders. Even pool halls that did not serve alcohol were regarded as dens of iniquity where young men were led astray by evil companions, learned to gamble, smoke, drink, and were routinely cheated by "pool sharks." Coarse language and obscene raillery were popularly thought to prevail in such venues.

Rites of Passage
In the 1800s and early 1900s many unmarried men relied on pool halls or saloons as places to meet and socialize after work. Living in rooming houses or

boarding with a family, single workingmen had no parlor or semipublic space to call their own. Married men also often preferred the hearty male camaraderie found in such masculine venues to the feminizing domestic sphere presented by the idealized Victorian home. Outside the watchful eye of wife, children, or landlady, they could relax, unwind, try their skills, and gamble money and honor.

For lower-class young men, the pool hall was a venue for a rite of passage into adulthood. Learning the game and its rituals constituted the ritual structure. As the decades passed, pool fell from favor and workingmen began to accept the middle-class imperatives of marriage and more respectable leisure. Pool, except for a minor resurgence in the early 1960s, has never recovered the prominence it enjoyed in the 1920s. Part of this is the failure of women to become attracted to the pastime, or due to their reluctance to invade such a prototypically male space.

Players congregated not only after work but frequently at lunch or during work hours, sometimes drawing the ire of employers. Hustlers, businessmen, and sporting men would meet to play and watch especially skilled players. Matches and tournaments could command large purses and took place at decidedly upscale establishments. Few such establishments exist today.

Wrath of Reformers

According to reformers and popular media portrayals, which explicitly link pool to the "seamy side of life," most pool halls were and are, however, in less affluent neighborhoods. While many posh gentleman's clubs had billiards rooms and pool tables, workingmen also engaged in low stakes games and other forms of gambling and illegal hustles, typically in back rooms. This drew the ire of antigambling reformers who were appalled that money that should have gone to families and toward upward mobility was being frittered away in alcohol-fueled gaming. Therefore, groups that were specifically oriented toward closing pool halls came into being.

Reformers did not appreciate the reality that the pool hall, like the cockpit, afforded lower-class males a forum for achievement and self-direction outside of their normally limited economic and social sphere, and that it reinforced male sociability. The pool hall was a retreat where the workingman

could enjoy the perquisites of "permanent bachelorhood" and live, if only for a few hours, outside the strictures of feminizing Victorian society. While it is impossible to know how many pool halls existed in the United States in the Victorian Era, there were 140 official pool halls in Chicago at the turn of the century.

But billiards and other games played in pool halls require skill; today a few men support themselves through pursuing as a livelihood what most men considered a mere pastime. Pool "hustlers" often invite unsuspecting victims into playing a few games for small amounts of money. The hustlers purposely lose a few games early in the series, thus inflating the victim's sense of skill and ego. Then the hustler proposes raising the stakes, wins, and take the victim for all he is worth. This classic pool hall hustle, noted by British novelists in the early 1800s, continues to the present.

Criminogenic Aspects

In his *Albany Trilogy*, William Kennedy writes about pool halls in New York State of the 1920s and 1930s as "hot spots" where organized crime figures, sporting men, gamblers, hard-bitten members of the press and local small businessmen and local toughs mingled with lower-class males and lower-middle-class boulevardiers. In such contexts bets, contacts were established and deals were made—all involving the demimonde. Crimes were planned and reputations were won and lost. This was decidedly male space and any demimondaine who might enter was assumed to be a prostitute or loose-living female.

Today's few remaining pool halls are often targeted by police as criminogenic venues. Besides the similarities to bars and taverns—late hours, free admission, alcohol service, quasianonymity—some pool halls have become the default hangouts of street gangs. In Los Angeles, for example, researchers documented the proclivity of young Filipino men to make pool halls among their chosen informal social headquarters beginning in the 1970s and well into the 1990s. While the pool halls themselves may not have been incubators of crime, they were easily identifiable and accessible places where groups of men could gather, some of whom were engaged in small-scale criminal activity.

Other sociologists have pointed out that the friendly confines of pool halls where entry is free makes them attractive places for the underemployed. A casual session on a search engine on a computer will reveal hundreds of violent incidents which begin in pool halls. It may be that the media have a prevalent sensitivity to such locales or that they do, in fact, act as places where disputes over honor and skill can become violent and spill over into the street. Researchers such as Robert Crutchfield have posited that many underemployed or unemployed African American men who frequent pool halls become "suitable targets" in the terminology of routine activity theory. In other words, they are more likely to be victims of crime while in the pool hall environment. Such criminologic factors can be mitigated by various policing approaches, but remain a manifestation of the essential character of the pool hall as a low-cost hangout predominantly used by men.

Frederick Hawley
Western Carolina University

See Also: Bars and Pubs; Environmental Criminology; Loitering; Routine Activity Theory.

Further Readings

Alsaybar, Bangele Deguzman. *Youth Groups and Youth Savers: Gangs, Crews, and the Rise of Filipino American Youth Culture in Los Angeles.* Ann Arbor, MI: Proquest, 2007.

Chudacoff, Howard *The Age of the Bachelor: Creating an American Subculture.* Princeton, NJ: Princeton University Press, 1999.

Courtwright, David T. *Violent Land: Single Men and Social Disorder From the Frontier to the Inner City.* Cambridge, MA: Harvard University Press, 1998.

Crutchfield, Robert, et al. *Race, Labor Markets, and Neighborhood Violence.* Seattle: University of Washington Press, 2006.

Kennedy, William. *An Albany Trio.* New York: Penguin Books, 1996.

Polsky, Ned. *Hustlers, Beats and Others.* New York: Anchor Books, 1969.

Projects, The

Public housing, known in street vernacular as "the projects," is government-supported housing provided at little or no cost to very low-income residents. The U.S. government's housing program has gone through a number of changes since its development in the 1930s, but its eventual outcome of concentrating high numbers of the most disadvantaged in often poor quality housing located in neighborhoods already suffering from distress and social disorganization, is now generally acknowledged as flawed public policy.

Excessive costs, financial ills, poor design, management, maintenance, and extended poverty and social exclusion are all associated with public housing in the literature. However, the strongest association is probably that of being the focus of high crime and violence. This association is not without merit; research on public housing has shown that it does indeed have a strong relationship with street crime.

History of Public Housing

Public housing as a national policy originated with the Housing Act of 1937, when the U.S. government provided funding to build 114,000 low-rent housing units. Units were small scale in design, rarely over four stories high, and were rented to working-class families who often moved into the middle class by the end of World War II. After the war, the Housing Act of 1949 was passed, which provided large amounts of money for public housing and urban renewal projects aimed at the deteriorating downtown fringes of large American cities.

To reduce costs and house more of the urban poor, these projects were built as large, high-rise complexes, and were soon populated predominantly by female-headed minority families on welfare with little expectation of moving into the middle class. While the federal government provided the funding for building the housing projects, management and maintenance were left to local housing authorities who received their funding from rental payments.

Weak federal control on building quality, along with increasing maintenance and management costs that were not covered by rental payments, soon led to unsafe, deteriorating buildings. The 1972 implosion of the crime-ridden 3,000 unit Pruitt-Igoe housing complex in St. Louis, Missouri, after only 10 years of operation is generally seen as the beginning of the end of traditional public housing projects in the United States.

Today, the large, multistory public housing complexes are being phased out of use and demolished. In their place, two new federal housing programs are being utilized. The first is a voucher program originally authorized by Section 8 of the 1974 Housing and Urban Development Act. Under this program tenants pay up to 30 percent of their income for rent while the government pays local housing authorities or private apartment landlords the remaining difference between the tenant's contribution and a fair market rent.

The other program is HOPE VI, created by Congress in 1992, which provides funding and the legal authority to reform older public housing projects. Under this program, local housing authorities are demolishing their most distressed housing complexes and building mixed-income communities in their place. Typically a portion of the units in these small-scale projects or townhouse neighborhoods are provided to the extreme poor; others may be rented at reduced rates to low-income working families; while others may be sold to blue-collar families at below market rates. The goals for both the Section 8 voucher and HOPE VI programs are to disperse the extreme poor for the advantage of residents and the surrounding community, provide more choices for housing the disadvantaged, and encourage public–private partnerships in low-income housing.

Public Housing and Crime

The connection between traditional public housing and street crime is a strong one. Research shows that public housing projects tend to have significantly higher violent crime rates than the immediately surrounding neighborhoods and city,

The Frederick Douglass Houses are a public housing project in New York City named for civil rights pioneer Frederick Douglass. The complex is owned and operated by the New York City Housing Authority. The original complex completed in 1958 consisted of 17 buildings, up to 20 stories tall, with 2,056 apartments and some 4,588 residents. Today, only 4 of the original 17 still stand.

especially for aggravated assaults, assaults against women, and gun crimes. Housing projects are also seen as safe havens for gangs and drug trafficking. However, property crime rates are frequently lower in complexes than the surrounding neighborhood and city.

The impact of public housing on crime, however, does not stop at the property line. Research shows a diffusion of crime from the complex into surrounding neighborhoods that can extend out a distance of at least one mile. Both violent and property crime rates in neighborhoods immediately surrounding public housing are generally higher than overall city rates. Robbery rates in these neighborhoods are found to be higher than in the housing projects themselves, with both being substantially higher than overall city levels.

Not all public housing is alike in size, design, residents, or crime levels. In general, the larger the complex, the greater the crime level on both the property and distance over which surrounding neighborhoods will be impacted. Taller projects tend to experience more crime than lower-rise ones, especially in the interior public spaces (e.g., hallways and elevators).

Complexes that house the elderly exclusively have lower crime rates than family complexes, and also have no impact on surrounding neighborhoods. Although the data is sparse, the available research suggests small scale (fewer than five units), scattered public housing has little negative impact on neighborhood crime rates. And finally, growing anecdotal evidence in the media and among community groups, and at least one study, suggest that the Section 8 voucher program may be merely displacing crime from one place to another. Residents relocated under this program often move en masse to nearby struggling neighborhoods or apartment complexes where rents are low enough to fall within Section 8 criteria—bringing existing crime problems along with them. To what degree this occurs is still unknown.

National statistics on housing project crime are difficult to come by; most data is generated by city, county, and state police departments, and compiling these data is often not cost-effective. However, some local measures reveal the depth of experience that law enforcement and legislatures have in dealing with housing project-related crime. For example, after a significant, 2.3 percent rise in housing project crime rates in New York City in 2010, the state legislature in 2011 passed a $5 million grant bill to compensate landlords for part of the cost of installing new door lock swipe-key systems, while providing for increased property inspections and related public safety and security measures in public housing.

In another example, an Urban Institute study reported that crime rates in Chicago and Atlanta have declined dramatically since 2000, "particularly in areas where public housing was demolished." Independent of other factors, the researchers estimated that in Chicago a citywide 4.4 percent decrease in crimes committed with a firearm during 2000–08 (and a 1 percent drop in all violent crime) was associated with tearing down public housing and relocating residents with a voucher program. The similar program in Atlanta was credited with a 0.7 percent overall violent crime decrease.

Conclusion

Most criminologists explain the high crime levels associated with public housing projects as the result of undermined social control brought about by the concentration of poverty, unemployment, disrupted families, and racial segregation. Oscar Newman argues in his thesis on defensible space that tall, high-density projects inhibit the development of social networks among residents, thus reducing collective vigilance, surveillance, and community use of public spaces. Many however agree that it is not only the housing projects themselves that are responsible for increased crime levels, but also the struggling neighborhoods in which they are located.

Eric S. McCord
University of Louisville

See Also: Defensible Space Theory; Environmental Criminology; Routine Activity Theory; Urban Planning.

Further Readings

Goetz, Edward. "Where Have All the Towers Gone? The Dismantling of Public Housing in U.S. Cities." *Journal of Urban Affairs*, v.33/3 (2011).

Newman, Oscar. *Defensible Space*. New York: Macmillian, 1972.

NewsOne. "America's Most Famous And Now Extinct Housing Projects." October 6, 2011. http://www

.newsone.com/1567685/americas-most-famous-and-now-extinct-housing-projects (Accessed April 2012).

New York State Senate. "Public Housing Safety and Security Act of 2011." January 23, 2012. http://www.m.nysenate.gov/legislation/bill/S5284-2011 (Accessed April 2012).

Urban Institute. "Study Estimates Public Housing Transformation's Effect on Crime in Atlanta and Chicago, Advancing Understanding of Successes and Challenges." April 5, 2012. http://www.urban.org/url.cfm?ID=901492&renderforprint=1 (Accessed April 2012).

Prostitute/Streetwalker

Street-based prostitution or sex work involves someone who solicits or negotiates sex outdoors—for example, on the street or in some other public outdoor venue, such as a boardwalk, pier, or parking lot. Street-based sex work is stereotyped as the province of drug addicts and within the context of street crime, and many street areas include drug sellers and users. However, sex workers on the street are not always involved with drugs. The practice also is often associated with such terms as *transactional sex, survival sex,* or *outdoor worker,* as well as various slang terms such as *whore, ho,* or *crack ho.* Outdoor prostitution is more common in warmer climates.

Marginal Living

Street-based sex work often involves women, transgender women, and men for whom few other options exist. They may face more problems with substance dependency, poverty, and unstable housing, and may lack opportunities for mainstream employment of any kind, even sub-living-wage jobs. These vulnerabilities, coupled with these individuals' higher visibility, create an environment in which street-based sex workers are more likely to face problems such as violence, police harassment, and false arrest.

Street prostitutes/walkers/sex workers are some of the most marginalized and victimized people in society and in the sex industry. Their work involves real time and proximal contact with their customers, which implies varying levels of danger and risk. They make less money than higher-end sex workers, and they are often beaten, victimized, robbed, and raped—crimes that they have virtually no means to prosecute. They also have an increased risk of contracting sexual or drug-related illnesses due to unsafe sex practices and drug use. Their low social status within the hierarchy of sex work and within their communities as a whole, along with their lack of access to social and medical services, makes it difficult for them to leave street sex work for work that is deemed more "legitimate" and less risky.

A number of other factors keep people on the street, even when they would like to leave. Because both drugs and prostitution are illegal in most of the United States, people participating in street-based sex work are often pulled into the criminal justice system. Once arrested, they may spend time in jail or, less commonly, in drug treatment. As a result of the collateral consequences of incarceration, such as being barred from certain jobs and housing in addition to the lack of comprehensive and targeted drug treatment, the street-based sex worker often leaves jail with even fewer options or resources than before.

Terms and Connotations

Although quoted often as "the world's oldest profession," some scholars argue that the concept of prostitution is a social construction that is relatively modern, created as an identifiable concept only within the last 200 years. For example, Laura Agustín argues that the term and identification of the prostitute was invented to create a pathetic victim who required "saving." Today, the most common understanding of the word *prostitute* includes both concepts of "sex for hire" and as an identity—if a person uses his or her body to participate in sexual acts for material compensation, that person is identified as a prostitute. Agustín argues that when scholars do not question the construction of the term *prostitute,* they continue to reproduce the stigma associated with it and ultimately hurt the women and men who are participating in commercial sex.

The word *prostitute* was first recorded in written form in approximately 1530 and meant "to offer indiscriminate sexual intercourse (usually in exchange for money)". The use of this word as a noun is dated at 1613 from the Latin word *prostituta* or *prostitute,* the feminine version of *prostitutes.*

According to the *Online Etymological Dictionary*, the concept of "sex for hire" was not "inherent in the etymology, which rather suggests one 'exposed to lust' or sex 'indiscriminately offered." The passive voice constructs a prostitute as weak and helpless, and this powerless position is often equated with dehumanization because the individual is not viewed as a person who is capable of making his or her own choices, but is controlled by other forces.

In general, the term *prostitute* is largely equated with people, largely women, who work on or near the street to exchange sex for money or other gain. Although the term *prostitution* is common, the term *sex work*, initially coined by Carol Leigh in the late 1970s, is not as common. Leigh created this term as an attempt to reconcile her feminist goals with her lived reality. By creating this term, Leigh works to create an atmosphere of tolerance in the women's movement for people working in the sex industry.

Notably, many people who are identified as prostitutes or street sex workers do not identify as either. Rather than neatly categorizing the object of this discourse, the terminology used more accurately reflects the viewpoint of the speaker. Words such as prostitute, sex worker, or "victim of sexual exploitation," make it easy to identify and categorize certain activities in specific ways, maintaining a victim-versus-agent dichotomy. The language positions the speaker on one side or the other of the debate, while also positioning the object of the discourse as one who is acting or being acted upon. Neither "victim" nor "agent" allows for the myriad contradictions and lived realities of life on the street.

Prevalence and Characteristics

The prostitute label includes a wide variety of women and men. Discerning precise data about prostitution is difficult because it is illegal in the United States except for a few counties in Nevada, and the women and men who participate in prostitution are difficult to track. In spite of these difficulties, researchers have estimated that approximately 20 percent of the prostitution that occurs in the United States includes street prostitutes. Leigh argues that street prostitution comprises between 10 and 20 percent of all sex-for-hire arrangements in larger cities such as Los Angeles and New York. In small cities, Leigh estimates the percentage to be much higher, somewhere in the neighborhood of 50 to 70 percent in areas where there are limited indoor venues.

According to the Federal Bureau of Investigation arrest statistics, approximately 90,000 arrests are made in the United States each year for violations of prostitution laws. This number does not include the arrests that are also made for disorderly conduct and loitering, two of the crimes for which street prostitutes are often arrested. Street workers make up the vast majority of arrests. Leigh cites that 85 percent of those arrested work on the street. This number is disproportionate to the number of street workers, as 80 percent of sex workers work off the street in saunas, massage parlors, or as call/outcall escort services.

Hierarchies exist in prostitution, and street workers have the lowest status and are the objects of the most stigma within the sex industry. Street sex work is also stratified by race, age, appearance, and location of work—all of which affect the worker's earning potential. Women and men who exchange sex on or near the street have a much greater chance of experiencing exploitation and victimization while working, as assault and rape are common crimes that occur against prostitutes. Street-based prostitutes may be entirely independent and work only when they choose to do so, but their work can also be surprisingly structured. Some street-based sex workers are part of structured networks including coworkers and pimps or other people who are expected to assist in cases of assault or arrest. Such relationships vary and can be mutually beneficial, altruistic, or exploitative. The ratio of on-street prostitution to off-street venues (such as saunas, massage parlors, or incall/outcall escort services) varies in cities depending on local law, policy, and custom.

Drug use or addiction may be the motivating factor for involvement in street prostitution when a worker must trade sex for money or drugs to support his or her habit. Scholars and activists have extensively reported the commonalities between prostitution, drug use, and an increased risk of human immunodeficiency virus and acquired immune deficiency syndrome (HIV/AIDS). Drug addiction can undermine a worker's control while also making her less discriminating when it comes to clients and services. Researcher Wendy Chapkis argues that women who work primarily to support their drug habit are often viewed by others as lowering prices in the market because they may work below the going rate or offer unsafe sexual services, for example, not requiring that condoms are used during sex. Illegal immigrants and workers from other countries are also commonly seen as being the cause for lower prices.

Isolation is a problem in terms of authority and control. Due to the social stigma and criminal status of prostitution, many people are afraid to reach out for help or information. In general, street sex workers are more vulnerable to the loss of social services and the removal of their children and termination of parental rights because of prostitution and other related activities. Their situation is amplified when women have their children removed from them because they can slip deeper into substance use and therefore into trading sex for money or drugs. These circumstances may make it impossible for these women to return to more "legitimate" areas of work and lifestyles. All of these issues perpetuate the lowered social status of street workers both within the hierarchy of sex work and in society as a whole.

Street prostitution, as compared to indoor prostitution, affects the community in very direct ways. Street prostitution is more visible and many consider it to be disruptive of the peace, and it is therefore the subject of public awareness in a way that indoor prostitution is not. This awareness leads to not only the stigma that is present about sex workers, but also people actively working to remove street prostitution from their neighborhoods. Community concerns about nuisance crimes such as loitering and littering mean police aggressively target street prostitution. In some cities, even though police are aware of street-based prostitution, they will only act on it and make arrests if prompted by local residents. As a result, street prostitutes tend to move within a city or travel from one city to another in an attempt to avoid being arrested.

Conclusion

Because many street prostitutes do not identify as members of a profession or view their involvement in the sex trade as a temporary activity, they are less likely to devote time and energy to organizing. In the hierarchy of prostitution, street workers are more commonly found to exhibit significant psychological problems as compared to call girls, brothel workers, and massage parlor workers. Prostitution on the street, because of its visibility, often receives the most attention from the press, communities, police, and researchers. This research is problematic for some scholars, because they think

it calls too much attention to street work at the risk of making other sex work invisible.

Jill McCracken
University of South Florida, St. Petersburg

See Also: Alcohol and Drug Use; Homelessness; Immigrant Neighborhoods; "Johns"; Pimp; Prostitution, Houses of; Rape and Sexual Assault; Sex Crimes; Urban Ethnography; Women.

Further Readings

Agustín, Laura Maria. "Helping Women Who Sell Sex: The Construction of Benevolent Identities." *Rhizomes* (2005). http://www.rhizomes.net/issue10/agustin.htm (Accessed June 2012).

Chapkis, Wendy. "Power and Control in the Commercial Sex Trade." In *Sex for Sale: Prostitution, Pornography, and the Sex Industry*, Ronald John Weitzer, ed. New York: Routledge, 2000.

Leigh, Carol. "Inventing Sex Work." In *Whores and Other Feminists*, Jill Nagle, ed. New York: Routledge, 1997.

Leigh, Carol. "Prostitution in the United States: The Statistics." *Gauntlet*, v.1/7 (1994).

Porter, Judith, and Louis Bonilla. "Drug Use, HIV, and the Ecology of Street Prostitution." In *Sex for Sale: Prostitution, Pornography, and the Sex Industry*, Ronald John Weitzer, ed. New York: Routledge, 2000.

Prostitution, Houses of

When one considers categories of street crimes with rich histories in America, few compare with prostitution. At present across the United States, houses of prostitution—or brothels—are only legal in some counties of Nevada. Within the state, there are only eight rural counties with active brothels. Major cities, such as Las Vegas, Reno, and Carson City, have complete bans on all forms of prostitution.

Public-Order Crimes

Over time, prostitution has found itself classified differently in different areas. Originally, operating houses of prostitution was considered akin to vagrancy crimes. These crimes were vague and covered any type of activity associated with known

Cottontail Ranch was a legal, licensed brothel in Nevada that opened in 1967. Beverly Harrell was the madame and published a book about the ranch. It closed in 2004 when she retired and is now available for sale.

criminals (loitering and drunkenness, for example). Through vagrancy laws, police were able to arrest individuals for suspected crimes in an effort to assure the moral integrity of their communities. It was not until the 1960s that vagrancy laws were found to be in violation of the due process requirements of the Fourteenth Amendment. Since citizens were not told what behaviors would be illegal, the courts ruled that vagrancy laws had to be more clear and defined.

Instead of vagrancy laws, prostitution today is classified most regularly as a public-order crime. These crimes are defined by criminologist Larry Siegel as "crime which involves acts that interfere with the operations of society and the ability of people to function efficiently." Actions that violate public-order crime laws do so by being contrary to shared norms, social values, or customs. Public-order crimes include consensual and victimless crimes. Through modern efforts, authorities attempt to maintain both a legal and moral sense of order.

Historical Backdrop

This history of brothel prostitution in our country is one rich with stories and developments. In the 1800s, parlor house brothels throughout the United States served upper-class clients while bawdy houses did the same for the lower class. As we have seen in movie portrayals, concert saloons were popular among men as they could eat, listen to music, watch a brawl, or pay women for sex. While prostitution was technically illegal, the ban was not enforced and city officials were regularly bribed by those involved to look the other way. Even in this early period, we began to witness a socioeconomic divide regarding brothel prostitution with individuals in the upper echelons of society experiencing a more luxurious brothel experience.

Houses of prostitution spread westward with the profits of the gold rush in the latter half of the 19th century. While becoming more regulated by police, society, as a whole, became more aware of their existence. In 1836, Helen Jewett—who worked at a New York City brothel—was murdered by a client, raising public awareness of the existence of brothels to new highs. At the time of the Civil War, Washington, D.C., was home to some of the most toxic brothels in the country—in a neighborhood referred to as Murder Bay. Most of these brothels were created to serve the needs of General Joseph Hooker's Union Army. By the time development had ended, nearly the entire two blocks between Pennsylvania and Missouri Avenues had become occupied by lavish, high-end brothels largely catering to army officers.

Over time, other well-known brothels would be established. In 1881, the Bird Cage Theater opened in Tombstone, Arizona, and featured a brothel in the basement. The Dumas Brothel opened in Montana in 1890 and would later become the longest-running house of prostitution in the country before closing in 1982. Sidney Story—a city alderman in New Orleans—created The District in 1897. All prostitutes were forced to live and work in this small area; eventually there were over 200 operating brothels in it.

Over time, different states and localities continued experimenting with laws related to houses of prostitution. In 1967, for example, New York City eliminated license requirements for massage parlors, which permitted many to easily transform into brothels. Likewise, in 1970, the state of Nevada started regulating houses of prostitution. This decision led to the licensing of Mustang Ranch as the first of its kind within the state, and the legalization of brothel prostitution in 10 counties within the state.

Degrees of Enforcement

Brothel prostitution has presented a prime example of street-crime policing in the United States throughout its history. Prostitution has been deemed illegal nationwide for much of its history. Yet, it is also a crime that has typically been not stringently enforced. As with other so-called victimless crimes, the general lack of violence and public risk has led to houses of prostitution being largely ignored in some jurisdictions.

While the moral compass of a community is unquestionably important, cracking down on activities that violently threaten the physical well-being of otherwise uninvolved citizens are typically emphasized at the expense of crimes like prostitution that in many if not most cases involve a transaction between willing partners. Even victimless crimes such as illegal drug use are viewed as more concerning as there is a clearer pattern of violence associated with this activity than brothel prostitution.

Perhaps the most concerning aspect of brothel prostitution in the United States is the presence of massage parlors, saunas, and spas that serve as fronts for prostitution—particularly in major cities. While statistics on legal brothels in Nevada can be found (the number of brothels in operation generally ranges from 25–30), the nature of the illegal commercial sex trade makes documenting such businesses difficult if not impossible to track.

Even though most citizens are aware of the activities that often take place within such institutions, there is rarely much pressure to investigate or shut down said businesses. To some extent, the public argument seems to center on the notion that prostitution cannot be eliminated from our country and it is better to make some allowances in order to keep prostitutes off of the street.

The punishment for prostitution varies by state, yet a first-time offender typically will only be charged with a misdemeanor and face a fine (on average, from $500 to $2,000) and the potential for jail time (from 15 days up to a year). In 2009, Rhode Island closed legal loopholes that had essentially decriminalized indoor prostitution for three decades. It is clear that states are interested today in working to prevent brothels from expanding and growing in a way that negatively impacts society—yet just as clear that authorities sometimes remain willing to "look the other way."

Conclusion

Whether the practice is legal or not, prostitutes can typically be found in any country around the world. In the American context, prostitution has been deemed illegal in nearly all geographic areas. It is a matter of how willing police are to seek out and shut down their operations that determines for how long they can be active. Houses of prostitution, however, are deemed to be more societally concerning than individual prostitutes, because of their structure and formality. Prostitution has long been a concern for societies and will continue to be, as is the international plague of sex trafficking that forces some individuals into prostitution work.

William J. Miller
Flagler College

See Also: Children, Commercial Sexual Exploitation of; "Johns"; Massage Parlors; Peep Shows; Pimp; Prostitute/Streetwalker; Risky Lifestyles; Sex Crimes; Women.

Further Readings

Felson, Marcus. *Crime and Nature.* Thousand Oaks, CA: Sage, 2006.

Heyl, Barbara Sherman. *The Madam as Entrepreneur: Career Management in House Prostitution.* New York: Transaction, 1978.

Keire, Laura Mara. *For Business and Pleasure: Red-Light Districts and the Regulation of Vice in the United States, 1890–1933.* Baltimore, MD: Johns Hopkins University Press, 2010.

Ringdal, Nils Johan. *Love for Sale: A World History of Prostitution.* New York: Grove, 2005.

Sanger, William W. *The History of Prostitution.* New York: Nabu, 2010.

Shaner, Lora. *Madam: Inside a Nevada Brothel.* Las Vegas, NV: Huntington, 2003.

Racial Assault

For almost 20 years, the U.S. Department of Justice though the Federal Bureau of Investigation (FBI) has been documenting the number and characteristics of known racial and ethnically motivated assault offenses in the United States. This entry will focus on crimes that are motivated entirely or in part by the race or ethnicity of the victim.

Racially Motivated Hate Crimes

It has long been noted that race and ethnicity are social constructs. What makes one person "black" and another "white" is much more a function of social mores than of biology; however, for this entry race and ethnicity will be used as outlined in statutes intended to criminalize this behavior. The U.S. government collects information on hate crimes and reports it in the FBI's annual Hate Crime Statistics report, which includes information about the victims, offenders, and category of each known offense in a given year. This FBI data will inform this entry.

Racial and ethnic assaults, like other bias-motivated crimes, are distinct from other assault incidents because they are motivated at least in part by certain characteristics of the victim (in this case, race) involved in the crime. It is important to note that the FBI only documents crimes reported to the police. If an individual victimized by a hate crime victim chooses not to report the crime for fear of retaliation or because of a belief that the police would do nothing about it, that incident would not be included in the national statistics.

In 2009, there were 4,925 hate crimes in the United States motivated by the race or ethnicity of the victim. Rates of racially and ethnically motivated offenses far exceeded those motivated by other characteristics including religion, sexual orientation, or disability—with just over 60 percent of all hate crimes reported in 2009 motivated by race or ethnicity. Of these racially and ethnically motivated hate crimes, 1,698 of them involved either aggravated or simple assault. Recorded biases in 2009 included assaults that were antiwhite, anti-black, anti-Hispanic, anti-American Indian, anti-Asian, and antimultiple races. Antiblack bias is consistently the most commonly reported hate crime motivation in the United States.

Although definitions, legal prohibitions, and standards for reporting and recording incidents of hate crime differ around the world, the patterns of racially motivated crimes in the United States are similar to the international experience, as measured by the Organization for Security and Co-operation in Europe's (OSCE) Office for Democratic Institutions and Human Rights. OSCE's 2009 annual report on hate crimes revealed that over 32 nations reported collecting data on the ethnicity of victims of crime, while 30 nations reported collecting data on the race of victims of crime. The exact number of crimes, and specifically assaults, involving racial bias is hard to know because information is submitted to the OSCE by contributing nations' governments, nongovernmental organizations (NGOs), and international governmental organizations (IGO's). However, we do know that in Britain in 2009, 43,426 racist hate crimes were recorded by police in England and Wales, while police in Scotland recorded 6,590 racially motivated crimes. While exact numbers of racial assaults internationally are unclear, what is clear is that racially motivated offenses remain a significant problem both in the United States and abroad.

Hate Crime Defined

In the United States, a hate crime is defined as a criminal act motivated by bias against victims because of their actual or perceived membership in a certain group. The FBI definition of hate crime reads: "A hate crime, also known as a bias crime, is a criminal offense committed against a person, property, or society that is motivated, in whole or in part, by the offender's bias against a race, religion, disability, sexual orientation, or ethnicity/national origin."

In the United Kingdom, the Crime and Disorder Act of 1998 made hateful behavior toward a victim based on the victim's real or perceived membership in a racial or religious group an aggravating factor in sentencing for specified crimes. The definition of race is broad; it can be used to describe a person's race, color, nationality, citizenship, or ethnic or national origins. The same law protects people from religiously-based discrimination. In 2003, the Criminal Justice Act extended protection to victims discriminated against based on sexual orientation or disability. Also, it is interesting to note that in England the determining factor in whether a crime is investigated as a hate crime is the perception of the victim—if a victim thought a crime was motivated by bias, the police will investigate it as a bias crime. In the United States, the determination of bias motivation is made by the police after an investigation. The victim's perception is only one element of this investigation.

Racial Assaults by Citizens

Racial assaults by citizens are often difficult to recognize as motivated by bias and labeled as hate crimes. Intrinsic qualities of racially motivated assaults, such as the fact that they are, on average, more violent than other assaults and tend to occur between strangers rather than acquaintances, are factors that the literature has found to be associated with bias-motivated assaults. When hate crimes do occur and are identified by public officials, the public reaction to these hate crimes can be powerful enough to lead to significant legislative and policy changes.

The extremely violent story of the murder of James Byrd, Jr., illustrates this. On June 7, 1998, three young white men offered Byrd, a 49-year-old African American man, a ride home in the town of Jasper, Texas. Instead of taking him home, however, they drove to a remote country road outside of town and beat him severely before chaining him by the ankles, attaching him to their pickup truck, and driving their pickup truck over three miles before Byrd was decapitated when his body hit a culvert in the road. Forensic evidence suggests that Byrd maintained consciousness for most of that drive, although parts of his body were found at 81 places along the route. The perpetrators then dumped the rest of his mutilated body in front of an African American church in town. Byrd's murder was identified as a hate crime for several reasons, one of which being that two of the men involved were known white supremacists.

Reactions in the town of Jasper, the state of Texas, and the country in general were predictably and justifiably emotional. But surprisingly, the lasting outcome of this emotion was positive: the major immediate reaction was a call for substantial racial healing in the United States. Several speakers at Byrd's funeral said his death should bring whites and blacks together in mutual outrage and determination to end violence. At his funeral, the Reverend Jesse Jackson suggested that, "Brother Byrd's innocent blood alone could very well be the blood that changes the course of our country, because no one has captured the nation's attention like this tragedy."

The event inspired conversation about race relations, discrimination, and inequalities in the United States and motivated many people to challenge the status quo. Locally, the community came together to honor an innocent man murdered for no reason other than his skin tone. At the state level, the James Byrd, Jr., Hate Crime Act was passed in 2001, distinguishing crimes motivated by bias from other crimes. At the national level, the 2009 Matthew Shepard and James Byrd, Jr., Hate Crimes Prevention Act expanded the 1969 federal hate crime legislation.

Racial Assaults by Police

The hate crime statistics gathered by the FBI do not count every bias-motivated crime in the United States; many hate crimes are not reported. In addition to the reasons for not reporting cited above, some racial and ethnic assaults are not committed by community members and thus not counted in the statistics. In the United States, racial assaults by police have been an ongoing problem for most of our history. Unlike racial assaults by citizens, which are labeled hate crimes and condemned almost uniformly in society, racial assaults by police present a different type of challenge—in description, in recognition, and in response.

Consider, for example, the case of Sean Bell. On November 25, 2006, Bell and two of his friends were leaving Bell's bachelor party at a strip club in Queens, New York. A plainclothes police officer from the New York City Police Department (NYPD) allegedly thought he heard one of Bell's friends say that he was going to get his gun. It is unclear exactly what ensued in the following moments, but in the parking lot, the plainclothes officer and three of his colleagues from the NYPD managed to shoot 50 bullets into the air, the street, adjoining buildings, and the car that Bell and his friends were in. Although the police officers claimed that they had reasonable suspicion that there was a gun in the car, no weapon was found. Instead, they killed Bell and seriously injured the other two men in the car.

Reactions to this purported racial assault were quite different. Thousands of people protested the amount of force used, and rather than coming together in the spirit of unity, they came forward angry with the police as an institution. Even though many politicians gave statements denouncing the amount of force used, including New York City mayor Michael Bloomberg and former New York State governor George Pataki, protestors insisted that governing agencies did not protect their communities from acts of racially motivated violence.

The days after the shooting were filled with angry exchanges between protestors and authorities, best exemplified by multiple threats of retaliatory shootings of NYPD police officers, so presumably feasible to police that patrol officers were taken off of their walking beats in the vicinity, and patrol was limited to cars. Although no retaliatory violence ever took place, this illustrates the severe impacts that racial assaults by police can have on communities and our society as a whole: our trust in the police is shattered, and this is threatening to the amount of authority individuals will grant police agencies.

Symbolism

Research has found that among some groups in society, the police are thought to reflect the dominant ideology of society as a whole. Consistently, members of the African American and Latino groups rate their trust and confidence in the police as much lower than do Caucasian community members. If the police engage in acts of intimidation or violence motivated by bias, the faith in the police by members of the community of color will be further eroded.

If victims of racial or ethnically motivated violence feel they cannot go to the police for protection and assistance, to whom can they turn? When the police are unavailable to victims, victims are faced with three untenable choices: retaliate on their own against their attackers; hide from future attacks which might include staying away from work, school, or places of recreation; or move away from the community in which they live. Innocent members of our society should never be faced with such unreasonable choices.

Conclusion

Hate crimes are symbolic crimes and they can have dramatic and far-reaching effects on the victims. Racial and ethnically motivated hate crimes are the most frequent category of all hate crimes and they can threaten the very core of any society. By sending a message that "you are not welcome in our community," racially and ethnically motivated assaults can significantly disrupt any policies to promote a diverse society. Similar assaults committed by the police can further undermine any attempts to promote diversity in a city or nation, by sending an additional message to members of minority groups that "not only do we not want you here, but we will not protect you if others target you for violence and intimidation." By taking racially and ethnically motivated assaults and other hate crimes seriously and offering real emotional support and assistance to the victims of these assaults, societies can take a significant step to becoming more diverse and tolerant communities.

John (Jack) McDevitt
Rebecca D. Pfeffer
Northeastern University

See Also: Hate Crime; Immigrant Neighborhoods; Police (Overview); Racial Profiling; Urban Incivility.

Further Readings

Chakroborti, Neil and John Garland. *Hate Crime: Impact, Causes, and Responses.* Thousand Oaks, CA: Sage, 2009.

Federal Bureau of Investigation. "2009 Hate Crime Statistics." Washington, DC: U.S. Department of Justice, 2010.

Levin, Jack and Jack McDevitt. *Hate Crime: America's War on Those Who Are Different.* New York: Basic Books, 2002.

Organization for Security and Co-operation in Europe (OSCE). "Hate Crimes in the OSCE Region—Incidents and Responses: Annual Report for 2009." Vienna, Austria: OSCE Secretariat, 2010.

Racial Profiling

There are many definitions of racial profiling in the scholarly literature, but basically the term refers to situations where law enforcement or other persons of authority (e.g., retail store mangers) make decisions based on the race or ethnicity of an individual rather than any behavior or prior intelligence that the individual is involved in criminal activity. Groups that have been alleged to engage in racial profiling include lawyers (jury selection), prosecutors (filing charges), store managers, airline security officials, real estate agents, and law enforcement officials. The most public debate about racial profiling has involved alleged profiling by the police.

Utility of Racial Profiling

It has been argued by some in law enforcement that racial profiling is a rational practice that stems from differential rates of criminal offending by certain groups. This may be true if one looks at certain crimes (e.g., robbery) but not if one considers other crimes (e.g., fraud). Even if there were a rational basis for selecting one group over another for increased law enforcement scrutiny, there would be a cost of such a policy. The targeted group would legitimately feel that the police are disproportionately looking for members of that group, believing that they are involved in criminal activity—and thus

In 2012 in Arizona, Maricopa County Sheriff Joe Arpaio was accused of unfairly targeting Latinos for detention and arrest and engaging in what the U.S. Justice Department termed unconstitutional policing.

the trust and confidence in the police among this group would decrease.

If certain groups in a community do not trust the police it can have the exact opposite effect from that intended by the police. If members of the group being profiled do not trust the police they will not report crime to the police, and they will not assist the police in investigations and prosecutions. Subsequently, overall crime may increase.

History of Profiling Claims

While claims of disparate treatment by police toward certain racial or ethnic groups have been around since the police themselves were formed, in the 1990s the claims came to national attention. A series of traffic stops involving the New Jersey State Police and the Maryland State Police brought the practice of racial profiling to national attention.

The practice of profiling African American or Latino drivers, a practice termed *driving while black* or *driving while brown,* appears to have come in part from a series of national trainings offered to local law enforcement by the Drug Enforcement Administration (DEA) that included a description of something DEA officials referred to as a Drug Courier Profile. This profile described characteristics of individuals who may be involved in drug transportation from southern U.S. states to northern cities. This profile included descriptions of the type of vehicle used, the character of the driving, and in some trainings, a description of those involved, which included race and ethnicity. According to criminologist David Harris, by one estimate, 27,000 law enforcement officials participated in this training, many of whom attempted to implement this profiling in their jurisdictions.

Research on Racial Profiling

Initially, there were many claims by members of the African American and Latino communities that racial profiling by police was a widespread practice. These claims were regularly disputed by members of law enforcement. There was a need for scientific research to determine if in fact African Americans and Hispanics were being disproportionately targeted. The initial research was conducted in Maryland and New Jersey along the Interstate-95 corridor, finding that nonwhite drivers were more likely to be stopped in comparison to white drivers.

Specifically, research by John Lamberth in New Jersey found that African Americans made up 13.5 percent of the drivers on the New Jersey Turnpike but made up 35 percent of the drivers stopped by the New Jersey State Police and made up 73 percent of drivers arrested in traffic stops. It is important to note that a racial or ethnic disparity does not mean racial profiling is ongoing; a number of legitimate explanations may exist for these disparities, such as deployment decisions, or programs targeted toward specific criminally involved groups.

It appeared that traffic stops were not the only areas of enforcement in which African Americans and Latinos were disproportionately subject to law enforcement investigative activity. In New York in the 1990s, the New York Police Department began a policy of aggressively stopping and frisking pedestrians who they thought might be engaged in criminal activity. In 1999, a report by New York State Attorney General Elliott Spitzer found that African Americans were 23 percent more likely than whites to be stopped by the police, and Latinos were 39 percent more likely to be stopped.

This early research has come under some criticism on methodological grounds, but as more and more research has been undertaken, it appears that African Americans and Latinos are consistently more likely to be searched than whites in traffic or pedestrian stops. The research to date has not found consistent patterns of disparate treatment in the practice of stopping vehicles; however, research has found consistent patterns of disparate treatment in what have been called poststop decisions, such as the decision to search a driver and the decision to give a ticket or warning to that driver.

A recent study by the U.S. Bureau of Justice Statistics found that African Americans, Latinos, and whites were stopped by the police at similar rates, but African Americans and Latinos were two to three times more likely to be searched. There are a number of explanations offered for these disparities, including the fact that members of these groups may be more likely to live in high-crime areas and be subject to increased overall police enforcement; that members of these groups may be more likely to engage in illegal behaviors (e.g., speeding), or that police officers, like most other members of our society, hold unconscious biases that influence behavior in ways we seldom realize.

Eliminating Racial Profiling

While it is important to note that racial disparities do not necessarily indicate that an officer is engaged in racial profiling, if members of the community believe that officers from a law enforcement agency are engaged in racial profiling there will be negative consequences in terms of community trust and confidence in the police. To reduce these perceptions, law enforcement organizations have taken steps in three major areas: training, monitoring, and community dialogue.

A common response to allegations of racial profiling involved offering training to officers in an agency. This training came from many different sources and was of widely varying quality; consequently it was not always well received by law enforcement officers. The best training involved understanding how racially disparate treatment might be occurring even by nonbiased, well-meaning officers. This kind of training, particularly when it included a discussion of unconscious bias, seemed to help officers understand the potential for bias in their actions without singling them out and labeling them racist.

One area in which agencies have changed their operations is to monitor the traffic enforcement behavior of officers. Before the issue of racial profiling became a public controversy in the 1990s, very few law enforcement agencies collected any information about the traffic enforcement behavior of their officers. This is in sharp contrast to the amount of information collected by departments on crime in their community and arrests made by their officers. While the number of agencies collecting data on traffic enforcement has declined recently, in 2004 there were approximately 4,000 agencies collecting this information. These agencies were able to monitor the actions of their officers while also demonstrating to the public that they were looking for any allegations of racial profiling by members of their organization.

Conclusion

One of the most effective approaches to community concerns about racial profiling appears to be to engage in a community dialogue about these concerns. Engaging in such a community dialogue presents an opportunity to those law enforcement officials who have chosen to collect data on the race and ethnicity of persons stopped, to include that data in a conversation about how the department is attempting to assess if any racial profiling occurs in their agency. Even in those agencies that do not collect data, engaging in a dialogue demonstrates to members of the community that they are concerned about any perceptions of profiling and that leadership in the agency will not tolerate any instances of racial or ethnic profiling in their agency.

John (Jack) McDevitt
Northeastern University

See Also: Community Policing; Police (Overview); Racial Assault; Stop and Frisk; Urban Ethnography.

Further Readings

Durose, Matthew R., Erica L. Smith, and Patrick A. Langan. "Contact Between the Police and the Public, 2005." Washington, DC: Bureau of Justice Statistics, 2007.

Fagan, Jeffrey. "Law, Social Science, and Racial Profiling." *Justice Research and Policy,* v.4/4 (2002).

Farrell, Amy, Jack McDevitt, and Michael E. Buerger. "Moving Police and Community Dialogues Forward Through Data Collection Task Forces." *Police Quarterly,* v.5/3 (2002).

Fridell, Lorie. "By The Numbers: A Guide for Analyzing Race Data From Vehicle Stops." Washington, DC: Police Executive Research Forum, 2004.

Harris, David A. *Profiles in Injustice: Why Racial Profiling Cannot Work.* New York: New Press, 2002.

Rape and Sexual Assault

This entry addresses sexual violence as an act that can and does occur both in public arenas as well as in the privacy of one's home.

Prevalence and Definitions

Sexual violence continues to be a serious problem in the United States. Multiple studies provide evidence indicating that women are at exceedingly high risks for sexual violence from someone they know as opposed to a stranger. Sexual violence often victimizes people well after the act itself. Victims of such crimes are more likely to perpetrate other crimes and have a multitude of issues relating to the incident. Violent acts of a sexual nature toward women can be traced back in history. Although it is typically thought of as an act perpetrated on stranger, recent studies suggest that it happens more often by someone known to the victim. Multiple terms for sexual violence have emerged and "marital rape," for example acknowledges that women (and men) can, in fact, be raped by their spouses.

Although seemingly less severe, sexual discrimination and sexual harassment are additional actions that are often seen as precursors to sexual violence. Sexual violence is an act involving aggression or discrimination against a woman or less commonly a male victim. This act may involve physical, sexual, emotional, or financial abuse resulting in injury to the victim. There are multiple theories of sexual violence that involve such factors as sexual motivation, socialization, masochism, biological indicators, psychological indicators, and the culture of violence. There are also multiple typologies of rape, a form of sexual violence—power rapes and anger rapes being the most common types.

It is equally as important to mention that although the issue is a serious one, the extent of the problem with sexual violence may be difficult to study, given three common challenges. First, there are definitional issues. The term *rape* is often used where sexual assault may be more appropriate, and vice versa. Next, the actual definition of the terms varies from one source to another, making it difficult to gather adequate information. And finally, medical professions view sexual violence from different perspectives (e.g., physicians view it as a medical problem, psychologists view it as a mental health issue, etc.).

The common challenges mentioned have led organizations such as the World Health Organization (WHO) to attempt to more clearly define the circumstances of sexual violence. According to the *World Report on Violence and Health,* funded by the WHO, any number of circumstances may be characterized as sexually violent acts including, but not limited to: rape within marriage or dating relationships; rape by strangers; systematic rape during armed conflict; unwanted sexual advances or sexual harassment, including demanding sex in return for favors; sexual abuse of mentally or physically disabled people; sexual abuse of children; forced marriage or cohabitation, including the marriage of children; denial of the right to use contraception or to adopt other measures to protect against sexually transmitted diseases; forced abortion; violent acts against the sexual integrity of women, including female genital mutilation and obligatory inspections for virginity; and forced prostitution and trafficking of people for the purpose of sexual exploitation.

A number of other organizations have sought to debunk common myths associated with rape, sexual assault, or intimate partner violence. Many of these myths can be found through university Web sites, various domestic violence advocacy groups, and child protection agencies to name a few. It is not uncommon for the target population of this information to be women as they are the greatest number of victims of sexual violence. According to the National Crime Victimization Surveys (NCVS), there is little variation among race, but low socioeconomic status appears to be associated with rape and sexual assault. Males are less often victimized—and they are almost exclusively the perpetrators in these cases.

The topic is discussed in the literature more today than ever before. Sexual violence and similar terminology are no longer taboo in everyday conversations. Studies have shown that this has led to more women having the confidence to report their victimization, and also to aid a friend in her quest for help. Next, the history and definition specifically of sexual assault and rape will be discussed in further detail.

Sexual Assault

The term *sexual assault* includes such acts as rape (by stranger, acquaintance, or marital), incest, molestation, and other unwelcome forms of sexual victimization. Sexual harassment definitions often overlap, but the distinction is when contact occurs it then becomes sexual assault. The prevalence and definition of sexual victimization is often misunderstood. There are numerous definitions of sexual victimization; reports vary in terms of statistics on the topic. It should be noted that sexual victimization crimes are among the most underreported of the crimes compiled by the Federal Bureau of Investigation (FBI), making it hard to gather accurate information on the issue. One reason in particular for this is that the victim often knows the perpetrator—making it difficult to prosecute him or her. Sixty percent of victims of rape or sexual assault identify their relationship with the offender as a nonstranger (intimate, relative, friend, or acquaintance).

Definitions of sexual victimization as determined by police departments vary, specifically with regard to sexual assault, and they are often under dispute. Since the mid-1970s attempts have been made to unify terminology, increase awareness, and better understand the issue and those impacted.

Typically women and children are victims of sexual victimization, but these crimes do not discriminate. According to the NCVS, in 2010, 5 percent of males said they were victims of intimate partner violence, compared to 22 percent of females. Much of the literature refers to women and children as victims of sexual assault primarily because the reported cases of male victims and survivors is extremely low. However, recent reports of same-sex violence have been significant. The treatment of these victims has improved since the mid-1970s when many new service agencies opened their doors, but the issue is so often underreported that many go on without any counseling or understanding of the crime that has victimized them.

Understanding the causes and how to prevent sexual assault are commonly debated, but it is generally agreed upon that is one of the nation's major criminal and social problems. Many victims and survivors of sexual assault are young (under age 18), leaving traces of bitterness and resentment. There are various types of sexual assault, and to better understand the definition of these crimes, a distinction of the various types should help to clarify.

Rape

Rape had been historically defined as an attack by a stranger upon an adult woman, using force. Broad definitions such as this claim that children and men could not be raped and that someone they know could not rape them. In addition, forced oral and anal penetration was not covered under traditional definitions. Other definitions began to include some of these other categories, but maintained that it could only happen to a woman without her consent by a man and that it was a woman who was not his wife. Unfortunately these definitions fell short in acknowledging rape within a domestic partnership (marriage, cohabitation) and rape with a same-sex partner, and the focus remained around her consent rather than his force. In addition, some forms of rape were taken more seriously than others, using a subjective manner to decide one's fate.

By the mid-1970s to the early 1980s rape legislation had changed significantly and the legal definition of sexual victimization, specifically rape, in many jurisdictions included principles such as gender-neutrality, other acts of penetration, degree of force, threatening behavior, and incapacitated victims (e.g., the mentally ill or substance abusers). Michigan and Illinois statutes had become the national models for inclusive definition of rape with the advent of the Criminal Sexual Conduct Statute of 1975. The criminal statutes still differ greatly from state to state, but the Federal Criminal Code for sexual assault has historically had a broad definition to include rape. In 2012, with the landmark Violence Against Women Act (VAWA) at the federal level raising awareness, Attorney General Eric Holder revised the FBI's definition of rape to include a more comprehensive definition: "The penetration, no matter how slight, of the vagina or anus with any body part or object, or oral penetration by a sex organ of another person, without the consent of the victim."

Several states more commonly use the term *sexual assault* and categorize rape (forced intercourse)

within the parameters of sexual assault. Rape is often further categorized into two terms that describe the relationship between the attacker and their victim. *Stranger rape* is a term associated with someone who is unknown to the victim. Acquaintance rape is associated with someone who is known to the victim. There are many examples of acquaintance rape, which include but are not limited to friends, lovers, former lovers, dates, spouses, colleagues, neighbors, etc. Some categories that are not mentioned here are marital rape, incest, and child abuse.

Girls are taught from a young age about the lurking rapist in the alley, but contrary to those beliefs, stranger rape is far less common than acquaintance rape. Research supports that 80–90 percent of rape victims know their attacker. It is important to note, however, that reports vary based on the method of obtaining information. Research on sexual victimization that is reported to police varies from that obtained from anonymous surveys. It is also known that most incidents of sexual assault are never even reported.

Geographic Impact of Rape and Sexual Assault

Data on the frequency of rapes and sexual assaults vary for a number of reasons. The most compelling reason is that the data sources are compiled in different ways. For example, The Uniform Crime Report (UCR) and the National Crime Victimization Survey (NCVS) are the two major national sources for violent and property crime in the United States: one analyzes data gathered from law enforcement agencies and the other is a survey administered to households. Both produce national statistics on victimization, however, their definitions of rape and sexual assault vary.

In addition to the differences in how the information is gathered, the definitions used by the agencies for "rape" and "sexual assault" vary. The definition used by the UCR until 2010 was defined as "carnal knowledge of a female forcibly and against her will." The definition originally excluded a number of forms of sexual victimization by other means of force that many states' laws include in their respective criminal codes. In 2013, the definition was expanded to the "penetration, no matter how slight, of the vagina or anus with any body part or object, or oral penetration by a sex organ of another person, without the consent of the victim."

In addition, this provides concern for data reported on this topic as it may be misleading in the trends for rape and sexual assault victims. For example, according to a report published by the FBI in 1999, 7 percent of women are sexually assaulted each year. A report published in 1997 by the NCVS stated that 37 percent of women are sexually assaulted annually. In both cases, the figures that they report may be misleading. Many women do not report victimization. This is especially true if the assailant is known to the victim.

Crime rates in general tend to be higher in urban areas than suburban areas. This difference is attributed to a number of factors. According to scholars, this is often attributed to increased population density, transient lifestyles, high levels of poverty and unemployment, and lower levels of education. However, in suburban or rural areas where the population may have a higher number of acquaintances, more isolation, and a culture that uses greater informal social controls (such as religion, school, etc.) there may be less reported incidents of rape and sexual assault. Victims of rape and sexual assault are more likely to be victimized by someone known to them (family, friend, acquaintance) and less likely to report the incident in these cases for both urban and suburban victims.

In a study conducted by C. Rennison, W. S. DeKeseredy, and M. Dragiewicz using NCVS data for 1992–2009, the authors found that the number of rapes and sexual assaults by intimate partners was higher in suburban areas (46.1 percent) and less in urban (30.4 percent) and rural areas (23.5 percent). These findings are consistent with earlier works that contended that certain geographic area may indicate higher percentages of rape/sexual assault.

More Findings

Much attention has turned toward intimate partner violence (IPV) in recent years, as the number of women victimized by loved ones, regardless of sexual orientation, has increased. In a 2000 study conducted by Ann Coker, Paige Smith, Robert McKeown, and Melissa King, the authors were searching for a better understanding of the frequency of IPV among women. Their findings indicated that 55 percent of women had experienced some type of IPV whether it was in current or past relationships. They also found that women in a relationship with a man were more likely to be victimized.

Women who experience substance abuse either directly or indirectly were more at risk than those who were not exposed to it. Another risk factor often discussed in the literature is that women who have children are more likely to become victims of IPV. This phenomenon is currently being explored more, but remains in the forefront of sexual violence literature today.

A number of studies seek to calculate the actual costs of victimization and in particular sexual violence. Quantifying the costs associated with street crime, specifically sexual offenses, is daunting, but important. In a 2004 study conducted by Andrew Morrison and Maria Orlando, the data show an increase in gender-based violence is an international phenomenon and is not unique to the United States. Although their research focus was international, the findings indicate that across the board the costs were similar to societies. These costs may be monetary or direct costs (i.e., health care, judicial services, and social services) and nonmonetary or indirect costs (i.e., loss of life, insurance, or employment due to injury). Typically a combination of both is evident among victims. Sexual victimization leaves behind survivors who often have issues ranging from mild immediate trauma to much more severe long term effects from the event. Families of both victims and survivors often suffer alongside them after the event. For those families forced to go on without their loved one in most capacities, the grieving could be substantial. In addition to the number of consequences, survivors of sexual victimization may have significant financial burdens.

Both nationally and internationally, the issue of sexual violence is existent and problematic. The challenges in studying the issue make information gathering a difficult process. Research analyzing the topic of sexual violence should be viewed critically to avoid bias on the topic.

Susan V. Koski
Central Connecticut State University

See Also: Children as Victims; Domestic Violence; Homophobic Assault; Juvenile Offending; Pimp; Prostitute/Streetwalker; Sex Crimes; Women.

Further Readings

Bachman, Ronet, Raymond Paternoster, and Sally Ward. "The Rationality of Sexual Offending: Testing a Deterrence/Rational Choice Conception of Sexual Assault." *Law & Society Review,* v.26/2 (1992).

Coker, Ann L., Paige H. Smith, Robert E. McKeown, and Melissa J. King. "Frequency and Correlates of Intimate Partner Violence by Type: Physical, Sexual, and Psychological Battering." *American Journal of Public Health,* v.90/4 (2000).

Finkelhor, David. *Child Sexual Abuse: New Theory and Research.* New York: The Free Press, 1984.

Jasinski, Jana L. and Linda M. Williams. *Partner Violence: A Comprehensive Review of 20 Years of Research.* Thousand Oaks, CA: Sage, 1998.

Kelly, Liz. *Surviving Sexual Violence.* Minneapolis: University of Minnesota Press, 1988.

Meloy, Michelle L. *Sex Offenses and the Men Who Commit Them: An Assessment of Sex Offenders on Probation.* Lebanon, NH: Northeastern University Press, 2006.

Morrison, Andrew R. and Maria Beatriz Orlando. *The Costs and Impacts of Gender-Based Violence in Developing Countries: Methodological Considerations and New Evidence.* Washington, DC: World Bank, 2004.

Park, R. and E. Burgess. *Introduction to the Science of Sociology.* Chicago: University of Chicago Press, 1921.

Raphael, S. and M. Sills. "Urban Crime, Race, and the Criminal Justice System in the United States." In *Companion to Urban Economics,* Richard J. Arnott and Daniel P. McMillan, eds. Malden, MA: Blackwell Publishing, 2006.

Rennison, C. "Criminal Victimization 2001: Changes 2000–01 With Trends 1993–2001. Washington, DC: Bureau of Justice Statistics National Crime Victimization Survey, NCJ 194610, 2002.

Rennison, C., W. S. DeKeseredy, M. Dragiewicz. "Urban, Suburban, and Rural Variations in Separation/ Divorce Rape/Sexual Assault: Results From the National Crime Victimization Survey." *Feminist Criminology,* v.7/4 (2012).

Shaw, C. and H. McKay. *Juvenile Delinquency and Urban Areas.* Chicago: University of Chicago Press, 1969.

Truman, Jennifer L. "National Crime Victimization Survey: Criminal Victimization 2010." Washington, DC: U.S. Department of Justice, Bureau of Justice Statistics, 2011.

Wallace, Harvey and Cliff Roberson. *Victimology: Legal, Psychological and Social Perspectives.* 3rd ed. Upper Saddle River, NJ: Prentice Hall, 2011.

Williams, Kirk R. and Nancy G. Guerra. "Epidemiology, Victimization Patterns by Age, Gender, Ethnicity, Socioeconomic Status." In *Encyclopedia of Interpersonal Violence.* Thousand Oaks, CA: Sage, 2008.

Williams, Linda M. "Researcher-Advocate Collaborations to End Violence Against Women: Toward Liberating Methodologies for Action Research." *Journal of Interpersonal Violence,* v.19/11 (2004).

World Health Organization (WHO). "Sexual Violence." In *World Report on Violence and Health.* New York: WHO, 2002.

Risky Lifestyles

Participation in risky lifestyles—including homelessness, prostitution or street hustling, frequent alcohol or drug use, frequent bar and nightclub patronage, and gang activities—is linked to both increased participation in street crimes and increased likelihood of victimization. This relationship is generally explained by a combination of opportunity and learning processes. Those who engage in risky lifestyles also may be isolated from the protections of conventional support systems (e.g., family members, friends, neighbors, clergy members, police, or social workers) because of shame or distrust, further increasing their vulnerability on the street.

Further, evidence suggests that participation in risky lifestyles may not fully be a matter of choice. Social location appears especially influential, as suggested by patterns of risky behavior that vary by gender, race, age, socioeconomic status, and geographic location. Cultural messages transmitted through mass media lend support for public suspicions of those who engage in risky lifestyles and encourage holding some individuals responsible for their own victimization.

Patterns of Offending and Victimization

Offenders and victims of street crime are overlapping populations and cannot be discussed as if they were separate groups. One of the most consistent findings in the literature on street crime is that victims and offenders share similar demographic characteristics, suggesting that lifestyle dynamics are highly influential in one's propensity to become involved in street crimes. In particular, individuals who are male, young (under 25), unmarried, members of a racial or ethnic minority group, low-income earners, and those who live in urban areas have higher risks of exposure to street crime than other groups (e.g., those who are older, female, white, or live in rural areas), which increases their likelihood of becoming offenders and victims.

Most scholars who seek to explain the link between risky lifestyles and patterns of offending and victimization emphasize a combination of opportunity and learning environments. According to both the "lifestyles explanation" and routine activity theory, individuals' risk of victimization and likelihood of offending depend on their exposure to criminal offenders, and that exposure depends on individuals' lifestyles and routine activities. Risky lifestyles generally expose associated individuals to unconventional others and situations.

Street criminals and their victims tend to live in socially disorganized neighborhoods (e.g., areas with trash on the streets and run-down buildings); exhibit low parental attachment, educational achievement, and career aspirations; and engage in risky lifestyles and offending behaviors in similar proportions. Routine behaviors that increase exposure to crime—and are associated with members of particular groups—include spending large amounts of time away from home (especially at nighttime); frequently visiting bars or nightclubs; using public transportation; and hanging out in public areas like parks, parking garages, and parking lots. In sum, when potential victims and willing offenders interact during times of reduced supervision (e.g., at night) and in settings where individuals engage in risky behaviors (e.g., in bars or nightclubs), the opportunities for offending and the risks of victimization increase.

A young homeless man sleeps on a Louisiana street, covered in newspapers to try to keep warm. Younger people and racial minorities are more likely to engage in risk-taking behaviors and to experience unemployment, serious illnesses, domestic violence, and imprisonment, which increases their risk of becoming homeless or engaging in street crime for survival.

In addition, it has been suggested that the presence of a criminal subculture, also known as "street culture" or the "code of the streets," can explain criminal offending and victimization. Offenders involved in risky lifestyles may learn criminal techniques, as well as norms, attitudes, and rationalizations, through their associations with other lifestyle participants, and they may receive support for their criminal activities through membership in deviant subcultures.

Further, life on the streets or within risky lifestyles or criminal subcultures may isolate individuals from conventional social attachments and the development of attitudes that are favorable to crime. In addition to increased exposure to crime, people who engage in risky lifestyles frequently lack social support systems (e.g., family members, conventional friends, and neighbors) that could shield them from harmful effects. Social supports consistently have been shown to improve physical and mental health in the general population, and negative life events and risky lifestyle choices may play a role in eroding such supports.

Some people who routinely engage in risky behaviors isolate themselves from social supports because of shame or fear of disapproval, and some isolate themselves from official sources of support (e.g., police officials and social workers) because of a general distrust of authority figures. They are reluctant to report their victimization because they do not trust that officials will take them seriously, or they may be fearful of drawing attention to their activities. This makes them attractive targets for crime because they can be victimized with little chance of legal repercussions. Some live secret lives, with pseudonyms, temporary dwellings, and few close friends, making their behaviors—and victimization—more difficult to detect.

Understanding Risk-Taking Behaviors

Speaking of risky lifestyles suggests an element of choice. While some individuals do choose to engage in routine risky behaviors and shun more conventional options, the social position of others may limit what options are available to them. Characteristics like gender, race, age, and socioeconomic status represent life chances, as they reflect the social structure that establishes what life choices are available to members of groups defined by these demographic categories. Lacking

conventional sources of power, younger people, racial minorities (particularly those of African American or Hispanic background), those with less education, and those of lower socioeconomic status are more likely to engage in risk-taking behaviors that compromise physical safety and well-being. These groups also tend to experience more negative life events (e.g., unemployment, serious illnesses, domestic violence, and imprisonment), which increase their risk of homelessness (itself a risky lifestyle) and involvement in other risky lifestyles (e.g., prostitution, drug using/selling, or gang membership) or street crime for survival. In addition, the Uniform Crime Reports and National Crime Victimization Survey both show a greater prevalence of serious crime in urban areas, suggesting the influence of geographic location in exposure to crime, as well as socioeconomic status, as individuals in poor and working classes disproportionately reside in urban areas.

Although far more men participate in routine risky ventures and street crime than women, men enjoy more power on the streets and are less vulnerable to assaults and exploitation. When women enter street life, frequently it is a result of a lack of opportunities and protections in conventional life. There are few legitimate opportunities for poorly educated, unskilled women, and the inability of public programs to support women and children at a livable standard may push some women into risky lifestyles in an effort to support themselves and their children. For example, the patriarchal structure of American society, along with the sexualization and objectification of women's bodies, leads some women into prostitution. This activity not only allows women some means of economic stability, but it also provides an amount of personal protection and a sort of support system through associations with others on the streets.

Yet, street life, too, is male dominated, and women who participate in risky lifestyles continue to be victims of an unbalanced power structure. A 1989 study of female "street hustlers" (prostitutes) by Kim Romenesko and Eleanor M. Miller found that it is necessary for these women to associate with a man for protection; female hustlers without a male associate are referred to on the streets as "outlaws" and frequently are subject to harassment, robbery, and sexual exploitation. But affiliation with men on the streets does not provide full protection. A 1998 study of female gang members by Jody Miller found that the women received, through their gang affiliation, protection from outside gang violence and harassment, but they were constantly vulnerable to routine physical and sexual assaults by fellow gang members.

Street crime itself involves risk-taking. As such, it may be an appealing pursuit for those who regularly participate in other risky activities. Sociologists Stephen Lyng and Jack Katz offer theoretical models that help explain risk-taking behaviors and conceptualize the often thrilling nature of criminal offending. Lyng has extensively explored high-risk pursuits and the appeal for some people of risk-taking and thrill-seeking activities. Although Lyng mostly focuses on activities such as rock climbing, skydiving, stock trading, unprotected sex, and sadomasochism, his concept of "edgework" helps explain why some people engage in risky lifestyles in general. It also can be used to understand the link between participation in both risky lifestyles and street crime. As in the commission of street crimes, edgework activities generally include a clear, serious threat to the participant's physical or mental well-being, and successfully conquering this threat is thrilling to participants. But participants also frequently claim a high level of expertise and control in their risky pursuits. The view that their activities are an exercise of skill, rather than risk-taking, encourages their continued practice, as well as the formation of supportive lifestyles.

For edgeworkers—and street criminals—their activities are not only thrilling, but also a source of satisfaction and pride. Routine risk-takers may also pursue perilous activities as a reaction to constraints they feel as part of their position in the power structure and exclusion from aspects of conventional social life. Lyng argues that the alienating nature of modern, industrialized society leads some people to participate in risky ventures because they offer the illusion of control and the opportunity to express a more "authentic" self. The modern world is full of uncertainty and dangers that generally are beyond our control, but participation in risk-taking behaviors—including street crime—may create a sense of greater control in such a threatening environment.

Of course, the need to express a "real self" outside of an alienating labor force does not push everyone into routine risk-taking. Many people experience self-actualization in their commitments to family, occupation, or religious beliefs, and others may gravitate to high-risk subcultures (e.g., biker groups) or work in high-risk occupations (e.g., police work, firefighting, and combat soldiering).

Focusing specifically on risky behaviors associated with criminal offending, Katz emphasizes the criminal experience, or the "seductive" or attractive components of crime, which can be "moving" and "thrilling" for some. Some people commit criminal offenses (or engage in risky lifestyles), not because of feelings of powerlessness or economic insecurity, but because they are excited by those behaviors. In this way, Katz places risk-associated criminal offending in the same realm as other risky ventures, which frequently include an emotional process that offers its participants distinctive rewards and sensations.

Representations and Reactions

Mass media accounts send messages about the typical characteristics and behaviors of offenders and victims. Criminals frequently are described in news and popular media as gripped by participation in risky lifestyles, which makes them unpredictable, uncontrollable, and compassionless. These portrayals—especially their emphasis on risk-taking behaviors of offenders—help separate offenders in the mind of the public from "the rest of us" and cast them as "other." In addition, media portrayals of victims who are members of vulnerable populations (who have fewer life chances and a greater likelihood of participation in risky lifestyles) frequently are negative and tend to attribute their disadvantaged status to individual flaws or mistakes, which is consistent with messages in American culture.

For example, women who violate traditional gender expectations by participating in risky behaviors (e.g., alcohol or drug use, stripping, prostitution, running away, promiscuity, dressing or acting provocatively, or staying out late) do not fit feminine ideals of innocence and submissiveness, and these victims frequently are discredited or even blamed for the crimes committed against them. Finally, references to risky lifestyles of victims and the absence of humanizing information (e.g., information about their families, friends, and goals) weaken the audience's ability or willingness to identify with the victims. This creates blindness to the victimization of some groups—as well as the crimes committed against them—and may increase the likelihood of victimization for already vulnerable segments of the population.

Julie B. Wiest
High Point University

See Also: Alcohol and Drug Use; Code of the Street; Drug Dealing; Gangs (Street); Homelessness; Prostitute/Streetwalker; Routine Activity Theory; Street Crime.

Further Readings
Anderson, Elijah. *Streetwise.* Chicago: University of Chicago Press, 1990.

Daday, Jerry K., Lisa M. Broidy, Cameron S. Crandall, and David P. Sklar. "Individual, Neighborhood, and Situational Factors Associated With Violent Victimization and Offending." *Criminal Justice Studies*, v.18/3 (2005).

Jacobs, Bruce A. and Richard Wright. "Stick-Up, Street Culture, and Offender Motivation." *Criminology*, v.37/1 (1999).

Katz, Jack. *Seductions of Crime: Moral and Sensual Attractions in Doing Evil.* New York: Basic Books, 1988.

Lyng, Stephen, ed. *Edgework: The Sociology of Risk-Taking.* New York: Routledge, 2005.

Road Rage

Road rage is a condition characterized by angry, aggressive, threatening, and potentially violent behavior exhibited by drivers of motor vehicles. Extreme cases of road rage have resulted in homicide. Road rage can emanate from a driver's angry and impulsive response to stressful road conditions caused by the real or perceived inconsiderate, careless, reckless, or aggressive behavior of others, although not all people who experience the occasional frustration associated with driving engage in road rage.

Retaliatory Behavior
Behaviors that have prompted some individuals to engage in road rage have included failure to use directional signals, abrupt lane changes, weaving in and out of traffic, cutting in front of others, passing on the shoulder of the road, failing to yield to others who have the right-of-way, disregarding a traffic signal, speeding, tailgating, and flashing one's lights; the inattentive, inconsiderate, deliberate, or antagonistic behavior of pedestrians or bicyclists; or any other inconsiderate, careless, or reckless driving actions.

Road rage can ensue when such driving behaviors incite others to respond angrily and irrationally with similar antagonizing, retaliatory, or otherwise aggressive driving that escalates and leads to verbal insults and threats, confrontational gestures, and/or physical threats and assaults. News reports abound describing incidents of road rage that have all too many times resulted in serious injury and even death whether attributable to motor vehicle collisions or criminal assaults.

Organizations such as the National Highway Traffic Safety Administration differentiate aggressive driving from road rage. While the former entails operating a motor vehicle in a manner that endangers or is likely to endanger another person or property, road rage, by contrast, constitutes an elevated degree of aggressiveness and violent behavior, to a degree that constitutes a criminal offense. Incidents of road rage have led to drivers brandishing and employing weapons including firearms, either while their motor vehicles were in operation, or when confronting others when their vehicles have come to a stop.

Road rage has led to motor vehicle accidents, collisions, and criminal assaults, many of which have resulted in bodily and serious bodily injury, and even death. In 2012, authorities addressing the implications of road rage have suggested that it has caused more than 3 million injuries, 27,000 deaths, and cost drivers over $150 billion. It has also been estimated that two-thirds of all fatalities which occur on U.S. roads are at least partly caused by road rage.

Traits and Characteristics
Road rage can be prompted by a continuum of actions—ranging from the unintentional, inadvertent, and carelessness of some drivers, to the deliberate, reckless, antagonistic, and aggressive behavior of others. Factors that can contribute to road rage may include (1) frustration and anger attributable to traffic delays and congestion; (2) running late

Road rage is an aggressive behavior by a driver of a motor vehicle, which may include deliberately driving in an unsafe manner. It is believed that traffic congestion could be a major cause of road rage.

for work, appointments, or other scheduled events; (3) personalizing another's inattentive, inconsiderate, careless, reckless, or aggressive driving; (4) competitiveness and a need to be first; (5) having a sense of anonymity within one's motor vehicle; and (6) physical or emotional stress.

Research suggests three principal factors bear upon road rage, namely demographics, character traits, and the situational settings. Demographically, male drivers between the ages of 18 to 34 are more likely to engage in aggressive driving and road rage than women and older men. When examining the character traits of drivers who engage in aggressive driving and road rage, research reveals that exposure to protracted stressful driving conditions, along

with being under constant pressure for time, are key contributors to aggressiveness and road rage.

Some psychologists suggest that road rage is an expression of a latent and underlying pathology that is exhibited by driver's aggressiveness, as in the form of tailgating, threatening gestures, and even worse, physical confrontation and assault. It has also been suggested that it is a form of "intermittent explosive behavior"; that it represents a form of retaliatory behavior to another driver's careless or reckless driving and thus countered by their own aggressiveness.

By contrast, other researchers suggest that road rage is not necessarily symptomatic of an underlying pathology; rather, it is due to heightened levels of stress, anxiety, and anger associated with congested roads, coupled with the psychological dynamics associated with being inside one's vehicle—suggesting that a driver's personality, mind-set, and disposition changes and consequently one makes decisions that they would not otherwise act upon. This has been illustrated by pointing to the behavior of someone waiting in a grocery store check-out line and having someone cut into line. Research indicates that individuals who have admittedly engaged in road rage would not necessarily respond aggressively to such a person; rather, they would politely point out that they were waiting in line.

Research also reveals that men who exhibit a macho personality and who purchase vehicles based on their size, speed, color, design, and enhanced performance, are more prone to engage in aggressive driving and road rage than those who purchase a vehicle based on safety and reliability. Lastly, it is the influence of the situational setting, not only in terms of road conditions and traffic congestion, but a sense of autonomy and anonymity that aggressive drivers seem to enjoy within their vehicles, especially those in vehicles with tinted windows.

Resources, Treatment, Prevention

As with many negative habits and behaviors, it is important that individuals who engage in aggressive driving and road rage acknowledge their behavior as a bona fide problem and that they can tap into many resources and treatments to overcome such dangerous driving. This may include but is not limited to developing stress, anger, and time management techniques; depersonalizing others' poor and aggressive driving behaviors;

developing coping techniques such as relaxation and deep breathing exercises; and changing one's belief system.

Recommendations by the Automobile Association of America for dealing with aggressive drivers and to avoid the potentially dangerous consequences of road rage include (1) avoid cutting drivers off and apologize if you do, (2) avoid tailgating and honking the horn, (3) avoid making inappropriate or offensive gestures, (4) steer clear of aggressive drivers, (5) avoid making eye contact, (6) seek help if you're being followed, by driving to a safe/crowded location or by dialing 911, (7) leave yourself enough time rather than trying to "make good time," (8) put yourself in the other driver's shoes, and (9) take a deep breath and remember escalating a situation will only make things worse.

Despite the inevitable frustration that all drivers experience on the road, whether due to the unintentional, inconsiderate, careless, reckless, or aggressive behavior of others, the key to maintaining one's safety and reducing stress is to avoid personalizing their behavior and allow them to continue on their way in the hope that they don't injure others or themselves.

Robert F. Vodde
Fairleigh Dickinson University

See Also: Alcohol- and Drug-Testing, On-Scene; Alcohol and Drug Use; Guns and Weapons; Motor Vehicle Theft; Patrol Cars; Urban Incivility.

Further Readings
Eberle, James. *Terror on the Highway—Rage on America's Roads.* Amherst, NY: Prometheus Books, 2006.

Garase, Maria L. *Road Rage.* El Paso, TX: LFB Scholarly Publishing, 2006.

James, Leon and Diane Nahl. *Road Rage and Aggressive Driving: Steering Clear of Highway Warfare.* Amherst, NY: Prometheus Books, 2000.

Taylor, Paul, Cary Funk, and Peyton Craighill. *Americans and Their Cars: Is the Romance on the Skids?* Washington, DC: Pew Research Center, 2006.

Walters, Carol H., Valmon J. Pezoldt, Katie N. Womack, Scott A. Cooner, and Beverly T. Kuhn. *Understanding Road Rage: Summary of First-Year Project Activities.* College Station, TX: Texas Transportation Institute, 2000.

Routine Activity Theory

Routine activity theory is a criminological theory of offending that proposes that crime occurs when motivated offenders converge with suitable targets without the protection of capable guardians. The chances of a crime occurring increase or decrease based on the routine activities of our everyday lives. These activities include our work habits, family lives, recreational experiences, and consumption practices.

Routine activity theory is an essential tool for scholars who research street crime in America because it allows researchers to better understand predatory victimization and crime prevention tactics. The routine activity approach is often referred to as a situational theory of crime. Lawrence E. Cohen and Marcus Felson first presented the routine activity theory to analyze the crime rate increases that occurred in America throughout the post–World War II era (1947–74). The public did not expect the crime rate increases, but rather had anticipated a period of increased peace and prosperity after the war. The authors suggested that changes in the labor market, such as female participation in the labor force and single-parent households, resulted in higher crime rates.

Cohen and Felson argued that changes in our daily activity patterns influenced crime based on the convergence of three elements. A likely, or motivated, offender is an individual who intends to commit a crime. A suitable, or attractive, target is something or someone presenting an opportunity to be victimized. If no other person is present to observe or prevent the crime, then there is an absence of capable guardianship. According to routine activity theory, these three elements of suitable target, motivated offender, and a lack of capable guardianship must all converge in space and time for a crime to occur. If one component of routine activity theory is missing, then crime is not likely to be committed.

Vantage Point on Street Crime

Most criminological theories focus on the factors that motivate individuals to participate in criminal activities. Routine activity theory, on the other hand, focuses on factors that make the opportunity to engage in crime more readily available or appealing. The theory dictates that an absence of guardianship, coupled with suitable targets, creates the opportune moment for a crime to occur. Varying rates of crime are seen as a function of changes in the number of potential victims, the number of possible offenders, and the absence of guardians capable enough to protect against the occurrence of crime.

As street crime is often defined as taking place in public spaces, its incidence can to some degree be predicted, monitored, and prevented by applying routine activity theory. For example, different types of street environments precipitate varying quantities of potential victims, as well as creating the conditions for different sized pools of possible offenders. Similarly, the guardian component of the population can prevent many types of street crime, making them more or less prevalent and more or less visible, depending on the variables of a given rural or urban infrastructure, neighborhood, or building.

Routine activity theory has been used to explain crime increases after World War II, geographic crime rate differences, sociodemographic differences in crime rates, and individual experiences with crime. Furthermore, the routine activities approach has helped explain crime-specific victimization rates, urban homicide rates, and police "hot spot" areas that produce a disproportionate number of calls to law enforcement officials. In sum, routine activity theory complements traditional criminological theories by explaining more than just the motivations of offenders.

Integrating Theories and Critiques

There is an assumption in routine activity theory that motivated offenders exist, but the theory does not explain the exact motivations of criminal offenders. Terance D. Miethe and Robert F. Meier acknowledged this limitation, and developed an integrated theory explaining both opportunity and offender motivations. Furthermore, the authors addressed prior criticisms of routine activity theory by suggesting that other conventional theories of crime ignored the conditional nature of the relationships between offenders, targets, and guardians. In other words, conventional theories concentrate more significantly on criminality, criminal behavior, and other triggers that motivate individuals to commit crime.

Another expansion of the routine activity approach has been an integrated feminist routine activities theory, developed initially to examine sexual assaults on college campuses throughout Canada. The results of that initial study strongly indicated that the peers of sexually abusive males had encouraged them to assault their girlfriends. This indication suggests that a relationship exists between an absence of guardianship and offender motivations. This integrated routine activity approach allows researchers to better understand the nature of certain relationships between motivated offenders, potential victims, and possible guardians.

Conclusion

The many elaborations and integrations of the routine activities perspective displays that it remains popular, and it has further demonstrated modest empirical support since its original conception. Theoretical integration has allowed scholars to examine beyond the basic motivations of offenders, and also analyze relationships between the offenders, victims, and possible lack of guardianship. The routine activity theory continues to be used by modern researchers to analyze homicide rates, urban crime rates, and even sexual assaults.

The future development of this approach through theoretical integration may allow scholars to one day better understand the relationships between street crime offenders and the victims of street crimes. If we are able to better understand the conditional relationships between offenders, targets, and guardians, then we may be able to implement situational crime prevention tactics in response that could dramatically decrease the likelihood of crimes occurring.

Christopher Mullins
Daniel Kavish
Southern Illinois University, Carbondale

See Also: Crime Prevention, Situational; Environmental Criminology; Hot Spots; Rape and Sexual Assault; Street Crime Defined; Urbanization; Women.

Further Readings

Andresen, Martin A., Paul J. Brantingham, and J. Bryan Kinney. *Classics in Environmental Criminology*. Boca Raton, FL: CRC Press, 2010.

Cohen, Lawrence E. and Marcus Felson. "Social Change and Crime Rate Trends: A Routine Activity Approach." *American Sociological Review*, v.44/4 (1979).

Miethe, Terance D. and Robert F. Meier. *Crime and Its Social Context*. New York: State University of New York Press, 1994.

S

San Francisco, California

Founded by the Spanish in 1776 and passed to Mexican rule in 1821, hispanic San Francisco was a tiny settlement called Yerba Buena (Good Grass) in the 1830s, which abutted a government presidio. In 1846, the United States seized the Mexican state of which it was a part, as spoils of the Mexican War. When gold was discovered in 1848, the city's population exploded. The "forty-niners" of lore and song came from all over the world, creating a combustible mix of diverse languages, ethnicities, and creeds.

The military, in charge of keeping the peace, was singularly unprepared to deal with law enforcement issues and was spread too thin to cover the many mining camps and prospector digs. In the absence of sufficient numbers of constituted legal agents, disorder, heavy drinking, crime, prostitution, and political violence became endemic. A supposedly legitimate political machine was established in San Francisco, but its purported corruption and links to Australian gangs led to said elected government being overthrown by self-appointed vigilantes with their own private army and a probusiness agenda. Curiously, in popular history accounts, the vigilantes of the 1850s emerged as heroes rather than as seditionists.

Gold Rush and Vigilante Days

The first committee of vigilance was constituted in 1851; its purported mission was to deal with the problems of burglary, murder, and arson. The city, entirely made up of wooden structures, had suffered several catastrophic fires. It was alleged that the Sydney Ducks, a gang of mostly Irish Australian ex-convicts, were the agents of a major fire that had swept the downtown area in 1849. While it was by no means clear that the fires were arson events, a moral crusade began, touted by newspapers and nativists (such as those in the Know Nothing political movement) and seized on the pretext of crime-fighting to persecute and expel as many Australians as possible. Many of the Ducks left the city to avoid persecution; some were compelled to take ships to other ports.

There is no doubt that many of these alleged gangsters were, in fact, involved in theft, intimidation, and other forms of crime. However, several innocents were almost hung due to cases of mistaken identity. At this time, nativism was rising as a political force in the United States in other cities as well.

In 1856 the vigilance committee was reconstituted. As in New Orleans and New York in the same period, a type of civic warfare broke out between factions, gangs, and private armies. San Francisco's case became among the most well known in popular history. Seizing arms from the national and state government, the vigilantes inaugurated a reign of terror against reputed criminals, the law enforcement community, elected Democrats, and anyone else who opposed them. This seditious activity was supported by some local newspapers and many contemporary historians, most of whom cited rampant corruption as a sufficient rationale for armed rebellion. However, shorn of the hyperbole of lionizing historians, it is apparent today that struggle involved seizing control of municipal government, as in 1851, from elected officeholders. The People's Party of the vigilantes mounted a coup, taking control from the Democratic administration and then, in time, merged with the Republican Party. While crime was a serious problem in the chaos following the Gold Rush, an overlying struggle was political. Similar scenarios played out in several other cities across the country. Mercantile interests were to prevail as popularly elected Democratic urban machines, including Tammany Hall in New York City, were dismantled or were brought under the control of the commercial class.

The Barbary Coast

Undeniably vice and crime were an ongoing problem in the area. Bars, bordellos, dance halls, "cow yards" (low-end bordellos), and gambling halls flourished in the permissive atmosphere of the "city by the bay" following the gold rush. Women from all over the world rushed in to exploit—and to be exploited by—the opportunity. The first to arrive were Chilean prostitutes and pimps. They were cruelly harassed by nativist American gangs such as the Hounds. Later, women and girls from Europe and the eastern regions of the United States began to flood into the area. Many had been prostitutes in their former haunts.

The influx of representatives of the vice industry, and patterns of heavy drinking and gambling, combined to produce an explosive combination. Crimes of violence, frequently over the favors of a dance hall girl or prostitute, were common. Pimps victimized their charges and became involved in robbing or defrauding customers. Some unlucky "johns," or prostitution customers, were drugged or knocked out and shanghaied, that is, kidnapped and made to work as sailors on undermanned ships leaving port. The unfortunate victim woke up many miles from shore and found himself involuntarily impressed into maritime servitude. Street criminals preyed on drunks and drugged johns as they staggered from bar to bar. Frequently, drunk customers were involved in fights over gambling debts, politics, or mining claims. These quarrels often ended with an assault or worse. Thefts from businesses

and common burglary were common. Insane, drunk, diseased, and homeless men, their luck in the gold fields nonexistent or played out, roamed the streets, speaking gibberish into their unwashed beards. They were frequently victims of criminals, or conversely, turned to crime to survive in a highly inflationary environment.

The situation of the common prostitute was pitiable. Disease flourished; the women were frequently poorly fed and were generally only afforded a single day off per week. Girls as young as 12 were auctioned off to special customers, then later returned to the brothel for a career of sexual servitude. Such events were common in the neighborhoods of Chinatown, where Chinese "crib girls" predominated, and in the Barbary Coast and Tenderloin districts.

Protection money paid to numerous politicians, judges, and law enforcement officials allowed this to persist. There was also little public outcry, except from clergy, against this major tourist attraction and local industry. A major disruption was the San Francisco earthquake and fire of 1906. The vice districts were destroyed almost uniformly; Chinatown never recovered as a vice center. Most of the Barbary Coast and Tenderloin were rebuilt. The overall pattern of protected or tolerated vice continued from approximately 1849 to 1917, when the city, pushed by a media-engendered moral crusade, finally closed down much of the various vice districts. However, one of the historical concentrations of vice, the Tenderloin area, remains a nucleus of violent crime, vice, and victimization to the present day.

The Beat and Hippie Eras

In the late 1940s, a small group of intellectuals began to gather in San Francisco's North Beach neighborhood, much as was happening in New York City's Greenwich Village. San Francisco's reputation for tolerance and diversity attracted those interested in living in or around this relatively small city with its lively cultural and intellectual life. In the late 1950s and early 1960s, coffeehouses, jazz clubs, inexpensive living conditions, cheap food, a mild climate, and unconventional bookstores attracted the so-called Beats to the North Beach area in particular.

Cannabis and various hallucinogens were popular among this group as they sought to find meaning outside the normal parameters of 1950s Eisenhower America. Beats were eventually driven from North

Beach by tourism and the commercialization of the area. By the mid-1960s the scene had shifted to the Haight-Asbury neighborhood.

This area, formerly working class, became a vibrant and exciting youth mecca. Drugs, including cannabis and various hallucinogens, were widely available. The disaffected youth of America, would-be "hippies," flocked into the small district in the summer of 1967, creating numerous problems. Young people with no accommodations were sleeping on the streets, panhandling, and begging for "Spare change, man." Sadly, predatory criminals and pimps entrapped some of these young people into a life of hard drug use and degrading sex work. Hard drugs and hallucinogens of suspect provenance created breakdowns and contributed to an atmosphere of chaos and disorder. The Summer of Love was over; many who had been spared the worst aspects of the decline of the area returned home, went to college, or moved to rural communes.

Street Crime Today

The city today retains a sizeable countercultural atmosphere and contingent, but it is no longer centered in the Haight, which remains a high-crime corridor with issues involving drunken violence from the homeless, drug sales, theft from cars, and pickpocketing. Despite the crime, it remains a tourist destination, and the streets are lined with boutiques and bars. In a return to its roots as a major player in the sex industry, San Francisco became nationally prominent as the locale where topless dancing originated in the early 1960s. Centered on the northern edge of Chinatown, the Condor Club gained international fame in this regard. Other clubs of the same ilk sprang up, along with adult

The hippie subculture was originally a youth movement that arose in the United States during the mid-1960s. Hippie Hill, shown here in 2010, is a small hill at the eastern end of Golden Gate Park in San Francisco, that is still a popular spot for concerts and smoking marijuana. Hippies often gathered there for that purpose during the 1967 legendary Summer of Love.

bookstores, peep shows, adult cinema, and other sexually explicit exhibitions and industries. The Tenderloin, to the west and south, also became a sex district and remains so to this day.

The Tenderloin remains the city's main crime neighborhood—a distinction that the general area has held since the city's beginning. Street crimes of every nature occur there with predictable regularity. Frequently unwary and intoxicated and unwary tourists and conventioneers stumble into the area looking for sexually oriented entertainment, or sex itself, and find themselves victimized by predatory criminals. It is also the nucleus of thefts from autos, public intoxication, street-level drug crimes, assaults, larceny with contact (pickpocketing, purse snatching) and other public order offenses.

This historic "skid row," although targeted by police actions such as Operation Matrix, and located near the upscale tourist and convention district, remains true to its rough and ready roots in the criminal past of the city. North Beach and Chinatown, immediately to the north of this area, is also a tourist destination and remains a secondary target for crimes which impact tourists; that is, thefts from cars, pickpocketing and sex industry-related crimes. The Haight, like the Tenderloin, has a large population of homeless and street people. Many of them live in and around Golden Gate Park and frequently appear drunk and disorderly in the Haight Street shopping and entertainment area. Street drug use and gang-related crime is increasing in this area and especially in the Mission District.

Although the San Francisco Police Department has a reputation for tolerating minor street crimes and minor incidents involving intoxicated homeless people, they have had to deal with increasing gang populations in recent years.

Asian gangs, some of which were enforcement arms of Asian family combines, have been noted in San Francisco since the 1800s. Often these operate as simple street-level shakedowns, but at other times may represent attempts by multinational organizations to gain or dominate a particular market or industry within the Asian American commercial community. Asian American street-level violence and gang activity is generally confined to businesses and areas that are Asian-owned. However, on rare occasions, tourists have been collateral casualties in shootings stemming from Asian American gang

wars. African American and Hispanic gangs have gained a foothold in the Bay Area as well.

Street crime in middle-class residential zones is almost nonexistent outside of those previously mentioned areas. Much lower crime rates are found in western areas of the city, which are increasingly Asian American and residential. Police in San Francisco are frequently called upon to deal with crimes against tourists, some of which seem to be brought on by tourists using poor judgment: leaving valuables in parked cars, stopping and conversing with individuals in "sex districts" while looking for sexual entertainment or opportunities, or not guarding wallets, cameras, or purses diligently. During the 1960s, the police had a reputation for being hard on labor, youth, minorities, and dissent but in succeeding decades their public posture and professionalism has much improved.

Violent crime (e.g., homicide, rape, robbery, aggravated assault) dropped almost 50 percent between 1995 and 2011, according to Uniform Crime Reports (UCR) data from the Federal Bureau of Investigation (FBI). Nonviolent street crime (e.g., larceny, arson, auto theft, burglary) was down about 40 percent in the same period. Still, street crime remains a serious problem in particular areas of the city.

Operation Matrix

Elected in 1991, San Francisco Mayor Frank Jordan launched Operation Matrix to attack the city's street crime epidemic, which was seen as stemming in large part from homelessness, public drunkenness, and related "nuisance crimes." At that time, the city had an estimated homeless population of 12,000. Coupled with an abundant base of shelters and subsidized housing, the Operation Matrix block by block crackdown on street crimes—as many as 14,000 quality-of-life summonses were issued in 1997—helped the city trim the amount of serious crimes reported by as much as 25 percent within a few years.

Jordan's successor as mayor, Willie Brown, however, opposed Operation Matrix, in particular against aspects that were seen by many voters as heavy-handed or wasteful. Much of the program was subsequently dismantled. The city's enforcement of "victimless" crimes began to drop off—ironically, this occurred just as California's state-wide Three Strikes law, aimed at implementing mandatory incarceration for repeat offenders, took effect. The city's stance was in stark contrast to statewide attitudes at the time.

Frederick Hawley
Western Carolina University

See Also: Asian Gangs; Gangs (Street); Homelessness; Prostitution, Houses of; Skid Row.

Further Readings
Asbury, Herbert. *The Barbary Coast*. New York: Knopf, 1933.

Brown, Richard M. *Strain of Violence: Historical Studies of American Violence and Vigilantism.* New York: Oxford University Press, 1977.

Courtwright, David T. *Violent Land: Single Men and Social Disorder From the Frontier to the Inner City.* Cambridge, MA: Harvard University Press, 1998.

Joe, Karen. "The New Criminal Conspiracy? Asian Gangs and Organized Crime in San Francisco." *Journal of Research in Crime and Delinquency*, v.31/4 (1994).

Lane, Roger. *Murder in America: A History.* Columbus: Ohio State University Press, 1997.

Richards, Leonard. *The California Gold Rush and the Coming of the Civil War.* New York: Knopf, 2007.

San Francisco Police Department CompStat. "CompStat Reports." http://www.sf-police.org/index.aspx?page=3255 (Accessed July 2012).

Waldorf, D. "When the Crips Invaded San Francisco: Gang Migration." *Gang Journal*, v.1/4 (1993).

Seattle Crime Places Study

While some criminologists in the 1800s were interested in the relationship between crime and places (e.g., the statistician Adolphe Quetelet and the social researcher Andre-Michel Guerry), it was not a focal point of the discipline. Until the latter part of the 20th century, criminologists were predominantly concerned with the examination of individual explanations for criminality and community crime rates. This focus changed after theoretical expansions in the field of criminology including Lawrence Cohen and Marcus Felson's 1979 Routine Activity theory. The routine activities perspective allowed criminologists to shift their focus from traditional modes of crime inquiry and examine the situations in which crimes occur. Specifically, many criminologists were now examining specific locations within the larger context of a community.

The Seattle Crime Places study is a 14-year study of crime within specific street segments in the city of Seattle that was conducted by David Weisburd and colleagues. This study found that crime reduction efforts focused on a small but active area ("hot spot") of criminal activity can effectively reduce crime there and in nearby areas as well. This entry devotes discussion to the prior research on crime locales, as well as a review of literature on street crimes in Seattle.

Research on Crime Locales
Prior to Cohen and Felson's introduction of Routine Activity theory in 1979, in which attention was focused on the locations where crime can occur, previous researchers had already begun to examine the environments where crime occurred. One of the earliest empirical examinations into crime concentrations in Seattle was conducted by Calvin Schmid in 1960. Schmid examined the crimes of homicide, rape, robbery, and burglary in two census tract zones in Seattle over a two-year period. He found that zones high in crime remained high during this period while those zones low in crime remained low during the time span. Throughout the 1970s to the 1990s, subsequent researchers examined street segments, addresses, or street blocks in various cities in the United States (e.g., Minneapolis, Philadelphia, Jersey City, Bronx, Baltimore, Boston) and found that crime is clustered in certain pockets, or hot spots, in a given city. The overwhelming finding that crime was concentrated in small sections of cities caused researcher Lawrence Sherman in 1995 to ask, "Why aren't we thinking more about wheredunit, rather than just whodunit?"

Seattle Crime Places Study Findings
While research has been available on where crime occurs in various cities, much of the early research did not examine the stability of crime in the concentrated crime areas. In fact, most of the previous research on the topic was based on cross-sectional data. Hence, researchers did not have a firm grasp on whether high or low crime rates were stable in these areas of a city over a longer period of time.

The Seattle Crime Places study by David Weisburd and colleagues in 2004 sought to overcome the flaws in the previous research. This was the first study to examine crime trends in microcrime places over this length of time, using a group-based statistical technique drawn from developmental criminology called trajectory analysis, which is able to show distinctive trends in the development of crime at places over time. The researchers utilized police incident report data to pinpoint crime locations as well as crime types.

Based on the incident report data, they were able to categorize crimes as follows: (1) property crime, (2) disorder, drugs, prostitution, (3) person crimes (homicide, assault, rape, robbery, kidnapping), (4) other nontraffic crime-related events (e.g., weapon offenses, warrants, domestic disputes), (5) traffic-related (hit and run, drunk driving, accidents with injuries), and (6) unknown (accounting for 1 percent of crime total). In their 14-year longitudinal study of the distribution of crime in street segments in Seattle, they found that crime is concentrated in specific street segments and that crime rates in these areas are stable ove time. Specifically, the results showed that 50 percent of crime was committed in approximately 4.5 percent of Seattle street segments.

This work supports the call for greater tailoring of police efforts coupled with creativity of approach and expansion of police practices in combating crime; it has been widely cited as a framework for evidence-based policing. Subsequent research by Weisburd and colleagues in 2009 utilizing Seattle Crime Places Study data examined the concentration of juvenile crime in Seattle and found that crime for juveniles is also geographically concentrated. Elizabeth Groff and colleagues in 2010 extended the study period two more years for a 16-year-longitudinal study; they found street-to-street variability in concentration of crime over time. This research suggests that strategies by law enforcement and city agencies need to focus on very small areas, such as a problem block.

Conclusion

The emerging literature on the concentration of crime in specific areas of cities has contributed to crime prevention policies such as targeting hardening and police patrol. For example, if police can better identify specific areas in a city that are crime prone, they can concentrate their patrol efforts more heavily in these specific areas. In Seattle specifically, the identification of hot spots of crime has emerged (e.g., the Pike/Pine/Belltown corridor), and the police, city council, business owners, and community members have utilized the Seattle Crime Places Study and the evidence-based policing approach to inform public safety decisions and to develop strategies to focus on high-crime places and street-to-street heterogeneity in crime trends.

Elaine Gunnison
Jacqueline B. Helfgott
Seattle University

See Also: Crime Mapping; Crime Patterns; Hot Spots; Routine Activity Theory; Urbanization.

Further Readings

City of Seattle, Office of the City Auditor. "Addressing Crime and Disorder in Seattle's 'Hot Spots': What Works." March 29, 2011. http://www.seattle.gov/audit/docs/2011Mar29_HotSpotsWhatWorks.pdf (Accessed April 2012).

Groff, Elizabeth R., David Weisburd, and Sue-Ming Yang. "Is it Important to Examine Crime Trends at a Local 'Micro' Level?: A Longitudinal Analysis of Street to Street Variability in Crime Trajectories." *Journal of Quantitative Criminology*, v.26/1 (2010).

Weisburd, David, Nancy A. Morris, and Elizabeth R. Groff. "Hotspots of Juvenile Crime: A Longitudinal Study of Arrest Incidents at Street Segments in Seattle, Washington." *Journal of Quantitative Criminology*, v.25/1 (2009).

Weisburd, David, Shawn Bushway, Cynthia Lum, and Sue-Ming Yang. "Trajectories of Crime at Places: A Longitudinal Study of Street Segments in the City of Seattle." *Criminology*, v.42/2 (2004).

Security, Private

Many urban neighborhoods have large and very visible populations of the homeless, substance abusers, persons with mental illness, unruly groups of adolescents, and aggressive panhandlers. While police historically managed these individuals, this task is increasingly becoming the responsibility of private security officers. This is an emerging trend in all developed nations, as security officers play a larger role in monitoring our behaviors on closed-circuit television (CCTV), engage in crime prevention activities, respond to offenses, investigate crimes, and apprehend suspects. Furthermore, their roles are becoming more police-like, and in many jurisdictions they are armed and wear uniforms that make them almost indistinguishable from police officers. While these private security officers augment the police, some are critical of this changing role and point out that these officials are often hired with less scrutiny, receive little training, and only act in the interests of the organizations that pay their salaries.

Scope and Status

Private security has played an increasing role in crime control activities in the past three decades. The Bureau of Labor Statistics, for example, reported that there were 1,066,600 security guards, private detectives and gaming investigators employed throughout the U.S. in 2011 and only 850,380 police officers. Some researchers believe that the actual number of these officers is higher and that there are two of these officials for every police officer. These officers are hired by individuals, community associations, nonprofit organizations (such as colleges and hospitals), as well as small businesses and large corporations. Given the large number of security officers, types of employers, and the fact that their actions are regulated by state and local legislation, their authority, accountability, and job tasks vary considerably.

Private security officers most often deal with the prevention of or intervention in crimes against property, burglary and larceny, minor traffic infractions, a range of juvenile offenses, and some forms of cybercrime or identity theft, and also frequently serve as deterrents to more serious crimes such as rape and assault. Depending on their duties and patrol areas, they often come into proximity of such potential street crimes as drug trafficking, prostitution, illegal gambling, and a variety of "quality of life" crimes.

Regardless of their roles or responsibilities, the one consistent factor in the private security industry is that these officers are paid to act in the interests of their employers, such as creating a more favorable climate for business. Consequently, the individuals who employ security officers can influence how high-visibility populations and minor street crimes in some communities are managed. Their

priorities, or the methods that these officers use, however, might not always be valued by the public.

Contrasts with Public Forces

As they are responsible for paying security officer salaries, organizations are apt to deploy these employees based on the actual threat of crime, rather than other considerations. Rick Ruddell, Matthew Thomas, and Ryan Patten found that the number of security officers employed increased in urban areas with the highest levels of crime, but this was not the case for deploying police officers. This is because government officials must include economic and political considerations in their decisions to hire and deploy officers. Police chiefs, for example, may be under pressure to increase patrols in neighborhoods where crime is rare, but the residents are very vocal.

In the past, many were critical of the competence of security officers. There was a basis in reality to that observation, and in many jurisdictions a person can become a security officer with a week or two of training. One hazard of hiring less skilled or less trained individuals is that these officers often interact with high-risk individuals and this can lead to escalating rather than preventing problems. In addition, security officers often undergo less rigorous background investigations and some would not be hired by law enforcement organizations. As a result, a growing number of organizations are recruiting security officers with law enforcement or military backgrounds. In many jurisdictions, for instance, off-duty police officers work in security-related jobs. Other organizations hire retired law enforcement or military personnel. While it is possible to save money by hiring less qualified officers, employing skilled and knowledgeable individuals results in fewer problems and less exposure to litigation for the organization.

Conclusion

Altogether, there are a growing number of private security officers who are responding to urban disorder, incivility, and crime, and their roles on the streets augment the activities of the police, especially in the largest urban areas. Their presence is an important aspect of crime control, as they free up the police to engage in more critical activities. Although private security officers have not always been highly regarded, there is acknowledgment that they will play a more important role in the future as the boundaries between public and private policing become less distinct and cash-strapped governments cut back on policing expenditures.

Rick Ruddell
University of Regina

See Also: Bar Personnel; Closed-Circuit Television; Community Policing; Neighborhood Watch; Urban Incivility.

Further Readings
Beckett, Katherine and Steve Herbert. "Dealing with Disorder: Social Control in the Post-Industrial City." *Theoretical Criminology*, v.12/1 (2008).

Bureau of Labor Statistics. Occupational Employment Statistics, 2011" (2012). http://data.bls.gov/oes (Accessed October 2012).

Fritsch, Eric J., John Liederbach, and Robert W. Taylor. *Police Patrol Allocation and Deployment*. Upper Saddle River, NJ: Pearson, 2009.

Ruddell, Rick, Matthew O. Thomas, and Ryan Patten. "Examining the Roles of the Police and Private Security Officers in Urban Social Control." *International Journal of Police Science and Management*, v.13/1 (2011).

Serial Killers, Spree Killers, and Mass Murderers

Most murders in the United States involve one victim and one killer, and in more than half of all of the homicides, there was a known relationship between the victim and the offender. These relationships included family members, friends, acquaintances, and neighbors. Other instances involve multiple victims whether or not known to the offender. These types of homicides can fall into descriptive categories, such as mass murder, spree killings, or serial murder.

Definitions and Differences
Mass murders are typically defined as four or more killings by the same perpetrator or participants in the same perpetrator group without a cooling-off period of time between the murders, but other definitions exist. Mass murder may include killings committed by terrorists, government agents (including members of armed forces operating unlawfully), and individuals. Well-known murders include the 1929 St. Valentine's Day Massacre in Chicago, when outside gangsters operating at the behest of Al Capone murdered rival gang members. Dressed like uniformed Chicago police officers and detectives, the killers, believed to be connected to Detroit's Purple Gang, lined up members of the Bugs Moran or North Side gang, and riddled their bodies with rounds fired from Thompson submachine guns.

In contrast, spree killings involve two or more locations within a short period of time. Like mass murders, there is no cooling-off period of time between the killings. An example of a spree killing is the Virginia Tech massacre in 2007 in Blacksburg, Virginia, when Seung-Hui Cho killed 32 individuals moving from one location to another on the campus over a period of less than three hours.

One accepted definition of serial murder is two or more murders that are separate events, occurring at different times by the same offender. At a symposium sponsored by the National Center for the Analysis of Violent Crime, located at the Federal Bureau of Investigation (FBI) Academy at Quantico, Virginia, a group of researchers, academics, police investigators, and FBI special agents met to discuss serial and related murders. It was agreed by the group that most relevant killings would be best placed in two categories: mass or serial murders. It was the view of these professionals that the classification of spree murders was difficult to capture precisely, and in any event, unnecessary for the efforts of law enforcement and medical practitioners as well as academics. Thus, the Virginia Tech massacre, which could quite possibly be categorized as both a mass murder and a spree killing, would be classified only as a mass murder.

The discussion that follows relates to those mass murderers, serial killers, and individuals involved in spree killings that are most closely aligned with street crime. Mass murders that occur in the context of terrorist activities, such as the 1963 16th Street Baptist Church bombing in Birmingham, Alabama, that killed four young African American girls, and the 1995 Oklahoma City Bombing, in which 168 lives were taken, will not be discussed. Similarly, mass murders and spree killings that take place in the context of cult activities, war crimes, crimes against humanity, or genocide are excluded.

Familicide, such as the case of James Rupert, who in 1975 killed 11 of his family members (the Easter Sunday Massacre), and so-called angels of death, who intentionally kill hospital patients with various motivations, are also not subject to this discussion.

The focus, to the extent possible, will be on those relevant killings that take place on or near city, suburban, or rural thoroughfares; thus, placing the offenses as close as possible within the context of street crime. This approach is necessary because there is no precise way to label any of these forms of homicides as street crimes per se. Indeed, serial killers and mass murderers, just like other criminals, operate under different motivations, mental conditions, and personality disorders that may have little or nothing to do with the locus operandi, the location where the crime is committed.

For example, a serial killer could take the life of one victim at location X (on the street) and another victim at location Y (in a private residence). There could be several different reasons for the two different locations, none of which necessarily bear any relationship to the offender being a "street criminal." Reasons for the differences between the locations of the crimes could include victimology (the relationships and interactions between the victims and the offender), opportunity, or an evolution of the modus operandi (M.O.) by the offender. Even when considering killings that occur on the street, definitional problems arise. For example, the question could be raised as to whether a particular mass murder constituted a street crime when the killings were actually racially or politically motivated.

It is equally important to delineate what is included in discussions relating to mass, spree, and serial killings. While there is a clear legal distinction between homicide and murder, most homicides that occur within the context of mass, spree, and serial killings should be discussed. A simple legal definition of homicide is the killing of one human being by another. Homicides can be lawful or unlawful. Lawful homicides are usually classified as justifiable or excusable. Unlawful homicides, depending on the jurisdiction, are generally classified either as manslaughter or murder. Murder often has different degrees depending upon the specific intent of the offender, the circumstances surrounding the killing, and the jurisdiction within which the homicide takes place. Thus, all murders are homicides, but not all homicides are necessarily murders.

A serial "killer" is a much more accurate description of an offender than a mass "murderer." A person who kills several people during one incident could be justified, excused, legally insane, or reckless. None of those circumstances would legally constitute the crime of murder. For purposes of this discussion, however, all unlawful homicides, including instances in which the actor is legally insane or operating under some form of diminished responsibility that might constitute "manslaughter," will be considered. Hence, the term *mass murderer* may be used, even when the killing cannot legally be classified as murder.

High Visibility Cases

Mass murders and spree killings are often associated with workplace and school violence. For those killings occurring in the workplace, profiles of the offenders are often nondescript other than being male and often veteran employees. Termination, reduction of benefits, and layoffs are frequent contributing factors. But grudges that are developed over the years also account for those incidents that emerge into deadly confrontations.

The Edmond Post Office Massacre, as it has been called, was one of the largest mass murders in the United States; in it, 14 postal workers were killed by a letter carrier in 1986. Over the next 20 years, there were several other incidents involving postal workers that could be classified as mass murder or spree killings. In spite of the fact that empirical research has shown that the levels of workplace violence are actually less associated with the U.S. Postal Service than in other types of employment, the term *going postal* has become associated with violent killings perpetrated by employees in the workplace.

Shootings and massacres on high school and college campuses and streets have received a lot of attention in recent years. In 1966, Charles Joseph Whitman, a former marine, shot and killed 16 people during a time period of just over 90 minutes from the top of a tower located on the campus of the University of Texas at Austin. The 1999 Columbine High School massacre, where 12 students and one teacher were killed, is often in the forefront of discussions related to this type of violent crime.

Gang-Related Cases

One category of street crime that is very closely associated with spree killings and mass murders involves gang violence and drive-by shootings.

Murders committed by drug dealers on America's streets often involve multiple suspects and multiple victims. Even if each offender kills only one victim during the incident, it could still be classified as a mass murder (dependent upon which definition is used) if four or more victims are killed collectively by members of the gang. From a legal perspective, this rationale would hold true if the killers were acting pursuant to a single common purpose, as members of a criminal enterprise, or were active participants in the crime (in some jurisdictions called principals in the first and second degree).

Gang activities of this nature are often associated with urban areas, but it is well documented that this is no longer the case. Gang related drive-by shootings now take place in suburban and rural areas in the United States, but the prevalence of such occurrences remain in urban areas. In 2010, for example, a mass shooting left one dead, and a short time later, three others were also killed when an argument over a missing piece of jewelry led to the shooting and killing of a young man on the streets of southeast Washington, D.C. The killers came back a few days later, looking for friends associated with the initial victim, and continued their killing rampage. Officers of the Metropolitan Police of the District of Columbia were quickly on the scene, gave chase, and eventually captured several of the perpetrators.

Gang-related killings are also taking on a new form of abduction-murder on the streets of American cities, which depending upon the circumstances, could constitute a form of serial murder. Mostly surrounding narcotics, the victims are abducted off street corners, transported to other locations, and executed. Police believe that the victims typically owe money to drug dealers or were witnesses to narcotics violations or related violent crimes including murder.

Regardless of the nonlegal classification attributed to the succession of these types of crimes by one or more perpetrators, these are still multiple murders occurring on the street and worthy of the same attention from the police and the public as any other so-called mass, spree, or serial killings.

Prostitutes and Mass Killings

Serial murders with prostitutes both as victims and offenders are by no means uncommon. A 2002 study by criminologist Jonathan Dudek indicated that many offenders who commit a single act of killing a prostitute do so as a result of a street dispute over payment for sex services, during the commission of robbing the prostitute, or as a result of a narcotics rip-off. In contrast, offenders who killed more than one prostitute were typically more sexually motivated.

Male prostitutes who are transvestites or who are transgendered can become more violent toward their male customers, known on the street as "johns." Sometimes violence erupts and turns to homicide after the "trick" (often used to refer to the act of sex with a prostitute) when the customer learns that he was having sex unwittingly with a man. In 1986 in Philadelphia, two transvestite prostitutes were brutally murdered. Their legs were cut off, and their bodies were dumped at a secondary crime scene and set on fire. Although no one has been convicted of the murders, detectives believe that the two men were murdered after the johns, believed to be members of an outlaw motorcycle gang, learned the prostitutes were indeed men.

The violence can go either way. At other times, male prostitutes, just like their female counterparts, rob or attempt to rob the unsuspecting johns. In late 2010, Philadelphia police arrested a transgendered prostitute and charged him with murder. The prostitute, who may have been a serial killer, apparently entered the victim's hotel room as a guest, and thereafter strangled, killed, and robbed the victim.

Conclusion

Understanding the mind or motivation of the killers, to the extent possible, is often useful as an investigative technique in an effort to identify the offender or link the killing to other crimes. This is true because there typically is no known relationship between the offender and the victim. But this is by no means an easy undertaking for a number of reasons. There may be multiple offenders each with different motivations, and there may be more than one motivation by an individual offender.

In the United States, the investigation of mass murders and serials killers, like virtually all other homicides, rests primarily with the jurisdiction of local law enforcement. Police departments in major cities such as New York, Los Angeles, Chicago, and Detroit need little help, if any, from outside agencies. For police agencies who need additional resources, the FBI has several dedicated units that provide training, research, and consultation to assist in the successful investigation of mass murderers and serial killers. The federal Bureau of Alcohol, Tobacco, Firearms and Explosives (ATF) is also available to provide expert assistance to other law enforcement agencies in the area of firearms analysis and tracing.

John R. Cencich
California University of Pennsylvania

See Also: Child Molesters; Crime Patterns; Hate Crime; Kidnapping; Mental Illness; Murder/Homicide; Police Detectives; Prostitute/Streetwalker; Rape and Sexual Assault; Sex Crimes; Stalking.

Further Readings

Block, Carolyn Rebecca and Richard Block. "Street Gang Crime in Chicago." Washington, DC: U.S. Department of Justice, National Institute of Justice, 1993.

Davis, Roger H. "Cruising for Trouble: Gang-Related Drive-By Shootings." *FBI Law Enforcement Bulletin*, v.64/1 (1995).

Dudek, Jonathan A. *When Silenced Voices Speak: An Exploratory Study of Prostitute Homicide.* Philadelphia: College of Nursing and Health Professions, 2002.

Hazelwood, Roy and Stephen G. Michaud. *Dark Dreams: Sexual Violence, Homicide, and the Criminal Mind.* New York: St. Martin's Press, 2001.

Holmes, Ronald M. and Stephen T. Holmes. *Serial Murder.* 2nd ed. Thousand Oaks, CA: Sage, 1998.

Jacobs, Bruce. "A Typology of Street Criminal Retaliation." *Journal of Research in Crime and Delinquency*, v.41/3 (2004).

Morton, Robert J. and Mark A. Hilts, eds. "Serial Murder: Multidisciplinary Perspectives for Investigators." Washington, DC: Federal Bureau of Investigation, National Center for the Analysis of Violent Crime, 2008.

Sex Crimes

There are many different types of sexual street crimes. Public exhibitionism is intentional and deliberate indecent exposure in a public location. Voyeurism is the act of spying on an individual engaged in intimate acts such as undressing, bathing, or having sex. Voyeurs are sometimes referred to as Peeping Toms. Sexual assault involves the use of threats, coercion, or other violent means to force an individual to participate in sexual acts, including kissing, fondling, sexual touching, and rape. Rape is a form of sexual assault in which sexual intercourse occurs.

Prostitution is the exchange of sex for money, drugs, or other payment. Survival sex is a form of prostitution in which sexual acts are exchanged for material items or for personal protection. Sex trafficking is the use of force, coercion, or fraud in order to sexually exploit a person. This entry summarizes several different types of sexual street violence, many of which are discussed in greater detail in this volume.

Public Exhibitionism

There are many types of public exhibitionism, including engaging in overt sexual behaviors (including sexual intercourse and masturbation) in a public place, and flashing. Flashing is the exposure of an individual's genitals to another person. The unwillingness of the victim or target to view the act is a key consideration in defining flashing. It is rare for the exhibitionist to desire actual physical contact with the victim. Flashing has a high rate of recidivism, and has been known to be a "gateway" offense into more violent sexual crimes.

Exhibitionism is also considered a psychological disorder, and in the mental health field, two types of exhibitionists are considered. The first type tends to be inhibited, anxious, and feel guilt rather than pleasure while flashing. In direct contrast, the second type of offender is more likely to have psychological issues and experiences sexual arousal while exposing himself or herself. It is this latter type of exhibitionist who is more likely to progress to more serious sexual offenses.

Voyeurism

Voyeurism is observing a person in a private act, without the consent of the observed person, for sexual purposes. It is considered a criminal offense due to the violation of the victim's right to privacy. In some instances, voyeurism is considered a sex crime, although this classification varies from state to state. Voyeurs, also referred to as Peeping Toms, are primarily male and their victims are most often minors or women. In 2004, the United States enacted the

Video Voyeurism Prevention Act, outlawing video voyeurism. Under this act, it is illegal for a person to "capture an image of a private area of an individual without their consent, and knowingly does so under circumstances in which the individual has a reasonable expectation of privacy."

Prostitution

Prostitution is perhaps the most common sexual street crime. Some individuals engage in prostitution voluntarily and prefer the term *sex worker.* Others are controlled by pimps. Still others are trafficked by large and small criminal organizations and forced into prostitution. Finally, some individuals engage in "survival sex," trading sexual acts for food, shelter, or other necessities. The proportion of sex workers within each subtype is unknown. The vast majority of sex workers are female, though male sex workers do exist. Additionally, a disproportionate number of sex workers are transgender. The role of the male in prostitution is most commonly relegated to "john" or "pimp." Johns, or "dates," are those who patronize individuals engaged in prostitution. Pimps are men who act as agents for prostitutes and live off of the money the prostitutes earn by exchanging sex. Both being a pimp or a john is illegal.

Prostitution occurs in a number of milieus. These include brothels, massage parlors, crack houses, some strip clubs, and on the street. All forms of prostitution are illegal, with the exception of brothel prostitution, which is legal in some rural counties in Nevada. Those engaged in street-level prostitution experience high levels of crimes committed against their person. They are subject to high incidences of physical violence, rape/gang rape, robbery, and threats of violence at the hands of their dates, as well as physical and sexual assault from their pimps in order to control them.

Street-level prostitutes are at greater risk of physical and sexual assault at the hands of dates, pimps, and law enforcement officers than those engaged in indoor prostitution. The likelihood that a street-level prostitute will experience physical or sexual violence is increased by engaging in substance abuse, by engaging in sexual transactions with young strangers, and by traveling with a date to an unfamiliar place. In addition, female street-level prostitutes have a higher risk of becoming homicide victims than women who are not engaged in prostitution and, of those serial homicides that

have been solved, prostitutes compose a significant proportion of those victimized by serial killers.

Violence against sex workers is often not reported, as street-level sex workers often perceive that law enforcement believes that being raped or beaten is a consequence of engaging in prostitution, and therefore not a reportable offense. There is also a disincentive for sex workers to report sexual victimization because it occurred during an illegal activity for which the victim could potentially be arrested.

There have been some legislative attempts to make it easier for individuals who engage in prostitution and have been sexually assaulted to report and prosecute their offenders. Rape shield laws were enacted at the state and federal levels in the 1970s. These laws sought to limit the instances in which attorneys for those accused of rape could introduce the sexual histories of alleged rape victims. However, several states have exceptions and loopholes to rape shield laws that allow for evidence that a rape victim has engaged in prostitution to be introduced—regardless of whether or not it pertains to the case at hand. This may prevent rape victims who have been engaged in prostitution from reporting being sexually assaulted.

Legalization of prostitution is a divisive issue. There are those who believe that there is no such thing as voluntary sex work and that all prostitution is sexual violence against women. Others believe that legalizing sex work would allow for sex workers to organize and unionize, which may reduce the amount of sexual and physical violence that those engaged in prostitution experience from both pimps and johns.

National Federal Bureau of Investigation arrest statistics relating to prostitution and commercial vice (which includes both indoor and outdoor prostitution as well as transporting an individual for the purposes of prostitution) show a steady decrease in prostitution-related arrests from 2005 to 2010.

Survival Sex

Survival sex is a form of sexual exploitation in which individuals barter sex for necessities, such as food, shelter, or protection. Homeless youth are especially vulnerable to being exploited within survival sex transactions, and within the homeless youth population African American; gay, lesbian, and bisexual; and substance abusing youth are more likely to engage in survival sex. Homeless gay, lesbian, bisexual, transgender, and transsexual youth and adults are also especially vulnerable to being victimized by physical and sexual violence.

Young men who engage in survival sex have higher risks of human immunodeficiency virus (HIV) infection than those who have never engaged in survival sex. Male survival sex workers also are more likely to engage in more sexual risk-taking and to have histories of drug injection and injecting drugs with partners, which contributes to their risk of HIV infection. For females that engage in survival sex, substance abuse increases their risk of contracting a sexually transmitted infection or HIV infection, and is associated with increased violence and exploitation.

Sex Trafficking

Sex trafficking refers to the recruitment of individuals by force, coercion, or through false promises for the purposes of sexual exploitation. Sex trafficking often involves women and young girls from Third World or politically and economically unstable countries. Sometimes these individuals are kidnapped or sold by their families to traffickers. Many

Gary Haugen, with U.S. Secretary of State Hillary Rodham Clinton, is the president of International Justice Mission, a human rights agency that rescues victims of violence, sexual exploitation, slavery, and oppression worldwide.

times, sex traffickers use trickery, promising well-paying jobs or educational opportunities in more prosperous countries in order to convince individuals to travel with them.

While most definitions of sex trafficking specify movement across international or interstate borders, it is important to note that under federal law in the United States any person under the age of 18 involved in prostitution is considered a trafficked individual. Trafficked individuals are extremely vulnerable and have often been subjected to severe human rights abuses such as sexual assault, forced confinement, and indentured servitude. They are also unlikely to report being victims of sex trafficking to authorities as they have often been threatened, or had their families threatened. In addition, victims of trafficking may be in the country illegally and may be afraid that reporting their status to the authorities will result in their deportation.

The U.S. Justice Department, in a 2012 report on human sex trafficking, estimated that in 2012 approximately 300,000 American youths were "at risk of becoming victims of commercial sexual exploitation." The report stated that the average age at which girls first become victims of prostitution is 12 to 14, while boys and transgender youth enter into prostitution between the ages of 11 and 13 on average. The U.S. Department of State, meanwhile, estimates that from 40,000 to 50,000 women and children are smuggled into the country each year. Researchers Richard J. Estes and Neil Alan Weiner project that about one third of these persons are under 18 years of age, and that at least half of that youth cohort become victims of commercial sexual exploitation.

In 2000, Congress passed the Trafficking Victims Protection Act (TVPA) to address issues related to human trafficking and sex trafficking. TVPA is the first significant piece of legislation to address human trafficking since the White Slave Act of 1910. TVPA allows some victims of sex trafficking who are not U.S. citizens to receive special T-visas which grant them temporary residency in the United States and eligibility to receive benefits and services such as access to victim's rights funds.

Rape and Sexual Assault

There are different categories of street-based sexual assault. Most rapes and sexual assaults are committed by an individual who is known to the victim. However, stranger rape represents a small proportion of rapes and sexual assaults that occur. Stranger rape is forced, nonconsensual sex on an individual to whom the perpetrator is unknown. Most victims of stranger rape are women. "Blitz rape" refers to a person being ambushed on the street and then sexually assaulted in a nearby location. Perhaps one of the most well-known instances of blitz rape is the case of the Central Park Jogger. Contact sexual assault refers to a perpetrator meeting a victim and attempting to gain that individual's trust in order to lure the victim somewhere and to sexually assault the person.

Frotteurism is a type of sexual assault in which an individual becomes sexually aroused by rubbing up against or touching a nonconsenting person. Frotteurs often act in public where it is difficult for victims to respond. Women and children are more likely to be victims of this type of sexual assault.

Conclusion

There are many types of sexual street violence with varying degrees of severity. Women and homeless youth are more likely to be victims of most types of sexual street violence. Many types of sexual street crimes, such as prostitution, survival sex, and sex trafficking also result in increased risk to individuals involved in contracting sexually transmitted infections or HIV infection.

Abby Bandurraga
L. Kris Gowen
Portland State University

See Also: Central Park Jogger Incident; Exposure, Indecent; "John"; Peeping Tom; Pimp; Prostitute/ Streetwalker; Prostitution, Houses of; Rape and Sexual Assault; Stalking; Tawana Brawley Incident; Women.

Further Readings

Anderson, Michelle. "*The Legacy of the Prompt Complaint Requirement, Corroboration Requirement, and Cautionary Instructions on Campus Sexual Assault.* Villanova, PA: Villanova University School of Law, 2004.

Civic Impulse, LLC. "S. 1301 (108th): Video Voyeurism Prevention Act of 2004." December 23, 2004. http:// www.govtrack.us/congress/bill.xpd?bill=s108-1301 (Accessed April 2012).

Dalla, Rochelle, Yan Xia, and Heather Kennedy. "'You Just Give Them What They Want and Pray They Don't Kill You'—Street-Level Sex Workers' Reports of Victimization, Personal Resources, and Coping Strategies." *Violence Against Women*, v.9/11 (2003).

Meyer, Robert G., E. Rhett Landis, and James Ray Hays. *Law for the Psychotherapist*. London: W. W. Norton, 1988.

Schauer, Edward and Elizabeth Wheaton. "Sex Trafficking Into The United States: A Literature Review." *Criminal Justice Review*, v.31/2 (2006).

U.S. Department of Justice. "UCR Program Changes Definition of Rape." March 2012. http://www.fbi.gov/ about-us/cjis/cjis-link/march-2012/ucr-program -changes-definition-of-rape (Accessed April 2012).

Shoplifting

Shoplifting generally implies the taking of merchandise from a retailer during the regular working hours while the business is open to the public. Statutes for shoplifting usually fall under the general category of larceny, with the monetary value of the items taken determining the severity of the offense; that is, misdemeanor or felony. Shoplifting is distinguished from theft after business hours. This criminal activity falls under the legal category of burglary.

Another source of considerable cost to businesses that involves concealment of illicitly gained property is that of employee theft. Employee theft differs from shoplifting in that the offender is employed by the business.

Cost and Demographics

Given the cost to businesses, shoplifting charges often include more than a disorderly conduct charge coupled with reimbursement for the lifted item. Many chain stores, which regularly have to contend with merchandise theft losses at a level of as much as three percent or more, insist on criminal prosecution for those caught shoplifting or for concealment, if only as a deterrent to potential shoplifters. Accessory before or after shoplifting are additional charges sometimes leveled against those involved in shoplifting schemes. Synonyms for shoplifting include five finger discount, jacking, nicking, boosting, and snitching. Shoplifting is a complex phenomenon that falls on a legal/clinical continuum that transcends its simple legal definition of absconding with goods without paying for them. Regardless of the type of or reason for shoplifting it remains a costly crime, one that actually impacts the costs of goods and services, especially among chain stores where security devices and personnel add to the cost of doing business. According to the National Learning and Resource Center of the National Association for Shoplifting Prevention (NASP), more than $13 billion worth of goods are lifted from retailers annually, with more than 10 million people caught shoplifting within the last five years. This includes taking goods from smaller shops, supermarkets, drug stores, and even thrift stores and libraries.

In its Uniform Crime Reporting summary, *Crime in the United States 2000,* the Federal Bureau of Investigation (FBI) noted that shoplifting made up 13.8 percent of the larceny-thefts nationally, or approximately 966,000 offenses. In its report for 2010, the FBI stated that shoplifting had risen to 17.2 percent of larceny-thefts, or more than one million offenses. The demographics of shoplifters are about equal among men and women, with 25 percent being children and youth, and 75 percent adults. For most of these offenders, shoplifting is a spontaneous, or impulsive, act. Yet, about 3 percent of shoplifters are professionals, including drug addicts who use this method to fund their habit. Such "professional" shoplifters account for about 10 percent of the total monetary loss associated with this crime. The NASP report indicates that shoplifting, regardless if it is impulsive or planned, is profitable in the aggregate for the offenders in that few are caught, and among those caught, they have a 50 percent chance of being turned over to the police for prosecution.

Boosters and Snitches

Researcher Mary Owen Cameron, in her classic work on shoplifting, makes a distinction between commercial shoplifters, or boosters, and those who steal for the thrill of it, or snitches. Boosters generally plan their crime, hence this type of shoplifting involves a greater degree of premeditation and often involves gang activity. Interstate booster gangs can result in investigation by federal law enforcement agencies. The gang effort features lookouts and drivers in addition to the person lifting the merchandise.

A common practice is to conceal stolen items in a booster bag, a backpack, purse, or loose-fitting clothing (sometimes a woman wearing maternity clothing), any of which can be lined with aluminum foil secured with duct tape, allowing the booster to pass electronic security detectors. Items are targeted for their resale value with the booster team often taking the items, with their electronic security tags intact, to another store for a full-cash return. This practice typically targets the major chain stores with numerous locations within a given region.

Conversely, Cameron terms snitches as pilferers—those who steal for the thrill of it. Transitory impulsive urges to take something for the excitement of taking it, and not for the purpose of resale, is a common developmental phenomenon afflicting children and youth. Clearly, such acts can be exacerbated by peer pressure. These activities usually occur during the period between puberty and the completion of the person's prime neurological development, generally around age 18. This is the neural developmental period of dendrite pruning and neuronal myelination—the insulation of the neural network in the frontal lobes. Most people who occasionally shoplifted as a youth lose this impulsive incentive once they reach adulthood, posing a dilemma for retailers and law enforcement regarding sticking these people with the stigma of a criminal conviction, in most cases a misdemeanor.

At the other end of this continuum is the mental illness kleptomania, which afflicts adults with a pervasive impulse control disorder associated with the irresistible urge to steal items for the excitement of the act itself. Situational kleptomania can also present as an associated feature of acute anxiety, often illustrated by a prominent person being charged with shoplifting of an inexpensive item of little value to him or her. A diagnosis of kleptomania reflects a major mental health disorder and needs to be separated from both the professional shoplifter and teen pilferers.

Laurence Armand French
University of New Hampshire, Durham

See Also: Arrest; Burglary; Juvenile Offending; Theft and Larceny.

Further Readings

Abelson, Elaine S. *When Ladies Go-A-Thieving: Middle-Class Shoplifting in the Victorian Department Store.* New York: Oxford University Press, 1989.

American Psychiatric Association (APA). *Diagnostic and Statistical Manual of Mental Disorders.* 4th ed.,

Text Revision (DSM-IV-TR). Washington, DC: APA, 2000.

Cameron, Mary Owen. *The Booster and the Snitch: Department Store Shoplifting.* New York: Free Press of Glencoe, 1964.

Clark, John P. and Richard C. Hollinger. "Theft by Employees in Work Organizations." Washington, DC: U.S. Government Printing Office, 1980.

Edwards, Loren E. *Shoplifting and Shrinkage Protection for Stores.* Whitefish, MT: Literary Licensing, 2012.

Klemke, Lloyd W. *The Sociology of Shoplifting: Boosters and Snitches Today.* Westport, CT: Praeger, 1992.

Sennewald, Charles A. and John H. Christman. *Shoplifting.* Oxford, UK: Butterworth-Heinemann, 1992.

Skid Row

Skid row is an expression that refers to a rundown part of town or to a slum, or, metaphorically, to a situation in life in which one has "hit the skids" or is in financial and/or moral trouble.

Historic Roots

Skid row is a variation of the lumber industry term *skid road*, broadly used in the Pacific Northwest to denote the rough roads where men "greased the skids" of wood slides to facilitate the sliding of logged timber to a sawmill for processing and shipment. As such it was frequented by loggers, and like many other boom town environments across North America, became a masculine-oriented slum, replete with bordellos, fleabag hotels or "flop houses," gambling joints, greasy spoon cafes, barber colleges (where a haircut could be had inexpensively), tobacconists, cheap clothing stores, saloons, and quite often a great many men without work. Skid rows were often near railroad yards or waterfront facilities, for industrial convenience—and also allowing easy access to tramps, hobos, seasonal migrant workers, and sailors.

The term *homeless*, when used in the late 1800s, had a different meaning than it does today. It meant that the single men who lived along the skid road were transient migrant laborers, often fruit pickers, laborers, lumberjacks, cowboys, or sailors. Such men, considered, "homeless," lived in boarding houses and cheap hotels; they were not necessarily hobos, tramps, or unemployed. Still, over time, the existence of such skid row environments across the nation—and their association as breeding grounds for street crimes both petty and serious—led to the nomenclature becoming synonymous with a vice-ridden slum.

This was recognized as a social and criminological problem as early as the beginning of the Progressive era. In the early years of the 20th century, the expansion of boom towns was explosive, as cheap labor was needed in the fields, mills, mines, and the lumber industry, to work on railroads, and to pick fruit. The number of bachelors living on skid rows in the early 1900s was probably in the millions: New York City's Municipal Housing Lodge House, for example, provided over 250,000 accommodations during a six-month period in 1915 for men who lacked the wherewithal to obtain even the crudest form of shelter. Though normally a ready source of tractable labor for mercantile interests, skid row residents became problematic to city leaders (as well as the small town and rural law-and-order forces) whenever they drank too much, turned to crime, or became engaged in the populist and Industrial Workers of the World (IWW) labor union movement in this era.

The Great Depression put many out of work and sent many on the road. By 1933 the number of transients recorded by the census was 1.25 million—a gross underestimate of that population in virtually every researcher's view. (As transients, they were seldom in one place long enough to be tallied by census takers.) By 1935, Chicago, a skid row and transient gathering place due to its massive railroad junctions, was providing 400,000 people with lodgings.

The pervasive economic boom associated with World War II at last put many of these single men in uniform—and many married in haste—during and following the war. The sorts of industries that employed single men also matured or fell into decline; the relative sizes and spread of skid row neighborhoods, in general, decreased. The boom that had required single workers was over; the age of the married suburban family man was at hand. Though skid row was in eclipse, it remained, and remains, in at least 50 cities in North America today. Skid row residents, predominantly male, remain poor and single.

Skid Row Today

Throughout the country, many urban skid rows, as characterized by the cheapest, short-term rental apartments and hotels, have shrunk into mere shadows of their former sizes and quite a few have ceased to exist. That notwithstanding, downtown skid rows persist in such cities as San Francisco (the Tenderloin district) and Seattle (Pioneer Square), while others have shifted to suburban areas, as in Atlanta and Detroit. Not all of these areas have historic or even present-day levels of street crimes high enough to draw specialized law enforcement responses. Still, the link is certain in more than one case. San Francisco's Tenderloin is a persistent location of violent and predatory crime. Part of the reason is opportunity; tourists and conventioneers looking for peep shows, pornography, and other forms of commercial sex are engaging in risky behavior and often become victims of assault or of theft from their person or auto. Drug and alcohol use are endemic, lending to the atmosphere of lower thresholds of violence and higher motivation to steal for ready cash.

Broad changes in the national economy, social structure, and urban geographic trends—including gentrification or rehabbing and upscaling of former skid row neighborhoods—affect the nature and crime-relatedness of former skid row areas as we know them today. The National Alliance to End Homelessness put the estimated number of homeless persons in the United States at approximately 655,000 as of January 2011. The figure is based on definitions of homelessness developed by the U.S. Department of Housing and Urban Development, as employed by survey counts conducted by shelters, missions, public officials, and social service groups across the country at a single point in time.

Many of the individuals counted in this way are part of family units and not the homeless or transient single male of skid row's past. Also, many of the new homeless are living in areas other than a true skid row or slum neighborhood. However, social and law enforcement bodies tasked with assessing risk and combating criminogenic features of today's urban concentrations of homeless people can use a knowledge of the skid rows of past decades in devising contemporary measures.

Frederick Hawley
Western Carolina University

See Also: Alcohol and Drug Use; Crack House; Crime Mapping; Homelessness; Panhandling or Begging; Risky Lifestyles; San Francisco, California; Urban Incivility.

Further Readings

Anderson, Nels. *The Hobo: The Sociology of the Homeless Man.* Chicago: University of Chicago Press, 1923.

Bahr, Howard M., ed. *Disaffiliated Man: Essays and Bibliography on Skid Row, Vagrancy, and Outsiders.* Toronto: University of Toronto Press, 1971.

Ellickson, Robert C. "Controlling Chronic Misconduct in City Spaces: Of Panhandlers, Skid Rows, and Public-Space Zoning." *Yale Law Journal*, v.105/1 (1996).

MacDonald, Heather. "The Reclamation of Skid Row." *City Journal*, v.17/4 (2007).

National Alliance to End Homelessness. "The State of Homelessness in America 2012." Washington, DC: National Alliance to End Homelessness, 2012.

Wallace, Samuel. *Skid Row as a Way of Life.* Totowa, NJ: Bedminster, 1965.

Skinheads

The "skinhead" gang provides a nexus between street gang culture and race-related activism. Skinheads are identifiable via their distinctive haircuts (shaved heads or closely cropped stubble) and pseudo-working-class clothing, particularly Doc Martens-style boots and suspenders. They can also be identified by their music, which evolved out of reggae into "Oi!" punk, and white supremacist rock music. Their uniform sets them apart from other street gangs, while their propensity for frequent violence sets them apart from many white supremacist and neo-Nazi organizations.

Origins in London

Skinheads first appeared in London during the 1960s as an outgrowth of the "mods" subculture. They clustered in neighborhood pubs and claimed specific territory as their own. They were typically undereducated children of working-class parents and saw themselves as representatives of the workers in an ongoing class struggle.

During the late 1970s and early 1980s, skinheads increasingly perceived immigrants as competition

Originally, the skinhead subculture was not based on politics or race. However, attitudes toward race and politics have become factors by which some skinheads align themselves, ranging from far right to the far left.

for factory jobs; the movement took a racist turn toward right-wing political leanings. By the late 1980s most skinheads were ideologically driven white supremacists who focused their violence on immigrants and minorities. During this same period, the movement crossed the Atlantic and caught on in the United States, particularly on the West Coast.

Structure and Activity

Skinhead gangs tend to organize around a specific neighborhood or school; attempts to organize larger groups have been largely unsuccessful. All too frequently, by the time law enforcement intelligence units have identified a specific gang, that gang has already fragmented. Skinhead gang violence often involves mass assaults against lone victims or smaller groups. Skinheads remain a danger to minorities and immigrants, but much of their violence today is committed against rival skinhead gangs. This is particularly true of West Coast and other gangs with close ties to prison gangs—such as the Aryan Brotherhood, the Aryan Circle, or Public Enemy Number 1 (PEN1)—for whom they act as distributors and enforcers in the methamphetamine trade. The relatively easy money of the illegal drug business has seduced an increasingly large number of skinheads since the mid-1990s. As such, skinheads are identified as involved with violent street crimes including aggravated assault, extortion, robbery, and homicide.

Conclusion

Reliable data concerning skinhead violence and criminal activity is difficult to obtain because of fragmented law enforcement jurisdictions and varying levels of concern. For example, Orange County, California, is known as a center of skinhead activities. At least 25 separate law enforcement agencies operate in this county, in addition to state and federal agencies. Joint task forces help alleviate this problem, but do not provide consistent oversight focusing on the skinhead gang problem; nor do these teams generate standard statistical data that can be compiled on a national basis. In time, more comprehensive figures will likely become available from federal antiterrorism agencies and federal prosecution efforts against hate crimes.

It is clear, however, that skinheads are overwhelmingly male; the few women involved tend most often to be treated as sexual objects or property. An occasional exception to this can be found in older female activists who are considered as surrogate mothers to a group or gang.

During the 1990s, a rival skinhead movement arose in opposition to the white supremacists, the self-styled antiracist skinheads. Members of both movements claimed to be "true" skinheads, and both movements use extreme violence to express their ideologies. The nonracist skinheads are collectively known as SHARPS (Skin Heads Against Racial Prejudice) or ARA (Anti-Racist Action).

J. Keith Akins
University of Houston, Victoria

See Also: Gangs (Street); Hate Crime; Homophobic Assault; Immigrant Neighborhoods; Racial Assault; Terrorism; Urban Ethnography.

Further Readings

Anahita, Sine. "Blogging the Borders: Virtual Skinheads, Hypermasculinity, and Heteronormativity." *Journal of Political and Military Sociology,* v.34/1 (2006).

Berlet, Chip and Stanislav Vysotsky. "Overview of U.S. White Supremacist Groups." *Journal of Political and Military Sociology,* v.34/1 (2006).

Blee, Kathleen M. *Inside Organized Racism: Women in the Hate Movement.* Berkeley: University of California Press, 2003.

Christensen, Loren. *Skinhead Street Gangs.* Boulder, CO: Paladin Press, 1994.

Dentice, Dianne. "The Nationalist Party of America: Right-Wing Activism and Billy Roper's White Revolution." *Social Movement Studies,* v.10/1 (2011).

Hamm, Mark. *American Skinheads: The Criminology and Control of Hate Crime.* Westport, CT: Praeger, 1993.

Jipson, Art. "Introduction to the Special Issue: Influence of Hate Rock." *Popular Music and Society,* v.30/4 (2007).

Sarabia, Daniel and Thomas E. Shriver. "Maintaining Collective Identity in a Hostile Environment: Confronting Negative Public Perception and Factional Divisions Within the Skinhead Movement." *Sociological Spectrum,* v.24/3 (2004).

Speakeasies (1920s)

A speakeasy was a clandestine bar, saloon, nightclub, or other similar establishment that illegally sold alcohol for consumption during America's era of Prohibition (1919–33). Influenced by America's temperance movement of the late 19th and early 20th century, which denounced and attributed the consumption of alcohol to many of the country's social ills, there was a concerted effort to rid society of alcohol and its ill effects. Members of the movement argued that the consumption of alcohol led to drunkenness and disorderly conduct, destitution, spousal abuse, debauchery, prostitution, and criminality. Because of the influence of the movement, by 1916, 23 out of 48 states banned bars and saloons—the traditional venues where alcohol was sold and consumed.

The momentum of the temperance movement eventually led to a national prohibition of alcohol and the ratification of the Eighteenth Amendment to the U.S. Constitution, which stated that "no person shall manufacture, sell, barter, transport, import, export, deliver, or furnish any intoxicating liquor" (January 16, 1919). While the Eighteenth Amendment ushered in the era of Prohibition, it was the National Prohibition Act (Volstead Act), enacted October 28, 1919, that provided for its enforcement.

Prohibition and the Birth of Speakeasies

Despite the well-intentioned goal of Prohibition (which was later referred to by President Herbert Hoover as the Noble Experiment), the demand for alcohol never abated among America's growing population. While Prohibition forced bars and saloons to close, by doing so it gave birth to underground bars, saloons, and other establishments that illegally sold and served alcohol, often referred to as speakeasies. The characterization of a speakeasy suggested that one was to "speak easy," coming from the practice of speaking quietly about such establishments while in public, or when inside of one, so not to alert neighbors or the police.

Despite the influence of the temperance movement, more commonly advanced by evangelical preachers, Protestant religious groups, progressives, and women who advocated abstinence from alcohol, speakeasies flourished throughout the country and were as popular in rural towns as they were in such major cities as Chicago, Detroit, and New York. While some were described as simple "hole-in-the-wall joints" behind storefronts with opaque painted windows, others sprung up in the basement apartments of brownstones, behind legitimate businesses' storefronts, and still others were located within elegant restaurants—all of which often required a special code or password to gain entry.

Their clientele included people of all walks of life, from the poor immigrant laborer to more high flying society people. Ironically, and in stark contrast to the activities of groups such as the Christian Women's Temperance Union, speakeasies were particularly popular among liberated women. Prior to Prohibition it would have been in extremely poor taste for a woman to be seen in a bar or saloon, but the cultural popularity of speakeasies, and perhaps the illicit and provocative nature of their activities, attracted as many women as they did men. In stark contrast to the goal of Prohibition, on the day it started it was estimated that New York City alone boasted approximately 15,000 drinking establishments, and within a few years thereafter, it had over 32,000, all of them illegal. By 1925, it has been estimated that New York City had anywhere from 30,000 to 100,000 speakeasies.

Crime and Corruption

While speakeasies contributed to the era of looser social mores, which featured ethnic and racial mixing, the rise of jazz music, and other cultural changes associated with the Roaring Twenties, their illicit nature led to personal exploitation and, even more seriously, ushered in a wide range of criminal activity. Prohibition provided profitable opportunities, albeit illegal, to many entrepreneurs, contributing to the rapid growth of organized crime. While the speakeasy predecessor—saloons—predominately served whiskey and beer, speakeasies' new female clientele gave rise to the cocktail, a drink in which hard liquor was sweetened with ginger, tonic, fruit juices, or sugar water.

Given their promiscuous, provocative, and permissive atmosphere, speakeasies also provided additional sources of temptation and entertainment in the form of drugs such as narcotics, hashish, and marijuana. Many speakeasies were either supplied by, or operated by, crime syndicates and gangsters who would smuggle alcohol from the Caribbean or Europe, hijack whiskey (when whiskey cargo is stolen from a truck or other vehicle after forcing it to stop) out of Canada, and oversee the manufacture, transportation, and sale of moonshine—alcohol made in clandestine stills during the night, and hence, by the light of the moon.

Bootlegging, gambling, prostitution, corruption, bribery, protection rackets, extortion, and brutal and murderous gang wars over turf and control over illegal businesses and speakeasies were some of the crimes related to prohibition and the operation of these establishments. While the Volstead Act was the enabling legislation for the enforcement of the Eighteenth Amendment, local, state, and federal agencies simply did not have the resources for carrying out their duties, and in many cases, the desire of individual officials was undermined through well-funded corruption.

Infamous Criminals

Infamous gangsters such as Al "Scarface" Capone, "Lucky" Luciano, "Bugs" Moran, and "Dutch" Schultz, known for their extravagant lifestyle and attire, were ruthless in maintaining control of their illicit speakeasy and liquor supply businesses. Not only were these gangsters at war with one another, but also with federal prohibition agents, such as the renowned Eliot Ness and his team of Bureau of Prohibition (U.S. Treasury Department) agents. The agents were nicknamed the "Untouchables" because they could not be influenced by bribery and corruption. The Bureau of Prohibition was formed in 1920 in response to the National Prohibition Act of 1919. It was initially a branch of the Bureau of Internal Revenue and later the Department of Treasury. Gangland warfare that employed all sorts of

weapons, including pistols, shotguns, machine guns, and hand grenades, wreaked havoc, as did the government's attempt to control, infiltrate, and destroy illegal operations. Further exasperating the climate created by Prohibition, police and government officials were readily bribed in an effort to safeguard the operation of speakeasies, thus breeding a creeping contempt for government at large.

While Prohibition may have been a well-intentioned, even noble initiative, it ultimately proved a dismal failure, as witnessed by its many unintended consequences, not the least of which was the birth and rise of speakeasies and the consequential spread of crimes that they bred.

Robert F. Vodde
Fairleigh Dickinson University

See Also: Alcohol and Drug Use; Bars and Pubs; Bootleggers; Drinking Establishments, Unlicensed; Gangs (Street); Organized Crime and Violence.

Further Readings

Badal, James Jessen. *In the Wake of the Butcher: Cleveland's Torso Murders.* Kent, OH: Kent State University Press, 2001.

Hamm, Richard. *Shaping the Eighteenth Amendment: Temperance Reform, Legal Culture, and the Polity, 1880–1920.* Chapel Hill: University of North Carolina Press, 1995.

Hirschfeld, A. *Speakeasies of 1932.* Milwaukee, WI: Glen Young Books, 2003.

Moray, Alistair. *The Diary of a Rum-Runner.* Mystic, CT: Flat Hammock Press, 2007.

Okrent, D. *Last Call: The Rise and Fall of Prohibition.* New York: Scribner, 2010.

Pietrusza, David. *1920: The Year of the Six Presidents.* New York: Carroll & Graf, 2007.

Pinney, Thomas. *A History of Wine in America: From Prohibition to the Present.* Berkeley: University of California Press, 2005.

St. Louis, Missouri

St. Louis—known for its baseball and breweries, timeless architecture and toasted ravioli, city appeal and small-town flavor—sports a history rooted in its placement on the Mississippi River and the benefits it provided the burgeoning fur trade of the 18th and 19th centuries. It is also a city that rapidly became the first major navigable port west of Pittsburgh, thus attracting both business and immigration. As commerce grew so, too, did the city's population. Attracted to the possibilities of lucrative employment, many both immigrated and migrated to St. Louis. Primary among these immigrants were the Irish Catholics whose early presence remains a constant in 21st-century St. Louis.

Reminiscent of the city's early history is its continuing appeal to immigrants of many backgrounds and its willingness to welcome them with open arms. Thus, contemporary St. Louis has truly become the melting pot of the midwest as Italians, Germans, Hispanics, Asians, Bosnians, and those of various backgrounds have come to call the city home. This is not to imply all has been or is well within the city and its 91 surrounding municipalities. In recent years, St. Louis has twice ranked at the top of the country's most violent cities—a dubious honor disputed by many city officials and local scholars.

In order to understand this less than admirable designation one must examine the city's history. As early as the 1600s, French explorers readily saw the value in the land surrounding what is now called St. Louis, in the territory that would become the state of Missouri. Founded by violence against the Native Americans who had long called the land home, the bloodshed did not end when the United States succeeded in becoming its own nation. Rather, the Civil War fought in the 1860s split the state of Missouri, with much effort given to securing the port of St. Louis.

Organized Crime

Although an independent city since its cessation from St. Louis County during the Civil War, the city has some peculiar direct ties to the state. For example, the St. Louis Metropolitan Police Department remains under the control of the state. Periodically city leaders attempt to wrest control of its police department from the state—a move strongly opposed by members of local law enforcement, who question the underlying reason behind these efforts and how such a move would affect their livelihoods. The long-standing designation of St. Louis as a major metropolitan city with a state-controlled police department not only sets it apart from other major urban areas, but also in some ways contributes to a larger culture of discontent affecting police-community relations as a whole.

The 20th century witnessed dramatic changes to the types of crime plaguing the city of St. Louis. Continuing migration, combined with nationwide changes to the legal system, made St. Louis a ripe location for the Mafia Family—a collection of five competing Mafia strongholds named the Sicilian Green Ones, the Pillow Gang, Egan's Rats, the Hogan Gang, and the Cuckoos—to make and leave its mark on the city. As many Italians moved northward from New Orleans to St. Louis, the criminal elements among them brought their organized crime ways and means. Rooted in Sicily, honed in New Orleans, and now calling St. Louis home, this branch of the Mafia used Prohibition to its benefit in the city often referred to as the beer capital of the country.

Establishing their original foothold in the neighborhood that is still called The Hill, the gangs not only extorted local businesses by imposing taxes on all salable goods, but also were soon at war with one another. The Green Ones established their superiority with three notable and gruesome acts of violence. Headed by Vito Giannola, the Green Ones expanded their operations to include control of the wholesale meat industry—a move challenged by one local distributor. The distributor's brutally slain body was soon found and its message to others was clear. Soon after, the husband and wife duo of John and Catherine Gray were similarly slain and their car set afire after refusing to comply with the gang's control over the purchase of liquor necessary for the success of the resort they owned and operated. Perhaps the most gruesome of the three examples cited here was the brutal murder of two police officers who were beat into unconsciousness and later forced to watch as their own graves were dug prior to their killing and burial.

These brutalities exacted upon citizens and police officers of St. Louis represent merely the tip of the iceberg as the ultimate number of victims defies documentation. Not only were law-abiding individuals and law enforcement agents victimized by specific gangs, so, too, were separate gangs at war with one another. As the influence of the Mafia waned in the latter half of the 20th century, a new threat was emerging on the scene that would bring with it its own threat to the citizens of St. Louis—the youth street gang.

Kids, Gangs, and Violence

St. Louis is now a metropolis seen by some as under siege by its youth. The Federal Bureau of Investigation (FBI) and local law enforcement have documented the presence of 92 separate gangs in St. Louis; the number of youth who belong to these gangs is in the thousands. Both the number of gangs in St. Louis proper and gang membership are both on the rise. These numbers escalate when one takes into account gang activity in the city's 91 surrounding municipalities. The local office of the FBI has estimated that 80 percent of all crime—from petty theft to homicide—in the area is gang-related.

Once considered a North City neighborhood problem, street gangs have now infiltrated most areas of the community and prey on the most vulnerable when recruiting new members. Furthermore, once considered a stronghold of the black community, new gangs and increased violence are emerging as the result of continued immigration into St. Louis. Ethnic ties and issues of territoriality now pit the newly formed Bosnian, Asian, and Hispanic gangs against those with long-standing claims to specific areas of the city. Thus, the efforts of law enforcement to identify specific gangs and place a number on gang membership is made more difficult, and efforts to deter their crimes need to keep changing.

Although guns, drugs, and violence have been constants in St. Louis and were once the trademark of organized crime dating to Prohibition, they are now daily fixtures of the youth street gangs. Research findings have consistently indicated that one most often joins a gang for protection, feelings of belonging to a family, or as an escape from poverty. As of 2009, approximately 31 percent of all St. Louis residents fell below the poverty level, with racial and ethnic minorities making up the vast majority of the city's poor. Concomitantly, 41 percent of all children lived in poverty. These children grow up seeking the same material goods as their counterparts in the middle and upper classes—homes, automobiles, and lucrative careers. Yet opportunity evades them. So, too, do active role models for achieving success in mainstream society. What is readily available are the opportunities provided by gang membership—feelings of belonging, protection, and financial success. Unfortunately, these come at the expense of community safety and the lives lost to violence and despair.

All too often ignored in studies and scholarly discussions is the mind-set one develops after joining a gang—the quiet acceptance that one will eventually spend time behind bars or face death at the hands of another. In many ways this belief has its roots in the larger culture of violence that is part and parcel of the city's history, from its early settlement days through the era of Mafia control, to the contemporary violent street crime.

Rankings, Reactions, and Reality

In 2006 and 2008, St. Louis was ranked by Cable News Network (CNN), *U.S. News and World Report,* and Morgan Quitno (a research publisher) as the most dangerous city among all major metropolitan areas in the United States. In 2007, it held the number-two spot, second only to Detroit. Needless to say, these reports evoked strong reactions from local law enforcement and political leaders alike. City officials cited the negative effect these widely publicized rankings might have on tourism, while local scholars called into question the methodologies employed by the researchers, the underlying reasons for publishing the reports, and the efficacy of the studies' findings.

The utmost concern to city officials and local scholars alike was twofold in nature. First, standardization of reporting crime is absent among law enforcement agencies from city to city. Second, at the discretion of the researchers some cities were not included in the studies due to the jurisdictional reporting, or lack thereof, of crimes occurring in their municipalities. Such is the case with Chicago, which was left out of the rankings due to its unorthodox manner of reporting rape.

Of further concern to local scholars was the fact that Morgan Quitno imposed a fee on any individual or group seeking access to its full report—from the methodology, to the cities included in its study, to the way in which rankings were assigned. It has long been accepted that research and its ultimate findings are the property of the larger scientific community in communal efforts to enhance cumulative knowledge and work toward cooperative change. Profiteering in any manner thus reduces the trust one is able to place on any research findings, let alone those that may negatively impact the economic base of an entire metropolitan area.

Without a doubt, these represent genuine concerns among both city leaders and policy makers alike. A larger methodological question arises that carries with it the ability to further mislead the general public when presented with misleading reports that extend beyond the ones cited above.

Uniform Crime Reports (UCR) data utilized for these studies were egregiously skewed as a result of the researchers' self-imposed boundaries set for the city of St. Louis. The data selected for these studies included the entire St. Louis metropolitan region—including the surrounding 92 Missouri municipalities, as well as those cities referred to as the East Side, all of which are located in Illinois. Thus, the UCR data used in the research—and claimed to be representative of the city of St. Louis—in reality represent the entire metropolitan area. This region sports a population of 2,824,159 while the city of St. Louis proper maintains a population of 320,454. While it is clear St. Louis has a long-standing history of street crime and one that shows no promise of an easy fix, it is imperative that accurate information be provided to policy makers and the general public alike.

According to initial UCR 2011 reports, St. Louis (population 320,454) experienced 113 murders, 188 rapes, 2,127 robberies, 7,015 aggravated assaults, and 3,369 motor vehicle thefts. Although more than problematic in nature for a city of its size, these data represent a far cry from statistics presented by research organizations whose methodological standards are questionable at best.

Conclusion

It goes without saying St. Louis is a city with a long standing and ongoing history of street crime that affects all in its midst—its residents, its public school system, its tourism, its economic basis, its infrastructure, and its hope for the future. In short, the street crimes plaguing the city of St. Louis have been long in the making and will not be easily cured.

St. Louis is a city whose historical culture has contributed to both its reputation and reality of a street crime ridden city. Although city leaders, policymakers, and police officers alike are working diligently to alter these problems, they will not change overnight. It will also need the efforts of its citizens if real changes are to occur. No longer can the city leaders and its police officers afford to merely be reactive in nature. In reality, an entire cultural mindset must change. Difficult? Yes. Impossible? That remains to be seen.

Martha L. Shockey-Eckles
Saint Louis University

See Also: Broken Windows Theory; Environmental Criminology; Gangs (Street); Guns and Weapons; Immigrant Neighborhoods; Juvenile Offending; Murder/Homicide; Police (Overview); Vandalism; Victims, Tourist.

Further Readings

Bogan, Jesse. "Girl's Burial Spotlights a Culture of Violence." *St. Louis Post-Dispatch* (March 20, 2011). http://www.stltoday.com/news/local/metro/article_26bd5032-f188-514a-ba93-1e9ac727e745.html (Accessed May 2012).

Ferguson, Kristin M., Jina Jun, Kimberly Bender, Sanna Thompson, and David Pollio. "A Comparison of Addiction and Transience Among Street Youth: Los Angeles, California, Austin, Texas, and St. Louis, Missouri." *Community Mental Health Journal*, v.46/3 (2010).

Garrison, Chad. "Back on Top: St. Louis Named Most Dangerous City in 2010." *Riverfront Times* (November 22, 2010). http://www.blogs.riverfronttimes.com/dailyrft/2010/11/st_louis_named_most_dangerous_city_2010.php (Accessed May 2012).

John Perry, a deputy U.S. marshal, died from gunshot wounds while serving an arrest warrant in St. Louis, Missouri, in March 2011. Above, a member of the St. Louis Police Department folds an American flag to be presented to Perry's mother.

Kurtzleben, Danielle. "The 11 Most Dangerous Cities." *U.S. News and World Report* (February 16, 2011). http://www.usnews.com/news/articles/2011/02/16/the-11-most-dangerous-cities (Accessed May 2012).

Stalking

"I have an obsession with the unattainable. I have to eliminate what I cannot attain." These were the words of Robert John Bardo as he wrote to his sister mere hours before murdering actress Rebecca Schaeffer on July 18, 1989. Bardo's crime motivated California lawmakers to create the first antistalking law in the United States. Subsequently, the National Institute of Justice tasked the National Criminal Justice Association (NCJA) to create a Model Anti-Stalking Code with which all U.S. state legislatures could follow in creating their own stalking statutes. By 1993, all 50 states and the District of Columbia had enacted their own stalking laws.

Statutes and Statistics

One of the largest areas of difference within the United States concerning stalking is the various legal, academic, and clinical definitions. Such variety carries much differentiation and some confusion from state to state when creating legislation or conducting research. The NCJA code referred to a stalker as any person who engaged in directed contact that results in the fear of bodily injury to themselves or members of their immediate family, and included a need for intent and knowledge on the part of the perpetrator. Any remaining variance of these laws among states typically include issues such as behavior patterns, fear, and threat levels. Three years after the model was created, President Bill Clinton signed a rigid antistalking bill that gave federal law enforcement jurisdiction over any incident of stalking which crossed state lines. The bill, sponsored by a recently stalked congresswoman, made federal stalking punishable by up to five years in prison for harassment, and up to life in prison if such behavior resulted in bodily harm.

Given the relative infancy of the criminalization of stalking in the United States, there are few empirical studies available on its true prevalence. Those studies attempting to determine prevalence estimate that approximately 8 percent of women and 2 percent of men have experienced stalking at some point in their lives. A vital concern raised within other studies was that between 50 and 80 percent of people stalked actually report such behavior to law enforcement. Of those reported, only an estimated 12 percent resulted in a conviction, according to research conducted by Katrina Baum et al.

Previous and ongoing studies indicate a high correlation between stalking and the occurrence of associated crimes, including street crimes. It is estimated that approximately 80 percent of all stalking cases are a product of a previous or current intimate relationship, and that nearly 90 percent of intimate partner violence was preceded by stalking. The U.S. Department of Justice further estimates that between 25 percent and 35 percent of murdered females were victims of battery, the majority of which were preceded by stalking behaviors. Recent research found that 40 percent of stalking victims experienced violence (e.g., being pushed or shoved, hit with a fist, grabbed, or slapped) consequent to stalking behavior.

Psychological Motivations

Stalking behavior is most commonly constructed in the literature as an artifact of a failed ongoing sexual relationship or as the result of rejected romantic overtures from an undesired suitor. Regardless of the specific relational context in question, stalking behavior becomes the way in which the spurned individual responds to this experience of rejection and loss. Unlike most individuals, those prone to stalking are unable to psychologically accept romantic loss or the rejection normally found in divorce, the ending a long-term relationship, or otherwise unrequited romantic overtures. With such individuals, stalking behavior comes to represent the desperate attempt to regain that which was "taken" from them.

It should not be surprising then that subsequent stalking behavior often commences after the breakup of a physically abusive relationship. The proximity of control used by many physically and psychologically abusive partners simply cannot be maintained once the actual relationship has been terminated by the victimized partner. In an attempt to regain lost control, the abusing partner resorts to various stalking behaviors. Researchers have found a strong correlation between the need for control and "breakup anger" by the rejected partner with subsequent stalking behaviors. It is also argued that this type of relational stalking may be viewed as an ongoing abusive event that does not necessarily end with the termination of the relationship.

Though the presence of relational abuse is often present with individuals who resort to stalking behavior, an ongoing relationship is certainly not a prerequisite for this type of abusive experience. The presence of control issues and "object loss" often manifest within the clinical context of personality pathology. Substance-related issues may also become the psychological pretext by which these types of loss are constructed and resolved. The attempt to pursue the lost object of one's desire, whether real or imagined, comes to represent the desire to once again achieve a sense of psychological wholeness at the expense of the individual who has been deemed as essential to that process.

The experience of stalking may take place within the context of an ending relationship or as a result of unrequited love; such behavior emerges as an artifact of a variety of psychological variables that must be included in any attempt for law enforcement officials to get a better understanding of this phenomenon. Though empirical studies often focus upon the frequency of stalking behavior, which appears variable across populations and individual perpetrators, more needs to be understood concerning the specific psychology of this experience. The fact that the vast majority of these types of cases emerge as the result of a formerly ongoing and now failed intimate relationship points to a variety of developmental factors within the individual that appear central to stalking behavior.

Conclusion

Attachment histories and the developmental processes these evoke seem foundational to stalking behavior. To be obsessed with that which one cannot attain is indeed at the center of this complex set of relational experiences. The better able we are to understand the driving force behind this obsession, the better able we will be to spare those who get caught up in its overwhelming shadow.

David Polizzi
William Mackey
Indiana State University

See Also: Alcohol and Drug Use; Domestic Violence; Kidnapping; Mental Illness; Murder/Homicide; Rape and Sexual Assault; Sex Crimes; Women.

Further Readings

Baum, Katrina, Shannon Catalano, Michael Rand, and Kristina Rose. "Stalking Victimization in the United States." Washington, DC: Bureau of Justice Statistics, 2009. http://www.ovw.usdoj.gov/docs/stalking -victimization.pdf (Accessed July 2012).

Boychuk, M. Katherine. "Are Stalking Laws Unconstitutionally Vague or Overbroad?" *Northwestern University Law Review*, v.15/4 (1994).

Coleman, Frances L. "Stalking Behavior and the Cycle of Domestic Violence." *Journal of Interpersonal Violence*, v.12/3 (1997).

Melton, Heather C. "Predicting the Occurrence of Stalking in Relationships Characterized by Domestic Violence." *Journal of Interpersonal Violence*, v.22/1 (2007).

Saunders, Rhonda. "The Legal Perspective on Stalking." In *The Psychology of Stalking: Clinical and Forensic Perspectives*, J. Reid Meloy, ed. San Diego, CA: Academic Press, 1998.

Tjaden, Patricia and Nancy Thoennes. "Stalking in America: Findings From the National Violence Against Women Survey." Washington, DC: U.S. Department of Justice Press, 1998.

Vitello, Corey J. "Stalking Laws, Therapeutic Jurisprudence, and Peacemaking Criminology: A Radical Law-Psychology Inquiry." *Journal of Forensic Psychology Practice*, v.3/2 (2003).

Sting Operations

A sting operation is a deception wherein police provide individuals with the opportunity to get caught committing a crime. Sting operations target particular crimes and crime areas; they are reactive to a selected crime problem, and proactive as they attempt to ferret out current and future criminals. In some uses, sting operations may also represent a "con game," a "confidence scheme," or similar fraud conducted by criminals against a variety of different targets from private citizens to other criminals.

Sting operations are an integral part of law enforcement operations throughout the world, and they are very effective at reducing crime. The essence of a sting operation is that law enforcement provide a setting, target, and opportunity for a specific type of crime, thus creating the chance to catch a criminal in the act. In such a situation, things are not always what they appear to be, as police play a role in the crime scenario.

Sting operations are used in combatting a range of crimes: bribery and corruption, sale of stolen property, fraud, prostitution, illicit drug sales, tax evasion and money laundering, illegal gun sales, auto theft, etc. Sting operations have been established to catch fugitives and bail jumpers. They are sometimes also an effective tool in fighting terrorism. Proactive sting operations seek to identify those who are involved in or attempt to develop a particular criminal enterprise.

Sting operations have been an effective tool in fighting street crimes. With early sting operations, police would develop relationships with individuals who purchased stolen goods, commonly known as "fences." A fence, acting as an informant, would provide information to the police about criminals and the items they stole, in return for leniency on pending criminal charges or even in exchange for cash payments. This type of relationship has worked well for police detectives; by extension, it sometimes evolved to where undercover police would play the role of the fence, no longer dealing with a person in that role who was also a criminal.

Police in setting up this type of sting would set up a legitimate "front" business as would a typical fence, either selling secondhand goods or as a pawnshop. The word would travel around the community, sometimes through the use of informants, that there was a place that would buy a variety of stolen items. While they would not ask too many questions, they would pay cash. The object was to lure the criminals who were already involved with robbery and theft into the store where police would identify them with fingerprints on the items they sold and photographs from a concealed camera.

These sting operations were usually reactive, in response to a particular crime problem. Often, a community would be experiencing a growing problem of burglaries, car thefts, car part thefts, hijackings, or robberies. Since the products of these offenses were rarely currency, the items would have to be sold; a storefront-fencing operation would be the perfect way to identify the culprits. Whether it

was a pawnshop, chop shop, electronics store, adult bookstore, or just a backroom where the goods could be sold, the sting was often very successful.

There are other crimes in which undercover police play a different role. Prostitution and drug sales are two common street crimes. Prostitution, a petty offense in most street situations, is another crime targeted by sting operations. Here, the police will play the role of either the prostitute or the "john," the purchaser of the sexual favors. Unlike the storefront operation that may last for a year or more before arrests are made, the suspected prostitute or "john" is arrested immediately for solicitation of prostitution.

Illegal drug sales (both prescription drugs and contraband drugs such as heroin, cocaine, LSD, methamphetamine, etc.) on the street are handled in a similar manner, with the police officer playing the role of the either the dealer or buyer; the offenders are usually arrested as they leave the area, to preserve the identity of the undercover officer. Similar methods are used when police target vendors who sell alcohol and cigarettes to underage individuals or counterfeit identification documents to minors or illegal aliens. Federal Bureau of Investigation (FBI) sting operations in 2010 involved several task forces that targeted the sex trafficking of children. This sting campaign started with the targeting of areas such as truck stops, Internet sites, and known street locations.

Grand theft auto is not just the name of a popular video game, but also a felony. Each year a different automobile may make the list of the most stolen vehicle. In every city and town there is an area where cars are more likely to be stolen; these can be ideal locations for police sting operations. Police will place a bait or decoy vehicle that they will use to catch the car thief. The state-of-the-art car will usually have tracking devices, video and audio recording devices, and even remote controls in the hands of law enforcement; this means that the thief travels only as far as the police permit him to travel. As the thief learns very quickly, there is very little joy in the short ride, and as the crime is a felony, he will have little time to worry about renewing his driver's license.

Targeting Corruption

Gaining convictions and uprooting corruption by street or beat police officers or sheriffs can actually be more difficult than penetrating higher level crimes. In these situations, the corruption may be the free meal, the stealing of money and drugs from the drug dealer, sexual favors from the prostitute, or other forms of extortion. In most situations the corrupt officers believe that there is nowhere that the victim can really go to report the theft of the fruit of the victim's illegal activity. This is where the sting will be run by internal affairs agents, another state or local department, or a federal agency where the law enforcement personnel will not be known to the locals.

The FBI and the Drug Enforcement Administration have worked together in stings to catch corrupt law enforcement officers who in some cases see nothing wrong with robbing drug dealers. The police who choose to take advantage of the street criminals may be more careful than the criminals themselves might be—and take care to check for surveillance and recording devices. But the combination of stealth on the part of the sting team, and the deployment of newer technological methods not widely known among the rank and file, can often yield the desired result and cut out police corruption.

Defenses

Because law enforcement sets the stage, writes the rules, and controls the events, stings result in extremely high conviction rates. In some cases the defendants may show some hesitation and will ask the undercover officer "if she is a cop." Having watched too many episodes of *Dragnet, CSI* or *Law & Order*, he mistakenly believes that if the officer lies about her status as an officer, he cannot be prosecuted because she must tell the truth. As he will soon learn, he is wrong!

Another popular defense is entrapment. In this situation, the defendant will argue that he was enticed into the criminal act by the government. This defense is rarely successful. The key to this defense in most jurisdictions depends on the predisposition of the defendant to commit the crime; this is known as a subjective standard.

The other side of entrapment and one that is likely to be successful is the objective standard for entrapment. In this case the defendant does not have that predisposition but the government makes the crime so attractive that he could not resist the temptation. In most street crime situations, especially in cases involving drugs or prostitution, it is the defendant who initiates the contact, exhibiting his predisposition to purchase the drugs or the sex.

Popular Perception

Sting operations play into the scripts of numerous television shows and movies. At the top of the list was *The Sting,* a film starring Paul Newman and Robert Redford. Two hucksters attempted to deceive a mob boss with a very sophisticated confidence game. In this case it was one criminal taking advantage of another criminal. While it is not what we normally consider a sting operation in the law enforcement community, who is to say how often such an operation has actually happened?

Keith Gregory Logan
Kutztown University

See Also: Arrest; Blackmail; Courts; Police Corruption, Street-Level; Policing, Problem-Oriented; Prostitute/Streetwalker; Terrorism.

Further Readings
Crockett, James R. *Operation Pretense: The FBI's Sting on County Corruption in Mississippi.* Jackson: University Press of Mississippi, 2003.

Dodge, M. "Puttin' on the Sting: Women Police Officers' Perspectives on Reverse Prostitution Assignments." *International Journal of Police Science and Management*, v.7/2 (2005).

"Federal Bureau of Investigation Arrests 22 in Bribery Sting Operation." *DISAM Journal of International Security Assistance Management*, v.32/1 (2010).

Glazer, Craig and Sal Manna. *The King of Sting: The Amazing True Story of a Modern American Outlaw.* New York: Skyhorse Publishing, 2010.

Jae Woong, S. "Punishing Disposition: Sting Operations on the Internet." *Open Communication Journal*, v.518/22 (2011).

Meyers, Michael A. "Police Practice." *FBI Law Enforcement Bulletin*, v.2000/5 (2000).

Moore, R., T. Lee, and R. Hunt. "Entrapped on the Web? Applying the Entrapment Defense to Cases Involving Online Sting Operations." *American Journal of Criminal Justice*, v.32/1–2 (2007).

Newman, Graeme R. and Kelly Socia. "Sting Operations: Response Guide No. 6." Madison, WI: Center for Problem-Oriented Policing, 2007.

Sullivan, T. P. "The Trial of My Life: Behind the Scenes at Operation Greylord." *Update on Law-Related Education*, v.23/1 (1991).

Tuohy, James and Rob Warden. *Greylord: Justice, Chicago Style.* New York: Putnam Adult, 1989.

Wilson, James Q. "The Changing FBI: The Road to ABSCAM." *National Affairs*, v.59/1 (1980).

Stop and Frisk

Stop and frisk is an important investigative tool used by law enforcement to fight street crime. A stop is a temporary detention for investigative purposes. A frisk is a pat down of the outer garments for weapons. Analysis of stop and frisk begins in this entry with a review of the U.S. Supreme Court decision *Terry v. Ohio,* which established the legal basis and constitutional standard for stop and frisk. Then an examination is made to distinguish stop and frisk from arrest and other police-citizen encounters, followed by examination of the standard of proof necessary to justify a stop and frisk and the types of evidence which would meet this burden. Finally, civil rights and policy implications of stop and frisk are explored.

Terry v. Ohio

The U.S. Supreme Court acknowledged the need for police to investigate suspicious individuals and set the legal standard for stop and frisk in *Terry v. Ohio.* Briefly, the facts of the Terry case are as follows: Detective McFadden, a 39-year veteran of the Cleveland (Ohio) Police Department assigned to plainclothes patrol of downtown Cleveland, observed Terry and another individual, Chilton, pacing back and forth, peering into a store window, and conferring on a nearby corner. At some point, the two were joined by a third individual who also conferred with them briefly. This went on for a period of at least 10 or 12 minutes.

Detective McFadden, believing that the three were casing the store for a robbery, stopped the three individuals and, fearing they were armed patted down their outer garments to determine if they were armed. He recovered revolvers from Terry and Chilton's overcoat pockets. The third individual, Katz, was not armed. Terry and Chilton were

charged with and convicted of concealed weapons violations in the Ohio state courts. Katz was not charged with a crime. Terry and Chilton claimed that they were detained and searched in violation of the Fourth Amendment.

The U.S. Supreme Court held that the Fourth Amendment applied to field stops of suspicious individuals and established legal standards for stop and frisk, balancing the relative rights of police and citizens. The court established reasonable suspicion based upon articulable facts as the legal standard for a stop. It held that since a temporary stop was less intrusive than an arrest, probable cause was not required for stop. The court also permitted a frisk or pat down of the outer garments if the police reasonably believed that the person stopped was armed. Similarly, because a frisk is not as intrusive as a search, probable cause was not required for a frisk. The U.S. Supreme Court was well aware of the legal and practical issues associated with stop and frisk, particularly the potential for harassment of minorities.

Stops and Reasonable Suspicion

Fourth Amendment requirements apply when an individual is stopped or detained. In other words, a reasonable person would feel that he or she is not free to leave. Police officers have the right to approach citizens, talk to them, and ask them questions. As long as individuals are free to leave, officers do not need reasonable suspicion or other justification to approach someone. This type of police-citizen interaction is often referred to as an encounter or accosting and occurs in a wide variety of contexts including business checks, canvassing an area for witnesses to crimes, and informal interactions between citizen and police on patrol. Many of these interactions are routine and non-confrontational—and Fourth Amendment issues do not arise.

However, when police accost or encounter suspects, the first legal issue that must be addressed is whether the individual is free to leave. This will be determined based upon all of the facts and circumstances surrounding the interaction. See, for example, *U.S. v. Mendenhall,* which enumerated factors to consider in determining whether or not a stop had occurred, and *Florida v. Rodriguez,* involving a consensual airport encounter. If an individual is not free to leave, then the police must have reasonable

A silent protest march through the New York City neighborhood of Harlem in June 2012. Several thousand residents marched to protest the New York Police Department's "Stop and Frisk" policy, which critics charge amounts to racial profiling. New York's Mayor Michael Bloomberg believes that the policy reduces crime and helps remove guns from the streets.

suspicion based upon articulable facts that criminal activity may be afoot.

The determination of reasonable suspicion is based upon the facts and circumstances of each particular case. Reasonable suspicion is derived from officers' personal knowledge; what they see, hear, smell, and touch; and information derived from third parties, citizens, witnesses, and criminal informants. Court decisions vary widely among and within jurisdictions. Types of conduct that have been held to justify reasonable suspicion include: bulges indicative of weapons, inappropriate conduct or clothing, furtive movements, and fitting the description of a wanted person.

In *Illinois v. Wardlow*, the U.S. Supreme Court held that while mere presence in a high crime area is not reasonable suspicion, coupled with unexplained flight it did constitute reasonable suspicion. Typically, reasonable suspicion does not result from any one factor but a combination of factors that together amount to reasonable suspicion. Association with known narcotics addicts does not constitute reasonable suspicion, as was demonstrated in *Sibron v. New York*. There must be specific, articulable facts that criminal activity is afoot at the time.

Specific Aspects

Anonymous tips without further information do not justify a stop and frisk, as was made clear in *Florida v. J.L.*, involving an anonymous call describing a young black male dressed in a plaid shirt who was standing on a particular corner and was said to be armed. The U.S. Supreme Court held that an anonymous tip such as this was not sufficiently reliable to justify a stop. There was concern that this decision would adversely impact law enforcement's ability to investigate crime. This fear largely did not materialize. An officer would respond to the call; he or she then either makes their own observations that might constitute reasonable suspicion, or approaches the individual and asks him or her questions, provided the individual was free to leave.

There is no set time limit concerning the length of the stop. Typical stops are often concluded within 15 or 20 minutes. Detention must be temporary and last no longer than necessary to effectuate the purpose of the stop, as noted in *Florida v. Royer.* Stops that exceed the permissible scope of a Terry stop may amount to seizure tantamount to arrest, which was laid out in *Dunaway v. New York.*

The frisk must initially be limited to the pat down of the outer garments for weapons. Only if an officer feels an object that might be a weapon can it be retrieved to determine if it is a weapon. Frisks are for weapons which may pose a threat to a police officer, not evidence. However, if during a pat down, it becomes immediately apparent that an individual possesses contraband, it may be seized pursuant to the plain feel doctrine, an extension of the plain view doctrine. This was examined in *Minnesota v. Dickerson.*

Racial Profiling Questions

Use of stop and frisk tactics has grown as cities have adopted CompStat and aggressive enforcement strategies targeting quality of life offenses and violent crime. Stop and frisk has been the subject of extensive complaints by minorities and civil rights advocates who claim the broad discretion given to police officers leads to racial profiling. While much of the racial profiling literature concerns traffic stops, the Rand Corporation conducted an analysis of stop and frisk in New York City in 2006. Eighty-nine percent of the approximately one-half million stops in 2006 involved nonwhites: 53 percent were African American, 29 percent were Hispanic, 10 percent were white, and 3 percent were Asian.

Michael M. Berlin
Coppin State University

See Also: Arrest; Broken Windows Theory; CompStat; Police Detectives; Racial Profiling.

Further Readings
Dunaway v. New York, 442 U.S. 200 (1979).
Ferdico, John N., Henry F. Fradella, and Christopher D. Totten. *Criminal Procedure for the Criminal Justice Professional.* 10th ed. Belmont, CA: Wadsworth Cengage Learning, 2009.
Florida v. J.L., 529 U.S. 266 (2000).
Florida v. Rodriguez, 469 U.S. 1 (1984).
Florida v. Royer, 460 U.S. 491 (1983).
Illinois v. Wardlow, 528 U.S. 119 (2000).
Minnesota v. Dickerson, 508 U.S. 366 (1993).
Ridgeway, Greg. *Analysis of Racial Disparities in the New York Police Department's Stop, Question, and Frisk Practices.* Santa Monica, CA: Rand Corporation, 2007.
Roberson, Cliff, Harvey Wallace, and Gilbert B. Stuckey. *Procedures in the Justice System.* 9th ed. Upper Saddle River, NJ: Prentice Hall, 2010.
Sibron v. New York, 392 U.S. 40 (1968).
Skolnick, Jerome H. *Justice Without Trial: Law Enforcement in a Democratic Society.* Hoboken, NJ: John Wiley & Sons, 1966.
Terry v. Ohio, 392 U.S. 1 (1967).
U.S. v. Mendenhall, 446 U.S. 544 (1980).

Street Art

Part of the urban experience in most American cities is the existence of graffiti and street art. Some experts suggest that "street art" is the encompassing term, and that graffiti is subsumed by street art. Others will argue that all unsanctioned art that is not graffiti and is applied to outdoor surfaces is street art.

Regardless, street artists consist of individuals who create stencils to paint them on the walls. They also include people who affix sticker art, and individuals known as wheat-pasters who put non-advertising–based posters on walls. Some recent developments also include knitters who affix their work to public objects (e.g., sculptures, parking meters, bike racks, etc.). Street art is usually affixed to the same locations that graffiti is, but there are some unique places where it appears. Although an increasing amount of scholarly attention and some public policy efforts have been spent on addressing street art, most of the attention has been on graffiti. Although street art is considered vandalism by local law enforcement and departments of public works, the degree of damage it creates to property varies based on the type of application. Some types of street art can be removed with a minimum of difficulty, while others are more difficult.

Nongraffiti–based street art has noticeable benefits for the artists. It often takes less time to put the piece up, and thus the possibility of either being detected and reported to the authorities or the authorities responding is less. The artists also do not have to inhale the fumes of the aerosol can. As compared to graffiti, it may not need large surfaces; most of the preparation work can be done in advance, off-site, and then applied later during an opportune time. Some of these works have explicit political kinds of messages, while others are simply tags placed on stickers. Others are simply works that seem to be scrawled in hip-hop style, while still others are elaborate images. Some street artists focus on getting one or more images that appear in the three different kinds of media. Street art can be placed on top or beside already existing graffiti. In general, there are four types of nongraffiti street art: stenciling, stickers, posters/postering (i.e., wheat-pasting), and installations. The balance of the entry will briefly explain each of these types of street art.

Stenciling and stickers are typically a hybrid form of the silk-screen method and can be painted or spray-painted depending on the artist's preferences. This can be as simple as a tag or an image that is stenciled on the side of a building. Artists may have a way of putting this together so that they layer a series of stencils one on top of each other or on top of portions of the existing images. Stickers are often placed on the front or back of traffic and parking signs. The images on the stickers are either ones that have been created on a computer or they have used stickers from the post office that you would attach to envelopes or parcels. Sometimes artists have written their tag on the larger art piece on the sticker as well. There are numerous free stickers that both public and private sector organizations produce that are then repurposed by street artists.

In other contexts, street artists will paste posters to surfaces. This is done with a wheat paste mixture. The image is typically produced on a photocopy machine or silk-screened and then affixed to a wall. Artists may do a run of the image in different colors. This is done to provide diversity in their content.

Periodically street artists will create structures that have a provocative message. They may be difficult to disassemble and be intended to be more permanent. There are also more involved kinds of street art. For example, Banksy, one of the most preeminent graffiti/street artists in the world, and his assistants have built and erected elaborate kinds of structures. These structures were documented in his movie *Exit Through the Gift Shop.*

All of these methods can be combined together to make even more complicated and nuanced creative works. Street artists are not simply content to focus on street art per se. They may also do graffiti or they move back and forth between the two media. Like graffiti, the application of street art must take into consideration weather, lighting, and security conditions. In other words, rain and snow are suboptimal conditions for installing the street art—as are dark conditions, but not so problematic as it is for graffiti artists. Posters are easiest to remove by the department of public works or owners of buildings; this may be one of the reasons why street artists may decide to do this kind of activity rather than the other options. Although posters and stickers can be removed with a high-velocity pressure washer, stencils are more difficult.

It requires a certain amount of talent to produce a piece that is attractive. Sometimes the perpetrators are high school or art students, with many being political activists trying to get their message through somehow to the passers by. The quality of the images usually get better over time through trial and error and proper mentorship.

Jeffrey Ian Ross
University of Baltimore

See Also: Broken Windows Theory; Gangs (Street); Graffiti; Juvenile Offending; Vandalism.

Further Readings

Banksy. *Exit Through the Gift Shop*. Film. Oscilloscope Laboratories, 2010.

Carlsson, Benke and Hop Louie. *Street Art Cookbook: A Guide to Techniques and Materials.* Arsta, Sweden: Dokument Press, 2010.

Howze, Russell. *Stencil Nation: Graffiti, Community, and Art.* San Francisco, CA: Manic D Press, 2008.

Lewisohn, Cedar. *Street Art: The Graffiti Revolution.* London: Abrams, 2008.

Streetsy. Posting Graffiti Since 2005. http://www .streetsy.com (Accessed July 2012).

Street Corner Society

Street Corner Society: The Social Structure of an Italian Slum, written by the sociologist William Foote Whyte, is considered a classic ethnographic study of an immigrant urban neighborhood, including some of its criminogenic aspects such as youth street gangs. Based on fieldwork conducted from 1937 to 1940, the book's first printing was in 1943 by the University of Chicago Press. The neighborhood, initially called Cornerville to protect the identities of those studied, was revealed in later editions as Boston's North End, an area then characterized as a slum inhabited mostly by Italian immigrants. Within the larger context of Boston, the neighborhood was considered to be a problem area, mainly because of the prevalence of street crime, poverty, corrupt politicians, and racketeers. To a lesser extent, the neighborhood was suspect because some Italian immigrants at the outset of World War II were suspected of being sympathizers of Benito Mussolini's fascist regime in Italy.

Well over a half century after its publication, *Street Corner Society* continues to be relevant. The work is considered a foundational study in ethnography, particularly for its neighborhood-level focus. Whyte's detailed discussion of his methodology of participant observation is also an important legacy (an expanded discussion of which was included in the 3rd [1980] and 4th [1993] editions). The study is also considered of seminal import for those interested in studying street gangs, and particularly for its focus on both their internal organization and external linkages with larger-scale criminal organizations and political environments.

In the tradition of ethnographic research in the social sciences, Whyte affords his readers an insider's view into a social world (and now a slice of history) to which they would not normally have access. As Whyte wrote in the Introduction (page xvi), "the middle-class person looks upon the slum district as a formidable mass of confusion, a social chaos. The insider finds in Cornerville a highly organized and integrated social system." Rather than disregarding the relevance of social life in a troubled neighborhood by making the assumption that the environment lacks social organization, Whyte demonstrated that the social environment in Cornerville was in fact highly organized. An important legacy of *Street Corner Society* is that in the book

Whyte translates the important social organizations of Cornerville in a way accessible to outsiders.

Motivation and Nature of the Individuals

The book is divided into two main sections, the first examining the social life of two groups observed in Cornerville: the "corner boys" and the "college boys." Social relations among young men in Cornerville were characterized as a competition for local dominance of street corners, with a different youth gang controlling each corner or city block. Rival youth gangs sometimes violently clashed with one another, but also competed for local control of social resources and both legitimate and quasi-legitimate financial influence.

Whyte befriended a key informant who was then the leader of a corner gang, and through this association, he learned about the social organization of gangs, which is based on a set of informal (often tacit) obligations. Involvement in gangs often develops out of childhood networks, and corner boys maintained loyalty to the associations developed in youth, often persisting well through their 20s or 30s. In contrast, college boys were a smaller segment of the young male population in Cornerville, and via their investment in higher education, were engaged in building professional careers affording them upward mobility.

Another key informant, this one among the college boys, helped Whyte to understand that this youth group, though similar in organization to that observed among corner boys, was more broadly interpreted as legitimate and constructive, because it sought higher education and legitimate employment. Although the corner boys and the college boys seemed at times to differ greatly in their world views, there was nonetheless some interaction between the individual members, including at times the overlap of membership.

Higher Tiers of Organization

The second section of the book examines the broader connections of racketeers and politicians within and affecting Cornerville, and in particular how these were linked to smaller-scale corner boy groups. Racketeers, though active in liquor distribution during the Prohibition era, by the late 1930s were primarily involved in illegal gambling. One of the most important findings of Whyte's work was that politicians, racketeers, and corner boy groups were linked in a larger social hierarchy, with politicians at the top, racketeers in the middle, and corner boy groups at the bottom. In addition, these hierarchies connected members involved in legitimate and illegitimate activities, and the individuals and groups within the hierarchy were tied to one another via informal reciprocal expectations, similar to the informal expectations that typified the social organization of corner boy groups. Thus, rather than examining street gangs as isolated phenomena, Whyte revealed that the corner boys were part of a broad social context involving numerous parties, and which included a variety of criminal and normative activities.

Glenn W. Muschert
Miami University

See Also: Bootleggers; Boston, Massachusetts; Code of the Street; Gambling, Street; Gangs (Street); Immigrant Neighborhoods; Juvenile Offenders; Organized Crime and Violence; Racial Profiling; Urban Ethnography.

Further Readings
Adler, Patricia A., Peter Adler, and John M. Johnson, eds. "Street Corner Society Revisited" [Special Issue]. *Journal of Contemporary Ethnography,* v.21/1 (1992).
Whyte, William Foote. "Revisiting Street Corner Society." *Sociological Forum,* v.8/2 (1993).
Whyte, William Foote. *Street Corner Society: The Social Structure of an Italian Slum.* 4th ed. Chicago: University of Chicago Press, 1993.

Street Crime (Online Game)

While street crime has been a societal problem for decades, the rise of video games depicting it in a positive manner has been equally concerning. Commercially successful games such as *Grand Theft Auto,* for example, demonstrate street violence and gang participation as an exciting, enjoyable experience. The *Street Crime* game presents another troublesome depiction of these activities in an online game setting. *Street Crime* is a browser-based, free multiplayer, role-playing game conducted online in which players immerse themselves in the world of

street crime in order to gain money and power. The game was initially released in 2007 and has grown in popularity since. At present, there are three versions of the game available for free online play.

Game Structure

Like most online games, *Street Crime* uses basic concepts to measure success. Players collect money in order to advance to further levels. At the beginning, players are given $5,000 in cash which is to be used to help them purchase tools that can be used in their criminal life. Ultimately, the tools are supposed to lead to large returns as the game progresses. With tools at hand, the actual game begins. The player's character is asked to commit a number of various crimes. Each crime is given a level of difficulty. and the amount of money players receive for successful completion depends on the difficulty. The harder the crime is to commit, the more the character will receive in compensation for completing it.

The game does not simply allow street criminals to commit crimes without the fear of consequences, however. During the commission of a crime, players must be concerned about the possibility of being arrested and serving time in jail. When players first begin playing *Street Crime,* the punishments they face are relatively low. This reflects the idea that since they have little criminal notoriety, they will merely be viewed as petty street criminals.

However, as players become more well known, their punishments will likewise become more

The Entertainment Software Association, the leading lobby of the video game industry, states that 20 percent of video game players are boys under the age of 17.

severe. Given the first-person play nature of *Street Crime*, jail time is served out in real time. Rather than seeing the fictional character sentenced to two years in jail, for example, the player is sentenced to 10 hours in jail, and is effectively banned from taking part in any game activities for that period.

While the player is in jail, there are options to avoid the full sentence. For example, players can ask their friends on the game to help them break out, and the player can offer bribes to jail staff to be freed. Or players can use tools they collect throughout the game to try to break free on their own. To discourage this behavior, unsuccessful attempts result in extended jail sentences.

Levels of Dubious Achievement

Another important element to consider about *Street Crime* is how a player moves up throughout the game. At the beginning, players are at the rank of mere Hobos. At this level, they are able to commit petty theft and other low-level crimes. With time, however, they can reach the rank of Godfather—the highest level possible in *Street Crime*. As the levels increase, so, too, do the available crimes to be committed. With added difficulty comes greater potential for more money and more jail time. The real shift comes when players advance to levels where they can begin running legitimate fields of business. At different points, players will find themselves in control of casinos and working on the stock market.

The game has no actual conclusion. At no point do players reach a place where they have completed everything. Instead, *Street Crime* uses incentives to keep players active, along with adding new content and versions of the game so that even the most successful players continue encountering new challenges. The game is fairly successful, with over 40,000 registered users. Of those, 344 have advanced to the level of Godfather. Approximately 300 people play the game on a daily basis. Beyond the actual gameplay, there is a thriving online community where players interact with one another. Through live chats and personal messages, players can determine ways to team together in order to best accomplish their aims and goals.

Questions of Effect

The game has received attention due to the fact that it is a first-person role-playing game located online that cannot accurately determine the age of players. When someone goes to sign up and join the game, he is greeted with the following message: "Register now to start a life of crime, killing, girls, and money. Join thousands of others in the biggest and best free online gangster game on the web."

Because there is no monetary fee for playing, and no disc or download of software is needed, one concern is that this eliminates at least one possible barrier to younger children or adolescents taking part in the game. While *Street Crime* may not reach the stratospheric popularity of such games as the *Grand Theft Auto* series, it nevertheless serves as another item on the list of questionable entertainment products that have the potential to desensitize its users to violence and a depraved morality.

Street Crime producers are aware of many concerns voiced by members of the public. The disclaimer visible as participants register reads:

Street Crime accepts no responsibility for the actions of its members i.e. Self harm, Vandalism, Suicide, Homicide, Genocide, Drug abuse, Changes in sexual orientation, Bestiality. Street Crime will not be held responsible and does not encourage any of the above actions or any other form of anti social behaviour. Although Street Crime is highly addictive we encourage you to spend time with your family and loved ones, do not forget them. Remember Street Crime is just a game, if you hit someone with a hammer in real life, they may not just go to hospital.

The reach of *Street Crime* has grown in recent years. The game is now able to be played through Facebook and has its own Twitter feed through which updates are sent to followers.

William J. Miller
Flagler College

See Also: Code of the Street; Drive-By Shooting; Gangs (Street); *Grand Theft Auto* (Video Game); Juvenile Offending; Risky Lifestyles; Street Crime, Popular Portrayals of; Television Shows.

Further Readings
Bytewire, Ltd. "Street Crime: Rule the Underworld." 2008. http://www.street-crime.com (Accessed April 2012).

McKegg, Conan. "Facing Challenges: Morality and Roleplaying Games." October 8, 2004. http://www.rpg.net/news+reviews/columns/stairs08oct04.html (Accessed April 2012).

Turkle, Sherry. *Alone Together: Why We Expect More From Technology and Less from Each Other*. New York: Basic Books, 2011.

Vega, Nora. "12 Most Controversial Video Games." February 17, 2010. http://www.oddee.com/item_96977.aspx (Accessed April 2012).

Street Crime, Popular Portrayals of

The way that we interpret and understand the world is based on our experience with both direct and indirect forms of communication. Because the mass media is a vital source of indirect communication, its messages are tremendously influential in the way we think about ourselves and the world around us. These media messages, or narratives, impact not only our sense of who and what we are but also the interactions we have with other people and social institutions, and our wider social and political contexts.

The portrayal of street crime, both real and fictional, is a central theme in a great deal of mass media narratives, including those that we consume through television programs, feature films, video games, advertisements, popular music, Web sites, and the news. At the first level of approximation, these mediated texts are the social reality of crime; in essence, they are stories that a society tells itself about crime. As a mediated reality, crime becomes a "product" through which producers, writers, reporters, editors, and other personnel in the culture industries draw the attention of television viewers, theatergoers, videogamers, radio listeners, Internet browsers, newspaper readers, and other audiences. By playing to emotions and traits such as fear, sadistic pleasure, voyeurism, loathing, and vengeance, these popular portrayals of street crime inform and reinforce public (mis)understandings of crime and transgressive behavior.

In other words, what people think they know about crime, criminals, and the criminal justice system; their fears of violent victimization; and their general feelings of personal vulnerability are all significantly influenced by popular culture's crime narratives. Hence, one of the most potentially illuminating areas of criminological inquiry lies in an analysis of popular portrayals of street crime.

Crime as News

The regular portrayal of crime as a newsworthy topic has its roots in early-19th-century newspapers. By 1830 coverage of crime was becoming a standardized component of news narratives, though it was not until the turn of the 20th century that crime took on the character of the salable commodity we know it to be today. According to sociologist Ray Surette, the mid-20th century saw the increasingly aggressive marketing of crime news through specialized crime beat reporting. The result was more sensationalistic coverage of crime that relied ever more heavily upon the police, prosecuting attorneys, and other criminal justice officials for commentary and analysis. The news media has since become a central conduit for the production and filtering of popular portrayals of crime.

However, criminologists have long recognized that news organizations do not simply report the news but rather determine the news. For example, Stuart Hall and his colleagues' comprehensive study of the ways in which the media presented a mugging as indicative of a national crisis illustrates that crime news is the end product of a media process that involves the systematic organization of events and topics in ways that conform to dominant social fears and anxieties.

This mediated construction and marketing of crime and crime control issues as news reveals the class-biased and racialized underpinnings of a host of street crime narratives. In their study of the news media, Stanley Cohen and Jock Young demonstrate that crime stories about drugs, sex, and violence—particularly those involving the poor, youths, racialized people, immigrants, or other socially disenfranchised groups—always make for compelling narratives and hence disproportionately make up the negotiated accomplishment that is the "crime news." Similarly, in his study of crime wave reporting, Mark Fishman found that violent crimes such as robberies, random shootings, stabbings, and other assaults constituted the majority of crime news—despite the fact that they made up only a very small percentage of all criminal activity.

Crime news promulgates and reinforces simplistic images of crime and criminality as a monopoly of the poor, racialized people, and other "dangerous classes." These narratives are not about the reality of crime, but instead constitute crime as a reality through narrative contextualization that mirrors the hegemony of late modernity.

The news media's coverage of crime is likely the single most influential factor in what criminologists refer to as a moral panic, or collective overreaction to some perceived crime threat. While it is only part of a larger process, the media's role in the orchestration of unrealistic and unsubstantiated public fear should not be underestimated. News coverage of certain kinds of criminal and transgressive behavior serve to inflate the seriousness of the incidents, making them appear more heinous and frequent than they truly are. Public anxiety is inflamed through the use of journalistic techniques. "Special Cover Story," "Breaking News," or "Investigative Report" coverage employs dramatic photos, video, and sound bites along with highly moralistic editorializing. Under such strictures, alienated and frustrated youth are transmogrified into "teen superpredators," small cohorts of young people into "rampaging mobs," protesters into "agitators" (or worse, "anarchists"), minor property damage into "wholesale destruction," and scuffles into "riots."

The news media typically view drama, violence, and physical harm as hallmarks of newsworthiness and hence play to the fears, both real and imagined, of the audience. The exploitative and sensationalistic media coverage of crime that we are today accustomed to is not so much designed to inform audiences as it is to entertain and sell (both advertising space and a value system). Gregg Barak theorizes that contemporary crime news acts as a buffer of social reality, converting criminal events into crime-infotainment. Hence, more than simply lucrative packages of "what society tells itself about crime," news coverage of crime omits, suppresses, and homogenizes inequality and human suffering.

One of the consequences of this myopic crime narrative is a distorted picture of crime and criminality. Unfortunately the news media's coverage of crime leaves little room for the audience to consider other forms of crime, such as those committed by the corporations, the state, and international financial institutions.

Crime as Entertainment

While some schools of criminology have examined portrayals of street crime in the news media since the 1970s, it has only been since the late 1990s that criminologists have seriously investigated the entertainment media's treatment of crime. Although crime as a form of entertainment is a somewhat more recent media foray than crime as news, only coming to first prominence in the latter part of the 19th century, it has increasingly cemented itself as a hallmark of popular culture, and an ever more salient component of cultural and economic brokerage.

Some of the earliest instances of crime as entertainment came in the form of serialized fiction in newspapers and magazines. For example, tales of the world's most famous detectives, Sherlock Holmes and Dr. Watson, first appeared in a British magazine in the late 1880s, and American readers were introduced to a series of no-nonsense sleuths, tough lawmen, and desperate criminals in nickel weeklies and dime store novels during this same period. And although English-language novels about detectives have arguably existed since the 18th century, as a popular genre detective fiction is a product of Depression-era America. Similarly, while some literary critics point to earlier examples, the emergence of the true-crime genre is often traced to the publication of Truman Capote's *In Cold Blood* in the mid-1960s.

Today, fictional portrayals of crime in the suspense, mystery, legal, and detective genres by authors such as Agatha Christie, James Ellroy, Sue Grafton, Patrica Highsmith, Walter Mosley, and Ian Rankin regularly top best seller lists. So, too, the general public hungrily consumes true crime's lurid tales of serial murder, child abduction, and organized crime. The public's appetite for information on bizarre and vicious crimes has spawned a plethora of books on everything from megacases such as the Manson Family, O. J. Simpson, JonBenét Ramsey, the Columbine Massacre, and the Chandra Levy disappearance, through the banal tragedies of high-priced sex trade workers, outlaw motorcycle clubs, drug-addicted cosmetic surgeons, and murderous philanderers.

In addition to the explosion in crime fiction publishing that occurred in the 1930s, that decade also witnessed the birth of radio crime dramas featuring programs such as *Calling All Cars, Crime Doesn't*

Pay, and *Police Headquarters.* These and other similar dramas were explicitly and unapologetically pro-law and order, presenting entertaining, though one-dimensional, images of wicked criminals and noble law enforcement officials.

Technological advances in the post–World War II period provided increasing outlets for fictionalized portrayals of street crime, first through Hollywood films, and later in the form of television programs such as *Dragnet, Highway Patrol, Perry Mason, 77 Sunset Strip, The FBI,* and *Hawaii Five-0.* For most of the 1970s and 1980s television's fictionalized portrayals of street crime were action packed, but relatively light, hour-long dramas featuring patrol-level police officers, detective partners, or private investigators—such as *CHiPs, Cagney & Lacey, Starsky and Hutch, Miami Vice, Charlie's Angels, Magnum P.I.,* and *Simon and Simon.*

First airing in 1981, *Hill Street Blues* proved to be a notable exception which heralded many of the medium's contemporary offerings. Set in the Hill Street police precinct of a major (but unspecified) urban center, the program dealt with grittier themes in a more nuanced fashion than did its predecessors. Topics such as poverty, urban blight, police use of force, political corruption, police-community relations, substance abuse, and others were explored thorough a large ensemble of characters including police officers, civilian police employees, community activists, gang members, prosecutors, legal aid counsels, and city officials.

Over the course of the past two decades this genre has expanded exponentially. Immensely popular and often graphic programs such as *Criminal Minds* and the multiple incarnations of *CSI* and *Law & Order* enthrall audiences by celebrating the investigative, scientific, and retributive components of the criminal justice system, while programs such as *The Sopranos, Dexter,* and *Sons of Anarchy* titillate by presenting the trials and decadent pleasures of lifeworlds revolving around crime, vigilantism, and transgression.

Crime Vérité

As in the case of crime-centric magazines and novels spawning true crime books, the progeny of television's fictionalized portrayals of crime is crime-based reality TV. Born in the late 1980s and truly taking form in the decade of the 1990s, this televisual circus is comprised of several subgenres,

including talk shows, one-time specials, "political affairs" programs, documentaries, and cinema vérité whose themes range from the simply outrageous and exploitative through the punitive and vengeful. *COPS,* which was one of the first forays into crime vérité, combines dashboard-mounted and portable handheld cameras to (re)create the experiences of moralizing patrol officers as they pursue and arrest suspects. First aired in 1989, the program inspired numerous imitations such as *To Serve and Protect, Police Women* (with several different series set in Broward County, Florida; Cincinnati, Ohio; and Memphis, Tennessee), *Dallas SWAT* (and its spinoffs *Detroit SWAT* and *Kansas City SWAT),* and variations on the theme, such as *Dog the Bounty Hunter.*

Likewise, a host of programs such as *American Justice* and *The First 48* present highly stylized versions of criminalistics and psychological profiling by creatively blending elements of documentary, docudrama, and investigative report styles. Though less obviously "trash-TV," the latter programs unfortunately do not provide a more realistic image of crime.

An equally sensationalistic approach coupled with a more openly retributive theme is evident on *America's Most Wanted.* Interspersing the host's presentation of "the facts" with dramatic recreations, the program purportedly seeks viewers' help in apprehending suspects believed to be responsible for the most heinous crimes. Similarly, a host of ultraconservative TV commentators such as Nancy Grace, Bill O'Reilly, and Geraldo Rivera regularly address gruesome (but statistically rare) crimes such as stranger abductions, sexual torture, and murder, employing the veneer of "victims' rights" to sheath their vituperative calls for retribution.

Conclusion

American culture's fascination with crime and retributive justice is perhaps best understood using criminologist Mike Presdee's analogy to the board game Monopoly. According to his model, crime, like monopoly capitalism, is dehistoricized, whitewashed, and transformed into mass-marketed pleasure.

Stephen L. Muzzatti
Ryerson University

See Also: Fear of Crime; *Grand Theft Auto* (Video Game); Risky Lifestyles; *Street Crime* (Online Game); Suite Crimes Versus Street Crimes; Television Shows.

Further Readings

Barak, Gregg, ed. *Media, Process, and the Social Construction of Crime.* New York: Garland, 1994.

Cohen, Stanley and Jock Young, eds. *The Manufacture of News.* Beverly Hills, CA: Sage, 1973.

Colaguori, Claudio. "Prime Time Crime Programming and the Formation of Authoritarian Attitudes Among Viewers." *Critical Criminologist,* v.20/1 (2011).

DeKeseredy, Walter and Molly Dragiewicz, eds. *The Handbook of Critical Criminology.* London: Routledge, 2011

Dowler, Ken, et al. "Constructing Crime: Media, Crime and Popular Culture." *Canadian Journal of Criminology and Criminal Justice,* v.48/6 (2006).

Fishman, Mark. "Crime Waves as Ideology." *Social Problems,* v.25/5 (1978).

Jewkes, Yvonne. *Media and Crime.* 2nd ed. London: Sage, 2010.

Muzzatti, Stephen. L. and Richard Featherstone. "Crosshairs on Our Backs: The Culture of Fear and the Production of the D.C. Sniper Story." *Contemporary Justice Review,* v.10/1 (2007).

Surette, Ray. *Media, Crime and Criminal Justice: Images, Realities, and Policies.* 4th ed. Belmont, CA: Wadsworth, 2011.

Street Crime Defined

At first glance, the term *street crime,* often considered a form of predatory crime, appears to be a relatively straightforward crime categorization. However, as a popular term among scholars, criminal justice practitioners, and the general public, there is no definitive definition of street crime. Even the nation's clearinghouse for the compilation and dissemination of criminal statistics, the Federal Bureau of Investigation (FBI), has no criteria in the categorization of specific crimes to be designated or defined as street crime.

Category Descriptions

Street crime involves those crimes customarily referred to as the "crime problem," and perpetrators of street crimes represent the prototypical criminal in the United States. A unifying theme of street crime is that it occurs in public space, usually in metropolitan and urban areas. The Uniform Crime Reports (UCR) program of the FBI that records all crimes known to the police typically defines street crimes as those offenses that occur on streets, highways, parking lots, and other salient public realms. Crime in this street context has generally been divided into two categories: violent crime and property crime.

Within the UCR, violent crime is composed of four offense categories: murder and nonnegligent manslaughter, forcible rape, robbery, and aggravated assault. Violent crimes are defined in the UCR program as those offenses that involve force or the threat of force against a person or persons. In contrast, the UCR defines property crimes as the offenses of burglary, larceny-theft, motor vehicle theft, and arson. (Shoplifting and vandalism are also property crimes but are not reported in the UCR.) According to the UCR definition, these property crime categories do not involve force or threat of force against victims, and their purpose is generally to acquire a person's money or property. Other street crimes may include possessing and/or distributing illegal drugs, prostitution, public disorder, aggressive begging, the creation of graffiti, vandalism, vagrancy, public intoxication, and related crimes that occur in public space.

Volume Trends of the Crimes

According to the 2010 UCR, an estimated 1,246,248 violent crimes occurred nationwide, or 403.6 violent crimes per 100,000 inhabitants—a decrease of 6 percent from the 2009 estimate. This 2010 estimated violent crime total was 13.2 percent below the 2006 level, and 13.4 percent below the 2001 level. In 2010, aggravated assaults accounted for the highest number of violent crimes reported by law enforcement at 62.5 percent, followed by robbery (29.5 percent), forcible rape (6.8 percent), and murder (1.2 percent).

In the 2010 UCR, there were an estimated 9,082,887 property crime offenses in the United States, or 2,941.9 per 100,000 inhabitants. In 2010, property crimes decreased 2.7 percent compared to 2009, and decreased 9.3 percent from 2006. Larceny-theft accounted for 68.1 percent of all property crimes in 2010, followed by burglary (23.8 percent) and motor vehicle theft (8.1 percent). Some major police jurisdictions have not reported arson in their filings with the FBI, so this makes arson tracking in the UCR problematic.

Neighborhoods and Gangs

It should be noted that not all violent or property crimes occur in the public sphere or in the street context. However, the vast majority of these crimes in the United States are street crimes that occur in large urban cities and in the poorest neighborhoods. Violent street crime tends to be located in communities plagued by extreme poverty and unemployment. In these socioeconomically disadvantaged neighborhoods, working-class and less affluent Americans are also more victimized by street crime.

Urban communities that offer residents economic and social opportunities have lower rates of street crime (i.e., property crime and violent crime). Overall, reduced wages, high unemployment rates, and lower government benefits all play crucial roles in the rise and persistence of street crime in disenfranchised communities across the United States.

A substantial portion of street crime located in poor urban communities is perpetrated in the context of gang violence. Gangs typically exist in high-crime, socially disadvantaged neighborhoods and become "institutionalized" when core social institutions function poorly (i.e., families, schools, economic systems). In contrast to popular belief, most street gangs are loosely structured, with transient leadership and membership. These so-called gangs are essentially informal street groups that perpetrate an overwhelming share of street crime in the United States. Much of this gang-related street crime is a result of a street culture involving feuds, vendettas, retribution, and violent displays of masculinity and one-upmanship.

Studies of large urban areas show that gang activity is largely responsible for the street crimes committed in those areas where they are prevalent. The U.S. Department of Justice has noted that gangs account for as much as 80 percent of street crime in some urban communities. Research has also estimated that over half of the nationwide killings counted in the FBI UCR are due to gang-related street crime.

The Drug Vector

A further cause of street crime in America is the violence and property violations caused by drug prohibition. This intrinsic violence of the illicit

A fingerprint scanning device is used on a suspect. Suspects often give false names when questioned and this technology foils that avoidance tactic by transmitting images of a suspect's fingerprints to the in-car computer where they are run through a database.

drug market, often referred to as systemic violence, is responsible for much street-related crime in the United States. Due to the fact that individuals involved in the illicit drug market cannot defer to formal control agents to solve disputes or handle wrongdoings they resort to forms of street crime to even debts and maintain order.

Street crime related to the drug market arises from disputes over drug territory, as a means of enforcing normative codes, retaliation for drug robberies, elimination of informers, punishment for adulterated drugs, and from the social ecology of drug-using areas. To a much lesser extent, some individuals addicted to drugs may resort to theft and other property crimes to support their habits, while others may commit acts of violence due to the pharmacological effects of certain drugs.

Media Depiction

When the majority of Americans think of crime, they think of street crime involving acts of personal violence or crimes against personal property. Many Americans believe that street crime is an increasingly widespread social problem despite the continual decline in U.S. crime rates. These perceptions of violent street crimes are reinforced by the news media and serve to amplify Americans' fears about their personal safety and possessions.

Both television crime dramas and news coverage depict the rarest and most sensational forms of street crime, such as street murders by strangers with unusual victims. The majority of victims and offenders of street crime are African American men, aged 12–24, and living in households with the lowest incomes. Aside from the crime of rape, men are much more likely to be both the victims and perpetrators of violent street crime. Furthermore, rates of street crime are higher in the southern region of the United States; evidence suggests that higher temperatures make people more agitated and prone to impulsive acts, while warmer weather allows for more opportunity as people are more likely to leave possessions outside and windows open

Patrick K. O'Brien
University of Colorado Boulder

See Also: Arrest; Code of the Street; Crime Patterns; Fear of Crime; Gangs (Street); History of Street Crime in America; Street Crime, Popular Portrayals of.

Further Readings

Federal Bureau of Investigation. "Uniform Crime Reports, 2010." 2011. http://www.fbi.gov/about-us/cjis/ucr/crime-in-the-u.s/2010/crime-in-the-u.s.-2010 (Accessed October 2011).

Hallsworth, Simon. *Street Crime*. Portland, OR: Willan Publishing, 2005.

LaFree, Gary. *Losing Legitimacy: Street Crime and the Decline of Social Institutions in America*. Boulder, CO: Westview Press, 1998.

Street/Block Parties

Block parties are neighborhood gatherings in which individuals organize collectively to eat, socialize, and take part in various forms of entertainment. These events can take place in a nearby local park or even in the neighborhood streets themselves. They can be relatively small events, but may also be large events organized by a neighborhood association or watch program.

Often, in areas that strongly practice community policing, law enforcement officials may attend or help sponsor the event. The purpose of block or street parties is to provide a prosocial networking atmosphere for the neighborhood residents. This allows individuals to meet and familiarize themselves with their neighbors.

Community Within a Community

Many contextual factors are of interest to researchers attempting to explain street crime in America. But perhaps none are more important than the context of "neighborhood." The neighborhood often serves as a community within a community. The wide-scale implementation of community policing policies by law enforcement agencies can be perceived as anecdotal evidence of the criminal justice system's prescription on the importance of the neighborhood. Subculture, conflict, and social disorganization theorists often focus on the context of neighborhoods when examining street crime. In other words, theorists have used neighborhood-level measurements, such as a census tract's median income, to help explain individual relationships with street crime and overall crime rates for specific areas.

Block parties have periodically been examined by researchers and criminal justice officials because of the possibility that they play a role in neighborhood crime reduction. Block parties are commonly used by Neighborhood Watch organizations for the purpose of disseminating information, and more importantly, creating a stronger sense of community among the neighborhood's residents. Block parties create a stronger sense of community by bringing neighbors together collectively, opening lines of communication among neighbors, and increasing awareness about criminal activities potentially taking place within the neighborhood.

Increased communication and awareness among neighbors has potential crime-reducing effects because neighbors may be more inclined to intervene, assist, or call the police for a neighbor they are more socially connected to. At the very least, it may create an atmosphere where neighbors talk to the police and support local law enforcement efforts to control crime. The hypothesis that block parties have crime-reducing effects may not be conclusively supported by research, but recent empirical examinations of collective efficacy produce supportive findings.

Collective Efficacy

Collective efficacy, that is, social cohesion facilitating a willingness to intervene on behalf of the common good, is hypothesized to reduce violence and crime. Increased levels of social cohesion in a neighborhood are empirically tied to reduced levels of violence. Block parties are often mentioned as way to increase neighborhood social cohesion. These events provide neighbors with the unique opportunity to better familiarize themselves with the other residents. If individuals become more familiar with their neighbors, then they may be more willing to intervene during or after a future criminal event that may take place.

Increased intervention among neighborhood residents combined with increased levels of social cohesion can possibly help reduce neighborhood levels of street crime. In sum, block parties may indirectly influence levels of street crime in the United States by increasing neighborhood levels of collective efficacy, which in turn has been shown empirically to be a robust predictor of levels of violence and street crime.

Need for Research

If block parties have potential to increase levels of collective efficacy in neighborhoods, then their role in Neighborhood Watch programs may be warranted. However, this further raises the level of importance for empirically testing the effects of not only levels of collective efficacy on crime, but also the effects of Neighborhood Watch programs. Block parties, collective efficacy, and Neighborhood Watch programs are interconnected ideas for potentially reducing neighborhood-level crime, but further research may be needed to determine the true effectiveness of block parties and Neighborhood Watch organizations.

Contemporary research findings steer clear of directly linking block parties to crime reduction. Rather, block parties and watch programs are seen as influencing neighborhood levels of collective efficacy, thus indirectly linking them to crime reduction. The effectiveness of using block parties to reduce neighborhood levels of crime is questionable and continues to be examined by scholars. Despite the state of empirical evidence, creating a stronger sense of community is still commonly perceived as a worthwhile Neighborhood Watch activity.

Daniel R. Kavish
Christopher W. Mullins
Southern Illinois University, Carbondale

See Also: Bystander Apathy; Community Policing; Neighborhood Watch; Street Crime Defined; Urban Ethnography.

Further Readings

Morenoff, Jeffrey D., Robert J. Sampson, and Stephen W. Raudenbush. "Neighborhood Inequality, Collective Efficacy, and the Spatial Dynamics of Urban Violence." *Criminology*, v.39/3 (2001).

National Sheriff's Association. "Neighborhood Watch Manual: USAonWatch—National Neighborhood Watch Program." Alexandria, VA: National Sheriff's Association, 2010.

Sampson, Robert J., Stephen W. Raudenbush, and Fenton Earls. "Neighborhoods and Violent Crime: A Multilevel Study of Collective Efficacy." *Science*, v.277/5328 (1997).

Suite Crimes Versus Street Crimes

When it comes to crime, criminality, or criminals, the majority of the public are concerned with street crime (e.g., burglary, rape, homicide). This type of crime remains the dominant focus of the media, politicians, the general public, and criminologists. Data are provided by governments that give us yearly breakdowns of the types of crimes committed, and studies have attempted to quantify the costs of crime in the United States and other advanced industrialized countries. Yet, in these discussions of crime, what is more often than not ignored are what have been labeled "suite crimes."

Crime on the Job

Suite crimes typically refer to white-collar crimes—offenses committed by individuals during the course of their occupation for the goals of, or in the name of, the organizations for which they work. This does not imply that such crimes omit those that are committed by people for their own personal interests as a result of their profession (i.e., occupational crimes), but that it generally also benefits the organization directly or indirectly (organizational crimes). Suite crimes include those referred to as corporate crime, crimes of the powerful, state-corporate crime, and state criminality. The latter two tend to have been the most often overlooked, ignored, and understudied by criminologists.

In all, suite crime is far more devastating and costly than all street crime combined. Consider the latest U.S. data provided by the Bureau of Justice Statistics, which estimates that during 2009 there were 15,241 homicides, 4.3 million violent crimes, 115.6 million property crimes, and 133,000 personal thefts. During that same year, the United Kingdom reported 648 homicides (England and Wales specifically), 4.45 million violent crimes, 44.61 million property crimes, and 103,600 personal thefts. These examples pale in comparison to the grand scope of suite crimes that are committed yearly by corporations, states, and international financial organizations. While there are no comprehensive statistics available, there are many documented cases, as illustrated below.

While such figures look staggering at first glance, consider that the numbers of civilians that have been killed, maimed, raped, tortured, or displaced by governments' policies far exceed those committed on the streets (e.g., Sudan's killing of the Darfurians, the U.S. invasion and occupation of Iraq, the numbers of civilians killed by Libyan forces during the Arab Spring protests, the massive human rights violations in Uganda, or the ongoing conflict in the Democratic Republic of the Congo). Likewise, corporate crimes have resulted in significant economic costs that far exceed those typically associated with the "high cost of crime."

One needs only to recall the recent economic housing market woes due to corporate mortgage fraud, kickbacks, market manipulation, embezzlement, falsification of financial statements, and securities and exchange improprieties. For example, a total of 592 corporate fraud cases are currently being investigated by Federal Bureau of Investigation field offices that have resulted in economic losses that individually exceed $1 billion. When one adds the environmental harm from suite crime to the table, costs are more often than not immeasurable. Consider the illegal toxic dumping by corporations into open waters or into other countries, or the improper storage of nuclear waste that has decades-long costs to surrounding citizens, the environment, and to future generations.

Given the financial, physical, and environmental costs and widespread nature of suite crime, the ongoing marginalization of the topic by the media, politicians, and criminologists is regretful. Yet, over the course of the past century or so, there have been some who have dedicated their careers to researching and/or exposing such crimes. The following section provides a brief overview of this history.

Historical Overview of the Concept

Suite crime has been recognized and reported on since the late 19th century. For example, in 1898 a French judge, Louis Proal, wrote *Political Crime*, a book focusing on the crimes of politicians and statesmen. The first regulations aimed at limiting monopolies and cartels occurred in 1890 with the Sherman Anti-Trust Act. Investigative journalists, also known as muckrakers, frequently wrote about suite crime, though without the labels given today. For example, in 1906 Upton Sinclair wrote the classic book *The Jungle*, describing the conditions and work practices in the meat industry. In 1934, Matthew Josephson wrote *The Robber Barons: The Great American Capitalists, 1861–1901*.

It was during this time that the first criminological attention to suite crimes was given. In 1939, Edwin Sutherland gave his presidential address to the American Sociological Society, wherein he called attention to a then-neglected form of crime, namely the crimes of "respectable people" in the context of a legitimate occupation, and of corporations. He referred to this as "white-collar crime." For several decades, there was little additional attention given to this form of criminality.

This changed in the 1970s; since then, there has been a fairly rich body of literature on suite crime. While there are various terminologies used to describe these forms of white-collar crimes, including crimes of the powerful and elite deviance, the promotion of the concept of suite crime can be attributed in part to Colin Goff and Charles Reasons's 1978 book on corporate crime in Canada.

As research on white-collar crime began to increase, the early works of the 1970s through the early 1990s were plagued by definitional quagmires. There were long debates and discussions of what constituted these crimes of the powerful, from standards to define the behaviors as criminal, to definitional issues of who were the criminals: an individual focus or that of a corporation. The literature began to be divided by those who studied occupational crimes, often referred to as middle-class crimes, and those who researched what became known as organizational crimes. Consequentially, the contemporary interest in white-collar crime, or suite crime, is reflected in the steady stream of books and articles ranging in focus from research on occupational crimes committed by individuals for their own benefit (e.g., fraud, tax evasion) to organizational crimes committed on behalf of organizational interests and goals (e.g., corporate crime, state-corporate crime, crimes of the state, and crimes of globalization).

Later Developments

The study of corporate crime was continued after Sutherland—in what is referred to as the "big chill" period of scholarship on these types of crimes—primarily by researchers Donald Cressey, Peter Yeager, and Gil Geiss. The origin of the field of state-corporate crime can be attributed to Ron Kramer and Raymond Michalowski's 1990 presentation at the American Society of Criminology conference. With the concept of state-corporate crime, a delineation of the role of the state in crimes of omission or crimes of commission was conceptualized. Since then, a full body of case studies exploring the intersection of corporate crime and states' roles has been produced, including the classic works on the NASA Challenger explosion, the ValuJet crash, and more recent cases including the companies Bridgestone Tire and Halliburton.

In 1989, William Chambliss gave his presidential speech to the American Society of Criminology in which he suggested criminologists should turn their attention to state-organized crimes. This resulted in yet another branch within the umbrella of white-collar crime to include what is now called state crime: those crimes committed by agents of the state that violate domestic and international laws. This includes those actions and policies that directly and indirectly result in criminality. Here again the field has developed a well-rounded body of literature that explores case studies from the production of and/or threat to use nuclear weapons, the Holocaust, the war on Iraq, and cases of genocide in Rwanda and Darfur.

Conclusion

Given the vast costs and harms of crimes of the suites, it seems that mainstream and criminological attention is inadvisably dominated with a focus on traditional street crime. While there is a growing and full body of literature on white-collar crimes, it still remains marginalized within the broader scope of criminology. Having said this, there is the National White-Collar Crime Center and the Federal Bureau of Investigation unit for white-collar crime. In both cases, however, the focus is predominantly on those crimes considered to be occupational crimes. Since the economic crisis and housing market woes of the past few years, there is a more widespread growth in attention by the media and politicians to crimes committed by corporations. Nonetheless, one need only turn on the television, news, pick up a newspaper, or do a quick Internet search on crime and those crimes that occur the least and are less costly to society remain highlighted.

Dawn L. Rothe
Victoria Ellen Collins
Old Dominion University

See Also: Environmental Criminology; Police Corruption, Street-Level; Street Crime, Popular Portrayals of; Street Crime Defined.

Further Readings

Barak, Gregg. *Crimes by the Capitalist State: An Introduction to State Criminality.* Albany: State University of New York Press, 1991.

Chambliss, William. "State Organized Crime." *Criminology*, v.27/2 (1990).

Clinard, Marshall Barron and Peter C. Yeager. *Corporate Crime.* New York: The Free Press, 1980.

Friedrichs, David O. *Trusted Criminals: White Collar Crime in Contemporary Society.* Belmont, CA: Wadsworth, 1996.

Josephson, Matthew. *The Robber Barons: The Great American Capitalists, 1861–1901.* New York: Harcourt, Brace and Co., 1934.

Michalowski, Raymond J. and Ronald C. Kramer, eds. *State-Corporate Crime: Wrongdoing at the Intersection of Business and Government.* New Brunswick, NJ: Rutgers University Press, 2006.

Proal, Louis. *Political Crime.* New York: D. Appleton, 1843.

Rothe, Dawn L. and Christopher W. Mullins. *State Crime, Current Perspectives.* New Brunswick, NJ: Rutgers University Press, 2011.

Sutherland, Edwin. "Presidential Address, American Sociological Society: White-Collar Criminality." *American Sociological Review*, v.5/1 (1939).

Swarming

An emerging trend in illegal youth group activity has been witnessed on our cities' streets: swarming. The act of swarming (sometimes referred to by commentators as wilding, flash mobs, crime mobs, or flashrob events) has captured the interest of urban communities, policing officials, news media, business owners, and criminologists. In his 2006 article "Swarming and the Social Dynamics of Group Violence," Rob White noted that swarming behaviors typically consist of a group of people (often youths) gathering in urban public places. Thus, the phenomenon of swarming is not typically found in rural areas; hence, it's truly an urban street crime activity.

Definition and Prevalence

Criminologists engaged in the study of swarming are interested in group processes whereby youths identify and surround a victim(s) to confuse or disorientate them in order to rob their possessions or to assault the victim during the swarming criminal event. In the victim selection process, typically an easy target is selected; the intimidation and/or overpowering of the victim is the goal, attained either with threats or actual violence. The rationale to swarm can be for a specific purpose or simply as a random-act assault by the group which may result in violence, intimidation, robbery, and occasionally the formation of criminal mobs. Finally, swarming events most commonly occur during warmer months, and the presence of large crowds in public places observing and milling around the swarming event may work to heighten aggressive behaviors by the criminal group.

The scholarly study of swarming is not a new phenomenon. Researchers studying group violence and conflict have long recognized similar activities within the gang literature. In fact, organized youth gangs are often the perpetrators of swarming crime events for the purposes of committing robbery on easy targets.

Moreover, evidence from offenders and victims suggests that swarming can be understood theoretically from a collective behavior approach in that during the swarm event, crime roles, cues, and normative group structure persist as the swarm is undertaken. Scholars have also sought to explain swarming from the contexts of group conflict, group crime, gang violence, school violence, robbery, youth culture, or victimization. Another line of inquiry has examined the use of technology resources (e.g., cell phones, iPods, Twitter, the Internet, and other social media usage) to assess how these are deployed in the formation of groups and coordinating their street activities, some illegal. Given the use of these technologies by youths, researchers and law enforcement officials continue to learn and understand how swarm groups use technology to organize activities by time, location, and purpose.

Growing in popularity in the late 1990s, particularly in Canadian cities, the trend of youths swarming victims to commit crimes has increased. A growing trend in U.S. cities is the swarming of businesses, usually retailers, by large groups intending to shoplift merchandise. Within these crime situations, the group's tactic is to very rapidly swarm a location, steal, assault if necessary, and flee with robbed or stolen items. In this context, the pack mentality is to overwhelm business owners and clerks—whereby perpetrators feel safer committing crimes in a fast-moving group because they believe they are less likely to be identified or prevented from stealing, and can more easily get away with the crime. However, accounts from police investigators and prosecutors have noted that swarming victims are often able to successfully identify their assailants. Accordingly, the successful rate of apprehension and prosecution of swarming offenders has led law enforcement to step up their efforts.

Media Depictions

Recently in American cities (for instance in Las Vegas, New York, and Philadelphia) the news media has increased reporting of swarming events, which result in Internet postings of offenders emptying out the shelves and merchandise of stores. In these group crimes, typically video footage shows an organized group of youths converging on a business, stealing, and abruptly departing together. The videos, often spreading virally via You Tube, may encourage further such events. These crime events have resulted in businesses and the police working together to find solutions that will help prevent and deal with future criminal swarming events. In terms of nonbusiness victims, however, one of the challenges of addressing swarming attacks is that many victims (especially youthful swarming victims) do not report these crimes to police.

Conclusion

Recent research by Mercer Sullivan would suggest that those interested in the study of swarming should also look beyond common understandings of traditional gangs' illegal activities. An insightful sociological approach undertaken by Dennis Mares in the study of homicide types and gangs illustrates how neighborhood contexts (effects of social disorganization and local social ecological factors) work to shape or structure crime outcomes and behaviors that groups engage in. Perhaps these considerations will help scholars, practitioners, and the criminal justice system find ways to better understand and curb this form of crime and disorder in our cities' streets.

Velmer S. Burton, Jr.
University of Minnesota, Twin Cities

See Also: Chicago, Illinois; Community Policing; Flash Mobs; Gangs (Street); Mobs and Riots; New York City; Philadelphia, Pennsylvania; Washington, D.C.

Further Readings

Mares, Dennis. "Social Disorganization and Gang Homicides in Chicago: A Neighborhood Level Comparison of Disaggregated Homicides." *Youth Violence and Juvenile Justice*, v.8/1 (2010).

Steel, Kevin. "Back-Stabbed by a Youth-Mob For a Pager." *Alberta Report/Newsmagazine*, v.25/17 (1998).

Sullivan, Mercer. "Maybe We Shouldn't Study 'Gangs': Does Reification Obscure Youth Violence." *Journal of Contemporary Criminal Justice*, v.21/2 (2005).

White, Rob. "Swarming and the Social Dynamics of Group Violence." *Trends and Issues in Criminal Justice*, v.326/1 (2006).

Tawana Brawley Incident

On November 28, 1987, a 15-year-old African American female, Tawana Brawley, was found in a garbage bag outside her former residence in Wappingers Falls, New York (situated in Dutchess County, north of New York City), allegedly kidnapped and raped by six Caucasian males. Civil rights activist Reverend Al Sharpton advocated in support of Brawley throughout her subsequent ordeal, helping draw national attention to the case.

Case and Cover-Up

Brawley had disappeared from her nearby home four days prior to her discovery. A missing persons report was not filed by her mother until day four of her disappearance, as Brawley had a pattern of running away from home. When found, Brawley was dazed, barely conscious, covered in feces and urine, and wearing burnt and torn clothing. Racial slurs were found written on her clothing and body suggesting a racially motivated attack. She was rushed to St. Francis Hospital in Poughkeepsie, New York, for evaluation and treatment.

Upon arrival at the hospital, doctors examined Brawley for evidence of an attack, rape, and sodomy; no physical injuries or evidence of rape or sodomy were found. When racial slurs were discovered on Brawley's body by medical personnel, the Federal Bureau of Investigation (FBI) was called in to investigate the possibility of federal civil rights violations. Shortly after, Brawley's mother Glenda and her aunt Juanita arrived at the hospital and were horrified when they discovered Tawana's condition. Later, they insisted she be interviewed only by a African American officer, as Tawana had responded with fear when white police officers attempted to interview her.

At the time of the attack, there were no full-time African American deputies employed by the Dutchess County Sheriff's Department. Eventually, the department was able to locate one of four African American part-time deputies to come to the hospital and interview Brawley. The deputy was a patrol officer with little or no experience interviewing crime victims. Nonetheless, he attempted to interview the traumatized girl. During the interview, Brawley was unable to speak to answer the officer's questions but managed to scribble "white cop" in his notebook with a pen. In subsequent interviews, Brawley responded with a series of nods, grunts, and scribbles on paper. Her family soon came to believe that she had been kidnapped and sexually assaulted by white police officers and that the sheriff's department was attempting to engage in a cover-up. This was the catalyst that sparked one of the largest race-related scandals and media circuses in New York history.

The Brawley family contacted the media and some of the most prominent African American attorneys and activists in the country about the attack and what they suspected was a conspiracy to cover it up. Sharpton became the Brawley family's public spokesperson, teaming up with attorneys Alton H. Maddox, Jr., and C. Vernon Mason. The family claimed that Tawana had been dragged into a dark car occupied by two white police officers and taken to the woods, where four other white men were waiting. She allegedly was then sexually assaulted and gang-raped, while the men were screaming racial slurs at her; she also claimed the men had urinated in her mouth. However, at the hospital, doctors noted that her teeth had recently been brushed and that she showed no signs of malnourishment, dehydration, or exposure to the elements, inconsistent with having been kept outdoors in cold weather. Brawley maintained that she had no recollection of what happened in the days following the attack or how she ended up in the garbage bag. At the eventual grand jury hearings, however, a witness said Brawley had herself climbed into the garbage bag outside her former residence; this witness also had heard noises coming from the apartment during the days Brawley was missing.

Eventually, Brawley's attorneys claimed she was kidnapped, raped, sodomized, and left for dead by six white men, including some members of the Dutchess County criminal justice community, who then conspired in a cover-up. Implicated directly was Steven Pagones, an assistant district attorney. Others named by Brawley in some relation to the alleged offenses included Harry Crist, Jr., a part-time police officer, who committed suicide during the early days of the investigation (his suicide note cited personal and career-related issues); Frederick Scoralick, the Dutchess County sheriff; and Tommy Masch, a volunteer fireman who loosely matched the description of an officer with a badge who had allegedly snatched Brawley from the street. All men had concrete alibis for the four days Brawley was missing.

Grand Jury

Several members of law enforcement, some community residents, and members of the press questioned the veracity of Brawley's claims. Nonetheless, Dutchess County District Attorney William Grady convened a special grand jury with the purpose of hearing testimony and evaluating evidence in the case. Brawley's attorneys and Sharpton insisted that the case be handled by an independent special prosecutor with no ties to Dutchess County.

Governor Mario Cuomo then assigned state attorney general Robert Abrams to step in as the special prosecutor. On advice from counsel, Brawley and her family refused to testify before the grand jury. Her mother was subpoenaed, yet failed to show up for her court date and later did not to explain why she had failed to comply; she was found in contempt of court with a penalty of 30 days in jail and a $250 fine. She sought sanctuary in a church, arranged by Sharpton, to avoid arrest.

The 23-member grand jury convened for more than 300 days, listened to testimony from 180 witnesses, viewed 250 exhibits of evidence, and finally concluded that no crime had occurred and that evidence indicated Brawley's condition had been self-inflicted. Evidence from the rape kit taken at the hospital along with Brawley's clothing, fingernail clippings, and other items collected near the scene were analyzed by the FBI laboratory. No evidence of a physical attack or rape such as blood or semen was found; nor was plant material present, inconsistent with an attack in the woods. Even more troubling, the FBI laboratory discovered that singed pieces of cotton and black matter found on gloves in the garbage bag and underneath Brawley's fingernails had been used to write the racial slurs on her body, ultimately leading to the conclusion that Brawley had written upon herself. Witnesses also testified to seeing Brawley out partying during the days she was missing. With the grand jury report, one of the most vitriolic hoaxes in New York State history was revealed.

A former boyfriend of Brawley, Daryl Rodriguez, later came forward claiming Brawley confided in him about what actually happened. On November 24, he said, Brawley returned home late after visiting the former boyfriend in jail and feared she would be beaten by her stepfather, Ralph King, who had murdered his previous wife and had beaten Tawana in the past. That same night she snuck out of the house and hid in the family's former apartment, then vacant, where she was later found on the front lawn in the garbage bag. The rape plot was essentially hatched to prevent King from harming Brawley for running away.

Reverend Al Sharpton

During the 1980s, Sharpton, an American Baptist minister, became known for holding marches and protests to demand legal actions in controversial cases where he asserted that the civil rights of

African Americans had been violated by whites and when criminal justice decisions appeared racially biased. As a young child, Sharpton had begun preaching and touring with gospel singers; as a young adult he worked on concert promotions for singer James Brown. At different points, Sharpton has been embroiled in controversy, including accusations by other African American activists that he was an informant for the FBI. In 2009 he agreed to pay $285,000 in civil penalties in a settlement with the Federal Election Commission for using contributions to his 2004 presidential campaign organization, the National Action Network, for his personal use.

Prior to the Tawana Brawley incident, Sharpton's efforts helped obtain a federal civil rights investigation of the 1985 Bernhard Goetz subway shootings case (the investigation found that Goetz was not reacting to race but to attempted robbery); Sharpton also galvanized community response to the 1986 Howard Beach manslaughter-by-mob of Michael Griffin, in which his efforts helped persuade Governor Cuomo to appoint a special prosecutor.

Sharpton is known as a street smart African American political leader, sometimes taking satisfaction in being labeled "radical" by critics. An intense and boisterous speaker, Sharpton has attracted broad media attention during his speeches and protests. He is known for popularizing the slogan "No Justice; No Peace," often chanted at marches he has led.

Aftermath
Under Sharpton's leadership, a range of public support events were held in support of Brawley's cause. One rally in Newburgh, New York, was attended by more than 1,000 African American individuals, who traveled from all over the country to unite against racism. Sharpton was arrested twice during tumultuous protests on behalf of Brawley; along with the attorneys in the case he claimed it was not possible for African Americans to receive justice in a white-dominated country. Sharpton compared the treatment of African Americans by the white government in New York to that of racism in Mississippi and South Africa.

In the aftermath of the Brawley case, Sharpton along with Maddox and Mason were successfully sued by Steven Pagones for slander and ordered to pay $345,000 in damages. Pagones was implicated by Sharpton and Brawley's attorneys as one of the rapists and claimed to have evidence; there was none.

To date, Sharpton and Tawana Brawley still maintain that she was attacked. Sharpton remains active in politics, having run for mayor of New York City, the U.S. Senate, and president; he has yet to hold any political office. In 2012, Sharpton hosted the news show *PoliticsNation* on MSNBC.

Amy Hyman Gregory
Central Connecticut State University

See Also: Crime Scene Investigation; Goetz, Bernhard; Kidnapping; Racial Assault; Rape and Sexual Assault.

Further Readings
Belknap, Joanne. "Rape: Too Hard to Report and Too Easy to Discredit Victims." *Violence Against Women*, v.16/12 (2010).
Markovitz, Jonathan. *Legacies of Lynching: Racial Violence and Memory*. Minneapolis: University of Minnesota Press, 2004.
McFadden, Robert D., Ralph Blumenthal, Myron A. Farber, E. R. Shipp, Charles Strum, and Craig Wolff. *Outrage: The Story Behind the Tawana Brawley Hoax*. New York: Bantam Books, 1990.
Sharpton, Al. *Go and Tell Pharaoh: The Autobiography of Reverend Al Sharpton*. New York: Doubleday, 1996.
Taibbi, Mike and Anna Sims Phillips. *Unholy Alliances: Working the Tawana Brawley Story*. San Diego, CA: Harcourt, 1989.

Television Shows

Crime dramas and reality programs are currently two of the most popular television genres. Public obsession with crime as entertainment, as reflected in the popularity of a host of crime-related television programs, is not a new phenomenon. Both crime dramas and reality shows most often take place in urban settings.

From the dawn of the printing press, crime has been a staple of news, novels, magazines, comic books, and later radio, film, and television. Mid-20th-century American radio programs like *The Shadow* and *Dragnet* quickly evolved into the crime drama genre. TV programs like *Cops* and *Real Life Stories of the Highway Patrol* were among the precursors to today's shows, which include *CSI, NYPD Blue, Law & Order, The Shield, Homicide: Life on the Streets, The Wire, The Closer, The Mentalist,* and many other popular programs. All promise to give viewers an inside window into the operations of the criminal justice system and, in many cases, the world of street crime.

Some scholars argue that crime shows are both a cultural reflection of our collective feelings about crime and justice, and an important factor in public responses to crime. These programs may help construct race and gender dynamics in society, shape public perceptions of the criminal justice system, reinforce stereotypes of offenders and victims, and, to some degree, even alter behavior of some viewers.

Social researcher Ray Surrette explained that much of our fascination with crime stories is because their focus is on backstage behavior, or behavior that occurs behind closed doors, shielded from public view, often with nefarious intent. These crime stories often fit quite easily into a formulaic presentation of the battle between good and evil, which culminates with a resolution that severely punishes evil offenders and sanctifies the behavior of the hero. Frequently, as Surrette pointed out in his book *Media, Crime, and Criminal Justice,* crime stories begin with the antagonist committing a crime, most often a violent crime, and tell the story of the protagonist (either a victim or their representative) seeking justice. The twists and turns in the story are designed to dramatically take viewers into the complicated world of crime, where most misdeeds are planned by offenders and utilize elaborate schemes to commit and cover up. Audiences enjoy contemplating behavior that they, most likely, would not commit and delving into the

A scene from Criminal Minds, *a police procedural television show that follows a team of profilers from the FBI's Behavioral Analysis Unit (BAU) based in Quantico, Virginia. The BAU is part of the FBI National Center for the Analysis of Violent Crime. The show differs from many procedural dramas by focusing on the criminal rather than the crime itself.*

pathology driving such behavior. These programs offer a glimpse into the psychology, technology, science, and artful detective work needed to successfully solve crimes in the real world. In doing so, crime shows provide the viewer with an opportunity to play armchair detective and vicariously solve cases in the pursuit of justice.

History of Crime Dramas

The introduction of television in the late 1940s allowed programmers to combine the drama and visual effects of the movies with the episodic nature of radio programming, particularly detective shows. Television's foray into non-news crime programming began with westerns in the 1950s and evolved into modern police and legal dramas. These fictional portrayals focus primarily on violent offenders and their interactions with the criminal justice system. The perspective of either law enforcement officials or prosecutors provides the lens for viewers to witness the action. A dominant theme of all of these programs is "justice," brought about by an offender being caught and punished for a crime. While these programs are fictional, they frequently borrow and sensationalize story lines from newspaper and television news headlines. For example, *Law & Order* advertises that it uses real-life crimes for script inspiration. A defining characteristic of the genre is an attempt to mirror reality and to give viewers an inside view of criminal justice officers.

The scholar Michael Arntfield, writing in the *Canadian Review of American Studies,* described three periods in American crime dramas, dubbed the Golden Age, the Gilded Age, and the Dark Age, each identifiable by character archetypes and their relationship to technology. His Golden Age (1967–75) is characterized by programs like *Dragnet* and *Adam-12,* which depict police officers as professional, operating within a strict, paramilitary hierarchy, bound by the crime fighting technologies of the day, and lacking exciting backstories in their own personal lives. Because of this myopic focus on police procedure and mechanization used to solve individual cases, issues of race, gender, and political unrest remain uncovered. These shows frequently depict street crimes, as characterized by the mix of violent and property crimes committed in a range of public places such as highways, parking lots, industrial and commercial areas, housing complexes, and sometimes involving drug-related offenses.

Programs during the Gilded Age (1975–92), like *Starsky and Hutch, Kojak,* and *Miami Vice,* emphasized the complexity of policing and presented character backstories that added to the lure of genre. Murder and other violent crimes predominate. In these programs there is a gray area in morality, which is reflected, both in the police investigations and the characters personal lives. Police officers are often placed in the role of vigilante or rogue officers who must defy the system in order to fight crime. Police technology and gadgetry play a central role in these dramas. Despite their imperfections and the limitations of the legal system, these vigilante law enforcers are shown defending the moral boundaries of society. The crimes depicted often take place in either degraded urban environments, as the setting for street crimes, or more flamboyant backdrops for more high level, "white collar" or syndicated crime.

The Dark Age (1993–present) began with programs like *Law & Order, NYPD Blue,* and *Homicide: Life on the Street.* Each of these programs focused on the gritty, working-class nature of crime fighting. Characters were driven by the demons of their pasts, human frailty, and a sense of isolation from the general public who do not deal with violence and depravation on a daily basis. Frequently, characters were drawn to the criminal justice profession because of a history of victimization. For example, Olivia Benson (a detective on *Law & Order: SVU*) has a backstory that includes being the victim of a violent rape. During the Dark Age, coroners and forensic scientists began to take a more prominent role in the story plots. This trend was further developed in *CSI: Crime Scene Investigation* and its spinoffs, in which a forensic team supplants the role of the traditional police detectives. Science and technology offer stability and answers in the chaotic world of crime and crime fighters, as the laboratory helps police extend their enforcement of justice and order upon a troubling milieu of private and corporate corruption mixed with raw street crime. Arntfield concluded that programs like *The Shield* may represent the next era of crime dramas, in which vigilante cops are no longer bound by morality or technological restraints.

History of Reality Justice Shows

In 1989, both *Cops* and *America's Most Wanted* aired their first episodes. These programs ushered in a new era of reality programs that focused on police officers, correctional officers, and detectives. The popularity of these programs and the genre is evidenced by the fact that both programs were still airing new episodes in 2011, and the fall 2011 television season contained a host of other reality criminal justice programs. Criminal justice reality programs almost universally represent the crime control and law and order model perspectives of justice. All stories are framed from the perspective of police officers or other criminal justice officials. In many cases, due process is shown as a hindrance to officers trying to apprehend offenders; the public is often encouraged to participate in the criminal justice process by increasing their own vigilance or phoning in if they have information related to a particular crime.

Reality criminal justice programs cover almost all aspects of the criminal justice process with programs aimed at policing (e.g. *Cops, Real Life Stories of the Highway Patrol, K-9 Cops*), corrections (*Lockdown*), bounty hunting (*Dog the Bounty Hunter*), courts (the *People's Court, Judge Judy, Court TV*), and private investigator/detective reality programs (*America's Most Wanted, Unsolved Mysteries; First 48*). These programs offer viewers a chance to watch a "real" criminal justice process, but the cases are handpicked by producers for their violence, sensationalism, humor, or bizarre nature. The "reality" of reality TV is that it represents a major distortion of the crime problem and the operation of the criminal justice system.

Infotainment

These two genres, crime dramas and reality police programs, fall under an umbrella category of "infotainment," or programs that blend news or factual presentation with entertainment. Each liberally borrows elements from the other genre to increase the sense of reality (e.g., shaky camera footage, documentary style) on one hand, and the sensationalism or entertainment factor (e.g., memorable music score, focus on bizarre or unusual crimes) on the other hand. The ratings and profits garnered by both television and cable networks from infotainment programs demonstrate their popularity. What these numbers can't tell us is how infotainment programs have changed public perceptions of the criminal justice system, offenders, and public policy.

Depictions of Justice

In the 1970s George Gerbner and his colleagues with the Cultural Indicators Project posited that watching television creates a "mean world view" among viewers because much of the content is violent and reinforces traditional notions of power linked to race and social status. In many ways, television content has not changed significantly since these observations. Crime, particularly violent crime, is still dominant in network and cable television content and violence is often used to resolve conflict. Both crime drama and criminal justice reality programs are prime examples.

To compound this issue, the new infotainment trend, which links fictional stories to sensational crimes in the news and uses advertising that promotes the "realistic" nature of these programs, may lead viewers to believe these programs mirror crime in the United States. If viewers perceive crime dramas and criminal justice reality programs to be realistic, then these programs are more likely to shape viewers' perceptions of the crime problem, their interpretations of the Bill of Rights, and their sense of the meaning of justice.

Depictions of Stereotypes

Crime dramas and criminal justice reality programs inundate viewers with stereotypical presentations of what justice should look like and what justice means. Included in these portrayals are racialized and gendered images of victims and offenders. Consistent themes in crime dramas and criminal justice reality programs are that crime, particularly violent crime, is out of control and increasing rapidly, could happen anywhere and to anyone, and is a result of individual pathology rather than socioeconomic conditions such as poverty, inequality, and racism. These themes to some degree turn the reality of offense patterns and the operation of the criminal justice system on their head. A prolaw enforcement message resonates throughout these programs, and as a result the crime control activities of the criminal justice system are emphasized and the due process and crime prevention roles of the system are minimized. A viewer might logically conclude from watching these types of programs that law enforcement agencies are an effective and efficient solution to the crime problem, due process guarantees (like those found in the Bill of Rights) often get in the way of crime fighting, and more punitive laws are needed to combat the crime problem.

Contrary to popular belief, with a few exceptions like *The Wire*, most crime dramas predominantly depict offenders as middle-aged, middle-class males. They also depict most police officers, prosecutors, and judges as white males, followed by white females. The "street" of most crime dramas is much whiter than the actual streets of most American cities. This trend is changing with the introduction of more minority criminal justice characters on television, but their representation is still quite limited. Additionally, the roles that minorities play are often support roles, with less complicated story lines than their majority counterparts. For example, Lieutenant Arthur Fancy, an African American character in a leadership position on *NYPD Blue,* was largely devoid of a backstory. Minorities, who have much higher actual victimization rates than whites, are less proportionately shown as victims on crime dramas. Those minorities who are shown as victims are more likely to remain nameless throughout the program and to be shown in a group victimization scene as one of multiple victims. Many feminist scholars have argued that whiteness is often used symbolically to represent the innocence of a victim, while minority victims are more likely to be shown contributing to the circumstance that led to the crime.

Given these trends, where do the stereotypes of minority offenders come from? Although whites are shown more frequently in all roles on crime dramas, if one examines the portrayals within races, minorities are much more likely to be shown as offenders relative to their portrayals as victims or criminal justice officials. The opposite is true for whites—whites are much less likely to be shown as offenders relative to their frequent portrayals as victims or criminal justice officials. Therefore, it may not be the number of offenders that one sees on television, but the proportion of offenders to sympathetic roles within a racial category that shapes public perceptions of typical offenders and victims. This same trend, yet even more pronounced, can be found in reality police programs. These depictions have often been criticized for perpetuating stereotypes about white police officers and minority offenders.

Women, especially white women, have made considerable gains in representation in crime dramas and reality police programs (with *Police Women of Broward County* now focusing solely on women) since the days of *Dragnet* and *The Untouchables.* Popular crime dramas such as *Cagney & Lacey; The Closer; Saving Grace; Crossing Jordan;* and *Cold Case* each featured female leads, and most

current crime dramas include an ensemble cast that includes at least one woman and often minority representation, as well. Consistent with this trend, women's depictions as offenders have increased as well. A recent study of *Law & Order: Special Victims Unit* by Sarah Britto and her colleagues found that women were disproportionately shown as sex offenders, relative to low actual offense rates in reality, and female offenders where particularly cruel and manipulative relative to their male counterparts on TV. Although men are the most frequent victims on television and reality, the proportion of female victims of homicide is highly exaggerated on crime dramas. What is still missing from most crime dramas and reality police programs are portrayals of minority women, especially positive portrayals.

Effects

Many scholars have paid considerable time and attention to the connection between watching television crime programming and fear of crime, use of protective measures, perceptions of the criminal justice officials, expectations of the criminal justice system, jury behavior, assessment of important community problems, and punitive attitudes. While many nuanced theoretical explanations of the relationship between media, public perceptions, and behavior exist, they generally fall on a continuum between those who argue that viewing crime-related programming is entertaining and produces few effects other than enjoyment—and those who argue that continual bombardment with images of seemingly random violent crime increases viewers' fear of crime, punitive attitudes, and use of protective measures (gun ownership, dog ownership, lights, locks, security systems, restricted movement, etc.), all of which have deleterious effects on an individual's psyche, economic situation, willingness to discriminate, ability to trust, and effective participation in one's community.

Empirical evidence has not been consistent in testing these opposing perspectives. Some studies have found both enhanced entertainment and reduced fear of crime, while other studies have found a connection between viewing and agenda setting, fear of crime, support for punitive measures, and social trust. Still other studies have shown no relationship between viewing and these measures. Recent research has found that the relationship between media, perceptions, and behavior is much more complicated than originally thought and varies based on the characteristics of the audience member, contextual variables such as neighborhood crime levels, racial characteristics of the viewer's neighborhood, and the specific media content. Future work should control for these factors when testing media effects.

A much talked about phenomenon is the "CSI effect," named after *CSI: Crime Scene Investigation*. Evan Durnal, writing in *Forensic Science International*, explained that this effect refers to a multitude of changes in attitudes, behaviors, and expectations of the criminal justice system that occur as a result of viewing forensic crime dramas. He argued that jurors now regularly expect forensic proof of a crime, rather than just circumstantial evidence, in order to return convictions in a trial, which has made the job of prosecutors and police officers more difficult. Victims are often disappointed with the criminal justice system when they compare the attention given to their cases with their television counterparts. Furthermore, if a victim's case does not result in a conviction, which most cases do not, public confidence in the criminal justice system may plummet. Finally, Dennis Stevens, author of *Media and Criminal Justice: The CSI Effect*, argues these programs also encourage police officers to be aggressive, cut procedural corners that may violate an individual's civil rights, and tolerate this behavior from other officers in order to live up to police depictions on television and public expectations. Research in this area is still in its infancy and more empirical studies are needed to verify the CSI effect.

Sarah Britto
Prairie View A & M University

See Also: Fear of Crime; Murder/Homicide; Police (Overview); Police Brutality/Excessive Force; Street Crime, Popular Portrayals of.

Further Readings

Arntfield, Michael. "TVPD: The Generational Diegetics of the Police Procedural on American Television." *Canadian Review of American Studies*, v.41/1 (2011).

Britto, Sarah, Tycy Hughes, Kurt Saltzman, and Colin Stroh. "Does 'Special' Mean Young, White and Female? Deconstructing the Meaning of 'Special' in *Law & Order: Special Victims Unit*." *Journal of Criminal Justice and Popular Culture*, v. 14/1 (2007).

Durnal, Evan. "Crime Scene Investigation (As Seen on TV)." *Forensic Science International*, v.199/1 (2010).

Gerbner, George and Larry Gross. "Living With Television: The Violence Profile." *Journal of Communication*, v.26 (1976).

Stevens, Dennis. *Media and Criminal Justice: The CSI Effect.* Sudbury, MA: Jones and Bartlett, 2011.

Surrette, Ray. *Media, Crime, and Criminal Justice: Images and Realities.* Belmont, CA: Wadsworth/Cengage Learning, 2011.

Terrorism

Terrorism and street crime are both violent activities, but they often occur in separate arenas. Street crime often has a predominately financial goal, while one of the key characteristics of the violence associated with terrorism is that the violence occurs in pursuit of political objectives. Terrorism is also designed to generate fear, involves organization and a target audience beyond the immediate victims, and is normally used by groups too weak to attain their political goals in other ways.

Even with these differences, connections between street crime and terrorism exist. First, some street crime involves attacks that would be considered hate crimes, with the violence being directed against minorities. Second, street crime can provide a source of funding for terrorist activities, albeit only a portion. Third, street actions can reinforce group solidarity in terrorist groups just as it can in gangs that have no political objectives. There is a final, less direct connection. Some individuals involved in street crime will, of course, be arrested, charged, convicted, and serve time. Prisons have served as a recruiting ground for new members of various kinds of terrorist groups.

Crime Against Minorities

The most obvious form of street violence linked to terrorism occurs when individuals are targeted because of their ethnic or religious heritage. The United States has a history of urban violence that is directed against minority communities. Before the Civil War, free blacks, Irish, Mormons, and Catholics suffered from such attacks. After the Civil War freed slaves, the Chinese immigrants became new

The Day of Silence is the Gay, Lesbian, and Straight Education Network's annual day of action to protest the bullying and harassment of lesbian, gay, bisexual, and transgender (LGBT) students and their supporters.

victims that were added to the list of targets. With increasing migration from southern and eastern Europe in the late 1800s, Jews joined Catholics as religious targets for urban violence. These attacks were often intended to drive the targeted groups away or to keep them politically inactive.

Even now attacks against minorities continue. The heritage of individuals may be obvious to the attackers from their attire or other visible characteristics, or they may be selected for assaults because they can be identified due to their presence in certain buildings such as synagogues, temples, mosques, or cultural centers. The groups behind such attacks may be attempting to persuade the victims and the target audience to move out of an area; such violence can be seen as a very basic form of ethnic cleansing.

A variety of right-wing extremist groups have been involved in these kinds of activities. African Americans have often been targeted by elements of the majority community for assaults and even

lynchings. The attacks have been used to send a message to the entire minority community about its status and have served as a form of social control. While this type of targeted violence against African Americans has decreased, hate crimes still continue and can be part of a general, even if vague, plan to force a minority community to leave a particular area.

A variety of other groups have become targets for similar street violence in today's world. Arab Americans and other persons from the Middle East and South Asia, as well as American Muslims, became targets in the aftermath of the 9/11 terrorist attacks in New York City and Washington, D.C. Although some assaults were uncoordinated reactions to the events of that day, others were part of efforts to force "foreign" elements to leave a city or the country.

Antigay street crime would also fall into this category of targeting minorities. The criminal actions in this case reflect prejudice and hatred toward gays—and sometimes a fear of homosexuality—but the attacks at some level are designed to force gays to leave or give up their lifestyle. This type of street violence also reflects the unwillingness of the assailants to accept that the target groups have basic political and personal rights that have been recognized and presumably protected in the political system.

Types of Attacks

Assaults have been a frequent type of street violence. In some cases the attacks may be combined with theft when property is taken, but the victims are chosen because of their ethnic or religious heritage, and not because of the prospect of economic gain. Property crimes and vandalism directed against religious or cultural centers may also occur, and such incidents would clearly suggest that the choice of targets is cultural rather than economic in origin. On rare occasions, individuals linked to extreme right-wing groups have gone on shooting sprees in which they have targeted nonwhites or Jewish residents on the streets. These attacks have clearly been intended to send a message to all members of the target audiences that they are in danger. In effect, these kinds of attacks are being used to encourage members of minority groups to leave the neighborhood or city, if not the country.

Groups that engage in terrorism may use street violence and petty crime as a means of funding their activities. Terrorist groups in Europe have frequently done so, and it has likely been used on occasion in the United States. The targets in this case may include anyone who is vulnerable regardless of cultural or ethnic heritage, although it is possible that minority groups would be the preferred target. It is difficult to determine how prevalent such activities have been since anyone arrested for such crimes would be unlikely to confess that the criminal activity is intended to finance terrorist attacks. Similarly, local police are not likely to routinely question persons arrested for street crime about any connections to political terrorism.

Individual Motivations

Street crimes that are directed against foreigners or minorities may also provide a means for enhancing solidarity within an extremist group. Individuals become accepted members of the group after violations of the law; additionally, they become more closely linked to other members. Street violence, even actions unrelated to target groups, may also be used as tests, initiations, or as part of an effort to increase group solidarity. The street violence organized by groups may have an additional effect of encouraging lone wolf attacks by individuals with similar political views. These individuals will choose to attack members of minority communities because they see themselves as militant patriots fighting against foreign cultural invasions. When other attacks have been occurring, they can see their own efforts as part of this broader cause.

Recruiting in Prison

A final area in which street crimes and terrorism may intersect occurs in a quite different context. Street criminals with no connections to extreme political groups will often be caught and spend time in jail. In prison they can be recruited into organizations with extreme political viewpoints. Prison provides an ideal setting for recruitment since it is a situation in which individuals are vulnerable to appeals that promise to provide them with support in a troubling and dangerous environment. Individuals in prison are removed from familiar social frameworks and support networks, and thus they become more open to appeals that promise to provide a new support structure—both inside prison and frequently after release. Individuals in prison can be especially susceptible to recruitment since it is not difficult to convince them that the political, social, and economic systems have

failed them. Ideological or religious extremists can provide the new recruits with a ready-made reason that explains their own failures and provides a plan of action that will supposedly reverse the negative situation in which they have found themselves. The explanations frequently identify a variety of minority groups as the cause of the problems.

Extreme right-wing racist groups have often been able to attract recruits from the prison population, and when individuals are released they become participants in street violence with political motivations or become involved in other forms of terrorism. Extreme Islamic groups have also been able to recruit from prison populations, often first converting inmates to Islam. The new recruits may become involved in street violence, and they may have been involved in more serious terrorist plots.

Conclusion

Even though terrorism does not always involve street crime, some activities by terrorist groups do. The criminal acts are linked to a broader purpose—usually convincing some minority group to exit from a particular area—or even from the United States. Such actions are much more likely in an urban or suburban setting, since that is where the minority communities are likely to be located and where there are sufficient like-minded individuals who will join groups that are willing to use criminal activity in the streets to further their (often vague) political objectives. While criminal activity linked to such political objectives is only a small portion of street crime, it is a disturbing element since it can be part of a process of moving toward more violent activities in other arenas.

James M. Lutz
Brenda J. Lutz
Indiana University–Purdue University Fort Wayne

See Also: Gangs (Street); Hate Crime; Homophobic Assault; Organized Crime and Violence; Racial Assault.

Further Readings

Hamm, Mark. *Terrorism as Crime: From Oklahoma City to Al-Qaeda and Beyond.* New York: New York University Press, 2007.

Kaplan, Jeffrey. "Islamophobia in America? September 11 and Islamophobic Hate Crime." *Terrorism and Political Violence*, v.18/1 (2006).

Lutz, Brenda J. and James M. Lutz. *Terrorism in America.* New York: Palgrave Macmillan, 2007.

Silber, Mitchell D. and Arvin Bhatt. *Radicalization in the West: The Homegrown Threat.* New York: New York Police Intelligence Division, 2007.

Theft and Larceny

Larceny-theft is a prevalent form of street crime in the United States. The Federal Bureau of Investigation (FBI) Uniform Crime Reporting (UCR) Program typically defines street crime as those crimes that occur on streets, highways, parking lots, and in other salient public realms. Crime in this street context has generally been divided into two categories: violent crime and property crime. Larceny-theft is a property crime, or a crime that does not involve force or threat of force against victims, and the purpose is generally to acquire a person's money or property. (In contrast, robbery is a violent form of theft, or a theft that involves force or threat of force against a person or persons.) Street thefts constitute a considerable portion of all thefts in the United States. For example, in 2010, according to the UCR, nearly half of all robberies in the United States were street robberies.

Definitions

In some jurisdictions, theft is synonymous with larceny; in others theft has replaced larceny as the term describing the unauthorized taking of a person's property. The act of theft has been known by many terms, such as stealing, thieving, and filching, and a person who carries out theft is known as a thief. The *actus reus* of theft is generally stated as the "unauthorized taking, keeping, or using of another's property." The act must also be accompanied by a *mens rea*, or the criminal intent or dishonesty of the perpetrator knowing that the act to deprive a person of his or her property is wrong.

In the United States, two categories of theft exist: petit larceny and grand larceny. The distinction rests in the value of the property involved in the theft. Grand larceny, sometimes referred to as felonious larceny, is a felony, while petit larceny is a misdemeanor. Although many jurisdictions across the United States have abandoned the petit/grand terminology, the fair market value, or the value of the property at the time and place it was taken, is still used to classify the theft as a misdemeanor or a felony.

Generally, there are fundamental elements involved in larceny-theft. First, larceny is a crime against possession, and the victim must demonstrate actual control and possession over the property when it was taken. Second, the offender must take physical control over the property; said another way, the offender must gain control of the victim's possessions during the theft, if only for a moment. Third, the perpetrator must move the property from its original position; the slightest movement is deemed sufficient. Fourth, the property involved in the theft must be tangible, with a physical or corporeal existence (The FBI has extended larceny-theft to include theft of intellectual property and identity theft, but these are typically not related to street crime.).

Fifth, the theft must occur without the consent of the owner; this means the theft is achieved by stealth, force, threat of force, or deceit. Sixth, the perpetrator needs to take the property with the intent to steal it (i.e., *animus furandi*). Historically, this has meant the offender intends to dispossess the owner of their property with no plan to return the property in a reasonable time. Finally, the property involved in the theft must typically have monetary or economic value.

Elements of Street Theft

Specifically, certain characteristics need to be present for a crime to be categorized as a street theft. First, the offender targets a victim. Second, the victim is typically a pedestrian and a stranger. Third, the offender attempts or completes a theft of cash or property. Fourth, the offense typically happens in a public or semipublic realm, such as a street, alley, parking lot, public park, near public transit, or near housing or apartments. However, there is often a gray area in this realm of street crime. For example, the perpetrator may also target a residence or a business as a victim because looting, shoplifting, and burglary are sometimes categorized as street theft. Furthermore, if the theft is classified as a robbery, a fifth characteristic must involve the offender using threat of force or actual force against the victim. Although a weapon does not need to be involved, and the victim does not need to be injured, force or threat of force necessitates a street robbery.

Certain street thefts are difficult to categorize. For example, purse snatching or snatch-theft involves the taking of a person's money or property (i.e., street larceny-theft), but may involve some force or threat of force (i.e. street robbery) to take the person's property. If the victim was unaware of the theft, and the offender stole by stealth, however, the crime may be categorized as street theft (i.e. pickpocketing). If the offender violently snatches property away from the victim, even if no weapon was used or injury ensued, the theft had elements of force and may be recorded as street robbery.

Thus, the distinctions between street larceny-theft and street robbery are sometimes difficult to define. The UCR defines larceny-theft as the unlawful taking, carrying, leading, or riding away of property from the possession or constructive possession of another. Examples may include thefts of bicycles, motor vehicle parts and accessories, shoplifting, pickpocketing, or the stealing of any property or article that is not taken by force, violence, or fraud. In contrast, street robbery, sometimes referred to as mugging, is an extremely common form of street theft.

According to the FBI, robbery is a particularly violent variety of theft, typically viewed as a combination of assault and battery along with larceny, often termed *aggravated larceny*. Robbery is typically defined as the taking away of valuable items or goods from the victim in a potentially lethal manner; the UCR defines robbery as the taking or attempting to take anything of value from the care, custody, or control of a person or persons by force or threat of force or violence and/or by putting the victim in fear. Although force, threat of force, and fear seem to be the difference between classifying larceny-theft from robbery, these criteria are often difficult to establish when classifying various street thefts.

Thief and Victim Demographics

Research and crime data have offered the typical demographic characteristics of street thieves. First, street theft is predominant among youth, with the vast majority of U.S. offenders in their late teens and early 20s. According to the UCR, in 2010 individuals under the age of 25 accounted for 42.1 percent of all arrestees, constituting 43.1 percent of those arrested for violent crime and 53.7 percent of those arrested for property crime. In the United States,

those under 25 years of age accounted for 64.2 percent of all robberies and 52.7 percent of larceny-thefts.

Second, the overwhelming majority of street thieves are male. The UCR reports that in 2010, 87.8 percent of all robberies were perpetrated by men (12.2 percent by women), though men were responsible for only 56.1 percent of larceny-thefts in 2010, leaving female perpetrators at 43.9 percent. Finally, in 2010, blacks composed 55 percent and whites 43.3 percent of those arrested for robbery, while whites represented 68.9 percent and blacks only 28.3 percent of those arrested for larceny-theft. It should be noted that blacks are over-represented in both arrest rates and incarceration rates for all street crimes.

Street thieves target potential victims who appear to possess money or other valuables. Offenders search for victims who seem vulnerable, such as people alone at night or under the influence of alcohol, or those who appear lost or unaware of their immediate surroundings. Perpetrators target victims who may possess cash, purses, wallets, credit cards, mobile phones, MP3 players, jewelry, or other small electronic devices. A street thief typically targets items that can be concealed once taken, items that are effortlessly removed from the victim, items that are both valuable and enjoyable, and finally items that can be easily sold or traded in the street context.

Street theft generally occurs at night, especially street robbery. However, thefts from the elderly generally occur in the morning and afternoon, while theft from youth typically occurs in the hours following school dismissal. Street theft more often than not occurs on the weekend.

Rates and Types

According to the UCR, larceny-theft accounted for 68.1 percent of all property crimes in 2010, constituting roughly 6,185,447 of the property crime offenses in the United States that year. In 2010, there were approximately 2,004 larceny-thefts per 100,000 inhabitants. The number of larceny-thefts dropped 3 percent from 2009 to 2010; this was part of a decade long decrease of 19.4 percent from 2001 through 2010. The average value of property taken during larceny-thefts in 2010 was $988 per offense, costing victims nationally over $6 billion dollars.

According to the FBI, nationwide in 2010 there were 367,832 robberies, estimated at approximately

119 per 100,000 inhabitants in the United States. The UCR reported a 10 percent decrease in robberies from 2009 rates, part of an 18.1 percent decrease from 2006 rates. An estimated $456 million in losses were attributed to robberies in 2010, with an average dollar value of property stolen per reported robbery at $1,239; banks lost the highest dollar amount, with the $4,410 average per offense greatly outweighing the average street robbery. Firearms were used in 41.4 percent of 2010 robberies according to the UCR, nearly equal to the percentage (42.0) of robberies reporting strong-arm tactics, followed by robberies with knives and cutting instruments (7.9 percent), and other dangerous weapons (8.8 percent).

Street robberies accounted for nearly half of all U.S. robberies in 2010 at 43.2 percent, followed by robberies of a residence (17.3 percent), commercial house (13.2 percent), miscellaneous (16.6 percent), banks (2.2 percent), gas/service stations (2.3 percent), and convenience stores (5.2 percent).

Motivations

Researchers have always been interested in the motivations behind street theft and robbery. Some take a structural perspective and propose that young offenders are a product of a society in which the consumption of material goods is widely desired. For those socioeconomically disadvantaged in society, street theft may be an avenue to attain goods and money when legal consumption avenues are blocked. These suppositions also explain why street theft and robbery is over-represented in impoverished communities with high unemployment, minority discrimination, and minimal social or economical outlets. Other researchers take a cultural perspective (i.e., values, norms, beliefs) and examine the cultural functions of street theft for the perpetrator such as enhancing the status of the offender, generating a reputation for toughness, responding to challenges of masculinity, obtaining an outlet for aggression, and a means for retaliation and revenge. Still others have taken an interactionist perspective, citing an offenders' socialization into street culture (often experienced by urban youths), in which they learn the techniques and rationalizations that serve to legitimate street theft.

Finally, rational choice perspective has been widely cited in explaining street theft and robbery. Rational choice focuses on the decision-making process as the goal-oriented offender focuses on the successful completion of the crime. It should be noted that the motives for street theft are wide ranging and no single explanation can encompass the complexity of factors involved.

Street theft, especially street robbery, is a major source of fear among the public because victims face an unexpected threat to life, a loss of control, and an assault of personal space. Street theft is an especially fear-inducing crime because of the circumstance in which it is prone to occur—during the course of a person's normal routines. The annual National Crime Victimization Survey consistently finds that the majority of street thefts occur when victims are on their way to work, school, shopping, or running errands. The risk of injury or death, especially during a street robbery, further serves to instigate public fears of street crime generally.

Patrick K. O'Brien
University of Colorado Boulder

See Also: Burglary; Crime Patterns; Fear of Crime; History of Street Crime in America; Mass Transit, Crime on; Mugging; Pickpocketing; Urbanization.

Further Readings

Hallsworth, Simon. *Street Crime*. Portland, OR: Willan Publishing, 2005.

LaFree, Gary. *Losing Legitimacy: Street Crime and the Decline of Social Institutions in America*. Boulder, CO: Westview Press, 1998.

U.S. Department of Justice. "Bureau of Justice Statistics, 2010–2011." http://www.bjs.ojp.usdoj.gov/index.cfm (Accessed October 2011).

Wright, Richard T. and Scott H. Decker. *Armed Robbers in Action: Stickups and Street Culture*. Lebanon, NH: Northeastern University Press, 1997.

Tompkins Square Riots/Tent City

Tompkins Square Park in Manhattan's East Village has been an important gathering place for local residents for generations. In 1874, it was the site of a riot making it a location of lasting symbolic significance for the labor movement and the political left. A century later, during the mid-1980s, as homelessness grew in cities across the United States as a result of recession, growing unemployment, and cuts to social services, Tompkins Square Park became a gathering space and residence for some homeless and "street-involved" people, some of whom were living in tents and shacks erected in rubble-strewn vacant lots nearby. It also became a haven for illegal drug use and associated petty and felony-level street crime. The riot that broke out there in the summer of 1988 has become a focal point of studies in urban crowd control, police community relations, and related policies.

Restrictions and Riot

Residents and neighbors were divided over the use of the park and future maintenance of the 10.5-acre park, a rather typical neighborhood oasis, featuring paved pathways, fountains, children's play areas, and wrought iron fencing, set in a densely residential section of New York City. Most neighbors, along with poor people's movements, antipoverty activists, and associations such as Friends of Tompkins Square Park, preferred that the park remain open as a community resource and public space. Business owners and their advocates in associations like the Avenue A Block Association meanwhile lobbied for a strict curfew over the park. The park, which had previously been open 24 hours a day, was subjected to a 1:00 A.M. curfew imposed by the governing Manhattan Community Board 3 on June 28, 1988. On July 11, police moved to restrict homeless people to the park's southeast section while evicting youth from the park.

Residents of the area viewed the police efforts as an attempt to remove the park from public use and diminish its place in the life of the neighborhood.

The Tompkins Square Riot of 1874 occurred in the middle of the Panic of 1873, a depression that began in 1873 and lasted for several years. Movements throughout the United States had begun to demand that the government ease the strain of the depression. Over 7,000 people had gathered at Tompkins Square Park when police entered the square and dispersed most of the crowd, using brutal force and beating people with clubs.

As a result of restrictions placed on park usage, community members organized a protest for July 31 to assert opposition to the curfew and policing practices. During this protest, police entered the park and several clashes between demonstrators and police occurred. Several people were injured and four demonstrators were arrested. Witnesses claimed that police initiated the conflict.

A follow-up rally was organized for August 6 to continue protesting the curfew, to open access to the park, and to express concerns about police behavior during the July 31 event. Around 11:30 P.M., approximately 200 people marched into the park. Police rushed the demonstrators, setting off a battle that would last until 6:00 A.M. By the end of the fracas, at least 38 people were injured, including uninvolved journalists and bystanders who had been harmed by police. Nine people were arrested on charges ranging from assault to participating in a riot.

Following the August 6 riot, the primary focus shifted to a concern about police brutality, police racism, and excessive use of force by police. The riot showed the emerging significance of personal videorecordings being used at such events, as numerous videos and photographs surfaced showing the use of violence by police against people who appeared to pose no threat to officers or to anyone else. Video footage of the riot showed police attacking African American bystanders; witnesses reported that police also hurled racist epithets at African Americans. This would provide an early example of what has become a more common occurrence during alternative globalization protests and riots and the Occupy movement. Citizens, in some cases, were able to provide video footage that showed convincingly that police, not protesters, had initiated or escalated aspects of the riot.

Charges and Reports

Overall, approximately 100 formal complaints of police brutality were investigated by the Civilian Complaint Review Board. In the end two officers were charged with excessive use of force, a number which infuriated residents who believed more charges should have resulted. A city report concluded that there had been numerous improprieties engaged in by police during the night of the riot, and also found a series of communication and leadership breakdowns during the crisis, both at the precinct level and more broadly within the police department, and also in the department's liaison with the mayor's office. Police Commissioner Benjamin Ward issued a report placing responsibility for the riot solely with the officers of Precinct 9.

In the wake of his department's report, Commissioner Ward compelled the retirement of Deputy Chief Thomas Darcy, who had left the scene at a critical juncture. Ward also had Deputy Inspector Joseph Wodarski transferred, and ordered the retraining of Captain Gerald McNamara, the highest-ranking officer on site after the abrupt departure of Darcy. The report, going beyond individual police performance, noted that the department itself was deficient in the training of its force on such functions as crowd control and basic supervision at the street level.

To properly contextualize the riot, it must be situated within the developing moral crisis around homelessness and squatting in New York City during the mid- to late 1980s. During the period leading up to the riot there were growing calls for the criminalization of various activities that homeless people relied on for survival. Street involved people were increasingly portrayed as threats to public safety by politicians and media. Mayor Ed Koch had claimed that homeless people were using the park as a toilet and claimed sandboxes contained feces and urine. He later admitted to personally having seen no evidence of this.

Tompkins Square had been a gathering place for political activists, particularly anarchists and punk musicians who opposed gentrification and the criminalization of poverty. That some neighbors viewed the park as a site of struggle against economic inequality and injustice is reflected in the fact that during the riot a luxury high-rise was targeted for property damage and calls of "Die Yuppie Scum!" went up. Banners during the initial march proclaimed, "Gentrification is Class War."

The 1988 riot has taken on its own political significance, as the 1874 riot did before it. Anarchist graphic novelists and artists such as Seth Tobocman have referenced the Tompkins Square Riot in their works. Concerts commemorating the riot have been held regularly with participation by anarchist and punk bands. The musical *Rent* echoes several key issues of the riot, its setting, and the strained urban environment of the time, including "street people," rough relations with the police, and apartment building squatting.

Jeff Shantz
Kwantlen Polytechnic University

See Also: Homelessness; Loitering; Mobs and Riots; New York City; Panhandling or Begging; Police Brutality/Excessive Force.

Further Readings

Abu-Lughod, Janet. *From Urban Village to East Village: The Battle for New York's Lower East Side*. Oxford: Blackwell, 1995.

Mele, Christopher. *Selling the Lower East Side: Culture, Real Estate, and Resistance in New York City*. Minneapolis: Minnesota University Press, 2000.

Ross, Jeffrey Ian. *Making News of Police Violence: A Comparative Study of Toronto and New York City*. Westport, CT: Praeger, 2000.

Sites, William. *Remaking New York: Primitive Globalization and the Politics of Urban Community*. Minneapolis: University of Minnesota Press, 2003.

Tobocman, Seth. *War in the Neighborhood*. New York: Autonomedia, 2000.

Truancy

Truancy, which is purposeful absenteeism from school, that is, skipping school or "playing hooky," is a major problem for school administrators, teachers, parents, society, and for the students themselves. Generally absenteeism from school on any specific day varies from 10 percent to 30 percent, although in some schools it may range as high as 40 percent. This is financially problematic for schools, as state funding is based on actual school attendance. Moreover, absenteeism and tardiness are rated as the two most prevalent and problematic discipline issues by school administrators.

Children who skip school inevitably fall behind in their classes, and, being without adult supervision, are susceptible to peer pressure to commit delinquent acts and have ample opportunity to commit them. Since truancy takes place during the workday, when most people are out of the house, many targets for criminal activity in public or private spaces are vulnerable, with opportunities for vandalism, drug use, property offense, and underage sex among the more frequent types. Moreover, habitual truants are more likely than other students to eventually drop out of school entirely—and it is well established that higher rates of criminality prevail among dropouts. For example, 1997 data from the U.S. Department of Justice revealed that 41.3 percent of the incarcerated population lacked a high school diploma or its equivalent, in contrast to 18.4 percent of the general population. The proportion of jailed persons who were dropouts had risen to 44 percent in 2002, the Justice Department reported.

Truancy and Street Crime

Truancy provides both time and opportunity for young people to commit delinquent acts. Frequently juveniles not only commit minor acts of deviance but get involved specifically in street crime. Grand juries in Florida found that one of the main factors tied to serious juvenile offenders was truancy. Moreover, almost 60 percent of convicted juvenile murderers in New York had extensive histories of truancy. When North Miami instituted a "truancy center" and began taking truants into custody, residential burglaries and thefts from cars both decreased about 20 percent. While other factors are doubtlessly involved. truancy has also been found to be a major contributor to delinquency, providing minors with both discretionary time and opportunity to facilitate middle-school drug use.

Thus, habitual truancy is considered both a contributing factor to street crime at the time the truancy is being committed and as a developmental factor in later potential street crimes. A delinquent jas the opportunity to commit a crime during the hours that he or she would normally be under adult supervision at school. Additionally, being a habitual truant contributes to poor performance in school and is evidence of a poor attachment to teachers and schoolmates, a lack of commitment to the long-term goals that school entails, and a lack of involvement in the whole panoply of school events and activities. Such a disengaged young person will often have a problematic trajectory into a delinquent adolescence and become a low-achieving adult.

Characteristics of Truants

Children who are habitual truants are more likely to: be from a minority background, have unemployed or underemployed fathers, have parents with criminal records, have delinquent siblings, have parents with marital conflict, and have been subjected to poor child-rearing practices. Adults who report being frequently truant as teenagers are more likely to be in low-income jobs, have either or both mental and physical health issues, live below the poverty level, be at increased risk of incarceration, and to, in turn, have children with behavioral issues.

Students frequently skip school because of being bullied, having personality issues with teachers, or due to discouragement about the institutional environment in general. In this light it is worth noting that truancy is especially high at large, impersonal urban schools where classes are large and consistent and personal intervention by counselors is less likely. It is particularly discouraging to such marginal students in these large schools to see an inordinate amount of institutional resources devoted to athletes and exceptional students, while they themselves, at a particularly vulnerable time of their lives, are seemingly invisible to both counselors and peers.

Legal Status

Compulsory school attendance became a concern to reformers in the late 1800s. Membership in gangs, lingering in pool halls, and general idleness were seen as highly problematic behaviors peculiar to undersocialized immigrant youth. The agenda of groups like the Child Savers included putting an end to child labor, prostitution, and delinquency. Having children in a socializing, Americanizing institution during the workday served a number of these seemingly worthy goals. Moreover, just keeping youth occupied and learning useful skills for the workplace also removed them from the corrupting influences of the street.

By 1918, every state had enacted compulsory attendance laws that basically mandated attendance up to 14 or 16 years of age. Some states required completion of a certain grade, usually sixth or eighth, irrespective of age. Completing high school in that still largely rural milieu was not required; as late as 1914 more than 60 percent of children dropped out after completing sixth grade. Enforcement of truancy laws was always uneven and depended on the emphases placed by individual juvenile courts and local school systems.

Today, enforcement remains spotty and is generally only invoked when truancy occurs in tandem with other more problematic offenses or with other status offenses, such as running away or incorrigibility. Police officers in general do not intervene in truancy cases unless their department has made a particular issue out of enforcement. Juvenile probation officers frequently cite truancy, however, as a point in violation of the conditions of juvenile probation when they consider revoking a delinquent child's probation. If it is suspected that the probated juvenile is using his truant time to deal drugs, commit burglary, or shoplift that is seen as particularly problematic and an appropriate context for invoking truancy statutes and sanctions by the court.

Role of Parents

Parents, however, not the juvenile, bear the ultimate legal liability for their ward's truancy. Parents are enjoined to get their children to school by reasonable means; the juveniles are generally only punished when the parents have demonstrated that they have been unable to obtain the juvenile's compliance. Having children stay home to take care of siblings or pets or putting them to work in a family business during school hours are not acceptable rationales for parents disregarding truancy laws. It must be allowed that some parents, often due to subcultural imperatives, do not regard standard schooling as useful or necessary.

Parents are often informed about an episode of truancy, or unexcused absence, by means of an automated telephone message from the school, school board, or rarely, from a formal notice from the juvenile court. Without a valid excuse, the parents and juvenile may have to go to the school or school board office to deal with a vice principal or, in the latter case, a truant officer. Truant officers are functionaries of the court, school board, or local police dedicated to the enforcement of compulsory attendance laws. If the parents and/or juvenile are recalcitrant, the school or truant officer may refer the child to juvenile court or a truancy service center. The latter are community-based resources with services ranging from counseling, mentoring, tutoring, and mediation, to educational testing.

In some cases, the juvenile may elect to attend an alternative school where structure is not as rigid (and conformity is not as strict) as in conventional educational environments. In cases where severe personality conflicts with teachers have occasioned truancy episodes, the student may be allowed or encouraged to take the problematic course or courses online. Children who persist in truancy may be declared a child in need of supervision (CHIN), removed from the custody of lackadaisical or incompetent parents, and placed in foster care or in the care of relatives.

Solutions

Some experts believe that compulsory school attendance is highly symptomatic of the failure of schools to be relevant, and that troubled truant teenagers should be allowed to drop out. It is thought that they will experience less frustration and strain in the workplace than in school, and thus be less likely to be delinquent. This assumption is highly dubious and is not generally supported by research. The dominant school of thought holds, however, that juveniles need to adjust to this important part of socialization and should be encouraged, even coerced if necessary, to attend classes.

Clearly more resources need to be dedicated to dealing with the closely connected problems of truancy and dropping out, in part as a means to forestall opportunities and proclivities for street crime from developing. Habitual truants, as potential dropouts, need counseling, a supportive environment, and to be surrounded by adults and peers who regard school as relevant and necessary for success in the "real world." Communities that can reduce truancy will be more likely to gain in their quest to reduce gang activity, drug offenses, and general delinquency.

Frederick Hawley
Western Carolina University

See Also: Bicycle Theft; Graffiti; Juvenile Offending; Pool Halls; Shoplifting; Vandalism.

Further Readings
Goode, Erich. *Deviant Behavior.* 8th ed. Upper Saddle River, NJ: Prentice Hall, 2007.
Heilbrunn, Joanna Zorn. *Pieces of the Truancy Jigsaw: A Literature Review.* Denver, CO: National Center for School Engagement, 2007.
Lawrence, Richard. *School Crime and Juvenile Justice.* New York: Oxford University Press, 2007.
Minnesota Office of the Revisor of Statutes. *2011 Minnesota Statutes—Chapter 260A—Truancy.* https://www.revisor.mn.gov/statutes/?id=260 a&view=chapter (Accessed April 2012).
National Center for Mental Health Promotion and Youth Violence Prevention. "Truancy Prevention." http://www.promoteprevent.org/publications/ prevention-briefs/truancy-prevention (Accessed April 2012).
National Center for School Engagement. "What Is Truancy?" http://www.schoolengagement.org/ TruancypreventionRegistry/Admin/Resources/ Resources/40.pdf (Accessed November 2012).
Shoemaker, Donald J. *Juvenile Delinquency.* Lanham, MD: Rowman & Littlefield, 2009.

Urban Ethnography

Urban ethnography, also known as street ethnography and/or fieldwork, is the "cornerstone of American social science," as noted by criminologist Wilson Palacios. This research method motivated sociologists during the early part of the previous century, who had been prone to armchair theorizing, to actually observe individuals, groups, and social processes and collect firsthand data about them. Unlike journalism, which is often conducted in a relatively random fashion with respect to the information that reporters gather and the people whom they interview, ethnography, when conducted properly, is a more systematic and self-reflective approach to gathering and interpreting data than that used by the news media.

Urban Focus

Ethnography is a type of qualitative methodology that depends on descriptive analysis. There is no cookbook approach to conducting ethnography. In order to properly do ethnography, budding researchers must experience the process and actively work on improving their technique and ability. According to Palacios, "Unfortunately, individuals seeking 'how-to' manuals for qualitative research methods are often perplexed, and at times frustrated, by what seems to be a lack of standardization across the field, leading them to conclude that such methodological steps comprise nothing more than a pseudo-social science."

Urban ethnography "is most appropriate for studying members of a 'hidden' vulnerable population. They are hidden in terms of the inherent difficulty in locating them and establishing their true numerical estimates," Palacios noted. Members of a hidden population pose challenges for social researchers because it is difficult to get enough members to study to make appropriate generalizations; the samples tend to be too small. According to researcher Michael Brown, "The most important use of observation . . . is to provide detailed descriptions of a particular social phenomenon and to use these descriptions to develop theories and formulate hypotheses which can be tested with other methods."

History of Ethnography

At the turn of the 20th century, ethnography was the principal method of anthropologists such as Bronislaw Malinowski. Many researcher, mainly men, would travel to a "foreign land . . . and . . . study exotic cultures, languages, customs, beliefs, and behaviors of 'natives,'" said Palacios. Soon, he remarked, researchers from the University of Chicago School of Sociology "rejected the degree of formalism promoted by anthropological ethnography and sought to implement a form of fieldwork, street ethnography, that encapsulated the social-cultural milieu of Chicago neighborhoods and its residents."

During the early 20th century, street ethnography was primarily used to study "marginalized groups such as the homeless person, the drug user/addict, the prostitute, the juvenile." Over time, the subjects and contexts have expanded. At its core, however, is "working within, giving prominence (voice) to people who are" typically perceived to be marginalized members of society. These individuals are usually "socially, politically, and economically disenfranchised," said Palacios. Starting in the 1960s a small but growing number of criminologists started using ethnographic methods to observe criminal justice practitioners (e.g., police, correctional, probation, and parole officers) as they conducted their jobs. These studies were relatively rudimentary at first, but over time grew in sophistication. Some of the studies looked primarily at neighborhoods and the individuals who worked and lived there that had criminogenic elements/features.

Methods

Although ethnographic research can include the collection of documents, reviewing materials in archives, the administration of questionnaires, photography, and video, there are three principle methods used in ethnography: observation, participant observation, and interviewing.

First, unlike casual observation, ethnographic observational research is typically a systematic method in which the researcher pays attention not only to who the players or actors are, but also to subtle nuances in their behavior, mannerisms, the words they choose, and their tone. Second, with respect to participant observation, researchers like Raymond Gold have outlined numerous types of participation. Gold identified a four-part schema with different levels of researcher involvement: complete observer, participant-as-observer, observer-as-participant, and complete participant.

Studying individuals and organizations that engage in deviant and/or illegal practices presents numerous challenges when the ethnographer engages in participant observation. The researcher, as Palacios points out, must carefully negotiate and balance issues such as "access, entrance, reciprocity, time, confidentially, personal biography, rapport, and resources, etc." that may impact the scope and duration of study. Moreover, just because you are a researcher does not give you immunity from being questioned, searched, arrested, or prosecuted by law enforcement authorities. History is littered with examples of people who do illegal things under the guise of ethnographic research.

Most field researchers take "field notes." This can be done in a notebook or on a computer. Regardless, it is a centralized place where the researcher can contextualize "field events, meanings, and social-physical environment of a study's setting and its people and their respective behaviors. . . . From jottings to more formal entries consisting of analytical memos, taxonomies, social network mapping, journal blogs, and video, field notes facilitate the systematic collection and analysis of participant observation," as noted by Palacios. Also important in this context is interviewing. Although observation is important, unless you ask the participants what they are doing and how they feel about what they are doing, a researcher may lose important aspects of the subject and setting. Again, Palacios stated:

All interviews are, in essence, conversations. In the field, these casual conversations are often a prelude to specific types of themes to be formally explored at a later point in time. Such casual conversations are often useful in developing rapport with prospective interviewees, establishing social boundaries concerning the appropriateness of the setting of certain topics/themes highlighting potential ethical dilemmas not previously considered, identifying key informants who may later facilitate the recruitment of interviewees, and creating a qualitative interview approach that is appropriate for the research setting, its scope, and the objectives.

Interviewing, he concludes, "can range from a series or combination of open-ended yet topically guided questions to inquiries with more of a substantive frame, such as semi-structured or structured interview protocols." Sometimes, with the subjects' permission, the researcher audio- or videotapes the subject who is interviewed. The goal for the researcher in these contexts is to get a sense of the subjective meanings that those being interviewed attach to their actions. Because of changes in technology and opportunities to publish, the way that ethnographies are conducted has subtly shifted. No longer are researchers confined to writing their notes by hand in field books, but can now do so with the aid of computer software that increases the rigorousness of the methodology. Moreover, investigators can record their observations via a number of relatively inexpensive methods, including smart phones, concealable handheld video cameras, etc. Nevertheless, many scholars that use street ethnography complain that there are not many outlets for the publication of their research, particularly on deviant and criminological practices. Indeed, in the field of criminology/criminal justice although there is a journal of quantitative criminology, no comparable journal exists for qualitative criminology/criminal justice. This may change as some university programs in criminology and criminal justice realize the benefits that can be achieved by using ethnographic research. Finally, properly conducted urban ethnographies are typically resource intensive as they take considerable time for the researchers to build rapport with their subjects and develop intimate knowledge of the environment.

Jeffrey Ian Ross
University of Baltimore

See Also: Code of the Street; Crime Patterns; Fear of Crime; History of Street Crime in America; Policing, Problem-Oriented; Street Crime, Popular Portrayals of; Street Crime Defined; Urbanization.

Further Readings
Brown, Michael K. "Direct Observation: Research in a Natural Setting." In *Empirical Political Analysis*, Jarol B. Manheim, et al., eds. New York: Longman, 1986.

Clifford, James and George E. Marcus, eds. *Writing Culture: Poetics and Politics of Ethnography*. Berkeley, CA: University of California Press, 1986.

Gold, Raymond L. "Roles in Sociological Field Observations." *Social Forces*, v.36/3 (1958).

Hobbs, Dick and Richard Wright, eds. *Sage Handbook of Fieldwork*. Thousand Oaks, CA: Sage, 2006.

Palacios, Wilson R. "Fieldwork: Observations and Interviews." In *21st Century Criminology*, J. Mitchell Miller, ed. Thousand Oaks, CA: Sage, 2009.

Urban Incivility

If crime and criminality are the hallmarks of criminological enquiry, then concerns over urban incivility (or disorder), which came into the limelight beginning in the 1970s, drastically altered the face of the field. These concerns also reflected a sense of panic and even hysteria concerning public spaces, leading to a rigorous crackdown, which in turn gave rise to numerous social, legal, and ethical implications.

The 1970s and Broken Windows
Urban incivility is a vague term that refers to myriad types of disorderly behavior (e.g., panhandling, squeegeeing, loitering, or public drinking) and material conditions (e.g., abandoned or dilapidated buildings, litter, or graffiti). Often, these are differentiated as social and physical disorder. These are not new problems in cities; many of these issues were of great concern in the past, evinced in the spate of historical vagrancy legislation which addressed similar urban challenges.

The 1970s, however, was a defining moment in this history. In particular, concerns over the fear of crime would give birth to concerns about urban incivility. Criminologists and other scholars began paying attention to matters over and beyond crime and criminality, the perhaps mundane but nevertheless pervasive everyday activities that they attributed to in explaining the rising fear in cities. Incivility, they argued, was the causal (or at least, a key contributing) factor of fear. It was however, the work of James Q. Wilson and George Kelling, who coauthored the now heavily influential Broken Windows Theory, that drastically changed the scope of urban governance and approaches to criminology itself.

Wilson and Kelling hypothesized that disorderly behavior is sequentially linked to urban decline. Disorderly behavior incites fear in people, and therefore, people who are afraid will tend to avoid public spaces and contact with others. This means that informal social control, which is primarily responsible for regulating behavior in public, will lose its potency because law-abiding citizens would no longer be on the streets to enforce the appropriate rules of conduct—and even if they were, would be afraid to so do. Public spaces would then become susceptible to further disorderly behavior, which in turn would erode their vitality, leading citizens to take flight to the suburbs and businesses to invest in more orderly locales. The sequence of this decline would eventually culminate with serious violent crime.

Wilson and Kelling highlighted several reasons for the growth of disorder, but one in particular

Urban decay results from a combination of interrelated socioeconomic conditions, including urban planning decisions, poverty, and construction of roads and rail lines.

was singled out: the erosion of civility as a means of informal social control. In that sense, they were making two important distinctions, one about a problem (disorder) and the other about the causes of it (the lack or deterioration of civility). In the wake of Broken Windows Theory, however, there has been a tendency to conflate disorder and the problems associated with the absence of civility; hence, the generic reference to incivility. Conceptually, however, this conflation has the effect of blurring and muddying the historicity of the production of incivility so that it becomes difficult to appreciate the trajectories that gave rise to its birth.

Other Approaches

This can be appreciated by exploring the birth of civility which has been vividly narrated by sociologist Norbert Elias in his classic *The Civilizing Process.* Elias documents the way the 16th- and 17th-century nobility in western Europe consciously sought to distance themselves from what they saw as disreputable conduct, in this case, the activities largely engaged in by the plebeian masses. In so doing, particular behavior hitherto considered normal and acceptable, such as eating with one's hands, slowly became subjected to microscopic regulation, thereby giving rise to civilized conduct.

More recently, the work of researchers Timothy Phillips and Philip Smith has explored some of these themes by moving discussions of incivility away from strictly criminological, and in particular, Broken Windows-inspired, analyses. Focusing exclusively on rude behavior, their work highlights

the manner in which rudeness is a product of everyday life and situations. Incivility, their work suggests, is everywhere and among everyone; thus it makes little sense to locate it solely among particular groups, that is, a criminal class, and in so-called dangerous spaces.

However, in public policy and in academia generally, discussions of incivility continue to be heavily tied to Broken Windows. And while the deleterious effects of incivility were repeatedly and vividly highlighted in that theory, subsequent research has been unable to conclusively verify many of these claims. In particular, it is still largely unclear whether incivility leads to crime, including serious violent street crime. However, research has convincingly established a link between incivility and fear.

Seeming Solutions

Two solutions put forward by Wilson and Kelling (which later underwent numerous metamorphoses) related to (1) equipping the police with the appropriate tools to tackle incivility—they called for the reintroduction of vagrancy legislation; and (2) that policing practices be reoriented toward more proactive means and be in tune with the needs of the community—they called for community policing. Many cities followed suit by enacting a spate of law-and-order type legislation to tackle incivility. Concomitantly, policing practices were reconfigured to be more proactive.

The quality-of-life campaigns undertaken in the New York City in the 1990s during the tenure of Mayor Rudolph Giuliani and Police Commissioner William Bratton, though not exactly following the model proposed by Wilson and Kelling, is nevertheless a famous example. With other cities soon following suit, and a general decline in crime rates which began in the mid-1990s, many argued that these programs were responsible for the reduction of crime and incivility.

These programs, however, are not without their critics. Many accusations have been leveled against them for being overly zealous in their efforts to clean up the streets; for focusing exclusively on the poor and vulnerable, including particular racial groups; and with it, trammeling constitutional rights. In addition, however, research has been unable to conclusively verify the effect of law-and-order programs in reducing crime and incivility, thereby further bringing these programs into disrepute.

Conclusion

In the end, however, whether incivility is linked to urban decline and crime, and whether law-and-order programs have reduced incivility and crime rates is perhaps irrelevant. Broken Windows serves as a self-fulfilling prophecy so that the very discussion and concern about incivility opens up a space for and creates its own momentum, logic, and rationality for its crackdown. Incivility, in other words, becomes a problem in and of itself, regardless of its putative effects.

Not only has the concern about incivility drastically shaped the way law and order is now thought about and put into practice, but it has also dramatically shaped the nature of criminology, expanding its focus to the mundane and otherwise minor matters that have great significance in the lives of people.

Prashan Ranasinghe
University of Ottawa

See Also: Bratton, William; Broken Windows Theory; Community Policing; Fear of Crime; Giuliani, Rudolph; Graffiti; New York City; Policing, Problem-Oriented.

Further Readings

Elias, Norbert. *History of Manners.* Vol. 1 in *The Civilizing Process,* Edmund Jephcott, trans., from 1939 edition. New York: Urizen Books, 1978.

Kelling, George L. and Catherine M. Coles. *Fixing Broken Windows: Restoring Order and Reducing Crime in Our Communities.* New York: The Free Press, 1996.

Skogan, Wesley. G. *Disorder and Decline: Crime and the Spiral of Decay in American Neighborhoods.* New York: The Free Press, 1990.

Smith, Philip, Timothy L. Phillips, and Ryan D. King. *Incivility: The Rude Stranger in Everyday Life.* Cambridge: Cambridge University Press, 2010.

Urban Planning

Urban planning is a process of design and regulation that seeks to improve the built, economic, and social environments of cities. Planning deals with physical aspects, such as the placement and design of new buildings and infrastructure, as well as the regulation of these places after they are built. Practiced in both government and private sectors, urban planning activities focus on land use, transportation, water and sewage, education, social services, recreation, and entertainment.

Modern planning practices also include concerns for the aesthetics of the built environment, preserving natural ecosystems, reducing social inequality, and collaborating with residents on decision-making processes. Urban planning thus plays an important role in shaping the physical and social surrounds of cities. Because street crime is the product of physical and social environments, urban planning has an important, if often overlooked, impact on the location, level, and prevention of street crime within communities.

Extent of Planning Activities

Examining urban planning more closely reveals the vast extent of its activities in molding physical and social environments. These activities occur at four interrelated levels of aggregation; macro, meso, micro, and design.

At the macrolevel, urban planning deals with the structure of the city as a whole. Included are such planning decisions as where city boundaries will end, which types of transportation systems are more desirable (private versus public transit), where major roads will be placed, economic activities that should be emphasized over others (service versus high-technology or blue-collar industries), and how different land uses should be separated through a broad system of zoning.

Meso-level planning focuses on discrete areas within the city, such as neighborhoods and districts. It attaches future community goals to current conditions of housing mix, traffic, industry, and commercial activities. Meso-planning brings about changes mostly through the development of vacant land or the redevelopment of existing uses. Decisions concerning the placement and design of new schools needed to keep up with changing demographics, and the approval of a new shopping center to better meet the needs of the community, are examples of meso-level planning.

Microlevel planning is concerned with the development of individual sites. Newly proposed developments are evaluated in terms of whether they conform to existing zoning rules and other pertinent regulations. City administrators refusing to allow a bar to open on land zoned for residential use, or barring an adult sexually oriented business to be built within 500 feet of an elementary school, are examples of urban planning decisions made at the microlevel of planning.

Design is the most detailed level of planning and centers on the specifics of the buildings and landscaping that will occur on an individual lot. The exterior design of buildings, required minimum lighting levels in parking facilities, amount and type of greenery on the site, and even the quality of locks on windows and doors can all fall within the purview of design planning activities.

Urban planning activities also include extensive regulatory processes. City administrators are permitted by law to impose restraints on the use and activities of both public and private property as long as they are in the interests of the public's "health, safety, morals, or general welfare." These regulations can be in the form of federal or state laws, city ordinances, the community's land use master plan, or stipulations added to business or special licenses such as liquor and live entertainment licenses. Regulations can include hours of operation, age restriction on customers, the number of people allowed in buildings, requirements that bars serve drinks in plastic cups, "don't touch" and no-alcohol rules for strip clubs, and mandates for security guards at large public performances and sporting events. Nuisance laws can also be used to shut down businesses that adversely affect the "use and enjoyment" of nearby property owners through excessive noise, odor, crime, or disorder.

Urban Planning and Street Crime

Urban planning incorporates the needs, concerns, and desires of local politicians, governmental agencies, private developers, business owners, and residents. It also must consider the economic, social, and legal issues surrounding each proposed project. Crime is but one outcome of planning decisions and is frequently overshadowed, if considered at all, by these other concerns.

Many urban planners have little understanding of how design and regulation impact crime levels. Recognizing this, many communities across the United States and abroad have specially trained police officers that review all new development plans as part of the community's development review process. Private architects and landscapers often utilize the services of consultants trained in crime prevention when potential crime impacts are being considered.

Urban planning processes must recognize and mitigate the impact of criminogenic land uses. Research shows that the presence of retail alcohol outlets, public transportation stops, adult businesses (strip clubs, adult video/book stores), public high schools, shopping centers, budget motels, and large public housing projects are related to increased street crime. Not only may these locations experience high crime, but they can also add additional crime problems to the surrounding neighborhood. This can occur when drug dealers locate near subway stops to ply their trade, street robbers target intoxicated patrons walking home from local bars, or neighborhoods surrounding public high schools experience high crime due to the many students of crime-prone age that travel through them each day. Additionally, studies show that mixed land use (e.g., commercial land use in predominantly residential areas) is related to both higher crime and disorder levels in neighborhoods.

Street design decisions can also be related to crime. Neighborhoods designed with traditional street grid systems tend to experience more crime than less permeable neighborhoods containing fewer entrances and more dead-end streets. Meta-analyses of the numerous studies examining the impact of street lighting also indicate that crime is reduced, and contacts among neighbors may increase, with appropriate levels of street lighting.

Crime prevention through environmental design (CPTED) and defensible space theories explain how site and architectural design is related to crime. Building placement, the location of entrances and windows, and exterior lighting levels can increase informal surveillance of a property and reduce opportunity for crime. Fencing, trespass signage, quality window and door locks, and well-placed thorn bushes can reduce unauthorized access to the property and targets contained within. Territory markers can be used to show ownership and control and remove excuses. These can include landscaping that delineates public from private property, good maintenance, and properly placed signage that announce rules for use of the property while meeting legal standards to assist law enforcement with offenders.

Regulation and Control

Regulatory powers that are part of the urban planning process also have their part to play in controlling crime. Because even criminogenic land uses often have their place in society, regulation is used, often in conjunction with physical design, to help reduce the negative or "secondary effects" of business activity that include crime and disorder. Reasonable controls on the use and activities associated with businesses can be attached to licenses or permits when issued; enforced via local, state, or federal laws; or agreed upon between city administrators and business owners during special license approval processes.

For example, stipulations attached to a nightclub's liquor license might require beverages to be served in plastic cups to prevent injuries from assaults, doors to remain closed during business hours to prevent noise from disturbing the surrounding neighborhood, and the presence of bouncers or security officers to handle disruptive or violent patrons. City ordinances may require liquor and convenience stores to have two clerks on duty during nighttime hours to reduce robberies or prevent the sales of single cans of beer and malt liquor to avoid attracting transients into neighborhoods. Game halls and arcades may be prohibited from allowing youths into the businesses during school hours or unaccompanied by an adult after curfew hours.

Eric S. McCord
University of Louisville

See Also: Crime Prevention, Environmental Design and; Defensible Space Theory; Environmental Criminology; Projects, The.

Further Readings

Clark, Lynn. "Ghost Neighborhoods—CPTED and the Foreclosure Crisis." http://www.cpted.net/PDF/newsletters/Jan2010.pdf (Accessed April 2012).

Crowe, Timothy. *Crime Prevention Through Environmental Design.* 2nd ed. Oxford: Butterworth-Heinemann, 2000.

Miller, Lori Ella. "Building a Safe, Sustainable Community in Central Woodward." http://www.detroit-lisc.org/news/892 (Accessed April 2012).

Newman, Oscar. *Design Guidelines for Creating Defensible Space.* Washington, DC: U.S. Department of Justice, 1976.

Reynard, Daniell M. and Henk Elffers. "The Future of Newman's Defensible Space Theory: Linking Defensible Space and the Routine Activities of Place." *European Journal of Criminology,* v. 6/1 2009.

Schneider, Richard and Ted Kitchen. *Planning for Crime Prevention: A Transatlantic Perspective.* London: Routledge, 2002.

Zelinka, Al and Dean Brennan. *Safescape: Creating Safer, More Livable Communities Through Planning and Design.* Chicago: Planners Press, 2001.

Urbanization

For well over 100 years, researchers have examined the association between urbanization and crime. The scientific method has been applied in a variety of ways to examine the social phenomenon of urban crime, with the aim of understanding that crime is not randomly distributed in space, but is associated with causal mechanisms associated with rural and urban spaces. Quantitative data methods have led to, and been further augmented by the development of, theoretical explanations that focus on the characteristics of cities and neighborhoods.

Cities and Criminality

The Sourcebook of Criminal Justice Statistics, produced by the U.S. Department of Justice, reports that in 2010, residents of cites and statistical metropolitan areas were twice as likely to be the victims of a violent crime as those living in rural communities. Further, they were slightly less likely than that to be victims of a property crime. When specific crimes are examined, the rate based on a population of 100,000 shows that robbery victimizations in cities are nine times that experienced in rural communities, 138 to 16, respectively. The rates for aggravated assault of 280 in cities to 154 in rural communities are reflective of nearly double the risk of being the victim of an assault.

When examining property crime rates, citizens living in a rural community are slightly less likely to have their home burglarized, comparing the burglary rates of 708 to 559. However, city dwellers have their cars stolen at three times the rate of rural residents, 282 to 101. It is no surprise that crime occurs at a greater rate in cities; however, the link between urban living and crime is one that bears exploring.

Crime that occurs in cities is often attributed to the presence of so-called dangerous classes of people that live within them. Dangerous classes of people are seen as embodying moral depravity. Their immoral behavior contributes to a variety of social ills; crime is one of those ills. Adolphe Quetelet, a statistician living in the early 1800s, measured the distribution of moral statistics (arrests) in France. He concluded that the degree of formal and informal control present in society helped explain the distribution of criminal behavior. In places where immoral people lived, he reported that crime flourished because of a lack of control and the exercise of free will. This position rests on a basic assumption that people in an urban setting are inherently prone to bad behavior.

Building on Quetelet's work from the 1830s, Andre-Michel Guerry used cartography to study the distribution of such moral statistics across France; he reported several important findings. First, crimes against persons and property were distributed differently. Property crimes occur in urban areas where there is more opportunity for these crimes to occur. On the other hand, the highest rates of crimes against persons proportionate to the local population were clustered in rural areas. However, both property and person crimes were far more prevalent in urban areas. The results of the study are roughly replicated in the contemporary sourcebook data on crime and place. The import of Guerry's work was to illustrate the distribution of crime in geographic space, with an emphasis on its occurrence in varying population concentrations.

Social Structural Theories

It was not until the 1920s that attention to place became a central dimension of criminological thought. Robert Park and Ernest Burgess, scholars at the Chicago School of Sociology at the University of Chicago, used models originally developed to study the ecological distribution of animal and plant life to study the development of cities. Their concentric zone theory suggested that the initial habitation of an area occurred around the means of production, and through time the city would grow in size moving outward from that center.

Sociologists Clifford Shaw and Henry McKay, who started working in the 1940s with crime data compiled in previous decades, used the concentric zone model as a template to study patterns of crime in Chicago. Using official data and arrest records, they charted the distribution of crime in the city. They reported that the further one went from the center of the city, the less crime appeared to occur. Conversely, in the interstitial area near the industrial center and in the area immediately next to it crime seemed to flourish. There were dense clusters of arrest that occurred there, and over time crime was a constant in these areas no matter what ethnic group lived there. They concluded that these areas were "natural areas" of crime, suggesting that place—not population—was the linchpin in understanding crime causation.

Shaw and McKay's theory is known as Social Disorganization. Social disorganization is associated with high levels of poverty, residential instability and transience, disrupted families, population heterogeneity, and a lack of informal and formal social control. Their research included neighborhoods that were filled with immigrants from western European countries who had come to America to make a new life. The flow of new residents coming and older residents leaving created a community of strangers. Their lack of community connection, common language, and shared culture led to isolation and an inability to take on the challenges of community—including but not limited to crime. Urban living, coupled with lower social class affiliation and social disadvantage, contributed to attenuated relationships characterized by this anonymity and isolation. The clustering of people who did not know or relate to each other, often possessing different cultural norms or values, contributed to criminal subcultural development, they surmised

Social disorganization has been a mainstay of criminological theory. Robert Bursik and Harold Grasmik added to this essential model in their work during the 1970s and 1980s by suggesting that neighborhoods were further attenuated due to their lack of connection to institutional structures and resources. These social institutions could have provided support and assistance to people who had substantial needs due to social disadvantage and isolation. Hence, not only were the communities extremely isolated and disadvantaged by the social structure; the structure systematically and institutionally perpetuated their relegation to the bottom of the social hierarchy.

Robert Sampson and other scholars associated with the Project on Human Development in

Chicago Neighborhoods, begun in the 1990s, have led to a further refinement of the role of urban living on criminality. Sampson and colleagues in their recent work argue that neighborhoods maintain significance due to their concentration of socially disadvantaged individuals. The concentrations are not random but result from historic patterns of racial segregation and isolation.

Although urban crime is often found to be highly correlated with the percentage of the population that is African American, for example, these scholars argue that the variable has historic meaning and reflects more than a binary association. The clustering in America's urban core of citizens who have been resource-deprived or consistently underserved results in social isolation, a lack of collective efficacy, little or no social capital, and an overall reduced level of formal and informal social control.

These conditions limit the capacity of individuals within these communities, and in turn limit the communities themselves to alter their basic fabric. The situation perpetuates criminal offending, gang formation, drug market development, and the presence of violence.

Urban Subcultures

The development of subcultures in lower-class urban communities has a long history in criminological thought. Walter Miller saw lower-class culture as contributing to the formation of gangs. Urban poverty left idle youth with little more to do than engage in nonutilitarian violence and criminal behavior. According to Miller, crime of lower-class urban youth had no economic utility since it was not resultant from poverty, but rather a need for belonging among peers. Instead of poverty, Miller argued that

Isolated, underserved urban communities have been found to perpetuate criminality, gang presence, drug dealing, and violence. It is common in American cities, as in this crime scene documented in San Pedro, California, for crime to be highly concentrated in a few, often economically disadvantaged areas where crime may remain a constant no matter which ethnic group lives there.

it was the focal concerns of lower culture that generated crime. Youth in lower-class communities honored toughness, trouble, smartness, fate, and autonomy. These values were the source of their esteem.

Another cultural theory that sought to explain high levels of violence in African American communities was developed by Marvin Wolfgang and Thorsten Sellin. They argued that subcultures of violence emerge in urban African American neighborhoods due to historic socialization and modeling of southern conceptions of chivalry and honor. Violence was compared to the dueling that occurred between southern gentlemen over insults and slights; disrespect as it were. In other words, the behavior of the black population was a mimicking of the masters that had owned them. While this explanation for urban crime did not find long-term support, another subcultural development, by Elijah Anderson, has gained tremendous support.

Anderson argues that competing cultures exist within urban African American communities, between the "decent" and "street" families. The "code of the street" conflicts and competes with the values of decent families, who struggle to maintain values consistent with the larger society. The street culture and its codes require specific responses to insults and challenges to manhood based on a conception of honor and respect. These responses are often violent and are designed to maintain street reputation and presence. Challenging street people or failure to honor the code of conduct that is promoted leads to marginalization and victimization.

Ongoing Research

More than a century of research has shown that official incidents of crime, that is arrests, are not randomly distributed. From the work of Quetelet and Guerry to the work of contemporary criminologists, arrest data for violent and property crimes occur disproportionately in urban centers. They also tend to occur more in poor communities where minority group members, ethnic groups, and racial concentrations reside. Although self-report studies provide evidence that crime occurs everywhere, official records consistently show a clustering of arrests for crime in cities.

Crime and urban settings seem to be inextricably linked. A variety of explanations are offered to describe the reasons for this pattern. Included in these are concerns with police bias toward poor minority group members. It has also been argued that the observed differences in arrest data are the result of arrestable conduct by members of minority groups. Finally, there are discussions of inherent inequality that leads to greater disadvantage in minority communities and in turn greater stress to survive. The connection is consistent, and the pattern of factors that contribute to its occurrence endures.

Norman A. White
Saint Louis University

See Also: Broken Windows Theory; Crime Mapping; Environmental Criminology; Hot Spots; Kerner Commission on Civil Disorders; Projects, The.

Further Readings

Anderson, Elijah. *Code of the Street: Decency, Violence, and the Moral Life of the Inner City.* New York: W. W. Norton, 2000.

Beirne, Piers. "Adolphe Quetelet and the Origins of Positivist Criminology." *American Journal of Sociology*, v.92/5 (1987).

Bursik, Robert and Harold Grasmick. *Neighborhoods and Crime: The Dimensions of Effective Community Control.* New York: Lexington Books, 1983.

Friendly, Michael. "Andre-Michel Guerry's 'Moral Statistics of France': Challenges for Multivariate Spatial Analysis." *Statistical Science*, v.22/3 (2007).

Sampson, Robert. *Great American City: Chicago and the Enduring Neighborhood Effect.* Chicago: University of Chicago Press, 2011.

Vandalism

The crime of vandalism varies greatly. However, most vandalism occurs against property that is on street level. Vehicles, warehouses, residential and commercial property, as well as street signs and the streets themselves, are all targeted for vandalism. The street is the common denominator in most vandalism, either as it provides access or is the physical location of the vandalism. This entry discusses what vandalism is, why it occurs, and its effect on the community.

Nature of the Crime

In its most simplistic explanation, vandalism is the intentional destruction or damage of public or private property. However, vandalism takes many forms. Vandalism encompasses everything from broken windows in occupied and abandoned property, arson, the keying of an automobile, or the slashing of the upholstery on a bus, to graffiti and street art created or installed without the permission of the owner of the property or the city.

Vandalism is a simple crime to commit. It does not take any special equipment or skill. A rock, a can of spray paint, a bumper sticker, a house key, a permanent marker—all of these items can be used to engage in vandalism. The ease with which someone can engage in vandalism also results in a wide range of individuals engaging in this crime and not identifying the behavior as deviant or criminal. Vandalism can be a by-product of the commission of another crime or as a crime unto itself. Vandalism is especially prevalent during riots, when property is damaged throughout the riot location.

Vandalism takes place everywhere. Vandalism can be found in urban and rural areas and in locations of high, middle, and low socioeconomic status. Vandalism is engaged in by individuals from all backgrounds, from the very young to those well into adulthood, the educated and the uneducated, rich and poor. Any available surface can be targeted for vandalism. Once a location has been the target of vandalism, more vandalism can be expected to occur in the same area. That is to say, once one person carves his or her name into a bench at a bus stop, more carvings and writings are likely to follow.

In contrast to the wealth of statistics available on violent crimes and major property crimes, there is a dearth of regular, reliable reporting on vandalism. However, the U.S. Department of Education pointed out that more than one-third of all 84,000 schools in the United States reported at least one case of vandalism in a recent year. Researchers for the National Education Association estimated that the physical property cost of vandalism in U.S. schools was about $200 million in 1970.

A study through the National Association of School Psychologists increased the estimate to

$600 million in 1990. In addition to the hard fiscal costs of school vandalism, there are associated negative affects to morale and social cohesion in schools and their communities. The same can be said for vandalism that occurs in public spaces beyond the school environment.

Underlying Motivations

The reasons behind vandalism are as varied as the actions that fall under this criminal designation. Vandalism can be used by individuals or groups as a means to "send a message" to a target group, usually stigmatized groups (e.g., minorities, homosexuals, or various religious groups). In these situations, the target location is chosen for the greatest impact, such as vandalism in a cemetery. Vandalism in most of these situations is used as a tool in intimidation campaigns. In these situations property is damaged and often graffiti, in the form of slurs or threats, is applied to the property or to property within the lines of sight of the primary target location, such as anti-Semitic graffiti on a wall across from a

Serious forms of vandalism may take place during public unrest, which can involve the willful destruction of property. Glass is strewn on the sidewalk in Oakland, California, after the police shooting of a young African American man.

synagogue. In some of these cases, the vandalism is a warning that more serious crimes may follow.

For others, vandalism is engaged in out of boredom, or for thrills. An abandoned vehicle may be completely destroyed by vandals, simply because it is available and no one seems to care about its condition. In these situations, the earliest vandals may be those who break windows of the vehicle to remove a stereo or other valuable parts. After the first incident of vandalism against the vehicle, others may follow further destroying the vehicle. In some areas, where vandalism is more prevalent than others, this destruction may take place rather quickly; in others it may take several days or weeks before the vandalism starts. Some engage in vandalism for revenge or out of emotional distress. In these cases the vandal and the property owner are usually known to each other and have had some form of falling-out, an argument or the end of a relationship, romantic or otherwise. Vandalism may be used in these situations to destroy property that was to be divided, due to divorce or settlement.

Vandalism can be used as a form of protest or to make a political statement. In these situations, billboards are a popular target, especially if they portray the business, individual, or political or social issue that the protester wishes to address. Some vandalism has become ritualized, in which a location has been set aside in a community after the location has been repeatedly targeted. An example would be a rock or wall that is repeatedly covered with graffiti during a pledge week in a college town. In these situations, the relative acceptability of the vandalism can change at any point, but is typically ignored by the community, despite the lack of overt permission.

Vandalism can also be used as a component of fraud. In these situations the owner of the property or a coconspirator damages or destroys their own property. Individuals hoping to cash in on insurance fraud against a vehicle, for instance, may abandon the vehicle in a neighborhood and begin the vandalism against the vehicle themselves, hoping that others will follow suit before the vehicle is recovered.

Consequences and Countermeasures

In attempts to prevent or decrease vandalism, closed-circuit television (CCTV) is often installed in areas that have been heavily vandalized. Signs are posted to remind potential vandals, especially those engaging in graffiti, of the illegal nature of their behavior. Some communities have placed age restrictions on the purchase of spray paint and paint markers. Other communities have policies in place to fine individuals who abandon vehicles or do not insure abandoned property. These policies are an attempt to decrease the availability of targets for vandalism by holding their owners accountable.

Vandalism is a crime under-reported to law enforcement, though it is one of the most recognizable crimes. It is also one of the more prevalent crimes. The clean-up and repair of vandalism can constitute a serious expense for individuals, when private property is targeted, as well as communities, when the target is public. The prevalence of vandalism in a community can alter resident's perceptions of their security and the prevalence of crime. The more vandalism a community experiences, the more that community is likely to perceive that it has problems with more serious crimes, such as illegal drug markets. This perception can also increase fear of crime or decrease a community's faith in the legitimacy of law enforcement.

Though the punishments vary by location, most vandals are sentenced to community service and ordered to pay restitution to the owner of the damaged property or the city. In some jurisdictions, when the vandals are juveniles, additional fines may be leveled against the parents of the juveniles. This often depends on the extent of the vandalism or its location, such as a school. Sentence enhancements can be applied, in some jurisdictions, for repeat offenders or because of the nature of the vandalism, such as vandalism that is identified as a hate crime.

Clairissa D. Breen
Cazenovia College

See Also: Arson; Broken Windows Theory; Graffiti; Hate Crime; Juvenile Offending.

Further Readings

Dedel, Kelly. *School Vandalism and Break-Ins.* Guide No. 35. Madison, WI: Center for Problem-Oriented Policing, 2005.

Goldstein, Arnold. *The Psychology of Vandalism.* The Springer Series in Social Clinical Psychology. New York: Plenum Press, 1996.

Shinn, Mark R., Hill M. Walker, and Gary Stoner. *Interventions for Academic and Behavior Problems II: Preventive and Remedial Approaches.* Bethesda, MD: National Association of School Psychologists, 2002.

Ward, C. *Vandalism.* London: Architectural Press, 1973.

Zimbardo, Philip. *The Lucifer Effect: Understanding How Good People Turn Evil.* New York: Random House, 2007.

Victims, Immigrant

Historically, scholars have paid relatively little attention to the criminal victimization of immigrants. Immigration scholars have focused on assimilation, or immigrant incorporation into society in ways that mostly ignored crime; criminology emphasizes immigrants as perpetrators through theories of how subcultures and cultural conflict lead to street crime. But immigration involves factors like race, citizenship, immigration status, fluency in English, religion, and income that can all relate to victimization. Such factors also relate to perceptions of, and actual experiences with, the criminal justice system as a source of support or revictimization. Immigrants can be the targets for hate crimes and are susceptible to victimization based on their generally vulnerable status as non-native born citizens. The latter includes predatory victimization at the hands of individuals, groups, or businesses seeking to exploit or oppress individuals, and due process victimization by the criminal justice system through profiling and detention.

Data on immigrant victimization is scarce. The Bureau of Justice Statistics Web site has no data on immigrants as victims. The National Crime Victimization Survey and the Federal Bureau of Investigation's Uniform Crime Reports (UCR) contain data on race and ethnicity, which includes multigeneration citizens as well as new arrivals. Both sources generally exclude undocumented immigrants, who are at the highest risk for victimization. There are some surveys from specific cities that assess victimization of immigrants but researchers cannot generalize these finding back to larger populations

Immigrants and Criminology

Early work on crime and genetics was done by whites whose research typically supported a form of white supremacy and thus concluded that non-whites, including many immigrants, were inferior races that needed to be excluded or subject to greater social control. Other research claimed that immigrant groups had "cultural predispositions" to crime. Drawing on research findings that community disorganization, poverty, and a high concentration of young males are related to higher crime rates, some criminologists hypothesized that immigrant communities would have higher crime rates because these factors were prevalent.

However, numerous studies have shown that immigrants have a similar or lower crime rate than native-born Americans. The 1931 *Report on Crime and the Foreign Born* (Wickersham Report) found that proportionally, immigrants commit fewer crimes than native-born Americans. Criminologists Clifford Shaw and Henry McKay came to a similar conclusion, noting that criminality correlated with social disorganization in certain areas of the city—not race, nationality, or how long people had been in the United States. Modern scholarship finds that immigrant arrests tend to be for immigration offenses, not for property or violent offenses. Further, the time during the 1990s when America experienced its strongest growth in both the Hispanic and undocumented immigrant populations was when crime rates fell significantly.

More critical scholarship adds that the first immigrants were European settlers who victimized Native Americans and took their land during colonization. Subsequently, Africans experienced forced immigration and the victimization of American slavery, which allowed for the assault, rape and murder of blacks with little or no legal consequence. Groups like the Chinese and Irish were welcomed when the United States sought cheap labor to complete the transcontinental railroad—but were then the subject of criminal laws—especially drug laws—to control them when the project was done. Organized crime (the Mafia) and street crime gangs formed partly in response to blocked opportunities for legitimate economic advancement. Finally, immigrant patterns of arrest reflect not just the prevalence of crime but heightened police scrutiny and less likelihood of informal sanctions in particular neighborhoods.

Immigrants and Victimization

Immigration laws influence victimization by altering the routine activities of immigrants as well as reducing the likelihood that the police will be involved. Furthermore, both actual and perceived immigration status shape interactions by creating an unequal power dynamic between immigrants and native-born, as well as among immigrants with different immigration statuses.

Nonimmigrants are generally less susceptible to status-based victimization—victimization that is linked to one's official immigrant or citizenship status—than are immigrants, with naturalized immigrants (citizens) the least vulnerable and undocumented immigrants the most. This dynamic is distinct from hate crimes, which are based on an ideology of white supremacy, which frequently seeks to make the United States a homeland for whites. Status-based victimizations are not based on bias, but a perpetrator's assumption that the prospective victim will not call the police and/or that the police will investigate the victims' immigration status rather than the crime. For example, perpetrators may target immigrants (especially undocumented ones) for theft because they will not report the loss to police and carry attractive amounts of cash if they do not have bank accounts. Some rapists target immigrant women because they believe they are more likely to get away with it. A batterer may tell a woman he is abusing that she will be deported if she seeks help for domestic violence..

While all immigration policies are by nature restrictive, they vary greatly in the degree to which immigrants can enter a country and participate in society. Countries that are restrictive will have a larger number of status-based offenses than those with more open policies. Recent U.S. immigration policy has generally been restrictive; enforcement draws increasingly upon a criminal justice model. Together, policy and enforcement facilitate the generalized "othering" and "criminalization" of immigrants, which leads to increased status-driven victimization. Immigrants are vulnerable because restrictive laws and practices deny them equal protection.

With undocumented immigrants, power differentials between them and those with legal status are at a maximum. Undocumented immigrants live in constant fear of arrest, detention, and deportation, making them more vulnerable to predatory offenses. Immigration raids are common, local police often work with immigration and border patrol agents, and documented cases of police interrogation and arrest of immigrant victims who have called for assistance all bolster immigrant fears. Thus, undocumented immigrants are unlikely to report victimization to the police, leaving them without protection and vulnerable to criminal harm.

Predatory Victimization

Assaults on immigrants and threats of violence against them frequently result from immigrants protesting predatory victimization. This is done by individuals, groups, and businesses who purposefully exploit an immigrant because that immigrant will not report them for fear of immigration status consequences, lack of communication skills, or lack of knowledge about their rights. Such victimization includes common discrimination or differential treatment; harassment; interpersonal crimes like blackmail and extortion. Employment abuse includes some of the above plus violations of labor law (lack of benefits or breaks), wage theft (sublegal wages, nonpayment of overtime, or nonpayment), unsafe working conditions, and even slavery. Perpetrators are likely to be somewhat close to victims, and may be romantic partners, family members, bosses, coworkers, business associates, neighbors, friends, or even lawyers. Because immigrants generally have fewer employment opportunities, employment-related victimization is likely the most widespread form of victimization experienced by immigrants, especially those who lack legal permission to work. Even those working legally may be unfamiliar with U.S. labor laws and how to pursue grievances. Labor-law enforcement has also been a low priority in recent federal administrations, so employment of immigrants is rife with illegal and unsavory activities, with many serious abuses, for example, in agriculture and the meatpacking industries.

Due Process Victimization

Due process victimization refers to offenses committed by criminal justice actors—such as police and agents of immigration agencies—who violate the rights of immigrants. This encompasses racial profiling; verbal harassment; excessive use of force; abuse (physical, psychological, or sexual); unreasonable searches, seizures, and arrests; failure to uphold basic civil rights as outlined by the Constitution; and not maintaining appropriate standards of confinement for immigration detention. The major difference distinguishing due process offenses from predatory offenses—other than the perpetrator's identity as a criminal justice employee—is that due process

perpetrators are not acting for personal gain and may indeed be following institutional procedures, objectives, and occupational norms.

While these issues occur in other contexts in the criminal justice system, they are more prevalent in immigration enforcement. Specifically, the adoption of a criminal justice model within immigration policy since the early 1990s has eroded due process protections and made it more difficult to challenge improper treatment against immigrants and refugees. Studies show that not only are deportees subject to verbal harassment, procedural failings, and excessive use of force, but also that force is more commonly used against deportees than citizens. Even the federal government has acknowledged several instances of detainee mistreatment and neglect—including inadequate health care, environmental health and safety concerns, and noncompliance with detention confinement guidelines.

Maya Pagni Barak
American University
Paul Leighton
Eastern Michigan University

See Also: Blackmail; Courts; Hate Crime; Jails; Police Brutality/Excessive Force; Racial Profiling.

Further Readings

Bacon, David. *Illegal People: How Globalization Creates Migration and Criminalizes Immigrants.* Boston: Beacon Press, 2008.
Boswell, Richard A. *Immigration and Nationality Law—Cases and Materials.* 4th ed. Durham, NC: Carolina Academic Press, 2010.
Lucas, Anne. "Huddled Masses: Immigrants in Detention." *Punishment and Society,* v.7/3 (2005).
Martinez, Ramiro, Jr. *Latino Homicide: Immigration, Violence, and Community.* London: Routledge, 2002.
Weissinger, George. *Law Enforcement and the INS.* Lanham, MD: University Press of America, 2005.

Victims, Senior

While the elderly are certainly thought to be more frequent victims of street crime than other age groups, that is not necessarily the case. Except for personal larceny, such as purse snatching, the elderly are the least frequent victims of street crime. Bureau of Justice Statistics reports reveal that people over 65 have the lowest rate of violent victimization—3.2 incidents per 1,000 people. This rate is three times lower than the nearest age group. Of all groups in the population, elderly, white females, followed by males in the same age group, have the least likelihood of violent victimization. Senior-aged black females are the next least-likely group to be crime victims. By way of contrast, the rate of victimization per 1,000 for those aged 12 to 15 is 10 times higher—38.6.

The low likelihood of victimization of the elderly is mainly due to the fact that they avoid contact with high-risk contexts, such as frequenting bars late at night, and do not associate with risky actors, such as rowdy young men. However, they are at high risk from fraud, con games, door-to-door scam artists, and abuse from family and health care workers. Federal and state agencies have recently become more focused on fraud and abuse against seniors

Crime and the Fear of Crime

Although in general terms the elderly are among the least likely violent crime victims (for example, those 65 and older have the lowest rate of homicide), if assaulted they have a higher risk of death than do younger people. They are less likely to be the victims of gun-related violence but are more likely to be bludgeoned to death than those who are younger. The elderly are more likely to be killed in the circumstances of the commission of another felony.

Because of their physical vulnerability, age, and gender, elderly women are among the most fearful of crime. However, they are no more likely to be the victims of robbery or larceny than are elderly males. In the case of younger people, males are much more likely to be victimized. Assaults against the elderly are more likely to be committed by offenders known to victims, as opposed to strangers. When injured, moreover, elderly women are much more likely to require medical care than are younger women.

That notwithstanding, in part because of their sedentary lifestyle, they are among the least at-risk populations in the United States. However their fear of crime is exaggerated, it nonetheless is a major factor contributing to their isolation from the world around them and to their retreat from constructive participation in their communities. Their movements become ever more constricted and they may become pathologically reclusive. Lamentably, most assaults against the elderly take place in private rather than public contexts.

Elderly women are the most fearful of victimization. This is in part due to socialization as females in a society that views women as more vulnerable than men. The elderly living in urban communities are generally more fearful of crime than those in the suburbs or rural areas. Being in poor health also increases the fear of crime among the elderly. Counterintuitively, being inveterate consumers of media and televised news does not seem to increase the fear of crime in the elderly population. However, hearing personal accounts of victimization from their peers is a strong fear stimulus

Living in a neighborhood dominated by minorities and the poor also increases elders' fears. This is true because these neighborhoods are often characterized, in their minds at least, by rowdy and uncivil (and, hence, unpredictable) behavior by youth and street people. It is not the actual presence of minorities or the poor that is problematic; it is the corrosive effects of poverty on the population and on the physical reality of the neighborhood that so troubles the elderly. But to older Americans in our society, the presence of minorities is a signifier of that actuality.

Awareness and Challenges

Elders living on their own may be subject to being defrauded by door-to-door scam artists, who specifically target and prey on older citizens. Frequently attractive and charismatic, they may sell older folks a decade's worth of dancing lessons, overpriced insurance and cemetery lots, or may simply defraud them using simple con games. When, and if, elders realize that they have been victimized they frequently avoid reporting this to family or police due to fear of being thought incapable of independent living. They are also subject to other crimes, such as burglary. In some cases of fraud, theft, and burglary, they may be totally unaware of having been victimized. Some of the most flagrant thefts may be committed by homecare workers or friends and family of said workers, or by family members of the elders. The crimes are falsely attributed to housebreakers and the perpetrators are never brought to justice.

Social service agencies and police departments have limited resources to help the elderly. In some urban areas and retirement havens, special victim assistance units have been formed to help the elderly work their way through the criminal justice process. Lack of funding hampers expansion of these services to a growing sector of the population, however.

Frederick Hawley
Western Carolina University

See Also: Burglary; Domestic Violence; Door-to-Door Scam Artists; Drugs, Prescription; Fear of Crime; Mental Illness; Theft and Larceny.

Further Readings
Bachman, Ronet and Michelle Meloy. "The Epidemiology of Violence Against the Elderly: Implications for Primary and Secondary Prevention." *Journal of Contemporary Criminal Justice*, v.24/2 (2008).

Rothman, Max, B. Dunlop, and P. Entzel. *Elders, Crime and the Criminal Justice System: Myths, Perceptions, and Reality in the 21st Century*. New York: Springer, 2000.

Snyder. David. *Elder Crimes, Elder Victims*. Burlington, MA: Jones and Bartlett Learning, 2014.

Truman, Jennifer and Michael Rand. "Criminal Victimization, 2009." October 13, 2010, U.S. Department of Justice. http://bjs.gov/index.cfm?ty=pbdetail&iid=2217 (Accessed June 2012).

Victims, Tourist

Tourism is a worldwide phenomenon and a $919 billion industry. About 940 million people engaged in leisure travel in 2010, even with a still-depressed worldwide economy. All that travel is not without consequences, though.

Nature and Extent of Victimization
There is substantial empirical evidence that the amount of crime experienced by tourists is higher than that experienced by the local population. This phenomenon has been documented in several tourist destinations across the globe. Researchers Meda Chesney-Lind and Ian Lind found that tourists in Honolulu and Kauai, Hawaii, were more likely to be victims of larceny, robbery, and rape than local residents. Criminologist Dee Wood Harper, Jr., compared the crime experience of tourists and nontourists in New Orleans, Louisiana; Honolulu and Kauai, Hawaii; Malaga, Spain; Barbados in the Caribbean; and Miami, Florida. He found that tourists were targeted for both property and violent crime significantly more often than locals in all of these locations except Miami. Moreover, as overall local crime rates increased, the victimization of tourists also increased.

According to Valaer Murray on Forbes.com, the 10 most-visited locations in the United States in 2010 were, in descending order of number of visitors: Orlando, Florida; New York City; Chicago, Illinois; Orange County, California; Miami, Florida; Las Vegas, Nevada; Atlanta, Georgia; Houston, Texas; Philadelphia, Pennsylvania; and San Diego, California. Though research has shown that tourists experience more crime than locals, it remains difficult for researchers to uncover the extent of tourist crime in some of these cities; certainly any publication demonstrating potential danger to tourists is not in these cities' interest and officials may be reluctant to open up records as a result.

Vulnerability Factors
The specific targeting of tourists is certainly a major factor in their increased vulnerability. Another factor that must be considered is tourists' naiveté about the locations they are visiting and their lack of knowledge about the dangerousness of some people and neighborhoods. The characteristics of the tourists themself must be considered, as must what the tourist is trying to accomplish from a theoretical perspective. Dean MacCannell has compared modern tourism with the earlier religious pilgrimage, both of which he concludes constitute a search for an "authentic" experience. It is not just the institutionalized tourism sites that tourists want to see; they often have a desire to get "backstage" and see how the real locals live. The temporal and physical features of the location where robberies and muggings occur are also factors that must be considered. Behavior of tourists (e.g., drinking too much and carousing) often places them in what has been described by researcher Jack Katz as contextual weakness. This occurs at many levels: The potential victim is in a strange city, late at night, most likely fatigued, and under the influence of alcohol.

Harper's study of New Orleans, a popular tourist destination in its own right, is useful in putting the above factors in context. He found that tourist victims tend to be male. Crimes against tourists tend to be concentrated in areas peripheral to the main tourist attractions, which suggests that at least some of the victims may have been looking for backstage excitement, perhaps in the form of illicit drugs or sex. These areas can become tourist robbery and mugging "hot spots." They are off the beaten path of popular attractions and distant from the guardianship typically provided by police and other security forces at tourist sites. Crimes against tourists tend to occur in the late night and early morning hours; disorientation of victims, due to drinking or other intoxicants as well as due to unfamiliarity with the area, are likely factors in their victimization.

In a substantial number of cases, the victims may have unwittingly collaborated in their own victimizations. The opportunity for the victimization was largely created by the choices the victim made. This type of vulnerability would not be likely to occur if the victim was on his or her home turf. By their actions in the tourism context, however, victims place themselves in a contextually weak position in three ways: being a stranger, being isolated in an unfamiliar place, and being there in search of some form of overindulgent or illicit action. Considering this motivation on the part of tourists, it is likely that a larger number of crimes against tourists go unreported to the police. Finally, being a nonpermanent member of the community adds yet another dimension to contextual weakness of the tourist victim. Even when an arrest is made in the incident, prosecution is unlikely because the victim has returned home, and unless there was serious loss or injury, is not likely to return and assist in the prosecution of the offender.

Street Criminals' Strategies and Tactics

Tourist victimization tends to reflect a decision-making process on the part of the would-be predator and a body of knowledge about the scene and the behavior of the soon-to-be tourist victim. Based on interviews conducted with former street robbers, researchers have learned that robbers seem to be conversant with how to identify, target, and rob a tourist and with what to look for in a potential target. In some instances, robbers will develop a relationship with the target, using an incentive such as the promise of drugs or sex to place the soon-to-be victim in a physical location favorable to committing the robbery. They then commit the robbery and

make good on their escape. Moreover, the predator is well versed in the habits of tourists, the sights and sounds they want to experience, their desire to party, and sometimes their desire for illicit action.

Choosing to mug or rob comes easily to an offender if he needs fast cash. Jacobs and Wright believe that people who engage in robbery often find themselves in a lifestyle of expensive habits, such as gambling, drugs, and heavy drinking, that require a steady flow of cash. Robbery then is understandable because it produces the cash that is immediately translated into the desired lifestyle. At the street culture level, preying on and ripping off tourists is seen as "legitimate."

Aggressive begging and panhandling is commonplace at tourist sites throughout the world. The beggar/panhandler begins by violating the personal space of his or her target by holding, touching, and pushing, often with a pathetic mien and an underlying threat of violence if the target does not comply quickly. Older couples who appear well-off but physically unintimidating are often targeted with this aggressive form of begging, which could also be legally classified as simple robbery. Stealing from tourists can include grabbing jewelry (gold chains, watches, etc.), purse snatching, taking uncontrolled property, breaking into cars with out-of-state license plates, pickpocketing, and armed robbery. At the level of street culture, all of these actions are viewed as at least quasi-legitimate because of the great naiveté of the tourist and the need or desire for a quick return. In their interviews with robbers, criminologists Richard Wright and Scott Decker found that in addition to the financial rewards, the robbers noted that committing robberies gave them a sense of control in a world where they otherwise had none.

Street criminals rarely work alone. Typically, pickpockets and muggers worldwide usually come in threes, and the would-be victim should assume that at least one of them is armed. A common ploy employed by criminals is to ask directions to a street location that would be likely known by a native but not by a tourist, or they might make a civil request, for a cigarette light for example. These ploys allow the criminal to size up his potential target and his civility lulls the victim into dropping his or her guard. What follows occurs in rapid secession. One perpetrator grabs and holds the victim while the second takes his or her billfold, wallet, purse, watch, and other jewelry; the third serves as a lookout and/or monitors the assault. Once the assault is underway, it usually lasts only a few seconds and the victim is safe from serious injury if he or she does not resist.

Thieves are always on the lookout for casually attended or unattended property such as purses, luggage, backpacks, cameras, phones, and laptops. Anything that is likely to contain cash or property that is easily convertible to cash is always on thieves' radar. Criminals are commonly in the business of distracting tourists just for a few seconds in order to steal their belongings.

Countermeasures

From the perspective of the tourist, the first and most important countermeasure is to be very alert to what is going on in the vicinity, even in areas that appear safe such as the hotel lobby, near a bureau de change or automated teller machine (ATM), the lobbies of airports, bus stations, train stations, and taxi stands. Most people perceive these locations to be safe but they are rendered less safe because the potential victim may be fumbling for money to pay fares or exchange currencies, alerting would-be predators to how much money the would-be victim is carrying. It is also smart to avoid wearing flashy clothes or jewelry, as this can attract unwanted attention. Before undertaking a sightseeing outing, consult with the hotel concierge or the hotel security office about areas of the city that are unsafe and should be avoided. When sightseeing, do so in groups if possible. Starting with a group of three, each additional member of the group lowers the likelihood of being a victim of street crime. If a particular tourist site is not located in a "safe" area of the city, the visitor should confine his or her visit to that site to daylight hours, preferably mornings, the period of the day when street criminals are the least active.

To reduce the likelihood of injury or even death when confronted by an armed robber or someone who implies having a weapon, it is safest to offer no resistance. Do not look the perpetrator directly in the face, and immediately hand over all cash and valuables. The robber is likely to quickly leave the location and will empty and then dispose of the wallet or purse. In some instances, the robber will also discard pieces of his own clothing, such as a T-shirt or cap, in order to reduce the likelihood of being quickly identified. A passport is a document that should be carefully guarded and should be locked in the hotel safe. If it is necessary for identification purposes, simply carry a photocopy of it. In many countries, particularly developing nations, it is also a good idea to register with your country's embassy upon arrival. Most strategies for avoiding victimization as tourists require simply using common sense.

Dee Wood Harper, Jr.
Loyola University New Orleans
Kelly Frailing
Texas A&M International University

See Also: Hot Spots; Mugging; New Orleans, Louisiana; Panhandling or Begging; Pickpocketing; Theft and Larceny.

Further Readings

Botterill, David and Trevor Jones. *Tourism and Crime.* Oxford: Goodfellow Publishers, 2010.

Chesney-Lind, Meda and Ian Y. Lind. "Visitors as Victims: Crimes Against Tourists in Hawaii." *Annals of Tourism Research*, v.13/2 (1986).

de Albuquerque, Klaus and Jerome McElroy. "Tourism and Crime in the Caribbean." *Annals of Tourism Research*, v.26/4 (1999).

Harper, Dee Wood, Jr. "The Tourist and His Criminal: Pattern in Street Robbery." In *Tourism, Security and Safety: A Case Approach*, Yoel Mansfield and Abraham Piazam, eds. Burlington, MA: Butterworth-Heinemann, 2005.

Jacobs, Bruce and Richard Wright. "Stick-Up: Street Culture and Offender Motivation." *Criminology*, v.37/1 (1999).

MacCannell, Dean. "Staged Authenticity: Arrangements of Social Space in Tourist Settings." *American Journal of Sociology*, v.79/3 (1973).

Washington, D.C.

Not far from the typical tourist attractions and the political controversy of the week, Washington, D.C., or the District, as natives prefer to call it, is a city that has a relatively steady amount of street crime. News of shootings, sexual assaults, and robberies occupy the first few pages of the metro section of the *Washington Post* and the daily local 11 o'clock P.M. television newscasts.

If the crimes are gruesome enough, and/or the editorial staff perceive that they may shock the conscience of Washingtonians (or the nation), then these stories are given more prominence. Occasionally the criminal acts include drive-by shootings and gang violence involving multiple victims on the same night.

Crime Rates and Gentrification

The amount of street crime in the District varies based on the time frame and geography of the city. Since the 1968 riots, there has been an outmigration of middle-class individuals, particularly whites, from Washington to the neighboring counties in Maryland (i.e., Montgomery and Prince George's) and Virginia (i.e., Arlington and Fairfax). The number of homicides was at its highest in 1991 with 479 people killed, leading D.C. to be called the Murder Capital of the United States. In 2011, there were a total of 35,358 index crimes (i.e., homicide,

forcible rape, robbery, aggravated assault, burglary, larceny-theft, motor vehicle theft, and arson). Granted, not all index crimes are street crimes, and this amount is approximately 10,000 incidents less than reported in 2001. Noticeable decreases have been witnessed in the homicide, forcible rape, and robbery cases over the past decade. The number of homicides in 2011 was 108.

The population of D.C. has fluctuated from a high of 802,000 people in 1950 to a low of 606,900 in 1990. As of 2010, there were approximately 617,000 people living in the District, and since 2000 the number has increased by about 5 percent. These population trends have been related to both the nature and amount of street crime.

Since the early 2000s, there has been considerable gentrification in selected D.C. neighborhoods including Columbia Heights, Adams Morgan, Mount Pleasant, Logan Circle, the U Street corridor, H Street, and Capital Hill areas. Not only does this gentrification apply to residences, but it has led to the creation of a vibrant nightly entertainment scene in these neighborhoods. Predictably, there has been an increase in street robberies and property crimes in these areas as the new residents, visitors, and properties are perceived by street criminals as acceptable targets for victimization.

Nevertheless, in the mid-2000s the crime rates dropped to some of their lowest levels. Since 1995 the amounts of violent and property crimes have just about halved. Whether this is the result of demographics or law enforcement practices is hard to say.

Geography and Street Crime

The District is shaped like a diamond that is bisected into four quadrants: northwest, northeast, southwest, and southeast. Each of these parts of the city is noted for different patterns of street crime.

One of the safest parts of the city is the Northwest District. This area has the greatest number of shopping areas, better public schools, and highest amount of personal wealth. Residents are disproportionately white, middle class, or upper class. This does not mean that there are no pockets where crime and violence occur.

Two of those areas are Columbia Heights and the Trinidad area. The area is geographically separated by Rock Creek Park and Parkway from the other quadrants of the District. This affects the city in terms of patterns of crime, with neighborhoods east of the park reporting considerably higher rates of street crime and those west of the park experiencing lower levels of crime and violence. Although gang violence is minimal in this area, the majority of it is caused by Latino gangs in competition with the declining African American ones who live there.

Not as affluent as Northwest, the Northeast District of Washington has its fair share of street crime. Long a bastion of middle-class African Americans, certain neighborhoods are known for their crime and violence, especially the areas close to Union Station and along the still-gentrifying H Street Corridor. As gentrification around these closer-to-downtown neighborhoods has increased, so have street crimes.

Physically the Southwest is the smallest quadrant in the District. It is bounded along the west and south by the Potomac River with its nightclubs, all-you-can-eat buffet style restaurants, and fish market. In the heart are housing projects and the National Defense University. Until the construction of the new major league baseball stadium just across South Capitol Street, the area had a reasonably high amount of street crime. The stadium's initiation led to a considerable amount of property speculation, and then construction of condominiums. This area is now a place where there are often easy pickings for street criminals victimizing people attending games at the stadium. The Southeast District, especially the area east and south of the Anacostia River, is rife with street crime. Although pockets of the Anacostia neighborhood are inhabited by middle-class African Americans, this part of D.C. is disproportionately poor with various places that most observers would describe as a ghetto. Numerous gangs and open-air drug markets characterize this area.

Law Enforcement Reaction

Washington, D.C., unlike many other urban centers in the United States, is literally awash in law enforcement agencies. Close to 23 different municipal and federal police departments operate in this city. With respect to street crime, each police chief has had his or her approach to fighting crime. Over the past two decades, the Metropolitan Police Department of the District of Columbia (MPDC) has been plagued with controversies and persistent public criticism in the way it has chosen to fight street crime (e.g., crime emergencies, gang intervention projects, and police checkpoints in certain neighborhoods).

Some of these challenges have been seen as a result of the contrast in the racial makeup of the city, which several decades ago was more than 70 percent African American, while the MPDC rank and file was nearly all white. Today the District and MPDC's demographics have dramatically altered; the city population is about 55 percent African American, while the police department is approximately 58 percent African American.

Another part of the solution to easing the tension was the hiring of Chief Charles Ramsay in 1998 as the first African American chief of police. After eight years of service, he was replaced by Cathy Lanier, a 20-year veteran of the MPDC who is its first female chief of police, and who is white.

Conclusion

Because Washington, D.C., is a large urban center, street crime is not restricted to the streets and back alleys. A considerable amount of this activity occurs on the Metro bus and subway system. In recent years, this includes the theft of smart phones by juveniles. There has been concerted gentrification in D.C., and where this has occured, there has been an uptick in street robbery. Because of the gentrification and demographic changes, street crime has been displaced disproportionately to Prince George's County adjoining the Anacostia area.

Jeffrey Ian Ross
University of Baltimore

See Also: Gangs (Street); Murder/Homicide; Police (Overview); Routine Activity Theory; Urban Ethnography.

Further Readings
Altschuler, David M. and Paul J. Brounstein. "Patterns of Drug Use, Drug Trafficking, and Other Delinquency Among Inner-City Adolescent Males in Washington, D.C." *Criminology*, v.29/4 (1991).
Hagelin, John S., et al. "Effects of Group Practice of the Transcendental Meditation Program on Preventing Violent Crime in Washington, D.C.: Results of the National Demonstration Project, June–July 1993." *Social Indicators Research*, v.47/2 (1999).
La Vigne, Nancy G. "Visibility and Vigilance: Metro's Situational Approach to Preventing Subway Crime." *National Institute of Justice Research In Brief*, v.11/1997.
Metropolitan Police Department. "Citywide Crime Statistics Annual Totals, 1993-2011." 2012. http://www.mpdc.dc.gov/mpdc/cwp/view,a,1239,q,547256,mpdcNav_GID,1556.asp (Accessed June 2012).
Weitzer, Ronald. "Racialized Policing: Residents' Perception in Three Neighborhoods." *Law & Society Review*, v.34/1 (2000).
Weitzer, Ronald, Steven A. Tuch, and Wesley G. Skogan. "Police-Community Relations in a Majority-Black City." *Journal of Research in Crime and Delinquency*, v.45/4 (2008).

Weed and Seed

Initiated in 1991 by the U.S. Department of Justice, Operation Weed and Seed (later to be known simply as Weed and Seed) was not a specific program, rather it was designed as an approach to making improvements in specifically targeted high-crime neighborhoods through the assistance of federal grant money. Weed and Seed was one of several federally funded programs launched in the 1990s to address concentrated crime areas, known as "hot spots."

Community-Based Concept

As noted in an evaluation of the program published in 2010, Weed and Seed did not change very much over the 20-plus years that it was funded by the federal government. The basic structure of Weed and Seed was that communities that suffered from high crime, illegal drug trade, gangs, and other social problems would create strategies to address those problems, and through the combined efforts of many different groups, problems could be solved in a way that would survive when federal monies ceased to support the operations.

As is apparent from its name, Weed and Seed focused on two main areas. The "weed" aspect focused on the elimination or reduction of crime in the designated area through the coordinated efforts of local, state, and federal law enforcement. Federal prosecution of suspected criminals was a key component of most of the local Weed and Seed communities.

The "seed" aspect focused on putting in place programs designed to address the perceived problems that fostered the crime in the area. Examples of "seeding" activities would be the creation of supervised after-school facilities for youth, drug and alcohol treatment centers for addicted individuals, and job training activities. One of the necessary elements of Weed and Seed was that the local police departments with jurisdiction over the target area adopt the community-oriented method of policing. Thus, the local law enforcement agencies were to be the link between the weed aspect and the seed aspect.

Objectives and Funding

The stated objectives of Weed and Seed were threefold. The first goal was to develop a plan that would bring together multiple agencies—both public and private—to address as completely as possible the problems of illegal drug use, street crime, and delinquency.

The second objective was to identify as many existing resources, stakeholders, community agencies, services, and service providers at the federal, state, and local levels and to focus those resources into the designated area. The third objective was to get residents of the target area to participate in the program by assisting in both the weed aspect as well as the seed aspect.

In its inaugural year, three sites received funding, and eventually well over 200 sites became designated Weed and Seed communities. Applications could be made to renew funding on an annual basis. Eventually, a five-year limit was placed on financial eligibility; recipients were funded up to approximately $1 million over that five-year period.

Because there was no specified "correct" way to implement Weed and Seed, each community grantee was able to create both weed and seed strategies that were appropriate for their neighborhoods and to create or utilize services that addressed their unique problems. One of the features of all of the Weed and Seed sites was the presence of a Safe Haven. This Safe Haven could be located anywhere in the community, such as an already existing YMCA, or within a church, school, or community center—so long as a variety of recreational programs and services were offered in a place that was safe and secure. This served to buttress the seed aspect of the campaigns.

Evaluations and Conclusion

Several evaluations of the program were performed, and each individual site was required to conduct self-evaluations. Both process and outcome evaluations were conducted. An evaluation of the original 19 programs, conducted in 1996 by the National Institute of Justice, found that the majority of the monies spent were for support of the community policing (on average about 39 percent) activities and other components of the weeding aspect (on average about 37 percent) of the program. Conversely, the seeding aspect garnered, on average, about 23 percent of the funds. As the program evolved, greater proportions of the funding began to be spent on the seeding aspect of the program.

Although a review of the effectiveness of Weed and Seed by the U.S. Office of Management and Budget rated the program as adequate, funding for the program was negatively impacted by across-the-board federal budget cuts in 2010. The last Weed and Seed grants were awarded in 2009; funding for new grant sites ended in June 2011. Nevertheless, over the course of the program, nearly 270 communities in 45 states (every state except Minnesota, North Dakota, South Dakota, Utah, and Vermont)

and two U.S. territories received funds and participated in Weed and Seed.

Patti Ross Salinas
Missouri State University

See Also: Alcohol and Drug Use; Broken Windows Theory; Community Policing; Crime Prevention, Situational; Drug Markets, Open-Air; Gangs (Street); Graffiti; Hot Spots; Juvenile Offending; Policing, Problem-Oriented; Zero-Tolerance/Saturation Policing.

Further Readings

Dunworth, Terence, Gregory Mills, Gary Cordner, and Jack Greene. "National Evaluation of Weed & Seed: Cross-Site Analysis." National Institute of Justice. 1999. https://www.ncjrs.gov/pdffiles1/176358.pdf (Accessed September 2011).

O'Connell, Jack, Matthew Perkins, and Jim Zepp. "Weed and Seed Crime Pattern Data Analysis." Washington, DC: Justice Research and Statistics Association, 2004.

Roehl, Janice, Robert Huitt, Mary Ann Wycoff, Antony Pate, Donald Rebovich, and Ken Coyle. "National Process Evaluation of Operation Weed and Seed." Rockville, MD: National Criminal Justice Reference Service, 1996.

Trudeau, James, Kelle Barrick, Jason Williams, and Jan Roehl. "Independent Evaluation of the National Weed and Seed Strategy." 2010. http://www.weedandseed.info/docs/reports/WnS_Final_Evaluation_Report.pdf (Accessed September 2011).

Women

There are probably two observations about female criminality with which many people will be familiar. First, and perhaps the best known, is that over long periods of time and in many differing judicial systems, women have a consistently lower rate of officially recorded crimes than men. Females are not only much less criminal than males, they are so much less criminal that whereas convictions are, statistically at least, "normal" for males, they are very unusual for females.

The second observation which has been increasingly stressed by feminist and other commentators since the 1960s is that this low criminal-participation rate has not been sufficiently remarked upon nor studied. Indeed, one of the key points made by feminist theorists and gender researchers studying crime is that female behavior, when not neglected, is explained using traditional theoretical approaches based on male behavior, rather than considering the unique ways that gender may affect crime and criminal justice experiences. Together, these observations have been noted as contributing to the "invisibility" of women in social science research and social policy related to female criminality.

While change has been slow, our knowledge about fundamental issues in the study of gender and crime has expanded greatly with the proliferation of studies over the past several decades. More than 40 years of feminist research has produced a substantial body of empirical research on female offenders and their experiences in juvenile and adult justice systems. It is clear, however, that there continues to be a need to study the ways in which different life experiences and circumstances of females and males—including gender differences in type, frequency, and context of criminal behavior—can lead to important theoretical insights and ultimately influence design of system-wide programs and services that match women's specific strengths and needs.

Female Criminality: What we Know

While males continue to constitute the majority of criminal offenders, the number of female offenders involved in the criminal justice system continues to grow at a much faster rate. Currently, women represent the fastest growing segment of prison and jail populations in the United States even though their crime rate is not increasing dramatically. As noted in the Bureau of Justice Statistics' *Prison and Jail Inmates at Midyear 2007* report, the number of women being held in the nation's prisons has increased 50 percent since 1995 and at year-end 2007, a total of 115,779 women were imprisoned in state or federal prisons, 6.9 percent of the total prison population.

The profile of the typical female prisoner has changed little over the years. Current research has established that incarcerated women are characteristically women of color, undereducated, typically low-income, unskilled with sporadic employment histories, and single mothers of young children. Moreover, imprisoned women tend to

have fragmented families, other family members involved with the criminal justice system, significant substance abuse issues, and multiple physical and mental health problems. Women in prison have typically experienced some form of abuse in their lifetime, including sexual assault, domestic violence, and sexual, physical, and psychological abuse.

The question of whether the increased involvement of women in the criminal justice system reflects actual changes in their involvement in an expanding range of activities considered criminal—or changes in law enforcement and sentencing policies and practices—has received some attention. The 1970s saw a great deal of debate in the media over whether the women's movement for equal rights would produce an era of "liberated" women criminals who would venture into serious, violent criminal activities.

Some academics claimed that increased arrests of women were evidence that the feminist movement was driving new trends in women's involvement in crime. Others countered that close analysis of arrest data indicated that increased arrests of women were largely occurring in categories conceived as traditionally female, such as shoplifting, prostitution, and passing bad checks. Even if women are having more opportunities—or greater need—to fall into crime, it is also true that the reality of women's criminality has far less to do with captivating images of corporate chieft executive officers, femmes fatales, and high-class madams beloved by newspaper tabloids and the movies and far more with the dreary exigencies of petty thievery and low-level drug dealing.

Violent Crimes Committed by Women

Over the past several decades, the popular press has warned periodically of a changing female criminal, one who is more violent than her predecessors. Although some researchers believe that women and girls are becoming more violent than in the past, their statistical contribution to murder, robbery, rape, and kidnapping has been remarkably stable. And, women are barely represented in the crime categories of hostage-taking or terrorism.

Not only does female crime continue to lag far behind that of males but the degree of harm inflicted by female offenders on others by their criminal behavior is lower: Women are much less likely than men to have committed violent offenses. This general tendency toward nonviolent offenses extends to the prison setting: Women offenders are generally less dangerous while incarcerated than male offenders.

Women's contributions to the total numbers of arrests for assault and aggravated assault do seem to be increasing for the 18–24-year-old group; however, many argue that these increases are largely due to reporting and system practice changes (i.e., girls and women are more likely to be arrested today than in past years for the same behaviors). When women do commit violent crimes, their victims tend to be family members, acquaintances, and intimates, especially in the context of intimate partner violence and/or psychological abuse; though in some highly publicized cases of women killing their children, postpartum syndromes and/or undiagnosed or untreated mental illnesses have been raised during legal proceedings and impacted sentencing decisions.

A minority of women have served as accomplices to men who abuse or kill other women or children.

Here, when women are involved in violence toward a child, particularly a sexual attack, these women are regarded as much more deviant than men and their actions are seen as a crime against nature as it is presumed to be such an unnatural thing for a woman to do. It should be noted that abuse and neglect of women's needs sets into motion a complex set of problems including depression, low self-esteem, and drug and alcohol use which can, over time, become the major focal point of female criminal offending and other crimes (e.g., theft and prostitution) that are a means to obtain drugs.

The limited availability of community resources and social support that would otherwise enable them to leave threatening situations and/or receive needed mental health care contributes to the law-violating choices made by many of these women. Thus, contrary to some exaggerated portrayals of women offenders, there is no new violent/dangerous female criminal. This mythical image, however,

A Chesapeake, Virginia, police officer fingerprints a young girl as part of a safety program focused on teaching children to be safe going to and from school, riding school buses, and how to handle school bullying. It has been reported that some girls are bullied into providing sexual favors in exchange for protection as gang culture continues to infiltrate inner-city school systems.

is used to influence public and judicial opinion and justify increasing harshness toward female prisoners. A good example is female gangs. Research shows the amount and activities of female gangs are no different now than they were in the past, even if reports on the nightly news disagree. Women rarely act as ringleaders of gang activity or organized crime syndicates.

Economic Crimes Committed by Women

Despite media portrayals of hyperviolent women offenders, women's crime patterns have not become like men's in type or amount. With few exceptions, national crime rates for female offenders are much lower than for males. Substantial arrest gains for females are limited largely to less serious, nonviolent property crime categories (larceny and fraud), and even in these categories, the main increase is because of traditional offenses like shoplifting or passing bad checks.

There are even gender differences in the ways in which males and females engage in shoplifting. Females tend to steal more items, steal from several stores, and steal items of lesser value—while males are considered to be "commercial shoplifters" and typically steal items that they can resell. Women tend to be motivated by economic concerns and tend to steal items they need or feel they cannot afford, while men are motivated by power and control as part of a broader display of masculinity.

Prostitution is a crime dominated by females. Research has focused mostly on street prostitution, which is considered the lower strata of the profession. However, the most prevalent type of prostitution is indoor work in such settings as escort services, brothels, and massage parlors. While there is a discrepancy in the types of prostitution, it is clear that this is a criminal act that cuts across ages, racial and ethnic groups, and socioeconomic status. These demographics can influence a prostitute's daily experiences. The limited research that has been conducted on this particular type of sex work suggests that prostitution can be an economic means to support a drug addiction, might enable women to financially support themselves and their families, or some combination thereof. Economic alternatives must be created so that women and girls do not have to prostitute themselves as a means to cope with high levels of unemployment and poverty in big cities, different regions, and foreign countries.

With respect to women and girls' involvement in relatively low-level drug offenses, they are highly vulnerable to involvement with drugs to generate income to support self-medicating addictions resulting from prior incidents with victimization. Because women are more low level with respect to their role in this crime (typically as accomplices) and the amounts dealt, they are more likely to get caught. While drug arrests have increased substantially for both women and men, the impact has been greater for women and has fueled much of the increase in women's incarceration. Nearly half of all women in prison are currently serving a sentence for a nonviolent, drug-related crime.

"Get tough" policies intended to target drug dealers and so-called kingpins have resulted not only in more women being imprisoned, but also in women serving longer and harsher prison sentences. Often, they get harsher prison sentences because they are used as mules, or drug carriers—a low-level job in drug dealing that often meets with strict sentences because it involves larger quantities of the drug than someone selling on the street carries at any one time. Direct sales to users are a predominately male offense. Women may also get harsher sentences in the federal system because they have nothing with which to bargain. A drug salesperson or kingpin, in contrast, might have names or connections to offer in exchange for a lighter sentence.

Contemporary Criminalization of Women

Women are often perceived primarily as victims, not perpetrators, of crime. No matter the data source, sexual victimization and intimate partner violence disproportionately affect women. While such violence has historically been perceived as a private matter best resolved by the persons involved, since the passage of the Violence Against Women Act in 1994 and other legislation, changes in law and practice have promoted (and in some cases mandated) more active involvement in domestic disputes by law enforcement and justice system officials.

Declining rates of intimate partner violence are a promising sign not only for women themselves but also for children who may be exposed to the violence. It should also be noted that crime rates vary by regional and local conditions and by type of crime. Rape, for example, is among the most under-reported crimes in America. According to the National Crime Victimization Survey, between

2004 and 2008, police were not notified of approximately half of all incidents of rape. While this figure may be shocking to some, it does not take into account the "dark" or "hidden" figures of this crime category that are committed beyond "the street" and in other settings (e.g., women's jails, prisons, or juvenile facilities).

Disgust at the violence committed against women and girls is heightened by the culture of impunity that allows some perpetrators of these crimes to go free without condemnation or punishment. That culture also turns victims into criminals, such as the girls and women in the United States who are sold for sex. Many of the females who fall prey to the sex trade are runaways from fragile families or communities who are lured, tricked, or coerced by pimps who promise them love and safety; they are the new commodities that traffickers and gangs are selling.

The perpetrators of this new form of modern slavery in America continue to operate without fear of punishment as there is no "war on trafficking" or any similar culture of crime and punishment for selling a 12-year-old girl for sex. Perversely, it is the girls—not the men—who suffer from criminalization by being restrained or arrested for prostitution after being repeatedly raped or forced into providing sex to grown men. Rather than feeling rescued from a torturous situation and placed in safety, many are reviled and publicly humiliated in a court of law where they are treated as criminals not victims. There are few safe-haven programs for girls or women who are trafficked; therefore their ability to leave this dangerous situation is virtually impossible.

With the advent of technology, cybercrime and victimization of women is on the increase and it poses a major threat to the security of a person as a whole. The new cybercrime of cyberviolence against women, including cyberstalking, e-mail harassment and using the Internet to publish obscene information to exploit or embarrass women is taking alarming proportions. Statistically, most cyberstalkers are men; however, there are reported cases of women cyberstalking men and same-sex cyberstalking. Victims can be any age.

Domestic violence victims are one of the groups most vulnerable to traditional stalking due to the rigid control and fear that they have lived with, so it is not a surprise that they are vulnerable to cyber-stalking and the resulting trauma. Cloaked behind a username and an account—which might

be repeatedly changed—stalkers can be difficult to identify. And while most states, and various federal statutes, now have laws that explicitly include electronic forms of communication within stalking or harassment laws, victims are often afraid to proceed with complaints as that could lead to exposure and social humiliation; hence, they are not interested in proceeding with complaints.

For women, if economic necessity, self-defense, punishing their abuser through their children, or being sold into the sex trade doesn't land them in jail or prison, the criminalization of pregnancy might. A new trend in the "war on drugs" is accusing pregnant drug addicts of fetal abuse, a notion that is legally unclear. Pregnant women who are turned in by doctors when traces of drug use show up in tests are being hit with charges that range from illegal transport of narcotics (through the umbilical cord), child abuse, assault with a deadly weapon, and even first-degree murder. In states that have enacted laws which criminalize drug-dependent expectant mothers, if prosecuted, they may be sentenced to lengthy prison terms based on their use of legal and illegal drugs while pregnant. The crusade to criminalize drug-dependent expectant mothers began in the late 1980s, and the prosecution of women who used cocaine while pregnant has accelerated in intensity and scope. Pregnant women are uniquely vulnerable to criminal justice involvement, and the criminalization of pregnant women is not only an affront to women's rights but also puts both mother and fetus at greater risk by erecting barriers to drug treatment and prenatal care.

The increasing criminalization of forms of girls' (and women's) minor violence that was once ignored is now being criminalized with serious consequences, particularly for females of color. The "gender neutral" relabeling of girls' victimization in schools, a site of much violence against girls, is extremely problematic. Renaming "sexual harassment" as "bullying" tends to psycho-pathologize gender violence while simultaneously stripping girl victims of powerful legal rights and remedies under civil law, particularly federal law Title IX. As a consequence, while girls' violence has actually been decreasing, girls' arrests for this behavior have been increasing, fueled by a series of policy changes that are criminalizing girls. Closer analysis of the impact of these practices show that, contrary to the notion that these arrest trends reflect girls' "masculinization," they instead reflect emerging practices focused on control of girls in family and school settings.

Conclusion

Research on female criminality highlights the challenges women and girls have faced prior to their arrest and incarceration. Most women and girls who get caught in the web of the criminal justice system are, throughout their lifetimes, pushed away from legitimate paths such as school and work. Family and social networks, if not positive forces, typically result in various forms of victimization due to poverty, addiction, and violence. Crime, for many, is a by-product of victimization in these women's lives. Understanding the life circumstances around which women make choices to commit crime—including what crime is committed, their motivation for crime commission, the role they play in the criminal act, weapon use—helps us to understand the crossroads at which choices are made and the types of things that may help the women to make better choices.

The criminal justice field has been dominated by the rule of parity: Equal treatment is to be provided to everyone. However, this does not necessarily mean that the exact same treatment is appropriate for both women and men. The data are very clear concerning the distinguishing characteristics of men and women offenders. They come into the criminal justice system via different pathways; respond to supervision and custody differently; exhibit differences in terms of substance abuse, trauma, mental illness, parenting responsibilities, and employment histories; and represent different levels of risk within both the institution and the community. If criminal justice policies continue to ignore these realities, the system will remain ineffective in targeting the pathways to offending that both propel women into, and return them to, the criminal justice system. An investment in gender-responsive policy can produce both short- and long-term dividends for the criminal justice system, the community, and female offenders and their families.

Barbara H. Zaitzow
Appalachian State University

See Also: Alcohol and Drug Use; Black Market; Children, Commercial Sexual Exploitation of; Children as Victims; Domestic Violence; Gangs (Street); Homelessness; Juvenile Offending; Prostitute/ Streetwalker; Prostitution, Houses of; Rape and Sexual Assault; Risky Lifestyles; Sex Crimes; Stalking.

Further Readings

Adler, Freda. *Sisters in Crime: The Rise of the New Female Criminal*. New York: McGraw-Hill, 1975.

Alder, Christine and Anne Worrall *Girls' Violence: Myths And Realities*. Albany: State University of New York Press, 2004.

Bloom, Barbara, Barbara Owen, and Stephanie Covington. "Gender-Responsiveness Strategies: Research, Practice, and Guiding Principles for Women Offenders." Washington, DC: U.S. Department of Justice, 2003.

Chesney-Lind, Meda and Randall G. Shelden. *Girls, Delinquency, and Juvenile Justice*. 3rd ed. Belmont, CA: Wadsworth, 2004.

Egley, Arlen, Jr., Cheryl L. Maxson, Jody Miller, and Malcolm W. Klein. *The Modern Gang Reader*. 3rd ed. Los Angeles, CA: Roxbury Publishing, 2005.

Zaitzow, Barbara H. and Jim Thomas, eds. *Women in Prison: Gender and Social Control*. Boulder, CO: Lynne Rienner, 2003.

Z

Zero-Tolerance/ Saturation Policing

Zero-tolerance policing is most commonly referred to as a policing strategy in which police resources are used to aggressively enforce criminal (and in some situations civil) laws. Zero-tolerance policing goes by a variety of different labels including, but not limited to, quality-of-life policing, incivilities policing, broken-windows policing, and order-maintenance policing.

Typically, zero-tolerance policing finds its theoretical and philosophical support from the Broken Windows Theory. The Broken Windows Theory was first published in a 1982 article by James Q. Wilson and George L. Kelling. Wilson and Kelling argued that there is a theoretical link between minor disorder and more serious forms of crime. More specifically, when minor forms of disorder and incivilities are left unaddressed, informal social control within the community is weakened. With a reduction in informal social control within the community, disorder and incivilities have the opportunity to grow, which reinforces the loss of informal social control. As this spiral of decay occurs, the community becomes more susceptible to criminal invasion, which leads to more serious forms of street crime. Zero-tolerance policing is often seen as the appropriate strategy to support a Broken Windows approach to crime. Using a zero-tolerance policing strategy, police organizations can target forms of social and physical disorder within the community and prevent serious crime that follows unchecked disorder and incivilities.

In the Field

Zero-tolerance policing, when compared to other policing innovations such as community-oriented policing and problem-oriented policing, tends to reflect a much more traditional approach toward policing. Because of the emphasis on aggressive enforcement of the law, line-level officers tend to have very limited discretion in their decision making. Additionally, organizational communication under a zero-tolerance philosophy is primarily downward (from management to line-level officers). Activities such as arrests and citations, and stops are often used as measures of the implementation of zero-tolerance strategies.

Qualitative measures are important as well. A study by the Police Foundation evaluated a Safe and Clean Neighborhoods initiative by the police department in Newark, New Jersey, and other municipalities in that state during the 1970s. The Safe and Clean Neighborhoods program was built upon a dramatic increase in foot patrols by officers, and more enforcement of vagrancy, drunkenness, and antiloitering statutes, and so forth. Residents surveyed in the evaluation described their areas as becoming more safe and themselves as becoming less fearful and more secure. While the police force was mainly made up of white men and the residents were overwhelmingly black, the surveyed residents indicated they were more satisfied with police activity during the initiative than they had been before—even though arrest rates were not dramatically higher.

Zero-Tolerance and the NYPD
Zero-tolerance policing was widely used by the New York City Police Department (NYPD) under Police Commissioner William Bratton. Zero-tolerance policing in New York was first applied to the New York subway system in order to address a variety of quality-of-life issues such as fare evasion and public urination in the New York subway system. Starting around 1993, Bratton applied the zero-tolerance philosophy to a broader set of disorder issues: prostitution, panhandling, public drunkenness, public urination, loitering, and, most infamously, squeegee men.

A variety of studies indicate that after these interventions, the New York crime rate significantly decreased. Between 1993 and 1997, overall felony complaints in New York decreased by around 44 percent, murder and nonnegligent homicide dropped by about 60 percent, and robbery and burglary dropped by around 48 percent and 45 percent, respectively.

However, some evidence calls into question the true effectiveness of zero-tolerance strategies in New York and the causal links between NYPD aggressive enforcement and the reduction in serious crime. National data indicate that significant crime reductions occurred virtually nationwide during the mid-1990s. This indicates that the crime drops in New York may have been caused by other factors unrelated to the zero-tolerance interventions by NYPD. Additionally, other departments during this same time period used other types of police interventions (for example, problem-oriented policing) and attained similar crime reductions. To date, the evidence is best described as mixed.

Other scholars have also found that police strategies that focus on minor crime can have impacts on more serious forms of crime. Scholars used county-level data from California to look at the impact of misdemeanor arrests on more serious types of crime. The findings indicated that increases in misdemeanor arrests were associated with decreases in assault, burglary, and larceny.

Zero-Tolerance Policing in Other Areas
While the experience of zero-tolerance policing in New York is likely one of the most widely publicized and studied applications of zero-tolerance policing in the United States, it is by no means the only application. A variety of other jurisdictions have applied zero-tolerance policing tactics to try and bring about overall crime reductions. Indianapolis, Indiana, has experimented with using focused traffic stops in order to target weapons to bring about crime reductions. Baltimore, Maryland, has focused on a variety of strategies to increase minor arrests in order to impact overall crime rates. Additionally, the use of zero-tolerance policing is not isolated to the United States—other jurisdictions have applied zero-tolerance strategies, including Hartlepool and Liverpool in England and Strathelyde in Scotland.

Cautionary Aspects
Besides crime reductions, other outcomes have been associated with zero-tolerance policing. A handful of scholars have commented that zero-tolerance policing strategies can often result in higher levels of citizen complaints against police officers. Some evidence of this does exist in the social science literature. However, scholars like Robert Davis and colleagues have argued that proper training and better community-police relations can reduce these complaints.

In addition to complaints against police, some academics have pointed out that zero-tolerance policing can be criticized as being discriminatory. Some accounts have indicated that zero-tolerance policing may be more likely to occur in low socioeconomic status or minority neighborhoods. Because of this, individuals in these communities may disproportionately be exposed to this policing tactic. In the long term, this can easily create resentful opinions toward police; it is also a factor in heated civil discussions among legislative bodies in many jurisdictions whenever the topic of zero tolerance comes up. In many cases—Chicago, for example—school departments have applied their own forms of zero tolerance within their domains, even as their city government has decided not to implement such a policy through its police department as a whole.

Cody Stoddard
Central Washington University

See Also: Bratton, William; Broken Windows Theory; CompStat; Fear of Crime; Giuliani, Rudolph; New York City; Panhandling or Begging.

Further Readings

Davis, Robert C., Pedro Mateu-Gelabert, and Joel Miller. "Can Effective Policing Also Be Respectful? Two Examples in the South Bronx." *Police Quarterly*, v.8/2 (2005).

Dennis, Norman and George Erdos. *Cultures and Crimes—Policing in Four Nations.* London: Institute for the Study of Civil Society, 2005.

Greene, Judith A. "Zero Tolerance: A Case Study of Police Policies and Practices in New York City." *Crime and Delinquency*, v.45/2 (1999).

Harcourt, Bernard E. "Reflecting on the Subject: A Critique of the Social Influence Conception of Deterrence, The Broken Windows Theory, and Order-Maintenance Policing New York Style." *Michigan Law Review,* v.97/2 (1998).

Rosenfeld, Richard, Robert Fornango, and Andres F. Rengifo. "The Impact of Order-Maintenance Policing on New York City Homicide and Robbery Rates: 1988-2011." *Criminology,* v.45/2 (2007).

Sousa, William H. and George L. Kelling. "Of 'Broken Windows,' Criminology, and Criminal Justice." In *Police Innovation: Contrasting Perspectives*, David Weisburd and Anthony Braga, eds. Cambridge, MA: Cambridge University Press, 2006.

Taylor, Ralph B. "Incivilities Reduction Policing, Zero Tolerance, and the Retreat From Coproduction: Weak Foundations and Strong Pressures." In *Police Innovation: Contrasting Perspectives*, David Weisburd and Anthony Braga, eds. Cambridge, MA: Cambridge University Press, 2006.

Wilson, James Q. and George L. Kelling. "Broken Windows: The Police and Neighborhood Safety." *Atlantic Monthly*, v.249/3 (1982).

Glossary

AMBER alerts: Message system used to spread alerts about missing children or young people by disseminating information through media, electronic billboards, and the Internet. The alerts are initiated immediately after a disappearance is reported because the first hours are considered the most critical in locating a missing person's whereabouts and apprehending kidnappers.

America's Most Wanted: Long-running television show that has helped apprehend more than 1,100 wanted criminals who were being sought in connection with crimes such as murder, rape, child molestation, and gang violence. Fox announced in May 2011 that the last regular show would be aired on June 18 but assured fans that reruns would continue to air, supplemented by periodic specials. Host John Walsh started the show in 1988 following the kidnapping and murder of his 7-year-old son Adam. That case is still unsolved.

Arrestee Drug Monitoring Abuse Program (ADAM): Federal drug abuse monitoring program that replaced Drug Use Forecasting (DUF) program in 1998. Continuing through 2003, the U.S. Department of Justice used ADAM to collect samples and oral responses from arrestees at targeted sites for purposes of tracking drug use and identifying relevant behavioral patterns.

Arrestee Drug Abuse Monitoring Program (ADAM II): Federal drug abuse monitoring program instituted in 2007 that continues the work of ADAM I while gathering new data on methamphetamine usage.

Bloods: Gang that started in South Central Los Angeles in the early 1970s to combat the growing power of the Crips. In 1998, the Bloods were propelled into the public eye as a result of the movie *Colors* starring Sean Penn and Robert Duvall.

Blue laws: Laws enacted to enforce moral codes that range from restrictions on the sale of alcohol to the banning of all commerce on Sundays.

Bootlegging: Illegal production, transport, and sale of controlled or illegal substances including but not limited to alcohol, firearms, and illegally copied music and movies.

Bounty hunters: Individuals who track down fugitives for monetary gain. In practice, modern bounty hunters are most often used to track down anyone who has skipped bail or who has failed to show up for scheduled court appearances.

Broken Windows Theory: A theory introduced in a 1982 article by James Q. Wilson and George L. Kelling that argued that the appearance of disorder and neglect in a neighborhood (e.g., presence of broken windows in a building), was associated with and encouraged increased vandalism and other criminal activity.

Burglary: A crime defined by the Federal Bureau of Investigation's (FBI's) Uniform Crime Reporting program as involving unlawful entry into a structure to commit a theft or felony; the use of force is not required.

Bystander effect: The social-psychological phenomenon that dictates that members of a large group of witnesses to a crime are less likely to offer assistance than members of smaller groups witnessing a crime.

Child molester: Generally carrying connotations of sexual deviance, a child molester is literally one who annoys, interferes, or meddles with a minor with the intention of troubling or harming him or her.

Code of the street: An unwritten but widely accepted code of behavior that often prevents witnesses and other criminals from testifying against perpetrators of crimes because of the fear of physical retaliation against themselves or others.

Community policing: Partnerships established between law enforcement officials and the public that focus on reducing crime and improving the quality of life in particular cities and neighborhoods.

CompStat: A computer analysis program started by Deputy Police Commissioner Jack Maple and others in New York City in 1984 to identify high crime areas where potential crimes were likely to occur and prevent them from taking place. Other cities subsequently adopted the model for their own use.

Confidence game: Fraudulent activities in which deception is used to deprive a person of items of value by exploiting that person's confidence or trust. Con games are generally assumed to exploit the dishonesty or greed of the victim as well, for instance, by promising to let in on a scheme that will reward them with a large sum of (unearned) money.

Crips: Predominately African American gang founded in Los Angeles in 1967 by Raymond Washington and Stanley Tookie Williams III that has evolved into a loose network of gangs. Their chief rival is the Bloods.

Cultural transmission: A socialization process by which particular group norms and values become internalized by individual members of a group. The term has been used to explain the adherence of members to norms and values established by particular street gangs.

Deterrence: The use of punishment to prevent criminal offenses. This assumes that potential and actual perpetrators knowledge of possible criminal sentences prevent them from committing crimes; the punishment of a criminal offender prevents recidivism; and the incapacitation of a criminal offender, for instance by incarceration, in order to prevent his further criminal activity.

Drive-by shooting: A term used to describe the hit-and-run tactics of modern gang members who use them to retaliate against other gang members but who often kill innocent bystanders.

Drug courts: Special courts established to deal with problems that derive from alcohol and drug addiction among criminal offenders and parents whose welfare cases are pending.

Drug subculture: Countercultures associated with use of a particular drug such as cannabis or marijuana. These subcultures may also be associated with other subcultures as in the case of the perceived association between certain types of music such as reggae, hip hop, or rave.

Drug Use Forecasting program (DUF): A program used by the federal government between 1987 and 1997 that gathered data on self-reported drug use of juveniles and adults who had been arrested at targeted sites.

Eighteenth Amendment: Prohibition amendment ratified in January 1919. Once it became effective in January of the following year, it prohibited the manufacture, sale, and transportation of intoxicating liquor throughout the United States. It was the first and only time in history that an amendment restricted the behavior of Americans rather than protecting their rights or changing the way in which the national government worked. With legal access to liquor blocked, many Americans procured it by illegal means, and organized crime flourished.

Excessive bails and fines: The Eighth Amendment to the U.S. Constitution protects those accused of crimes from being charged with excessive bails and fines. Courts have generally interpreted this to mean that the punishment must fit the crime. They also take into account such factors as the seriousness of the crime in question, the financial status of the accused, and the flight risk of the accused.

Felony crimes: Established at the state level, felony crimes may vary among jurisdictions, but generally they involve crimes carrying penalties that can range from six months in prison to the death penalty. Since 1963 with *Gideon v. Wainwright*, the Sixth Amendment to the U.S. Constitution has been interpreted to require that courts must appoint attorneys in felony cases in which individuals are unable to afford legal representation.

Gang Prevention and Effective Deterrence Act of 2005: With bipartisan support, the act enhanced support for fighting gang activity in the United States. It also increased criminal penalties while directing additional resources to protecting the public and expanding prevention programs.

Grand Theft Auto **video game:** Controversial from the outset of its 1997 debut, the video game sets the players against law enforcement by allowing them to attack police officers, shoot them, set them on fire, or even decapitate them. While continuing their spree of street crime, players are free to attack other characters at will. The game's creators have been accused of promoting violence through the original game and in several sequels.

Guardian Angels: Founded in 1979 to fight rampant crime in the Bronx as a group of 13 unarmed volunteers. By the early 21st century, the group had grown to 140 chapters throughout the world and had updated its mission statement to target bullying in schools and making cyberspace safe in addition to the ongoing battle against street crime.

Harrison Narcotics Act of 1914: Act in which Congress attempted to identify anyone involved in importing, exporting, manufacturing, or distributing either opium or cocaine by requiring such individuals to register with the federal government and pay taxes on their activities.

Hate crime: Threats, harassment, or violent acts that target victims because of their race, color, religion, national origin, ethnicity, sexual orientation, or mental disability. While hate crimes have been committed throughout American history, the term only came to be used popularly in the 1980s following a wave of such crimes.

Hells Angels: Popular motorcycle gang that was established as the result of a bitter gang rivalry between existing groups that had surfaced in the wake of World War II when army surplus made motorcycles easily affordable to veterans craving adventure. The name was derived from the nickname used for bomber squadrons during the two World Wars.

Jacob Wetterling Crimes Against Children and Sexually Violent Offender Registration Act: Federal law named in honor of 11-year-old Jacob Wetterling who was kidnapped from his Minnesota home in 1989 and never seen again. The law attempted to bring state laws in line with federal standards on sex-offender registration by withholding funds from states that failed to comply.

LA Noire: Rockstar's video game in which the player fights street crime in the role of a detective for the Los Angeles Police Department. Achievements include killing 100 "bad guys" and shooting 30 of them in the head.

Larceny: The crime of taking possession of the personal property of another person.

Legalized gambling: Practice of making gambling activities such as lotteries, betting, bookmaking, slot machines, and video poker legal within specific jurisdictions in order to mitigate effects of illegal gambling and increase public income through either taxes or direct profits, as is the case with state lotteries. Those profits may be earmarked for specific programs such as education.

Loitering laws: State laws and local ordinances that ban hanging around in public places in the absence of valid reasons. Such laws are regularly used to limit street crimes such as gang-related activity, drug dealing, prostitution, begging, public drunkenness, and solicitation. Courts have frequently found loitering laws unconstitutional because they are deemed vague, unclear in their interpretation, and limit the freedom of ordinary citizens to engage in normal activity.

Megan's Laws: A series of state and federal laws that honor Megan Kanka, a 7-year-old New Jersey girl murdered by a known sex offender who lived in her neighborhood. The laws call for the registration of such offenders whenever they move into a neighborhood and require the police to alert members of the local community to their presence.

"Minnesota Strip": Section of New York's Eighth Avenue that in the late 1960s and early 1970s came to be heavily identified with young runaways from the midwest, particularly Minnesota, who were solicited for the purposes of prostitution and sexual exploitation as soon as they arrived in the city.

Miranda v. Arizona: A decision by the U.S. Supreme Court in 1963 establishing that persons held in police custody must be informed of their rights to legal counsel and to refrain from making statements ("the right to remain silent") that might incriminate them.

Misdemeanor crimes: Generally a less serious crime, typically punishable with a fine and/or incarceration for one year or less to be a misdemeanor.

National Center for Missing and Exploited Children (NCMEC): Resource center and clearinghouse that assists families and law enforcement agencies in searching for missing children and young people and in working to prevent the sexual exploitation of children. By 2011, NCMEC had handled 675,000 sexual exploitation cases, many which were identified through the CyberTipline, and had helped recover 135,000 missing children and youths.

National Night Out: Annual event that since 1983 has brought individuals, civic groups, businesses, neighborhood organizations, and local officials together to work toward crime and drug prevention at the local level.

NCVS: The National Crime Victimization Survey, a method of measuring the incidence of crime using sampling and surveys of crime victims, begun in 1972 to address perceived shortcomings of the Uniform Crime Report.

Nuisance laws: Umbrella term for laws dealing with health, morals, safety, comfort, convenience, and the overall well-being of local communities. Depending on the severity of the offense in question, nuisance laws are punishable by fines, jail sentences, or both. Nuisance laws are regularly employed to limit gang activity and control illegal gambling. Courts have frequently found that they are unconstitutional because the need to cover general offenses results in vague language being employed.

Pandering: Violation under state law that deals with procuring customers for prostitutes. Efforts to clean up prostitution rings frequently result in pimps being charged with pandering violations.

Pedophile: From a psychological viewpoint, a pedophile is one who has fantasies, urges, or behaviors of a recurrent, intense, and sexually arousing nature that involve children 13 or younger. The term is sometimes used interchangeably with child molester among the general public.

Police observation devices (PODs): Commonly known as "blue light" surveillance because of their flashing blue lights, PODs are remote-controlled surveillance devices with zoom capability that have been used in large cities to combat drug and gang activity. Critics have questioned their use as crime deterrents and insist that they violate the right to privacy.

Prohibition: The banning of the manufacture, transportation, and sale of all alcoholic beverages other than those used for medicinal or religious purposes. In the United States, the passage of the Eighteenth Amendment established Prohibition in 1920, resulting in an upsurge in organized crime. Prohibition ended with the ratification of the Twenty-First Amendment in 1933.

Prostitution: The act of accepting financial remuneration for engaging in sexual acts. In the United States, prostitution is illegal in all states except Nevada, where it is strictly regulated and controlled.

Since the passage of the Mann Act in 1918, it has been illegal in the United States to transport individuals across state lines for the purposes of prostitution, debauchery, or other immoral activities.

"Prowling by Auto": Local laws that ban the use of motorized vehicles in the wandering and strolling of public streets without a clear and lawful purpose or objective in mind. Such laws are often used in conjunction with vagrancy and loitering laws to keep gang members and drug dealers off the streets in order to reduce incidences of street crime.

Racial profiling: The controversial practice by which law enforcement targets groups of individuals simply because they are believed to be likely to commit certain types of crimes because of their race, ethnicity, religion, or national origin. Racial profiling has been used to target African Americans driving in areas that are associated with drug running and Arab Americans because of the perception that they may be involved in terrorist activity.

Recreational drugs: Substances containing pharmacologic characteristics that are ingested for the purposes of personal pleasure or individual satisfaction rather than for medical reasons. Alcohol, barbiturates, amphetamines, cocaine, and heroin all come under the label of recreational drugs, as do caffeine and cola products.

Road rage: Aggressive or violent behavior in which motorists engage after they become angry at other drivers for activities such as cutting in front of them, following too closely, or failing to yield the right of way. The National Highway Traffic Safety Administration stipulates that the action in question must involve a combination of three or more moving vehicles in which life and property are endangered.

Robbery: A crime of theft by force, threat of force, or by putting the victim in fear.

Sexual exploitation of children: General term for offenses against minors that include using them in sex rings, portraying them in child pornography, and forcing them to participate in sex tourism or engage in child prostitution. The term also includes using various forms of technology, such as the Internet, to violate the rights of minors for sexual purposes.

Sexual victimization of children: A term that encompasses sexual abuse, sexual exploitation, sexual assault, and sexual abduction of minors.

Speakeasies: Institutions that sold illegal liquor during the Prohibition era that were frequently associated with racketeering and organized crime.

Speak-outs: Public meetings at which people gather to express their views on particular issues. Speak-outs were widely used by feminists of the 1960s and 1970s to focus public attention on the need to make public streets safe for women. They argued that simply telling females to stay off the street was punishing them rather than would-be rapists and predators.

Stonewall: The Greenwich Village bar in which rioting took place in 1969 and which provided the impetus for the gay rights movement. On June 28, 1970, the first anniversary of the rioting, the first Gay Rights Parade was held in New York City.

Stop and Frisk: A physical search of an individual suspected of carrying a concealed weapon by a police officer in cases where the suspect has not been formally arrested. The search is usually conducted by an officer "patting down" a person's outer garments.

"Stop Snitching" movements: Efforts to intimidate potential witnesses to crimes and paid police informers to keep them from testifying against modern criminals such as drug dealers and gang members. The "Stop Snitching" logo has become so common on T-shirts and hats that such items have been banned in courtrooms throughout the United States.

Stranger danger: Popular myth promoted by the Federal Bureau of Investigation in the 1950s and 1960s that all child molesters were evil-looking strangers who lurked behind trees and lured children into traps by offering them candy.

***Street Crime*:** Popular role-playing video game in which the player takes on the role of gangsters, casino owners, gamblers, prostitutes, pimps, or drug traffickers.

Street gangs: While experts do not always agree on what constitutes a gang, street gangs are generally conceived of as groups of young people who hang out in particular neighborhoods where they are recognized according to a self-proclaimed identity by both members of the street gang and by those who observe them. The term also carries the assumption that members have committed various criminal offenses that cause them to be viewed in a negative light by both police and the neighborhood at large.

Streetwalker: A prostitute who solicits customers by standing on or walking the streets. Most streetwalkers habituate particular areas.

***Super Columbine Massacre* video game:** Controversial online video game in which the player takes on the role of the two teenagers who engaged in a killing spree at Columbine High School in 1999. Players are required to kill classmates that are perceived of as "enemies."

Sutton's Law: According to American legend, when notorious bank robber Willie Sutton was asked why he continued to rob banks, he replied "because that's where the money is." The phrase became an integral part of popular culture, and the medical community adopted it for use in training medical students to look for the most obvious causes first when diagnosing medical problems.

Tammany Hall: Headquarters of the Democratic political machine that operated in New York from the 1790s to the 1960s, exerting tight control on all elements of city politics. The most well-known of the Tammany political bosses was William M. "Boss" Tweed.

Three Strikes law: A statute enacted by some state governments that requires a greater sentence (typically, a life sentence) for the third instance of a serious criminal offense.

Terry Stop: In 1968 in *Terry v. Ohio*, the Supreme Court held that stop and frisk searches are not a violation of the Fourth Amendment's protection against unreasonable searches and seizures. This ruling allows police officers to engage in such searches in cases where they have probable cause to suspect that a crime is about to be committed even if the search is conducted without first obtaining a search warrant.

Turf wars: Battle for control of a particular neighborhood area or of certain rackets such as gambling or the drug market. The term is believed to have originated in the late 19th century to describe battles over control of gambling activity in horse racing.

Twenty-First Amendment: The amendment that ended Prohibition. Fulfilling a campaign promise, President Franklin Roosevelt asked Congress to authorize the sale of 3.2 percent beer in early 1933. By the end of the year, enough states had ratified the Twenty-First Amendment to the Constitution to officially end Prohibition and establish an environment that was less conducive to the widespread criminal activities that had flourished throughout the Prohibition years.

UCR: The Uniform Crime Report, a reporting system for crimes, created in the United States in 1930. State and local law enforcement agencies provide data to the FBI, which then aggregates it and publishes the results. The reports are used to track the incidence of crime in different locations.

Unreasonable search and seizure: Because the Fourth Amendment to the U.S. Constitution guarantees that Americans must be "secure in their persons, houses, papers, and effects," the Supreme Court determined in *Mapp v. Ohio* in 1961 that the police may not use evidence in court that has been obtained during illegal search and seizures. Subsequent decisions have given the police considerable leeway in conducting searches in which they have probable cause to suspect individuals of committing particular crimes.

Vagrants: Individuals with no permanent residence who roam the streets without a clear purpose or objective in mind. Vagrancy laws are generally employed at the local level to keep individuals off the streets in order to prevent them from committing street crimes or from acting as public nuisances.

Vehicle prowling: Criminal acts in which perpetrators unlawfully enter vehicles for the purposes of theft or other criminal activity. Such crimes are frequently committed by gangs who become highly proficient in carrying out their crimes. These gangs are so skilled that they can break into a vehicle within 30 seconds and complete the commission of their crimes within two minutes.

Violence Against Women Act: Act passed in 1994 to protect the civil rights of women. An amendment in 2000 established the Office on Violence Against Women, which has a major role in establishing policies that affect the safety of women in the United States.

Weed and Seed: A strategy sponsored by the U.S. Department of Justice that brings law enforcement and local communities together to reduce violent crimes and control drug abuse and gang activity in areas that have been identified as high-crime neighborhoods. The "weeding" involves removing criminals and criminal activities from the designated areas, and "seeding" is carried out by involving social service agencies in activities such as prevention, intervention, treatment, and neighborhood restoration in order to generate an environment in which criminal activities are unable to thrive.

Wild One, The: Marlon Brando epic film of 1953 in which the actor plays Johnny Strabler, the leader of the 40-member motorcycle gang, The Black Rebels, who terrorize a small town after losing a motorcycle competition.

Wyos: Violent street gang that terrorized New York in the mid-1800s.

Elizabeth Rholetter Purdy
Independent Scholar

Resource Guide

Books

Abelson, Elaine S. *When Ladies Go-A-Thieving: Middle-Class Shoplifting in the Victorian Department Store.* New York: Oxford University Press, 1989.

Abu-Lughod, Janet. *From Urban Village to East Village: The Battle for New York's Lower East Side.* London: Blackwell, 1995.

Adler, Freda and Herbert Marcus Adler. *Sisters in Crime: The Rise of the New Female Criminal.* New York: McGraw-Hill, 1975.

Almquist, Laura and Elizabeth Dodd. *Mental Health Courts: A Guide to Research-Informed Policy and Practice.* New York: Council of State Governments, 2009.

Anderson, Elijah. *Code of the Street: Decency, Violence, and the Moral Life of the Inner City.* New York: Norton, 1999.

Anderson, Nels. *The Hobo: The Sociology of the Homeless Man.* Chicago: University of Chicago Press, 1923.

Arrestee Drug Abuse Monitoring Program II. Washington, DC: Office of National Drug Control Policy, 2009.

Ayers, Edward L. *Vengeance and Justice: Crime and Punishment in the 19th Century American South.* New York: Oxford University Press, 1984.

Barak, Gregg. *Class, Race, Gender, Crime: The Social Realities of Justice in America.* Lanham, MD: Rowman & Littlefield, 2007.

Barak, Gregg. *Crimes by the Capitalist State: An Introduction to State Criminality.* Albany: State University of New York Press, 1991.

Barak, Gregg, ed. *Media, Process, and the Social Construction of Crime.* New York: Garland, 1994.

Barrett, Wayne. *Rudy: An Investigative Biography of Rudolph Giuliani.* New York: Basic Books, 2000.

Barrett, Wayne and Dan Collins. *The Untold Story of Rudy Giuliani and 9/11: Grand Illusion.* New York: HarperCollins, 2006.

Bernstein, Elizabeth and Laurie Schaffner, eds. *Regulating Sex: The Politics of Intimacy and Identity.* New York: Routledge, 2005.

Best, Joel. *Threatened Children: Rhetoric and Concern About Child Victims.* Chicago: University of Chicago Press, 1993.

Bierne, Piers and Nigel South, eds. *Issues in Green Criminology: Confronting Harms Against Environments, Humanity, and Other Animals.* Portland, OR: Willan Publishing, 2007.

Blakely, Edward J. and Mary G. Snyder. *Fortress America: Gated Communities in the United States.* Washington, DC: Brookings Institution, 1997.

Boger, John Charles. *Race, Poverty, and American Cities.* Chapel Hill: University of North Carolina Press, 1996.

Bratton, William. *Turnaround: How America's Top Cop Reversed the Crime Epidemic.* New York: Random House, 1998.

Brown, Richard M. *Strain of Violence: Historical Studies of American Violence and Vigilantism.* New York: Oxford University Press, 1975.

Bullard, Robert D., ed. *Unequal Protection: Environmental Justice and Communities of Color.* San Francisco: Sierra Club Books, 1994.

Bumgarner, Jeffrey, ed. *Icons of Crime Fighting: Relentless Pursuers of Justice.* Westport, CT: Greenwood Press, 2008.

Burnett, Betty. *St. Louis: Yesterday and Today.* Lincolnwood, IL: Westside, 2011.

Burns, Ronald G. and Michael J. Lynch. *The Sourcebook on Environmental Crime.* New York: LFB Publishers, 2004.

Burt, Martha R. *Over the Edge: The Growth of Homelessness in the 1980s.* Thousand Oaks, CA: Sage, 1992.

Butts, Jeffrey A. and John Roman, eds. *Juvenile Drug Courts and Teen Substance Abuse.* Washington, DC: Urban Institute Press, 2004.

Cameron, Mary Owen. *The Booster and the Snitch: Department Store Shoplifting.* New York: Free Press of Glencoe, 1964.

Carson, Rachel. *Silent Spring.* Boston: Houghton Mifflin, 1962.

Chesney-Lind, Meda and Randall G. Shelden. *Girls, Delinquency, and Juvenile Justice.* 3rd ed. Belmont, CA: Wadsworth, 2004.

Chin, Lo-Lin. *Chinatown Gangs: Extortion, Enterprise, and Ethnicity.* New York: Oxford University Press, 1996.

Christensen, Loren. *Skinhead Street Gangs.* Boulder, CO: Paladin Press, 1994.

Clark, John P. and Richard C. Hollinger, *Theft by Employees in Work Organizations.* Minneapolis: University of Minnesota Press, 1983.

Coblenz, Stanton. *Villains and Vigilantes.* New York: Thomas Yolseloff, 1936.

Cohen, Albert K. *Delinquent Boys: The Culture of the Gang.* New York: The Free Press, 1955.

Cohen, Stanley and Jock Young, eds. *The Manufacture of News.* Beverley Hills, CA: Sage, 1973.

Courtwright, David T. *Violent Land: Single Men and Social Disorder From the Frontier to the Inner City.* Cambridge, MA: Harvard University Press, 1998.

Cullen, Francis T. and Pamela Wilcox, eds. *The Handbook of Criminological Theory.* New York: Oxford University Press, 2011.

Davis, Kenneth Culp. *Police Discretion.* St. Paul, MN: West Publishing, 1975.

Decker, Scott H. and Barrik van Winkle. *Life in the Gang: Family, Friends and Violence.* New York: Cambridge University Press, 1996.

DeKeseredy, Walter and Molly Dragiewicz, eds. *The Handbook of Critical Criminology.* London: Routledge, 2011.

Denno, Deborah W. *Biology and Violence: From Birth to Adulthood.* Cambridge: Cambridge University Press, 1990.

Eck, John E. and William Spelman. *Problem-Solving: Problem Oriented Policing in Newport News.* Washington, DC: National Institute of Justice, 1987.

Eck, John E. and David L. Weisburd, eds. *Crime and Place: Crime Prevention Studies.* Monsey, NY: Criminal Justice Press, 1995.

Eck, John E., et al. *Mapping Crime: Understanding Hot Spots.* Washington, DC: National Institute of Justice, 2005.

Edwards, Loren E. *Shoplifting and Shrinkage Protection for Stores.* Springfield, IL: Charles C. Thomas, 1970.

Egley, Arlen, et al, eds. *The Modern Gang Reader.* 3rd ed. Los Angeles: Roxbury Publishing, 2006.

Ellsworth, Scott. *Death in a Promised Land: The Tulsa Race Riot of 1921.* Baton Rouge: Louisiana State University Press, 1992.

Farrell, Kathleen L. and John A. Ferrara. *Shoplifting: The Antishoplifting Guidebook.* Westport, CT: Praeger, 1985.

Farrell, Ronald and Carole Case. *The Black Book and the Mob.* Madison: University of Wisconsin Press, 1995.

Farrington, David P. and Brandon C. Welsh. *Making Public Places Safer.* New York: Oxford University Press, 2009.

Feldman, Leonard C. *Citizens Without Shelter: Homelessness, Democracy, and Social Exclusion.* Ithaca, NY: Cornell University Press, 2006.

Ferdico, John N., et al. *Criminal Procedure for the Criminal Justice Professional.* 10th ed. Belmont, CA: Wadsworth Cengage Learning, 2009.

Ferrell, Jeff. *Crimes of Style.* Lebanon, NH: Northeastern University Press, 1996.

Ferrell, Jeff, et al. *Cultural Criminology: An Invitation.* London: Sage, 2008.

Fleisher, Mark S. *Beggars and Thieves: Lives of Urban Street Criminals.* Madison: University of Wisconsin Press, 1995.

Fleisher, Mark S. *Dead End Kids: Gang Girls and the Boys They Know.* Madison: University of Wisconsin Press, 1998.

Fletcher, George P. *A Crime of Self-Defense: Bernhard Goetz and the Law on Trial.* New York: The Free Press, 1988.

Fox, James A. *Forecasting Crime Data: An Econometric Analysis.* Lexington, MA: Lexington Books, 1978.

Friedrichs, David O. *Trusted Criminals: White-Collar Crime in Contemporary Society.* Belmont, CA: Wadsworth, 1996.

Fritsch, Eric J., et al. *Police Patrol Allocation and Deployment.* Upper Saddle River, NJ: Pearson, 2009.

Gardiner, Richard. *Design for Safe Neighborhoods: The Environmental Security Planning and Design Process.* Washington, DC: Department of Justice, 1978.

Garrelts, Nate, ed. *The Meaning and Culture of Grand Theft Auto: Critical Essays.* Jefferson, NC: McFarland & Company, 2006.

Garrison, Chad "Back on Top: St. Louis Named Most Dangerous City in 2010." *Riverfront Times* (November 22, 2010).

Garrison, Chad. "Battle Lines: Gangs Keep Their Murderous Hold on the Streets of St. Louis and Kids Like Lil' Robert Walker Pay the Price." *Riverfront Times* (August 23, 2006).

Goldkamp, John S. *Two Classes of Accused: A Study of Bail and Detention in American Justice.* Cambridge, MA: Ballinger, 1979.

Gowan, Teresa. *Hobos, Hustlers, and Backsliders: Homeless in San Francisco.* Minneapolis: University of Minnesota Press, 2010.

Graham, Hugh Davis and Ted Robert Gurr. *The History of Violence in America: A Report to the National Commission on the Causes and Prevention of Violence.* New York: Bantam, 1969.

Graham, Kathryn and Ross Homel. *Raising the Bar: Preventing Aggression in and Around Bars, Pubs, and Clubs.* Devon, UK: Willan Publishing, 2008.

Grimes, William. *Straight Up or on the Rocks: The Story of the American Cocktail.* New York: North Point Press, 2001.

Groenveld, Richard F. *Arrest Discretion of Police Officers: The Impact of Varying Organizational Structures.* New York: LFB Scholarly Publishing, 2005.

Hagedorn, John M. *People and Folks: Gangs, Crime, and the Underclass.* Chicago: Lakeview Press, 1988.

Harper, Dee Wood and Kelly Frailing, eds. *Crime and Criminal Justice in Disaster.* Durham, NC: Carolina Academic Press, 2010.

Harris, David A. *Profiles in Injustice: Why Racial Profiling Cannot Work.* New York: New York University Press, 2002.

Hayden, Tom. *Street Wars: Gangs and the Future of Violence.* New York: The New Press, 2004.

Hayward, Keith. *City Limits: Crime, Consumer Culture, and the Urban Experience.* London: Glasshouse Press, 2008.

Hobsbawm, Eric. *Primitive Rebels: Studies in Archaic Forms of Social Movements in the 19th and 20th Centuries.* New York: W. W. Norton, 1965.

Hogg, Ian. *Guns and How They Work.* Secaucus: NJ: Chartwell Books, 1984.

Hogg, Ian. *Small Arms: Pistols and Rifles.* Barnsley: UK: Greenhill Books/Lionel Leventhal, 2001.

Howell, James C. *Preventing and Reducing Juvenile Delinquency: A Comprehensive Framework.* 2nd ed. Los Angeles: Sage, 2009.

Howell, James C. *Youth Gangs: An Overview.* Washington, DC: Department of Justice, Office of Juvenile Justice and Delinquency Prevention, 1998.

In Harm's Way: The Toxic Threat to Child Development. Boston: Boston Physicians for Social Responsibility, 2000.

Ivkovic, Sanja Kutnjak. *Fallen Blue Knights: Controlling Police Corruption.* New York: Oxford University Press, 2005.

Jacobs, Jane. *The Death and Life of Great American Cities.* New York: Random House, 1961.

Janness, Valerie and Kendal Broad. *Hate Crimes: New Social Movements and the Politics of Violence.* New York: Aldine de Gruyter, 1998.

Jeffrey, C. Ray. *Crime Prevention Through Environmental Design.* Thousand Oaks, CA: Sage, 1971.

Jenkins, Philip. *Moral Panic: Changing Concepts of the Child Molester in Modern America.* New Haven, CT: Yale University Press, 1998.

Jewkes, Yvonne. *Media and Crime.* 2nd ed. London: Sage, 2010.

Josephson, Matthew. *The Robber Barons: The Great American Capitalists, 1861–1901.* Boston: Harcourt, Brace. 1934.

Katz, Jack. *Seductions of Crime.* New York: Basic Books, 1988.

Kelling, George and Catherine Coles. *Fixing Broken Windows: Restoring Order and Reducing Crime in Our Communities.* New York: The Free Press, 1996.

Kelling, George and Mark Moore. *The Evolving Strategy of Policing.* Washington, DC: U.S. Department of Justice, 1988.

Kelling, George, et al. *The Kansas City Preventive Patrol Experiment: A Summary Report.* Washington, DC: Police Foundation, 1974.

Kenney, Dennis J. *Crime, Fear, and the New York City Subways: The Role of Citizen Action.* Westport: CT: Praeger, 1987.

Kerner Commission. *Report of the National Advisory Commission on Civil Disorders.* New York: Bantam, 1968.

Klemke, Lloyd W. *The Sociology of Shoplifting: Boosters and Snitches Today.* Westport, CT: Praeger, 1992.

Knapp Commission. *Commission to Investigate Allegations of Police Corruption and the City's Anti-Corruption Procedures: The Knapp Commission Report on Police Corruption.* New York: George Braziller, 1972.

Knight, Nick. *Skinhead.* New York: Omnibus Press, 1983.

Lane, Roger. *Murder in America: A History.* Columbus: Ohio State University Press, 1997.

Lavigne, Yves. *Hells Angels: Into the Abyss.* Toronto: HarperCollins, 1996.

Lawrence, Richard. *School Crime and Juvenile Justice.* New York: Oxford University Press, 2007.

Leap, Jorja. *Jumped In: What Gangs Taught Me About Violence, Drugs, Love, and Redemption.* Boston: Beacon Press, 2012.

Leo, Richard A. and George Conner Thomas III. *The Miranda Debate: Law, Justice, and Policing.* Lebanon, NH: Northeastern University Press, 1998.

Levin, Jack and Jack McDevitt. *Hate Crimes Revisited: America's War on Those Who Are Different.* Boulder CO: Westview Press, 2002.

Linn, Edith. *Arrest Decisions: What Works for the Officer?* New York: Peter Lang, 2009.

Logan, Samuel. *This Is for the Mara Salvatrucha: Inside the MS-13, America's Most Violent Gang.* New York: Hyperion, 2009.

Long, Patrick Du Phuoc with Laura Ricard. *The Dream Shattered: Vietnamese Gangs in America.* Lebanon, NH: Northeastern University Press, 1997.

Low, Setha. *Behind the Gates: Life, Security, and the Pursuit of Happiness in Fortress America.* New York: Routledge, 2003.

Lupo, Lindsey. *Flak-Catchers: One Hundred Years of Riot Commission Politics in America.* Lanham, MD: Lexington, 2010.

Lutz, Brenda J. and James M. Lutz. *Terrorism in America.* New York: Palgrave Macmillan, 2007.

Lynch, James P. and Lynn A. Addington, eds. *Understanding Crime Statistics: Revisiting the Divergence of the NCVS and UCR.* New York: Cambridge University Press, 2007.

Lyon, Danny. *The Bikeriders.* San Francisco: Chronicle Books, 2003 [1968].

Mackay, Charles. *Extraordinary Popular Delusions and the Madness of Crowds.* New York: Farrar, Straus, & Giroux, 1960.

Manning, Peter K. *Technology of Policing.* New York: New York University Press, 2008.

Mansfield, Yoel and Abraham Piaza, eds. *Tourism, Security and Safety: A Case Approach.* Burlington, MA: Butterworth-Heinemann, 2005.

Maple, Jack. *The Crime Fighter: How You Can Make Your Community Crime-Free.* New York: Broadway Books, 1999.

Marshall, George. *Skinhead Nation.* New York: S. T. Publishing, 1996.

Mays, G. Larry and L. Thomas Winfree. *Juvenile Justice.* New York: McGraw-Hill. 2000.

McDonald, Phyllis. *Managing Police Operations: Implementing the New York City Crime Control Model-CompStat.* Belmont, CA: Wadsworth/Thomson Learning, 2002.

McIllwain, Jeffrey Scott. *Organizing Crime in Chinatown: Race and Racketeering in New York City, 1890–1910.* Jefferson, NC: McFarland, 2004.

Mele, Christopher. *Selling the Lower East Side: Culture, Real Estate, and Resistance in New York City.* Minneapolis: Minnesota University Press, 2000.

Michalowski, Raymond J. and Ronald C. Kramer, eds. *State-Corporate Crime: Wrongdoing at the*

Intersection of Business and Government. New Brunswick, NJ: Rutgers University Press, 2006.

Miethe, Terance D. and Robert Frank Meier. *Crime and Its Social Context.* Albany: State University of New York Press, 1994.

Miethe, Terance D., et al. *Crime Profiles: The Anatomy of Dangerous Persons, Places, and Situations.* Los Angeles: Roxbury, 2006.

Mitchell, Don. *The Right to the City: Social Justice and the Fight for Public Space.* New York: Guildford, 2003.

Mollen Commission. *Commission to Investigate Allegations of Police Corruption and the Anti-Corruption Procedures of the Police Department: Commission Report: Anatomy of Failure: A Path for Success.* New York: City of New York, 1994.

Morris, Dashaun Jiwe. *War of the Bloods in My Veins: A Street Soldier's March Towards Redemption.* New York: Scribner, 2008.

Nagle, Jill. *Whores and Other Feminists.* New York: Routledge, 1997.

Natapoff, Alexandra. *Snitching: Criminal Informants and the Erosion of American Justice.* New York: New York University Press, 2009.

Neely, Richard. *Take Back Your Neighborhood.* New York: Donald I. Fine, 1990.

Newman, Oscar. *Defensible Space: Crime Prevention Through Environmental Design.* New York: Macmillan, 1972.

Norton, Peter D. *Fighting Traffic: The Dawn of the Motor Age in the American City.* Cambridge, MA: MIT Press, 2008.

Paradise, Paul R. *Trademark, Counterfeiting, Product Piracy, and the Billion Dollar Threat to the U.S. Economy.* Westport, CT: Quorum, 1999.

Payne, Brian K. *Crime in the Home Health Care Field.* Springfield, IL: Charles C. Thomas, 2003.

Pearson, Geoffrey. *Hooligan: A History of Respectable Fears.* New York: Palgrave Macmillan, 1983.

Pennell, Susan, et al. *Guardian Angels: An Assessment of Citizen Response to Crime.* Washington, DC: U.S. Department of Justice, National Institute of Justice, 1986.

Pennsylvania Crime Commission. *Report on Police Corruption and the Quality of Law Enforcement in Philadelphia.* Saint Davids, PA: Commonwealth of Pennsylvania, 1974.

Perry, Barbara. *In the Name of Hate.* New York: Routledge, 2001.

Phillips, Susan A. *Wallbangin'.* Chicago: University of Chicago Press, 1999.

Phillips, Tim. *Knockoff: The Deadly Trade in Counterfeit Goods.* London: Kogan-Page, 2005.

Pogrebin, Mark, et al. *Guns, Violence, and Criminal Behavior: The Offender's Perspective.* Boulder, CO: Lynne Rienner Publishers, 2009.

Pollack, Otto. *The Criminality of Women.* Philadelphia: University of Pennsylvania Press, 1950.

Polsky, Ned. *Hustlers, Beats and Others.* New York: Anchor Books, 1969.

Price, Barbara Raffel and Natalie Sokoloff, eds. *The Criminal Justice System and Women: Offenders, Victims, and Workers.* New York: McGraw-Hill, 2004.

Punch, M. *Police Corruption: Deviance, Accountability and Reform in Policing.* Portland, OR: Willan Publishing, 2009.

Rafael, Tony. *The Mexican Mafia.* New York: Encounter Books, 2007.

Ramiro, Martinez and Abel Valenzuela, eds. *Immigration and Crime: Race, Ethnicity, and Violence.* New York: New York University Press, 2006.

Rehder, William J. and Gordon Dillow. *Where the Money Is: True Tales From the Bank Robbery Capital of the World.* New York: W. W. Norton, 2003.

Richards, Leonard. *The California Gold Rush and the Coming of the Civil War.* New York: Knopf, 2007.

Roberson, Cliff, et al. *Procedures in the Justice System.* 9th ed. Upper Saddle River, NJ: Prentice Hall, 2010.

Ross, Jeffrey Ian. *Making News of Police Violence: A Comparative Study of Toronto and New York City.* Westport, CT: Praeger Publishers, 2000.

Ross, Jeffrey Ian and Stephen C. Richards. *Beyond Bars: Rejoining Society After Prison.* New York: Alpha/Penguin, 2009.

Ross, Jeffrey Ian and Stephen C. Richards. *Behind Bars: Surviving Prison.* New York: Penguin, 2002.

Ross, Jeffrey Ian and Stephen C. Richards. *Convict Criminology.* Belmont, CA: Wadsworth, 2003.

Rousey, Dennis C. *Policing the Southern City: New Orleans, 1805-1889.* Baton Rouge: Louisiana State University Press, 1996.

Rubin, Lillian B. *Quiet Rage: Bernie Goetz in a Time of Madness.* Berkeley: University of California Press, 1986.

Sennewald, Charles A. and John H. Christman. *Shoplifting.* Oxford: Butterworth-Heinemann, 1992.

Shantz, Jeff. *Active Anarchy: Political Practice in Contemporary Movements.* Lanham, MD: Lexington, 2011.

Sheldon, Randall G., et al. *Youth Gangs in American Society* Belmont, CA: Wadsworth, Cengage Learning, 2004.

Sherman, L. W. *Scandal and Reform: Controlling Police Corruption.* Los Angeles: University of California Press, 1978.

Shoemaker, Donald J. *Juvenile Delinquency.* Lanhan, MD: Rowman & Littlefield, 2009.

Shoemaker, Donald J. *Theories of Delinquency: An Examination of Delinquent Behavior.* New York: Oxford University Press, 1990.

Skogan, Wesley. G. *Disorder and Decline: Crime and the Spiral of Decay in American Neighborhoods.* New York: The Free Press, 1990.

Silber, Mitchell D. and Arvin Bhatt. *Radicalization in the West: The Homegrown Threat.* New York: New York Police Department Intelligence Division, 2007.

Silverman, Eli B. *NYPD Battles Crime: Innovative Strategies in Policing.* Lebanon, NH: Northeastern University Press, 1999.

Simon, Rita James. *Women and Crime.* Toronto: Lexington Books, 1975.

Simpson, Colton with Ann Pearlman. *Inside the Crips: Life Inside L.A.'s Most Notorious Gang.* New York: St. Martin's Press, 2005.

Singer, Audrey. *The Rise of New Immigrant Gateways.* Washington, DC: Brookings Institution, 2004.

Sismondo, Christine. *America Walks Into a Bar: A Spirited History of Taverns and Saloons, Speakeasies, and Grog Shops.* New York: Oxford University Press, 2011.

Sites, William. *Remaking New York: Primitive Globalization and the Politics of Urban Community.* Minneapolis: University of Minnesota Press, 2003.

Skolnick, Jerome H. *Justice Without Trial: Law Enforcement in a Democratic Society.* Hoboken, NJ: John Wiley & Sons, 1966.

Skolnick, Jerry and David Bayley. *The New Blue Line: Police Innovation in Six American Cities.* New York: The Free Press, 1986.

Snyder, Gregory. *Graffiti Lives.* New York: New York University Press, 2009.

Snyder, Howard N. and Melissa Sickmund. *Juvenile Offenders and Victims: 2006 National Report.* Washington, DC: U.S. Department of Justice, Office of Juvenile Justice and Delinquency Prevention, 2006.

Stevens, Dennis. *Media and Criminal Justice: The CSI Effect.* Sudbury, MA: Jones & Bartlett, 2011.

Stewart, George Rippey. *Committee of Vigilance: Revolution in San Francisco, 1851.* Boston: Houghton Mifflin, 1964.

Sugrue, Thomas J. *The Origins of the Urban Crisis: Race and Inequality in Postwar Detroit.* Princeton, NJ: Princeton University Press, 2005.

Surrette, Ray. *Media, Crime and Criminal Justice: Images, Realities, and Policies.* 4th ed. Belmont, CA: Wadsworth, 2011.

Taylor, Ralph. B. *Breaking Away From Broken Windows: Baltimore Neighborhoods and the Nationwide Fight Against Crime, Grime, Fear and Decline.* Boulder, CO: Westview Press, 2001.

Thompson, Edward Palmer. *Whigs and Hunters: The Origins of the Black Act.* New York: Pantheon, 1975.

Thompson, Hunter. S. *Hell's Angels: A Strange and Terrible Saga.* New York: Random House, 1966.

Tobocman, Seth. *War in the Neighborhood.* New York: Autonomedia, 2000.

Trojanowicz, Robert and Bonnie Bucqueroux. *Community Policing: A Contemporary Perspective.* Cincinnati, OH: Anderson, 1990.

Tuttle, William M. *Race Riot: Chicago in the Red Summer of 1919.* Urbana-Champaign: University of Illinois Press, 1996.

Wacquant, Loïc. *Punishing the Poor: The Neoliberal Government of Social Insecurity.* Durham, NC: Duke University Press, 2009.

Walker, Lenore E. *The Battered Woman.* New York: Harper & Row, 1979.

Wallace, Harvey. *Victimology: Legal, Psychological and Social Perspectives.* Upper Saddle River, NJ: Pearson, 2007.

Wallace, Samuel. *Skid Row as a Way of Life.* Totowa, NJ: Bedminster. 1965.

Weeks, John and Ian V. Hogg. *Pistols of the World: The Definitive Illustrated Guide to the World's Pistols and Revolvers*. Iola, WI: Krause Publications, 2004.

Weitzner, Ronald, ed. *Sex for Sale: Prostitution, Pornography, and the Sex Industry*. 2nd ed. London: Routledge, 2010.

Whiteacre, Kevin and Raeann Howes. *Scrap Yards and Metal Theft Insurance Claims in 51 U.S. Cities*. Indianapolis: University of Indianapolis Community Research Center, 2009.

Wilcox, Pamela, et al. *Criminal Circumstance: A Dynamic Multi-Contextual Criminal Opportunity Theory*. New York: Walter de Gruyter, 2003.

Williams, Stanley Tookie. *Blue Rage, Black Redemption: A Memoir*. New York: Touchstone Books, 2004.

Wilson, Charles Reagan and William Ferris, eds. *Encyclopedia of Southern Culture*. Chapel Hill: University of North Carolina Press, 1989.

Wilson, James Q. *Thinking About Crime*. Rev. ed. New York: Basic Books, 1983.

Wilson, William J. *When Work Disappears: The World of the New Urban Poor*. New York: Alfred A. Knopf, 1996.

Wright, Richard T. and Scott H. Decker. *Armed Robbers in Action: Stickups and Street Crime*. Lebanon, NH: Northeastern University Press, 1997.

Wyatt-Brown, Bertram. *Southern Honor*. New York: Oxford University Press, 1982.

Yesil, Bilge. *Video Surveillance: Power and Privacy in Everyday Life*. El Paso, TX: LFB Scholarly Publishing, 2009.

Yin, Peter. *Victimization and the Aged*. Springfield, IL: Charles C. Thomas, 1985.

Zaitzow, Barbara H. and John Thomas. *Women in Prison: Gender and Social Control*. Boulder, CO: Lynne Rienner, 2003.

Journals

Albany Law Review
American Journal of Orthopsychiatry
American Journal of Psychiatry
American Journal of Public Health
American Journal of Sociology
American Psychologist
American Sociological Review

ANNALS of the American Academy of Political and Social Science
Annals of Tourism Research
Archives of Pediatric Adolescent Medicine
Child Maltreatment
City
Clinical Child and Family Psychology Review
Corporate Crime
Counter-Terrorist
Crime, Law, and Social Change
Crime and Delinquency
Crime and Justice
Crime Prevention Studies
Criminal Justice and Behavior
Criminal Justice Policy Review
Criminal Justice Research
Criminology
Criminology and Public Policy
Critical Criminologist
Deviant Behavior
Forensic Science International
International Journal of Law and Psychiatry
International Journal of Offender Therapy and Comparative Criminology
Journal of Aggression, Conflict and Peace
Journal of Applied Behavior Analysis
Journal of Applied Econometrics
Journal of Church and State
Journal of Clinical Psychology
Journal of Community Psychology
Journal of Contingencies & Crisis Management
Journal of Criminal Justice and Popular Culture
Journal of Criminal Law and Criminology
Journal of Current Issues in Crime, Law, and Law Enforcement
Journal of Drug Education
Journal of Drug Issues
Journal of Experimental Criminology
Journal of Forensic Psychiatry
Journal of Interpersonal Violence
Journal of Men's Studies
Journal of Prevention and Intervention in the Community
Journal of Quantitative Criminology
Journal of Quantitative Research
Journal of Research in Crime and Delinquency
Journal of Sex Research

Journal of Social History
Journal of Social Issues
Journal of Studies on Alcohol
Journal of Substance Use
Journal of the American Academy of Child and Adolescent Psychiatry
Journal of the American Medical Association
Justice Quarterly
Justice Research and Policy
Juvenile and Family Court Journal
Juvenile Justice Bulletin
Law and Human Behavior
Law and Policy
Lincoln Law Review
Ohio State Journal of Criminal Law
Police Forum
Police Quarterly
Policing: An International Journal of Police Science and Management
Property Management
Psychiatric Services
Seattle University Law Review
Social and Legal Studies
Social Forces
Social Inquiry
Social Policy and Administration
Social Problems
Social Service Review
Social Work
Sociological Quarterly
Sociology
Sociology and Social Research
Sociology Compass
Substance Use and Misuse
Technology and Culture
Terrorism and Political Violence
Theoretical Criminology
Theory, Culture, and Society
Trends in Organized Crime
Tulane Law Review
Urban Studies
Vanderbilt Law Review
Violence Against Women
Youth Violence and Juvenile Justice

Internet

2009 National Crime Victimization Survey
www.icpsr.umich.edu/icpsrweb/ICPSR/studies/28543

2010 Federal Bureau of Investigation Bank Crime Statistics
www.fbi.gov/stats-services/publications/bank-crime-statistics-2010/bank-crime-statistics-2010-q1

2010 Federal Bureau of Investigation Latest Hate Crime Statistics
http://www.fbi.gov/news/stories/2010/november/hate_112210/hate_112210

2011 Neighborhood Watch Manual
www.usaonwatch.org/assets/publications/0_NW_Manual_1210.pdf

Addressing Crime and Disorder in Seattle's Hot Spots: What Works
www.seattle.gov/audit/docs/2011Mar29_HotSpotsWhatWorks.pdf

Analysis of Racial Disparities in the New York Police Department's Stop, Question and Frisk Practices
www.rand.org/pubs/technical_reports/2007/RAND_TR534.sum.pdf

By the Numbers: A Guide for Analyzing Race Data From Vehicle Stops
www.cops.usdoj.gov/html/cd_rom/mayors72nd/pubs/ExecutiveSummaryBytheNumber.pdf

Child Maltreatment
www.ncvc.org/ncvc/main.aspx?dbName=DocumentViewer&DocumentID=38709

Comparison of Hate Crime Rates Across Protected and Unprotected Groups
www.centeronhalsted.org/programs/Williams_Institues_Hate_Crimes_Report.pdf

Confidence Games on Canal Street: The Market for Knockoffs in New York City
csrn.camden.rutgers.edu/newsletters/6-2/Carducci.html

Contact Between the Police and the Public
bjs.ojp.usdoj.gov/content/pub/pdf/cpp05.pdf

Controlling Chronic Misconduct in City Spaces: of Panhandlers, Skid Rows, and Public-Space Zoning
digitalcommons.law.yale.edu/fss_papers/408

Dangerous by Design: Solving the Epidemic of Preventable Pedestrian Deaths
4america.org/docs/dangerousbydesign/dangerous_by_design.pdf

Economic Impact of Counterfeiting and Piracy:
Executive Summary
www.oecd.org/dataoecd/13/12/38707619.pdf

Gender-Responsiveness Strategies: Research,
Practice, and Guiding Principles for Women
Offenders
static.nicic.gov/Library/020419.pdf

Homicide Trends in the U.S.: Weapons Used
bjs.ojp.usdoj.gov/content/homicide/weapons.cfm

Kidnapping of Juveniles: Patterns from NIBRS
www.missingkids.com/en_US/documents/
kidnapping_juveniles.pdf

Miranda v. Arizona
www.law.cornell.edu/supct/html/historics/
USSC_CR_0384_0436_ZS.html

National Association of Shoplifting Prevention
www.shopliftingprevention.org/main.asp

National Crime Victimization Survey (NCVS):
Weapon Use by Offense Type
bjs.ojp.usdoj.gov/index.cfm?ty=tp&tid=43

National Drug Court Institute
www.ndci.org/ndci-home

National Estimates of Missing Children:
An Overview
www.missingkids.com/en_US/documents/
nismart2_overview.pdf

National Gang Threat Assessment 2009
www.justice.gov/ndic/pubs32/32146/index
.htm

Neighborhood Crime and Travel Behavior:
An Investigation of the Influence of Neighborhood
Crime Rates on Mode Choice
www.transweb.sjsu.edu/mtiportal/research/
publications/summary/0702.html

Police Observation Devices
https://portal.chicagopolice.org/portal/page/
portal/ClearPath/About%20CPD/POD%20
Program

Pretrial Release of Felony Defendants in
State Courts
bjs.ojp.usdoj.gov/content/pub/pdf/prfdsc.pdf

Problem-Oriented Guides for Police, Number 33:
Illicit Sexual Activity in Public Places
www.popcenter.org/problems/illicit_sex

Problem-Oriented Guides for Police, Number 47:
Drive-By Shootings
www.cops.usdoj.gov/files/ric/Publications/
e02072864.pdf

Problem-Oriented Guides for Police, Number 48:
Bank Robbery
www.cops.usdoj.gov/files/RIC/Publications/
e03071267.pdf

Problem-Oriented Guides for Police, Number 58:
Theft of Scrap Metal
www.popcenter.org/problems/pdfs/metal_theft
.pdf

Security vs. Status: The Two Worlds of Gated
Communities
www.scribd.com/doc/8414774/Security-Versus-
Status-The-Two-Worlds-of-Gated-Communities

Shot Spotter
www.wired.com/wired/archive/15.04/
shotspotter.html

United States v. Salerno
www.oyez.org/cases/1980-1989/1986/1986_86_87

Video Surveillance of Public Places
www.cops.usdoj.gov/files/ric/Publications/
e02061006.pdf

What's Wrong with Public Video Surveillance?
www.aclu.org/technology-and-liberty/whats
-wrong-public-video-surveillance

Appendix

Street Crime Trends in America's 25 Largest Cities Over the Past 24 Years

Official records of street crime in the 25 largest cities in the United States have largely been documented within the Uniform Crime Reporting (UCR) Program, which has served as a primary source of the country's street crime statistics since its inception in 1929. The UCR was developed as a source of reliable information about crime committed in the United States. The Federal Bureau of Investigation (FBI) began collecting and managing this information in 1930 and continues to do so today. The FBI's collection of UCR data serves as a reliable publicly available source of information to examine street crime trends in America's cities.

The offenses reported in the UCR primarily contain serious offenses because these are most likely to be reported with some regularity, especially across multiple jurisdictions, to police. Defining these crimes is also extremely important because standardized definitions of each type of offense must be in place for law enforcement authorities to accurately categorize recorded crime. The UCR offenses for each of the top 25 largest cities in the United States covered here are broken into two categories: (1) crimes committed against persons and (2) property-related crimes.

Crimes committed against persons include (1) murder and non-negligent manslaughter, which includes "the willful (non-negligent) killing of one human being by another. Deaths caused by negligence, attempts to kill, assaults to kill, suicides, and accidental deaths are excluded"; (2) forcible rape: "the carnal knowledge of a female forcibly and against her will. Rapes by force and attempts or assaults to rape, regardless of the age of the victim, are included. Statutory offenses (no force used—victim under age of consent) are excluded"; (3) robbery: "the taking or attempting to take anything of value from the care, custody, or control of a person or persons by force or threat of force or violence and/or by putting the victim in fear"; and (4) aggravated assault: "An unlawful attack by one person upon another for the purpose of inflicting severe or aggravated bodily injury. This type of assault usually is accompanied by the use of a weapon or by means likely to produce death or great bodily harm. Simple assaults are excluded," according to the U.S. Department of Justice in 2011.

Property-related crimes include (1) burglary: "the unlawful entry of a structure to commit a felony or a theft. Attempted forcible entry is included (also known as breaking and entering)"; (2) larceny-theft: "The unlawful taking, carrying, leading, or riding away of property from the possession or constructive possession of another. Examples are thefts of bicycles, motor vehicle parts and accessories, shoplifting, pocket-picking, or the stealing of any property or article that is not taken by force and violence or by fraud. Attempted larcenies are included. Embezzlement, confidence games, forgery, check fraud, etc., are excluded"; (3) motor vehicle theft: "The theft or attempted theft of a motor vehicle. A motor vehicle is self-propelled and runs on land surface and not on rails. Motorboats, construction equipment, airplanes, and farming equipment are specifically excluded from this category"; and (4) property crime, which is a total crime index based on the sum of burglary, larceny-theft, and motor vehicle theft, according to the U.S. Department of Justice in 2011.

This review of street crime in the 25 largest U.S. cities was based on the rate of each of these types of crime. These rates were calculated by taking the total number of a given type of crime, dividing this number by the population of the appropriate city, and then multiplying by 100,000. This calculation adjusts each city's number of crimes to a number of crimes relative to the size of the population of that city. Although this procedure produces a rate of a crime according to a city's population and these rates can be used to track trends in crime within a certain city, these calculations should not be used as direct comparisons between cities, for several reasons, according to the U.S. Department of Justice in 2011. One reason to avoid direct comparisons using these crime rates is related to each city's unique characteristics that cannot be equally compared to others. This can include differences in historical development, expansion, and geographic size. Cities are also likely to have minor variations in their law enforcement practices and they may allocate varying levels of resources toward law enforcement practices. Both of these factors can directly affect the number and type of crimes reported and investigated by the police. Considering these cautionary notes, the crime rates reported here have been used to observe trends within the top 25 cities for the 24-year period spanning 1985–2009.

Figure 1 Crimes committed against persons: national estimates

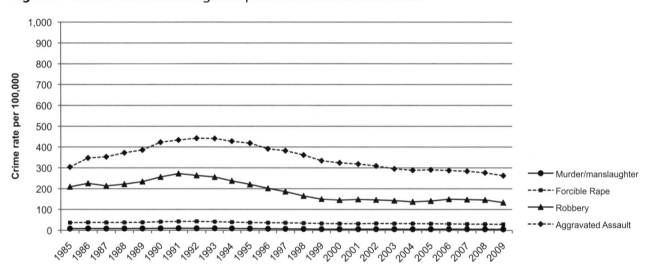

Sources: FBI, Uniform Crime Reports, National Archive of Criminal Justice Data

Figure 2 Property-related crime: national estimates

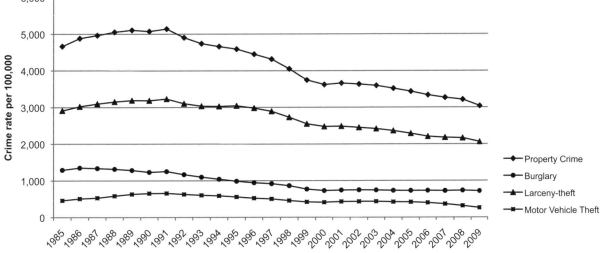

Sources: FBI, Uniform Crime Reports, National Archive of Criminal Justice Data

The street crime rates in the top 25 largest cities in the United States come together to create national trends in these crimes (Figures 1 and 2). The trends in all four measures of street crime committed against persons declined over this 24-year period. Aggravated assault, the most prevalent street crime committed against another person, dropped 14 percent from a rate of 304 per 100,000 in 1985 to 263 per 100,000 in 2009. Robbery declined 36 percent in 24 years from 209 per 100,000 in 1985 to 133 per 100,000. The 22 percent decrease in forcible rape rates resulted in a drop from 37 per 100,000 in 1985 to 29 per 100,000 in 2009. A 38 percent decline was observed with murder and non-negligent manslaughter over this time period dropping from 8 to 5.

Property-related street crime also exhibited a downward trend during this period. The overall national property crime rate dropped from 4,666 per 100,000 in 1985 to 3,036 per 100,000 in 2009. Larceny-theft, the most prevalent type of property-related crime, fell 29 percent over this period from 2,911 per 100,000 in 1985 to 2,061 in 2009. A larger drop was observed for motor vehicle theft, falling 44 percent from 464 per 100,000 in 1985 to 259 in 2009. Burglary dropped 45 percent from 1,292 per 100,000 in 1985 to 716 in 2009.

These national trends have been associated with trends of the same forms of street crime in American cities. David McDowall and Colin Loftin have shown larger U.S. cities (i.e., those with a population greater than 500,000) to have crime rates which were more likely to be accounted for by the national trend compared to smaller cities (those with a population smaller than 250,000). Individual city trends have also been matched to an overall national trend with estimates predicting anywhere from 54 percent to 75 percent of Americans, depending on the size of the city they lived in, would experience the national trend in street crime.

Table 1 Population change of 25 largest U.S. cities from 1985 to 2009

City	1985 Population	2009 Population	Percent change
1. New York City, NY	7,183,984	8,400,907	17%
2. Los Angeles, CA	3,186,459	3,848,776	21%
3. Chicago, IL	2,998,841	2,848,431	-5%
4. Houston, TX	1,746,375	2,273,771	30%
5. Phoenix, AZ	890,746	1,597,397	79%
6. Philadelphia, PA	1,640,102	1,547,605	-6%
7. Las Vegas, NV	456,749	1,377,282	202%
8. San Antonio, TX	862,878	1,373,936	59%
9. San Diego, CA	988,284	1,314,773	33%
10. Dallas, TX	997,467	1,290,266	29%
11. San Jose, CA	706,062	954,009	35%
12. Detroit, MI	1,090,581	908,441	-17%
13. Honolulu, HI	817,083	907,124	11%
14. Indianapolis, IN	471,656	813,471	72%
15. Jacksonville, FL	601,007	810,064	35%
16. San Francisco, CA	733,456	809,755	10%
17. Charlotte, NC	335,690	777,708	132%
18. Austin, TX	406,469	768,970	89%
19. Columbus, OH	565,682	759,391	34%
20. Fort Worth, TX	424,449	723,456	70%
21. Memphis, TN	654,626	667,421	2%
22. Baltimore, MD	771,097	638,755	-17%
23. Louisville, KY	*	631,260	*
24. Boston, MA	573,131	624,222	9%
25. El Paso, TX	474,870	618,812	30%

*Louisville merged with Jefferson County, KY in 2003 making 1985 population estimates incomparable.
Sources: FBI, Uniform Crime Reports, National Archive of Criminal Justice Data

Although American cities may follow the national trend in street crime there are many advantages to examining them individually, especially since no two American cities are exactly alike. Although the majority of America's largest cities have experienced some degree of growth in the past 24 years, for example, others have decreased in size (as seen in Table 1). This review of the distinct trends of street crime in each of the top 25 U.S. cities offers a snapshot of each city's changes in crime during this time period.

Figure 3 Crimes committed against persons: New York City

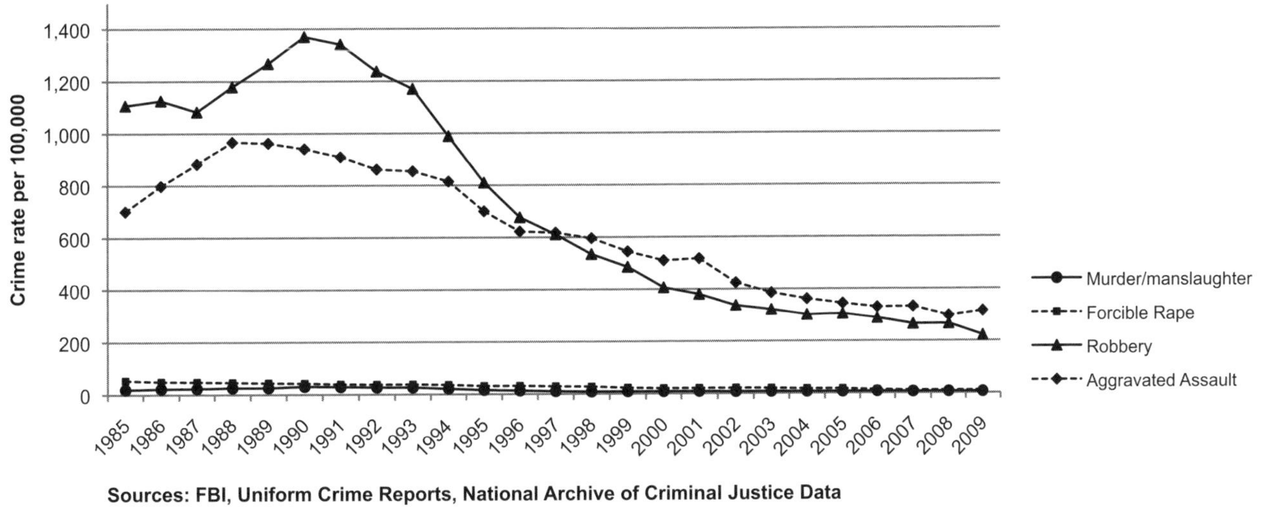

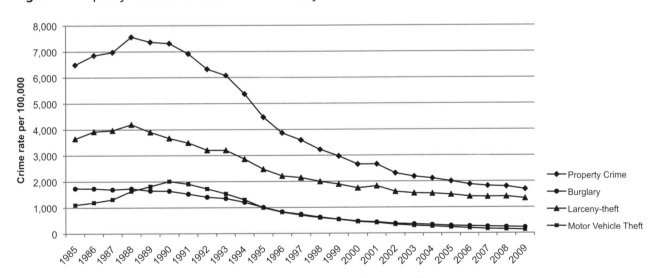

Sources: FBI, Uniform Crime Reports, National Archive of Criminal Justice Data

The patterns for street crime committed against persons in New York City are presented for this time period in Figure 3. The largest drop occurred among forcible rape with an 82 percent reduction from 54 per 100,000 in 1985 to 10 per 100,000 in 2009. Despite the peak robbery rate of 1,370 per 100,000 in 1990, there was an 80 percent decrease in the city's robbery rate from 1,107 in 1985 to 221 in 2009. Murder and non-negligent manslaughter also peaked in 1990 at 31 per 100,000 with a 71 percent drop from 19 in 1985 to 6 in 2009.

Figure 4 Property-related crime: New York City

Sources: FBI, Uniform Crime Reports, National Archive of Criminal Justice Data

Similar downward trends were also observed among property-related crimes during this period in New York City (Figure 4). Overall, there was a 74 percent drop in rates of all property crime. More specifically, the motor vehicle theft rate declined 88 percent from 1,106 per 100,000 in 1985 to 127 per 100,000 in 2009. The burglary rate dropped from 1,738 in 1985 to 224 per 100,000 in 2009: an 87 percent decrease. The larceny-theft rate, which peaked at 4,199 per 100,000 in 1988, steadily decreased to 1,340 per 100,000 in 2009.

Figure 5 Crimes committed against persons: Los Angeles, California

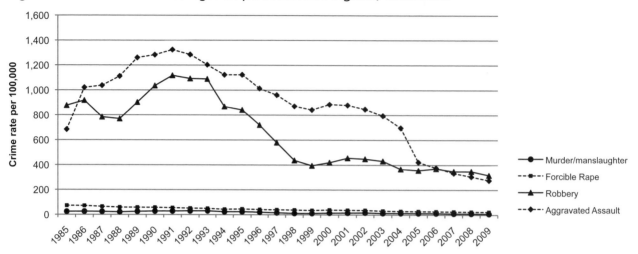

Sources: FBI, Uniform Crime Reports, National Archive of Criminal Justice Data

In Los Angeles, California, the second-largest city in the United States (Figure 5), the robbery rate and the aggravated assault rate reached their heights in 1991 at 1,118 per 100,000 and 1,324 per 100,000, respectively. There was a 64 percent overall drop in the robbery rate from 1985 to 2009 and a 60 percent overall drop in aggravated assault over this 24-year span. Murder and non-negligent manslaughter peaked later, in 1993 at 31 per 100,000, but still exhibited an overall decline of 67 percent, from 24 per 100,000 to 8 per 100,000 from 1985 to 2009. The forcible rape rate was highest in 1985 at 73 per 100,000 and steadily decreased to 24 per 100,000, resulting in a 68 percent drop.

Figure 6 Property-related crime: Los Angeles, California

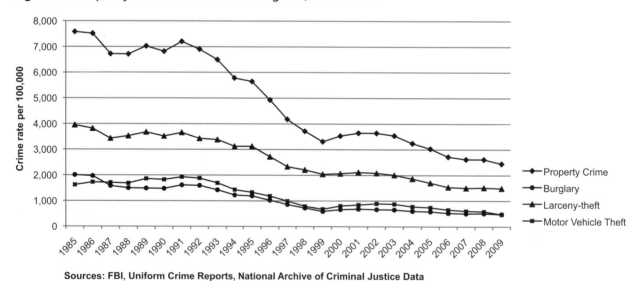

Sources: FBI, Uniform Crime Reports, National Archive of Criminal Justice Data

Figure 6 shows the overall property crime rate in Los Angeles in 1985 was 7,581 per 100,000 during this year and dropped to 2,449 in 2009: a 68 percent decrease. The burglary rate and the larceny-theft rate displayed similar patterns. There was a 76 percent decline in burglary dropping from a rate of 2,007 per 100,000 in 1985 to 479 per 100,000 in 2009. The rate of larceny-theft fell 62 percent from 3,953 per 100,000 in 1985 to 1,492 in 2009.

Figure 7 Crimes committed against persons: Chicago, Illinois

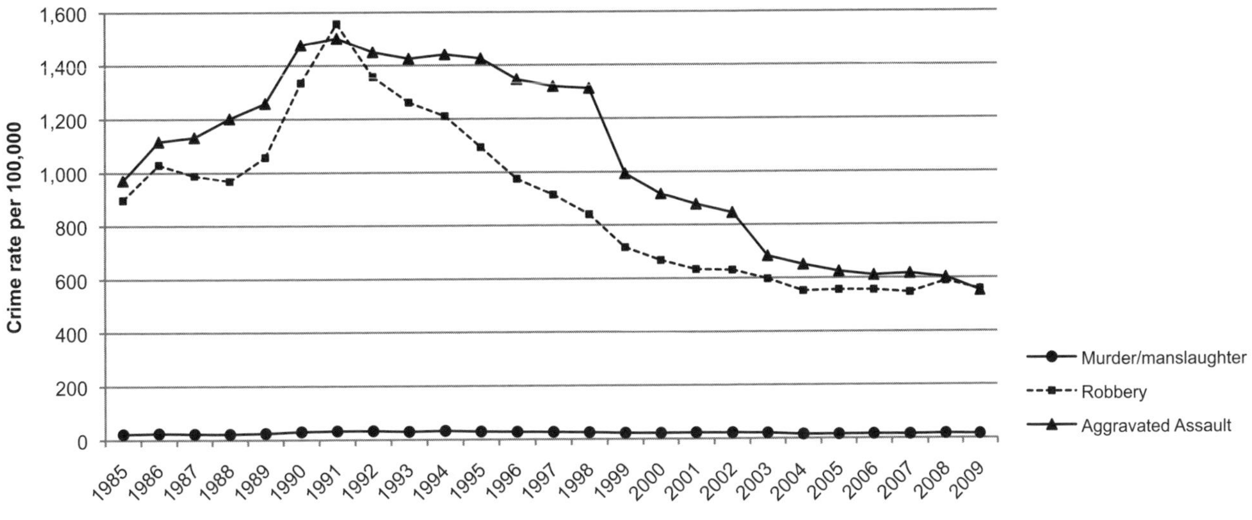

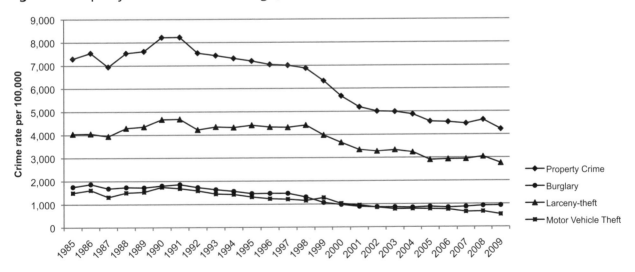

Note: Data on forcible rape was not collected
Sources: FBI, Uniform Crime Reports, National Archive of Criminal Justice Data

After peaking in 1991, the rate of aggravated assault in Chicago, Illinois (the third-largest city in the United States), and the rate of robbery both steadily dropped (Figure 7). The rate of aggravated assault fell 63 percent from 1,502 per 100,000 in 1991 to 552 per 100,000 in 2009. There was a nearly identical 64 percent drop in the robbery rate from 1,557 per 100,000 in 1991 to 557 in 2009. Murder and non-negligent manslaughter peaked in 1992 at 33 per 100,000 and fell 51 percent to 16 per 100,000 by 2009.

Figure 8 Property-related crime: Chicago, Illinois

Sources: FBI, Uniform Crime Reports, National Archive of Criminal Justice Data

Chicago's property-related street crime rates exhibited slightly different trends (see Figure 8) compared to the city's rates of crimes against persons. The rate of burglary, for example, fell 52 percent from 1,756 per 100,000 in 1985 to 847 per 100,000 in 2004, but increased slightly to 930 per 100,000 by 2009. The larceny-theft rate reached its peak in 1991 at 4,684 per 100,000 and dropped 41 percent to 2,754 per 100,000 in 2009. The rate of motor-vehicle theft followed a similar decline.

Figure 9 Crimes committed against persons: Houston, Texas

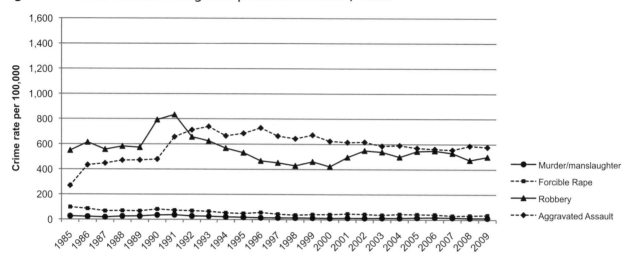

Sources: FBI, Uniform Crime Reports, National Archive of Criminal Justice Data

Houston, Texas, was America's fourth-largest city in 2009 with a population over 2 million (Table 1). The rates of street crimes against persons fluctuated from 1985 to 2009 (Figure 9). The rate of aggravated assault, for example, was 269 per 100,000 in 1985, swelled to a high of 739 per 100,000 in 1993, and settled at 577 per 100,000 in 2009: an overall increase of 114 percent. In contrast, the prevalence of the other three types of street crime committed against persons in Houston largely decreased during this time. The rate of robbery was 549 per 100,000 in 1985 and, after peaking at 833 per 100,000 in 1991, it decreased to 500 per 100,000 in 2009. The rate of forcible rape also decreased, dropping 63 percent from 98 per 100,000 in 1985 to 36 per 100,000 in 2009. Lastly, murder and non-negligent manslaughter also fell from a rate of 26 per 100,000 in 1985 to 13 per 100,000 in 2009.

Figure 10 Property-related crime: Houston, Texas

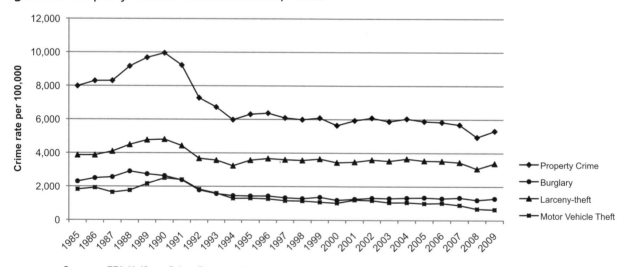

Sources: FBI, Uniform Crime Reports, National Archive of Criminal Justice Data

Property-related street crime rates in Houston all followed similar downward patterns (Figure 10). The largest decrease was in the rate of motor vehicle theft, dropping 65 percent from 1,817 per 100,000 to 642 per 100,000. The burglary rate dropped from 2,302 per 100,000 to 1,288 per 100,000 and the larceny-theft rate displayed the smallest decline (12 percent) from 3,865 per 100,000 to 3,389.

Figure 11 Crimes committed against persons: Phoenix, Arizona

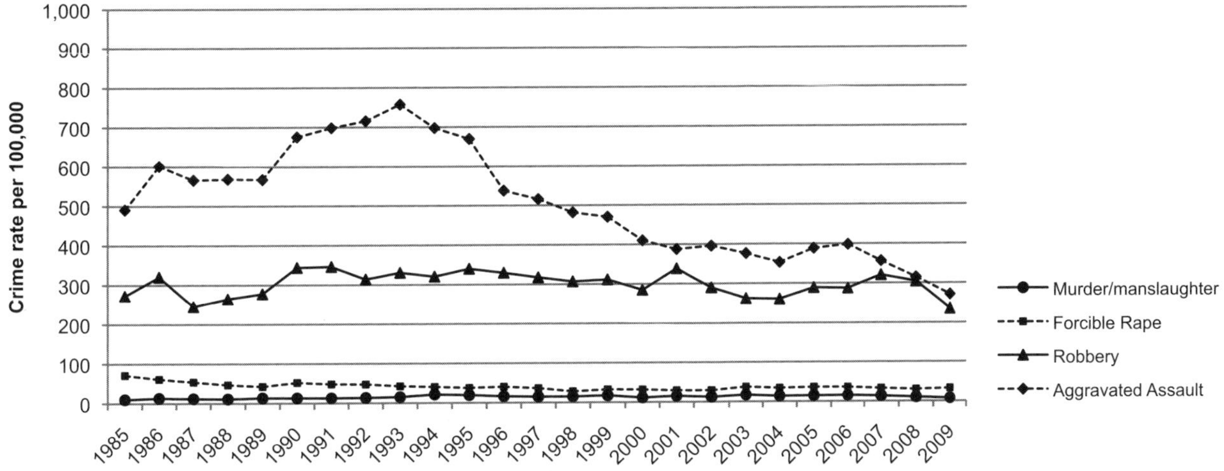

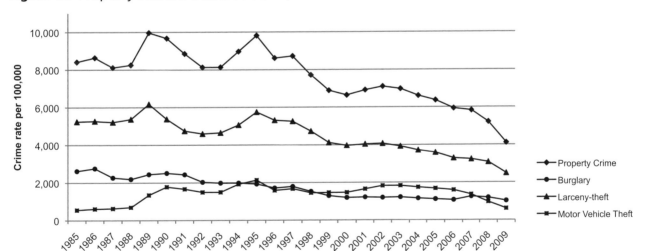

Sources: FBI, Uniform Crime Reports, National Archive of Criminal Justice Data

The population of Phoenix, Arizona, grew to over 1.5 million, nearly an 80 percent increase, to achieve the status of America's fifth-largest city in 2009 (Table 1). Despite the growth experienced by this city, the rates of street crime against persons declined over this 24-year period (Figure 11). The smallest decline occurred in the rate of robbery (14 percent), falling from 272 per 100,000 in 1985 to 235 per 100,000 in 2009. Murder and non-negligent manslaughter dropped 24 percent from 10 per 100,000 in 1985 to 8 per 100,000 in 2009. The forcible rape rate decreased from 71 per 100,000 in 1985 to 33 per 100,000 in 2009, and the rate of aggravated assault also fell from 491 per 100,000 in 1985 to 271 per 100,000 in 2009.

Figure 12 Property-related crime: Phoenix, Arizona

Sources: FBI, Uniform Crime Reports, National Archive of Criminal Justice Data

Motor vehicle theft in Phoenix (Figure 12) fluctuated somewhat erratically. Starting at 552 per 100,000 in 1985, the motor vehicle theft rate almost quadrupled to 2,133 per 100,000 in 1995, subsided quickly, and then surged again to 1,828 per 100,000 in 2003. Shortly thereafter, the motor vehicle theft rate dropped to 607 per 100,000 in 2009. Multiple peaks in the larceny-theft rate also emerged: one in 1989 at 6,174 per 100,000 and another in 1995 at 5,749 per 100,000 before dwindling to 2,482 by 2009. The rate of burglary exhibited a fairly steady decline with a 61 percent drop from 2,621 in 1985 to 1,019 per 100,000 in 2009.

Figure 13 Crimes committed against persons: Philadelphia, Pennsylvania

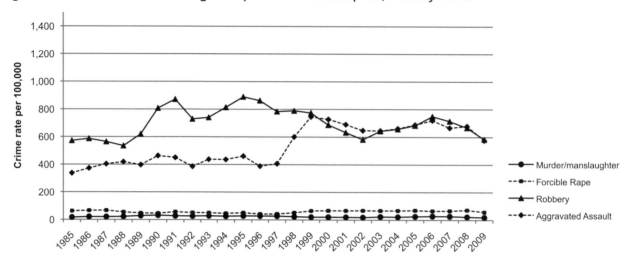

Sources: FBI, Uniform Crime Reports, National Archive of Criminal Justice Data

Philadelphia, Pennsylvania, was among the few of the largest cities in the United States to experience a decrease (6 percent) in population from 1985 to 2009 (Table 1). The shrinking population of the city occurred at a time when several types of street crimes against persons were on the rise (Figure 13). The robbery rate grew the least (2 percent) from 572 per 100,000 in 1985 to 584 per 100,000 in 2009, despite spiking up to 890 in 1995 and again up to 749 in 2006. The murder and non-negligent manslaughter rate also grew modestly (17 percent) from 17 per 100,000 in 1985 to 20 per 100,000 in 2009. The rate of aggravated assault grew the most (71 percent) from 337 per 100,000 in 1985 to 577 per 100,000 in 2009. The forcible rape rate was the only one to decrease in comparison, dropping 7 percent from 62 per 100,000 to 58 per 100,000.

Figure 14 Property-related crime: Philadelphia, Pennsylvania

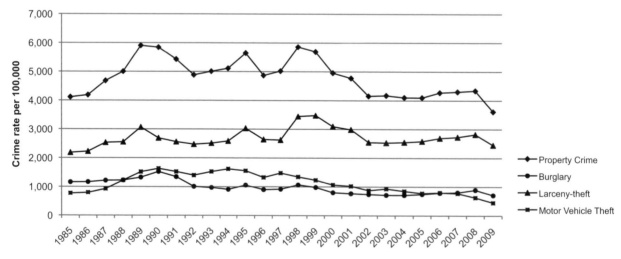

Sources: FBI, Uniform Crime Reports, National Archive of Criminal Justice Data

Some property-related street crime also increased in Philadelphia during this time (Figure 14). The larceny-theft rate increased a total of 12 percent from 1985 to 2009 with three distinct peaks: 3,063 per 100,000 in 1989, 3,029 in 1995, and 3,475 in 1999. On the other hand, the burglary rate declined 39 percent from 1,159 per 100,000 to 709 per 100,000 while the motor vehicle theft rate declined 41 percent from 770 to 451 during this time period.

Figure 15 Crimes committed against persons: Las Vegas, Nevada

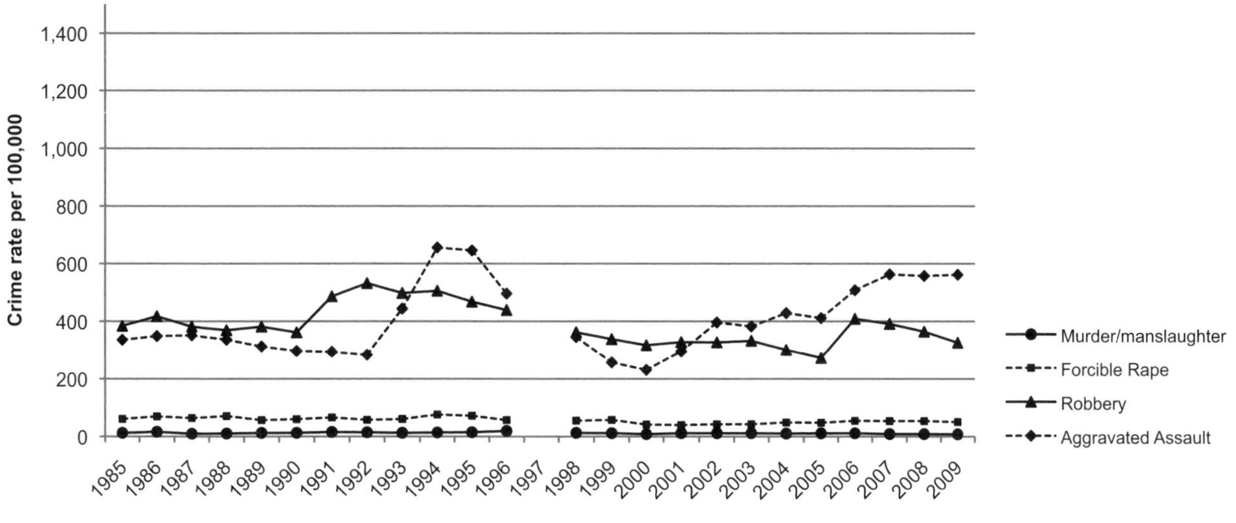

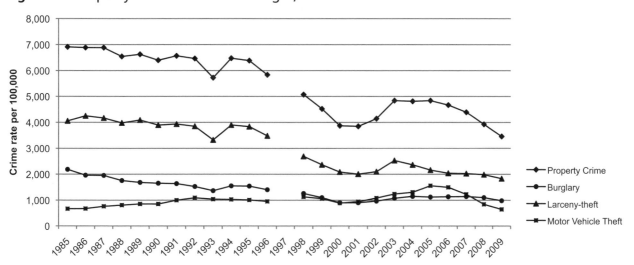

Note: 1997 data were not reported
Sources: FBI, Uniform Crime Reports, National Archive of Criminal Justice Data

Both population and the rate of aggravated assault in Las Vegas, Nevada, exhibited growth, although not to such a great extent, with a 67 percent rise from 336 per 100,000 in 1985 to 562 per 100,000 in 2009 (Figure 15). In comparison, the other three types of street crime committed against persons declined. Murder and non-negligent manslaughter displayed the largest drop (35 percent), followed by a 17 percent drop in the forcible rape rate (from 61 per 100,000 in 1985 to 51 per 100,000 in 2009), and a 15 percent decline (384 per 100,000 in 1985 to 326 per 100,000 in 2009) in the robbery rate.

Figure 16 Property-related crime: Las Vegas, Nevada

Note: 1997 data were not reported
Sources: FBI, Uniform Crime Reports, National Archive of Criminal Justice Data

The most prominent spikes in Las Vegas, Nevada, appear in the pattern of motor vehicle theft, which stood at 670 per 100,000 in 1985 (Figure 16). This rate oscillated just over 1,000 per 100,000 from 1992 through 1995, reaching a peak of 1,557 in 2005. The motor vehicle theft rate then fell 57 percent in four years to 648 per 100,000 in 2009. The burglary rate dropped 55 percent from 2,184 per 100,000 in 1985 to 981 per 100,000 in 2009 while the larceny-theft rate also fell 55 percent from 4,058 per 100,000 to 1,832 per 100,000.

Figure 17 Crimes committed against persons: San Antonio, Texas

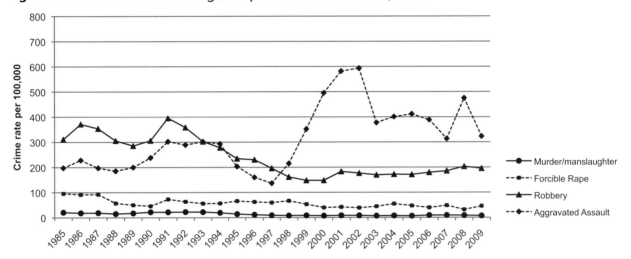

Sources: FBI, Uniform Crime Reports, National Archive of Criminal Justice Data

San Antonio, Texas, also experienced a sizable (59 percent) amount of growth from 1985 to 2009. During this time, aggravated assault increased 63 percent, peaking in 2002 at 593 per 100,000 before dropping to 323 per 100,000 in 2009 (Figure 17). In contrast, the murder and non-negligent manslaughter rate steadily declined after peaking in 1993 at 22 per 100,000 to 7 per 100,000 in 2009. The robbery rate also steadily declined to 148 per 100,000 in 2000 after peaking at 395 per 100,000 in 1991, but then the rate rose again to 195 per 100,000 in 2009. The forcible rape rate was at its peak in 1985 at 96 per 100,000 before dropping to a low of 39 per 100,000 in 2002 and rising slightly to 46 per 100,000 in 2009.

Figure 18 Property-related crime: San Antonio, Texas

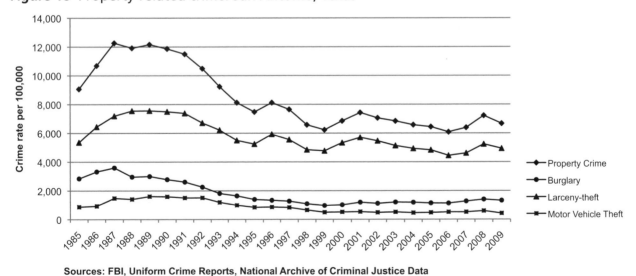

Sources: FBI, Uniform Crime Reports, National Archive of Criminal Justice Data

Property-related street crime in San Antonio generally declined over this 24-year period (Figure 18). Larceny-theft displayed the smallest overall decrease (8 percent) declining slightly from 5,350 per 100,000 in 1985 to 4,926 per 100,000 in 2009. The motor vehicle theft rate dropped more dramatically (51 percent) from 1985 to 2009, after peaking at 1,607 per 100,000 in 1989. The burglary rate also declined sharply from a high of 3,591 per 100,000 in 1987 to 1,322 in 2009.

Figure 19 Crimes committed against persons: San Diego, California

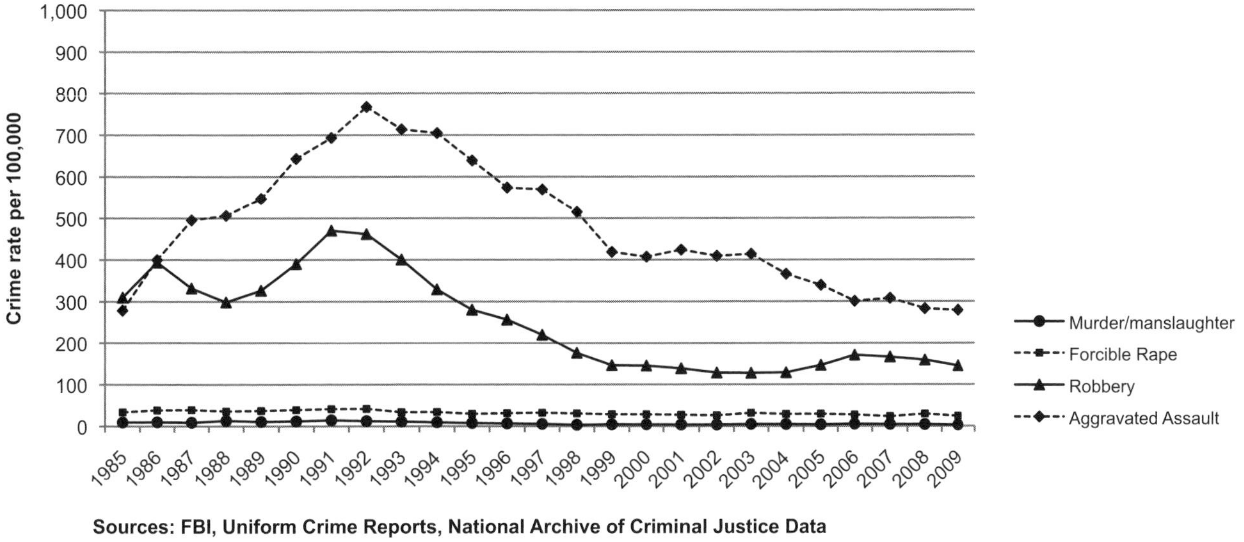

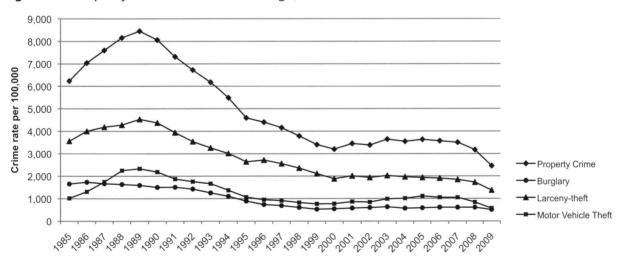

Sources: FBI, Uniform Crime Reports, National Archive of Criminal Justice Data

The rates of street crimes committed against persons in San Diego, California, peaked in the early 1990s and steadily declined afterward (Figure 19). The rate of aggravated assault, for example, peaked in 1992 at 768 per 100,000 and dropped to 279 per 100,000 in 2009. The rate of forcible rape also peaked in 1992 at 42 per 100,000 and fell to 24 per 100,000 in 2009. The robbery rate reached its apex one year earlier in 1991 at 470 per 100,000 and dropped to 145 per 100,000 in 2009. The rate of murder and non-negligent manslaughter followed a similar trend, peaking in 1991 at 15 per 100,000 and steadily decreasing to 3 per 100,000 in 2009.

Figure 20 Property-related crime: San Diego, California

Sources: FBI, Uniform Crime Reports, National Archive of Criminal Justice Data

Property-related street crime in San Diego reached its height in 1989 (Figure 20). The overall rate of property crime peaked at 8,453 per 100,000 in 1989 and fell 71 percent to 2,453 per 100,000 in 2009. The burglary rate, which crested at 1,592 per 100,000 in this same year, dropped 68 percent to 509 per 100,000 in 2009. The same trend was observed with the rate of larceny-theft falling 70 percent from a high of 4,532 per 100,000 in 1989 to 1,373 per 100,000 in 2009. The rate of motor vehicle theft was also at its climax of 2,329 per 100,000 in 1989 before it dropped 76 percent to 570 per 100,000 in 2009.

Figure 21 Crimes committed against persons: Dallas, Texas

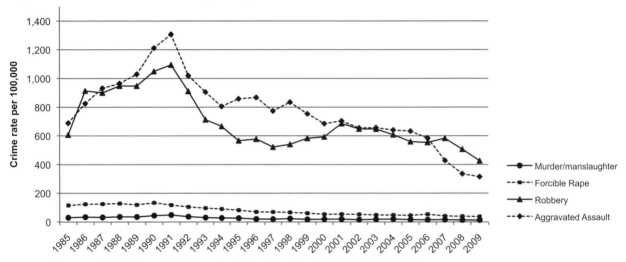

Sources: FBI, Uniform Crime Reports, National Archive of Criminal Justice Data

Street crime rates related to crimes against persons reached their height in Dallas, Texas, in the early 1990s (Figure 21). The rate of murder and non-negligent manslaughter reached its apex in 1991 at 49 per 100,000 and declined relatively steadily to 13 per 100,000 in 2009. The rate of robbery also peaked in 1991 at 1,094 per 100,000 and dropped 61 percent to 426 per 100,000 in 2009. The observed trend in the aggravated assault rate reached its climax in 1991 at 1,308 per 100,000 prior to falling 76 percent to 315 per 100,000 in 2009. The rate of forcible rape reached its height in 1990, at 134 per 100,000 and steadily declined to 38 per 100,000 by 2009.

Figure 22 Property-related crime: Dallas, Texas

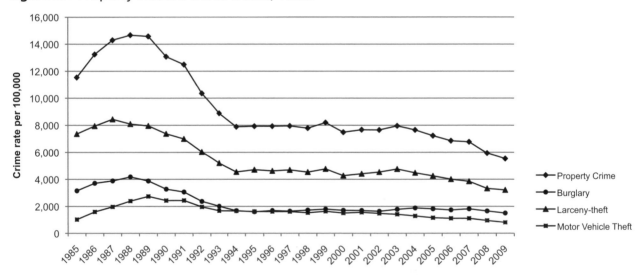

Sources: FBI, Uniform Crime Reports, National Archive of Criminal Justice Data

Property-related street crime trends in Dallas were similar to crimes against persons, but property-related street crimes were at their height slightly earlier in comparison (Figure 22). The rate of larceny-theft, for example, was 7,359 per 100,000 in 1985, rose to 8,442 per 100,000 in 1987, and dropped to 3,215 per 100,000 in 2009: an overall decrease of 56 percent. The burglary rate peaked just one year later, in 1988, at 4,180 per 100,000 prior to falling to 1,506 per 100,000 in 2009. The motor vehicle theft rate reached its height in 1989 at 2,740 per 100,000 before it fell to 810 per 100,000 by 2009.

Figure 23 Crimes committed against persons: San Jose, California

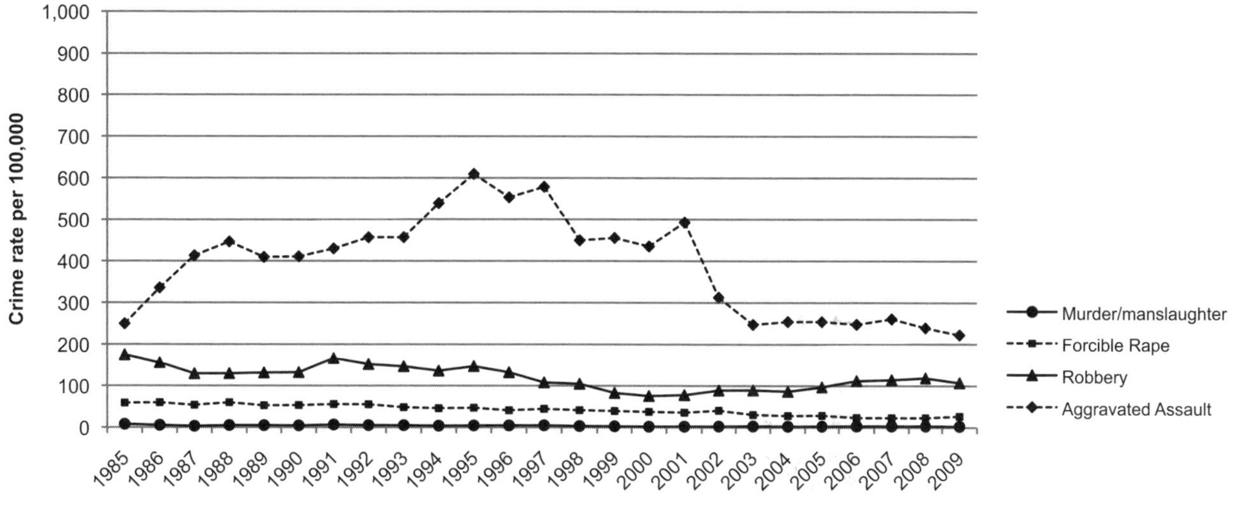

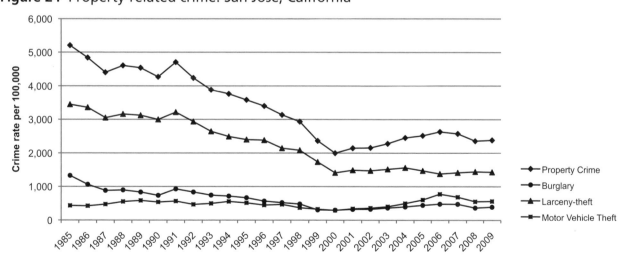

Sources: FBI, Uniform Crime Reports, National Archive of Criminal Justice Data

The aggravated assault in San Jose, California, rate rose from 250 per 100,000 in 1985 to a high of 610 per 100,000 in 1995, decreased slightly before rising again to 493 per 100,000 in 2001, and dropped to 223 per 100,000 by 2009 (Figure 23). The robbery rate also oscillated over this period, dropping from 175 per 100,000 in 1985 to 76 per 100,000 in 2000, before rising to 107 per 100,000 by 2009. In contrast, the forcible rape rate exhibited a fairly steady 54 percent decline from 59 per 100,000 in 1985 to 27 per 100,000 in 2009. The murder and non-negligent manslaughter rate declined 63 percent from 1985 to 2009.

Figure 24 Property-related crime: San Jose, California

Sources: FBI, Uniform Crime Reports, National Archive of Criminal Justice Data

The overall property crime rate, the burglary rate, the larceny-theft rate, and the motor vehicle theft rate in San Jose all dropped from 1985 to 2000 (Figure 24), when they reached their lowest levels. From 2000 onward, the burglary rate rose 31 percent from 298 per 100,000 to 392 per 100,000 by 2009. The larceny-theft rate also rose slightly (2 percent) during this decade from 1,407 per 100,000 in 2000 to 1,429 per 100,000 in 2009. The motor vehicle theft rate rose dramatically (93 percent) in the 2000s from 292 per 100,000 in 2000 to a high of 776 per 100,000 in 2006 before decreasing slightly to 564 per 100,000 in 2009.

Figure 25 Crimes committed against persons: Detroit, Michigan

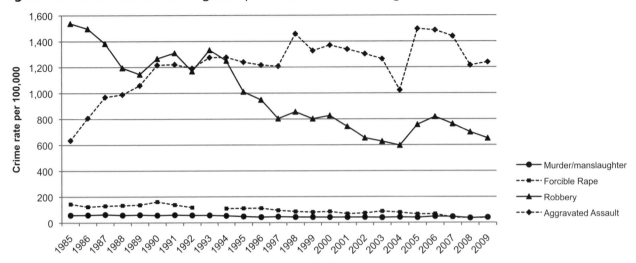

Note: 1993 data on forcible rape was not available
Sources: FBI, Uniform Crime Reports, National Archive of Criminal Justice Data

Detroit, Michigan, was tied with another city (Baltimore, Maryland) for the largest population loss from 1985 to 2009 (Table 1). Three of the four measures of street crime rates committed against persons declined in Detroit during this time (Figure 25). The murder and non-negligent manslaughter rate dropped 31 percent from 58 per 100,000 in 1985 to 40 per 100,000 in 2009. The forcible rape rate fell 74 percent from 144 per 100,000 in 1985 to 37 per 100,000 by 2009, while the robbery rate decreased 58 percent from 1,538 per 100,000 in 1985 to 651 per 100,000 in 2009. In stark contrast, the aggravated assault rate increased 136 percent from 635 per 100,000 in 1985 to a high of 1,496 per 100,000 in 2005 before dropping slightly to 1,239 per 100,000 in 2009.

Figure 26 Property-related crime: Detroit, Michigan

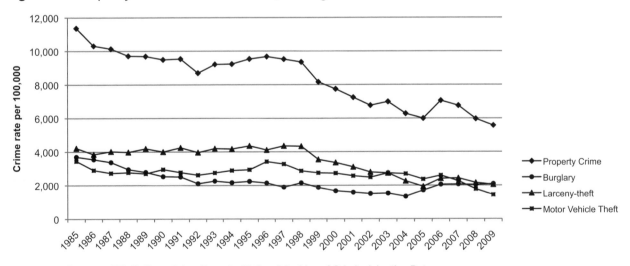

Sources: FBI, Uniform Crime Reports, National Archive of Criminal Justice Data

Fairly consistent decreasing trends emerged among property-related street crime rates in Detroit (Figure 26). The motor vehicle theft rate dropped 59 percent from 3,452 per 100,000 in 1985 to 1,432 per 100,000 in 2009, the larceny-theft rate fell 52 percent from 4,219 per 100,000 in 1985 to 2,045 per 100,000 in 2009, and the burglary rate decreased 44 percent from 3,703 per 100,000 to 2,091 per 100,000.

Figure 27 Crimes committed against persons: Honolulu, Hawai'i

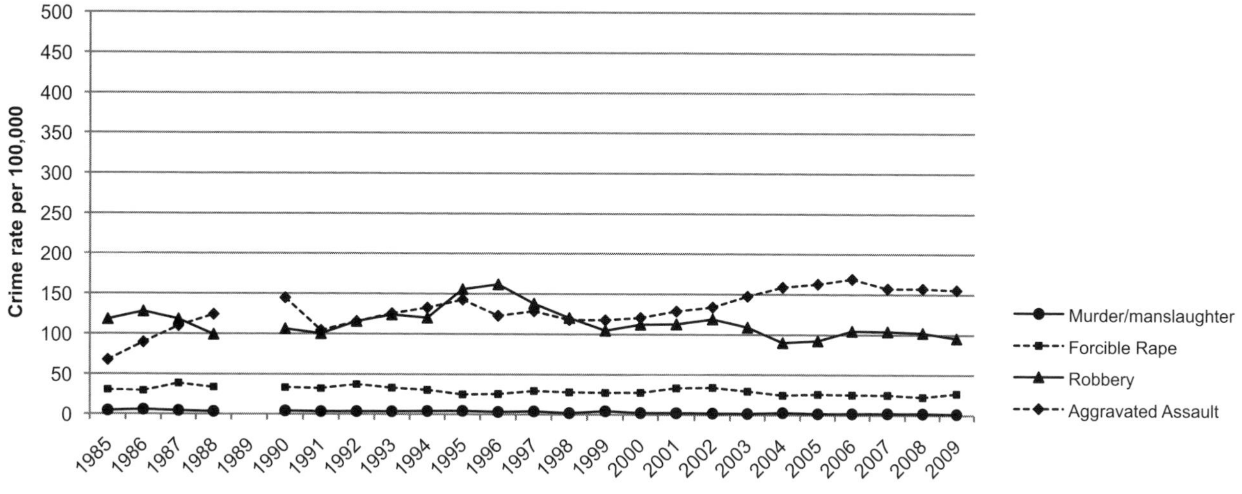

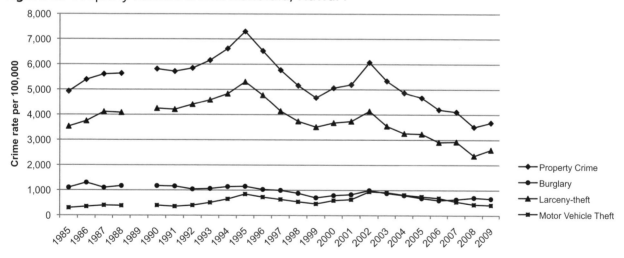

Note: 1989 data were unavailable
Sources: FBI, Uniform Crime Reports, National Archive of Criminal Justice Data

Three of the street crime rates committed against persons declined in Honolulu, Hawai'i, from 1985 to 2009 (Figure 27). The murder and non-negligent manslaughter rate decreased by about half from 4 per 100,000 in 1985 to 2 per 100,000 in 2009. The drop in the forcible rape rate was more modest (12 percent) declining from 30 per 100,000 in 1985 to 27 per 100,000 in 2009. The robbery rate also fell during this time from 118 per 100,000 to 96 per 100,000. The aggravated assault rate, in direct contrast, more than doubled from 68 per 100,000 in 1985 to 156 per 100,000 in 2009.

Figure 28 Property-related crime: Honolulu, Hawai'i

Note: 1989 data were unavailable
Sources: FBI, Uniform Crime Reports, National Archive of Criminal Justice Data

Property-related crime rates in Honolulu appeared to spike twice (Figure 28): first in 1995 and the second time in 2002. The burglary rate reached its peak in 1995 at 1,150 per 100,000 before rising again to a rate of 992 per 100,000 in 2002. The larceny-theft rate also reached its height in 1995 at 5,305 per 100,000 and surged again in 2002 to 4,137 per 100,000 before dropping to 2,607 per 100,000 in 2009. The motor vehicle theft rate followed a similar pattern, peaking at 845 per 100,000 in 1995, swelling again to 943 per 100,000 in 2002 prior to resting at 411 per 100,000 in 2009.

Figure 29 Crimes committed against persons: Indianapolis, Indiana

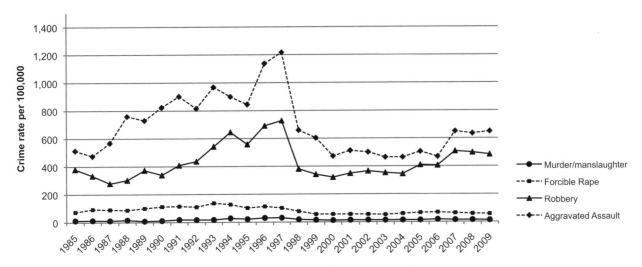

Sources: FBI, Uniform Crime Reports, National Archive of Criminal Justice Data

Indianapolis, Indiana, is another U.S. city that experienced a significant amount (72 percent) of growth in the past 24 years (Table 1). The trends in street crime rates committed against persons in Indianapolis were mixed: the rates of two types of crime increased while two decreased (Figure 29). There was a slight (2 percent) overall decrease in the murder and non-negligent manslaughter rate, after reaching a peak of 31 per 100,000 in 1997. The forcible rape rate also exhibited an overall decline (23 percent) settling at 57 per 100,000 in 2009. The robbery rate, in comparison, increased 27 percent from 381 per 100,000 in 1985 to a high of 728 in 1997, and then declined to 483 per 100,000 in 2009. The aggravated assault rate also increased, reaching its height of 1,217 per 100,000 in 1997 before falling to 648 per 100,000 in 2009.

Figure 30 Property-related crime: Indianapolis, Indiana

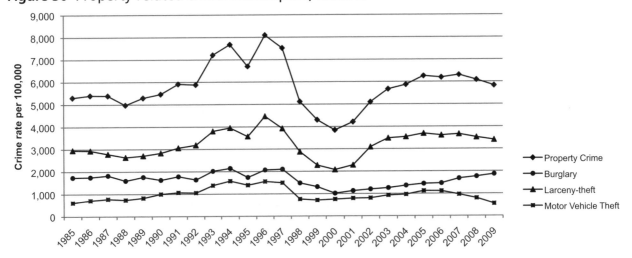

Sources: FBI, Uniform Crime Reports, National Archive of Criminal Justice Data

There were similar mixed trends in property-related street crime rates in Indianapolis (Figure 30). The burglary rate grew slightly (7 percent) from 1,741 per 100,000 in 1985 to 1,871 per 100,000 in 2009. The larceny-theft rate also grew modestly (15 percent) from 2,953 in 1985 to 3,407 per 100,000 in 2009. In contrast, the motor vehicle theft rate fell slightly (10 percent) from 613 per 100,000 in 1985 to 551 per 100,000 in 2009.

Figure 31 Crimes committed against persons: Jacksonville, Florida

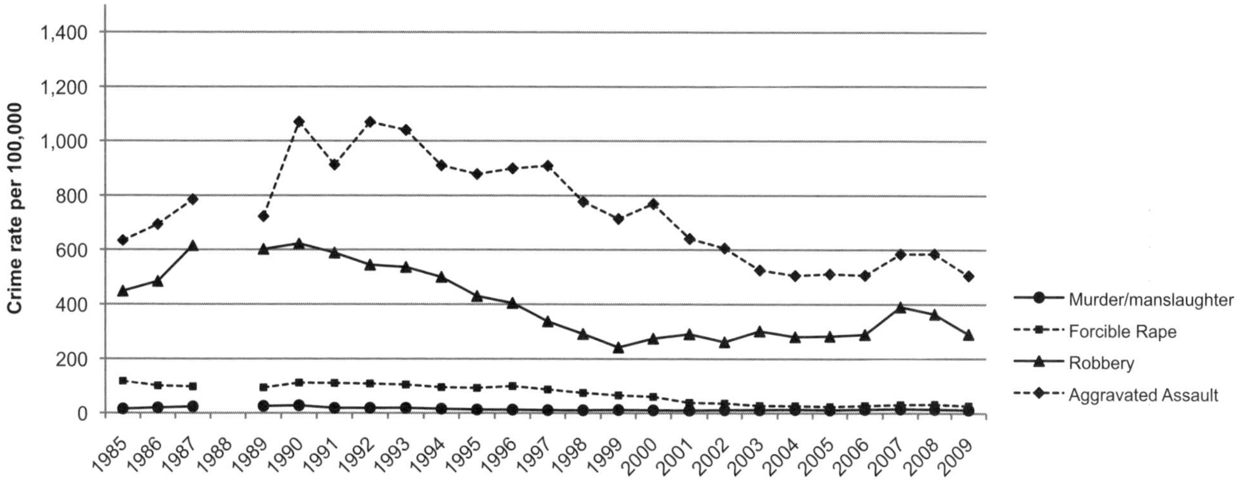

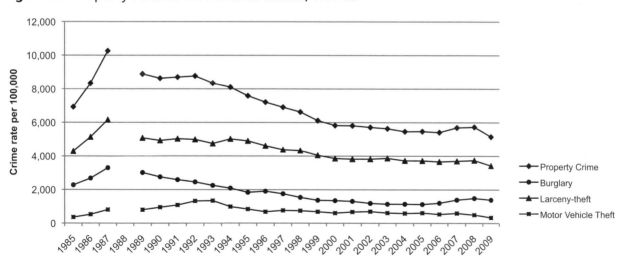

Note: 1988 data were unavailable
Sources: FBI, Uniform Crime Reports, National Archive of Criminal Justice Data

Generally, the trends in street crime committed against persons in Jacksonville, Florida, increased from 1985 to 1990, but decreased steadily until 2009 (Figure 31). The aggravated assault rate increased from 634 per 100,000 in 1985 to 1,070 per 100,000 in 1990 and fell to 506 per 100,000 by 2009. The robbery rate followed a similar pattern increasing from 448 per 100,000 in 1985 to 622 per 100,000 in 1990 and falling to 291 per 100,000 in 2009. The forcible rape rate also peaked in 1990 at 111 per 100,000 and fell to 27 per 100,000 in 2009. The murder and non-negligent manslaughter rate reached its height at 28 per 100,000 in 1990 and fell to 12 per 100,000 in 2009.

Figure 32 Property-related crime: Jacksonville, Florida

Note: 1988 data were unavailable
Sources: FBI, Uniform Crime Reports, National Archive of Criminal Justice Data

Similar patterns were revealed in the rates of burglary and larceny-theft in Jacksonville (Figure 32). The burglary rate reached its climax in 1987 at 3,293 per 100,000 and fell consistently to 1,396 per 100,000 in 2009. The larceny-theft rate also reached its height in 1987 at 6,163 per 100,000 and dropped fairly steadily to 3,426 per 100,000 in 2009. In comparison, the motor vehicle theft rate did not reach its peak of 1,344 per 100,000 until 1993, but it decreased similarly to 336 per 100,000 in 2009.

Figure 33 Crimes committed against persons: San Francisco, California

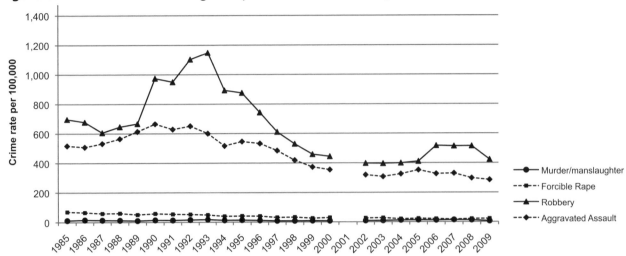

Note: 2001 data were unavailable
Sources: FBI, Uniform Crime Reports, National Archive of Criminal Justice Data

Although the street crimes committed against persons in San Francisco, California, seemed to followed a downward trend, the rate of each type of crime rose and fell at different times (Figure 33). The murder and non-negligent manslaughter rate, for instance, reached its high of 18 per 100,000 in 1993 and then fell to 6 per 100,000 in 2009. The forcible rape rate was highest in 1985 at 70 per 100,000 and dropped 68 percent to 22 per 100,000 in 2009. The robbery rate rose from 697 per 100,000 in 1985 to 1,148 in 1993 and declined to 423 per 100,000 in 2009. The aggravated assault rate rose from 517 per 100,000 in 1985 to 665 per 100,000 in 1990 and then decreased to 285 per 100,000 in 2009.

Figure 34 Property-related crime: San Francisco, California

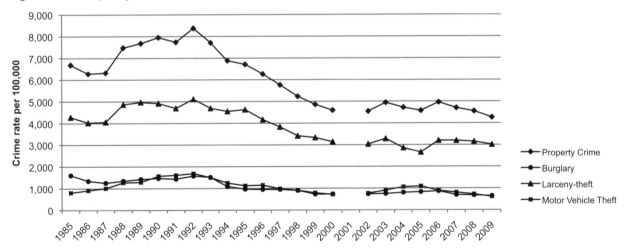

Note: 2001 data were unavailable
Sources: FBI, Uniform Crime Reports, National Archive of Criminal Justice Data

In contrast to crime rates for offenses committed against persons, the rates of property-related crime in San Francisco reached their highest values in the same year: 1992 (Figure 34). The burglary rate reached a high of 1,576 per 100,000 in 1992 before falling to 642 per 100,000 in 2009. The larceny-theft rate peaked at 5,111 per 100,000 in 1992 and dropped to 3,013 in 2009, while the motor vehicle theft rate dropped from 1,687 per 100,000 in 1992 to 607 per 100,000 in 2009.

Figure 35 Crimes committed against persons: Charlottee, North Carolina

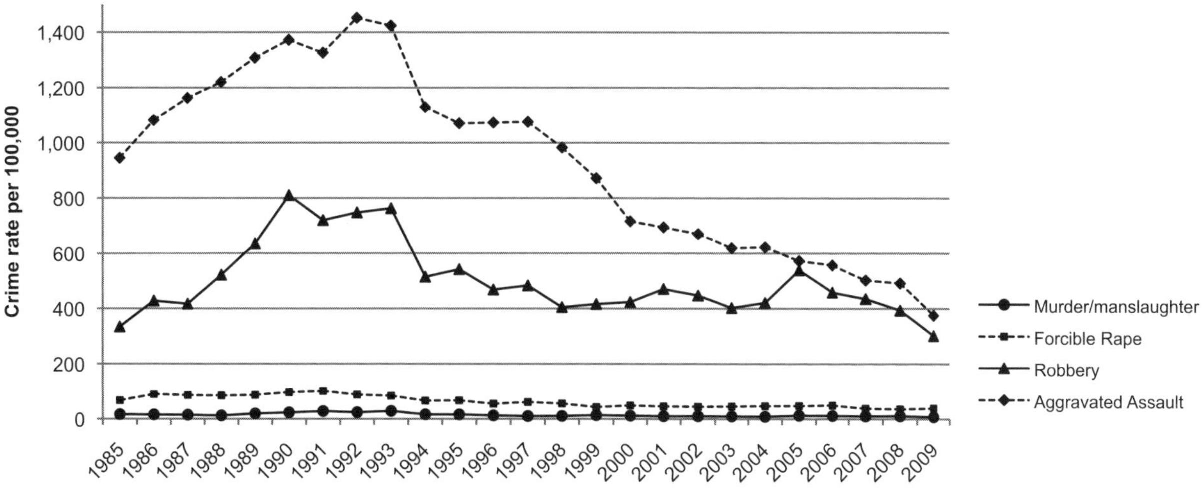

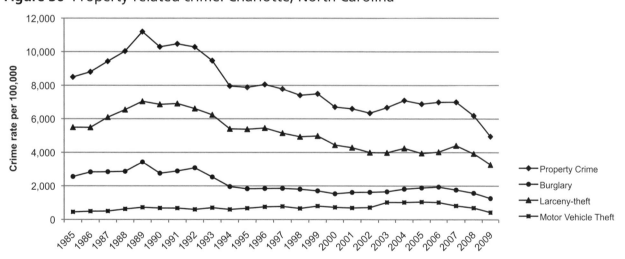

Sources: FBI, Uniform Crime Reports, National Archive of Criminal Justice Data

The rates of street crime committed against persons in Charlotte grew into the early 1990s, but then steadily declined from that point forward (Figure 35). The murder and non-negligent manslaughter rate, which was 17 per 100,000 in 1985, swelled to 29 per 100,000 in 1993, and eventually fell to 8 per 100,000 in 2009. The forcible rape rate was 67 per 100,000 in 1985 and grew to 101 per 100,000 in 1991 before dropping to 39 per 100,000 in 2009. Similarly, the robbery rate in 1985 was 334 per 100,000, which increased to 810 per 100,000 in 1990, and dropped to 302 per 100,000 in 2009. The aggravated assault rate was 945 per 100,000 in 1985, peaked at 1,452 per 100,000 in 1992, and decreased to 375 per 100,000 in 2009.

Figure 36 Property-related crime: Charlotte, North Carolina

Sources: FBI, Uniform Crime Reports, National Archive of Criminal Justice Data

Property-related street crime rates in Charlotte exhibited slightly varied trends relative to one another (Figure 36). For instance, the burglary rate, which was 2,551 per 100,000 in 1985, swelled to 3,428 per 100,000 in 1989 before eventually dropping to 1,262 per 100,000 in 2009. In contrast, the motor vehicle theft rate grew from 1985 (447 per 100,000) to 2005 (1,048 per 100,000) prior to falling below its 1985 value in 2009 (429 per 100,000). The larceny-theft rate increased from 1985 (5,495 per 100,000) to 1989 (7,039 per 100,000) and decreased from this point through 2009 (3,263 per 100,000).

Figure 37 Crimes committed against persons: Austin, Texas

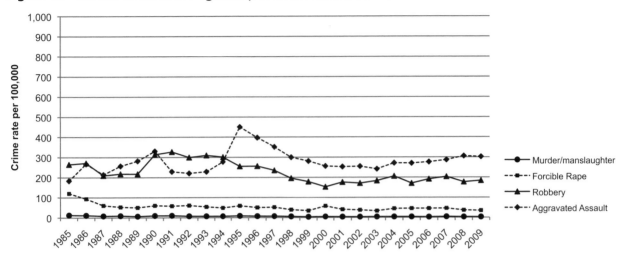

Sources: FBI, Uniform Crime Reports, National Archive of Criminal Justice Data

Some of the rates of street crime committed against persons in Austin, Texas, steadily decreased during this period while others fluctuated (Figure 37). For example, the murder and non-negligent manslaughter rate declined 77 percent from 1985 (13 per 100,000) to 2009 (3 per 100,000) while the forcible rape rate exhibited a similar 71 percent decline from 120 per 100,000 in 1985 to 35 per 100,000 in 2009. In contrast, the robbery and aggravated assault rates vacillated quite a bit. The robbery rate increased from 265 per 100,000 in 1985 to 327 per 100,000 in 1991 and then dropped to 184 per 100,000 in 2009. The aggravated assault rate displayed a similar pattern as it increased from 184 per 100,000 in 1985 to 451 per 100,000 in 1995 before falling to 302 per 100,000 in 2009.

Figure 38 Property-related crime: Austin, Texas

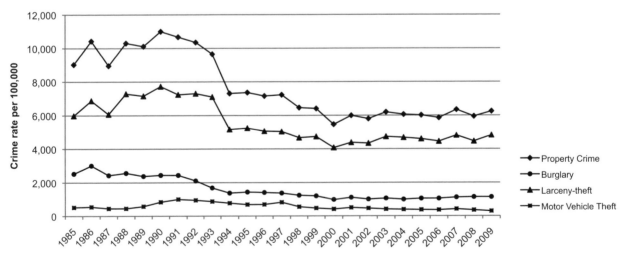

Sources: FBI, Uniform Crime Reports, National Archive of Criminal Justice Data

The property-crime rates in Austin followed similar trends during this time (Figure 38). Although the larceny-theft rate dropped 19 percent from 5,980 per 100,000 in 1985 to 4,819 per 100,000 in 2009, it swelled to 7,722 in 1990. In a similar manner, the motor vehicle theft rate, which was 520 per 100,000 in 1985, increased to 997 per 100,000 in 1991 before falling to 289 per 100,000 in 2009. The burglary rate fell 55 percent from 2,524 per 100,000 in 1985 to 1,138 per 100,000 in 2009.

Figure 39 Crimes committed against persons: Columbus, Ohio

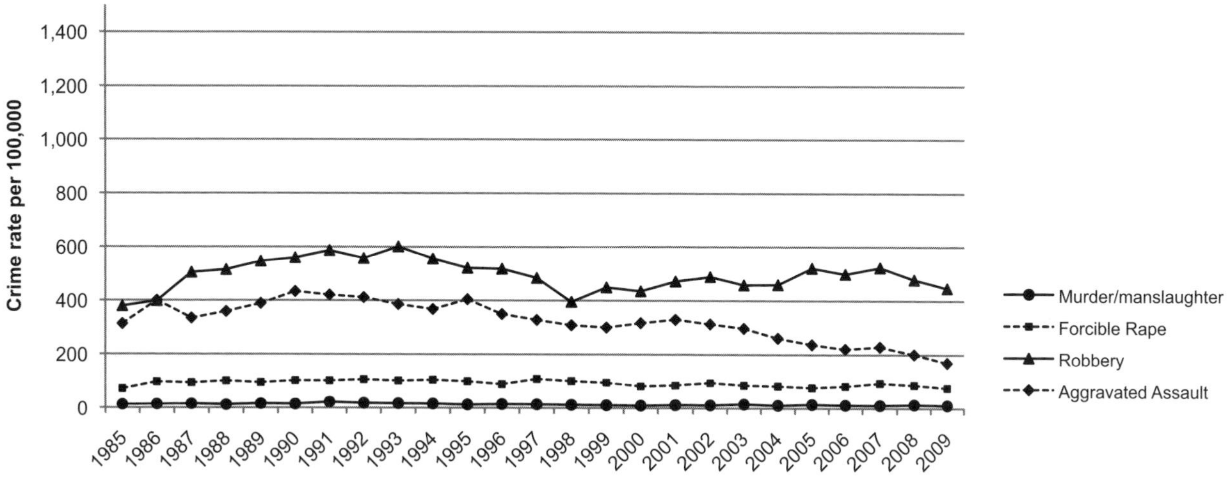

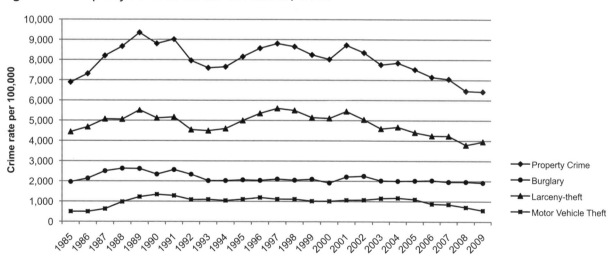

Sources: FBI, Uniform Crime Reports, National Archive of Criminal Justice Data

Columbus, Ohio, experienced some interesting trends in street crime committed against persons from 1985 to 2009 (Figure 39). The forcible rape rate marginally increased (5 percent) from 72 per 100,000 in 1985 to 76 per 100,000 in 2009. The robbery rate also increased modestly (18 percent) from 379 per 100,000 in 1985 to 447 per 100,000 in 2009. The aggravated assault rate, in comparison, decreased (46 percent) from 313 per 100,000 in 1985 to 170 per 100,000 in 2009. The murder and non-negligent manslaughter rate followed a similar downward trend decreasing 14 percent from 13 per 100,000 in 1985 to 11 per 100,000 in 2009.

Figure 40 Property-related crime: Columbus, Ohio

Sources: FBI, Uniform Crime Reports, National Archive of Criminal Justice Data

The property-related street crime rates in Columbus exhibited less stable patterns during this period (Figure 40). The motor vehicle theft rate peaked earliest, at 1,338 per 100,000 in 1990, before eventually falling to 551 per 100,000 in 2009. The larceny-theft rate increased from 4,435 per 100,000 in 1985 to a high of 5,595 per 100,000 in 1997 and dropped to 3,956 per 100,000 in 2009. The burglary rate also initially grew from 1,962 per 100,000 in 1985 to its highest value of 2,631 per 100,000 in 1989 and slowly declined to 1,920 per 100,000 in 2009.

Figure 41 Crimes committed against persons: Fort Worth, Texas

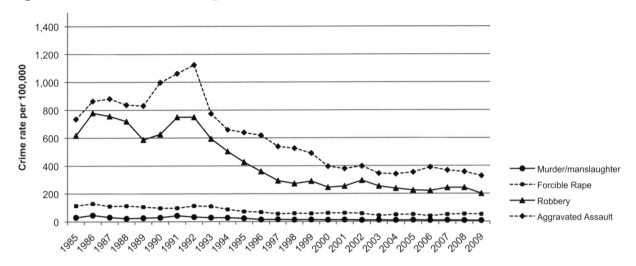

Sources: FBI, Uniform Crime Reports, National Archive of Criminal Justice Data

Fort Worth, Texas, rounded out the top 20 largest cities in the United States with a 70 percent increase in population from 1985 to 2009. The trends in Fort Worth's street crime rates committed against persons were fairly similar to one another (Figure 41). The rates of murder and non-negligent manslaughter (46 per 100,000), forcible rape (129 per 100,000), and robbery (780 per 100,000) peaked in 1986 and followed a general downward trend until 2009. The rate of aggravated assault, which was 735 per 100,000 in 1985, grew to 1,123 per 100,000 in 1992 before dropping to 328 per 100,000 in 2009.

Figure 42 Property-related crime: Fort Worth, Texas

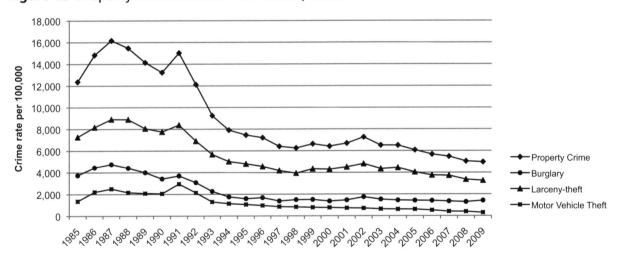

Sources: FBI, Uniform Crime Reports, National Archive of Criminal Justice Data

A similar pattern was observed among property-related street crime in Fort Worth (Figure 42). The rates of burglary (4,758 per 100,000) and larceny-theft (8,904 per 100,000) peaked in 1987 and began to trend downward. The rate of motor vehicle theft, on the other hand, rose from 1,356 per 100,000 in 1985 to 2,946 per 100,000 in 1991 before falling to 295 per 100,000 in 2009.

Figure 43 Crimes committed against persons: Memphis, Tennessee

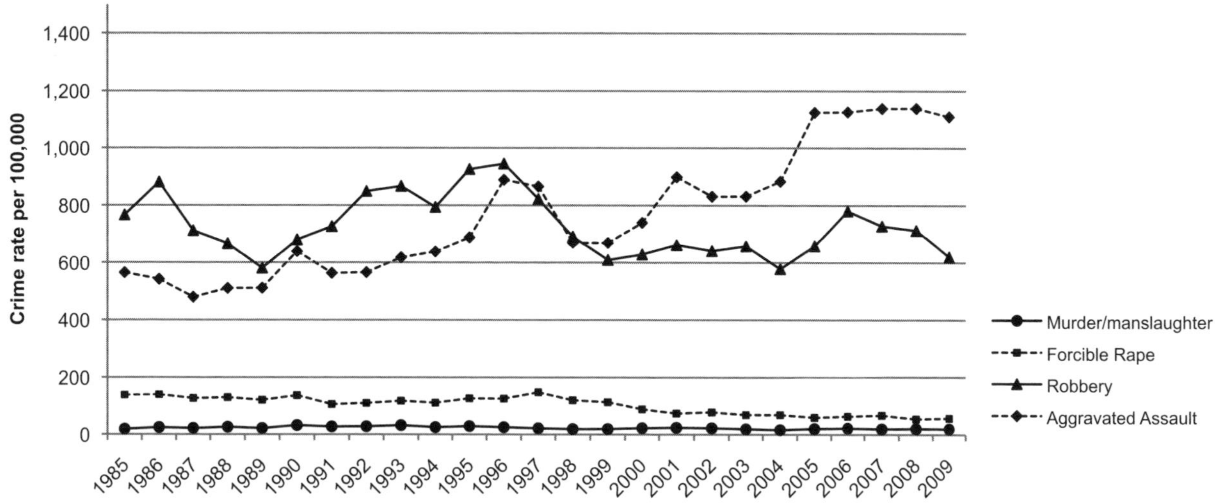

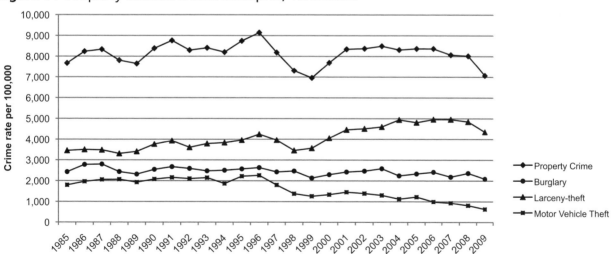

Sources: FBI, Uniform Crime Reports, National Archive of Criminal Justice Data

The population of Memphis, Tennessee, remained fairly stable from 1985 to 2009, and although some street crime rates for crimes committed against persons remained constant, others fluctuated a fair amount (Figure 43). The murder and non-negligent manslaughter rate was one that remained somewhat stable, growing only 6 percent from 19 per 100,000 in 1985 to 20 per 100,000 in 2009. The aggravated assault rate, on the other hand, increased dramatically (96 percent) from 565 per 100,000 in 1985 to 1,109 per 100,000 in 2009. Despite an overall 59 percent reduction, the forcible rape rate rose from 138 per 100,000 in 1985 to 147 per 100,000 in 1997 before dropping to 57 per 100,000 in 2009. The trend in the robbery rate was similar, swelling from 766 per 100,000 in 1985 to 945 per 100,000 in 1996 and dropping to 620 per 100,000 in 2009.

Figure 44 Property-related crime: Memphis, Tennessee

Sources: FBI, Uniform Crime Reports, National Archive of Criminal Justice Data

There were divergent trends in property-related street crime rates in Memphis during this time (Figure 44). Although the motor vehicle theft rate declined 65 percent from 1,794 per 100,000 in 1985 to 628 per 100,000 in 2009, the larceny-theft rate increased 26 percent from 3,452 per 100,000 in 1985 to 4,354 per 100,000 in 2009. The burglary rate exhibited a modest decline (14 percent) from 2,427 per 100,000 in 1985 to 2,089 per 100,000 in 2009.

Figure 45 Crimes committed against persons: Baltimore, Maryland

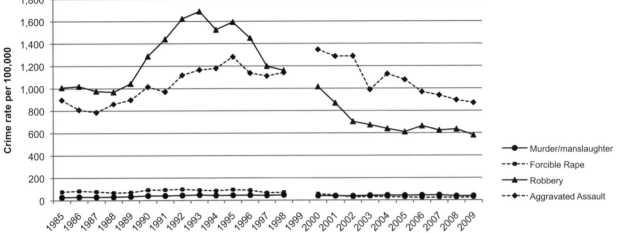

Note: 1999 data were unavailable
Sources: FBI, Uniform Crime Reports, National Archive of Criminal Justice Data

Baltimore, Maryland, was tied with Detroit as the other city with the largest population reduction (17 percent) from 1985 to 2009. One of the street crime rates for those committed against persons remained stable during this period while the others grew or fell (Figure 45). The aggravated assault rate exhibited a minor overall change (3 percent) from the 1985 rate of 898 per 100,000 to the 2009 rate of 871 per 100,000. The murder and non-negligent manslaughter rate, in contrast, rose 35 percent from 28 per 100,000 in 1985 to 37 per 100,000 in 2009. The forcible rape rate and the robbery rate both declined, with the forcible rape rate dropping from 77 per 100,000 to 25 per 100,000 while the robbery rate decreased from 1,008 per 100,000 in 1985 to 580 per 100,000 in 2009.

Figure 46 Property-related crime: Baltimore, Maryland

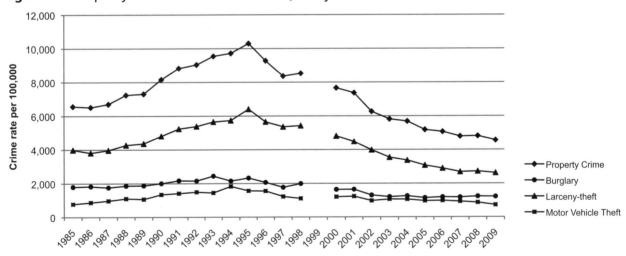

Note: 1999 data were unavailable
Sources: FBI, Uniform Crime Reports, National Archive of Criminal Justice Data

The property-related crime rates in Baltimore followed patterns similar to one another (Figure 46). The burglary rate swelled from 1,799 per 100,000 in 1985 to its peak of 2,442 per 100,000 in 1993 before falling to 1,221 per 100,000 in 2009. Similarly, the larceny-theft rate grew from 3,986 per 100,000 in 1985 to 6,405 per 100,000 in 1995 before dropping to 2,621 per 100,000 in 2009. The motor vehicle theft rate increased from 781 per 100,000 in 1985 to a high of 1,831 per 100,000 in 1994 before falling to 724 per 100,000 in 2009.

Figure 47 Crimes committed against persons: Louisville, Kentucky

Note: Data prior to 2004 were unavailable and reporting practices changed in 2005
Sources: FBI, Uniform Crime Reports, National Archive of Criminal Justice Data

Louisville, Kentucky, merged with Jefferson County in 2003, which prohibited accurate comparison of the city's 1985 population with the new 2009 geography of the city. This merger made observing trends in street crime during this period virtually impossible. The trends in street crime rates related to crimes committed against persons based on the available data are presented in Figure 47. Louisville experienced slight increases in three measures of street crime committed against persons. The murder and non-negligent manslaughter rate increased 11 percent from 9 per 100,000 in 2005 to 10 per 100,000 in 2009. The forcible rape rate also increased (9 percent) from 34 per 100,000 in 2005 to 36 per 100,000 in 2009. The aggravated assault rate was the third measure to increase slightly (4 percent) during this time from 290 per 100,000 in 2005 to 302 per 100,000 in 2009. In contrast, the robbery rate decreased (15 percent) from 292 per 100,000 to 249 per 100,000 in 2009.

Figure 48 Property-related crime: Louisville, Kentucky

Note: Data prior to 2004 were unavailable and reporting practices changed in 2005
Sources: FBI, Uniform Crime Reports, National Archive of Criminal Justice Data

The patterns of property-related crime rates for Louisville are presented in Figure 48. The motor vehicle theft rate decreased 46 percent from 505 per 100,000 in 2005 to 274 per 100,000 in 2009. The burglary rate remained fairly stable (2 percent decline) from 1,146 per 100,000 in 2005 to 1,122 per 100,000 in 2009. The larceny-theft rate increased slightly (4 percent) from 2,750 per 100,000 in 2005 to 2,866 per 100,000 in 2009.

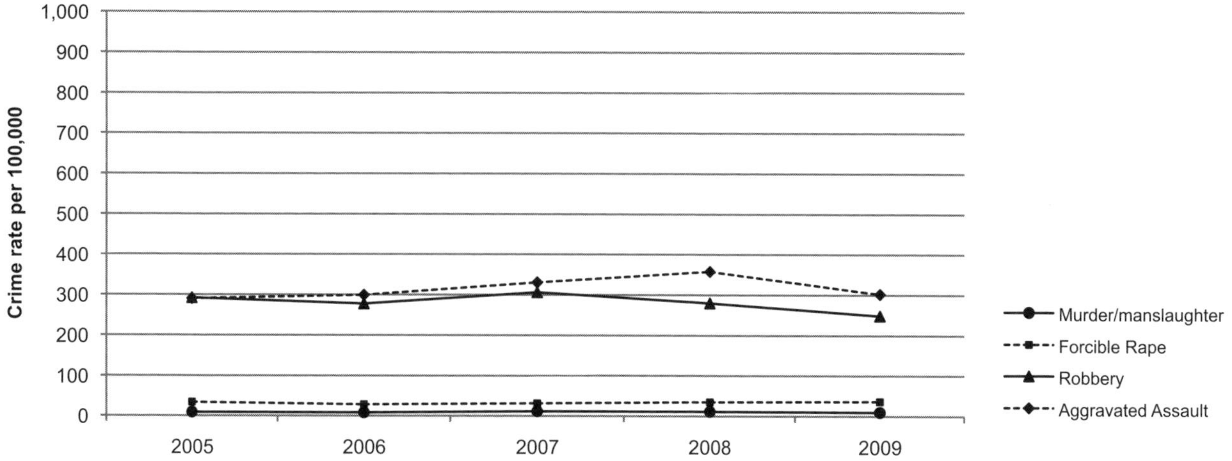

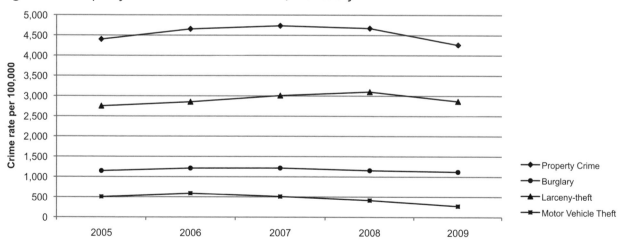

Figure 49 Crimes committed against persons: Boston, Massachusetts

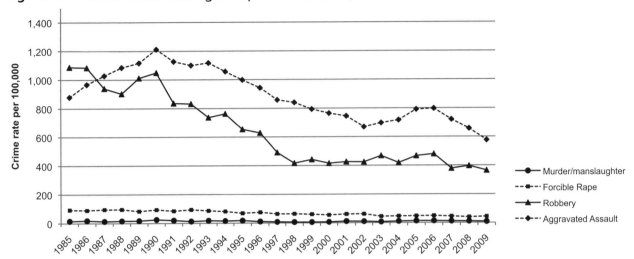

Sources: FBI, Uniform Crime Reports, National Archive of Criminal Justice Data

Boston, Massachusetts, generally exhibited a downward trend in rates of street crimes committed against persons from 1985 to 2009 (Figure 49). The city's robbery rate steadily declined from its peak of 1,087 per 100,000 in 1985 to 365 per 100,000 in 2009. The aggravated assault rate increased from 879 per 100,000 in 1985 to its height in 1990 (1,212 per 100,000) before falling to 576 per 100,000 in 2009. A similar trend was observed among murder and non-negligent manslaughter, which grew from 1985 (15 per 100,000) to 1990 (25 per 100,000) before dropping to 8 per 100,000 in 2009. The forcible rape rate decreased 54 percent, from 93 per 100,000 in 1985 to 43 per 100,000 in 2009.

Figure 50 Property-related crime: Boston, Massachusetts

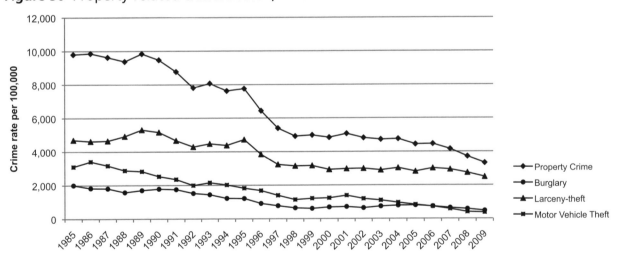

Sources: FBI, Uniform Crime Reports, National Archive of Criminal Justice Data

The property-related crime rate trends in Boston all followed a general downward trajectory (Figure 50). The burglary rate steadily decreased 76 percent from 2,001 per 100,000 in 1985 to 473 per 100,000 in 2009. The larceny-theft rate also steadily decreased after it peaked in 1989 (5,308 per 100,000) to 2,484 per 100,000 in 2009. The motor vehicle theft rate reached its height in 1986 (3,410 per 100,000) and steadily declined through 2009 (366 per 100,000).

Figure 51 Crimes committed against persons: El Paso, Texas

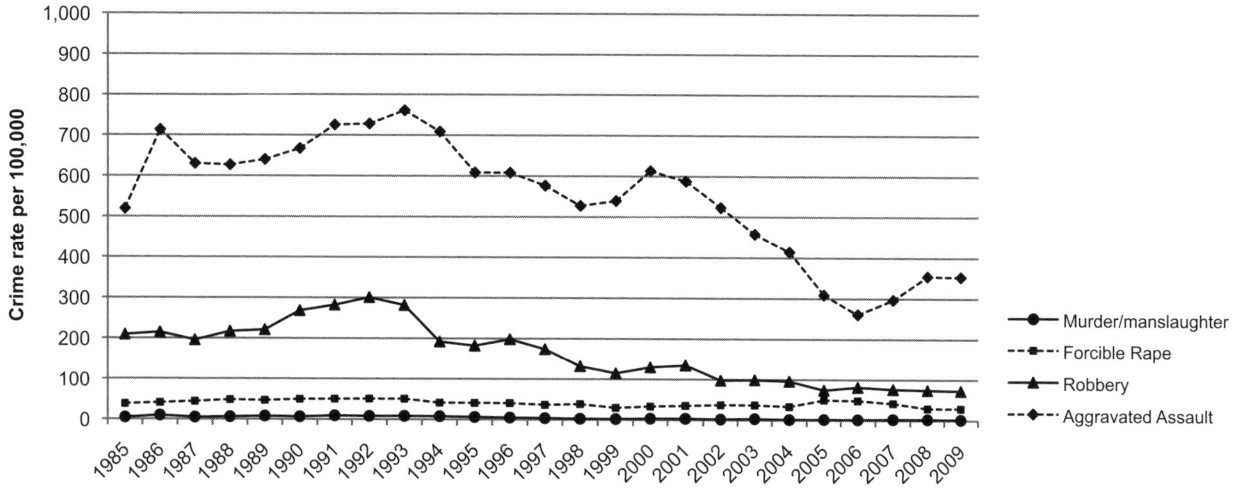

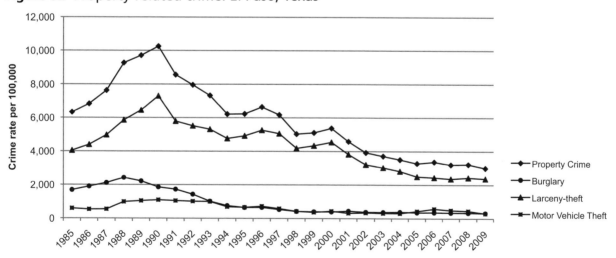

Sources: FBI, Uniform Crime Reports, National Archive of Criminal Justice Data

El Paso, Texas, rounded out the top 25 largest U.S. cities in 2009. Overall, the city's street crime rates for those committed against persons declined from 1985 to 2009 (Figure 51). The murder and non-negligent manslaughter rate fell 59 percent from 5 per 100,000 in 1985 to 2 per 100,000 in 2009, and the robbery rate dropped 65 percent from 209 per 100,000 to 73 per 100,000 in 2009. The forcible rape rate decreased more modestly (23 percent) from 38 per 100,000 in 1985 to 29 per 100,000 in 2009, and the aggravated assault rate fell 32 percent from 519 per 100,000 in 1985 to 353 per 100,000 in 2009.

Figure 52 Property-related crime: El Paso, Texas

Sources: FBI, Uniform Crime Reports, National Archive of Criminal Justice Data

The property-related street crime rates in El Paso fluctuated a fair amount from 1985 to 2009 (Figure 52). The burglary rate, for instance, swelled from 1985 (1,686 per 100,000) to 1988 (2,425 per 100,000) before falling to 340 per 100,000 in 2009. The larceny-theft rate followed a similar trajectory, increasing from 1985 (4,045 per 100,000) to 1990 (7,298 per 100,000) before dipping to 2,367 per 100,000 in 2009. The motor vehicle rate also grew from 1985 (594 per 100,000) to 1990 (1,094 per 100,000) and then steadily declined to 305 per 100,000 in 2009.

Contributions to Cities' Street Crime Increase in the 1980s

This close examination of street crime trends shows that most of the 25 largest U.S. cities experienced similar patterns in these crime rates. Street crime appeared to increase during the latter portion of the 1980s into the first part of the 1990s, with a steady pattern of decline taking place from that point forward. Although many explanations have been offered to account for the observed increase in the late 1980s, the simplest is related to the enhanced reporting efficiency that began to emerge at the time. Robert O'Brien demonstrated that the height of street crime prevalence peaked at a time when the reliability of official recording of criminal incidents increased dramatically. The advent of reliable computer databases, for example, helped streamline and organize the recording process. In addition to these improved recording tools and techniques, the National Crime and Victimization Surveys (NCVS) also show that the offender-generated rates (i.e., self-reported offending) of street crime generally began declining in the early 1990s. Crime was being recorded with greater reliability and there was also a marked decreased in actual offenses taking place.

The burgeoning crack cocaine trade also played a significant role in the increase in urban street crime in the 1980s. Crack cocaine is a crystalline form of cocaine. It is usually smoked and produces a quickly realized (due to its route of administration through lung tissue) yet short-lived high. Crack gained recognition as a popular street drug in the latter half of 1985 and early 1986 as it emerged in the largest cities on each coast (i.e., Los Angeles and New York). The intense yet relatively brief physiological effects of the drug contributed to strong reinforcement for continued use, leading to assertions such as, "Try it once and you're hooked for life!" However, James Inciardi found only a minority of those who did smoke crack cocaine engaged in consistent use on a daily basis. Despite the reality of the low numbers of regular crack cocaine users, the media latched on to the story and crack cocaine monopolized news headlines for an extended period of time.

The great deal of media attention devoted to the crack epidemic, as it has come to be known, eventually demanded criminal justice and public policy responses aimed at the amelioration of the crime wave that had taken hold of America's cities. Sensationalized stories about babies born to mothers who smoked crack cocaine and the uncontrollable increase in the number of impoverished inner-city residents, mostly African American, who were addicted to the substance dominated the airwaves in the late 1980s. These stories ultimately supported harsher sentencing structures for those arrested for possession of crack (versus powder cocaine), and they supported justifications for steady increases in antidrug program funding. Law enforcement and public school programs ranging from government-funded sources to corporate enterprises, such as the Partnership for a Drug-Free America, became fully dedicated to the complete eradication of crack cocaine from America's cities.

These dramatized media claims and the accompanying political rhetoric also singled out crack cocaine as the primary cause of the drastic spike in urban street crime. In reality, crack cocaine appeared most often in disenfranchised inner-city neighborhoods already suffering from high unemployment rates and few opportunities for economic advancement: settings likely to foster drug use and street crime at any given time. In other words, the neighborhoods where crack cocaine appeared and use was most prevalent were already susceptible to high rates of street crime. Therefore, there were many possible causes of increases in crime at the time and crack cocaine, which cannot be singled out as the sole culprit, was certainly a contributing factor.

In fact, research conducted in New York City in 1988, the peak of the crack cocaine era, identified how crack cocaine may have played a significant role in the escalation of violent street crime. For instance, slightly over half (52.7 percent) of homicides that occurred in 1988 in the study's sample were in some way drug-related. Examining these data more closely revealed about one-fourth (26 percent) of drug-related homicides were related specifically to crack cocaine sales, with the most common cause being attributed to territorial disputes between rival crack dealers. These disputes may have come at a time when young, inexperienced crack dealers were competing for a share of the crack market. Semiautomatic handguns were also becoming more available on the streets during the late 1980s, which undoubtedly allowed these disputes to easily escalate to the point of violence.

The Street Crime Decline in America's Top 25 Cities

Several innovative policing practices were adopted in direct response to the relatively high levels of urban street crime recorded in American cities in the late 1980s. At least two of these practices have been acknowledged as significant factors in the reduction of street crime, especially in New York City. The first was implemented as a targeted approach to reduce gun-related violence and came in the form of "hand gun checks." Police on patrol would initiate contact with anyone appearing to have a "suspicious bulge" in their clothing. After approaching persons with this noticeable protrusion in their clothing, police would ask them to explain the reason for it. If the bulge was, in fact, due to the concealment of a handgun, police would be able to address the situation accordingly and proactively remove at least one variable likely to foster violent street crime. Similar patrols directed specifically at firearm reduction in Indianapolis also resulted in a decrease in the number of homicides where these patrols took place.

The second practice came in the form of general quality-of-life enforcement procedures, which were also intended as more proactive approaches to street crime suppression. Police in New York City became much more focused on routinely stopping anyone on the street who was suspicious of having committed any of a variety of minor offenses. Suspects would be asked to provide identification, and police officers would subsequently perform a check for outstanding arrest warrants and address the suspects as their past criminal justice involvement dictated.

It was also during the early to mid-1990s when many police departments, including San Diego and Baltimore, began implementing variations of problem-oriented policing models. This policing approach focuses police attention toward resolving issues within the community rather than on police administration. This model also places a high value on evaluating problems relative to a wide variety of potential solutions while collecting feedback from key players outside of the police organization. Problem-oriented policing's concentration on positive policing outcomes as opposed to policing processes has differentiated this approach as an effective crime control strategy.

Although police practices and their outcomes enjoy positive valuation for their successful approaches to reducing street crime in the 1990s, these may not be the only factors that bolstered the continued downward trend that has largely lasted into the 2000s. For example, the 1994 omnibus crime bill led to a 14 percent increase (approximately 50,000–60,000) in the number of police officers per capita during this time period. It is estimated that this increase in the number of police officers subsequently led to an estimated reduction in crime by 5 to 6 percent. These additional police forces also likely contributed to the growth in incarceration rates during the same period. The U.S. incarceration rate more than doubled from 200 per 100,000 in 1985 to 502 per 100,000 in 2009. The added number of police officers and the incapacitation of such a significant proportion of offenders likely accounted for at least some portion of the drop in crime during the period.

Researchers have also investigated other explanations for the steady decline in national street crime rates during this period. Some of the large-scale policy-driven explanations include the positive effects stemming from increased levels of education in the United States, a healthy economy, the benefits of welfare programs, and the changing age structure (i.e., "aging out" of the developmental period of high proclivity toward crime). However viable these explanations may be, it is unlikely any one worked independently of the others. It is instead more likely that a combination of criminal justice factors, public policy initiatives, and individual-level variables continue to influence the steady decrease in street crime into the new millennium.

Index

Index note: Article titles and their page numbers are in **boldface**.

A

ABA (American Bar Association), 7
abduction. *See also* **kidnapping**
  children as victims, 72
  National Incidence Studies of Missing, Abducted,
    Run-Away, and Throwaway Children
    (NISMART-I), 233
Abel, I. W., 231
abortion clinics
  bombings, xxxi
  murders, xxxi, xxxiv, xxxv, xxxvi
Abraham, Jauhar, xxxvi
abuse. *See also* **domestic violence**; **sex crimes**; violence
  ADAM II, 5
  Anti-Drug Abuse Act, xxxii
  CAPTA, 71
  child molester, 462
  children as victims, 71
  National Institute of Drug Abuse, xxxi
  NCANDS, 71
  sexual exploitation of children, 465
access control, 115
accountability, 331–332
ACLU (American Civil Liberties Union), xxxi, 80, 305
acquaintance kidnapping, 234
activities. *See also* **routine activity theory**
  Asian gangs, 13
  La Eme (Mexican Mafia), 236
  MS-13, 275
  skinheads, 380
  street gangs, xxxvi, 168–169
activity support, 115–116

ADAM (Arrestee Drug Abuse Monitoring Program),
  461
Adam-12, 413
ADAM II (Arrestee Drug Abuse Monitoring Program), 5
Addams, Jane, 256
administrative function of jails, 215–216
African Americans, xxviii. *See also* **Crips**; **racial
  assault**; **racial profiling**
  causes of death, xxxvi
  driving while black, 348–349
  gangs, xxxv
  riots, xxx
  underage drinking, 143
aggravated larceny, 420
Agustin, Laura, 340
Albany Trilogy (Kennedy), 336
alcohol and drug testing, on-scene, 1–3.
  See also **open-container laws**
  blood alcohol level, 2
  DUI, 1
  DWI, 1
  motor skills testing, 1–2
  technologies for, 2–3
alcohol and drug use, xxviii, xxxv, **3–5**. *See also* **bars
  and pubs**; cocaine; **drinking, underage**; **drinking
  establishments, unlicensed**; heroin; **needle
  exchanges**; **open-container laws**; Prohibition;
  speakeasies (1920s)
  ADAM II, 5
  Alcohol, Tobacco, Firearms and Explosives (ATF),
    373

crime and, 3–4
data, 5
diversionary and specialty court programs, 5
drug-defined offenses, 3
drug-related offenses, 3
drug-using lifestyle, 4
mental illness and, 255
shaping perceptions, 4
sociological models and crime policy, 4–5
street matrix, 5
subculture theories, 4
alienation, 82–84
ALKQN (Almighty Latin King and Queen Nation), 238–239
Allen, Barry, 179
Almighty Latin King and Queen Nation (ALKQN), 238–239
AMA (American Motorcycle Association), 272
AMBER Alert system, xxxv, xxxvi, 461
American Bar Association (ABA), 7
American Civil Liberties Union (ACLU), xxxi, 80, 305
American Federation for Social Hygiene, xxviii
American Kin, 137
American Me, 236
American Motorcycle Association (AMA), 272
American Psychological Association, 65
American Purity Alliance, xxviii
American Vigilance Committee, xxviii
America's Most Wanted, 399, 413, 414, 461
Anderson, Elijah, 82–83, 279, 436
Anglin, D., 146
Annie E. Casey Foundation, 18
Anthony, Carmelo, 81
Anti-Drug Abuse Act, xxxii
anti-Filipino riots, xxviii
anti-gambling vigilante groups, xxvii
anti-graffiti campaigns, 181–182
anti-homosexual attacks, xxxiv
anti-Semitic attacks, xxxiii
appeals system, 95–96
Araujo, Cheryl Ann, 54
Arizona v. Grant, 7
Arntfield, Michael, 413
arrest, 6–8. *See also* **alcohol and drug testing, on-scene; bail; courts; jails; Miranda warnings; police (overview); stop and frisk**
ADAM II, 5
arson, 10
definitions and probable cause, 6
LAPD Crime and Arrest Weekly Statistics Report, 244
literature, 7–8
post-arrest matters, 7
stop and frisk, 6
warrants and misdemeanors, 6–7

Arrestee Drug Abuse Monitoring Program (ADAM), 461
Arrestee Drug Abuse Monitoring Program (ADAM II), 5, 461
arson, 8–11
arrests, 10
incidence, 8
investigations, 10
patterns, 9
types, 8–10
The Art of Jail Admissions and Processing (McLaughlin), 57
Aryan Brotherhood, 236, 380
Aryan Circle, 380
Asian Boyz, 225
Asian gangs, 11–14
Chinese gangs, 12
demographic diversity, 11
ethnic identity and image, 11–12
historical influences, 12–13
Indochinese gangs, 12
Japanese American street gangs, 12
Korean gangs, 12
law enforcement response, 13–14
research, 13
structure and activities, 13
assassination
Kennedy, John F., xxx
King, Martin Luther, Jr., 231
assault. *See* **homophobic assault; racial assault; rape and sexual assault**
ATF (Federal Bureau of Alcohol, Tobacco Firearms, and Explosives), 373
Atlanta Child Murders, xxxi
Atlantic Monthly, 46, 292
attitudes, counterfeit goods, 91
Atwater v. city of Lago Vista, 7

B
bail, 15–17. *See also* **arrest; courts**
development, 43
excessive bails and fines, 463
industry size, 17
nonfinancial, 16
options, 15–16
origins, 15
preventive detention, 16
Bail Reform Act of 1984, 16
Baltimore, Maryland, 17–19
Annie E. Casey Foundation, 18
gun buyback program, 18
police and law enforcement, 18
police corruption, 18
structural concerns, 17

Bandidos, 272
bank robbery, **19–22**. *See also* **theft and larceny**
 definition and history, 19–20
 in Great Depression, 20
 in popular culture, 20–21
 scope and character, 21
Banksy, 393
bar personnel, **22–25**. *See also* **alcohol and drug use**;
 bars and pubs
 door culture and bouncers, 23
 instigators of violence, 22
 research, 22–25
 servers and intoxication, 23–24
Barbary Coast, 364
Barger, Ralph ("Sonny"), 273
Barker, Thomas, 326
Barrio Azteca, 236
Barrios, Luis, 237
Barrow, Clyde, 20
bars and pubs, **26–28**; *See also* **alcohol and drug use**;
 drinking establishments, unlicensed; **speakeasies**
 (1920s)
 environments, 26–27
 key factors to target, 27
 research, 26
The Battered Woman (Walker), 138
Bayard, John, xxxiv
Beach, Howard, xxxii
Beat era, 364
begging. *See* **panhandling or begging**
behaviors
 risky lifestyles, 356–357
 road rage, 358
Bell Sean, 347
benign flash mobs, 163
Best, Joel, 60
bicycle theft, **28–30**
 extent, 28
 outstanding questions, 29
 prevention, 29
 victimization, 28–29
Big Five, 272
Big Four, 272
The Bikeriders (Lyon), 272
Bingo, xxix
biological warfare agents, 3
Birmingham church bombing, 1963, xxx, 370
black bloc anarchists, 269
Black Guerrilla Family, 236
black market, **30–32**. *See also* **counterfeit goods**
 causes and costs, 31
 persistent plague, 30–31
 prostitution and sex trafficking, 31–32
 research, 30

blackmail, **32–34**. *See also* extortion
 attack on respectability, 33
 bribery and, 33
 extortion and, 33
 gang fealty, 33–34
 prevalence and history, 33
 research, 33
 victimizing dependency, 34
Blakely, Edward J., 172
Blink (Gladwell), 137
blitz rape, 376
Block, Richard, 250
blood alcohol level, 2
Bloods, xxx, **34–36**, 225, 291, **461**
 leadership, 36
 origin in strive, 35
 structure and crime impact, 35–36
Bloomberg, Michael, 185
blue laws, xxvii, xxix, xxxvi, **36–38**, 461
 corruption and, 38
 current thinking, 37–38
 origin and resistance, 36–37
 Supreme Court and, 37
bombings
 abortion clinics, xxxi
 Birmingham church bombing, 1963, xxx, 370
Bonnie and Clyde, 20
Booker, Cory, 292, 293
boosters, 377
bootleggers, **38–39**, 382. *See also* **alcohol and
 drug use**; **drinking establishments, unlicensed**;
 Prohibition; **speakeasies (1920s)**
 current, 39
 in entertainment industry, 39
 famous bootleggers, 39
 history, 38
Boston, Massachusetts, **40–43**. *See also* **Operation
 Ceasefire**
 Boston Police Department (BPD), 40–42
 current crime problems and control efforts,
  41–43
 Operation Ceasefire, 40–41,
  299–300
 Operation Night Light, 40–41
Boston Police Department (BPD), 40–42
Boston Strangler, xxx
bouncers, xxvii, 23
bounty hunters, **43–45**, 461
 bail and surety development, 43
 image, 44
 impetus to professionalize, 44
 PBUS, 44
 ROR, 43–44
 Supreme Court on, 44

Bowery Boys, xxvii
Bowie, James ("Jim"), 186
Boyum, David, 151
BPD (Boston Police Department), 40–42
Braga, Anthony, 41, 300
Brando, Marlon, xxix, 467
Bratton, William, 45–46, 48, 178–179
    career steps, 45
    impact on crime, 46, 248
Brawley, Tawana. *See* **Tawana Brawley incident**
breathalyzer, 2
Brehm, Sharon S., 137
bribery, 33, 382
Bringer v. United States, 6
Britto, Sarah, 415
Broadway Boys, xxvii
Broken Windows Theory, 47–49, 132, 201
    critics, 48
    disrupting the spiral, 47–48
    in Newark, New Jersey, 292
    revolution and reaction, 48
    urban incivility and, 429–430
Brooke, Edward, 231
Brotherton, David, 237
Brown, Byron W., 50
Brown, James, 411
Brownstein, Henry, 150
Budd, Grace, xxix
Buerger, M., 205
Buffalo, New York, 49–51
    response of law enforcement, 50
    street crime trends, 49–50
Bullard, Robert, 155
bullet-lead analysis, 122
bullying, xxxvi, 120
Bureau of Justice Statistics, 3
Burgess, Ernest, 61, 434
burglary, 51–54. *See also* **bank robbery; bicycle theft;**
  credit card theft; metal theft; motor vehicle theft;
  mugging; theft and larceny
    burglar preferences, 52–53
    motivation and target selection, 51–52
    NCVS data, 51
    prevention and deterrence, 53
    rate of incidence, 51
    UCR data, 51
Burns, Sarah, 60
Bursik, Robert, 434
Bush, George W., xxxvi
Byrd, James, 346
bystander apathy, 54–55
    examples, 55–56
    historical example, 54
    research, 54–55

bystander effect, 462
bystander psychology, 173–174

C
Cabey, Darrell, 179
Cagney & Lacey, 399, 415
Calling All Cars, 398
Cameron, Mary Owen, 377
Campus P.D., 2
Campus Sexual Assault Victims Bill of Rights, xxxiv
Canty, Troy, 179
Capone, Al, xxviii, 39, 382
CAPTA (Child Abuse Prevention and Treatment Act), 71
Cardenas-Guillen, 302
carjacking, 270–271
Carlin, Leo, 291
Caro-Quintero, 302
Cashman, Brian, 33
Casolaro, Peter, 60
Caulkins, Jonathan, 151
CCTV. *See* **closed-circuit television**
CDR (child death reports), 71
Cellular, 87
Centers for Disease Control and Prevention, xxxvi, 223
central booking, 57–58. *See also* **arrest; bail; courts;**
  jails
    problems and resolutions, 57
    sequence and process of jail admissions, 57
The Central Park Five (Burns), 60
Central Park jogger incident, 58–61, 376.
  See also **rape and sexual assault**
    aftermath, 60
    Central Park Five, xxxvii, 58, 60
    confessions and convictions, 59
    convictions vacated, 60
    DNA evidence, 60
    response, 59–60
    wilding, 60
    writing and analysis, 60
Chamberlain Kahn bill, xxviii
Chambliss, William, 405
Charlie's Angels, 399
Chen, Vincent, xxxii
Chermak, Steve, 212
Chesney-Lind, Meda, 443
Chicago, Illinois, 61–65
    anti-gang ordinance, xxxiv
    Chicago Eight, 64
    Chicago School, 61–62
    corruption, 64
    Democratic National Convention of 1968 police riot,
      63–64
    Division Street riot, xxx
    Franks murder, 63

homicides, 63
    law enforcement, 64
    loitering, 240–241
    race riot of 1919, 62–63
    St. Valentine's Day massacre of 1929, 63
Child Abuse Prevention and Treatment Act (CAPTA), 71
child death reports (CDR), 71
child in need of supervision (CHIN), 425
Child Maltreatment 2009, 71
child molesters, 65–66, 462
    community and, 65–66
    evolution of, 65
    managing, 66
    sex crimes against youth, 65
Child Savers, 425
children, commercial sexual exploitation of, 66–70
    defined, 66
    nature and extent, 67–68
    pimps and, 68–69
    prevention and intervention, 69
    research, 68
    as social problem, 67
    violence and, 69
children as victims, 70–74
    Amber Alert system, xxxv, xxxvi, 461
    Atlanta Child Murders, xxxi
    child molester, 462
    Department of Justice on, 72
    Jessica's Law, xxxvi
    Megan's Law, xxxiv, xxxv, xxxvi
    Missing Children's Assistance Act, xxxii
    Missing Children's Day, xxxi
    National Center for Missing and Exploited Children, xxxi, xxxii
    National Resource Center and Clearinghouse on Missing and Exploited Children, xxxii
    NCMEC on, 72
    NCVS on, 70
    non-family abduction, 72
    offense categories, 70–71
    online, 73
    physical abuse and neglect, 71
    property crimes, 71
    research, 73
    sexual exploitation of children, 465
    sexual victimization, 465
    St. Louis, Missouri, 384
    UCR on, 70
Chimel v. California, 7
CHIN (child in need of supervision), 425
Chinchesters, xxviii
Chinese gangs, xxvii, 12
CHiPs, 399

Cho, Seung-Hui, 370
Christ, Harry, Jr., 410
Christie, Agatha, 398
Cicero, Theodore, 148
Cincinnati, Ohio, 74–76
    challenges and history, 74
    crime spike of 2001 to 2002, 75
    gun violence, 76
    law enforcement response, 75–76
    street crime, 74–75
cities, 114, 131. *See also specific cities*
    Safer Cities Initiative, 176
    urbanization, 433–434
City of Chicago v. Morales, xxxiv
Civil Rights Act of 1968, 64
Civil War, U.S., 37, 147, 187, 227, 343, 383
The Civilizing Process (Elias), 430
Clarke, Ronald, 118–120
Cleveland, Ohio, 76–79
    persistent crime, 78
    police department strife, 76–78
Clinton, Bill, xxxiv, 41, 386
closed-circuit television, 79–81, 250, 369
    development and spread, 79–80
    probing effectiveness, 80
    for vandalism, 438
The Closer, 411, 415
cocaine, xxxii, 3, 5, 86, 104. *See also* **alcohol and drug testing, on-scene; alcohol and drug use; crack house; drug dealing; drug markets, open-air;** heroin
code of silence/stop snitching, 81–82
    riding social wave, 81
    sliding scale, 81
    social pressure and response, 81–82
code of the street, 82–84, 462
    academic and policy responses, 84
    alienation and approaches, 82–84
Code of the Street (Anderson), 279
Cohen, Albert, 4
Cohen, Lawrence E., 360
Coker, Ann, 353
Coker v. Georgia, xxxi
Cold Case, 415
Colombo organization, 178
Colors, 461
Colquhoun, 256
Columbine High School killings, xxxv, 371
Commission on Public Health, xxxiii
communications, patrol cars, 306–306
community. *See also* **gated communities;** neighborhoods; **neighborhood watch; street/block parties**
    child molesters and, 65–66
    juvenile offending programs, 225

Milwaukee, Wisconsin, problem-solving, 261
Strategic Approaches to Community Safety Initiative (SACSI), 41
Weed and Seed, 449
community policing, xxxiv, **84–86**, 462
    background, 84–85
    philosophy, 85
    theory and practice, 85
Community Resources Against Street Hoodlums, 86–87
    legacy, 87
    mission, 86
    Rampart scandal, 86–87
complete streets, 219
CompStat, xxxv, **87–90**, 280, 462
    crime mapping, 88–89
    developments since, 89
    Indianapolis, Indiana, 213
    NYPD and, 89
    street crime and, 90
confessions, 59
Connally, John, xxx
Connery, Sean, 244
conscience collective, 267
Constitution, U.S., 6, 15, 332, 466. *See also specific amendments*
convictions, 59–60
Copes, H., 141
Cops, 2, 411, 413, 414
Cordner, Gary, 85
Corman, James, 231
The Corner (Simon), 17
corporate corruption, 413
corruption, 198, 394. *See also* **blackmail**; extortion; **police corruption, street-level**
    blue laws and, 38
    Chicago, Illinois, 64
    corporate, 413
    environmental criminology and, 156
    Giuliani targeting, 178
    Miami, Florida, 258
    NYPD, 327–328
    organized crime and violence, 301
    RICO, 236, 301
    San Francisco, California, 363
    speakeasies, 381–382
    St. Louis, Missouri, 382
    sting operations and, 388–389
costs. *See also* economics
    black market, 31
    drug courts, 99
    metal theft, 256–257
    shoplifting, 376–377
    vandalism, 438

counterfeit goods, **90–92**. *See also* **black market**
    combating, 92
    immigration and globalization, 91
    imports and attitudes, 91
    types, 90–91
countermeasures
    bank robbery, 21–22
    door-to-door scam artists, 140–141
    fear of crime, 162
    murder/homicide, 279–280
    tourist victims, 444–445
    vandalism, 438–439
County of Riverside v. McLaughlin, 7
Court TV, 414
courts, 92–97. *See also* **arrest; bail; central booking;** Supreme Court, U.S.
    appeals system, 95–96
    case volume, 93–94
    diversionary and specialty programs, 5
    drug courts, 462
    procedures and processes, 94
    sentencing, 95
    tiers and jurisdictions, 93
    trial ways and means, 94–95
courts, drug, 97–100
    costs and benefits, 99
    future challenges, 100
    juvenile, 99–100
    origins, 97
    teams and treatments, 97–99
courts, mental health, 100–103
    concept, 100–101
    judges and, 102
    regional differences, 101
    research, 101–102
COYOTE, xxxi
Cozens, Paul, 117
CPTED (crime prevention through environmental design), 432
crack house, 103–105. *See also* **alcohol and drug use;** cocaine; **drug dealing; drug markets, open-air**
    levels of enforcement, 104–105
    scales of crime and disorder, 103
    violence and women, 103–105
crackdowns
    credit card theft, 106–107
    massage parlors, 252–253
CRASH. *See* **Community Resources Against Street Hoodlums**
credit card theft, 105–107
    FBI crackdowns, 106–107
    identify theft, 106
    industrial scale, 106–107
Cressey, Donald, 405

crime. *See also* **mass transit, crime on**; property
  crimes; **sex crimes**; violence
    alcohol and drug use and, 3–4
    Baltimore, Maryland, 18
    Boston, Massachusetts, 41–43
    Bratton's impact on, 46
    Cleveland, Ohio, 78
    crack house, 103
    Detroit, Michigan, 133
    guns and weapons and, 190
    Indianapolis, Indiana, 212
    juvenile offending, 224–225
    Minneapolis, Minnesota, 263
    Newark, New Jersey, 291–292
    peep show connections, 308
    in the projects, 338–339
    public-order, 342–343
    sociological models and policy, 4–5
    speakeasies, 381–382
    state, 198–199
    Washington, D.C., 447–448
    white collar, 403–405
  crime, displacement of, 107–109
    empirical evidence, 108–109
    types and levels, 108
  Crime Concern, 249
  Crime Doesn't Pay, 398
  crime fighters, 322
  crime mapping, 109–111
    applicability to criminology, 110–111
    CompStat and, 88–89
    history and development, 109–110
  crime patterns, 111–114. *See also* **crime patterns**
    arson, 9
    explaining trends, 113–114
    individual, spatial, temporal, 113
    individual crime, 113
    juvenile offending, 224–225
    models, 113
    observing, 111–112
    risky lifestyles, 354–356
    spatial crime, 113
    temporal crime, 113
    theory, 114
    underage drinking, 142–143
  crime prevention, environmental design, 114–118
    access control, 115
    activity support, 115–116
    empirical evidence, 116–117
    image, 115
    key aspects, 115–116
    limitations, 117
    surveillance, 115
    target hardening, 116

    territoriality, 115
    theoretical development, 114–115
  crime prevention, situational, 118–120
    categories, 118
    hot spots, 119
    locations, 118
    offenders, 118–119
    opportunity reduction, 118
  crime prevention through environmental design
    (CPTED), 432
  crime scene investigation, 120–123
    CSI syndrome, 122
    history and development, 121
    procedure, 122
    technology, 121–122
  crime–consumerism nexus, 123–126
    conception and context, 123–124
    engagement with risk, 124–125
    hyper strain, 124
    insatiability of desire, 124
    instant gratification or impulsivity, 125
  Crimes Against Children Research Center, 70
  Criminal Justice Act, 346
  Criminal Minds, 399
  criminality
    urbanization, 433–434
    women, 451–452
  criminalization
    decriminalizing prostitution, xxxi
    homelessness, 200–201
    mental illness, 253–254
  criminology, 61. *See also* **environmental criminology**
    crime mapping and, 110–111
    immigrant victims, 439–440
    murder/homicide, 279
    pool halls, 336–337
  Crips, xxx, 34–35, **126–128**, 225
    defined, 462
    national and global influence, 127
    origins and symbols, 126–127
  Cromwell, Oliver, 37
  Crossing Jordan, 415
  CSI, 389, 399, 411
  CSI syndrome, 122
  Cuckoos, 383
  Culhane, Dennis, 254
  cultural transmission, 462
  culture. *See also* popular culture
    alcohol and drug use, 4
    bar personnel, 23
    door, 23
    murder/homicide perspective, 279
    subculture theories, 4
  Cuomo, Mario, 178, 410, 411

Curtis, Rick, 68
Curtis, Robert, 175
cyberbullying, 120
cyberstalking, 120

D
Dabney, Dean, 119
Dallas SWAT, 399
Dalton gang, 19
Darley, John M., 54–55
Darrow, Clarence, xxix, 63
Davis, Kenneth Culp, 7
Davis, Sean, 250
day reporting center, 129–130
    advantages, 130
    jurisdictional differences, 130
    range of service types, 129–130
de la Beckwith, Byron, xxx
The Death and Life of Great American Cities (Jacobs, J.), 114, 131
Defensible Space (Newman), 115
defensible space theory, 130–133
    background, 131–132
    public space as private trust, 132
    social control dynamics, 132
deinstitutionalization movement, 254
demographics
    Asian gangs, 11
    shoplifting, 376–377
    theft and larceny, 420
Department of Energy, 257
Department of Justice
    on children as victims, 72
    National Gang Threat Assessment Report, xxxvi
    Prevention and Control of Urban Disorders, 258
    on sex trafficking, 375
    Violent Gang Sage Streets Task Force, 14
Department of Transportation (DOT), 1
destructive flash mobs, 163
deterrence
    burglary, 53
    Gang Prevention and Effective Deterrence Act, xxxvi, 463
Detroit, Michigan, 133–135, 399
    image, 135
    law enforcement, 134–135
    riots, xxx
    street crime, 134
    violent crime, 133
Detroit SWAT, 399
Developmental Victimization Survey, 73

Dewey, Thomas, xxix
Dexter, 399
Diagnostic and Statistical Manual of Mental Disorders, 65
Diallo, Amadou, xxxv, **135–137**
    background and incident, 135–136
    investigation and trial, 136
    protests and legacy, 136–137
Diallo, Sankarella, 137
Diaz, Jose, xxix
Dillinger, Clyde, 20
Dinkins, David, 60, 136, 178
displacement, 175–176
DNA evidence, xxxvi, 60
Dog the Bounty Hunter, 16, 399, 414
Dombrink, John, 259
domestic violence, xxxiv, **137–139**.
    See also **rape and sexual assault**
    cycle of causes, 138–139
    nature of abuse, 137–138
    research, 138
Donnelly, Patrick G., 117
door culture, 23
door-to-door scam artists, 140–141.
    See also **victims, senior**
    obstacles to study, 141
    structure and countermeasures, 140
    victims, 141
DOT (Department of Transportation), 1
Doyle, Arthur Conan, 203
Dragnet, 389, 399, 411, 413, 415
drinking, underage, 142–144. *See also* **alcohol and drug use**
    African Americans, 143
    age and ethnic patterns, 142–143
    consequences, 143
    Hispanics, 143
    prevention, 143
    research, 142
drinking establishments, unlicensed, 144–145.
    See also **alcohol and drug use; bootleggers; speakeasies (1920s)**
    investigations and enforcement, 144–145
    origins, 144
drive-by shooting, 145–147, 462. *See also* **terrorism**
    gang use, 146
    history and modern era, 146
    incidence, 146
    research, 146
driving under the influence (DUI), 1
driving while black, 348–349
driving while intoxicated (DWI), 1
drug cartels, 302
drug courts, 462

drug dealing, xxvii, **147–150**. *See also* **alcohol and**
    drug use; cocaine; **crack house**
    historic and current profiles, 147–148
    illicit channels for prescription drugs, 148–149
    Miami, Florida, 260
    Milwaukee, Wisconsin, 261–262
    New Orleans, Louisiana, 285–286
    New York City, 289
    research, 148
    shifts in cause and effect, 149
Drug Enforcement Administration, 14
Drug Enforcement Agency, 148
drug markets, open-air, **150–151**
    hot spots, 151
    origins and interventions, 150–151
    regulatory enforcement, 151
    research, 151
drug subculture, 462
Drug Use Forecasting program (DUF), 462
drugs, prescription, **151–154**
    changing enforcement trends, 152
    clinical street setting, 152–153
    criminal justice response, 153
    nonclinical street setting, 153
    numbers, 152
due process victimization, 441
DUF (Drug Use Forecasting program), 462
DUI (driving under the influence), 1
Dunaway v. New York, 6, 392
Durkheim, Émile, 267
Durnal, Evan, 416
Duvall, Robert, 461
DWI (driving while intoxicated), 1
Dynes, Russell, 242–243

E

Easy Rider, 272
Eck, John, 333
Eckstein, M., 146
economics. *See also* costs
    mobs and riots, 267
    Philadelphia, Pennsylvania, 310
Economist, 316
ECPAT (End Child Prostitution in Asian Tourism), 72
edgeworkers, 357
Edmond Post Office Massacre, 371
Egan's Rats, 383
Eighteenth Amendment, xxviii, xxix, 37, 39, 462
Eighth Amendment, 15, 16
Eisenhower, Dwight, 364
EJ (Environmental Justice), 155
Elias, Norbert, 430
Ellroy, James, 398
Emanuel, Rahm, 64

End Child Prostitution in Asian Tourism (ECPAT), 72
End Demand campaigns, 221
enforcement. *See also* law enforcement
    crack house, 105
    Drug Enforcement Administration, 14
    Drug Enforcement Agency, 148
    environmental criminology, 157
    hate crime, 195–196
    houses of prostitution, 343–344
    ICE, 14, 215, 218
    "johns," 220–221
    open air drug markets, 151
    prescription drugs, 152
    regulatory, 151
    unlicensed drinking establishments, 144–145
English Bill of Rights, 15
Entrapment, 244
environmental criminology, **155–158**
    corruption and, 156
    injury and death, 157
    scope of green damage, 156
    toxic effects on youth, 156–157
    unequal distributions of toxins, 155–156
    unequal environmental enforcement, 157
Environmental Justice (EJ), 155
Erasistratus, 121
Establishment Clause, 37
Estes, Richard, 68
Eterno, John, 7
ethnography. *See* **urban ethnography**
Evers, Medgar, xxx
evidence
    crime prevention, environmental design, 116–117
    in displacement of crime, 108–109
    DNA, xxxvi, 60
    immigrant neighborhoods, 210
excessive bails and fines, 463
exhibitionism, 373
Exit Through the Gift Shop, 393
exposure, indecent, **158–159**
    flashers, 158
    research, 158
    variables and profiles, 158–159
    victims and consequences, 159
extortion, 33, 382. *See also* **blackmail**; corruption
Exxon Valdez oil spill, 156

F

Facebook, 164
familicide, 371
family kidnapping, 233–234
Faristen, Linda, 60
Faster, 87
FBI. *See* Federal Bureau of Investigation (FBI)

The FBI, 399
fear of crime, 161–162
    effects, 161
    senior victims, 441–442
    trends and countermeasures, 162
    vulnerability, 161–162
Federal Bureau of Alcohol, Tobacco Firearms, and
   Explosives (ATF), 373
Federal Bureau of Investigation (FBI). *See also* Uniform
   Crime Reporting (UCR)
    bullet-lead analysis, 122
    credit card theft crackdown, 106–107
    on gangs, xxxvi
    Hate Crime Statistics, 202
    National Center for Analysis of Violent Crime, 370
    on organized crime and violence, 300–301
    Organized Crime Unit, 290
    prostitution statistics, xxxiv
    Supplementary Homicide Reports, 70
Federal Lottery Act, xxviii
Fein, Steven, 137
felony crimes, 463
Felson, Marcus, 360
feminists, xxxi
fences, 388
Fidelis, Fortunato, 121
Fifth Amendment, 266, 332, 467
Finkelhor, David, 70, 73
First Amendment, 37
Fish, Albert, xxix
Flamingo Casino, xxix
flash mobs, 162–164
    benign or destructive, 163
    legislative and police response, 163–164
flashers, 158
Florencia 13, 225
Florida v. J.L., 391
Florida v. Rodriguez, 390
Florida v. Royer, 392
Fly Boys, xxvii
Flying Tigers, 273
Flynn, Edward, 261–262
Forbes, 13, 227
Forecasting Crime Data (Fox), 113
Forensic Science International, 416
forensics, 121, 416
Forty Thieves, xxvii
41 Shots (Roy), 137
Fourteenth Amendment, 467
Fourth Amendment, 6, 332, 390, 466, 467
Fox, James Allen, 113
Frank, Leo, xxviii
Franks, Bobby, 63
Fresno Bulldogs, 225

Friedli, Otto, xxix
"From Arrest to Inmate to Release," 57

G
Gambino organization, 34, 184
gambling, general, 382
    banned in Boston, xxvii
    Bingo, xxix
    horse racing, xxx
    legalized, 463
    lotteries, xxvii, xxx, xxxi
    mob involvement, xxix
    Nevada legalizing, xxix
    pari-mutuel betting, xxix
    Pittsburgh, Pennsylvania, 317–318
gambling, street, 165–167
    anti-gambling vigilante groups, xxvii
    dangers, 167
    shell game, 167
    street craps, 165–166
    Three-Card Monte, 166–167
gang injunction, 36
Gang Prevention and Effective Deterrence Act, xxxvi,
   463
gang rape, xxxii
gangs (street), xxvii, **167–172**, 466. *See also* **Asian
   gangs**; **Bloods**; **Crips**; **juvenile curfews**; **juvenile
   offending**; **MS-13**; **skinheads**; *specific gangs*
    activity, xxxvi, 168–169
    African American, xxxv
    causes and conditions, 171
    Chicago ordinance, xxxiv
    Chinese, xxvii
    defined, 168
    in defining street crime, 401
    drive-by shooting usage, 146
    ethnic, xxvii
    FBI on, xxxvi
    graffiti and, 181
    Hispanic, xxxiii, xxxv
    juvenile offending, 225
    LAPD units, 246
    Los Angeles, California, xxxi, 245–246
    mental health, 169–170
    Milwaukee, Wisconsin, 261–262
    mixed ethnicities, xxviii
    murder/homicide, xxxvi, 278
    National Gang Intelligence Center, 224–225
    New York City, 289–290
    Pittsburgh, Pennsylvania, 317–318
    prevention, 170
    seeking solutions, 170–171
    serial killers, spree killers, and mass murderers,
      371–372

St. Louis, Missouri, 384
Supreme Court on, xxxv–xxxvi
in urban schools, xxxiii, xxxv
violence, 168–169
Violent Gang Sage Streets Task Force, 14
The Gang (Thrasher), 62
Garafalo, James, 283
Gardiner, Richard, 116
Gartin, P., 205
gated communities, 172–173. *See also* neighborhoods;
  neighborhood watch
    concepts and rationales, 172
    history, 172–173
    Lifestyle Communities, 172
    Prestige Communities, 172
    Security Zone Communities, 172
    who lives where, 172
Gates v. Illinois, 6
gay, lesbian, bisexual, transgender, and transsexual
  youth, 374
gay riots, xxx
Geiss, Gil, 405
General History of Connecticut, xxvii
General Social Survey (GSS), 162
genocide, 405
Genovese, Kitty, xxx, **173–174**
    bystander psychology, 173–174
    front page tragedy, 173
    witness confusion, 174
Genovese organization, 178
gentrification, 174–177, 314, 423
    displacement and informal control, 175–176
    law enforcement effects, 176
    research, 175
    viewpoints, 174–175
    violence and, 176
    Washington, D.C., 447–448
geographic information systems (GIS), 109
George II, 256
Gerbner, George, 414
Gerstein v. Pugh, 7
Ghost Rider comic series, 272
Giannola, Vito, 383
Gideon v. Wainwright, 463
GIS (geographic information systems), 109
Giuliani, Rudolph, 46, 48, 60, **177–179**,
  185, 430
    corruption and, 178
    crime policies, 248
    first years, 177
    homelessness and, 201
    legal career, 177
    policing and, 178–179
    political career, 178

Gladwell, Malcolm, 137
globalization
    counterfeit goods and, 91
    protests, 423
Glock, Gaston, 188
Goetz, Bernhard, xxxii, **179–180**, 411
    media portrayals, 179
    self-defense assertion, 180
    subway vigilante, 179–180
Goff, Colin, 404
Gold, Raymond, 428
Gold Rush, 363–364
Goldstein, Herman, 85, 332–333
Goldstein, Paul, 150
Goldwater, Barry, xxx
Gordon, Dina, 197
Gotti, John A., 184
Grace, Nancy, 399
Grady, William, 410
graffiti, 180–182. *See also* **juvenile offending; street
  art; vandalism**
    anti-graffiti campaigns, 181–182
    gang aspects, 181
    identity and status, 181
    tagging the heavens, 181
    writers and crews, 181
Grafton, Sue, 398
Graham, K., 22, 23, 26
Grand Theft Auto (**video game**), xxxv, xxxvi, 87,
  182–183, 463. *See also* *Street Crime* (**online game**)
    evolution and revenues, 182
    youth influence and reaction, 182–183
Grasmik, Harold, 434
gratification, 125
Great Depression, xxix, 64
    bank robbery in, 20
    skid row and, 378
Green, Esmin, 54
Green, Stuart, 242
green damage, 156
Griffin, Michael, 411
Griffith, Michael, xxxii
Groeneveld, Richard, 7
Groff, Elizabeth, 368
GSS (General Social Survey), 162
Guardian Angels, 183–186, 463
    CyberAngels, 185
    expansion, 185–186
    origin and principles, 183–184
    safety patrols, 185
    troubled history, 184–185
guerrilla bands, 147
Guerry, Andre-Michel, 434, 436
Gunn, David, xxxiv

guns and weapons, 186–190
clubs and knives, 186–187
crime and, 190
firearm types, 188–190
flintlocks to revolvers, 187–188
gun buyback program, 18
gun violence, 76
Gun-Free School Act, xxxiv
guns in schools, xxxiii, xxxiv
NCVS on, 190
gunshot detection system, 190–192
capabilities and utility, 191
ideal case, 191
technology, 191
Gurr, Ted, 196
Gypsies, 221

H
Hagerman, Amber, xxxv
Halderman, Robert, 33
handguns, xxxvii
Haracopos, A., 150
harm reduction, 281–282
Harper, Dee Wood, Jr., 443
Harris, Eric, xxxv, xxxvi
Harris, Fred R., 231
Harrison Narcotic Act, xxviii, 463
hate crime, xxxii, xxxv, **193–196**, 345–346.
See also **racial assault**
defined, 463
definitions and implications,
193–194
enforcement, 195–196
forms of violence, 194
legislation, 195
motivations, 194–195
Supreme Court on, xxxiv
Hauptmann, Bruno, xxix
Hawaii Five-0, 399
Hawkins, Yusef, 60
Hayward, Keith, 123
Hells Angels, xxix, 168, 272–273, 463
Hells Angels: A Strange and Terrible Saga
(Thompson, H. S.), 272
Henderson, Russell, xxxv
heroin, xxxiii, 17, 133, 149, 152–153, 289. *See also*
alcohol and drug use; cocaine; **drug dealing; drug
markets, open-air**
Highsmith, Patricia, 398
highway patrol, 321–322
Highway Patrol, 399
Hill Street Blues, 316
hippie era, 364–365
Hirschfield, Alex, 119

Hispanics. *See also* **Latin Kings**
gangs, xxxiii, xxxv
underage drinking, 143
history of street crime in America, 196–199
1960s, 197
1970s, 197–198
1980s, 198
1990s, 198
2000s, 198
criminal justice responses, 198
state crime and, 198–199
HIV/AIDS
Miami, Florida, 259
needle exchanges and, 281
prostitute/streetwalker, 341
testing of prostitutes, xxxii
Hobbs, D., 23
Hodge, D, 32
Hogan Gang, 383
Holliday, George, 324
Hollinger, Richard, 119
Hollister Riots, 272
Holocaust, 405
homelessness, 199–201. *See also* **panhandling or
begging**; poverty; **risky lifestyles; skid row**
clinging to commons, 201
criminalizing, 200–201
Giuliani and, 201
housing as human right, 200
mental illness and, 254–255
National Coalition for the Homeless, 201
National Law Center on Homelessness and Poverty,
201
panhandling or begging and, 303–304
Homicide: Life on the Street, 17, 411, 413
homicides. *See* **murder/homicide**
homophobic assault, 201–203
characteristics of offenses and offenders,
202–203
law enforcement, 203
Hooker's Ball, xxxi
hooliganism, 203–205
Europe origins, 203–204
moral panics, 204–205
street fights, 203
U.S. sports troubles, 204
Hoover, Herbert, 381
horse racing, xxx
hot spots, 109, 110, **205–206**
crime prevention, situational, 119
drug markets, 151
mapping down, 206
Minneapolis, Minnesota, 263
patrol cars, 306–306

police response, 206
   research and theories, 205
   Weed and Seed, 449
Hough, M., 150
Housing Act of 1937, 337
housing as human right, 200
Hurricane Katrina, 286–287
Hutson, H., 146
hyper strain, 124

I

I Am the Central Park Jogger (Meili), 60
ICE (Immigration and Customs Enforcement), 14, 215, 218
identity
   Asian gangs, 11–12
   graffiti and, 181
identity theft, 106
Illinois v. Perkins, 266
Illinois v. Wardlow, 391
image
   Asian gangs, 11–12
   bounty hunters, 44
   crime prevention, environmental design and, 115
   Detroit, Michigan, 135
   motorcycle clubs, 272
   Newark, New Jersey, 292–293
IMF (International Monetary Fund), 205
immigrant neighborhoods, 207–211.
   See also **victims, immigrant**
     changing nature, 207–208
     current controversy, 209–210
     evidence, 210
     research, 207, 210
     street crime, 210–211
     traditional theory, 208–209
immigration, xxvii, 14
   Chinese, xxviii
   counterfeit goods and, 91
Immigration and Customs Enforcement (ICE), 14, 215, 218
imports, 91
impulsivity, 125
Inciardi, James, 148
incidence
   arson, 10
   burglary, 51
   drive-by shootings, 146
   National Incident-Based Reporting System (NIBRS), 71, 224
   National Incidence Studies of Missing, Abducted, Run-Away, and Throwaway Children (NISMART-I), 233

Indianapolis, Indiana, 211–213
   CompStat, 213
   crime, 212
   law enforcement, 211–212
   public safety, 212–213
individual crime patterns, 113
Indochinese gangs, 12
informal control, 175–176
Innocence Project, 60
institutionalization
   deinstitutionalization movement, 254
   juvenile offending, 225–226
intelligent fingerprinting, 3
Internal Revenue Service (IRS), 14
International Monetary Fund (IMF), 205
International Narcotics Control Board, xxxiv
intervention
   commercial sexual exploitation of children, 69
   open air drug markets, 151
investigations. *See also* **crime scene investigation**
   arson, 10
   Diallo, 136
   police detectives, 331
   serial killers, spree killers, and mass murderers, 372–373
   unlicensed drinking establishments, 144–145
Iraq War, 405
IRS. *See* Internal Revenue Service (IRS)
isolation, 342
Italian Mafia, xxviii

J

Jackson, Jesse, 136, 346
Jacob Wetterling Crimes Against Children and Sexually Violent Offender Registration Act, xxxiii, 463
Jacobs, Jack, 238
Jacobs, Jane, 114–115, 131
jails, 215–218. *See also* **arrest; bail; central booking; courts**
   administrative function, 215–216
   contemporary America, 215
   historical development, 217–218
   racial inequality, 216
   social function, 216
   Survey of Jail Inmates, 254
James, Sly, 229
James gang, 19–20
Janssen, John, 260
Japanese American street gangs, 12
jaywalking, 218–220
   onrush of automobiles, 218–219
   regulatory change, 219
Jean, Wyclef, 137
Jeffrey, C. Ray, 114

Jencks, Christopher, 197
Jenkins, Herbert, 231
Jenkins, Philip, 65
Jessica's Law, xxxvi
Jews, 221
"johns," 220–221. *See also* **pimp**; prostitution
    End Demand campaigns, 221
    schools, 220
    sex workers, 220
    shifting enforcement, 220–221
    targeting demand, 220–221
Johnson, Lyndon B., xxx, 231, 467
Johnson, Sylvester, 311
Jordan, Frank, 366
Josephson, Matthew, 404
Juarez cartel, 302
Judge Judy, 414
judges, 102, 414
Julius Caesar, 121
The Jungle (Sinclair), 404
Junk Dealing and Juvenile Delinquency, 256
juvenile curfews, 221–223. *See also* **gangs (street)**
    contending perspectives, 222
    development and aims, 221–222
    effectiveness, 222
Juvenile Delinquency and Urban Areas (Shaw, McKay), 61, 207, 210
juvenile drug courts, 99–100
juvenile offending, 223–226. *See also* **Bloods**; **Crips**; **gangs (street)**
    community-based programs, 225–226
    crimes and patterns, 224
    data sources, 223–224
    gang offenses and make-up, 224–225
    laws and institutionalization, 225–226
    National Incident-Based Reporting System (NIBRS) on, 223
    Uniform Crime Reports (UCR) on, 224

K
K-9 Cops, 414
Kanka, Megan, xxxiv, 464
Kansas City, Missouri, 227–229
    law enforcement, 228–229
    street crime, 227–228
Kansas City Preventive Patrol Experiment, 229–231
    evaluation and impact, 230–231
    structure, 229–230
Kansas City Star, 227
Kansas City SWAT, 399
Kassin, Saul, 137
Katz, Jack, 357
Keep Talking, 82
Kelling, George, 46, 292, 429–430

Kelly, Raymond, 60
Kennedy, David, 300, 318
Kennedy, John F., xxx
Kennedy, Robert F., 63, 178
Kennedy, William, 336
Ker v. California, 6
Kerley, K., 141
Kerner, Otto, Jr., xxx, 231
Kerner Commission on Civil Disorders, xxx, **231–233**
    debate over, 232
    recommendations and responses, 232
    "separate and unequal," 231–232
kidnapping, 233–234. *See also* abduction
    acquaintance, 234
    family, 223–234
    research, 233–234
    stranger, 234
    types, 233
Kiladelphia, 312
Kimble, Charles E., 117
King, Martin Luther, Jr., 63, 231
King, Melissa, 353
King, Ralph, 410
King, Rodney, xxxiii, 324
Klaas, Polly, xxxiv
Klebold, Dylan, xxxv, xxxvi
Kleiman, Mark, 151
Klein, Malcolm, 237
kleptomania, 377
Knapp, Whitman, 327
Knapp Commission, 327–328
Knight, Suge, 87
Know Nothing Party, xxvii
Knox, George, 237
Koch, Ed, 184
Kojak, 413
Korean gangs, 12
Kramer, Ron, 405

L
La Cosa Nostra, 236, 316
La Eme (Mexican Mafia), 168, 235–236
    enterprises and activities, 236
    origins and characteristics, 235
    structure, links, rivals, 235–236
LA Noire, 463
La Nuestra Familia, 236
Lanier, Cathy, 448
LAPD. *See* Los Angeles Police Department (LAPD)
Latané, Bibb, 54–55
Latin Disciples, 225
Latin Kings, 168, 225, 236–240. *See also specific gangs*
    ALKQN, 238–239
    danger of, 240

geographic growth, 238
ideology, 239–240
organizational structure, 239
secret society, 238–239
LaVigne, Nancy, 250
Law and Order, 389, 399, 411, 413, 415
law enforcement
    Baltimore, Maryland, 18
    Buffalo, New York, 50
    Chicago, Illinois, 64
    Cincinnati, Ohio, 75–76
    crack house, 104–105
    Detroit, Michigan, 134–135
    gentrification, 176
    hate crime and, 195–196
    homophobic assault, 203
    Indianapolis, Indiana, 211–212
    Kansas City, Missouri, 229
    neighborhood watch, 282
    response to Asian gangs, 13–14
    skinheads and, 380
    Washington, D.C., 449
laws
    juvenile offending, 225–226
    loitering, 463–464
    nuisance, 432, 464
    stalking, 386
    Sutton's Law, 466
leadership, 36
Ledonne, Danny, xxxvi
legalized gambling, 463
Leigh, carol, 341
Leopold, Nathan, 63
Letterman, David, 33
Levin, Jack, 193
Levine, Ned, 249
Levy, Chandra, 398
Lewis, Jerry, 204
Lifestyle Communities, 172
Lindbergh, Charles, xxix
Lindsay, John, 231, 327
Linn, Edith, 7
Liquor Control Commission, 144
Lizarraga, Ana, 236
Loeb, Richard, 63
loitering, 240–241
    Chicago and Supreme Court,
        240–241
    laws, 463–464
    racial profiling and, 241
Long Bridge Boys, xxvii
Loo, Jim, xxxiii
looting, xxviii, **242–243**
    concept and debate, 242

prevention, 243
    verified instances, 242–243
Los Angeles, California, 243–246
    city of contradictions, 243–244
    gang crimes, 245–246
    property crimes, 244–245
    Safer Cities Initiative, 176
    street crime, 246
    violence, 244
    zero-tolerance policing, 176
Los Angeles Police Department (LAPD), xxxiii, 21,
    45–46. *See also* **Community Resources Against
    Street Hoodlums**
    gang units, 246
    LAPD Crime and Arrest Weekly Statistics Report, 244
Los Angeles Times, 36
lotteries, xxvii, xxx, xxxi
Louima, Abner, 137
Loukaitou-Sideris, Anastasia, 251
Lowney, Shannon, xxxiv
Luciano, Charles ("Lucky"), xxix, 382
Luckenbill, David, 279
Lunsford, Jessica Marie, xxxvi
Lynch, Michael, 157
lynching, xxviii, 194, 417
Lyon, Danny, 272
Lyng, Stephen, 357

M
MacCannell, Dean, 443
The Mack, 315
MacMahon, Lloyd F., 177
MADD (Mothers Against Drunk Driving), 1
Maddox, Alton H., Jr., 410–411
Mafia, 178. *See also* **La Eme (Mexican Mafia)**;
    organized crime and violence
    Italian, xxviii
    Texas Mexican, 236
Magnificent 13, xxxi
Magnum P.I., 399
Malinowski, Bronislaw, 427
Manhattan Bail Project, 16
Mann, James R., xxviii
Mann Act, xxviii
Maple, Jack, xxxv, **247–248**, 462
    career, 247–248
    early years, 247
    impact on crime, 248
Mapp v. Ohio, 96, 467
Mara Salvatrucha, 225, 273. *See also* **MS-13**
Marcos, Imelda, 178
Mares, Dennis, 407
Marijuana Tax Act, xxix
Marsh, James, 121

Marxism, 269
Maryland v. Shatzer, 266
Mason, C. Vernon, 410–411
Mason, K., 141
mass transit, crime on, **249–251**
    local, 250
    prevention, 250
    research, 250
    situational analysis, 249–250
    whole journey approach, 249
    women's security, 251
massage parlors, **251–253**. *See also* **prostitution, houses of**
    prostitution, 251–252
    raids and crackdowns, 252–253
Massie, Thalia, xxix
Maxson, Peter, 249
McCarthy, Garry, 64
McCoy, William S., 39
McCray, Antron, 58–60
McCulloch, William, 231
McDevitt, Jack, 193
McGarrell, Edmund, 212
McGowan v. Maryland, xxix, 37
McKay, Henry D., 61–62, 207, 210, 434, 440
McKeown, Robert, 353
McKinney, Aaron, xxxv
McKnight, A. James, 23
McLaughlin, Tom, 57
McLeod, Maureen, 283
McNamara, Joseph, 231
Media, Crime, and Criminal Justice (Surrette), 411
Media and Criminal Justice (Stevens), 416
media depictions. *See also* popular culture; **television shows**
    Goetz, 179
    street crime, 401–402
    swarming, 406–407
Megan's Law, xxxiv, xxxv, xxxvi, 464
Meier, Robert F., 361
Meili, Trisha, xxxiii, xxxvi, xxxvii, 58–60. *See also* **Central Park jogger incident**
Melvin, Frank, 184
Menino, Thomas M., 41–42
mental health, 169–170. *See also* **courts, mental health**
mental illness, **253–256**
    criminalization and victimization, 253–254
    homelessness and, 254–255
    perfect storm, 255
    response, 255–256
    substance use and, 255
    Survey of Jail Inmates, 254
Merton, Robert, 124

metal theft, **256–257**
    causes and prevention, 257
    history, 256
    prevalence and cost, 256–257
Miami, Florida, **258–260**
    corruption, 258
    HIV/AIDS, 259
    illicit drug capital, 260
    policing model, 269
    street crime components, 258–259
    street crime impact, 259–260
Miami Vice, 399, 413
Michalowski, Raymond, 405
Miethe, Terance D., 361
Milam, J. W., xxix
Milk, Harvey, xxxi
Miller, Christopher, 57
Miller, Eleanor M., 356
Miller, Walter B., 4, 435
Milwaukee, Wisconsin, **260–262**
    community problem-solving, 261
    gangs and drug trade, 261–262
    modern era, 261
    police history, 260–261
Milwaukee Journal-Sentinel, 261
Minneapolis, Minnesota, **263–265**
    crime trends and hot spots, 263
    Murderapolis, 263
    police, 263–264
    prevention blueprint, 264–265
"Minnesota Strip," xxx, 464
Minnesota v. Dickerson, 392
Miranda v. Arizona, 7, 96, 266
Miranda warnings, **265–267**
    constitutional grounds, 266
    exceptions and controversy, 266
    impact, 266
misdemeanor crimes, 6–7, 464
Missing Children's Assistance Act, xxxii
Missing Children's Day, xxxi
Mississippi Burning, xxxiii
Mitchell, Todd, xxxiii
mobs and riots, **267–269**
    African Americans, xxx
    anti-Filipino, xxviii
    black bloc anarchists, 269
    Chicago Division Street, xxx
    Chicago race riot of 1919, 62–63
    conscience collective, 267
    Democratic National Convention of 1968 police riot, 63–64
    Detroit, xxx
    gay, xxx
    Hollister Riots, 272

nature of, 267–268
Newark, xxx, 291–292
politics, race, economics, 267
primitive rebellion, 269
race, xxviii
regular occurrences, 269
targets, 267
Tompkins Square Park, xxxii
Watts, xxix, xxx
WTO meetings, 269
Mollen, Milton, 328
Mollen Commission, 328
Moore, Devin, 182
Moral Panic (Jenkins), 65
moral panics, 65, 204–205
Moran, Bugs, 382
Morgenthau, Robert, 60
Morrison, Andrew, 353
Moscone, George, xxxi
Mosley, Walter, 398
Mosley, Winston, xxx, 173
Moten, Ronald, xxxvi
Mothers Against Drunk Driving (MADD), 1
motivation
    burglary, 51–52
    hate crime, 194–195
    stalking, 386
    Street Corner Society (Whyte), 394
    terrorism, 418
    theft and larceny, 421
    vandalism, 438
motor skills testing, 1–2
motor vehicle theft, 269–272
    anatomy of, 270
    carjacking, 270–271
    organized, 271
    security measures, 270
    UCR on, 269–270
motorcycle clubs, 272–273. *See also* **bars and pubs;
    drug dealing; gangs (street); mobs and riots**
    Big Five, 272
    Big Four, 272
    criminal minority, 272–273
    Hells Angels, 272–273
    history and image, 272
    Hollister Riots, 272
    Sons of Silence, 272
    weekend warriors, 272
motorcycle gangs, 225
Mozer, Robert, 54
MS-13, 225, **273–275**
    characteristics, allies, rivals, 274–275
    enterprises and activities, 275
    origins, 274

mugging, **275–277**
    current trends, 276
    targets, 275–276
    UCR on, 276
    variations, 275–276
    victims and degrees, 275
    violence, 276
murder/homicide, xxxiii, 17, **277–280**. *See also* **serial
    killers, spree killers, and mass murderers**
    abortion clinic murders, xxxiv, xxxv, xxxvi
    Atlanta Child Murders, xxxi
    Chicago, Illinois, 63
    countermeasures, 279–280
    criminological viewpoints, 279
    culture and subculture perspectives, 279
    drugs and, 277–278
    felony related, 277
    New Orleans, Louisiana, 285–286
    New York City, 288
    research, 279
    Sleepy Lagoon Murder, xxix
    street gangs, xxxvi, 278
    Supplementary Homicide Reports, 70
    tourist robbery, 286
Murrow, Edward R., xxix
My Heart Will Cross This Ocean (Diallo, Wolff), 137

N
Narcotic Drugs Import and Export Act, xxviii
NASP (National Association for Shoplifting
    Prevention), 377
National Association for Shoplifting Prevention
    (NASP), 377
National Center for Analysis of Violent Crime, 370
National Center for Missing and Exploited Children
    (NCMEC), xxxi, xxxii
    on children as victims, 72
    CyberTipline, 464
National Child Abuse and Neglect Data System
    (NCANDS), 71
National Coalition for the Homeless, 201, 304
National Crime Victimization Survey (NCVS), xxxiii, 276
    burglary data, 51
    on carjacking, 270–271
    on children as victims, 70
    on guns and weapons, 190
    implementation, 112, 197
    on rape and sexual assault, 351
    on risky lifestyles, 356
    on theft and larceny, 421
    tracking, 74
National Criminal Intelligence Service, UK, 301
National Criminal Justice Association (NCJA), 386
National Domestic Violence Hotline, xxxiv

National Drug Intelligence Center (NDIC), 290

National Gang Intelligence Center, 225

National Gang Threat Assessment Report, xxxvi

National Incidence Studies of Missing, Abducted, Run-Away, and Throwaway Children (NISMART-I), 233

National Incident-Based Reporting System (NIBRS), 71, 223

National Institute on Drug Abuse, xxxi, 223

National Insurance Crime Bureau (NICB), 257

National Law Center on Homelessness and Poverty, 201, 304

National Night Out, xxxii, xxxiv, xxxvii, 464

National Opinion Research Council, xxxiii

National Organization for Women, xxxi

National Resource Center and Clearinghouse on Missing and Exploited Children, xxxii

National Sheriff's Association, 282

National Youth Gang Survey, xxxv

Native American Party, xxvii

Nazi Party, 203

NCANDS (National Child Abuse and Neglect Data System), 71

NCJA (National Criminal Justice Association), 386

NCMEC. *See* National Center for Missing and Exploited Children (NCMEC)

NCVS. *See* National Crime Victimization Survey (NCVS)

NDIC (National Drug Intelligence Center), 290

Neathway, Louise, 33

needle exchanges, 281–282. *See also* **alcohol and drug use**

    harm reduction, 281–282

    HIV/AIDS and, 281

    research, 282

neglect, 71

neighborhoods. *See also* **immigrant neighborhoods**; **projects**; **street/block parties**

    in defining street crime, 401

    PSN, 41

    turf wars, 467

    urban planning, 432

neighborhood watch, 282–285

    development and variations, 282–283

    law enforcement, 282

    limitations, 284

    research, 282–283

New Orleans, Louisiana, 285–287

    changes since Hurricane Katrina, 286–287

    drug-related and retaliatory murder, 285–286

    rape in, 287

New York City, 287–291

    anti-crime initiatives, 289

    drug crime, 289

    encouraging trends, 287–289

    gang activity, 289–290

    murder/homicide, 288

New York Police Department (NYPD)

    CompStat and, 89

    corruption, 327–328

    crime reporting and management, 289

    racial assault, 347

    zero-tolerance/saturation policing, 458

New York Times, 173

New York v. Quarles, 266

Newark, New Jersey, 291–294

    Broken Windows Theory in, 292–293

    crime, 291–292

    perception and statistics, 292–293

    renaissance, 291–292

    riots, xxx, 292

    today, 293–294

Newark foot patrol experiment, 294–295

    criticisms, 295

    study design and findings, 294–295

Newman, Andrew, 119

Newman, Oscar, 114–115, 118, 131–132

Newman, Paul, 389

NIBRS. *See* National Incident-Based Reporting System (NIBRS)

NICB (National Insurance Crime Bureau), 257

Nichols, Leanne, xxxiv

NISMART-I. *See* National Incidence Studies of Missing, Abducted, Run-Away, and Throwaway Children (NISMART-I)

Nixon, Richard, xxx, xxxi

nonfinancial bail, 16

Notorious B.I.G., 87

nuclear weapons, 405

nuisance laws, 432, 464

Nutter, Michael, 311–312

NW. *See* **neighborhood watch**

NYPD. *See* New York Police Department (NYPD)

NYPD Blue, 411, 413, 415

O

Obama, Barack, 42, 203

objectivist model, 4

obsessive compulsive disorder (OCD), 159

OECD (Organisation for Economic Co-operation and Development), 90

Office for Security and Co-operation (OSCE), 345–346

Office of Drug Control Policy, U.S., 5

Office of Juvenile Justice and Delinquency Prevention (OJJDP), 223

Office of National Drug Policy Control, xxxii

OJJDP (Office of Juvenile Justice and Delinquency Prevention), 223

Olmos, Edward James, 236
Olsen, Arvid, 273
Olsen, Robert K., 323
O'Malley, Martin, 248
Omnibus Crime Control and Safe Streets Act of 1968, 300
online child victimization, 73
open-container laws, 297–299. *See also* **alcohol and drug testing, on-scene; alcohol and drug use**
    global opposition, 298
    local preferences, 297–299
Operation Ceasefire, 40–41, **299–300**.
    See also **Boston, Massachusetts**
    evaluation, 300
    structure and implementation, 299–300
Operation Matrix, 366–367
Operation Night Light, 40–41
Opium Poppy Control Act, xxix
opportunity reduction, 118
order maintenance, 322–323
O'Reilly, Bill, 399
Organisation for Economic Co-operation and Development (OECD), 90
organized crime and violence, 34, **300–302**.
    See also **La Eme (Mexican Mafia)**; Mafia
    bosses, 302
    corruption, 301
    definitions and derivations, 300–301
    drug cartels, 302
    FBI on, 300–301
    Gambino organization, 34, 184
    Genovese organization, 178
    La Cosa Nostra, 236, 316
    racketeering, 301–302
    research, 302
    St. Louis, Missouri, 383
    types and patterns, 301–302
organized motor vehicle theft, 271
Orlando, Maria, 353
OSCE (Office for Security and Co-operation), 345–346
Oswald, Lee Harvey, xxx
O'Toole, Ottis, xxxi
outdoor worker, 340
Outlaws, 272

P
Pagans, 272
Pagones, Steven, 410–411
Palacios, Wilson, 427–428
pandering, 464
panhandling or begging, 303–306.
    See also **homelessness; risky lifestyles; skid row**
    homelessness and, 303–304
    prevention, 305

prohibitions, 304–305
research, 304–305
tourist victims, 444
Para, F., 146
Pare, Ambroise, 121
pari-mutuel betting, xxix
Park, Robert, 61, 434
Parker, Bonnie, 20
Parks, Gordon, Jr., 315
patrol cars, 306–307
    communications and hot spots, 306–306
    driving and walking beats, 306
Patten, Ryan, 369
patterns. *See* **crime patterns**
Patz, Etan, xxxi
PBUS (Professional Bail Agent of the United States), 44
Peden, Graham, 231
pedophiles, 65, 464
peep shows, 307–308
    crime connections, 308
    early versions, 307
    modern versions, 307–308
Peeping Toms, 309–310
    definition and aspects, 309
    video voyeurism, 309
PEN1 (Public Enemy Number 1), 380
Penn, Arthur, 20
Penn, Sean, 461
People's Court, 414
Perez, Rafael, 86
PERF (Police Executive Research Forum), 323, 333
perfect storm, 255
Perry, Barbara, 193
Perry Mason, 399
Peruggi, Regina, 177
Peters, Samuel, xxvii
Philadelphia, Pennsylvania, 310–313
    disrupted economic base, 310
    Kiladelphia, 312
    Philly Rising, 312
    police tactics and programs, 310–311
    stop and frisk, 311–312
    Terry stops, 311
    violence, 312
Phillips, Timothy, 430
physical abuse, 71
Piche, Lloyd, xxxiii
Piche, Robert, xxxiii
pickpocketing, 313–314
    dramatic decline, 314
    prototypical youth street crime, 313
    techniques, 313–314
Pillow Gang, 383

pimp, 68–69, **314–316**. *See also* **"johns"**; prostitution
  pimpmobile, 315
  in popular culture, 315–316
  power over work and relationships, 315
Piru, 35
Pittsburgh, Pennsylvania, 316–318
  allies, 318
  gambling and gangs, 317–318
  history and current profile, 316–317
  police cooperation and key targets, 317
PODs (police observation devices), 464
police (overview), 318–323
  Baltimore, Maryland, 18
  brief history, 318–320
  Cleveland, Ohio, 76–78
  contemporary society, 320
  crime fighter, 322
  highway patrol, 321–322
  hot spots response, 206
  Milwaukee, Wisconsin, 260–261
  Minneapolis, Minnesota, 263–264
  order maintenance, 322–323
  Philadelphia, Pennsylvania, 310–311
  Pittsburgh, Pennsylvania, 317
  racial assault, 347
  recruiting and training, 320–321
police brutality/excessive force, 323–326
  lethal and less-lethal force, 325
  necessity of control, 324–325
police corruption, street-level, 326–329
  Baltimore, Maryland, 18
  drug-related, 328–329
  NYPD corruption, 327–328
  types of, 326–327
police detectives, 329–332
  accountability, 331–332
  investigations, 331
  requirements for, 329–330
  role and responsibilities, 330
  Supreme Court and, 332
Police Executive Research Forum (PERF), 323, 333
Police Headquarters, 398
police observation devices (PODs), 464
Police Women, 399
Police Women of Broward County, 415
policing. *See also* **community policing; zero-tolerance/
  saturation policing**
  Giuliani and, 178–179
  Miami model, 269
  zero-tolerance, 176
policing, problem-oriented, 332–335
  coining, 332–333
  models, 333–335
  premises and principles, 333

Political Crime (Proal), 404
politics
  Giuliani, 178
  mobs and riots, 267
  political patronage, xxvii
pool halls, 335–337
  criminogenic aspects, 336–337
  male youth magnet, 335–336
  reform, 336
  rites of passage, 335–336
popular culture. *See also* **Grand Theft Auto (video
  game)**; media depictions; *Street Crime* **(online game)**;
  television shows
  bank robbery in, 20–21
  pimp in, 315–316
poverty. *See also* **homelessness; panhandling or
  begging; skid row**
  National Law Center on Homelessness and Poverty,
    201
  war on, xxx, 467
predatory victimization, 441
Presdee, Mike, 399
President Truman, xxxiii
Prestige Communities, 172
prevalence
  blackmail, 33
  metal theft, 256–257
  prostitute/streetwalker, 341–342
  rape and sexual assault, 350–352
  swarming, 406
prevention
  bail as preventive detention, 16
  bicycle theft, 29
  burglary, 53
  CAPTA, 71
  commercial sexual exploitation of children, 69
  CPTED, 432
  Gang Prevention and Effective Deterrence Act,
    xxxvi
  looting, 243
  mass transit crime, 250
  metal theft, 257
  Minneapolis, Minnesota, 264–265
  OJJDP, 223
  panhandling or begging, 305
  preventive detention, 16
  road rage, 359–360
  street gangs, 170
  underage drinking, 143
Prevention and Control of Urban Disorders,
  258
primitive rebellion, 269
Principles of Criminology (Sutherland), 61
prison gangs, 225

Proal, Louis, 404
probable cause, 6
Professional Bail Agent of the United States (PBUS), 44
Prohibition, 38, 39, 144, 464. *See also* **alcohol and drug use**; **bootleggers**; Twenty-First Amendment; Volstead Act
    end of, 466
    Noble Experiment, 381
    speakeasies and, 381
Project Safe Neighborhoods (PSN), 41
projects, the, 337–340
    crime, 338–339
    history, 337–338
property crimes, 174
    children as victims, 71
    Los Angeles, California, 244–245
prostitute/streetwalker, 340–342, 466
    hierarchies, 341
    HIV/AIDS, 341
    isolation, 342
    marginal living, 340
    prevalence and characteristics, 341–342
    serial killers, spree killers, and mass murderers and, 372
    terms and connotations, 340–341
prostitution, xxviii, 151, 220, 382. *See also* **"johns"**;
  pimp
    anti-prostitution laws, xxx
    auto impoundment and, xxxiii
    black market, 31–32
    decriminalizing, xxxi
    FBI statistics, xxxiv
    HIV/AIDS testing, xxxii
    massage parlors, 251–252
    pandering, 464
    sex crimes, 374
prostitution, houses of, 342–344.
  See also **massage parlors**
    enforcement, 343–344
    historical backdrop, 343
    public-order crimes, 342–343
protection rackets, 382
prowling by auto, xxxi, 465
Pryor, Richard, 315
PSN (Project Safe Neighborhoods), 41
Psychological Bulletin, 55
Public Enemy Number 1 (PEN1), 380
public health, 256
public safety
    Indianapolis, Indiana, 212–213
    street crime and, 256
public space as private trust, 132
public-order crimes, 342–343
purse snatching. *See* **theft and larceny**

Q
Quantrill's Raiders, 147
Quarantelli, Enrico L., 242–243
Quetelet, Adolphe, 434, 436
Quitno, Morgan, 384–385

R
rabble, 216
race, 267
racial assault, 345–348
    by citizens, 346
    NYPD, 347
    by police, 347
    racial hate crimes, 345–346
    symbolism, 347
racial inequality, 216
racial profiling, 4, **348–350**, 465
    driving while black, 348–349
    eliminating, 349–350
    history, 349–350
    loitering and, 241
    research, 349
    stop and frisk and, 392
    utility of, 348–349
Racketeer Influenced and Corrupt Organizations Act (RICO), 236, 301
racketeering, 236, 301, 301–302
raids, 252–253. *See also* **sting operations**
Rampart scandal, 86–87
Ramsay, Charles, 448
Ramseur, James, 179
Random Violence (Best), 60
Rankin, Ian, 398
rape and sexual assault, xxviii, xxix, xxx, xxxiii, xxxvi, **350–354**. *See also* **Central Park jogger incident**; **domestic violence**; **Genovese, Kitty**
    blitz rape, 376
    gang rape, xxxii
    geographic impact of, 352–353
    National Crime Victimization Surveys (NCVS) on, 351
    New Orleans, Louisiana, 287
    prevalence and definitions, 350–352
    research, 352–353
    sex crimes, 375–376
    Uniform Crime Report (UCR) on, 352
Rappaport, Helen, 33
Rational Choice Theory, 257
Rats, xxvii
R.A.V. v. St. Paul, xxxiv
Reagan, Ronald, xxxi, xxxii, 4, 178
Real Life Stories of the Highway Patrol, 411, 414
Reasons, Charles, 404
recreational drugs, 465

Redford, Robert, 389
Reed, Zack, 164
reform
    Bail Reform Act of 1984, 16
    pool halls, 336
regulatory enforcement, 151
Reitz, Kevin, 196–197
release on recognizance (ROR), 16, 43–44
Reno, Janet, 41
Repetto, Thomas, 108
research. *See also* **Newark foot patrol experiment**;
    Seattle Crime Places Study; **urban ethnography**
    Asian gangs, 13
    bar personnel, 22–25
    bars and pubs, 26
    black market, 30
    blackmail, 33
    bystander apathy, 54–55
    children as victims, 73
    commercial sexual exploitation of children, 68
    domestic violence, 138
    drive-by shootings, 146
    drug dealing, 148
    drug markets, 150–151
    gentrification, 175
    hot spots, 205
    immigrant neighborhoods, 207, 210
    indecent exposure, 158
    kidnapping, 233–234
    mass transit crime, 250
    mental health courts, 101–102
    murder/homicide, 279
    needle exchanges, 282
    neighborhood watch, 282–283
    organized crime and violence, 302
    panhandling or begging, 304–305
    racial profiling, 349
    rape and sexual assault, 352–353
    risky lifestyles, 356
    road rage, 359
    shoplifting, 377
    swarming, 407
    television shows, 416
    underage drinking, 142
    urbanization, 436
    women, 455
response
    academic and policy, 84
    Buffalo, New York, law enforcement, 50
    Central Park jogger incident, 59–60
    code of silence/stop snitching, 81–82
    flash mobs, 163–164
    in history of street crime in America, 198
    hot spots, 206

Kerner Commission on Civil Disorders, 231–233
    law enforcement to Asian gangs, 13–14
    mental illness, 255–256
    prescription drugs, 153
Revolutionary War, xxvii
Reyes, Matias, xxxvi, 60
Rhode Island v. Innis, 266
Richards, James, 184
Richardson, Kevin, 58–60
RICO (Racketeer Influenced and Corrupt Organizations
    Act), 236, 301
rights. *See also* Constitution, U.S.; **courts**; Supreme
    Court, U.S.
    Campus Sexual Assault Victims Bill of Rights, xxxiv
    Civil Rights Act of 1968, 64
    English Bill of Rights, 15
    housing as human right, 200
right-wing groups, 417
Riis, Jacob, 256
riots. *See* **mobs and riots**
risk, 125
risky lifestyles, 354–358
    behaviors, 356–357
    National Crime Victimization Survey (NCVS) on,
        356
    patterns and victimization, 354–355
    representations and reactions, 357–358
    research, 356
    Uniform Crime Report (UCR) on, 356
Rivera Geraldo, 399
road rage, xxxii, xxxv, **358–359**, 465
    research, 359
    resources, treatment, prevention, 359–360
    retaliatory behavior, 358
    traits and characteristics, 358–359
robbery, 286. *See also* **bank robbery**; **theft and larceny**
The Robber Barons (Josephson), 404
Roberson, Michelle, 119
Roberts, J., 24–25, 27
Rodriguez, Daryl, 410
Roe v. Wade, xxxi, 461
Roebuck, Julian, 326
Romenesko, Kim, 356
Roosevelt, Franklin, 466
ROR. *See* release on recognizance (ROR)
Rosenbaum, Yankel, xxxiv
routine activity theory, 150, 257, **360–361**
    integrating theories and critiques, 361
    as street crime tool, 360
    vantage point, 360–361
Roy, Beth, 137
Ruddell, Rick, 369
Rupert, James, 371
Ruth, Henry, 196–197

Ryan, Nancy, 60
Rydon, Phillip, 23

S
SACSI (Strategic Approaches to Community Safety Initiative), 41
Safer Cities Initiative, 176
safety weeks, 219
Salaam, Yusef, 58–59
Saloman, Arthur K., xxxii
Sampson, Robert, 434–435
San Francisco, California, 363–367
    Barbary Coast, 364
    Beat era, 364
    corruption, 363
    Gold Rush and vigilante days, 363–364
    hippie era, 364–365
    Operation Matrix, 366–367
    street crime, 366–367
Sanderson, Robert, xxxv
Santana, Raymond, Jr., 58–60
Saville, Greg, 117
Saving Grace, 415
Schele, Carl Wilhem, 121
Schiengold, Stuart, 196
school shootings, xxxv, 371
school vandalism, xxvii
Schultz, Dutch, 291, 382
SCWG (Street Crime Working Group), 255–256
Seale, Bobby, 64
Seattle Crime Places Study, 367–368
security, private, 368–370
    contrasts with public forces, 369
    scope and status, 369
Security Zone Communities, 172
self-defense, 180
Sellin, Thorsten, 436
sentencing, xxxvi, 95
serial killers, spree killers, and mass murderers, 370–373. *See also* bombings; school shootings
    definitions and differences, 370–371
    Edmond Post Office Massacre, 371
    familicide, 371
    gang-related, 371–372
    high visibility, 371
    investigations, 372–373
    prostitutes and, 372
    St. Valentine's Day massacre of 1929, 63, 370
    Virginia Tech massacre, 370
77 Sunset Strip, 399
sex crimes, 373–376. *See also prostitute/prostitution references*
    public exhibitionism, 373
    rape and assault, 375–376

    sex trafficking, 375
    survival sex, 374–375
    voyeurism, 373–374
sex offenders, xxxiv, xxxv, xxxvi
sex trafficking, 31–32, 375
sex workers, 220
sexting, 158
sexual deviation, xxix
sexual exploitation of children, 465
sexual victimization, 352–353, 465
The Shadow, 411
shared space, 219
SHARPS (Skin Heads Against Racial Prejudice), 380
Sharpton, Al, 136. *See also* **Tawana Brawley incident**
Shaw, Clifford, 61–62, 207, 210, 434, 440
shell game, 167
Shepard, Matthew, xxxv
Sherman, Lawrence, 151, 205, 231
Sherman Anti-Trust Act, 404
The Shield, 87, 411, 413
shoplifting, 376–378
    boosters and snitches, 377
    cost and demographics, 376–377
    kleptomania, 377
    research, 377
Sicilian Green Ones, 383
Siegel, Benjamin ("Bugsy"), xxix
Silverman, Eli, 7
Silverman, Ira, 57
Silway, Curtis, xxxi, 183–185
Simon, David, 17
Simon and Simon, 399
Simpson, O. J., 398
Sinclair, Upton, 404
skid row, 378–379. *See also* **homelessness; panhandling or begging; risky lifestyles**
    current, 379
    Great Depression and, 378
    history, 378
Skin Heads Against Racial Prejudice (SHARPS), 380
skinheads, 379–381
    fragmented law enforcement, 380
    origins, 379–380
    SHARPS, 380
    structure and activities, 380
Skinners, xxvii
Slaton, John, xxviii
Sleepy Lagoon Murder, xxix
Slepian, Barnett, xxxv
SLPDC (street-level prescription drug crime), 151–153
Smith, Paige, 353
Smith, Philip, 430
Smith's Vly gang, xxvii
snitches, 377

snitching. *See* **code of silence/stop snitching**

Snyder, Mary Gail, 172

SOAP (stay-out-of-areas-of-prostitution), 31

social control dynamics, 132

social disorganization theory, 61, 174–176, 209, 434

social function of jails, 216

social pressure, 81–82

social structure theories, 434–435

SODA (stay-out-of-drug-use-area), 31

solutions

    street gangs, 170–171

    truancy, 425–426

    urban incivility, 430–431

Sons of Anarchy, 399

Sons of Silence, 272

The Sopranos, 399

Sourcebook of Criminal Justice Statistics, 259

Southby, Richard, 57

Spartican Army, xxx

spatial crime patterns, 113

speakeasies (1920s), 381–382, 465. *See also* **alcohol
and drug use; bars and pubs; bootleggers; drinking
establishments, unlicensed; organized crime and
violence**

    crime and corruption, 381–382

    criminals, 382

    Prohibition and, 381

speak-outs, 465

Spellman, William, 333

Springsteen, Bruce, 137

St. James, Margo, xxxi

St. Louis, Missouri, 382–385

    corruption, 382

    kids, gangs, violence, 384

    organized crime, 383

    rankings, reactions, reality, 384–385

    street crime, 385

St. Valentine's Day massacre of 1929, 63, 370

Stack v. Boyle, 15

stalking, 386–387. *See also* **kidnapping; rape and
sexual assault**

    motivations, 386

    statutes and statistics, 386

Starsky and Hutch, 399, 413

state crime, 198–199

stay-out-of-areas-of-prostitution (SOAP), 31

stay-out-of-drug-use-area (SODA), 31

stereotypes, 414–415

Stevens, Dennis, 416

sting operations, 387–390. *See also* **arrest**; raids

    basic and variations, 387–388

    corruption and, 388–389

    defenses, 389

    targets, 387

Stonewall, 465

stop and frisk, 6, 311–312, **390–392**. *See also* **arrest;**
Terry stops

    defined, 465

    key aspects, 391–392

    racial profiling question, 392

    reasonable suspicion, 390–391

    Terry v. Ohio and, 390

Stop Snitching movements, 465

Strain Theory, 124

stranger danger, 465

stranger kidnapping, 234

stranger victimization, 4

Strategic Approaches to Community Safety Initiative
(SACSI), 41

street art, 392–393. *See also* **graffiti**

***Street Corner Society* (Whyte), 394–395**

    higher tiers of organization, 394–395

    legacy, 394

    motivation, 394

street craps, 165–166

***Street Crime* (online game), 395–397**, 465.
See also ***Grand Theft Auto* (video game)**

    achievement levels, 396

    effects, 396

    structure, 395–396

street crime, general. *See also* **history of street crime
in America; suite crimes versus street crimes;**
specific topics

    Buffalo, New York, 49–50

    Cincinnati, Ohio, 74–75

    CompStat and, 90

    Detroit, Michigan, 134

    immigrant neighborhoods, 210–211

    Kansas City, Missouri, 227–228

    Los Angeles, California, 246

    Miami, Florida, 258–259

    public safety and, 256

    San Francisco, California, 366–367

    St. Louis, Missouri, 385

    urban planning and, 432

    Washington, D.C., 448–449

street crime, popular portrayals of, 397–400

    crime as entertainment, 397–398

    crime as news, 397–398

    crime vérité, 399

street crime defined, 400–402

    category descriptions, 400

    drug vector, 401

    media depiction, 401–402

    neighborhoods and gangs, 401

    volume trends, 400–401

Street Crime Working Group (SCWG), 255–256

street fights, 203

street hustlers, 356
street/block parties, 402–403
    collective efficacy, 402–403
    community within community, 402
    crime reduction and, 403
street-level prescription drug crime (SLPDC), 151–153
streetwalker. *See* **prostitute/streetwalker**
Stretesky, Paul, 157
strip clubs, 432
subculture
    drug, 462
    murder/homicide, 279
    theories, 4
    urbanization, 435–436
suite crimes versus street crimes, 403–405
    crime on the job, 403–404
    historical overview, 404–405
Sullivan, Mercer, 407
Sullivan, Timothy, 60
Super Columbine Massacre video game, xxxvi, 466
Super Fly, 315
Supreme Court, U.S., xxvii, xxix, xxxi, 266, 467.
    See also specific cases
    blue laws and, 37
    on bounty hunters, 44
    on force, 325
    on gangs, xxxv–xxxvi
    on handguns, xxxvii
    on hate crime, xxxiv
    on loitering, 240–241
    police detectives and, 332
    on probable cause, 6
    Terry stops and, 311, 390
Sureños and Norteños, 225
surety, 43
Surrette, Ray, 411
surveillance, 115. *See also* **sting operations**
Survey of Jail Inmates, 254
survival sex, 340, 374–375
Sutherland, Edwin, 61
Sutton, Willy, 19–20, 466
Sutton's Law, 466
swarming, 406–407
    definition and prevalence, 406
    media depictions, 406–407
    research, 407
symbolism
    Crips, 126–127
    racial assault, 347
syphilis, xxviii

T
tagging the heavens, 181
Tale-Yax, Hugo Alfredo, 54

Tammany Hall, xxvii, 466
Tango Blast, 225
target hardening, 53, 116
targets
    bars and pubs, 27
    burglary, 51–52
    johns, 220–221
    mobs and riots, 267
    mugging, 275–276
    Pittsburgh, Pennsylvania, 317
    sting operations, 387
    theft and larceny, 419
Tawana Brawley incident, xxxii, **409–411**
    aftermath, 411
    case and cover-up, 409–410
    grand jury report, 410
    Sharpton and, 410–411
technology
    crime scene investigation, 121–122
    gunshot detection system, 191
Tejada, Charles J., 60
television shows, 411–416. *See also* media depictions;
    popular culture; *specific television shows*
    depictions of justice, 414
    depictions of stereotypes, 414–415
    effects, 415
    history of crime dramas, 413
    history of reality justice shows, 413–414
    infotainment, 414
    research, 416
Temperance Movement, 37
temporal crime patterns, 113
territoriality, 115
terrorism, 416–419. *See also* **drive-by shooting; gangs
    (street); hate crime; racial assault**
    crimes against minorities, 416–417
    individual motivations, 418
    recruiting in prison, 418
    right-wing groups, 417
    types of attacks, 417–418
Terry stops, 311, 390, 466
Terry v. Ohio, 6, 96, 311, 390, 466
Texas Mexican Mafia, 236
Texas Syndicate, 236
theft and larceny, 419–421. *See also* **bank robbery;
    bicycle theft; burglary; credit card theft; metal
    theft; motor vehicle theft; pickpocketing;
    shoplifting**
    aggravated larceny, 420
    definitions, 419
    identity, 106
    motivations, 421
    NCVS on, 421
    rates and types, 420–421

targets, 419
thief and victim demographics, 420
UCR on, 420
theory. *See also* **Broken Windows Theory; crime–consumerism nexus; defensible space theory; research; routine activity theory**
community policing, 85
crime patterns, 114
hot spots, 205
immigrant neighborhoods, 208–209
Rational Choice Theory, 257
social disorganization, 61, 174–176, 209, 434
social structure, 434–435
Strain Theory, 124
subculture, 4
Thomas, Matthew, 369
Thompson, Hunter S., 272
Thompson, Jack, 182
Thornton, Charles, 231
Thrasher, Fredric M., 62
Three-Card Monte, 166–167
Thurman v. City of Torrington, 139
Till, Emmett, xxix
Tiller, George, xxxvi
TIME magazine, 46, 178
Timmendequas, Jesse, xxxiv
Tiny Rascal Gangsters, 225
To Serve and Protect, 399
Toffolon-Weiss, M., 155
Tompkins Square riots/Tent City, xxxii, **421–424**
charges and reports, 423–424
restrictions and riot, 422–423
tourist robbery, 286
toxins, unequal distribution, 155–156
transactional sex, 340
Treatise on the Police of the Metropolis (Colquhoun), 256
trends. *See also* **crime patterns**
Buffalo, New York, street crime, 49–50
crime patterns explaining, 113–114
fear of crime, 162
Minneapolis, Minnesota, crime, 263
mugging, 276
New York City, 287–289
prescription drugs, 152
volume in street crime, 400–401
tricks, 220
Trojanowicz, Robert, 85
truancy, **424–426**
characteristics, 424–425
legal status, 425
role of parents, 425–426
solutions, 426
turf wars, 467
Turnaround (Bratton), 45

TVPA (Victims of Trafficking and Violence Protection Act), 67, 375
Twenty-First Amendment, xxix, 39, 144, 466.
See also Prohibition
Twitter, 164

U
UCR. *See* Uniform Crime Reporting (UCR)
undesirables, 216
Unequal Verdicts (Sullivan), 60
Uniform Crime Reporting (UCR), 41
burglary data, 51
cataloged offenses, 196
on children as victims, 70
development, 111
on juvenile offending, 223
management, 64
on motor vehicle theft, 269–270
on mugging, 276
on risky lifestyles, 356
on theft and larceny, 420
tracking, 74
United States v. Salerno, 16
unreasonable search and seizure, 466
Unsolved Mysteries, 414
The Untouchables, 415
urban ethnography, **427–429**
history, 427–428
methods, 428
urban focus, 427
urban incivility, **429–431**
1970s, 429–430
approaches and solutions, 430–431
Broken Windows Theory and, 429–430
urban planning, 219, **431–433**
CPTED, 432
extent of, 431–432
neighborhoods, 432
regulation and control, 432–433
street crime and, 432
urbanization, **433–436**
cities and criminality, 433–434
ongoing research, 436
social structure theories, 434–435
urban subcultures, 435–436
U.S. News and World Report, 384
U.S. v. Mendenhall, 390
U.S. v. Watson, 6

V
Vagrancy Act of 1824, 303
vagrants, 303, 466
Valencia-Corneili, 302
Van Wyk, J., 141

vandalism, 437–439. *See also* **graffiti; juvenile offending**
    CCTV for, 438
    consequences and countermeasures, 438–439
    costs, 438
    motivations, 438
    nature of, 437–438
    occurrence, 437
    school, xxvii
VAWA (Violence Against Women Act), xxxiv, 352, 467
Vega, Manuel, 57
vehicle prowling, 466–467. *See also* prowling by auto
Venkatesh, S. A., 30
Vera Foundation, 16
Vice Lords, 168, 225
victimization. *See also* National Crime Victimization Survey (NCVS)
    bicycle theft, 28–29
    blackmail, 34
    Developmental Victimization Survey, 73
    due process, 441
    mental illness, 253–254
    online child, 73
    predatory, 441
    risky lifestyles, 354–355
    sexual, 352–353
    stranger, 4
victims, general. *See also* **children as victims**
    Campus Sexual Assault Victims Bill of Rights, xxxiv
    door-to-door scam artists, 141
    indecent exposure, 159
    mugging, 275
    theft and larceny, 420
victims, immigrant, 439–441
    criminology, 439–440
    due process victimization, 441
    predatory victimization, 441
victims, senior, 441–443. *See also* **door-to-door scam artists**
    awareness and challenges, 442–443
    crime and fear of crime, 442
victims, tourist, 443–445
    begging and panhandling, 444
    countermeasures, 445
    nature and extent, 443
    strategies and tactics, 444-445
    vulnerability, 443–444
Victims of Trafficking and Violence Protection Act (TVPA), 67, 375
video voyeurism, 309
Video Voyeurism Prevention Act, 374
vigilantes
    anti-gambling vigilante groups, xxvii
    San Francisco, California, 363–364

violence, xxxiv, xxxvi, 60. *See also* abuse; **domestic violence; murder/homicide; organized crime and violence**
    bar personnel, 22
    commercial sexual exploitation of children, 69
    crack house, 103–105
    crack house and, 103–105
    gentrification and, 176
    gun, 76
    hate crime, 194
    Los Angeles, California, 244
    mugging, 276
    National Center for Analysis of Violent Crime, 370
    Philadelphia, Pennsylvania, 312
    St. Louis, Missouri, 384
    street gangs, 168–169
    Violence Against Women Act (VAWA), xxxiv, 352, 467
    Violence Policy Center (VPC), 146
Violence Against Women Act (VAWA), xxxiv, 352, 467
Violence Policy Center (VPC), 146
Violent Gang Sage Streets Task Force, 14
Virginia Tech massacre, 370
Volstead Act, 38, 381
voyeurism
    sex crimes, 373–374
    video, 309
VPC (Violence Policy Center), 146
vulnerability
    fear of crime, 161–162
    tourist victims, 443–444

W
walkability, 219
Walker, Lenore, 138
Walsh, Adam, xxxi
warrants, 6–7
Warren, Michael, 60
wars
    Civil War, U.S., 37, 147, 187, 227, 343, 383
    on drugs, xxxii, 82
    Iraq War, 405
    on poverty, xxx
    Revolutionary War, xxvii
    turf, 466
    World War I, xxviii
Washing Away of Wrongs, 121
Washington, D.C., 447–449
    crime and gentrification, 447–448
    geography and street crime, 448
    law enforcement, 448
Washington Examiner, 250
watch your back, 279
Watts riots, xxix, xxx

WB (World Bank), 205
weapons. *See* **guns and weapons**
Weed and Seed, 449–450, 467
    community-based, 449
    evaluation, 450
    hot spots, 450
    objectives and funding, 450
weekend warriors, 272
Weiner Neil, 68
Weisburd, David, 108, 231
Weiss, Alex, 212
Wells, H. G., 203
Wells, S., 22
Wetterling, Jacob, xxxiii, 463
White, Dan, xxxi
White, Rob, 406
white-collar crime, 403–405
White Slave Act of 1910, 375
white slavery, xxviii
WHO (World Health Organization), 255, 351
Who Killed Michael Farmer, xxix
whole journey approach, 249
whore, 340
Whyte, William, 394–395
Wickersham Report, 440
The Wild One, xxix, 272, 467
wilding, 60
Wilkins, Roy, 231
Williams, Stanley ("Tookie"), 126
Williams, Wayne, xxxi
Willie Dynamite, 315
Wilson, J. Q., 7, 46, 125, 292, 429–430
The Wire, 411, 414
Wise, Kharey, 58–59

Wolff, Craig, 137
Wolfgang, Marvin, 436
women, 399, 415, **450–455**
    contemporary criminalization, 453–455
    crack house and, 103–105
    criminality, 451–452
    economic crimes by, 453
    mass transit security, 251
    National Organization for Women, xxxi
    Violence Against Women Act (VAWA), xxxiv, 352, 467
    violent crimes by, 451–452
World Bank (WB), 205
World Health Organization (WHO), 255, 351
World Trade Organization (WTO), 205, 269
World War I, xxviii
Wright, James D., 304
WTO (World Trade Organization), 205, 269
Wyos, xxviii, 467

Y
Yeager, Peter, 405
Younger gang, 19–20

Z
Zacchia, Paolo, 121
zero-tolerance/saturation policing, 46, **457–459**
    cautionary aspects, 458
    in field, 457–458
    Los Angeles, California, 176
    NYPD, 458
Zielonko, Mary Ann, 174
Zone of Transition, 61
zoot suit, xxix

Photo Credits

Library of Congress: 1,422; U.S. Department of State: 37 (Kay Chernush), 375; U.S. Department of Defense: 178; Federal Emergency Management Agency: 141 (Michael Medina); U.S. Navy: 452 (Jessica Pounds); U.S. Department of Transportation: 2; National Archives and Records: 38, 208; Federal Bureau of Investigation: 274; Kansas City, Missouri, Police Department: 228 (Darryl Forté); Thinkstock: 24, 30, 47, 98, 107, 189, 359; CrimeView: 88; U.S. White House: 194 (Pete Souza); West Midland Police Department: 121; StockXchange: 104 (Rotorhead) 298; NC PDB Archives: 156; Flickr: 42, 52 (Salim Virji), 112, 126 (Sheila Steele), 131 (Elvert Barnes), 145, 163 (Steven Polunsky), 171 (Javi Velazquez), 175, 264, 319 (Kate Sheets), 385 (Shane T. McCoy), 395, 401, 435 (Marshall Astor); Wikimedia Commons: 9, 18, 20, 35, 59 (Thomas Good), 62, 72, (Bob Bobster), 92, 131, 166, 185, 198, 213, 217, (Andrew Bardwell), 237 (Javier Ramirez), 242, 249, 254 (Elena Chochkova), 259, 268, 278, 283, 288, 293, 304, 311, 313, 324, 329, 334, 338, 343, 348, 355, 365, 380, 391 (Thomas Good) 412, 417, 430, 438.